Chambers' Corporate Governance Handbook

Sixth Edition

Professor Andrew Chambers

Academic Director,
FTMSglobal
www.ftmsglobal.com

Bloomsbury Professional

Bloomsbury Professional Ltd
Maxwelton House
41–43 Boltro Road
Haywards Heath
West Sussex
RH16 1BJ

Bloomsbury Professional Ltd is an imprint of Bloomsbury Publishing plc

British Library Cataloguing-in-Publication Data

A CIP Catalogue record for this book is available from the British Library.

ISBN: 978 1 78043 482 7

Typeset by Phoenix Photosetting, Chatham, Kent
Printed and bound in Great Britain by CPI Group (UK) Ltd, Croydon, CR0 4YY

Preface

The first edition of this Handbook appeared 12 years ago in 2002. Each new edition has been a substantial amendment, so that this sixth edition is almost unrecognisable from the first and substantially revised from the fifth edition.

For this edition several chapters and appendices have been replaced and there has been comprehensive updating of others, to bring the Handbook fully up to date. So as to address important contemporary issues, we have new chapters on:

- evaluating board effectiveness;
- corporate social responsibility, integrated reporting and sustainability;
- culture, ethics and the board;
- the new British Governance Standard;
- board risk committees;
- current developments in internal auditing and new enhanced guidance for internal audit;
- the three lines of defence;
- the external auditor and the global capital markets.

The fifth edition went to print at the end of 2011 just as we appeared to be emerging from a global financial crisis. Many of its UK references were to the 2010 Corporate Governance Code which was current at the time, though we had some indications of changes that would be made in the 2012 version of the Code. It is the current 2012 version of the Corporate Governance Code that we use in this edition of the Handbook, as well as the 2012 version of the UK Stewardship Code, targeted mainly at institutional investors. With permission we reproduce these codes at Appendices 1 and 2.

The UK Corporate Governance Code and Stewardship Code are due for further amendment in 2014, keeping to the Financial Reporting Council's (FRC) schedule of reviewing the Code every two years. The FRC's aim is to have the revised texts by the end of July 2014, subject then to consultation. These anticipated versions of the two Codes are likely to apply from 1 October 2014 with companies expected to follow them for the first time for their years ending on or after 30 September 2015.

The FRC has started it consultation on guidance to replace Turnbull and its aim is to publish the guidance by March 2014; it would then take effect in April 2014 or possibly October 2014 to coincide with the updated version of the UK Corporate Governance Code.

When we went to print with this Handbook, the FRC had no plans to further update its Guidance on Audit Committees, but will look again once the revised codes are in place.

Readers should refer to the FRC's website to keep abreast with these changes (www.frc.org.uk).

Another significant change in the UK occurred when in 2013 the Financial Services Authority was replaced by the Financial Conduct Authority (FCA) and by the Prudential Regulation Authority (PRA). The FCA, a company limited by guarantee, now regulates financial firms providing services to consumers and maintains the integrity of the UK's financial markets; it focuses on the regulation of conduct by retail and wholesale financial services firms. The PRA is a wholly owned subsidiary of the Bank of England; it carries out the prudential regulation of deposit-taking institutions, insurers and designated investment firms (financial firms, including banks, investment banks, building societies and insurance companies.

These have been turbulent times for corporate governance. The global financial crisis was first a failure of business but it was also a failure of what John Coffee, presciently in 2006, called the 'gatekeepers' – outside or independent watchdogs or monitors who screen out flaws or defects and verify compliance with standards or procedures (see Coffee, John C. (2006) *Gatekeepers – The Professions and Corporate Governance*, Oxford University Press, p 2.) Coffee focused on the roles and performance of auditors, corporate lawyers, securities analysts and rating agencies. This Handbook focuses on the roles of boards, regulators of corporate governance and, yes, both external and internal auditors.

Undoubtedly corporate governance failed. It failed to prevent the financial crisis. It also largely failed to see it coming – despite outliers such as Enron, WorldCom and Tyco. More recently it can be argued that it has failed to improve standards of corporate governance as many scandals post-2008 have already surfaced. Perhaps it is not surprising that concerted efforts have been made to pin the blame on owners of companies for not being sufficiently active to make their voices heard by boards. But the primary responsibility must be with boards. Even in the UK, where shareholders' powers are relatively strong, they are grossly inadequate to determine the corporate governance conduct of companies. The FRC takes the view that boards are responsible for corporate governance.

While drawing attention to the unfortunate limitations of shareholder powers, this Handbook seeks to show how boards can be more effective. Much of the practical content of this Handbook has been suggested by experience of working on corporate governance projects for a wide variety of clients over the past thirty or so years, and from involvement as a member of boards of listed and unlisted companies, charities and of public sector entities.

As a source of reference I am mindful more of the Handbook's omissions than of any inaccuracies — though there are likely to be some of these too. I have attempted to make full acknowledgement of the sources I have used and to obtain their permission where appropriate: I regret if I have erred in any respect and will endeavour to rectify any omission at the earliest opportunity.

We are very grateful to IDDAS for permission to reprint its excellent guidance in Chapters **B2**, **B3**, **B4** and **B5**.

Clare Chalmers, Chief Executive of IDDAS, would be pleased to hear from readers with any inquiries about this guidance. She can be contacted at IDDAS, IDDAS House, 74 New Cavendish Street, London, W1G 8TF (tel: +44 (0)20 7436 0101; email: clare.chalmers@iddas.com; website: www.iddas.com).

Based in London, IDDAS specialises in providing board effectiveness, mentoring and coaching, leadership facilitation and executive assessment services for chairs, CEOs and main board directors, as well as for those who aspire to non-executive roles. IDDAS has an established reputation for its quality, innovative, supportive and flexible approach.

The IDDAS documents being reproduced are:

- Board Dynamics: Evaluating Board Effectiveness (Chapter **B2**)
- Board Dynamics: A Female Perspective (Chapter **B3**)
- Board Dynamics: The Chairman's Perspective (Chapter **B4**)
- Board Dynamics: The Non-Executive Director's Perspective (Chapter **B5**)

I am also grateful to the publishers for putting a fascinating opportunity my way, and for their impressive work on the production side of this volume.

We would like to hear from those who use this Handbook, with comments and suggestions.

Andrew Chambers
March 2014

About Andrew Chambers

Eur Ing ANDREW D CHAMBERS, BA, PhD, CEng, FCCA, FCA, FBCS, CITP, FRSA, FIIA

Twice mentioned in House of Lords' debates as an authority on corporate governance and internal auditing and by *The Times* as '*a worldwide authority on corporate governance*', in 2008 Andrew received the Institute of Internal Auditors' (UK) Distinguished Service Award. Also author of *Operational Auditing Handbook – Auditing Business & I.T. Processes* (2nd edn, 2010, Wiley), and *Tolley's Internal Auditor's Handbook* (2nd edn, 2009, LexisNexis), Andrew has been a non-executive director of a FTSE250 financial institution, a well-known mutual, small software companies, an NHS acute hospital trust and a well-known charity – usually having chaired their audit committees. He was Dean of what is now the leading Cass Business School where he is professor emeritus and until 2013 was Professor of Corporate Governance at London South Bank University. In 2010 he was appointed as the Specialist Advisor to the House of Lords' Economic Affairs Select Committee's Inquiry into *Auditors: market concentration and their role*. Andrew was a member of the UK committee that in 2013 published *Internal Audit Guidance for Financial Services*. He has been a member of the UK FRC's Auditing Practices Board (2006–09) and member and deputy chair of FEE's Corporate Governance and Company Law committee (2008–13). Andrew is a judge for the Hawkamah Bank Corporate

Governance Awards in the MENASA region (Middle East, North Africa and South Asia) and the ICSA Hermes Transparency in Governance Awards. He is now Academic Director for FTMSglobal.

Andrew Chambers,
Management Audit LLP,
Moat Lane, Old Bolingbroke, Lincolnshire,
PE23 4ES, UK
Email: ac@m-a.myzen.co.uk
Website: http://www.management-audit.com
Tel: +44 (0)207 099 9355
Fax: +44 (0)207 099 3954

Foreword

Since I started writing the Foreword to the *Chambers' Corporate Governance Handbook* in 2012, there has been a seismic shift of interest in and relevance of corporate governance; this goes way beyond the technical trenches of the strongly committed and has moved governance into the mainstream as never before. There has been a consequent rise in the profile of the profession of corporate governance and the increased visibility, centrality and influence of the chairman and the supporting company secretariat role.

I wrote in the last Foreword of the external board review as a catalyst for focusing on board performance and the need for this process to be socialised with chairmen, who at the time were somewhat ambivalent as to the value of the process. The desire of chairmen to 'discover' a board evaluation process which reflected value and development was clearly drawn in the Board Dynamics research commissioned by me in my previous company, reproduced in this Handbook at **B2** to **B5**. Chairmen were looking to get to grips with board evaluation as a meaningful way to drive the development of their boards and while the external board review has certainly established a very strong base camp, there is still much to do. The Financial Reporting Council's (FRC) Developments in Corporate Governance report (December 2013), cites Grant Thornton research which reported that in the last three years 94 per cent of FTSE 350 companies reported that they had carried out an externally facilitated board review (34 per cent in 2013, 35 per cent in 2012 and 25 per cent in 2011). The report, while reflecting directors' views on the positive impact of external board reviews, also raised concerns about the variable quality of the service provided by external practitioners and stated that it is difficult to differentiate between providers.

The increasing exposure of chairmen and non-executive directors (NEDs) to the media spotlight, is an evident trend, 'fuelled' by further corporate 'mishaps' and what appears to be some boards 'sleeping on the job'. The board chairman and remuneration committee chairman are increasingly preparing for their '15 minutes of fame' as they appear before Select Committees and the media. That corporate governance is now commentated on and followed on 'Twitter' is testament to its increasing profile; it does however further increase the impact and speed with which boards are required to act and react. The reality of journalists and politicians making instant comment on the latest corporate 'crisis' is a new and demanding challenge for chairmen and NEDs at a personal and business level.

All this indicates and underpins the rapidly shifting view of board governance which has been growing and developing momentum over the past four years. The external independent board review every three years is now the *de facto* standard. This has created a significant growth in the practitioner market and stimulated the debate on standards and consistency of approach to the board review. As an increasing number of regulators, investment bodies and other stakeholder groups become more 'reliant' on an objective and robust review process, their ability to 'trust' in a systematic and structured process is all the more important.

Diversity on boards has also increased in significance over the past few years, with female diversity driven by the Davies Report and its goal of 25% female representation by 2015. This has also given a general boost to the issues of diversity in all its forms. A key board review criterion in looking at a board is their diversity of thinking, skillset and resistance to 'groupthink', the latter having been put into play by the FRC in its 2011 Guidance on Board Effectiveness. While achievement of the Davies' targets started slowly, it has gathered momentum and more importantly has changed the mindset amongst chairmen as they design and craft the composition of their boards. Chairmen are for the first time seeing the positive impact of a diversity of viewpoints on their boards. From my own observations, reinforced from conversations with chairmen and company secretaries, where there are two or more women on the board there is a fundamental shift in the board dynamics for the better, with increased effectiveness of the challenge and engagement with the executive team and across the organisation as a whole.

At a strategic level there is also an increasing realisation of the board as a catalyst which goes beyond the creation of a strategic business plan and speaks to the longevity of the organisation. This leads the board to take a much more active role as the guardian and promoter of the strategic values of the organisation, with boards taking a much more serious and closer look at the culture and succession of the business which translates into the need to evaluate the future talent and capability of the organisation. This perspective is focused on both the specific issue of the executive pipeline for women, and the depth of talent and capability of the organisation to 'survive' beyond the tenure of a specific chief executive officer (CEO) and executive team.

All these influences create an environment where the external independent board review takes a pivotal position in the governance arena. The FRC's Developments in Corporate Governance report (December 2013), raised important issues around the standards for undertaking an external board review. It marks the developing maturity of this practitioners' market and that the issue of standards is increasingly to the fore.

At this point I must declare a personal interest in the development of standards over the years. In my current position as chairman of Advanced Boardroom Excellence, we have launched a draft Code of Practice for external independent board reviews (the draft code of practice is set out in this Handbook at **App9**). It is my hope that the Code will be picked up by the industry, and following a consultation process run by the Institute of Chartered Secretaries and Administrators (ICSA), will become an established Code of Practice for the delivery of external Independent board reviews.

It was my view (shared by Sir David Walker) that interested practitioners needed to create a process of best practice which will create an uplifting, challenging and positive experience for the chairman and the whole board – a 'box ticking' exercise will not achieve this. Also with positive progressive examples of 'Codes' from such as the search and remuneration consultancy markets, how can we, the evaluators who seek to evaluate the performance of others, remain exempt?

As the board evaluation market has become more mainstream this need for a Code of Practice for board evaluations which responds to the need for greater clarify for chairmen and company secretaries, is necessary to provide a platform for developing and increasing standards in the board evaluation sector.

Having launched the draft Code of Practice through Advanced Boardroom Excellence, we supported a process of extensive consultation with providers, investors, regulators and interested parties to expand upon our initial code of practice document. The response from a range of interested parties was hugely productive with a growing sense of need to establish a 'benchmark' in what is becoming a much more mature market. The outcome of this was the production of the draft Code of Practice which seeks to begin the discussion to address and resolve this perceived lack of market confidence and instil a more coherent framework to allow companies and consultants to work more effectively together.

With reference to the FRC's guidance on Board Effectiveness, the Code sets out the issues which should drive a high quality board evaluation – professionalism of approach; competencies and capabilities; expectations of the clients by the consultant and clarifying the terms of engagement.

Key features of the Code, which is designed to lead to a significant increase in standards, include proposals for amongst other things:

- not pursuing more than two consecutive assignments in order to remain independent;
- avoiding, or resolving, conflicts of interest;
- being suitably qualified and experienced to conduct an evaluation credibly;
- agreeing with the client how sensitive issues are handled effectively;
- ensuring the outcome of a board evaluation is disclosed in an appropriate manner.

The draft document suggests a mechanism for providing oversight of the application of, and adherence to the Code. The Code will be subject to a process of public consultation to which all market participants and interested participants will be invited to contribute. In a supporting statement for the code, Sir David Walker author of the Walker Report and now chairman of Barclays commented:

> 'The performance of boards is critical to the performance of the entities that they direct and the regular appraisal process will only be value-additive if done to a high standard. This proposal for a Code of Conduct for professional evaluators is a very welcome and timely initiative. Attestation that an evaluation process has been conducted to the standards of the Code should become a valuable ingredient in assuring shareholders and other stakeholders that the process has been insightful and substantive.'

The emergence of the external independent board evaluation is a critical development for the governance community as a truly effective board is one that is open to scrutiny on its effectiveness at a process, skills and behavioural dynamic level. This demands that the effective practitioners use a diverse set of abilities, capabilities and behavioural understanding, to 'benchmark' boards not only on their processes and procedures but also for the interpersonal dynamics of the board.

The independent external board evaluation at least every three years as suggested by the UK Corporate Governance Code (albeit there is a growing view that annually would be more beneficial), arose from the recognition, following the Walker Report, of the systemic failure of boards to effectively oversee their organisations. The Walker Report, also raised the spectre of board behaviour as the marker of an effective board, with the procedural aspects being important, but only a foundation of an effective board.

This critical behavioural aspect was captured well in the FRC's guidance on Board Effectiveness in March 2011, which signposted a shift in the required standards for a board evaluation, with a skilled assessment and understanding of board behavioural dynamics and the artful feedback of development needs, becoming a key skill practised by the best providers in the market. This FRC guidance brought into the board effectiveness evaluation the language of behavioural team dynamics, with the now ubiquities 'group think' taking centre stage, moving on from what had often been more characterised by an audit checklist approach of policies and procedures.

While the board evaluation market has some long established practitioners with this more rounded approach, there has been a significant influx of new practitioners from a range of quarters. The board evaluation market also suffers from a lack of clarity as to what chairmen and company secretaries can expect from a board evaluation, as clearly indicated in a range of research. The perspective from these insights was one of little history of the positive benefits of an external board review and a confusion and lack of clarity amongst chairmen as to the added value an external independent board evaluation could bring.

As chairmen deal with the challenges of the capability, diversity and commitment of their boards, they are looking for an approach which supports and develops both individual directors and the collective board team. Recognising true board effectiveness is not just a matter of governance, important though that is, but of addressing boardroom behaviour at an individual and collective level.

The board is increasingly engaged with ensuring it is able to oversee the organisation to meet the immediate needs of effective performance within an ethical and cultural framework, while at the same time ensuring future strategic building blocks of the organisation are in a place to safeguard the long term development of the organisation.

Being on a board requires a level of sophistication – not just in an interpersonal sense – but a capability to cope with ambiguity, an intellectual acuity to understand quickly what the key issues are, the implications of those issues and how to steer the executive through the appropriate decision making process and execution model. Directors are then required to apply the required level of oversight to ensure all is on course, the risk profile is appropriate and the business has the right people at the leadership level also ensuring the depth of emerging talent below. This latter element of executive succession and development sometimes seems to have fallen down the board agenda of late, pushed aside by more immediate significant issues such as risk – in IT, financial and reputational terms, not to mention the perils of remuneration decisions. It is however, one of the key strategic functions of a board to ensure the stability and continuity of the organisation beyond the tenure of a specific executive cadre.

How can a board ensure it has the robustness and resilience to survive through the various potential challenges thrown their way? Recent corporate history has demonstrated the varied 'slings and arrows of outrageous fortune' which they can encounter. The reality is that the board can never truly anticipate and prepare for all eventualities, but needs to be constantly vigilant, have a fair and transparent process for decision making and manage its key stakeholders at all levels. Little wonder that NEDs now need to put in an average of three times more time than before the financial crisis, with increasing accountability and especially in financial services a constant engagement and dialogue with regulators.

A principal way of preparing and developing boards is assessing the performance of the board and its dynamic, as opposed to the company performance (albeit these two are intrinsically linked – certainly in the mind of the City), with an effective board evaluation which provides a developmental platform for the board. Board evaluation as set out in the corporate governance code with a 'comply or explain' philosophy has moved more consistently to 'comply'. Boards need to become increasingly focused upon their policies, processes and performance. The general counsel/company secretary once viewed as a 'back office' or ancillary function, is now viewed as a vital function for keeping the board on track. The company secretary is increasingly becoming the chairman's right hand person.

A truly effective evaluation requires a high level of skill as it examines all aspects of the board's performance and turns a 'spotlight' on the dynamic processes and governance. This is not however the full picture, it is the skill of the chairman and breadth of capabilities of the NEDs that will dictate whether the board dynamics will deliver the appropriate behaviours to ensure the board is operating at its optimum. The composition of the board is therefore key, the right skills and capabilities need to be present and then 'artfully orchestrated'. The 'heavy lifting' of a board's work is usually done in the committees. Ensuring the interface of the committees and the engagement and explanation of the decisions to the whole board is crucial. This ensures the delegated authority is being exercised appropriately; and terms of reference are key, as they provide the framework for effectiveness.

Evaluating a board effectively is therefore a complex 'art and science', with chairmen seeing the external independent evaluation as a serious and important aspect of their own and collective team 'professionalism'. All of which has created a concern, need and momentum for standards of quality and engagement within the board evaluation marketplace. Additionally the pressure from chairmen, NEDs, regulators and the investor community for a credible board evaluation process has made the integrity of this process increasingly important.

As we move into the future of corporate governance, the issue that continues to exercise chairmen and their boards is the effective development of the board to meet its emerging challenges. The challenge of diversity, as mentioned previously, is ever present, not just in relation to genetics but more broadly in relation to skill set and diversity of thought. Many chairmen would like NEDs who have CEO experience; however, recruiting serving CEOs can present conflicts regarding time, availability and priorities. The landscape is changing so quickly that retired CEOs' currency may not remain relevant for very long. Issues such as cyber-crime, IT issues, digitisation, customers and culture now feature heavily on boards' agendas alongside strategy, financial performance and risk.

Chairing remuneration committees is also beginning to be viewed as not only a reputational risk but also in some regulated businesses a 'poisoned chalice'. Public stakeholdings in major banks have fettered those organisations' autonomy in relation to pay and rations, with much public backlash whenever the thorny topic of 'bankers' bonuses' is raised.

The issue of succession both of the executives and NEDs also remains a key challenge. The need to avoid 'group think' is to the forefront of many chairmens' minds. Whilst this can be addressed on many boards by hiring a diverse range of people, in regulated entities the regulators frequently insist on industry knowledge. It could be argued therefore that by definition these boards will become homogeneous and prone to the very malaise chairmen seek to avoid.

Against this background, directors and corporate governance specialists must set the bar of their own understanding of corporate governance issues even higher than ever before. As ever this Handbook provides the essential and up-to-date reference guide in a user-friendly way that is accessible to an ever increasing range of interested readers.

Helen Pitcher
Chairman, IDDAS
www.iddas.com

Contents

Part B: Guest Chapters

Part C: Understanding Corporate Governance

Appendices

Table of Statutes

References are to paragraph number and Appendix. References in **bold** *indicate where material is set out in part or in full.*

Table of Statutory Instruments

References are to paragraph number and Appendix. References in **bold** *indicate where material is set out in part or in full.*

Table of Cases

References are to paragraph number.

ADVANCED BOARDROOM
EXCELLENCE

Advanced Boardroom Excellence is a board effectiveness consultancy dedicated to individual and collective director effectiveness.

We are passionate about the development and improvement of boardroom standards, behaviour and ethics. Our experience as a leading business effectiveness consultancy is focused on supporting chairmen, CEO's and directors and is underpinned by continuous research. We utilise the skills required by all directors by challenging, supporting, directing and executing, coupled with intellectual rigour and behavioural sensitivity.

This is achieved through:

BOARD DYNAMICS AND GOVERNANCE ALIGNMENT: an industry leading approach to independent board reviews and governance best practice including board behavioural development, board level reputational and cultural management.

TRANSFORMATIONAL PERFORMANCE COACHING: a dynamic and strategic approach to executive coaching, direct level assessment-development, and career management.

LEADERSHIP EFFECTIVENESS AND IMPACT: supporting boards and leadership teams to embed and accelerate their impact on the organisation, covering board and leadership team alignment, leadership impact programmes and emerging talent development.

Part A:
Effective Boards and Directors

Chapter A1

The Effective Board

The importance of quality information for the board A1.1

There are many lessons to be learnt from the global financial crisis. One is that frequently boards did not adequately understand the risks their companies were running. In part that was a consequence of the ineffectiveness of individual non-executive board members, whether due to inadequate experience, inadequate time commitment or lack of willingness to challenge robustly; as well as a consequence of a wide willingness to take uncontrolled risks which should have been unacceptable. Then there was the problem of executive board members acting more like executives than as board members, always carefully falling into line behind the chief executive at board meetings.

An important contributor to the crisis was the poor quality of information coming to the board. Boards were insufficiently able to discern whether the policies of the board were being implemented by management. Bad news tended to be suppressed from coming to the board, or was given a gloss which misrepresented it. Boards were in the dark about 'banana skins', known or not to management, that were deflecting the company from achieving its goals, or were at risk of doing so in the future.

A key issue is how boards get the assurance they need. An open, constructive dialogue with management together with free flow of information from management to the board, is the first essential.

There is a type of circular process as illustrated in Figure 1. From available data, information may be drawn. Information should be analysed and the analysis used as a basis for decision taking. Decisions lead to actions and data is collected on the results of those actions. And so it cycles round.

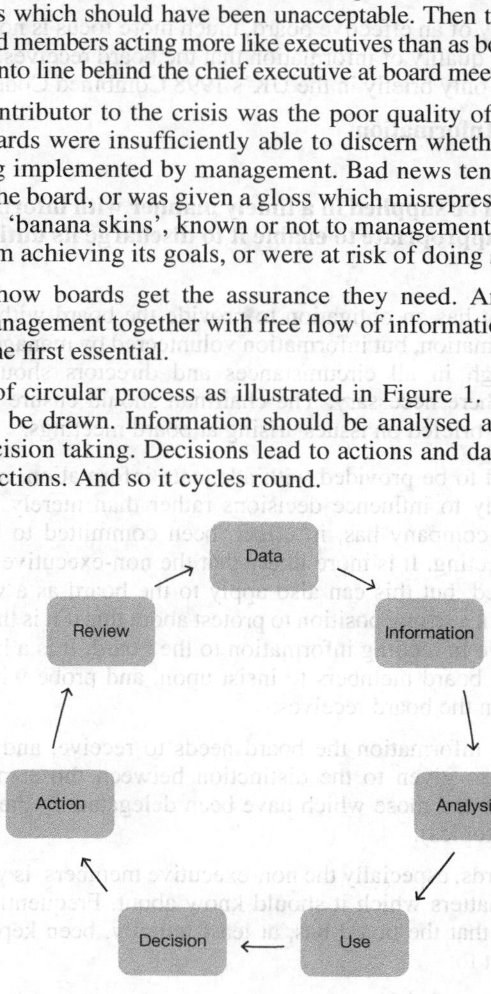

Some entities have a surfeit of data, but inadequate information drawn from that data[1]. Some have abundant information, but inadequate analysis using that information. Some entities suffer from abundant analysis, but a relative inability to make decisions based upon that analysis. Others may be quite good at making decisions, but poor at ensuring that the requisite action flows from the decisions that had been made. If action is not taken well, then results are unlikely to be up to expectations. Certainly all of these elements need to be present proportionately to each other; and each should be a sound basis for the element which follows it.

Management teams and boards should consider whether they have the balance right between the components in Figure 1. Equally important is the quality of each of these components and their seamless relationship with each other. This is important at executive levels across the business. It is also important for the board to consider whether the balance, quality, content and relationship of these components are carefully engineered to meet the board's needs.

As an essential quality of an effective board, much more focus is now being given to the importance of the quality of information that the board receives. Just a few years ago this was covered only briefly in the UK's 1998 Combined Code, as follows:

> **'A.4 Supply of Information**
>
> **Principle**
>
> **The board should be supplied in a timely manner with information in a form and of a quality appropriate to enable it to discharge its duties.**
>
> **Code Provision**
>
> A.4.1 Management has an obligation to provide the board with appropriate and timely information, but information volunteered by management is unlikely to be enough in all circumstances and directors should make further enquiries where necessary. The chairman should ensure that all directors are properly briefed on issues arising at board meetings.'

Board members need to be provided with adequate information, made available to them in time properly to influence decisions rather than merely to ratify courses of action which the company has, in effect, been committed to by the executive prior to the board meeting. It is more likely that the non-executive directors will be inadequately informed, but this can also apply to the board as a whole. Executive directors may not be in a strong position to protest about this if it is the chief executive who is being selective in feeding information to the board. It is a key responsibility of the non-executive board members to insist upon, and probe with respect to, the quality of information the board receives.

In determining what information the board needs to receive, and the timing of it, consideration needs to given to the distinction between those matters which are reserved to the board and those which have been delegated by the board (**A1.10** to **A1.17** address these topics).

A key anxiety of boards, especially the non-executive members, is whether the board is informed on all matters which it should know about. Frequently there are cases where it is apparent that the board has, at least initially, been kept in the dark, for instance, with respect to:

- internal and external risk;
- off balance sheet transactions;
- contingent liabilities;

- expected or current litigation;
- contractual breaches;
- compensation claims;
- undisclosed liabilities;
- late payment of tax;
- unprovided losses;

and so on. Once the bond of trust has been broken between, on the one hand, the chief executive and finance director in particular and, on the other hand, the non-executive directors, it is very hard to mend. The bond is threatened both by withholding information from the board and also by providing the board with information which subsequently is shown to have been unreliable. Non-executive directors have a solemn responsibility to ask the right questions, to probe when they have concerns and not to be content with unclear explanations.

It may not be that the executive is deliberately misleading the board: it might be that the executive is not in possession of the information the board needs to know. What is not clearly understood cannot be clearly expressed. Or the executive may be guilty of oversight or denial. Boards, as well as board committees, are likely to need to ensure they receive advice from independent, external parties to supplement the information and views they obtain from the executive team.

Audit committees may review the quality of information that the board receives:

> 'One of the major requirements for good corporate governance is that the board of the company receives the information it needs to take the decisions it has to take; that this information is reported in a digestible form and that it is accurate. This is something the audit committee looks at on a regular basis, though it is equally a concern of the whole board who take great interest in this matter.'[2]

This chimes with the 1998 Hampel Committee's observation that:

> 'We endorse the view of the Cadbury committee (Report 4.14) that the effectiveness of non-executive directors (indeed, of all directors) turns, to a considerable extent on the quality of the information they receive.'[3]

However, beyond highly specific obligations to review information (for instance, with respect to the financial statements of the company, or with respect to whistleblowing), neither the latest version of the UK Corporate Governance Code (set out in full at **App1**) nor the FRC's guidance on audit committees gives the audit committee a specific remit to review the quality of information which the board receives. This is not to say that the audit committee should not undertake this.

With respect to information on internal control, in the US the Public Oversight Board advised that audit committees should:

> 'obtain a written report from management on the effectiveness of internal control over financial reporting and establish specific expectations with management and the internal and external auditors about the qualitative information needs of the committee related to internal control. Discussions of internal control should include the effects of technology on current and future information systems.'

In Chapter **G1**, we suggest that, especially in the context of implementing Turnbull, the board should receive regular information on the performance of the entity with respect to the key risks of the business. This is in addition to regular management accounting information which should come to the board.

Good practice is for an attractively presented, bound set of management accounts to be produced monthly and to be circulated to board members. If the board meets monthly, this management accounting pack ('MAP') can be presented to the board monthly by the finance director. (We consider MAPs further in **A1.2**.) We suggest it is likely that it should include the sections shown below.

Contents of MAP for the board A1.2

- Performance summary.
- Key financial indicators, including liquidity and solvency indicators.
- Key risk indicators.
- Group profit and loss.
- Segmental profit and loss.
- Margins analysis.
- Cashflow analysis.
- Headcount.
- Health and safety statistics.
- Avoidable losses.
- Other financial information.
- Performance summary for each business segment.
- Treasury.
- Share performance and market comparables.

Each section should commence with a narrative summary highlighting the main points and trends contained within the data which should follow. The use of colour and graphical representations will improve the clarity of the MAP, and is to be recommended.

As with other board papers, it is important that board members receive the MAP a few days before the board meeting so that they can prepare themselves properly.

Categories of information the board needs A1.3

In today's environment the information the board needs goes well beyond conventional management accounting information, important though that is. Sometimes other forms of information are even more important. Of these, there are four categories which stand out in terms of being essential, but all too often are inadequate:

- Key performance indicators (KPIs) designed to enable the board to monitor the success of the executive in managing the risks which the board considers to be the major risks facing the business.
- Information on board performance. Other categories of information (such as management accounting information, risk management KPIs, and the type of information discussed in this section) all throw light on board performance. In addition the board needs information more directly focused on how the board conducts itself – such as the attendance record of individual directors.

- Information which tracks corporate reputation and the quality and importance of relationships with stakeholders (see **C3.20** to **C3.23**). For a listed or other company, the principal stakeholder is the shareholder (see below).
- Information which tracks the board's success in delivering value to the shareholders, which is the subject of this section.

We recommend that the traditional MAP which the board regularly receives should be extended to include key information in the above categories. If this information is not reaching the board, it is likely that the board is not giving these important matters sufficient focus. One can measure the importance which the board is giving to a matter by the quality of the information the board receives regularly on it, and the extent to which that information is discussed at the board.

A quick self-test, that any director can do, is to consider whether he or she knows how the company shapes up with respect to the performance measures on delivering value to shareholders discussed in this section.

Historic data, projections and peer group data **A1.4**

Beyond bringing information to the board about shareholder value, the board should set targets to achieve in this area, approve strategy designed to deliver on these targets, and monitor success in doing so.

Much more so than with conventional management accounting information, measures on delivering value to shareholders are particularly illuminating when historical data stretching back a number of years[4] and forward projections[5] are placed before the board alongside current information. Care must be taken to account for the distortion of the statistics which may result, for instance, from an acquisition, a change in the issued share capital, and so on. We should also be alert to the sensitivity of the numbers to the particular date on which the data is struck – for instance, market capitalisation can fluctuate widely in response to volatility of share price. Share price volatility in turn may be a consequence of low volumes of trading when there are not many buyers or sellers in the market.

Much of the information on shareholder value discussed in this section is more informative if comparable data of a peer group of companies is also presented. This is particularly the case with respect to information on current and projected performance.

There are many different facets to measuring shareholder value. As with so many performance measures, it is necessary to look at performance across an array of pertinent measures, as relative success in one may be at the expense of relative failure in another – it is the entire tapestry that gives the picture, not the individual threads.

Graphical representations of shareholder value **A1.5**

Graphical representations provide a useful visual impression. In Chart 1, for a hypothetical listed company we show past trends in market capitalisation,[6] P/E ratio[7] and profit before tax.

Chart 1 A1.6

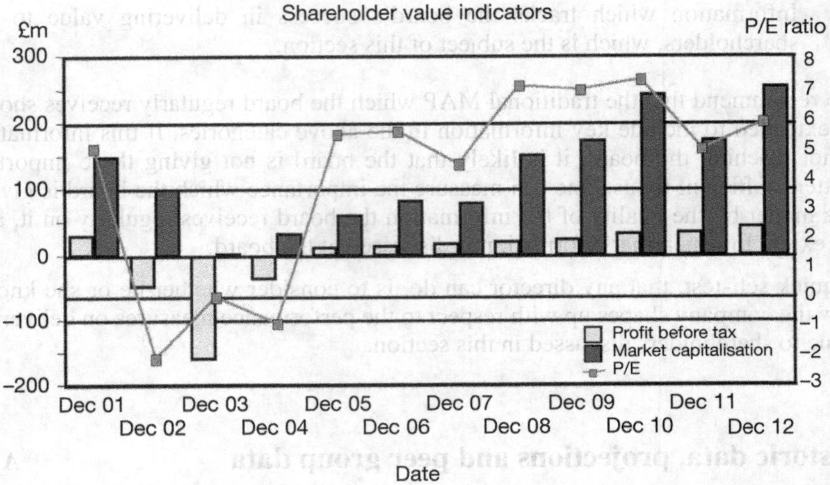

The same basic data is presented in a different way in Chart 2 to reveal how closely, for this fictional company, share price tracks profitability. The charts also show that profit before tax has, for this company, grown quite steadily.

Chart 2 A1.7

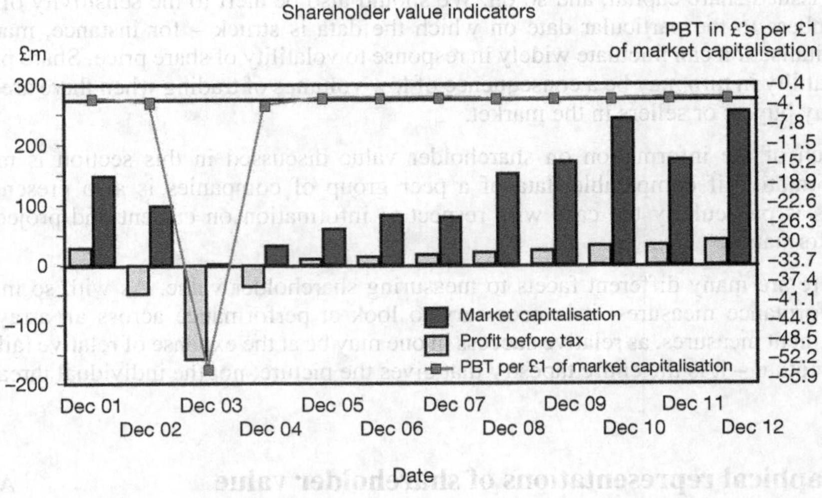

Information on shareholder value **A1.8**

We give below a checklist of information which relates closely to whether the board is delivering value to shareholders. Our suggestion is that boards select, from these types of information, the information they will monitor and interpret regularly in order to satisfy themselves that they are performing well in terms of shareholder value. Most of these measures should be applied over time, with historical data going back four years or so, and projections forward also by four years or so.

1. General company performance data which impacts directly or indirectly on shareholder value

1.1 Profit before tax
1.2 Profit after tax
1.3 Net assets (per balance sheet)
1.4 Total shareholder value
1.5 Cost to income ratio
1.6 Share of market
1.7 Revenue gains plus cost savings
1.8 Free cash
1.9 Projected tax rate
1.10 Peer group comparisons with respect to most of the above.

2. Share information

2.1 Shareholder concentration (50% in hands of top 5 institutional investors; 75% in hands of top 15)
2.2 Volumes of trading in shares (share price volatile if volumes small)
2.3 Peer group comparisons with respect to the above.

3. Share performance

3.1 Share price
- Graph showing monthly movements for the last four years
- Graph showing 90-day average movements over last four years

3.2 Earnings per share (EPS) – P/E ratios (based on profit before tax) – and minimum and maximum P/E ratios over the past 12 months
3.3 Projected growth rate in earnings per share
3.4 Price to book (market capitalisation, divided by net worth – a common measure in financial companies)
3.5 Net assets per share (excluding goodwill)
3.6 Return on equity (RoE) (profit after tax divided by opening shareholder funds (capital and reserves) at the start of the period)
3.7 Declared dividend
3.8 Yield (total dividend as a percentage of market capitalisation)
3.9 Total shareholder return (comprises yield (annualised dividend yield over time, at present value), plus movement in market capitalisation (annualised change in 'share price x number of shares on issue' at present value, after adjusting for the impact of new share issues during the measurement period), adjusted for changes in share capital either by new issues or company buy back of its share capital apportioned annually over the measurement period, expressed at present value)
3.10 Peer group comparisons with respect to most of the above.

4. **Brokers' reports** (brokers' forecasts can be shown separately and also the consensus view of the brokers taken together)
   - 4.1 Brokers' forecasts of target market price of shares over the next three years
   - 4.2 Brokers' forecasts of profit before tax over the next three years
   - 4.3 Brokers' forecasts of earnings per share over the next three years
   - 4.4 Brokers' forecasts of target price in 12 months time
   - 4.5 Brokers' recommendations on 'Strong buy', 'Buy', 'Add', 'Hold' or 'Sell' etc
   - 4.6 Brokers' recommendations on whether 'Undervalued' …
   - 4.7 Plot for comparable group the P/E ratio (vertical axis) against EPS increase (% – horizontal axis)
   - 4.8 Peer group comparisons with respect to most of the above.

Shareholder value information which could usefully appear in the MAP which the board receives A1.9

1. Commentary (anything on movements, comparables etc):
   - Major movements in the month
   - New/exiting institutional investors
   - New broker reports
   - Comparables moves.
2. Measures, selected from the Table (above).
3. Comparables.

With respect to comparable companies (peer group) six-month relative price movements, price:book, prospective P/E and projected EPS growth rates.

Schedule of matters to be reserved to the board A1.10

It is good practice for a company to know what decisions need to be made by the board itself. As far back as 1992 the Cadbury Code of Best Practice for corporate governance included a Code Provision that stated:

> 'The board should have a formal schedule of matters specifically reserved to it for decision to ensure that the direction of the company is firmly in its hands.'[8]

After the Hampel Committee reported,[9] the Cadbury Code was replaced in the UK by the 1998 Combined Code which included a Code Provision that stated:

> 'The board should have a formal schedule of matters specifically reserved to it for decision.'[10]

Provisions of the Combined Code are subordinate to overarching Principles. In this case, the 1998 Principle was:

> 'Every … company should be headed by an effective board which should lead and control the company.'[11]

The latest version of the UK Corporate Governance Code (**App1**) now expresses it like this:

'SECTION A: LEADERSHIP

A.1 The Role of the Board

Main Principle

Every company should be headed by an effective board which is collectively responsible for the long-term success of the company.

Supporting Principles

The board's role is to provide entrepreneurial leadership of the company within a framework of prudent and effective controls which enables risk to be assessed and managed. The board should set the company's strategic aims, ensure that the necessary financial and human resources are in place for the company to meet its objectives and review management performance. The board should set the company's values and standards and ensure that its obligations to its shareholders and others are understood and met.

All directors must act in what they consider to be the best interests of the company, consistent with their statutory duties.[12]

Code Provisions

A.1.1 The board should meet sufficiently regularly to discharge its duties effectively. There should be a formal schedule of matters specifically reserved for its decision. The annual report should include a statement of how the board operates, including a high level statement of which types of decisions are to be taken by the board and which are to be delegated to management.'

Strictly, all of the above applies only to UK public companies with a premium listing, those companies being required by the listing rules to disclose in their annual reports how they are ensuring they apply the Main Principles of the UK Code (**App1**) and whether or not they comply with the Provisions (and, if not, why not). But the Code is sound counsel even for listed companies with a standard listing, AIM companies, non-listed and smaller companies as well as other types of organisation, if applied flexibly; and certainly the sentiments reproduced in bold above are important even for the smallest non-listed company.

Company law dictates that some matters are the responsibility of the board (see Chapter **D1**). Good corporate governance dictates that further matters also should be. Companies' own memoranda and articles of association and shareholders agreements may add further matters.

The two examples given at **A1.12**, of schedules of matters reserved to the board, are attempts to produce practical, useful guidance. They are not complete lists of the important responsibilities of a board although they relate very closely to these. The responsibilities of a board include those matters which the board may delegate to others – authority, not responsibility, is delegated. The lists are restricted to those matters which it is likely that a board will decide not to delegate – in other words, those matters on which the board is likely to wish to reserve to itself the powers of decision.

General responsibilities of boards A1.11

More general, more comprehensive advice on the responsibilities of boards can be found elsewhere.[13, 14] For instance, a board's responsibilities include:[15]

- the legal requirement for directors to prepare financial statements for each financial year which give a true and fair view of the state of affairs of the company (or group) as at the end of the financial year and of the profit and loss for that period;
- the responsibility of the directors for maintaining adequate accounting records, for safeguarding the assets of the company (or group), and for preventing and detecting fraud and other irregularities;
- confirmation that suitable accounting policies, consistently applied and supported by reasonable and prudent judgements and estimates, have been used in the preparation of the financial statements; and
- confirmation that applicable accounting standards have been followed, subject to any material departures disclosed and explained in the notes to the accounts.

Neither should these example lists be interpreted as comprehensive guides to the responsibilities of individual directors.

Schedules of matters reserved to the board A1.12

Example 1

This schedule was drafted by a recently appointed non-executive chairman, for his second board meeting. At that meeting the suggested schedule was adopted by the board.

At a meeting of the board on [date] it was resolved by the board that only the board can approve:

	Reserved items:
1. Strategy	
1.1	Strategic decisions which are, or may be significant, in terms of future profitability.
1.2	Any decision to commence, discontinue or modify significantly any business activity or to enter or withdraw from a particular market sector.
2. Capital and finance	
2.1	Decisions on share capital changes (authorised and/or issued).
2.2	Decisions on investments or capital projects by the company or its subsidiaries where the principal sum or cost exceeds *£n*.
2.3	Decisions to acquire or dispose of company assets where the acquisition cost, disposal proceeds or profit or loss on disposal exceeds *£n*, or which would be likely to be regarded as significant by the board.

2. Capital and finance – *contd*	
2.4	Decisions over new borrowing or significant amendments to the terms and conditions of existing borrowings.
2.5	Decisions on the adoption of treasury and risk management policies.
3. Terms of reference etc	
3.1	Decisions on the wording of any changes to be recommended to the memorandum and articles of association and any other constitutional documents of the company.
3.2	Decisions on the creation, maintenance, terms of reference, leadership and membership of board committees.
3.3	Initial consideration of any matter (such as a company name change) which has to be decided by special resolution of the company.
4. Delegation of authority	
4.1	Deciding delegation of authority to board and other committees such as an Assets & Liabilities Committee.
4.2	Decisions to grant, or vary, power, role, responsibilities and authority levels to individual directors, especially the chairman and the managing director; and in so doing to specify by implication the ones that the board reserves to itself.
5. Appointments	
5.1	Decisions to appoint or remove a member of the board, or the company secretary, or the head of the internal audit function, following proper procedures agreed by the board.
5.2	Decision to appoint or remove a director from the chairmanship of the board.
5.3	Decisions to appoint or remove the auditors or other professional advisors.
6. Contracts and transactions etc	
6.1	Decisions to commit the company to directors' contracts, including the terms of their appointment and remuneration.
6.2	Decisions to enter into any other significant contracts.
6.3	Significant decisions relating to any transaction in which a director has a direct or indirect material interest.
6.4	Any matter where a director's (or directors') personal interests might conflict with his or her duty to the company. eg a political donation.
6.5	Significant decisions on any contract or transaction material to the company falling outside the above categories.

7. Disclosure	
7.1	Decisions to adopt financial information for publication (eg the annual financial statements, prospectuses etc).
7.2	The presentation of reports and accounts to shareholders at the Annual General Meeting.
7.3	Decisions on anything that is likely to generate significant publicity and affect the image of the company.
8. Meetings	
8.1	Deciding policy governing the frequency, notice, purpose, conduct, duration and reporting of board meetings; and, especially, the setting of agendas.

Example 2

In compliance with Provision A.1.1 of the UK Corporate Governance Code, it was resolved by the board that:	
1.	Only the board can approve:
1.1	The acquisition and disposal of group assets where the acquisition cost, disposal proceeds or profit or loss on disposal exceeds £5m, or would be likely to be regarded as significant by the board.
1.2	Strategic decisions which are, or may be significant, in terms of future profitability.
1.3	Investments or capital projects by a member of the group where the principal sum or cost exceeds £5m.
1.4	Any decision to commence, discontinue or modify significantly any business activity or to enter or withdraw from a particular market sector.
1.5	Any significant contracts.
1.6	Decisions over new borrowing or significant amendments to the terms and conditions of existing borrowings.
1.7	The appointment or removal of auditors or other professional advisors.
1.8	Any transaction in which a director has a direct or indirect material interest.
1.9	Anything which is likely to generate significant publicity and affect the image of the group.
1.10	Any transaction material to the Group falling outside other categories.
1.11	The granting to, or variation of, authority levels for executive directors.

1.12	The implementation or operation of group treasury and risk management policies including the delegation of authority to an Assets & Liabilities Committee.
1.13	The appointment or removal of a member of the board or the company secretary.[16]
2.	Any three of the chairman and the non-executive directors be appointed a Nomination Committee.[17] Only candidates nominated by the Committee shall be appointed as members of the board.
3.	That, in addition to any expenses payable in accordance with the Company's Articles of Association, the Company will reimburse directors for the reasonable costs of obtaining independent professional advice on matters directly connected with their directorship of the Company up to a limit of £5,000 per director per annum (or such greater sum as the Chairman may approve).[18] See also **A2.20**.
4.	That the Terms of Reference of the Audit Committee, as approved by the board on [date] should be extended by including the following: 'The Committee is able to obtain outside professional advice and, if necessary, to invite outsiders with relevant experience to attend its meetings.'[19]
5.	It was noted that in compliance with the Code, James Green has been nominated the senior non-executive member of the board.[20]

Delegation of authority guidelines **A1.13**

Delegation of authority guidelines (which, alternatively, may be called authorisation guidelines or concurrence guidelines) are the policies of the company on delegation of authority. They specify where decisions should be taken on important matters and whether these decisions are to be taken upon the recommendation of another or after consultation with another. That they are adopted by formal board resolution is a valuable way of contributing to the board being in effective overall control of the business. We suggest they should be reviewed by the board annually – both to remind the board of what is board policy and to provide an opportunity for amendment.

How authority guidelines follow corporate governance best practice **A1.14**

When considering the necessity and justification for establishing and implementing a policy on delegated authorities, the overall requirement to create a valid and realistic risk management and internal control environment should be borne in mind. The board needs to know that there is effective risk management and internal control, even though it is unusual for a listed company board to publish an overall opinion on this.

Approach to developing guidelines A1.15

The nature and form of any business organisation is naturally subject to ongoing development and change; accordingly, the contents of these authority delegation policies should be subject to periodic review in order to ensure that they remain relevant and realistic.

Guidelines such as these may usefully be classified into major areas and documented in table form (with a table for each major area).

While it is important that companies make sure that any guidelines they develop are tailored to their requirements, the following example may be a useful starting point.

Example of authority guidelines A1.16

The following tables represent the Board Policies on Delegation of Authority recently drafted for use within a large company. They have been developed in relation to both the prevailing organisational structure and the spirit of the company's original 'Concurrence guidelines'. The relative financial limits have also been reviewed and updated where necessary. The old Concurrence guidelines indicated that concurrence was not required with respect to transactions and decisions which had already been approved as part of a budget or business plan; that concept, though entirely valid, has not been carried through to these guidelines. The company was a German-based multinational, and the two-tier board structure shows through to a limited extent – requiring minor modifications (referred to in the footnotes) for a unitary board situation. The German approach to directing and managing tends to be more thoroughly controlled than the UK approach, but UK companies should consider whether they might benefit from adopting a rather similar approach.

In this example, the nominated authorisation responsibility for each of the noted activities can be defined under any of the headed columns which the tables use. The nature of the responsibility is denoted by use of the alphabetic coding which is explained in the following paragraph. Whenever necessary, the coding is augmented by specific, stated limit values or by more discursive explanatory notes.

The alphabetic codes, used in the authorisation responsibility columns, have the following meanings:

O – Originated by	This denotes the potential point of origin for a requirement, transaction etc. It is possible to use this code in combination with others where alternative courses of action are possible. Additionally, a specific economic event may have a number of potential points of origin within the organisation. Where there are either a number of potential points of origination or all the points may apply, we have avoided illustrating every combination for the sake of clarity.

R – On recommendation of	This normally relates to a proposal or activity, which may have originated elsewhere, which should be subject to formalised assessment and authorisation before progressing to the next authority stage. An example would be the recommendation of an appropriate committee prior to submission to the board of directors for final sanction.
C – After consultation with	At any stage prior to final concurrence it may either be desirable or necessary to obtain the views of affected parties. Beyond the obvious benefit of involving and motivating those affected, this process can add quality to the understanding of the relative situation and the solution being proposed.
D – Decision	The use of this category indicates where the responsibility for the final decision lies. Ideally there should be a formal process of signifying and documenting that actions, transactions, projects etc are officially authorised to proceed.

The delegations of authority have been classified into nine sets, each corresponding to one of the tables. The tables are as follows:

Table 1	Board affairs
Table 2	Strategy
Table 3	Communications
Table 4	Accounting and variances
Table 5	Published statements and other key documents
Table 6	Audit and control
Table 7	Personnel
Table 8	Appointments

Authorisation tables

Table 1

Board affairs

1.	Board Affairs	Chairman	Board	Board Committee	Executive Committee	Country Manager	Divisional Manager	Regional or Functional Head
1.1	Amendments to the company's constitution (Memorandum & Articles of Association, or equivalent)		R Decision of members in general meeting					
1.2	Whether the posts of Chairman and Chief Executive should be combined or separate[1]		D					
1.3	Where the posts of Chairman and Chief Executive are combined, which director is to be the recognised senior member[2]		D of non-executive directors only					

[1] Where a board is entirely non-executive, this is not an issue. The *Combined Code* (1998) read:
'A2 Chairman and CEO
Principle There are two key tasks at the top of every public company – the running of the board and the executive responsibility for the running of the company business. There should be a clear division of responsibilities at the head of the company which will ensure a balance of power and authority, such that no one individual has unfettered powers of decision.
Code Provision:
A.2.1 A decision to combine the posts of chairman and chief executive officer in one person should be publicly justified. Whether the posts are held by different people or the same person, there should be a strong and independent non-executive element on the board, with a recognised senior member other than the chairman to whom concern can be conveyed. The chairman, chief executive and senior independent director should be identified in the annual report.'

[2] To review all policy matters not specifically reserved to the Board or to another Board Committee.

1.	**Board Affairs**	**Chairman**	**Board**	**Board Committee**	**Executive Committee**	**Country Manager**	**Divisional Manager**	**Regional or Functional Head**
1.4	The appointment and replacement of the Chairman of the Board		D					
1.5	The number of non-executive and executive main Board directors		D with effective ratification by members					
1.6	The appointment and removal of a Board director, together with severance terms		D with effective ratification by members					
1.7	Severance terms on removal of a director		D					
1.8	What shall be the standing committees of the Board, eg: – Audit committee – Assets & Liabilities committee		D in all cases					

1.	Board Affairs	Chairman	Board	Board Committee	Executive Committee	Country Manager	Divisional Manager	Regional or Functional Head
	– Chairman's committee – Community Affairs Committee – Group Operations committee – Ethics committee – Finance committee – Nominations committee – Personnel committee – Standing Orders committee							
1.9	Who shall be the Chairman of the Board committees	(R)[3]	D	(D or R)[3]				
1.10	Who shall be the members of the Board committees	D						

[3] Board may wish to consult with, or follow the recommendation of (a) the Chairman of the Board, or (b) the committee itself. Sometimes, the committee itself is authorised to appoint its own Chairman.

1.	Board Affairs	Chairman	Board	Board Committee	Executive Committee	Country Manager	Divisional Manager	Regional or Functional Head
1.11	Policy on Board members, as individual directors, seeking outside professional advice, including the financial limits set to this		D					
1.12	The frequency and scheduling of the meetings of the Board	D						
1.13	The frequency and scheduling of the meetings of the Board's committees			D by the committee chairman				
1.14	Agenda of Board meetings	D						
1.15	The appointment and removal of the secretary to the Board		D					

Table 2

Strategy

2.	Strategy	Chairman	Board	Board Committee	Executive Committee	Country Manager	Divisional Manager	Regional or Functional Head
2.1	Major decisions on strategy, reorganisations/ restructuring		D		R			
2.2	Board policies on delegation of authority		D		C			
2.3	The nature of the business, including adoption of new technologies		D		R			
2.4	Approval of significant transactions which have material financial, political, commercial, legal, employee relations or environmental implications now or in the future		D	R	R			

2.	Strategy	Chairman	Board	Board Committee	Executive Committee	Country Manager	Divisional Manager	Regional or Functional Head
2.5	Transactions which have a significant effect on entities outside the Area executing the transaction				D			
2.6	Policy re future acquisitions and divestments		D		R			
2.7	Actual acquisitions, mergers and divestments		D		R			
2.8	Significant disposals of assets		D	R Assets & Liabilities Committee	C			
2.9	Management buy-outs		D	R[4]	C			
2.10	Business principles and ethics, including approval of a written Code of Corporate Conduct		D	R[5]	R/C			

[4] Only if the Board has an Ethics committee.
[5] Only if the Board has an Ethics committee.

2.	Strategy	Chairman	Board	Board Committee	Executive Committee	Country Manager	Divisional Manager	Regional or Functional Head
2.11	Insurance cover policy:							
	1 Directors' liability insurance		D	R Finance committee				
	2 Officers' liability insurance		D	R Finance committee				
	3 Fidelity bonding insurance (limit of cover, and posts to be covered)			D	R Finance committee			
	4 Key person cover							
	5 General insurance		D	R Finance committee	D			
2.12	Arrangements for the management of land, buildings and other assets					D		
2.13	Management and control of stocks							D
2.14	Health and safety arrangements		D		R			

Table 3

Communications

3.	Strategy	Chairman	Board	Board Committee	Executive Committee	Country Manager	Divisional Manager	Regional or Functional Head
3.1	Communication of policies (especially those covered in Table 2)				D	R	R	
3.2	Determining the Terms of Reference for each of the Board committees		D	R[6]				
3.3	Determination of Minutes of Board meetings		D					
3.4	Management and control of computer systems and facilities				D			R Head of I.T. etc
3.5	Data protection arrangements							R Head of I.T.

[6] Optional to ask for Recommendation of the committee itself.

Table 4

Accounting and variances

4.	Strategy	Chairman	Board	Board Committee	Executive Committee	Country Manager	Divisional Manager	Regional or Functional Head
4.1	Review and acceptance of outturns, in general				D[7]	D[7]	D[7]	D[7]
4.2	Post investment appraisal				D[7]	D[7]	D[7]	D[7]
4.3	Post project evaluation				D[7]	D[7]	D[7]	D[7]
4.4	Negative variances of > 5% from the net income of an approved budget or business plan: – > $1 million[8]				Must be specifically identified and brought to the attention of the Executive Committee			

[7] Depending upon their nature and scale.

[8] Previous Concurrence Guidelines required concurrence of the Executive Committee upon identification if >5% of net income, and additionally required it to be brought to the attention of the Board if >10% of net income.

4.	Strategy	Chairman	Board	Board Committee	Executive Committee	Country Manager	Divisional Manager	Regional or Functional Head
	–>$1 million			Must be specifically identified and brought to the attention of the Board Executive Committee B				
4.5	Excess from an approved capital investment budget:[9]							
	–>10%				D			
	–>20%			D				
4.6	Consideration as to whether the company remains a going concern		D	R Finance committee				

[9] Previous Concurrence Guidelines required concurrence of the Executive Committee upon identification if variance was >10%, and additionally it had to be brought to the Board's attention if >20%.

Table 5

Published statements and other key documents

5.	Strategy	Chairman	Board	Board Committee	Executive Committee	Country Manager	Divisional Manager	Regional or Functional Head
5.1	The time of publication of published statements		D	R Finance committee				
5.2	The time of statutory general and other shareholder meetings		D		C			
5.3	Approval of the confidential annual report and accounts		D	R Audit committee				
5.4	Approval of any other published reports and accounts – such as prospectuses		D	R Audit committee				
5.5	Approval of the less confidential Annual Review		D	R	C			
5.6	Signing and sealing of documents				D10	D[10]	D[10]	D[10]

[10] Depending upon their nature and the size of any commitment which is involved.

Table 6

Audit and control

6.	Strategy	Chairman	Board	Board Committee	Executive Committee	Country Manager	Divisional Manager	Regional or Functional Head
6.1	The appointment and removal of the Group Chief Internal Auditor			D Audit committee				
6.2	The appointment and removal of the external auditors		D to be ratified by the members	R				
6.3	Compensation for the external auditors		D to be ratified by the members					
6.4	Review and approval of the plans, scope, quality and report of the external auditors			D Audit committee				
6.5	Plans and scope of internal audit work			D Audit committee				R Chief Internal Auditor

6.	Strategy	Chairman	Board	Board Committee	Executive Committee	Country Manager	Divisional Manager	Regional or Functional Head
6.6	Review of the adequacy of the company's systems of internal control, including computerised information system controls and security			D Audit committee	C			C Chief Internal Auditor
6.7	Review and acceptance of the external auditors' management letters			D Audit Committee				
6.8	Review and acceptance of the results of internal audit work			D Audit Committee	C	C	C	C

Table 7

Personnel

7.	Strategy	Chairman	Board	Board Committee	Executive Committee	Country Manager	Divisional Manager	Regional or Functional Head
7.1	The appointment and removal of the Chief Executive, together with severance terms		D	C Personnel and Nominations committee				
7.2	Approval of Chief Executive's expenses claims	D[11]						
7.3	Approval of expenses of the Chairman of the Board			D by chairman of the Remuneration committee				
7.4	Approval of expenses of directors	D						

[11] Or by chairman of the Remuneration committee, or another non-executive director approved for this purpose by the Board.

7.	Strategy	Chairman	Board	Board Committee	Executive Committee	Country Manager	Divisional Manager	Regional or Functional Head
7.5	Compensation packages of non-executive directors: – Service contracts – Fees – Other benefits	D[12]						
7.6	Personnel policies to be used for determining pay and other terms and conditions of key staff			D Personnel committee	R			
7.7	Actual salaries and emolument packages of executive directors: – Service contracts – Salaries – Profit sharing – Bonuses – Other incentives – Pension contributions – Other benefits							

[12] Where the Board has executive directors it would be usual that the latter would recommend on this to the Board.

7.	Strategy	Chairman	Board	Board Committee	Executive Committee	Country Manager	Divisional Manager	Regional or Functional Head
7.8	Salaries and emolument packages of senior executives:[13] – Service contracts – Profit sharing – Bonuses – Other incentives – Pension contributions – Other benefits			D Remuneration committee				
7.9	General staff bonus schemes			D Remuneration committee				
7.10	Engagement in, or having an interest in, any business similar to the company's business or representing a potential conflict of interest, by:							
	– a director		D					
	– a member of the Executive Committee		D					
	– another		D		D			
7.11	Significant redundancies		D Personnel committee	R	C	C	C	

[13] Where the Board has executive directors, it would be usual that the latter, with the chairman of the Board, would recommend on these matters to the Board.

Table 8

Appointments

8.	Strategy	Chairman	Board	Board Committee	Executive Committee	Country Manager	Divisional Manager	Regional or Functional Head
8.1	Appointment of the official stockbroker to the company		D	R Finance committee	C			
8.2	Appointment of the principal form of lawyers to the company		D	C				
8.3	Appointment of the company's merchant bankers			D Finance committee	C			
8.4	Issuing, receiving and opening of tenders, appointment of contractor(s), and post tender negotiations				D	D	D	D

Shadowing of executive directors by non-executive directors **A1.18**

Some boards apply the practice, formally or informally, of nominating a non-executive director to 'shadow' a particular executive director.

If the board is a balanced board numerically, between executive and non-executive directors, then a fairly comprehensive system of shadow partnering can usually be worked out. Each executive director can be 'shadowed' by a non-executive director.

A 'shadow director' **A1.19**

This is, of course, completely distinct from the concept of a 'shadow director' which occurs when the board is customarily inclined to follow the direction of a party, such as a major shareholder, who has not been formally appointed to the board. Such a party may be held to have the same responsibilities and potential liabilities as the directors who have been formally appointed to the board. Neither is this type of shadowing (partnering) related to the situation which occurs when someone passes him or herself off as being a board director of the company and thereby may assume the responsibilities of a director and incur the potential liabilities.

Section 251 of the Companies Act 2006 defines 'shadow director' as follows:

'(1) In the Companies Acts "shadow director", in relation to a company, means a person in accordance with whose directions or instructions the directors of the company are accustomed to act.

(2) A person is not to be regarded as a shadow director by reason only that the directors act on advice given by him in a professional capacity.

(3) A body corporate is not to be regarded as a shadow director of any of its subsidiary companies for the purposes of—
Chapter 2 (general duties of directors),
Chapter 4 (transactions requiring members' approval), or
Chapter 6 (contract with sole member who is also a director), by reason only that the directors of the subsidiary are accustomed to act in accordance with its directions or instructions.'

Section 251 of the Insolvency Act (1986) defines 'shadow director' as:

'"shadow director", in relation to a company, means a person in accordance with whose directions or instructions the directors of the company are accustomed to act (but so that a person is not deemed a shadow director by reason only that the directors act on advice given by him in a professional capacity).'

Example **A1.20**

For instance, a non-executive director might shadow the finance director: he or she would be chosen for his or her financial acumen; would focus on financial, accounting and audit issues; and would be relied upon by the board to have prepared, particularly thoroughly, for any board agenda items in these areas. This 'shadow' might, for instance, receive a full copy of each internal audit report whereas the other directors on the audit committee might usually receive very high-level summaries only. This 'shadow' would routinely discuss issues of concern with the finance director prior to board and audit committee meetings – which can be an excellent way of ensuring that the non-executive directors become more fully involved and better informed.

Approach to 'shadowing' A1.21

Generally, the approach to follow is that, if the 'shadow' has any particular queries on agenda items relating to the work of the executive director being shadowed, then in advance of the board or board committee meeting these should be raised and discussed (usually with that executive director) to the shadow's satisfaction.

Pros and cons of 'shadowing' A1.22

This 'shadowing' approach provides an excellent opportunity for non-executive directors to get actively involved – not as executives, but in an active non-executive capacity. It avoids inactivity of non-executives between board meetings. It assists a new non-executive director to get 'up to speed' quickly.

The 'shadow' can be a valuable ally and source of counsel and advice for the executive director being shadowed. The approach can contribute to team building at the level of the board, but, of course, there is a risk that it could contribute to divisive coalitions forming.

'Shadowing' in this way has to be handled carefully. In some circumstances a 'shadow' may be held to be more culpable for any negligence of the board in the area being 'shadowed'. So the 'shadow' must be chosen with care. The rest of the board should understand that a 'shadowing' arrangement does not absolve them, collectively and individually, of their usual responsibilities: there will always be a risk that the other directors might tend to assume that the non-executive 'shadow' can be relied upon to keep on top of issues within his or her area of 'shadowing' responsibility – even to the extent that the rest of the board might be inclined to neglect to master those agenda items so thoroughly.

Prioritising shareholder value A1.23

In an individual case, the right decision for a board to come to may not be the decision which maximises shareholder value. This may be so, for instance, when the decision which might maximise shareholder value would be in breach of a law, a regulation or a covenant entered into by the company under the terms of a contract. If a company is in breach of a funding covenant, it is right that the board should disclose this to the parties involved rather than pretend that the problem does not exist – even if, in extreme cases, this might cause the collapse of the share price and even of the company itself. It may be the right decision for a board to take, in the best interests of the shareholders, to allow the company to be in breach of a contract and to face up to the requirement to compensate the damaged counterparty.

Directors are in an invidious position if they are facing a possible need to take a course of action which will damage shareholder value. If the action were ill-founded, they could find themselves sued by the shareholders for the value lost. On the other hand, if they fail to act in accordance with law, regulation or covenant, they are likely to be in breach of their duty to so act and thus vulnerable to action from other parties.

Clearly the board needs to weigh things up very carefully and will probably need expert advice. Unfortunately a board is more likely to be faced with this challenge when the company is in particular difficulty and careful stewardship of funds is extra important. Nevertheless the board may need to take even costly independent advice when confronted by such a dilemma. If a board acts in accordance with the best possible professional advice, it is less likely that its directors could be successfully sued by shareholders or other parties, as the directors should be able to show that they had been diligent and careful about the action they decided upon.

So it is true that, in an individual case, the right decision for a board to come to may not be the decision which maximises shareholder value. However, in the generality of board decisions taken over time, and also with respect to the majority of individual decisions the board makes, the guiding principle above all others should be the intention of the board – the firm determination and indeed the effect – to maximise shareholder value while acting 'within the rules of the game'. In the words of Milton Friedman:

> 'There is one and only one social responsibility of business – to use its resources and engage in activities designed to increase its profits so long as it stays within the rules of the game …'

Almost certainly the board will fail in this if the information it receives on shareholder value is inadequate. This useful schematic expresses well the relationship between 'information' and 'shareholder value':

> Data > ('informationalise') > Information > Knowledge > Strategy > Action > Shareholder value

Company secretarial function checklist A1.24

Objective

To ensure that the board and its committees are served by competent secretarial assistance in general and with regard to meetings and statutory/regulatory matters.

Checklist

1. Key issues

1.1 Is the board and its committees provided with adequate secretarial support?

1.2 Do the secretarial arrangements for the board and its committees preserve due business confidentiality?

1.3 Is there maintained satisfactorily by the secretarial function a guide (or guides) accessible to members to regulate the conduct of board and committee business, covering terms of reference, standing orders, resolutions of continuing significance etc?

1.4 Do minutes sufficiently and promptly record the discussion and resolutions of meetings, are they signed by the chairman, and are they maintained in an orderly, accessible yet secure fashion?

1.5 Are there procedures which ensure that statutory and regulatory returns are submitted correctly and on time?

1.6 Do board members and senior executives receive appropriate and timely advice on matters of a statutory or regulatory nature?

2. Sound arrangements for meetings

2.1 There should be a meetings calendar so that business is executed at appropriate times.

2.2 Board committees should meet approximately ten days before the associated board meeting so that the draft minutes of a committee meeting can be an agenda paper at the following board meeting.

2.3 Adequate notice of meetings should be given so as to ensure good attendance.

2.4 Draft agenda should be approved by the committee chair before issuance.

2.5 Agendas and agenda papers should be approved by the board or committee chairman and circulated to members at least one week in advance.

2.6 Agenda papers should be fully informative.

2.7 Draft minutes should be approved by the board or committee chairman before issuance.

2.8 The approval of minutes should be taken seriously, will usually occur at the next meeting of the board or committee concerned and will be indicated by the dated signature of the board or committee chairman on a copy of the approved minutes.

2.9 Minutes should fully describe the discussion which ensured at the meeting.

2.10 Follow-up of committee and board decisions is the responsibility of the committee or board concerned, and is facilitated by careful attention to 'matters arising' and by carrying forward open items to the agendas of subsequent meetings.

2.11 Chairs of meetings should not stifle contributions from members, but should facilitate full discussion of agenda items to the satisfaction of the board or committee members.

2.12 A copy of all agendas, agenda papers and approved minutes should be retained indefinitely in a secure and accessible place.

The importance of an independent element on the board **A1.25**

Independence is considered in more detail in Chapter **A3**.

Except in the most general of terms, even Cadbury in 1992 sold the pass on defining independence, explaining only that independent directors are 'independent of management and free from any business or other relationship which could materially interfere with the exercise of their independent judgement' and that 'it is for the board to decide in particular cases whether this definition is met'.[21] In 1998 the Hampel Report concurred, adding that the board 'could be called on to justify its decision'.

> 'The Cadbury Committee recommended that a majority of non-executive directors should be independent, and defined this as "independent of management and free from any business or other relationship which could materially interfere with the exercise of their independent judgement" (report 4.12). We agree with this definition, and after careful consideration we do not consider that it is practicable to lay down more precise criteria for independence. We agree with Cadbury that it should be for the board to take a view on whether an individual director is independent in the above sense. The corollary is that boards should disclose in the annual report which of the directors are considered to be independent and be

prepared to justify their view if challenged. We recognise, however, that non-executive directors who are not in this sense "independent" may nonetheless make a useful contribution to the board.'[22]

Sir Adrian Cadbury has said (1998):

> 'The presence of independent members of boards does not imply that they have inherently higher standards of morality than their executive colleagues. It is simply that it is easier for them to take an objective view of whatever matters are under review. They stand further back from the action, they bring outside standards to bear on the issues and their interests are less directly at stake. The argument for independent members of professional disciplinary bodies rests on the same grounds.'

There is nothing quite like the notion of 'independence' to rattle the timbers of the non-executive director. To pin it down has been like nailing a jelly to the ceiling. Higgs noted that so many different and often inconsistent lists of criteria of independence had been developed by institutional investors and others that, by 2003, it had become time to incorporate a standard list of independence criteria into the 2003 revision of the Combined Code, rather than being content with the rather general wording which used to be contained within Provision A.3.2 of the 1998 Code:

> 'The majority of non-executive directors should be independent of management and free from any business or other relationship which could materially interfere with the exercise of their independent judgement. Non-executive directors considered by the board to be independent in this sense should be identified in the annual report.'

It was notable that absent from the 2003 specific independence criteria was the age bar (age 70) which many other lists of criteria had included, but which the Higgs report had not recommended (see **C2.19** and **F2.11** for further discussion of this).

Revisions of the Code until the present have made no further changes to the section on independence.

All directors must exercise independent judgement A1.26

One of the codified duties of any director, as set out in the UK's Companies Act 2006, is to exercise independent judgement. The 2006 Act makes no distinction between executive and non-executive directors, nor between non-executive directors who are regarded as independent and those who are not. As far the Act is concerned, there are no distinctions between directors, and all are expected to exercise independent judgement.

This is often much more difficult for an executive director to achieve than for an 'outside director'. An executive director may find his or her judgement to be coloured by their specific executive responsibilities, or by the steer they receive from the chief executive. Many top executive teams have a pre-board meeting when they decide the line that the executive directors will take at the board meeting. Even so, it is incumbent upon an executive director to participate in decision making at the board by exercising and articulating his or her judgement independently as to what is in the best interests of the company, not what is in the best interests of his or her executive area of responsibility and not according to the instructions of the chief executive.

This means that, when an executive joins the board, the transition to being a board member will not be easy. Whereas non-executive directors joining the board will need induction training that focuses on the company's business, executives joining the board will need induction training on the distinctive duties of directors in contrast to the duties of executives, and how to manage the conflicts between those duties. Chief executives need to understand that executive directors are not ciphers for the chief executive. Of course, boards will not welcome an executive director team that is strongly and consistently divided, and it is likely to be appropriate for that team usually to have a pre-board meeting. But where there is a genuine difference of view amongst the executive directors, there should be freedom to express that difference at the board meeting. An open dialogue between board members has been said to be the most important ingredient of a successful board.

Directors' handbook **A1.27**

A major challenge for most boards is for their members to be able readily to recall all past resolutions of the board. Usually these were originally resolved upon for good reason and after careful consideration: not only should they be regarded as binding upon the board until rescinded but they are likely to represent prudent practice. Of equal difficulty is for the board to be sure that they are fully aware of all material contract terms which the entity has entered into and which, if breached, would place the company and the board in default of their duties – either by virtue of the breach or by failure to disclose the breach to the other parties. An example would be a clause in a financing agreement which requires any 'material adverse change' to be drawn to the attention of the other party(ies). Another, sometimes related, example would be a clause in a contract which makes it an automatic breach of the terms of the contract if an accommodation is made with a party to another contract, or if a disclosure is made to a party to another contract of a material adverse change.

It is sound practice for each director to have an up-to-date directors' handbook giving them ready access to documents and information of continuing importance to the board. The handbook will be maintained by the company secretariat function. Here we suggest the contents of this manual.

Example contents of the directors' handbook/manual **A1.28**

1. A copy of the constitutional documents of the entity (memorandum of association, articles etc).
2. A copy of the terms of reference of all board committees.
3. A copy of policy statements such as the entity's statement of corporate principles, code of business conduct, code of ethical conduct, fraud policy statement and environmental policy statement.
4. A copy of the resolution authorising board members to take individual professional advice at the company's expense.
5. A copy of all other resolutions of the board with continuing effect.
6. A précis of all decisions of continuing significance made by the board under their reserved powers.

7. A copy of any established delegation of authority guidelines (see **A1.13–A1.17**).
8. Terms of appointment of board members: an up-to-date and complete copy of the service and employment contracts with the company of all directors.
9. A statement of the general and specific responsibilities of the directors.
10. A copy of declared (a) conflicts of interest and (b) related party transactions of directors and senior executives.
11. A copy of the key terms of the contracts between the company and its professional advisors.
12. Details of key contract terms the breach of which could conceivably lead to action against the directors.
13. The calendar of future company, board and board committee meetings and, where appropriate, an outline of their planned agendas.
14. Details of contingent liabilities of the company.
15. A schedule setting out the composition of the shareholders of the company, especially naming the principal shareholders.

Directors' need to know contractual terms of their co-directors **A1.29**

There are conflicting issues in play here. 'A director is a director'. Company law imposes a duty on all directors, *including executive directors*, to exercise independent judgement (Companies Act 2006, s 173). All directors are jointly and severally responsible for all board decisions. The remuneration committee is just a sub-committee of the board with no powers superior to the board itself. To adhere to the principle that no director shall be involved in determining his or her own remuneration, this is assigned to the board's remuneration committee. The board notes, but does not reopen, remuneration committee decisions – subject to board override in extreme cases. It is bad form for the board to revise decisions that the remuneration committee has come to. But if the remuneration committee is clearly acting (or has acted) dysfunctionally, in extreme cases the board may ask the remuneration committee to reconsider, or the board may make changes to the remuneration committee.

There have been too many cases of boards, especially their outside directors, being taken by surprise when they have learnt retrospectively about the contractual terms usually of their executive directors – often when severance payments are having to be made under terms of which the board had been unaware.

The decisions of the remuneration committee should be transparently and promptly communicated to the whole board. That is what we should aim for. The reasoning behind the decisions may need to be nuanced – for instance, in the interest of personal privacy. The reaction of an executive director to this information must be the reaction that is appropriate of a director *acting in the best interests of the company*, rather than the reaction of an executive serving his or her own personal or executive interests. Likewise, subsequent use of that information by the executive should not be for their own advantage, and directors must of course preserve due confidentiality.

Outside directors have a particular independent oversight role, and so it is important that, whether or not they are members of the remuneration committee, they are all fully appraised of the contractual arrangements that apply to the executive directors, and also to each of the NEDs. This is one reason why best practice suggests that they themselves should not be personal beneficiaries of performance-related or pension schemes.

Is it reasonable to withhold detailed information about an executive director's package from other executive directors? Usually, 'No!'. But this puts an onus upon the executive directors to respond in a mature way. This will usually mean that they will note but not challenge the decisions made by the remuneration committee. Rare cases of challenge would only be justified if in the best interests of the company and would be a matter for the board as a whole.

Companies listed on the main market have to make the contractual terms of directors available to shareholders on request. It is therefore inconceivable that this information is not also available to all the members of the board.

Each director is responsible for his or her conduct as a director, and the cohesiveness of the board is important. The chairman of the board is overall responsible for the effectiveness of the board and may need, from time to time, to point out to board members that their behaviour is unhelpfully discordant. For instance, strictly speaking any director could insist on attending a meeting of any board committee, but best practice corporate governance suggests that only members of the remuneration committee should attend its meetings, unless others are invited to do so. The chairman of the board would make it clear to an executive director who insisted on attending a remuneration committee that this was unacceptable conduct, and that director's tenure on the board would be at risk. Similarly, if there were a good reason for temporarily withholding from the full board information about executive director remuneration, then the chairman should make it clear to the director concerned that his or her demand for this information is unhelpful.

Readers may like to consult **App5** for guidance on the role of the chairman.

Main Principle D.2 of the UK Corporate Governance Code (**App1**) states that there should be a formal and transparent procedure for developing policy on executive remuneration and for fixing the remuneration packages of individual directors. Paragraph 6.2 of the terms of reference for remuneration committees[23] published by the Institute of Chartered Secretaries and Administrators (ICSA) stated that draft minutes of committee meetings shall be circulated promptly to all members of the committee and that, once approved, minutes should be circulated to all other members of the board *unless it would be inappropriate to do so*. Paragraph 8.1 stated that no director or manager shall be involved in any decisions as to their own remuneration. Paragraph 9.1 stated that the committee chairman shall report to the board on its proceedings after each meeting on all matters within its duties and responsibilities, and paragraph 9.2 that the committee shall make whatever recommendations to the board it deems appropriate on any area within its remit where action or improvement is needed. Both the Code and paragraph 1.2 of ICSA's terms of reference state that only members of the committee have the right to attend committee meetings.

A new director has a right to see minutes and agenda papers of past board and board committee meetings.

Achieving a high degree of board openness is clearly a very good thing.

Auditing the board **A1.30**

It is a paradox of business that, while nothing is more important to the success of the business than the conduct of the board, the board itself is possibly the least likely of all parts of the business to be subject to independent review. But it can be done! We discuss board evaluation in Chapter **B2**.

And it should be done. The board sets the tone for the business. Tight control should not be regarded as an irksome and counterproductive impediment for the board, while being an important feature for the rest of the business. Neither need control impede the flair of boards; rather, board internal control provides the framework in which board creativity can blossom to its fullest extent.

While it is true that the board is subject to external control by the stakeholders, this does not diminish the need for it to have effective internal control for its own purposes. Whatever the business activity, the primary justification for a satisfactory system of internal control is to ensure that the activity is likely to be done well; the secondary justification is to provide reassurance to those external to the activity that the task is under control. Either way, the board needs good internal control. And we now understand that the review, or monitoring, of internal control is an essential feature of an effective system of internal control.

Where auditing the board does occur, it is likely to be occasional rather than continuous. As such, it is likely to be only reactive to a particular concern about board performance rather than being a periodic 'health check' of an unlimited scope ultimately determined by the reviewer.

In these respects, it is often very different from the classic model of an internal audit which suggests that, after consultation, internal audit determines its programme of work having regard to risk. So management consultants and external auditors rather than internal auditors will often be used for this purpose. The checklist we provide here is intended as an *aide memoire* for whichever agency is entrusted with the task.

Board evaluation best practice **A1.31**

Readers may like to consult Chapter **B2** and **App5** for further performance evaluation guidance.

Since 2003, the UK Combined Code required that companies observing the Code should assess the performance of the board. The requirement of the current UK Corporate Governance Code is that the performance of the board, its committees, individual directors (both executive and independent) and the chairman of the board should be evaluated at least annually with independent, external facilitation of the evaluation at least once every three years. 2011 saw an amendment to the Code to capture within the board evaluation the hot issue of board diversity, including gender; Supporting Principle B.6 (**App1**) now reads as follows:

> 'Evaluation of the board should consider the balance of skills, experience, independence and knowledge of the company on the board, its diversity, including gender, how the board works together as a unit, and other factors relevant to its effectiveness'.

In the author's experience, board evaluations are often incomplete. They may, for instance, exclude an evaluation of the performance of individual directors or of the chairman of the board. They may exclude an evaluation of board committees or of the chairs of those committees. They may fail to determine the impressions of board performance of top management below the level of the board.

A task for internal audit? A1.32

The UK Code (**App1**, Provision B.6.2) requires that the evaluation of large company boards should be externally facilitated at least once every three years:

> 'Evaluation of the board of FTSE 350 companies should be externally facilitated at least every three years. The external facilitator should be identified in the annual report and a statement made as to whether they have any other connection with the company.'

At a minimum, the use of an external party at least once every three years is in a facilitation role, which does not exclude making use of internal resources when an external facilitator is also involved. The traditional rationale for not using internal audit for this review centres upon the position of internal audit within the business. To be most effective, internal audit needs to be independent. Of course, there is no such thing as complete independence.

One important aspect of effective independence is that the most senior point to whom internal audit reports must be able to be confident of the objectivity which underpins the determination of (a) audit scope, and (b) the content and emphasis of audit reports. That means, for instance, that it must be confident that the scope of internal audit reviews has been the professional judgement of the internal auditor. If, for instance, internal audit reports to an audit committee, that committee must be confident that no one beneath the audit committee has been unduly influential in deflecting internal audit away from investigating certain areas and into other areas against internal audit's better judgement. It also means that the most senior point to which internal audit reports must be confident that the content of internal audit reports is determined by internal audit and not, in effect, censured, by anyone beneath the level of the audit committee which relies upon the objectivity of internal audit.

Certain safeguards can provide reassurance to the audit committee as to internal audit independence, but these safeguards will not necessarily ensure effective independence for internal audit from the board itself and from the audit committee.

Reporting arrangements for internal audit A1.33

The management grade of the head of internal audit is a factor in influencing the likely effectiveness of internal audit's review of board level matters. The Chartered Institute of Management Accountants (CIMA), in its submission to Hampel, went as far as to suggest to Hampel that heads of internal audit should have equal status with executive directors. ICSA asserted to Hampel that in many companies the company secretary, particularly if a chartered secretary, is probably the most suitable officer to head up the internal audit function. On the other hand, there can be a conflict if the head of internal audit is also secretary to the audit committee of the board, one of whose responsibilities is to monitor on behalf of the board the effectiveness of internal audit.

Neither CIMA's nor ICSA's suggestion was picked up by Hampel.[24]

In 2013, the UK's enhanced guidance for internal audit in the financial sector[25] recommended that the head of internal audit should attend board committee meetings and some board meetings and should have a status equivalent to that of members of the executive committee (Exco) of the entity. This guidance recommended that the head of internal audit should have the right to attend Exco meetings. Furthermore, the guidance recommended that the head of internal audit might report for all purposes to the chair of the audit committee or even to the chairman of the board, and that if there were a secondary reporting line it should be to the CEO. It is now widely held that internal audit is the third line of defence, or at least an important part of the third line (see Chapter **G3**), whereas the chief risk officer and the head of compliance head up important parts of the second line of defence which are closer to management. These enhancements of internal audit independence and status, where they are in place, make it more feasible for internal audit to play a key role in evaluating the board, at least to the same extent as the company secretary might do so.

While most heads of internal audit report to the board or to the board's audit committee on the results of internal audit work, and on the professionalism of the internal audit function, administrative reporting by internal audit (for 'pay and rations') is still most frequently to management. The snag with this arrangement is that 'he who pays the piper calls the tune'. Gradually this is being recognised, as more internal audit heads report to the chair of the board and the cost of the internal audit function thus becomes regarded as one of the costs of running the board. This approach strengthens the ability of internal audit to provide valuable, independent assurance to the board. It means that internal audit can fill more of a board's assurance vacuum than would otherwise be the case. It does not mean that such an internal audit function is a less useful source of assurance to management: arguably, assurance is better if the provider of the assurance is more independent of those to whom the assurance is provided. Certainly it is far from ideal for the board to rely on assurance from an internal audit function that reports for 'pay and rations' at an executive level *below* the board. Where it is considered inappropriate to sever the umbilical cord between the executive team and the internal audit function, there may be reasonably satisfactory fallback compromises available. For instance, if the company secretary reports for 'pay and rations' to the board, internal audit might report for 'pay and rations' to the company secretary. Another approach is for the audit committee of the board to satisfy itself on such matters as the appointment, retention and dismissal of the chief audit executive and his or her remuneration, and to inquire of the chief audit executive whether he or she is experiencing any threats to internal audit independence. Internal audit should never subordinate their professional judgement to that of others.

A checklist for auditing the board **A1.34**

Control Objectives: To ensure the enterprise has a high quality board of directors. To ensure that the board effectively sets the strategic direction of the business and is in control of its execution. To ensure effective corporate governance within the business. To ensure that board business is conducted efficiently. To ensure that overall board costs are reasonable.

Key issues		**Illustrative scope or approach**
	Risk/control issue	**Current control/measure**
1.1	How does the board ensure that its constitution, composition and organisation address its responsibilities effectively? (see also 1.2 below)	Terms of reference of the board, explicitly adopted by the board and reviewed periodically. Appropriate main board committees with terms of reference which have been explicitly adopted by the board and are periodically reviewed by the board. Appropriate mix of executive and non-executive directors as members of the board and its committees. A formal and appropriate selection and performance review process re: the chair of the board, including approval by the board. A formal and appropriate selection and performance review process of chairs for the board committees, including approval by the board of these appointments.
1.2	How does the board address the matter of ensuring that its membership is suitable (in its size, composition and other respects) to the needs of the business? (see also 1.1 above)	Formal contracts for all directors. Directors' contracts are for a satisfactory fixed term. There is a board nominations committee which: ● determines board need; ● is responsible for succession planning; and ● recommends appointees to the board. A sufficient degree of independence amongst the non-executive directors. The record shows that the board determines that the majority of its audit committee members are regarded by the board as being independent. Analysis of need, and a matching of background and skills to need. The board itself resolves on appointments and terminations of board members. Periodic comparison of board composition with that of similar enterprises. A record is kept of attendance of directors at board and board committee meetings, tabled to the board periodically. Attendance has been good (better than 80%).

Key issues		**Illustrative scope or approach**
	Risk/control issue	**Current control/measure**
1.3	How does the board ensure that there is not excessive concentration of power at or near the top of the business?	● Separation of the roles of chief executive and chair of the business; or ● nomination of a suitable non-executive director to be the senior non-executive director. Non-executive directors meet alone from time to time, in addition to their time together at certain board committee meetings. Sufficient access for the board and its members to management, in addition to the managing director. Close liaison between the chairs of board committees and the relevant, responsible manager(s) and/or other parties – for instance, between: ● the chair of the audit committee; ● the head of internal audit; ● the head of compliance (if applicable); and ● the external auditor. The record shows that board members at board meetings are encouraged to challenge management proposals.
1.4	How does the board ensure it has taken charge of the ethical values of the business?	The board has adopted, as corporate policy statement(s), one or more of the following, as appropriate: ● statement of corporate principles; ● code of business conduct; ● code of scientific conduct; ● code of ethical conduct; ● code of environmental conduct; and ● fraud policy statement.

Key issues		Illustrative scope or approach
	Risk/control issue	**Current control/measure**
1.4 – *contd*		The board sets an appropriate and consistent example. The board follows the principle of openness, and the other Nolan Principles where appropriate. There is a satisfactory policy and procedure for taking ethical violations to the board. The board is in overall control of the business's policy and practices with respect to equal opportunities.
1.5	How does the board ensure that its business is conducted efficiently and effectively, both at the board and in committee?	Scheduling of board and board committee meetings ensures that board committee minutes (at least in draft) are promptly available to the board as board agenda papers. Chairs of board committees speak to their committee minutes at board meetings. Adequate time is allowed for board and board committee meetings, and apt allocation of time between agenda items. There are sufficient refreshment breaks within long meetings, and between meetings which follow on from each other. Adequate notice of board and board committee meetings. Future schedule of meeting dates prepared and issued to members on a rolling annual basis. Adequate timing of distribution of agenda papers, for members to prepare thoroughly. Quality of agenda papers, including their reliability, sufficiency and clarity. Freedom of undue filtering of information placed before the board. Avoidance at the board of excessive involvement in detail and in management matters.
1.6	How does the board ensure that the total compensation packages of executive and non-executive directors are appropriate?	An effective remuneration committee of non-executive directors to determine executive directors' compensation. Non-executive directors' compensation determined by the executive directors.

Key issues		**Illustrative scope or approach**
	Risk/control issue	**Current control/measure**
1.7	How does the board ensure that the right items are placed on board agendas, on a timely basis?	The board has an agenda committee (or a chairman's committee with, inter alia, agenda-setting responsibility).
1.8	How does the board ensure that matters which require board approval are brought to the board?	Regular written reports from each executive director to the board, presented orally by the director and fully discussed at the board. Maintenance of a formal schedule of matters reserved to the board for its decision (see 1.11 below).
1.9	How does the board ensure that its members are fully appraised of the continuing information they need to discharge their responsibilities as directors effectively?	There is a tailored, ongoing induction and training programme for each board member. Regular presentations are made to the board of important aspects of the business. Each director has a copy of a directors' manual containing, inter alia, a copy of: ● the memorandum of association; ● the articles of association; ● each director's contract; ● the terms of reference of board committees; ● delegation of authority guidelines; ● standing orders; ● all past board policy decisions not yet rescinded (see 1.10 below); ● essential extracts from all critical contracts, including significant covenants in financing and other agreements;[26] and ● copy of policy statement on directors taking independent professional advice (see 1.14 below).

Key issues		Illustrative scope or approach
	Risk/control issue	**Current control/measure**
1.10	How does the board ensure that earlier formal resolutions it has taken will always be recalled, when appropriate, as being board policy – until rescinded or replaced?	There is a complete and up-to-date guide to board policy decisions which have not been rescinded (see 1.9 above). Minutes are thorough. Matters arising from past minutes are identified and carried forward until addressed fully.
1.11	How does the board ensure that it is in control of the business?	There is a formal schedule of matters reserved to the board for its decision (see 1.8 above). There are delegation of authority guidelines, and they are clear and comprehensive. Do the right things get placed on board and board committee agendas – in time to determine outcomes? The board receives a regular management accounting pack (MAP) which allows board members to monitor performance against plan, in all areas of the business. The MAP is: ● comprehensive; ● reliable; ● clear; ● timely; and ● not misleading.
1.12	How does the board ensure its decisions are implemented?	There is a monitoring procedure for follow-up of decisions, which is applied. It includes a schedule of decisions whose implementation must be ensured. There is evidence that this monitoring procedure is being applied.

Key issues		**Illustrative scope or approach**
	Risk/control issue	**Current control/measure**
1.13	How does the board ensure that its business, and that of its committees, is managed efficiently and effectively?	A qualified company secretariat, independent of other responsibilities, services the board and its committees.
1.14	How does the board ensure that directors have adequate access to information and advice?	The company secretariat is available to the board, its committees and to individual board members in order to provide information and address issues of concern brought to the secretariat. Board members need access to members of management in addition to the chief executive. Board committees and individual board members are formally empowered to take independent, professional advice at the business's expense (see 1.16 below).
1.15	How does the board ensure it is appraised of shareholder, customer, supplier and other stakeholder complaints and concerns?	There is an established reporting system through to the board on these matters. Non-executive directors serve on panels which deal with these matters. These panels have appropriate terms of reference and standing orders, and their proceedings are thoroughly minuted. Records of these panels show they work well.
1.16	How does the board protect itself and its members against the risk of negligent performance and/or possible litigation?	Thorough minuting of all board and board committee meetings. Directors' liability insurance. At their own discretion, individual directors and board committees (per their terms of reference) are authorised to take professional advice at the business's expense, on matters relating respectively to their duties as directors or to their committee responsibilities (see 1.14 above).

Key issues		Illustrative scope or approach
	Risk/control issue	**Current control/measure**
1.17	How does the board secure its records?	Permanent retention of 100% of board and board committee agenda papers and minutes. Duplicate (separate and secure) storage of these records. Records are readily accessible by those who are authorised to access them, but safeguarded against unauthorised access. Access to records is logged, and the log is kept secure. Storage method(s) is proof against deterioration. Archives are inspected for quality periodically. Electronic records are checked periodically for continued accessibility and are refreshed periodically to avoid deterioration.
1.18	How does the board monitor that the business continues to be a going concern?	The MAP (see 1.11 above) covers this with respect to liquidity, solvency etc. The audit committee of the board regularly addresses going concern. The board, or the audit committee on behalf of the board, reviews the adequacy of the business's disaster recovery plan.
1.19	Is the board determining effectively the nature and content of corporate information which is published?	The audit committee considers the reliability of all information from the directors which is published. The board consciously determines its policy with respect to the content of the annual report and accounts – particularly with regard to disclosures over which there is no mandatory requirement, such as: • environmental statements; and • corporate governance statements beyond minimum requirements.

Key issues		**Illustrative scope or approach**
	Risk/control issue	**Current control/measure**
1.20	Is the board approaching its legal responsibilities effectively?	The board has appointed a senior executive as compliance officer. The board, through its audit committee, ensures that there is an effective internal audit, including: • staff and other resources; • qualifications; • reporting relationships; • programme of audits; • completion of planned programme of audits; and • content of audit reports. The board, through its audit committee, ensures that there is an adequate external audit, headed by an appropriate audit partner. In non-financial, non-accounting respects, the information and reporting system through to the board is sufficient to enable its directors to be reassured that they are meeting their legal responsibilities. The code of business conduct, approved by the board, specifically bans illegal acts by representatives of the business.
1.21	Is the board pro-active?	The board and its committees (such as the audit committee) must consider future issues. Significant time at meetings should be spent on future prospects.
1.22	Are board members properly prepared for their duties?	There should be a tailored induction programme for each new board member, covering: • the affairs of the business; and • the characteristics of this board. The responsibilities, duties and practice of directors (except for already experienced directors).

Qualifications for directors **A1.35**

In the UK a taxidermist, specialising in stuffing dead animals, must be trained and registered. There is no such requirement for directors of companies or other organisations. In part this is because people come to this role relatively late in their careers when they have less appetite for study and for obtaining additional qualifications.

If directors had to be qualified in directorship, there would undoubtedly be a dearth of available directors. Even so, in today's world there is a need to recognise that many will change careers during their working life, and it would be unacceptable if the assumption was that in their later roles there was no need to become qualified.

Certainly it is important for each company to identify the training needs of its directors, which will vary according to their background and board roles, and then to have a budget to provide that training. While training may need to be provided early after a director's appointment to the board, companies should recognise that it must be ongoing and tailored for each director. This initiative should be spearheaded by the company secretary and overseen by the chairman of the board who is responsible for the effectiveness of the board.

In one leading Far East country, they bravely attempted to remedy this deficit. Directors of listed companies were required to attend six three-hour modules of training in directorship and to register with the registrar of companies that they had completed this programme. The programme was dropped – in part when it was discovered that directors were checking in for this training and then departing, leaving their drivers to attend on their behalf.

There is one glowing exception. The UK Institute of Directors has developed a qualification in directorship, for executive and non-executive directors, which leads to the designation CDir (Chartered Director). It has become widely accepted across the world. Of course, it is not a mandatory requirement anywhere. We provide details of the CDir programme at **App3**.

Notes

1 Chambers, A.D. (2009) *Tolley's Internal Auditing Handbook*, 2nd edn (LexisNexis Butterworths Tolley), pp 378–379.
2 John Baden, ex Chair, Alliance & Leicester's audit committee.
3 Final Report of the Committee on Corporate Governance (the 'Hampel Committee'), p 17.
4 For about four years.
5 Also perhaps for four years.
6 Total issued shares, multiplied by today's market price.
7 The number of times market capitalisation exceeds annual profit.
8 Report of the Committee on the Financial Aspects of Corporate Governance, chaired by Sir Adrian Cadbury (the 'Cadbury Report') (1 December 1992).
9 Final Report of the Committee on Corporate Governance, chaired by Sir Ronald Hampel (January 1998).
10 Committee on Corporate Governance, The Combined Code (June 1998), Provision A.1.2.
11 1998 Combined Code, Principle A.1.

12 For directors of UK incorporated companies, these duties are set out in Companies Act 2006, ss 170–177.

13 See eg Institute of Directors in association with Henley Management College *Good Practice for Directors – Standards for the Board* (1995).

14 Sir Adrian Cadbury *The Company Chairman* (Director Books in association with the Institute of Directors, 1990).

15 Drawn from the Cadbury Report, p 66.

16 UK Corporate Governance Code, Provision B.5.1 reads:

> 'All directors should have access to the advice and services of the company secretary, who is responsible to the board for ensuring that board procedures are complied with. Both the appointment and removal of the company secretary should be a matter for the board as a whole.'

17 UK Corporate Governance Code, Provision B.2.1 reads:

> 'There should be a nomination committee which should lead the process for board appointments and make recommendations to the board. A majority of members of the nomination committee should be independent non-executive directors. The chairman or an independent non-executive director should chair the committee, but the chairman should not chair the nomination committee when it is dealing with the appointment of a successor to the chairmanship. The nomination committee should make available its terms of reference, explaining its role and the authority delegated to it by the board.' [The requirement to make the information available would be met by including the information on a website that is maintained by or on behalf of the company.]

18 UK Corporate Governance Code, Provision B.5.1 reads:

> 'The board should ensure that directors, especially non-executive directors, have access to independent professional advice at the company's expense where they judge it necessary to discharge their responsibilities as directors. Committees should be provided with sufficient resources to undertake their duties.'

See also **A3.20–A3.22**.

19 Curiously, the Hampel Committee was silent on this, although the 1998 Combined Code specified that the remuneration committee should be empowered to seek outside advice. On the other hand, the earlier Cadbury Committee had recommended that audit committees should be able to seek outside advice, and we assume that not to do so was an oversight of the Hampel Committee. The 2010 version of the UK Corporate Governance Code also does not specifically state that audit committees should be empowered to seek outside advice, although Provision B.5.1 states in more general terms that board committees should be provided with sufficient resources to undertake their duties. Provision B.2.4 states that there should be an explanation in the annual report if neither an external search consultancy nor open advertising was used to assist the nomination committee in the appointment of a chairman or a non-executive director.

20 Although some had considered that the Cadbury Code guidance on this could lead to divided boards, the Hampel Committee continued with the guidance in the Combined Code, and indeed strengthened it, so that, even when the posts of chairman and chief executive are not combined, it is recommended that there should be a recognised senior non-executive director. Despite opposition to Higgs' proposals on this, the 2003 Combined Code strengthened the role of the senior non-executive director still further. Since 2003 the Code has included the Provision:

> 'The chairman should hold meetings with the non-executive directors without the executives present. Led by the senior independent director, the non-executive directors should meet without the chairman present at least annually to appraise the chairman's performance and on such other occasions as are deemed appropriate.' (now Provision A.4.2)

and

> 'The board should appoint one of the independent non-executive directors to be the senior independent director to provide a sounding board for the chairman and

to serve as an intermediary for the other directors when necessary. The senior independent director should be available to shareholders if they have concerns which contact through the normal channels of chairman, chief executive or other executive directors has failed to resolve or for which such contact is inappropriate.' (now Provision A.4.1)

21 Report of the Committee on the Financial Aspects of Corporate Governance (December 1992), paras 4.12 and 4.13.

22 Final Report of the Committee on Corporate Governance, the Hampel Committee, chaired by Sir Ronald Hampel (January 1998), para 3.9.

23 See the ICSA website.

24 Final Report of the Committee on Corporate Governance, the Hampel Committee, chaired by Sir Ronald Hampel (January 1998).

25 Effective Internal Audit in the Financial Services Sector: Recommendations from the Committee on Internal Audit Guidance for Financial Services, Chartered Institute of Internal Auditors (CIIA), July 2013, available at http://www.iia.org.uk/media/354788/0758_effective_internal_audit_financial_webfinal.pdf, accessed 14 July 2013.

26 Just one example here would be financing contracts which contain clauses that the board must disclose any material adverse change in the business's circumstances to the other parties to the contract, and perhaps that such a material adverse change represents a breach in the terms of the contract. The key point here is that the board needs to be confident that it is keeping on top of the business's contracting arrangements – at least to the extent that they have a potential material impact upon the welfare of the business.

Considering Joining a Board

Joining a board – how to decide A2.1

In this section we suggest a careful approach a prospective director might follow if invited to join a board of directors. At **A2.18** is a checklist which summarises the main points made. **A4.2** also discusses due diligence when considering joining a board. Our recommendation is that prospective directors weigh up the offer carefully before deciding, and use their own judgement as to whether the advice given in this section of the handbook is directly applicable to the circumstances.

How should you react to an approach to join a board? Of course, you may be flattered and keen to accept the challenge for the experience that it promises to bring. You should not allow that excited reaction to colour your judgement.

On the other hand, if you are predisposed to decline the invitation, probably you should heed your inclination if it has anything to do with a lack of motivation, for, certainly, being a successful director requires more commitment, energy and focus (not to mention skills, experience and integrity) than you might at first anticipate.

But if your cautious reticence is a matter of concern about the risks you may be taking, then there may be much you can do to allay or confirm your anxieties before you have to make a decision. No worthwhile company would wish you to give a snap response and, if circumstances mean that time is the essence, then a worthwhile company will be keen to address the issues you raise quickly, before you have to make your decision.

Readers may also consult **App5** for guidance on the role of the non-executive director.

What can you bring to the board? A2.2

Your analysis will need to have two facets. First, will you be able to make the contribution to the board that the board believes you can? Secondly, can you afford to take the risk of joining the board? The two are connected, as the risk will be greater if you find yourself unable to devote the requisite time to the responsibility.

Time commitment varies considerably from company to company, from one directorship to another within the same company, and from time to time. It should be possible to estimate in advance the range of the likely time commitment, and the letter of appointment should set out what it is expected to be. Typically a non-executive director may expect to need to devote between 30 and 35 days a year, divided fairly equally between meetings and site visits on the one hand, and background work and preparation for meetings on the other hand. The chair of the board may need twice as much time at least, though there are some chairmen who are almost full time. Board committee responsibilities will increase the time commitment, which will be further increased by any committee chairmanship responsibilities.

On the contribution to the board that the board believes you can make, you already have an indication that someone (perhaps a number of people) believes you are likely to be the right person. It seems you have a good reputation, which takes time to build but can be quickly lost. But you may know more about yourself than others do! You should know more than most others about your personal impediments to being an effective director at this time and on this board. Especially, you more than anyone are privy to your present and future circumstances and to those aspects of your business and personal life which are currently unfolding. For instance, if the board is intent upon you being one of their independent directors, do you know of any present or likely future impediment to you being so regarded?

While there is much contemporary criticism of how boards are perceived to select directors from a rather 'incestuous' closed circle of cronies, there is an almost forgivable rationale for this. Prospective directors have to be very careful about what boards they join, and companies equally have to be very cautious as to whom they welcome on to their boards. When the parties have known each other for a long time, they are less likely to make mistakes. When most of the parties are relative strangers, then there is a need for extra caution.

Being a director carries weighty responsibilities. In principle, each director is fully responsible for the direction and control of the company and for breaches in company and other law by the company. It is true that, when courts apportion damages between directors, they may take account of a director's background, qualifications and expertise which he or she held out as having. For instance, if you are a qualified accountant you may be judged as having a special responsibility for the financial and accounting affairs of the company, notwithstanding that you might be inclined to plead that you were 'only' a non-executive director. The law makes no distinction between executive and non-executive directors.

If you are being invited to join a board because of your professional qualifications, you must consider whether you really do have the skill sets associated with those qualifications. It is less likely that you will if you qualified a long time ago, have not practised for a while, or have not kept abreast with your continuing professional development. Your letter of appointment should set out the nature of the expertise that the company is presuming you have.

Risk A2.3

By joining a board, you are risking your fortune as well as your reputation. You could find yourself party to behaviour which also could lead you to being disqualified from being a director. If you are already active in business, you will know that you are often required to fill in forms which inquire whether you have been a director of a company that has gone into liquidation.

It may be appropriate for you to make arrangements to place your assets beyond the reach of any who may have claims against you for your involvement as a director of this company. In some circumstances, transfer of assets into a trust fund or into the name of your partner or spouse may achieve this, although perhaps not without some disadvantages and usually involving a time delay before this transfer is effective. Such a transfer will be ineffective if it is designed to put your assets beyond reach of a court action when a specific incident has occurred, so it is preferable to make such arrangements before an incident arises.

From your experience of running a business, you know that management is not about taking no risks, but about taking risks in a controlled way. A prerequisite is to know what are the risks. You should follow this line of inquiry before accepting a position on a board.

The risk you will be taking in joining a board will be all the greater if the company has no directors' indemnity insurance cover in place: you should inquire about this, the terms of the insurance policy and also consider whether the limit of the cover is likely to be sufficient. Indeed, available cover is unlikely to be sufficient to cover all circumstances: the directors of Equitable Life were sued for £1.7 billion.

It would be wise to ask for a copy of the policy. When you have joined the board, you should inquire regularly to ensure that this insurance cover remains in place. A good company secretary will be proactive in confirming to the directors regularly that the policy remains in force. Some non-executive directors arrange their own insurance cover.

Blue chip companies may be very well run and almost risk free for their directors, in comparison with small, private or start-up companies. Nevertheless, there have been many examples of very large companies that have failed. It is usually true that the smaller company is unable to remunerate its directors (especially its non-executive directors) to the same extent as the blue chip company, despite the bigger risks which may be involved for each director.

The insolvency risk **A2.4**

Most directors who end up in court are directors of small companies being sued for allegedly allowing their companies to continue trading when insolvent – often small, inadequately capitalised companies, perhaps recent start-ups which have been over-trading. An aspect of your risk assessment before you agree to join the board should be to make a judgement about the quality of the management accounts and whether you can be confident that they will clearly indicate to you the trends into or away from insolvency. A company is insolvent if it is unable to pay its debts when they fall due or if it has a negative balance sheet where liabilities exceed assets – unless the board is able to come to a careful decision at that time that the apparent insolvency is likely to be rectified in a timely way, perhaps by a planned injection of new capital or by a significant payment from a long outstanding debtor. Directors are potentially jointly and severally liable for losses incurred by parties doing business with the company after the point in time that the company is judged to have become insolvent.

Reward **A2.5**

Best practice is that directors' remuneration is proportionate to the expertise and experience the director brings to the board, and to his or her time commitment. It is not necessary that all non-executive directors receive the same remuneration, although it is not uncommon that they do. Frequently a non-executive director will receive extra for membership or chairmanship of a board committee.

Total boardroom costs should be proportionate with other business costs and with company performance. The prospective director should learn about these matters before accepting an appointment on a board and shy away from board involvement where the board is rewarding itself extravagantly.

You need to know what salaries and other elements of compensation the other directors receive. You should also know about any outstanding loans to directors and whether any directors have unreasonably large outstanding expenses advances or significant unexplained company credit card transactions which may indicate an anarchic situation.

The solution for the small company which is unable to afford to compensate its non-executive directors for the extra risks they are taking, and perhaps for the extra involvement they are expected to make, is often to allocate to a new director a small proportion of the company's equity. So, for instance, whereas a large listed company might pay a non-executive director an annual fee of £50,000 to £80,000, a very small company might pay an annual fee of £5,000 or £10,000 and provide an equity stake of between 1% and 3% of the issued share capital. It would be reasonable for the company to reserve the right to buy back this equity stake from the new non-executive director if his or her appointment on the board was terminated early due to unsatisfactory performance, but it is important that the terms of this buy-back are set out in advance. The director who is allocated this small equity stake will need to have a exit route defined which will allow him or her to realise the value of these shares at some future date.

A rough and ready way to assess what would be a typical fee for a non-executive director of a particular company is to calculate the average daily remuneration (excluding performance-related and pension elements) of the board's executive directors including the chief executive, based on a national time commitment of 200 days per year. This daily figure is then multiplied by the estimated time commitment expected of the non-executive director to arrive at the annual fee to be paid. The result is that companies are obtaining the services of non-executive directors at a considerable discount to the cost of, for instance, retaining the services of an equivalent level accountant or lawyer from a professional firm.

Tax implications A2.6

You should budget personally for any income tax implications of receiving an equity stake in the company in lieu of director's fees. The tax authorities are likely to value this stake for income tax purposes according to their estimate of its value at the time it was allocated to you, which is not easy to determine for a company that is not listed. Any other purchases of shares in the company by other people at about the same time may be held by the tax authorities as an indication of the value of your stake – so be aware of the possible implications of the value of your small stake if any investor has invested heavily in the company recently but been granted only a modest equity stake – as may be the case if a new executive director has recently joined the board.

The UK tax authorities take the view that a company should deduct at source income tax and national insurance from non-executive directors' fees, even though the contract is a contract for service rather than a contract of employment, and even in the case of those with plural directorships.

Because tax authorities may query whether some of the non-executive directors' reimbursed expenses represent a taxable benefit, some companies 'gross up' expenses and then deduct tax at source. This is, however, an extravagant way of unnecessarily rewarding the tax authorities. It also carries the disadvantage that a non-executive director's fee disclosed in the annual report will be exaggerated, as it will incorporate the 'grossed up' expenses in addition to the fee itself.

Shareholders' agreement **A2.7**

The issue of shareholdings in private companies should be covered in the shareholders' agreement. For instance, this agreement will set out the circumstances and terms under which a shareholder's shares will be bought back from the shareholder in the event that the person's involvement with the company is ended. The right time to ensure that there is a satisfactory shareholders' agreement is when the company is set up in the first place, and a prospective director should be very cautious about accepting a position on the board if there is no shareholders' agreement, or if it is inadequate. So the prospective director should be given a copy of the shareholders' agreement and should study it before accepting a position on the board – whether or not he or she is being offered a shareholding. The prospective director should similarly require and study a copy of the memorandum and articles of association.

Learning about the company **A2.8**

You need to learn as much as you can about the company that wants you on its board, before you decide whether to accept its invitation. This is your 'due diligence'. Some prospective non-executive directors seek professional advice in their due diligence.

As soon as the invitation reaches you, you should not overlook that, in the invitation itself, you are starting to learn significant things about the company. First, who was it who invited you to join the board? If it were not the chairman, was there a good reason why the task was deputed to another? Or does it mean that the chairman is not in control of the board, which is possibly indicative of a poorly run, disunited board. If it is the chairman who has approached you, try to ascertain whether the rest of the board has given prior concurrence to the approach: if not, it could be a warning that all is not well with the board. It could indicate dominance of the board by the chairman. Usually, directors are appointed initially by board resolution, and the appointment is confirmed by the shareholders at the next general meeting.

In some circumstances the shareholders will initiate a board appointment, voting on it at a general meeting of the shareholders.

Readers may like to consult **App5** for a pre-appointment due diligence checklist for new board members.

The commitment **A2.9**

If, however, the way the overture has been made to you does not sound any alarm bells as a bad omen for the future, you can immediately pursue the matter further by inquiring why the board wants you to join them. No worthwhile company will approach someone to join the board without very careful analysis of the company's requirements and the qualities of the prospective director. In your estimation, do you fit that profile? There should be an essential reason why the company needs you, or someone with similar credentials, as a member of the board.

You should not be put off if you are one of a shortlist being approached about just one vacancy on the board – this reveals prudent caution by the board and a determination to have both the strongest and most compatible board possible.

You should also be able quickly to get a feel as to why the board thinks you are the right person. What particular skills and experience of yours are they looking for? You need to learn about the skills and experience of the other board members and satisfy yourself that what you will bring to the party is not already provided in abundance by other board members. This gives you the opportunity, too, to satisfy yourself that the board is a balanced board which is likely to meet the needs of the business into the future.

Skills and responsibilities A2.10

Apart from the skills and experience that the board is looking for in yourself, the board may also be intending that you take on special responsibilities, such as the chairing of a board committee, and you should consider whether their intention, and the timing of it, are appropriate in view of your strengths, weaknesses and initial time availability. Furthermore, if there are other members on the board who appear to have the requisite skills and experience for this additional responsibility, what is the significance of their being passed over?

It is not ideal for a new non-executive director to assume immediate responsibility for chairing a board committee, although there will be occasions when that is necessary. It should, however, be mentioned at an early stage and not sprung upon the new director when he or she has indicated their likely acceptance of an invitation to join the board.

Time commitment A2.11

Clearly, you need to assess the time commitment which will be involved. In addition to scheduled board meetings and board committee meetings, there are likely to be unscheduled board meetings and informal board meetings to attend, and you may be required to attend at the company for other reasons and to make site visits. For instance, the chairman of the audit committee may wish to meet with internal and external auditors and with the secretary of the committee between meetings on occasion. If a change of external auditor is contemplated, there are likely to be presentations to attend from the firms tendering for the work and so on. Many companies have a weekend away for the board once a year to consider strategy.

A practical problem may be that you have other regular commitments which clash with the company's standard date for board meetings, for example, too many companies seem to choose the last Friday of the month for this purpose! If you are right for the company and the company needs you, then the company is likely to be willing to try to rearrange its preferred date for board meetings so as to avoid clashes with your prior appointments. It is not unreasonable for you, as a prospective director, to point out that you have diary clashes, at least initially. It is certainly important that you 'come clean' in advance of accepting a board position, if it appears that there will be significant clashes with other commitments into the future, and this needs to be resolved before you accept the invitation to join the board. It is a sensible idea for the company to issue its planned board and board committee dates on a rolling basis for at least a full year forward. You will find as a director that careful diary maintenance is important.

The quality of the board and the company **A2.12**

In getting to grips with the issue as to whether you will be able to give the company the attention you should, you will also be able to assess whether the board meets sufficiently often to discharge its responsibilities thoroughly, which is essential. This will vary between companies, but a fairly standard norm is a monthly board meeting, or possibly a formal board meeting every other month alternating with an informal board meeting in each of the intervening months. Audit committees which meet fewer times than four a year may be ineffective, and it is certainly unwise that they should meet, for instance, at nine in the morning before the main board meets on the same morning at ten.

You would be imprudent not to inquire whether any of the directors has a criminal record or has in the past been a director of a company that has failed, or has been declared bankrupt or come to an arrangement with his or her creditors. This is one of the many issues you will want clarification about before you join the board, and will need to have it in writing for it to be worthwhile.

Succession planning **A2.13**

If from your inquiries you form the view that the board is being forward-looking in its succession planning, then this is good news. The corollary will be concerning: a board that has no planned turnover of its membership is likely to be an ossified, unbalanced board. So it is reasonable to inquire about planned board succession, and about the duration and end dates of directors' contracts.

In general, a well-run board will have arranged things so that something like one-third of the board appointments come up for termination or renewal annually, and it would be a matter of concern if a director's contract allowed compensation amounting to more than one year's compensation. You should inquire as to the significant terms within each director's contract, and ascertain whether, when you join a board, a copy of each director's contract will be made available to you.

The UK Corporate Governance Code (set out in full at **App1**) states at Provision B.7.1 that all directors of FTSE 350 companies should be subject to annual election by shareholders, and that all other directors should be subject to election by shareholders at the first annual general meeting after their appointment, and to re-election thereafter at intervals of no more than three years.

Financial and management accounting matters A2.14

Once you are a member of the board, you will quickly appreciate how important the accounting processes and accounting information of the business are to its board of directors. 'Flaky' management accounts can mean that the board is uncertain whether or not the business is solvent and thus whether the company is trading illegally – which is a solemn responsibility of each director to avoid (see **A3.5**). 'Flaky' management accounts will be an inadequate basis for decision-making at the board and will almost inevitably lead to the decline of the company.

There is much that you can do before you join the board to assess whether you are likely to have problems with management accounts and financial statements when you are a member of the board. It would be sensible to ask for a copy of the last two sets of audited financial statements; this will give you comparative figures for the past three years.

Of course, you will endeavour to interpret the audited financial statements. Any qualification to the audit opinion or emphasis of matter statement within the audit report will weigh upon you. If the date of the audit report is more than three months after the end of the year, you may interpret this as being inefficient and worrying: if such a practice continued after you joined the board, it would mean that you would be delayed in getting the reassurance that the audited financial statements may give you. You will look for trends over the years for which you have been given the figures. You will observe the level of profitability of the company and the extent to which its assets exceed its liabilities, having regard to the size of the business. It would be wise, if possible, to work out a few key accounting ratios and to observe the trends in these over time. If you decide to join the board, you can be surprisingly effective at board meetings if you continue to monitor changes in these key ratios over time.

The quality of the regular monthly management accounts is very important. You should ask to see examples from the recent past, including the most recent. For a small company, at a minimum they should include an up-to-date balance sheet, profit and loss account, and cash flow projection; and, for each of the important items for this company, the management accounts should show monthly results and 'cumulatives' for the year-to-date compared to budgets, with projected outturns for the financial year.

You should have regard for how long it appears to take to produce these monthly accounts, whether a following month's management accounts appear to start with the closing figures reported for the previous month, and for the quality of the chief accountant's or financial director's narrative interpretation of these figures. Be particularly wary of any indications that the company has become too tightly extended with regard to its cash flow: indications of this may include the factoring of its debts, high levels of loans, overdue accounts etc. Although it should not be your chief concern, if cash flow is unhealthy it could mean that you will experience difficulty in extracting from the company your agreed director's fees. It would be sensible to ensure that you have in writing what your remuneration will be and the dates on which payment will be made.

You should be worried if tax payments are being delayed: check if the company is incurring any penalties from the taxation authorities. What you are less likely to learn about from scrutiny of management accounts is the possibility of unrecorded liabilities, but you can ask the chief executive and the finance director directly for assurances on this score. You should also check if the company is engaged in any significant legal disputes or is aware that it has breached any covenants in its contracts or of any significant claims made, or likely to be made, against the company. Ask the company if it has a disputed accounts file and, if so, request to peruse it. Be wary of accounting practices which seem dubious and too clever by half.

Remember, financial statements which are published are the directors' financial statements (not the auditors') and so, if you join the board, you will shortly be subscribing to a set of annual financial statements. You should be very cautious about joining if the monthly accounts to the board give you little confidence about the company's capability to prepare reliable accounts.

The value of the audit **A2.15**

If the company has a small turnover, in some legislations it may choose not to have an annual audit, in which case this leaves you, as a prospective director, in a vulnerable position unless you can satisfy yourself in other ways as to the reliability of the financial statements. Currently, companies that fall within the European Community's small companies regime may opt out of an annual audit unless their shareholders insist. The threshold for what constitutes a small company is raised periodically, and currently is when two of the following three criteria apply: fewer than 50 staff, turnover of less than £6.5 million and total assets of less than £3.26 million. 'Mid-tier companies' are larger but with a turnover less than or equal to £25.9 million and total assets less than or equal to £12.9 million.

The European Commission recently proposed also removing the audit requirement from these mid-tier companies, and in 2011 a UK government minister expressed the view that the UK government believed there was a strong case for taking away the mandatory requirement for an audit from these medium-sized companies, thus removing the audit requirement from a further 32,000 companies.[1]

Without an audit, all you can be reasonably sure about is that the financial statements which have been returned to the authorities are compiled consistently with the underlying accounting records, not that those accounting records are reliable.

Except for the smallest of companies, it should not improve your confidence if the annual audit has been done by a very small firm, or perhaps by a sole practitioner. On the other hand, there is wide agreement that even large quoted companies do not necessarily need to be audited by one of the largest firms of public accountants. Most FTSE 100 and FTSE 250 companies are audited by a 'Big Four' audit firm (see Chapter **H2**).

Conduct of board meetings **A2.16**

When being invited to join a board, in general it should be entirely reasonable for you to ask to see the agenda papers and minutes of recent board meetings. You may leave this request until just before you are ready to accept the invitation to join the board, as companies may reasonably be reluctant to share this information with a distant, uncommitted suitor. There may be justification for certain items to be omitted from what you are permitted to see, but it is desirable that you know the general nature of these and the reasons why they were omitted. For instance, one agenda item is likely to have been the board's consideration of the pros and cons of inviting you to join the board; you should be concerned if that were not the case, as it means that the board minutes are an incomplete record of the directors' deliberations on board business.

When you study these agenda papers and minutes, you will learn much about the affairs of the company which will help to get you up to speed more quickly, and further questions to ask will spring to mind. You will also have the opportunity to conclude much about how the board conducts its business by asking the following questions:

- Do agenda papers reach board members in sufficient time before meetings for them to be thoroughly prepared?
- Do the executive directors regularly provide written reports to the board within the agenda pack which is circulated to directors in good time in advance of the meetings?
- Do agenda papers appear to be competently written and cover in sufficient detail the items upon which the board needs to be informed and as a basis for the decisions to be taken?
- Do the board agenda papers include minutes of the board committees?
- Are the right sort of items on the agendas of board meetings? For instance, is the board attending to its core business or is it preoccupied with other matters, such as new ventures etc?
- Are the minutes of the board issued reasonably promptly?
- Do the board minutes and board committee minutes appear to cover in sufficient detail the key points of discussion that took place in the meetings, in addition to decisions arrived at?
- Do later meetings appear adequately to follow up items outstanding from earlier meetings and decisions taken at earlier meetings?
- Is attendance by directors good?

Every board should have a schedule of matters reserved to the board, and this should have been adopted by formal board resolution. Provision A.1.1 of the UK Code reads:

> 'The board should meet sufficiently regularly to discharge its duties effectively. There should be a formal schedule of matters specifically reserved for its decision. The annual report should include a statement of how the board operates, including a high level statement of which types of decisions are to be taken by the board and which are to be delegated to management.'

You should ask for a copy of this schedule and ask yourself whether there are any significant omissions from it. See **A1.12**. Bear in mind that matters not contained therein may be matters which will not come to the board for decision. The board needs to be in control of the company.

Some companies get into difficulties through failing to keep abreast with statutory requirements such as registering promptly with the authorities any changes in board membership, failing to issue share certificates in accordance with board decisions to issue shares, and failing to lodge annual financial statements within the stipulated time. Your own search where financial statements etc are lodged may be informative.

Meeting the directors **A2.17**

You will wish to meet most or all of the directors individually before you accept the invitation to join the board. They should wish to meet you. Try to discern if there is tension between board members; a board riven with dissent is best avoided. Discreetly try to gauge the opinions of board members as to the calibre and commitment of their colleagues.

Clearly you will need to see and finalise your director's contract before joining the board. This should not be a problem, but if it is then there is probably a deeper problem within the company.

Induction training **A2.18**

Readers may also like to consult **App5** for another induction checklist.

If you decide to join the board, you will probably be aware of your limitations as a new board member. With the chairman and chief executive, you should endeavour to identify the training you need and obtain their agreement to that taking place. It may involve attendance at outside courses, not just initially but at other times during the tenure of your directorship. You should also ask that an induction programme for you should be arranged, so that you can meet the key players within the company and visit the key operations within the first month or two of you joining the board.

Considering joining a board? Checklist of matters to be considered **A2.19**

Readers may also wish to refer to **B5.8**.

Suggested principal method of inquiry:	**Y =**	**Your responsibility to ascertain/decide**
	W =	**In writing from the company**
	V =	**Verbally from the company**

		Timing and method of inquiry		
	Issue to be addressed	**At outset**	**During negotiations**	**Before acceptance**
1.	**You personally**			
1.1	Ascertain why you are being asked to join the board.		W	
1.2	If you are being sought because of a particular expertise, will you be able to give that expertise to the company in the way they need it?			Y
1.3	Have you the motivation for this appointment?			Y

		Timing and method of inquiry		
	Issue to be addressed	**At outset**	**During negotiations**	**Before acceptance**
1.4	Will you be able to devote the required time, not just for meetings but for preparation as well?			**Y**
1.5	Obtain dates of future meetings and check and resolve any significant diary clashes.		**W**	
1.6	Do you think you have, or can acquire, the skills you will need?			**Y**
1.7	Is there anything in your background which makes you unsuitable to accept a directorship?	**Y**		
1.8	Is there anything in your circumstances which you writing) should draw to the attention of the board before accepting, such as a potential conflict of interest?		**Y (in writing)**	
1.9	If the board is relying upon you to be an independent non-executive director, would that be the case?		**Y**	
1.10	Are your personal assets sufficiently protected from being claimed against in the case of legal actions against the directors of the company whose board you are considering joining?			**Y**
1.11	Have you planned for your tax liabilities which may result from accepting this position (eg liability to pay tax on any share allocation you may be granted)?			**Y**
1.12	Does the company have sufficient directors' indemnity insurance cover?			**W**
2.	**Your duties and your development**			
2.1	Are you clear, and are you satisfied, as to the board's intentions of the contribution you can make?		**W**	

		Timing and method of inquiry		
	Issue to be addressed	**At outset**	**During negotiations**	**Before acceptance**
2.2	Have you been told which board committees you will be asked to belong to, and whether it is the intention that you will chair any of these, initially or later?		V	
2.3	Is the company arranging an induction programme for you?		V	
2.4	Is the company committed to developing you through training courses, and have your development needs been identified?		V	
2.5	Even as a non-executive director, will your performance be subject to annual appraisal?		V	
3.	**Contractual matters**			
3.1	Is the intended compensation package for you (fees, allocation of shares etc) appropriate?			Y
3.2	Is there a written contract covering your post as director, and is it satisfactory?			W/Y
3.3	Does the intended contract specify the duration of your appointment and whether it is open to renewal thereafter?			W
3.4	Does the intended contract specify the fees you will receive and their dates of payment?			W
3.5	Are there any matters in the contracts of other directors of the company which cause you concern?		W/Y	
3.6	Is there a shareholders' agreement, and is it satisfactory?			W/Y
4.	**The company**			
4.1	Are you clear as to the principal risks the company faces?			Y

		Timing and method of inquiry		
	Issue to be addressed	**At outset**	**During negotiations**	**Before acceptance**
4.2	Have you visited the company and its key sites?			**Y**
4.3	Have you inspected the constitutional documents of the company (eg memorandum and articles of association)?			**Y/W**
5.	**The board**			
5.1	Was it the board that decided you should be invited to join the board?	**Y**		
5.2	Have you met the board members prior to making a decision to join the board, and learnt about their backgrounds?			**Y**
5.3	Do you consider the board to be balanced, competent and committed?		**Y**	
5.4	Does the board have proper succession planning for board positions?		**Y/V**	
5.5	Does the board and its committees meet sufficiently frequently and for sufficient time?		**Y**	
5.6	Is there a schedule of matters reserved to the board, and does it seem appropriate?		**W/Y**	
6.	**Board meetings and board information**			
6.1	From what you have seen, does attendance at board meetings seem good?		**Y**	
6.2	Do agenda papers appear to reach board members in sufficient time before meetings for them to be thoroughly prepared?		**Y**	

		Timing and method of inquiry		
	Issue to be addressed	**At outset**	**During negotiations**	**Before acceptance**
6.3	Do the executive directors appear to regularly provide written reports to the board – within the agenda pack which is circulated to directors in good time in advance of the meetings?		**Y**	
6.4	Do agenda papers appear to be competently written and cover in sufficient detail the items upon which the board needs to be informed and as a basis for the decisions to be taken? Do the board agenda papers include minutes of the board committees?		**Y**	
6.5	Are the right sort of items on the agendas of board meetings? For instance, is the board attending to its core business, or is it preoccupied with other matters – such as new ventures etc?		**Y**	
6.6	Are the minutes of the board issued reasonably promptly?		**Y**	
6.7	Do the board minutes and board committee minutes appear to cover in sufficient detail the key points of discussion that took place in the meetings, in addition to decisions arrived at?		**Y**	
6.8	Do later meetings appear adequately to follow up items outstanding from earlier meetings and decisions taken at earlier meetings?		**Y**	
7.	**The finances of the company**			
7.1	Have you seen and studied the last two years' audited financial statements, and do they indicate any matters of concern?		**Y**	
7.2	Are total boardroom costs reasonable?		**Y**	

		Timing and method of inquiry		
	Issue to be addressed	**At outset**	**During negotiations**	**Before acceptance**
7.3	Are there any outstanding loans and advances to other directors which should cause you concern?			**W/Y**
7.4	Does the board receive regular, up-to-date, sufficient and apparently reliable management accounts with a narrative interpretation of their key points?		**Y**	
7.5	Do the financial statements and the latest management accounts of the company indicate a healthy position and prospects?			**Y**
7.6	Does the company have any significant outstanding claims or contingent liabilities?			**W/Y**
7.7	Does the company have a cash flow problem?		**Y**	
7.8	Is the company solvent?		**Y**	
7.9	Is the company up to date with its payment of tax liabilities?			**W/Y**

Outside advice for directors at the company's expense **A2.20**

Main Principle A.1 of the UK Corporate Governance Code (**App1**) now reads:

> 'Every company should be headed by an effective board which is collectively responsible for the long-term success of the company.'

The Main Principles and Supporting Principles within the UK Corporate Governance Code (set out in full at **App1**) are intended to be followed by UK companies with a premium listing. The more detailed Provisions of the Code, which nest below the Principles, are intended to have a 'comply or explain' status. The UK Listing Rules require a statement in the annual report explaining how the Main Principles have been applied. The Listing Rules (previously at rule 12.43A, then rule 9.8.6; and, from 2010, rule 9.8.6 (5) and (6)) also require a statement explaining whether or not all of the Provisions have been observed and, if not, which Provisions have not been followed, and why not:

> 'In the case of a listed company incorporated in the United Kingdom, the following additional items must be included in its annual financial report:
>
> …

(5) a statement of how the listed company has applied the Main Principles set out in the UK Corporate Governance Code, in a manner that would enable shareholders to evaluate how the principles have been applied;

(6) a statement as to whether the listed company has:

(a) complied throughout the accounting period with all relevant provisions set out in the UK Corporate Governance Code; or

(b) not complied throughout the accounting period with all relevant provisions set out in the UK Corporate Governance Code and if so, setting out:

(i) those provisions, if any it has not complied with;

(ii) in the case of provisions whose requirements are of a continuing nature, the period within which, if any, it did not comply with some or all of those provisions; and

(iii) the company's reasons for non-compliance.'

For most companies, observing the Provisions is likely to be appropriate as contributing to applying the Principles, although as far back as 1998 the Hampel Committee warned that 'box ticking' compliance with Provisions would not amount to adherence to the Principles. Nevertheless, most companies take the line that compliance with the Provisions is sensible. Indeed, in the 1992 Cadbury Code there was no distinction between Principles and Provisions, and the items in that Code carried the same optional status as the Provisions in the Combined Code.

The development of guidance on independent advice commencing 1992 **A2.21**

It is good practice that board committees and individual directors should be empowered to take independent professional advice at the company's expense on matters relating to their responsibilities. Provision B.5.1 of the UK Corporate Governance Code reads:

> 'The board should ensure that directors, especially non-executive directors, have access to independent professional advice at the company's expense where they judge it necessary to discharge their responsibilities as directors. Committees should be provided with sufficient resources to undertake their duties.'

The arrangements for this should be set out in a formal board resolution. Features of this resolution might include:

- the circumstances in which such advice might be sought;
- the nature of such advice that is included within this authority;
- the annual financial limit of the cost of this advice without specific board or chairman approval;
- arrangements for payment, and whether disclosure of the nature of the advice sought and given is required;
- whether the chairman should be consulted first; and
- that the choice of professional advisor is at the discretion of the individual director or the board committee seeking the advice.

Some companies require the approval of one of the independent directors before such advice may be sought.

To obtain an understanding of what is regarded as best practice, it is still necessary to draw upon both the Cadbury and Hampel Committee Reports and their 1992 and 1998 Codes respectively. This is in part because it appears that Hampel omitted, while not apparently intending to overturn, certain content of Cadbury, which we refer to below. Of course, it is also necessary to draw upon the Financial Reporting Council's latest version of the UK Corporate Governance Code (**App1**).

Note that the first part of Provision B.5.1 is targeted at each individual director – whether executive or non-executive, but especially the non-executive directors. Note, too, that there are also other Provisions designed to ensure that individual directors perform in a competent way; a major feature of the Codes from 2003 onwards is the new stress that is placed on the selection, competence, commitment and evaluation of the performance of individual directors.

Note further that board committees, not just individual directors, should be mandated to seek independent advice in the furtherance of their responsibilities. However, there was no reference in any part of the 1998 Combined Code, nor in the Hampel Report itself, to the nominations and audit committees needing to be empowered to take outside professional advice, though such authority would certainly be desirable. On the other hand, the Cadbury Report (though not its Code of Best Practice[2]) contained the following:

> 'The audit committee should have explicit authority to investigate any matters within its terms of reference, the resources which it needs to do so, and full access to information. The committee should be able to obtain external professional advice and to invite outsiders with relevant experience to attend if necessary.'

and, within the specimen terms of reference for an audit committee, which the Cadbury Report recommended:

> 'The Committee is authorised by the Board to obtain outside legal or other independent professional advice and to secure the attendance of outsiders with relevant experience and expertise if it considers this necessary.'

and, for remuneration committees:

> 'We recommend that boards should appoint remuneration committees, consisting wholly or mainly of non-executive directors and chaired by a non-executive director, to recommend to the board the remuneration of the executive directors in all its forms, drawing on outside advice as necessary.'

Chapter **E10** discusses remuneration committees and **App4.9** provides illustrative terms of reference for a board remuneration committee. Readers may like to consult **App5** for a summary of the principal duties of remuneration committees.

In one respect the 1998 Combined Code was an advance from the earlier Cadbury Code. While there were these recommendations within the body of the Cadbury Report that remuneration and audit committees should be empowered to take outside advice at the company's expense, there was no provision on this in the Cadbury Code, whereas the Hampel Committee's 1998 Combined Code did provide for this, but only in the context of remuneration committees, a provision carried through into the latest version of the UK Corporate Governance Code for remuneration committees.

The 1998 Combined Code Provision A.1.3 statement that:

> 'There should be a procedure agreed by the board for directors in the furtherance of their duties to take independent professional advice if necessary at the company's expense.'

represented a sharpening of the wording of the equivalent Provision in the 1992 Cadbury Code, which had read:

> 'There should be an agreed procedure for directors in the furtherance of their duties to take independent professional advice if necessary, at the company's expense.'[3]

So, by 1998 it was clear that the procedure must be agreed by the board in some way. The Cadbury Report had indicated as much in the body of that report, though not in the Cadbury Code, in wording (or equivalent wording) which was absent from the Hampel Report, namely:

> '**Professional Advice**
>
> Occasions may arise when directors have to seek legal and financial advice in the furtherance of their duties. They should always be able to consult the company's advisers. If, however, they consider it necessary to take independent professional advice, **we recommend** that they should be entitled to do so at the company's expense, through an agreed procedure laid down formally, for example in a Board Resolution, in the Articles, or in the Letter of Appointment.'[4]

Readers may like to consult **App5** for a sample letter of non-executive appointment.

The 1998 Code (Provision B.2.5) with respect to remuneration committees had stated:

> 'Remuneration committees should consult the chairman and/or chief executive officer about their proposals relating to the remuneration of other executive directors and have access to professional advice inside and outside the company.'

But this specific wording had been lost from the 2003 Code, where Provision A.5.2 merely stated (see above):

> '... Committees should be provided with sufficient resources to undertake their duties.'

It is true that the Smith Report, in guidance which has not been incorporated into the Codes from 2003 to the present, stated (at para 2.15):

> 'The board should make funds available to the audit committee to enable it to take independent legal, accounting and other advice when the audit committee reasonably believes it necessary to do so.'

and the 2003 Code included, in its 'Summary of the principal duties of the nomination committee':

> 'The committee should make a statement in the annual report about its activities; the process used for appointments and explain if external advice or open advertising has not been used ...'

and in a similar section on remuneration committees, that:

> 'The committee should be exclusively responsible for establishing the section criteria, selecting, appointing and setting the terms of reference for any remuneration consultants who advise the committee.'

The 2012 UK Corporate Governance Code has replaced the above two wordings in Provisions B.2.4 and D.2.1, which read respectively:

> 'A separate section of the annual report should describe the work of the nomination committee, including the process it has used in relation to board appointments. This section should include a description of the board's policy on diversity, including gender, any measurable objectives that it has set for implementing the policy, and progress on achieving the objectives. An explanation should be given if neither an external search consultancy nor open advertising has been used in the appointment of a chairman or a non-executive director. Where an external search consultancy has been used, it should be identified in the annual report and a statement made as to whether it has any other connection with the company.'

and

> 'The board should establish a remuneration committee of at least three, or in the case of smaller companies two, independent non-executive directors. In addition the company chairman may also be a member of, but not chair, the committee if he or she was considered independent on appointment as chairman. The remuneration committee should make available its terms of reference, explaining its role and the authority delegated to it by the board. Where remuneration consultants are appointed, a statement should be made available of whether they have any other connection with the company.'

Readers may like to consult **App5** for a summary of the principal duties of nomination committees.

Deciding directors' remuneration independently **A2.22**

The key principle is that no director should participate in the determination of his or her own compensation package. Thus, the compensation of executive directors should be recommended to the board by a remuneration committee of independent, non-executive directors; and the fees of the non-executive directors should be recommended to the board by a committee of executive directors and the chairman, though this committee is not a formal a requirement of the UK Corporate Governance Code. The remuneration committee of the board may also be charged with the responsibility to determine the remuneration of the most senior executives below the level of the executive directors.

Example policies on independent advice **A2.23**

At **A2.24**, we reproduce the policy statement which one UK listed company has developed to cover the issue of individual directors taking independent professional advice if necessary at the company's expense. The Notes that follow it at **A2.25** are our elaboration upon some of the content of the policy statement, but they did not form part of the policy statement itself. In particular, we draw readers' attention to footnote 2 on whether the scope of the advice which may be sought under this policy should be restricted in any way – perhaps to advice on one's responsibilities in law as a director, or advice only of legal and accounting matters in general.

Frequently, board policies on individual directors seeking external advice require that prior approval should be obtained from one of the independent directors, who should not be the director intending to seek the advice. The policy should cover both executive and non-executive directors. Note that this Provision within the Code is no longer one that the external auditor reviews in the course of the external audit (see **H1.7**).

Example 1 on independent professional advice for directors A2.24

(Adapted from existing guidelines of a major multinational company.)

1. The board recognises that as is recommended in corporate governance best practice, directors should be able to take independent professional advice, at the expense of the company, in the event that circumstances warrant it.
2. This facility is intended to provide directors with a 'safety net' to be used when they feel that a second opinion is necessary on a particular matter, over and above the advice available to them through the normal channels.
3. This facility should not be used lightly, and consequently it is difficult to anticipate all the circumstances under which a director would find it necessary to seek independent counsel. Whilst it is not mandatory, a director who finds him or herself in a position which, in the director's judgement, warrants independent advice being taken, should consider first raising the matter with the chair of the audit committee who may be in a position to resolve the matter through the channels of that committee.
4. The limit on the amount of costs which may be incurred by any director on an annual basis is £10,000. This amount may be varied at any time by board resolution.
5. There is no obligation for a director to disclose the nature of the advice sought or given. He or she is only obliged to confirm that the advice was sought in the context of his or her position as a director of XYZ Ltd.
6. A director who seeks to invoke this policy should instruct the independent advisor (law firm etc) to address invoices to: c/o the Secretary to the Audit Committee, The Group Chief Audit Executive, XYZ Ltd, (Address)

Notes on Example 1 A2.25

1. In this policy statement, the term 'directors' referred exclusively to members of the board of XYZ Ltd and not to directors of any other group companies.
2. It was the Cadbury Code of Best Practice which first used the expression 'independent professional advice' (Provision 1.5 at **App6.1**) in this context, but elsewhere in the Cadbury Report (para 4.18) this was referred to as 'legal or financial advice'. It is up to boards to decide whether the scope of this advice should be broader than legal and financial: in view of the terms of reference of Cadbury, it is reasonable to take the view that Cadbury's recommendation was limited to 'legal and financial' advice, but this is not to say that Cadbury would have disapproved of a company broadening the scope beyond 'legal and financial'. It may be, for instance, that a director in the furtherance of his

or her duties might feel a need for independent advice on human resource or IT issues: couching the query in legal and/or financial terms, he or she could consult lawyers and/or accountants to obtain this advice. They in turn might consult other specialists. Or authority might exist for the director to consult the appropriate specialist directly.

3. Resolution in this way may either be that the audit committee takes the professional advice itself (perhaps by action of the chair) or that the chair prevails upon the director concerned that the advice should be taken openly at the company's expense and available to all board members.
4. In addition, some companies permit a higher spend, subject to prior approval of the company chairman.
5. The implication of this address is that the secretary to the audit committee is the group chief audit executive. Ideally, the secretary of the audit committee should be the company secretary as (a) the committee is a committee of the main board and (b) it is preferable that the secretary to this committee is not a person whose performance it is critical that the audit committee appraises.
6. It is not necessary that the audit committee need be involved as per paragraph 3 (above) or with respect to payment. It could alternatively be the company chairman, or the senior non-executive director (where there is one) or the company secretary.

Notes

1 Mr Ed Davey, UK government minister in the Department of Business, Innovation and Skills, expressed this view on 25 January 2011 to the House of Lords Economic Affairs Select Committee's Inquiry into Audit Market Concentration – see Qs 522, 523 and 524 in the Evidence Volume (Volume II of the Report (30 March 2011), HL Paper 119-II, ISBN 978 0 10 947325 8, £27.50; also available on the Parliament website). Volume 1 is the report of the Inquiry (30 March 2011), HL Paper 119-I, ISBN 978 0 10 847326 5, £13.50.

2 The Cadbury Code of Best Practice (1992) (**App6.1**), the predecessor of the UK Corporate Governance Code (**App1**) is generally regarded as having been the world's first corporate governance code.

3 Report of the Committee on the Financial Aspects of Corporate Governance (1 December 1992) ('The Cadbury Committee Report') (Gee, ISBN 0 85258 915 8), Code Provision 1.5 at p 58.

4 The Cadbury Committee Report (above), para 4.18 at p 24.

Independence Issues

Introduction A3.1

Certain independence aspects were introduced at **A1.25** to **A1.26**. Chapter **A9** deals with independence and conflict of interest implications of company loans to directors. At **C2.19** we discuss independence as one of the hallmarks of effective corporate governance. The UK Corporate Governance Code covers independence at Provision B.1.1 (**App1**).

Commencing with Cadbury on Independence A3.2

When the Cadbury Committee reconvened to review compliance with its Code, it cited the following barriers to independence while conceding that this view of independence might run contrary to the views of some boards and their auditors:

- a close relative of an executive director;
- a connection with the company exceeding 20 years;
- formerly an executive director; or
- an employee of the company.

Its survey also concluded rather bravely that the majority of non-executive directors were independent.

In the interests of pragmatism, Cadbury had compromised on the principle of independence by conceding that independent directors might hold shares in the enterprise and receive directors' fees – a concession which rightly endures to today.

Of course, there are examples of non-executive directors receiving no fee. Take, for instance, those on the boards of Training and Enterprise Councils which existed until 2001, and on the boards of many charities. With respect to the former, it is difficult to avoid the conclusion that the government deemed it unnecessary to offer them fees as many TEC directors had an interest in their TEC through their positions in the local community – often as directors of major, local business partners of their TEC though being large local employers. While TEC directors were non-executive, many of them could not be regarded as independent.

Cadbury had declined to specify the criteria that could impede a director from being classified as an independent director. The 1992 Cadbury Code merely stated:

> 'The majority [of non-executive directors] should be independent of management and free from any business or other relationship which could materially interfere with the exercise of their independent judgement, apart from their fees and shareholding. Their fees should reflect the time which they commit to the company.'

Subsequently, various bodies developed their lists of independence criteria. While they had significant common ground, they were not identical. Thus, Sir Derek Higgs recommended that the UK's 2003 Combined Code should incorporate an agreed list of criteria (**A3.13**). This was done and the list has remained unchanged since then.

In our experience, directors who do not conform to the standard independence tests would nevertheless fiercely defend their independence – especially if they were non-executive. Indeed, as we shall see, company law requires all directors to exercise independent judgement. In 1998, Sir Adrian Cadbury said:

> 'The presence of independent members of boards does not imply that they have inherently higher standards of morality than their executive colleagues. It is simply that it is easier for them to take an objective view of whatever matters are under review. They stand further back from the action, they bring outside standards to bear on the issues and their interests are less directly at stake. The argument for independent members of professional disciplinary bodies rests on the same grounds.'[1]

He might have added that it is also a matter of perception – that stakeholders can have more confidence that decisions have not been made in a self-interested way if the board has a majority of independent directors. Perception has a reality of its own.

Defining independence criteria A3.3

One of the criteria that failed to make it to this agreed list of independence critieria was the criterion that someone over the age of 70 should not be regarded as independent. It was never a very valid criterion, but it became more unacceptable as 'ageism' became recognised as a form of discrimination. Such validity as this criterion had was predicated on the assumption that an elderly person would realise that his or her chances of getting another board appointment were very limited, thus discouraging them from taking an independent line on any issue if to do so might mean that they were more likely to lose their board appointment. But it is apparent that elderly people frequently exhibit the quality of stubbornness which is not too far removed from independence.

On the other hand, younger non-executive directors, anxious to please their peers and with much of their career in front of them, might be unwilling to take an independent line on a board matter for fear of alienating their colleagues upon whom their future careers may depend. Another perceived justification for the 'age 70' criterion was that declining mental acumen might make it more difficult for them to reason when and how they should take an independent position on an issue. But 'today's 70 is yesterday's 60'. It is no longer a company law requirement for directors over the age of 70 to stand for annual re-election to the board rather than once every three years. For FTSE 350 companies the UK Corporate Governance Code (set out in full at **App1**) states that best practice is that all directors should come up for re-election annually (Provision B.7.1) – a recent innovation which has been criticised as possibly encouraging board short-termism, despite the Code's emphasis elsewhere on the importance of the long-term view.

Independence of audit committee and risk committee members A3.4

Note that the 2003 Combined Code included, at the level of a Provision, for the first time a 'requirement' that every member of the audit committee should be an independent director, whereas previously, while all should have been non-executive, only a majority were 'required' to be independent.

The 1998 Combined Code (Provision D.3.1) stated:

> 'The board should establish an audit committee of at least three directors, all nonexecutive, with written terms of reference which deal clearly with its authority and duties. The members of the committee, a majority of whom should be independent non-executive directors, should be named in the report and accounts.'

Now the UK Corporate Governance Code, at Provision C.3.1 (**App1**), has been further modified to permit the chairman of the board (who is not counted as one of the independent directors) to be a member but not the chairman of the audit committee of a company below the FTSE 350, so long as he or she were independent at the time they became the chairman of the board; and the audit committee of a company outside the FTSE 350 may now have only two members:

> 'The board should establish an audit committee of at least three, or in the case of smaller companies two, independent non-executive directors. In smaller companies the company chairman may be a member of, but not chair, the committee in addition to the independent non-executive directors, provided he or she was considered independent on appointment as chairman. The board should satisfy itself that at least one member of the audit committee has recent and relevant financial experience.'

The 2003 UK Combined Code considerably expanded upon the audit committee content of its predecessor 1998 Combined Code. Since then, the content within the Code on audit committees has been changed only by the addition in 2012 of C.3.4 (see **App1**) and by the addition of the first two bullets at C.3.8. (see **App1**). Commencing 2003, the Code introduced the possibility of boards having risk committees (see Chapter **E9** and **App4.18**). Risk committees of the board should not be confused with risk committees that may exist at executive level. The relevant wording of Provision C.3.2 of the current Code says:

> 'The main role and responsibilities of the audit committee should be set out in written terms of reference and should include:
>
> ...
>
> to review the company's internal financial controls and, *unless expressly addressed by a separate board risk committee composed of independent directors, or by the board itself, to review the company's internal control and risk management systems*;' (emphasis added)

This 100% independent composition of the board's risk committee is inconsistent with the Code at Provision C.3.1 which, as we have seen, endorses the possibility that the company chairman of a smaller company may sometimes belong to the audit committee, whereas he or she is implicitly excluded from belonging to the risk committee of a board that is complying with the Code.

We should note too that, while the Code's guidance is that every member of a board risk committee that assumes responsibilities that would otherwise be carried by the audit committee should be an independent director, this is not in line with the 2009 Walker Review guidance[2] which required only that most members should be non-executive directors (not necessarily independent) and that the chief finance officer (CFO) may also be a member:

> 'The board risk committee should, like the audit committee, be a committee of the board and should be chaired by a NED with a majority of non-executive members, but additionally with the CFO as members or in attendance and with the CRO invariably present (see next section on the independence of the risk function). Whether the CEO should be present will be for decision between the chairman of the committee and the CEO. But the CEO will invariably be involved in deliberations of the full board on risk matters and there may be merit for the board risk committee in having an open and wide-ranging discussion without the sometimes dominating presence of the CEO.'

There must be a possibility that the expected 2014 update of the UK Corporate Governance Code might require a board to have a board risk committee to the same extent that an audit committee is required.[3]

The special circumstances of some large financial institutions make the Walker guidance appropriate for them. Some are subsidiaries of overseas parents. These subsidiary boards may have insufficient non-executive directors who pass the independence tests to populate their UK subsidiary board risk committees. Some of these non-executive directors are likely to be executives within the overseas parent and thus not to be regarded as independent. It is also wise advice to require the finance director to be a member of a bank's risk committee of the board, although his or her general attendance at meetings, though not as a member, might be a better approach.

On the other hand, Walker (at Recommendation 23) is more forthright than the Code, in that Walker is not offering the alternative of the board's audit committee overseeing the issues which would otherwise be addressed by a risk committee of the board:

> 'The board of a FTSE 100-listed bank or life insurance company should establish a board risk committee separately from the audit committee. The board risk committee should have responsibility for oversight and advice to the board on the current risk exposures of the entity and future risk strategy, including strategy for capital and liquidity management, and the embedding and maintenance throughout the entity of a supportive culture in relation to the management of risk alongside established prescriptive rules and procedures. In preparing advice to the board on its overall risk appetite, tolerance and strategy, the board risk committee should ensure that account has been taken of the current and prospective macroeconomic and financial environment drawing on financial stability assessments such as those published by the Bank of England, the FSA and other authoritative sources that may be relevant for the risk policies of the firm.'

The extra independence of complete outsiders A3.5

We sometimes use the expression 'outside director' to lay emphasis upon the independent credentials of most non-executive directors. We should not forget, however, that *all* directors have a statutory obligation to exercise independent judgement.[4] In some contexts the complete outsider (who is not also a director) may bring an even greater degree of independence. For instance, for several years until 2002 the audit committee of the Church Commissioners had a chairman who was not a member of the board. The chairs of many audit committees in the public sector are often not members of the board, and indeed the responsibilities carried collectively by the board of a company are often enshrined within the personal responsibilities of a single accounting officer. But neither Cadbury, Hampel nor more recent versions of the UK Corporate Governance Code made provision for any non-director to be a member of an audit committee.

Undoubtedly, the complete outsider who is not a member of the board brings to bear an extra degree of independence, but has the disadvantage of not necessarily being privy to all aspects of board business, and thus facing an extra challenge to be fully aware of all the issues which may be of importance to the audit committee. The complete outsider also is perhaps less motivated by the solemn responsibilities of being a director, though caution would need to be exercised to avoid the risk of such a person being held to be a shadow director (see **A1.19**). Such an independent chairman of the audit committee would need to be 'in attendance' at board meetings, or parts thereof, in order to present the report of the audit committee. Many audit committees report to the board by tabling their minutes as part of the board agenda papers, or by the chair of the audit committee preparing a special report of the audit committee as an agenda paper for the board meeting. In addition, or alternatively, audit committees may make to the board an annual report of the audit committee or a six-monthly report (see Chapters **E1** to **E8** on audit committees).

It is considered that an independent director is always, by definition, a non-executive director. It is implied as being axiomatic that being an executive may cloud one's independence of judgement, though in reality this may depend more upon personality, attitude of mind, background, ability and access to information. At the board, every director is required to put partisan executive interest to one side. The true independence of the executive director may only become apparent following resignation on a point of principle. Here we reach another truism: independence is in the eye of the beholder; independent directors must be seen and believed to be independent. Of course, no one would argue that an executive director is entirely independent of the executive, but many would argue that there is no such thing as complete independence for anyone and that independence depends upon much else besides the formal role of the individual concerned.

Assessing director independence **A3.6**

Most understand that the independent director is something more than a non-executive director. What exactly, defies definition. However, since 2003 we have had a standard list of criteria in the UK's Corporate Governance Code which has not been modified since (see **App1**, Provision B.1.1, and **A3.13**). We might cheerfully conclude that the non-executive director who is the spouse of the chief executive is not independent of the executive; but who is to say? What of the non-executive director who went to school or college with the chief executive; or who is the godmother of the chief executive's daughter; or who is an executive director on a second board to which the chief executive of the first board belongs in a non-executive capacity?

In truth, non-executive directors who fail most of the formal tests of independence may still be the most independent of directors who are often much more capable of standing up to over-powerful, misguided executives. Their closer social ties to one or more executives may have removed their fear of taking a stand at odds with the viewpoint of those people; and personality and other personal attributes can in practice by far outweigh impediments to independence posed by social and other ties.

Contrariwise, the non-executive director who has no links with any executives may in practice be far from independent. This might be so if he or she did not have the personal courage to stand up and be counted; possibly through a meek temperament or on account of significant dependence upon the income which the directorship attracts.

The Higgs Report, which was very influential on the wording first introduced into the 2003 UK Combined Code, expressed the view that:

> '… it is important that a non-executive director is not so dependent on the income from their role or shareholding as to prejudice independence of judgement, and I would expect boards to take this into account in determining independence.'[5]

The Tyson report, also published in 2003, said:

> '… the perception of a possible conflict between NED compensation and NED independence may be a possible constraint on the selection of NED candidates from non-traditional talent pools. Currently, average annual NED remuneration is about £44,500 for FTSE 100 firms, £34,800 for FTSE 250 firms, and £23,221 for other listed companies. These are relatively small amounts compared to the annual compensation levels of chief executives, top-level management and other business professionals. But NED compensation levels may be quite large compared to the annual incomes of NED candidates drawn from non-traditional sources such as the non-commercial sector and academia. Institutional investors and other company stakeholders might wonder whether a NED can be truly independent if NED compensation represents a substantial fraction of his or her total annual income.'[6]

Despite the risks involved in being a non-executive director, there is no shortage of those who would like such positions who are often those for whom the non-executive director's fee is an attraction. The preferred candidates for non-executive positions are often those with significant executive director experience in other companies, or similar business experience, and there is a relative shortage of supply of such candidates for whom the non-executive director's fee is often relatively immaterial for them and they judge that the risk-reward ratio is not right. A non-executive director carries broadly the same board responsibilities and risks as an executive director, but for a much more modest financial reward, albeit a much smaller time commitment. The supply of experienced executive directors for non-executive positions is small, as many executives would find the time commitment excessive. For instance, Code Provision B.3.3 states that the board should not agree to a full-time executive director taking on more than one non-executive directorship in a FTSE 100 company nor the chairmanship of such a company.

Not least of the threats to effective independence is an incapability to master the issues that confront the board. This leads to dependency upon the executive who may be pulling the wool over that director's eyes. Failure to master issues may be a consequence of several factors. Incomplete information may be given to the board which could be too late to influence decisions: in such cases, executive directors may be better placed than non-executive directors to form objective judgements. So, independence does not necessarily enhance objectivity, though it is largely for that reason that independence is valued. So much information might come to the board that core issues are obscured. The background of the non-executive director may be inappropriate to master technical fundamentals. Or the non-executive director may be unwilling or unable to put in the time to master the affairs of the business and the business of board meetings. Note that a statutory duty of any director is to exercise reasonable care, skill and diligence (as would be expected of a reasonably diligent person carrying out the functions of the director, as well as based on the director's actual knowledge, skill and experience).[7]

The UK Corporate Governance Code, guided by the 2003 Higgs Report, endeavours to cover these concerns in Provision B.1.1 by stressing that, in addition to the given list of independence criteria, an independent director is one who is 'independent in character and judgement' and that it is 'for the board to determine' this based, of course, upon their knowledge of the personal attributes of the individual director concerned. A practical though difficult implication of this is that, at recruitment time, a board should weigh up the character and personality of a candidate for a board position, gauging whether he or she is likely to be able to exercise independent judgement at board meetings. Another practical implication is that a board should assess whether all of its board members, especially those that are designated as independent, are conducting themselves in ways which assert their independence of judgement. These practical implications, especially the second, which should be part of the annual board evaluation, are difficult to exercise and tend to be honoured more in the breach. The UK Code requires disclosure in the annual report of each director that the board considers to be independent (Provision B.1.1).

An appropriate capacity to exercise independent judgement also includes the ability to judge when it is necessary to do so. After all, an equally important though sometimes diametrically opposed quality sought after in each director is the ability to act as a member of the team which is the board. In the normal course of events, a cohesive board performs better. Proximity to the executive also may impede effective independence. We are all social animals and value our membership of groups. While the chairman is responsible for the effectiveness of the board, all directors share this responsibility – by their personal conduct as board members and by their contribution to ensuring the board operates well as a team.

A non-executive director who passes these tests with flying colours as far as main board business is concerned may fail lamentably when it comes to the intricacies of audit committee business. Of course, it is true that those with a non-financial, non-accounting background can achieve a workable degree of independent judgement even when quite technical accounting matters are being debated and decided upon. Yet, audit committees are frequently addressing frontier issues, for instance, the impact of new accounting standards, and it may be too much to expect the lay person to follow the arguments. Indeed, if lay people insist on preserving their independence by taking advice from no one, they may be more likely to come to wrong conclusions, and, in a sense, as soon as we open our mouths we have lost a degree of independence. It is not without significance here that the 1992 Cadbury Code and the UK Codes thereafter have provided for directors to take independent professional advice if necessary, at the company's expense in the furtherance of their duties (**A2.20** to **A2.21**).

Effective director independence requires at least that directors know the right questions to ask and can understand and weigh the answers given. Knowing the right questions to ask may require them to take advice on what are the important issues. Independence is different from expertise. The expert director is able to articulate the questions that need to be asked, and to answer them for himself or herself. Independent directors are not expected to have that level of expertise unless they are on the board in part because they are expert. For instance, the UK Corporate Governance Code states that the board should satisfy itself that at least one member of the audit committee has recent and relevant financial experience. The US Sarbanes-Oxley Act (2002) ('SOX') introduced a broadly similar requirement for companies with primary or secondary listings in the US, and mandated the Securities and Exchange Commission ('SEC') to introduce 'rules' to define the meaning of this (SOX section 407). In response the SEC has defined an 'audit committee financial expert' as a person with all of the five following attributes:

- an understanding of generally accepted accounting principles and financial statements;
- the ability to assess the general application of such principles in connection with the accounting for estimates, accruals and reserves;
- experience preparing, auditing, analyzing or evaluating financial statements that present a breadth and level of complexity of accounting issues that are generally comparable to the breadth and complexity of issues that can reasonably be expected to be raised by the registrant's financial statements, or experience actively supervising one or more persons engaged in such activities;
- an understanding of internal controls and procedures for financial reporting; and
- an understanding of audit committee functions.

The SEC stipulates that in order to qualify as an 'audit committee financial expert' a person must have acquired the above listed attributes through any one or more of the following:

- education and experience as a principal financial officer, principal accounting officer, controller, public accountant or auditor or experience in one or more positions that involve the performance of similar functions;
- experience actively supervising a principal financial officer, principal accounting officer, controller, public accountant, auditor or person performing similar functions;
- experience overseeing or assessing the performance of companies or public accountants with respect to the preparation, auditing or evaluation of financial statements; or
- other relevant experience; and, if other relevant experience is what qualifies the director, that experience must be described.

It may sometimes be unrealistic to expect that all the necessary financial expertise can be vested in just one member of the audit committee. For instance, it is likely that an insurance company's audit committee will need one expert on actuarial matters and another on financial reporting and audit matters.

Possible conflict between being a member of both the audit and the remuneration committee **A3.7**

See also **E2.6**.

It has been suggested that an audit committee's governance brief should cover monitoring the role of the remuneration committee and that this will be made more difficult if there is overlapping membership between the two committees.

We do not consider that an audit committee conventionally has a general governance brief, unless it has been given a wider remit by the board than is typical. Some boards will have a separate governance committee or a chairman's committee with more general governance oversight responsibilities on behalf of the board. The NYSE corporate governance standards give more general corporate governance responsibilities to the 'nominating/corporate governance committee'.

It can only be the case that there is a conflict between being a member of both the audit and the remuneration committees if it can be demonstrated that both committees focus on one or more of the same issues, and need to do so independently from each other. Their core roles are different, as one would expect. In brief, remuneration committees determine the remuneration of executive directors and perhaps that of senior, key executives not on the board; they may also set the bands within which executives at lower levels shall be remunerated. The main 'independence' issue about remuneration committees is to ensure that executive directors do not participate in decisions about their own remuneration. Audit committees advise the board on the reliability of information that is published in the name of the board, on the effectiveness of risk management and internal control, and on the appropriateness of external and internal audit provision.

The audit committee does not make decisions about executive remuneration; neither does it second-guess the decisions about executive remuneration that the remuneration committee has come to. It might be construed that there is an overlap in that the audit committee gives assurance to the board that financial information which is published in the board's name is reliable: the published information about executive remuneration is financial information. That is a very small area of overlap and is only of concern if there is a possibility that the information might not be accurate. The remuneration committee does not determine how executive remuneration is disclosed in the financial statements.

It should be possible to rely upon the independence of the members of board committees to manage things adroitly in the unlikely event of any real or perceived conflict. We can also gain a measure of reassurance in that the committees themselves are distinct from each other with their own terms of reference and most probably different chairmen, even if their membership overlaps. The potential problem would be more serious if it were the same committee that deliberated on both executive remuneration matters and also on audit matters – which nobody is suggesting.

Being pragmatic, the majority of boards today are typically small (say eight to ten members) and typically balanced in membership between executive and non-executive directors. Under the UK Corporate Governance Code, the remuneration committee of a FTSE 350 company should have *at least* three members and all should be non-executive directors who are judged by the board to be independent directors; remuneration committees of smaller FTSE companies may have just two members who must also be independent directors. An audit committee also has to have *at least* three non-executive director members, all of whom should be independent directors, except in the case of smaller FTSE companies which may have just two independent directors as members and on which the chairman of the board may serve, but not as chairman of the audit committee, if independent at the time he or she was appointed chairman of the board.

On some boards, not all non-executive directors can be classified as independent. This means that it would not be possible for many boards to find suitable directors to belong to the audit committee and another clutch of suitable directors for the remuneration committee. Companies have to be concerned about 'total boardroom costs'; also, small boards are arguably more effective than large ones.

There are many aspects of the financial statements which have the potential to be disclosed in misleading ways and which will consume audit committee attention. The audit committee's focus on remuneration disclosures should be sufficient for the audit committee to be able to advise the board that these disclosures are in accordance with accounting standards and are not misleading. Financial information about executive remuneration is not in any case prepared by the remuneration committee: it is prepared by the finance director and accountants of the company – none of whom are members of the audit or remuneration committees.

It is possible that a remuneration committee may have made arrangements for elements of executive remuneration not to be disclosed transparently in the annual report. If there is no cross-membership between the audit and remuneration committees, it may be less likely that the audit committee will be aware of this issue. For instance, one or more executive directors of Company A may be receiving additional remuneration through a joint venture Company B that is not controlled by Company A. Not being controlled by Company A, Company B may not be consolidated into the financial results of Company A, and so this additional joint venture remuneration may not be revealed in Company A's annual report. It is conceivable that the audit committee of Company A may not be aware of this. If the audit committee were aware of this, the audit committee may judge Company A's disclosure to be misleading and in need of greater transparency. This particular issue could be avoided if best practice corporate governance were followed by ensuring that all fees to executives for serving joint ventures were paid to Company A and that Company A would recompense those executives appropriately.

A rare example of audit committee involvement in the reliability of disclosures on executive remuneration occurred at the Medical Defence Union with respect to their annual report for the year ended 31 December 2005. All four outside, independent directors resigned after the year-end when the board had rejected the advice of its audit committee to enhance the clarity of disclosure of remuneration of Medical Defence Union executives in connection with their joint venture responsibilities. They were audit committee and remuneration committee members. Cross-membership of the remuneration and audit committees did not impede those independent directors from taking an independent stance. Those directors took the view that it is a serious matter when a board rejects the advice of its audit committee on matters of disclosure and transparency. Although it appeared that those independent directors had failed to persuade the board, nevertheless the Medical Defence Union's following annual report, for the year ended 31 December 2006, had much greater clarity of disclosure, even beyond that which the audit committee had been calling for a year earlier.

Being a member of all three board committees A3.8

Where a company follows the guidance within the UK Corporate Governance Code, it will have at least three board committees (nomination, audit and remuneration), and the main burden of committee membership will fall upon the independent directors. The fourth and last board committee referred to in the Code is the board's risk committee (see **App1**, Code Provision C.3.2, and **D4.7**). Except in smaller companies where it is permissible for the chairman of the board to belong to the audit committee (see **A3.4**), all members of the remuneration and audit committees will be independent directors. A majority of members of the nomination committee will be independent non-executive directors. The chairman or an independent non-executive director will chair the nomination committee, but the chairman should not chair the nomination committee when it is dealing with the appointment of a successor to the chairmanship.

We have to allow that an independent director might belong to more than one board committee, even if there may be potential overlap between the two committees. The fact that they are 'independent' directors should give us less concern about any potential conflict due to belonging to two or three committee at the same time.

Note, however, that the 2003 Higgs Report recommended against a non-executive director belonging to all three of the principal board committees:

> 'No one non-executive director should sit on all three principal board committees (audit, nomination and remuneration) simultaneously.'

and:

> 'When appointing committee members, boards should draw on the independent non-executive directors with the most relevant skills and experience. Consideration should also be given to rotating committee members. In order not to concentrate too much influence on one individual. **I consider it undesirable for any one individual to be on all three principal board committees at the same time**.'

The bolding (above) is Higgs', which he uses when he is expressing a firm recommendation. However, his suggested Code Provision on this did not see the light of day. The nearest the Code came to it is one of the Supporting Principles at A.3 (2003 and 2006) and at Supporting Principle B.1 in the current Code, which since 2003 has read:

> 'The value of ensuring that committee membership is refreshed and that undue reliance is not placed on particular individuals should be taken into account in deciding chairmanship and membership of committees.'

Higgs had not thought of the idea of 'Supporting Principles', so they were absent from his proposed revision of the 1998 Combined Code. Supporting Principles were introduced for the first time into the 2003 Combined Code that appeared after the Higgs and original Smith reports were published. The Supporting Principle quoted above is clearly all that eventually became of Higgs' suggested Code Provision A.3.7. His proposed Code Provision A.3.7 would have read (p 82):

> 'Unless a company is small, no individual should sit on all three principal board committees at the same time.'

The UK Corporate Governance Code and its predecessor Codes have not been mandatory, though most listed companies try to observe the Code and also many entities that are not listed (see **F2.4**). And this particular recommendation of Higgs, that a director should not belong to all three committees at the same time, never quite made it to the Code – so it is certainly not obligatory. It was clearly deliberately not adopted. Nevertheless, it would count as wise advice in most circumstances.

Threats to independence from significant shareholdings A3.9

The Code's non-exhaustive list of criteria that may be relevant to a board's determination as to whether a non-executive director should be regarded as independent (Provision B.1.1) includes 'if the director represents a significant shareholder'. By implication, this would also include the case where the director himself or herself is the significant shareholder. What level of shareholding should be regarded as 'significant' is not well articulated. Possibly a director who owned, or represented those who owned, more than 1% of the equity of a company with a full listing, or more than 3% if AIM-listed, should not be regarded by the board as independent.

A further consideration should be the market value of the shares the director holds: possibly a £25,000 shareholding could affect one's independence of judgement, and even many wealthy people might start to get irrationally concerned when more than £50,000 of their own wealth might be at stake! It may be that a company wishes its non-executive directors to have a larger stake in the company; and an individual NED might wish to have a larger shareholding more in line with that of other directors, for instance. Within reason, we would not think that would be an independence issue so long as the shareholding were not higher than 1% of the equity (if listed) – but it should be for the board to decide. Since those directors that the board decides are independent are, per the Code, disclosed as such in the annual report – which would also show the shareholdings of individual directors – the owners of the company will be well informed and in a position to try to influence the board if they are concerned. Under the Code, a company would need to draw attention to the matter and explain why they regarded a non-executive director as being independent, notwithstanding a sizeable shareholding – similarly if any of the other independence criteria are not conformed to (Provision B.1.1).

Best corporate governance requires that the controlling shareholder is not also the chairman A3.10

Stelios Haji-Ioannou, the founder of easyJet, announced on 18 April 2002 that he was standing down as chairman of easyJet. Sir Colin Chandler became deputy chairman for a year before succeeding Haji-Ioannou as chairman at the company's next AGM in March 2003. On Sky News, Haji-Ioannou said 'Best corporate governance requires that the controlling shareholder is not also the chairman'. easyJet was Europe's second largest low-cost carrier, after Ryanair: on 18 April 2002, easyJet had a market capitalisation of £1.49 billion, while Ryanair's market cap was larger than British Airways.

This is an interesting case of the need to make changes in order to introduce best practice corporate governance in enterprises built up rapidly by successful entrepreneurs.

It is also an interesting case of the practical impact on corporate governance of judgements being made by interested parties about adherence with the Code 'Principles' – even though in this case none of the more detailed 1998 Code 'Provisions', which are interpretative of the 'Principles', had been breached. For instance, Haji-Ioannou was not both chairman *and* chief executive. Institutional investors are (as they are entitled to do) making their own interpretations as to whether 'Principles' have been violated, and are not content to use the 'Provisions' as a sufficient guide of this.

In part, this change shows that modest pressure from institutional and major investors can influence the composition of boards: only a handful of shareholders voted against Haji-Ioannou at the March 2002 AGM. Indeed, it is apparent that easyJet was already looking for a new chairman before that AGM – no doubt in part in anticipation of modest shareholder disapproval.

At easyJet's March 2002 AGM, of the institutional investors it was only one with a small holding (the Co-operative Insurance Society with 17,205 shares out of the total issued shares of 292 million) that had voted against easyJet's report and accounts because of concerns about easyJet's corporate governance – both the independence of non-executive directors and the ability of Haji-Ioannou's easyGroup, the biggest shareholder with 58.5% of the equity, to appoint the chairman. However, it is thought that other shareholder groups may have exerted 'behind the scenes' pressure on easyJet – which might have become more vociferous at the next AGM, had Haji-Ioannou not acted.

One wonders whether the decision of institutional investors to take a stand might have been accentuated by the colourful non-establishment personality at the top of easyJet, and whether it would have been the same had easyJet's leader been more conventional.

More recent events have shown the special challenges faced by the chairman of a board when a large block of shares are closely held – the new chairman may not find it easy to exert his independence. However, Haji-Ioannou also announced his intention to offload some of his easyJet stock, saying: 'I need to sell my past to finance my future', and that starting a company 'requires a very different skill set to those needed to chair a major plc and I consider my strengths are in the former. I am a serial entrepreneur.' It is to his credit that he has this insight which is so sorely lacking in many successful entrepreneurs.

Subsequent to Haji-Ioannou's departure from easyJet's board he has shown, for better or for worse, how a major shareholder can impact upon the board, for instance with respect to strategy and dividend policy.

Nominated directors' conflict of loyalty between their nominator and the company **A3.11**

While there are notable examples of investment institutions which are active shareholders but would not seek to place their people on the boards of companies in which they invest, this is not always the case. Pension funds, insurance companies and some other institutional investors may prefer to retain the freedom which comes from not having their representatives on the boards in which they are investing significantly. But venture capitalists, private equity firms and banks very frequently make board appointments and are quite pragmatic about being there to protect their investments. They might argue that it would be negligent to take a major stake in a company and not to use this opportunity to steer and monitor it. Protecting the stakes of shareholders and other investors can, however, be done in other ways than by having one or more seats on the board (eg by careful monitoring from outside, by applying the law, by the stakeholder clearly making known its viewpoint as an active shareholder, etc). Care needs to be taken to ensure that the interests of minority shareholders are not trampled over.

A broadly parallel situation exists when a representative of a dominant shareholder (perhaps a family or founder of the company) sits on the board; or when one or more members of a board sit on the board of a subsidiary company which is listed.

Where the practice of nominating directors for boards is followed, the nominating institution is likely to be nervous about conflicts of interest but to take the view that these rarely occur and can be managed when they do, especially if the investing institution has a clearly worked-out policy on this matter.

There is a fundamental flaw in the concept of nominated directors on boards of publicly held companies. The flaw exists when the intention or the effect is to make inside knowledge available to the investing institution so as to optimise their potential to safeguard their interests.

In the UK, Part X of the Companies Act 1985 stipulated that directors should seek shareholder approval in circumstances where a director's personal interests might conflict with his or her duty to the company. More generally, a board of directors is accountable to the shareholders as a whole for its stewardship of the company. The Companies Act 2006 is more specific on the duties of directors to avoid conflicted situations (see **D1.5**, **D1.9** and also **A3.12** to **A3.17**).

If, as we shall suggest later, it is necessary for a nominated director not to participate in board business where there is a conflict of interest, then (assuming this is successful) the presence of the nominated director cannot serve the intended purpose. Paragraph 8 of the Preamble to the 2003 and 2006 Combined Codes acknowledged that all shareholders should have similar access to information:

> 'Nothing in this Code should be taken to override the general requirements of law to treat shareholders equally in access to information.'

The 'Sample letter of non-executive director appointment', drawn from the Higgs Report (see **App5**), reminded non-executives directors that:

> 'All directors must take decisions objectively in the interests of the company.'

and:

> 'It is accepted and acknowledged that you have business interests other than those of the company and have declared any conflicts that are apparent at present. In the event that you become aware of any potential conflicts of interest, these should be disclosed to the chairman and company secretary as soon as apparent.'

and:

> 'All information acquired during your appointment is confidential to the Company and should not be released, either during your appointment or following termination (by whatever means), to third parties without prior clearance from the chairman.
>
> Your attention is also drawn to the requirements under both legislation, and regulation as to the disclosure of price-sensitive information. Consequently you should avoid making any statements that might risk a breach of these requirements without prior clearance from the chairman or company secretary.'

Note that acting in the interests of the company is not always the same as acting in the best interests of the shareholders as a body, let alone the best interests of a faction of shareholders. Sometimes, boards have to make decisions which do not maximise shareholder value – for instance, when it is a matter of observing the law or observing terms entered into by the company in contracts.

The focus of much of the UK Corporate Governance Code on careful selection of board members, using a nomination committee, makes no allusion to the circumstances in which a third party nominates its representative(s) to join the board, and indeed the general tenor of the Code (especially with respect to independence) does not provide any support for nominee directors. The Code is, of course, targeted primarily at listed companies, but has been adopted much more widely. The concerns about nominated directors do not apply only to listed companies, although they are more pronounced for companies which are not closely held.

Motivations of nominee appointments **A3.12**

A key question is the motivation to nominate a director. If the motivation is to ensure that the company has scarce expertise available to it, then that is less problematic than certain alternative motivations. But it would be disingenuous to suggest that the scarce expertise sought is only available in the form of a nominated director. There is an understandable resistance by prospective non-executive directors to accepting board positions in order to supply a company with an essential expertise it would otherwise lack, as this implies an executive or a professional advisory role rather than a board role. Nevertheless, this is the most often mentioned justification that small companies make for inviting non-executive directors onto the board. If the motivation is that the company has at least one director who is well informed about the policies of a major shareholder, then that could also be construed as desirable. But chairmen and chief executives of companies without nominated directors resort to other much more effective ways of sounding out the opinions of their major shareholders. If the motivation is that the nominating entity thereby gains inside and fast-track knowledge of the affairs of the nominee company, that is less defensible. Any non-executive director must ensure that he or she manages potential conflicts between the interests of the company on whose board he or she serves and the interests of those who nominated him or her. Perhaps it is impossible to manage the conflict if the director also serves on the board of the entity which nominated him or her.

To some extent, where nominee directorships pertain, some reliance can be placed on the fact that the directors were elected by the shareholders in general meeting. If, at that time, the shareholders were clear as to the nominee relationship, it could be harder for those shareholders subsequently to object to the conduct of the nominee director when he or she appeared to be placing first the interests of the nominating company. But that would not, in all circumstances, be an adequate defence in an action against the nominee director for breach of trust. In practice, an action may be by the company against the board of directors as a whole; such an action may be inspired by the conduct of the individual nominee director if that is construed as having been against the interests of the shareholders or against the interests of the company. There is also the matter that the board initially appoints the director and it is only later that the shareholders vote to confirm his or her appointment: so there is a period of time when the shareholders have not been consulted about the appointment, during which the board might be vulnerable to shareholder action because of the effect of its decision to welcome the nominee on to the board.

Board balance, independence and nominee directors A3.13

It needs to be understood that a nominee director may be non-executive but is certainly not independent. It would be ironic if investment institutions, which exert pressure on companies to conform to corporate governance best practice, were to make it harder for companies to do so by nominating non-executive directors who are not independent to the boards of companies in whom they have invested. Many investment institutions today insist that companies in which they are invested comply with the UK Corporate Governance Code in most respects – extending required compliance with the Provisions and their own interpretations as to what are the criteria to be applied in determining whether the Provisions are being complied with.

We reproduce here the Code's independence criteria (see Provision B.1.1), which include whether the director:

'• has been an employee of the company or group within the last five years;
- has, or has had within the last three years, a material business relationship with the company either directly, or as a partner, shareholder, director or senior employee of a body that has such a relationship with the company;
- has received or receives additional remuneration from the company apart from a director's fee, participates in the company's share option or a performance-related pay scheme, or is a member of the company's pension scheme;
- has close family ties with any of the company's advisers, directors or senior employees;
- holds cross-directorships or has significant links with other directors through involvement in other companies or bodies;
- represents a significant shareholder; or
- has served on the board for more than nine years from the date of their first election.'

Two of these independence criteria are likely to disqualify a nominee director from being considered by the board to be independent. The nominee director may be an executive or otherwise be significantly associated with a related party (for instance, an investor or a parent company) (second criterion above). The nominee director is also likely to represent a significant shareholder (sixth criterion above). The fifth criterion above may also be breached.

A slightly different slant was given by the Cadbury Committee, who used the phrase 'related party transactions' as an indicator as to whether a non-executive director should be regarded as independent. Association with a significant supplier of the company would mean that the director was linked with a related party and thus not independent. An investing institution is clearly a related party as a supplier of capital to the company.

In our view, it is likely to be impractical for companies to find much space on their boards for nominee directors since they cannot be regarded as independent. Modern boards are modest in size – both in the interests of effectiveness and in order to control total boardroom costs. Total boardroom costs are related to board size, and an investing institution or parent company should be reluctant to burden the company with extra board costs. Except for companies outside the FTSE 350, at least half of the board, excluding the chairman, are to be independent, as per Code Provision B.1.2:

> 'Except for smaller companies, at least half the board, excluding the chairman, should comprise non-executive directors determined by the board to be independent. A smaller company should have at least two independent non-executive directors.'

The Code also states within Supporting Principles B.1 on 'The Composition of the Board' that:

> 'The board should include an appropriate combination of executive and non-executive directors (and, in particular, independent non-executive directors) such that no individual or small group of individuals can dominate the board's decision taking.'

and:

> 'the board … should not be so large as to be unwieldy.'

While the Code is strictly applicable to listed companies, and not to their subsidiaries or to those companies in which a listed company has investments (unless listed), it is regarded as best practice much more generally. We should say here that, under the Listing Rules, it is the Main Principles, and not the Supporting Principles or the Provisions, which should be regarded as mandatory (although there is no evidence that they are enforced by the regulators). Listed companies may depart from the Provisions if they disclose and explain their departures. The relevant Listing Rule is reproduced at **D3.3**.

In general, it is not best practice to appoint non-executive directors to the board who cannot be regarded as independent at the time of their appointment. Since today's board is usually small, and there will be a need to have a proportion of the board today who satisfy the independence tests into the future, it is likely to be problematic to appoint non-executive directors who are not independent even at the time they are appointed. A strict reading of Provision B.1.1 would allow that a non-executive director could become independent when particular impediments to that director's independence no longer apply; but that is unlikely and, where it could be held to apply, it would not do so for long as a director is not to be regarded as independent if he or she has served on the board for longer than nine years since first appointed. Indeed, under Code Provision B.2.3 …

'Any term beyond six years for a non-executive director should be subject to particularly rigorous review, and should take into account the need for progressive refreshing of the board.'

We should also not overlook that some directors appointed as independent may lose that status in the future and yet still be desirable members of the board. In practice, therefore, it is not easy for board composition to be managed in order to ensure an adequate independent element, and new appointments that may impede this objective (such as of non-executive directors who are not independent when appointed) are usually best avoided.

Close family ties[8] **A3.14**

The UK Corporate Governance Code (2012) Provision B.1.1 (see **App1**) indicates that one of the criteria that a board should use in their determination of whether a director can be regarded as an *independent* director, is as follows:

> 'has close family ties with any of the company's advisers, directors or senior employees'

This wording was first used in the 2003 Combined Code.

We are not aware that the FRC or any other party has indicated the meaning they attach to the phrase 'close family ties' – either by defining it or referring to a definition elsewhere. No doubt it is intended that this is an aspect of director independence that 'the board should determine'[9].

By way of guidance, content within the following approximate, though not exactly to what must be intended by 'close family ties' in a UK 'independent director' context:

1. Financial Services and Markets Act 2000;
2. Companies Act 2006;
3. Criminal Justice Act 1993, Pt V;
4. FSA Code of Conduct.

We shall look at each of the above four in turn.

1. The Financial Services and Markets Act 2000 (Amendment) Regulations 2009, at Pt 1, s 3 defines 'family members' as follows:

   '(1) This paragraph defines what is meant by references to members of a manager's family.

   '(2) The members of a manager's family are – (a) the manager's spouse or civil partner; (b) any relative of the manager who, on the date of the transaction in question, has shared the same household as the manager for at least 12 months; (c) the manager's children or step-children under the age of 18.'

   An adjacent section also defines 'connected persons'.

2. Section 253 of the 2006 Companies Act reads:

'Members of a director's family

(1) This section defines what is meant by references in this Part [of the Act] to members of a director's family.

(2) For the purposes of this Part the members of a director's family are—

(a) the director's spouse or civil partner;
(b) any other person (whether of a different sex or the same sex) with whom the director lives as partner in an enduring family relationship;
(c) the director's children or step-children;
(d) any children or step-children of a person within paragraph (b) (and who are not children or step-children of the director) who live with the director and have not attained the age of 18;
(e) the director's parents.

(3) Subsection (2)(b) does not apply if the other person is the director's grandparent or grandchild, sister, brother, aunt or uncle, or nephew or niece.'

An adjacent section of this Act also defines 'connected persons'.

3. The Criminal Justice Justice Act 1993, Pt V deals with insider dealing and defines a connected person as:

'Your Spouse, civil partner, children or step children under 18, parents, any other person with whom you

4. The FSA Code of Conduct, as revised in 2012, uses the above definition (3) above).

The nominee's duties to the nominator A3.15

The issues of conflict, which we are discussing here, apply whether or not the nominee director is also a director of the entity which nominated him or her. Where the individual is also on the board of the entity which nominated him or her, an additional conflict factor comes into play. It is that the director is likely to have inside knowledge of the affairs of the company on whose board he or she has been nominated to sit (whether a subsidiary (which may be listed separately from the parent) or a company invested in by an investment fund). The director may find that he or she is unable to discharge his or her duties to the latter nominating company, due to unwillingness to make disclosure to that board of matters relating to the former company.

A board and its individual members must act in the interests of all the shareholders, and not preferentially in the interests of any group of shareholders. Minority shareholders, for instance, need their interests to be looked after by the board; but, again, not preferentially. No director is to use inside knowledge for his or her personal benefit or for the benefit of others with whom they are associated, or indeed for the benefit of other parties. There should be no director (or director-inspired) dealings in shares of the company when inside knowledge applies or may apply (eg during a close period). This would apply to dealings in the investor company shares when that company's appointee had inside knowledge about the company on whose board he or she sits. Having a nominee on the board can cramp the style of the investment institution, who may feel unable to deal in the shares, or to act in other ways, because of its inside position on the board of the company.

Creating a shadow director situation A3.16

We should not overlook that, in some circumstances, if a lender interferes in the direction of company in which the lender has invested, the lender could be construed as at least a shadow director, and the loan might then regarded as equity. Prima facie this situation is more likely to pertain when the lender has a representative on the board (see **A1.13**).

Components of compensation as factors affecting independence A3.17

It is regarded as best practice that non-executive directors' compensation should be limited to the fee they receive for being a non-executive director, though in the UK the 1998 Hampel Report saw no objection to a proportion of their compensation being in the form of shares in the company. Unlike US practice, participation by non-executive directors in share option schemes is not approved in the UK on account of the risk that the 'leverage effect' of these schemes could cloud the exercise of independent judgement by non-executive directors when making decisions, especially decisions that impact upon share price or on the option schemes themselves. Another reason is that boards need some of their directors to be independent of performance-related reward schemes and pension schemes so that they can view these dispassionately. However, it is accepted that UK non-executive directors may (but are not required to) hold shares in the company and that this can be positively desirable, as it will mean that the directors identify more closely with the interests of the shareholders. But it should be pointed out that the right decision for a board to come to is not always the decision that maximises share price (as, for instance, when the board decides it should disclose that it is probably in breach of a key funding covenant).

The 2003 and 2006 Codes, reflecting Higgs' recommendations, made two changes to this. First, commencing 2003, it has not been inconsistent with the Code for non-executive directors to have share options, although the Code is restrictive about the circumstances in which this would be reasonable; the Code also suggests that the possession of share options would probably mean the board should not regard the director as an independent director. Provision D.1.3 reads:

> 'Levels of remuneration for non-executive directors should reflect the time commitment and responsibilities of the role. Remuneration for non-executive directors should not include share options or other performance-related elements. If, exceptionally, options are granted, shareholder approval should be sought in advance and any shares acquired by exercise of the options should be held until at least one year after the non-executive director leaves the board. Holding of

share options could be relevant to the determination of a non-executive director's independence (as set out in Provision B.1.1).'

Secondly, since non-executive directors' fees should be proportionate to their responsibilities and their time commitment, it is in order for supplements to be paid for belonging to and chairing board committees. Total compensation should always be known to the board and disclosed in the annual report.

Some companies pay non-executive director fees according to their attendance record. Rare in the UK, where this applies it is designed to more closely align non-executive director rewards to the contribution that they make, and to encourage good attendance. In the UK, we rely on the requirement to disclose in the annual report the attendance record of each director at board and board committee meetings to foster responsible behaviour. The UK view would also be that a director's responsibilities are not diminished by a poor attendance record. Even with respect to meetings a director is unable to attend, the director has a responsibility to address the agenda items. A good chairman of a board, or of a board committee, will endeavour to liaise with an absent director to ensure that his or her inputs are addressed and that the board's decisions are communicated to that director.

Elements of a policy for handling these conflicts of loyalty **A3.18**

- Accept the need at times formally to declare an interest, and ensure the declaration is minuted.
- On occasion, exercise the option of not voting on an issue.
- Even, on occasion, exercise the option of not attending a board or board committee meeting, or part of such.
- In the case of a smaller, non-listed company, make sure the shareholders' agreement gives shareholders the right to see all information made available to the directors; and make sure there is a mechanism in place that allows for a flow of information from subsidiaries/investee companies to the main board, so that the type of situation where a representative director is privy to information at subsidiary/investee company level that he or she might not feel comfortable to disclose to the parent company/majority shareholder should not arise. This mechanism has to accommodate the need for outside shareholders to be privy to the same information if it is price sensitive with respect to the share price.
- Make it clear that the director must resolve any conflict in favour of the company on whose board he or she sits at the time, although he or she must take into account the impact on shareholders/other group companies.

Notes

1 Sir Adrian Cadbury's 1998 lecture to Gresham College in London, delivered at Mansion House, London.

2 The Walker Review on Financial Sector Corporate Governance (November 2009), para 6.15.

3 Audit committees are referred to in the Code only at the level of 'comply or explain' provisions. Hence, strictly speaking, they are not mandatory.

4 Companies Act 2006, s 173 states the now codified independence duty of a director as follows:

'Duty to exercise independent judgment

(1) A director of a company must exercise independent judgment.

(2) This duty is not infringed by his acting–

(a) in accordance with an agreement duly entered into by the company that restricts the future exercise of discretion by its directors, or

(b) in a way authorised by the company's constitution.'

The list of general duties of directors now codified in this statute are:

1. to act in accordance with the company's constitution and to act within the company's powers (s 171; see also s 257);
2. to promote the success of the company for the benefit of its members as a whole, and in doing so have regard *inter alia* to specified matters (s 172);
3. to exercise independent judgment (s 173);
4. to exercise reasonable care, skill and diligence (as would be expected of a reasonably diligent person carrying out the functions of the director, as well as based on the director's actual knowledge, skill and experience) (s 174);
5. to avoid conflicts of interest (s 175);
6. not to accept benefits from third parties (s 176); and
7. to declare interests in a proposed transaction or arrangement with the company (s 177).

5 Higgs, Sir Derek (January 2003): The Role of the Non-Executive Director, para 9.14.

6 Tyson, Laura (June 2003): *The Tyson Report on the Recruitment and Development of Non-Executive Directors*, on widening the director recruitment gene pool', p 16.

7 Companies Act 2006, s 174.

8 The author is grateful to Nick Mangwana who kindly researched into the likely meaning of 'close family ties'.

9 2012 Code Provision B.1.1.

Chapter A4

Resigning a Directorship

Introduction A4.1

Here we focus, largely but not exclusively, on resignations by directors, whether executive or non-executive, on matters of principle over which the board is divided. Directors should not rely on this guidance in lieu of seeking legal advice according to their particular circumstances when facing the prospect of resigning and their need to manage that process and its aftermath appropriately.

Throughout this chapter, we refer frequently to the UK's Corporate Governance Code which we reproduce at **App1**.[1] Other Codes, applicable elsewhere, are not identical. The UK Listing Rules allow companies wide flexibility in applying the Code (see **D2.3**). While the Code has been developed for listed companies with a premium UK listing, it is seen more generally as being best practice, with wider applicability to other types of entity (see **F2.4**).

Due diligence when joining a board A4.2

Even when considering whether to join a board (see Chapter **A2**), a prospective director should have in mind the possibility of resignation at some time in the future. It is as well to appreciate that it may not be straightforward to resign from the board. The prospective director's initial due diligence should be targeted partly at minimising the potential need for resignation later and also partly at establishing the particular process to be followed by a member of this board should resignation become necessary.

In part because it may not be straightforward to resign from the board, it makes eminent sense to undertake one's general due diligence thoroughly and carefully before accepting an invitation to join a board. Ensuring that the due diligence uncovers what might later become a resignation issue is not straightforward and cannot be guaranteed to be successful, especially when it is unrelated to the recent departure of another director.

Uncovering the potential resignation issue at the due diligence stage may enable it to be addressed in a non-contentious way before accepting an invitation to join the board. For instance, there may be no board policy empowering individual directors to take outside advice at the company's expense should the need arise (see **A2.20** to **A2.25**), as compliance with UK Corporate Governance Code Provision B.5.1 requires,[2] but the board may be willing to rectify that omission. In another example, the chair of an audit committee was advised by the company chairman that, under board standing orders, he had no authority to convene a meeting of the audit committee: all meetings of board committees had to be convened by the company secretary, and the chairman of the board disagreed that a special meeting of the audit committee was required. Had the chair of the audit committee studied the board's standing orders before he joined the board, he or she could in all probability have negotiated a change to those standing orders before the matter became enmeshed within a board dispute.

A prospective director's due diligence should, *inter alia*, also involve obtaining an awareness of other matters that might bear upon subsequent resignation. These will include the existing polices of the board, the articles of the company and the terms of reference of board committees. An appreciation of the financial statements of the company over the past few years and a review of up-to-date management accounts are also essential. Not only will this work have the potential to highlight the key areas of weakness and strength; it will also enable the prospective director to identify key performance indicators he or she will be able to track over time after joining the board.

Boards that are hidebound by complex standing orders are likely to be problematic boards to belong to: certainly, the standing orders should be understood before joining the board. Even more important are the articles of association, especially those articles which deal with the composition of the board and resignation from the board. Prospective new directors should also ask to review recent minutes of the board and board committees as well as key supporting agenda papers.

The prospective director should enquire directly why he or she is being invited to join the board. Enquiry should be made as to how the board vacancy has arisen. It is partly a matter of ensuring that the prospective director can bring to the board the skills and commitment that are being sought. The prospective director should use his or her best endeavours to meet separately with each member of the board, executive and non-executive, before accepting an invitation to join the board. It would be a matter of concern if they saw no need to meet up. He or she should also make enquiry of recent past directors, especially of the director, if any, who is being replaced. The purpose, of course, is to learn directly their reasons for leaving the board – especially whether it were a matter of principle – and the substance of that disagreement, so as to ascertain whether there are grounds for declining to join the board. In some cases, it may be possible for the incoming director to negotiate changes in board policy or practice that remove the causes of the previous director's resignation and thus enable the invitation to join the board to be accepted.

Consideration should also be given to arranging to speak to the audit engagement partner, particularly when someone with financial and accounting experience or responsibilities is being invited to join the board.

While careful due diligence can significantly reduce the likelihood of later finding oneself in a resignation situation, it will not eliminate the risk. There may be a reluctance on the part of the company to be fully open with a prospective director until he or she has accepted the invitation to join the board. Issues may only come to light in the course of the first few board meetings thereafter.

Apart from teasing out specific issues, careful due diligence along the lines suggested above should also be used to try to gauge the integrity of the board and of the senior management team. There may be no apparent specific issues but just an uncomfortable feeling which should not be put to one side.

Senior executive directors being sought for non-executive roles in other companies may, by agreement with the company whose board they may be joining, delegate some of the due diligence to their staff or to a firm of accountants.

Due diligence enquiries that may alert you to extra risks of later resignation (not exhaustive):

1. Is there anything in the Articles of Association that you are uncomfortable about?

2. Is there anything in the Board's Standing Orders, the Director's letter of Appointment or within the Terms of Reference of the board's committees with which you are uncomfortable about?

3. Does the company have any policies that require directors to resign in particular circumstances?

4. Do your discussions with directors and your review of recent board agenda papers and minutes indicate:
   - a divided board?
   - a balanced board?
   - a poorly led board?
   - doubtful board values?
   - excessive concentration of power?
   - a company in serious difficulty?

5. Does your review of past published financial statements and recent management accounts and forecasts raise serious concerns that remain unsatisfied?

6. Have you asked if there are any significant disputes affecting the company and are you satisfied that the board's stance on these is ethical?

7. Are you clear why you are being invited to join the board and are you confident you can bring to the board what the board is expecting – in terms of:
   - time commitment?
   - skills?
   - care?
   - diligence?
   - inter-personal relationships?

8. Has the company adequate directors' insurance in place?

9. Why did recently departed directors resign from the board?

When joining a board, be clear about your possible resignation exist strategy (not exhaustive):

1. Is there anything in the Articles or in your Letter of Appointment that could restrict your freedom to resign?

2. What is the company's laid down procedure for a director to resign?

3. Does the company have a protocol for notifying shareholders promptly when a director resigns?

4. Is there a satisfactory board policy for directors to take independent professional advice at the company's expense, and would this cover costs associated with resignation?

5. Are you confident that the company secretary can be relied upon when necessary to keep matters confidential between the two of you?

6. Do you have the contact details of all members of the board and of the company secretary?

7. Do you know which specialist lawyer you could turn to in case of need with respect to resignation?

8. Are the above matters, to the extent appropriate, set out in writing so that you will be able to refer to the policy?

9. Is there a risk that your dependence on the income that comes with this board appointment could cloud your judgement when deciding whether to resign?

Dialogue, advice and the role of the chair **A4.3**

Dialogue and taking advice are powerful means of resolving issues impacting the board.

Just as all political careers are said to end in failure, so all directors in time will leave their boards. Resignation over a matter of principle is usually, in a very real sense, a tacit acknowledgement of failure – possibly a failure to carry the board on a particular issue by the director(s) who resign(s), albeit an issue which has led the board to follow a course of action which the dissenting director considers to be fundamentally wrong or misguided. It is not uncommon for several contentious issues to coalesce so that, together, they amount to grounds for resignation.

Director resignation is also often linked to a failure of chairmanship. Those who chair boards are responsible for the effectiveness of their boards. Good chairs of boards interpret their role as being to chair the *whole board*, not of a particular group of directors on the board. Yet, frequently, chairs of boards tend to side with the same faction of directors on the board, often the executive directors but possibly with the independent directors, to the detriment of board cohesion. Biased alignment by the chairman with the executive is less likely if the chairman were independent at the time he or she were appointed chairman, as the UK Code counsels.[3] When divisions threaten a board, the chair, as leader of the board, has a key role to heal these rifts, but may not always be successful despite the best of endeavours. The UK Code provides that the chairman should hold meetings with the non-executive directors without the executives being present; and also that, led by the senior independent director, the non-executive directors should meet without the chairman present on such other occasions as are deemed appropriate.[4]

An effective chair of the board will ensure that all directors know that they are at liberty to discuss their concerns at any time, not only with the chair of the board and with other directors, but also with senior executives, the external auditor, the head of internal audit and the company secretary. The company secretary must serve the board as a whole. It may be helpful to view the company secretary as the agent of the board rather than as a member of the executive team. The chair of the board should make it clear to the company secretary that the confidence should be respected of a director who asks the company secretary for advice, and should not be relayed directly to the executive team where that would undermine the director concerned.

To safeguard the independence of the company secretary, the practice is developing whereby the company secretary reports for all purposes, including for 'pay and rations', to the chairman of the board. The company secretariat function is then regarded as one of the costs of running the board and the budget for the company secretariat is provided and overseen by the chairman of the board. These arrangements make it that much easier for the company secretary to be a trusted advisor to the directors. This can also be utilised to improve the independence of the internal audit function, whose chief audit executive may report for 'pay and rations' to such an independent company secretary rather than to a senior executive such as the finance director or the chief executive: 'he who pays the piper calls the tune'. While company secretaries should be relied upon, when requested, to respect the confidentiality of any discussions they have with individual directors, they cannot provide absolute assurances that they may not communicate the essence of these discussions to the chairman of the board. They should, however, be trusted to be very discreet in disclosing the essence of these discussions to the executive, including to executive directors.

The UK Code counsels that directors, especially non-executive directors, should have access to independent professional advice at the company's expense where they judge it necessary to discharge their responsibilities as directors (**A2.20** to **A2.25**).[5] It is a moot point as to whether this facility should be available, if necessary, in connection with a director's resignation and also whether it should extend to support from, for instance, a communications consultant in handling relationships with the media post-resignation. The policy on independent advice should make the position clear on this. As part of a prospective director's due diligence when being invited to join a board, it is wise to establish whether the provision of this financial support has been approved by formal board resolution and whether it will be available, according to the director's judgement of need, to cover professional fees relating to a resignation, both before and after the resignation.

Such policies often require that one other director, usually an independent director, should approve the utilisation of this facility by the director. Even if the policy does not cover resignation *per se*, it may be a valuable means of resolving a contentious issue so as to make resignation unnecessary. For instance, if a director has an anxiety about the reliability of financial reporting, which it has not been possible to resolve through the normal channels to the director's satisfaction, taking independent outside advice may be sufficient to allay the director's concerns. Nevertheless, in most cases a concerned director should be able to persuade his or her colleagues that the board should collectively seek this outside advice.

Quite closely related to resigning on a matter of principle is the resignation prompted by concern about the personal risk of continuing on the board of a company that is in difficulty. Both are in a sense exceptional, in that they are unrelated to the normal turnover of members of the board. While an ex-director has no responsibility for the consequences of decisions of the board or for the actions of the company after his or her resignation, the ex-director continues to have the usual joint and several liability for the consequences of what occurred before his or her resignation. In practice, it will be unusual for a resigning director not to have accrued a degree of potential culpability for the issue(s) that eventually led to his or her resignation since these types of matter often have a long fuse, but tend to start in an anodyne, often unnoticed way:

> 'A failure to act appropriately in the face of knowledge inevitably leads to the conclusion that directors have become part of the problem instead of the solution. If the other directors will not act, resignation is often the only alternative. A director who finds himself or herself in that position should consult independent counsel immediately; the danger of being perceived by regulators, the SEC, or a jury as one who has been drawn into wrongdoing can escalate very quickly.'[6]

The many members of boards of UK central government organisations, such as government departments and agencies and non-departmental bodies, usually do not have joint and several liability in a legal sense, except in the few cases where the organisation is incorporated as a company. The likelihood of their being taken to court is small and would probably only apply if there were a suspicion of corruption. So, directors of these entities should not be concerned about the personal risk of continuing on such a board – except from the perspective of personal reputation. Due to the absence of joint and several liability, directors of these public bodies are usually not covered by directors' liability insurance, as they do not need to be. The UK Code provides that this insurance cover should be in place for directors of listed companies.[7]

Agendas and minutes A4.4

The records of board meetings may later turn out to be important evidence as to why a director resigned, and so we deal with this at some length here. A director who is considering resignation should be careful to check that board minutes accurately record the matter which may lead to his or her resignation, as subsequently they are likely to be held to be the true record.

The UK Code provides that, where directors have concerns that cannot be resolved about the running of the company or a proposed action, they should ensure that their concerns are recorded in the board minutes.[8] It is important that dissenting views are recorded, particularly regarding matters where there are statutory offences for non-compliance or inaction. This is because frequently the statutory rules on liability apply to every director who was at fault, or otherwise base liability on whether a director took all reasonable steps to ensure compliance with the matter in question. The director may be able to avoid or limit personal culpability by ensuring that his or her dissent is recorded within the board minutes. Ideally, this should be done every time the subject has been discussed at the board, to avoid the risk that the cumulative record might imply that, while at one stage the director had dissented, nevertheless at later meetings the director appeared to go along with the matter. If the minutes cross-reference to a supporting agenda paper that contains detail about the dissent, that would be sufficient so long as the supporting paper were accessible and retained – which, of course, would not be something that the dissenting director could ensure, except with respect to his or her own copy of the minutes and agenda papers.

There are no legal rules that address the not-unknown scenario whereby the company declines to agree to record in the board minutes a director's dissent; but best practice requires minutes to be clear, concise and unambiguous, which would invariably require dissent to be recorded when a director insisted. Failure to record an objection at a director's insistence would probably cause a loss of confidence in the way that the board was being run. The minutes are the legal responsibility of the directors, with the company secretary being the servant of the board in this respect.

In practice, it is quite likely that a director may fail to ask for his or her concerns to be minuted. Initially, the eventual significance of the matter may not have been appreciated, and it is divisively confrontational to demand that one's dissent is always recorded. The subsequent effect may be that the director feels obliged to stay on the board to play a part in extricating the company from the difficulties it finds itself in.

Under s 248 of the Companies Act 2006, UK law requires[9] records of board and shareholder resolutions and of meetings to be kept and retained for ten years. The Act does not make any distinction between board meetings and board committee meetings. The courts are likely to interpret this section as extending to board committee meetings as well as board meetings: if a committee comprises members of the main board, then its meetings will be meetings of (some of) the company's directors. Given that a board committee almost certainly will have delegated powers from the main board to act, and will have the power to commit the main board, it would in any case make sense for the committee's deliberations and decisions to be recorded in the same way as those of the main board and to be reported to the board. While there is no express requirement within the Act to retain agendas or agenda papers, keeping these in some recorded form will be highly advisable as especially important when a minute cross-refers to a paper on the agenda of the meeting concerned, but does not reproduce that text within the minute.

Making the resignation decision **A4.5**

Of course, not every board disagreement is a resignation issue! A hallmark of a successful board is open, lively dialogue between board members. This in itself makes it less likely that board factions will develop and assume polarised positions. Board members need to be good team workers. A resignation on a point of principle draws attention to a divided board, diverts management and board attention to handling the resignation and its aftermath, and can damage the company commercially. So, resignation may be the Exocet option – to be used very reluctantly. Not entirely unreasonably, directors who have resigned may, like whistleblowers, be viewed with some suspicion by other boards as being potentially too difficult as colleagues to welcome on board.

'A director is a director is a director'. While many board responsibilities are held in common by all the members of the board who have joint and several responsibility, non-executive directors fulfil certain roles that are different from those of executive directors, and non-executive directors who are independent are different again. Whether a resignation should be judged appropriate may vary according to the role of the director on the board. For instance, independent directors should consider the implications if their resignation would be likely to result in a weakened independent element on the board.

Many family businesses across the world are in the process of going public. In these cases, the chairman of the board may, for instance, be the family member who ran the business before a proportion of its equity was floated. The independent directors might have been found by the company's chairman. If the chairman departs, there remains the question as to whether the independent directors should also resign. One commentator has observed that:

> 'The departure of a non-independent chairman should not be a good reason for an independent director to exit as he is not expected to be aligned to the previous or current majority shareholder and chairman.'[10]

It has been said that:

> 'It would be appropriate for independent directors to resign when their views are consistently and fundamentally different from the board's.'[11]

Of course, all the relevant factors have to be weighed carefully before a director makes this decision. It will be damaging to the company if the board is seriously and continuously divided on fundamental issues, such as the strategy of the company. If a board is so divided, there is little point in dissenting directors remaining, and resignation should probably be carefully planned with respect to succession and as amicable and 'quiet' as possible. The much more difficult issue, and hopefully less common one, is where there is suspected or known breaking of law, regulations, accounting standards or similar: then the resignation should most likely be much higher profile and 'noisy'.

While 'a director is a director is a director', the long-standing principles of skill and care mean that more is expected from a director with particular skills and experience than from one without those skills and experience. Under the Companies Act 2006, this will develop significantly: in future, the law will expect a certain standard of skill and care from all directors and will additionally take into account the particular functions that an individual director is carrying out. This will raise the bar of conduct generally, almost certainly leading to an elaboration of the standards expected of non-executive directors vis-à-vis executive directors. This will certainly be taken into account in determining responsibility for damages purposes.

If it is clear that a director does not have the skills needed to discharge his or her particular roles on the board, then the director should resign unless the roles can be revised. Similarly, if the director is unable to put in the time needed, then resignation usually becomes appropriate. Annual evaluation of the performance of each director may be a means of addressing these issues in a timely way so that resignation is not necessary. If the time requirements have proved significantly greater than expected when the appointment was accepted, and the board is unable to rectify the problem nor is the director able to devote the requisite amount of time that circumstances are proving to be necessary, then it is hard to avoid the logic that the appropriate course of action is likely to be to resign from the board appointment. It would be unsatisfactory to soldier on as a director, with all the obligations that directors have, if one were unable to devote sufficient time to the responsibility.

Resignation is the usual and most discreet course of action in cases of unsatisfactory performance by a director to the extent that he or she should leave the board. The chairman of the board will encourage the director to take that course of action and to synchronise it with other considerations that the chairman needs to keep in mind, such as succession or the making of other announcements simultaneously. The alternative approach of asking the shareholders to vote to remove the director is likely to be reputationally damaging, delayed and uncertain.

The 2010 version of the UK Code dropped reference at the level of a Supporting Principle to the importance of a candidate for a board position having sufficient time. Supporting Principle at A.4 of the 2008 Code had stated:

> 'Appointments to the board should be made on merit and against objective criteria. Care should be taken to ensure that appointees have enough time available to devote to the job. This is particularly important in the case of chairmanships.'

The current Code does, however, set out at the level of a 'comply or explain' Provision that the letter of appointment of a non-executive director should indicate the expected time commitment and that the non-executive director should undertake that he or she will have sufficient time to meet what is expected.[12] The issue of time availability is also pertinent for chairs of boards and for executive directors. Until 2010 the UK Code stated that 'no individual should be appointed to a second chairmanship of a FTSE 100 company', but this has now been removed[13] although this Provision is in place:

> 'For the appointment of a chairman, the nomination committee should prepare a job specification, including an assessment of the time commitment expected, recognising the need for availability in the event of crises. A chairman's other significant commitments should be disclosed to the board before appointment and included in the annual report. Changes to such commitments should be reported to the board as they arise, and their impact explained in the next annual report.'[14]

The latest version of the Code continues with the guidance that an executive director of a FTSE 100 company should not accept more than one non-executive directorship nor the chairmanship of such a company.[15]

A Supporting Principle of the UK Code is that all directors must act in what they consider to be the best interests of the company consistent with their statutory duties.[16] Similar requirements apply across the world. For instance the Singapore Companies Act, s 157 states that:

> 'a director shall at all times act honestly and use reasonable diligence in the discharge of the duties of his office.'

There could be circumstances where a director's culpability or liability is the greater because of his or her resignation; that is, the court might take the view that the director should have stayed on the board to try to sort out the mess for which he or she was partly responsible. Where the company faces probable insolvency, a director is required to take every step to minimise losses to creditors; otherwise, he or she will face personal liability for the company's ongoing debts. So, a director who jumps ship rather than staying to sort out the mess in the interests of creditors is likely to be in a worse personal position than one who stays and tries to do the right thing. Stephen Friedman has said:

> 'Directors are elected by shareholders to, among other things, protect the company from the potential damage that management misjudgment … can create. There is little doubt that the right thing to do is to talk to other directors, bring the company's counsel and auditors to board meetings, and stop the improper conduct.'[17]

Insolvent liquidation **A4.6**

Section 214 of the Insolvency Act 1986, on wrongful trading, states that if, in the course of the winding up of a company, it appears that s 214(2) applies in relation to a person who is or has been a director of the company, the court, on the application of the liquidator, may declare that that person is to be liable to make such contribution (if any) to the company's assets as the court thinks proper. Section 214(2) applies in relation to a person if (a) the company has gone into insolvent liquidation, and at some time before the commencement of the winding up of the company, (b) that person knew or ought to have concluded that there was no reasonable prospect that the company would avoid going into insolvent liquidation, and (c) that person was a director of the company at that time.

The court shall not make a declaration under this section with respect to any person if it is satisfied that, after the condition specified in (b) above was first satisfied in relation to him or her, that person took every step with a view to minimising the potential loss to the company's creditors as (assuming him or her to have known that there was no reasonable prospect that the company would avoid going into insolvent liquidation) he or she ought to have taken. The facts which a director of a company ought to know or ascertain, the conclusions which he ought to reach, and the steps which he ought to take are those which would be known or ascertained, or reached or taken, by a reasonably diligent person having both the general knowledge, skill and experience that may reasonably be expected of a person carrying out the same functions as are carried out by that director in relation to the company, and the general knowledge, skill and experience that that director has. The functions carried out in relation to a company by a director of the company includes any functions which he or she does not carry out, but which have been entrusted to him or her. A company goes into insolvent liquidation if it goes into liquidation at a time when its assets are insufficient for the payment of its debts and other liabilities and the expenses of the winding up.

Deciding objectively **A4.7**

Directors may need to be firm with themselves not to allow their pecuniary interests in the company to interfere with making the correct decision regarding whether to resign. The UK Higgs and Tyson reports both indirectly addressed the risk that a non-executive director's fee might influence his or her resignation decision:

> '... it is important that a non-executive director is not so dependent on the income from their role or shareholding as to prejudice independence of judgement, and I would expect boards to take this into account in determining independence.'[18]

and:

> 'The perception of a possible conflict between NED compensation and NED independence may be a possible constraint on the selection of NED candidates from non-traditional talent pools ... These are relatively small amounts compared to the annual compensation levels of chief executives, top-level management and other business professionals. But NED compensation levels may be quite large compared to the annual incomes of NED candidates drawn from non-traditional

> sources such as the non-commercial sector and academia. Institutional investors and other company stakeholders might wonder whether a NED can be truly independent if NED compensation represents a substantial fraction of his or her total annual income.'[19]

So, best practice is suggested as being that the board, when making an appointment, should consider whether the director's fee will make such a significant impact on the director's standard of living as to potentially colour his or her judgement and make it impractical for the director to contemplate resignation objectively. This has been a contentious recommendation, as there are many people who would like to be non-executive directors, for whom the fee would make a significant difference and is a large part of the attraction. Many of them would argue that they would be quite capable of acting objectively on points of principle.

Furthermore, it is not just non-executive directors who may be faced with resignation, and the remuneration of executive directors (for their executive role as well as their board role) has much more potential to colour their judgement. However, the special role of *independent* directors on the board is safeguarded when their pecuniary interest in the company is not at a level which interferes, or might be seen as potentially interfering, with their exercise of independent judgement.

There is little or no risk that members of councils of charities who provide their services without financial reward, as well as members of the boards of many public bodies whose fees are very modest, would be influenced by pecuniary considerations when they decide whether or not to resign from the board.

Possible resignation issues **A4.8**

As an aid to deciding whether to resign, we invite use of the following questions (which do not comprise an exhaustive list of possible issues):

1.	Are you sure that the board has taken a fundamental decision with long-term impact, perhaps on long-term strategy, that you are convinced is wrong and that you will not be able to support going forward?	
2.	Can you see clearly that the company is embarked upon a policy that will lead to a future crisis and from which you have been unsuccessful in persuading the company to pull back?	
3.	Is the board acting dishonourably by supporting, or conniving in, a significant course of action in breach of: ● covenants entered into with a third party (without sufficient restitution)? ● the duties of directors? ● the law?	
4.	Is there a breakdown of trust and confidence between members of the board which has proved impossible to resolve, but which your resignation is the best way to resolve?	

5.	Has the board rejected the advice of a committee of the board on a significant matter that the committee considers it cannot compromise over; and have all means to resolve the disagreement been exhausted?	
6.	Is it apparent that you are unable to make an effective contribution as a director?	
7.	Do you have irresolvable concerns about disclosure and financial reporting to the extent that you consider published results to be misleading?	
8.	Have you finally failed to get action to align the financial interests of top management with the interests of the company's members?	
9.	Have you failed to persuade the board to address your significant concerns about the quality of the company's corporate governance?	
10.	Have you lost confidence in the integrity of colleagues on the board, with no real potential of being able to address this successfully?	
11.	Have you lost confidence in the competence or integrity of non-board management, for actions that you as a director will be held responsible but which you as a director have been unable to resolve?	

Users of this table must apply their own judgement when weighing up whether their answers to these, and other, questions amount to a case for resigning.

Making the resignation **A4.9**

Most directors ultimately leave the board through resignation. The other exit route is when shareholders decline to re-elect a director or when they vote to remove a director from the board. That exit route may have been instigated by a shareholder vote at a general meeting of the company, perhaps on a resolution of the board to remove the director. Even in these cases, it is usual for the departing director to formally submit his or her resignation following the vote.

Companies may have policies that require directors to resign if particular circumstances arise. For instance, a chief executive may be required to resign from the board if he or she loses the position of chief executive. Or a director may be required to resign if a significant shareholder sells their stake in the company. It would no longer be legal, under UK law, for the policy of the company to require a director to resign upon reaching a certain age.[20] Setting out in advance what some of the resignation circumstances are, and thus when a resignation letter is expected, will help to avoid the acrimony that may result if a director has to be removed in another way.

Written resignation is effective when it has been despatched by the departing director and it is prudent that proof of despatch is retained. Oral resignation at a board meeting will be effective if that resignation and its effective timing were clear and unambiguous; but it is wise to follow up an oral resignation with written confirmation to the company chairman or to the company secretary or as required by the articles.

If a director resigns at a board meeting, it is as well for that director to make it clear whether the resignation is with immediate effect from the end of the meeting. A board member is a party to the decisions of the board up until the moment in time that he or she resigns.

Undated resignations should be avoided. Where a notice is not dated, then if a company follows Table A (1985), which says that a notice is deemed to have been received 48 hours after it was posted, the company would be entitled to record the resignation as of the date of receipt or, if earlier, 48 hours from any verifiable time of dispatch. There will be very few circumstances where undated resignations might be appropriate – deliberate omission of a time and date of resignation would arguably suggest uncertainty as to the director's intentions. Conceivably, an undated resignation might be something to consider in situations where a board needs to ratify a resignation for it to be effective – in that sort of situation, an undated resignation might be presented as a threat designed to force an issue and reach a compromise – but it would still be a risky move since the board could accept it anyway. The chairman would not have authority to depart from the rules of procedure as set out in the articles on this matter.

New model articles have been introduced under the Companies Act 2006 which state:

> 'the resignation of a director shall take effect in accordance with the terms of the notice of resignation.'

This implies that the contents of the notice of resignation shall be definitive as regards the effective date and status of the act of resignation. Note that the new model articles do not apply automatically to existing companies.

Acceptance of a resignation, usually by the chairman on behalf of the board, is not a prerequisite for the resignation to be effective – unless the articles stipulate otherwise.

Directors need to be aware of what, if anything, the articles of the company set out with regard to how a resignation should be made. The case where a company's articles require the board to approve any resignation before it is effective can be problematic; this emphasises the importance of a prospective director undertaking a thorough due diligence, which takes in the articles of the company, before accepting an invitation to join the board.

Model articles or Table A apply where the company has not adopted its own tailored articles. Under 22(f) of the Model Articles for UK public companies, a person ceases to be a director as soon as notification is received by the company from the director that the director is resigning from office as director, and such resignation has taken effect in accordance with its terms. There are other model articles for private companies limited by shares and companies limited by guarantee. The old Table A has been replaced for new companies by these simplified and modernised Companies Act 2006 Model Articles which came into force on 1 October 2009. However, Table A remains the default model articles of association for companies incorporated under the Companies Act 1985 in the form it existed at the time of incorporation of the company. Table A says that a director may resign by giving written notice to the company. In practice, notice given to the company secretary or to the chairman of the board will be appropriate. Table A also says that proof of an envelope having been properly addressed, pre-paid and posted will be conclusive evidence that the notice of resignation was given, and it will be deemed to be given 48 hours after it was posted. So, if the resignation is not personally presented, it would be sensible for the director to send the notice by recorded delivery and to retain the proof of posting. If personally presented, it may be prudent to obtain a receipt if the resignation is being effected in contentious circumstances.

The significance of Form TN01 (previously 288b) is only that it fulfils the company's obligation to place the amended details of the board's membership on the public record – it has no direct implications for the validity of the resignation. The resigning director cannot personally submit Form TN01 to Companies House, as it requires the signature of a current director. If the company fails to submit Form TN01, this does not mean that the director who has submitted his or her resignation is still a member of the board. A director who has resigned may, however, wish to check with Companies House that Form TN01 has been submitted.

After resignation A4.10

In practice, the exclusion of the departed director from the future business of the board can lead to concern as to whether his or her resignation is being explained and interpreted appropriately. The UK Code states that, on resignation, a non-executive director should provide a written statement to the chair of the board, for circulation to the board, if the director resigned over any concerns.[21] We would say that the same should also apply to an *executive* director who resigns on a matter of principle. It may be prudent for the resigning director to personally copy this statement to each member of the board if there is any question as to whether the chair of the board will do so. As a practical matter, it is therefore important, for this and other reasons, that each member of the board has at all times up-to-date contact details for each of the other directors on the board. If the resignation was discussed at a board meeting attended by the resigning director, then he or she can make an appropriate statement to the board and require that this be minuted.

A director who has resigned at a board meeting should ask to receive a copy of the minutes of the board meeting at which the director resigned. This ensures that the departed director can make representations if the board minute referring to the resignation is, in his or her view, inaccurate or incomplete. There is a risk that those minutes will not be received since that director is no longer a member of the board. While a director has no legal entitlement to receive a copy of board minutes which apply to board business *after* his or her resignation, we suggest it would be good practice for boards to ensure that they are supplied.

A director will still have legal rights up to the time that his cessation of office takes effect. Under case law precedent, if the director resigns at a meeting 'herewith' and all directors present accept the resignation, then it is effective immediately. Therefore the director will no longer have legal rights to inspect the minutes or do anything else as a director. If the director announces an intention to resign as per the formal procedure in the articles, he or she will technically still be a director until the procedure is complied with, and so will be able to see the minutes of the meeting up until that time. If the minutes are not available until some time after the meeting and after the formal date of resignation, the ex-director would not have a right of access to them. There is no express right for an ex-director to see the minutes of the meeting at which he or she (definitively) resigned. He or she can of course always check with Companies House that Form TN02 has been filed and can ask the company for formal assurance that the resignation has been recorded and notified to Companies House. While it would seem good practice for a company to give this assurance, it is not a legal matter.

When directors resign on a point of principle, it will be prudent for them to retain their personal copies of board and board committee papers relating to the resignation issue so that they have their own independent evidence of what those papers contained. Other board papers may be disposed of. An effective way of doing this may be to return them personally to the company secretary for secure disposal. Alternatively, the ex-director has the responsibility to ensure that they are disposed of securely.

After resignation, some care may need to be taken so as to avoid passing off as still being a director. Once a director has resigned, his or her responsibilities will cease as at the date and time of his resignation – so long as he or she does not continue to act as a director. The UK definition of 'director' is based on activity rather than title, so it is conceivable that a person who formally resigns as director may continue to act as such or as a shadow director. A person will only be a shadow director if he or she issues directions or instructions which would customarily be issued by a director. In respect of their statutory functions, shadow directors can find themselves with the same liability as directors.

Where a director has resigned, he or she will still be subject to certain fiduciary responsibilities towards the company, so the director should be careful to conduct him or herself carefully. He or she should not act in any way which could be construed as damaging the company and, in particular, it is advisable to exercise care not to make any statements which might all too easily be interpreted as impugning the integrity of past colleagues within the company. While bearing these considerations in mind, it is reasonable to make a statement, perhaps a letter to shareholders or a press release, announcing the resignation and the reason(s) for it. While directors do not have to give a publicised reason for resigning, it should be possible to do so without adverse legal ramification. The publicised reason should be as accurate as possible. The use of phrases such as 'for personal reasons' or 'to spend more time with the family' should be used only if they are correct. One authority has suggested:

> 'It is acceptable if someone is resigning due to reasons of illness, bereavement or other genuine personal difficulties, but we propose that anyone who uses the 'personal reasons' excuse should, if they have other listed directorships, be required to explain in the same announcement why these 'personal reasons' do not make it necessary to resign from those positions, too.'[22]

The director who has resigned has no general right to insist that the company releases an announcement of the resignation: the company may prefer to delay the announcement perhaps until the time it next reports to the members in the form of an annual report; Form TN01 will, of course, be on the public record; and, for a listed company, there are requirements to inform the market of various issues, although there is no specific requirement to do so in respect of changes in directors.

However, a chief executive's resignation from a listed company is an 'announceable' event. For market reasons, it is likely to be unwise to announce the departure of a chief executive until the company is also able to announce his or her replacement. So it is usual for a chief executive to advise the board of his or her *intention* to resign, so that the later announcement of the resignation can be contemporaneous with the announcement of who the successor will be. This approach may also be applied so as to limit the damage to a company when one or more directors, perhaps non-executive directors, resign.

It is reasonable for a director who has resigned to press the company to ensure that the Form TN01 notice is placed on the public record promptly and to inform him or her that this has been done. There are currently limited powers for Companies House (on approach by an interested party or otherwise) to amend information on the public record if it is incorrect or no longer correct, although this has changed under the Companies Act 2006. The director who has resigned may also require the company to desist from referring to him as a director in any official company publication. If it came to it, he or she could consider taking out an injunction against the company to compel it to stop referring to him or her publicly as a director. But the failure on the part of the company to file Form TN01 does not affect the validity of the director's resignation (assuming the resignation is valid, in that it has been made in a way consistent with the requirements of the company's articles).

It is unlikely to be in the best interests of the company for the members of the company not to be informed promptly of the resignation of a director. While 'the company' has its own corporate personality, its members are, after all, a hugely important part of the company. While the fundamental reason for the resignation may have been a disagreement on a point of principle, much of the impact of the resignation will be lost if the members of the company remain unaware of it. It would be regrettable if the company were to decline to ensure that members became aware promptly of a director's resignation on a point of principle. The ex-director should find a way of ensuring that the members are informed promptly.

Prior to resignation, it is advisable that the director who is considering resignation avoids making commitments of any sort about his or her intentions following resignation. It is preferable to keep all options open, as the director concerned cannot possibly know how affairs will unfold following the resignation. For instance, an undertaking not to issue a press release or not to speak to journalists may inhibit the resigned director from correcting misinformation after he has left the board.

In tense situations, it may be helpful for the leaving director to retain a firm of communications consultants and to refer all enquiries about his or her resignation through that firm.

It is quite likely that a director who has resigned will be approached by someone who is being invited to replace him or her on the board, to enquire the circumstances surrounding the resignation and whether there are any reasons why this candidate should not accept the role. Again, this requires circumspection. If the enquirer is unknown to the ex-director, care must be taken to guard against the risk of discussing company affairs with an impostor who has a private agenda. It is safer ground to stick to factual material, especially that which is in the public domain, leaving the candidate to draw his or her own conclusions. You may also safely correct misinterpretations of material that is within the public domain.

Scenarios **A4.11**

1. The articles require the approval of the board before you can resign as a director. If you noted this before you joined the board, how would you react? How would it affect your approach to resigning?
2. You are resigning on a matter of principle. The board refuses to notify the members of the company about your resignation until the next annual report reaches the members in several months' time. What would you do?
3. Can you anticipate a situation in which it would be in the best interests of the company for the board not to inform the shareholders promptly of the resignation of a director on a matter of principle?
4. If the majority shareholders oust the chairman of the board, does that justify the subsequent resignation of the independent directors?
5. A company nears collapse under a mountain of debt after former management had defrauded clients and shareholders. What should determine whether or not the independent directors stay on the board to try to save the company?
6. If a director resigns from a board and blows the whistle to the Serious Fraud Office or to the Financial Services Authority on the accounts, might it be reasonable for that person to seek immediate reinstatement under legal protection afforded to those who come with information to the authorities, or compensation for loss of office?
7. If a non-executive director resigns because the time commitment has proved significantly greater than that set out in his or her letter of appointment, and it has not been possible to resolve the matter, might it be appropriate for the director to sue the company for loss of office?
8. Do you consider that the board's policy that authorises a director to seek outside advice at the company's expense on matters to do with his or her role as a director, should extend to advice relating to designation from the board – both prior to resignation and subsequent to it?
9. The board has declined to accept the advice of the audit committee, which you chair, on improving the clarity of disclosure on executive remuneration within the annual report and accounts. In the audit committee's view this means that the annual report and accounts are misleading. However, they have been prepared in accordance with the law and with applicable accounting standards and the external auditors accept how they have been prepared. Would you resign over this matter?

Notes

1 Financial Reporting Council, The UK Corporate Governance Code (June 2010, ISBN 978-1-84798-323-7), available on the FRC website.

2 The UK Corporate Governance Code: 'The board should ensure that directors, especially non-executive directors, have access to independent professional advice at the company's expense where they judge it necessary to discharge their responsibilities

as directors. Committees should be provided with sufficient resources to undertake their duties.'

3 The UK Corporate Governance Code, Provision A.3.1: 'The chairman should on appointment meet the independence criteria set out in B.1.1 below. A chief executive should not go on to be chairman of the same company. If exceptionally a board decides that a chief executive should become chairman, the board should consult major shareholders in advance and should set out its reasons to shareholders at the time of the appointment and in the next annual report.'

4 The UK Corporate Governance Code, Provision A.4.2: 'The chairman should hold meetings with the non-executive directors without the executives present. Led by the senior independent director, the non-executive directors should meet without the chairman present at least annually to appraise the chairman's performance (as described in A.6.1) and on such other occasions as are deemed appropriate.'

5 The UK Corporate Governance Code, Provision B.5.1: 'The board should ensure that directors, especially non-executive directors, have access to independent professional advice at the company's expense where they judge it necessary to discharge their responsibilities as directors. Committees should be provided with sufficient resources to undertake their duties.'

6 Freidman, Stephen J, 'Resigning from the board', *Directors & Boards* (1996, Vol 20, Issue 2, p 30(3)).

7 The UK Corporate Governance Code, Provision A.1.3: 'The company should arrange appropriate insurance cover in respect of legal action against its directors.'

8 The UK Corporate Governance Code, Provision A.4.3: 'Where directors have concerns which cannot be resolved about the running of the company or a proposed action, they should ensure that their concerns are recorded in the board minutes. On resignation, a non-executive director should provide a written statement to the chairman, for circulation to the board, if they have any such concerns.'

9 This provision came into effect in October 2007.

10 Tan Lye Huat, CEO of HIM Governance, quoted in 'When is it OK for directors to quit', *The Business Times*, Singapore (28 November 2006).

11 Penelope Phoon, head of ACCA in Singapore, quoted in 'When is it OK for directors to quit', *The Business Times*, Singapore (28 November 2006).

12 The UK Corporate Governance Code, Provision B.3.2: 'The terms and conditions of appointment of non-executive directors should be made available for inspection [The terms and conditions of appointment of non-executive directors should be made available for inspection by any person at the company's registered office during normal business hours and at the AGM (for 15 minutes prior to the meeting and during the meeting).]. The letter of appointment should set out the expected time commitment. Non-executive directors should undertake that they will have sufficient time to meet what is expected of them. Their other significant commitments should be disclosed to the board before appointment, with a broad indication of the time involved and the board should be informed of subsequent changes.'

13 The 2008 Combined Code, Provision A.4.3: 'For the appointment of a chairman, the nomination committee should prepare a job specification, including an assessment of the time commitment expected, recognising the need for availability in the event of crises. A chairman's other significant commitments should be disclosed to the board before appointment and included in the annual report. Changes to such commitments should be reported to the board as they arise, and included in the next annual report. No individual should be appointed to a second chairmanship of a FTSE 100 company.'

14 Code Provision B.3.1 (**App1**).

15 The UK Corporate Governance Code, Provision B.3.3: 'The board should not agree to a full-time executive director taking on more than one non-executive directorship in a FTSE 100 company nor the chairmanship of such a company.'

16 The UK Corporate Governance Code, Supporting Principle A.1, and Companies Act 2006, ss 170–177.

17 Freidman, Stephen J, 'Resigning from the board', *Directors & Boards* (1996, Vol 20, Issue 2, p 30(3)).

18 Higgs Review of the Role and Effectiveness of Non-Executive Directors (January 2003), a report commissioned by the Department of Trade & Industry, §9.14.

19 Tyson Report on the Recruitment and Development of Non-Executive Directors (June 2003), a report commissioned by the Department of Trade & Industry, p 16.

20 The age limit of 70 for has been taken out of UK company law by the Companies Act 2006, and that repeal came into effect on 6 April 2007. The age discrimination rules brought in in 2005 extend to company directors as well as the employment situation.

21 The UK Corporate Governance Code, Provision A.4.3: 'Where directors have concerns which cannot be resolved about the running of the company or a proposed action, they should ensure that their concerns are recorded in the board minutes. On resignation, a non-executive director should provide a written statement to the chairman, for circulation to the board, if they have any such concerns.'

22 David Webb, editor of governance website Webb-site.com, quoted in: 'What other countries say', *The Business Times*, Singapore (28 November 2006).

Chapter A5

Board Committees

Introduction A5.1

This handbook carries sample terms of reference for board committees, as follows:

- audit committee: **App4.1–App4.7**;
- remuneration committee: **App4.8–App4.10**;
- nominations committee: **App4.11–App4.12**;
- finance committee: **App4.13–App4.14**;
- HR/personnel committee: **App4.15–App4.16**;
- standing orders committee: **App4.17**; and
- risk committee: **App4.18**.

The Institute of Chartered Secretaries and Administrators ('ICSA') has published excellent pro forma terms of reference for the four board committees referred to in the UK Corporate Governance Code (set out in full at **App1**) – audit, risk, remuneration and nominations. They can be found on the ICSA website.[1]

ICSA was asked by the Financial Reporting Council to update the 2003 Higgs guidance on the role of the non-executive director, which they have done in the form of another excellent publication titled 'Improving Board Effectiveness', to be found on the ICSA website.

'Improving Board Effectiveness' is significantly different in scope from the Higgs guidance, which had an almost exclusive focus on non-executive directors and contained a large number of specific recommendations for revisions to the UK Corporate Governance Code current at that time, many of which were incorporated into the 2003 Combined Code.

Many UK entities deem the gender-specific term 'chairman' to be both acceptable and indeed required, but progressive companies might alternatively opt for the rather ungainly expression 'chairperson' or just 'chair'.

The committee oversight role of the chairman of the board A5.2

While the chairman of a board committee is responsible for the effectiveness of that committee, it is wise to consider this to be responsibility arising from authority delegated by the chairman of the board. The chairman of the board is overall responsible for the effectiveness of the board and that must include the effectiveness of its committees. A good, open working relationship between the chairman of the board and the chairman of the board's committees is essential. It is up to both chairmen to work on ensuring that this is achieved. Much depends upon the extent and quality of an open, ongoing dialogue between the two chairmen.

It is much easier for the board committees that rely significantly on independent directors to work closely with the chair of the board if he or she were independent when appointed. An extreme example of this was an occasion when the audit committee needed to investigate the conduct of the chief executive: not least because the chairman of the board was independent when he had been appointed chairman, the audit committee had confidence in keeping the chairman of the board fully informed during the progress of the investigation which in due course led to the chairman of the board dismissing the chief executive. Had the chairman of the board been closely aligned with the executive, perhaps through having been a member of the top executive team when appointed chairman of the board, it would have been much more difficult for the audit committee to have handled this investigation successfully.

It is general practice that the board determines who shall be the chairman of these board committees, often on the recommendation of the chairman of the entity whose overall responsibility it is to ensure the effective functioning of the board and its committees. A usually less satisfactory alternative would be for the committee itself to select its own chairman from those appointed by the board to be members of the committee.

A notable feature of the ICSA terms of reference is that they each assume that the nominations committee of the board, after consulting the chairman of the board committee concerned, will make the recommendations to the board on who should be appointed to each of the board committees, and that these decisions will then be made by the board. While ICSA makes no mention of any role for the chairman of the board in this process, the UK Corporate Governance Code does, however, allow that the chairman of the board may be a member of, and may chair, the nominations committee. As best practice guidance, this is ahead of its time in the sense that nominations committees are not always involved in the process of choosing board committee members. It is, however, logical, not least because one of the responsibilities of the nominations committee is to undertake succession planning to ensure that the board is refreshed with the competencies it needs, including the competencies needed at the level of the board committees.

It is usual that the chairman of a board committee is approved by the board on the recommendation of the chairman of the board. Of course, chairing a board committee is not just about turning up to chair meetings to an agenda prepared by the company secretary: it entails proactively assuming the responsibility of ensuring the committee is effective in all respects.

The rationale for board committees **A5.3**

Standing committees of the board are a useful means of ensuring that the board gives in-depth consideration to all matters for which it is responsible. The time available at board meetings may make this difficult or impossible to achieve at meetings of the board itself. The appropriate timing when matters need to be considered and decisions made may make it more efficient for certain matters to be considered first by a board committee rather than by the board as a whole. Some matters, such as the remuneration of executive directors, may be best determined by a committee comprising only some of the board members.

Committees are not mentioned at the level of the Main Principles of the UK Corporate Governance Code. The implication is that boards may be able to apply the Main Principles in ways that do not require reliance on board committees.

It is only the remuneration committee that has any of its responsibilities referred to at mid-level of a Supporting Principle in the UK Code, the others being referred to only at the lesser level of 'comply or explain' Provisions:

> 'The remuneration committee should judge where to position their company relative to other companies. But they should use such comparisons with caution, in view of the risk of an upward ratchet of remuneration levels with no corresponding improvement in performance.
>
> 'They should also be sensitive to pay and employment conditions elsewhere in the group, especially when determining annual salary increases.'[2]

Deciding what board committees to have **A5.4**

Boards should be economical in the number of board committees they establish. Half a dozen is likely to be on the high side – especially for anything other than very large companies with large boards. Those which are appropriate will vary according to statute, regulation, nature of business, corporate culture and the inclination of the principal players.

Specifying in a committee's terms of reference that committee duties are additional duties for directors makes it practical for supplementary fees to be paid to directors for their committee duties, where appropriate. This is likely to be appropriate in the case of non-executive directors. A further supplement may be paid for chairing a board committee. Some companies settle for paying a supplementary fee only to their chairs of board committees, and then only where they are non-executive. Other companies pay no supplementary fee for board committee duties, on the basis that these are shared out fairly between the non-executive directors over time; but this is becoming a less usual practice.

An audit and finance committee of the board? **A5.5**

A key point to remember is that an audit committee should be as independent as is practical of finance and accounting decisions. It is therefore unsound in principle for there to be a single 'finance and audit committee' or for any other committee to have oversight of both (a) investment and other financial matters *and* (b) audit matters.

Board committees serving more than one board **A5.6**

Caution should be exercised in making arrangements for a single committee to serve the needs of more than one board – perhaps in the interests of economy and efficiency. *Prima facie* this may appear appropriate where a committee has oversight of a number of special vehicle entities or subsidiaries set up by a company; or it may be an option for an audit committee of company A to also be the audit committee of a partly owned joint venture company B. In the latter case, difficulties might arise as follows:

- If the membership of the audit committee is drawn from the boards of both companies, a decision of the audit committee might not be made in the best interests of one or other of the companies.
- It will be difficult or impossible for the audit committee to address issues which need to be confidential to either company A or B, and in particular issues which relate to concerns about the conduct of the other company.
- Communicating the results of audit committee business to the respective boards will be more difficult. For instance, the chair of the audit committee may not be a member of both boards. Best practice is that all members of board committees are also members of their boards.

The 'downside risk' of board committees A5.7

Board committees are intended to make boards more effective in particular areas, but can perversely effectively exclude the board from taking a real interest in issues that the board has delegated to its committees. When most UK companies set up audit committees in the 1990s, this was welcomed by many as indicating that, at last, boards were taking more interest in audit matters. But in some companies it has had the perverse effect that their boards have assumed that financial reporting, internal and external auditing, risk management and internal control matters are in the safe hands of their audit committees and that the board can focus on other things. So it is essential that the board engages appropriately in the important work of its committees, rather than assuming that the board can leave those issues entirely to their committees. This means that there must be proper reporting by board committees to the board and adequate discussion of committee business at the board, which discussion should be minuted.

Board delegation to committees, not abdication A5.8

Boards delegate to board committees what would otherwise have to be done at the level of the board itself. Delegation does not, of course, mean abdication. Although not referring specifically to the board's reliance upon board committees, a UK court on two occasions, with respect to Barings Bank, set out this position:

> 'Whilst directors are entitled (subject to the articles of association of the company) to delegate particular functions to those below them in the management chain, and to trust their competence and integrity to a reasonable extent, the exercise of delegation does not absolve a director from the duty to supervise the discharge of the delegated function. No rule of universal application can be formulated as to the [foregoing]. The extent of the duty, and the question whether it has been discharged, must depend on the facts of each particular case, including the director's role in the management of the company.'[3]

and the court later held:

> 'The extent to which a NED may reasonably rely on the executive directors and other professionals to perform their duties is one which the law can be fairly said to be developing and is plainly 'fact sensitive'. It is plainly arguable, I think, that a company may reasonably at least look to NEDs for independence of judgement and supervision of the executive management.'[4]

The direction and oversight role of board committees A5.9

We must also distinguish between the responsibilities of board committees for particular issues and the responsibilities of the executive for the same issues. Generally, board committees are responsible to the board for the development of policy on particular issues, and for oversight of implementation of those policies, whereas the executive (rather than the board or the board committee) is likely always to be responsible for the implementation of that policy which has been developed.

In **App4** the proposed draft terms of reference of the audit (second example) and remuneration committees include wording which specifies the committee is not an executive committee. Further consideration would need to be given as to whether the distinction between 'executive' and 'non-executive' in the context of committee powers, responsibilities and duties is valid, and, if so, which (if any) committees are to have executive powers.

Since board committees are comprised largely or exclusively of outside directors, it would be particularly inappropriate if they were to act as if they were part of the executive apparatus of the company. Boards direct and oversee. Boards may delegate to their committees certain powers to direct and oversee within the scope of their roles and responsibilities. These roles and responsibilities should be set out in terms of reference for each standing committee of the board, approved by the board and regularly reviewed by both the board and the committee. The equivalent to terms of reference for an ad hoc board committee (see **A5.12** below) will be the minuted resolution of the board setting up the ad hoc committee.

Just as the board directs and the executive executes, so board committees should avoid treading on executive toes by assuming executive responsibilities. Often, the right approach for a board committee is to err on the side of advising the executive on what the committee considers an appropriate course of action. The executive should be wise enough to take note of the guidance. The executive knows that, if necessary, the issue can be taken to the board for resolution if there is disagreement between the executive and the committee. This advisory style would not be the case for the remuneration committee, which should set executive performance targets and determine executive performance-related rewards in a very definite way.

Mandatory or discretionary board committees A5.10

It is not mandatory for a UK listed company to have any particular board committee, unless it is set out in the articles of the company. The UK Corporate Governance Code (**App1**) is discretionary. Although the Main Principles of the Code are meant to be applied by all public companies with a premium listing in the UK, the enforcer of the UK Listing Rules has never enforced the Principles of the Code upon companies. The Provisions within the Code only have 'comply or explain' status. The UK regulator of financial institutions may impose a mandatory obligation upon a regulated entity to have certain board committees. The New York Stock Exchange corporate governance Standards are intended to be mandatory for companies listed on that Stock Exchange, and thus certain board committees should be regarded as mandatory for these companies (nominations, compensation and audit).

The most common board committees A5.11

Entities in compliance with all the UK Corporate Governance Code will have an audit committee, a remuneration committee and a nominations committee. They may also have a risk committee of the board, unless the audit committee of the board or the board itself has the responsibility to review all of the company's internal control and risk management systems (Provision C.3.2). Beyond that, entities will need to exercise their discretion to determine whether further board committees are appropriate.

Temporary, ad hoc board committees A5.12

Apart from standing committees, boards may resolve from time to time to set up temporary ad hoc committees comprising some board members with delegated power from the board to progress an issue between board meetings, within parameters that the board has set as guidance for the ad hoc committee. Usually the board will ratify any decisions made by an ad hoc committee at the next meeting of the full board. Ad hoc committees with a longer life span may be set up to work on behalf of the full board on special projects – such as a takeover, a rights issue or a crisis.

Other board committees A5.13

Here we list some of the committees we have noted as being in place in medium to large corporations. It would be exceptional for a board to have more than five or six board committees:

- Acquisitions and disposals
- Agenda
- Appraisal and remuneration
- Assets and liabilities (ALCO)
- Audit
- Board business
- Capital resources
- Chairman's
- Community affairs
- Compliance
- Corporate governance
- Compliance
- Due diligence
- Environmental
- Ethical
- Ethics and standards
- Group operations
- Health and safety
- Human resources
- Legal
- Management development
- Manufacturing
- Marketing (domestic)

- Marketing (overseas)
- Nomination(s)
- Personnel
- (New) product development
- Remuneration
- Risk/risk management
- Resources
- Standing orders
- Strategic planning
- Treasury.

Non-board committees of the company **A5.14**

There will most likely be a number of committees within a business that are not committees of the board. It would be a committee of the board if it were established as a board committee by the company's articles or by formal board resolution. Whether or not the committee reports to the board (for instance, its minutes or a tailored committee report are an agenda paper for the board) and whether or not the committee is comprised wholly or partially of directors are not the crucial determinants of whether it should be regarded as a board committee.

Assistance for board committees **A5.15**

In most cases, it is sound that secretarial support for committees of the board should be provided by the secretary of the board, but it would be acceptable, if necessary, for someone such as the assistant company secretary to act as secretary to a board committee. It would not, for instance, be sound for the head of internal audit to act as secretary of the audit committee.

Increasingly, board committees are being empowered to take outside professional advice at the company's expense in connection with the discharge of their responsibilities. Board committees may also commission work to be done directly on their behalf by executives of the business. A 1997 survey found that audit committees of a sample of multinational companies typically commissioned one assignment each year to be conducted directly on the committee's behalf by the company's internal audit function.[5] However, in many cases it will be normal practice for a board committee to work through the responsible executive directors to arrange for specific tasks to be undertaken to meet the committee's needs. The nominations and remuneration committees are likely to need to conduct their business discreetly.

Not being executive committees, board committees are highly dependent on the quality of information they receive. They should place priority on ensuring that they are serviced with high-quality, timely, relevant and clear information. The frontline responsibility for servicing board committees is with the company secretary who services the board. UK Code Supporting Principles at B.5 puts it like this:

> 'Under the direction of the chairman, the company secretary's responsibilities include ensuring good information flows within the board and its committees and between senior management and non-executive directors, as well as facilitating induction and assisting with professional development as required.

The company secretary should be responsible for advising the board through the chairman on all governance matters.'

Membership of board committees A5.16

The bias in board committee membership towards independent directors is for two reasons. First, outside directors are particularly challenged to develop and maintain an adequate understanding of the affairs of the company. Membership of board committees assists them to be on top of their brief. For instance, the root reason for the wide establishment of audit committees in the 1990s was that outside directors needed a forum to scrutinise draft financial statements before publication, since in UK law they have joint and several liability for the reliability of those financial statements. The second related reason is that effective board oversight of many of the matters entrusted to board committees needs a perspective that is independent of the executive: this is particularly the case with respect to the remuneration committee's determination of executive compensation.

Independent directors on board committees A5.17

Where it is necessary for committee members to be chosen from amongst the independent directors, as is stipulated in most cases by the UK Corporate Governance Code for listed companies, it may be significant that one of the criteria for determining whether a director is independent is that he or she has not been a member of the board for more than nine years. The Code also includes other criteria to assess whether a director is independent.[6]

The UK Corporate Governance Code states that the members of the remuneration and audit committees, and also of the risk committee of the board if there is one, should all be independent directors, and that a majority of the members of the nominations committee also should be independent directors. The Code allows that the chairman of the board of a company outside the FTSE 350 may be a member of the audit committee (but not its chairman) if he or she were independent when appointed as chairman of the company. The Code also allows that the chairman of the board may belong to and chair the nominations committee, but should not chair it when the committee is dealing with the appointment of a successor to the chairmanship (Provision B.2.1). Although the Code recommends that the chairman of the board should be independent at the time he or she is appointed as chairman of the board, it is generally regarded that the chairman of the board is not thereafter regarded as independent. The Code does not exactly endorse that; the reasoning for this interpretation of the Code is to be found in the wording of Provision B.1.2:

> 'Except for smaller companies [a smaller company is one that is below the FTSE 350 throughout the year immediately prior to the reporting year], at least half the board, excluding the chairman, should comprise non-executive directors determined by the board to be independent. A smaller company should have at least two independent non-executive directors.'

Chapter **A3** deals with independence in more detail.

Executives as members of board committees **A5.18**

The UK Code sets out that all members of the nominations, audit and remuneration committees will be directors and, indeed that they will all be independent non-executive directors – with the exception of the nominations committee where just the *majority* of members are to be independent non-executive directors. Board committees for companies not subject to the Combined Code, and other board committees for public companies subject to the Combined Code, may include committee members who are executive directors, executives below the level of the executive directors and also complete outsiders who are neither executives nor members of the board.

The Walker Report (November 2009)[7] took a modified view, in stating firmly that banks and financial institutions should definitely have a separate risk committee of the board in addition to an audit committee, but Walker allowed that its members may be non-executive though not necessarily independent, and that the executive finance director may also be a member. Many companies have risk committees at executive level. It is important to understand that these are no substitute for risk committees at board level. Conceivably, there could be committees comprising solely executive directors that are considered by the board to be committees of the board, but this would be unusual.

Outsiders on board committees **A5.19**

Not all members of board committees will necessarily be members of the board. There have been examples of audit committees chaired by complete outsiders who attend meetings of the board just to present the report of the audit committee. The extra independence of complete outsiders is discussed in detail at **A3.5**.

Potential liability **A5.20**

When complete outsiders, or executives of the entity who are not members of the board, belong to board committees, there is a risk that they could be held to have acted in the capacity of being a director, and thus have assumed the potential liabilities of a member of the board. The risk can be guarded against if the outsiders are clearly in attendance but not as members, or if the committee is clearly established as a committee of the company but not of the board. See also **A3.5**.

Care, skill and diligence **A5.21**

Section 174 of the Companies Act 2006 replaced the old, traditional 'subjective' standard of skill and care with a new objective standard which legal commentators have said enshrines in statute law the position the courts have already reached:

> 'A director of a company must exercise reasonable care, skill and diligence. This means the care, skill and diligence that would be exercised by a reasonably diligent person with:
>
> - the general knowledge, skill and experience that may reasonably be expected of a person carrying out the functions carried out by the director in relation to the company, and
> - the general knowledge, skill and experience that the director has.'

Before agreeing to join a board or a board committee, a prospective member should determine what qualities it is being assumed that he or she will be able to competently bring to the board or to the board's committee and be satisfied that he or she has the ability to deliver as expected. A professionally qualified person will be expected to have the professional knowledge and skill associated with a competent member of that profession who has kept up-to-date with professional developments.

Attendance at committee meetings **A5.22**

No director should insist on his or her right to attend a board committee meeting unless a member of it. The UK Corporate Governance Code has Supporting Principles at B.1 that state:

> 'The value of ensuring that committee membership is refreshed and that undue reliance is not placed on particular individuals should be taken into account in deciding chairmanship and membership of committees.'

and

> 'No one other than the committee chairman and members is entitled to be present at a meeting of the nomination, audit or remuneration committee, but others may attend at the invitation of the committee.'

and with respect to the chairman's involvement with the nomination committee, Code Provision B.2.1 states:

> 'There should be a nomination committee which should lead the process for board appointments and make recommendations to the board. A majority of members of the nomination committee should be independent non-executive directors. The chairman or an independent non-executive director should chair the committee, but the chairman should not chair the nomination committee when it is dealing with the appointment of a successor to the chairmanship. The nomination committee should make available its terms of reference, explaining its role and the authority delegated to it by the board.'

Arguably, any director has the theoretical right to attend any board committee meeting. But the chairman of the board will make it clear, to a director who inappropriately insists on doing so, that his or her future as a member of the board is in doubt.

Attendance by non-members at board committee meetings **A5.23**

It is usually the case that board committees will need non-committee members to attend for all or part of their meetings. Thus, for instance, audit committees may require the head of internal audit, the chief risk officer, the head of compliance, the finance director and the external auditor to be in attendance at least from time to time.

On the other hand, it is usually also the case that a board committee will function more effectively if directors who are not members of the board committee do not attend its meetings. For instance, the presence of the chairman of the board at a meeting of the audit committee might cramp the style of the audit committee's chair. Or the presence of executive directors at remuneration committee meetings will impede that committee whose main brief is to determine the remuneration of the executive directors.

Where a committee, such as the audit committee, has a role in providing assurance, it can be argued that the assurance given is likely to be better if it was arrived at independently of those to whom the assurance is given. Thus, the chairman of the board and other members of the board who are not members of the audit committee could with advantage not be involved routinely in audit committee meetings. In the public sector, this would suggest that the accounting officer should neither be a member nor routinely be in attendance at audit committee meetings.

The chairman of a board committee should proactively arrange for appropriate executives to be in attendance, or not to be in attendance, for specific agenda items. The assumption and practice that certain non-members will always be in attendance should be avoided if this means it becomes embarrassing and impractical for the committee to require the absence of an executive when that is appropriate for the agenda item being discussed. Executive attendance or absence should be arranged before the meeting takes place.

In some cases, executive attendance would clearly be counterproductive, as, for instance, the attendance of an executive director at a remuneration committee which is determining his or her compensation package. Best practice is that no director should participate in the determination of his or her own remuneration.

Committee terms of reference **A5.24**

See **A5.1** for further discussion of committee terms of reference.

To remove any ambiguity, we recommend that all board committees have terms of reference formally adopted by the board, and that the articles of the company set out that these terms of reference, current at any time, are binding. The terms of reference can address who is entitled to attend each board committee and who can be required by the committee to attend, but the committee should have an override on attendance by those who are not members of the committee. Board committees should be empowered to require any executives to attend for particular agenda items.

The authority, responsibilities and membership of each board committee should be outlined in the committee's terms of reference which should be adopted by the board. It should be the board that determines the terms of reference of its board committees – although this may sometimes be delegated by the board to the committee itself. It is good practice for each board committee to review its own terms of reference annually and propose any changes to the board. This has the advantage of reminding committee members what their role is, and also ensures that the terms of reference are kept up to date.

The membership of a board committee should be set out in its terms of reference, which will also cover its responsibilities and membership. The terms of reference should be adopted by the board. The terms of reference are likely to empower the chairman of the committee to invite others who are not members (whether other directors, senior and other executives or outsiders) to be in attendance for part or all of meetings, and should empower the chairman to require those in attendance to leave the meeting when he or she considers it appropriate. While technically within his or her rights, any director who was not a committee member and yet insisted upon attending against the wishes of the chair should be brought to realise that he or she is also acting against the wishes of the board and should be prepared to face the consequences.

Some companies make provision in their constitutional documents for the existence of a remuneration and some other standing committees of the board; others make provision by detailing the membership and responsibilities of these committees in minuted board resolutions.

Sample terms of reference **A5.25**

Under each of the sample terms of reference of board committees reproduced in **App4: Board Committees – Terms of Reference**, the committee is authorised to engage professionals as the committee sees fit, to provide independent counsel and advice and to assist in any review or investigation on such matters as the committee deems appropriate. A related topic is that individual directors should be empowered to obtain independent professional advice in the furtherance of their responsibilities as directors; advice on the standing guidelines that regulate the conduct of board business may be shown as a responsibility of the standing orders committee, which may also be the committee with the responsibility to ensure that there is maintained an up-to-date board manual, available to all board directors. The standing orders committee is also shown as being responsible to advise the board on matters to be reserved to the board and on delegation of authority guidelines.

In **App4**, we reproduce sample terms of reference for board committees developed in draft for one client. In their draft form, there is some overlap between the terms of reference of three of the committees – nominations, personnel and remuneration. Here we summarise the overlap contained within these three draft terms of reference. With the client for whom these terms of reference were developed, the suggestion arose internally for a personnel committee, and this has been developed into proposed terms of reference which include certain duties also within the recommended terms of reference of the remuneration and nominations committees. This overlap would need to be corrected if the board decided to go ahead and establish a personnel committee of the board.

Potential overlap between the nominations, remuneration and personnel committees can be summed up as follows.

- From the **nominations committee** draft terms of reference:

  '6.6 Nominating suitable people for the most senior executive positions, including that of chief executive.'

- From the **remuneration committee** draft terms of reference:

  '6.1 The committee's purpose is to ensure that the … senior executives are fairly rewarded for their individual contributions to overall performance …

  6.2 The duties of the committee shall be to recommend to and advise the board on the remuneration (in all its forms) and associated matters of the … senior executives. This requires the committee to:

  1. Determine appropriate remuneration in all its forms (including pension arrangements within the discretion of the company's

scheme) of the … senior executives, as defined from time to time. This will bear in mind differentials between levels of personnel and market relativities.

2. Ensure there is good succession planning and management development at senior executive levels, and to review specific development plans for the top *n* executives in the group.
3. Measure the performance of key senior executives as a prelude to determining their annual remuneration, bonus rewards and award of long term incentives.
4. See that, in exercising the rights to performance related compensation, benefits are related to the performance both of individuals and the group, and that they provide a long-term incentive.
5. Ensure that the committee only makes recommendations which it can justify to shareholders and staff alike and that the criteria on which performance is measured can be clearly explained.'

- From the **personnel committee** draft terms of reference:

'1. Ensure that the company has a satisfactory personnel function covering all aspects of personnel management including succession planning and career development.

…

6. Ensure there is good succession planning and management development at senior executive levels; and review specific development plans for the top executives in the group.
7. Recommend to and advise the board on the remuneration (in all its forms) and associated matters of the senior executives.
8. Review the performance of key senior executives.
9. Ensure that, in exercising the rights to performance related compensation, benefits are related to the performance both of individuals and the group, and that they provide a long-term incentive.
10. Ensure that the committee only makes recommendations which it can be justified to shareholders and staff alike and that the criteria on which performance is measured can be clearly explained.
11. Nominate suitable people for senior executive positions.'

Board and board committee authority **A5.26**

In the UK, care has been taken to ensure that board committees are always sub-committees of the board, with no superior powers to those of the board. That is not to say that the board may not delegate powers to a board committee and then routinely decline to reopen decisions that the board committee makes.

In the US, an exception is the audit committee of the board of a US quoted company, which has overall responsibility for the appointment of the auditors and for deciding their remuneration. In the UK, the guidance in the Corporate Governance Code

(Provision C.3.7) is only that the audit committee recommends to the board who should be the external auditors and that the board should explain in the annual report what the audit committee's advice was and why the board did not follow it, if that was so:

> 'The audit committee should have primary responsibility for making a recommendation on the appointment, reappointment and removal of the external auditor. FTSE 350 companies should put the external audit out to tender at least every ten years. If the board does not accept the audit committee's recommendation, it should include in the annual report, and in any papers recommending appointment or re-appointment, a statement from the audit committee explaining the recommendation and should set out reasons why the board has taken a different position.'

At present in the UK, it is formally the board that reports on the work of each of its board committees within a company's annual report, rather than being a report from the committee. The board committee does not have the final say on its wording. Furthermore, at a general meeting of the shareholders of a UK company, the shareholders do not have a general right to insist that a question is answered by the chair of a particular board committee: it is up to the chairman of the general meeting to decide whether and by whom a question will be answered.

For board committees to function well, it is in certain circumstances inappropriate for the board to reopen conclusions arrived at by a board committee, although ultimately it has the power to do so. For instance, the performance targets and the performance-related bonuses set by the remuneration committee of independent directors should not be subject to reconsideration at the whole board when executive directors will be present and able to influence the outcome.

Meetings of board committees, and committee minutes A5.27

Adequate time must be allowed for board committee meetings, adequate notice given and adequate agenda papers circulated sufficiently in advance to allow for thorough preparation by the committee members.

Generally, board committees should schedule their meetings so that their draft minutes are available to become agenda papers of an appropriate main board meeting, unless the chairman of the board committee prepares a special written report of the committee for the board. Either way, it is likely to be appropriate for board committee meetings to be scheduled shortly before the associated board meeting so that the board has timely feedback from its board committees. Thus, for instance, the audit committee will meet shortly before the board approves the financial statements for publication.

It is not ideal for board committees to meet on the same day as the board itself, although non-executive directors will often try to contrive such an arrangement in the interests of their time. It would mean that the meetings on that day would be rushed, meeting fatigue would set in, and there can be no written agenda paper to the board meeting about the work of the committees that met earlier on the same day.

Committee reporting to the board **A5.28**

In practical terms, it is usually best to schedule board committee meetings to take place about two weeks before a board meeting. That allows the minutes of the committee to be drafted by the committee secretary and checked by the committee chair before being included in the agenda pack of board papers.

Committee minutes **A5.29**

While this means that the committee minutes will usually reach the board in draft form, since the committee will not have met again to ratify those minutes, this is usually sufficient for the board – especially if all the members of the committee are also board members. If there is anything wrong about the draft minutes, they can point this out at the board meeting. It is much to be preferred that board committees report promptly to the board than wait for a further committee meeting to take place, perhaps three months hence in the case of an audit committee, to ratify the committee minutes before they go to the board.

Companies can, however, follow a practice of confirming by chairman's action the minutes of the board and its committees at any time after they have been drafted, although this is rarely done. Section 249 of the Companies Act 2006 means that authentication of draft minutes by the chairman of the meeting is sufficient[8] evidence of the proceedings of the meeting; and, until the contrary is proved, that the meeting was duly held and convened, that all the proceedings duly took place, and that all appointments made at the meeting were valid.

In the case of important board committees – and most are important – the report from the committee will be an item for discussion at the board, not merely for noting. The report may be in the form of the committee minutes, or in the form of a special report prepared for the board.

Special and annual committee reports to the board **A5.30**

Practice may be for a special report to the board to be drafted by the chair of the board committee, rather than relying on the minutes of the board committee. It is also likely that the committee, additionally, will provide an annual report to the board, summarising the work the committee has done over the year, highlighting any issues, and providing overall committee conclusions. Thus, for instance, the audit committee's annual report to the board will provide the committee's overall conclusions on the reliability of the financial statements to be published, on the effectiveness of risk management and internal control, on the adequacy of the internal audit function (if any), and on the appointment of the external auditors.

Reporting committee business to the board **A5.31**

The chairman of a board committee will usually speak to the committee's minutes that are tabled at the board meeting. Frequently, these will be draft minutes since, by then, the committee may not have met subsequently to approve those minutes, but in practice this is rarely an impediment to the efficient conduct of business.

Usually the members of board committees will also be members of the board – so a committee member will be able, if necessary, to use the board meeting to dissent from a committee minute which is tabled to the board in draft form.

An alternative to using the draft minutes of a committee as an agenda paper for the board meeting is for the chair of the board committee to prepare a special report for the board. If this approach is taken, the minutes of the board committee can come to the board at a later stage, when they have been confirmed by the next meeting of the board committee, at which point it is likely that they will be tabled at the board for information only, not for discussion.

Board committee minutes, as well as board minutes, should be sufficiently comprehensive to be an adequate record not only of recommendations made to the board but also of the process followed in arriving at those recommendations. There may be a need to refer back to minutes to show that the committee, and thus the board, had conducted its affairs diligently and not negligently.

Occasionally, there may be outside membership of a board committee, and there are even instances where the chair of the audit committee is not a member of the board.

Because board committees are established to assist the board to despatch board business efficiently and effectively, their decisions are only advice to the board, potentially to be overturned at that level. Yet it would not be appropriate to have such committees if the main board routinely reopened all matters which had been considered at committee meetings.

In some cases, it may even be regarded as preferable that the board routinely opts for *the decisions themselves* of a committee (such as the remuneration committee's determination of executive compensation) not even to be disclosed to the board. Of course, there is no doubt that the board always has a right to this information, but the board may choose not to ask for it. In a culture of openness and fuller public disclosure, it is less likely that there will be matters to be decided in this way.

The example of BP A5.32

We have said elsewhere that we consider it is insufficient for a board to have effective oversight if it meets much less than monthly. Listed UK companies' annual reports disclose the number of board meetings and board committee meetings, as well as the attendance record of members at these.

The incidence of BP's meetings, as reported in its annual reports, is interesting. It was in 2005 that BP experienced its Texas Oil refinery explosion and the Prudoe Bay, Alaska pipeline leakage – the same year that the board met only seven times.

BP's 2010 Gulf of Mexico disaster occurred well into the year, meaning that the board must have met some 18 times in the second half of 2010 (**Table 1**). This is a good example of prospective non-executive directors, in assessing whether they have sufficient time to assume the role, needing to ensure that they have a margin of spare available time should circumstances demand. It was not just that the board met approximately every week or two in the second half of 2010; a crisis board committee was formed to oversee the Mexican Gulf rescue project, meeting more than once a month thereafter during 2010 (**Table 1**).

It is strikingly impressive, as well as unusual, how often BP's audit committee has met over the past several years at least (**Table 1**). Audit committees are finding they need to meet more frequently than previously, and each time for longer, but five or six times a year now is not untypical. It is not clear from BP's annual report whether its reported number of audit committee meetings includes site visits by the audit committee, although it is clear that these visits take place. It is understood that BP's audit committee meets twice with respect to each quarterly public reporting requirement, once near the commencement of the process of preparing the report, and again shortly before its adoption and publication.

Table 1

BP: reported number of meetings of its board, audit committee and Gulf of Mexico committee

	2003	2004	2005	2006	2007	2008	2009	2010	2011	2012
Board	8	8	7	9	12	9	12	25	15	19
Audit committee	9	13	12	12	14	13	13	15	11**	11**
Gulf of Mexico committee								9*	16	23

* The Gulf of Mexico spillage commenced on 20 April 2010.
** Includes one joint meeting of the Board's Safety, Ethnic and Environment Assurance Committee (SEEAC) at the start of each year to review BP's risk management and internal control systems of the previous year and to review the coming year's forward programme of audit work. The general auditor (head of internal audit) reviews his team's findings and management's actions to remedy significant issues identified in that work. His report includes information on the results of audit work undertaken by the safety and operational risk audit team and reviews by the group's finance control team.

In its 2008 and 2009 annual reports, BP was transparent about the allocation of its audit committee's agenda time and disclosed that this excluded site visits time (**Table 2**). It was not clear whether 'Internal controls and audit' time included the audit committee's time overseeing the external statutory audit, or whether that time was reported within the financial reporting time.

Table 2

BP: reported allocation of audit committee time

Allocation of audit committee agenda time*	2008	2009	2010–12
– Financial reporting	34%	31%	Information not publicly available
– Monitoring business risk	36%	28%	
– Internal controls and audit	26%	36%	
– Other	4%	5%	

* BP's reported allocation of audit committee time excluded site visits.

Almost all BP's board committees meet at least six times a year, and often much more frequently – either routinely or in response to special circumstances (**Table 3**). For instance, the Nomination Committee met 15 times in 2009 when BP was searching for a new chairman. Late in 2011, BP reported that its chairman was taking on the additional chairmanship of Volvo. Both Volvo and BP are experiencing challenging times, and although the chairman's commitment to BP is understood to be three days a week, one wonders whether this allows enough latitude to cope with possible future crises. Nevertheless, it was reported that BP's board is fully behind its chairman with respect to this additional responsibility.

BP's Safety, Ethics & Environment Assurance Committee (SEEAC) corresponds quite closely to a board risk committee. BP was in front of best practice in setting up this risk committee of the board. Recognising that there is an overlap between SEEAC and its audit committee, these two committees have at least one joint meeting each year.

On 9 November 2010, Baroness Hogg, chairman of the UK's Financial Reporting Council, recommended to the House of Lords Economic Affairs Select Committee Inquiry that not only should boards of FTSE 350 companies have risk committees, but also that these committees should receive independent advice from a party or parties other than the company's external auditors. Since BP's board accepted a recommendation of the Baker Panel's report, commissioned by BP's board following the Texas City and other 2005 operational failures, this has been the case for BP. Again, BP has been ahead of emerging best practice. So it is disappointing that this attempt to ensure the board is better informed about operational risks was unsuccessful at avoiding the Gulf of Mexico disaster.

Table 3

BP: reported number of meetings of its board's other committees, and number of directors

	2008	2009	2010	2011	2012
Remuneration Committee	6	8	6	7	5
Safety, Ethics & Environment Assurance Committee (SEEAC)	?	7	9	9	6
Nomination Committee	6	15	8	5	4
Chairman's Committee	4	5	8	9	8
Number of directors:					
Chairman	1	1	1	1	1
Non-executive directors	9	9	11	11	11
Executive directors	4	5	3	4	4
Total	**14**	**15**	**15**	**16**	**16**

The composition of BP's board quite closely resembles that of a US listed company, although the common US weakness of combining the roles of chief executive and board chairman is avoided by BP. With so few executives on the board, there is a greater risk that the flow of information to the board is over-dependent on the chief executive. A key governance issue is 'how do boards get the assurance they need that the policies of the board are being implemented by the executive, and that there are no "banana skins" (known or not to management) which the company risks slipping over in the future?'.

The UK Corporate Governance Code states very flexibly, at the level of a Main Principle, that best practice is to have a balanced board and, at a Supporting Principle at B.1, that:

> 'The board should include an appropriate combination of executive and non-executive directors (and, in particular, independent non-executive directors) such that no individual or small group of individuals can dominate the board's decision taking.'

Notes

1 https://www.icsa.org.uk/about-icsa/latest-from-icsa/article/icsa-publishes-new-terms-of-reference (accessed 27th December 2013).

2 Supporting Principles at D.1.

3 *Re Barings plc (No 5)* [2000] 1 BCLC 523, Court of Appeal.

4 *Equitable Life Assurance Society v Bowley* [2003] EWHC 2263 (Comm); action ultimately withdrawn.

5 Management Audit Ltd 'Health Care Companies' Internal Audit Survey (1997). Tel: +44 (0)1790 763350, email: email@management-audit.com.

6 Code Provision B.1.1: 'The board should identify in the annual report each non-executive director it considers to be independent. The board should determine whether the director is independent in character and judgement and whether there are relationships or circumstances which are likely to affect, or could appear to affect, the director's judgement. The board should state its reasons if it determines that a director is independent notwithstanding the existence of relationships or circumstances which may appear relevant to its determination, including if the director:

- has been an employee of the company or group within the last five years;
- has, or has had within the last three years, a material business relationship with the company either directly, or as a partner, shareholder, director or senior employee of a body that has such a relationship with the company;
- has received or receives additional remuneration from the company apart from a director's fee, participates in the company's share option or a performance-related pay scheme, or is a member of the company's pension scheme;
- has close family ties with any of the company's advisers, directors or senior employees;
- holds cross-directorships or has significant links with other directors through involvement in other companies or bodies;
- represents a significant shareholder; or
- has served on the board for more than nine years from the date of their first election.'

7 The Walker Review on Financial Sector Corporate Governance (November 2009), Recommendation 23, para 6.12.

8 'Sufficient evidence' in Scotland; 'evidence' elsewhere.

Chapter A6

Board Policies and Policy Statements

Oversight and control – board policy statements A6.1

A sound control environment is now universally recognised to be an essential component of effective management[1] or, put another way, an essential contribution to giving reasonable assurance that corporate objectives will be achieved. Included within what is termed 'the control environment' is the example set by the board of directors. It should go without saying that the board must display impeccable standards of integrity in the ways it conducts itself, collectively and individually. It is also important that the board and its members are consistent, not least in their dealings with staff and business partners, and in how they react to wrongdoing. Readers may wish to refer to Chapter **C6** – Culture, Ethics and the Board.

PCAOB's Auditing Standard No 2, 'An audit of internal control over financial reporting performed in conjunction with an audit of financial statements' (2004, www.pcaobus.org), ran to 185 pages and 25 pages of preamble. In May 2007 it was replaced by a simplified Auditing Standard No 5, running to 118 pages. Both Standards placed special emphasis upon the control environment which, in Standard No 2, was usefully elaborated upon as encompassing:

'
- Integrity and ethical values;
- Commitment to competence;
- Board of directors or audit committee participation;
- Management's philosophy and operating style;
- Organisational structure;
- Assignment of authority and responsibility; and
- Human resource policies and procedures.'

PCAOB Auditing Standards No 2 and 5 were developed to guide external auditors on the approach they must take to attesting to the CEO's and CFO's certification of the effectiveness of internal control over financial reporting, required by section 404 of the 2002 Sarbanes-Oxley Act. We discuss this in Chapter **E3** – Audit Committees and Sarbanes-Oxley in the UK. Both the SEC Rule, on how the CEO and CFO should approach this, and the PCAOB Standard require that 'the control environment' should be within the scope of section 404 compliance: it is not just a matter of being satisfied that appropriate control procedures (activities) are in place. All the essential components of internal control need to be in place. Too often, section 404 compliance and auditing work place disproportionate stress on control procedures, important though they are, to the exclusion of the other essential components of effective systems of internal control.

The five essential components of internal control, according to the Committee of Sponsoring Organizations (COSO), are:[2]

- the control environment;
- information and communication;
- risk assessment;

- control activities; and
- monitoring.

More and more businesses are developing a code of business conduct, which Turnbull in the UK and COSO in the US both regard as part of the 'control environment' of a business. Doing so provides a good opportunity to crystallise a business's attitudes and practices with respect to many matters that have ethical implications. While often the result will be a formalisation of what is already custom and practice, it is surprising how the development of a code is likely to confront the organisation with anomalies and dilemmas to be resolved before consensus emerges. A code of business conduct can provide an agreed, communicable and understandable framework to govern the conduct of staff and contractors. So long as it is communicated effectively, everyone knows where they stand. They know what is expected of them. They know what their responsibilities and opportunities are to raise matters of concern.

Of course, it is important that the code is developed through a process of wide consultation. The well-meaning sentiments of a consultant or even of the chairman of the board will be quite inadequate. The code should encapsulate the practical values of the business as a whole. While the development of the code will undoubtedly give some opportunities to improve on current practice, fundamentally it should be a code which reflects the best practices and the best principles currently at work within the enterprise. Of vital importance is that it is applied consistently in practice. The code and its application should be reviewed regularly.

While a code may have real value in public relations terms, it should not be seen as a promotional tool to be ignored in practice. It can be an integral part of the open, empowered, participative and motivated enterprise. In developing a code which can be workable in practice, it may be necessary to settle for something less than the ideal. We believe that this is preferable to developing a code which in some respects is an aspiration only, intended to be honoured in the breach rather than the observance.

We recommend that the code of business conduct should be adopted by formal board resolution as the policy of the board for the company as a whole.

Examples A6.2

It is, of course, at the discretion of the board to decide what policy statements should be developed, adopted by the board and effectively communicated and followed throughout the business and by business partners such as contractors. In the following sections, we give examples of these policy statements:

- Vision, promise and values (**A6.3–A6.4**).
- Who are our stakeholders and what do they want? (**A6.5–A6.6**).
- Statement of corporate principles (**A6.7**).
- Code of business conduct (**A6.8**).
- Code of ethical conduct on scientific and environmental matters (**A6.9**).
- Product supply chain ethical principles (**A6.10**).
- Risk strategy policy statement (**A6.11**).
- Internal audit charters (**A6.12–A6.15**).
- Whistleblowing (**A6.16–A6.22**).
- Harassment (**A6.23–A6.24**).

- Environment and health (**A6.25**).
- Information security (**A6.26–A6.28**).
- E-mail internet and telephone (**A6.29**).
- Fraud (**A6.30**).

The statement of corporate principles, code of business conduct and code of ethical conduct on scientific and environmental matters were developed as a set for a multinational pharmaceutical group whose board considered there was an overarching requirement for a statement of principles, to be interpreted separately with respect to commercial and scientific rules of conduct. This approach is discussed in more detail in the preamble to the statement of corporate principles at **A6.7**.

Statements of vision, promise and values **A6.3**

XYZ Group plc **A6.4**

Vision

- To become the UK's most highly rewarded specialist provider of finance for people.
- As such, we will assist our customers to achieve their lifestyle ambitions and be an organisation of which employees can be proud.

Promise

- Deliver product value with excellence.
- Work together as a team.
- Invest in staff to enable them to achieve their career potential.
- Seek constant improvement – never being satisfied.
- Produce value and results that are both pleasing and rewarding to shareholders.

Values

- **Team work**
  To work in harmony in our respective teams and collectively towards the delivery of the overall objectives.
- **Creativity**
  To identify and create new business opportunities and to apply creative and effective solutions to problems.
- **Integrity**
  To be ruthlessly honest and open in everything we do.
- **Respect**
  To treat people as individuals and to listen to their views.

- **Commitment**
  To drive the business forward with determination and to do so with effort and enthusiasm.
- **Professionalism**
  To maintain the highest standards and to deliver our products and services with care and accuracy.
- **Humour**
  To ensure we have fun while achieving success.

Who are our stakeholders and what do they want? A6.5

ABC plc A6.6

See also C.3.22.

Major stakeholders	What do they want?
Shareholders	Depends on shareholder Generally above average earnings per share growth over time
Staff Directors	Security Job satisfaction Rewards
Customers	Service Relationship
Suppliers	Future business Paid on time
Funders	Low risk Additional business

Statement of corporate principles A6.7

A multinational pharmaceutical company set to work to develop its code of business conduct. It was not long before it determined that its approach should be to develop an overarching statement at the level of general principles to which the business subscribed, which it called its statement of corporate principles. We reproduce it here. It then developed two codes at a lower level. The two codes were more at the level of being rules to be followed, and were intended to be consistent with the overarching principles. They were:

- code of business conduct; and
- code of ethical conduct on scientific and environmental matters.

These are reproduced in **A6.8** and **A6.9**.

Space does not allow us to analyse in detail the statement of corporate principles and the code of business conduct. We would say that the company intended to develop a code which really could be observed in practice rather than being a statement of theoretical aspiration to be used for PR purposes, with no intention that it should be complied with in reality. In view of this, the reader may think that some ethical compromises have been made. For instance, there is no unequivocal statement that company personnel would never break the law in the context of their activities. Neither do staff have a stated duty to report on wrongdoing unless they are personally involved in it; if they are not personally involved, they are accorded a right rather than a duty. Codes of business conduct in other companies make it a duty in both cases.

XYZ

XYZ London Limited
150 River Walk
London WC2 3XD

(Chairman's name)

Chairman

(Date)

Statement of corporate principles

This policy statement addresses the general principles of our corporate life. Our separate code of business conduct sets out the rules which govern our application of these principles. Our code of ethical conduct applies our policy principles to scientific and environmental issues in particular. You will find some wording in common between the statement and the two codes where similar principles and practices are set out.

Copies of these three documents are available to all staff – from regional and country managers, and from divisional and business unit heads. They are also available from environmental affairs staff or through internal audit locally or at group level, from whom guidance on interpretation and application may be sought.

XYZ operates responsibly and with integrity, avoiding even the suggestion of impropriety. There should be no risk to our reputation if any details about our affairs became public knowledge. It is our policy to operate worldwide in a manner which protects the environment and the health of our employees and of those in the communities where we have an impact. We conduct our business honestly, scrupulously and free of deception or fraud. We observe applicable laws and regulations. We endeavour to ensure that equivalent standards are followed in companies in which XYZ has an interest but does not have control and also in those businesses with whom XYZ has contractual relationships.

The board of XYZ regards it as the duty of every individual employed by or acting for XYZ to observe the principles set out here. Any individual has a right to raise concerns about apparent breaches of these principles directly with senior management or with the group director of internal Audit.

Conflicts of interest

XYZ's staff are to avoid any real or apparent conflict between their personal interests and those of XYZ. XYZ's assets and other resources are for use in XYZ's business only.

Business gifts, favours and entertainment

XYZ does not encourage the practice of giving or receiving gifts, even of nominal value. This also applies to gifts etc made indirectly by another on XYZ's behalf. We believe that commercial criteria, rather than the influence of gifts, etc, best serve XYZ's interests. When gifts etc are made they should be lawful and ethical, necessary and appropriate, of nominal or moderate value, capable of reciprocation, and properly authorised and recorded. They should not be interpretable as an improper inducement, nor be extravagant or too frequent.

Confidentiality

XYZ's information is handled with discretion. It is not to be misused nor disclosed so as to place XYZ at a potential or actual commercial disadvantage, or for the benefit of another who is not entitled to receive it. Rights and responsibilities under privacy and other data legislation are to be observed.

Internal control

XYZ acknowledges its duty to maintain an effective system of internal control which provides reasonable assurance of the achievement of business objectives, of the reliability of information used for reporting, of the safeguarding of resources, and of compliance with laws and regulations.

Operational and accounting records

It is company policy (a) that the operational records and accounts of the business are to be reliable, truthful, accurate, complete, up-to-date and in compliance with prescribed standards and regulations, and (b) that there shall be no falsification. There are to be no secret or unrecorded activities, bank accounts, funds of money or other assets; no liabilities are to go knowingly unrecorded or unprovided for; and there are to be no off-books transactions.

Relationships with suppliers

The viability of our suppliers is a key concern of XYZ. We set out to observe the terms of purchase orders and contracts, including the payment of suppliers according to agreed payment terms. We give weight to the quality of past service to XYZ while ensuring that transactions are justified on commercial grounds, and while actively considering alternative sources of supply. We avoid excessive dependence upon particular sources of supply when possible.

Political activities and contributions

XYZ companies are authorised to make political donations in the countries where they operate in so far as the objective is to facilitate a healthy political process and to the extent that the contributions are lawful and meet our other criteria relating to purpose, amount, transparency and authorisation.

We have an interest in communicating relevant, reliable and responsible information and views on issues of public concern which impact upon our business.

XYZ strives to be a good employer with regard to individual staff who are actively involved in politics as private individuals.

Conduct towards employees

XYZ is committed to its employees. We seek to maximise the extent to which employees achieve their personal potential through their work with XYZ. We do this in part through appropriate commercial policies so that employees share in the company's success, and in part through policies which relate to health and safety. We believe in the inalienable right of every person to their personal dignity and do not allow practices which infringe upon this. All XYZ employees have equal opportunity in their employment. Staff are recruited for their relevant aptitudes, skills, experience and ability. Discrimination or harassment on grounds of race, colour, marital status, religion, sex, sexual orientation, ethnic or national origin, or legal political activity is not permitted. Treatment at all times shall be fair in terms of compensation, job security, work experiences, recognition of achievement and opportunities for advancement.

Conduct in the community and charitable contributions

Our business is dedicated to the well-being of individuals. We have a duty to avoid conduct prejudicial to the communities where we do business and to enhance community life where practical. Our community support is targeted to improve economic or social well-being.

Customer relations and product quality

We strive to ensure that our products and services meet or exceed customer and statutory requirements at economical price; that our product information is reliable, and that we are responsive to customers' enquiries.

Please use your best endeavours to bring this statement to the attention of all personnel and to any with whom we are associated or do business.

Code of business conduct **A6.8**

This code is one of a set of three statements reproduced in this handbook, the others being the statement of corporate principles (at **A6.7**) and the code of ethical conduct on scientific and environmental matters (at **A6.9**).The relationships between the three are explored in the preamble to the former.

We consider this code of business conduct is strong in the avenues of communication which staff are authorised to use in order to express their concerns on matters of conduct. For instance, they may by-pass their immediate boss; or they may communicate directly with the head of internal audit.

Notice the efforts that this company is taking to endorse this code at the highest level and to ensure that it is disseminated throughout the business. Note, too, that they expect their contractors and business partners to comply with this code.

XYZ

XYZ London Limited
150 River Walk
London WC2 3XD

(Chairman's name)

Chairman

(Date)

Code of business conduct

XYZ is a major multinational corporation whose business partners range from governments and multinationals through to small suppliers, and whose ultimate customers are the many individuals who rely on the quality of our products for their well-being. So it is appropriate that we are seen to operate responsibly and with ethical integrity in our business conduct and in our corporate governance – to a standard which would usually be associated with the major public, listed companies who are so often our competitors; and we should avoid even the suggestion of impropriety. This should be so even when the law is permissive. In principle, there should be no risk to our local or international reputation if any details about our business affairs were to become public knowledge. At all times our business must be conducted honestly and scrupulously, free of deception and fraud.

To these ends, this code provides detailed guidance on the application to issues of business conduct of the policies outlined in XYZ's statement of corporate principles. A separate code of ethical conduct applies those policies to scientific and environmental issues in particular. You will find some wording in common between the statement and the two codes where similar principles and practices are set out.

Copies of the three documents are available at all locations to all staff, from regional and country managers, and from divisional and business unit heads. They are also available from environmental affairs staff or through internal audit locally or at group level, from whom guidance on interpretation and application may be sought by staff.

This document has been approved by the executive committee and adopted by the board of XYZ. The executive committee reviews annually the code's appropriateness and effectiveness, and advises the board accordingly. As part of this review, line managers annually are required to formally monitor their and their staff's performance in observing the requirements of this code within their areas of responsibility and, where judged appropriate, to develop initiatives to provide reasonable assurance of future compliance.

The board places particular importance upon timely actions to be taken whenever necessary to identify, contain and eliminate illegal acts.

A fundamental principle of the way XYZ conducts its business affairs is that applicable laws and regulations are to be scrupulously observed at all times.

Practical difficulties may arise in many cases, such as when there are conflicts between the law of different countries, when local business custom and practice is inconsistent with local law or when there is ambiguity as to the legal position. Any case of actual or prospective non-compliance with law should be raised urgently with management and, if material, with the group chief executive.

The XYZ person responsible should endeavour to ensure that equivalent standards to those set out in this code are followed in companies in which XYZ has an interest but does not have control and also in those businesses with whom XYZ has contractual relationships. Where they are not, the XYZ person responsible should refer the matter upwards within XYZ.

The board of XYZ regards it as the duty of every individual employed by or acting for XYZ to follow all the requirements of this code. Any proposed action which appears to be in breach of any requirement of this code should not be progressed without full disclosure to and prior approval of the group chief executive or as delegated to the group financial controller or the group director of internal audit. Appropriate behaviour by individuals which is in compliance with this code and also specifically approved departures from this code will be supported by the company under the principle of collective responsibility.

Your duty to comply with this code includes a duty both to yourself and to XYZ to raise any concerns you may have on any matter of business conduct which appears to be a violation of this code and in which you are actively involved. In addition you have a right to raise similar concerns about the conduct of others even where you are not directly involved. Usually you should first raise a matter of concern with your line manager and you should do so at the earliest opportunity. At your discretion you may raise your concerns directly with senior management, with local internal audit or with the group director of internal audit and you should do so where an issue remains unresolved to your satisfaction after you have consulted your immediate management about it.

Conflicts of interest

Directors and employees of XYZ are responsible to avoid any real or apparent conflict between their own personal interests and those of XYZ. This may be at risk with respect to:

- dealings with suppliers, customers and other parties doing, or seeking to do, business with XYZ;
- transactions in securities of XYZ or of any company with whom XYZ has or is likely to have a business relationship; and
- acceptance of outside positions whether or not for a fee.

In appropriate circumstances XYZ encourages its directors and staff to be active outside the company.

XYZ's assets and other resources should not be used for any purpose other than for XYZ's business. They are not to be used for personal gain. These resources include but are not limited to staff time, materials, property, plant, equipment, cash, software, trade secrets and confidential information.

In cases of doubt, an employee should discuss the matter with his or her manager.

Business gifts, favours and entertainment

XYZ operates in many host countries of the world with widely differing laws, regulations, customs and business practices. As a multinational XYZ is expected by its host in each case to conform to local societal norms and values whether enshrined in their laws, regulations, customs or business practices. Ethical dilemmas abound and have to be managed in harmony with the requirements of this code.

By way of illustration these may be some of the dilemmas:

- inconsistency between different applicable laws within one country;
- inconsistency between the laws of different countries involved in a transaction;
- inconsistency between law on the one hand and customs and practice on the other hand;
- an opportunity to achieve a considerable social good (such as by successfully marketing an effective product) but only at an ethical cost (such as by making a facilitating payment);
- the difficulty of distinguishing convincingly between on the one hand facilitating payments which may in some circumstances be permissible (to facilitate a legal right which might otherwise be withheld or delayed) and bribes which should not be permissible even when legal (to influence a business decision or gain an unfair commercial advantage which is not a right); or
- at what level a payment becomes extravagant.

As a general rule XYZ does not encourage the practice of giving or receiving gifts, even those of nominal value. Employees should use their best endeavours to ensure so far as is possible that commercial criteria, rather than the influence of gifts, favours or entertainment, best serve XYZ's business interests and their ongoing maintenance.

In determining whether any given or received business gift, favour and/or entertainment is permissible under this code each occurrence (and all connected ones taken together) are required to pass all of the following tests unless a requirement is specifically waived by the group chief executive or his or her delegatee. These tests should also be applied equally to gifts etc made indirectly by another party such as by an agent using funds which could be construed as having originated in XYZ.

The tests:

- It could not be interpreted reasonably as an improper inducement.
- It is necessary.
- It would be considered nominal or moderate, and neither extravagant nor too frequent.
- It would be considered appropriate to the business responsibilities of the individual concerned.
- In the case of a gift etc received, it would be capable of reciprocation as a normal business expense.
- Unless of nominal value, there is appropriate prior specific approval usually of regional management.
- It is properly recorded, whether given or received.

- The group financial controller and the group director of internal audit have both been made fully aware of it beforehand.
- It is lawful and ethical.

Confidentiality

All of XYZ's employees and contractors have a general duty to ensure that all XYZ's data and information which they encounter is handled with discretion.

XYZ personnel are not permitted to use confidential price sensitive information or to engage in other ways with competitors or others to fix the market price for products.

XYZ's information (whether technical, commercial, financial, personnel or other) must not be disclosed so as to place XYZ at a potential or actual commercial disadvantage, or for the benefit of another party who is not entitled to receive it.

Employees and contractors must ensure they act so as not to jeopardise (a) the rights of staff and others under privacy legislation and (b) the responsibilities and restrictions which apply to XYZ under data protection and other legislation.

Internal control

All businesses and projects owned, managed or controlled by XYZ must maintain an adequate system of internal control which is in accordance with XYZ's control policies. Management and staff are responsible to ensure that, within their respective areas of responsibility, necessary arrangements at acceptable cost are in place and are complied with to give reasonable assurance that the objectives of internal control are met. These objectives include:

- the achievement of business objectives efficiently and economically;
- the reliability of information used internally and for external reporting;
- the safeguarding of corporate resources; and
- compliance with laws, regulations and policies of the company.

The necessary arrangements comprise proper attention to:

- the control environment;
- information and communication;
- risk analysis;
- control activities or procedures; and
- monitoring.

All incidents involving a breakdown of control leading to any actual or potential losses should be reported upwards immediately to management and to internal audit. For companies in which XYZ has an interest but does not have control, the XYZ person responsible should endeavour to ensure that equivalent standards are applied and should refer the matter upwards within XYZ when they are not.

Operational and accounting records

Responsible staff must ensure that all the operational records and books of account of the business represent a reliable, truthful, accurate, complete and up-to-date picture in compliance with prescribed corporate procedures and external standards and regulations; and that they are suitable to be a basis for informed management decisions. The prompt recording and proper description of operations and of accounting transactions is a duty of responsible staff. Falsification of records and books is strictly prohibited.

No secret or unrecorded bank accounts, funds of money or other assets are to be established or maintained; no liabilities should knowingly go unrecorded or unprovided for; and there should be no off-books transactions.

Relationships with suppliers

It is as important for XYZ to secure satisfactorily its sources of supply as it is for XYZ to achieve and maintain market penetration. To this end, the viability and wellbeing of XYZ's suppliers must be a key concern of XYZ's management and staff. Employees have a duty to ensure that XYZ observes the terms of purchase orders and contracts, including the payment of suppliers according to agreed payment terms.

While it is appropriate that due weight be given to the quality of past service to XYZ rendered by a supplier, the placing of an order for goods or services should always be demonstrably defensible on commercial grounds, and as a general principle XYZ's employees should be active in seeking new sources of supply. Excessive dependence upon particular sources of supply should be avoided whenever possible.

Political activities and contributions

XYZ recognises that a healthy political climate is, in the long-term, an essential attribute of a prosperous and stable society as well as a key ingredient for the long-term success of XYZ whose mission is to improve the quality of life of ordinary people through the responsible application of its expertise. XYZ acknowledges that a healthy political climate depends in part upon adequate funding of the political process, upon there being active participation by many in the political process, and upon open and well informed debate on societal issues.

XYZ group companies are authorised to make political donations in the countries where they operate in so far as the objective is to facilitate a healthy political process by contributing to the adequacy of funding, by raising the level of participation or by enhancing the quality of informed debate on issues related to the XYZ business; but only to the extent that such contributions are:

- entirely lawful;
- in the public domain;
- modest in amount and not disproportionate in size to local conditions and to XYZ's public profile;
- not designed to prejudice political or commercial outcomes;
- properly recorded in the accounting records; and
- authorised in advance by the appropriate managing director.

XYZ has an enlightened self interest in communicating information and views on issues of public concern which have an important impact upon the XYZ business: management should be active in looking for appropriate opportunities to do so. The information and views so communicated must be relevant, reliable and responsible.

XYZ strives to be a good employer with regard to individual staff who are actively involved in politics. Accordingly XYZ management should facilitate and not unnecessarily impede the process when individual XYZ staff exercise their legal rights to become actively involved in local or national politics. In turn, staff who are politically active, or minded to become so, should be candid with their XYZ management so that management are best able to be cooperative and difficulties are more likely to be avoided. Staff so involved have an obligation to XYZ to weigh carefully their obligations to XYZ when actual or potential conflicts of interest arise; in their use of time, in campaigning of issues of relevance to the XYZ business, and so on. Employees engaging in political activity do so as private individuals and not as representatives of XYZ.

Conduct towards employees

XYZ is committed to its employees. An underlying principle is to maximise the extent to which all employees have the opportunity to achieve their personal potential through their work with XYZ. XYZ believes that it succeeds through the dedication of all its employees. Their motivated involvement, work satisfaction and security are high priorities. In part this depends upon the implementation of appropriate commercial policies so that employees share in the company's success; in part upon policies which relate to health and safety. Apart from the inalienable right of every person to their personal dignity, practices which intentionally or unintendedly infringe upon personal dignity are likely to interfere with an individual's work performance.

In the conduct of his or her business responsibilities, every XYZ employee is expected to apply the principle of equal opportunity in employment. No member of staff shall discriminate so that another member of staff (or a member of staff of a contractor, supplier or customer) is victimised or less favourably treated than another on grounds of race, colour, marital status, religion, sex, sexual orientation, ethnic or national origin, or legal political activity. Treatment shall at all times be fair in terms of compensation, job security, work experiences, recognition of achievement and opportunities for advancement.

Staff shall be recruited for their relevant aptitudes, skills, experience and ability; and their advancement shall be on the same grounds according to the opportunities available within XYZ.

Employment practices including recruitment practices, contract terms and working conditions shall be sensitive to the culture of the country concerned so as to ensure that company conduct does not contribute to unacceptable social tensions or malaise. At the same time, care must always be taken to ensure so far as is reasonably possible (a) that no harm occurs to those whose services the company employs while they are engaged in work-related activity, and (b) that the equal opportunity principles outlined in the preceding two paragraphs are applied.

XYZ seeks to ensure that employees have and exhibit mutual respect for each other at all times, both at work and also at business-related functions. XYZ staff are expected to behave in this way towards other employees, contractors, suppliers and customers. Harassment is unacceptable. Discrimination, in action, writing or through remarks, is a form of harassment. Unwelcome verbal and physical advances and derogatory remarks are other forms of harassment. It is a duty of all XYZ employees to ensure that their behaviour at no time contributes towards the creation of an intimidating, offensive or hostile work environment.

For staff to identify with XYZ and for XYZ to benefit most from the potential within its staff, the approach to their staff of XYZ's managers and supervisors must be as open and candid as possible. Staff also must be made to feel that they can communicate upwards without formality, rebuff, rancour or victimisation. While not abdicating their personal responsibility, managers should delegate downwards to as great an extent as possible so as to empower and develop their staff. Rigid hierarchical styles of management should be discouraged and staff may address any issues directly above the level of their immediate supervisor if they judge this to be appropriate.

Conduct by people acting on XYZ's behalf

In the introduction to the code I indicated that the XYZ person responsible should endeavour to ensure that equivalent standards to those set out in this code are followed in companies in which XYZ has an interest but does not have control, and also in those businesses with whom XYZ has contractual relationships. I also stated that it is the policy of the board of XYZ that those employed by or acting for XYZ should follow all the requirements of this code. For instance, contractors working on behalf of XYZ must ensure they act in accordance with this code with respect to confidentiality, conflicts of interest, the making and receiving of gifts and with respect to their and their employees' conduct towards XYZ's employees and towards those whom the contractors employ on XYZ's business.

It is not accepted that management and staff of XYZ circumvent their obligations under this code by deputing unacceptable practices to intermediaries acting directly or indirectly on XYZ's behalf so that XYZ may achieve a desired end while endeavouring to avoid any opprobrium.

Conduct in the community and charitable contributions

XYZ accepts that it has community obligations where it does business. We have a general duty to avoid conduct prejudicial to the best interests of the communities where we do business. We have a positive duty as well as a self interest, as corporate citizens committed within our business to improving the well-being of individuals, to use our best endeavours to enhance community life. Apart from altruistic motivations which are important, we believe that a positive approach to our community relations is in the best long-term interests of our company, of those who work within it, and of our present and future customers.

Staff are asked to assist XYZ to be proactive in searching out appropriate opportunities to contribute positively to community affairs and staff will be encouraged by XYZ to do likewise as individuals. Our contributions may be in leadership by initiating or steering community projects; they may be supportive in terms of donations of facilities, equipment, materials, time or cash.

To avoid waste, our community support should be targeted to improving economic or social well-being in demonstrable ways with a particular emphasis upon improving the quality of life of ordinary people. In nature and scale our support should be appropriate in each community while bearing favourable comparison with other companies of similar standing. Our support should be consistent with XYZ's business interests and corporate image, and should have a clear potential to enhance both of these.

Customer relations and product quality

XYZ has no future unless it continues to satisfy customer needs in a competitive environment characterised by rapid technological advances. The company acknowledges the primacy of the following business principles which it expects its staff, as of duty, to apply consistently in practice and to encourage those who supply our ultimate customers to do likewise:

- We strive to ensure that the specifications of our products meet or exceed customer requirements at economical price.
- We strive to provide services which are excellent value-for-money and are delivered courteously and with sensitivity to our clients' requirements.
- We endeavour in all circumstances to ensure that all information about our products and services is reliable and a sufficient basis for fully informed customer decision making and customer use.
- We will be truthful and not misleading in our public relations, marketing and advertising.
- We are committed to satisfying enquiries, complaints and suggestions thoroughly and promptly.
- We are committed to meeting or exceeding all statutory requirements with regard to our products and services as well as to their marketing, sale, distribution and subsequent after-sales support.

Grievance procedures

Every XYZ operating unit must have in place and comply with suitable procedures to ensure that the concerns of staff on any issue related to this code are considered promptly and thoroughly, and that remedial action is taken where appropriate.

Please use your best endeavours to bring this code appropriately to the attention of all personnel, to all new employees, to our business partners and contractors as well as their staff and to any others with whom we are associated or do business.

Code of ethical conduct on scientific and environmental matters **A6.9**

This code is one of a set of three statements reproduced in this handbook, the others being the statement of corporate principles (at **A6.7**) and the code of business conduct (at **A6.8**). The relationships between the three are explored in the preamble to the former.

XYZ

XYZ London Limited
150 River Walk
London WC2 3XD

(Chairman's name)

Chairman

(Date)

Code of ethical conduct on scientific and environmental matters

XYZ is a major multinational corporation operating in many countries, impacting upon the environment in many ways, employing many people and whose ultimate customers are the many individuals who rely on the quality of our products for their well-being. So it is appropriate that we are seen to operate responsibly and with ethical integrity in our scientific conduct and our environmental responsibility.

Our guiding principle is that we should endeavour at all times to maximise community benefit while never doing any harm. We should avoid even the suggestion of impropriety. This should be so even when the law is permissive. There should be no risk to our local or international reputation if any details about our affairs were to become public knowledge. We should aim to adopt the highest available scientific and environmental standards. At all times our business must be conducted honestly and scrupulously free of deception.

To these ends, this code provides detailed guidance on the application to issues of scientific and environmental responsibility of the policies outlined in XYZ's statement of corporate principles. A separate code of business conduct applies those policies to commercial issues in particular. You will find some wording in common between the statement and the two codes where similar principles and required practices are set out.

Copies of the three documents are available at all locations to all staff; from regional and country managers, from divisional and business unit heads. They are also available from environmental affairs staff or through internal audit locally or at group level, from whom guidance on interpretation and application may be sought by staff.

This document has been approved by the executive committee and adopted by the board of XYZ. The executive committee reviews annually the code's appropriateness and effectiveness and advises the board accordingly. As part of this review, line managers annually are required to formally monitor their and their staff's performance in observing the requirements of this code within their areas of responsibility and, where judged appropriate, to develop initiatives to provide reasonable assurance of future compliance. Line managers are responsible to foster a sense of responsibility for the environment amongst employees at all levels. The board places particular importance upon timely actions to be taken whenever necessary to identify, contain and eliminate irresponsible or illegal acts; especially having regard to changes in technology, industrial practices, product design and trends in legislation.

A fundamental principle of the way XYZ conducts its affairs is that applicable laws and regulations are to be scrupulously observed at all times. Practical difficulties may arise in many cases, such as when there are conflicts between the law of different countries, when local business custom and practice is inconsistent with local law or when there is ambiguity as to the legal position. Any case of actual or prospective non-compliance with law should be raised urgently with management and, if material, with the group chief executive.

The XYZ person responsible should endeavour to ensure that equivalent standards to those set out in this code are followed in companies in which XYZ has an interest but does not have control and also in those businesses with whom XYZ has contractual relationships. Where they are not, the XYZ person responsible should refer the matter upwards within XYZ.

The board of XYZ regards it as the duty of every individual employed by or acting for XYZ to follow all the requirements of this code. Any proposed action which appears to be in breach of any requirement of this code should not be progressed without full disclosure to and prior approval of the group chief executive or the group head of environmental affairs. Appropriate behaviour by individuals which is in compliance with this code and also specifically approved departures from this code will be supported by the company under its principle of collective responsibility.

Your duty to comply with this code includes a duty both to yourself and to XYZ to raise any concerns you may have on any matter of scientific or environmental conduct which appears to be a violation of this code and in which you are actively involved. In addition you have a right to raise similar concerns about the conduct of others even where you are not directly involved. Usually you should first raise a matter of concern with your line manager and you should do so at the earliest opportunity. At your discretion you may raise your concerns directly with senior management, with local internal audit or with the group head of environmental affairs and you should do so where an issue remains unresolved to your satisfaction after you have consulted your immediate management about it.

Conduct in the community

XYZ accepts that it has community obligations wherever XYZ sources its supplies, conducts its business and where its products are used. We have a general duty to avoid conduct prejudicial to the best interests of these communities. We have a positive duty as well as a self interest, as corporate citizens committed within our business to improving the well-being of individuals, to use our best endeavours to enhance community life. Apart from altruistic motivations which are important, we believe that a positive approach to our community relations is in the best long-term interests of our company, of those who work within it, and of our present and future customers and users of our products.

Staff are asked to assist XYZ to be proactive in searching out appropriate opportunities to contribute positively to community affairs and staff will be encouraged by XYZ to do likewise as individuals. Our contributions may be in leadership, by initiating or steering community projects; they may be supportive, in terms of responsible donations of facilities, equipment, materials, time or cash.

To avoid waste, our community support should be targeted to improving economic or social well-being in demonstrable ways with a particular emphasis upon improving the quality of life of ordinary people. In nature and scale our support should be appropriate in each community while bearing favourable comparison with other companies of similar standing. Our support should be consistent with XYZ's business interests and corporate image, and should have a clear potential to enhance both of these.

XYZ has an enlightened self interest in communicating information and views on scientific and environmental issues which should be of public concern which have an important impact upon the XYZ business: management should be active in looking for appropriate opportunities to do so. The information and views so communicated must be relevant, reliable and responsible. We should seek to co-operate with official bodies and technical organisations in the formulation of standards and the means of complying with them.

XYZ strives to be a good employer with regard to individual staff who are actively involved in community life, including involvement in politics. Accordingly, XYZ management should facilitate and not unnecessarily impede the process when individual XYZ staff exercise their legal rights to become actively involved in local or national affairs and politics. In turn, staff who are so active, or minded to become so, should be candid with their XYZ management so that management are best able to be co-operative and difficulties are more likely to be avoided. Staff so involved have an obligation to XYZ to weigh carefully their obligations to XYZ when actual or potential conflicts of interest arise; in their use of time, in campaigning on issues of relevance to the XYZ business, and so on. Employees engaging in political activity do so as private individuals and not as representatives of XYZ.

Business and product development

The environmental impact and potential health effects of all new corporate activities, acquisitions, projects, processes, products and services shall be assessed in advance by responsible staff. XYZ accepts a responsibility to evaluate the 'cradle-to-grave' impacts of our products and services. All investment decisions are to take account of environmental and health considerations. There is an a priori assumption that clean technologies shall be chosen. The environmental impact of facilities shall be assessed with regard inter alia to site appearance, effect on local and remote ecological systems, and storage safety and access. XYZ's transport strategy shall be determined having due regard to its environmental soundness.

Conduct towards employees

XYZ is committed to its employees. An underlying principle is to maximise the extent to which all employees have the opportunity to achieve their personal potential through their work and in the rest of their lives. XYZ believes that it succeeds through the dedication of all its employees. Their work satisfaction, security and safety are high priorities. In part this depends upon the implementation of appropriate policies which relate to health and safety.

Employment practices including recruitment practices, contract terms and working conditions shall be sensitive to the culture of the country concerned so as to ensure that company conduct does not contribute to unacceptable social tensions or malaise. At the same time, care must always be taken to ensure so far as is reasonably possible that no harm occurs to those whose services the company employs while they are engaged in work-related activity.

For staff to identify with XYZ and for XYZ to benefit most from the potential within its staff, the approach to their staff of XYZ's managers and supervisors must be as open and candid as possible. Staff also must be made to feel that they can communicate upwards without formality, rebuff, rancour or victimisation. While not abdicating their personal responsibility for scientific and environmental matters, managers should delegate downwards to as great an extent as possible so as to empower and develop their staff. Rigid hierarchical styles of management should be discouraged and staff may address any issues directly above the level of their immediate supervisor if they judge this to be appropriate.

Supply

XYZ is concerned about the sources and methods of production of the raw materials and components it acquires, and the environmental conditions of service providers. XYZ subscribes to the principle of sustainable development, development which meets the needs of the present without compromising the abilities of future generations to meet their own needs. Wherever possible we use renewable, recycled and recyclable materials and components. Responsible XYZ staff should enquire so as to ascertain the extent to which elements of XYZ's suppliers' environments, products and services are hazardous, toxic, over-packed, non-renewable or not reusable.

Production and administration

In designing and operating production and administrative processes, XYZ staff shall endeavour to maximise efficiency by minimising or eliminating waste in all parts of the business with respect to materials, supplies, energy and other inputs and processes. Excess production is to be avoided. Where available 'waste free' processes and business practices shall be chosen in preference to others. Wherever possible XYZ reuses and recycles by-products of production. Hazardous substances, discharges, emissions, activities, practices and equipment are formally identified and necessary measures (including satisfactory plant maintenance and quality control) introduced and followed to prevent unwanted outcomes.

Product quality and customer relations

XYZ aims to provide eminently usable products which function for users efficiently and reliably and without harmful effects. They are, where possible and appropriate, to be reusable and repairable. At the time of production there must be sufficient opportunities to ensure ultimate safe and environmentally friendly disposal of our products and their parts including packaging; and wherever practical our products and their components shall be recyclable.

Appropriate advice shall be provided to customers on all relevant environmental aspects of the handling, use and disposal of the products made or distributed by the company.

XYZ has no future unless it continues to satisfy customer needs in a competitive environment characterised by rapid technological advances. The company acknowledges the primacy of the following environmental and technical principles which it expects its staff, as of duty, to apply consistently in practice and to encourage those who supply our ultimate customers to do likewise:

- We strive to maximise the operational efficiency and reliability of all products we supply.
- We strive to eliminate all possible hazards arising from the use of the products we supply.
- Wherever possible we intend to provide products which are environmentally friendly through their reliability, reparability, reusability and recyclability.
- We ensure that our products and packagings can be disposed of safely.

- We endeavour in all circumstances to ensure that all information about our products and services is reliable and a sufficient basis for fully informed customer decision-making and customer use.
- We are committed to satisfying enquiries, complaints and suggestions thoroughly and promptly.
- We are committed to meeting or exceeding all statutory requirements with regard to our products and services as well as to their marketing, sale, distribution and subsequent after-sales support.

Internal control

All businesses and projects owned, managed or controlled by XYZ must maintain an adequate system of internal control which is in accordance with XYZ's control policies. Management and staff are responsible to ensure that, within their respective areas of responsibility, necessary arrangements at acceptable cost are in place and are complied with to give reasonable assurance that the objectives of internal control are met. These objectives include:

- the achievement of business objectives efficiently and economically;
- the reliability of information used internally and for external reporting;
- the safeguarding of corporate resources; and
- compliance with laws, regulations and policies of the company.

The necessary arrangements comprise proper attention to:

- the control environment;
- information and communication;
- risk analysis;
- control activities or procedures; and
- monitoring.

All incidents involving a breakdown of control leading to any actual or potential breaches of the code should be reported upwards immediately to management and to internal audit. For companies in which XYZ has an interest but does not have control, the XYZ person responsible should endeavour to ensure that equivalent standards are applied and should refer the matter upwards within XYZ when they are not.

Records

Responsible staff must ensure that all the operational records of the business represent a reliable, truthful, accurate, complete and up-to-date picture in compliance with prescribed corporate procedures and external standards and regulations; and that they are suitable to be a basis for informed management decisions. The prompt recording and proper description of operations is a duty of responsible staff. Falsification of records is strictly prohibited.

No secret or unrecorded scientific activities are to be established or maintained.

Conduct by people acting on XYZ's behalf

In the introduction to this code I indicated that the XYZ person responsible should endeavour to ensure that equivalent standards to those set out in this code are followed in companies in which XYZ has an interest but does not have control, and also in those businesses with whom XYZ has contractual relationships. I also stated that it is the policy of the board of XYZ that those employed by or acting for XYZ should follow all the requirements of this code. For instance, contractors working on behalf of XYZ must ensure they act in accordance with this code.

It is not accepted that management and staff of XYZ circumvent their obligations under this code by deputing unacceptable practices to intermediaries acting directly or indirectly on XYZ's behalf so that XYZ may achieve a desired end while endeavouring to avoid any opprobrium.

Grievance procedures

Every XYZ operating unit must have in place and comply with suitable procedures to ensure that the concerns of staff on any issue related to this code are considered promptly and thoroughly, and that remedial action is taken where appropriate.

Please use your best endeavours to bring this code appropriately to the attention of all personnel, to all new employees, to our business partners and contractors as well as their staff and to any others with whom we are associated or do business.

Example of product supply chain ethical principles A6.10

Introduction

This document details the ethical principles of the ABC Group in respect of the product supply chain. It should be read in conjunction with the 'code of business conduct', the 'environmental protection principles and guidelines' and the group personnel policies (this latter document currently under development). These four policy statements together dictate our behaviour towards our stakeholders, competitors, customers and the community in general.

We are a unique healthcare company and proud of our tradition of supplying high quality products and services developed through the application of our scientific and technical expertise.

As a general principle, the safety of our end users is of paramount importance and decisions in respect of all of all products and services we supply are taken with safety as the overriding criteria.

The embodiment of current best practices within ABC into these principles, demonstrates the importance that the top management of our group give to the ethical principles of our product supply chain. All our people are required to live these principles. These principles were developed by a working party which included representation from the ultimate holding company of the ABC Group.

Part A – Summary

A.1 Research and development

Research and development carried out by the ABC Group is directed at new products which serve the health of our customers.

Our goal is to offer extensive health concepts for disease management, from research to routine applications, covering diagnosis through to therapy, monitoring and patient training.

The use of biotechnology is particularly important for this and we are aware of the concerns that some people have in respect of this subject. We therefore attach great importance to behaving in a responsible and ethical manner in this, as well as all other areas.

A.2 Products and services

ABC is involved in some or all stages of development, manufacture, marketing and sale of therapeutic, diagnostic and biochemical products and services. These products and services are aimed at improving the quality of life of the individuals who are treated with them.

A.3 Production

Quality, a high degree of employee and plant safety, and respect for the environment, are the cornerstones of our manufacturing philosophy. We have mechanisms in place to ensure that our production processes are critically examined to keep risks as low as is possible. In addition, we recognise that different types and levels of risk will exist in different geographic and cultural environments and we will balance these with the techniques used in our production facilities.

A.4 Marketing and customers

The ABC Group markets a range of high-quality diagnostic, therapeutic and biochemical products and services of high value to our customers.

These products are aimed at improving the well-being and quality of life of a variety of end users and are developed and produced in an ethical manner.

A.5 Other policies

ABC is committed to environmental protection, and our policy in this respect is detailed in a separate document entitled 'Environmental Protection Principles and Guidelines' issued in June 1995.

In addition to the importance that we place on acting responsibly and ethically in respect of our Product supply chain, and Environmental matters, we also have a 'code of business conduct', issued in October 1996 which describes our standards in respect of the conduct of our business affairs.

ABC is also in the process of developing 'personnel policies' which will codify our principles in respect of personnel matters.

Part B – Detail

B.1 Research and development

B.1.1 Introduction

Research and development with the ABC Group is aimed at using our technological and scientific expertise to meet current and future needs for high quality products and services to improve the well being and quality of life of our various end users.

The scientific standards that we apply are amongst the highest in our industry, taking into consideration the competitive environments that exists.

We undertake to communicate any research results which are of direct significance to our customers without delay. However, the scientific knowledge gained through our research forms the basis for the development of new products and the international competitive situation requires us to treat this information confidentially. We are aware of the contradiction between the economic need for confidentiality and giving appropriate access to the results of research and we acknowledge our obligations in this respect.

The following statements refer to some specific aspects of research and development within the ABC Group.

B.1.2 Gene technology

Methods such as gene technology, which are enhancing our knowledge on the causes of illnesses, are being used to develop methods of diagnosis and treatment. In addition, gene technology also enables us to produce proteins and other biological substances with increased efficiency and in an environmentally friendly manner. Gene technology is also essential in the production of many human proteins which are used for therapeutic purposes. Furthermore, it has become possible to modify the DNA sequence coding for proteins, thereby resulting in improvements to aspects of the product such as the pharmacological properties.

ABC is aware of the concerns associated with gene technology and this technology is used responsibly and ethically in the field of medicine with the clear objective of increasing our ability to improve the health, well-being and quality of life of our customers.

B.1.3 Gene therapy

The development of somatic gene therapies to treat genetic diseases is one of the main focuses of our work. The dignity of human life is paramount and at ABC we are opposed to any form of interference in the human genotype.

B.1.4 Animal experiments

Animal experiments are essential for the development and introduction of new therapeutic products. In many countries, it is a legal requirement for new products to have been tested on animals, prior to their being registered and sold in the marketplace. Animal experiments are used to evaluate dangers, side effects and risks to humans and to test the efficacy of the product.

At ABC we have undertaken to carefully review the necessity for animal experiments, to limit animal experiments in research and development of new drugs and treatments to a bare minimum, and to resort to alternative test procedures wherever possible. We also make every effort to use alternatives which contribute to a reduction in animal experimentation, and wherever possible to develop alternatives to animal experimentation ourselves.

B.1.5 Transgenic animals

Transgenic animals make possible the creation of more specific and accurate pathological models than previously available, and therefore lay the scientific foundations for the future treatment of illnesses such as cancer and cystic fibrosis.

Furthermore, the use of transgenic animals allows a drastic reduction in animal experiments.

B.1.6 Technology transfer

Technology transfers and co-operation with research institutes and universities is a major key to our success. For this reason, it is extremely important for the ABC Group to allow our joint-venture partners an appropriate share of this success. This is also true of scientific publications and patents. The terms and conditions of such ventures are negotiated fairly and in a timely manner with our partners.

B.1.7 Resources from developing countries

The use of biological resources, including those from developing countries, makes an important contribution to our research for new medical substances. We do of course observe all legal requirements in each of the countries concerned and ensure that we deal with any joint-venture partners equitably and reward them fairly for their assistance. We also act in full awareness of the importance of preserving biodiversity and strive to pass this awareness on to our joint-venture partners.

B.1.8 Risk/benefit analysis

We try to analyse potential risks and dangers which could arise in the development or later application of our products before they are developed. We only develop a product when the expected benefits outweigh the potential risks.

B.2 Products and services

B.2.1 Introduction

As a unique healthcare company, our aim is to improve the quality of life of the persons being treated with our products and services through the application of our scientific and technical expertise.

Our business comprises diagnostic, therapeutic and biochemical products.

B.2.2 Diagnostics

The ABC Group is involved in the development and sale of diagnostic products for various illnesses. Ethical problems do exist in certain areas of this science, for example tests for the diagnosis of non-treatable diseases, the area of genetic diagnosis (also known as DNA diagnosis), or tests which indicate increased disposition to illnesses. For this reason, we will only work in these areas if we, or other firms, are also working on the development of treatments for the diseases concerned, or if the tests for diseases with no means of treatment are still of high value, for example proof of pathogens in stored blood.

B.2.3 Therapeutics

In the development of therapeutic products the guiding principle of the ABC Group is to offer a high degree of efficacy together with the highest possible safety.

In the therapeutics division we have established principles that we are involved in the development of drugs and services which provide the population with good and affordable health care; and our products are aimed at the prevention and/or treatment of illnesses.

We aim to prevent off-label use of our products by the provision of clear and comprehensive information. Any side effects, contra-indications and possible dangers of off-label use of our products are explained in unambiguous terms.

B.2.4 Biochemicals

At the ABC Group, we also undertake manufacture and sale of biochemical products which are needed for research and medical application. We are aware that these reagents can also be used for purposes other than those intended by us and we therefore reserve the right to refuse to sell these products if there is reasonable grounds for suspicion that their ultimate use will not be in accordance with our ethical principles.

B.3 Production

We continually strive to improve our production processes, for example by reducing energy consumption. In the manufacture of our products, we try to use scarce resources with care and we develop processes for recycling raw materials wherever practical. It is our stated objective to keep environmental impact caused by production to the minimum possible.

In respect of plant safety, our production sites are governed by standards which satisfy all legal requirements, and exceed them wherever practical and possible.

When building new production sites we choose suitable sites world-wide which meet economic, social and ecological criteria, taking into consideration factors such as the impact on the community and existing workforce, the existing infrastructure, waste disposal capacities and the availability of suppliers.

B.4 Marketing and customers

Our objective is to offer high quality health-care products of the maximum possible customer value, which have been developed and produced in an ethical manner.

We carry out targeted market research which guarantees that the products which we develop are oriented to the needs and wishes of our customers.

We strive to bring new diagnostic and therapeutic principles to the market as quickly as possible, without compromising safety or quality. We undertake not to delay the market launch of new developments which could contribute to better health care solely for business reasons.

Information about our products will be scientifically accurate, open, and easy to comprehend. We will inform customers and end-users honestly about any risks in respect of our products, particularly in the case of misuse.

Our products will meet and, wherever possible, exceed all legal requirements in respect of safety of use both for the consumer and for the environment. Our products are subject to continuous quality control to ensure that this requirement is met.

Employees with an appropriate degree of technical knowledge will be available to answer any legitimate questions concerning our products. Complaints will be promptly investigated and courteously resolved.

We offer our customers an extensive service oriented towards their needs including training for doctors and patients, provision of comprehensive information material, and consultation in respect of problems, servicing of appliances etc.

We conduct ongoing reviews with the objective of determining ways by which our products can be further improved so as to provide increased value to our customers and end-users.

Risk strategy policy statement A6.11

Today, the conscious focus of boards and management is very much on risk strategy and risk management. Turnbull stipulates a 'top down' assessment of risk and control starting at the level of the board, and that processes for the review of risk and control should be embedded within the business and reviewed by the board. New, consultant-driven approaches to 'enterprise risk management' ('ERM') are being rolled out – with the contemporary accent of the gurus now being more on 'enterprise risk management' than on 'control risk self-assessment'. ERM is the new bandwagon to jump on!

So it is appropriate, indeed necessary, that the board formulates a policy on risk for the enterprise. This statement is contributed by Kelsey Beswick.

Background

Risk is defined as 'Any event or action that effects Network's ability to meet its key business objectives and deliver its strategies effectively'.

Housing Corporation requirements – Regulatory Code

'Housing Associations must operate a framework which effectively identifies and manages risks … identifying all risks which might prevent it achieving its objectives … with the necessary arrangements to manage risks and mitigate their effects.'

The risk assessments usually cover about an 18-month period. However, medium-terms risks also need to be considered.

Risk appetite

Network's risk appetite centres on the types and level or risk the organisation is prepared to take. It is based on the premise that calculated risk-taking is essential for ongoing success and that prudence is naturally required in situations where there are uncertainties over the outcome and where public money is at stake.

The types of risks Network is willing to take are covered by the organisational objectives. We will not take risks which fall outside of our objectives without prior board approval. Our approach remains one where significant new types of risk will be managed by creating specialist teams or subsidiaries when the activity level is sufficient to warrant such action.

Each year we will review our business activities and the board will decide whether it is appropriate to set activity limits to determine the level of risk we are prepared to take. Consideration will be given to turnover, property numbers, subsidy and resource capability.

Network will use external scanning and market analysis tools to identify risk areas and long term financial modelling to quantify financial risks.

The risk management framework

Managing risk is a continuous process which needs to be embedded into Network's systems to aid decision-making, accountability and systems improvement.

Risks are identified and prioritised at two key stages during the year, before and after the production of the business plan and monitored regularly to take into account the impact of new risks and changes in priority.

An assessment of the effectiveness of the controls in place to mitigate risks is carried out as an integral part of the process and actions to correct weaknesses are identified and implementation monitored.

The risk management framework and outputs are reviewed by the risk panel and by the group audit committee reporting to the board.

Responsibilities

The table below shows responsibilities for Network Housing Association. The group strategy board and group management team responsibilities are also noted to demonstrate how group risks are managed. The risk panel may be asked to co-ordinate group risk management activities.

Strategic approach to risk management

Network will employ the following strategies to ensure effective risk management:

- Carry out risk assessments before and after the production of the business plan, taking into account external and operational risk factors.
- Carry out half-yearly reviews of the risk assessment recording changes in risks and priorities.
- Monitor actions agreed to improve control effectiveness on a half-yearly basis.
- Provide an annual evaluation of control effectiveness to the board via the group audit committee.
- Carry out annual departmental risk assessments.
- Carry out risk assessments on all significant projects.
- Monitor overall impact to ensure that we do not attempt to introduce too many risks at once.
- Implement a policy on reporting control failures.
- Maintain the risk map and risk strategy on @Work (intranet).
- Carry out risk/control workshops with board and managers.
- Focus committee papers on risk issues where relevant.
- Register our risk management procedures to ISO9001.
- Identify group and cross-collateral risks and monitor.

Internal audit charters **A6.12**

The Code of Ethics and the Standards of the Institute of Internal Auditors are at **App7** and **App8**.

Standard 1000 'Purpose, Authority and Responsibility' reads:

> 'The purpose, authority and responsibility of the internal audit activity must be formally defined in a charter, consistent with the Definition of Internal Auditing, the Code of Ethics, and the *Standards*. The chief audit executive must periodically review the internal audit charter and present it to senior management and the board for approval.'

Standard 1000.A1 reads:

> 'The nature of assurance services provided to the organization must be defined in the internal audit charter. If assurances are to be provided to parties outside the organisation, the nature of these assurances must also be defined in the charter.'

and Standard 1000.C1 reads:

> 'The nature of consulting services must be defined in the audit charter.'

The Glossary to these Standards defines 'charter' as:

> 'The internal audit charter is a formal document that defines the internal audit activity's purpose, authority, and responsibility. The internal audit charter establishes the internal audit activity's position within the organisation; authorises access to records, personnel, and physical properties relevant to the performance of engagements; and defines the scope of internal audit activities.'

and 'board' is defined to include audit committees working on behalf of boards and also sole individuals in whom are vested the responsibilities more usually carried by directors collectively, namely:

> 'The highest level of governing body charged with the responsibility to direct and/or oversee the activities and management of the organization. Typically, this includes an independent group of directors (e.g., a board of directors, a supervisory board, or a board of governors or trustees). If such a group does not exist, the "board" may refer to the head of the organization. "Board" may refer to an audit committee to which the governing body has delegated certain functions.'

Example 1 A6.13

Here we provide a revised charter for an internal audit activity,[3] giving effect to the requirement that the nature of consulting services provided by an internal audit activity should be defined in the charter.

Internal Audit Charter 1

ABC Holdings plc

CHARTER

OF

GROUP INTERNAL AUDIT

In this charter the following words and terms have these respective meanings.

'The Entity' The group of businesses within this plc;

'The board'	The board of directors of the entity;
'The group'	All operations, investments and obligations which are the responsibility of the board;
'Audit committee'	A committee of directors of the entity appointed by the board as provided for in 'Terms of Reference of the Audit Committee' formally adopted by the board; and
'Group Internal Audit'	The function which provides internal audit services to group management and to the board through the audit committee.

This charter identifies the purpose, authority and responsibility of the group internal auditing unit.

Purpose

The group internal auditing unit is responsible to advise all levels of management, and the board through its audit committee, on the quality of the group's operations with particular emphasis on systems of control. It is a review activity which does not relieve line management of their responsibility for effective control. It functions by conducting independent appraisals leading to reports on its findings and recommendations addressed, as appropriate, to (a) the levels of management who need to know and are capable of ensuring that appropriate action is taken, and (b) the audit committee of the board.

Subject to not prejudicing its assurance activity, the internal auditing unit may undertake consulting engagements the nature and scope of which are agreed upon with management and which are intended to add value and improve the organisation's operations. Such consulting engagements will generally apply internal audit's competence in risk management, internal control and/or governance, and involve the provision of counsel, advice, facilitation, process design and/or training.

The board requires the group internal auditing unit to function professionally, adhering to the Code of Ethics, Standards and Guidelines of The Institute of Internal Auditors and meeting the requirements of regulatory authorities in those areas which are within the group internal auditing unit's responsibility.

Authority

The group internal auditing unit derives its authority from senior management and from the board to whose audit committee it has open access. The entity has also given the group internal auditing unit, for the purpose of its audit work, unrestricted access at any time to all the records, personnel, property and operations of the entity with strict responsibility for safekeeping and confidentiality.

The audit committee of the board reviews the scope and nature of the work of the group internal auditing unit to confirm its independence, and receives and reviews its reports to the committee.

The group internal auditing unit does not perform line tasks as this would impair its objectivity; neither has it any direct responsibility for, nor authority over, the activities it reviews.

Responsibilities

The group head of internal audit is responsible for determining the group internal auditing unit's programme of work, so that management and the board can have assurance as to the objectivity of audit reports. To provide this reassurance to management and the board, the scope of the group internal auditing unit's work includes ascertaining, at home and abroad and at all levels of the entity, that the assets of the group are being safeguarded; that operations are conducted effectively, efficiently and economically in accordance with group policies and procedures as well as with laws and regulations; and that records and reports of the group are accurate and reliable. The review of systems under development is part of the group internal auditing unit's responsibilities. In addition the group internal auditing unit may perform special reviews requested by management or the Board.

The group internal auditing unit is not relieved of its responsibilities in areas of the group's business which are subject to review by others; but should always assess the extent to which it can rely upon the work of others and co-ordinate its audit planning with those other review agencies.

[Signed]

Example 2 A6.14

Internal Audit Charter 2

Purpose and scope of work

The purpose of the Internal Audit service is to provide independent, objective assurance and consulting services designed to add value and improve the organisation's operations. It helps the organisation accomplish its objectives by bringing a systematic, disciplined approach to evaluate and improve the effectiveness of risk management, control and governance processes.

The scope of work of the Internal Audit service is to determine whether the organisation's network of risk management, control and governance processes, as designed and represented by management is adequate and functioning in a manner to ensure:

- risks are appropriately identified and managed;
- significant financial, managerial and operating information is accurate, reliable and timely;
- employees' actions are in compliance with policies, standards, procedures and applicable laws and regulations;
- resources are acquired economically, used efficiently and adequately protected;
- programmes, plans and objectives are achieved;
- quality and continuous improvement are fostered in the organisation's control process;
- significant legislative or regulatory issues impacting the organisation are recognised and addressed appropriately; and
- opportunities for improving management control, profitability and the organisation's image may be identified during audits. They will be communicated to the appropriate level of management.

Accountability

The head of audit and consultancy is accountable to management and the group audit committee to:

- provide annually an assessment on the adequacy and effectiveness of the organisation's processes for controlling its activities and managing its risks in the areas set forth under the Purpose and Scope of Work;
- report significant issues related to the processes for controlling the activities of the group, including potential improvements to those processes and provide information concerning follow up and implementation of agreed action;
- periodically provide information on the status and results of the annual audit plan and the sufficiency of department resources; and
- co-ordinate with and provide oversight of other control and monitoring functions (risk management, external audit, internal quality auditing).

Independence

To provide for the independence of the Internal Audit service, staff report to the head of audit and consultancy, who in turn reports functionally and administratively to the chief executive, and periodically to the group audit committee (see Accountability section). Included in the reporting is a regular report to the group audit committee on internal audit staff resources.

Responsibility

The head of audit and consultancy and staff of the Internal Audit service have responsibility to:

- develop a flexible annual audit plan using an appropriate risk-based methodology, including any risks or control concerns identified by management and submit that plan to the audit committee for review and approval as well as periodic updates;
- implement the annual audit plan, as approved, including as appropriate any special tasks or projects requested by management and the audit committee;
- maintain a professional audit staff with sufficient knowledge, skills, experience and training to meet the requirements of this charter;
- evaluate and assess significant new or changing services, processes, operations and control processes coincident with their development, implementation and/or expansion;
- issue periodic reports to the group audit committee and management summarising results of audit activities;
- keep the group audit committee informed of emerging trends and successful practices in internal auditing;
- provide significant performance measurement targets and results to the group audit committee;
- assist in the investigation of suspected fraudulent activities within the organisation and notify management and the group audit committee of the results; and
- consider the scope of work of the external auditors, internal quality auditors and regulators, as appropriate, for the purposes of optimal audit coverage, to the organisation at a reasonable overall cost.

Authority

The head of audit and consultancy and staff of the Internal Audit service are authorised to:

- have unrestricted access to all functions, records, property and personnel;
- have full and free access to the group audit committee;
- allocate resources, set frequencies, select subjects, determine scopes of work and apply the techniques required to accomplish audit objectives; and
- obtain the necessary assistance of personnel in departments of the organisation where they perform audits, as well as other specialised services from within or outside the organisation.

The head of audit and consultancy and staff of the Internal Audit service are *not* authorised to:

- perform operational duties inconsistent with the audit and consultancy role for the association or the group; or
- initiate or approve accounting transactions external to the audit and consultancy department.

Standards of audit practice

The Internal Audit service will meet or exceed the Standards for the Professional Practice of Internal Auditing of The Institute of Internal Auditors and abide by the Code of Ethics.

SIGNED ________________

Head of Audit and Consultancy

SIGNED ________________

Chief Executive

SIGNED ________________

Chair of Group Audit Committee

Example 3 **A6.15**

This is the sample internal audit department charter of The Institute of Internal Auditors Inc.

Mission and scope of work

The mission of the internal audit department is to provide independent, objective assurance and consulting services designed to add value and improve the organisation's operations. It helps the organisation accomplish its objectives by bringing a systematic, disciplined approach to evaluate and improve the effectiveness of risk management, control and governance processes.

The scope of work of the internal audit department is to determine whether the organisation's network of risk management, control and governance processes, as designed and represented by management, is adequate and functioning in a manner to ensure:

- risks are appropriately identified and managed;
- interaction with the various governance groups occurs as needed;
- significant financial, managerial, and operating information is accurate, reliable, and timely;
- employees' actions are in compliance with policies, standards, procedures, and applicable laws

and regulations;

- resources are acquired economically, used efficiently, and adequately protected;
- programmes, plans and objectives are achieved;
- quality and continuous improvement are fostered in the organisation's control process; and
- significant legislative or regulatory issues impacting the organisation are recognised and addressed appropriately.

Opportunities for improving management control, profitability and the organisation's image may be identified during audits. They will be communicated to the appropriate level of management.

Accountability

The chief audit executive, in the discharge of his/her duties, shall be accountable to management and the audit committee to:

- provide annually an assessment on the adequacy and effectiveness of the organisation's processes for controlling its activities and managing its risks in the areas set forth under the mission and scope of work;
- report significant issues related to the processes for controlling the activities of the organisation and its affiliates, including potential improvements to those processes, and provide information concerning such issues through resolution;
- periodically provide information on the status and results of the annual audit plan and the sufficiency of department resources; and
- co-ordinate with and provide oversight of other control and monitoring functions (risk management, compliance, security, legal, ethics, environmental, external audit).

Independence

To provide for the independence of the internal auditing department, its personnel report to the chief audit executive, who reports functionally to the audit committee and administratively to the chief executive officer in a manner outlined in the above section on Accountability. It will include as part of its reports to the audit committee a regular report on internal audit personnel.

Responsibility

The chief audit executive and staff of the internal audit department have responsibility to:

- develop a flexible annual audit plan using an appropriate risk-based methodology, including any risks or control concerns identified by management, and submit that plan to the audit committee for review and approval as well as periodic updates;

- implement the annual audit plan, as approved, including as appropriate any special tasks or projects requested by management and the audit committee;
- maintain a professional audit staff with sufficient knowledge, skills, experience and professional certifications to meet the requirements of this charter;
- evaluate and assess significant merging/consolidating functions and new or changing services, processes, operations and control processes coincident with their development, implementation, and/or expansion;
- issue periodic reports to the audit committee and management summarising results of audit activities;
- keep the audit committee informed of emerging trends and successful practices in internal auditing;
- provide a list of significant measurement goals and results to the audit committee;
- assist in the investigation of significant suspected fraudulent activities within the organisation and notify management and the audit committee of the results; and
- consider the scope of work of the external auditors and regulators, as appropriate, for the purpose of providing optimal audit coverage to the organisation at a reasonable overall cost.

Authority

The chief audit executive and staff of the internal audit department are authorised to:

- have unrestricted access to all functions, records, property and personnel;
- have full and free access to the audit committee;
- allocate resources, set frequencies, select subjects, determine scopes of work and apply the techniques required to accomplish audit objectives; or
- obtain the necessary assistance of personnel in units of the organisation where they perform audits, as well as other specialised services from within or outside the organisation;

The chief audit executive and staff of the internal audit department are not authorised to:

- perform any operational duties for the organisation or its affiliates;
- initiate or approve accounting transactions external to the internal auditing department; or
- direct the activities of any organisation employee not employed by the internal auditing department, except to the extent such employees have been appropriately assigned to auditing teams or to otherwise assist the internal auditors.

Standards of audit practice

The internal audit department will meet or exceed the *Standards for the Professional Practice of Internal Auditing* of The Institute of Internal Auditors.

SIGNED________

Chief Audit Executive

SIGNED______
Chief Executive Officer

SIGNED______
Audit Committee Chair

Dated______

Whistleblowing and whistleblowing policy statements **A6.16**

At **A6.22**, we provide an example of a whistleblowing policy statement.

The UK Public Interest Disclosure Act 1998 **A6.17**

The Public Interest Disclosure Act 1998 ('PIDA 1998') came into effect on 1 July 1999. UK employers risk heavy penalties and media attention if they discourage or attempt to cover up staff warnings about malpractice.

Under PIDA 1998, employees are able to claim full compensation if they are sacked or otherwise victimised for disclosing perceived malpractices to their employer or to an approved outside organisation. As there is no limit imposed on the level of compensation that can be awarded by a tribunal, the government hopes that this may encourage senior managers to blow the whistle on unscrupulous employers.

The purposes of PIDA 1998 are: to protect an individual who makes certain disclosures of information in the public interest; and to allow such an individual to bring action (including claims for compensation for wrongful dismissal) in respect of victimisation on the ground that the worker has made a protected disclosure. The relevant failure may have occurred within the UK or elsewhere, and the law applying to it may be the law of any country.

A qualifying disclosure to a person other than to the worker's employer is regarded as a disclosure to the employer if it is in accordance with a procedure authorised by the employer. The same rights apply to workers in government bodies if the disclosure is made to a minister or to a person prescribed for the purpose by the Secretary of State.

Under this Act, contractual duties of confidentiality are void insofar as they purport to preclude a worker from making a protected disclosure. Section 43K of PIDA 1998 extends the Act in certain circumstances to freelance workers, contractors and subcontractors and those on work experience etc.

PIDA 1998 uses the expressions 'qualifying disclosure', 'relevant failures' and 'protected disclosures'. A 'qualifying disclosure' is any legal disclosure of information which, in the reasonable belief of the worker making the disclosure, tends to show one or more of these 'relevant failures':

(a) that a criminal offence has been committed, is being committed or is likely to be committed;
(b) that a person has failed, is failing or is likely to fail to comply with any legal obligation to which he or she is subject;

(c) that a miscarriage of justice has occurred, is occurring or is likely to occur;
(d) that the health or safety of any individual has been, is being or is likely to be endangered;
(e) that the environment has been, is being or is likely to be damaged; or
(f) that information tending to show any matter falling within any one of the preceding paragraphs has been, is being or is likely to be deliberately concealed, unless the disclosure is made by a person to whom the information has been disclosed in the course of obtaining legal advice, about which a claim to legal professional privilege could be maintained in legal proceedings.

A 'protected disclosure' is a 'qualifying disclosure' made by the worker in good faith to his or her employer, or in some cases to another, so long as the following apply:

(a) the worker makes the disclosure in good faith;
(b) he or she reasonably believes that the information disclosed, and any allegation contained within it, are substantially true;
(c) he or she does not make the disclosure for purposes of personal gain;
(d) a number of conditions are met; and
(e) in all the circumstances of the case, it is reasonable for him or her to make the disclosure (what constitutes reasonableness is spelt out in PIDA 1998, s 43G(3)(a)–(f)).

UK whistleblowing cases following the Public Interest Disclosure Act 1998 A6.18

Employees are protected if they make a qualified disclosure in good faith.

Other workers (such as subcontractors) must also pass the test that the disclosure was based on a reasonable belief in the truth of the matter disclosed.

A qualifying disclosure is one which tends to show (a) that a criminal offence is being or will be committed, (b) some other legal obligation such as a statutory duty or contract is being or will be breached, (c) the health and safety of a person is being or will be put in danger, (d) the environment is being or will be damaged, or (e) any of the above are the subject of a cover-up.

Fernandes v Netcom Consultants (UK) Limited A6.19

An industrial tribunal awarded compensation of £293,441 to Fernandes, who was dismissed after blowing the whistle to Netcom's parent company that £300,000 of expenses claims by the managing director of Netcom did not have the necessary supporting documentation. The tribunal judged that the reasons given for Fernandes' dismissal were a smokescreen, and the intention was to cover up the financial irregularities which had taken place.

Azmi v Orbis Charitable Trust A6.20

Mrs Azmi's appointment was not confirmed. This occurred after she had disclosed her concern about allegedly improper payments to (a) the external auditors, (b) the charity commissioners, (c) the charity's US associate organisation, and (d) Orbis' executive director. The tribunal found that (a) and (b) did not amount to a protected disclosure as (a) and (b) had been careful to ensure that they kept her disclosures to them confidential. Point (c) was also not a protected disclosure because (c) was a separate organisation, not the parent of Orbis. But (d) was a protected disclosure and so Mrs Azmi won her case, the tribunal not believing Orbis' explanation for her termination.

Bladon v ALM Medical Services Limited **A6.21**

A matron disclosed his concern about the standard of nursing care to (a) management, and then, when no action followed, to (b) Social Services, who investigated and found the allegations largely justified. The tribunal found that he was entitled to go outside the organisation in view of the nature of the complaint, the lack of action and the fact that the employer had no disclosure policy operating to act as guidance. If there had have been such a policy which was being followed, the employer may have been able to argue that the disclosure was unprotected, or the damages awarded may have been less. His disclosure was protected, as he had first brought his concerns to the attention of his employer. The tribunal dismissed as 'fabricated' the employer's given reasons for dismissing him for 'dereliction of duty'. Damages of £23,000, including £10,000 for aggravated damages, were awarded.

Whistleblowing policy statement – 'doing the right thing' (Network Housing Association) A6.22

Here we reproduce a whistleblowing policy statement by Kelsey Beswick and her colleagues in Network Housing Association, with the assistance of the charity Public Concern at Work.

There are a number of key elements to this policy statement.

The scope of the statement is given and covers frauds, corruption and malpractice, criminal or illegal behaviour, miscarriage of justice, danger to health and safety, abuse or neglect of vulnerable people, failure to deliver proper standards of service, damaging personal conflicts at senior level and bullying, discrimination, harassment or victimisation in the work place. The organisation commits generally to the highest standards and specifically to involve staff in the development of its procedures on confidential reporting. It undertakes to monitor the policy, keeping confidential records of all matters raised through the whistleblowing policy and ensuring that an appropriate committee receives reports with an assessment of the effectiveness of the policy and any emerging patterns.

The policy encourages employees to express concerns suggesting they might like to come forward with a colleague or another person. There is a promise of support and confidentiality where possible, and describing it as a disciplinary offence to discourage staff from expressing concerns or victimisation following expression of a concern. There is specific commitment to ensuring that expressing concerns will not affect careers.

Staff are encouraged to 'blow the whistle' within the organisation rather than overlooking a problem or raising the issue outside. Staff are reminded that organisational rules require staff not to disclose confidential, false or misleading information. So, in considering whether to take a concern outside the organisation, staff are reminded of their duty of confidentiality and that they should ensure that the matter is raised without confidential information being divulged. The policy statement points out that PIDA 1998 gives legal protection to whistleblowers who honestly and reasonably believe that the information they disclose, or the allegations they make, are substantially true.

A flexible route for communicating concerns is allowed for, in most cases to the immediate manager but with allowance for the concern to be expressed, at the discretion of the concerned person, direct to the internal audit service, or to a senior officer, or to the central services director, or even to the chief executive. Staff are given the right to ask a for confidential meeting, and are reminded that both parties should treat such contacts in confidence.

There is specific reference to the view that, if the organisation's policy and procedures are working properly, there should be no need to contact one of the organisation's board members, or some external agency, to express concerns. But it is recognised that there may be exceptional or urgent circumstances where it might be best to contact an external agency, and examples are given of the circumstances and what external people might be contacted. Reference in this context is made to Public Concern at Work who assisted this organisation to draw up this policy statement. Staff are, however, reminded that abuse of this confidential reporting process, for instance, by maliciously raising unfounded allegations, will be treated as a disciplinary matter, but the statement seeks to reassure that no one who comes forward in good faith will have anything to fear.

The conduct of an investigation is covered within the general assurance that it will be looked into carefully and thoroughly, and acted upon appropriately. Provision for either internal or independent investigation is made. Fairness to all parties is warranted. If requested, the organisation agrees to try to let the concerned person know the results of the investigation and the action proposed.

The policy provides that concerns which fall within the scope of an established procedure will be referred for consideration under those procedures.

The organisation commits to acknowledging a communicated concern within seven days, with an indication of how the organisation proposes to deal with the matter and likely timescale. If a decision is made not to investigate, the reasons will be given. The concerned person is assured of as much information as possible on the outcomes of the investigation, subject to certain constraints.

1. Introduction

1.1 Network Housing Association is committed to the highest standards of quality, probity, openness and accountability.

1.2 As part of that commitment, we encourage employees or others with serious concerns about any aspect of our work to do the right thing and come forward and express those concerns. In many cases, concerns or complaints will be dealt with through our normal procedures. However, in some cases, we recognise that employees will need to come forward on a confidential basis. We want to make it clear that they can do so without fear of reprisal or victimisation.

1.3 This statement to our employees is intended to underline our commitment, and our support to those who come forward to express their concerns. Staff are often the first people who realise that there may be something seriously wrong within the organisation, but may not express their concerns. This could be for a number of reasons; because speaking up might be regarded as disloyal by colleagues or the organisation, because of fear that they may be victimised, doubts about reporting what might only be a suspicion, or because it might seem easier to ignore it and not get involved.

1.4 'Whistleblowing' is often understood as reporting a concern outside the organisation because, for various reasons, the employee does not wish or feel able to raise the matter internally. This whistleblowing policy aims to encourage and enable staff to raise serious concerns by 'blowing the whistle' within the Association, rather than overlooking a problem or raising the issue outside.

1.5 There are existing procedures in place to enable staff to raise concerns (the fraud policy), be it about the conduct of a service, or in order to protect service users from abuse and other forms of ill treatment. In addition, there are procedures to enable staff to complain on behalf of service users on more general matters relating to the provision of services. This policy has a wider application and is intended for any form of malpractice and cover-up of any of these.

2. Consultation and information

2.1 We will consult and involve you as we develop our procedures and practices on confidential reporting. We will also consult the staff association and recognise trades unions, as well as using our normal staff briefing and consultation procedures. We hope to get wide backing for and promotion of our approach.

2.2 Through our staff induction and briefing, we will make sure that you know how to recognise the following problems, and that you understand the effects they may have on the organisation, your job and the service you provide:

- Frauds, corruption and malpractice;
- Criminal or illegal behaviour;
- Miscarriage of justice;
- Danger to health and safety;
- Abuse or neglect of vulnerable people;
- Failure to deliver proper standards of service;
- Damaging personal conflicts at senior level; and
- Bullying, discrimination, harassment or victimisation in the workplace.

2.3 We will make sure that you know what is expected of you, and what practices you regard as unacceptable. You should study our staff guidance carefully, and discuss anything that seems unclear with your manager. If you are not sure what to do in a given situation, ask before taking any action.

2.4 When we find a problem, we will always deal with it seriously. We know that we cannot expect you to practise higher standards than those we apply. We will always pursue fraud and serious abuse as vigorously as possible through our disciplinary procedures, or if necessary, through the courts; frauds are always reported to the police. We hope that you will feel confident in doing the right thing by coming forward, that we share your sense of right and wrong and act on what you tell us.

3. Confidential reporting

3.1 We know that it is never easy to report a concern, particularly one which may relate to fraud or corruption. We urge you to come forward with any concerns at an early stage, and before problems have a chance to become serious.

3.2 If you prefer, we are happy for you to come forward with another colleague, a friend, trades union representative or other advisor to report a concern.

3.3 We will support concerned employees and protect them from reprisals or victimisation. If you come forward with a concern, you can be confident that this will not affect your career, or your enjoyment of your job. This applies equally if you come forward in good faith with a concern which turns out later not to be justified.

3.4 We will do anything we can to respect your confidentially, if you have requested this.

3.5 If anyone tries to discourage you from coming forward to express a concern, we will treat this as a disciplinary offence. In the same way, we will deal severely with anyone who criticises or victimises you after a concern has been expressed.

3.6 The association's disciplinary rules and staff conduct requires that you do not disclose confidential, false or misleading information. In considering taking a concern outside the association you should be aware of your duty of confidentiality and ensure that the matter is raised without confidential information being divulged.

3.7 The Public Interest Disclosure Act 1998 (which came into force in January 1999) gives legal protection to whistleblowers who honestly and reasonably believe that the information they disclose or the allegations they make are substantially true.

4. Who to contact

4.1 In most cases, you should be able to raise your concerns with your immediate manager or his supervisor. If for some reason this is not possible, you should speak to the internal audit service, a senior officer, the central services director or the chief executive. If necessary, you should ask for a confidential meeting. All such contacts should be treated in confidence.

4.2 If our policy and procedures are working properly, you should not need to contact one of the organisation's board members, or some external agency, to express concerns. But there may be exceptional or urgent circumstances where it might be best to contact an external agency. It is not possible to give precise examples but, for instance, relevant situations might be:

- if the problem involved very senior member of the organisation, the chair or another board member;
- in the case of a criminal offence, the police;
- in the case of abuse of vulnerable people in a residential home;
- the local authority social services department;
- in the case of abuse of public funds, the Housing Corporation, which is responsible for regulating all registered social landlords;

- In the case of any fraud, the association's external auditors; or
- regional office of the Housing Corporation.

We hope that none of these will ever prove necessary.

4.3 You can also approach Public Concern at Work for confidential and independent advice at the following address: Lincoln's Inn House, 42 Kingsway, London WC2B 6EX. E-mail: whistle@pcaw.demon.co.uk.

4.4 Performance audit staff in the relevant regional office of the Housing Corporation are also able to advise on a confidential basis if you are not sure whom to contact about a particular problem. As regulators, they may need to follow up on any potential problems identified.

5. Network's response

5.1 If you come to us with a concern, we will look into it carefully and thoroughly. We have to be fair to you, but also to any other person involved. If someone is potentially being accused of misconduct, we have to find out their side of the story as well. In our investigation, we will respect any concerns you have expressed about your own safety or career.

5.2 If you request, we will try to let you know the results of our investigation and about any action that is proposed. However, in doing this, we have to respect the confidentiality of other employees as well.

5.3 The action that will be taken by Network will depend on the nature of the concern. The matters raised may be investigated by management, by internal enquiry or through the disciplinary process. Alternatively, they may be subject to independent enquiry. Relevant matters may also be subject to investigation by the police. However, in order to safe guard both Network and individuals, initial enquiries will be made to determine whether the commitment of resources to any form of investigation would be appropriate. These initial enquiries would also assist in determining the most appropriate process for the consideration of the concern. Any necessary action that is required urgently would be carried out ahead of any assessment/investigation process.

5.4 Concerns or allegations raised which fall within the scope of established procedure will be referred for consideration under those procedures.

5.5 A referral of a concern will be acknowledged within seven days, with an indication of how the association proposes to deal with the matter and likely timescale. If it is not possible to complete the initial enquiries within the seven days, the letter of acknowledgement will explain. If a decision is made not to investigate, the reasons will be given.

5.6 Some matters may be investigated without the need for initial enquiries to be made. Similarly, some concerns may be capable of resolution by agreed action without the need for investigation.

5.7 The level of contact between you and whoever is considering the issues will depend on the nature of the matters raised, the potential difficulties involved as well as the clarity of the information provided. Further information may be sought from you.

5.8 The association will take appropriate steps to minimise any difficulties that you may experience as a result of using the whistleblowing policy.

5.9 You will be given as much information as possible on the outcomes of the investigation, subject to the constraints of the association's duty of confidentiality to service users, staff or board members or any other legal constraint. The objective of the various responses would be to assure you that the matter has been addressed.

5.10 If you have abused the confidential reporting process, for instance by maliciously raising unfounded allegations, we will treat this as a disciplinary matter. But no one who comes forward in good faith has anything to fear.

6. Monitoring the policy

6.1 Confidential records will be kept of all matters raised through the whistleblowing policy and the appropriate Network committee will receive reports with an assessment of the effectiveness of the policy and any emerging patterns.

Harassment policies **A6.23**

Increasing attention is being given to the need to make the workplace a safe and supportive environment. Here we reproduce a harassment policy, together with guidelines for managers investigating allegations of harassment, which has recently been agreed between management and trades union colleagues, and formally adopted by the board.

The underlying theme is that harassment as defined is unacceptable, whether by other staff or by representatives of business partners (especially suppliers and customers) or by other parties (for instance, visitors). The policy and guidelines reproduced here define the action which will be taken where inappropriate behaviour is found to have taken place.

In this organisation, the board considered harassment to be a priority area for action, including the need for the implementation of policies and procedures to tackle harassment and for arrangements to monitor progress. They have arranged that the policy and guidelines will be reviewed periodically and performance will be monitored.

Readers should note that harassment is not the same thing as victimisation. The word 'harassment' appears 27 times but 'victimisation' only twice. Arguably, this or another statement should also address victimisation to a greater extent.

Readers of this statement have pointed out that the requirement to write a letter could be difficult, even intimidating, in these circumstances, and that perhaps a form could be designed to be used instead. Another observation on this statement is that the phrase 'putting someone down' is ambiguous.

A practical suggestion is that this statement would be improved if the organisation's policy provided for a 'mediation service' to resolve tensions, especially where complaints appear to be malicious or otherwise unjustified, and if this mediation service was covered within this statement.

Harassment – policy statement **A6.24**

Introduction

The company believes that employees have the right to be treated with dignity and respect at work and to carry out their employment without any form of harassment.

This policy applies to all persons employed by the company and also to those other persons who work within the company and make decisions on behalf of the company, where such decisions affect any matter set out within this policy and could give rise to any unacceptable practice.

The company will not condone or accept trade union, employment agency or service contractor policies and practices which it considers constitute any form of harassment.

The company also considers that all employees, customers, suppliers and associates have a responsibility to treat others with consideration, dignity and respect.

What is 'harassment'?

Harassment is behaviour which may involve unwelcome, unreasonable and offensive physical, verbal or non-verbal conduct, where the individual is intimidated, humiliated, threatened, bullied, abused, patronised or where their privacy is invaded in some way. This may be on the grounds of race, gender, sexuality, religion, ethnic origin, marital status, disability, age, expired convictions or health.

Harassment is defined by the impact on the recipient not the intention of the perpetrator. The person whose course of conduct is in question ought to know that it amounts to harassment of another, if a reasonable person in possession of the same information would think the course of conduct amounted to harassment of the other.

It may be the result of a single act or repeated inappropriate behaviour.

Examples

- Unwanted physical contact, including unnecessary touching, patting or pinching, brushing against another person's body;
- Shouting or swearing at someone;
- Assault;
- Personal insults;
- Coercing sexual intercourse, unwelcome sexual advances;
- Suggestive remarks, innuendoes, lewd comments, discriminatory or personal remarks;
- Treatment detrimental to professional status and credibility;
- Display of racist, pornographic or sexually suggestive pictures, objects or written materials;
- Leering, whistling or making sexually suggestive or insulting gestures;
- Non-co-operation or exclusion from conversation and activities; or
- Putting someone down.

Informal remedy

Employees who are victims of harassment should make it clear to the harasser that the behaviour is unacceptable and must stop. The employee may wish to seek advice from their manager, personnel officer or staff side representative before doing so.

Formal procedure

If the informal remedy fails to resolve the situation or the harassment is too serious to be dealt with this way, the victim should submit a formal written complaint to their immediate manager, or their staff representative may do it on their behalf. This should contain:

- the name of the harasser;
- the nature of the harassment;
- dates and times when harassment occurred;
- names of witnesses to any form of harassment; and
- any action taken by the complainant to stop the harassment.

In some circumstances it may not be appropriate to send this complaint to the immediate manager and if this is the case it should be submitted to a more senior line manager or to a personnel manager.

As harassment is a disciplinary offence, the complaint should be investigated and dealt with under the company's disciplinary procedure. Whilst an investigation is taking place it may be necessary to suspend the alleged harasser from duty or remove them to a different area of work. However, a person accused of harassment may not necessarily be guilty and has a right to support and to know of what they are accused.

The complaint should be investigated within ten working days wherever possible. All employees involved in the investigation will be expected to maintain confidentiality. Failure to do so may be considered a disciplinary offence.

An employee who makes a complaint will not suffer victimisation for having done so. However, if the complaint is untrue and has been made in a malicious way, disciplinary action will be taken against the complainant.

Alleged harassment of staff by representatives of customers and suppliers, and by visitors

Staff have the right to be treated with respect and dignity at all times and it is unacceptable for others external to our company to harass staff.

Staff should initially raise any concerns they may have about harassment from this source with the appropriate manager. The content of any discussion should be kept confidential unless further action is considered necessary. Staff may also discuss the matter in confidence with their personnel officer or staff representative to obtain further advice. The manager should carry out a full investigation and keep a written record which may be used in evidence in case the member of staff complaining of harassment becomes the subject of a complaint by the other party. Where the problem is of a serious or persistent nature the alleged harasser of the member of staff must be made aware that such behaviour is unacceptable and that the company may take legal action. In some cases it may be appropriate to review the company's business relationship with a supplier or customer or to arrange for changes in personnel to minimise the future risk.

Duty of supervisors and managers

All supervisors and managers have a duty to take all reasonable action to ensure that harassment does not occur in work areas for which they are responsible.

Managers should be responsive and supportive to any members of staff who complain about harassment, provide full and clear advice on the procedure to be followed, maintain confidentiality and ensure there is no further problem or any victimisation after a complaint has been resolved.

Duty of employees

All employees have a clear role to play in creating a climate at work in which harassment is unacceptable. They must take all reasonable steps to prevent this through awareness and sensitivity towards the issue and by ensuring that standards of conduct and behaviour for themselves and for colleagues do not cause offence.

Appropriate disciplinary action, including dismissal for serious offences, will be taken against any employee who breaches this policy.

Review

Implementation of this policy will be monitored by personnel and a review undertaken from time to time to ensure that it continues to meet the needs of the company and its staff.

Management of harassment guidelines for managers investigating allegations of harassment

Complaints should be investigated in accordance with the company's disciplinary procedure, within ten working days of the complaint being made.

Interviewing the complainant

- Explain the process to be followed and reassure them regarding confidentiality;
- Allow plenty of time and be prepared for the complainant to become emotional;
- Do not express any personal views or opinions;
- Try to establish:
  - what actually took place, where and when;
  - the frequency of the alleged harassment;
  - whether there were any witnesses;
  - what was said or done by whom and to whom;
  - how the complainant felt at the time;
  - what the complainant has done to stop the alleged harassment;
  - whether they have notes or copy letters to support the allegations or demonstrate any action they have taken;
  - whether they have discussed the alleged harassment with anyone else; and
  - whether they are aware of anyone else being subjected to the same treatment.

Finally, reassure the complainant and clarify the process again, and retain full and clear notes which reflect the discussion.

Interviewing the alleged harasser

- Explain the allegations that have been made against them and the process to be followed;
- Reassure them regarding confidentiality;
- Allow plenty of time and be prepared for the individual to become emotional or aggressive;
- Listen with an open mind and remain impartial;
- Try to establish and corroborate the facts;
- Give the individual adequate opportunity to respond to all the allegations;
- Clarify the process again for the individual; and
- Retain full and clear notes which reflect the discussion.

Policy statement on environment and health A6.25

XYZ will ensure that all its activities worldwide are conducted safely; the health of its employees, its customers and the public will be protected; environmental performance will meet contemporary requirements, and that its operations are run in a manner acceptable to the local communities.

In particular we will:

- comply with relevant laws and regulations and take any additional measures we consider necessary;
- ensure that all our activities are being carried out in accordance with the XYZ Group safety, health and environment standards;
- set demanding targets and measure progress to ensure continuous improvement in safety, health and environmental performance;
- require every member of staff to exercise personal responsibility in preventing harm to themselves, others and the environment, and enable them to contribute to every aspect of safety, health and environmental protection;
- manufacture only those products that can be transported, stored, used and disposed of safely;
- seek to develop new or modified products which assist in conserving the environment and lead to sustainable development;
- provide appropriate safely, health and environmental training and information for all our staff, contractors and others who work with us, handle our products, or operate our technologies;
- communicate openly on the nature of our activities and report progress on our safety, health and environmental performance;
- promote the interchange of safety, health and environmental information and technology throughout the XYZ Group and make our expertise and knowledge available to relevant statutory authorities; and
- encourage, through positive interaction within the industry, the worldwide development and implementation of the principles of the International Chamber of Commerce's 'Business Charter for Sustainable Development'.

This policy applies throughout XYZ and our subsidiaries worldwide.

We encourage our related companies to adopt policies which accord with this policy.

Information security policy statements **A6.26**

In the following two sections of this handbook we provide example IT security guidelines for staff (at **A6.27** and **A6.28**) and an example of an e-mail, internet and telephone usage policy statement (at **A6.29**).

The UK's Department of Trade and Industry (DTI) gave us permission to reproduce its 'boilerplate' information security policy statement.

The DTI pointed out that an information security policy provides an opportunity for top management to set a clear direction and demonstrate their support for and commitment to information security. It should complement the organisation's 'mission' statement and reflect the desire of the business to operate in a controlled and secure manner.

As a minimum, the information security policy should include guidance on the following areas:

- The importance of information security to the business process;
- A statement from top management supporting the goals and principles of information security; and
- Specific statements indicating minimum standards and compliance requirements for:
  - legal, regulatory and contractual obligations;
  - security awareness and educational requirements;
  - virus prevention and detection;
  - business continuity planning;
  - definitions of responsibilities and accountabilities; and
  - details of the process for reporting suspected security incidents.

Information security policy statement **A6.27**

Policy

The purpose of the policy is to protect the company's information[4] assets from all threats, whether internal or external, deliberate or accidental.

- The chief executive has approved the information security policy;
- It is the policy of the company to ensure that:
  - information will be protected against unauthorised access, and
  - confidentiality of information will be assured;[5]
- Integrity of information will be maintained;[6]
- Regulatory and legislative requirements will be met;[7]
- Business continuity plans will be produced, maintained and tested;[8]
- Information security training will be available to all staff;
- All breaches of information security, actual or suspected, will be reported to, and investigated by the information security manager;

- Standards will be produced to support the policy which may include virus control, passwords and encryption;
- Business requirements for the availability of information and information systems will be met;
- The role and responsibility for managing information security, referred to as the information security manager, will be performed by whom;[9]
- The information security manager has direct responsibility for maintaining the policy and providing advice and guidance on its implementation;
- All managers are directly responsible for implementing the policy within their business areas, and for adherence by their staff; and
- It is the responsibility of each employee to adhere to the policy.

Objective

The objective of information security is to ensure business continuity and minimise business damage by preventing and minimising the impact of security incidents.

Signed:_____

Title: _____

Date:

(The policy will be reviewed by the information security manager, usually plus one year from the date signed.)

Information security – guidelines for staff A6.28

We provide another example, information security policy statement, at **A6.27**; we provide an example of an e-mail, Internet and telephone policy statement at **A6.29**.

Introduction

The growth of PCs, networks, applications and data accessible to employees means that information is available to a wide audience in XYZ plc. It is essential that this information is kept:

- confidential; and
- protected from damage or abuse.

The company managers are clearly accountable for ensuring that there is a secure process for staff to operate; however, there are some things for which every employee must take individual accountability.

Objective

The objective of this leaflet is to set out for XYZ's employees and associated staff, the standards and practices for which they must take personal accountability and where failure to observe them will be regarded as a serious breach of trust.

Security policy

XYZ maintains as information security policy, agreed by the directors, that embodies industry best practice. Some of the requirements in the policy are repeated in this booklet. Others are the responsibility of identified directors or managers.

You are responsible for reading and understanding the policy and bringing to your manager's attention any serious breach of its requirements. The policy can be obtained via your manager.

You are responsible for understanding and adhering to any formal procedures that are put in place and documented or the implementation of the policy.

Taking care of assets

Most staff have important assets in their personal custody. Typically these are such things as:

- personal computers (equipment, files, software) and documents;
- security 'tokens' (keys, access cards, passwords, etc); and
- mobile phones.

You are responsible for ensuring these items are not:

- passed to third parties;
- misused or damaged;
- used for the purposes other than XYZ's business; or
- removed from company premises without authority.

Access

Many operational areas have special access rules. You are responsible for abiding by them.

You must ensure the following points are carried out.

- Escort any external visitor until they leave or are handed over to another member of staff;
- Challenge unauthorised 'intruders' or report them to the manager of the area; and
- Lock away confidential items (documents, PC diskettes etc) when the area is unattended. No business information should be available for casual inspection by visitors. Workstations should not be left unattended in a state where applications could be accessed by unauthorised individuals.

A 'clear desk' policy is followed by XYZ.

Operating procedures

Operating procedures are written to help safeguard XYZ's assets. You are responsible for following them and bringing to your manager's attention any errors they contain.

Viruses

Viruses and other types of malicious software are a serious threat, particularly to personal computers.

You must not carry out the activities below.

- Load illegal copies of software or any games or 'shareware' on to any computer. Even spreadsheets or documents are a risk. If you are importing files from third parties raw data files are preferable.
- Use any disk that you know has not been virus checked.

- Interrupt the 'boot-up' sequence.

You must ensure the following.

- Report any symptom that might indicate your PC is 'infected'.
- Understand and adhere to the company's formal virus avoidance procedure. This will include the procedure for implementing legal code (eg software fixes) from insecure sources (eg the Internet).

Communications

Most public communication services (eg email, telephone) are inherently insecure. When using the Internet add the following text to any of your emails which might amount to 'business letters':

XYZ plc

Registered office:

[Address]

Registered in England no. XXXXX

This basic corporate information is required by law to be given on business letters and order forms. When sending e-mails which contain sensitive information, it is worth adding the following text:

> This e-mail is confidential and may contain privileged information. If you are not the addressee it may be unlawful for you to read, copy, distribute, disclose or otherwise use the information in this e-mail. If you are not the intended recipient please notify us immediately.

System access controls

All applications should have access controls (eg passwords) to prevent unauthorised use or access to data. This applies equally to personal computer applications.

You must not:

- use another employee's password or user identity without management authority;
- access or change any application or data that you are not authorised to do;
- input information that you know to be incorrect; and
- write down, display or disclose your user identity or password.

You must:

- adhere to password standards, eg:
  - use more than six characters;
  - change it regularly varying at least three characters;
  - do not use user-ID or name;
  - avoid all numeric passwords where possible;
  - get your user-ID deleted if you no longer need it; and
  - report any violation of these guidelines or any attempt to persuade you to provide access or information to an unauthorised person.

Purchasing

XYZ has a formal purchasing process. This requires that goods and services that are required are sourced and provided by the IT department.

Legislation and contracts

XYZ is committed to adhere to legislation and contract conditions.

You must not:

- create unauthorised copies of copyright software, documents or customer data;
- hold personal data other than is allowed by our entry on the data protection register, as held by group secretariat; or
- use software except as allowed under the terms of the license purchased.

As an individual, the following legislation applies to you personally:

- the *Copyright, Designs and Patents Act 1988* (this outlaws illegal copying of software);
- the *Computer Misuse Act 1990* (this defines 'hacking' and deliberate virus contamination as criminal offences); and
- the *Data Protection Act 1998* (this covers the conditions under which personal data can be held).

Housekeeping

Data owners are responsible for deleting unnecessary files to avoid retention of out-of-date information and wasting of vulnerable storage resources. For individuals this is particularly relevant for their C, D and network drives.

The IT department take back up copies of all data stored on the network drives every night but individuals have the responsibility for ensuring that proper back-ups of their data stored on local drives (C or D) are taken and securely stored.

Insurance

The use of equipment at home for XYZ work should be notified to your household buildings and contents insurers as this may well affect the cover under your policy.

Internet

Access to the Internet must be authorised by a head of department and must be used for company purposes only.

Email, Internet and telephone policy statement **A6.29**

In the previous two sections of this handbook, we provide an example of general IT policy statements (at **A6.27**), and of guidelines to staff on IT security (at **A6.28**).

This statement of policy aims to explain briefly:

- how employees are allowed to use email, telephones and the Internet using the company's facilities;

- how employees or the company may be liable in law for misuse of email or the Internet; and
- how the employee's interests and the company's interests can be protected.

This policy is not a definitive statement of what the company's facilities must not be used for. Employees must conduct themselves in a trustworthy and appropriate manner so as not to discredit or harm the company or its staff and in accordance with the spirit of this policy statement.

This policy applies to all telephone and computer users within the company (including, without limit, all directors, employees and third parties) who use email, bulletin boards, the worldwide web and the Internet through computers based at the company's premises or through any computers located at other sites (including private equipment) via the company's network or using the company's telephone lines. A breach of or refusal to comply with this policy is a disciplinary offence and is liable to result in disciplinary penalties including instant dismissal.

Authorised use

Email and Internet

The company encourages staff to use email as a method of communication in appropriate circumstances within the office and with third parties by the Internet. It will not always be appropriate to communicate by email and staff should always consider whether there is a more suitable method (for example, in circumstances where there is a need to preserve confidentiality or in the case of sensitive issues which should be communicated face-to-face).

Employees' use of e-mail and the Internet is only authorised for bona fide purposes directly connected with employers' work or the company's business. Employees are expected to exercise responsible and appropriate behaviour when using the company's computers and when sending email, whether internally within the company or externally using the Internet.

Unauthorised use of the Internet may expose both employees personally and the company to court proceedings including criminal liability. An employee will be held responsible for any claims made against the company arising out of any legal action brought as a result of the employee's unauthorised use of the internet. Unauthorised use of the internet and the company's computer system or breach of this policy is a disciplinary offence, which may lead to dismissal.

Telephone use

No personal calls should be made or received except in an emergency, when permission should be first obtained from a manager.

Employees should be aware that mobile telephones can be disrupting and distracting, and personal mobile phones should either be turned off or diverted during working hours.

Monitoring

The company reserves the right to listen to or have access to read any communication made or received by an employee using its computers or telephone system without notice for the following purposes:

- to establish the existence of facts;
- to ascertain compliance with regulatory or self regulatory practices;
- for quality control and staff training purposes;
- to prevent or detect crime;
- to investigate or detect unauthorised use of the company's telecommunication system;
- to intercept for operational purposes, such as protecting against viruses and making routine interceptions such as forwarding emails to correct destinations; or
- to check voice mail systems when staff are on holiday or on sick leave.

The company also reserves the right to make and keep copies of telephone calls or emails and data documenting use of the telephone, email and the internet systems, for the purposes set out above, and if it sees fit to use the information in disciplinary proceedings against employees. The company may bypass any password you set. You may only set passwords and security codes for your computer, the system or any part of it or documentation held on it in accordance with company policy from time to time.

All communications and stored information sent, received, created or contained within the company's systems are the property of the company and accordingly should not be considered as private.

Software

The company licenses computer software from a variety of outside sources. The company does not own this software or related documentation and, unless authorised by the software developer, does not have the right to reproduce it. The software used on the local area network or multiple or individual machines should have the appropriate licence(s) and employees should only use it according to the licence agreement.

Employees should notify their departmental manager or the IT manager of any misuse of software or associated documentation.

Security

The accessibility of the Internet is both an advantage and disadvantage of the system. Whilst employees can access a huge amount of information via the Internet, information and emails sent across the Internet may be read by persons unknown to the sender. Potentially anyone could read private and confidential information transmitted on the Internet. Even if some information has been deleted from your screen it may not necessarily be deleted from the Internet system which provides back up saving mechanisms. It is therefore essential that you notify any third party with whom you are communicating via the Internet that any email exchanged is transmitted over the Internet in an interceptable form. Any message or information requiring security or confidentiality should be distributed by an alternative means of communication.

Employees must not put on the Internet any material which incites or encourages or enables others to gain unauthorised access to the company's computer system. It is vital that all staff take all necessary steps to safeguard the company's computer system from viruses. Accordingly, employees should not exchange executable programs using Internet email and discard any documents or attachments which employees receive unsolicited. Employees must not introduce new software on to the company's system without written authorisation from the IT department and employees must always ensure that the appropriate virus checking procedures have been followed.

Courtesy

As emails can easily be misconstrued, employees must consider carefully whether email is the appropriate form of communication in particular circumstances and if employees decide that it is, consider carefully the content of the e-mail and who the recipients should be. It is inappropriate to send emails and/or attachments to people (whether they are other employees of the company or third parties) if the email does not relate to them or if the attachment cannot be read by them. In addition, sending emails needlessly to other people wastes their time and needlessly sending long files or attachments will cause delays in the system.

Defamation

The Internet is considered to be a form of publication and accordingly is within the scope of legislation relating to libel. Both words and pictures produced on the Internet are capable of being libellous if they are untrue, ridicule a person and as a result damage that person's reputation. Employees must not put any defamatory statement on to the Internet or on the company's computer system. As well as the employee being liable, the company can also be liable as an online provider.

Obscenity

The Internet has been abused by the distribution of child and other pornography. It is an offence to publish or distribute obscene material and this includes possessing, showing or distributing any indecent photographs or pseudo-photograph of a child (this includes a computer-generated photograph on the Internet). It is also an offence to display indecent material in public. The Internet qualifies as a public place. Employees must not send any such material using the company's system.

Discrimination and harassment

The company does not tolerate discrimination or harassment in any form whatsoever. This principle extends to any information distributed on the company's system or via the Internet. Employees may not put on either system any material which discriminates or encourages discrimination or harassment on racial or ethnic grounds or on grounds of gender, sexual orientation, marital status, age, ethnic origin, colour, nationality, religion or disability. To do so will lead to disciplinary action up to and including dismissal. Please also bear in mind the company's policy on discrimination and harassment.

Data protection

If employees are required to put information (including photographs) on to the company's system or the Internet containing personal data other than their own, employees must have the express written consent of the individuals to whom the personal data relates.

Board policy statement on fraud **A6.30**

The XYZ Group will deal with fraud within the framework of its statement on business ethics, and its security policy, which require a secure working environment to protect people, capital information and the assets from the risk of deliberate harm, damage or loss.

In particular:

- we require all employees to act honestly and in the best interests of the company at all times, and to ensure that XYZ acts with integrity in its dealings with third parties;
- we will ensure that effective controls and procedures are in place for preventing, detecting and dealing with fraud;
- we will ensure that all employees are aware of their responsibility to report details immediately to their line manager (or next most senior person) if they suspect that a fraud has been committed or see any suspicious acts or events;
- we will ensure that the controller is advised of any significant fraud or attempted fraud;
- we require management to investigate any allegations or evidence of fraud in consultation with the relevant security adviser and internal audit manager;
- we require employees to assist in investigations by making available all relevant information and by co-operating in interviews; and
- in appropriate cases, and after proper investigation, we will dismiss without notice employees who are found to be defrauding the company and, where appropriate, press for criminal prosecution and to seek financial recovery through civil proceedings.

All businesses and subsidiaries shall establish, and audit, procedures to ensure that this policy is fully implemented.

Notes

1 See eg ICAEW Internal Control and Financial Reporting – Guidance to Directors of Listed Companies Registered in the UK (December 1994).

2 COSO (1992, 2004 and 2013): Internal Control – Integrated Framework (1992 and 2013), and Enterprise Risk Management (2004), www.coso.org.

3 Note that the terminology of the post-2001 Standards means that 'an internal audit' is no longer an internal audit 'activity', it is now an 'engagement'. New terminology uses 'activity' in a different context, dispensing with terms such as 'Unit' or 'Department' in favour of:

'Internal Audit Activity – A department, division, team of consultants, or other practitioner(s) that provides independent, objective assurance and consulting services designed to add value and improve an organisation's operations. The internal audit activity helps an organisation accomplish its objectives by bringing a systematic, disciplined approach to evaluate and improve the effectiveness of governance, risk management and control processes.'

(Glossary of Terms to the new Standards of the Institute of Internal Auditors – see **App8**).

4 Information takes many forms and includes data stored on computers, transmitted across networks, printed out or written on paper, sent by fax, stored on tapes and diskettes, or spoken in conversations and over the telephone.

5 The protection of valuable or sensitive information from unauthorised disclosure or intelligible interruption.
6 Safeguarding the accuracy and completeness of information by protecting against unauthorised modifications.
7 This applies to record keeping, and most controls will already be in place; it includes the requirements of legislation such as the Companies and Data Protection Acts.
8 This will ensure that information and vital services are available to users when they need them.
9 This may be a part-time or full-time role for the allocated person.

Chapter A7

Family Firms and their Governance

> *'For the family-owned business, good governance makes all the difference. Family firms with effective governance practices are more likely to do strategic planning and to do succession planning. On average, they grow faster and live longer.'*
>
> John L. Ward, Clinical Professor of Family Enterprises at the Kellogg School of Management

Introduction A7.1

It is axiomatic that there is a family connected to most business start-ups. The parallel family commitment of the entrepreneur means the family interest in the business is quite likely to persist. Hence, some 75% of UK businesses are said to be family enterprises. The proportion is even higher in less mature economies – 95% in India, Latin America, the Middle East and the Far East.

Separation of ownership from control A7.2

Separation of ownership from control is less pronounced in family businesses than with listed companies. Indeed, there may be no separation of ownership from control. Some degree of separation will occur when subsequent generations of the family inherit shares within the business, and some of those family members are likely to be inactive in the direction and management of the business – a situation that can cause tensions which we discuss later.

While a likely lack of separation between ownership and management has its challenges, it can make decision-making more straightforward. When more generations of the family become involved in the business and more non-family members are amongst the management team, then there will be an increasing need for formal systems and a logical organisational structure.

Some degree of separation may also occur when the family floats a proportion of the equity of the business to unlock some of the value within the business for the benefit of the family, or to acquire additional capital for the benefit of the business. A problem can then arise that the new investors in the business may be minority shareholders with perhaps only 20% of the equity and with the family still controlling the other 80%. It is an obligation of the board to run the business in the best interests of the company and all of its shareholders, but the founder of the business or his or her successors may be psychologically unable, or may be unwilling, to make the transition from running the business in their own interests to now understanding that there is a clear distinction between the interests of the family and the interests of the company. Questions are currently being asked whether a free float of just 20%

should be sufficient for a company to be listed, or whether a free float of closer to 50% should be required.

General similarities between businesses of all forms A7.3

All companies – large or small, private or public – need effective management, including effective internal control and risk management. All must observe company and other law and regulations. But many of these requirements vary according to company size and depending upon whether the company is private or public.

Long-term thinking A7.4

Successful family businesses may be characterised by longer-term thinking than listed companies, where the priority of maintaining a good share price may encourage short-termism. Agency theory would suggest that the management of a public company may be less willing to forgo personal financial rewards than would be the case of a family business where the principals are also the management. Families are often willing to inject additional capital at no cost to the business from their own resources to keep a family business afloat, or when the family can see long-term potential in the business. So the cost of capital for a family business can be effectively lower than for a listed company. On the other hand, a listed company can have better access to both equity and loan capital: the more liquid the capital market in which it is listed, the lower its cost of capital. Clearly, the higher the cost of capital, the lower will be shareholder value.

Long-term thinking is likely to be a relative strength of a family business that is intent on building the business for future generations. The founding values are likely to give the business a strong identity. There is likely to be a strong commitment to making a success of the business, with business and family life being wrapped up with each other. Initially at least, the business and the family hierarchy are likely to be aligned. Family businesses often display a notable degree of paternalism towards their non-family employees, not too dissimilar to the traditional care by landed families of their workers. These qualities have often resulted in conspicuous levels of loyalty by non-family employees, with often entire families for several generations working for such family companies.

Of course, not all family businesses are characterised by long-term thinking. Many fail, perhaps early in their life, when the family takes too much value out of the business for its own benefit. Others fail through overtrading early in their life and running into liquidity problems. Some fail for both these reasons.

Trust A7.5

Although trust can break down for family businesses, especially when some family members feel disenfranchised despite being shareholders, generally they are run internally rather more on the basis of trust than on the basis of formal, laid-down procedures. This is particularly the case for family businesses that are small. A challenge is to introduce more necessary formality as the business grows, without losing the valuable flexibility associated with less bureaucracy. Failure to run the business more scientifically may result in the business failing or being acquired by new owners who see an opportunity to run the business more profitably.

Regulation **A7.6**

While it varies according to sector, in general small businesses suffer from less external regulation. Flying under the regulatory radar screen can be a strategic benefit. Growing the business above the level that attracts regulatory attention, requirements and costs can be a significant step change for the family business. Strategically, it may justify calling a halt to growth. Or it may suggest diversification so as to maintain the different business streams at a level which avoids costly regulation. What must be avoided is to ignore regulations which growth has made the company subject to. This is often the stage when the company looks for a buyer. Buyers may be willing to pay a considerable premium in order to 'take out' a company that threatens to acquire significant market share, or in order to acquire intellectual capital which enables the acquirer to maintain its position or to diversify. Although there can be economies of scale, the overheads associated with keeping a larger business under effective control may be unattractive, and not something that the entrepreneurial founder(s) of the business may be suited to achieving.

Private companies experience less public scrutiny. Their filed annual reports and financial statements are required to disclose much less. Small companies can avoid the requirement to have an annual audit, and the threshold which determines this is being raised regularly (see **D1.13**). They can run their businesses behind closed doors to a greater extent. Any obligations of their necessary membership of trade associations and professional bodies will tend to diminish this advantage, as will disclosure requirements when tendering for business. As they fall within the scope of regulation, more is likely to be in the public domain.

Growing a family business **A7.7**

While many family businesses make conscious or tacit decisions not to grow beyond a certain level of activity, others are more expansionist. Growth requires capital, in the form of loans or equity, when the growth cannot be financed from retained profits or from a positive cash flow. Even without the ambition of growth, or in parallel with it, there is likely to come a time when the founder or parts of the wider family wish to unlock some of their value in the business. If this is done through an initial public offering, owners from outside the family may become significant parties. The challenge then is for the entrepreneur and the wider family to adjust to the legitimate interests of the wider body of stakeholders, rather than running the business as before, when they may have made little distinction between their personal interests and those of the business. Founder entrepreneurs usually find it hard to adjust to this transition of partial ownership external to the family, and retaining a majority of shares within the family makes it easier to ride roughshod over the interests of outside providers of capital.

Solvency **A7.8**

When an ambitious young business seeks to expand organically without injection of new equity capital, there is often a risk of overtrading. Most cases when directors end up in court are to answer allegations of trading when insolvent. The majority of these involve directors of family businesses, and their family wealth is generally at stake. A director may be personally liable for losses incurred by third parties as a consequence of the business continuing to trade after it became insolvent. One of the challenges for a small family business is to ensure that the quality of management accounting information is of a high standard, so that at any time it is clearly apparent whether the firm is solvent or not. Another challenge is to interpret the insolvency tests correctly. A business is insolvent if it is unable to pay its debts when they fall due. A business is also insolvent if its balance sheet has negative value. If either is the case, the firm may continue trading if there is a reasonable expectation that rectification will occur in a timely way – for instance, through the injection of new capital. But this needs to be a considered judgement which can be defended in court. The understandable temptation is to soldier on, more in hope than expectation, not least because apparently similar crises may have resolved themselves on previous occasions. The risk is all the greater as many small firms in such circumstances may not have effectively functioning boards.

The life cycle of a frog **A7.9**

An illuminating analogy has been drawn between family businesses and the life cycle of a frog (tadpole, drowned frog, boiled frog and bull frog). Like the majority of *tadpoles*, many family businesses fail to survive because they are basically unhealthy businesses with an unsound business idea or a lack of requisite business acumen. Often these are founded on an emotional, rather irrational whim, and no amount of commitment can paper over the fundamental flaws. Then there is the *drowned frog* syndrome of the family business that fails because of over-ambitious management. Next is the *boiled frog*. It is said that if you drop a frog into a pan of boiling water it will immediately try to jump out, but if you place it in a pan of cold water which you then heat up slowly to boiling point, the frog will not notice the change and so will not try to escape its predicament. The equivalent to the 'boiled frog' is the family business that fails to adapt to change, because either it does not notice that the world is moving on or it lacks the motivation to adjust. Finally, there is the *'bullfrog'* family business where a dominant manager, usually but not always the founder entrepreneur, drives the business forwards and brooks no debate or dissent, with the consequence that terminal decline can set in. The 'bullfrog' is often associated with the occurrence of fraud or unethical behaviour. It will be apparent that the strategic advice that a properly functioning board of directors can give can be an effective antidote to these risks of failure, though not easy to achieve for small family businesses.

The generational ageing process **A7.10**

All businesses are at risk of an ageing process – of becoming set in their ways and not noticing the need for change. It takes time to establish a business approach and to establish business processes, and there can be a reluctance to reinvent these, or even a failure to see the need to do so. Family businesses have often floundered as one generation hands over to another. The second generation was brought up to appreciate, by observation and participation, the sterling efforts that the founder entrepreneur and perhaps his or her immediate relatives expended to build the business from scratch, and their total commitment to making a success of it. As such, the second generation is quite likely to have what it takes to move the business forward when the founder steps down. Indeed, the risk may be that the second generation is motivated to outperform the first generation, replacing prudence with excessive risk-taking in order to impress. The third generation, born with a silver spoon in their mouths and likely to have enjoyed a relatively pampered existence, may be less understanding of what it takes to run a successful business or less willing to expend the same energy.

Dissent **A7.11**

By the time the third generation is in charge, by inheritance, there are also likely to be many family owners who are not involved in the management of the family business and are suspicious and critical of those who are actively involved – on the basis that they appear to be running the family business to feather their own nests rather than to provide a reasonable return to the family members who are not active in managing the business. The non-active family members are likely to 'want out', particularly if the returns on their shareholdings are small or non-existent and the constitution of the business makes it difficult or impossible for them to dispose of their shares at what they consider to be fair value. So, at the risk of over-generalisation, family businesses are particularly vulnerable to decline or takeover when the third generation is in control:

> 'Those managing the firm may well feel that they are keeping the remainder of the family in the state to which they have become accustomed. They see themselves as doing the work and carrying the responsibility, while their relations enjoy the results and are free to criticise their efforts into the bargain. Equally, the members of the family who are owners but not managers may consider on their side that their interests as shareholders are being subordinated to the interests of those managing the firm.'

Objective management **A7.12**

It is therefore particularly important for family businesses to have a performance-based promotion policy, with objective performance appraisals, and to be open to recruiting non-family management. There needs to be fairness of rewards between active family members and those who are solely shareholders, as well as for non-family members of the management team.

Family councils **A7.13**

A family council, separate from the board, that meets regularly to discuss family and business issues, can be an excellent way to moderate dissent. Such a council may become a properly constituted family assembly over time. It will be necessary to set out who is entitled to membership: for instance, is membership open to family members by marriage? It will also be necessary to determine how the chair of the family assembly is chosen and who will speak for the family to the family business.

The importance of boards for family businesses A7.14

In general terms, corporate governance is the system or process by which entities are directed and controlled. More specifically, good corporate governance requires that owners and other stakeholders are well informed about the business so that they can exercise appropriate control from outside. In the case of a company, owners do this by electing the directors to the board, by voting on resolutions at general meetings, by making their voices heard to the board between general meetings, and by making informed decisions with respect to buying, holding and selling their shares in the business. Boards are responsible for setting direction, including future strategy, and overseeing the implementation of their direction by management. The board directs and oversees; management manages.

It is apparent, therefore, that the existence of a properly functioning board is essential if the corporate governance of a family firm is to be effective. Many founder entrepreneurs fail to appreciate the value of such a board, considering that it distracts management from focusing on day-to-day operations and represents an unnecessary overhead cost. Certainly, firms should monitor their total boardroom costs. Many founder entrepreneurs are reluctant to cede responsibility for running the board to someone else, such as an independent chairman, with the consequence that they run both the business managerially and also the board. The question arises as to whether this constitutes excessive concentration of power at the top of the business – all the more so when ownership is dispersed.

Non-executive directors of small businesses A7.15

There is also concern about whether outside, non-executive directors add value in a tangible way. A non-executive director who is a significant provider of capital to the family firm is likely to be tolerated, even welcomed; independent outside directors less so. Family businesses are likely to expect non-executive directors to bring to the business expertise that is otherwise lacking internally. This blurs the distinction between being non-executive and assuming executive responsibilities. The concern of management is likely to be the cost-benefit of having one or more non-executive directors on the board, and there may be a preference to structure non-executive rewards to track the future growth in the value of the company rather than to be paid in terms of directors' fees, which cash flow considerations are quite likely to mean that the business can ill afford. A family business needs to generate a lot of sales in order to retain enough funds to pay a non-executive director a fee of, say, between £20,000 and £30,000 a year plus expenses. So the family business may need to be willing to concede a small equity stake to its non-executive directors. It also needs to surmount the problem that at any time it is hard to place a value on the shares of a private company, and to realise that value at any future date may be problematic, as there may be no market even amongst existing shareholders.

While family businesses may be reluctant to appoint outside directors, such potential directors themselves should be cautious about accepting such appointments. 'A director is a director' and in many ways there are extra risks in becoming a director of a small business. The time commitment of a non-executive director on a small company board will not be much different from that on the board of a large listed company. The risks include poor quality information flow to the board, trading when insolvent, acting in the best interests of individual key managers rather than in the best interests of the company as a whole – and so on. It will probably be much more difficult to undertake an effective due diligence of a small family business, before accepting an invitation to join the board, than of a well-run listed company.

In many cases, the first non-executive director that a family business appoints is asked to establish an effective board and to chair that board.

Further reading

Neubauer, Fred and Alden G. Lank, (1998) *The Family Business – Its Governance for Sustainability* (Macmillan Business), foreword by John L. Ward who is Clinical Professor of Family Enterprises at the Kellogg School of Management.

Bollen, Dr. L.H.H., Prof. Dr. G.M.H. Mertens, Prof. Dr. R.H.G. Meuwissen, Dr. J.J.F. van Raak, Dr. C. Schelleman (October 2005): *Classification and Analysis of Major European Business Failures* [Research commissioned by the European Contact Group, based on original research by Argenti (1976)].

Cadbury, Sir Adrian, (2000) *Family Firms and their Governance – Creating Tomorrow's Company from Today's* (Egon Zender International).

Clarke, Philip, (1972): *Small Businesses – How they Survive and Succeed* (David & Charles).

Harvey-Jones, Sir John, (1988): *Making it Happen: Reflections on leadership* (Collins).

Chapter A8

Governance of International Organisations

Introduction A8.1

Many large companies started when an entrepreneur with a bright idea persuaded just a lone or few wealthy individuals, or more recently an investment fund, to back the idea with capital. This single owner, or small number of owners, would meet at intervals with the entrepreneur, who acted as the general manager, to make it clear how their investment should be used (ie to set the 'direction') and to check on management's process ('oversight'). But as, over time, the number of shareholders became greater, it then became necessary for the shareholders to elect from their number a small group to provide direction and oversight on behalf of all the 'company of shareholders'. Hence, the board of directors came to be.

Now, in the UK, it is no longer a requirement that directors should be found from amongst the company of shareholders. Furthermore, it is understood that 'the company' has a personality that is distinct from its shareholders, so the expression 'company of shareholders' is passé. Nevertheless, the shareholders comprise a most important element of what is the company. However, directors must act in the best interests of the company which may not, in individual cases where decisions are made, necessarily coincide with the best interests of the shareholders. The duties of directors are codified in the UK's Companies Act 2006, which gives emphasis to the wider range of responsibilities of directors. When a company is insolvent, the directors are responsible to run the company ion the interests of the creditors.

Separation of ownership from control A8.2

Thus, albeit largely by necessity rather than design, the separation of ownership from control came about. Boards of such companies became better able to resist pressure from individual shareholders, or from informal coalitions between small groups of shareholders. Minority shareholders' rights became better protected. The board became better able to concentrate upon building overall shareholder value in the medium to long term, relatively unimpeded by factional pressure from amongst the owners.

Of course, there have been challenges in this. For instance, the importance of the board accounting transparently to the company's owners has become a crucial plank of corporate governance. The ability of the owners to exercise effective control from outside has become a matter of concern. Frequently, it appears that the board of directors and senior management are running the company for their own personal benefit, especially with respect to the levels of executive remuneration and continuity of employment. To keep the shareholders quiet, the temptation of management has often been to go for short-term corporate advantage rather than managing for long-term success.

Agency (ie principal, agent) theory has been developed to give us a better understanding of the tensions between shareholders and management. Some, especially lawyers, regard the board of directors as the apex of management whereas, in a corporate governance context, it is better to consider the board as holding the ring between (executive) management and the owners.

The private equity case A8.3

The buyout of listed and large private companies by private equity firms has, in many cases, reversed the separation of ownership from control in the for-profit sector. Private equity groups claim to be much closer to management and to be better able to achieve a close alignment between board policy, management practice and owners' interests. Private equity firms usually are driven by their desire to exit their investment after a short period, perhaps of five years. They have been criticised therefore for pursuing a short-term strategy associated with aggressive cost cutting and asset stripping, etc. Their counter-argument is that there will be no buyers to enable their exit strategy unless they have kept real value within the company. But it is likely that under-performing assets will have been eliminated, meaning that the company no longer has any 'fat' to act as a buffer against future bad times.

Member states' representatives as board members A8.4

Where do international organisations fit within this range of corporate governance arrangements? They are set up by treaty or convention and represent a pooling of some sovereignty for a particular purpose or purposes as set out in the convention. While there are variations between the international bodies, the starting point is usually that each participant nation nominates one person to be that nation's representative on the governing body of the international organisation. Invariably the representative will be a citizen of the nation concerned and is likely to be a national specialist in the technical activity that is the business of the international body. Thus, almost all members of the Administrative Council, as the governing body is called, of the European Patent Office (EPO) are heads of their national patent offices.

Power to make policy, to set direction and to oversee the executive is vested in the governing body of the international organisation – but subject strictly to the provisions set out in the relevant convention.

Unlike with large public companies, there is thus no effective separation of ownership from control. The governing body is, in effect, the 'owners' of the international organisation – although 'owners' may not be quite the right word. Each member of the governing body is likely to have been nominated by one of the members of the international body, and each will regard it as his or her primary duty to represent the interests of his or her nation in the deliberations and decisions of the international body. On particular issues, informal coalitions are likely to be formed to force through the governing body decisions that suit some of the members.

Lack of independence A8.5

While the governing body of an international organisation is likely to be 100% non-executive, it is also likely that none of its members are independent, since one of the formal tests of independence is that the member of the governing body does not represent a significant 'owner' of the organisation.

The corporate governance deficit of international bodies **A8.6**

It is a moot point as to whether such a governing body of an international organisation corresponds more closely to the general meetings of members of a company, or to the meetings of a company's board. Broadly speaking, while such a governing body is likely to seek to discharge both roles, it is ill-equipped to do the latter for the following reasons:

- Inadequate independent oversight and judgement by members of the governing body.
- Inadequate influence by the organisation over the choice of membership of the governing body.
- Lack of balance of skills between governing body members. Technical competence (whether diplomatic, in the case of the UN, or patents experience in the case of the EPO, for instance) is likely to be present in abundance. But other requisite skills are more likely to be relatively absent from the governing body – such as financial, HR, strategy, risk management, public relations, corporate governance, board and committee chairmanship skills and experience). Governing body members are selected by the member states for their representational quality, not by the organisation in order to achieve a balance of competence on the governing body.
- The governing body is likely to spend inordinate time wrangling between the different interests of its member states, and too little time setting an effective direction for management to implement and supporting management to do so.

With respect to the third list item above, engineering companies have learnt that they can have too many engineers on their boards, and university governing bodies should not comprise an excessive number of academics. 'Leaving the lunatics to run the asylum' springs to mind as an analogy.

It is hard to avoid the conclusion that the system by which an international organisation is directed and controlled is deficient on account of the inability of the governing body to act as an effective board – to direct and oversee in the best interests of the entity. We have to accept that, while international organisations may be effective political organisations, they are unlikely to be effective and efficiently run businesses. Their costs compared to the economic value of their outputs are likely to be excessive.

Countermeasures **A8.7**

There are, however, measures that may be taken to mitigate these risks. Some of these measures, in some international organisations, would require modifications to the conventions that govern those organisations. Possible measures include:

- Appointing a number of external, independent members to the governing body.
- Appointing a number of external, independent members to committees of the governing body, such as to the audit committee.
- Contracting out to the private sector the delivery of some of the services for which the international organisation is responsible.
- Governing body succession planning, with top management lobbying of member states to communicate the organisation's competence gaps at governing body level.

- In an international body, it is particularly important for internal audit to be independent of the executive and to report directly to the board. Boards in international bodies (tending to be entirely or almost entirely non-executive, meeting only very infrequently and with members focusing on getting the best deal for those they represent) are not well placed to ascertain that their policies are being implemented by the executive and that there are no significant risks of which the board is unaware. These boards need independent assurance, and in part this can come from internal audit, if internal audit is sufficiently independent of the executive.

Further reading

de Cooker, Chris (editor), (2005): *'Accountability, Investigation and Due Process in International Organizations* [Martinus Nijhoff Publishers, Leiden/Boston, ISBN 90-04-14793-4].

Committee chaired by Sir Franklin Berman, (2004): 'Accountability of International Organisations' [to the 2004 International Law Association Berlin Conference, 2004, published in *International Organizations Law Review*, vol 1, pp 221–293, 2004].

Lewin, David, (2001): 'IR and HR perspectives on workplace conflict: what can each learn from each other?', *Human Resource Management Review* [Pergamon,11 (2001) pp 453–485 (www.HRmanagementreview.com)].

Chapter A9

Directors with Company Loans: Independence and Conflict of Interest Implications

Introduction A9.1

Here we draw on law, regulation and best practice from Europe, the UK, the US and Canada, to explore the legitimacy of granting loans to directors and the consequences in terms of director independence and board effectiveness and with respect to the roles to be discharged by independent directors only, such as membership of audit or remuneration committees.

Across the world, there are tight restrictions and requirements, often enshrined within law, on the granting of loans to directors and their associates. Rightly so, as loans to directors can abuse the interests of shareholders in general. It would be best to avoid loans and similar arrangements for directors. If they are to be made, it is strongly desirable that they are disclosed to the members of the company. Of course, the interests of confidentiality may mitigate against disclosure; but, where that is so, it amounts to a further reason for not granting the loan. Certainly, there should always be open disclosure to the board itself.

It is when the company's business includes money lending that directors' loans and similar arrangements of material size are likely to be allowed by law and regulation. Even so, directors and boards should consider carefully that it will usually be preferable for directors to arrange their credit requirements with other lending institutions. A contrary, traditional argument has sometimes been that a company prefers the credit needs of those associated with the company to be provided by the company itself, so as to avoid reputational damage should a breach of the terms of the loan occur, and to enable the company to monitor the financial conduct of its servants. This paternalistic argument, which falls foul of certain contemporary values, may have a degree of merit with respect to employees but not with respect to non-executive directors.

In some circumstances, the acceptability of a loan to a director may hinge on its materiality. Materiality should be considered from the perspective of the individual borrowing director as well as from the perspective of the company, and it should be reassessed periodically over the life of the loan.

Unless there is specific approval by the members of the company, loans to directors by a money-lending company should be made on terms available to the public at large, and the borrower should meet or exceed the standard credit criteria that the company applies. This should apply at the inception of the loan and be reassessed throughout its life. Otherwise, apart from other considerations, the director may be in receipt of a benefit – either from commencement of the loan or at some point during the life of the loan. An appropriate test to apply is whether the director could at any time move the loan to another lender on similar terms.

A director may become 'locked in' to the company for the purposes of the loan, perhaps due to a deterioration of the director's credit worthiness or a general tightening of the availability of credit in the market, neither of which, under the terms of the loan agreement, may require redemption of the loan. In such circumstances, the director would be unable to take his or her borrowing elsewhere. We are uneasy about the implications of this with respect to whether it should be deemed there is benefit to the director that should be quantified and disclosed, and whether there may be a further impact upon the director's independence in such circumstances. There may be tax implications as well.

For various reasons, we would say that a non-executive director in receipt of a loan or a similar arrangement should not be regarded by the board as being one of the board's independent directors. A board should come to this conclusion whether or not the loan includes an element of preference not available to the public at large, but particularly where it does include such a benefit. The most telling reason for our conclusion is that the board (and, in particular, the board of a money-lending company) must have a significant element of independent directors who are capable of viewing the company's financial services and other financial matters in an entirely disinterested, objective way; hence the disapproval of independent directors participating in performance-related remuneration schemes or belonging to the company's pension scheme (Financial Reporting Council, 2008).[1]

US regulation (New York Stock Exchange, 2003)[2] and UK best practice (FRC, 2008)[3] stipulate that half or more of the board of a listed company should comprise directors assessed by the board as being independent. US law and UK best practice both require for listed companies that each member of the board's audit committee should be an independent director;[4] and US (NYSE, 2003)[5] and UK (FRC, 2008)[6] best practice make a similar requirement for members of remuneration committees. The UK requirements are not so stringent for listed companies outside the FTSE 350.[7] UK mandatory regulation, in line with EC requirements, is less demanding than UK best practice guidance, the former only requiring that a listed company must have a body performing equivalent functions to an audit committee, with at least one independent director as a member (Financial Services Authority, 2008).[8]

Context **A9.2**

Whether, and in what circumstances, loans to directors are permissible or desirable will vary according to legal, regulatory and best practice requirements of nation states to whom companies are subject – as well as to the specific constitution of the company concerned. The extent to which a company has a policy of observing the highest standards of corporate governance is also relevant.

Statute law, mandatory regulation (such as listing rules) and codes of best practice are where we may expect the issues of loans to directors and directors' independence to be addressed. The extent to which this is so, and indeed the rigour with which this issue is addressed, varies significantly between nation states. Here we make use of a small number of these authoritative sources, from the UK, the EC and the US.

Legal requirements take precedence over the strictures of best practice guidance. Best practice is usually enshrined within corporate governance codes of best practice or within standards – for instance, the Corporate Governance Rules of the New York

Stock Exchange. While best practice may be enforced by listing rules, this is not invariably so. The Financial Services Authority, the 'enforcer' of the UK Listing Rules, interprets the FSA's main listing rule on the UK Corporate Governance Code as being merely a requirement for a listed company to disclose whether or not they comply with the main principles and the provisions of the Code.[9] On the other hand, as we shall see, the NYSE regards its Corporate Governance Rules as mandatory for listed companies, with the potential sanction of delisting for violations of those Standards.[10]

Law on loans to directors **A9.3**

Under the US Sarbanes-Oxley Act (2002), applicable to companies with primary or secondary listings in the US, a loan to a director is generally not permitted unless it is granted by a money-lending company so that the loan is in the ordinary course of the consumer credit business of the company, of a type that is generally made available by the company to the public, and is made on terms that are not more favourable than those offered to the general public.[11]

The UK Companies Act 2006 does not exclude, in all circumstances, directors receiving loans from their companies or benefiting from other types of financial arrangement such as quasi-loans, transactions with persons connected to directors or credit transactions.[12] But there are strict rules and a director who fails to observe these rules may be required to compensate the company. The rules are stricter for listed companies. In general, the transaction must be approved by a resolution of the company's members, although there are some derogations from this basic rule, such as if the value of the loan is small or if the company is a 'money-lending company', in which case a transaction with a director in the ordinary course of business and of a value not greater, nor on terms more favourable, than it would be reasonable to expect the company to extend to a person unconnected with the company does not need members' approval, whereas other loans to directors would require members' approval.[13] In cases where member approval is not required, it would be best practice to ensure that the board is fully informed.

It is widely the case, across legislations, that all directors have a general duty to act in the best interests of the company and not to benefit at the company's expense, although receiving a fee for being a director and holding shares in the company are generally regarded as permissible, even desirable. In the UK, the traditional duties of directors, vested in common law, have for the first time been codified within the Companies Act 2006.[14] The duty to act in the best interests of the company is expressed as to promote the success of the company for the benefit of the members as a whole. Other codified general duties (incumbent upon all directors, not just those deemed to be independent) include to exercise independent judgement and to avoid conflicts of interest.

Implications of financial distress or insolvency of the company **A9.4**

A director in receipt of a loan from the company could be in a difficult position if the company were insolvent at the time the loan was granted or became insolvent during the life of the loan. While this would more commonly be a problem for directors of small, private companies, we know, of course, that even very large companies become insolvent. When this happens, whether or not a new team or an insolvency practitioner replaces the old board, there is then an obligation to act first in the best interests of the company's creditors, and sentiment cannot be the determinant. So, for instance, Equitable Life sued the directors who were no longer on the board for £1.7 billion in an action that failed; and, in 2008, the new board of Northern Rock announced that it was taking legal advice as to whether there were grounds for the company to sue its previous directors. In neither of these cases was it loans to directors that were the issue; but, in other circumstances, loans to previous directors could provide a basis for the action.

All loans are, of course, a debt owed to the company and repayable as such. Any insolvency practitioner would pursue repayment accordingly. In the UK, if the loan were granted when the company was already insolvent (or became so within two years), the debt would also probably be recoverable as a preference to a connected person under section 239 of the Insolvency Act 1986. The insolvency practitioner might also consider whether the director's conduct amounted to misfeasance or a breach of fiduciary duty, which are grounds for disqualification of a director as being unfit to be a director of a company.

Law on independence — A9.5

While loans to directors may in some circumstances be legal, that is not of course to say that such a loan to a director may not impact upon the director's independence.

Except for section 173 of the Companies Act 2006, which requires *all* directors (whether executive or non-executive) to exercise independent judgement, UK law is silent on the criteria that should be applied in determining whether a particular director is independent. In the UK, this issue of 'independence' is addressed in some detail at the level of best practice guidance (see **App1**). US law, an EC Directive and the UK Listing Rules all draw a distinction between the director who is independent and the director who is not independent.

The US Sarbanes-Oxley Act (2002) sets out that all members of audit committees of quoted companies shall be independent[15] and provides two simple independence criteria, the first of which may make it inappropriate for members of audit committees to be beneficiaries of company loans or similar financial arrangements. This first SOX criterion is that an independent director shall not accept any consulting, advisory, or other compensatory fee from the issuer; the second criterion is that an audit committee member shall not be an affiliated person of the issuer or any subsidiary thereof. If a loan to a director is on preferential terms, its effect is equivalent to a 'compensatory fee'. Even if a loan to a director were not made on preferential terms, there is a risk that the director's judgement might be coloured by self-interest when the board is making decisions relating to the company's credit policy – in other words, that the director's independence may be impaired.

The 8th Directive of the European Union[16] requires only that at least one member of the audit committee of a public interest entity[17] shall be independent,[18] but independence is not defined in this Directive or elsewhere – for instance, in the revised 4th and 7th Directives.[19]

It is at least as important that members of remuneration committees should be free of significant borrowings as it is that audit committee members should be. It should be unacceptable to have significant borrowers determining the remuneration package and bonuses of the CEO on the one hand, and the CEO determining or agreeing the terms of their borrowings on the other hand.

Mandatory regulation on loans to directors **A9.6**

Unlike the UK's Corporate Governance Code, the New York Stock Exchange's Corporate Governance Rules are intended as mandatory for companies listed on that Exchange. Each listed company CEO must certify to the NYSE each year that he or she is not aware of any violation by the company of NYSE Corporate Governance Rules,[20] and the NYSE may issue a public reprimand letter to any listed company that violates a rule. If companies repeatedly or flagrantly violate NYSE listing rules, suspension and delisting remain the ultimate penalties.[21]

The NYSE Corporate Governance Rules require listed companies to adopt and disclose a code of business conduct and ethics for directors, officers and employees covering, *inter alia*, the handling of potential conflicts of interest, and to promptly disclose any waivers of this code for directors or executive officers.[22] NYSE Commentary on this rule refers to loans to directors in stating:

> 'A "conflict of interest" occurs when an individual's private interest interferes in any way – *or even appears to interfere* – with the interests of the corporation as a whole. A conflict situation can arise when an employee, officer or director takes actions or has interests that may make it difficult to perform his or her company work objectively and effectively. *Conflicts of interest also arise when an employee, officer or director, or a member of his or her family, receives improper personal benefits as a result of his or her position in the company. Loans to, or guarantees of obligations of, such persons are of special concern.* The company should have a policy prohibiting such conflicts of interest, and providing a means for employees, officers and directors to communicate potential conflicts to the company.' (italics added)

Mandatory regulation on independence **A9.7**

Another of the NYSE Corporate Governance Rules would specifically disallow a director to be regarded as independent if he or she were associated with a loan or other arrangement where he or she is an executive officer or an employee, or whose immediate family member is an executive officer, of a company that makes payments to, or receives payments from, the listed company for property or services in an amount which, in any single fiscal year, exceeds the greater of $1 million, or 2% of such other company's consolidated gross revenues.[23]

These NYSE Rules recommend that a board adopt and disclose categorical standards to assist it in making determinations of independence and then makes a general disclosure whether a director meets these standards. Any determination of independence for a director who does not meet those standards must then be specifically explained.

The independence definition under the NYSE Rules[24] requires that the board of directors affirmatively determines the following for each director:

1. No material relationship with the company (either directly or as a partner, shareholder or officer of an organization that has a relationship with the company). Material relationships can include commercial, industrial, banking, consulting, legal, accounting, charitable and familial relationships, among others.
2. Not an employee, nor whose immediate family member is an executive officer, of the company.
3. Does not receive, nor whose immediate family member receives, more than $100,000 per year in direct compensation from the listed company, other than director and committee fees and pension or other forms of deferred compensation for prior service (provided such compensation is not contingent in any way on continued service).
4. Is not affiliated with or employed by, nor whose immediate family member is affiliated with or employed in a professional capacity by, a present or former internal or external auditor of the company.
5. Not employed, or whose immediate family member is not employed, as an executive officer of another company where any of the listed company's present executives serve on that company's compensation committee.
6. Is not an executive officer or an employee, nor whose immediate family member is an executive officer, of a company that makes payments to, or receives payments from, the listed company for property or services in an amount which, in any single fiscal year, exceeds the greater of $1 million, or 2% of such other company's consolidated gross revenues.

(The above monetary amounts change from time to time.)

An 'immediate family member' is defined as including a person's spouse, parents, children, siblings, mothers and fathers-in-law, sons and daughters-in-law, brothers and sisters-in-law, and anyone (other than domestic employees) who shares such person's home. We are not aware that the 'close family' independence criterion within the UK's Combined Code has been defined,[25] so it might not be inappropriate for UK companies to be guided by this NYSE's definition. For further discussion of 'close family ties', readers should refer to **A3.13** to **A3.14** of this Handbook.

Best practice guidance on loans to directors and the potential impact upon their independence A9.8

To the best of our knowledge, the UK's Corporate Governance Code (set out in full at **App1**) gets closest to addressing this issue. Not only does it set out that an audit committee should comprise exclusively of directors who are independent, but it also sets out how a board should determine whether a director should be regarded by the board as an independent director. Companies compliant with this Code will ensure that at least half their board, excluding the chairman of the board in this count, is independent. In the case of companies smaller than the FTSE 350, the Code sets out that at least two of the directors should be independent.

The Cadbury Report (Cadbury, 1992), which gave us the world's first code of best practice for corporate governance, accepted for pragmatic reasons that neither receiving a fee for being a non-executive director nor holding shares in the company should invalidate a director's claim to being independent. Although clearly both of these might threaten to inappropriately colour a director's judgement on certain issues, it would be impractical to bar either. The UK Code regards a 'significant' shareholding as a criterion to apply when determining independence, and no beneficiary relationship (other than holding shares and receiving a director's fee) are ruled in for independent directors.

While Cadbury accepted that independent directors should be allowed to receive a fee for being a non-executive director and also to hold shares, both are nevertheless to be disclosed to members. Also disclosed to members is whether or not a director is deemed by the board to be independent. There is therefore a strong argument that loans to directors, if permissible and given, should also be disclosed to the members. The principal is the same and the UK approach to corporate governance is principles-based (Cadbury, 1992). Furthermore, if, notwithstanding a loan, the board concludes that the director should be regarded as independent, the board should explain their reasoning.[26]

The existence of a loan to a director, or a similar arrangement, is not specifically referred to within the UK Corporate Governance Code as a criterion to be applied in determining independence. Since other criteria given in the Code may challenge a director's effective independence in the same ways as might loans, we may reasonably conclude that boards should take account of directors' loans in determining independence and thus of suitability for membership of board committees, such as audit and remuneration, that require independence on the part of their members. Provision B.1.1 makes it clear that the given list of criteria for determining independence is not intended to be an exhaustive list. Beyond the given list of criteria, the Code also requires the board to consider whether an individual director is independent in character and judgement.

The rationale for our contention that a director's loan is an implicit independence criterion per the UK's Code is summed up as follows:

1. The board's assessment of a director's independence is required to consider 'independence of ... judgement', not just specific independence criteria.
2. The specific independence criteria listed in the Code are stated in the Code as not being an exhaustive list. Rather, the board should consider whether there are *any* relationships or circumstances which are likely to affect, or could appear to affect, the director's judgement, *including* those criteria listed in the Code.
3. The receipt of a loan or similar arrangement from the company may amount to 'a material business relationship with the company either directly, or as a partner, shareholder, director or senior employee of a body that has such a relationship with the company' which the Code specifically refers to. 'Material' is not defined by the Code. As we have stated, we can reasonably take it that materiality is from the perspective of the director rather than from the perspective of the company, since it is within a criterion for assessing the director's independence.
4. If the director's loan were not made on an arm's-length commercial basis, or if its continuation represented a benefit not available to the market generally,

then it would amount to the director having received, and continuing to receive, additional remuneration from the company apart from a director's fee. This is another Code criterion to be applied in assessing a director's independence.

Considerations might therefore include whether, when the loan was taken out, could the director have arranged it elsewhere and on similar terms? And, at any time during the currency of the loan, could the director obtain similar terms elsewhere? If the answer to the latter is negative, it might exacerbate the independence challenge beyond what it was at the time of the inception of the loan.

If the terms of a loan to a director are more beneficial to the director than the terms available to other customers with similar financial circumstances (ie if the terms were not at arm's length), the question arises as to whether the director has received an increased fee versus other directors (which can perhaps be dealt with through disclosure), whether he or she has obtained an illegal loan, and whether some executives in the company may have acted illegally.

The 2003 UK Higgs Report on the role of non-executive directors, as well as the 2003 UK Tyson Report on widening the gene pool from which non-executive directors may be recruited, both drew attention to the possibility that non-executive director fees, though modest for some, might be material for others, for whom they may have the potential to compromise director independence. Higgs (2003) put it that:

> 'it is important that a non-executive director is not so dependent on the income from their role or shareholding as to prejudice independence of judgement, and I would expect boards to take this into account in determining independence.'

and Tyson (2003) said:

> 'Institutional investors and other company stakeholders might wonder whether a NED can be truly independent if NED compensation represents a substantial fraction of his or her total annual income.'

Thus, if a loan or similar arrangement to a non-executive director, or to others closely associated with the director, is significant in the context of the personal circumstances of the director, then there is a stronger case for the board to regard the arrangement as meaning that the director should not be regarded as one of the members on the board who meets the independence tests.

The essence of materiality from the perspective of the company and the director may be captured within the concept of 'significant borrower'. For instance, two Canadian banks define a 'significant borrower' as one whose indebtedness to the bank exceeds 1/50th of 1% of the bank's regulatory capital if a natural person or, in the case of loans to entities, the greater of 1/20th of 1% of the bank's regulatory capital and 25% of the value of the entity's assets. Both these banks would consider a director as not being independent if he or she, as a natural person, were a significant borrower in these terms. In addition, one of these two Canadian banks would not consider a director independent if the director or the director's spouse controls, had a material influence over or was an employee or executive of an entity that was a significant borrower, or had an investment in such an entity equal to more than 15% of his or her net worth. If a loan below the level which would be caught by the 'significant borrower' criterion was 'not in good standing', then both banks would regard this as disqualifying the director from being considered independent.

References

Cadbury, Sir Adrian (1992) *Report of the Committee on the Financial Aspects of Corporate Governance* chaired by Sir Adrian Cadbury, 'The Cadbury Report', London: Gee & Co.

Financial Services Authority (FSA) (2008): *Implementation of the 8th Company Law Directive – Feedback on CP07/24 and final rules*. London: FSA.

Higgs, Derek (2003): *Review of the Role and Effectiveness of Non-Executive Directors*. London: The Department of Trade and Industry, chapter 9 on 'Independence'.

New York Stock Exchange (NYSE), (2003) *Corporate Governance Rules*. New York.

Tyson, Laura (June 2003): *The Recruitment and Development of Non-Executive Directors*, chaired by Laura Tyson, 'The Tyson Report', London: The Department of Trade & Industry, see Part X (p 16) on 'Constraints on Creating More Diverse Corporate Boards'.

Notes

1 UK Corporate Governance Code, Provision B.1.1:

'… The board should state its reasons if it determines that a director is independent notwithstanding the existence of relationships or circumstances which may appear relevant to its determination, including if the director: …

- has received or receives additional remuneration from the company apart from a director's fee, participates in the company's share option or a performance-related pay scheme, or is a member of the company's pension scheme; …'

2 Corporate Governance Rules of the New York Stock Exchange (approved by the SEC on 4 November 2003), Rule 1:

'Listed companies must have a majority of independent directors.'

3 UK Corporate Governance Code, Provision B.1.2:

'Except for smaller companies [outside the FTSE 350], at least half the board, excluding the chairman, should comprise non-executive directors determined by the board to be independent. A smaller company should have at least two independent non-executive directors.'

4 A slight watering down of the UK Corporate Governance Code requirement, that each member of the audit committee should be independent, is to be found in the Code Provision re-worded in June 2008 to read:

'The board should establish an audit committee of at least three, or in the case of smaller companies two, independent non-executive directors. In smaller companies the company chairman may be a member of, but not chair, the committee in addition to the independent non-executive directors, provided he or she was considered independent on appointment as chairman. The board should satisfy itself that at least one member of the audit committee has recent and relevant financial experience.'

The previous wording of this Provision had been:

'The board should establish an audit committee of at least three, or in the case of smaller companies two, members, who should all be independent nonexecutive directors. The board should satisfy itself that at least one member of the audit committee has recent and relevant financial experience.'

'Smaller companies' are those outside the FTSE 350. While revised Provision C.3.1 only countenances the chairman of a small company being appointed to the audit committee if he or she were independent when appointed as chairman of the board, one interpretation of Code Provision B.1.2 is that, after appointment as chairman of the board, he or she should no longer be considered as one of the independent directors. Provision B.1.2 reads:

'Except for smaller companies, at least half the board, excluding the chairman, should comprise non-executive directors determined by the board to be independent. A smaller company should have at least two independent non-executive directors.'

5 Corporate Governance Rules of the NYSE, Rule 5 (a):

'Listed companies must have a compensation committee composed entirely of independent directors …'

6 UK Corporate Governance Code, Provision D.2.1:

'The board should establish a remuneration committee of at least three, or in the case of smaller companies two, independent non-executive directors. In addition the company chairman may also be a member of, but not chair, the committee if he or she was considered independent on appointment as chairman. …'

7 See, for instance, the UK Corporate Governance Code, Provisions C.3.1 and D.2.1.

8 Financial Services Authority (June 2008): *Implementation of the 8th Company Law Directive – Feedback on CP07/24 and final rules* [R = Rule; G = Guidance]:

'7 Corporate governance

7.1 Audit committees

Audit committees and their functions

7.1.1 R An *issuer* must have a body which is responsible for performing the functions set out in *DTR* 7.1.3R. At least one member of that body must be independent and at least one member must have competence in accounting and/or auditing.

7.1.2 G The requirements for independence and competence in accounting and/or auditing may be satisfied by the same member or by different members of the relevant body.

7.1.3 R An *issuer* must ensure that, as a minimum, the relevant body must:

(1) monitor the financial reporting process;

(2) monitor the effectiveness of the *issuer's* internal control, internal audit where applicable, and risk management systems;

(3) monitor the statutory audit of the annual and consolidated accounts;

(4) review and monitor the independence of the *statutory auditor*, and in particular the provision of additional services to the *issuer*.

7.1.4 R An *issuer* must base any proposal to appoint a *statutory auditor* on a recommendation made by the relevant body.'

[Note: Article 41.3 of the *Audit Directive*]

9 That this is so is indicated by this exchange between the author of this handbook and the FSA:

QUESTION TO THE FSA: 'Is there anywhere an indication of your policy with respect to enforcement of 12.43(a)? Does the FSA ever admonish or sanction a listed issuer for (i) providing insufficient explanation, or (ii) not applying the principles (eg Morrisons with respect to 2003 Code Principle A.3)? Or are the Principles, in effect, discretionary?'

ANSWER FROM KEN RUSHTON OF FSA ON 10 SEPTEMBER 2003: 'On monitoring and enforcement our powers are limited. We look at a sample of Annual Reports to check they include a corporate governance disclosure statement in line with the Code, but I expect you appreciate we make no judgement on the quality or accuracy of these statements. This is a matter for investors to determine. We could take enforcement action against companies that refused to make any disclosure but this has not proved to be necessary. We have spoken to one or two companies whose statements were considered inadequate and they have done better next time.'

10 Corporate Governance Rules of the NYSE, Rule 13:

'The NYSE may issue a public reprimand letter to any listed company that violates a NYSE listing standard.

Commentary: Suspending trading in or delisting a company can be harmful to the very shareholders that the NYSE listing standards seek to protect; the NYSE must therefore use these measures sparingly and judiciously. For this reason it is appropriate for the NYSE to have the ability to apply a lesser sanction to deter companies from violating its corporate governance (or other) listing standards. Accordingly, the NYSE may issue a public reprimand letter to any listed company, regardless of type of security listed or country of incorporation, that it determines has violated a NYSE listing standard. For companies that repeatedly or flagrantly violate NYSE listing standards, suspension and delisting remain the ultimate penalties. For clarification, this lesser sanction is not intended for use in the case of companies that fall below the financial and other continued listing standards provided in Chapter 8 of the Listed Company Manual or that fail to comply with the audit committee standards set out in Section 303A.06. The processes and procedures provided for in Chapter 8 govern the treatment of companies falling below those standards.'

11 Section 402: Enhanced conflict of interest provisions

'(a) PROHIBITION ON PERSONAL LOANS TO EXECUTIVES.—Section 13 of the Securities Exchange Act of 1934 (15 U.S.C. 78m), as amended by this Act, is amended by adding at the end the following:

''(k) PROHIBITION ON PERSONAL LOANS TO EXECUTIVES.—

(1) IN GENERAL.—It shall be unlawful for any issuer (as defined in section 2 of the Sarbanes-Oxley Act of 2002), directly or indirectly, including through any subsidiary, to extend or maintain credit, to arrange for the extension of credit, or to renew an extension of credit, in the form of a personal loan to or for any director or executive officer (or equivalent thereof) of that issuer. An extension of credit maintained by the issuer on the date of enactment of this subsection shall not be subject to the provisions of this subsection, provided that there is no material modification to any term of any such extension of credit or any renewal of any such extension of credit on or after that date of enactment.

(2) LIMITATION.—Paragraph (1) does not preclude any home improvement and manufactured home loans (as that term is defined in section 5 of the Home Owners' Loan Act (12 U.S.C. 1464)), consumer credit (as defined in section 103 of the Truth in Lending Act (15 U.S.C. 1602)), or any extension of credit under an open end credit plan (as defined in section 103 of the Truth in Lending Act (15 U.S.C. 1602)), or a charge card (as defined in section 127(c)(4)(e) of the Truth in Lending Act (15 U.S.C. 1637(c)(4)(e)), or any extension of credit by a broker or dealer registered under section 15 of this title to an employee of that broker or dealer to buy, trade, or carry securities, that is permitted under rules or regulations of the Board of Governors of the Federal Reserve System pursuant to section 7 of this title (other than an extension of credit that would be used to purchase the stock of that issuer), that is—

(A) made or provided in the ordinary course of the consumer credit business of such issuer;

(B) of a type that is generally made available by such issuer to the public; and

(C) made by such issuer on market terms, or terms that are no more favorable than those offered by the issuer to the general public for such extensions of credit.

(3) RULE OF CONSTRUCTION FOR CERTAIN LOANS.—Paragraph (1) does not apply to any loan made or maintained by an insured depository institution (as defined in section 3 of the Federal Deposit Insurance Act (12 U.S.C. 1813)), if the loan is subject to the insider lending restrictions of section 22(h) of the Federal Reserve Act (12 U.S.C. 375b).''.'

12 Companies Act 2006; see these sections:

s 197: Loans to directors: requirement of members' approval;
s 198: Quasi-loans to directors: requirement of members' approval;
s 199: Meaning of 'quasi-loan' and related expressions;

s 200: Loans or quasi-loans to persons connected with directors: requirement of members' approval;
s 201: Credit transactions: requirement of members' approval;
s 202: Meaning of 'credit transaction';
s 203: Related arrangements: requirement of members' approval;
s 204: Exception for expenditure on company business;
s 205: Exception for expenditure on defending proceedings etc;
s 206: Exception for expenditure in connection with regulatory action or investigation;
s 207: Exceptions for minor and business transactions;
s 208: Exceptions for intra-group transactions;
s 209: Exceptions for money-lending companies;
s 210: Other relevant transactions or arrangements;
s 211: The value of transactions and arrangements;
s 212: The person for whom a transaction or arrangement is entered into;
s 213: Loans etc: civil consequences of contravention; and
s 214: Loans etc: effect of subsequent affirmation.

13 Companies Act 2006, s 206.

14 Companies Act 2006; see these sections:
s 170: Scope and nature of general duties;
s 171: Duty to act within powers;
s 172: Duty to promote the success of the company;
s 173: Duty to exercise independent judgment;
s 174: Duty to exercise reasonable care, skill and diligence;
s 175: Duty to avoid conflicts of interest;
s 176: Duty not to accept benefits from third parties; and
s 177: Duty to declare interest in proposed transaction or arrangement.

15 Section 301: Public company audit committees:

'Section 10A of the Securities Exchange Act of 1934 (15 U.S.C. 78f) is amended by adding at the end the following:

"(m) STANDARDS RELATING TO AUDIT COMMITTEES.—

(1) COMMISSION RULES.—

(A) IN GENERAL.—Effective not later than 270 days after the date of enactment of this subsection, the Commission shall, by rule, direct the national securities exchanges and national securities associations to prohibit the listing of any security of an issuer that is not in compliance with the requirements of any portion of paragraphs (2) through (6).

(B) OPPORTUNITY TO CURE DEFECTS.—The rules of the Commission under subparagraph (A) shall provide for appropriate procedures for an issuer to have an opportunity to cure any defects that would be the basis for a prohibition under subparagraph (A), before the imposition of such prohibition.

(2) RESPONSIBILITIES RELATING TO REGISTERED PUBLIC ACCOUNTING FIRMS.—The audit committee of each issuer, in its capacity as a committee of the board of directors, shall be directly responsible for the appointment, compensation, and oversight of the work of any registered public accounting firm employed by that issuer (including resolution of disagreements between management and the auditor regarding financial reporting) for the purpose of preparing or issuing an audit report or related work, and each such registered public accounting firm shall report directly to the audit committee.

(3) INDEPENDENCE.—

(A) IN GENERAL.—Each member of the audit committee of the issuer shall be a member of the board of directors of the issuer, and shall otherwise be independent.

(B) CRITERIA.—In order to be considered to be independent for purposes of this paragraph, a member of an audit committee of an issuer may not, other than in his or her capacity as a member of the audit committee, the board of directors, or any other board committee—

(i) accept any consulting, advisory, or other compensatory fee from the issuer; or

(ii) be an affiliated person of the issuer or any subsidiary thereof.

(C) EXEMPTION AUTHORITY.—The Commission may exempt from the requirements of subparagraph (B) a particular relationship with respect to audit committee members, as the Commission determines appropriate in light of the circumstances.

(4) COMPLAINTS.—Each audit committee shall establish procedures for—

(A) the receipt, retention, and treatment of complaints received by the issuer regarding accounting, internal accounting controls, or auditing matters; and

(B) the confidential, anonymous submission by employees of the issuer of concerns regarding questionable accounting or auditing matters.

(5) AUTHORITY TO ENGAGE ADVISERS.—Each audit committee shall have the authority to engage independent counsel and other advisers, as it determines necessary to carry out its duties.

(6) FUNDING.—Each issuer shall provide for appropriate funding, as determined by the audit committee, in its capacity as a committee of the board of directors, for payment of compensation—

(A) to the registered public accounting firm employed by the issuer for the purpose of rendering or issuing an audit report; and

(B) to any advisers employed by the audit committee under paragraph (5).''.'

16 Revised version adopted in 2006.

17 The EC allows that member states may determine what shall be regarded as a public interest entity. The UK has limited this to listed companies.

18 European Commission, 8th Directive, Article 41:

'Audit committee

1. Each public-interest entity shall have an audit committee. The Member State shall determine whether audit committees are to be composed of non-executive members of the administrative body and/or members of the supervisory body of the audited entity and/or members appointed by the general meeting of shareholders of the audited entity. At least one member of the audit committee shall be independent and shall have competence in accounting and/or auditing …'

19 Also revised in 2006.

20 Corporate Governance Rules of the NYSE, Rule 12:

'(a) Each listed company CEO must certify to the NYSE each year that he or she is not aware of any violation by the company of NYSE corporate governance listing standards.

Commentary: The CEO's annual certification to the NYSE that, as of the date of certification, he or she is unaware of any violation by the company of the NYSE's corporate governance listing standards will focus the CEO and senior management on the company's compliance with the listing standards. Both this certification to the NYSE, and any CEO/CFO certifications required to be filed with the SEC regarding the quality of the company's public disclosure, must be disclosed in the company's annual report to shareholders or, if the company does not prepare an annual report to shareholders, in the companies annual report on Form 10-K filed with the SEC.

(b) Each listed company CEO must promptly notify the NYSE in writing after any executive officer of the listed company becomes aware of any material noncompliance with any applicable provisions of this Section 303A.'

21 See note 10 above.

22 Corporate Governance Rules of the NYSE, Rule 10.

23 Corporate Governance Rules of the NYSE, Rule 2.

24 Corporate Governance Rules of the NYSE, Rule 2.

25 UK Corporate Governance Code, Provision B.1.1 includes this criterion which should normally preclude a director from being regarded as independent:

'has close family ties with any of the company's advisers, directors or senior employees.'

For discussion of 'close family ties', readers may refer to **A3.13** to **A3.14**.

26 UK Corporate Governance Code, Provision B.1.1:

'... The board should state its reasons if it determines that a director is independent notwithstanding the existence of relationships or circumstances which may appear relevant to its determination, including if the director ... represents a significant shareholder; ...'

Part B:
Guest Chapters

Chapter B1

Avoiding the Pitfalls in Running a Private Company

Introduction B1.1

We are very grateful to the Institute of Chartered Accountants of Scotland for permission to reprint this guidance. No responsibility for loss occasioned to any person acting or refraining from action as a result of any material in this publication can be accepted by the authors or the publishers.

Alice Telfer would be pleased to hear from readers with any inquiries about this guidance. She is Assistant Director, Business Policy and Public Sector, The Institute of Chartered Accountants of Scotland, CA House, 21 Haymarket Yards, Edinburgh, EH12 5BH.

AVOIDING THE PITFALLS IN RUNNING A PRIVATE COMPANY: A PRACTICAL GUIDE FOR DIRECTORS

The members of the Institute's Business Law Committee who took part in this initiative were:

Lorraine Bennett
KPMG LLP

Andrew Brown
Baker Tilly International, Brussels

Chris Fletcher
Baillie Gifford & Co

Kenneth Gilmour (Convener)
Standard Life plc

Paul Hally
Shepherd and Wedderburn LLP

John Langlands
British Polythene Industries PLC

Robin McGregor
Christie Griffith Corporate Ltd

John Moffat
Grant Thornton UK LLP

Robert Pattullo
Archangel Informal Investment Ltd

Greig Rowand
Henderson Loggie

Becky Woodhouse
PURE Spa

Charlotte Barbour (Secretary)
The Institute of Chartered Accountants of Scotland

It should be noted that the members of the Committee were acting in their personal capacity and were not representing the organisations for which they work.

Foreword

By Jim Mather CA MSP
Minister for Enterprise, Energy and Tourism
The Scottish Government

In order to manage and grow a company successfully the members of the board need to know what is expected of them, both individually and collectively, and how to measure the achievement of these expectations. Using the well-established principles of corporate governance which have developed in the UK over the last fifteen years for listed companies, this booklet sets out a framework of governance suitable for private companies. It shows how this can be applied in a positive way, based upon the size of the company and the nature of any external investment.

This guide is designed to be practical and to assist directors when establishing or reviewing the company's governance procedures. It can also be used by someone who is asked to become a director, to help him or her in evaluating whether or not to join the company board.

I am pleased to support this publication by the Institute of Chartered Accountants of Scotland. It reinforces the reputation of ICAS as a provider of useful guidance to both its members and the wider business community.

Jim Mather
April 2008

Introduction

Good governance focuses on the relationships between board members, evaluating internal controls and it should support the leadership of the company by setting good standards of business behaviour. In doing so, it should improve the long term value of the company and assist in bringing discipline and accountability.

The Institute of Chartered Accountants of Scotland is pleased to publish this guide for the use of individual directors and for boards of private companies. Although corporate governance codes have been developed for publicly listed companies, we believe that the key principles and benefits are important to businesses of all sizes.

The Combined Code on Corporate Governance (the Code) sets out principles that need to be applied, and provisions with which listed companies are expected to comply, or to explain why they have not. However, for a smaller, private company, compliance with some or all aspects of the Code may not be practical or even appropriate. This guide considers those principles of the Code that we believe are the most relevant to private companies and discusses the manner in which they might be usefully applied. The main principles of the Code are included in Appendix E for information.

This guide is for:

- directors of a company who wish to apply a sound system of management and control as the company grows and develops
- individuals who are asked to join a business as a director to help them to assess the level of governance in the business
- shareholders of privately owned companies to benchmark the governance in the company against best practice
- external investors to assess what might be an appropriate level of governance for unlisted companies.

This guide is not intended to be prescriptive but simply to suggest ways in which private companies may develop good practice in governing their affairs. The board is responsible on a collective basis for ensuring that the company is well run on a day to day basis and is meeting its short and long term priorities. For the growing company the guide also provides a pathway to the framework set out in the Combined Code. The guide considers the collective responsibilities of the board, the role of each director, and risk management and internal controls. The practical implications of how each topic can be applied depending on the company's ownership are also considered.

The different stages of ownership of a company specifically identified in this guide are:

1 100% private ownership, either start-up or mature situation, i.e. the owner-managed company

2 100% private ownership, but with external commitments such as bank loans

3 Private ownership but with some shareholders who are not involved in the management

4 No longer in private ownership, for example, due to an AIM or full listing.

This guide focuses on the first three stages and Appendix B provides a brief series of questions designed to encourage debate about how a company is governed and whether oversight processes could be improved.

1 THE COLLECTIVE RESPONSIBILITIES OF THE BOARD

'Every company should be headed by an effective board, which is collectively responsible for the success of the company', according to the Combined Code. This is equally relevant for the private company. The board needs clarity of its role and responsibilities. The simplest way of doing this is to set these out in a board 'charter' which can be monitored and revisited on an ongoing basis. The responsibility of the board is to direct the affairs of the company to maximise its value for its shareholders and stakeholders as a whole. In doing so, the board must ensure the company complies with its articles as well as relevant legal, regulatory and governance requirements. The following paragraphs outline the collective responsibilities of a board and how they may apply in practice to the private company.

The Responsibilities of the Board

The board's key responsibilities are to:

- establish clear purpose, vision and values
- set appropriate strategy and structure
- delegate day-to-day authority to manage the business to management, monitor management's performance and hold them to account
- establish proper risk management and internal control frameworks
- provide leadership.

Practical considerations for the private company:

- In an owner-managed company the distinction between the board and the management may be blurred or non-existent. Nevertheless, time should be allowed for consideration of purpose, strategy and structure, risks and internal control.
- The growing company, with increasing staff numbers and external financing, should be encouraged to formalise the key responsibilities by discussing the board's role and setting it out in a clear statement.
- Any non-executive directors on the board should lead the monitoring of management performance, the challenge to the vision, values, strategy, risk management and internal controls, and should ensure that the board provides appropriate leadership.
- A company is unlikely to remain static and therefore its strategy and direction will evolve, meaning that the key responsibilities should be revisited on a regular basis.
- The board should have appropriate documentation to reflect and communicate the company's mission, business plan, and delegations. Appendix A shows a list of the range of documents that may be appropriate.

Matters Reserved for the Board

To make sure the board can exercise its oversight responsibilities, it retains approval authority for certain specific matters. These should be formally documented in a schedule of matters reserved and, in our view, would reserve to the board the approval of:

- changes to capital
- payment of dividends
- corporate objectives, strategies and structure
- corporate plans and all material changes to the corporate plans
- operating and capital budgets and all material changes to these budgets
- material transactions (e.g. acquisitions, disposals, starting or ceasing a business activity)

- the financial statements
- any borrowings or guarantees
- relevant external communications e.g. with any regulator or shareholders
- the appointment and remuneration of directors
- any authorities delegated to management
- political and charitable donations
- company policies
- compliance with legislation, for example in the areas of company law, employment, environmental matters, health and safety, wrongful trading and competition laws.

Practical considerations for the private company:

- Arguably, the smaller the company, the more important it is to identify someone else, such as the person providing company secretarial services, who can undertake the necessary oversight and operational decisions if need be, or in case of an emergency such as when the director(s) are not available. Alternatively, the owner manager may wish to appoint a power of attorney in case of such emergencies.
- In an owner-managed company those responsibilities undertaken by the owner manager and those delegated to staff should be clearly distinguished and understood.
- As the company grows there should be a regular review of which matters are reserved and which authorities are delegated.

Delegations of Authority

Operational matters need to be delegated in order to ensure the smooth running of the business and to allow the board to focus on its primary role. A schedule of delegations of authority should be established, which sets out the parameters of the delegated authority and particularly any financial limits. Areas that could be covered in the scheme of delegation include:

- opening bank accounts and authorising payments
- general purchasing powers/budgets
- signing of leases
- signing of regulatory documents
- powers of attorney
- external communication
- staff recruitment and remuneration
- health and safety operations
- compliance with current legislation, in particular, employment, health and safety and tax.

Practical considerations for the private company:

- In a smaller company the owner-manager usually retains responsibility for many of the above matters. It should be clear what areas are delegated, if any.
- As the company grows the owner/board needs to develop a systematic means of delegating authority and formalising this.
- Delegated authorities ought to be reviewed periodically to ensure that they are complied with and that the authorities remain appropriate for the size of the enterprise and its management structure.

Board Meetings

The board should meet often enough to complete its statutory and regulatory responsibilities and to exercise its oversight role properly. Good practice can be summarised as:

- an agenda should be prepared by the chairman and company secretary
- the agenda and any supporting papers should be circulated with sufficient time to allow directors to prepare for the meeting
- formal minutes of the meeting should be taken, ensuring all decisions are recorded and giving a flavour of the challenges and questioning raised by directors
- the minutes should include an action plan to ensure decisions are followed up in a reasonable timescale
- the meeting should monitor progress against the approved plans and budgets and ensure proper coverage of the matters reserved.

Practical considerations for the private company:

- In an owner-managed company it is good practice to set aside time for regular formal board meetings (and not just extend informal management meetings), at least to consider those aspects set out above.
- As a company grows, and particularly when external finance is introduced, the board may be expected to meet more frequently; for example on a monthly basis or around times when key reporting requirements are to be met (e.g. completion of annual report).
- It is also helpful to have documented procedures to deal with urgent issues which require board approval and arise between timetabled board meetings.
- Despite the Companies Act 2006 no longer requiring a private company to hold an AGM, companies with shareholders who are not involved in the management of the business may benefit from the discipline of a formal meeting to review the past year's activities and results, and the future prospects of the company.

Implementation and Compliance Schedules

The company should prepare, and keep updated, implementation schedules which show when the various financial, legal and regulatory requirements require to be completed and who is responsible for completing them. The schedules may include:

- preparation of accounts and their approval by the board
- filing accounts with Companies House and HMRC
- tax returns and payments
- preparation and submission of annual return to Companies House
- health and safety reviews and risk assessments
- employment matters.

Practical considerations for the private company:

- These principles are relevant regardless of the size or ownership of the company.
- Matters to be addressed in a compliance schedule are included at Appendix A.
- A specific individual should be responsible for monitoring the compliance schedule on a monthly basis. It is important to be aware that criminal penalties can arise from failure to comply with the submission deadlines. It is the directors who are responsible for company compliance and passing this work on to an adviser does not transfer this responsibility.

2 THE ROLE AND RESPONSIBILITIES OF INDIVIDUAL BOARD MEMBERS

An effective board should have a balance of skills and experience that is appropriate for the size and requirements of the business. In the smallest owner-managed companies it is probable that all responsibilities will fall on one or two people but as the company grows, so should the board. At the stage when a company wishes to list, the Combined Code expects a balance of executive and non-executive directors, and that the chairman should be separate from the chief executive. The following paragraphs outline the individual board members' responsibilities and how they may be undertaken in the private company as it grows and develops.

The Chairman

The chairman is appointed by the board and his duties include responsibility for:

- leadership of the board
- setting the board agenda and ensuring that directors have accurate and clear information
- the effectiveness of board meetings, including the induction, training and development of members of the board

- ensuring the company has an appropriate strategy, objectives, and risk controls
- communications with the shareholders.

Practical considerations for the private company:

- In a private company without external shareholders it is unusual to find the roles of chairman and chief executive as separate appointments. However, the individual fulfilling these two roles should remember that the responsibilities of each are separate and distinct.
- An independent chairman may be best practice but in a small company this is unusual and may not be commercially justifiable.
- Once a company has external financing and/or shareholders who are not involved in the management, it should have a chairman who is separate from the chief executive.

The Chief Executive

The chief executive is appointed by the board, and is responsible for managing the day to day business of the company and should have clear authority from the board to do so.

Practical considerations for the private company:

- A smaller company is usually run by its owner who assumes a range of roles. As the company grows it is best practice for the decision-making in the company to be spread between several (executive) directors or management.
- When a company seeks external financing, the role of the chief executive should be more clearly defined to be responsible for overall management of the business. With external financing there are new responsibilities on the management team and the board should consider whether it needs to recruit new directors.
- Once a company has shareholders who are not involved in the management, the chief executive should have a clearly defined role reporting to a board of directors.

The Secretary

Despite the fact that under the 2006 Companies Act a private company no longer needs to appoint a company secretary, the functions that the company secretary carries out remain. These consist of fulfilling the legal necessities and administration associated with running the company.

Practical considerations for the private company:

- In an owner-managed small company it may appear unnecessary to appoint a secretary; however, all the associated tasks should be included on a compliance schedule (see Appendix A) and allocated to a specific individual or individuals.
- A private company with only one director should consider appointing a company secretary so that there is more than one officer of the company in order to act if the director is incapacitated.
- With external shareholders, one person should have overall responsibility for shareholder information and dealing with shareholder communications.

Executive Directors and Non-Executive Directors

Executive directors have day-to-day management responsibilities, in addition to their responsibilities as members of the board. They are usually employed on a full-time basis by the company.

The role of non-executive directors is to participate fully in the functioning of the board, advising, supporting and challenging management as appropriate. They may be independent with no other links with the company (see Appendix C for the definition of an independent director). In particular, a non-executive director should:

- have suitable experience
- challenge and contribute to the development of strategy
- scrutinise the performance of management against the objectives of the company
- seek to ensure the integrity of financial information
- determine appropriate levels of remuneration and consider succession planning.

Practical considerations for the private company:

- In an owner-managed company a non-executive director may bring different experience and an external, more objective, viewpoint to the board.
- As a company grows, with wider responsibilities and external commitments, this should be reflected by giving consideration to introducing and/or increasing the number of non-executive directors.
- External investors will frequently insist on a non-executive director and the investor may assist in the appointment.

The Appointment of Non-Executive Directors

In selecting someone for appointment as a non-executive director, it is appropriate to consider the following:

- skills and experience
- professional qualifications
- references
- other appointments
- potential conflicts of interest
- sufficient time available to devote to the role
- likely remuneration package
- role and specific responsibilities on the board.

There should be a formal letter of appointment of the non-executive director which should detail the amount of time expected to be committed to the company and the basis of remuneration. (An executive director should have a service contract detailing his or her terms and conditions.)

Practical considerations for the private company:

- Points that may be addressed in a letter of appointment are noted in Appendix C.
- Period of appointment: Companies may appoint a non-executive director for a fixed period such as an initial three-year period, which can be renewed for further three year periods, as recommended in the Code. However, other companies may prefer the flexibility of an open ended agreement and this is common in private companies.
- The overall length of service should be carefully considered from the points of view of external perceptions and value to the company. In a highly specialised industry it may take a period of time for a non-executive director to become familiar with the business.

3 RISK AND INTERNAL CONTROL

The board's responsibilities identified earlier include the key elements of risk management and internal controls. Risk is an inherent part of being in business, and risk management is concerned with identifying, assessing, monitoring and mitigating risk, not necessarily removing it. An effective system of internal control is key to robust risk management. There should be a set of clearly documented procedures that tell those responsible what they must do or not do and, as part of an effective control system, there need to be regular checks to ensure that the procedures are operating effectively. The Combined Code states 'the board should maintain a sound system of internal control to safeguard shareholders' investment and the company's assets'.

The following paragraphs outline key aspects of risk management and internal control and how these may apply in the private company. The practical application will depend on a number of factors including the number of employees, the levels of delegation, the nature of the business and geographical spread, and the complexity of the company's practices and procedures.

Risk Management

A company should ensure that it has a continuous risk management process. This involves:

- agreeing the company's appetite for risk, for example, in some industry sectors the business model may be based on taking a higher degree of risk than competitors in order to achieve a premium price or other market advantage
- identifying the risks in the company's strategy; including strategic, operational, financial, regulatory, environmental or political risks
- taking appropriate measures to mitigate the risks identified
- establishing controls and review procedures to ensure that risk management is effective, and
- updating and improving these processes in the light of experience.

Practical considerations for the private company:

- In an owner-managed company risk management is generally addressed by the owner but is rarely documented, although making notes of even simple assessments can provide a focus to decision making and risk mitigation.
- A simple SWOT (strengths, weaknesses, opportunities and threats) analysis can be beneficial to identify key risks and opportunities.
- Understanding risk should be a company-wide responsibility but often in a smaller company it will be either the chief executive or finance director who will shoulder most of this responsibility. Where possible, involvement of other staff will almost always add to the effectiveness of the process.
- Professional advisers may be of assistance in identifying key risks and controls.
- In the growing company, reporting and monitoring procedures should be put in place so that the senior management team, board, and ultimately the shareholders, can be confident that risks are being properly identified and managed.
- In larger companies the creation of a risk management committee involving senior managers and directors should create the basis for more effective analysis of risks.
- A risk management policy needs to be regularly revisited to ensure that the company learns from its own experience, makes use of relevant industry knowledge, and takes account of changes in the external business environment.

Company Policies and Internal Controls

Company policies and procedures set out standards of behaviour and responsibilities for staff and the internal controls are the checks to ensure they are being properly applied. Policies are likely to be required across all aspects of the business to varying degrees depending on the scale and nature of the company's operations. These policies may cover the following:

- anti-fraud
- anti money-laundering
- business continuity
- internal and external communications
- human resources, remuneration, allowable expenses, and compliance with current legislation
- information security and reliability
- outside appointments
- purchasing/procurement
- records management
- regulatory compliance
- health and safety compliance

An internal control system should consist of policies, procedures, allocation of responsibilities, and checks to ensure these are functioning. The system is unlikely to remain effective, however, unless it is reviewed regularly, and developed as the business grows to take account of new and emerging risks, control failures and market expectations or changes. Internal controls should include some or all of the following:

- Authorisation limits
- Segregation of duties
- Accounting reconciliations and monitoring of cash flow
- Suitable qualifications and training
- Budgetary controls
- Controls over incoming funds, expenditure and access to bank accounts
- Security of premises and control over assets

Practical considerations for the private company:

- Smaller owner-managed companies with few employees handle risks and controls quite informally but as a company grows a more formal system of internal control will become necessary.
- Basic control policies usually start with financial controls, insurance requirements, and health and safety.
- Strong financial controls and the ability to monitor any covenants will be essential if external financing is sought.
- Without regular review and monitoring of cash management, particularly in cash strapped companies, there may be exposure to wrongful trading or insolvency.
- As the company grows, the basic controls can be extended and, thereafter, the company should evaluate the level of risk attached to the above topics and the way in which these are controlled.

Business Continuity

A continuity plan should identify the key people and processes in an organisation which could place the company at risk if they were not available for whatever reason. The key areas are likely to include:

- key personnel – directors, managers, staff with specific skills, knowledge or licences
- premises
- IT systems
- supply chain
- customer, staff and supplier communication channels
- payroll, banking and financial systems.

The continuity plan should include an action plan for the company to continue to operate if something should happen in one of the identified key risk areas, including a timescale within which a back up resource must be made available. Reasons could include:

- unexpected death or serious illness of a key member or members of staff
- IT system crash or virus attack
- an unforeseen incident at any point in a company's supply chain
- loss of a single supplier, distributor, or customer
- payroll or financial system crash
- fire at company's premises.

The company should consider back-up procedures, which could include:

- regular back-up to a remote server for IT systems

- delegating key tasks to nominated alternative company personnel in the event of an emergency, with training to ensure alternative personnel are well briefed and competent
- ensuring that key company processes do not rely solely on one person within the organisation especially, for example, access to the company bank account or payroll system
- documenting emergency plans and alternative procedures if a company's supply chain or customer communications is affected, to minimise down-time, or if a company's premises are destroyed or otherwise unavailable.

Practical considerations for the private company:

- These principles are relevant to all private companies.
- In an owner-managed company, whilst it is good practice and advisable to consider business continuity this is not always undertaken due to time and cost restraints. Nevertheless a basic plan covering the key areas could possibly save the company if something unexpectedly goes wrong.
- Any business plan should be tested to establish as far as possible whether it works in practice, with any learning points identified in the test reflected in a revised plan. Testing might usefully involve third parties who have been identified as key elements of the continuity strategy.
- Many well run companies have a company manual, which consists of a documented record of the elements which have been discussed in this section, including key personnel and their responsibilities, the main company policy documents, and a risk register. Creating a comprehensive manual, and then reviewing it regularly, assists the board in governing the company in a structured manner. A company manual should also enable a person to cover someone else's responsibilities if necessary and therefore provide part of the contingency planning.
- In any private company, and in particular in an owner-managed company, it is important to consider a succession plan. This may need to be revisited periodically and plans are required to work towards its fulfilment. For example, will a younger member of the family take over, or do the owners have an ambition to sell to a rival, or float on AIM? If a company is seeking external investment or for the shareholders to sell out it is beneficial to have had, for example, a non-executive director, minuted board meetings, regular budgeting and so on to show that there is a proven record from which to negotiate.

Code of Business Conduct

Successful companies benefit from the highest standards of professional and ethical conduct from all directors and employees. A code of business conduct sets out these standards and supports and enhances a company's core values and culture. The existence of such a code also presents the company favourably externally. The principles of effective business conduct include:

- compliance with all applicable laws, regulations, and professional conduct standards
- high standards of service
- avoiding personal or financial conflicts of interest
- not being compromised through any unwarranted preferential treatment given to or accepted from customers, suppliers, or others
- communicating honestly and accurately with all stakeholders
- integrity and honest, ethical business practice
- contributing to the social and economic wellbeing of the community
- treating customers, suppliers and employees fairly and supporting employees' learning and development.

Practical considerations for the private company:

- Whilst this may initially appear to be an exercise for the larger company, all companies can benefit from formally considering and documenting the manner in which they wish to conduct their business and ensuring the company's values are applied in all the company's operations.
- With increasing numbers of staff it is useful to have the ethos of the company clearly expounded for induction, training and even disciplinary action purposes.

APPENDICES

Appendix A: Company Documents and Compliance Schedule

Company Documents

Written statements, in the form of company documents, help the board to clarify what it is doing and provide essential communications to staff and others. This allows all interested parties to know what is expected of them, the company's objectives, and how each party is expected to meet the objectives. Equally, funders and external stakeholders may wish to see the company objectives. The following company documents may be helpful:

Strategy and planning

A statement of the company's strategy may set out the overall aims and objectives, and can be supported by a business plan with the key objectives for the coming year. A medium term, two to five year plan may also be considered. These plans may consist simply of business objectives or they may also include financial plans.

Company manual

The company manual is a vital part of the internal controls and should document all policies and procedures including:

Operating policies and procedures

Staff policies and procedures

Job descriptions

Organisational chart

IT policies, procedures and backup procedures

Health and safety policies, and

Legal and regulatory compliance schedule – see below.

Board statement

A board statement should consist of the board's responsibilities, reserved matters, and delegated authorities.

Compliance Schedule

The directors are responsible for ensuring that the company meets its legal and regulatory commitments so systems and timetables need to be in place. Reliance on advisers will not remove the directors' responsibility.

The following matters need to be considered:

Accounts

Preparation of annual accounts

Board review and agreement of accounts

Copy of accounts to members

Filing of accounts with Companies House – within 10 months of year-end but the deadlines are being reduced to 9 months with the new Companies Act 2006, which will be effective for accounting periods commencing on or after 6 April 2008

Filing of accounts and tax return with HMRC – within 12 months of year-end.

Annual Return

Check, amend if necessary, sign and return to Companies House within 28 days of receipt, along with fee.

Tax Compliance

Corporation tax – for small and medium sized companies corporation tax needs to be paid within 9 months of the year-end and the return and accounts filed within 12 months. Large companies will need to make payments on account

VAT – quarterly returns to be prepared and paid within one month

PAYE – by 19th of each month, plus annual compliance following tax year-end

P11Ds by 6 July following the relevant tax year

Companies House Compliance

Details of the following need to be returned to Companies House within set deadlines:

Changes to the company's articles

Certain resolutions

Changes in directors and/or their details

Change in company secretary and/or his details

Change to the registered office

Details of charges.

Banking facilities and covenants

Reporting requirements for company funding need to be met.

Health and safety compliance

A full health and safety policy should be in force at each location where the company operates with clear guidelines for staff and documentation of staff responsible for compliance.

Full risk assessments including fire risk assessment should be undertaken and reviewed at least annually. Compliance with daily, monthly, and yearly safety checks eg first aid, fire alarms

Insurance

Annual review of insurance to ensure relevance to business and all areas covered, especially public and employer liability.

Appendix B: Questions: How is the Company Governed?

Provided below are a series of questions designed to encourage debate about how a company is governed and whether oversight processes could be improved. The questions should be considered in relation to the size and nature of the company, as discussed in the previous sections. Answers to these questions, together with a copy of the company's key policy statements, can be used to form the basis of a tailored company manual.

The Board Role

1 Is the board clear what the business is supposed to achieve for its owners?

2 Has it set goals to be achieved?

3 Has it determined the values and policies that will be adopted by the business?

4 Has it reviewed the strategic options available, selected those to be followed and decided how they will be implemented and resourced?

5 Does it ensure that policies and plans are implemented and reviewed regularly?

Responsibilities of Board Members

1 What is the job specification of each director?

2 Collectively, what skills do the board require to run the company effectively?

3 Are there any skills overlaps? Gaps?

4 Is any training required, how is this identified and organised?

5 How are new directors appointed, reappointed and, if necessary, removed?

6 Is there a succession plan?

7 Is there a person nominated to understudy key functions?

Matters reserved for the Board

1 Are corporate plans, operating and capital budgets prepared on a regular basis, for example, an annual cycle that ties in to the board calendar of meetings?

2 Who is responsible for instigating, preparing, reviewing and authorising of corporate plans and budgets?

3 Does the board undertake subsequent evaluations of plans to ensure they were adequately prepared, and follow up action for future plan preparation if necessary?

4 How does the board decide when dividends are to be recommended, how much they should be, and who organises their payment?

5 What is the board's definition of a material transaction, for example, acquisitions, disposals, starting or ceasing a business activity?

6 Who is responsible for instigating any material transaction?

7 How is a material transaction evaluated and does the board take a collective decision about its final authorisation?

8 Are there subsequent evaluations of material transactions?

9 Is there a business plan, a budget, and forecasted cash flow for the company and are these regularly monitored and, when necessary, updated?

10 Are actual results compared to budgets with variances investigated?

11 What are the procedures for preparing the annual financial statements?

12 Is the documentation and related information relating to all borrowings and guarantees up to date, reviewed regularly, and is each board member aware of the company commitments?

13 Are all covenants reviewed regularly to ensure that they are not breached?

14 Are borrowings as cost efficient as possible or should they be renegotiated?

Delegated Authorities

1 Are company policies current, clear and consistent, compliant with legal requirements and detailed in the company manual? Who is responsible for these policies?

2 Who can open bank accounts and sign cheques, and what are the limits on these authorities?

3 Which members of staff have authority for general purchasing, what are the relevant procedures, and what are the limits of their authority?

4 Who can sign regulatory documents and are there procedures in place to check these have been reviewed prior to submission?

5 Who is responsible for authorising the recipients and amounts of political and charitable donations?

6 Who has authority to represent the company or to issue external communications?

7 What are the procedures for recruiting staff?

8 Who has the ability to commit the company to signing of leases?

Board Meetings

1 Is the number of meetings appropriate and is there an annual calendar of board meetings?

2 How many directors are required for a valid (quorate) meeting?

3 Does the chairman set the agenda and can other directors add relevant business?

4 Is the management of meetings satisfactory with agenda papers sent out on a timely basis, sufficient time given to discuss all business, and minutes circulated promptly afterwards?

5 Are there suitable quality control checks in place to ensure that board papers contain appropriate, high quality, timely information to permit discussion and sensible decisions?

6 Do the minutes provide an adequate record of each meeting?

7 Are tasks allocated among directors, and how are these and any action points followed up?

8 What is the process for decision making, and is there a procedure for dealing with decision making between board meetings?

Compliance Schedule

1 Have external advisers and service providers, e.g. an accountant, pension adviser, auditor, been appropriately appointed with an engagement letter that details the required services, a commencement date, the basis of fees, and reporting requirements?

2 Is there a timetable and project plan in place for producing the annual report and (audited) accounts within the regulatory deadlines for their submission to Companies House and HMRC?

3 Do the timetables and project plans detail what is to be done so that any replacement person could undertake the tasks?

4 Do all the directors have sufficient opportunity to review the draft financial statements before they are signed?

5 Which government departments need to be dealt with, e.g. HMRC, Health and Safety, DWP, which director is responsible for these contacts, and what are the timetables for doing so?

Appendix C: Director's Appointment Letter, Induction, and the Definition of an Independent Director

Each director needs to be aware of his or her responsibilities, both the legal duties defined in various acts and those associated with his or her role in the company.

Director's Appointment Letter

The following aspects may be addressed in the director's letter of appointment:

- the date from which the appointment is effective
- whether there should be a fixed period of appointment and, if so, for how long (eg three years)
- state whether it is a contract for services (non-executive directors) or a contract of employment (executive directors)
- termination procedures, for example, at the discretion of either party with one/three months' notice
- the expected time commitment, of x number of days per annum, including attendance at all board meetings
- the legal responsibilities of a director
- the specific responsibilities expected in this appointment
- fees and expenses, and the basis of payment
- outside interests, and management of any potential conflicts of interest
- confidentiality during and after the period of the contract
- an anti-competitive clause both during and after the period of the contract
- induction procedures
- insurance: directors' liability insurance.

Director's Induction

New directors should be aware of the responsibilities associated with their appointment and be given as much background information about the company as possible. This allows them to make an effective contribution as early as possible. On the appointment of a new director the following should be addressed:

- announcement of appointment – e.g. press release, update the website, inform staff
- grant of share options – consider if any award is to be made and, if so, put in place

- register of outside appointments – ensure a record is kept and updated periodically
- notify Companies House of the appointment within 14 days
- there may be other regulatory requirements, for example, FSA requirements
- any background checks required, for example, Disclosure Scotland Form
- issue contractual terms of appointment
- complete a confidentiality agreement including a restriction on joining competitors
- check if there are any conflicts of interest or the possibility of related party transactions
- directors' liability insurance – prepare and issue an indemnification certificate
- access to financial statements, previous board minutes, company strategy and plans etc
- prepare any introductory meetings with staff, other directors, visits to the company (headquarters and operational sites).

After induction, there should be a formal programme of training and development for directors.

The Definition of an Independent Director

An Independent Director is someone outwith the company and, more specifically:

- has not been an employee of this company in the last five years
- has not had a material business relationship with the company in the last three years
- does not hold cross directorships or have significant links with other directors through involvement in other companies or bodies
- does not represent a significant shareholder
- has not received additional remuneration from the company apart from a director's fee, and does not participate in any company share option scheme, performance related pay scheme, or the company's pension scheme
- does not have close family ties with the company or the company's advisers, and
- has served on the board for less than nine years.

(Definition extracted from the Combined Code.)

Appendix D: Directors' Duties

The Companies Act 2006 has codified the duties of directors. These statutory duties are applicable to all directors regardless of the size of the company. There are seven general duties for directors:

- a director must act in accordance with the company's constitution and only exercise powers for the purpose for which they are conferred
- a director must act in the way he considers, in good faith, would be most likely to promote the success of the company for the benefit of its members as a whole, and in doing so have regard (amongst other matters) to the interests of employees, the community and the environment
- a director must exercise independent judgement
- a director must exercise the care, skill and diligence of a 'reasonably diligent person' having both the general knowledge, skill and experience reasonably expected of a director in his position (objective test), and the general knowledge, skill and experience which he actually has (subjective test)
- a director must avoid a situation in which he has, or can have, a direct or indirect interest that conflicts, or possibly may conflict, with the interests of the company
- a director must not accept any benefit connected with his role as a director from a third party unless it cannot reasonably be regarded as likely to give rise to a conflict of interest
- a director must declare the nature and extent of any personal interest in a proposed transaction with the company to the other directors before the company enters into the transaction.

The directors may wish to be able to demonstrate that they are acting 'in a way that promotes the success of the company' in which case this should be reflected in the board minutes.

There are other duties such as

- filing accounts and complying with Companies House requirements
- an awareness of the Insolvency Act 1986 in relation to fraudulent and wrongful trading and when to take advice on this. Board minutes are also crucial in establishing fraudulent or wrongful trading or otherwise, as the case may be.
- awareness of the Directors Disqualification Act 1986.

Appendix E: The Combined Code's Main Principles

The Combined Code is for public listed companies. Some, or aspects of, the main principles are relevant for private companies as discussed in the first part of this guide. The principles are reproduced here in order that any private company with ambitions to list in the future is aware of this governance code. The full code is available on the Financial Reporting Council website.

A1 – Every company should be headed by an effective board, which is collectively responsible for the success of the company.

A2 – There should be a clear division of responsibilities at the head of the company between the running of the board and the executive responsibility for the running of the company's business. No one individual should have unfettered powers of decision.

A3 – The board should include a balance of executive and non-executive directors (and in particular independent non-executive directors) such that no individual or small group of individuals can dominate the board's decision-making.

A4 – There should be a formal, rigorous and transparent procedure for the appointment of new directors to the board.

A5 – The board should be supplied in a timely manner with information in a form and of a quality appropriate to enable it to discharge its duties. All directors should receive induction on joining the board and should regularly update and refresh their skills and knowledge.

A6 – The board should undertake a formal and rigorous annual evaluation of its own performance and that of its committees and individual directors.

A7 – All directors should be submitted for re-election at regular intervals, subject to continued satisfactory performance. The board should ensure planned and progressive refreshing of the board.

B1 – Levels of remuneration should be sufficient to attract, retain and motivate directors of the quality required to run the company successfully, but a company should avoid paying more than is necessary for the purpose. A significant proportion of executive directors' remuneration should be structured so as to link rewards to corporate and individual performance.

B2 – There should be a formal and transparent procedure for developing policy on executive remuneration and for fixing the remuneration packages of individual directors. No director should be involved in deciding his or her own remuneration.

C1 – Financial Reporting: the board should present a balanced and understandable assessment of the company's position and prospects.

C2 – Internal Control: the board should maintain a sound system of internal control to safeguard shareholders' investment and the company's assets.

C3 – Auditors: the board should establish formal and transparent arrangements for considering how they should apply the financial reporting and internal control principles and for maintaining an appropriate relationship with the company's auditors.

D1 – There should be a dialogue with shareholders based on the mutual understanding of objectives. The board as a whole has responsibility for ensuring that a satisfactory dialogue with shareholders takes place. D2 – The board should use the AGM to communicate to investors and to encourage their participation.

Appendix F: Other Sources of Useful Information

Financial Reporting Council (FRC): www.frc.org.uk

The FRC is the UK's independent regulator responsible for promoting confidence in corporate reporting and governance. The FRC publishes the 'Combined Code on Corporate Governance'. It also has further guidance such as the Turnbull Report 'Internal Control: Guidance for Directors on the Combined Code', which has subsequently been revised and reissued by the FRC; and 'Good Practice Suggestions from the Higgs Report', which covers the role and effectiveness of non-executive directors.

Institute of Chartered Secretaries and Administrators (ICSA): www.icsa.org.uk

The ICSA provides guidance to company secretaries and senior administrators across all sectors.

The Institute of Directors (IOD): www.iod.com

The IOD supports, represents and sets standards for directors.

Quoted Companies Alliance: www.quotedcompaniesalliance.co.uk

The Quoted Companies Alliance (QCA) is a not-for-profit organisation that was formed solely to represent the interests of smaller quoted companies on the Main List, AIM and PLUS. It provides guidance on a range of topics including corporate governance.

Her Majesty's Revenue and Customs: www.hmrc.gov.uk

Guidance can be found regarding tax matters such as PAYE, corporation tax and value added tax.

Health and Safety Executive www.hse.gov.uk

The HSE provides information about, and ensures compliance with, health and safety matters

Business Gateway www.bgateway.com

The Business Gateway provides general business help and guidance for businesses in Scotland

Business Link www.businesslink.gov.uk

The Business Link provides general business help and guidance for businesses in England and Wales

The Advisory, Conciliation and Arbitration Service (ACAS) www.acas.org.uk

Acas aims to improve organisations and working life through better employment relations. It provides information, independent advice, high quality training and works with both employers and employees to solve problems and improve performance.

International Federation of Accountants (IFAC) www.ifac.org/paib

The International Center for Professional Accountants in Business, hosted by IFAC's Professional Accountants in Business (PAIB) Committee, provides resources and facilitates the exchange of knowledge and best practices among the more than one million professional accountants worldwide employed in commerce, industry, the public sector, education, and the not-for-profit sector.

Chapter B2

Board Dynamics: Evaluating Board Effectiveness

Introduction **B2.1**

We are very grateful to IDDAS for permission to reprint this excellent guidance, and also three others in their series, which we reproduce at Chapters **B3**, **B4** and **B5**. No responsibility for loss occasioned to any person acting or refraining from action as a result of any material in this publication can be accepted by the authors or the publishers.

Clare Chalmers, Chief Executive of IDDAS, would be pleased to hear from readers with any inquiries about this guidance. She can be contacted at IDDAS, IDDAS House, 74 New Cavendish Street, London, W1G 8TF (Tel: +44 (0)20 7436 0101; Email: clare.chalmers@iddas.com; Website: www.iddas.com).

Based in London, IDDAS specialises in providing board effectiveness, mentoring and coaching, leadership facilitation and executive assessment services for chairs, CEOs and main board directors, as well as for those who aspire to non-executive roles. IDDAS has an established reputation for its quality, innovative, supportive and flexible approach.

Board Dynamics

Evaluating Board Effectiveness

The Art and Science of Board Effectiveness, Development and Transition
A member of the Savile Group plc

Contact: Helen Pitcher, IDDAS, Iddas House, 74 New Cavendish Street, London, W1G 8TF

T: +44 (0)20 7436 0101 | E: helenp@iddas.com | W: www.iddas.com

Published 2012.

Foreword

When I presented my review of corporate governance in the UK banking industry in 2009, it seemed to me that many boards, not only in banking but also more widely, were not according evaluation of their own performance the attention it deserved.

I am pleased to note that the situation appears to have improved over the past two to three years, with some form of annual evaluation now an accepted fixture in the boardroom calendar of many more of our largest companies.

But while welcome progress has been made, there is still more to be done to ensure that the evaluation process itself is rigorous enough to add real value. In particular there is need for better understanding of what makes an evaluation process effective, and whether and how an external facilitator might contribute to this. On the latter, I have suggested that a potentially valuable initiative would be for advisers committed to the highest standards in the difficult and sensitive role of external facilitation to draw up a code of practice, both to boost confidence in boardrooms in appointing them and to increase the readiness of major shareholders to call for such professionalism in evaluation of board performance in the companies in which they invest.

In the meantime, this report is a valuable contribution to the body of knowledge available to boards and shareholders. I hope that its findings will encourage boards that have not yet used external facilitation to be ready to do so, if only initially on an experimental basis. They would be likely to find that the independence, experience and skill introduced by a high-quality external facilitator greatly enhances the yield of the whole process.

Sir David Walker

Introduction

It is almost a decade since the Higgs Report mooted the idea of board evaluations and three years since Sir David Walker recommended external evaluation every two or three years for banks and financial institutions.

In 2010, the revised UK Corporate Governance Code gave further momentum to external evaluation by recommending that all FTSE 350 boards undertake an external review at least every three years.

The direction of regulatory travel is clear. Yet the practice of board evaluation, particularly external evaluation, is still very much in its infancy. During three years of interviewing chairmen and non-executive directors for our Board Dynamics research series, it has become clear to us that there is still a wide range of opinions on the value of board evaluations.

Some chairmen and directors remain sceptical – often as a result of bad experiences. Others can see the benefits of a properly conducted review in enhancing board effectiveness and improving board dynamics.

Our interviewees told us that the greatest value from an external evaluation comes from a skilled outsider's ability to address behavioural issues. The objectivity they bring allows them to do this in a way that is rarely possible in an internal review.

As with all our research, it is rooted in the voices of people with first-hand experience.

Whatever their views, many directors are eager for information on what good evaluation, internal or external, looks like, how to go about implementing it, and where to turn for expert advice.

It was with this in mind that we chose to investigate directors' and providers' actual experience of board evaluation for our fourth Board Dynamics research report. At the same time, we were invited by Sir David Walker to start a dialogue among providers of external board evaluations on creating a 'Gold Standard' within the industry.

This report draws together both those pieces of work and is intended as a resource for anyone involved with or interested in board evaluation.

As with all our research, it is rooted in the voices of people with first-hand experience. They include chairmen, non-executive directors and consultants engaged in board evaluation. All are very busy people who found space in their diaries to take part in a series of roundtable discussions or one-to-one interviews. We would like to thank them again for giving their time so generously. Their insightful observations give a unique flavour of the issues at stake in this important debate.

Helen Pitcher

Chairman, IDDAS

Executive Summary

Performance review is a sensitive subject at the best of times.

Even after 10 years of regulatory prompting, some boards are still complacent about their own performance and harbour a belief that evaluation is no more than a burdensome requirement of compliance. Yet those who have experienced good evaluations speak highly of the benefits.

We asked chairmen and directors about the purpose of evaluation and what they thought it should cover. We explored their views on the internal/external debate and asked what makes or breaks a review. We probed them on the challenge of assessing individual board members and on the link if any between board performance and company performance. Finally, we attempted to create a picture of the market for external board evaluation– something in which our interviewees showed considerable interest.

General findings

- Our survey of 77 top 200 companies showed that a third had carried out external evaluations in 2010/11 – a substantial increase on the previous year.
- A good evaluation can make any board more effective. Chairmen reported that they discovered things they were not aware of.
- There is no agreement on whether board performance should be linked to company performance.
- Both internal and external evaluation have their place.
- Assessing board dynamics and behaviour is the hardest part of an evaluation but has the potential to bring the greatest benefit. Addressing procedures is easier but has relatively minor impact.
- External evaluation is better for exposing difficult issues, particularly people issues, as board members generally speak more frankly to an independent outsider.

Towards best practice

It is too early for a comprehensive definition of best practice. However, a consensus is emerging on certain issues.

- Buy-in from the whole board is critical to success and can be achieved by upfront discussion of the purpose and process of evaluation.
- The evaluation should cover both individual and collective board performance and both executive and non-executive directors should be individually appraised.
- One-to-one interviews promote engagement, and elicit the most insightful information; comments made in interviews should be kept anonymous in feedback.
- Questionnaires can be useful if carefully designed and completed with sufficient consideration. However, they are susceptible to being rushed.
- Discussion of an evaluation's findings is essential. Change will only take place if these lead to an action plan, with subsequent review of progress.
- The quality of the evaluator, whether internal or external, is crucial.

External evaluators

- Providers of external evaluation fall into a number of categories: board effectiveness consultancies, specialist individual consultancies, professional services firms, membership organisations, and headhunters or their spinoffs.
- A significant number of companies use the board evaluation arm of headhunters but it is plainly important in such cases that conflicts of interest are avoided.
- External consultants bring knowledge of how other boards work.
- Some boards see benchmarking as a key advantage of external evaluation. However, benchmarking should not lead to complacency about performance.
- Repeated use of the same reviewer may lead to staleness and a loss of independence.

The Findings in Detail

We took as our starting point the board evaluation experiences of chairmen and directors themselves and attempted to draw lessons from their stories.

Our research in context

Board effectiveness has remained high on the corporate agenda since the credit crunch of 2008. Our three previous research reports about women on boards, chairmen and non-executive directors revealed strong interest in the characteristics of an effective board. These were neatly summarised by the Institute of Chartered Secretaries and Administrators (ICSA) in 2010 into the following key themes:

- the critical role of the chairman
- the importance of the board's role in building a culture that creates value while minimising risk

- the need for challenge in the boardroom
- the importance of high-quality board decision-making
- the role of board composition and diversity in delivering an effective board
- the advantages of good training and development for board directors
- the benefits of regular evaluation to explore how well the board is functioning.

It is this last theme that is the subject of our present report. Information on the market for external evaluation services is scarce and indeed there has been relatively little research on the whole business of how effectiveness is best evaluated. We took as our starting point the board evaluation experiences of chairmen and directors themselves and attempted to draw lessons from their stories.

Understanding the purpose of evaluation

For any group of people, reviewing their own performance has the potential to be an uncomfortable experience.

"It is not designed to make you happy, but to ensure for the shareholders, suppliers and customers that the board is effective."

"It is a spur: are we doing the things we should be?"

Board evaluation is about improving performance. No organisation is perfect and even if things are working well there is always room for improvement.

One of the advantages of the new regulatory environment, which promotes more frequent and far-reaching reviews for all boards, is that it stops evaluation being seen as a remedial exercise for poor performers. A good evaluation can make any board more effective – as many of our interviewees commented.

For any group of people, reviewing their own performance has the potential to be an uncomfortable experience. If the group is made up of very senior individuals, used to being recognised as leaders in their own right, it can be even harder to acknowledge that something isn't working well, has not been resolved through informal channels, or could be done better.

"There are some who still say: 'This is a waste of time; the chairman and CEO need to get on,' or, 'We should all be able to do this over coffee. People will say if there is a problem.'"

And yet issues do arise on boards. One FTSE 350 director said there were people on his board who were "worthless" and "everyone knows who they are". Others spoke about overbearing chief executives or directors whose personal style alienated colleagues. Several mentioned executive directors who never spoke outside their functional expertise.

"It is extraordinary how the group on a board can get into ways of working which they don't recognise or talk about, and which make the working of the board less effective. Certain no-go areas might have emerged, and there is a failure to discuss better ways of working, whether in process (how the papers are presented, how long they are, etc.), or in the approach, or in interpersonal relationships."

"The point is to try to improve the way the board functions in future, for the shareholders and all other parties. A review that has been done well will lead to changes."

"No-one would ever say we don't need management accounts, and it would be extremely odd not to conduct a formal review of management and employees. Why should the situation be any different for the board?"

First-hand experiences

Most of our interviewees made the point that open-ended questions and discussions are more enlightening than the tick-box answers on questionnaires.

We asked our interviewees about the evaluations they had led or experienced. They described a variety of processes from the highly structured to the very general. One chairman insisted that people put their names to their comments to avoid "creepiness". Another said that he never gave individual feedback to directors. A third had a highly structured approach to individual appraisal of all directors and expressed horror of boards where appraisals do not take place.

"I have always believed in annual appraisals. Each year I do my own appraisal of the performance of the CEO, and of each executive and non-executive director. In a measured fashion, I always talk to members of the board about their fellow directors. I end up with a piece of feedback, which I give personally to each one. I start with my views, and then a synopsis of what I have learned from others. In a board that knows each other well, and operates well, these can be swift conversations. In other situations, they can be quite challenging and tortuous. The SID does the performance review of me as chairman. I have a two-day board meeting in January and give individual feedback."

"I have always done assessment of NEDs in a group situation. I have never sat down with NEDs individually to give a formal assessment. I have occasionally given verbal feedback. I get feedback on my own performance from the SID and one other NED – I choose one of the newer, younger NEDs."

"I put the questionnaire together with the company secretary and HR director [including] a section at the bottom requesting comments. Then I circulate the responses to everyone, with names on them, so everyone can defend or explain what they have said. I then allocate one hour at the board meeting to discuss the results, and whether we have to make changes. At the six-month stage, we review against the agreed actions to cover the issues. I also sit down with the SID, and the chairman of Remcom, to ask for feedback on myself. I think this all works well: it is open, there is no creepiness, and it allows opinions to be voiced."

Most of our interviewees made the point that open-ended questions and discussions are more enlightening than the tick-box answers on questionnaires. This is where the most useful information is drawn out.

"I asked each board member to write half a page on the board and its members. There was no format, and really interesting points came out. Some came as a complete surprise. It made me recognise that individuals have different perspectives. As a chairman, it is sometimes important to be reminded that not everyone is in the same knowledge position. The review made me recognise that there are times when discussion has to be allowed to flow. I believe that this learning would not have emerged through a tick-box approach."

"In one case where I was chairman, from informal feedback the question arose: 'Did you know that three out of your four NEDs are a bit concerned about the fourth?' They hadn't raised it with me; now I could sort it out. Otherwise the fungus can grow."

"The more useful sessions are when NEDs get together and talk together on how well the board is working. I have participated in some good discussions over the years."

Internal vs external: the pros and cons

Internal or external is not the main issue: it is the quality of the evaluator that is most important.

About half of our interviewees had experience of external as well as internal evaluations, and a number were expecting to have their first external review in the next year. It was clear that both types of evaluation have their place, and those who had experienced good evaluations, particularly good external evaluations, were very enthusiastic about the benefits.

Our interviewees made two main points about the relative merits of internal and external evaluation. First, external evaluation has a much better chance than internal evaluation of addressing difficult issues, especially people issues.

"The longer you work together, the harder it is to remain objective, and everyone is polite. A good external review will be able to bring an insight on how things are working which insiders might miss."

"If you have a difficult board situation where people are not working as a team, I can see that you would bring in a third party. If the board appears to be working well, I don't see the benefit of an external."

"Externals bring experience of observing and seeing how other boards work. With internal reviews, there are sometimes elephants in the room. An outsider can make this obvious and will push people to verbalise what they really think and feel."

"It is clearly a more thorough process if you bring in a third party – as long as you have all agreed – because you are forced into a greater degree of objectivity. The third party can facilitate more challenging discussion on an individual and collective basis. External is the way to go, but you mustn't do them too close together because this would lead to process overload."

"Internal reviews can be used to track progress between external reviews, and to chart the milestones."

The calibre of the reviewer

The second point our interviewees made was that internal or external was not the main issue. It is the quality of the evaluator that is most important: an internal evaluation conducted by an emotionally intelligent chairman/SID is better than an external evaluation conducted by a sub-par independent facilitator.

"A lot depends on whoever leads having the emotional intelligence to cover all the issues and the courage to say things which make people feel uncomfortable – particularly if those people are the chairman or CEO. In many ways, it should be possible to do internal reviews, but it is seen as easier to use an external. As the SID I have led a process, and found it quite difficult to deliver the messages. This is a big challenge. My conclusion was that an external should do it next time."

"The chairman did a so-called review, but it was absolutely useless because he put the board on the back foot, and when he had matters drawn to his attention he was not capable of dealing with them."

"The chairman's own review, when she did it, was more valuable than the external review. She said we're not challenging enough. It was her own format, and it was useful and led to her changing a couple of board directors. After that, people felt they could say things they couldn't say before."

"The external facilitator needs the necessary experience, perception and emotional intelligence to do it. If they tremble before great corporate giants, then they will confirm prejudices against going the external route."

"You have to have someone who is prepared to tell the chairman he's a turkey, or that the board is dysfunctional because you, you and you are always fighting and you are not contributing."

"If you go external, the chairman has to be very careful in weighing up which person to use, so the process of selection is very important. It mustn't be a mate; it must be someone who is impartial."

One interviewee made the important point that an external reviewer does not absolve the chairman of responsibility for ensuring a review's success.

Support for the internal option

Despite the consensus on external reviews being better for dealing with difficult relationship issues, several interviewees also highlighted potential advantages of internal reviews – and pitfalls with the external route.

"If you've got a couple of people who are prepared to ask awkward questions, it's easier to do a review internally. If you are truly functional you'd have an open discussion around the table anyway."

"The benefit of internal reviews is that you get the chance to talk in a way you wouldn't with an outsider. If you can do this in a relaxed fashion, you can allow the process to take longer; with an external partner, you have a constrained timeframe."

"If you use an independent reviewer too regularly, they may not remain independent. Every three years for an external review is right and this is the minimum under the Code."

"I don't think a consultant observing how the board works will gain a true picture. People won't be frank when they are being observed."

"An external review feels like an imposed process. Why are we paying money?"

One interviewee made the important point that an external reviewer does not absolve the chairman of responsibility for ensuring a review's success.

"The external reviewer is a facilitator, not a subcontracted chairman. The chairman may want to subcontract, but this is not appropriate."

What makes or breaks a review

"A bad review is worse than no review, because people think it's been done when it hasn't."

We talked to directors about what makes a review successful – and where things go wrong. Several interviewees said that it was important that everyone on the board knew the aims of the review, its scope and how it would be conducted.

Providers of external evaluation whom we spoke to emphasised the importance of buy-in from the whole board. The danger otherwise is that the evaluation becomes an empty compliance exercise rather than a mechanism for improving effectiveness.

"The review is most effective if the objectives are made very clear, and if there is discussion around the board table about what it is for, the method to be used and how things wil be actioned. Clarity beforehand is best."

"Agreeing the scope with the chairman is really important. Chairmen are the most sensitive to the review."

Discussion and follow-up

The most common complaint about reviews, however, was that boards do not sufficiently debate the findings, or follow through with actions. The frequency with which this point was made suggests that this is an area where many boards still struggle.

"If there is no feedback it makes the exercise invalid. I know that some shy away from doing this."

"At one company the internal board review process was fairly comprehensive, but then there was no debate. The feedback was largely done on paper so we didn't get the benefit because it was a one-way exercise."

"A dysfunctional board I was on had an independent review. It did open up questions but they were never resolved. So the issues sat on the table and created discomfort."

"It is very important for the chairman to say: 'There are three or four points I need to report back to you on,' in terms of collective board behaviour. Reporting back has to be handled carefully, with generalised conclusions, rather than verbatim comments."

Periodic review

It is what comes after the review that determines its success: an action plan with follow-up is essential.

Indeed, an effective evaluation should not be a once-a-year exercise. There must be an action plan that is periodically reviewed to ensure that things actually change.

"There is a trap you can fall into: that conducting a board effectiveness review changes things. It does not. Follow-up, with data, is extremely important and often under-cooked. People tend to settle back and return to business as usual. So follow-up is very important."

"You should discuss the results, and agree a series of actions as a board. Obviously it is easier when they are structural issues. Following up on behavioural issues comes down to the skill of the chairman and SID. If they are not dealt with effectively, it may underline the problem (possibly with the chairman him or herself) or the differences of opinion. In both cases, someone may have to leave the board."

"The critical thing is what comes afterwards. If it transpires that there are some shortcomings – someone talks too much, undermines others, knows too little of the business – then you have to make them aware of this, and you have to have development programmes. You mustn't shy away. If it is positioned that everyone can expect 'development for me', and all get it, then this is a helpful way to move forwards. If someone says: 'We knew this,' or 'I don't think that's true,' then nothing will move forward."

"The chairman should review after six months: 'When we had the last review, these items came up. Have we improved?'"

What needs to be covered

"Only 5% should be procedural. The rest has to be about behaviour."

Interviewees told us what they thought should be included in an evaluation. Four main areas emerged:

- leading the business
- board dynamics and behaviour
- board composition
- processes, procedures and structures.

Leading the business

Examining whether the board is focusing on the right business issues and looking ahead at opportunities and risks, emerged as a key concern amongst board members.

"This is going to sound a bit old fashioned, but the main thing to be covered is how effective the board is in achieving [business] objectives. There are three objectives: strategy, performance and talent. So, the review should be structured around these objectives. If you are not addressing them, then you are missing the point."

"The review should assess whether [the board] looks at the right issues, in a constructive way and with the right capability. Perhaps you have to focus on one or two things, and monitor these to ensure tough issues get onto the agenda."

"You must look at what the key issues are for the business, and how the board is helping on them, and assess how good the board is at looking ahead."

Board dynamics and behaviour

Many interviewees made the point that behavioural issues are central. This includes, for example, whether the chairman chairs effectively, whether the board is cohesive, whether people contribute and challenge, and how effectively relationships with executive management and other stakeholders are working.

"It is very important to cover: how the chairman chairs the board, how board members feel about this, are they able to contribute, can they speak openly? You do need to assess collective board effectiveness because the board is a 'cabinet-run show'. It has collective responsibility, and must have a single message."

"The real value is in the softer side. What is affecting the effectiveness of the board and the relationships on it? Both the structural and the interpersonal are important. Nothing should be off the table."

"Behaviour is important. I know a board where one individual is absolutely brilliant, but his behaviour is shocking. This has to be tackled."

"You need to look at whether the board sufficiently tests and challenges the executive team and whether members feel that they take part in the strategy debate, understand the direction of the company, and are happy with it."

"[The evaluation] should look at the quality of discussions, the contribution of individuals, the performance of the chairman and chairs of committees, and the relationships between the executive and non-executive directors."

"[What the evaluation should cover] depends on where the board thinks it is. For some boards you don't need a board effectiveness review; you need psychoanalysis."

Board composition and capability

Evaluating process and procedures is the easiest part of a review. Exposing behavioural issues demands more skill but is central to the exercise.

Interviewees made the point that the review is an opportunity to assess training needs and whether board members have sufficient knowledge, experience and skills to fulfill their role. It is also an opportunity to look at succession arrangements.

"It's important to make a proper assessment of how much the board members know about the business, and how much time they spend in the business. Not everyone needs to know everything, because they may bring other skills – but then they must apply them."

"The chairman must identify key issues that might be facing the board. It could be his or her own succession – does a plan exist, is it a good one? Chairmen can be very badly behaved on this for self interest."

Processes, procedures and structures

Interviewees agreed that this was the easiest part of an evaluation and should cover quality of papers, frequency and length of meetings, roles and responsibilities on the board and its committees, etc.

"You have to look at the nuts and bolts, e.g. that the paperwork is issued on time, is appropriate, covers all issues, that there is a good level of debate and that everyone is listened to and is involved in the debate, that they are visiting locations, etc. This is all the easy stuff."

"It's important to review how the committees are working and interacting with the main board and, in a plc, how decisions are made."

"Clearly, you [must examine] process – pedantic things, like the agenda, timing, papers, presentations, what your authorities are, and what has been delegated."

"The last question might be: 'What else would you like to say?' I would ask a general question: 'Do you want to step back and give an overall view of the board?' If this leads to issues, then you discuss them around the table."

Reviewing individual board members

One of the most delicate aspects of a board evaluation is reviewing the effectiveness of individual board members. Interviewees told us that it was important to do this, and that the contribution of executive directors to the board should be assessed separately from their functional performance.

Boards vary in their approach. On some boards, each member is asked to comment (usually, but not invariably, anonymously) on his or her colleagues, including the chairman. On others, it is the chairman alone who assesses individual members.

Everyone agreed, however, that it was the job of the chairman to feed back in person to individual directors and for the SID/company secretary to feed back the results of the individual assessment to the chairman. Many also acknowledged that chairmen often find this aspect of their role particularly difficult.

"People can fire a CEO, but find it difficult to say to an NED: 'You are not effective,' or 'We want you to contribute more.' This may be pretty bland, but chairmen are not prepared to do it. This is a real issue."

"It is the chairman's responsibility to be robust in feeding back individually to the board members. It has to be handled sensibly.

Some chairmen will not want to do this and may want the external reviewer to do it, but the fundamental role of the chairman is about the performance of the board.… There is no harm, on a confidential basis, in individuals having action plans arising from the review."

"A board is a number of individuals following constitutionalised procedures. It is not a concern if someone is quiet if their contributions are good. I think what a chairman needs to do, and the external reviewer helps, is give everyone a voice, including the executive directors. I have found that the executive directors are sometimes uncomfortable contributing generally. Typically, executives who aren't the CEO or CFO are only comfortable talking about their own patch. I understand this, but it doesn't help the dynamics of the board."

"Sometimes you get a surprise. A chairman can find it very useful to know how others see the members of the board, and their reactions to individual A, B, or C. They may not have noticed things which other members have."

"There must be an acceptance of the feedback, and personal learning. 'Thank you, I hadn't realised that I need to be more aware of Mr X's sensitivities re subject Y.' The follow-up is the responsibility of the chairman, who should look at performance quarterly. He/she should ask, 'How are we doing, do we need to take any other actions?' You do not want to leave it for 12 months to find out if the Remco chairman has been to the training programme."

The link to company performance

No-one had a clear idea about how to link board and company performance directly, though many felt the relationship could not be ignored.

We asked our interviewees whether board performance should be linked to company performance, and if so, how? Opinions were divided. Some were adamant that the two were entirely separate, others felt it was nonsensical to ignore the company's position or performance in the market. No-one had a clear idea about how to link the two directly, although some made the point that using the review to assess fitness for future purpose went part of the way. This might include succession planning, reviewing whether the skills needed on the board reflect market trends, or assessing fitness to deal with a future crisis in the wake of one that has just taken place.

"It is critical [to link board and company performance]. The value of the board is to make the company more effective. The board is there to enhance the company, otherwise it would just be governance, reported in the annual report."

"The company will deliver better performance if they have a strong board. I'm sure there is a strong correlation between an effective board and successful performance of the company."

"You can't conduct a review in isolation of how the company is performing. You absolutely cannot. If the company is performing badly, it is impossible to say the board is doing a good job. But how the two are linked is more difficult to assess."

"You only know how effective a board is when things are going badly wrong. The fault lines then appear. That's when you see if they are splitting or pulling together."

"In theory the two are linked. If the board is working effectively, it can affect performance. But I am not a scientist. There are a lot of other factors which come into play, therefore I don't know how we would make the link."

"The difficulty [with relating board success to company success] is you can be successful today and not successful tomorrow. Take the RBS example. From the outside, everyone would have said, 'It's a successful company, growing and growing', but still it was not an effectively functioning board."

"I don't think context should be taken into account. All companies go through cycles. The board should be as good in a good year as in a bad year. If there's a crisis, it's a good idea to do a post-crisis review. Did we have the systems in place, were we kept informed, if it happened again are we fit enough to deal with it?"

"A board can perform well when a company is performing badly. There is a distinction."

Tips and tools

In the course of our conversations, some interviewees gave us their personal tips on useful techniques and favourite questions.

"Add 15 minutes at the end of board meetings, which will not be minuted, when you discuss what members did or did not like in the meeting. You might query: 'Did we do a good job there?'"

"Separate the review of the committees and the external review of the board, because this gives you more time to debate the committees. If you do only one review, it tends to focus on the board, but committees are very important, and shouldn't be ignored."

"Have a scorecard for the board with six to 12 measures that are not just financial. If you've got data, you have a reference point for starting a conversation."

"Set up a phone call. Form-filling is a barrier."

"Ask yourselves: 'How many decisions have we made a difference to in the last year?' If none, then what are you doing there?"

"Say to the board: 'Tell me behaviours that might make this board more effective?' Get people to think about that beforehand."

"Ask the board: 'In a year's time, what are the couple of things that would take us to the next level?'"

"Ask the chair to reflect on how he/she provided leadership to the board."

Towards Best Practice

Given the youth of the board evaluation industry it is too soon to expect comprehensive best practice to have emerged.

Despite the lack of concrete information, some consensus is emerging on boards and among providers on what makes an effective evaluation.

Companies are still experimenting with different techniques and approaches in response to successive reports and codes.

Official sources of regulatory guidance are the UK Corporate Governance Code 2010, which describes the regulatory framework, and the FRC's Guidance on Board Effectiveness (see Annex) and Developments in Corporate Governance. The impact and implementation of the UK Corporate Governance and Stewardship Codes, which give recommendations on evaluation but do not attempt to prescribe how companies should go about it.

A framework for successful review

Despite the lack of concrete information, some consensus is emerging on boards and among providers on what makes an effective evaluation. Our research suggests that to achieve the best results an assessment should:

- be tailored to the company
- be driven by the chairman and owned by the whole board
- be used as a mechanism for improving board effectiveness – not just motivated by compliance or a desire to benchmark
- have a clear scope and process understood by the whole board
- be designed to cover the current and future needs of the board

- address behavioural issues as well as the focus of the board, its composition, processes and procedures
- cover both collective and individual effectiveness, including effectiveness of the chairman
- include feedback and debate by the whole board
- lead to an action plan with appropriate follow-up.

External review – the engagement process

Board agreement on external review	• Board briefing • Timeframe to fit with report and accounts publishing dates, board changes, etc.
Scope of the review	• Terms of reference, usually agreed by chairman, SID and company secretary • Must haves • Like to haves • Interesting to see
Formal tendering	• List of potential providers • Recommendations • Usually driven by company secretary
Proposal development	• Initial briefing, usually face-to-face • Outline of objectives of evaluation • Discussion of ideas and approaches • Formal proposal • Indicative costs
Timetable and schedule agreement	• Evaluation proposal • Meetings shortlist • Chairman and others meet consultants
Final clarification and engagement	• With chairman and company secretary • Final costs • Board "socialisation" and briefing on agreed approach

The diagram above outlines the steps a company may go through in engaging an external review specialist.

Source: IDDAS

The behavioural question

The FRC's Guidance on Board Effectiveness states: "Boards need to think deeply about the way in which they carry out their role and the behaviours that they display, not just about the structures and processes that they put in place."

Board evaluation started out by looking almost exclusively at process and procedure. Our research supports the FRC's view that in fact the real value in an evaluation comes from addressing behavioural issues. As one director put it, "The process stuff is a hygiene factor. There are things you can improve on and tweak, but it's not fundamental."

Given the difficulty of addressing behavioural issues at this level, board evaluation requires an individual with a particular set of skills and personal qualities. Reviewers must be:

- able to inspire confidence, put people at their ease and win trust
- independent
- well informed about the company and its operating environment
- familiar with the workings of boards and the issues that face them
- capable of gathering, absorbing and analysing large quantities of information, and able to present their findings in both written and verbal form
- emotionally intelligent, to be able to give sensitive feedback in a non-judgemental way.

Evaluation methodologies

Most board evaluation consultants believe that whatever the methodology, information should be used on a non-attributable basis so that participants speak freely.

External providers of evaluation use a variety of methodologies. Annual reports show widespread use of questionnaires in board review, particularly when the evaluation is conducted in-house. They can provide plenty of data, our interviewees told us, but without careful analysis their value is limited. They have most relevance for evaluating documents, processes and structures, but for more complex issues they are considered limiting, even when they include space for comments. As one of our interviewees remarked:

"Some people are very conscientious about adding comments, but others (including me) find the easiest way out: tick the boxes and don't make comments. With a board that is working well, it becomes a routine, and bland. If a board has issues, then a questionnaire will not work, and if the problem is the chairman himself, this will not emerge."

For this reason, external consultants prefer to use interviews, either alone or in combination with a questionnaire. Interviews are more open-ended and more likely to expose issues, particularly on sensitive subjects. Most board evaluation consultants believe that whatever the methodology, information should be used on a non-attributable basis so that participants speak freely.

The external review process

While each reviewer will approach the review differently, a typical IDDAS review might progress as follows:

Timetable and schedule agreement

This must accommodate the crowded schedules of all board members, some of whom will not be UK-based. Sufficient time must also be allowed for feedback and review sessions and for determining what is to be included in the annual report.

Past reviews and future capability needs

The reviewer will revisit earlier reviews and progress made on any recommendations. Particular attention will be paid to the impact of any future plans identified on board capability needs.

Desk research and review of board papers

This part of the review is to assess board papers related to the governance framework and to understand the corporate governance model in action.

Timetable and schedule agreement	Agreement on timetable, including feedback to chairman on director performance
Review history and future capability/skills needs	• History of board reviews if any and issues outstanding • Future skills and experience requirements
Desk research and review of board papers	• Company secretary interview • Review of board papers • Governance model review
Individual interviews	• Chairman • SID • NEDs • Executive directors as appropriate
Board and sub-committee observations	• Decision making • Challenge • Behavioural dynamics • Communication
Review report development	• Clarification and confirmation • Follow-up information
Draft report	• Draft report to chairman and company secretary • Agreement of facilitated discussion/feedback to the board • Individual development feedback to chairman
Final report and feedback	• Formal report • Report feedback to board • Behavioural dynamic facilitated session

Individual interviews

These should be face to face and confidential, typically using a structured questionnaire. IDDAS has its own well established Insight questionnaire, which then provides a platform for collective discussion/review by the board. In addition to covering all board members and the company secretary, it may also be appropriate to interview executive directors who are not on the board, such as the senior risk officer and the HR director.

Board and sub-committee observations

The purpose of attending meetings is to understand the challenge, clarity, interaction and dynamics in the boardroom.

Review report development

This stage includes obtaining clarification on any outstanding issues and agreeing a structure for the report.

Draft report

The reviewer will share the draft findings with the chairman and finalise feedback mechanisms.

Final report and feedback

The reviewer will facilitate a discussion of the findings, including behavioural dynamics in the boardroom.

The Board Evaluation Market

Virtually all of the UK's largest companies are now conducting some kind of annual evaluation.

The quality and quantity of the information companies disclose about evaluation in their annual reports has improved noticeably in the past year.

There is considerable variation in what they are doing and how, and how they report what they have done. Some have clearly embraced evaluation, seeing it as a real opportunity for improving the board's performance, while others have appeared to treat it simply as compliance, an annual box-ticking exercise. Among smaller companies and voluntary organisations, our research suggests board evaluation has yet to play a significant role.

Approaches to evaluation

The only public source of information about how evaluation has been approached to date is what companies write in their annual reports and, increasingly, what they put on their websites. But the usefulness of this information is dependent on the level of detail they give and what they choose to disclose. It is pleasing to note that both the quality and quantity of the information provided has noticeably improved in the past year.

According to Grant Thornton's *Corporate Governance Review 2011*, over half of all FTSE 100 companies gave full details of the evaluation process in the period covered. It further observed that 24% of its total study of 298 FTSE 350 groups provided 'strong description' of outcomes and action plans. The amount written about evaluation in the annual report is also interesting. This varies between nothing, through a few sentences to several detailed paragraphs. Examples of companies whose recent reporting has been substantial include Barclays, Centrica and Tate & Lyle.

At its most complete, the information given in the annual report provides:

- details of the evaluation process, including who and what was evaluated and how

- details of the findings, an action plan for the year ahead, and a report on progress against the previous year's action plan
- the name of any external provider and any conflicts of interest.

This shows a desire to treat board effectiveness as part of the overall assurance process, providing evidence to convince shareholders that the board is taking all necessary steps to optimise performance. Satisfactory individual performance evaluations are increasingly being cited in annual reports in support of a recommendation for the re-election of directors. In some cases, they are also mentioned in the Notice of AGM.

The following, by contrast, is an example of uninformative reporting, a handful of lines that gives little away but states that the board was judged effective.

"A review of the operation of the Board, its committees and the skills of the Directors was undertaken during the year. The form of this year's Board Evaluation was reviewed by independent consultants. The process was led by the Chairman. All Directors completed the wide-ranging appraisal questionnaire and the results were reviewed by the Board. The process confirmed the ongoing effectiveness of the Board."

Investors may draw their own conclusions as to why some reporting is brief. It could be that a perfectly acceptable review has taken place, but the lack of detail could just as well mask complacency on the part of the chairman, or cast doubt on the quality of the evaluation itself.

Our research suggests another reason for limited reporting: a fear that giving more detail might reveal commercially sensitive, confidential or embarrassing information. As it stands, boards are entirely free to decide whom they share the results of the evaluation with. In most cases, they keep them very close to their chests. One of our interviewees told us that she had asked to see a copy of the most recent evaluation before accepting a place on the board of a large plc, but her request had not been granted.

This may change with time if board evaluation becomes part of the assurance process. A small move towards greater openness is suggested by the FRC in its document, Developments in Corporate Governance 2011. This recommends that companies give the name of any external evaluator they use in their annual report. At the moment, a significant minority still fails to do this. As one evaluation provider remarked: "It's a misconception that we are part of assurance. We will be but not yet."

Who has gone the external route?

Our research suggests a significant increase in take-up of external review among FTSE 100 firms –but second-tier companies are some way behind.

Annual reports suggest that companies have, in the last year, started to embrace external evaluation more fully. The UK Corporate Governance Code's provision that FTSE 350 boards undertake an external evaluation at least every three years came into effect at the end of June 2010. In its Review of the UK top 200 companies 2010, ICSA reported that 33 companies or 17% of its study had conducted an evaluation with some sort of external involvement.

This was more or less in line with previous years (see graph).

There is evidence that there has been an upswing in external evaluations in the last year. Our analysis of the reporting of 75 top 200 companies which have published annual reports so far for 2011 showed that 25 – or one third – had carried out an external review. This suggests a substantial increase on the 17% recorded by ICSA in 2010. Interestingly, only eight of the 25 identified in our research were outside the FTSE 100, suggesting that the second tier of companies are some way behind in their take-up of external evaluation.

UK top 200 companies using some form of external involvement in board evaluation 2007–10

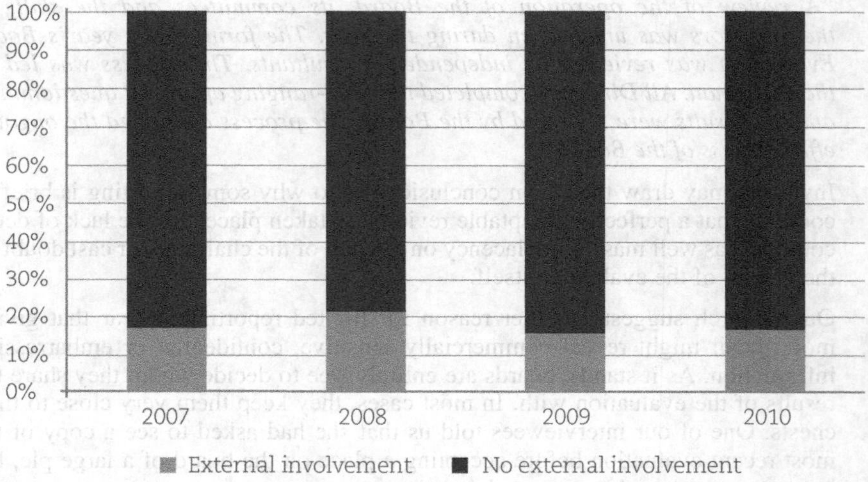

Source: ICSA Board Evaluation

Some companies acknowledge the Code change in their annual reports, but have put off external evaluation for another year. Sometimes the annual report states that an external review was postponed because of a change in board composition, or other upheaval. In other cases, boards took the opposite view, believing that there was much to be gained from an effectiveness review in times of change.

It may also be that external evaluations have been seen as remedial, or only carried out when the board has something to prove. The list of companies choosing external evaluation in 2010 was top-heavy with banks, engineering groups, oil and power companies, all of whom operate in high-risk sectors. Just under a third of them had used external evaluators in four out of the last five years, suggesting their choice had little to do with the new Code provision.

For the generality of companies who have not gone down the external route, another reason could be the lack of clarity about who the providers are and what the board can expect to get out of an external evaluation. As one of our interviewees commented:

"If you spend £100,000 on a review, what can you expect to benefit by in the course of the next three years? What's the value added? You don't buy a service from KPMG and not expect some value added. It's all very vague at the moment. What are we going to get out of our board review? We don't really know. How will we measure it?"

Indeed, cost is undoubtedly a factor inhibiting companies, particularly outside the FTSE 100, from using external consultants. Prices charged vary considerably. The norm is considered to be around £50–60k but fees of £100,000 are not unusual.

Providers argue that a successful external review brings objectivity to the evaluation and the benefit of knowledge and experience gained from evaluating many boards. One of the things that attracts some to external evaluation is the opportunity to benchmark their performance against others. As one provider pointed out, however, evaluation should not be seen merely as a benchmarking exercise: "We don't like to benchmark, because if you think you are doing OK you are not motivated to improve." The purpose of evaluation is to make the board's performance better in absolute terms, not just in relation to industry peers.

IDDAS analysis of a sample of 75 annual reports identified another 22 companies who used external providers in 2011 (see final column).

UK top 200 companies using external providers in 2010 and before

Company	2006	2007	2008	2009	2010	2011 *
3i Infrastructure						x
Aberdeen Asset Management					x	x
Alliance Trust		x			x	NR
Babcock International		x	x	x	x	NR
BAE Systems	x	x	x	x	x	NR
Balfour Beatty	x				x	NR
Barclays	x	x	x	x	x	NR
Berkeley Group Holdings						x
BG Group			x		x	NR
BHP Billiton						x
Burberry Group						x
Catlin Group					x	NR
Chemring					x	NR
Close Brothers Group				x	x	NR
Cobham				x	x	NR
Diageo						x
EasyJet					x	NR
Experian						x
G4S				x	x	NR
Great Portland Estates						x
Hays		x	x		x	NR
HSBC Holdings		x	x	x	x	NR
ICAP						x
Imperial Tobacco Group	x	x	x	x	x	NR
InterContinental Hotels Group			x		x	NR
International Power			x		x	NR
Johnson Matthey						x
Kazakhmys		x		x	x	NR
Kingfisher						x
Land Securities Group					x	x
Lloyds Banking Group		x	x	x	x	NR
Man Group						x
Marks & Spencer Group					x	x
Morrison (Wm.) Supermarkets						x
National Express Group		x	x	x	x	NR
National Grid						x
Old Mutual					x	NR
Petrofac		x			x	NR
Prudential	x	x	x	x	x	NR
PZ Cussons						x
Rolls-Royce Group					x	NR
Rotork			x	x	x	NR
Sage Group						x
Sainsbury (J)						x
Scottish & Southern Energy					x	NR
Shaftesbury						x
Shire Pharmaceuticals Group					x	NR
Smith and Nephew	x	x		x	x	NR
Smiths Group						x
SSE Plc						x
Tate & Lyle						x
TUI Travel						x
Victrex						x
Vodafone		x			x	NR
Wolseley				x	x	NR

It is hard to be sure who is providing evaluations to any great degree and to what standard.

Who are the evaluators?

Given the newness of the requirement for external evaluation, it is not surprising that the market is relatively undeveloped. Published information is scarce. It is hard to be sure who is providing evaluations to any great degree and to what standard. As one of our interviewees said,

"If you want to have a serious operation in America, you can look at which surgeons are rated and how they are rated. You ought to be able to do that for this sort of thing, [find out] who's good for big companies, who's good for small companies."

On page 36 is a list of UK external board evaluators, compiled from a combination of annual reports, internet research and our own market knowledge. The list is not definitive, but gives an indication of the range of providers in the market, including IDDAS.

We have grouped providers as follows:

- **Board Effectiveness Consultancies**, where external board reviews are a key part of their service offering
- **Individual Consultancies**, undertaking external board reviews primarily as a sole practitioner
- **Headhunting & Search Firms**, who undertake external board reviews as part of their service offering
- **Professional Services Firms/Partnerships**, including accountants and lawyers who undertake external board reviews as part of their service offering
- **Membership Organisations**, for example ICSA, who undertake external board Reviews as part of their services
- **Other Organisations**, including corporate governance consultancies.

A full evaluation of all aspects of board performance might call for the services of a specialist consultancy.

A selection of UK external board evaluators

Board Effectiveness Consultancies	
IDDAS	Helen Pitcher
Independent Audit	Jonathan Hayward
Armstrong Bonham Carter	Martin Armstrong
Bvalco	Brian Quinn
Individual Consultancies	
Boardroom Review	Dr Tracy Long
Sheena Crane Ltd	Sheena Crane
Stuart Timperley Associates	Professor Stuart Timperley
Professor Rob Goffee (London Business School)	Professor Rob Goffee
Professor Andrew Kakabadse (Cranfield School of Management)	Professor Andrew Kakabadse
Independent Board Evaluation	Ffion Hague (also an IDDAS mentor)
Headhunting & Search Firms	
Trust Associates	Richard Clarke
Egon Zehnder International	See website
JCA Group	Jan Hall
MWM Consulting	Anna Mann
Lygon Group	See website
Professional Services Firms/Partnerships	
Towers Watson	See website
Lintstock	Merlin Underwood
Praesta Partners	See website
Manchester Square Partners	See website
Membership Organisations	
ICSA Board Evaluation	Simon Osborne
IOD	See website
Other Organisations	
Equity Communications	See website
Law Debenture	Louise Redmond
Edis-Bates Associates	Jon Edis-Bates

Source: Compiled from a combination of annual reports, internet research and our own market knowledge. The list is not definitive, but gives an indication of the range of providers in the market, including IDDAS.

The choice of consultant depends on what the board wants to get out of the evaluation. A full evaluation of all aspects of board performance might call for the services of a specialist consultancy. If compliance is the main concern, a professional services firm or corporate governance consultancy may suit; or if the principal preoccupation is succession planning, a firm from a headhunting background may be the right choice. However, regulators and others warn of the danger of conflict of interest. The ABI believes this would “preclude those who provide other services, such as search agents who assist in the recruitment of directors, and remuneration consultants”.

Among the providers mentioned in annual reports, several were reappointed. Some of our interviewees commented that if the same consultants are used year after year, the process could become stale and they could get too close to the board, thus losing some of the independence which underpins their value.

This reflects the thinking behind the FRC's advice on the frequency of external evaluation.

As ever, much will depend on the integrity and objectivity of the evaluator and their ability to manage this sensitive process.

Annex and Resources

In its Guidance on Board Effectiveness, the FRC put forward guidelines on what an evaluation might cover:

- the mix of skills, experience, knowledge and diversity on the board, in the context of the challenges facing the company
- clarity of, and leadership given to, the purpose, direction and values of the company
- succession and development plans
- how the board works together as a unit, and the tone set by the chairman and the CEO
- key board relationships, particularly chairman/CEO, chairman/senior independent director, chairman/company secretary and executive/non-executive
- effectiveness of individual nonexecutive and executive directors
- clarity of the senior independent director's role
- effectiveness of board committees, and how they are connected with the main board
- quality of the general information provided on the company and its performance
- quality of papers and presentations to the board
- quality of discussions around individual proposals
- process the chairman uses to ensure sufficient debate for major decisions or contentious issues
- effectiveness of secretariat
- clarity of the decision processes and authorities
- processes for identifying and reviewing risks
- how the board communicates with, and listens and responds to, shareholders and other stakeholders
- approach to development of strategy, oversight of risk and control.

Resources

UK Corporate Governance Code 2010 pp 16–17 (FRC, June 2010)

Guidance on Board Effectiveness pp 11–12 (FRC, March 2011)

Developments in Corporate Governance 2011: The impact and implementation of the UK Corporate Governance and Stewardship Codes p 17 (FRC, December 2011)

Review of the UK top 200 companies 2010 (ICSA Board Evaluation, April 2011)

Corporate Governance Review 2011: A Changing Climate, Fresh Challenges Ahead pp 17–18 (Grant Thornton, November 2011)

Report on Board Effectiveness (Association of British Insurers, September 2011)

The Report Team

Helen Pitcher

Helen is recognised as a leading Board Effectiveness practitioner and facilitated the round tables for this research. She writes and presents regularly on the role of the chairman and NEDs in creating a high performance board culture and on the behavioural aspects of board performance.

Helen is chairman of IDDAS and a main board director of the Savile Group plc. Her career spans 30 years in both the business world and the consulting sector. She held a variety of senior roles in blue chip companies, then in her subsequent consulting career became CEO of CEDAR, which she built into one of the best regarded consultancies in the human capital world.

Helen is also a leading organisational performance coach and mentor, and works at the most senior level in FTSE 100 and international companies and in the public sector. She has a worldwide network of alumni whom she has coached over the years. Helen is chairman of the Selection Panel for Queen's Counsel, a panel member of the Employment Appeal Tribunal, chairman of KidsOut, and a trustee and fundraiser for several other charities. She was recently appointed to a Special Appeals Panel for returning Armed Forces veterans.

Helen holds an MA and an LLB, and is an alumna of the groundbreaking INSEAD Challenge of Leadership Programme. She is also an APECS-accredited coach, a qualified psychometric assessor and a Fellow of the IOD, CIPD and RSA.

Mark Winkle

Mark is an experienced Board Effectiveness consultant and executive coach whose experience covers a wide range of sectors, with a strong focus on financial services. His career spans consulting and executive management with ITT Financial Services, Chase Manhattan Bank, KPMG, GAN Financial Services, CEDAR TM and IDDAS.

Mark has particular expertise in creating a corporate governance assessment process, which captures the future focus of the organisation and provides a platform for active board development. He is adept at establishing the assessment frameworks, context and development to support the chairman and the board in creating a high performing board team.

Mark has over 15 years of coaching experience focused on performance development, working with a wide range of directors and senior executives across all disciplines.

This has included facilitating organisational strategies at individual and team level. He holds a BA in Law and an MBA from Roffey Park. He is a qualified NLP Practitioner, an APECS accredited executive coach and a qualified psychometric assessor. He is also certified in the process of Systemic Thinking.

Hilary Sears

Hilary is a senior IDDAS mentor and undertook all the interviews. She has extensive experience in executive search and board assessment, as a director and vice president in Carré Orban, Korn Ferry and AT Kearney. Hilary worked in the Cabinet Office on secondment to the Leadership and People Strategy Directorate. She is chairman of the MS Society and of KIDS, a national charity for disabled children, deputy chairman of the International Advisory Board of Cranfield School of Management, a director (and past chairman) of the Association of MBAs and past vice chairman of Forum UK. Hilary is a qualified NLP practitioner and coach.

Hashi Syedain

Hashi is a freelance business journalist with more than 20 years' experience of writing for national newspapers, business magazines and websites. She is a former deputy editor of Management Today and has worked as a journalist and editor in both Russia and Germany. Hashi is also a member (and past chairman) of the Independent Monitoring Board of Harmondsworth Immigration Removal Centre, which reports on standards of fairness and decency for asylum seekers and other immigration detainees.

Annabella Gabb

Annabella has worked as a freelance business editor and journalist for online and print publications for many years. She is a former Associate Editor of *Management Today*.

Susan Dudley

Susan's background is in HR, administration and project co-ordination. She provides project co-ordination and consultancy services to a number of corporate clients across various sectors, including utilities, telecommunications, retail and the NHS. Susan is a member of the CIPD and a qualified psychometrician.

IDDAS provides experience-based Board Effectiveness services, including Independent Board Reviews, Coaching, Business Mentoring, Leadership Facilitation, Assessment and Career Management Services to assist boards and senior executives with business and career transitions.

The IDDAS offering covers:

- Board Effectiveness
- Independent Board Reviews
- Executive Coaching
- Business Mentoring
- Leadership Facilitation
- Executive Assessment-Development
- Career Mentoring Transition

Board Effectiveness and Independent Board Reviews

IDDAS supports both the formal governance review of a board and the behavioural aspects of board effectiveness development, to create a powerful and valuable review process.

The IDDAS integrated approach is unique in that it looks not only at the formal board functioning against corporate governance standards, but also at the commerciality and performance of the board as a whole, and of individual board members.

IDDAS

The Art and Science of Board Effectiveness, Development and Transition

A member of the Savile Group plc

Chapter B3

Board Dynamics: A Female Perspective

Introduction **B3.1**

We are very grateful to IDDAS for permission to reprint this excellent guidance, and also three others in their series, which we reproduce at Chapters **B2**, **B4** and **B5**.

Clare Chalmers, Chief Executive of IDDAS, would be pleased to hear from readers with any inquiries about this guidance. She can be contacted at IDDAS, IDDAS House, 74 New Cavendish Street, London, W1G 8TF (Tel: +44 (0)20 7436 0101; Email: clare.chalmers@iddas.com; Website: www.iddas.com).

Based in London, IDDAS specialises in providing board effectiveness, mentoring and coaching, leadership facilitation and executive assessment services for chairs, CEOs and main board directors, as well as for those who aspire to non-executive roles. IDDAS has an established reputation for its quality, innovative, supportive and flexible approach.

IDDAS BOARD DYNAMICS: A FEMALE PERSPECTIVE – WOMEN ON FTSE 100 BOARDS

Foreword

The boardroom is under scrutiny as never before – and rightly so, given recent events. The bank failures of last year highlight the central importance of challenge and debate to a healthy organisation. Robust discussion requires careful facilitation and a range of contributions from people who bring different perspectives and complementary skills and experiences to the table.

This report focuses on the strengths that female non-executive directors bring to the boardroom. It offers a rare insight into the actual experience of women operating at this level – part of a tiny band of just 113 female directors who sit on FTSE 100 boards.

They make an enormous contribution to their respective boards for many reasons which have nothing to do with gender. And yet many in this elite group, who have worked successfully in male-dominated environments for much of their careers, also believe that women can and do bring something different.

The views and advice contained in this report will be of interest to women seeking to make their mark. More important is that the message is heeded by the boardroom majority, and by those responsible for boardroom composition.

Lord Freeman
Chairman, Savile Group Advisory Board

Introduction

The stimulus for this research was IDDAS's experience of coaching senior women. When we started the project at the height of the banking crisis, questions were being raised about the macho risk-taking culture which had fuelled the crisis and whether the more open, collective decision-making approach, typically ascribed to women, would have made a difference.

As we began conducting our interviews, Deputy Prime Minister Harriet Harman made the bold statement that a top political team should always consist of a man and a woman. Meanwhile, Home Secretary Jacqui Smith demonstrated an openness rarely shown by (mostly male) colleagues by stating that she would have liked some more training when she took over one of the biggest political jobs in the country.

We have since seen the publication of David Walker's review of corporate governance in UK banks and financial institutions. Walker concludes that the most important factor in ensuring long term corporate success for any organisation, *"is a highly effective executive team that is not dominated by a single voice; where open challenge and debate occurs; and yet the executive team is cohesive and collectively strong."*

The women who spoke to us – almost a fifth of all female board directors on FTSE 100 companies – felt that these were areas where their presence made a particular difference.

Our participants were frequently at pains to emphasise that the points they were making about the characteristics, skills or circumstances required for boardroom success are equally applicable to men and women. Nonetheless, there was broad agreement that gender remains an issue in the UK's boardrooms and that women at this level have to be extra careful and confident in the value they add, because they are such a visible minority.

Our interviewees are an exceptional group of women. We would like to thank them all for the time they gave us, despite their numerous commitments. Their insights make invaluable reading for existing and aspiring board directors, whether male or female, and for anyone involved in the appointment and development of board directors.

Helen Pitcher
Chairman, IDDAS

Executive summary

The progress of women up the UK corporate ladder has been painfully slow. Despite the recommendations of the Higgs and Tyson reports in 2004, The Female FTSE Report 2008 indicates that women make up just 11.7% of board directors, a small improvement on 6.9% ten years ago, but there are still 22 companies in the FTSE 100 with all male boards and of the 149 new appointees in the last year only 16 (10.7%) were women.

We set out to interview those women who have made it onto boards of FTSE 100 companies to understand what they bring to their boards and what they have done to maximise their success.

We probed their attitudes to challenge and debate and what role the chair plays in enabling them to be effective as non-executive directors (NEDs).

Finally, we explored how they were recruited, how they responded to being in a minority and how they coped with media attention.

Over the course of three months we conducted structured interviews with 24 women, a fifth of all female directors in the FTSE 100.

All are either the only woman on their board or one of a small minority, a fact that makes them highly visible and places them under considerable pressure to perform. Several spoke of having to work hard not to be seen as 'the woman' and said it was a relief when a second woman joined their board.

Many also felt that a balance of men and women improved board dynamics and the quality of discussion. In particular, the quality of questioning improved because women are more prepared to probe and clarify, if there is something they do not understand.

Our research revealed certain qualities that women at their best demonstrate. These are by no means exclusively female qualities, but areas in which the most successful women excel. Overall, women have usually had to work so hard to get to the board and are so well qualified and prepared that, "they raise the bar for everyone" as one interviewee put it.

Women at their best:

- Take their role as NED very seriously and choose carefully the right board to join.
- Are well qualified for the roles they take on and are proactive about plugging any gaps in their expertise.
- Often bring a different perspective to men.
- Are interested in building relationships and promoting good team dynamics on the board.
- Are not egocentric, focusing on the organisation's goals rather than their own agenda.
- Are adept at challenge and seek to do so in a non-threatening way.
- Bring great energy, drive and commitment to the role.

The central importance of the role of the chair in managing a board effectively was another key finding. While the benefits are clear, dealing with the individual and team dynamics is harder work with a diverse board because more effort is required to ensure everyone contributes and the team manages to gel. The behaviours of effective chairs – and the consequences of poor chairing are explored on page 24.

We found that there is an important role for organisations to play in growing executive women for NED board positions. The best companies have a clear strategy to develop their own talented women, and are selfless in accepting that this talent will be used in the service of global business generally. At the same time, organisations need to pay more attention to board development and assessment. Joining a board is the start of a journey, our participants told us, and they believe not enough weight is given to on-going learning and performance management. Their recommendations for induction, training and development are given on page 26.

Take their role as NED seriously and choose carefully which board to join

The women we spoke to see becoming a NED as an active career choice. They spend time finding out about a board before they join, make sure they know how they can add value and then commit themselves to learning about the company and staying abreast of the issues.

Several stressed, in particular, the time they spent reading board papers thoroughly.

"I screen the opportunity very seriously before pursuing it and will only go for opportunities which are interesting, where I can contribute and where the chemistry of the board will work."

"Can you look other NEDs in the eye and trust them? Is it right for you? Will the dates fit? All of this questioning makes you more rigorous in the process."

"This role is not an easy option; it involves a significant commitment, which can have a critical impact on work-life balance."

"I always do due diligence and have turned boards down. In the US, I turned one down because it did not feel right, and within weeks the CEO had sued the board for dismissing him!"

Are well qualified for the roles they take on and are proactive about plugging any gaps in their expertise

Like their male counterparts, the women we interviewed have years of executive experience, including specialist, operational and/or international roles, but they also have the confidence to seek out expertise or training, if they do not know about something.

"A NED needs to be forthright, and ask for what they need to know ... they should take responsibility for customising their own induction, including acknowledging their own background holes."

"I needed to learn about the actual business and organised my own induction. I had to be very pro-active in doing this."

"One shouldn't be embarrassed about asking and learning on the job. Finance was my shortfall, and I worked hard at applying myself to it."

Bring a different perspective to men

Our participants often felt that they brought a different approach to the table than the male majority and that this difference was beneficial to the board.

"The ability to think laterally, to see a shape that no-one else does, to see things differently."

"Women may approach things in a different way. Women are better at spinning many plates and having wider responsibilities and therefore perspectives. They may ask about different areas, rather than only focussing on one area."

"Women understand people better and are not embarrassed to talk about the issues. Men are less prepared to talk about individuals' needs. They talk more about the business issues, and outcomes and only then do they look at personnel, and reasons for particular performance."

"I religiously raise the human dimension and am well received."

Are aware of board dynamics and play an active role in building strong relationships and promoting good teamwork

Women recognise that building board relationships is very important. They are aware of boardroom dynamics and will give constructive feedback either to the chair or individual members to ensure the team works effectively. They come to the table with an appreciation that teams make better decisions than individuals.

"On the whole, women are good at reading reactions, at recognising the impact they will have on the feelings of the board. They can draw out a consensus where there is one to be had."

"It is not the role of an NED to sort out the dynamics amongst the executive team, but the one service you can provide is to point out to the chairman that someone in the team is stressed, that something isn't right. This is the softer side of what I do."

"One of my major contributions is helping the board to feel open and relaxed with each other. I will often be the one who finds a way through the blocks or the posturing."

"No-one really knows what strategic risk is, and no-one knows what risk is strategic. The current banking situation was never listed as a risk. Strategic risks usually emerge from discussion. It is not normally one person who raises it, but a number of them in discussion. I can't think of a single example of just one person demonstrating huge insight."

Are less ego-driven than men and committed to the organisation's goals rather than their own agenda

While acknowledging that women too can have large egos, most of our respondents felt that women were less prone to this failing than men and more committed to the organisation's goals as a result.

"In general, women have far fewer ego issues. At one organisation, I was on a board of strong personalities, opinions and egos. Some of the NEDs had joined because it was one of the big FTSE 100 boards to join, not because it was inherently interesting to them, or because they can add value. Individually they were nice, but there was definitely a culture of 'my car is bigger than your car'."

"I am mostly competitive with myself, not seeking to get ahead at the expense of other colleagues. I want to be associated with being part of the best organisations but I am very concerned about the whole and what we are doing for the whole."

"I have to be clear that it is about shareholder value and not for my own personal benefit. For instance, in evaluating an acquisition, I believe it needs to be for the good of the business, not for the good of the senior management."

Are adept at questioning and challenging and seek to do so in a non-threatening way

Women are not afraid to raise tough issues, but think carefully about how to do so in a constructive manner. They are also willing to probe and ask basic questions.

"Women ask questions that other people are not prepared to ask and have a strong sense of smell – knowing where there is a problem, from a little flicker."

"Women are less blunt, and therefore, in some ways, more effective. When you are NED, you are there to give advice and stop the company going off the rails (which happens relatively rarely!). You are talking finer shades of grey, and women are more gentle in their probing."

"I am not fussed about raising issues. What's the worst that can happen? You get shot down? NEDs should be ashamed if they don't seek more information. They are not fulfilling the role."

"Women can ask questions and disagree with grace. They get answers without putting people on the defensive."

Bring great energy, drive and commitment to the role

We were struck during our interviews by the focus, determination and drive that the women demonstrated. It stood out from the whole body of an interview how much thought, effort and sheer hard work a woman had put into arriving at this point in her career. Sometimes it came through in asides about domestic arrangements or sacrifices to personal life, and occasionally it was explicitly stated.

"This role is not an easy option, it involves a significant commitment which can have a critical impact on work-life balance."

"Women work hard and take their responsibilities very seriously. They come very well prepared. You can guarantee that they will have done their homework more thoroughly than the men."

Implications and conclusions

For women

Becoming a NED is a serious career choice, which needs careful consideration. It comes at a price in terms of work-life balance. Women, in particular, must plan well in advance to position themselves correctly, amass the right kind of experience and network strategically, especially if they take career breaks. They must be very clear about the value that they bring.

Although it may be hard to get appointed, women should choose carefully to make sure they join the right board and can deliver what is expected to a high standard. They must be particularly discerning about whether they can work with the chair, whose role will be critical in determining their future success.

Although many of the factors that lead to success are not gender specific, gender is nonetheless an issue in many UK boardrooms because there are still so few women at this level, placing them constantly in the spotlight.

For boards and organisations

Women make a significant difference to board effectiveness through their individual contributions and through their effect on board dynamics. Organisations should be creative in their approach to recruiting women and should evaluate the overall combination of skills, experience and personal qualities an individual brings to a particular board. The NED role requires different strengths to the executive – listening, probing, influencing and facilitation skills. These are areas in which women often excel.

Organisations can widen the pool of talented individuals suitable for board positions by grooming women and other under-represented groups and then actively encouraging them to find roles as NEDs with other organisations. Such individuals need to be carefully selected and assessed against a clear framework of technical and personal characteristics, but then actively helped to secure outside board positions.

Diverse boards are more effective, but successfully managing such a group requires greater skill on the part of the chair to ensure that everyone is included and that the more vibrant debate that characterises diverse teams can flourish. Chairs may need coaching to support them in this role.

Organisations and chairs should pay more attention to proper induction, training and development for NEDs, to help them become effective quickly and improve their overall performance. This should be a combination of orientation to the business, meeting key executives, spending time on role clarity with the chair and working with someone to evaluate contribution and performance. Chairs should spend time with NEDs and look at their personal development, including possible roles on committees. This is particularly important for women and other minorities.

Boards need to re-examine how they use their board evaluation data. Whilst it is laudable that boards are asking for external professional guidance to evaluate their performance, it is not clear that the data is used to develop board effectiveness and foster personal and collective learning and growth.

Some thoughts on Walker

The case for more diverse boards is both overwhelming and widely accepted. Yet the actual number of women reaching board level in the UK's largest companies is still tiny. The Walker Review notes the central importance of boards not being dominated by a single voice and of encouraging challenge and debate.

However, there is a danger that Walker's recommendation to place greater emphasis on experience versus personal qualities in choosing NEDs for financial institutions, will have the effect of excluding women further.

Although Walker's recommendations relate specifically to the finance industry, they nonetheless set the agenda for all NED appointments. Amassing the requisite experience is where women generally – with notable exceptions, of course – tend to do less well than men, because of the challenges of combining a high-powered career with childraising.

It would be unfortunate if the Walker review did have this no doubt unintended effect. Yet it is hard to see how it can be avoided unless organisations make strenuous efforts to groom and assist promising women in obtaining NED positions – or the UK adopts a radical Norwegian-style solution of imposing quotas for female board directors on the largest companies.

The findings in detail

In this section we explain how we did our research and present some of the data in more detail.

We start by examining the impact for female directors of being the only woman on the board. We go on to describe a set of four characteristics that successful female board directors demonstrate: social intelligence; courage and resilience; breadth of view; energy and drive and we set out what most often trips them up.

We show how successful women use these characteristics to challenge in a non-confrontational way and highlight the vital role of the chair in helping women make a full contribution. We also set out participants' views about the induction and training they have received – and would have liked to have received – to maximise their effectiveness.

In the final section we look at how our interviewees were recruited; their differing approaches to networking and their attitudes to the media – including advice on how to handle the attention.

We end with top tips gleaned from the women on how to succeed as a board director.

Methodology

We wanted to be able to explore issues in depth, in a way that would not be possible with a tickbox questionnaire. So we chose a qualitative approach, based on structured interviews, created from a pilot group of seven women.

In all, we interviewed:

- 24 women from FTSE 100 boards
- 21% of current FTSE women directors

Board roles:

- 14 have one or more NED positions, 5 have both executive and non-executive directorships, 4 are executive directors

Nationality

- 15 are British, 8 North American, 1 European

Education

- 5 hold MBAs, including 4 from American schools, 5 trained in law, 2 are qualified accountants, 2 have PhDs.

Age

- Their ages ranged from 44–68. 4 were in their 40s, 14 were in their 50s, 6 were in their 60s.

Sectors of operation

- They operate in sectors, including financial services, public services, utilities, retail, telecommunications and manufacturing.

Each interview lasted 60–90 minutes and was conducted either face to face or on the telephone. Respondents gave us their views about their own contribution and their views on female colleagues who they have worked with or met at board level. A guarantee that all answers would be unattributable led the women to be open and forthright in what they told us.

Being the sole woman on a FTSE board

Our interviewees are so used to being the lone woman in the room, or one of a tiny minority, that the situation feels quite normal to them. Yet as one interviewee pointed out, most corporate men have no idea what is it like to be routinely outnumbered twelve to one in a meeting.

Many – though not all – feel that being the only woman does make a difference to how they are perceived, that they are more likely to be seen as 'the woman' than as just another director, but most go on to say that they make sure it does not affect them or their contribution.

Nonetheless, several interviewees said that things do change when there are more women; the tenor of discussion can be quite different when a board is more balanced and even having a second woman at the table can make a big difference. Apart from the impact on board dynamics, it takes the spotlight off the lone female and normalises women as board members.

Taken as a whole, the comments show just how tough these women have to be in order to be able to shrug off their minority status.

"As the only woman you are in the spotlight. Men may get away with things but it is more visible for the woman."

"Women may be hindered by the expectations of the men on the board and, to some extent, by conforming to those expectations."

"Being the only woman can be a problem, because you can be made to feel the token woman and are treated like that."

"As the single woman, it would be very easy to feel excluded. I don't because I am determined not to be. I know what to do: I am prepared, I can smile and grimace at the right time, and I do go out of my way to establish strong relationships."

"Men see women as a category, not as an individual woman, and this blocks women's very independence."

"In principle, for those who are inclined to see how you act 'as a woman', then having more than one will show the differences between them. If people are not prejudiced, then it is not necessary."

"More than one woman does change the dynamics in the room. I don't see or feel it, because I have always been in a male dominated environment and boardroom, but when I do pay attention, there is a subtle change: it tends to make others more careful in their listening and general dynamics on the board. Women can raise the bar, because they are so well prepared."

"In a predominantly male boardroom there is less willingness to share lack of understanding."

"Having more than one woman on the board made things hugely much easier for the women. It made a big difference; we gave each other encouragement, smiled. As the only woman, you have to be quite brave to speak out."

"It's more comfortable for everyone [if there is more than one woman], because there is not such a spotlight. It doesn't mean that you have a closer relationship with the other woman or women, as that is all about what you have in common."

Some interviewees felt gender was not an issue

"I have no problems being the only woman. All the members are very down to earth and I am not singled out as a woman."

"I am not convinced that there is a tipping point – that having five instead of two women would really make a difference. It depends more on personal style, values and principles. More critical is the leadership as this sets the tone, agenda and ensures the cogs fit and are properly tuned."

"The views on this are a bit nebulous, as it is not women battling against men. It is much more subtle than that. In a group of 10–15 people, a woman is not an island unto herself."

The characteristics of successful (female) board members: the bright side

It is no surprise that most of our interviewees found it easy to think about the characteristics of successful women, bearing in mind how hard it is for them to get appointed to a FTSE 100 board.

We have clustered the success factors for effective performance into four main areas: **social intelligence, courage and resilience, breadth of view and energy and drive**. A fifth characteristic – **mental agility** – also came up but was largely taken as a given: you do not get to this level unless you have a sharp mind.

Social intelligence

Effective women board directors consider the environment in which they operate, use insight to consider the best time and forum to raise issues and do this in a way that does not break relations. They use skills of mediation and facilitation to maximise their influence.

"As a woman, people confide in you. The majority of men don't have the ability to 'endear', to form a relationship fairly quickly, and get people to talk. A woman can do this more naturally and comfortably. People are more apt to seek me out and talk."

"This is an extremely sexist observation, but women are able to listen without ego, and find patterns in behaviour and point them out. At board level everyone is successful, but I've had experiences where the men have been attempting to establish who was the most successful. Female directors seem to require less feeding of their egos."

"A board evaluation noted that women are better at picking up weak signals. One of the women NEDs in particular is very useful at throwing in a thought and picking up nuances that the men on the board would not naturally do."

"Women are capable of fitting in with the culture and at times are almost chameleon-like. They modify their approach and use their emotional intelligence to deal with different situations."

"Women use techniques of affiliation and support people behind the scenes, rather than the direct Maggie Thatcher style."

"Empathy, listening, sensitivity. Women have the ability to connect, to form those important relationships."

"Personal insights, intuition, greater flexibility. The ability to assess a situation, step back and look at what approach will work, not just take the same approach again."

"They have a distinctive ability to get on well with colleagues especially male colleagues and do not hold themselves apart."

"Women are quite good listeners and recorders and can be objective about flow and what has been agreed. They listen to others' opinions and can have a more practical perspective in questioning strategic options."

Courage and resilience

Effective board directors have self-confidence and emotional resilience. They can cope with robust discussion and isolation. Many interviewees said that women are less afraid of asking basic questions and seeking further clarification.

"A woman has to not find being in a minority daunting and have had enough exposure to male dominated teams. You need confidence in yourself and to have enough experience to have your own point of view and to be able to express that point of view persuasively."

"You have to have strength and tenacity."

"I am prepared to challenge, probe, take an argument to its conclusion. I'm prepared to say difficult things like: I didn't join this board to do that."

"Probably women are more prepared to get into an issue: 'Take me through that again, I don't understand.' Men don't do this – in the same way they don't like asking for directions at a garage."

"You need the courage to ask the questions, to know when to."

"You need a degree of confidence and bravery to be clear on what you are raising, and why. You must avoid trying to score a point, but must raise an issue when it is standing in the way of creating value."

Breadth of view

Directors at this level need the ability to see a broad macro economic perspective linked to the current business environment. They must bring in strategic insights from other commercial situations.

"I have the capacity to put the question concerned in a wider context: what is the strategic importance of this issue?"

"The more experience you have, then the more you can draw on this; you can see patterns. If you've done so many mergers, change programmes, IT upgrades, then you know what questions to ask. The more you do, then the more capable you become and the more confident. People listen to you more."

"You must prompt different perspectives and approaches around strategy, not about operations and detail. It involves putting forward views, and positions which are different. You must work to support the executive and the CEO. It doesn't mean talking all the time; you must be mindful where you place your comments."

"This is not a female thing, but a general comment: you are less successful if you tend to focus on minutiae, rather than on the long term needs of the business, and if you are strident."

Energy and drive

Women are well organised and disciplined with a strong work ethic and enormous commitment. They plan ahead, manage the diary and prioritise time and commitments. They demonstrate huge energy and drive and can withstand significant periods of pressure.

"Perhaps from years of competing, we tend to be better prepared. Women typically are also prepared to work hard, in order to understand at a fundamental level."

"I am very well prepared, and well organised. I plan my life two years ahead, and absolutely everything is scheduled (including vacations) within that timeframe."

"Women have organisational strengths, because they are used to juggling: they have to be good at organising their time."

"I allocate time to reading, as board packs are often meaty. For one board, there are six board meetings a year which last 2 days, so there is a lot of reading."

"I don't get sick. I've had only one half day off sick in nine years."

The characteristics of less successful (female) board members: the dark side

We asked our interviewees to tell us what may block or hinder the effectiveness of women and to describe the difference between those who are only moderately successful and the best. The most common derailers our interviewees cited were lack of **self-confidence and personal impact** and a **tendency to perfectionism**, but they also mentioned characteristics that are equally associated with less successful male NEDs, such as being **too aggressive or trying to do the job of the executives.**

Low self confidence and impact

The most common answers women gave to our questions about derailers related to issues of confidence or assertiveness. Low self-confidence, they told us, leads some women not to speak up, or to speak only on their specialist area. Lack of assertiveness may mean they do not fight their corner. Both inevitably reduce their impact on the board.

"In the early years of my NED career, I thought many things before I spoke, and then kicked myself when men brought them up instead of me. [Confidence] is more gender oriented than you would like and hope."

"I have seen it take women longer than their male counterparts to get comfortable to speak. In one case, I heard of a woman asked to leave as she was not challenging enough of the board."

"Being too passive, not speaking up on areas outside their specialist areas of expertise, letting go of their view too quickly."

"Women can let themselves down, by not standing their ground, not challenging."

"At board level it is important to take personal ownership. Although already successful, women need to acknowledge that they will hit obstacles but they need to remain assertive and get their point in the room, they must not let go of what they want to say."

"Women do have a tendency to defer to those with more experience."

"A hesitancy about making their mark, and turning their expertise and knowledge to good effect and in the process advancing their own reputation. Women are not as good as men at this."

"Some are too quiet and restrained in expressing views at all or about a particular topic. One female NED I worked with said nothing, except on personnel which was her background".

"They sit in their expert role, and don't advance into the full territory of debate."

"You are often the only woman on the board, and the others are not giving you the confidence. Also, most women are "slow burn"; they take time to learn their brief. You really have to get up to speed quickly, because the first impression is a lasting one, and is hard to change."

Telling executives how to do their job

Failing to understand the difference between executive and non-executive roles is a common pitfall for newly appointed NEDs, including some women.

"It is difficult being a NED while still holding a senior executive position, because it is difficult to step from one mode into the other. The danger is that you appear to be telling the executive how to do the job; you must instead query, be objective, coach and mentor. You must also not behave like a less informed executive, but if you wait until you have left your executive role and have no NED experience, then it is very hard to step onto the NED ladder."

"The biggest difference between executive and non-executive is that a totally different skill set is required. So, while your executive experience is valuable, the skills needed on the board are different. What are the important ones? The ability to influence. Successful executives sometimes struggle with the influencing skills needed, because they no longer have direct line, and cannot control in the way you can in an executive capacity."

Challenging or aggressive behaviour

Women, like men, sometimes speak inappropriately or out of turn.

"It can be tough being the only woman, you have to cope with a load of banter and not just talk for the sake of it. Women need to learn to listen and to pace. While men may get away with it because there are so many of them, a woman does not. She is in the spotlight."

"Of course, it is not necessarily a gender issue but more about how to raise issues and the need to influence and impact people in a way that it is not seen as confrontational, too clumsy and too brusque can be a problem."

"Some women can talk about items that they know nothing about and this reduces their standing. They do not appear responsible but rather egocentric, determined to advance themselves at the expense of the organisation if necessary."

"They feel they have to lose their temper and criticize management which is totally pathetic."

Perfectionism

Several interviewees mentioned that women are more likely than men to hold back, if they are not absolutely expert.

"Women often want to be master of everything and if they are lacking in a small area of technical skills they discount themselves and their contribution. In an alpha male type boardroom environment they may hold back from making a full contribution."

"Women worry about 'winging' it and aim to have mastery of the data; they need to learn to trust their instincts."

"The toughest part for women is to recognise that they are always learning and as such will never have absolute mastery of a subject."

Low interest in relationship building

Dealing with the reality of their minority status is something women must learn to do.

"Women can make some people less comfortable. They need to take on a responsibility to make sure relationships work and get past the first impediment."

How women raise tough issues successfully

Many of our interviewees spoke about the efforts they go to if they want to raise a contentious issue. This was an area we explored in detail, given the central importance of constructive challenge to a healthy boardroom and the potentially disastrous consequences when non-executives cannot hold their own.

They consider the best approach and make sure it's not a surprise

"I will get the board agenda ahead of time and alert the relevant person before the meeting if I'm raising a contentious issue. This gives them an opportunity to prepare a response. You don't want someone to look bad as a result of being caught off guard."

They get the chair on board

"If I have an issue with something in the board papers, I will raise it with the chairman beforehand. Often the chairman concurs with the point and I have never been put back into the box. If I had a real problem, I would 'phone the CEO, via the chairman, to pre-wire them on my thinking. That gives the executive the opportunity to answer. You don't just throw a bomb into the room. That would destroy trust and people would then withhold information."

They are less confrontational …

"A woman's approach can be different. A woman recognises the value of someone else's contribution before they tear it apart. This confirms it is not a personal attack but about an issue: "That is an interesting view point," whereas men are more ready to go for the jugular."

"I probe differently. I don't do the belligerent approach ever. If I'm asking a difficult question or expressing an unpopular view, I might do it almost with regret; I don't want it to be seen as criticism."

"Women are less blunt and, therefore, in some ways, more effective. When you are nonexecutive, you are there to give advice and stop the company going off the rails (which happens relatively rarely!). You are talking finer shades of grey, and women are more gentle in their probing."

… perhaps because they have to be

"I'm not sure that men like being challenged by women and so women have to make it palatable."

Or perhaps they are better placed?

"In my experience, most men are the sole breadwinner, and won't raise contentious issues – they don't want negativity after the event, or to affect their bonus. A woman can raise things in a more conciliatory fashion, 'I am wondering why we are doing this?'"

"Women may be more willing to take a risk and probe because they are not part of the club, so they don't have to worry about playing golf with the same colleagues afterwards."

The role of the chair

The chair has an enormous impact not only on the board but on ensuring a diverse board works effectively. For our interviewees the management of board dynamics was critical, and in fact women often turn down a position if they feel the chair will not actively support them and include diverse views and opinions. In other cases they have turned down a second term when they felt the chair did not manage the egos in the room or encourage an openness to alternative views.

A strong chair will discuss development with a female NED and, in particular, her appointment to committees. Taking on a committee role was found to be highly beneficial and increased both the credibility and confidence of women NEDs.

"Chairing a committee takes you to a different level of participation; you take a different position in the boardroom as you now report to the board and have others on your committee from the board reporting to you. This undoubtedly increases your expertise. However, it is not all about previous expertise but rather intelligence, commitment and analytical skills – often it is more about asking the right questions."

"The role [of the chairman] is critical for all directors, but even more so for women and ethnic minorities. It is essential for the chairman and CEO to work well together, especially on female development issues."

Chairs who are most effective at engaging diverse members of the board will:

- Show respect and actively include minority groups
- Listen to different perspectives
- Recognise the importance of their own role in building a strong team

Show respect and actively include women

"There is no question that the chairman – especially for women who have had limited exposure at board level – has to make particular effort to include them in conversations and solicit their views and opinions. If the chairman is not inclined to do this, it won't happen. I went to a women's network meeting at one of my companies, and was struck by a comment there: It's one thing to recruit, another to include."

"The way the chairman relates to women is very important. He needs to give them respect. There is a two-way responsibility. He sets the standard and allows contributions from men and women which will add value."

"Role of chair is crucial. They get it right when they invite comment, solicit input, and give visual cues of contact and interest."

Listen to different perspectives

"The chairman sets the tone for meetings, behaviours expected, and willingness of board members to listen to each other. It is critical that he guide the meetings."

"One of the important roles of the chairman is to get the best out of each of the board members and acknowledge what they bring to the discussion. For instance, some may be more able to contribute on brand strategy, while others move on the recommendation on the next dividend. Both are fundamental issues for the board, but different members will bring distinct experience. The chairman must recognise the respective experience, and get it onto the table to enrich the discussion. The chairman will seek a richness of views from the board."

"The chairman is key in terms of women contributing to the full, being even-handed in taking contributions from all NEDs. This is essential on policy and people issues. Part of his task is to listen to different perspectives. A poor chairman does not give sufficient weight to the NED perspectives, conversely giving too much to the executives."

Build a strong team

"The more I sit on boards and committees, the more respect I have for a good chairman and realise how difficult the role is. On a big board, managing the interaction of a number of highly opinionated people is a real skill. I'm cautious about generalities of gender – but noisier people dominate discussion; it is a failure of the chairman if they don't make sure everyone contributes."

"The chairman has to lead what typically is a group of disparate individuals, who have been brought together for the board. They will have different views, but the same objective to help the company."

"The role of the chairman is completely critical. It is very important to create space in meetings for everyone to contribute. There is always someone who jumps in first, and you really need to create space for all to make their point. This is the skill of the chairman."

"The chair should conduct evaluations and give feedback and look at the overall board dynamics at least once a year. The chair should consider how to promote women onto committees to raise their profile and prominence. The chair should do their background work before they get in the room and know who is keen on certain issues and then makes sure that these issues are surfaced. A good chair also spends time creating good social bonds and the space for networking."

"The chairman also needs to make sure of the fit on the board. You need to check this out beforehand. In my role on nominations committees, I try to get candidates in front of as many directors as possible, but it is up to the chairman then to create enough opportunities, face time, and relaxed face time for the board to gel and become a team."

Cautionary tales …

"At one company, I witnessed the chairman 'turning off', and then no-one controlled the CEO. This is when things can happen, and if you, as a woman, challenge this, the CEO may end up very much countering you and doing his own thing. The chairman is essential to keep control and be open-minded."

"One chair managed to call all of the three women by the wrong name. You let this kind of thing pass at your peril. I suggested at one meeting that he might call all of us Jane: I was fierce and furious!"

"I had an issue with a CEO who was not respectful, and would shut me up. The executive team said they really wanted to hear what I had to say; I had to be resilient."

Induction, training and development

Our interviewees were very clear that the journey does not end once you are appointed, but the amount of induction and training on offer, even in the largest companies, varies considerably, so you need to be a "self starter" to get the support you need.

There is no single answer to what will give a NED the most value, but options range from a discussion with the chair to clarify the role and expectations, to in-depth induction on the business, meetings with key advisers (auditors, lawyers, investment analysts) and opportunities to meet the top executives and to get to know other board colleagues.

Women said a new NED should be prepared to visit the different business sites, be it the mines, the nuclear reactor, the call centre or the production facility. Several women commented how much they had learnt from spending time with the company secretary.

Often the women had been active in arranging visits and meetings themselves but they emphasised that it works best when there is a partnership between the NED and the company in arranging support. It is also important that the NED is prepared to say what they do not know.

Many participants commented that they had not been offered coaching or mentoring but believed this would be beneficial.

They also mentioned the role of external training programmes and in particular the NED course at Cranfield School of Management. Such courses help to clarify the exact responsibilities, expectations and liabilities. They felt it was particularly important to understand the difference between NED and executive roles.

Training on media management and communications was considered vitally important (see page 30, section on impact of the media).

Our participants believe that there is more work to be done by companies to improve the level of support for NEDs – and to ensure on-going performance management and development, particularly in the light of increasing expectations being placed on this role.

"Induction courses are necessary, but you have to be prepared to say what you don't know. At one company I had to meet every director for 90 minutes, and it

was incredibly useful. I've subsequently made a point of asking for this whenever I join a board."

"Something resembling coaching would have been very useful – to have somebody on the board who will take a younger person under their wing. It happens more for the senior executives in the company, because they all know you. On the board, it is much more difficult, because you are there in an individual capacity, so it depends on how the interactions play out. You typically do not get feedback from your board colleagues."

"Support from the chairman is very important, plus practical support from company secretarial functions can make an enormous difference, as well as support in the form of further training and development."

"[You need] a really good induction, not just in governance, but into the business. An audit course might help some. NEDs tend to get less of an induction than an executive."

"I learned both from inside and outside – from suppliers, customers, research, etc. You have to understand the company's marketplace, its strategy and performance."

"One company paid for me to attend the NED training course at Cranfield, which was fabulous. It gave me a good understanding of the role, the differences between executive and non-executive, and of the role of the Company Secretary which doesn't exist in the US."

"Very few chairmen raise the spectre of how the board operates. Appraisals of the board are very cursory. Some take it more seriously: they employ consultants to speak with both the executive and non-executive director, but I'm not sure that they revisit and reassess against the recommendations. There is more to be done."

"Boards are not good at looking at their own performance and how they can develop skills. Board reviews are increasing and we need to look at performance going forward."

The recruitment process

Interviewees gave us encouraging feedback on the recruitment and selection process. It is clearly highly professional and involves a significant number of meetings with key personnel, which was appreciated by women. Our respondents believe that it is a two-way choice and that it is critical for both parties to make the right decision.

Headhunters are the most significant route to NED board appointment. Women also used networking to secure appointments but stressed that this was not like "an old boys club" but linked closely to their experience and performance. The speed of the appointment process varied from four weeks to six months.

"The recruitment process has been changing and improving. You used to meet just the headhunter and the CEO. Now there will be several meetings: the chairman, CEO, the Senior Independent Director and NEDs. It might be up to six people."

"A headhunter was involved in all my appointments. In two cases, I did not know the chairman or CEO at all beforehand. With another, I had been on the board

with someone who became a chairman elsewhere, and he instigated the approach, but still went through the headhunter."

"For one board I met the chairman, CEO, the chairman of the Nominations Committee, and another NED. This was followed by dinner with the whole board."

"Headhunters were involved in all of my appointments, and they have worked to a brief, and given structured interviews. In some cases, the client has been led by the chairman, in others the Senior Independent Director; in all cases I have been given exposure also to the senior management."

"When I've been recruited through my network, I would not describe it as the old chum network. I'm getting roles based on what I've done. I think it works differently for men, where the 'usual suspects' are placed. This doesn't happen for women."

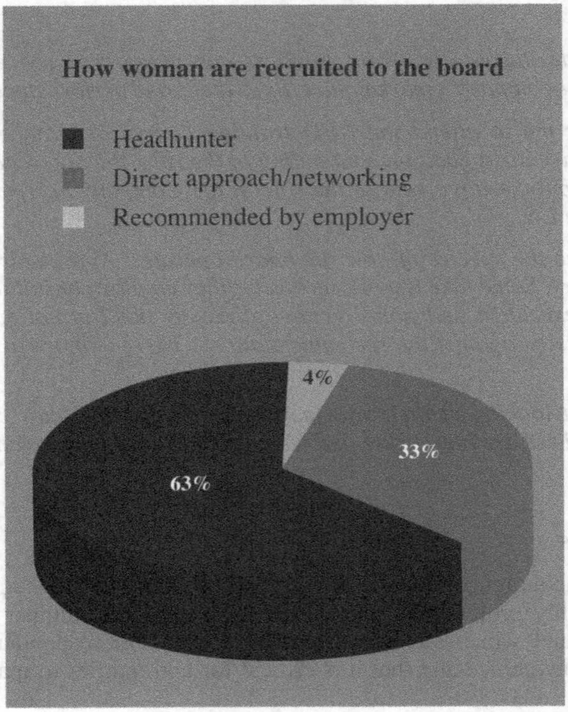

Women and networking

Our interviewees had wildly differing approaches to networking. Some were highly networked and placed considerable importance on maintaining a wide range of contacts. Others said they did very little, either because they lacked the time, but also because they did not enjoy it or see it as important.

Many of our participants are members of women only networking groups, the most common being Forum UK. They said such groups give them the opportunity to share learning and seek support in a safe environment. However, the strong networkers also spoke about the importance of cultivating a broad set of networking relationships, both male and female, across a range of organisations.

Several women also alluded to the fact that it can be harder to network with male colleagues, because their wives may be unhappy about them having dinner with a woman. However, women need to find a way around these problems as the benefits outweigh the initial barriers.

Our participants also recognise the power they have as positive role models and many of them take on a role as mentor to other women with board potential. The increasing length of maternity provision available to women makes networking critical to enable women to keep in contact and maintain their personal development.

Some women prioritise it

"Networking is important both to help you get into the boardroom and then to build credibility in the boardroom. It gives you people to call when you need to do due diligence. Formal networks can help build mentoring relationships and sometimes being able to share issues with similar types of people e.g. other women, can help, but you need a diverse set of networks not just women-only groups."

"It is important to be part of a number of different networks, women only groups can form a support system but you need to be part of other networks."

"Managing the work-life balance is difficult and critical. I have children, never took much time off and always worked more than fulltime. It is important for women to network and learn from each other how to manage. I don't know what will happen for women now they can have 12 months maternity leave. I would suggest that they don't have the time totally off and maintain any voluntary roles from which they can learn. This whole area has not been thought out."

"I have increased my networking, partly because I now have more time, and also I make time for it. I volunteer to be a speaker, attend coffee mornings and lunches with key people. I still network with financial services connections, and with the Big Four, as they have good insights into what is happening to the business and the market. KPMG NED breakfasts are good for meeting peers."

"I stay in contact with a wide network through business and NED connections. It is an enormous advantage being able to seek advice and to ask questions from a peer group. I try also to do things for younger women. I want to contribute to their futures."

"Women are good at helping to bring on other women … but if there is no culture for this in a company, then women can struggle and fail."

"I started a network for all the female directors in subsidiaries and business units around the world. This kind of networking is helpful for women and can help them understand how to manage their careers."

Others are less active

"I am not a member of a female network, or indeed any network. I don't like networking, and don't have time. I've got children and I work three days a week away from home, staying in a hotel."

"I'm not a member of any network of women board directors and have never felt the need. The need is to meet male board directors, not female. I chair the women's network at one of my companies and am involved in diversity and inclusion issues. I recently spoke at a NED programme, which was good, except the participants, aspiring NEDs, were all 'pale, stale and male'."

"I'm not part of a women's network although a senior female colleague recently tried to get me to join one. I'm nothing like the best at networking, but must be reasonably OK, to do the job and to make the links."

"I am not a member of a network. Partly it's lack of time, but also because I'm shy, an extreme introvert. I am one of the world's worst networkers. I find it horrible."

The impact of the media

We asked if the media put women off from taking on a NED role. Our interviewees do indeed feel that the media has a pervasive impact but they regard this as part of the territory and seek actively to manage the risk it can pose. Some also acknowledge that the media have had a positive impact in highlighting the importance of the NED role. More off-putting, they said, is the level of responsibility and the risk to reputation for very low pay.

"You will think twice now about joining a FTSE Board. It is very tough knowing how big, complex organisations work, and very difficult to perform your fiduciary responsibility."

"It has made me reflect more on the risk/ reward balance of doing the job particularly as I'm on the board of a bank. The responsibilities that go with it, and what is expected of a NED, make the equation a lot less balanced."

"Recent events have been very unfortunate. It is appalling that something as important as the role and responsibilities of the board has been made less attractive to good potential recruits. On the other hand, it is not an easy role, so maybe it's a good thing that this is understood. It is very, very responsible, particularly if things are going wrong. It is very time consuming."

"Media coverage doesn't put me off; in fact, it has emphasised how important effective corporate governance is. It ensures that the right things are discussed, including the risk register. It can be a shot across the bows of a very forceful CEO."

"As a minority it is all in your own hands. If you play on the fact that you are the only woman on a board, then they will come after you if you are in the public eye. You do get higher recognition as a woman and the papers write more about you."

Specific advice included:

Avoid life style articles

"I once gave an interview to the Sunday Telegraph and would never do it again. The questions were personal and family related, and would not have been asked of my husband. I found it demeaning."

"Avoid 'celebrity' coverage, unless you have an important message to get across for your cause. The press always know if you are trying to use them for your

own aggrandisement, to create a profile: stay away from this, and from lifestyle articles."

"There is a natural tendency here in the UK to be preoccupied with individuals, how they run their lives, what they like to do. I've been shocked by what has been published about me – with no foundation. This can be a complete turnoff for women. Shareholders and investors are not so naturally confident about women – so it's best to avoid publicity."

Think carefully about what you say

"On a personal level, I am very sensitive about not saying or doing anything which will attract attention to myself, to other NEDs or to the company."

"Remember that things can be misrepresented and misquoted."

Get professional media training from the beginning of your appointment

"If I was to do this again, I would want a PR consultant at my elbow from day one. You need training and mentoring. Women can be more sensitive and therefore need to think early about controlling the press. By the time of a crisis, it is often too late to control."

"In general, interviews are too superficial. Journalists can mess it up profoundly and no company should allow a board member to be interviewed alone without a press officer. This makes the interview more disciplined, and it protects the individual."

"I've certainly had negative press in the past and now know I need to be street smart. It is important to have media training."

Develop a thick skin

"I have been hero and zero and know what short memories papers have. I used to talk often to the press, but now have a press officer. I'm not bothered by the media, despite being set up by a journalist who told total lies. Now I just think: so be it."

"I just accept that women attract more attention and I live with the description they have of me."

"I'm used to bad press and manage the reputation. It's 'tall poppy syndrome', where people want to have a go at you for being at the top."

"I ignore the media, although I've been in their sights for years."

Top tips for board success

With so much experience under their belts, our interviewees are well placed to advise other women on building a successful board career. These are their top tips for aspiring directors.

Plan your career

"You need to be able to bring years of experience, either or both specialist and operational and often international."

"Build up 'baby NEDs' – voluntary, or subsidiary boards. Otherwise it is hard to be seen as credible for main boards. This will also help you network where you might be seen."

Pick wisely which boards to join

"Do your due diligence. The composition of the board is critically important when you are deciding. Meet up with as many people as possible. You don't want to make a mistake about the calibre and behaviour of the board; this will not be good for you."

"If you have any doubts about the chairman, then don't take the role."

Prepare your initial impact

"Think very carefully about how you present yourself the first time you meet the other board members – first impressions are everything. You must be able to hold your ground and remember the agenda when you are being interviewed."

"Don't say anything at the first meeting unless you have a real contribution to make; instead, tune into the conversation and say up front: 'I'm probably not going to say very much as I'm keen to absorb the issues and conversation.'"

"Work hard at having something important to say right from the beginning. It is part of your job to influence and impact. You are not there to keep the chair warm."

"Think about dress. Successful women should not look blousy. They must project the right image if they want to be taken seriously. There should be no cleavage in the boardroom."

Work out how you can add value

"Really think about the issues you are going to make your own. Do the homework; learn how it works, and how you can add value."

"Make sure you go onto a board where you can see for yourself what you can add: a specific background, experience, which will fit in with what the company does. The last thing you want is a crisis on what you can contribute. It can be anything, but it is important to know."

Get to know the business quickly

"Work hard in the first couple of months so that you can begin to contribute quickly. Don't be afraid to ask silly questions at this stage but hit the ground running. You can't sit back and wait while getting the feel, as you will be typecast as a pushover".

"The day you say yes, you have to start learning and meeting people. Make sure you build your own orientation programme, use the time wisely, ask questions, skull around."

Develop strong relationships with board members

"As in any other job, it is relationships with people which count, their respect, and their confidence."

"You need to build quasi-social relations with other directors, and to find common interests. You also need to be able to have an intellectual debate, which may not be a gender debate. What broke the ice for me was the after-meeting drinking. I also fly fish, and did once kill a moose: reciting this helped, as the others thought it was hilarious. They tell the story again and again, and it made a big difference."

Don't be pigeon-holed

"Directors are picked for specific attributes – speak on those, and be intelligent on others but avoid being stereotyped with soft stuff."

Follow Up

"Take questions off-line, if you are not able to contribute in a main meeting. Educate yourself and follow up later on a one to one basis."

Have confidence in yourself

"You are better than you think; you would not be here if someone had not recognised that you had something valuable to contribute. Don't undervalue your own position."

"Be yourself, don't try to compete on the board or emulate someone else, but remain true to yourself."

"Don't talk too much. You don't need to hear your own voice – this indicates insecurity."

Have fun

"Life is too short to take this role on and not enjoy it."

The project team

Helen Pitcher – Project Sponsor

Helen is Chairman of IDDAS. Her career spans 30 years in both the business world and the consulting sector. At the age of 27 she was appointed the youngest ever board director for a division of Grand Metropolitan. In her subsequent consulting career, she became CEO of CEDAR, which she built into one of the best-regarded consultancies in the human capital world.

Helen is recognised as a leading organisational performance coach and mentor, who works at the most senior level in FTSE 100 and international companies, as well as the public sector. She has a worldwide network of contacts and alumni whom she has coached and developed over the years. Helen is a panel member of the Employment Appeal Tribunal, Member of the Selection Panel for Queen's Counsel, Chairman of KidsOut and is also a trustee and fundraiser for several other charities.

Helen has a Law Degree and an MA, is an APECS accredited coach and qualified psychometric assessor. She is a Fellow of the IOD, CIPD and RSA and has worked across a range of sectors including financial services, utilities, media, leisure, telecommunications, retail and public sector.

Hilary Sears – Project Director

Hilary is a senior IDDAS mentor who undertook the majority of the interviews. She has extensive experience in executive search and board assessment, as a director/vice president in Carré Orban, Korn Ferry and AT Kearney. Hilary worked in the Cabinet Office on secondment to the Leadership and People Strategy Directorate. In 2007, she was appointed as Chairman of the Association of MBAs, which accredits MBAs internationally, and in 2008 as Chairman of KIDS, a charity for disabled children. She is on the board of Forum UK, part of the International Women's Forum.

Hilary has a BSc from UCL, an MBA from Cranfield, and the Certificate in Coaching from Henley Business School.

Adrienne Rosen – Design Consultant

Adrienne is a senior consultant at IDDAS, who designed the overall research, undertook the pilot interviews and wrote the research report. Adrienne has over 20 years of experience in leadership assessment, coaching, human resources and development as a practitioner and a consultant. Her area of expertise is in psychological assessment and personal development, specialising in leadership. Her areas of research have included the characteristics of successful chief executives and senior managers; what it takes to be a successful NED and evaluating high performance teams. Adrienne has a BA from Bristol University and an MBA from Cass Business School. She is a Fellow of the CIPD, an accredited coach and a visiting lecturer at Cass Business School.

Susan Dudley – Project Co-ordinator

Susan's background is in HR, consultancy, administration and project co-ordination. She provides project co-ordination and consultancy services to a number of corporate clients across various sectors, including utilities, telecoms, retail and the NHS. Susan is a member of the CIPD and qualified psychometrician.

Chapter B4

Board Dynamics: The Chairman's Perspective

Introduction B4.1

We are very grateful to IDDAS for permission to reprint this excellent guidance, and also three others in their series, which we reproduce at Chapters **B2**, **B3** and **B5**.

Clare Chalmers, Chief Executive of IDDAS, would be pleased to hear from readers with any inquiries about this guidance. She can be contacted at IDDAS, IDDAS House, 74 New Cavendish Street, London, W1G 8TF (Tel: +44 (0)20 7436 0101; Email: clare.chalmers@iddas.com; Website: www.iddas.com).

Based in London, IDDAS specialises in providing board effectiveness, mentoring and coaching, leadership facilitation and executive assessment services for chairs, CEOs and main board directors, as well as for those who aspire to non-executive roles. IDDAS has an established reputation for its quality, innovative, supportive and flexible approach.

IDDAS BOARD DYNAMICS: THE CHAIRMAN'S PERSPECTIVE

Foreword

I know from my own experience how challenging the position of chairman can be. It is a role that requires true leadership, including among other qualities, the ability to listen, build consensus, encourage others, act diplomatically and judge wisely.

At a time of great scrutiny of the chairman's role in ensuring effective governance, this report makes a valuable contribution to our understanding of the issues and challenges faced by chairmen.

Its strength lies in the detailed views it offers of what a group of chairmen, currently heading significant public corporations, think and believe about the job they do.

It will be of interest to many audiences. Serving chairmen will find it instructive to compare notes on the views of their colleagues. Those aspiring to chair a board at a future date will find invaluable advice and insights to help them decide whether the chairman's role is really for them, and what they can do to get there. Other board members, both executive and non-executive, can gain a better understanding of the very particular challenges of managing a group of peers.

Finally, anyone involved in the selection or development of chairmen or other board members will find much of interest to help them make intelligent and creative choices. As we reach for economic recovery, such choices will be vital for the health of corporate Britain.

John Allan
Chairman, DSG international

Introduction

Our desire to research the chairman's perspective of running a corporate board emerged long before we had even finished the first report in our Board Dynamics series, about women on FTSE 100 boards. As we interviewed the women directors, it became clear that the chairman plays an absolutely pivotal role in shaping an effective board. Again and again, we heard how it was the chairman who created the conditions for a board to operate effectively, or not, and how he – or occasionally she – was the key figure, setting both the agenda and the tone for the board's dealings. It was clear to us that we should make the chairman's perspective the subject of our next report and find out what new insights into the chairman's role our face-to-face interviews could bring to an existing body of research driven predominantly by a procedural and statistical approach.

As with the women in our first report, what was particularly fascinating was hearing directly the voices of chairmen who were in the thick of running some of our most significant boards. If one thing stands out, it is that these chairmen – all individuals with substantial careers to their names – had more to say about the people challenges they faced in their role than about strategic, financial or governance issues. Whenever we posed open questions about the most important aptitudes for chairing, or the greatest challenges faced in the role, or the best advice they could proffer to newcomers, the chairmen most often cited 'people skills', or issues to do with building productive relationships. There was a real sense that outside times of genuine crisis, this was what they grappled with most.

At the hub of it all was their relationship with the CEO. Many spoke of the time and effort it took to get this right – to achieve mutual trust and the right balance of support and challenge. If the relationship wasn't working it had to be 'fixed', they said, or someone had to go. Other themes that emerged included the importance of the unseen time and energy spent outside the boardroom creating and maintaining a cohesive team and the challenge of evaluating board and director performance.

This report is timely as it echoes the importance of the behavioural aspects of a board's functioning, a key theme of the new UK Corporate Governance Code which was published recently (see section on Behavioural leadership on page 11).

We were fortunate to be able to speak in depth to so many chairmen, and would like to thank them for their participation. Our interviewees are all people with exceptionally busy schedules and we are grateful to them for the time they gave us. Their insights will be invaluable not just for other chairmen, but also for board directors present and aspiring, and for those involved in hiring or developing them.

Helen Pitcher
Chairman, IDDAS

Executive summary

Our research comes at a time when the central role that chairmen play in the effectiveness of corporations has received greater attention than ever before.

Two major reports on corporate governance have been published in the past year: the Hogg Review of the Combined Code on Corporate Governance and the Walker Review of corporate governance in the UK banking industry. These culminated in the publication in May 2010 of the UK Corporate Governance Code, whose recommendations will be applied to accounting periods from 29 June 2010. The revised code creates a new main principle stating the chairman's responsibility for leading the board and reflecting Walker's belief in the importance of leadership skills.

Indeed Walker, who has been much quoted as emphasising the need for financial skills and experience on boards, actually places these second to "*convincing leadership experience*" in the chairman of a bank or financial institution, saying that "*financial industry experience without established leadership skills in a chairman is unlikely to suffice.*"

Our findings support this view. If there was one overriding message that came out of our interviews it was that the greatest skill of the chairman is in managing relationships between him or herself and the CEO, between executives and non-executives and between board members individually and as members of a team.

We probed our chairmen on their own path to chairmanship and the skills and experience they felt were most important. We asked about their approach to board performance and how they judged, evaluated and developed it. We also explored their views on training and networking and what they felt were the biggest challenges they faced.

Finally, we asked for their best advice to others seeking their first chairmanship.

Key findings

- The relationship between the chairman and CEO is the most important in the company and effective chairmen spend considerable time and effort getting this right. If they are not successful, their ultimate duty is to replace the CEO.

- The skill of the chairman lies in the ability to achieve influence without holding power. This involves balancing the needs and interests of multiple stakeholders and personalities; forging the board into a well performing team; running effective board meetings; and ensuring the right mix of people and skills around the board table.

- Our chairmen learnt how to chair primarily from observing good and bad practice in chairmen they had served under. Few had received mentoring or coaching for their first chairmanship or indeed subsequently, although some would have welcomed it.

- Chairmen find recruitment a significant challenge. They value diversity of skills, experience and perspective on their boards, but, don't necessarily believe this can be translated into a traditional diversity agenda.
- Board evaluation processes are not always felt to be effective and are sometimes conducted for the sake of compliance, rather than to improve performance. Shareholders show little interest in board evaluation.
- Being a chairman takes more time than expected and can be a lonely position. Chairmen have limited support networks for their chairing role.

Conclusions and implications

- A corporation should choose its chairman for his or her leadership and inter-personal skBills, rather than for a particular career background – a point acknowledged by Walker, and a key point in the new UK Corporate Governance Code.
- There is little prospect of the number of women on boards increasing significantly in the near future, if our chairmen's views are typical. Despite the wider debate about the need for more diversity and various initiatives to raise the profile of senior women, our chairmen believe that there are still not enough suitably qualified women available – and that they are already doing what they can to recruit them.
- There is a need for more research into effective board evaluation practices to fill the evaluation gap that some chairmen feel exists.
- Corporations should take a more realistic view of the time commitment involved in being a chairman.

Behavioural leadership and the new UK Corporate Governance Code

"Behaviour is at the heart of it"

The new code published in May 2010 places greater emphasis on the leadership role of the chairman and an environment that promotes constructive challenge. It calls for greater awareness among board members of their effectiveness both individually and collectively. This will pose a challenge for many UK directors, who are more comfortable reviewing process than focusing on the more emotive issue of behaviour.

In the light of the new code, directors should now consider the best way that their individual and collective behaviour can deliver robust strategic decision making, a challenging oversight of the company's risk management and genuine accountability to shareholders.

The code makes a number of specific recommendations:

Selection and diversity

- To encourage boards to be well balanced and avoid "group think", there are new principles on the composition and selection of the board. These include the need to appoint members on merit, against objective criteria and with due regard for the benefits of diversity, including gender diversity.

Challenge and debate

- To promote proper debate in the boardroom, there are new principles on the leadership of the chairman, the responsibility of the nonexecutive directors to provide constructive challenge and the time commitment expected of all directors.

Board development

- To help enhance the board's performance and awareness of strengths and weaknesses, the chairman should hold regular development reviews with directors. Board evaluation reviews in FTSE 350 companies should be externally facilitated at least every three years.

Annual elections

- To increase accountability to shareholders, all directors of FTSE 350 companies should be re-elected annually, and chairmen are encouraged to report personally on how the principles relating to the leadership and effectiveness of the board have been applied.

Risk and the business model

- To improve risk management, the company's business model should be explained and the board should be responsible for determining the nature and extent of the significant risks it is willing to take.

Performance pay

- Performance-related pay for executive directors should be aligned to the long-term interests of the company and its risk policies and systems.

Edited extract from an article in The Boardroom *magazine, June 2010. The author Sheelagh Duffield is an IDDAS mentor and part of the IDDAS Board Effectiveness team. She is also a founder of Savendie, a board compliance and governance consultancy.*

The findings in detail

How we did our research

Our research was based on in-depth, structured interviews with chairmen of large commercial organisations. We focused on open questions designed to encourage our interviewees to speak freely and widely. Interviews typically lasted an hour or more and were conducted in person or, occasionally, by telephone.

About our interviewees

Most of our chairmen were men in the latter stages of their careers. The youngest was 54, and 13 were over 60. The majority held one chairmanship and no executive positions, having consciously decided to move away from executive responsibilities.

Two of the chairmen interviewed were US citizens, and two were women.

Role held prior to becoming chairman

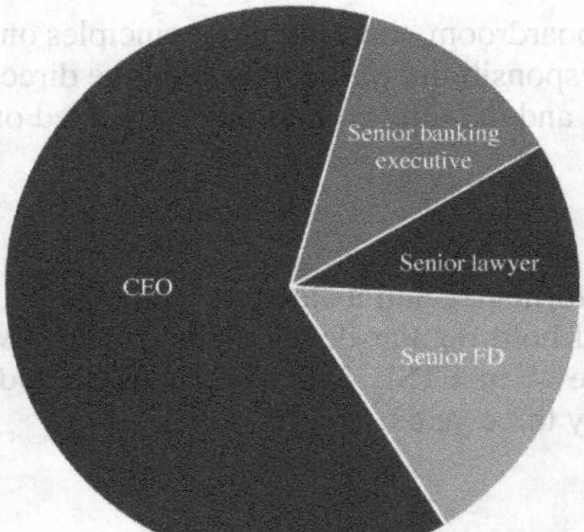

The chairmen represent

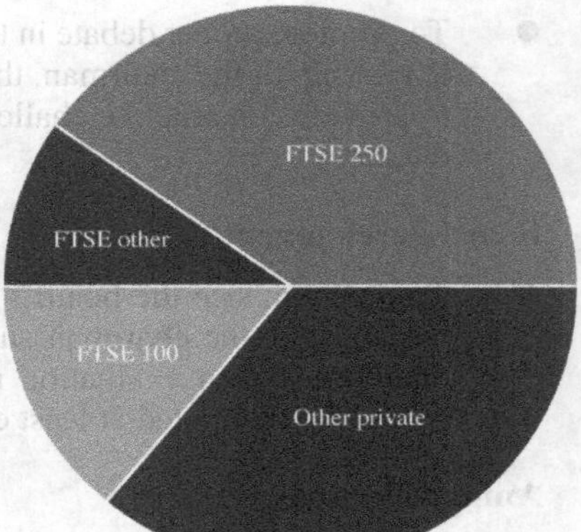

The chairmen's qualifications

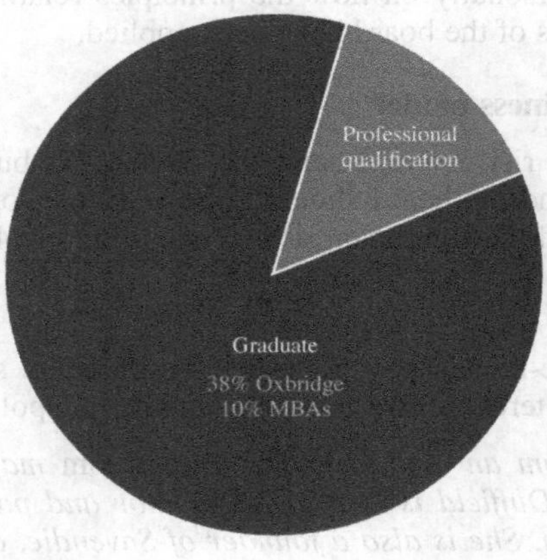

CEO and chairman: the most important relationship in the company

"The relationship between the CEO and chairman is absolutely critical. A company will malfunction if it is not correct."

It is impossible to overplay the importance of a productive relationship between chairman and CEO. Again and again our interviewees returned to this theme in their reflections on successful (and unsuccessful) chairmanship. The first pre-requisite, they told us, was to have clearly defined roles separating the responsibilities of the chairman and the CEO and abide by them. All else follows from this, one advised.

Even with clarity of role, getting the relationship right is not always easy. Indeed, in answer to our question, *"What are the three most difficult areas of your chairmanship?"* almost half of our interviewees cited issues relating to the CEO. For some, finding the right CEO was the hardest part, for others it was having to remove the CEO. But for most, simply building the right relationship with the CEO or keeping a close and effective relationship was their biggest challenge. One interviewee underlined the point, identifying getting the relationship with the CEO right as the first, second and third most challenging issue.

Ceding control

There is often a tension between the roles of chairman and chief executive, not least because many chairmen are former chief executives themselves. Our interviewees spoke of the importance of standing back and letting the CEO do his job, but it was clear that some found it hard to give way.

"The worst possible thing is NEDs wanting to take over. They must not, and they must not meddle or subvert management processes."

"I loved being an executive, and making executive decisions. Now I don't have the same power in the business as I had."

"I learned to keep my mouth shut and not to bawl out individuals about something I don't like – instead I go to the CEO."

"The CEO is usually the biggest ego round the board table and you can't have two!"

Notwithstanding any of the above, it is the chairman's duty to deal with an overbearing CEO.

"There is always a big challenge in dealing with a really dominant CEO. He might be good and creating lots of value, but too dominant and bullying, which might be destroying working lives, including good successors, who leave."

Almost half of our chairmen had previously held chief executive positions. They had reflected deeply on the difference between the two roles and on the transition from one to the other, which one summed up as *"like the parent to grandparent transition – no longer making decisions, but helping others to make them"*.

Others commented:

"I made a conscious decision a decade ago after being a CEO to take on chairing roles. I no longer wanted to run things. I had been an NED but the role didn't appeal. I found it unrewarding, insufficiently engaged with the business. The role of the chairman was an attractive half-way house, between the day-to-day executive role and the detached NED. There is more engagement."

"A key difference is that you are not on top of the business. You don't know what is happening; you are reliant on the executives."

"As a CEO, you have a lot of autonomy in decision-making, whereas as a chairman the role is about influencing, and helping good decisions to be made."

"You have to be more of a mentor, counsellor, challenger."

"You have to understand that your role as chairman is to lead, not 'to do'. This distinction is quite difficult but really, really important."

Adapting to the chair is easier if you have yourself been a CEO for a long time, said one interviewee, because over time you become less operational and more focused on strategy. *"This is important. As long as your interests and focus as CEO have made this transition, you can migrate."*

Investing time and building trust

Given the importance of the relationship between CEO and chairman, it was no surprise to learn that our chairmen spent a good deal of the time they gave to their role on building and nurturing that relationship.

Interviewees mentioned the importance of listening to the CEO, understanding his/her issues, and acting as a sounding board. Others spoke of the need to be in constant touch, usually by email, and to be available to the CEO on the phone 24/7. Several mentioned acting in a coaching or mentoring role to the CEO.

Trust also came up more than once, both in the sense of having an honest and open relationship, and in letting the CEO get on with the job, without undue interference.

"You just have to let the CEO run the company. You don't do that yourself. Once this is established, it should all fall into place."

"Whatever you hear from the executives and the NEDs, you religiously share with the CEO, and vice versa."

"The chairman should not try to be CEO, but must keep an eye on what is going on with others. If I see something I don't like, I alert the CEO."

Having made every effort to build a positive relationship, if things are not working, it's up to the chairman to take action – including getting rid of the CEO if all else fails.

"The chairman must be very supportive of the CEO, but you have to tell him when he is not performing."

"Get really excited and enthused by your CEO, or get your colleagues' agreement to fire him."

The skill of the chairman – influence without power

"It's a more subtle art form than being a CEO, because you haven't got authority."

We asked our interviewees about the key skills and experience needed to become a chairman, how these were acquired and what they found to be the most difficult aspects of the chairman's role. There was a strong (though not universal) consensus that you needed to have had executive board experience, or as one interviewee put it, *"to have been there, done it, fixed it, got it right."*

Among those interviewees who were ex-CEOs and ex-finance directors, many, unsurprisingly, thought you needed one of those two backgrounds to be an effective chairman – although others commented that former CEOs might find it hard to relinquish control. Equally, one former finance man felt a finance background was only an advantage if coupled with the right personality and approach.

"Finance directors vary dramatically. Some would not make good chairmen."

Only one interviewee referred to specific knowledge of the company or sector as a factor and that was to say that it wasn't particularly important.

"You don't really need to know the business you're going to chair, although there are some advantages if you know the sector. Witness the movement of NEDs and chairs among the plcs."

A delicate balancing act

Among the most frequently cited skills were listening, influencing, coaching, engaging (both executives and non-executives) and building consensus. You have to be versatile, interviewees said, because the style and techniques you need to employ will vary from situation to situation.

Soft skills: an essential ingredient for success

Our interviewees placed enormous emphasis on the importance of soft skills. Yes, you need to be able to grasp strategy, finance, risk and governance – and there's no substitute for operational experience – but because these have long been the essence of the 'day job' for the great majority of our interviewees, they perhaps took them for granted and focused their comments more on the softer skills involved.

"The hard, analytical skills are helpful, but EQ is more key in the role of chairman."

The word balance came up frequently – balancing interests, such as those of shareholders versus those of executives, balancing skills and personalities on the board and crucially, balancing support for the executives with the right amount of challenge. The latter, we found, was something many of our chairmen found *"bloody difficult"* to achieve.

"There is a need to find the balance between amicable board behaviour/team-building and the ability of the NEDs to ask, probe and challenge. If you're too aggressive in this, you won't get the information or co-operation from the executive directors. If you are too close as a team, you will be seen as (and may be) too soft."

"You have a balance to achieve, which is the toughest challenge for a chairman. You must create an atmosphere of open challenge, but you don't want it to become too aggressive; on the other hand, you have to avoid it becoming too 'clubbable' and lovey-dovey. If this happens, then people will not challenge because they don't want to be awkward and spoil the club atmosphere."

The tone set by the chairman plays a big part in how successfully this delicate balance is achieved.

"Style really matters."

"You must encourage people to speak up, and not punish them if they say something brave."

"You have to lead by example. Ask probing questions in the right style. If you do, most of the board will follow suit. What I love is when they have a debate with me. A board should have debates, as it brings the best questions to the table."

One chairman commented that women are often particularly adept at challenging in a non-threatening manner – something women NEDs had told us themselves in our previous research (see panel opposite, Women at their best).

"The best women directors, from my own experience, have very good inter-personal skills and influencing skills. They can challenge rigorously without causing offence, which men may fail to do."

If the right level of challenge is absent, it is up to the chair to do something about it.

"I must understand why [there is not enough challenge]. If it is because of low-quality NEDs, you have to change them. If the papers are not good enough, you ensure that they are better next time. It is your responsibility as chairman."

"Sometimes you can see if an individual is uncomfortable about a topic or debate. You either have to tease this out in the meeting, or talk outside the boardroom. A facilitator can be very helpful, either an external facilitator or the company secretary."

Women at their best

For our previous research, *A female perspective*, we interviewed a fifth of the women directors of FTSE 100 companies. Among the things they told us was that women at their best are adept at questioning and challenging in a non-threatening manner and are less ego-driven than male counterparts. They felt that women bring a different perspective to a board and play an active role in promoting good team dynamics. These views were endorsed by some of our chairmen.

Forging a team

The ability to achieve the right balance of support and challenge was down to how well the board works as a team.

"Boards are not natural teams, and unless you work at it, it's pot luck if they work together."

Several chairmen said getting the board together on an informal basis from time to time was vital to creating cohesion. Some had dedicated 'away days', others made a point of ensuring that some board meetings included an overnight stay, with dinner the night before.

"To ensure integration of all board members we have informal dinners twice a year where we include the chief executive."

"We will have an away day and dinner before every third board meeting."

Several chairmen spoke of creating a collegiate atmosphere, or striving for cabinet responsibility. Indeed, when we asked them to say what distinguished a superior board from the run of the mill, one chairman described it as follows:

"You know when a board is not working well when people only want to come [to a meeting] to make a point and then say the same thing over and over; or when someone seems to be hostile to another board member or senior executive,

when this is not justified; or when people are splitting into groups and not acting independently, as individuals. When a board is working well, you have a sense that however difficult the situation, everyone will work together to get through it; there is a sense of comradeship, which is very important."

The art of the board meeting

Running an effective board meeting is an art in its own right and takes practice and experience, our interviewees asserted. Success is heavily dependent on preparation, they told us, including having the right people around the table to start with. Our interviewees spoke of the importance of getting good-quality information well ahead of time – and making sure that they, and other board members, had read it all in advance of discussions (some chairmen found it a challenge to ensure NEDs were sufficiently engaged to do all their homework). Furthermore, where there were contentious issues to be discussed, chairmen would raise them before the meeting with the executives and other NEDs, in order to prepare the ground for the meeting itself.

It's about the team

"Devote effort to team-building, so that issues can be vigorously debated without people being defensive. A board needs to be able to pursue issues, not individuals, rigorously and therefore you also need good executives, who can respond appropriately to vigorous challenge and questioning."

Other advice for meetings

- Keep to time – set out time pressures at the beginning and be firm.
- Don't allow executives to fill all the time with presentations.
- Ensure that everyone contributes and no-one dominates.
- Try out different techniques, like a change in the running order or seating, to keep things fresh.

One chairman's description was a masterclass in effective chairing.

"If there's a big strategic investment, for example, I will engage the most knowledgeable NED in that area and also be involved myself to prevent a nuclear option. Then I engage the board in it, often at more than one meeting. When the matter comes to the board, I must know where people stand, and give them the opportunity to speak, so that there is open and balanced discussion. The board paper itself must have options, risks and rewards, not just one option. I also believe that you need independent advice. I believe that you must have the widest range of views; a lot of chairmen don't like this, because it takes time and effort."

Another suggested it was useful to practise chairing skills in a variety of settings.

"You can learn how to run meetings efficiently as an executive, or as a chairman or NED on other boards charity, not-for-profit, local authority, etc. You learn to handle people who want to grandstand, and how to reach decisions. If you have held a variety of roles, then you get used to the way an efficient board operates. It is good

to have operated in different settings and cultures and where expectations might differ; you can find ways to make it work, and to develop and command authority."

Learning by observing

The main way our chairmen learned what to do was by observing others and then practising themselves. When we asked what they would include in a training course for chairmen, the most common answers were case studies and the opportunity to speak to a peer group. They sought to copy the good and avoid the mistakes of the bad.

"There is a very wide gulf between effective and non-effective chairmen and boards."

"I primarily learned from the different chairmen I worked with what to avoid. One was disruptive with the management, and set them against each other; another had too short an attention span."

"I worked under three different chairmen on one board and saw very different styles: the first was very good, he kept us informed and engaged; the second was destructive – he was very bright, and drove us to do restructuring which was necessary, but he created an almost unworkable set of dynamics; the third has only been there for 10 months and the jury is still out. One of the chairmen I work with now is the best at making the board stay on target and in-bounds. He doesn't allow it to get into operating-level detail, and makes sure that NEDs understand that this should be left to the CEO."

A masterclass in effective chairmanship

"If there's a big strategic investment, for example, I will engage the most knowledgeable NED in that area, and also be involved myself to prevent a nuclear option. Then I engage the board in it, often at more than one meeting. When the matter comes to the board, I must know where people stand and give them the opportunity to speak, so that there is open and balanced discussion. The board paper itself must have options, risks and rewards, not just one option. I also believe that you need independent advice. I believe that you must have the widest range of views; a lot of chairmen don't like this, because it takes time and effort."

"The biggest lesson was how not to be a chairman: not to let the CEO run everything and accept his assurances that the board should not worry. This is the situation I experienced [as an NED] at one [FTSE 100] company, where the then CEO achieved disastrous results, while being highly paid. The chairman was too accepting, too nice. Both had to go."

Mentoring is rare

We asked our interviewees whether they had had any kind of mentor or coach when first becoming a chairman. The overwhelming majority had not, although several mentioned having someone they could use as a 'sounding board' or could turn to for informal advice.

"I didn't really have anyone. It's not that different from when I became a CEO – there are one or two individuals who are really sage. They might be in your bank, financial PR, law firm, etc. They are not mentors as such, but sages: if I had a road block, I asked their view, and they gave it without personal or financial gain involved."

"No. I'm not conscious that I felt the need."

"I did not have a formal mentor, which I think is a mistake. I believe strongly in mentoring, and act as mentor to a number of individuals."

"If you are a chairman, there are two independent people who can give you advice: the partners of your audit and law firms, because both have history with the company. This can help you understand how the business will react. It's sad that these two professionals have become more like technicians."

"No, but I did have lots of people I could turn to. You should be able to stand on your own two feet when you reach this position."

"I had various sounding boards, but most important of all was listening to my colleagues on the board, especially the SID [senior independent director]. You use them to get information, and advice."

One interviewee had a particular theory about why so few chairmen (including himself) had had a mentor.

"I think one of the problems in the UK, particularly in the public-school elite, is that they're taught to be self-sufficient, not to ask, not to expose lack of decisiveness. I believe that talking helps to sort out ideas and if you can do this with a mentor, then it is anonymous. If you do it with colleagues, you are concerned that it might be seen as a sign of weakness."

In praise of mentoring

One chairman was a particular fan.

"I did not have a formal mentor, which I think is a mistake. I believe strongly in mentoring, and act as mentor to a number of individuals."

Getting the right people around the table

"First of all, you have to be able to choose a broad body of skills that are required to run the company. You have to do the analysis, and then go out and find any skills which are missing."

Our chairmen were running boards that varied in size from 5–20 people, with 8–12 the most common range. Achieving the right balance of numbers, disciplines, executives and nonexecutives was something they thought carefully about. There was a general preference for smaller boards, as these were felt to be easier to run, but the size and nature of some businesses and the need to have enough members for committees, often made higher numbers necessary.

"I like boards where you can sit around the table and see everyone. The dynamics are better on a small board and I can call upon individuals to contribute."

"The benefit of a small board is that everyone has to work hard. There is no hiding place, everyone has to have read their papers, and this ups the game considerably."

Setting numbers is not a once and for all activity, however.

"I think that in a public company with big institutional shareholders one should look annually at the size and composition [of the board] and drivers of the business."

"You need to continuously define and upgrade the needs and so it is important to have a finite term on a board. The ideal might be to change two NEDs per year, depending on the number on the board. You have to build a long-term recruitment programme, looking at what skills/backgrounds you will require two to three years ahead, and approach potential candidates with this timeframe in mind."

There was less consensus on the appropriate mix of executives and non-executives (although agreement that the latter must outnumber the former). Several chairmen reported operating well with just two or three executive directors. Another felt, by contrast, that *"a board with less than four executive directors is probably not fit for purpose, because all you are hearing is the CEO's view."*

Recruiting the right skills and numbers

The business of actually recruiting NEDs was cited by several chairmen as one of the biggest challenges. Some took a very systematic approach, matching the skills they needed around the table with the needs of the business – although, as one chairman who adopted this approach observed, that doesn't necessarily give you a range of personality types, which is also desirable. Chairmen used a variety of methods to source potential candidates, including headhunters and personal networking.

Diversity matters

We asked about the importance of diversity on a board and found universal agreement that having an assortment of skills, experience and perspectives was vital for good performance.

"[Diversity] is extremely important, because what you want around the boardroom table is differing perspectives; if, for instance, you have 12 goalkeepers, then you won't let in many goals, but you won't score any!"

"Diversity of opinion is critical."

"I think if you get more minds looking at a problem from different perspectives this has to be good. Just as you don't want 10 FDs or marketing directors around the boardroom table, it is good to have a balance of perspectives. You don't want homogeneity."

"What you actually want on a board is a variety of people who have a variety of views, which may or may not be expounded by individuals of diverse backgrounds. Someone can be female, or from an ethnic minority background, or a different region or country and yet still have similar views... What I do believe is that you should look for NEDs far more widely, and not be prejudiced by culture to fill the role, or by narrow skill/industry sector boxes."

No place for tokenism

Despite their enthusiasm for diversity, several of our chairmen warned of translating this into a traditional diversity agenda for reasons of *"political correctness"*. They spoke about avoiding *"formulaic representation"*, *"dangerous quota-ing"*, or *"tokenism"*. One chairman said gender diversity was only important externally, in that you need to demonstrate it.

"Diversity of experience and wisdom is essential. Other types of diversity (ethnic background or sex) are completely irrelevant."

"All forms of diversity – be it women, or ethnic – can really enrich what a board does. But somehow this doesn't happen often, because women or ethnic minority appointees who reach the board have often compromised. For example, women have become more like men so they have succeeded in the same world as those they might be expected to have different views from. It doesn't mean that they are not good NEDs."

Notwithstanding the caveats, some interviewees were very robust about the need to have more women NEDs, particularly for companies with large numbers of female customers.

"On the male/female gender mix, it's fairly clear that if you have a customer-focused organisation, you need to represent that customer base."

"For a food company, it would be extraordinary to have a board which was all men. It would be bizarre, as we need to understand tastes, fashion, social trends. We must reflect our consumers."

"It is a bad idea to have clones, because you don't get challenged and so I am in favour of a mix. Sexual diversity is advantageous, but you should also have different nationals."

"If a board does not have a woman, it should seek one."

One interviewee made the point that the most important type of diversity was independence.

"It is far more important that the NEDs should be independent of each other. Once they form little cliques and have social connections (playing or talking golf with each other, for instance), then this is negative and excludes the executive. You want diversity through total independence and by having representatives of sections of society in which the company operates – which for most organisations means all sections of society. I regard independence as the key."

Although diversity in its broadest sense was welcomed by all, several chairmen pointed to the additional challenges involved in managing a diverse group of people.

"The diverse board is likely to be more effective but there must be something that binds them together, as effectively they will have started out as strangers. They have to be blended, and this takes time, trust and a willingness to compromise and to respect the opinions of others. Diversity may make it a harder journey."

"I do believe that it is important to consider diversity in gender, age and nationality/ international experience, especially as companies become more international. But there is a difficulty in going too far, in that you may lose the feeling of solidarity. You need cohesiveness in the group."

Succession planning and tenure

We also asked our chairmen about succession planning for their own role and about Sir David Walker's recommendation that chairmen of financial institutions be reappointed annually. Many conceded that succession planning was not always as efficient as it should be – although all said it was important.

"I think succession planning generally is not well done (whether for chairman or CEO). Is it important? Absolutely. What you do depends on what you want to achieve."

"It is vitally important for any board to have succession planning for the chairman and CEO roles. With the chairman's role, ideally you will have two options: someone who already knows the company and an outsider. If you do go internally, it is difficult to use the Nominations Committee, as the individual(s) may well be on it. You would establish through conversations with each NED if anyone would want to succeed you and would discuss their merits. If no-one is right, then you may recruit a possible successor early [from outside]."

"You obviously need to think about this, but it is quite difficult to deal with. For instance, there might be two potential candidates already on the board, or you might decide you have to go outside, because you do only have five to six people to choose from and they may not have the appropriate skills. Bringing in someone from outside is tough because they may not fit with the existing board."

"We have succession planning in place for when I step down. We know when I will retire and we have a shortlist of possible candidates already on the board. Unless something unforeseen happens, we have it planned."

Walker's recommendation of annual reappointment, meanwhile, got short shrift from most of our chairmen.

"He is recommending that they put themselves up for annual re-election, which is a very good idea, but the effect will be zero."

"This is crazy: reappointment every year? This shows ignorance of what the role of a chairman is all about, and is wholly inconsistent with the role responsibilities. No one will subject themselves to a regime of 12 months. You need consistency and continuity. Good boards don't just happen; it requires energy and tenacity."

"I think it is a load of nonsense and I have written as much. This is political correctness gone mad, and could make people too short-term in their actions/ decisions."

"I don't think there will be any impact. If a chairman is failing, then he should be voted out anyway. If the shareholders and board haven't sussed out that the chairman needs to go, then they should all go!"

"It will have either no impact whatsoever, or people will be less inclined to be chairman of banks and financial institutions."

However, several interviewees voiced support for fixed terms – and hinted at potential difficulties if these did not exist.

"Chairmen never like to think they've got to go. It is the responsibility of the SID to handle the situation, and the chairman should make it clear to the SID when he intends to go. He should not do more than two terms (six years)."

"I believe that the appointment to the position of chairman should have a clear time limit, of three years and two terms."

"For a chairman coming in from outside, creating a board that is really working well takes time. It needs to be seen as something that evolves. Think of these things over multi-year horizons. The term should be five to 10 years. If the change is more frequent, then the company is unlikely to have a truly effective board; by 10 years, the chairman is likely to be too slow!"

Assessing performance – more art than science

"We are all used to evaluating subordinates and in 360-degree appraisals, inviting evaluation of bosses. But peer evaluation is more problematic."

There was a wide range of views and a variety of practices for assessing board and individual director performance, but we came away with a sense that many felt they had not fully cracked this issue.

Almost all the boards had undertaken some kind of annual assessment of the performance of the board as a whole – although some chairmen were dubious about the usefulness of the exercise. Assessment techniques included self-evaluation questionnaires and group discussions, sometimes over a dinner.

As for individual director performance, this was normally assessed through one-to-one interviews with the chairman. Some used a systematic approach to such interviews, others were more informal in their methods.

"There is a useful checklist in the back of the Higgs Review. I use this as a good prompt for questions and answers. I do it on a one-to-one basis with all the NEDs. The CEO does the same for the executive directors. Some questions might be personal, some general, and the directors are given the opportunity to indicate matters they might like to discuss."

"I do it by gut feel and a good understanding of what I think they're doing. The CEO fills in annual goals. NEDs you evaluate on their helpful contributions – and if they don't make any, you make sure their contracts don't get renewed."

"You use human judgement about each individual's contributions, the quality and the frequency of them; and you note if they are mute or offer opinions."

"You have to listen very hard. You have to watch the body language of people, and watch the inter-relations between people to see if the chemistry is good. You have to see if some are talking too much. If they are, you have to mention this in their appraisal. I have done it in a humorous way, saying that they have saved the company money, as I don't need to pay for them to go on an assertiveness course."

However, several chairmen expressed the view that it is difficult to be entirely honest in these circumstances and that external evaluation might be more productive. About half of our chairmen had experience of using external evaluators and several more intended to try them. Apart from encouraging openness and honesty, external evaluation was felt to be useful in offering an outsider's opinion of the way a board operated.

"I find it quite challenging to ask board members to comment on the behaviour of colleagues around the table. Even when I do, I'm not sure they can be honest, and I find feedback difficult to do. This is because you are all part of the same team: it is easy to praise people who bring constructive ideas, but to comment on under-performance is more difficult. This is where third-party appraisers may get a more open dialogue."

"To assess board performance I would like to appoint someone to talk to each board member, including the chairman, sit in on two board meetings, and then provide advice on the content, papers, how advice is sought and given. It is sometimes easier for someone from outside to act as the mirror. And it would be easier to suggest that someone steps down after such an evaluation."

"At one company where I was a director, the external consultant was pretty forthright: the chairman had created an atmosphere which wasn't working and he subsequently left."

Changes in practice

When it came to implementing changes as a result of an evaluation, whether internal or external, our chairmen generally gave us examples of changes in practice or procedure, rather than changes in behaviour – which are notoriously difficult to achieve. One chairman concluded: *"You can only nudge people's behaviour a bit."*

"I think [evaluation] has changed the way we work, tightening up on board procedures. For instance, it pointed out where communication could be improved."

"It has [changed how we operate]. You pick out four of five of the most important things and then commit to having a discussion in the future about whether they happened. For instance, are NEDs making more consistent contributions around the table; are communications from the executive more open and more timely?"

"Yes, I always learn from every one, and I find them helpful. On all the boards, the feedback/ results have been used to improve managing the agenda and our interactions in a slightly different way."

Some interviewees gave tips about the use of external evaluation.

"The output from consultants is only as good as the input they receive/elicit."

"We took the selection of an external advisor very seriously. We interviewed four people for the job and each had a completely different approach. We chose someone whose approach was more traditional, not, for instance, online."

"Changes don't so much come out of the evaluation, but from the meeting-to-meeting process. I encourage a lot of communication between meetings (on the phone, or face to face). I also encourage NEDs to talk to the executives, to develop personal relationships and understanding."

Some chairmen, however, were entirely sceptical about the value of evaluation exercises, seeing them as something that needed to be done, rather than something that 'added value'.

"We hold an annual discussion around skill sets. On the whole, it has been a dilatory experience, and not very enlightening."

"[External evaluation] gets you off the corporate governance hook. I didn't learn anything new from it at [my previous board], but I will do it again [at the present one]. Essentially you want people to talk to you away from the board and appraisals."

"At one board I sat on, they did an external evaluation every three years, using consultants, who criticised the length of the meetings (4+ hours), the presentations, the detail. Nothing changed. But I suppose it doesn't do any harm."

"Where I have done it, it didn't add anything, and was very expensive. Here, I have asked the company secretary to look into different approaches."

Shareholders are not taking an active interest in board evaluation, according to our chairmen, so any changes in practice are likely to be internally driven.

"The shareholders are not fussed about how the board is performing and is evaluated; they are more concerned about the performance of the company and risk."

"Shareholders are so far off the pace on governance that I'm not sure they have clear expectations of an effective board. You will find disappointment among the chairmen, because we get very little input, advice or knowledge from our shareholders. I'm not sure their ideas are well thought through or worthwhile. Perhaps Walker is wanting more exposure on effectiveness, but this is nonsense because these are complicated matters with a high degree of subjectivity."

"Major shareholders are involved in many companies; they don't have the time to be involved [in driving better evaluation]."

How should the chairman be judged?

There are two criteria, said our interviewees, by which the chairman's performance may be assessed: the company's performance, either against its own strategy or compared to competitors and the chairman's style and personal effectiveness in running the board.

"Is the board being well run? Is it well respected? Alongside the CEO, you are the face of the company. If the company does badly, the chairman shares responsibility for this."

"The shareholders must feel that I'm doing a good job and the executives must feel they're getting the right support and challenge."

"[The chairman should be judged] by how the business is doing versus its comparators."

In almost all cases, our chairmen described a process that was led by the senior independent director who had either a group discussion with other board members about the chairman or one-to-one meetings.

"The SID/deputy chairman talks to all the board members and seeks their views on my performance and that of the board and [considers] how changes can be made in my performance and the management of the board."

"This is conventionally done by the SID, who solicits views from other board members."

"We have a process of having a dinner once a year with the NEDs. In the first half, I lead a discussion on the performance of the CEO; I then exit, and the senior independent director (who will already have talked with the executive directors) leads a discussion of my performance."

At the end of the process, it is usually the SID who faces the delicate task of feeding back to the chairman.

"It is one of the less welcome parts of the SID role. None of us is arrogant enough to think we are working perfectly."

"As a SID myself, I know this is difficult. I have a chairman who talks too much and I have fed this back to him more than once."

Not all of our chairmen were formally evaluated and one confessed that he hadn't had an appraisal of any kind since 1996. Others described a relatively informal process, or gave suggestions about how they could be better evaluated.

"The SID takes soundings from the other executive and non-executive directors on my performance and then gives me feedback."

"If I were slipping, they would tell me. After the [board evaluation] dinner, I leave the table and they talk about me."

"I believe it should involve an external evaluation (but I have never done this)."

"If you really want to do it, it would involve 360, and external evaluation and possibly soliciting shareholders' views to see if they feel they are being fed enough information."

Two chairmen shared feedback they had received about themselves.

"The criticism that I get of me is that I'm rather impatient and don't suffer fools gladly. I want to move things on and may cut off discussion. This has been fed back to me."

"I have a yearly assessment. The feedback has been that I am good at knowing what I am good at and drawing upon the experiences of others to fill in the gaps."

Final reflections

Being chairman of a large plc is a time consuming business. The old adage – about the CEO running the company and the chairman running the board – suggests that the job revolves around board meetings. Yet our interviewees made clear that chairing a board is about much more than the meetings.

"It is important to go to some trouble to know what's going on in the business, not just by reading but by visiting and meeting with executives. This should be continuous. You must walk about the sites, otherwise you miss things."

One interviewee said he budgeted one day each week on his work as chairman for six board meetings a year. Another observed that the time he spent as chairman had gone up to 70 days a year, compared to just 20 days five years ago. A third was in the organisation every day and said: *"It's always more time than you expect."*

"You should not underestimate the time needed. You definitely spend more time outside the boardroom than in it, working with the CEO, the executive team and the board."

As well as being time consuming, the role of chairman can be lonely. Several mentioned this explicitly, while others observed that there was no one obvious to turn to for advice or to act as a sounding board. To some extent this is inevitable. *"Any top job has the need for social distance,"* one chairman said. Others mentioned attending networking events for chairmen from time to time, usually hosted by consultants – but were lukewarm about the usefulness of these sessions.

"My network is not as deep or as supportive as I need on occasion. I do go to people, to friends who have been chairmen and to some consultants I know and I actually go to my board members, for instance the SID, who understand the particular challenge."

"I have a support network which I can call on but not specifically about my chairman role. If a friend knows the business, I might say that I need advice, but they would see themselves as a friend, rather than an advisor. The CEO is also very supportive."

"You can't be a loner, but I do find the chairman roundtables universally depressing, so I stir them up!"

"I want to develop this more; I need more contacts."

"I went to Big 4 briefings in the beginning, but not now."

"I do a bit of chairman networking. I go to courses given for NEDs, particularly on regulatory stuff and new challenges (perhaps I attend five or six a year). I also go to dinners held by people who want to get something from us, for instance the headhunters, accounting firms and PR companies. I might attend 10 a year."

Top tips from our chairmen

"Be humble."

"Remember that the main role of the chairman is to appoint or disappoint the CEO."

"Do thorough due diligence on the company you are considering, because once you're in it's too late."

"Make very sure you understand what you're letting yourself in for, and speak to a number of chairmen of similar institutions to check what they consider the most important issues."

"Talk to the previous chairman. Find out where the bodies are hidden."

"Have a skill plan: don't be afraid to admit things you need to know, e.g. corporate finance, the business itself, etc. Fix this by learning."

"Retain a sense of humour, because you'll need it."

"Use your ears more than your mouth, and your nose comes in helpful too!"

"Enjoy it – then you will do it rather better."

The report team

Helen Pitcher

Helen is chairman of IDDAS. Her career spans 30 years in both the business world and the consulting sector. She was appointed the youngest ever board director for a division of Grand Metropolitan. In her subsequent consulting career, she became CEO of CEDAR, which she built into one of the best-regarded consultancies in the human capital world.

Helen is recognised as a leading organisational performance coach, mentor and boardroom facilitator. Regularly coaching chairmen, CEOs and NEDs, she works at the most senior level in FTSE 100 and international companies, as well as the public sector. Helen has a worldwide network of contacts and alumni whom she has coached and developed over the years. She is a panel member of the Employment Appeal Tribunal, a member of the Selection Panel for Queen's Counsel, chairman of KidsOut, and a trustee and fundraiser for several other charities.

Helen is an APECS-accredited coach and qualified psychometric assessor. She is a Fellow of the IOD, CIPD and RSA and has worked across a range of sectors including financial services, utilities, media, leisure, telecommunications, retail and public sector.

Hilary Sears

Hilary is a senior IDDAS mentor and undertook the interviews. She has extensive experience in executive search and board assessment, as a director and vice president in Carré Orban, Korn Ferry and AT Kearney. Hilary worked in the Cabinet Office on secondment to the Leadership and People Strategy Directorate. In 2007, she was appointed chairman of the Association of MBAs, which accredits MBA programmes internationally and in 2008 she became chairman of KIDS, a national charity for disabled children. She is on the Advisory Board of Cranfield School of Management, is the final judge for the Women in The City Award, and is a past Vice Chairman of Forum UK, part of the International Women's Forum.

Hashi Syedain

Hashi Syedain is a freelance business journalist with more than 20 years' experience of writing for national newspapers, websites and business magazines. She is a former deputy editor of *Management Today* and has worked as a journalist and editor in both Russia and Germany. She has won several awards for her business writing and was highly commended in the Towers Watson HR Journalist of the Year Awards 2010.

Hashi is also chair of the Independent Monitoring Board of Harmondsworth Immigration Removal Centre, which reports on standards of fairness and decency for asylum seekers and other detainees in the centre.

Peter MacKenzie

Peter is director of executive development at IDDAS. He undertook the initial research into the background on chairmen's effectiveness and designed the research premise and questionnaires. Peter works with leaders on both their individual and their collective leadership development. He brings to this role 19 years of developmental experience, gained through senior in-house development roles, in the UK and internationally, as well as consultancy and collaborations with business schools.

Susan Dudley

Susan's background is in administration and project co-ordination. She provides project co-ordination and consultancy services to a number of corporate clients across various sectors, including utilities, telecommunications, retail and the NHS. Susan is a member of the CIPD and a qualified psychometrician.

Chapter B5

Board Dynamics: The Non-Executive Director's Perspective

Introduction **B5.1**

We are very grateful to IDDAS for permission to reprint this excellent guidance, and also three others in their series, which we reproduce at Chapters **B2**, **B3** and **B4**. No responsibility for loss occasioned to any person acting or refraining from action as a result of any material in this publication can be accepted by the authors or the publishers.

Clare Chalmers, Chief Executive of IDDAS, would be pleased to hear from readers with any inquiries about this guidance. She can be contacted at IDDAS, IDDAS House, 74 New Cavendish Street, London, W1G 8TF (Tel: +44 (0)20 7436 0101; Email: clare.chalmers@iddas.com; Website: www.iddas.com).

Based in London, IDDAS specialises in providing board effectiveness, mentoring and coaching, leadership facilitation and executive assessment services for chairs, CEOs and main board directors, as well as for those who aspire to non-executive roles. IDDAS has an established reputation for its quality, innovative, supportive and flexible approach.

IDDAS BOARD DYNAMICS: THE NON-EXECUTIVE DIRECTOR'S PERSPECTIVE

Foreword

The non-executive director's role has always been a coveted one. However, where it may once have been seen as icing on the corporate career, conferring more status than it required effort, the events of recent years have forced a fresh focus on the accountability of NEDs.

This is a good thing. It is good both for the health and success of UK corporations and for NEDs themselves, as they now have a stronger mandate than ever to use the skills and experience for which they are appointed.

This report draws on the views of non-executive directors in a range of organisations and sectors. It offers valuable insights into how the role is developing and the backgrounds, skills and experiences that are needed to discharge it.

Successive reviews of corporate governance and board effectiveness have called for what amounts to a significant cultural change for many boardrooms. This report suggests that key messages are getting through, particularly on effective challenge, the need for structured induction and training, and the importance of a balanced board composition. However, more progress is needed in implementation, particularly in getting women and candidates from ethnic minorities onto boards, if we are to avoid mandatory quotas in future.

Fulfilling the role of a non-executive director is not easy. It requires the subtle skills to influence and contribute without wielding power, to be respected as a challenging and credible individual. Many seek these positions, but few truly have the ability to fulfil them. This report is valuable reading for anyone who wishes to join their ranks.

Anne Minto OBE
Group Director, Human Resources, Centrica
Non-Executive Director, Shire PLC

Introduction

This third report in our Board Dynamics series looks at the role of the non-executive director a couple of years on from the financial crisis. We have now interviewed more than 60 board directors for this report and its predecessors, *The Chairman's Perspective* and *A Female Perspective*. In the process we have built up a comprehensive picture of the changing dynamics within British boardrooms.

Boards have now had a chance to absorb the recommendations of the Turner and Walker reviews, and the updated UK Corporate Governance Code has been in effect long enough for most to have completed a full reporting year under the new regime.

There has also been a renewed focus on improving the diversity of boards, in particular on attracting more women to the NED role. While we were conducting our research, Lord Davies published *Women on Boards*, in which he made 10 recommendations, one of which was that FTSE 100 companies should aim for a minimum of 25% female board members by 2015.

What do non-executive directors make of all these changes and recommendations? How much progress has been made in implementing them? Where do NEDs stand on quotas? These are some of the questions our research sought to answer.

As always, our focus has been on behaviours and attitudes. We have explored the transition from executive to non-executive, preparedness for the non-exec role, and the all-important issue of challenge. We asked about time commitment and responsibility in relation to pay and about ways of widening the pool from which NEDs are drawn.

Our findings suggest that today's NEDs are acutely aware of their increased accountability and are prepared to work hard. No one joins a board nowadays expecting an easy ride. Many would like to be better paid, but see no likelihood of this in the near future. They are instinctively opposed to quotas for women, but recognise the need for urgent action to address the current shortfall.

We also noted, alongside a general tendency for people to become NEDs at a younger age, an emerging cadre of highly accomplished individuals who are becoming portfolio NEDs in their 40s or early 50s as a deliberate career and lifestyle choice. This move reflects the fact that top-level executive careers are starting and ending earlier, and that the increased accountability of the NED role makes it a meatier, more challenging and ultimately more interesting proposition than it might have been in the past.

It is too soon to tell whether this is truly a trend, or just a re-alignment in response to the current changes. If it does take hold, it has the potential to bring more women onto boards – although it will certainly not be enough by itself, to redress the gender balance of the boardroom.

What is clear above all, however, is that this is a fascinating time in which to be an NED.

I would like to thank all the NEDs who participated in our research. They are busy people with packed schedules and we greatly appreciate the time they took to share their views. Their insights will be valuable to board directors and chairmen, current and aspiring, and to anyone involved in hiring or developing them.

Helen Pitcher
Chairman, IDDAS

Executive Summary

This research set out to explore key aspects of the role of the non-executive director.

We were interested in the skills and experience required to obtain an NED role, what enables an NED to operate effectively, and how board membership can be broadened.

NEDs are getting younger

Among the key findings detailed opposite, perhaps the most striking was the emergence of the career-choice NED. As executives get younger, and boards become more accountable and professional, having a portfolio of NED roles is being viewed as a viable career option for people in their 40s or early 50s, looking for a lifestyle change.

For those with the right kind of experience, building such a portfolio offers the possibility of an attractive alternative to staying on the executive treadmill.

It is too early to predict whether this is a development that will have a significant impact on the make-up of boards in the future. But it is arguably a logical consequence of the increased accountability and higher profile of the NED role. Most commentators have focused on the difficulty of attracting people, given the greater accountability and time commitment required. The flip side of these developments is that being an NED is now interesting and challenging enough to satisfy people still at the peak of their careers. This reflects IDDAS's experience of an increasing trend for full-time executives to seek NED positions as a valuable opportunity to broaden their capabilities for the top job and at the same time build a longer term portfolio career.

Key findings

- We are seeing the emergence of career-choice NEDs who deliberately step off the executive career ladder to take up NED roles.

- A non-executive directorship is a useful experience for most serving executives, but many feel that the time commitment makes it difficult to manage.
- The contrast in pace and style of contribution between an executive and a non-executive career is huge. Those leaving executive life particularly miss the administrative support systems they are used to.
- Although some NEDs feel that the pay they receive does not reflect the increased level of accountability demanded in recent years, this does not necessarily stop them seeking NED roles.
- Many NEDs, while instinctively against the introduction of mandatory quotas to bring more women onto boards, would reluctantly accept them if female representation did not increase significantly in the next few years.
- NEDs do not necessarily believe that a board should work as a team. What is important is that board members respect each other and work together effectively.
- NEDs are acutely aware of the issue of effective challenge in the boardroom. Trust in the capabilities and modus operandi of NEDs is an essential prerequisite to achieving this.
- The Financial Services Authority's focus on challenge has led to greater awareness, more process and different use of language. It is not clear whether it has led to more effective challenge.
- Committee work has become central to operating effectively as an NED – and adds significantly to their workload.
- NED induction is becoming increasingly professional, but some organisations could still do better.
- Internal board effectiveness reviews are patchy and arouse little enthusiasm. NEDs generally welcome external reviews.

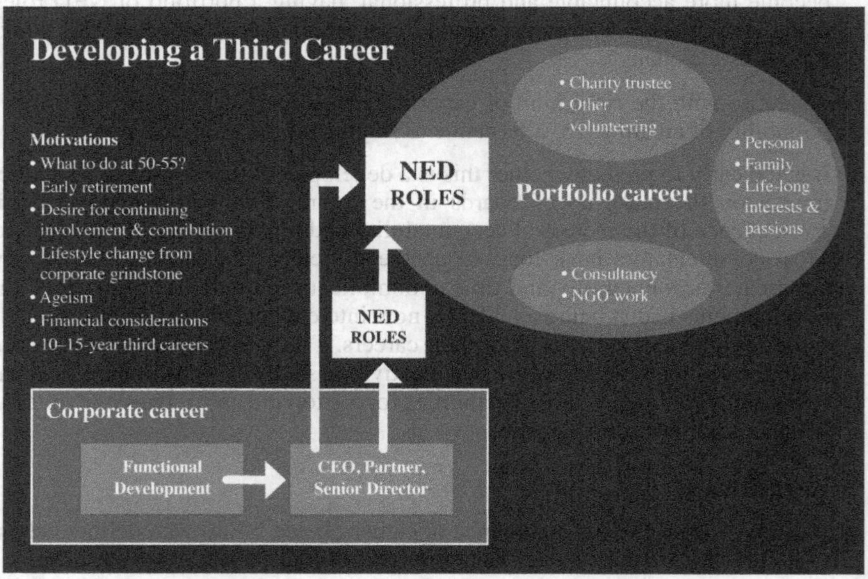

About our interviewees

Our research was based on in-depth, structured interviews with 26 non-executive directors. We mainly used open questions designed to elicit wide-ranging responses. Interviews typically lasted an hour or more and were conducted in person or, occasionally, by telephone.

Our interviewees came from various sectors including financial services, manufacturing, utilities, healthcare, transport, media, retail and leisure.

They held 66 non-executive directorships between them, involving the boards of eight FTSE 100 and nine FTSE 250 companies, and numerous other organisations.

- 6 still held an executive position.
- 15 held more than one directorship.
- 7 were women.
- 2 were American.
- 6 held an accounting qualification.
- 4 were former CEOs.
- 7 were former finance directors.
- The youngest was 39.
- The oldest was 66.
- The median age was 55.
- 7 were over 60.
- 16 were in their 50s.
- 2 were in their 40s.
- 1 was under 40.

Getting onto a Board

The classic NED used to be an ex-top executive or banker who took up one or two board positions after retiring from full-time employment in his 60s.

Very few of our sample fitted into this mould. Fewer than a third were over 60 and only two had been 60+ when they first became NEDs. Most had obtained their first NED position while still in an executive role, on occasion encouraged by their employer, who saw it as a development opportunity for top talent. The majority of the rest turned to nonexecutive positions after retiring in their 50s.

The career-choice NED

During our previous research with chairmen and female NEDs, we came across a third category of NED which we wished to explore further: the young professional, who makes a deliberate choice to abandon corporate life and pursue an NED portfolio career. These are people who have reached very senior executive positions relatively early in their careers and want a change of lifestyle. A small number of our sample fell into this category and several others had noticed it as a trend among colleagues.

"I still see two types of NED: the 60-year old who wants to keep active one day a week between golf and holidays; or the younger NED who has gone into it as a serious career choice, and who has a series of NED roles. I believe that the older version will say it has become too hard, with too much bureaucracy and risk. The younger guys see it as a legitimate career."

"We have young board members (I am the oldest at 64) who have all decided on plural because they don't want the weight of an executive role; most have made money, but still want to have involvement, and want to contribute."

"I left [the bank] when my daughter was one year old. I felt demoralised and didn't want to continue with 100-hour weeks. Frankly, I didn't need the money and I didn't need the lifestyle – the travelling, the limousines, the flights in seat 1A. My clients suggested that I look at non-executive directorships."

Although there was a wide consensus that NEDs are getting younger, not all agreed that it was necessarily a matter of career strategy. They observed the emergence of a 'third career' after a period in CEO and top leadership roles, filling the gap from the mid-50s onwards and creating an active and engaged career for an additional 10–15 years.

"There is more ageism now: we have to step down younger in the professional services sector. In law firms in the US you can keep going to 90, but not in the UK, where partners may be asked to leave at 50 and certainly 60. They are still in the prime of life, so they seek something else to do."

"A CEO who is past 60 is pretty unusual. He or she is more likely to be late 40s or early 50s. So those people who want to continue will make the move into non-executive directorship. I include myself in this group."

"An increasing number of people run out of road in their 50s in their corporate career. I see it as a proper third career. There is an emerging trend of professional NEDs, consultants, advisors in their early/mid-50s, who consider it worth doing and feasible."

"It is driven by a combination of earlier retirement dates, the reduction in the number of final salary pensions, and lower annuity rates – you look for additional income to help pay the bills. The tendency to have children later in life also means they are still in full-time education."

Most interviewees welcomed the trend towards more youthful NEDs – seeing it also as a natural development, given the increased time commitment and accountability involved in the role.

"NEDs are getting younger, which is good. It is very useful to have NEDs who have recently been doing what the CEO is doing. Probably as a result, there is wider experience and a group of people who have more time to give (as compared to the full-time FD who has limited time for an NED). The portfolio group is probably more professional."

"For those who opt to do it as a career, they will be working five days a week; I see myself somewhere in between. The more active an NED is mentally, the better for the company."

However, one interviewee sounded a note of caution about too much youth.

"I think the difficulty is experience. I have just met someone who is viewing it as a profession, and they just may not have the scar tissue and the experience which I believe you need. The theory of business is not complicated. Experience is what you give in this role."

Landing the first role

Our interviewees were, broadly speaking, people with a strong business or finance background – although some were younger than the classic NED. Nonetheless, almost half spoke of difficulties obtaining their first NED position, or commented that they had not achieved the level of directorship to which they aspired, or found it hard to build the balanced portfolio they wanted.

Participants variously told us that lawyers are not popular, HR directors are not popular, consultants are not popular, and that you cannot get onto a FTSE board if you don't have executive experience at FTSE-board level.

Among those who described a smooth passage to their first role, three had help from their companies. A further interviewee, who had had a stellar career but was younger than the traditional NED, said her most significant breakthrough came when a highly respected chairman championed her cause, by calling headhunters on her behalf.

Many commented that it was much easier to get offers once you were already on a board – and the most common advice to aspiring NEDs was to network diligently among contacts and headhunters and to do as much preparation as possible while you were still in your executive role.

Transition challenges

The non-executive role is fundamentally different to the executive. The former is about influence, and contributing at a strategic level only, helping the executives to be more effective and make the best decisions; the latter comes with power, day-to-day involvement, action, and detailed knowledge and understanding of the business.

Almost without exception, our interviewees told us that the differences between executive and non-executive life were huge. Many commented on the practical challenges of acting without the infrastructure to which they were accustomed – secretaries, IT support, pre-booked travel. One even suggested setting up the equivalent of a barristers' chambers for NEDs, offering support and a secretariat.

One spoke of "a monster life change", both in what you do and how, while another called the contrast "night and day". Apart from the lifestyle change, there is the challenge of stepping back and accepting less control.

"Every NED gets slightly frustrated: they can see issues which were they executive they would grab hold of, shake around and get solved. But as an NED you are there to help others make better decisions (they may not be what you would have decided)."

This sentiment chimed with our previous research on the chairman's perspective, which examined the subtle art of wielding influence without power.

"The worst possible thing is NEDs wanting to take over. They must not, and they must not meddle or subvert management processes."

Wearing two hats

We also asked whether having a non-executive role elsewhere was beneficial to someone in a CEO or senior executive position. There was an overwhelming feeling that it was, because of what you can learn from outside your own company or sector. As one interviewee commented, *"People who are mono-life can be pretty parochial; you can always learn from others."*

Nonetheless, interviewees acknowledged that it is very difficult to find time for both. One commented that you could only make it work if you had command of your own diary as an executive. Several also noted that they were not permitted by their employer to take on an NED role during their executive career, or that it would be seen as a negative step if they did. Only one interviewee expressed this view himself: *"I don't believe executives have time to do the job, and they are shortchanging their own shareholders if they do."*

"I believe that it is good for a CEO to undertake a non-executive directorship, as there are learnings you can bring back from a different company, industry, chairman, etc. But I wouldn't be happy if a CEO wanted to be chairman of another board, as this is too time-consuming."

"My view is that it should be beneficial. I wasn't allowed to have one, but had someone said to me 10 years ago that it would be good for me, I can see that it would have broadened my experience."

"I have always been supportive of executive directors having one non-executive directorship, whether on a company board, or 'great and good' not-for-profit. It is a refresher, it is recognition by their company, giving them an opportunity to grow without having to jump ship."

"We were not allowed to have a nonexecutive directorship, so I have no personal experience. However, where I have seen it, yes, it broadened the individual's experience. This is particularly good for CEOs and FDs."

"I have benefited so much – it has made me a better exec and added value to my organisation."

"I'd have to say yes, but it depends. It has an advantage because it enables the CEO to understand better the position and role of NEDs on his own board."

"I do think that a senior executive should have a non-executive directorship, but he/ she needs to be careful – about the nature of the business, how bumpy a ride it is likely to be, and certainly only one. There needs to be clear prior discussion on their own board, and an understanding that if they take on an extra role (for instance, chairman of the Audit Committee, or Remco) they could be distracted for a month."

"I really encourage people in the CEO position to fit in one NED position. It is very useful for them to see how other organisations operate. Yesterday I did appraisals, and I gave views based on what I had seen elsewhere. It was very useful."

"Yes, but I think the question is: how realistic is it for a corporate CEO to fulfil the requirement. Certainly more than one non-executive directorship would be too challenging."

"On balance, yes. I say 'on balance' because you are always torn, when you're a CEO or finance director, about time: you should be pretty tied up in what you are doing. But it gives you breadth, and prepares you for the NED role and transition."

One interviewee made the point that headhunters and coaches still categorise people as one or the other, executive or NED, which she believed was wrong.

"I see many similarities between executive and non-executive roles: you are part of a team, you still need a high work ethic and you still need a good brain."

The argument for quotas

The increasing youth of NEDs, and the emerging trend towards more professional career NEDs, could increase diversity on boards. But it hasn't done so yet, particularly in relation to women.

We asked our NEDs what was preventing boards from becoming more diverse and what they thought of recruiting from non-traditional backgrounds, such as academia or the media. We also asked them about quotas for female NEDs.

Only a small number of interviewees were completely dismissive of quotas.

"Nonsense. If somebody is good enough for the job, they should get it. The chairman should use his leadership to make sure it happens. I dislike being told that I have to do something."

"I do not subscribe to this. You want the best people. It leads to the belief that you need one of everything, but why?"

"I think quotas (ethnic, gender, sexuality) are wrong. You should pick the people who are right for the job."

"I do not believe in quotas. Talent will always come to the top. More women are rising on merit; the idea of a quota would cause resentment and it is not the way to do it."

Such strident views were not typical, however. The majority – including most of our female interviewees – remained against quotas for fear that they would lead to a lowering of the bar, or be seen as patronising to women; but they also stressed the need for change in recruitment practices, or expressed frustration with the lack of progress in this area.

"I don't like quotas. I would be mortified if I was there because I am a woman, and if it was thought I'd got there with lower capabilities. Most women feel the same. But if men are left to recruit in their own image, how do you get them to look at diverse issues? The mindset does need to change."

"It will lead to the view that women are at the board because of their gender rather than by their experience and skills. I believe that the answer to making this shift is through public pressure and better lists of potential women candidates from headhunters. The last thing one would want is to have substandard women on boards, as that would reinforce the male dinosaur view."

"I am deeply ambivalent. I'm not completely opposed but I would be very reluctant to adopt a quota at the moment. We should go to greater lengths to introduce more women and maintain five years of serious pressure (although I'm not sure it will work)."

"This is a hard question. I am never in favour of positive discrimination because if you lower the bar then a woman on the board is perceived to be there to make

up the numbers. However, given that nothing has changed over a long period now, I can see why quotas have come up."

"I have always been against quotas although I can see the frustration with the current situation. Women make most of the consumer decisions, and they should be the advocate of consumers on the board. Having this perspective is important. It's an amazing gap otherwise."

"I used to be completely against quotas of any kind. My worry however is that unless there is some form of aggressive action, it won't happen. Something does need to change – or force change."

Several interviewees had ideas for increasing the number of women.

"We have a policy of moving to a 50/50 split in gender. Our chairman believes we should be there in a year; the management's view is three years."

"We need to mine below the executive committees in big companies. Executives there hold far bigger jobs and responsibilities than people in smaller companies, but divisional executives have tended to be ignored."

"Boards should be stricter on wanting women on the shortlist: it is wrong of them to put the blame on headhunters."

"You need to look at where you are going to get really good women, and one answer is HR directors. But there is a reluctance to have HR at the board table, because the board does not see the role as strategic. In my opinion, this is wrong. I challenge strategy, structure, remuneration and organisational change: this is all about performance, and enhancing it. This is how HR relates to strategy. It is meat and drink for HR directors."

"We should examine why women are not getting to be CEOs. Perhaps greater education, coaching and mentoring of women to get to the top in the executive will lead to more of them becoming NEDs."

"There should be consideration [by a board] as to whether their modus operandi unconsciously militates against women. It would be interesting for the nominations committee from time to time to be obliged to survey or find out why they are getting a smaller pool of suitably qualified female candidates. Think of Parliament where the work starting at 3pm and going on late may make a difference."

Broadening the mix

Two of our (male) interviewees – who were against imposing quotas – nonetheless commented on the benefit to board dynamics of having a gender balance (a view that echoed our previous research into female NEDs).

"The mix is very important. Why? Because it changes the chemistry of the group, and this different chemistry seems to work better. We have benefited enormously from three women who absorb some of the machismo, make us behave differently, and in that difference, you get good things coming out."

"If you were to ask: 'Should there be more female NEDs?' then the answer is 'Yes, provided they are of the right quality.' Women bring something valuable: a different way of behaving which stops the male-dominated boards acting like

that. Women also tend to be more intuitive than their male counterparts, although I know this is a generalisation."

A handful of interviewees indicated that quotas might yet be justified if voluntary targets didn't succeed.

"If you give the board notice that you are expecting them to move and they don't respond, then you might impose a quota."

"Women have to be there, and I have been listening to the current arguments to get them there. If there is no improvement, then perhaps you resort to a quota."

"If necessary, then OK. But quotas really are the last resort."

One brave soul, however, did come out in favour of quotas now – just about.

"I'm probably marginally in favour to create the shift – but only marginally. You have to have the right quality of thinking. You would hope that thinking would embrace more women."

Is corporate experience a must?

Our interviewees had mixed views about whether those from outside the corporate world, such as academics or media people, should be considered for NED roles.

Some were unequivocally against, either on principle or because of bad experiences.

"This is a big mistake. They might challenge differently, but you are not there to be the corporate conscience; you are there for shareholder value."

"I have seen two NEDs who do not have classic backgrounds. Both have struggled, and it has been very hard to command respect. If you can't operate at the right level, it becomes a nightmare."

"I really do think this is absolute nonsense. The job is to look after the interests of shareholders, it is not about social engineering."

Those on bank boards said you definitely needed to have banking experience – although this requirement is making bank boards more homogenous than ever.

"The problem is not about being able to ask good questions (as a media personality or academic might be able to do), but being able to understand the answers. Financial services are just too complicated for a non-financial services person to be able to challenge the answers."

In less technical areas, on the other hand, it might be appropriate to look wider, according to some interviewees.

"It does depend on the type of business you are in. Perhaps if you are a retail business, a wider perspective might add value."

Those in favour of casting the net wider argued that personal qualities are more important than technical background – and that non-traditional backgrounds could form part of a balanced board, if others had more traditional skills.

"I interviewed someone today for a board who was not from the corporate sector. If they have got this far, then it is not about what is on the CV, but about what they

can bring to the board in terms of attitude, thought processes, intelligence and interpersonal skills."

"I think there is a need to widen the net. It can be powerful to have someone who can see other options. Committee members can jump to conclusions. A lot of people don't have P&L experience, but the question is: do you need to have owned a P&L? If you insist on this, then you will always end up with CEOs and finance directors. I think the majority of the board need this, but it doesn't have to be all."

"You have to be able to command respect for what you bring to the board. If Einstein had wanted to be on a board, then you might have been interested and therefore gone outside the normal pool, but you should not do this for the sake of simply widening the pool."

A couple of interviewees also commented on the need to recruit more widely from within the corporate sector.

"What you don't need are more financial people: you need marketing, HR. It is a big worry with the increasing regulations, the number of people who come from financial services and accounting, because they represent only one area of the business."

The question of pay

This issue split our interviewees. Almost all of them said that being an NED was more onerous than it used to be and that the time commitment was greater than they had anticipated – particularly when you added in committee work. Most put the workload at two to three times the number of days for board meetings, plus extra for committees.

Furthermore, accountability, while legally no greater than before, is now perceived to be much higher, and the risk to reputations is therefore more real.

Given these realities, about a third of interviewees felt the pay was too low – particularly in comparison to the risk/reward balance that existed in the past.

"I don't think the remuneration reflects the increasing demands. In a basic way, the daily rate is about half what I get as an advisor. I know a fellow board member who has restricted himself to just one nonexecutive directorship, because he can earn more elsewhere."

"Depending on the industry, the remuneration is not enough. You seriously do question: is it worth the liability and the aggro?"

"If you are going to have serious people on FTSE boards, then the fees should be around £5,000 per day (not £1,500)."

Public-sector boards – which pay a fraction of the private sector fees – will run into increasing difficulty in recruiting the right calibre of person, said several of those undertaking such roles. Smaller public companies also pay too little, commented one interviewee.

"The remuneration in FTSE 100 companies is probably fair, but it is not in FTSE 250 companies, where NEDs are paid £28–30,000. It does depend on the challenge, but this level of remuneration is a nonsense. Given the demands, and the time

requirement of 20–30 days, why would you take on a smaller plc non-executive directorship rather than one in a private company? The smaller plc involves a lot of hassle and governance. Private companies have less focus on governance, but could be just as interesting. This will be a challenge in the future – to find good NEDs for FTSE 250 companies – unless the remuneration issue is addressed."

However, about a fifth of our interviewees stated categorically that they felt well remunerated. Others acknowledged that it was politically difficult to raise NED fees in the current climate, or that money should not be a significant motivator. Furthermore, paying too much could compromise independence – and there is no shortage of candidates for NED positions.

"If you were to start to pay large sums of money, it would destroy the sense of detachment, which is the reason you want to do it. You can walk away. Compared to the average, you are getting a lot, but you are not dependent: ultimately you need to be able to walk away. If you get £40,000 now, would an additional £20,000 make a difference? It should be a reasonable amount for the time you spend, and the concentration you bring to it. People choose to do it, without day-to-day responsibility. I do think that the chairman of the Audit Committee should be paid a sum closer to that of the chairman, as there is a huge responsibility and time commitment."

"By any normal standards what you get paid for the time you do is probably generous, if you think of it as £40,000 for two to three days a month. Many outside the board environment would say: just give me that."

"Money should not be the driver. This is about: How is my life more interesting than it was yesterday?"

"As long as remuneration is pitched at a level that people don't feel out of pocket then that's fine. The minute an NED is not giving some discretionary time then there is something wrong. I'm there because I want to be."

"I am not aware of anyone saying 'No' to an offer because the fee is not sufficient."

"I think remuneration is completely irrelevant. There is a lot of competition for people to come to these roles."

Board Effectiveness

Challenge is the word of the moment. In the wake of the banking crisis, both the Walker Review and the Financial Services Authority emphasised the importance of challenging boardroom debate. Without it, they said, non-executives are not doing their job. When the FSA examines boardroom minutes or attends a bank's board meeting, robust challenge is one of the things it explicitly looks for.

The art of challenge

We asked our interviewees about their perception of challenge and how they go about challenging effectively without usurping the authority of the executive.

It was an issue that engaged many of them and the answers they gave were varied and nuanced. Several said that challenge was fundamental to the role of the non-executive director. But there is challenge and challenge – and more than one way to skin a cat.

For example, challenging in the sense of asking probing questions in order to understand the business, its strategy and the risks it faces, is crucial. Otherwise NEDs are failing to exercise good governance.

"There is a danger if you don't understand, and don't challenge, of a box-ticking corporate governance route, instead of a fact-based assessment. The job is to get the best decision from the information – ask if you need more."

"It is not acceptable to sit on a board when you don't understand the risks being faced by the company, when you can't therefore challenge, as these risks need to be identified and documented. You have a personal responsibility to do this."

Even questioning for information can be seen as hostile, said one interviewee.

"It takes time to learn what is seen as a challenge in an industry that is new to you, because you want to ask about KPIs, and issues and details. One chairman pointed out that this can be seen as threatening. So questions for knowledge can be seen as aggressive."

Asking searching questions to ensure the executives have thought things through fully or explored alternatives was also cited several times as a key part of the NED role.

"It is important for the executives to have someone really quiz them on strategy, or how they are pursuing the company objectives, so that they don't become complacent."

"Challenge involves being able to ask sufficiently probing questions to establish why the executive team have adopted particular strategic plans. It is trying to see if they have thought it through rather than adopting a fashionable view."

"The art is in knowing the right questions to ask. As an executive, you are aware of the two or three questions you would prefer not to be asked – good NEDs ask them."

No challenge without trust

Again and again participants told us that the board has to trust you, if you are to be in a position to challenge effectively. In particular, contentious rather than exploratory challenge needs to be preceded by trust. You earn trust, they told us, both for your technical expertise and for your approach or style. This means picking your battles and your language carefully.

"Challenge needs to be based on real understanding of the organisation and the context. Challenge also needs to be based on having secured a position of trust in relation to the company. Unless you have the understanding and the trust, your challenge will be destructive rather than positive."

"You do have to earn the right to challenge. I have watched some NEDs being downright unpleasant; this is not the role, and there is no need for this behaviour. You are a critical friend."

"You need to pick a few issues and be consistent. It is not helpful to nit-pick."

"I tend to stick to what I know. I will challenge big time if I am uncomfortable in the areas I know – if I challenge on health and safety, or operations, everyone listens."

"Ideally, you pick areas of activity where you are best equipped to comment. You go out and visit these areas, so that you have extra knowledge. You contribute to the discussions, but it is about style. You do not usurp the executive ground. When you speak, you flavour your comments with such expressions as: 'I wonder…'."

"It is important to challenge in a supportive way (which is a challenge in itself), not always criticising, not being a pain. Sometimes the challenge will not be worth pursuing; at other times, it is important to keep up the challenge. So, you must be clear on the focus, you mustn't get on your hobbyhorse. Above all, you must be respected."

"It is all about the way you phrase the question. You don't say: 'In my experience…', or 'Where I worked before…'. You ask: 'Have you considered…?' or 'What do you think about…?'."

Several interviewees talked about the central role of the chairman in effecting constructive challenge and in tackling contentious issues outside the board meetings. As one interviewee put it, *"The board is more effective if the executives have an answer – not when they haven't. It is not a matter of trying to catch them out."*

"The worst thing is to rely on doing the challenging at the board meetings. You have to invest time with the chairman, NEDs and EDs before the meeting. You raise issues, clarify perspectives in advance. This really helps, so that the issues are not brought up cold at the board meeting. Sometimes it still leaves you with different views from other NEDs, and you have to challenge at the board table."

"I think it is important to recognise the hierarchy of the executive and always work through that. At one company, we have oneto- one meetings between individual NEDs and the CEO. That's where you can be at your most challenging in a relatively safe environment."

"The chairman's role is absolutely key in this. Anyone who says, 'Here is my experience of this, this is what we should do,' may be entirely wrong and could bias the discussion. If something is difficult, the chairman should have had conversations off-line, in order to arrive at consensus."

"I had a situation on one board where, as chairman of the RemCo, I looked at the CEO's objectives and thought they were rubbish. So I spoke to the chairman who agreed to talk with him, and I suggested to the CEO that he might want to talk through his ideas with the chairman. When the item came up at the board, the CEO was able to say that he had decided he would like the opportunity of discussing it with the chairman before making a recommendation. This was a constructive intervention, with much more effect."

"The extent to which a non executive can challenge is determined by the chairman. If the chairman doesn't support me, say if I was challenging the CEO, then it is very difficult to do. The board dynamics overall dictate the level of challenge."

Some interviewees felt that all challenge has to take place outside the boardroom – or else it comes too late.

"If you have to challenge, it means that you got involved in the issue too late; it is a signal that the relationship has started to go wrong. If there is strong and

fierce challenge, it usually means that the relationship is breaking down. This is particularly true in smaller companies, where the role of the NED has to be more involved and more collaborative."

"In reality, NEDs do not get into real strategic discussions early enough to really impact the strategy. We pitch up for a set piece, and the executive members are not soliciting real input. In the longer term, strategy does not change that much; NEDs are always playing catch-up and it is quite uncommon to have the strategic discussion at the very beginning of these initiatives. In other words, they would not be brought to the board unless the executive wanted it, and therefore the goose has already been cooked."

"Ultimately, the board does one thing: choose or fire the CEO. Any board which does more than this is in danger of crossing the line between executive and non-executive. You are trying to do everything for the good of the company, and the challenge is intelligent questioning, rather than overt challenge. If an executive comes to the board and gets his proposal rejected, then it is almost a vote of no confidence."

Others were more sanguine about the potential for conflict, even in board meetings.

"Challenge is critically important. In fact, one of the most important things an NED can do is to provide challenge and critique of the executive management's activities. You have to understand that it will be inherently confrontational, but this can be handled by people working professionally. You must not be fobbed off: if something appears wrong, then it probably is."

But NEDs also need to know when to let an issue go.

"Recognise when you should back down, and accept that the point has been made."

"The executives are the ones with all the data, which they have analysed and from this analysis come up with logical conclusions. You can ask: 'Have you thought about doing it this way?' but if they come back with a logical answer, even if you don't agree, you can't do anything. You are there to safeguard the company assets, not to agree with everything they are doing – as long as what they are proposing is consistent with the strategy."

"You have to be open to the point that you could very well be wrong. This is particularly pertinent to NEDs working in broadly familiar territory. They need to recognise that things that may have worked for them in the past won't necessarily work this time. The experience should be used to inform but not as a blueprint."

In all cases, finding the right balance of challenge and support is critically important – and not always easy.

"NEDs are not the secret policemen or the in-house regulators. They are the friendly advisors to the executive. They act to check and test the thinking, and in that testing process they bring their own ideas. You could see challenge as part of a mentoring, coaching or detached advisory process. This has a richer, more nuanced feel than challenge. There is something confrontational in challenge; it may be part of what you are doing, but only a small part."

Challenge and the FSA

The NEDs on financial services boards were particularly aware of the need for the right level of challenge. But they were not entirely convinced that the FSA was barking up the right tree in the ways it seeks to monitor challenge.

"Challenge is a great Financial Services Authority word. They are always checking on whether there is sufficient challenge. You write in the minutes: 'The NEDs challenged this point.' It is an overworked term."

"I'm sure when the FSA come to observe our board they will want to see some tough questioning. But board meetings aren't meant to be an ordeal. They are meant to build confidence in the management."

"There is no doubt at all, especially in financial services, which are so regulated, that the importance of challenge has come to the fore since 2008. Minutes will now contain the word 'challenged', whereas previously they might have had 'said, remarked, stated'."

"The FSA has focused on whether NEDs are challenging enough. They read the minutes, but miss the point. Some questions could be totally irrelevant, but can be seen by the FSA as challenge. The FSA can't see the body language of the board, and whether trust is there."

Is a board a team?

We asked our interviewees how NEDs can be encouraged to work as a team. They aren't a team, nor should they be, said several interviewees, as that could get too cosy. Instead, it's about understanding each other and learning to work effectively, which needs to be done outside the boardroom.

"How close should the board be to each other as a team? Acting as a pack would be very extreme. On the other hand, it is much more difficult to cope with NEDs who all have different agendas. You do have to have a common thread and agenda, otherwise the board is dysfunctional, and this is horrendous. I have seen it. Cohesion is important, as is balance. This has an impact on recruitment: to recruit the right balance of skills."

"If being a team means consensus, then this is wrong. If it means that you listen to, discuss and communicate with each other, and come to a common decision, then this is as far as teamwork needs to go. It is about effectiveness, not teamwork. The objective is that NEDs add value to each other's contribution."

"There has to be a mutual trust in each other's capabilities. You need to understand those capabilities, and how to draw on the strengths of each other to achieve greater effectiveness."

"You need to understand why each of you is there, your distinctive experience, character, etc. That is the precursor to things working."

"You must have some interaction informally to talk about business, e.g. over breakfast, or dinner, where you have time to get to know each other in a more leisurely way. You don't see each other often, you come from different industries, and you didn't choose each other, so you have to decide how to be most effective."

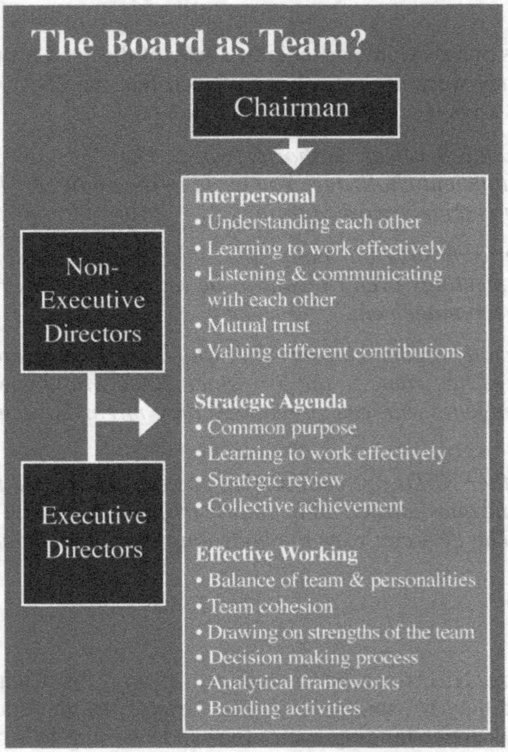

The Board as Team?
Chairman
Non-Executive Directors
Executive Directors
Interpersonal
• Understanding each other
• Learning to work effectively
• Listening & communicating with each other
• Mutual trust
• Valuing different contributions
Strategic Agenda
• Common purpose
• Learning to work effectively
• Strategic review
• Collective achievement
Effective Working
• Balance of team & personalities
• Team cohesion
• Drawing on strengths of the team
• Decision making process
• Analytical frameworks
• Bonding activities

"We have board dinners, and in October the chairman organised an afternoon tour of Boston, and then a dinner in the JFK Library with the founder, who is in his 80s. There were just the seven of us and we felt so privileged. It was a great idea."

"The best team-building is to do a task together. On one of my boards we have to meet with the Scottish Government every quarter. This meeting is a great team-building context."

Some interviewees thought that teamwork was relatively easy to achieve.

"Most NEDs, if they have been senior in business or whatever they've done in life, tend to be good team players, because they wouldn't have got where they are otherwise. Perhaps you meet someone who has worked alone (author, academic?), but this is very rare. Most have been senior managers, and so team working is not a problem: they know how to interact. It is a skill set."

Others saw it as harder.

"It is difficult. In most cases, it falls off the bottom of the To Do list. It has to be an investment of time by the NEDs with the EDs, and by the chairman with the NEDs. Committee meetings are periodic, so I wouldn't say they are team-building. A strategy Away Day does achieve something."

Whatever their interpretation of teamwork, everyone agreed that the role of the chairman was critical – including ensuring the right mix of people at the table.

"This is down to the quality of the chairman, and the chairman working to understand the NEDs as a body, helping them to understand each other and also the executives."

"The chairman must ensure balance. A whole board of extroverts, or of introverts, would be horrible. The chairman then has to make the balance work – for example, he must pull out the introverts, contain the extroverts."

"The chair must create the team atmosphere and validate that you are operating as part of a team. Otherwise, cliques and alliances form as you would find with any group of people."

"Well, it's back to the chairman – if you all conclude that the chairman is hopeless then you work together against him."

The importance of committees

The work of committees has become increasingly important in recent years and the great majority of our interviewees felt that being on committees was a vital component of being effective on a board.

"The committee is where the work is done. Committees are absolutely the key to the whole thing – where your personal exposure is most significant, for good or bad."

"It is extremely important, because effectively the board does much of the work through committees. If you are really going to get to grips with the company, you need to be on a minimum of one committee."

"Everyone has to go onto one committee – and in smaller companies, you go onto all of them. It helps you understand the business from either a financial or remuneration perspective, and helps you to make contributions in different ways. In fact, I believe it's better to be on all the committees, because then you have all the information. Being chairman of the Audit Committee is good for this."

There was one dissenting voice on the usefulness of committees.

"There is a proliferation of committees now (in financial services, you have audit and risk). It can be much too detailed. It's an argument I have had with the Financial Services Authority: we are in danger of second-guessing the executives too much, and are too much into the detail. It will take some of the satisfaction out of the executive roles."

Induction and training

Successive reviews of board performance have called for better induction and training. Our interviewees suggested that induction has got better but could still be improved. The elements mentioned most frequently were:

- **Structure.** Companies should offer a formal programme (with flexibility for individual tailoring), rather than relying on the NED to make up his or her own induction programme.
- **Meeting key people.** Induction should not be just a reading exercise or a series of presentations, but should include personal meetings with key executives from different parts and levels of the business.

- **External perspectives.** Induction should include views from or meetings with external stakeholders, such as investors or auditors.
- **Visits to the coalface.** Induction should include visiting key operational sites and talking to staff on the front line.
- **Personalisation.** The induction programme should take account of the needs and interests of the individual director.
- **Ongoing process.** You can't do induction in a day or a week. It needs to be spread over several weeks or months.

Interviewees told us:

"You need to understand what is happening at the coalface. If you are experienced, you know what happens at the top. Most of my time, I have sat with teams, talking to them about the risks they see, and I challenge them; this gives me a much better understanding. So get out and see things."

"You have to find a way of really knowing the business. It isn't about just 'the good and great occasions'. For instance, to increase my own knowledge, I will visit [shops] or phone the call centre."

"The reason people spend wasted time in the early stages is because they haven't spent time with the executives on a one-to-one basis. It is a huge education – even the glossary of terms, how the business talks about itself, the language and abbreviations it uses. There is an assumption of knowledge because of the NED's distinguished career, and deference to it, which you have to break down."

"One company chairman suggested that I had lunch with each of my fellow NEDs individually. This was very good advice, because I got to know them, and learned what they were concerned about."

"The induction from the company itself should be ongoing, not just at the beginning. I've been on one board for six months and we are now talking about the next phase of my learning."

Views about training were more mixed. Some had received very little training and felt no great need for it, stressing the value of experience and learning on the job.

"I would say that training for NEDs is completely useless. I think there is huge box-ticking and bureaucracy about corporate governance and it is useless."

"The best training is your executive experience, which you must be able to bring to bear to add value."

"I have not had any specific training. The biggest thing to learn is the demarcation line between ED and NED. Some people find it quite difficult, because you must not make decisions for executives."

Others were very keen to have ongoing training or personal development, and most mentioned attending seminars and workshops held by headhunters and consultancy firms, in order to keep up to date.

"In my mind, training is important, and I had it. Good governance encourages it. The NED role is incredibly subtle – you are not telling them what to do, but influencing. You are only telling in a crisis, so you do have to be very careful."

"I dedicate 20 days a year to development: I regularly attend the seminars/courses run by the accounting and law firms, for instance on remuneration, succession planning, risk and finance. This is far more training than I ever got in my executive capacity when you just don't have time."

Two interviewees mentioned having a coach, and both found it useful. In one case the coach was part-financed by one of companies on whose board she sits. *"I have found it absolutely transforming,"* she said. *"I am now clearer on what I have to offer."*

Judging board performance

Most (though not all) of our interviewees had experienced some form of board evaluation, but there were mixed views on the effectiveness of what they had been through. Overall, we had a sense that performance evaluation was more often seen as a regulatory requirement, rather than an opportunity to improve.

On the whole, those who had been involved in an external process found it more valuable than an internal review. Nonetheless, very few interviewees could cite examples of the impact of an evaluation exercise, and where they did, it was procedural rather than behavioural improvements they noted.

"I have seen the use of the internal questionnaire, when everyone says how wonderful we all are and everything is. I have also seen the use of an external consultant, and although my gut reaction is that one should use an external, as it should be more objective, I have seen it be very disruptive. If things are working well, then you really don't need the external acknowledgement. If things are not going right, it usually means that there is a problem with the chairman, or between the NEDs and the EDs, and you really need to sort this out yourselves. If you tell them via the third party, it has to be very skillfully handled."

"Questionnaires online I have found to be a good way to put down views, but slightly sterile for discussion. I think a board would benefit from external facilitated assessment. We all need a 'shrink' to know ourselves."

"Until last year, both companies did internal questionnaires, which I never thought were much cop. Last year, under pressure from the FSA, we did an external review, and it was extremely helpful. Having a third party to talk to made an enormous difference. Things came out and were explored. This should be done every three years. It's all about honesty, and that tone is set by the chair."

"I have been involved in professional, external board effectiveness reviews. I would prefer external consultants being used more often (perhaps every two years rather than three, because with three there is a long time between)."

"I believe it doesn't matter whether it is external, internal, formal or informal, but then I am forthright, and say what I think. I won't hold back the way some others may."

"It is least effective when the chairman asks what people think. Next least effective is when the chairman asks for an email contribution to be sent to the company secretary. Those I have done used a template/questionnaire adapted to the particular organisation, and sent to the other NEDs, including open questions."

"I would do away with it as it is useless. The chairman should know if things are working. I know that there is an argument for external consultants to be used, but I believe that it's a conspiracy of the headhunting firms out for the business."

Advice for aspiring NEDs

"Start early, while you are still employed, to build the bridges and networks. Convince your current board that this would be helpful in your current role and make personal relationships with headhunters. This takes time and you need to have credibility."

"Don't shoot for the moon and set your sights too high. Take something to get practice. It is easier then to trade up."

"Get your first NED role in a sector you know well, so that you can really add value."

"Get a view about how the company expects the NEDs to relate to the business – some have controlling CEOs who would want to know what conversations the NEDs might be having with the executive team."

"Don't get too obsessed about the size of the company as opposed to whether or not it will be interesting. Pick a company you're very interested in and where you can make a contribution, rather than being among talking heads. Like the people. I have turned down a board where I didn't care for the chairman or CEO, much to the surprise of the headhunter."

"If you want to take the plural route, don't rely on the headhunters. You will catch many more fish through your own network."

"Do what you might call self-analysis to determine if your strengths are suitable for this type of work. You need to establish if you have the qualifications needed to be an NED, and where you would fit. There is a big difference between a plc and a small company, and yet the role in both instances is called a non-executive director."

"Be very clear about what time you are going to allocate and err on the generous side. For example, if there are 12 board meetings a year, double that time commitment."

"Never be a sole NED (which is possible on a non-quoted board). You need someone alongside you. Being the only one is very difficult, very exposed, and dangerous."

"People told me a not-for-profit NED role would help. Not one headhunter has supported this. In fact, one of them told me to take it off my CV, as it's the commercial experience that the chairmen seek (and they see a charity role as a diversion). It doesn't carry any weight, or tick any of the boxes that are important to the chairmen. I would suggest that you only do it if you are truly passionate about the cause, not to help you get a non-executive directorship."

And finally…

"I hate the expression 'sitting on the board'. This evokes all the wrong images and feelings. You don't sit, you work, there's a lot to do, and you could go to jail."

The Report Team

Helen Pitcher

Helen is chairman of IDDAS and a main board director of the Savile Group plc. Her career spans 30 years in both the business world and the consulting sector. She held a variety of senior roles in blue chip companies. In her subsequent consulting career, she became CEO of CEDAR, which she built into one of the best-regarded consultancies in the human capital world.

Helen is recognised as a leading organisational performance coach and mentor, who works at the most senior level in FTSE 100 and international companies and in the public sector. She has a worldwide network of alumni whom she has coached over the years. Helen is a panel member of the Employment Appeal Tribunal, a member of the Selection Panel for Queen's Counsel and Chair of its Ethics and Integrity sub committee, chairman of KidsOut, and a trustee and fundraiser for several other charities. She was recently appointed to a Special Appeals Panel for returning Armed Forces veterans.

Helen is an APECS-accredited coach and qualified psychometric assessor. She is a Fellow of the IOD, CIPD and RSA and has worked across a range of sectors including financial services, utilities, media, leisure, telecommunications, retail and public sector.

Hilary Sears

Hilary is a senior IDDAS mentor who undertook all the interviews. She has extensive experience in executive search and board assessment, as a director and vice president in Carré Orban, Korn Ferry and AT Kearney. Hilary worked in the Cabinet Office on secondment to the Leadership and People Strategy Directorate.

Hilary is chairman of KIDS, a national charity for disabled children, deputy chairman of the International Advisory Board of Cranfield School of Management, a director (and past chairman) of the Association of MBAs and past vice chairman of Forum UK. Hilary is a qualified NLP practitioner and coach.

Hashi Syedain

Hashi Syedain is a freelance business journalist with more than 20 years' experience of writing for national newspapers, business magazines and websites. She is a former deputy editor of *Management Today* and has worked as a journalist and editor in both Russia and Germany. Hashi is also a member (and past chairman) of the Independent Monitoring Board of Harmondsworth Immigration Removal Centre, which reports on standards of fairness and decency for asylum seekers and other immigration detainees.

Susan Dudley

Susan's background is in HR, administration and project co-ordination. She provides project co-ordination and consultancy services to a number of corporate clients across various sectors, including utilities, telecommunications, retail and the NHS. Susan is a member of the CIPD and a qualified psychometrician.

Part C:
Understanding Corporate Governance

Chapter C1

Understanding Corporate Governance

'Governance', derived from Latin 'gubernare' – 'to steer'
'To han the gouernance of hous and lond'

'To have the governance of house and land'

Line 814 in Hengwrt *manuscripts* of
Canterbury Tales, Chaucer (1340–1400)

'The proper governance of companies will become as crucial to the world economies as the proper governing of countries.'

James D Wolfensohn, President of
the World Bank, c 1999

'There is one and only one social responsibility of business – to use its resources and engage in activities designed to increase its profits so long as it stays within the rules of the game, which is to say, engages in open and free competition without deception or fraud.'

Milton Friedman[1]

Introduction C1.1

Even Milton Friedman, the arch-advocate of companies concentrating solely on maximising the return to their shareholders, made the important qualification that they should stay within the rules of the game – a qualification often omitted when Friedman is quoted. He explained that, by the rules of the game, he meant:

> 'the basic rules of society, both those embodied in law and those embodied in ethical custom.'

It is more straightforward to show that failures of corporate governance are associated with adverse outcomes than to demonstrate that higher standards of corporate governance contribute significantly to corporate success. Almost invariably it is possible to point the finger at shortcomings in the corporate governance of an entity which has got itself into difficulties – not least because it is axiomatic in such a case that the system of corporate governance has not succeeded in delivering success. Corporate governance is now so broadly defined as to make it unlikely that deficiencies in corporate governance would not be involved when entities decline or collapse – and this will appear so particularly with the wisdom of hindsight.

Good governance means:

- substance, not just form;
- practices, not just policies; and
- performance, not just conformance.

Spectacular collapses C1.2

It is significant that the contemporary focus on corporate governance in the UK had its genesis in the spectacular collapses of listed companies – for instance, London & Commonwealth, Polly Peck, BCCI and Maxwell – the last two being mentioned by name in the Preface to the 1992 Cadbury Report.[2] The US Treadway Report,[3] which came five years earlier than the Cadbury Report, was commissioned through concern about the fraudulent financial reporting of Wall Street-listed companies. The common ground behind Cadbury and Treadway was, therefore, in the main, deceitful, untrustworthy, unreliable top managements and boards, or as Cadbury put it more diplomatically:

> 'It is, however, the continuing concern about standards of financial reporting and accountability, heightened by BCCI, Maxwell and the controversy over directors' pay, which has kept corporate governance in the public eye.'[4]

As far back as 1992, the Cadbury Report highlighted the controversy over top pay, an issue that then led in 1995 to the 39 Provisions of the Greenbury Code on Directors' Remuneration,[5] many of which were incorporated, with amendment, into the UK's 1998 Combined Code. Despite the focus on this issue over the years, it remains unaddressed in any effective way. Income Data Services reported that FTSE 100 executive directors saw their total earnings rise by 49% in the year 2010–11 alone – at a time of economic crisis when staff numbers and staff pay had been declining. While base salaries of FTSE 100 directors rose by only 3.2%, earnings were boosted by bonuses, pay-outs under long-term incentive plans and nominal gains on share options cashed in during the year.[6] The multiple by which chief executive pay exceeds average staff pay has widened annually and is now more than 100:1. For at least a generation, there has been a paralysis of inaction to rectify this extreme, socially divisive and continuous trend. When the matter is raised, it is brushed aside by those who benefit from it as just populist rhetoric. Meanwhile, the greedy continue to feather their nests with apparently scant regard for the morality of their behaviour.

It is arguable that the UK's focus for more than a generation on improving corporate governance has assisted the UK to weather the economic storms more effectively than would otherwise have been the case. Nevertheless, corporate governance failed in the sense that it failed to prevent the financial crises which started in 2007 – in the UK and across much of the world. In the past, it had been tempting to speculate that the avoidance by the UK of spectacular corporate collapses like Enron, WorldCom and Tyco had been attributable to a quite long-term, more balanced, mature approach to corporate governance within the UK. Against this needs to be set the obvious scope for more spectacular corporate debacles in the US, where the size of businesses tends to be much greater. Neither can it be claimed that the UK had emerged entirely unscathed. Marconi is a case in point. But, if it is possible to make the distinction, Marconi was more a failure of the board with respect to *strategy*, whereas the US failures have been a repeat of the old-fashioned (1980s and 1990s) failures of *internal control* allowing rampant fraudulent financial reporting by deceitful top management teams to go unchecked for long periods of time.

The more recent collapse of major UK banks and other financial institutions no longer allows the UK to claim that its corporate governance standards have been better than elsewhere or adequate.

Good governance as a driver of corporate success C1.3

When corporations succeed brilliantly, there is not the same incentive to attribute the success to exemplary corporate governance. Indeed, in such cases, protective corporate governance mechanisms, such as the assertiveness of the outside directors, will most probably not have been needed to be activated so obviously. There will have been other causes of success, apart from what we usually regard as 'good corporate governance' – such as technological innovation, changes in the environment, effective strategy, world-class management and so on. But the creation of these competitive advantages and the positioning of the entity to exploit these competitive advantages is to do with good corporate governance.

There is also the conundrum that a successful company is better placed to invest in high standards of corporate governance. It is often only when its circumstances change, and the company finds it has its back to the wall, that these quality corporate governance mechanisms will be tested. A failing company may feel it has neither the time nor the energy, nor the resources, to devote to improving its corporate governance processes – as it focuses single-mindedly on turning the company round. It is this conundrum which has led some to claim that audit committees work best in well-run companies which need them least, and are less likely to work well in the poorly run companies which need them most.

A less extreme view is that it is best to set up an audit committee before the bad times arrive, so that the committee is well placed to ensure that the company does not sail close to the wind when it is later tempted to do so. The same prudent approach should be applied to other aspects of corporate governance best practice; it is wise to establish effective mechanisms of corporate governance during the good times – not merely to encourage excellence and to avoid mistakes, but so that the bulwarks are in place in anticipation of the possibility that the business may enter harder times, when it could be tempted into disreputable decisions and practices in order to paper over the cracks rather than to correct the fundamentals. So good corporate governance is a means of more effectively achieving corporate objectives and a safeguard against future corporate malaise.

The efficacy of corporate governance has been suggested by studies which compare the market capitalisation of companies with similar fundamentals operating in economies with differing standards of corporate governance. It has been shown that market capitalisation is likely to be greater for companies in economies noted for high standards of corporate governance – not least for the greater confidence this gives to investors. But again, is it the better corporate governance that results in the higher market capitalisation, or is it the lower cost of capital which provides the opportunities for entities to invest in better corporate governance? In economies where corporate governance is a jungle, higher standards of corporate governance in one company might not contribute to corporate survival when pitted against the less impressive business practices of the local competition.

Correlating corporate performance with corporate conformance C1.4

Dulewicz and Herbert[7] found scant support for the more prominent theories of the board with respect to better corporate governance contributing to better corporate performance. They found no relationship between company financial performance[8] and the proportion of NEDs, the tenure of NEDs or the existence of audit and remuneration committees. Sales turnover tended to grow more slowly when there were more NEDs both as a proportion of the board and in absolute numbers. However, they found that companies with a non-executive chairman separate from the CEO tended to perform better, as did companies with more executive directors and companies whose directors owned more shares. However, this could have been a consequence of companies, as a crisis management measure, tending to combine these two roles when the company is performing badly.

These results support the UK corporate governance best practice of separating the chairman's role (which role they characterise as being 'pivotal') from that of the chief executive, and ensuring that the chairman is non-executive. But, at least in terms of company performance, the results question the perceived 'best practice' of perhaps half the board being non-executive, and for their tenure as well as their personal shareholdings to be limited.

Dulewicz and Herbert acknowledge that some corporate governance best practice may have an 'accountability' rather than a 'performance' purpose. We would say that, for instance, audit and remuneration committees are justified, in part at least, as tools of accountability. But in principle, better accountability should reduce the costs of capital (as investors have more confidence to invest capital). Lower costs of capital in turn should contribute to better financial performance, but there is nothing in Dulewicz and Herbert's study to show that this occurs. However, we should not overlook that all of their sample were UK companies: differences in accountability practices are more stark between countries than between companies within one country.

While Dulewicz and Herbert showed that several accepted criteria of good corporate governance had not contributed to corporate performance in their sample UK companies, we consider it is possible that these criteria may nevertheless have been a bulwark against corporate corruption and demise in some companies and had thus contributed to performance in that way. Dulewicz and Herbert's study was based on what happened to 86 of 134 companies which they had originally studied in 1997. The remaining 48 companies 'had gone into liquidation, been taken over, merged with another company, or broken up'. If it had been possible to factor in those 'failed' companies into Dulewicz and Herbert's 2003 study, it is perhaps possible that a correlation between good corporate governance and company performance might have emerged.

Is corporate governance a dangerous distraction? C1.5

As more formalised approaches to corporate governance emerged in the UK commencing in the 1990s, concerns were expressed as to whether these truly contributed to, or detracted from, building up great companies. Might it have been that an excessive board focus on corporate governance was distracting boards from building business prosperity? Alternatively, or additionally, might it have been that the emergence of codes of best practice for corporate governance merely encouraged a superficial 'box ticking' mentality?

The Hampel Report[9] commenced with the words:

> 'The importance of corporate governance lies in its contribution both to business prosperity and to accountability.'

The draft Hampel Report[10] had gone on to say that:

> 'In the UK the latter has preoccupied much public debate over the past few years *to the detriment of the former*.'

The emphasis is ours. The words in italic were dropped from the final Hampel Report which did, however, continue to say, as in the draft:

> 'We would wish to see the balance corrected.'

For our part we see this as a false dichotomy. Much of the present debate continues to be about improving the quality of accountability by boards to stakeholders – especially so that shareholders can make better investment decisions which are themselves essential prerequisites for building prosperous businesses. The 2010 and 2012 UK Stewardship Code (set out in full at **App2**) is part of this. Likewise, we see more effective internal control as contributing to, rather than being a drain upon, the bottom line. Indeed, so did Hampel, for instance, in his wording of the Combined Code's Principle on Internal Control:

> 'The board should maintain a sound system of internal control to safeguard shareholders' investment and the company's assets.'[11]

The equivalent wording is amended in the 2012 version of the UK Corporate Governance Code (Main Principle C.2) so that it now reads:

> 'The board is responsible for determining the nature and extent of the significant risks it is willing to take in achieving its strategic objectives. The board should maintain sound risk management and internal control systems.'

Entities of all sorts and types **C1.6**

We also believe the contention of superficial 'box ticking' has been overstated, and that the focus on corporate governance has immeasurably strengthened corporate entities in the UK. Nevertheless, the Hampel Committee set out to address the challenge of perceived 'box ticking' by deriving Principles, which all companies should apply, from the list of more detailed Provisions which were given only 'comply or explain' status. In this way, Hampel had the twin intentions of discouraging 'box ticking' and also ensuring that a single code could be regarded as applicable for all listed companies, whatever their size, age and other characteristics; and also likely to be broadly applicable to other types of entity, such as private companies, mutual societies or government agencies.

The principles of best practice for corporate governance should be regarded as having much wider applicability than just for listed companies. Most public companies are not listed, and many have not offered securities to the public. Only some 2,500 of the 12,000 UK public limited companies are listed.

Following on from Hampel, commencing with the 2003 version of the Combined Code a mezzanine level of 'Supporting Principles' has been introduced within the Code between the Main Principles and the Provisions, some of the previous

Principles being relegated to become Supporting Principles. The 2008 version of the Code removed the requirement for companies to report how they were applying these Supporting Principles and, in 2010, the relevant Listing Rule came in line and also removed the obligation with respect to the Supporting Principles. Only applying the Main Principles now has to be explained, and that only for companies with a premium, not a standard, listing. UK corporate governance has always been very light touch, and this makes it even more so.

Early work by ICSA C1.7

In parallel with the European and UK quality revolutions of the 1980s and 1990s, there has been a growing interest by governments and all industry sectors in governance and ethical issues. One of the earliest references to governance as an economic issue was in 1979. The Institute of Chartered Secretaries and Administrators (ICSA) published a series of papers on corporate governance and accountability, by distinguished contributors from industry and academia, introducing these with:

> 'In recent years, public debate has ranged over industrial democracy, audit committees, the duties and responsibilities of company directors, disclosure of information, accounting standards and other subjects but there has been little new thought about more fundamental aspects – the "why" and "how" of corporate governance.'

Two of the contributors, Sir Arthur Knight and, the then, Dr K Midgley, examined boardroom responsibilities, listing the claims of various groups that management needed to take into account in their decision making. These lists included most of the groups currently referred to as the organisation's 'stakeholders'. In ranking these groups, they identified consumers as '*Customers come first;* …'. They did not at that time see other groups (stakeholders) as customers. In listing groups with claims on an organisation, they both predated the current wide definition of 'stakeholder' (see Chapter **G3**). Conclusions reached by both contributors placed accountability clearly at the door of directors and profitability still the most reliable guide to management efficiency.

The meaning of 'corporate governance' C1.8

> 'Corporate governance is concerned with holding the balance between economic and social goals and between individual and communal goals. The governance framework is there to encourage the efficient use of resources and equally to require accountability for the stewardship of those resources. The aim is to align as nearly as possible the interests of individuals, corporations, and society.'[12]

Origins of 'governance' C1.9

The *Oxford New English Dictionary on Historical Principles* (1901) (OED) described governance as 'the action or manner of governing', or 'controlling, directing, or regulating influence; control, sway or mastery', or 'the manner in which something is governed or regulated; method of management, system of regulations'. It appears from the OED that the term 'governance' was initially applied in a divine context before being used in a slightly more temporal, ecclesiastical way. It was only a matter of time before these early auspicious uses[13] were to be joined by associating the word, quite recently, with systems of national regulation and now with corporate direction and control.

Governance of companies as important as governance of countries **C1.10**

Perhaps this journey reflects the changing preoccupations of the contemporary time when, by some methods of measurement, about half the largest economies of the world can now be said to be corporations, and suggests the gravity with which we should approach the challenges of corporate governance.

According to the United Nations Conference on Trade and Development, measured on the basis of value-added – the yardstick used to calculate countries' gross domestic product – the activities of the largest 100 companies accounted for 4.3% of world GDP in 2000, up from 3.5% in 1999. On that basis, 29 of the world's largest economic entities were then companies. Exxon, with an estimated value-added of £40 billion at that time, was larger than all but 44 national economies and the same size as Pakistan. Ford, DaimlerChrysler, General Electric and Toyota were comparable in size with Nigeria. Value-added can be construed as corresponding most closely to the GDP calculation.[14] It has been claimed that 51 of the 100 largest world economies in year 2000 were companies not countries; while, by 2004, the percentage had grown to 53%.[15] While some companies have declined since then, the strains on the global economy mean this is also the case for some countries.

Keys and Malnight[16] report that in 2012, 40% of the 100 largest economies were companies rather than countries (42% in 2010; 44% in 2009) which they reported was down 20% between 2000 and 2012. The percentage that are companies rose to 58% of the top 150 economies in both 2010 and 2012.

Origins of 'corporate governance' **C1.11**

It is not unusual for there to be chance occurrences of an expression before the expression develops as a fixed collocation – sometimes as a result of a book or film title, or a song, etc. For instance, there are examples of the phrase 'politically correct' from 1793, but no one is suggesting it had the same resonances then. There is an isolated instance of the phrase 'corporate governance' in 1953 (*Annals of the American Academy of Political and Social Science*, 1953, 290 33/1) where these words appear:[17]

> 'Flexibility in corporate governance would also be needed'.

After 1953, there appears to have been a gap until 1960 (*Harvard Law Review*, 1960, 74 202) in a review of the book *The Meaning of Modern Business* (1960), by R. Eells:

> 'One of the most thought-provoking sections of the Eells book […] is that dealing with corporate governance.'

The term 'corporate governance' seems to have found a firmer footing in the 1970s when it was quite widely used in the North American legal literature.[18] An early use outside specialist business and law journals was in 1970 (*Science*, 24 July 1970):

> 'It will add little to our comprehension of minority problems or corporate governance to confuse the two issues.'

Tricker – the father of corporate governance C1.12

Robert Tricker, to whom we refer below, was mentioned in a 1978 article in *The Times* (6 November 1978) which said both:

> 'Over here Mr Tricker wants a wider debate on 'corporate governance and not mere tampering',

and

> 'The introduction of audit committees will be neither because of carefully considered theories of corporate governance nor because directors feel they need independent monitoring.'

Indeed, in 1984 Tricker was first responsible for the very visible use of the term 'corporate governance' when it appeared as the title of a book[19] written by Tricker who, in echoes of Henri Fayol (often regarded as the Father of Management Theory) or of Frederick Taylor (the Father of Management Science), deserves the accolade 'the father of corporate governance'. As far back as 1976, the year that Harold Wilson's *The Governance of Britain* appeared, Tricker had used the expression 'corporate governance' in a book titled *The Independent Director*:[20]

> 'Our present models of management, the way we distinguish and typify corporate governance, are inadequate.'

In 1993, he was the founder editor of what has become a leading journal on corporate governance,[21] handing over this mantle in 2001.

He continues to be prolific on corporate governance well into the new millennium (Bob Tricker, 2009, *Corporate Governance Principles, Policies and Practices,* Oxford University Press, ISBN: 978-0-19-955270-2, 448 pages).

Defining corporate governance C1.13

In this handbook, we take the perspective of the Cadbury Report that, in essence, corporate governance is to do with the processes by which a corporate entity is directed and controlled. Governance is derived from the Greek word 'to steer' which neatly combines both 'direction' and 'control'. On the other hand, a 'governor' on a steam or other engine is a control device. Arguably too much of our corporate governance focus is on the control side of corporate governance, with too little emphasis on the board's responsibility for setting direction and agreeing strategy.

The draft Cadbury Report's definition of corporate governance was as follows:

> 'Corporate governance is the system by which companies are run. At the centre of the system is the board of directors whose actions are subject to laws, regulations and the shareholders in general meeting. The shareholders in turn are responsible for appointing the directors and the auditors and it is to them that the board reports on its stewardship at the Annual General Meeting.[22]

The final Cadbury Report has revised this to read:

> 'Corporate governance is the system by which companies are directed and controlled. Boards of directors are responsible for the governance of their companies. The shareholders' role in governance is to appoint the directors and

the auditors and to satisfy themselves that an appropriate governance structure is in place. The responsibilities of the board include setting the company's strategic aims, providing the leadership to put them into effect, supervising the management of the business and reporting to shareholders on their stewardship. The board's actions are subject to laws, regulations and the shareholders in general meeting.'

While we reproduce the 2012 version of the UK Corporate Governance Code at **App1**, we do not reproduce most of the material which is printed in the FRC's publication before and after the Code itself.[23] In the preamble to the 2010 Code, the FRC has included, for the first time since the 1992 Cadbury Report, the above Cadbury definition of corporate governance and continue to reproduce this in the preamble to the 2012 Code. The significance of the FRC doing so is that it wishes to emphasise the Cadbury view that it is the board that is primarily responsible for corporate governance, with shareholders having just very limited roles, but with the board being responsible for conforming to laws and regulations. We are dissatisfied with this perspective. Since the global financial crisis broke, and indeed before that, there has been much criticism of shareholders not being sufficiently engaged with the companies in which they are invested and therefore being responsible for the crisis. Shareholders have, in effect, shared much of the blame for the corporate governance failures of companies.

Undoubtedly, many shareholders, even institutional shareholders, have not been sufficiently active. The creation by the FRC of the UK Stewardship Code is an attempt to address this shareholder deficit. But until we formally adjust the balance of power more towards the shareholders, it is not reasonable to heap blame on shareholders. Boards have too much latitude to ignore shareholders on corporate governance matters. Shareholders have insufficient powers to dictate corporate governance standards within the companies in which they are invested. Some shareholder 'powers', such as their mandatory vote on the remuneration policy of the board, are advisory, and have not been significant powers at all. The advice has often been ignored by boards, though post-2013 UK changes make this shareholder vote binding. Other powers, such as electing the directors, are powers that shareholders are reluctant to exercise at variance with the intentions of the directors themselves, in view of the consequences that may follow. While technically the shareholders elect the auditors, it is almost always on the advice of the board, so that the auditors are more closely aligned with management than they are with the shareholders. The shareholders have no effective powers to approve or disapprove of the company not conforming to principles and provisions within the UK Corporate Governance Code, which itself is discretionary. Shareholders have no vote on whether the company should comply with the various parts of the Code.

While the above Cadbury definition of corporate governance ('Corporate governance is the system by which companies are directed and controlled') is a balanced definition, much of the emphasis within the Cadbury Report was on the control side of things – the monitoring of, and accounting for, the implementation of sound board policy – rather than on the formulation of policy and the development of strategy which are the starting points of good corporate governance. Indeed, some inappropriately consider that corporate governance is *only* to do with the control side. Take, for instance, the HM Treasury's control-oriented definition of corporate governance in the public sector as being:

'the system by which Accounting Officers carry out their responsibility for ensuring that effective management systems, including financial monitoring and control systems have been put in place.'

In this handbook we adopt the perspective that the board is at the pivotal point of corporate governance, looking outwards especially to the stakeholders of the entity who need to exercise effective external control, and looking inwards to oversee the execution of board policy.

The main link between the board and the shareholders is the reporting system through which the board accounts to them for the activities and progress of the company. The role of the auditors is to provide the shareholders with an external and objective check on the directors' financial statements which form part of that reporting. Although the reports of the directors are addressed to the shareholders, they are important to a wider audience, not least to employees whose interests boards have a statutory duty to take into account.'

Tricker (1984)[24] had a closely similar view in superimposing governance on management (see his diagram below), and describing the process of corporate governance as having four principal activities:

Direction:	Formulating the strategic direction for the future of the enterprise in the long term;
Executive action:	Involvement in crucial executive decisions;
Supervision:	Monitoring and oversight of management performance; and
Accountability:	Recognising responsibilities to those making legitimate demand for accountability.

The activities of governance and management compared (Tricker's 1984 diagram)

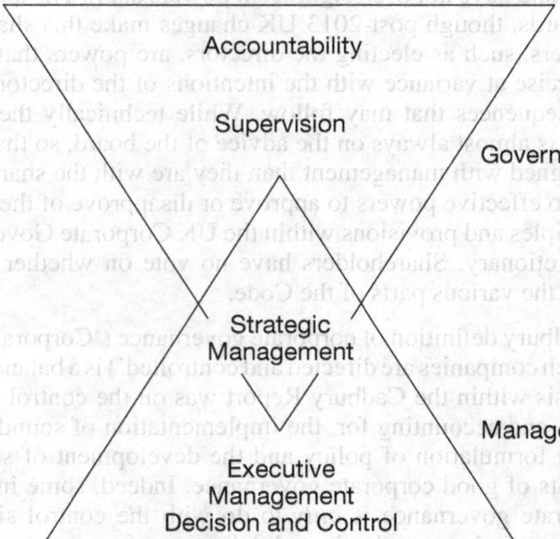

The OECD has achieved a good balance in its definition of corporate governance:[25]

> 'a set of relationships between a company's management, its board, its shareholders and other stakeholders. Corporate governance … provides the structure through which the objectives of the company are set, and the means of attaining those objectives and monitoring performance … Good corporate governance should provide proper incentives for the board and management to pursue objectives that are in the interests of the company and shareholders and should facilitate effective monitoring, thereby encouraging firms to use resources more efficiently.'

Summary of 'corporate governance' and 'board' definitions **C1.14**

Definitions of 'corporate governance'

	Date	Source	Definition
1.	1992	Cadbury Report	Corporate governance is the system by which companies are directed and controlled (for which the board of directors is responsible).
2.	1984 & 1994	R Tricker	[It] is concerned with the way corporate entities are governed as distinct from the way businesses within those companies are managed. Corporate governance addresses the issues facing boards of directors, such as the interaction with top management and relationships with the owners and others interested in the affairs of the company …
3.	1996	Bain & Bland	To add value to as many organisational stakeholders as possible.
4.	1999	OECD	A set of relationships between a company's management, its board, its shareholders and other stakeholders. Corporate governance … provides the structure through which the objectives of the company are set, and the means of attaining those objectives and monitoring performance … Good corporate governance should provide proper incentives for the board and management to pursue objectives that are in the interests of the company and shareholders and should facilitate effective monitoring, thereby encouraging firms to use resources more efficiently.
5.	2000	MacAvoy & Millstein	A set of structured relationships that determines authority and responsibility for the conduct of an organisation and its management.

	Date	Source	Definition
6.	c. 2000	HM Treasury (UK)	The system by which Accounting Officers carry out their responsibility for ensuring that effective management systems, including financial monitoring and control systems, have been put in place.
7.	2001	Institute of Internal Auditors (IIA) *Standards* Glossary definition (see **App8**)	Governance – The combination of processes and structures implemented by the board to inform, direct, manage, and monitor the activities of the organisation toward the achievement of its objectives.
8.		Institute of Chartered Secretaries (www.icsa.org.uk/about/govern.html)	The systems by which organisations are run and the laws, regulations and best practice with which they are required to comply.
9.		The Corporate Library (www.thecorporatelibrary.com/)	The relationship between the shareholders, directors and management of a company, as defined by the corporate charter, by-laws, formal policy and the rule of law.
10.		Institute of Chartered Secretaries (www.icsa.org)	Ensuring compliance with regulations and the implementation of appropriate administrative procedures.
11.	2002	Information Assurance Advisory Council	The management of risk within an organisation with a view to ensuring the continuity of that organisation's business and existence.
12.	2013	British Standard 13500 (see Chapter **D6**)	System by which the whole organisation is directed, controlled and held accountable to achieve its core purpose over the long term.

Definitions of 'the board'

	Date	Source	Definition
1.	1992	Cadbury Report	Boards of directors are responsible for the governance of their companies … The responsibilities of the board include setting the company's strategic aims, providing the leadership to put them into effect, supervising the management of the business and reporting to shareholders on their stewardship.
2.	2001	Institute of Internal Auditors (IIA) *Standards* Glossary definition (see **App8**)	Board – The highest level of governing body charged with the responsibility to direct and/or oversee the activities and management of the organisation. Typically, this includes an independent group of directors (eg, a board of directors, a supervisory board, or a board of governors or trustees). If such a group does not exist, the 'board' may refer to the head of the organization. 'Board' may refer to an audit committee to which the governing body has delegated certain functions.

Unitary and two-tier boards **C1.15**

The distinction between the responsibilities of the board and the responsibilities of management is potentially clearer in the case of two-tier boards, which are standard practice especially for public companies in many countries. German supervisory boards comprise 20 non-executive members, made up of investor, workforce and local community and other representatives. Under Germany's two-tier system, the supervisory board appoints members of the management board and supervises their actions. The management board runs the company's day-to-day business. The supervisory board is the board referred to in EC directives applicable across the EU for countries with both two-tier and unitary boards.

The board has overall responsibility for what happens within the entity and must therefore hold to itself the determination of overall policy and the oversight of its implementation. With respect to the latter, the board needs to put itself in the position of being reasonably certain that it knows 'where the company is at'. This includes the board forming a well-informed view about the effectiveness of internal control – since it should be a policy of the board that the entity has effective internal control. Effective internal control provides reasonable assurance of the achievement of corporate objectives.

Late in June 1999, having received inputs from both member and non-member countries as well as from the World Bank and the International Monetary Fund, the Organisation for Economic Co-operation and Development (OECD) published its 'Principles of Corporate Governance'.[22] The OECD had not been in a position to advocate a particular board structure, and indeed even the term 'board' was a bit of a challenge to it in view of the existence of both unitary and two-tier board structures in different countries. The OECD resolved this challenge by applying the term 'board' to the 'supervisory board' in a typical two-tier system, and the phrase 'key executives' to the 'management board' in a two-tier system. In 2014, OECD is reviewing its corporate governance principles with a view to updating them (http://www.oecd.org/corporate/).

In times of convergence towards globally accepted principles of corporate governance, it is interesting to see some convergence between the unitary and two-tier board structures. A unitary board is a single board comprising executive and non-executive members. Under a two-tier system the supervisory board is entirely non-executive, and the management board beneath it is entirely executive. Many, probably most, UK and US companies now have an executive board (or committee – EXCO) under the main (unitary) board; and the main board is tending towards greater independence from management. An executive board beneath a unitary board may be merely an informal arrangement whereby the chief executive manages the business and prepares for board meetings; or it may be established by the company's constitution. The unitary board may have a bias in its membership towards non-executive directors: this is more common in the US, where there may be just one or two executives on the board. Only 4 of the 16 members of BP's board are executive directors, although UK best practice corporate governance suggests that there needs to be a significant number of executives on the unitary board in order for it to be balanced. Many German companies are accepting that a supervisory board, comprising 'the great and the good' and representatives of key stakeholder groups, may not be an effective overseer of management. One indication of this is the creation of more and more audit committees of the supervisory board in German companies, where previously it had often been considered that the existence of supervisory boards obviated the need for audit committees.

The Cadbury (and now the UK Corporate Governance) Code provision, that listed companies should have audit committees comprising at least three non-executive directors, the majority of whom should be *independent* non-executive directors, has often had the indirect effect of bolstering the independent element on UK unitary boards – an element already taken care of in the case of two-tier board structures. But this is not to say that companies with two-tier boards have no need for audit committees. The need is largely the same as for unitary boards – financial statements which are to be published, risk management and internal control, as well as external and internal audit, need a degree of detailed scrutiny on behalf of the supervisory board, which that board is unlikely to be able to do when it is meeting in main session.

Risk management and internal control C1.16

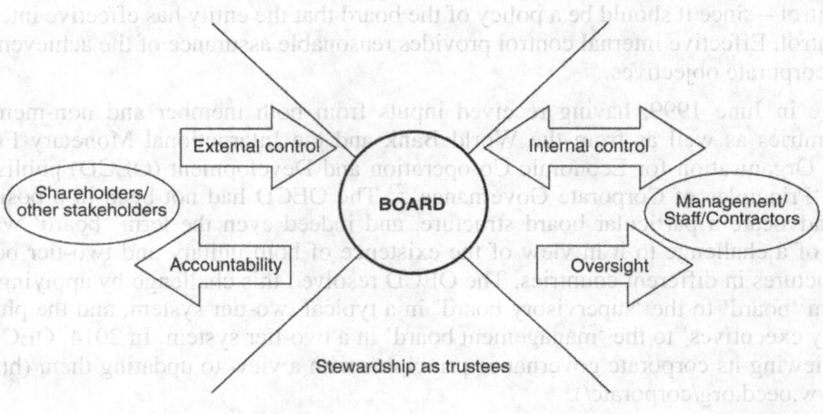

As we have indicated, our view is that corporate governance is to do with external as well as internal control – as illustrated in the diagram. It comprises the processes of accountability to, and oversight by, stakeholders – which provide the means by which external control can be exercised. And it comprises the processes of accountability to and oversight by the board – which are necessary if risk management and internal control are to be effective so that corporate objectives can be achieved.

The Hampel Committee's 1998 Combined Code's Principle on Internal Control was the first UK Code to state:

> 'The board should maintain a sound system of internal control to safeguard shareholders' investment and the company's assets.'

This wording was continued through into the 2008 Combined Code before being modified in 2010.

This was a non-standard statement as to the objectives of internal control. It also inappropriately gave the *board* a 'maintenance' rather than an 'oversight' responsibility, the former being a responsibility of management rather than of the board:

- The chairman runs the effectiveness of the board;
- The board runs the chief executive; and
- The chief executive runs the business.

Nevertheless, it made the point that internal control is central to the responsibilities of the board.

The Turnbull Report[26] expressed much better than the Code the respective responsibilities for internal control of the board, management and other personnel, namely:

> 'The board of directors is responsible for the company's system of internal control. It should set appropriate policies on internal control and seek regular assurance that will enable it to satisfy itself that the system is functioning effectively. The board must further ensure that the system of internal control is effective in managing risks in the manner which it has approved.'

and (at para 17):

> 'It is the role of management to implement board policies on risk and control. In fulfilling its responsibilities, management should identify and evaluate the risks faced by the company for consideration by the board, and design, operate and monitor a suitable system of internal control which implements the policies adopted by the board.'

and (at para 18):

> 'All employees have some responsibility for internal control …'

The Turnbull Report has now been included by the Financial Reporting Council (FRC) as part of the UK Corporate Governance Code framework.

So the board is at the pivotal point of corporate governance. Internal control is an essential part of corporate governance, and internal auditors are important players in corporate governance. Internal auditors, in their assessment of risk management and internal control, largely focus on the internal dimensions of corporate governance – but not exclusively so.

For more detailed discussion of internal control, please refer to **C2.24** and Chapter **G1**.

Internal audit **C1.17**

The Wall Street Journal Europe said, in a leading front page article entitled 'European Companies Shy Away From Issuing Profit Warnings':[27]

> 'Faced with a sudden cooling of the economy, North American companies have been churning out profit warnings. In Europe, however, only a few companies have admitted they won't live up to analysts' expectations.
>
> Why the ominous silence in Europe? The short answer is denial. Many companies seem to be hoping to avoid the global slowdown. Others appear unwilling to show their hands before regularly scheduled releases of results.
>
> Investors aren't waiting. These days, they dump shares on the mere suspicion that a profit warning is due, reasoning that if US competitors are issuing them,

> the Europeans must be sharing their pain. "It often seems that companies should have known their problems much earlier," grumbles Markus Straub of SdK, a shareholder-rights group in Germany. "*At best, you can say they need to improve their internal auditing; at worst it could be criminal.*" ' (italics added)

An interesting point here is that at least one corporate governance pressure group considers that internal auditors have a role to influence the reliability of disclosures to the market, and to prevent fraudulent financial reporting. A more cautious view would be that internal audit plays in a particular position on the corporate governance pitch – reserving itself to that part of corporate governance which takes place *within* the entity.

More recently, on 29 August 2007, the *Daily Mail* carried this comment in the context of Barclays Bank's challenges with respect to its reported European collateralised debt obligations:[28]

> '… one might have expected its internal audit department to have checked thoroughly all the potential deals that could go wrong and come up with a 'kitchen sink' measure for shareholders, in much the same way as HSBC did with its £5bn write-down of its US sub-prime interests.
>
> 'That has not happened, so there remains a suspicion that investors have not been told the whole story …'

Again, a commentator is giving internal audit a role in disclosures to the market, with just a suggestion that it should be a direct and independent reporting role for internal audit to the market.

There are indications that internal audit is moving across the divide between 'internal' and 'external' corporate governance, even though to date there is no general obligation for internal audit itself to report publicly within the annual report of the company. Examples are:

- assisting the board in formulating their published reports on internal control;
- contributing to the reliability of financial statements;
- involvement in environmental audit and reporting;
- assurances to the board on other operational analyses which are published, especially those not subject to other independent attestation;
- advising the audit committee on external audit;
- reports about internal audit, or from the chief audit executive, within the company's annual report and
- in some companies, providing secretariat and other services to the audit committee.

An interesting example of how internal audit may affect share price was reported in August 2003. The giant Australian insurer AMP was in talks with the Financial Services Authority (FSA) to safeguard UK policyholders' interests amid worries that its plans to pull out of Britain might leave more than 2 million savers high and dry. The company, which also had around 60,000 small shareholders in the UK, wanted to float its British operation in London. Doubts surfaced about the demerger, and AMP's share price plunged after it was learnt that a draft internal audit report had warned about shortcomings in its risk controls at one part of its UK operations – notwithstanding that AMP said the draft contained 'some inaccuracies'.

For more detailed discussion of internal audit, please refer to Chapters **G2, G3** and **G4**.

Notes

1 Friedman, Milton (1962) *Capitalism and Freedom,* University of Chicago Press; and Friedman Milton (1970) 'The Social Responsibility of Business is to Increase its Profits', *The New York Times Magazine*, 13 September.

2 *Report of the Committee on the Financial Aspects of Corporate Governance* (the 'Cadbury Report') (1 December 1992).

3 Committee of Sponsoring Organizations of the Treadway Commission *Internal Control – Integrated Framework* (AICPA, New York, September 1992).

4 The Cadbury Report, Preface, p 9.

5 Sir Richard Greenbury (17 July 1995): Directors' Remuneration: Report of a Study Group chaired by Sir Richard Greenbury.

6 Groom, Brian (28 October 2011): FTSE directors' total earnings rise 49%, *Financial Times*, p 4.

7 Victor Dulewicz and Peter Herbert 'Does the Composition and Practice of UK Boards Bear Any Relationship to the Performance of Listed Companies?' Henley Management College, Working Paper Series HWP 0304 (2003).

8 Based on cash flow return on total assets (CFROTA) and sales turnover.

9 Committee on Corporate Governance, chaired by Sir Ronald Hampel *Final Report* (January 1998). (This report does not include the Combined Code, which was developed in the following months and published separately.)

10 Committee on Corporate Governance, chaired by Sir Ronald Hampel; Committee Secretary John Healey *Preliminary Report* (August 1997). The *Final Report* was published in January 1998.

11 The 1998 Hampel Combined Code, Principle C.2.

12 Foreword by Sir Adrian Cadbury to Magdi R Iskander and Nadereh Chamlou *Corporate Governance: A Framework for Implementation* (World Bank Group, 1999).

13 Wyclif (c 1380); Chaucer (1391).

14 Guy Jonquières 'Companies Bigger Than Many Nations' (2002) *Financial Times*, 13 August, p 7; see also www.unctad.org.

15 Guy Jonquières 'Companies Bigger Than Many Nations' (2002) *Financial Times*, 13 August, p 7; see also www.unctad.org.

16 Keys, TS and Malnight, T (2013) 'Corporate Clout 2013: Time for Responsible Capitalism', http://www.slideshare.net/tskeys/corporate-clout-2013-time-for-responsible-capitalism, accessed 14 October 2013.

17 The author's thanks are due to Ivon Asquith (previously chief executive of the Oxford University Press) and to John Simpson, the Editor of the *Oxford English Dictionary*, for the discovery of these mentions of 'corporate governance'.

18 This was referred to in Smerdon, R (2004) *A Practical Guide to Corporate Governance*, Sweet & Maxwell, ISBN 042185300X, 2nd edn; and also by Arne Friese, Simon Link and Stefan Mayer (2008) 'Taxation and Corporate Governance – The State of the Art' in *MPI Studies on Intellectual Property and Competition Law*, Max Planck Institute for Intellectual Property, Competition and Tax Law, p 359.

19 Tricker, Robert I, *Corporate Governance – Practices, Procedures and Powers in British Companies and Their Boards of Directors* (Gower, 1984).

20 Tricker, Robert I, *The Independent Director – A Study of the Non-executive Director and of the Audit Committee* (Tolley Publishing, 1976), p 68.

21 *Corporate Governance – An International Review*, Blackwell.

22 The Committee on the Financial Aspects of Corporate Governance ('The Cadbury Committee') *Draft Report Issued for Public Comment* (27 May 1992) pp 7–8, paras 2.5, 2.6.

23 The full publication can be found on the Financial Reporting Council's website.
24 Robert I Tricker (1984), *Corporate Governance*, p 7.
25 Organisation for Economic Co-operation and Development (June 1999). The publication can be downloaded in html or pdf format from their website.
26 Financial Reporting Council (2005), Internal Control: Revised Guidance for Directors on the Combined Code, www.frc.org.uk, paras 15, 17 and 18.
27 (2001) *Wall Street Journal Europe*, 9 April.
28 (2003) *Daily Mail*, London, 12 August, p 6.

Chapter C2

Grand Themes in Corporate Governance

> *'... there are known knowns; there are things we know that we know. There are known unknowns; that is to say, there are things that we now know we don't know. But there are also unknown unknowns – there are things we do not know we don't know.'*
>
> United States Secretary of Defense, Donald Rumsfeld, 2002

Introduction C2.1

A challenge for boards is to direct entities in circumstances where the future is always uncertain, in circumstances where the future is at the beck and call of governments, of speculators and of almost chance happenings. The iron law of business is that the only certainty about the future is that the future is uncertain. It sometimes seems that, almost without exception, businesses plan for the future on the misguided assumption that current trends will continue, when the truth is that current trends will always terminate. Future dislocation, or future shock, is the backcloth against which corporate plans should be developed. Business developments must be planned so that survival, even success, is feasible when the traffic lights change from green to amber or even to red:

> 'The problem is not simply that we plan too little; we also plan too poorly.'[1]

Boards have twin corporate governance responsibilities – first for policy and overall strategy, and secondly for oversight and control. These two responsibilities are not mutually exclusive: entities need policies and strategies for good corporate governance; and good corporate governance reduces the risk of damaging decisions being made in medium- to long-term plans.

Here we highlight some fundamentals of good corporate governance practice that can be a bulwark against future shock.

So what are the ground rules for effective corporate governance? We offer a ten-point programme. Of course, it is the principles behind the prescription which are most important. It is the principles which should be achieved – the method is secondary. With some interpretation, we believe this prescription is broadly applicable to entities within both private and public sectors.

The ten 'principia' of good corporate governance C2.2

These are the ten 'principia' of effective corporate governance:[2]

1. Stakeholder control of the business (**C2.3–C2.12**).
2. Maximum and reliable public reporting (**C2.13–C2.14**).

3. Avoidance of excessive power at the top of the business (**C2.15–C2.16**).
4. A balanced board composition (**C2.17**).
5. A strong, involved board of directors (**C2.18**).
6. A strong, independent element on the board (**C2.19**).
7. Effective monitoring of management by the board (**C2.20–C2.22**).
8. Competence and commitment (**C2.23**).
9. Risk assessment and control (**C2.24**).
10. A strong audit and assurance process (**C2.25–C2.26**).

Stakeholder control of the business C2.3

First and foremost, the stakeholders must be in control of the entity. This is at least as vital, though harder to achieve, in cases where only a small percentage of the capital of a company has been floated. Outside investors should be particularly vigilant of the corporate governance arrangements of companies where a majority of shares are closely held – especially when those shareholders are members of the board and perhaps members of a single family.

Here we are addressing *external* control – which is the control of the stakeholders over their stakes in the business. Whether one conceives of the stakeholder constituency extending beyond the shareholding or other proprietors of the business is very much a matter of personal and corporate philosophy. Joseph Johnston, a US corporate lawyer, and the American Bar Association's expert on corporate governance, in a pamphlet published by the UK Social Affairs Unit, an independent think-tank, argued that:

> '[a broad view of] stakeholding is part of the European corporatist tradition but is alien to Anglo-American ideas of corporate governance.'[3]

Johnston concluded that directors should obey the law, but that their ethical obligation is to act in the exclusive interest of the shareholders, the people who risk their capital:

> 'every time company directors bow to stakeholder demands, they betray their duty to company shareholders.'

Safeguards in a free market C2.4

If this approach to accountability is to work for the greater good of society, it is reliant upon:

- legislation rather than corporate conscience dictating the social and environmental responsibility of firms;
- shareholder pressure for social and environmental responsibility perhaps in the form of ethical investment funds; and
- a long-term corporate perspective which perceives the enlightened self-interest of the corporation partly in terms of its social and environmental responsibility.

The global financial crisis whose symptoms showed up commencing in 2007, and the sovereign debt crisis which became a major issue commencing 2011, resulted in major financial bail-outs funded by taxpayers. In turn, this has lent weight to the argument that Milton Friedman's famous dictum, set out here, is seriously inadequate:

> 'There is one and only one social responsibility of business – to use its resources and engage in activities designed to increase its profits, so long as it stays within the rules of the game …'[4]

It is now more widely accepted that stakeholders in addition to shareholders have legitimate interests in how companies, sovereign wealth funds and other entities are being run. Board accountability should not be just to the shareholders. Other stakeholders have a stake, a form of ownership, in corporate endeavours. The Anglo-Saxon free capital markets model has surrendered ground, to some extent, to the European social markets model, which has a more balanced perspective on the interests of different stakeholder groups. Indeed, this shift was anticipated by the formulation of the enlightened shareholder value duty within s 172 of the UK Companies Act 2006, which imposes on directors a duty to promote the success of the company for the benefit of its members as a whole, and in doing so have regard (*inter alia*) to these specified matters:

- the longer term;
- the interests of the company's employees;
- the need to foster the company's business relationships with suppliers, customers and others;
- the environment;
- the impact of operations on the wider community; and
- the desirability of the company maintaining a reputation for high standards of business conduct and the need to act fairly between members of the company.

It is clear from the Act that this may not be an exhaustive list of matters that the board should have regard to. This duty does not put the interests of other stakeholder groups *pari passu* with the best interests of the shareholders, but it requires directors to consider the impact on other stakeholders of any decisions they are taking. It is a single duty rather than separate duties in relation to each of the parties listed. It codifies in law corporate social responsibility (CSR) to a small extent. It is a very modest move towards the European social markets model. But the courts will never second guess whether a board made a right decision in view of these 'specified matters' that the board should have regard to. A court could only find a board at fault if it could be shown that the board had not had regard to these 'specified matters' in coming to a particular decision. It is therefore wise for the record of board meetings to be sufficient to demonstrate retrospectively that the board considered these matters. Possibly the best way to do this is to ensure than a board agenda paper on an item that a board is to decide upon should have attached to it an impact assessment which covers these and other matters to the extent that they relate to the agenda item.

Note, too, that s 172 requires the board to have regard to the longer term. Not having such a regard was one contributory factor to the global financial crises.

A prerequisite of effective shareholder or broader stakeholder control is an informed shareholder/stakeholder body. This requires maximum, reliable reporting by the board to them.

One share, one vote C2.5

Opinions differ as to whether or not 'one share, one vote' is appropriate. In a free capital market, with the associated benefit of a lower cost of capital, it follows that owners who are taking an equal investment risk should participate equally in the control of their investments. It is argued that those who buy shares in a class with inferior voting rights should be fully aware of what they are doing when they make that buying decision and therefore should not complain: the price they paid when they acquired their shares was presumably discounted to reflect their relative lack of control over the company.

Having different classes of shareholder effectively disenfranchises some of those shareholders. Yet some would claim that it is positively desirable to protect a company from unwelcome takeover bids, by ensuring that the ultimate decision on whether to accept a takeover offer is vested in a particular class of shareholder who is likely to be a more long-term investor. But that begs the question as to whether an investor who is 'in for the medium to long term' should or should not have a greater influence upon the future of the company. The long-term investor, perhaps the residue of the family that established the company in the first place, may have his or her own agenda that does not prioritise maximising value for all shareholders.

Arguments against 'one share one vote' **C2.6**

1. Owners of companies have a perfect right to offer shares without votes. Buyers of those shares know what they are buying and the market determines the right price for those shares. If the shares are less valuable, they will be priced at a discount.
2. The class(es) of shareholders that retain control because they have voting rights can ensure that the longer-term interests of the company are safeguarded. Shareholders who are not 'in for the long term' have a shorter-term perspective which may not be in the interests of the company (and its staff, customers, suppliers, local community etc) in the longer term.
3. Different classes of shares may be appropriate in special circumstances. For instance, the 'golden share' held by UK government in newly privatised utilities protected them from premature hostile takeovers before they had established themselves as viable listed companies. Preference shares carry special rights to preferential distribution, etc, perhaps in return for weaker or no voting rights.

Arguments for 'one share one vote' **C2.7**

1. Those who take an equal risk should participate equally in the control of the company. If it is the case that classes of shareholder without voting rights are taking a lesser risk (perhaps because there is a more liquid market in their classes of shares and their shares can be bought and sold at a discount), this does not mean that they should not participate in shareholder decisions. Perhaps it might mean that each of their shares should have less influence, proportionate to their discount in the market.
2. Owners sometimes fail to appreciate that 'going public' means that they are ceding control to the body of shareholders as a whole – or, at least, they should be doing so. There are too many listed companies that are still being run as if they were the private property of the original owners.
3. Different classes of shares usually means that control of the company is determined by a minority of the total shareholder body, ie the holder of a particular class of shares. This may militate against a more successful management team of another company assuming control of a poorly performing

company. This dooms the body of shareholders (and the workers of the company, the customers and suppliers) to being managed by a second- or third-rate management team. In whose interests is this? Perhaps only the minority of shareholders who belong to the class of shareholders that can determine the future of the company. A free market in capital control is the most efficient way of optimising employment and returns to shareholders. Different classes of shares are poison pills which distort this free market.

4. The existence of different classes of shares in some companies but not in others creates an unlevel playing field.
5. It is unsustainable in the long term for a club to have different classes of member.

Appointment of directors C2.8

Of equal importance is effective control by the shareholders over the composition of the board of directors. It should be realistically feasible for the members of the company to remove one or more directors at any time by exercising their powers to ensure that meetings of the shareholders are convened and to ensure that the appointment and reappointment of directors is voted upon by the shareholders at the annual general meeting, with perhaps one-third of directors coming up for reappointment at each annual general meeting. For UK companies, the Companies Act 2006 requires that directors come up for re-election at least once every three years. Companies within the FTSE 350 and following the UK Corporate Governance Code will ensure that all their directors are subject to annual election (Provision B.7.1). Relevant requirements and powers will be laid down in the constitutional documents, such as the articles, of the company. Reappointment should not be automatic but should be on the basis of an assessment of the needs of the company and the anticipated contribution that the individual appointee will make in the future.

Remuneration of directors C2.9

Likewise, with respect to both executive and non-executive directors, the remuneration and other elements of compensation of directors, which should be fully disclosed, should be subject to approval by the shareholders in general meeting. Sections 439 and 440 of the UK Companies Act 2006 require a shareholder vote on this for listed companies. Until 2013 the legal requirement was that the vote was only advisory, not binding.

In 2003, prior to the 2006 Act, UK law was changed to require the remuneration report of a company with respect to its directors to be put to the vote at the company's AGM. This quickly led, in 2003, to GlaxoSmithKline's shareholders rejecting proposed severance pay arrangements for its chief executive (where concern was largely about the perception of 'rewarding failure'); to Tesco coming under renewed pressure to change directors' contracts (where the concern was their perceived excessive length beyond the acceptable 12-month term); and to Cable and Wireless suffering a sizeable revolt in protest at a share incentive scheme for five non-executive directors (where the concern was that non-executive directors, being involved in setting share performance targets for executive directors, should not have their independence compromised in this way). With respect to this last example, participation by NEDs in schemes where directors are incentivised through the opportunity to acquire shares on special terms, is acceptable in the US; best UK practice is that non-executive directors should only receive a fee for their non-executive directorship responsibilities, although part of that fee may be paid in shares acquired in the usual way in market at the price prevailing at the time. In 2009, an overwhelming majority of shareholders at the AGMs of Shell and RBS voted against the remuneration reports of those boards. The former was in protest that the remuneration committee had awarded the full performance-related bonuses to Shell's executives even though they had not met the performance targets set for them by the remuneration committee. The latter was in protest at the joining package of the new top executive team. Neither at Shell not at RBS did the majority dissenting vote make a difference to the outcome of what the shareholders were objecting to.

In the US, under the NYSE corporate governance standards, shareholders vote on executive share option schemes (ESOPs).

Directors' contracts **C2.10**

While most directors outside of the FTSE 350 will come up for reappointment perhaps once every three years, their contracts with the company generally should not exceed 12 months, though this 12 months may be on a rolling basis; very rarely indeed need they exceed 12 months for non-executive directors. This avoids the risk of directorship posts becoming too secure, to encourage the continuance of committed performance. It also significantly reduces the risk of excessive severance payments being required under the terms of the directors' contracts – a situation which can appear to reward, and therefore encourage, failure rather than success.

Directors' contracts of appointment should not be secret. Their full terms should be brought to the board and approved by the board in each case. Section 318 of the Companies Act 1985 required, with only incidental exceptions, a copy of each director's service contract to be available for inspection by members at the company's registered office; or if there is no such written contract, for a written memorandum of its terms to be kept and to be available for inspection. Section 229 of the Companies Act 2006 goes further and requires that hard copies of directors' service contracts should be sent on to a member within seven days of a request for payment of a fee, or be available free of charge for inspection by a member. Since directors' contracts are available for scrutiny by members, it follows that there can be no objection, indeed the opposite, to each director being privy to the terms within the service contracts of all the other directors; indeed, it would be negligent if this were not so. Yet it is surprising how frequently members of a board are unaware of the contractual terms of their colleague directors. We discuss this issue further at **A1.29**.

The fees of non-executive directors should relate to their contribution to the business and the time they devote to it. The compensation packages of executive directors should not exceed market rates, nor be more than the company needs to pay.

Where possible, there should be a planned, orderly turnover of directors so that the board is not denuded of too much experience at one moment in time. Non-executive directors should be chosen largely for the contribution they will be able to make and should generally not serve on the board for much more than six to nine years, so as to preserve the independence of judgement which the non-executive directors are able to bring to bear. One of the codified duties applicable to *every* director is to exercise independent judgement (Companies Act 2006, s 173). Beyond that, a special sort of independence is expected of non-executive, independent directors (UK Corporate Governance Code, Provision B.1.1). The Code counsels that any term beyond six years for a non-executive director should be subject to particularly rigorous review (Provision B.2.3), that non-executive directors (whether of FTSE 350 or of smaller listed companies) who have served longer than nine years should be subject to annual re-election (Provision B.7.1), and that the board is likely to judge that a non-executive director is no longer an independent director if he or she has been on the board for more than nine years since their first election (Provision B.1.2).

Retirement of directors **C2.11**

There is no longer a requirement within the Companies Act 2006 for directors beyond the age of 70 to come up for re-election annually, rather than once every three years. One major oil company was so aggrieved by that requirement that it put all of its directors up for re-election annually at the AGM so as not to discriminate against its more elderly members of the board. There used to be a view that non-executive directors over the age of 70 may have reduced independence, in view of the probability that they must know that the chances are not good of them being invited to join other boards. It is, however, risky to generalise, and if this is a potential impediment to effective independence, it is often more that counterbalanced by the extra willingness of people of advanced years to take independent positions on issues. Furthermore, younger directors, with much of their careers in front of them, may have a degree of reluctance to risk alienating their fellow directors by taking independent positions on issues. So the 'aged 70' threshold failed to make it into the indicative list of independence criteria contained, since 2003, within the Combined Code (now the UK Corporate Governance Code – see Provision B.1.1), although it had been in most of the equivalent lists (of PIRC, ABI, Hermes etc) that preceded these agreed-upon criteria.

Note that the Companies Act 2006 sets a minimum age for a director at 16 years.

Appointment and oversight of auditors **C2.12**

Different legislations vary as to whether the shareholders always have a regular opportunity to vote on the appointment and reappointment of the auditors of the business, and on their fee. In the UK, the board recommends to the shareholders the appointment of the auditors, and the shareholders vote to confirm their appointment. Having this opportunity increases the control of the shareholders over the business, and encourages the external auditors to be mindful that their client is the shareholders, not management nor the board. The published financial statements of the company are the statements of the directors, and it is reasonable that those to whom they are addressed should have a very significant part in determining who, as auditors, shall report to them, the shareholders.

Maximum and reliable public reporting **C2.13**

In the case of a public company, the market capitalisation (ie. today's quoted share price times the number of issued shares) should be capable of being rationally based on investors' informed judgments of the performance and prospects of the company. In the medium to long term, market capitalisation, and therefore the cost to the company of capital, is maximised by a policy of full, timely and reliable disclosure. The market will rightly become nervous of a company which is opaque, tardy, unreliable or surprising in its reporting. At the time of the crisis of the 'tiger economies' in the late 1990s, Singapore's Deputy Prime Minister Lee Hsien Loong pointed out to Singapore's Parliament that lack of disclosure by local banks had led people to fear the worst, even though the institutions were sound:

> 'The problem is we have not put out as much as we could have done, and as a result, even though the banks are sound, people fear the worst, which is not really justified.'[5]

Already, public companies are carrying their annual reports on the Internet. Eventually, modern IT will make it possible for companies to report in real-time, continuously updating their published reports monthly, weekly or even daily. We can expect those companies to become the favoured stocks of investors due to the transparency of information. Clearly, real-time reporting will have implications for the approach which will be required in accounting and in auditing.

The proprietors of private companies and other entities also need full, reliable information as a basis for rational investment decisions.

Non-standard and creative accounting policies are to be avoided. With the emergence of more multinational companies and international investment funds, published accounts really should accord with international financial reporting standards, even when there is a need for a second set to be produced to satisfy local legislative requirements. However, there should be only one set of books and no 'off balance sheet' transactions, assets or accounts.

Transparency C2.14

The annual report and accounts should make full disclosure of all elements of the compensation packages of the directors. Shareholders have a right and need for this information which should be held up to the light of day and justified. Total board costs need to be monitored carefully, compared with those of other similar enterprises, and justified fully. Excessively large boards are both unnecessarily costly and also less likely to be effective. Six to ten directors is likely to be adequate in most cases; although, of course, there may be a conclusive case for larger or smaller boards in particular instances. Sleeping directors should be avoided. Every director should serve an essential purpose on the board.

It is an aspect of transparency and accountability that the chair of the board and of its remuneration and audit committees, as well as the partner in charge of the external audit, should be available at general meetings of the members to answer questions put by shareholders. It is good practice that other directors should also be available at general meetings for this purpose.

Avoidance of excessive power at the top of the business C2.15

The choice of new board members should be a decision of the full board, subject to confirmation by the shareholders at the next general meeting. Alternatively, shareholders may appoint their own candidates. Reliance should be placed upon a nomination committee of the board which should be responsible for succession planning as well as for recommending to the board who should be appointed to the board. The board should not be presented with a virtual *fait accompli* by the chairman, the chief executive or any other party. If this occurs, it is likely that there is excessive concentration at the top of the business. Where a seat, or seats, on the board are to be nominated by a particular party or body,[6] it is still desirable that the board should concur in the appointment.

Prima facie there is likely to be excessive concentration of power at the top of the business if the roles of chairman and chief executive are combined.

There is a rather similar problem if the chairman is an *executive* chairman. This is not a matter of how the chairman's post is designated in terms of 'job title', but rather a matter of the reality. If the chairman is virtually full time, has an office adjacent to the managing director, shares secretariat support with the executive directors and has duties of an executive nature (with executives reporting to him or her in an executive capacity) – then such a chairman is an executive chairman, regardless of designation.

When the roles of 'chairman' and 'chief executive' are combined C2.16

There may be justification for combining the posts of chairman and chief executive. This may be so when particularly strong leadership is needed quickly at a time of crisis. Generally, it should be regarded as a temporary expedient to be rectified as quickly as practical. Where these two posts are combined, it is good practice for the board, on the advice of the non-executive directors, formally to designate one of the non-executive directors to be the senior non-executive director. Companies in compliance with the UK's Corporate Governance Code will have designated one of the non-executive board members as the 'senior non-executive director' – *whether or not* the posts of chairman and chief executive are combined (**App1**, Provisions A.1.2, A.4.1 and A.4.2); the equivalent 1992 Cadbury Code Provision had made this a requirement only when these two posts had been combined. This director leads the process of appraising the chairman's performance, has a special monitoring role with respect to the executive, and is a focal point for investors and non-executive directors to express their concerns.

It is good practice for all the non-executive directors of any board to meet from time to time informally without executive directors present (**App1**, Provision A.4.2). This should be additional to the meetings of the remuneration and audit committees – which may not involve all non-executive directors.

A balanced board composition C2.17

Balance is needed principally between:

- executive and non-executive directors;
- the functional areas and technical skills represented on the board; and
- age, gender, ethnic and other balance – as appropriate in particular cases.

A healthy board is likely to need an approximately even balance of executive and non-executive directors. This is a matter of balancing the number of these and also the strength of personality and the technical skills they possess.

Some boards apply the practice, formally or informally, of nominating each, or some, non-executive director to 'shadow' particular executive directors (**A1.17–A1.21**).

Ideally the non-executive members of the board should collectively possess the skills and experience that correspond to those principally needed by the top executive team, so that the board is able to be an effective challenge as well as an effective support to the executive.

A strong, involved board of directors **C2.18**

It is an absolute essential that the board and its individual members set the highest ethical standards. Their example will be noticed and emulated. Considerable emphasis should be placed by the nominations committee upon confirming the past record of probity of those whom the committee recommends for appointment to the board.

The board is responsible for ensuring that the business has an effective control environment. In part this includes the ethical example set by board members in their own conduct. It also includes promulgating appropriate, clear, ethical principles throughout the business.

Consistency is an important trait of a board. Not only must the personal example of directors be appropriate and consistent, but also the board collectively and its members individually must be consistent in their application of ethical and other principles to others. If not, staff and business partners will not know where they stand. The board should monitor that management too is consistent in the application of the ethical standards and rules of business conduct established by the board.

Ethical principles and rules of conduct must be observed by board members themselves, whose example is crucial if these principles and rules are to be observed by other staff. A clear, unambiguous signal needs to be given at all times. The 1992 Cadbury Committee's Report gave some emphasis to the part that internal rules should play in corporate governance, namely:

> 'It is important that all employees should know what standards are expected of them. We regard it as good practice for boards of directors to draw up codes of ethics or statements of business practice and to publish them both internally and externally.'

A strong, independent element on the board **C2.19**

We discuss independence in more detail in Chapter **A3**. Independence is hard to define but important to achieve. In essence, it means freedom from impediments to the exercise and expression of objective judgement. The 1998 Combined Code was no more prescriptive than the 1992 Cadbury Report had been, stating only that independence meant:

> 'independent of management and free from any business or other relationship which could materially interfere with the exercise of their independent judgement.'

but others had interpreted this general guidance in much more prescriptive ways. Indeed, because of the development of a number of differing lists of criteria intended to define director independence, the Higgs Report (2003) recommended that a standard list should be incorporated into the Code, which was done commencing with the 2003 Code. This list of criteria remains unchanged (Provision B.1.1).

Non-executive directors may bring the essential quality of independence to the board, but not all non-executive directors can be regarded as independent. Every board will benefit from a strong, independent element, and every public company or public sector enterprise should have this element of independence.

Because independence is so difficult to define in individual cases, the board should decide in each case whether a director is an independent director. It is best practice for the board to report publicly which directors it considers to be independent:

> 'The board should identify in the annual report each non-executive director it considers to be independent.'[7]

Being the spouse or close relative of an executive director or having previously been an executive in the business are, for instance, two attributes which should always be regarded as disqualifying the director concerned from being regarded as 'independent'. We discuss the meaning of 'close family ties' at **A3.14**.

Effective monitoring of management by the board C2.20

There is a crucial need for board members to be provided with adequate information, and for this information to be made available to them in time to influence decisions. In particular, it is likely that the non-executive directors will be inadequately informed, but this can also apply to the board as a whole. Executive directors may not be in a strong position to protest about this if it is the chief executive who is being selective in feeding information to the board. The confidence of board members can be irretrievably lost if suspicions develop amongst them that the board is not being kept properly informed.

In extreme cases, individual directors may become worried about whether the company is a going concern if they consider there are risks that the board is not being kept fully informed. Of particular concern is the risk of liabilities, contingent or actual, being kept from the board. For instance, the executive team may know that there is a potential claim from a customer for non-delivery under the terms of a contract, but this may be kept from the board. Or the financial circumstances of the company might have led to failure to pay a tax liability, but the board has not been informed. When suggestions of the withholding of information from the board become fixed in non-executive directors' minds, it can be almost impossible to restore their confidence. Of particular importance here is the degree of confidence that the board has in its finance director and that this confidence is well placed. Related to this is the confidence that the board has in the oversight by the chief executive of the finance director.

It is increasingly common for audit committees formally to consider, as an important agenda item at least once a year, the quality of information that the board receives.

Allied to these issues is the nature of the arrangements for the meetings of the board and its committees.

Directors' handbook C2.21

A major challenge for most boards is for their members to be able to recall readily all past resolutions of the board. Usually these were originally resolved upon for good reason and after careful consideration: not only should they be regarded as binding upon the board until rescinded but they are likely to represent prudent practice.

Of equal difficulty is for the board to be sure that they are fully aware of all material contract terms which the entity has entered into – especially those which, if breached, would place the company and the board in default of their duties – either by virtue of the breach or by failure to disclose the breach to the other parties. An example would be a clause in a financing agreement which requires any 'material adverse change' to be drawn to the attention of the other party(ies). Another, sometimes related, example would be a clause in a contract which makes it an automatic breach of the terms of the contract if an accommodation is made with a party to another contract, or if a disclosure is made to a party to another contract of a material adverse change.

It is sound practice for each director to have access, perhaps online, to an up-to-date directors' handbook for reference to documents and information of continuing importance to the board. The handbook will be maintained by the company secretariat function. The handbook will include, *inter alia*, a summary of resolutions of the board of continuing relevance and a summary of key covenants entered into by the company in contracts with other parties, particularly those at risk of being breached. Item 1.9 in the table at **A1.34** suggests a more comprehensive list of contents for a directors' handbook or manual.

Reserving matters to the board C2.22

There should be no ambiguity as to the matters which are reserved to the board. What these matters are should be the subject of a formal board resolution.

Many boards will have required and endorsed more elaborate guidelines on the delegation of authority, which will specify the levels of management authorised to make decisions up to certain authority limits and the required manner in which the decisions are to be arrived at. We discuss this in depth at **A1.10** to **A1.17**.

Competence and commitment C2.23

Directors, executive and non-executive, must know their general and specific responsibilities and it is wise that this is stated in writing rather than agreed verbally and then likely to be overlooked.

Directors should be chosen in part for the special expertise they can bring to the board. The board will require particular technical expertise in many cases. Beyond that, it will be necessary for directors to commit sufficient time to their directorship responsibilities so as to act on behalf of the business, to prepare thoroughly for meetings and to attend reliably and participate in meetings.

It is a good practice for directors' attendance records at board and board committee meetings to be kept and for a summary to be an agenda paper at a board meeting once a year. It is up to the chairman to ensure that board members' attendance is satisfactory. The chairman is responsible for the effective performance of the board. Excessive absence should require resignation.

Risk assessment and control **C2.24**

Risk assessment is now understood to be an essential component of an effective system of internal control (see Chapter **G1**). It is for the board to ensure that management has in place an effective system of internal control. One part of this is for the board to ensure that the business has in place effective ways of assessing and managing risk.

Many businesses have a committee of the board responsible for monitoring risk, overseeing risk management and reporting to the board on these matters. The UK Corporate Governance Code has for several years given this as a responsibility of the audit committee (see Chapter **E5**), unless the board has a separate risk committee comprising independent directors (Provision C.3.2). Where there is no such committee, the board must undertake more of the detail for itself.

The risks associated with proposed major capital commitments need to be assessed before commitment and thereafter revisited and reassessed. Likewise with other forms of major financial exposure. But it is important to recognise that the board is responsible for monitoring *all* types of risk. It is not just a matter of financial risk. Operational risks are at least as important. Thus, for instance, the board of a hospital is responsible for financial risk and control, but is also responsible for clinical risk and control.

An essential aspect of risk to be assessed by businesses is the risk factors associated with national economic and other policies. On the whole, external risks are harder to identify, assess and mitigate than internal risks. But it is important that an emphasis is placed on both external and internal risks. While it may be difficult to identify in advance the specific threats which represent external risks to be mitigated, it is easier to approach external threats by sketching out specific scenarios and then considering how they should be managed should they occur, and whether the business will be in a position to manage them should they occur. Thus, for instance, one specific threat might be a dirty bomb exploding in the centre of London. There are any number of other threats which could have closely similar consequences. So the practical approach is to focus on each scenario rather than upon the many threats. The scenario question here would be:

> Let us assume, for one reason or another, we were unable to use our central London HQ for (a) a day, (b) a week, (c) a month, or (d) a year or more. What would the consequences be for us? Would we be able to manage our way through this scenario if it occurred? What do we need to put in place now to enable us to manage our way through that scenario?

Forward projections on the basis of present trends continuing uninterrupted are always inadequate. Particular emphasis should be placed on the business consequences of possible future change; and, of course, great care should be taken to identify the possible future changes which have the potential to impact significantly upon the business.

Single point estimates of future outcomes are usually too simplistic to be a basis for decision making. The future impacts of different possible scenarios need to be assessed, and probabilities associated with each.

A strong audit and assurance process C2.25

Financial reporting concerns have been close to the centre of the developing corporate governance debate. This means that independent audit issues are not merely peripheral to the corporate governance debate. So it was disappointing that the issues within the Cadbury Code closest to the accounting and statutory auditing professions were the issues that caused the most trouble. Indeed, it was only those two Provisions within the Cadbury Code which were closest to the accounting profession (that directors should report on going concern, and that directors should report on the effectiveness of internal control), the implementation of which had to be delayed pending the development of guidance first for directors and then for auditors. External auditors have been very reluctant to become involved in attesting to directors' corporate governance assertions: only a very small proportion of directors' assertions on compliance with the UK Corporate Governance Code are subject to review by the external auditor.

The audit firm should be chosen for its ability thoroughly and effectively to audit the affairs of the business. In general, there are grounds for concern if a large business is audited by a small firm. Even where there is no legal requirement for an audit, or for a full audit, it is good corporate governance practice for a full annual audit to be conducted.

Internal audit plays a vital role in the corporate governance of the modern business. The review of risk management and internal control are themselves essential components of effective risk management and internal control; and this is the mission of the modern internal audit function. Line management and staff may neither have the time, inclination nor competence to undertake all of this monitoring. Internal audit does what management would do if management had the time and knew how. Primarily, internal audit is a service *for* management, but to an extent internal audit is also an audit *of* management when it reports to the audit committee of the board or directly to the board itself. Since as far back as 1978, the global Standards for internal auditing[8] have referred to internal audit as 'serving the organisation', not just serving management and certainly not just serving the accounting and finance functions.

The terms of reference, or 'charter' of the internal audit function should give internal audit unlimited scope and unrestricted access to information and staff at all times. The terms of reference of the audit committee of the board should require the committee to monitor the adequacy of internal audit, and should stipulate that the head of internal audit should not be appointed or removed without the prior concurrence of the audit committee.

The head of the internal audit function should have unrestricted access to the chair of the audit committee and to the committee itself at all times; the audit committee should meet with the head of internal audit from time to time, and upon his or her request, without executive management being present. Similarly, the audit committee should meet with the external auditors without any member of the executive being in attendance.

The principal responsibilities of the audit committee, on behalf of the board, are to satisfy itself as to:

(a) the reliability of financial reports for publication; and
(b) the effectiveness of risk management and internal control.

Arising from these responsibilities are the committee's responsibilities to monitor:

(c) the quality of the external audit; and
(d) the quality of internal audit.

The audit committee is a *sine qua non* of the modern enterprise. The best model for an audit committee is one which is entirely non-executive, with at least a majority of its members also being independent.

The board's black hole **C2.26**

There has been a long line of occasions when the board, or more precisely its non-executive directors, have been taken by surprise by a revelation of impropriety as to how the business has been run. The chairman should run the board, the board should run the chief executive, and the chief executive runs the business. Too often, we are finding much too late that there has been a disconnect between the policies of the board and the approach being followed by management. How can the board know whether its policies are adequate and whether they are being circumvented by management? What makes a board different from management is the non-executive element on it, who are hugely dependent on the information that flows from the executive to the board. Recent debacles have shown that chief executives too often control that information flow, so that our balanced boards are in reality little better than the US boards that may have only one executive on them – who may also be the chairman of the board.

One imperative is that internal audit functions should be independent of the executive, so that they do not subordinate their judgement on professional matters to that of anyone else. Another is that internal audit functions should adopt professional standards for internal auditing. In 2007 the Chartered Association of Certified Accountants adopted the global standards of the Institute of Internal Auditors as applicable to their members involved in internal auditing. In these ways, audit committees get more assurance from the results of internal audit work. Yet, typically, perhaps unbeknown to the audit committee, the head of internal audit's report for the audit committee passes across the desk of the finance director or the chief executive before it is approved for submission to the audit committee. It is true that the internal audit is an audit *for* management, but it should also be an audit *of* management *for* the board. Few companies have reached the point where it is the audit committee that appoints the head of internal audit and determines his or her remuneration; but this, or something very close to it, is essential if internal audit is to provide the independent assurance that boards need. There is also a need for a cadre of 'super internal auditors' capable of addressing the issues that should concern the board and of communicating on equal terms with directors.

While internal audit should be constituted to maximise the degree of independent assurance it can give to the board, it is unlikely that this will be sufficient assurance for the board. Meanwhile, boards, especially non-executive directors, are operating within an assurance vacuum largely dependent on what management decides to tell them. It is small surprise that boards or their committees have commissioned reports from outsiders in an attempt to fill this vacuum – the Davis Polke & Wardell Report for Shell's audit committee following the oil reserves crisis, the Baker Report for BP's board, and the Wolf Report for BAE spring to mind. But these shut the stable door after the horse has bolted.

What the board needs is regular, systematic, *ex ante*, independent assurance. The Baker recommendation, which BP's board agreed to, that the Baker Committee should approve the appointment of an external assessor for the board on health and safety for at least five years, shows that these external reviews can lead to arrangements that partially fill the vacuum. But what is needed is an expert team working continuously and capable of identifying any of the potential banana skins (not just health and safety) and then considering skilfully whether those risks are being mitigated effectively – and with the maturity to interface with the board on equal terms.

Notes

1 Alvin Toffler (1973) *Future Shock*, Pan.
2 A D Chambers (1998): 'A failure of governance?' *Corporate Governance*, March, newsletter for the Far East of FTMS Consultants (S) Pte Ltd.
3 Nils Pratley 'Directors must look exclusively to shareholders', review of pamphlet published by Social Affairs Unit, 26 January 1998 (1998) *Daily Telegraph*, 26 January, p 25.
4 Friedman, Milton (1962) *Capitalism and Freedom*, University of Chicago Press; and Friedman, Milton (1970) 'The Social Responsibility of Business is to Increase its Profits', *The New York Times Magazine*, 13 September.
5 Reported in (1998) *The Straits Times*, 15 January.
6 As with eg the composition of boards of subsidiary companies, of joint venture entities or of public bodies.
7 **App1**, Provision B.1.1.
8 The Standards of the Institute of Internal Auditors, at www.theiia.org.

Chapter C3

Applying the Theories that Underpin Corporate Governance

Introduction C3.1

In an important though brief article in July 2003, Sumantra Ghoshal, professor of strategy and international management at London Business School, challenged the frenzied development of new and redesigned courses on corporate social responsibility as business schools' responses to Enron and Tyco. Rather he laid the blame for corporate scandals on business schools' focus on agency theory, transaction cost economics and strategy theory – as well as their general tendency to treat business as a science:

> 'The problem is that, unlike theories in the physical sciences, theories in the social sciences tend to be self-fulfilling … A management theory, if it gains enough currency, changes the behaviour of managers. Whether right or wrong to begin with, the theory becomes "true" as the world comes to conform to its doctrine.
>
> That is why it is nonsense to pretend that management theories can be completely objective and value-free … By incorporating negative and highly pessimistic assumptions about people and institutions, pseudo-scientific theories of management have done much to reinforce, if not create, pathological behaviour on the part of managers and companies. It is time the academics who propose these theories and the business schools and universities that employ them acknowledged the consequences.'[1]

Berle & Means (1932) explored the significance of the separation of ownership from control, which we discuss later in this chapter. They have been more associated with stakeholder theory than with agency theory.[2]

While we touch on other theories, the focus of this chapter is on agency and stewardship theory, and their practical applications.

Agency theory C3.2

Adam Smith pointed out in 1776:

> 'The directors of such companies, however, being the managers rather of other people's money than of their own, it cannot well be expected, that they should watch over it with the same anxious vigilance with which the partners in a private copartnery frequently watch over their own … Negligence and profusion, therefore, must always prevail, more or less, in the management of the affairs of such a company.'[3]

Michael Jenson, who taught at Harvard, was an earlier writer on agency theory. Under this theory, shareholders are seen as *principals* and management are their *agents*:

> 'Agency theory argues that agents will act with rational self-interest, not with the virtuous, wise and just behaviour assumed in the stewardship model.'[4]

Greed as self interest C3.3

The 'agency problem' is a result of separation of management and ownership in large public companies. Consequently, the interests of owners and managers are likely to diverge:

1. Inside directors (ie corporate employees) tend to be self-serving by maximising their utility at the expense of non-management shareholders, through:
   - monetary compensation;
   - job stability; and
   - on-the-job prerequisites.
2. Inside directors are not likely aggressively to oversee the CEO (but perhaps outside directors may be even less critical of management?).

The dominant driver of self interest is, for many executives, greed. It has even been suggested that it is rational to take the position that 'greed is good'.[5] It has also been suggested that:

> 'It is not that humans have become any more greedy than in generations past. It is that avenues to express greed have grown so enormously.'[6]

Agency theory takes the view that people *cannot* be trusted to act for the public good in general, and in the interests of the shareholders in particular:

> 'managers could not be trusted to do their job – which of course is to maximise shareholder value'.[7]

Negotiating costs, and negotiating power C3.4

Managers need to be monitored and controlled to ensure compliance with good practice, and this results in *agency costs* which, the theory goes, should be incurred to the point at which the reduction of the loss from non-compliance equals the increase in enforcement costs.

Under agency theory, each group (the principals and the agents) wish to maximise their own return. The principals are relaxed about high rewards for the agents – so long as those rewards are commensurate with, and consequential upon, the returns that the principals are receiving. But agency theory leads us to understand that agents, because of their negotiating power, receive high rewards for failure, not just for success. Information asymmetry gives power to lower-order participants (ie the agents) in the negotiating process.[8] Continuously renegotiated contracts for the agents exacerbate this perversity.[9]

Agency costs have been described as the sum of:[10]

1. the monitoring expenditures of the principal (ie owner/shareholders);
2. the bonding expenditures by the agent (eg the cost of transparent reporting to the principal by the agent); and
3. the residual loss (ie 'the key feature'):

'residual loss is the reduction in the value of the firm that obtains when the entrepreneur dilutes his ownership. This shift out of profits and into managerial discretion induced by the dilution of ownership is responsible for this loss. Monitoring expenditures and bonding expenditures can help restore performance toward pre-dilution levels. The irreducible agency cost is the minimum of the sum of these three factors'.[11]

The role of the board **C3.5**

In the context of corporate governance, agency theory emphasises the need to:

'… control managerial "opportunism" by having a board chair independent of the CEO and using incentives to bind CEO interests to those of shareholders.'[12]

Indeed, investors and commentators often carelessly refer to 'the board' as 'management', betraying that they have given up on the board having a different role from management, believing that all too often management has captured the board.

The UK Corporate Governance Code (set out in full at **App1**) frowns on blurring the distinction between the board chair and the CEO:

'A.2 Division of Responsibilities

Main Principle

There should be a clear division of responsibilities at the head of the company between the running of the board and the executive responsibility for the running of the company's business. No one individual should have unfettered powers of decision.

Code Provision

A.2.1 The roles of chairman and chief executive should not be exercised by the same individual. The division of responsibilities between the chairman and chief executive should be clearly established, set out in writing and agreed by the board.

A.3 The Chairman

…

Code Provision

A.3.1 The chairman should on appointment meet the independence criteria set out in B.1.1 below. A chief executive should not go on to be chairman of the same company. If exceptionally a board decides that a chief executive should become chairman, the board should consult major shareholders in advance and should set out its reasons to shareholders at the time of the appointment and in the next annual report.'

The board under an independent chairman should hold the ring between the principals and the agents, trying to ensure fair treatment between both these parties, and representing the interests of each party to the other party. The board must try to ensure that the interests of both parties are as closely aligned as is practical. The board itself must try to ensure that its own orientation is independent between the two parties. It is not surprising that boards are often inclined towards the interests of management; here are some of the reasons:

1. The day-to-day relationship between the board and management is much more intimate and intensive than between the board and the shareholders.
2. The chairman of the board may be almost full-time, have an office adjacent to the chief executive and perhaps sharing the chief executive's secretarial support. It is important, for the effectiveness of the board, that the chairman of the board and the chief executive have a close working relationship.
3. The board relies upon the executive to implement the policies of the board and to deliver upon the strategy that the board has adopted.
4. Investors are often 'semi-detached' from the company. They may be short-term holders of the company's shares. Many of them may not wish to engage with the board, and this is particularly the case when shares are widely held (ie where the separation of ownership from control is great).

The 2010 introduction of the UK's Stewardship Code (the 2012 version is set out in full at **App2**) was intended to strengthen the relationship between the board and the company' shareholders. The UK Corporate Governance Code stresses the importance of a good dialogue between the board and the company's shareholders. For instance:

> **'Code Provision**
>
> A.4.1 The board should appoint one of the independent non-executive directors to be the senior independent director to provide a sounding board for the chairman and to serve as an intermediary for the other directors when necessary. The senior independent director should be available to shareholders if they have concerns which contact through the normal channels of chairman, chief executive or other executive directors has failed to resolve or for which such contact is inappropriate.'

Shareholder powers C3.6

The shareholder relationship is one of agency:

> '… a contract under which one or more persons (the principals) engage another person (the agent) to perform some service on their behalf which involves delegating some decision making authority to the agent. If both parties to the relationship are utility maximizers there is good reason to believe the agent will not always act in the best interests of the principal …'[13]

The 'agency problem' is a result of separation of ownership from management in large public companies, often termed the separation of ownership from control. The interests of owners and managers are likely to diverge. The separation of ownership from control has become greater due to greater dispersion of stock ownership. In the US, it led to the establishment of the Securities and Exchange Commission (SEC) to promote and oversee an efficient capital market in the absence of direct and effective involvement of the shareholders.

Internally, it is the board of directors and their oversight of executive remuneration which are relied upon to moderate the exercise of excessive executive self-interest. Externally, it is regulators (such as the SEC) and active shareholders who are relied upon to have a suitably ameliorating influence.

In the UK, shareholder powers are insufficient to create a level negotiating playing field between the principals (shareholders) and the agents (management). Quite intendedly it has been arranged thus. The introduction to the UK Corporate Governance Code leaves us in no doubt that the UK view is that the directors (some of whom, with unitary boards, will be executives), and not the shareholders, are responsible for corporate governance. The Cadbury Report included these paragraphs, dusted down by the FRC and reproduced in the introduction to their current and previous versions of the UK Corporate Governance Code:

> 'Corporate governance is the system by which companies are directed and controlled. *Boards of directors are responsible for the governance of their companies.* The shareholders' role in governance is to appoint the directors and the auditors and to satisfy themselves that an appropriate governance structure is in place. The responsibilities of the board include setting the company's strategic aims, providing the leadership to put them into effect, supervising the management of the business and reporting to shareholders on their stewardship. The board's actions are subject to laws, regulations and the shareholders in general meeting.
>
> *Corporate governance is therefore about what the board of a company does ...*'[14] (italics added)

Prior to the 2003 version of the UK Combined Code, it was a Code recommendation that members of listed companies should vote on the remuneration report of the directors. The apparent intention was to give shareholders an influential say in the determination of executive remuneration. But it was only an advisory vote which boards could ignore. And the vote took place usually after the remuneration committee had made the specific performance-related awards to the executives. So it was taken out of the Code and made a statutory requirement by means of a statutory instrument attached to the UK Companies Act current at that time. When the Act was replaced by the Companies Act 2006, the requirement for the shareholders to vote on the remuneration report of the directors was built into the new Act at section 439. But until 2013 it remained just an advisory, not a binding, vote. There has been a huge reluctance in the UK to give shareholders real powers. There are an increasing number of companies whose shareholders have voted in a majority against the remuneration report but it has not altered the remuneration granted to the executives. The UK has some appearance of shareholder power but with little of the substance.

Agency problems self-correcting over time **C3.7**

To some extent, agency problems and the fragmentation of share ownership seem to be self-correcting over time, but at the cost of continuous destruction of corporate value. Large public companies, with a large dispersed and largely disenfranchised shareholder body, perform sub-optimally for the owners, as managements are able to run those companies to serve their own agency interests. Over time, those shareholders withdraw their capital in disillusionment at the modest or negative shareholder return. It could be argued that this represents the capital markets functioning efficiently, but only in reaction to the destruction of corporate value.

The executives who ran those companies selfishly have long since gone, but others have replaced them. Even if the new executives were not tarred with the old brush, in a competitive market the potential to regain market leadership is heavily constrained.

Meanwhile, new companies emerge, initially with little or no separation of ownership from control and few agency issues. They steal market share or create new markets: they grow large and attract outside capital until, over time, they progressively succumb to the same malaise of their aged and declining rivals.

Agency theory and the corporate ageing process C3.8

It is hard to resist the conclusion that there is an ageing process at work in companies. It is a consequence of many factors. For instance, older companies become muscle bound by more rigid, extensive bureaucratic procedures. New companies have had no time to tie themselves up in such knots. Older companies tend to fail to see how the market is changing and find it harder to adapt. But another part of the corporate ageing process is explained to us by agency theory. Agency theory in practice plants the seeds of decay which in time will reap the grim harvest.

The theory of market for corporate control C3.9

Questions of control are interpreted as a tussle between management and shareholders, with the board of directors in the middle. Some would argue that management makes decisions in its self-interest, needing only to placate the owners of the company. The board of directors is a buffer that serves management interests and deflects shareholder demands. Since private property rights for shareholders are attached only to their certificates, and since ownership is so widely dispersed, management use of corporate assets is influenced little by shareholders. On the other side of the debate are those who argue that shareholders maintain control over the use of corporate assets through their behaviour in financial markets.[15] The buying and selling of stock as a reflection of shareholder control, it is argued, should not be minimised. 'Management that makes decisions contrary to shareholder interests is penalised, through the market, and thus risks its position in management. Boards of directors that ignore shareholder interests are similarly subject to the penalties of the market'.[16]

The theory of transaction cost economics C3.10

Developed by Oliver Williamson and taught at Berkeley and Stanford, this theory emphasises that managers should be strongly incentivised to ensure that staff are tightly controlled so that they do what is expected of them.

Theory of competitive strategy C3.11

Exemplified by Michael Porter,[17] this theory emphasises that companies need to compete effectively not just with their competitors but with other stakeholders, such as employees, suppliers and regulators. In essence, profits are made by the company that succeeds in restricting competition.

External and internal control **C3.12**

A fundamental purpose of corporate governance is to minimise the risk associated with the separation of 'ownership' from 'management'. So, corporate governance includes the control exercised by the legitimate stakeholders over their respective stakes in the entity; and the mechanisms (such as the accountability of the directors) that facilitate this external control. In part, it is also internal control which comprises the oversight of management by the board of directors, together with the internal control mechanisms which management implement and apply (including management's accountability to the board) in order that the board has reasonable assurance of the achievement of the entity's objectives.

There is a distinction, too often blurred, between the responsibilities of the board and the responsibilities of management. It is understandable that the distinction between the responsibilities of the board and those of management is the more blurred in the case of the Anglo-Saxon unitary board, which may be balanced in its membership between executives and non-executives. Nevertheless, an executive who is a board director is not acting in a managerial capacity when he or she participates in decision making at the board. He or she is acting in a managerial capacity when reporting to the board on the operation(s) for which he or she has executive responsibility.

Stewardship theory[18] **C3.13**

> 'The original corporate concept enshrined a philosophical assumption about the nature of man, one that has been reflected in subsequent developments of company law – a view that man is essentially trustworthy, able to act in good faith in the interests of others with integrity and honesty. This is implicit in the fiduciary relationship required of directors. This perspective has been termed 'stewardship theory.'[19,20]

Donaldson and Davis undertook an empirical study which came up with conclusions that would seem to us counter-intuitive ten years later:

> 'Stewardship theory stresses the beneficial consequences on shareholder returns of facilitative authority structures which unify command by having roles of CEO and chair held by the same person. The empirical evidence is that the return on equity (ROE) returns to shareholders are improved by combining, rather than separating, the role-holders of the chair and CEO positions. Thus the results fail to support agency theory and lend some support to stewardship theory. The safeguarding of returns to shareholders may be along the track, not of placing management under greater control, by owners, but of empowering managers to take autonomous executive action.'

Donaldson and Davis (1991) argued that managers can choose to act as stewards or as agents, depending upon their motivations and their perceptions of the situation. Likewise, principals also choose to create an agency or a stewardship relationship according to how they interpret the situation and how they assess management. Managers are more likely to take a stewardship perspective if they are motivated by a needs for achievement, responsibility, doing a good job, recognition (of achievement), altruism, self respect, respect for authority. The ideas of Maslow and Herzberg, which we discuss below, are relevant here.

Stewardship theory is consistent with McGregor's 'Theory Y' (see below). Stewardship theory takes the view that people *can* be trusted to act in the public good in general, and in the interests of the shareholders in particular.

Stewardship theory articulates that management are, or should be, the stewards of the owners of enterprises. The UK's Stewardship Code is misnamed, as it is targeted at the responsibilities of the owners rather than the managers.

Herzberg's theory of motivators and hygiene factors C3.14

> 'Job attitude data suggests that after the glow of the initial year on the job, job satisfaction plummets to its lowest level in the work life of individuals. From a life time of diverse learning, successive accomplishment through the various academic stages, and periodic reinforcement of efforts, the entrant to our modern companies finds that, rather than work providing an expanding psychological existence, the opposite occurs; and successive amputations of his or her self-conceptions, aspirations, learning and talent are the consequence of earning a living.'[21]

Herzberg considered certain attributes, all of which relate closely to the job itself, to be *motivators* (that is, *satisfiers*), whereas other attributes which relate more to the surroundings of the job (such as working conditions, salary, supervision, company policy and administration) he designated *hygiene factors* (that is, *dissatisfiers*). Herzberg's view was that no amount of attention to the hygiene factors would positively motivate an employee, although unsatisfactory hygiene factors would be a source of discontent. His was thus a two-factor hypothesis:

> 'Factors involved in producing job satisfaction were separate and distinct from the factors that led to dissatisfaction.'[22]

Hygiene factors also have a much shorter *half life* than motivators: for instance, the favourable impact of a salary increase wears off very quickly (implying that 'little and often' is more effective), whereas the impact of achievement, recognition of achievement or advancement last much longer.

A diagrammatic way of representing Herzberg's theory is given here:

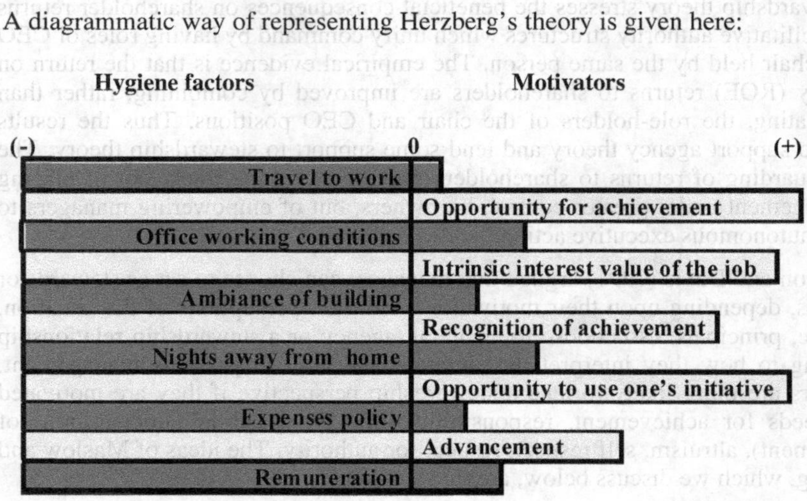

Maslow's hierarchy of needs **C3.15**

Maslow, a Harvard professor, had a unipolar view of fulfilment, unlike Herzberg's bi-polar view.[23] Maslow's hierarchy of personal needs can be visualised as a pyramid shown in this figure:

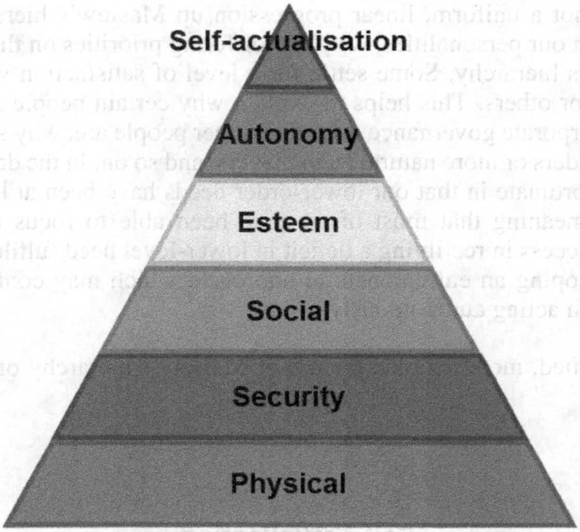

At the base of the pyramid are one's physical needs which, if they are not satisfied, are one's major preoccupation in order to stay alive in the short term, to the exclusion of being concerned with the higher-order needs shown further up the pyramid. If one's physical needs are satisfied, then we turn our attention to endeavouring to secure our physical needs in the medium to long term. This may lead us to relocate or to retrain.

The quality of our social life will be likely to be our principal preoccupation if our security needs are well under control, when concerns about social needs will take a lot of our attention until they are reasonably well satisfied.

Maslow's theory suggests that there are higher-order needs that consume our attention when the lower-order needs are under control. At the higher level, we may start to brood over our self-esteem, and endeavour to take measures to enhance it. Our self-esteem is profoundly influenced by the esteem in which others hold us – though that varies from person to person to some extent. If we consider we can hold our head high in terms of esteem, it may then become an issue for us whether we have true autonomy. Autonomy can be expressed as the ability to make decisions and to see the results that flow from the decisions we have made. At middle levels of management, this is often a problem – how many middle managers can attribute outcomes to their own decisions and actions? Many more consider they fail to get the credit for their achievements – both an esteem issue and a self-actualisation issue.

Should we be fortunate enough to have had all these personal needs satisfied to a reasonable degree, we may still experience a partial vacuum in terms of our general sense of self-fulfilment – what Maslow referred to as 'self-actualisation'. This sense of emptiness sometimes motivates us to make major life changes – which, if made rashly, can result in new and significant deficits in terms of Maslow's lower-order needs.

In reality it is not a uniform, linear progression up Maslow's hierarchy of needs. Depending upon our personalities, we place differing priorities on the various needs within Maslow's hierarchy. Some settle for a level of satisfaction which would be unsatisfactory for others. This helps to explain why certain people are more suited for particular corporate governance roles than other people are, why some people are more natural leaders or more natural team players, and so on. In the developed world, we have been fortunate in that our lower-order needs have been at least reasonably well satisfied, meaning that most of us have been able to focus on higher-level needs. Often, success in rectifying a deficit in lower-level need fulfilment can be the driver for developing an entrepreneurial approach, which may contribute to being comfortable with acting autonomously.

A slightly modified, more detailed picture of Maslow's hierarchy of needs is given here:

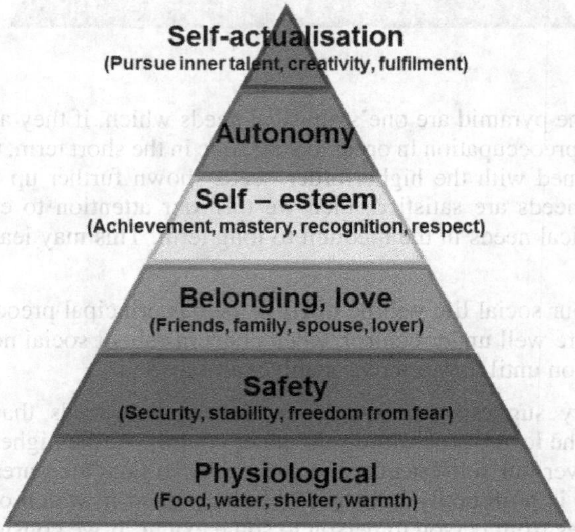

Douglas McGregor's Theory X and Theory Y[24] C3.16

> 'Theories X and Y are not strategies of managing: they are assumptions about the nature of people which influence the adoption of a strategy for managing.'

Theory X and Theory Y Assumptions

	Traditional view: Theory X		The more innovative view: Theory Y
1	*A proposition common in Theories X and Y*: Management is responsible for organising elements of productive enterprise – money, materials, equipment, people – in the interest of economic ends.		
2	With respect to people, this is a process of directing their actions, modifying their behaviour to fit the needs of the organisation.	2	People are not by nature passive, or resistant to organisational needs. They have become so as a result of experience in organisations.
3	Without this active intervention by management, people would be passive – even resistant – to organisational needs. They must therefore be persuaded, rewarded, punished, controlled – their activities must be directed. This is management's task. We often sum it up by saying that management consists of getting things done through people.	3	The motivation, the potential for development, the capacity for assuming responsibility, the readiness to direct behaviour toward organisational goals are all present in people. Management does not put them there. It is a responsibility of management to make it possible for people to recognise and develop these human characteristics for themselves.
4	The average person is by nature indolent – he or she works as little as possible.	4	The essential task of management is to arrange organisational conditions and methods of operation so that people can achieve their own goals *best* by directing *their own* efforts toward organisational objectives.
5	He or she lacks ambition, dislikes responsibility, prefers to be led.		
6	He or she is inherently self-centred, indifferent to organisational needs.		
7	He or she is by nature resistant to change.		
8	He or she is gullible, not very bright, the ready dupe of the charlatan and the demagogue.		

Stakeholders and Reputational Management C3.17

Reputational risk, reputational management and reputational audit are becoming an important area of focus for boards, senior managements and internal auditors. The spotlight is widening from the narrower focus of reputation to a broader spread on stakeholders. The goal should be that the stakeholder audit becomes part of every company's system of internal control. Handling stakeholder relationships well is 'key' to achieving vital organisational objectives, and knowing whether this is being done should be regarded as essential. Internal control is defined as the processes, effected by the board, management and other personnel, which give reasonable assurance of the achievement of objectives. The monitoring of internal control is one of the essential components of effective internal control which Rutteman and Turnbull both included amongst the criteria an organisation should use to assess whether there is effective internal control. Any who are responsible for implementing Turnbull in a state-of-the-art way are likely to find these challenging ideas of real value. In addition to chief executives, these issue are important for communication directors, strategy directors and finance directors.

Although here we take the 'for profit' company as the subject for a stakeholder audit, the approach is equally relevant for 'not-for-profit' organisations which, likewise, have their own but different bodies of stakeholders.

The stakeholder audit approach recognises that, increasingly, the worth of a company resides in its intangible assets. The Department of Trade and Industry (DTI) report, 'Creating value from your intangible assets' had this to say:

> 'The combined impacts of globalisation, new technology and increased competition [mean] that all companies are facing the prospect of continual incremental and, occasionally, radical change … ultimately, a company's ability to flourish in this environment will depend on its ability to create value from intangibles … Ultimately, the ability of your organisation to meet not only its current goals and objectives, but also to grasp future opportunities, will depend on its ability to create value from its intangible assets. It is only by identifying, managing and developing the full spectrum of intangibles that you will be able to unlock your full potential.'[25]

One of the greatest sources of intangible value resides today in a company's ability to *manage its relationships* with its various stakeholder groups. Relationships are the drivers of reputation. Failure to manage relationships effectively is a key area of risk that many companies are overlooking.

If further persuasion is needed, the DTI study went on to say:

> 'We … highlight the need for organisations to improve the quality of dialogue with a variety of stakeholders, in communicating risks and uncertainties. Ultimately the quality of dialogue affects both "licence to operate", which includes issues like consent to and support for activities from *non financial stakeholders*, and "cost of capital" which is influenced by the attractiveness of the overall business proposition to *financial stakeholders*.' (emphasis added)

and:

> 'A successful company is one that looks constantly to build on its existing relationships, be they *external* (customers, suppliers or anyone else whose ideas

and co-operation may assist in meeting goals and solving problems) or *internal* (different functions and their teams working together to seize opportunities and create value).' (emphasis added)

and:

> 'For your company to reach its full potential in this area it is essential that you not only consider how you can develop and improve your current relationships, but that you also carefully consider how you can develop and improve the relationships necessary for your future success.'

The stakeholder audit challenges us as to whether we can now answer these and other questions in the context of our businesses:

- Is responsibility for the management of stakeholder groups clearly delineated in the business?
- Do we know the state of health of each stakeholder relationship?
- Do we understand the risks inherent in these stakeholder relationships?
- Do we know which stakeholder groups represent the greatest opportunity for us?
- Is the amount of time and effort the business spends on managing stakeholder relationships roughly in proportion to their relative importance or intangible value?
- What listening mechanisms are in place to monitor these relationships on an ongoing basis?
- How well do we integrate stakeholder relationship management? (There is too much potential for companies to give out conflicting messages through a lack of stakeholder communications integration.)
- How effective is our communication with each group?
- Have we checked that there is consistency between the way we perceive each stakeholder relationship and how they see us?

Compete successfully by being ahead in management thinking C3.18

There are many battlefields on which companies compete. We compete aggressively for customers, for supplier commitment, for staff loyalty, for fast access to technology and innovation, and for many other valuable inputs and outcomes. There are also many different strategies for achieving competitive advantage – differentiation, price leadership and so on.

Even more fundamental today, in terms of competitive advantage, is the quality and style of management that companies apply in all their battlefields. Companies re-engineer their cultures to secure competitive advantage in a changing world, and management generally has become much more professional. It seems that constant change in the business environment forces constant change of managerial approach upon businesses. A competitive edge comes to the leading business that is proactive in adapting to changing needs, not to the trailing business that tries to play the game of catch up.

New insights into what is required to achieve corporate success come through in waves, that need to be harnessed quickly if a company is not to be left behind. Sometimes, more than one wave strikes simultaneously. In the 1990s, we experienced the waves of empowerment, business process re-engineering, delayering, downsizing, corporate governance, internal control and risk management. In a sense, each of these has been a new lens through which management has needed to train its eye so as to gain, retain or recover a competitive edge. More recently, there has been the lens of reputational risk, and the idea of reputational audit has been born.

The Provision in the UK Corporate Governance Code, that directors should report on internal control and risk management, together with the Turnbull guidance on how boards should set about doing this, have led to a sea change in the focus that boards are placing on risk. Formal 'top-down' assessments of risk, starting at the level of the board, are now commonplace. They should certainly embrace considerations of reputational risk, though many still do not. They should now be adapted to focus, not exclusively but importantly, on stakeholder risk.

'Top-down' assessments of risk C3.19

The obvious gap in most 'top-down' assessments of risk has been that they have not adequately reflected stakeholder risks. One of the greatest risks facing any business today is that of growing out of touch with, or otherwise failing to understand, what the market and other stakeholder groups expect, want and need. There have been a number of notable and dramatic cases recently, such as Marks & Spencer, BT and Railtrack, where a company appears to have grown out of touch with its various markets.

Now, the eye of the storm is shifting to focus more on the stakeholders themselves – and the very practical concepts of stakeholder risk, stakeholder control and stakeholder audit are moving centre stage. The stakeholder audit has been designed to meet boardroom and chief executive needs, for whom the interests of stakeholders of all sorts are becoming the major preoccupation.

Image as reality C3.20

For some years now, it has been accepted that intangibles, such as 'image', along with hard commercial fundamentals, are important ingredients for success. When we can look back, we may conclude that the year 2000 was about the time when perceptions of reality became the real reality, the main drivers of success and thus the necessary focus of successful management teams. There are already many businesses now whose market capitalisation owes more to brand image than to hard tangible assets.

So, building value for shareholders is becoming predominantly about developing and cherishing the corporate brand. In the last few years of the twentieth century, this became manifest in a focus on reputational management. In today's small, global, Internet business world – subjected to intense media scrutiny – there are no hiding places for disreputable business practices. Truth will out – and often rapidly so. In an affluent society, consumer perceptions of quality increasingly factor in perceptions of brand ethics. In a world of brands, a tarnished brand image enhances no consumer's life style – which is image based.

Today 'reputation risk', tomorrow 'stakeholder risk' C3.21

Risk management became reputational risk management. In a contemporary business, it has been argued, there are now no risks except for reputational risks – which need to be identified, assessed and managed. This has been interpreted as a matter of taking steps to enhance the corporate and product brand(s), to avoid events which would damage the brands, and to respond effectively and convincingly to crises which threaten the brands.

Now, the stakeholder audit is likely to take over from the reputational audit as the preferred approach for leading-edge companies to use. The reputational audit approach constructively focused on the criticality of reputation, but it targeted the different stakeholder groups only in a scattergun way. In our experience, some key stakeholder groups were often largely overlooked in the reputational audit approach. Another change is that the stakeholder audit focuses more on relationships as the drivers of reputation, rather than more exclusively on reputation itself.

The stakeholder audit is a strategic management tool which enables companies consciously to identify and understand who are their stakeholders; then to assess and monitor the health or otherwise of their relationship and reputation with each key stakeholder group; and then to design and implement the necessary measures to create a better state of health in the future. In this way, the stakeholder audit helps to control, and thereby reduce, risks arising from relationships with various stakeholder groups.

Few companies today systematically consider their relationships with their true body of stakeholders. The body of stakeholders might resemble that shown in Figure 1 below.

The stakeholder audit approach C3.22

See also **A6.5–A6.6**.

The stakeholder audit approach allows that this will vary from one company to another.

Whereas Figure 1 illustrates, for a hypothetical company, the assessed state of health with respect to each stakeholder relationship, Figure 2 additionally provides an indication of the relative importance to the company of each stakeholder relationship, on a numeric scale. Together they suggest where action is most needed and where are the best opportunities to leverage off relationships.

Companies need to achieve, preserve and enhance a strong reputation with each of their stakeholder groups. It is likely that even stakeholder groups not perceived as being 'key' can be serviced more satisfactorily to the long-term benefit of the company. You can never be sure when a particular stakeholder relationship will assume more importance; and when it does, it might be too late to put right the effect of past, and possibly long-term, neglect.

There is often a balance between satisfying the needs of different stakeholder groups. Company directors may not know how to reconcile the conflicting needs of their various stakeholders. Shareholders and customers appear to want completely

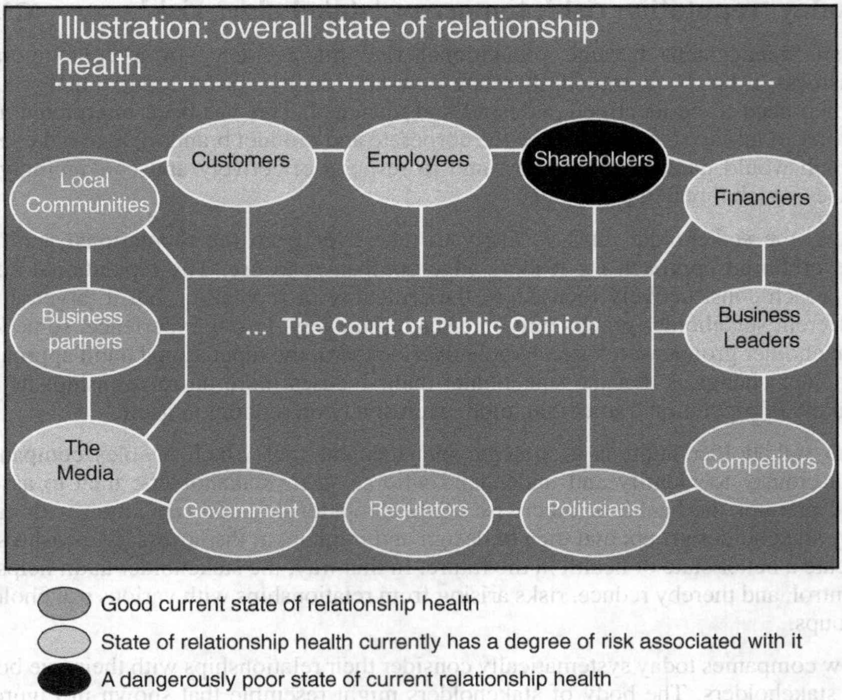

Figure 1

opposite things. How do you reconcile these conflicting needs and keep all happy? But opportunities to satisfy one stakeholder group are often missed, simply though lack of attention rather than because of any conflicts with the needs of other stakeholder groups.

In the last analysis, it is not too fanciful to suggest that the conflicting interests of different stakeholders can be harmonised. For instance, in the long term it is likely to be in the best interests of staff to work for successful companies, even if this means they experience the uncertainty of contested takeovers and other major changes. It is likely to be in customers' best interests to deal with suppliers who are generating a good return for their financial stakeholders. It is likely to be in an environmentally conscious community's best interests that a local employer is not having to cut corners to save costs. And so on. It is often a matter of managing stakeholder perceptions and expectations in order to reconcile conflicts between stakeholders for the better benefit of all; but, of course, a necessary prerequisite is to understand what it is that has to be managed.

Satisfying stakeholders' perceived needs is not always costly or resource intensive, but more a matter of doing 'appropriate things well' rather than 'inappropriate things badly'.

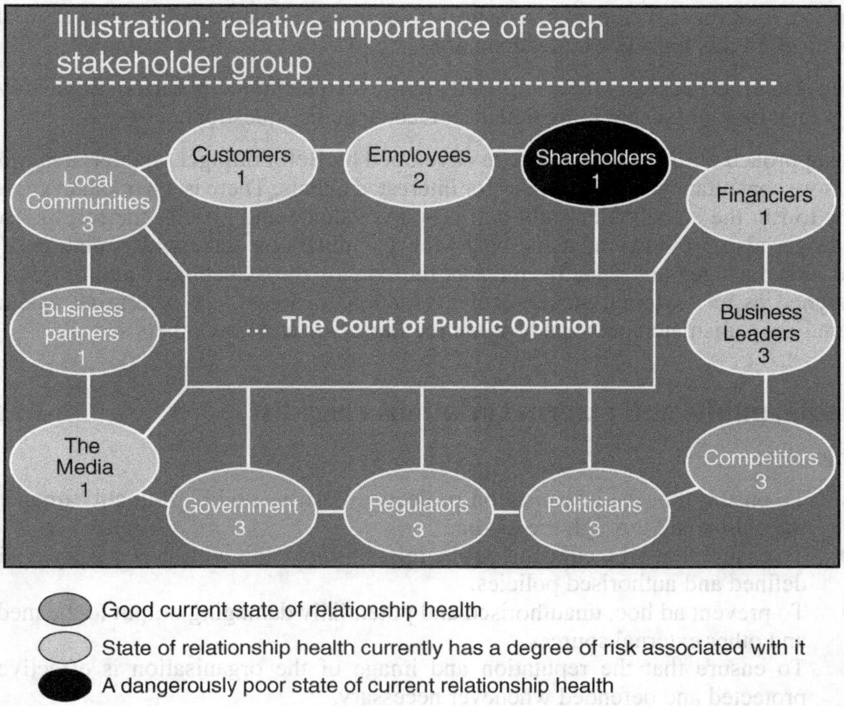

Figure 2

The stakeholder audit sets out to provide companies with an ongoing way of handling these challenges. It is designed to enable companies to strike the right balances between stakeholders. It should undoubtedly contribute to enhancing reputation across all stakeholder groups. Therefore, it optimises returns and creates conditions for sustainable success.

Identifying vulnerabilities in stakeholder relationships is important, as it is a prerequisite to developing strategies to improve things. But as least as important is to ensure that we are exploiting for competitive advantage the particular strengths that we have in our stakeholder relationships. Businesses achieve their goals more by exploiting strengths than by avoiding vulnerabilities. The stakeholder audit facilitates both. There is little point in having an excellent stakeholder relationship if that is not turned to commercial advantage in the best possible way.

The stakeholder audit is multi-faceted and multi-staged. Initially, there is the high-level introductory questionnaire which sets out the proposition and flags up areas of opportunity. The CEO or one of his or her colleague directors could quite quickly complete this questionnaire. Alternatively, and preferably, internal audit could complete it in consultation with directors and senior staff, using the questionnaire as the basis of an audit assignment. If time permits, internal audit in the traditional way can look for sufficient evidence prior to homing in on appropriate answers to the questions in this high-level questionnaire.

Areas identified as key in the completed high-level questionnaire can be drilled down in greater depth by using more detailed 'facet-specific' questionnaires.

The approach outlined here has been developed by Bell Pottinger, and has a number of more consultancy-based add-ons for interested clients. There is a workshop around how to run the stakeholder audit and how to evaluate and present the results. Bell Pottinger also provides intensive board-level seminars on stakeholder relationships and risk management. Finally, there is the part of the stakeholder audit which is designed as an 'external stakeholder evaluation' process – to determine whether there is any mismatch between how we see ourselves and how others see us.

Media, public and external relations checklist C3.23

Objectives

(a) To ensure that the organisation projects a positive and high-quality image to the public and through the media.

(b) To ensure that all media and public relations are dealt with in accordance with defined and authorised policies.

(c) To prevent ad hoc, unauthorised and potentially damaging output to the media and other external sources.

(d) To ensure that the reputation and image of the organisation is effectively protected and defended whenever necessary.

(e) To ensure that relevant members of management are suitably trained to deal with the media.

(f) To ensure that plans are developed effectively to handle crisis situations (ie strikes, product concerns etc).

(g) To ensure that the organisation fosters good relationships with local communities.

(h) To ensure that the organisation maintains an accurate awareness of relevant public opinion and takes the appropriate action.

(i) To ensure that the organisation's business interests are supported by active participation in relevant trade associations or standards bodies.

(j) To ensure that attempts to influence government policies and regulations are handled legally and effectively.

Checklist

1. Key issues

1.1 Has an agreed and authorised public and media relations policy been implemented, and if so how is management to be assured that the policy is always complied with?

1.2 Are the relevant employees and managers adequately trained to handle media and public relations, and how can management be sure that all external inquiries are correctly routed to the nominated individuals?

1.3 How does management remain aware of public opinion or media comment about the organisation, and what mechanisms are employed effectively to react to such comments?

1.4 Have contingency plans been developed in the event of crisis situations, and have specific responsibilities been allocated?
1.5 What steps does management take in order to remain aware of local community issues and to foster good relations with the local community?
1.6 What action does management take to ensure that the organisation is actively represented within the relevant trade and industry bodies?
1.7 Where there is a need to remain aware of, and attempt to influence, government policies in areas affecting the organisation, what steps are taken to ensure that lobbying is both legally conducted and effective?

2. Detailed issues

2.1 What mechanisms prevent unauthorised statements being made to either the media or another external body?
2.2 Are named individuals made responsible for handling media and public relations matters, and are they appropriately experienced and trained?
2.3 Are all other staff made aware that they should not make comments or statements about the organisation to media representatives?
2.4 How does the organisation maintain an awareness of its public image, and does it have a structured approach to the projection of a positive corporate image?
2.5 How is the success of public relations activities monitored and evaluated (eg through the use of market research techniques)?
2.6 Are all media and public relations stances agreed and authorised by senior management, and how is this evidenced?
2.7 Are all company statements authorised and issued through an appropriate press officer?
2.8 In order to engender good local community relations, does the organisation become involved in local events and issues (and is such involvement subject to adequate justification and authorisation)?
2.9 How does management ensure that the impact of the organisation on the local community (eg through the appearance of its buildings or any potential environmental influences) is minimised and dealt with?
2.10 How does management ensure that inquiries or complaints from the local community are appropriately dealt with?
2.11 What steps does the organisation take to ensure that its opinion is effectively directed to influence the appropriate trade and industry bodies?
2.12 Have clear (and documented) guidelines been established regarding the methods to employ when seeking to influence government policies which could affect the organisation's business interests?
2.13 How can management be assured that lobbying activities do not contravene either the law or ethical business practices?
2.14 Are all the costs associated with media, public and external relations accurately identified, authorised and reflected in the accounts?
2.15 Does management monitor the effectiveness of media, public and external relations in order to improve techniques and procedures?
2.16 How is the accuracy of data input from other systems (eg financial reporting) confirmed?
2.17 How is accuracy of data output to other systems (eg to industry regulators) confirmed?

Notes

1 Sumantra Ghoshal, 'Business schools share the blame for Enron' (2003) *Financial Times*, 18 July, p 192.
2 Berle, Adolf and Gardiner Means (1932), *The Modern Corporation and Private Property* (US, Transaction Publishers, ISBN 0887388876).
3 Smith, Adam (1776) *An Inquiry into the Nature and Causes of the Wealth of Nations*, Vol 2, Bk 5, Ch 1, Pt 3, Art 1.
4 See, for instance: Jenson, Michael and William Meckling (1976), Theory of the Firm: Managerial Behavior, Agency Costs and Ownership Structure, *Journal of Financial Economics,* October, 1976, Vol. 3, No. 4, pp. 305–360; reprinted in Michael C. Jensen, A Theory of the Firm: Governance, Residual Claims and Organizational Forms (Harvard University Press, December 2000); also published in Foundations of Organizational Strategy, Michael C. Jensen, Harvard University Press, 1998. Fama, Eugene F. (1980), Agency problems and the theory of the firm, *Journal of Monetary Economics*, 6(1), pp 39–57; Also *The Journal of Political Economy*, 88 (2), 1980. Fama, Eugene F. & Michael Jensen, 1983, Separation of Ownership and Control, *Journal of Law and Economics*, Vol. XXVI.
5 In a speech by Gordon Gekko in the film 'Wall Street'.
6 Alan Greenspan, Chairman of the US Federal Reserve, Testimony to Congress, 2003.
7 Tricker, Robert I. (1994) *International Corporate Governance* (Prentice Hall, Singapore), p 4.
8 Pettigrew, A.M. (1973) *The Politics of Organizational Decision-making*, Tavistock, ISBN 0422741205.
9 Fama, Eugene F. (1980), Agency problems and the theory of the firm, *Journal of Monetary Economics*, 6(1), pp 39–57. Also *The Journal of Political Economy*, 88 (2), 1980.
10 Donaldson, Lex and James H Davis 'CEO Governance and Shareholder Returns: Agency Theory or Stewardship Theory' (1988) Academy of Management Meetings, and offered to Australian Journal of Management in early 1990s (uncertain whether published).
11 Jenson, Michael and William Meckling, note 3 above.
12 Jenson, Michael and William Meckling, note 3 above.
13 Williamson, Oliver E (1998) 'Corporate finance and corporate governance', (XLII, 3) *J Finance*, July.
14 We reproduce the Code itself at **App1**. The full publication, including this quotation from the Introduction on p 1, can be found on the Financial Reporting Council's website.
15 Eg Nader, Ralph, Mark J Green and Joel Seligman (1976), *Taming the Giant Corporation*, Norton.
16 Eg Baysinger, Barry D and Henry N Butler (1985), 'Corporate Governance and the Board of Directors: Performance Effects of Changes in Board Composition', *Journal of Law, Economics and Organization,* 1(1): 101–124, Oxford Journals.
17 Eg Porter, Michael (1985) *Competitive Advantage: Creating and Sustaining Superior Performance* (The Free Press and Macmillan, London and New York, 1985); see also his *Competitive Strategy: Techniques for Analysing Industries and Competitors* (The Free Press, 1980).
18 A useful source is M Muth and L Donaldson, *Stewardship Theory and Board Structure – A Contingency Approach*, Corporate Governance (Blackwells, 1998) vol 6, no 1, pp 5–28.
19 Muth, M and L Donaldson, note 17 above.
20 Tricker, Robert I. (1994), note 6 above.
21 Herzberg, F. (1966) *Work and the Nature of Man* (World, Cleveland, Ohio); and F Herzberg (1959) *The Motivation to Work* (John Wiley & Sons, New York).
22 Herzberg, F. (1966) *Work and the Nature of Man* (World, Cleveland, Ohio).

23 Maslow, Abraham H. (1954): *Motivation and Personality*, New York: Harper; also (2005) Longman/Addison-Wesley.

24 McGregor, Douglas (1960) *The Human Side of Management* (McGraw-Hill, New York).

25 Department of Trade and Industry (DTI) 'Creating value from your intangible assets' (May 2001).

Chapter C4

Do Non-Executive Directors Add Value?

Introduction C4.1

This chapter is based on the full text of the professorial inaugural lecture given on 30 November 2004 by Andrew Chambers, author of this handbook, at London South Bank University, with minor updating. Its full title was *'A teddy bears' picnic or the lion's ring? – Do non-executive directors add value?'*. To retain its cohesion, no updates for post-2004 developments have been made. In the main, this means that references are to earlier versions of the UK Corporate Governance Code (then termed 'The Combined Code') rather than to the one current today and reproduced at **App1** of this handbook, and that the illustrations refer to pre-2005 examples only. Table 5 at **C4.17** has been updated.

> 'The board's role is to provide entrepreneurial leadership of the company within a framework of prudent and effective controls which enables risk to be assessed and managed. The board should set the company's strategic aims, ensure that the necessary financial and human resources are in place for the company to meet its objectives and review management performance. The board should set the company's values and standards and ensure that its obligations to its shareholders and others are understood and met.
>
> 'All directors must take decisions objectively in the interests of the company.
>
> **'As part of their role as members of a unitary board, non-executive directors should constructively challenge and help develop proposals on strategy. Non-executive directors should scrutinise the performance of management in meeting agreed goals and objectives and monitor the reporting of performance. They should satisfy themselves on the integrity of financial information and that financial controls and systems of risk management are robust and defensible. They are responsible for determining appropriate levels of remuneration of executive directors and have a prime role in appointing, and where necessary removing, executive directors, and in succession planning.'**[1]

The questions C4.2

'What is the effect of the non-executive director'? Considering the effect of the non-executive director is not quite the same as addressing 'the effective non-executive director'. Do non-executive directors have any effect and, if so, what are the effects and to what extent? Of course, positive answers to these questions would suggest tests to apply in determining whether someone has what it takes to make an effective contribution as a non-executive director. This would also assist in determining the scope of the evaluation of the performance of each non-executive director – which is now very much part of our new 2003 Combined Code on Corporate Governance.[2]

Assessing potential or actual contribution C4.3

Sir Derek Higgs has said that he considers his report's[3] main contribution in the long term would likely be seen to be in the area of board and individual director performance. Evaluating performance was addressed neither in the 1992 Cadbury Code[4] nor the 1998 Combined Code[5] (except in the context of determining executive remuneration, which is one of the responsibilities of outside directors). Neither was the issue of careful selection and training of directors covered significantly until 2003. Over half (52%) of UK boards now assess individual directors' performance regularly[6] and this could rise rapidly as 90% of UK directors consider it should be standard practice. Practice in the US (29%), France (23%) and Germany (1%) lags far behind.

While the question as to whether non-executive directors have any positive effect is a different question to what makes a non-executive director effective, the two are of course related. Assuming there is the potential to add value to the company it will not happen without adequate time commitment, thorough preparation for meetings, recent and relevant experience, an inquiring and independent mind and, not least, team working qualities.

A prospective non-executive director should always be clear in his or her mind what it is that a company is looking for in their new non-executive director, and be ruthless to ensure that he or she can live up to expectations. There is no room for passengers on a board. Total boardroom costs matter, should be tracked and will need to be contained. The larger the board, the more unwieldy it becomes.[7] Each member of a board should clearly be making an essential contribution: if not, what is the point? Conger and Lawler have put it well:

> 'The best boards are composed of individuals with different skills, knowledge, information, power, and time to contribute. Given the diversity of expertise, information, and availability that is needed to understand and govern today's complex businesses, it is unrealistic to expect an individual director to be knowledgeable and informed about all phases of business. It is also unrealistic to expect individual directors to be available at all times and to influence all decisions. Thus, in staffing most boards, it is best to think of individuals contributing different pieces to the total picture that it takes to create an effective board.'[8]

However, in today's more demanding world, it is unsafe to imply that non-executive directors can be routinely unavailable at times – a view which has recently been given some further currency within the Tyson Report on widening the gene pool from which non-executive directors are recruited.[9]

The uniqueness of the non-executive director's role C4.4

Non-executive directors are that extra board level ingredient, over and above the qualities of the top executive team. Some of the top executives will belong to the main board along with some non-executive directors: the UK, generally speaking, is committed to having

> 'a strong presence on the board of both executive and non-executive directors.'[10]

So, the essential difference between 'the board' and 'management' is the non-executive directors. Strip out non-executive directors from boards and boards become just another management forum – overlaid with the particular legal, regulatory and shareholder-driven responsibilities which boards have.

Many companies have a top-level executive committee below the level of the main board and chaired by the chief executive; this committee may even be called 'the executive board' but in reality it is a committee of the chief executive. Would such a company do as well without a main board – with all the decision-taking, all the oversight and all the accountability being entrusted to the executive? If so, then 'the board' would have no value and the contribution of the non-executive board members would be of no effect. On the other hand, if the board makes a valued contribution it must in large part be a consequence of the additional effect of the non-executive directors (that extra ingredient) who act out their role at that level, not at the executive level. A corollary of this is that non-executive directors are definitely not executive. This means, for instance, that the audit committee of the board should avoid creating the impression that it is an executive committee. Management should be left to manage. Some of the overload of audit committees might be avoided if audit committees took this to heart. Sometimes there is a failure to make the clear distinction between on the one hand the board of director's responsibility to set direction and oversee its execution by management and on the other hand the responsibility of management to manage. This is evident when the word 'management' is used loosely to refer collectively to the board and management – a slip of the tongue perhaps more frequently made in the US.

Morrisons is an interesting case. Their 2003 and 2004 annual reports showed that they had no non-executive directors, nor an audit committee, nor a usual remuneration committee (see Boxes 1 and 2). Management looked after everything. Yet the board met in full on over twenty occasions in each of those two financial years. Of course they have a board, but this was the senior executive team working collaboratively on board affairs. What value would non-executive directors bring?

Box 1

From the Directors' report within Morrisons' annual report for the year ended 2 February 2003

References within square brackets have been added for this article

'The company ensures that it recruits to the board only individuals of sufficient calibre, knowledge and experience to fulfil the duties of a director appropriately. There is no formal training programme for directors [A.1.6].

'The company does not have any non-executive directors on the board [A.2.1, A.3.1, A.3.2, A.6.1] as the board is currently of the opinion that there is no commercial benefit in appointing them. The directors are mindful of the code of best practice in this regard and will review the situation from time to time.

'The company's nomination committee is made up of the chairman and managing directors. There are no non-executive members on the committee [A.5.1].

'The company does not have a formal remuneration committee [B.1.1–3, B.1.9–10, B.2.1–6, C.2.3] but the emoluments of the directors are the subject of appraisal by the chairman and the managing directors taking into account individual performance and market conditions.'

Box 2

From the Directors' report within Morrisons' annual report for the year ended 2 February 2004

References within square brackets have been added for this article and are to the new 2003 Code. Changes from 2003 annual report are shown in italics (additions) or as strikeouts.

> 'The company ensures that it recruits to the board only individuals of sufficient calibre, knowledge and experience to fulfil the duties of a director appropriately. There is no formal training programme for directors [A.1.6].
>
> 'The company does not have any non-executive directors on the board [A.2.1, A.3.1, A.3.2, A.6.1] ~~as the board is currently of the opinion that there is no commercial benefit in appointing them~~. The directors are mindful of the *combined* code of best practice in this regard and ~~will~~ *regularly* review the situation ~~from time to time~~.
>
> The company's nomination committee is made up of the chairman and managing directors. There are no non-executive members on the committee [A.5.1].
>
> The company does not have a formal remuneration committee [B.1.1–3, B.1.9–10, B.2.1–6, C.2.3] but the emoluments of the directors are the subject of appraisal by the chairman and the managing directors taking into account individual performance and market conditions.'

It is true that a board has particular statutory and other responsibilities – for instance reporting responsibilities. But if these responsibilities could be discharged as effectively in other ways, for instance by the top management team acting alone, then it would be superficial to claim that the board, balanced between executive and non-executive members, were 'adding value' when the board does this. The question would then need to be asked whether the board, as it is at present, is worthwhile, and thus whether the non-executives make a valuable contribution.

How it all began C4.5

There was a time when there were just owner-managers. Then there were owners *and* managers. Those owners met occasionally with their managers to receive reports on progress and to direct and oversee their investment. Agency theory tells us that owners and managers each wish to maximize their own returns, and some even tell us that greed is good.

Over time ownership became more widely dispersed as more held shares in ventures. It became impractical for all of the shareholders of a joint stock company to participate directly in the oversight of management. So they elected from amongst their number just a few to meet on their behalf with the general manager and to report back to the other shareholders. In those days, except sometimes in family businesses, all of the directors would usually have been non-executive directors. They were able to hold the ring between the owners and management; and part of this was to ensure effective communication in both directions between shareholders and management. Shareholders needed to be informed of the progress of their company and they needed to be sure their voices were heard – by their board of directors and thence to management. This is still an essential and valuable service that non-executive directors provide, strengthened in the UK Corporate Governance Code.

It would not have been long before the board of directors would have suggested to the shareholders that a particularly good general manager should be elected to the board – so becoming the 'managing director'. Perhaps the managing director would later have suggested that the production manager and the finance manager should also be invited to join the board. Gradually the board pendulum swung in favour of management even to the extent that, in some companies, non-executive directors were crowded out altogether. Then there was no referee to hold the ring between shareholders and management. Even where there was some non-executive representation on the board, the balance of power might effectively have been with the management members of the board. Influence is not just a matter of a crude numerical headcount.

Executive directors need non-executive directors C4.6

Today a director no longer has to be a shareholder, but a director is still a trustee for the shareholders. This means that, subject to legal, regulatory and contractual obligations, directors should act in the best interests of the shareholders, and that no director should make personal gain at the shareholders' expense from his or her office as a director of the company. Strictly, what should guide a board's decision making is what is in the best interests of the company – which might not necessarily always coincide with the best interests of today's shareholders. 'A director is a director is a director' (whether executive or non-executive) but it must be particularly hard for directors who are also executives of the company, to ensure that they always have the interests of the company or the shareholders at heart. In this regard, executives (in their role as directors) benefit from the perspective that independent directors can bring.

In mid-2004 the founder and *executive chairman* of DFS, Lord Kirkham, was bidding to take DFS private and DFS's independent directors had to consider whether to give the go-ahead for Nomura, Kirkham's financial backer, to carry out 'due diligence' investigations of the company's books without committing themselves to acceptance of an offer. It is hard to see how a board without independent directors could ensure it acted in the best interests of all the shareholders in such a case.

Board balance as an antidote to executive excesses? C4.7

Referring to US corporate excesses, in 2003 Alan Greenspan told the US Congress:

> 'It is not that humans have become any more greedy than in generations past. It is that avenues to express greed have grown so enormously.'[11]

He might have had in mind an excess of *executive* power in the boardrooms of US and other corporates. Yet, how can that be the case when a typical US listed company may have just one or two executives on the board and a considerable majority of non-executive directors? But it is not just a matter of numerical balance. The UK's new Code of Best Practice on Corporate Governance states:[12]

> 'The board should include a balance of executive and non-executive directors (and in particular independent non-executive directors) such that no individual or small group of individuals can dominate the board's decision taking.'

and

> 'To ensure that power and information are not concentrated in one or two individuals, there should be a strong presence on the board of both executive and non-executive directors.'

While the CEO of a US company might be the only executive on the board, in the US it had become a macho thing, now being dismantled, for a prospective CEO to insist that he or she should also chair the board. If it is accepted that the chairman 'runs' the board, that the board 'runs' the chief executive and that the chief executive 'runs' the business (not forgetting also that the shareholders should 'run' the company – and some would say they run the chairman), then there are potential problems if the chairman and the chief executive are one and the same. Certainly, in such circumstances the US board needs to be heavily weighted numerically with non-executive members if there is to be any prospect of balance. (If the word 'run' is unacceptable, alternatives would be 'manages', 'is responsible for the effectiveness of' or 'is responsible for the leadership of'.)[13]

Prima facie it is strange that some institutional shareholders such as fund managers, who have championed effective corporate governance, are now outsourcing their corporate governance oversight to so called 'corporate governance businesses' such as EOS and 'Governance for Owners'. Candidate activities for outsourcing are those that do not need to be kept in house for strategic or security reasons and which could offer better value for money if assigned to an external service provider. It puts out the wrong signal for institutional investors to characterise their interface with corporate governance in such a diminutive way. It is true that pension funds outsource their fund management which is clearly strategically vital to the pension funds, but that is because they cannot hope to have the in-house competence to manage funds well for themselves. In contrast, it should be possible for institutional shareholders to oversee the corporate governance arrangements of the companies in which they are invested, and to act out their own important corporate governance roles without subcontracting that to third parties.

The new UK Code states:[14]

> 'There should be a clear division of responsibilities at the head of the company between the running of the board and the executive responsibility for the running of the company's business. No one individual should have unfettered powers of decision. The chairman is responsible for leadership of the board, ensuring its effectiveness on all aspects of its role and setting its agenda. The chairman is also responsible for ensuring that the directors receive accurate, timely and clear information. The chairman should ensure effective communication with shareholders. The chairman should also facilitate the effective contribution of non-executive directors in particular and ensure constructive relations between executive and non-executive directors. The roles of chairman and chief executive

should not be exercised by the same individual. The division of responsibilities between the chairman and chief executive should be clearly established, set out in writing and agreed by the board. The chairman should on appointment meet the independence criteria ... A chief executive should not go on to be chairman of the same company. If exceptionally a board decides that a chief executive should become chairman, the board should consult major shareholders in advance and should set out its reasons to shareholders at the time of the appointment and in the next annual report.'

A strategic or a monitoring role? C4.8

Enhancing the role of non-executive directors has been perhaps the most significant thread running through UK corporate governance developments since the Cadbury Code of 1992. Other significant, and often intertwined, threads are to do with more rigorous audit arrangements, the accountability of the board, more sophisticated board arrangements, and better shareholder control.

Cadbury defined corporate governance as:

> 'the system by which companies are directed and controlled'[15]

and went on to say:

> 'The emphasis in this report on the control function of non-executive directors is a consequence of our remit and should not in any way detract from the primary and positive contribution which [non-executive directors] are expected to make, as equal board members, to the leadership of the company.'[16]

The 1992 Cadbury Code said:

> 'Non-executive directors should bring an independent judgement to bear on issues of strategy, performance, resources, including key appointments, and standards of conduct'[17]

In 1998 the Hampel Committee concurred:

> 'Non-executive directors are normally appointed to the board primarily for their contribution to the development of the company's strategy. This is clearly right. We have found general acceptance that non-executive directors should have both a strategic and a monitoring function.'[18]

Expertise, mentoring and networking C4.9

Hampel added:

> 'In addition, and particularly in smaller companies, non-executive directors may contribute valuable expertise not otherwise available to management; or they may act as mentors to relatively inexperienced executives. What matters in every case is that the non-executive directors should command the respect of the executives and should be able to work with them in a cohesive team to further the company's interests.'

'Opening doors' is one service which is often sought from non-executive directors, and also even the prestige which they can bring to the board. For instance, more than a third of the 682 peers – that is, excluding bishops and law lords – who could sit on at least one board do so.[19] But a place on the board for the contacts one can bring is now rarely sufficient justification. In the words of the *Financial Times*:

> 'The fact that just 20 MPs and peers occupy nearly 200 seats on corporate boards sums up the non-executive directorship at its worst: a sinecure for superannuated politicians requiring an occasional glance at the books and an appetite for lunch.
>
> 'That may be a crude caricature. But too often non-execs are recruited for their ability to open doors rather than look out for shareholders. Stronger corporate governance requires higher quality non-execs who are willing to stand up to management.'[20]

In terms of a mentoring role for non-executive directors, there have been successful arrangements whereby a non-executive director 'shadows' a particular executive director. This facilitates the involvement of the non-executive director and contributes to keeping the non-executive element on the board well informed; and it provides practical and moral support for the executive directors. An ACCA study found that non-executive directors of SMEs had a significant mentoring role.[21]

SMEs

C4.10

Another ACCA-sponsored study in 2000,[22] which also focused on SMEs, found that a significant proportion of these companies then already had non-executive directors (see Table 1). The study was based on questionnaires sent to the managing directors of 5,279 UK SMEs, randomly selected. 1103 questionnaires were returned, representing a good 20.9% response rate. It is apparent that managing directors found their non-executive directors made a worthwhile contribution in both the oversight/control and the strategic aspects of their role (Table 2).

Table 1

SMEs with non-executive directors

Number of employees	Percentage with at least one non-executive director
1–10	20–22%
11–49	18%
50–99	33%
100–199	43%
200–499	47%

Table 2

Non-executive director contribution within SMEs

Contribution	All	1–49	50–499
Objectivity	73%	63%	80%
Strategic view	50%	48%	51%
Financial expertise	33%	34%	25%
Operational expertise	31%	29%	31%
Contact network	28%	18%	33%
Structure to board	28%	22%	31%

How chairmen and finance directors view the non-executive director C4.11

A further and major study in 2004 investigated whether good corporate governance improves a company's ability to generate wealth.[23] This study covered FTSE 100 (21% of those surveyed), FTSE 250 (31%) and other (48%) companies and respondents were either company chairmen or finance directors in equal numbers. Taking just one of the many issues being explored by this study, respondents were asked for their views on eight statements about non-executive directors with the preliminary results as shown in Table 3. This study shows there are mixed views about the contribution that non-executive directors make to wealth creation but very high levels of confidence that non-executive directors play a significant role in corporate governance terms. There is also a strong conviction indicated that being a non-executive director is becoming more demanding.

Table 3

How chairmen and finance directors view the non-executive director

		Disagree	Agree
1	Independent NEDs play an important role in the organisation's ability to create wealth	30%	36%
2	Independent NEDs play an important role in establishing effective corporate governance practice in the organisation	3%	78%
3	Independent NEDs should play a stronger role in corporate governance	24%	35%
4	It is difficult to appoint truly independent NEDs	45%	25%
5	Independence of mind (ie objectivity and integrity) is more important than independence in appearance (ie compliance with a checklist)	1%	91%

		Disagree	Agree
6	The role of independent NEDs is much more challenging now than it was three years ago	3%	88%
7	Institutional investors have too much influence over appointing independent NEDs	56%	8%
8	Independent NEDs do not devote enough time to their role in companies	46%	15%

Another 2004 survey[24] enquired about specific corporate governance contributions which non-executive directors make, again showing that non-executive directors are relied upon strongly in the area of corporate governance (Table 4).

Table 4

The effectiveness of independent directors

		Fully quoted			AIM/OFEX etc		
		Y	N	M	Y	N	M
Change under-performing directors?	%	80	4	16	72	14	14
Control directors' compensation?	%	87	7	6	77	10	13
Force a change of professional advisors?	%	80	4	16	65	11	24
Discuss concerns with shareholders?	%	75	10	15	74	7	19
Control a combined Chairman/ CEO?	%	82	9	9	72	15	13
Compliance with governance guidelines	%	96	1	3	85	10	5

Has corporate governance worked for the UK? C4.12

There has been speculation whether the Cadbury and post-Cadbury focus on the control side of governance has diverted boards' attentions away from direction and strategy. Many directors will concur with the sentiment that a greater proportion of their available time is now taken up with accountability, audit, risk management and control matters than was historically the case. In 1998, after six years of Cadbury, the Hampel Committee noted:

> 'The importance of corporate governance lies in its contribution both to business prosperity and to accountability. In the UK the latter has preoccupied much public debate over the past few years. We would wish to see the balance corrected.'[25]

If this has indeed diverted boards' attention away from direction and strategy – but to the relative benefit of control and oversight – then this could go some way to explaining the contention that the UK has largely avoided the spectacular corporate governance debacles of the US in recent years which on the whole have been a consequence of deficiencies of *control* and *oversight* rather than of direction and strategy.

Good corporate governance as a bulwark against management fraud C4.13

So, if corporate governance has worked well for the UK since 1992 it is likely, in part at least, to be the effect of non-executive directors. Prima facie, if good corporate governance makes it less likely that a company will collapse as a consequence of, for instance, dishonesty, then certainly the non-executive director as a contributor to good corporate governance, is adding value. In 1992 Cadbury memorably said that

> 'had a Code such as ours been in existence in the past, we believe that a number of the recent examples of unexpected company failures and cases of fraud would have received attention earlier. It must, however, be recognised that no system of control can eliminate the risk of fraud without so shackling companies as to impede their ability to compete in the market place.'

Cynics might counter by claiming, for instance, that audit committees are more likely to work well in companies that don't need them so much, and vice versa – but that is too simplistic. It is certainly much to be preferred for a well run company to establish its audit committee in good working order as a bulwark against future risks – for instance when the management team changes or when the company is finding it hard to turn in results up to market expectations. The audit committee can then serve the company well by deterring the company from sailing too close to the wind.

It was only in November 2003 that the US adopted their Mark I version[26] of the equivalent of the UK's code of best practice on corporate governance whereas the UK's 2010 Corporate Governance Code is our Mark VI version. So, has better corporate governance avoided the Polly Pecks and London & Commonwealths – both of which preceded Cadbury; or the Maxwells and BCCIs – which surfaced after the Cadbury Committee started its work in May 1991? Sir Adrian has pointed out that BCCI and Maxwell, especially Maxwell, widened the committee's remit beyond the 'financial aspects of corporate governance'[27] to how corporate governance worked more generally in the UK.

Failures of 'strategy', or failures of 'control'? C4.14

It is certainly true that our most spectacular recent debacle – Marconi – was more a failure of direction and strategy than of control. Were Marconi's non-executive directors asleep on their watch? Do boards let management steer the ship? Are non-executive directors effective at challenging the executive on strategy – to the point of putting their collective foot down? It would appear that they are at least sometimes better at taking the needed, drastic, remedial action when things have gone badly wrong than they are at preventing things going wrong in the first place. Or perhaps publicity is rarely made of the serious corporate debacles that non-executive directors have been instrumental in avoiding?

But there has been the Shell debacle – a matter of control and oversight failures rather than of wrong corporate direction and failed strategy. The collapses of Independent Insurance, and the Manchester-based Claims Direct, and the near-collapse of TeleWest were also more to do with failures of control than of strategy: they may not have been so high-profile as some of the US cases but then UK companies on average have lower market capitalisation. The higher you climb the further you fall. So, *has* our focus for a decade on corporate governance served us well enough to avoid the corporate debacles caused by deficient control?

Control and strategy inextricably linked C4.15

Even to discriminate between direction and control is perhaps superficial. As part of the board's direction role, the board must adopt appropriate board policies on risk and control – such as codes of business conduct and policies on risk management, whistleblowing, harassment, IT security – and so on. Conversely, policies and strategies themselves need to be developed in a well controlled way. So to attempt to separate the control side from the direction side doesn't entirely stack up. The two are the warp and the weft of the corporate governance tapestry: the one falls apart without the other.

Certainly there needs to be proper control over the development, adoption, implementation and review of strategy. COSO's new ERM study makes it clear that risk management should be applied to formulating strategy and to objective setting.

Drucker said:

> 'The main goal of a management science must be to enable business to take the right risk. Indeed, it must be to enable business to take greater risks – by providing knowledge and understanding of alternative risks and alternative expectations; by identifying the resources and efforts needed for desired results; by mobilizing energies for contribution; and by measuring results against expectations; thereby providing means for early correction of wrong or inadequate decisions. 'All this may sound like mere quibbling over terms. Yet the terminology of risk minimization does induce a hostility to risk-taking and risk-making – that is, to business enterprise.'[28]

and

> 'No entity operates in a risk-free environment, and enterprise risk management does not seek to move towards such an environment. Rather, enterprise risk management enables management to operate more effectively in environments filled with risk.'[29]

In my experience our current focus on risk management is seriously deficient in two respects and it is to be hoped that the current Turnbull review will address this.

First, risk management today focuses on downside risk – that is the identification of events which would be likely to have a negative impact on the business were they to occur, and so must be mitigated through carefully devised controls. There is little or no emphasis in our risk management on identifying future events which, if they occurred, would be worthwhile opportunities beyond the business plan if they could be exploited successfully – and thus deserve attention so as not to pass over these opportunities should they occur. What companies are doing is what Herbert Simon called 'satisficing' – being content with an outcome which achieves our plan, even though outcomes might have been significantly better than that. Secondly our risk management rarely considers that risk events are like London buses – they tend to come all at once. Companies tend to fail when they are hit on all sides at once. Our risk assessment tends to consider risks individually rather than assess the risk that several may impact simultaneously.

It would not be right to lay at the feet of non-executive directors the blame for any excessive concentration upon the control side of governance. There has been, and is, much else within our Codes of Best Practice on corporate governance which have laboured the control side – even apart from the enhanced role of the non-executive director. And the role of the non-executive director is to do with strategy as well as control.

Rewarding non-executive directors C4.16

By 1998 50% of directors of UK listed companies were by then non-executive directors, though not necessarily independent as is now 'required'. The average fee for a non-executive director of a large company with a turnover of more than £2bn was £27,800 in 1998 and the non-executive director of such a company devoted between 11 to 20 days each year to his or her duties.[30] The Tyson Report found that 2003 average annual non-executive director remuneration was about £44,500 for FTSE 100 firms, £34,800 for FTSE 250 firms, and £23,221 for other listed companies.

In 2004 two different surveys have indicated that UK non-executive directors of large companies devote between 28 and 43 days a year, including preparation time and 18 days a year for the smallest companies.[31, 32] The fee for a non-executive director of a company with a turnover of more than £1bn has risen to over £50,000 compared to less than £28,000 in 1998 for a company with a turnover then of £2bn.[33] The data shows that the *per diem* rates have barely changed whilst the time commitment has more than doubled, suggesting that further fee increases could be in the pipeline.[34, 35]

Even these enhanced fee levels are often proving unattractive in view of the risks that non-executive positions are perceived to have – at least by those favoured by companies for these positions who tend already to be quite well off. Korn-Ferry found that almost half of those approached had turned down a non-executive position within the past twelve months on account of it being too risky.

The Tyson Report pointed out:

> 'The perception of a possible conflict between NED compensation and NED independence may be a possible constraint on the selection of NED candidates

from non-traditional talent pools. … These are relatively small amounts compared to the annual compensation levels of chief executives, top-level management and other business professionals. But NED compensation levels may be quite large compared to the annual incomes of NED candidates drawn from non-traditional sources such as the non-commercial sector and academia. Institutional investors and other company stakeholders might wonder whether a NED can be truly independent if NED compensation represents a substantial fraction of his or her total annual income.'[36]

This quite controversial sentiment was shared by Derek Higgs:

'…it is important that a non-executive director is not so dependent on the income from their role or shareholding as to prejudice independence of judgement, and I would expect boards to take this into account in determining independence.'[37]

The seven specific criteria to be applied in determining independence were set out in detail for the first time in our Code[38] whereas formerly it was for the board to decide whether a non-executive director was 'independent of management and free from any business or other relationship which could materially interfere with the exercise of their independent judgement, apart from their fees and shareholding'.[39] Perhaps 'total income from all sources' should join 'aged over 70' in the trash can of independence criteria! Indeed, 'total income from all sources' gets no explicit mention amongst the seven independence criteria of the UK's new Combined Code.

Independence is still 'for the board to decide' but the board is now given more prescriptive guidance to assist it to decide. A Code-compliant board must also now explain its reasoning if it chooses to deviate from the independence criteria within the new Code.

It is at least as important for the board to determine whether a director is 'independent in character and judgement' (as our Code puts it) as to determine whether the seven specific independence criteria are met. For instance, a non-executive director may meet all the seven independence criteria but be unwilling or unable to 'master the brief' – in which case he or she will be dependent on explanations given by others and unable or disinclined to form an independent opinion.

Steadily increasing burden of compliance C4.17

The weight of our corporate governance requirements is progressively increasing. Table 5 summarises the extent to which adherence to UK corporate governance codes of best practice has become a more demanding business over the last decade or so.

Table 5

Number of Provisions and Principles in the UK Codes, over time

		Cadbury Code	**Greenbury Code**	**Combined Code**	**Revised Combined Code**	**UK Corporate Governance Code**	**UK Corporate Governance Code**	**UK Corporate Governance Code**
		1992	*1995*	*1998*	*2003, 06 & 08*	*2010*	*2011*	*2012*
Main Principles	General				14	18	18	18
	Addressed to institutional investors				3	0	0	0
	Total	0	0	0	17	18	18	18
Supporting Principles	General				21	24	25	28
	Addressed to institutional investors				5	0	0	0
	Total	0	0	0	26	24	25	28

Table 5 – *contd*

		Cadbury Code	**Greenbury Code**	**Combined Code**	**Revised Combined Code**	**UK Corporate Governance Code**	**UK Corporate Governance Code**	**UK Corporate Governance Code**
		1992	*1995*	*1998*	*2003, 06 & 08*	*2010*	*2011*	*2012*
Principles (Main and Supporting)	General			14	35	42	43	46
	Addressed to institutional investors			3	8	0**	0	0
	Total	0	0	17	43	42	43	46
Provisions	General	19	39	44*	48	52	52	53
	Addressed to institutional investors	0	0	3	0	0	0	0
	Total	19	39	47	48	52	52	53

* Excluding (a) the seven Schedule A Provisions on the design of performance related remuneration which were part of the *Combined Code* and (b) the seven Schedule B Provisions on what should be included in the Remuneration Report which are no longer in the *Code* but were made into separate regulations (The Directors' Remuneration Report Regulations 2002, S.I. no. 1986) and are now in the 2006 Companies Act.

** Excluding 3 Main and 3 Supporting Principles for Institutional Shareholders at Schedule C of the FRC's UK Corporate Governance Code publication (www.frc.org.uk) which have been superseded by the separate 2010 Stewardship Code.

Enhancing the part that non-executive directors play **C4.18**

The 1992 Cadbury Code, in 'requiring' that listed companies' audit committees comprised at least three non-executive directors,[40] was working in part to a hidden agenda – to ensure that boards had a significant element of non-executive membership. The Cadbury Code also 'required' that board remuneration committees should be made up wholly or mainly of non-executive directors.[41] The 1998 Combined Code turned the screw a bit tighter by 'requiring' that a majority of the non-executive audit committee members should also be independent[42] and that all members of the remuneration committee should be independent directors.[43] The screw was tightened still further commencing with the 2003 Code which 'requires' that *every* member of the audit committee should be an independent director,[44] and indeed that

> 'at least half the board, excluding the chairman, should comprise non-executive directors determined by the board to be independent'.[45]

The 1998 Code had just 'required' that at least one third of the board should be non-executive and the majority of those were to be independent.[46]

To intimate that our Code 'requires' something, warrants clarification: the 2003 Combined Code has 'Main Principles' and 'Supporting Principles' and a listing rule states that a company should explain how it applies both of these. It might be forgivable to assume therefore that they are intended to be mandatory – especially so as there are also 'provisions' which have a 'comply or explain' status. But the FSA, the enforcer of the listing rules, has never enforced a Principle upon a company. The FSA leaves it to the market to enforce. The FSA sees its enforcement role here as being to enforce *disclosure* rather than enforce *observance*. So if a company reports that it applies a Principle by ignoring it – that seems to be acceptable to the FSA.

Senior independent directors **C4.19**

The tightening of the defined roles of non-executive and independent directors has been accompanied by a similar progressive tightening in regard to the role of the senior independent director. The Cadbury Code[47] just required there to be a 'recognised senior [independent] member' when the chairman was also the chief executive. The 1998 Code[48] stipulated that *all* listed companies should have such a member who (as with the other independent directors)[49] was to be identified in the annual report. The 2003 Code went further (though not quite as far as Higgs proposed) by spelling out specific new duties for the senior independent director who should:

- Lead the other non-executive directors in a meeting, at least annually, to appraise the chairman's performance, and on such other occasions as are deemed appropriate[50] taking into account the views of the executive directors.[51]
- Be available to shareholders if they have concerns which contact through the normal channels of chairman, chief executive or finance director has failed to resolve or for which such contact is inappropriate.[52]
- Maintain sufficient contact with major shareholders to understand their issues and concerns,[53] attending sufficient meetings with a range of major shareholders to listen to their views in order to help develop a balanced understanding of the issues and concerns of major shareholders.[54]

In this area there has therefore been only a modest drawing back from Higgs proposals. Higgs proposed that the non-executive directors should meet *regularly* as a group without the executives present (and at least once a year without the chairman) and that the senior independent director should chair these meetings.[55] Higgs also proposed that the new Code should include an obligation for the senior independent director to communicate shareholders' views to the non-executive directors and, as appropriate, to the board as a whole.[56] Higgs further proposed that the chairman, while being a likely member, should not chair the nomination committee[57] but the Code allows that he or she might – except when it is dealing with the appointment of a successor to the chairmanship.[58]

So do non-executive directors improve company performance? C4.20

There may be no research proving unequivocally that non-executive directors lead to better company performance. It would be hard to demonstrate this. It may be that successful companies are better placed to invest time and other resources in improving their corporate governance – so if it were shown that good corporate governance is found in better performing companies, this would not necessarily mean that good corporate governance contributes to better performance. Based on the performance of 134 listed companies in 1997, 1998, 1999 and 2000, two researchers at Henley Management College found no relationship between company performance and (a) the proportion of non-executive directors, (b) the tenure of non-executive directors, or (c) the existence of audit and remuneration committees.[59] But the researchers were looking for differences in performance depending upon the proportion of the board which was non-executive (whether 33% or 50%): even if non-executive directors *do* result in better performance this would be unlikely to be so finely tuned to whether one third or one half of the board is non-executive.

It is much safer ground to assert that non-executive directors add value in providing oversight of management with respect to the accountability, control and corporate governance aspects of best board practice. Cars have brakes so that they can go faster. Again, this is hard to measure as there is likely to be no public awareness of most major or minor disasters that non-executive directors are instrumental in avoiding – only those which they fail to prevent, which one has to say, are not infrequent!

After pressure from their group audit committee, in January 2004, Shell reclassified as 'provable' rather than 'proven' its oil and gas reserves by 20% (3.9 billion barrels) and several further downwards adjustments have since been made. These led to the departure in March 2004 of its two most senior executives – the chief executive and the director of exploration and production. Shell's audit committee commissioned a review from Davis Polk & Wardwell, an American law firm leading to a 400 page report by the group audit committee to the board and resulting straightaway in the resignation of Shell's chief financial officer.

Shell's director of exploration claimed in March 2004 that he could not have bypassed the chief executive to take his concerns over reserving to the board or to the audit committee. He said:

'Because the unspoken rule within the company is that you are not supposed to go directly to individual board members or the group audit committee. I had to rely on the [chief executive] and chief financial officer to advise the group audit committee and assumed that happened in early December [2003].'[60]

However, at the end of April 2004, John Hoftmeister, Shell's director of human resources, reinforced the prevailing Shell board view that there was nothing wrong with Shell's unusual corporate structure, when he said:

'The way our processes are set up, it should have gone through audit, human resources or the non-executive function.

'It is our desire and intent that all Shell staff speak their mind on any issue that concerns them at any level if the Shell organization. HR processes ere intact and available for anyone to use.'[61]

Nevertheless, Shell has since announced a radical restructuring of their corporate governance.

It was also revealed in April 2004 that Shell's internal auditors had been aware of the reserves problem since February 2002.[62]

Criminal sanctions apply to Section 302 of the 2002 Sarbanes-Oxley Act and fines may be as much as $5m each as well as 10 years in jail for knowingly filed false accounts. Several directors signed Shell's annual report in the US for 2003. They each said:

'Based on my knowledge, this annual report does not … omit to state a material fact necessary to make the statements … not misleading.'

The Sarbanes-Oxley Act also requires the directors to disclose 'all significant deficiencies in the … operation of internal controls' and 'any fraud' – and they also certified to that.

Note that:

- The suggestion that an executive director did not consider he had the authority to take a matter directly to the board or to the group audit committee is astonishing; yet how often is it the case that junior, middle and even senior executives consider they cannot make waves with the chief executive?
- There is the question as to what internal audit did with the information they had since February 2002, and whether they also allowed their reports to the group audit committee to be influenced, against their best professional judgement, by senior executives.
- The independent element on the board influenced the investigation into oil reserves and the initial restatement downwards.
- The independent element on the board was able to ensure that appropriate top executive changes were made.
- The independent element on the board was able to ensure that investigations were made which were independent of the executive, including the retention by the audit committee of outside consultants.
- The independent element on the board has been instrumental in forcing through future changes in company structure/corporate governance arrangements.
- *But* the independent element on the board was unsuccessful in preventing these problems in the first place, or preventing their escalation into major problems.

Non-executive director impact on share price C4.21

Clearly, an important measure of success of any listed company is its share price. In this respect the presence of non-executive directors is often seen as an important element of good corporate governance. A 2002 global survey by McKinsey[63] found very strong evidence of investor willingness to pay a premium for shares in well-governed companies. That this willingness had diminished very slightly between 2000 and 2002 was probably a consequence of the bounce back of the 'Tiger economies' after their 1999 collapse.

> 'Corporate governance lies at the heart of prospects for growth and development, and will be a key determinant of a country's success. It's very simple, if you think someone is dishonest and not telling the truth, you don't give them the money. It's not a question of people, it's a question of intelligence. If you think someone is being honest, and is giving you a fair shake, a fair return, you do business with them.'[64]

and:

> 'If a country does not have a reputation for strong corporate governance practices, capital will flow elsewhere. If investors are not confident with the level of disclosure, capital will flow elsewhere. If a country opts for lax accounting and reporting standards, capital will flow elsewhere. All enterprises in that country – regardless of how steadfast a particular company's practices may be – suffer the consequences. Markets must now honour what they perhaps, too often, have failed to recognise. Markets exist by the grace of investors. And it is today's more empowered investors who will determine which companies and which markets will stand the test of time and endure the weight of greater competition. It serves us well to remember that no market has a divine right to investors' capital.'[65]

As the World Bank has said, now that more than 50% of the largest economies in the world are companies, not countries:[66]

> 'The proper governance of companies will become as crucial to the world economies as the proper governing of countries.'

Those charged with governance should not exclusively be those charged with management. Non-executive directors are a small price to pay to achieve some clarity in the distinction between management and the board.

Notes

1 The Combined Code on Corporate Governance, (July 2003), Supporting Principle A.1.

2 Section A.6 of the 2003 Code reads:

> **'A.6 Performance evaluation**
>
> **Main Principle**
>
> **The board should undertake a formal and rigorous annual evaluation of its own performance and that of its committees and individual directors.**
>
> **Supporting Principle**
>
> Individual evaluation should aim to show whether each director continues to contribute effectively and to demonstrate commitment to the role (including commitment of time for board and committee meetings and any other duties). The

chairman should act on the results of the performance evaluation by recognising the strengths and addressing the weaknesses of the board and, where appropriate, proposing new members be appointed to the board or seeking the resignation of directors.

Code Provision

A.6.1 The board should state in the annual report how performance evaluation of the board, its committees and its individual directors has been conducted. The non-executive directors, led by the senior independent director, should be responsible for performance evaluation of the chairman, taking into account the views of executive directors.'

3 Higgs, Derek, (January 2003): *Review of the role and effectiveness of non-executive directors* ('The Higgs Report'), DTI, Room 507, 1 Victoria Street, London, SW1H 0ET, Tel.: 020 7215 0409, www.dti.gov.uk/cld/non_exec_review.

4 Report of the Committee on the Financial Aspects of Corporate Governance ('The Cadbury Report') (December 1992).

5 Committee on Corporate Governance – The Combined Code, (June 1998), Gee Publishing, London, ISBN 1 86089 036 9.

6 The Korn/Ferry Boardroom Britain survey 2004, www.kornferry.com, p 4.

7 Supporting Principle A.3: 'The board should not be so large as to be unwieldy. …'

8 Jay A. Conger and Edward Lawler III, (2001) 'Building a High-Performing Board: How to Choose the Right Members,' *London Business School Business Strategy Review*, 2001, Volume 12.

9 The Tyson Report on the Recruitment and Development of Non-Executive Directors, (June 2003), A report commissioned by the Department of Trade & Industry following the publication of the Higgs Review of the Role and Effectiveness of Non-Executive Directors in January 2003.

10 Supporting Principle A.3.

11 Alan Greenspan, (2003): testimony to the US Congress, 2003.

12 The Combined Code on Corporate Governance, (July 2003), Main and Supporting Principles A.3 [The Financial Reporting Council, www.frc.org.uk/publications].

13 As our 2003 Code puts it with respect to the chairman's role.

14 The Combined Code, (July 2003), Main and Supporting Principles A.2 and Provisions A.2.1 and A.2.2.

15 Report of the Committee on the Financial Aspects of Corporate Governance ('The Cadbury Report') (December 1992), §2.5.

16 'The Cadbury Report', (1992), §4.10.

17 'The Cadbury Report', (1992), Provision 2.1 within the Cadbury 'Code of Best Practice'.

18 Committee on Corporate Governance: Final Report ('The Hampel Report') (January 1998), §3.8.

19 *Financial Times*, (13 August 2002), 'Companies still prefer to have a lord on the board', p 3.

20 *Financial Times*, (13 August 2002), 'Editorial', p 16.

21 David Deakins, Patrick Mileham and Eileen O'Neill, (1999): *Director or Mentor? The role of non-executive directors in the growth process of SMEs and comparisons with the role of mentors* (Certified Accountants Educational Trust).

22 Aiden Berry and Lew Perren, (2000), *The role of non-executive directors in United Kingdom SMEs* (Certified Accountants Educational Trust).

23 Paul Moxey, (November 2004): 'Corporate Governance and Wealth Creation'. The Association of Chartered Certified Accountants, ACCA Occasional Research paper No. 37, ISBN 1 85908 411 7, published by the Certified Accountants Educational Trust. Respondents were asked to indicate on a Likert scale of 1 to 5 their agreement or disagreement with 8 statements about non-executive directors where 1 is disagree strongly and 5 is agree strongly. All 91 respondents answered this question with the

following result. 'Agree' are those who scored '1' or '2'; 'Disagree' are those who scored '4' or '5'.

24 'Effectiveness of independent directors' (The Independent Director Survey), (2004), IRS with 3i, www.independentremuneration.co.uk, p 7.

25 'The Hampel Report', (1998), §1.1.

26 The New York Stock Exchange's corporate governance rules (often referred to by NYSE as 'standards') were finally approved by the SEC on November 4, 2003 – other than Section 303A.08 (on Shareholder Approval of Equity Compensation Plans), which had been approved by the SEC on June 30, 2003. These final rules have been codified in Section 303A of the NYSE's Listed Company Manual and can be downloaded from www.nyse.com.

27 Which was the formal title of the Cadbury Committee.

28 Drucker, P.F., (1977): *Management: Tasks, Responsibilities, Practices*, [1979 Pan UK edition, ISBN: 0 330 25638 6, p 433].

29 COSO ERM Executive Summary, p 2.

30 Joint Survey by Egon Zehnder International and ICAEW, (1998), reviewed in *Accountancy Age*, (5 November 1998, p 13).

31 (The Independent Director Survey (2004): IRS with 3i; www.independentremuneration.co.uk, p 7.

32 30th Korn/Ferry Annual Board of Directors Study (2003).

33 'The Tyson Report', p 16.

34 (The Independent Director Survey (2004): IRS with 3i; www.independentremuneration.co.uk, p 7.

35 30th Korn/Ferry Annual Board of Directors Study (2003).

36 'The Tyson Report', p 16.

37 'The Higgs Report', §9.14

38 Provision A.3.1.

39 Cadbury Code Provision 2.2. Similar wording was carried forward largely unchanged into the 1998 Combined Code (Provision A.3.2: 'The majority of non-executive directors should be independent of management and free from any business or other relationship which could materially interfere with the exercise of their independent judgement.') and into the 2003 Code (Provision A.3.1: 'The board should determine whether the director is independent in character and judgement and whether there are relationships or circumstances which are likely to affect, or could appear to affect, the director's judgement.').

40 Provision 4.3.

41 Provision 3.3.

42 Provision D.3.1.

43 Provision B.2.1.

44 Provision C.3.1.

45 The Combined Code on Corporate Governance, (July 2003), Provision A.3.2 – which goes on to say 'A smaller company should have at least two independent non-executive directors'. Consistent with this is that the Code allows the audit committee of a smaller company to comprise just two members (Provision C.3.1). Note that a 'smaller company' is one outside the FTSE 350 throughout the year immediately prior to the reporting year.

46 Provisions A.3.1 and A.3.2.

47 Provision 1.2.

48 Provision A.2.1.

49 Provision A.3.2.

50 Provision A.1.3.

51 Provision A.6.1.

52 Provision A.3.3.

53 Supporting Principle D.1.

54 Provision D.1.1.

55 Review of the role and effectiveness of non-executive directors ('The Higgs Report') (January 2003), proposed Provision A.1.5 (p 80).

56 Proposed Provision C.1.2 (p 88).

57 Proposed Provision A.4.1 (p 82).

58 Provision A.4.1.

59 Dulewicz, V and P. Herbert, (2003): 'Does the composition and practice of UK boards bear any relationship to the performance of listed companies?', Henley Management College Working Paper No. 0304. ISBN 1 86181 158 6.

60 *Financial Times*, (29 April 2004), 'Shell 'had systems in place' to hear fears over reserves', p 21.

61 *Financial Times*, (29 April 2004), 'Shell 'had systems in place' to hear fears over reserves', p 21.

62 Financial Times, (29 April 2004), 'Shell 'had systems in place' to hear fears over reserves', p 21.

63 McKinsey Global Investor Opinion Survey on Corporate Governance, 2002.

64 President of the World Bank, 2002 or 2003.

65 Arthur Levitt, former Chairperson of the US Securities and Exchange Commission, in December 2000 at a Manhattan conference sponsored by the Federal Reserve.

66 According to the United Nations Conference on Trade and Development, measured on the basis of value-added – the yardstick used to calculate countries' gross domestic product – the activities of the largest 100 companies accounted for 4.3% of world GDP in 2000, up from 3.5% in 1999. On that basis 29 of the world's biggest economic entities were then companies. Exxon, with an estimated value-added of £40bn at that time was larger than all but 44 national economies and the same size as Pakistan. Ford, DaimlerChrysler, General Electric and Toyota were comparable in size with Nigeria. Value-added can be construed as corresponding most closely to the GDP calculation. [See Guy Jonquières, (13 August 2002), 'Companies "bigger than many nations"', *Financial Times*, p 7; see also www.unctad.org.]

Chapter C5

Corporate Social Responsibility, Integrated Reporting and Sustainability

'Capitalism needs financial stability and sustainability to succeed. Integrated reporting will underpin them both, leading to a more resilient global economy.'

Jane Diplock, former Chairman, The International Organisation of Securities Commissions

'Integrated Reporting is a process founded on integrated thinking that results in a periodic integrated report by an organization about value creation over time and related communications regarding aspects of value creation.

An integrated report is a concise communication about how an organization's strategy, governance, performance and prospects, in the context of its external environment, lead to the creation of value in the short, medium and long term.'

International Integrated Reporting Council (IIRC) (http://www.theiirc.org/)

'Integrated Reporting builds on the practice of financial reporting, and environmental, social and governance reporting. It equips companies to manage their operations, brand and reputation strategically and to manage better any risks that may compromise the long-term sustainability of the business.'[1]

Professor Mervyn King, Chairman, IIRC and Chairman for the King Committee on Corporate Governance

Conventional paradigms of corporate social responsibility C5.1

Conventional paradigms of corporate social responsibility (CSR) are passé. How can this be? CSR implies overlaying an acceptance that businesses may draw unsustainably upon natural and social capital to deliver their profits through their core activities, supplemented by a sort of band-aid, piecemeal effort to demonstrate some responsibility.

A new approach would be to realise that, ultimately, business models are unsustainable unless they use resources which can be sustained and prevent themselves from overstepping environmental limits and causing social problems. Bottom line profits of corporations have not reflected the true social and environmental costs associated with running the business, as the corporation has not had to meet the full extent of these costs. Now, providing solutions to the problems we face is a massive opportunity for business. So – out with CSR as a band-aid, and in with 'sustainable business'. Jonathon Porritt, in his book *Capitalism as if the World Matters* (Porritt, 2005, ch 14), uses the 'band-aid' analogy and alludes to:

> 'the seductive illusion of CSR'.

He suggests that much, though by no means all, of conventional CSR toys around with the gap between regulatory minima, and genuine sustainability. He suggests (at p 242, end) that corporate responsibility or corporate social responsibility will only allow organisations:

> 'to reach the first base camp along the road to sustainability.'

Forum for the Future prefers to talk about 'sustainable business' as the end goal and 'sustainable development' as the process by which we get there. They too distinguish between CSR and sustainable development, characterising CSR as more of a band-aid approach and thus intrinsically inadequate (Draper, Hanson, Uren, 2006, p 6):

Corporate social responsibility:

- focuses on current 'issues';
- is reactive, reputation-driven;
- has limited reach into core business;
- tends to neglect strategic opportunities;
- tends to avoid material issues by diverting focus onto non-material areas.

Sustainable development:

- is about long-term continuity of global society;
- allows integrated approaches to social, environmental; and economic issues;
- business is a key actor (as well as government and civil society);
- will shape the future of the global economy;
- can offer insights to underpin the future viability of business models;
- provides context to examine inherent sustainability of products and services.

Similar arguments were made by a further research study (Spence and Gray, 2007). Their thesis is that almost all corporate social/environmental activity is conducted because it fits within the organisations' concept of 'the business case' – and if a proposed action does not fit, then it will not be undertaken. Thus there are important limits to corporate action – and although this should not detract from the 'goodness' of some of the things that businesses may decide to do, it means that there is usually no properly articulated link to the broader sustainability imperative; and thus real transformational steps are not taken.

Means deployed by businesses C5.2

The means that businesses may deploy to legitimately fulfil their purposes, for instance to maximise financial return to their owners, are being progressively curtailed. More and more of the means employed in the past are now perceived as being exploitive and are thus being challenged. Milton Friedman (1982), that arch doyen of the free market, famously claimed that:

> 'There is one and only one social responsibility of business – to use its resources and engage in activities designed to increase its profits'.

But even he added with his next breath:

> 'so long as it stays within the rules of the game …'[2]

Friedman's view is not a view that Cadbury (2006) shares. Cadbury says:

> 'the argument that all publicly-quoted companies should focus solely on making as much money for their shareholders as possible fails, because not all shareholders share the same aims and the aims of at least some of them will include social as well as financial considerations'.

Note that Cadbury is here presuming that it is the owners of the business who should determine its purpose(s) rather than any broader constituency of stakeholders, and also not the board of directors.

The 'rules of the game' are progressively and unremittingly being extended. Indeed companies themselves would argue that a prerequisite for truly responsible behaviour must be for laws and regulations to create a level playing field which is applied fairly to all entities in competition with each other. *Reductio ab absurdum*, harmonisation eliminates competition, depriving society of the economic advantages that flow from enhanced competition. If we harmonise taxes, state aid, working hours, greenhouse emissions, human rights, data protection, privacy rights, corporate governance and so on, we may achieve a level playing field but, in effect, the opportunities for one team to play better than another team have been eliminated largely. Have we destroyed the means of achieving competitive advantage and thus of increasing the productivity of capital and labour? If we are left only with competition between brands, then we might expect that the tyranny of brands will also lead to brand regulation. The rules of the game are not just being progressively extended to regulate further the exploitive character of corporate inputs – such as workers and raw materials – processes and outputs – such as emissions. The rules of the game regulate competition between brands – evidenced by the concerns about Tesco's dominance; and the rules of the game even extend to the regulation of profits themselves – evidenced by the concern about levels of taxation applying to, for instance, private equity and multinational internet businesses. It would seem that wherever there is an opportunity to compete profitably, it may be only a matter of time before that door is closed. Is this why CSR is being described as the new communism?

Exploitation is unavoidable, even desirable **C5.3**

A fourth contention is that exploitation is unavoidable, even desirable. Looking at things holistically, profit may always be regarded as the result of exploitation – exploitive of the environment, of the community, of staff, of customers, of shareholders – and so on. Someone has gained at someone else's expense. In many respects it is a zero sum game. Companies may compete on the quality of their innovation, but that only runs into superior profit when they induce customers to pay over the odds for those products or services.

Is profit always exploitive? Profit depends upon a positive margin between costs and income. That margin can only be achieved by containing costs and/or by achieving sales revenues so that the former is less than the latter. Companies that make impressive, increasing profits are either bearing down on costs or ratcheting up sales revenues, or both. This represents a transfer of resources to the company from suppliers or from customers or from both – and the bigger the profits, the bigger the transfer. Arguably there is a level at which the transfer – from suppliers or customers – becomes exploitive of suppliers or customers, or both. In a genuinely free and competitive market we could argue that the market would curtail transfers of resources at levels that could be characterised as excessive, or exploitive. But the market is neither sufficiently free nor sufficiently competitive to achieve that. While a genuinely free and competitive global market might avoid gross exploitation of the supply of labour, it cannot be relied upon to avoid gross exploitation of natural resources: many companies achieve their profits by acquiring natural resources at low price, or returning to the environment their effluent at less than the cost to the planet.

Aversion to risk taking **C5.4**

There can be unintended consequences of regulation and more and more regulation means more and more unintended consequences. The rise of a compensation culture (which may or may not be a good thing) leads to an aversion to taking so much risk. Aversion to risk taking is an undesirable consequence of more regulation.

Tony Blair (2005) quite recently had this to say (and I quote at some length):

> 'Public bodies, in fear of litigation, act in highly risk-averse and peculiar ways. We have had a local authority removing hanging baskets for fear that they might fall on someone's head, even though no such accident had occurred in the 18 years they had been hanging there. A village in the Cotswolds was required to pull up a seesaw because it was judged a danger under an EU Directive on Playground Equipment for Outside Use. This was despite the fact that no accidents had occurred on it.
>
> And in case we think we alone are subject to this, countless examples can be found even in the most 'open market' economies. The response of the US Congress to the Enron and Worldcom scandals shows what governments can do wrong. In 2002 the Sarbanes-Oxley Act was, in the words of The Economist, 'designed in a panic and rushed through in a blinding fervour of moral indignation.
>
> The point about Sarbanes-Oxley was not that the underlying problems it was addressing were not real. It was quite right to put some distance between a company's auditors and its managers, between whom a severe conflict of interest had arisen. The problem was that the Act was not limited to the remedy of that specific defect.
>
> Inspired by the need for Congress to be seen to do something dramatic, Sarbanes-Oxley has imposed the threat of criminal penalties on managers and substantial new costs on American business: an average of \$2.4m extra for auditing for each company. The burden is especially heavy on smaller companies, the real risk-takers in the market. Firms with a revenue of less than \$100m per annum now pay out more than 2.5% of turnover in compliance costs. Cumulatively the costs run into billions of dollars.

There is a delicious irony in this which illustrates the unintended consequences of regulation. Sarbanes-Oxley has provided a bonanza for accountants and auditors, the very professions thought to be at fault in the original scandals.'

With regard to 'risk', profit is the reward for taking risk. Drucker (1977) said:

> 'The main goal of management science must be to enable business to take the right risk. Indeed, it must be to enable business to take greater risks – by providing knowledge and understanding of alternative risks and alternative expectations; by identifying the resources and efforts needed for desired results; by mobilizing energies for contribution; and by measuring results against expectations; thereby providing means for early correction of wrong or inadequate decisions. All this may sound like mere quibbling over terms. Yet the terminology of risk minimization does induce a hostility to risk-taking and risk-making – that is, to business enterprise.'

But COSO (2004) takes a different view:

> 'No entity operates in a risk-free environment, and enterprise risk management does not seek to move towards such an environment. Rather, enterprise risk management enables management to operate more effectively in environments filled with risk.'

Necessity for laws and regulations **C5.5**

A further contention is that, of course, laws and regulations are often necessary to engender responsible behaviour by companies. For instance, where the opinions of owners cannot make themselves sufficiently felt, the gap needs to be filled by law and regulation (Cadbury, 1998). Of course, the issue arises as to whose opinions should be influential upon the conduct of a business. The Anglo-Saxon capital markets model stresses the need for a free market in capital and the primacy of the shareholders to control the businesses they own. The European social market model gives a role to other stakeholders to exercise control. The Companies Act 2006 moves the UK a little towards this European model. For the first time we have a codified statement of directors' general duties,[3] to replace the previous common law approach which drew upon the responsibilities of trustees in order to determine the responsibilities of directors. The second of the seven given responsibilities of directors, under the 2006 Act, is to promote the success of the company for the benefit of its members as a whole, and in doing so have regard (*inter alia*) to specified matters which are set out as being to have regard to:

- the longer term;
- the interests of the company's employees;
- the need to foster the company's business relationships with suppliers, customers and others;
- the environment;
- the impact of operations on the wider community;
- the desirability of the company maintaining a reputation for high standards of business conduct and the need to act fairly between members of the company;
- (not exhaustive).

But this is a single duty rather than separate duties in relation to each of the parties listed.

The operational and financial review (OFR) C5.6

In November 2005, Gordon Brown, then UK Chancellor, dropped the new statutory operational and financial review (OFR) statutory regulations which had been intended to take effect for financial years beginning on or after 1 April 2005. He dropped them arguing that they would have amounted to gold-plating European directives. EC Fourth and Seventh Directives require all companies other than small ones to publish a business review. The UK Government had given the Accounting Standards Board (ASB) of the Financial Reporting Council the statutory power to make reporting standards for OFR which had led to a highly acclaimed Standard being published in final form in January 2006,[4] having appeared first in draft in May 2005. UK businesses had been gearing up to implement OFR when the requirement was suddenly dropped. It is interesting to recall that there was widespread disappointment that the requirement was abandoned.

The requirement for companies to publish a business review is within the newly amended Fourth and Seventh Directives and is now reflected in the Companies Act 2006. Although the requirements of the business review are not so demanding as the requirements of the OFR would have been, the business review covers all companies except small ones,[5] whereas the OFR would have applied only to quoted companies.

The overriding purpose of the business review is to help shareholders assess how the directors have performed their new fundamental statutory duty to promote the success of the company. All companies other than small ones must give a 'balanced and comprehensive analysis' of the development and performance of the company's business and of its position at the end of the year *and must describe the principal risks and uncertainties facing the business*.

The business review requirements are extended for quoted companies who must disclose information about environmental, employee, social and community matters ('to the extent necessary for shareholders to understand the development, performance and position of the business') and to disclose the main trends and factors likely to affect the future development and performance of the business.

Responsibilities and accountabilities C5.7

The next contention is that where there are responsibilities there should be matching accountability obligations – otherwise irresponsibility, neglect and even corruption will tend to creep in over time. Thus, there is also a need for audit.

> 'Without audit, no accountability; without accountability, no control; and if there is no control, where is the seat of power? … great issues often come to light only because of scrupulous verification of details.'[6]

(I am not entirely convinced that accountants and auditors are rising to this challenge, an issue I intend to revert to later.)

Cadbury (2006) recently took a similar view:

'if shareholders, employees and the public are to be able to assess how far companies take social issues into account, they need detailed information about the ways in which companies arrive at their decisions over the allocation of their resources between competing interests and about the policies which guide them in so doing.'

Along similar lines Cadbury (1998) had earlier pointed out:

'Disclosure is the lifeblood of governance. … Openness by companies is the basis of public confidence in the corporate system and enables external governance forces to function as they should. … Provided those with interests in, or responsibilities to, companies know how they are directed and controlled they can influence boards constructively. Investors, lenders, employees and the public can only play their governance roles provided they have the information.'

In an increasingly complex society there are more responsibilities, more accountability and a pervasive requirement for assurance by audit. Audit is a *sine qua non* of social responsibility, an insight memorably captured by Professor Power of LSE in his seminal book *The Audit Society* (Power, 1997) and more recently in *Assurance of Performance* (Chambers, 2006). We should not underestimate the importance of audit to provide assurance of performance.

Does socially responsible behaviour improve performance? C5.8

A final contention is that socially responsible behaviour, whether it is behaviour that is sustainable or whether it is the application of high standards of corporate governance in general, does not necessarily improve the performance of companies as we measure it today. The idea that CSR is in the enlightened self interest of the company and adds to the profit bottom line is only 'sustainable' (if I may use that word) if it is the 'band-aid' type of CSR – the sort of CSR which is embarked upon for PR reasons and would not be embarked upon if it impacted negatively on bottom line economic performance. So we need to devise new ways to measure performance. A key question is whether accountants and auditors can step up to the challenge or will they cede the future to others?

The trouble is that companies do not survive on noble aspirations. They survive only if they have money in the bank. Socially responsible, alternative means of measuring performance may indicate that a company is remarkably successful in CSR terms while the company may be sliding down the slippery slope to liquidation. Alternative means of measuring company performance need to be attuned to market forces. The market in carbon credits is an example of this. Socially responsible corporate behaviour represents an on-cost and the logic is that this inevitably means that more companies will fail. To plagiarise a Thatcherism, perhaps those are not real jobs anyway?

Integrated reporting C5.9

Established in 2009, the International Integrated Reporting Council (IIRC) is sponsored and supported by large companies and professional bodies. IIRC's chairman is Professor Mervyn King, intimately associated with the South African

King Report on Governance[6] which has led the way in developing approaches to sustainability reporting for companies, and where integrated reporting has been mandatory since 2010–11.

The IIRC's work is the latest attempt to promote CSR reporting. The lack of traction achieved by many previous attempts does not auger well for this latest attempt. Following their consultation draft[7], the IIRC published their framework in December 2013[8]. We summarise later the main recommendations of the IIRC.

Early social audit initiatives C5.10

Early attempts date back to the 1970s, notably the work of Humble and others on social auditing[9, 10]. At that time Lessem had suggested a means of integrating CSR results into the double entry bookkeeping system and into the financial statements themselves[11]. IIRC is not suggesting that style of integration.

EC Directives and UK company law requirements C5.11

The EC requirement for a published business review was incorporated into UK law in s 417 of the Companies Act 2006. The requirement to publish a business review is extended for quoted companies. The business review of all companies, other than small ones, must give a balanced and comprehensive analysis of the development and performance of the company's business and of its position at the end of the year, describing the principal risks and uncertainties facing the business. The EC business review requirements are extended for quoted companies to include disclosure of information about environmental, employee, social and community matters ('to the extent necessary for shareholders to understand the development, performance and position of the business'), and to include the main trends and factors likely to affect the future development and performance of the business.

The Companies Act 2006 includes 'safe harbour' protection covering information in directors' reports and directors' remuneration reports. The business review, as part of the director's report is therefore covered by 'safe harbour' provisions. A director will be liable in relation only to statements that have proved untrue/misleading on a knowingly/recklessly basis, or if the director knew that an omission was a dishonest concealment. The aim of the 2006 Act here is to exclude the courts from developing a common law approach to directors' liability that goes any further than this statutory instrument. The overriding purpose is to help shareholders assess how the directors have performed their new fundamental statutory duty to promote the success of the company.

In addition, the 2006 Act for the first time codified the seven general duties of directors which had previously been based only on common law interpreted by case law. The second duty, described in s 172, known as the 'enlightened shareholder value duty' is particularly relevant to sustainability and integrated reporting. Under this duty, a director *has a duty to the company* to 'act in the way he considers, in good faith, would be most likely to promote the success of the company for the benefit of the members as a whole [i.e. shareholders].' This broadly replaces the previous fiduciary duty to act in the company's best interests. In acting to promote the success of the company for the benefit of the members as a whole, a director is required to have regard to:

- the longer term;
- the interests of the company's employees;
- the need to foster the company's business relationships with suppliers, customers and others;
- the environment;
- the impact of operations on the wider community;
- the desirability of the company maintaining a reputation for high standards of business conduct and the need to act fairly between members of the company.

This is not intended to be an exhaustive list. It introduces new new social responsibility factors, although the requirement to have regard to the interests of the company's employees dates back to the Companies Act 1985. The requirement for a director to have regard to these matters is a single duty rather than separate duties in relation to each of the parties listed.

The 2006 Companies Act also includes at ss 260–264 a statutory derivative action procedure, being a new statutory basis for a shareholder to take action against directors by means of the new extended right for shareholders to sue directors. The codified 'derivative claims' provisions make the criteria and procedure for minority shareholders to make a claim in the name of the company clearer, but includes protections to ensure that unmeritorious suits are quickly dismissed with costs falling to the person bringing the claim.' Protections include that before the shareholder(s) is allowed to proceed with an action the shareholder(s) will be required first to establish a prima facie case of breach and, second, to satisfy the court that the alleged conduct was inconsistent with the director's fundamental duty to act in a way which 'promotes the success of his company'. In addition, the court will be expected to take into account whether the petitioning shareholder(s) is acting in good faith, whether the conduct has been authorised or ratified by the company and any views expressed by 'independent' shareholders. A director will only be liable to the company (or its shareholders on behalf of the company) if the company can demonstrate that it has suffered loss as a result of the breach.

The directors' report in the annual report and accounts does not need to contain a business review if the company is 'subject to the small company's regime'. The small companies regime applies to a company for a financial year in relation to which the company qualifies as small and is not excluded from the regime under s 384 of the Companies Act 2006. However, the shareholders of a small company can choose to insist that the company does not avail itself of the dispensations that may apply. For instance, small companies need not have an annual audit, but the shareholders can insist that it does.

Main recommendations of IIRC **C5.12**

IIRC regards its fundamental concepts as being six 'capitals' – financial, manufactured, intellectual, human, social and relationship, and natural.

The IIRC proposes that an integrated report should answer the following questions:

- Organisational overview and external environment:
  What does the organisation do and what are the circumstances under which it operates?
- Governance:
  How does the organisation's governance structure support its ability to create value in the short, medium and long term?
- Opportunities and risks:
  What are the specific opportunities and risks that affect the organisation's ability to create value over the short, medium and long term and how is the organisation dealing with them?
- Strategy and resource allocation:
  Where does the organisation want to go and how does it intend to get there?
- Business model:
  What is the organisation's business model and to what extent is it resilient?
- Performance:
  To what extent has the organisation achieved its strategic objectives and what are its outcomes in terms of effects on the capitals?
- Future outlook:
  What challenges and uncertainties is the organisation likely to encounter in pursuing its strategy, and what are the potential implications for its business model and its future performance?

IIRC further proposes that the organisation should identify and disclose:

1. the organisation's materiality determination process;
2. the reporting boundary and how it has been determined;
3. the governance body with oversight responsibilities for integrated reporting;
4. the nature and magnitude of the material trade-offs that influence value creation over time;
5. the reason why the organisation considers any of the six 'capitals' to be immaterial given its particular circumstances, if that is the case.

Conclusions **C5.13**

The contentions of this chapter have been:

1. that conventional paradigms of CSR are passé;
2. that the means businesses may deploy to fulfil their purposes are being progressively curtailed;
3. that exploitation is unavoidable, even desirable;
4. aversion to risk taking is an undesirable consequence of more regulation;
5. that laws and regulations are often necessary to engender responsible behaviour by companies;
6. that socially responsible behaviour, whether it is behaviour that is sustainable or high standards of corporate governance does not necessarily improve the performance as we measure it today;
7. that where there are responsibilities, there should be matching accountability obligations;
8. that we need to devise new ways to measure performance.

While the arguments above have been largely from the perspective of the for-profit business entity, parallel contentions apply in the related fields of the human sciences, in health, in the arts – and so on.

Many companies have been publishing sustainability reports, usually separately from their annual report and accounts, but sometimes as a section therein. Notable UK examples of separate sustainability reports are those of Unilever, BT and then Co-op. It is widely understood that CSR goes much further than the making, and reporting about, charitable donations. It is a commendable proposal to make the reporting of CSR matters more integrated. Integrated reporting usefully suggests that organisations should give an explanation of factors that create or destroy intangible value. It remains to be seen whether it is sensible to regard anything other than finance as capital – the IIRC proposes that we should consider that there are six capitals – financial, manufactured, intellectual, human, social and relationship, and natural. It is the economic bottom lines that determine whether entities survive in the long term.

Research in 2012 by Blacksun, the corporate communications consultancy,[12] suggests that integrated reporting breaks down silos. Blaksun found that 93% of businesses believe integrated reporting helps to break down silos and connect departments; 98% agreed that the shift towards integrated reporting leads to a better understanding of how the organisation will create value over time; 74% agreed that it will lead to more consistency in external communications; 93% agreed that it leads to better quality data collection; 64% think that analysts will benefit significantly from integrated reporting in future; 95% think that employees will benefit, 28% are already seeing significant benefit to the Board from integrated reporting; 56% expected to see significant benefit to the board in future, with 97% anticipating positive change overall.

It is now generally accepted that the financial statements themselves do not give investors all the information they need to make informed investment decisions and to participate effectively ion the oversight of the companies they own. So there has been an emphasis upon the importance of narrative reporting for the benefit of market participants.[13] Integrated reporting attempts to take matter further by extending the extent to which published information by companies is addressed to categories of stakeholder other than shareholders.

References

Blair, T (26 May 2005), speech on compensation culture delivered at the Institute of Public Policy Research, University College, London, http://www.number10.gov.uk/output/Page7562.asp.

Cadbury, Sir Adrian (1998), *The future of governance: the rules of the game* (lecture to Gresham College, delivered at Mansion House, London), reprinted in Chambers, AD (2005) *Tottel's Corporate Governance Handbook*, ISBN 1-84592-082-1.

Cadbury, Sir Adrian (June 2006) *Corporate Social Responsibility, 21st Century Society* (Routledge and Academy of Social Sciences), Vol 1, No 1, pp 5–21.

Chambers, AD (2006): *Assurance of Performance*, *Measuring Business Excellence* (Emerald, ISSN 1368-3047), Vol 10, No 3, pp 41–55.

COSO (2004) Enterprise Risk Management, Executive Summary (US, Committee of Sponsoring Organisations, www.coso.org), p 2.

Draper, S, Hanson, L and Uren, S (March 2006) *Are you a Leader Business? Hallmarks of Sustainable Performance* (Forum for the Future, www.forumforthefuture.org.uk).

Drucker, PF (1977) *Management: Tasks, Responsibilities, Practices* (Pan UK edn, 1979, ISBN: 0 330 25638 6), p 433.

Friedman, M (1982) *Capitalism and Freedom* (Chicago, University of Chicago Press).

Mackenzie, JM in the foreword to EL Normanton (1966) *The Accountability and Audit of Governments* (quotation from foreword by Professor WJM Mackenzie p vii) (Manchester University Press. Also published by Frederick A Prager, New York (1966)).

Porritt, J (2005) *Capitalism as if the World Matters* (London, Earthscan, ISBN 1-84407-192-8).

Power, M (1997) *The Audit Society: Rituals of Verification* (Oxford University Press). Professor Michael Power is PD Leake Professor of Accounting at The London School of Economics.

Spence, C and Gray, R (2007) *Corporate Social Responsibility: Beyond the Business Case*, Association of Chartered Certified Accountants, Research Report no 98 (London, Chartered Accountants Educational Trust).

Notes

1 Quoted in Blacksun (2012) *Understanding Transformation: Building the Business Case for Integrated Reporting*, http://www.blacksunplc.com/corporate/iirc_understanding_transformation/index.htm, accessed 4 December 2013.

2 Friedman, M (1962) *Capitalism and Freedom* (University of Chicago Press) and Friedman, M (1970) 'The Social Responsibility of Business is to Increase its Profits', *The New York Times Magazine*, 13 September 1970.

3 The Companies Act 2006 sets out a statutory statement of a director's seven general duties, as follows:

1. to act in accordance with the company's constitution (s 257) and to act within the company's powers (s 171);
2. to promote the success of the company for the benefit of its members as a whole, and in doing so have regard (*inter alia*) to specified matters (s 172);
3. to exercise independent judgment (s 173);
4. to exercise reasonable care, skill and diligence (as would be expected of a reasonably diligent person carrying out the functions of the director, as well as based on the director's actual knowledge, skill and experience) (s 174);
5. to avoid conflicts of interest (s 175);
6. not to accept benefits from third parties (s 176);
7. to declare interests in a proposed transaction or arrangement with the company (s 177).

4 ASB (2006) Reporting Standard (RS) 1, Accounting Standards Board of the Financial Reporting Council, January 2006, http://www.frc.org.uk/Our-Work/Publications/ASB/UITF-Abstract-24-Accounting-for-start-up-costs/Reporting-Statement-Operating-and-Financial-Review.aspx, accessed 4 December 2013.

5 The directors' report in the annual report and accounts does not need to contain a business review if the company is 'subject to the small companies regime. The small companies regime applies to a company for a financial year in relation to which the company qualifies as small and is not excluded from the regime under s 384 of the Companies Act 2006.

The qualifying conditions are met by a company for a financial year in which it satisfies two or more of the following requirements:

- turnover – not more than £5.6m;
- balance sheet total – not more than £2.8m;
- number employees – not more than 50.

The qualifying conditions have, generally speaking, to be met in the relevant financial year and the preceding financial year (though the provisions are technically more complex than this).

Also a parent company can only qualify as a small company if the group headed by it qualifies as a small group and the qualifying conditions for that are as above, but with the figures for each member of the group being aggregated. The small companies regime does not apply to a company that is or was within the relevant financial year (*inter alia*), a member of an ineligible group and a group is ineligible if any of its members is, (*inter alia*), a public company.

However, the shareholders of a small company can choose to insist that the company does not avail itself of the dispensations that may apply. For instance, small companies need not have an annual audit, but the shareholders can insist that it does.

6 Professor Mackenzie, an eminent economist at Manchester University, coined these words as far back as 1966 in his Foreword to a book on auditing in governments by EL Normanton based on the latter's MPhil thesis which Mackenzie had supervised: Normanton, EL (1966) *The Accountability and Audit of Governments – A Comparative Study* (Manchester University Press; also published by Frederick A Prager, New York (1966)), p vii.

7 IoDSA (Institute of Directors in South Africa) (2009) *The King Report on Governance (King III)*, http://www.iodsa.co.za/?page=kingIII, accessed 10 September 2013.

8 IIRC (2013), *Consultation Draft of the International Integrated Reporting <IR> Framework*, April 2013.

9 IIRC (2013), *International Integrated Reporting (IR) Framework*, December 2013.

10 Humble, JW (1973) *Social Responsibility Audit: Tool for Survival* (Amacon).

11 Blake, DH, Crittenden, FW and Myers, MS (1976) *Social Auditing: Evaluating the Impact of Corporate Programs* (Praeger, ISBN 0275567001, 9780275567002).

12 Lessem, R (1977) 'Corporate Social Responsibility in Action: An Evaluation of British, European and American Practice', 2 (4) *Accounting, Organizations and Society*, pp 279–294.

13 Blacksun (2012) *Understanding Transformation: Building the Business Case for Integrated Reporting*, http://www.blacksunplc.com/corporate/iirc_understanding_transformation/index.htm, accessed 4 December 2013.

14 For instance, ASB (2007), *A Review of Narrative Reporting by UK Listed Companies in 2006*, January 2007.

8 IIRC (2013), *Consultation Draft of the International Integrated Reporting <IR> Framework*, April 2013.

Chapter C6

Culture, Ethics and the Board

Context C6.1

'The governing body should recognize that organizational culture, whether deliberately created or not, is a crucial determinant of everyone's behaviour. A good governance system demands good behaviour, but it cannot deliver good behaviour – only people can do that. Written policies can be powerful, but can also be displaced by unwritten rules. Similarly, from the perspective of stakeholders, an organization with a good governance system is more likely to be trustworthy, but only if everyone fulfils their respective accountabilities within it. Therefore, the governing body should deliberately create an effective governance culture'.[1]

Today one feels it would be inconceivable not to address this subject in a contemporary corporate governance handbook, and an admission of past inadequacy that this sixth edition is the first to dedicate a chapter to it, although ethical practices has been a thread woven through the tapestry of these handbooks since the first edition appeared in 2002. This gap in previous editions of this handbook has in part been a product of reluctance to pontificate on these vexed issues.

Since the global financial crisis broke there have been many strident, though too polarised, calls for radical reform. On the one hand, there has been the school of thought that has focused, and continues to focus, on the need to transform business ethics led by the board. On the other hand, there are those who place little faith in businesses becoming more ethical and who resort to calls for stronger regulation – whether in the financial or in other sectors.

There is more evidence that indicates that regulation has been strengthened than that business ethics have improved independently of enhanced regulatory requirements. Simply observing rules is not the same thing as making right moral judgement.[2] It is true that there has been much debate about business ethics, yet serious lapses continue to emerge with alarming regularity. We need to 'walk the talk' not just 'talk the walk'. George Weston, chief executive of Primark's parent, Associated British Foods, has said:

> 'We must get away from the days of the past where companies parade their ethics as a marketing tool [and actually change the way we work].'

Ethics and rules in tandem C6.2

We need a balanced, twin-prong approach that seeks to continue to fight to strengthen both business ethics as well as regulation. While this chapter places an emphasis on the 'softer' components which contribute to an effective culture, contrary to much current accepted wisdom it also stresses the importance of procedures, controls, rules and regulations as cultural influencers. It can be argued that today's cultural malaise in business is not so much a matter of a collapse in morality, but has been facilitated by a move away from traditional controls against wrong-doing. These controls used to be more rigorous both within businesses (for instance, through a stronger emphasis on preventative controls such as segregation of duties) and also over businesses (through the application of professional standards and regulation).

We started this chapter with a quotation from the British Standards Institution and have also quoted George Weston. Both, as well as many others, are optimists that culture, ethics and behaviour can change. Certainly it is not easily achieved and often not genuinely intended. Social anthropologists' ethnographic studies in the 1950s and 1960s of so-called primitive African tribes were justified in part as being necessary before the evidence was lost as those tribes broken down due to outside influences. Those studies were also justified as being suitable cases to use to obtain an understanding of how social groups behave as they were largely self-contained and cut off from external influences. Those anthropologists showed us that every society is an intricate combination of social, legal, economic, familial and other systems. Members are initiated into the norms of the society and tend to behave in a conformist way. Social re-engineering can have catastrophic and unintended consequences as it tends lead to a situation of anomie. The greatest of care is needed to understand the interconnectedness of different societal characteristics before change is embarked upon. And there will always be a high degree of resistance to change. Imposed changes have a high risk of failure.[3] More recently anthropologists are applying their insights to businesses.[4]

The subject of this chapter is bedevilled with 'management speak' pedalled by management gurus, and this chapter has not succeeded in avoiding its usage. We suspect that many in business do not understand the meaning of terms like 'culture', 'ethics' and 'behaviour' and tend to use them inconsistently. At the end of this chapter we have provided definitions of important terms.

Internal guides relating to culture and behaviour C6.3

Just as external regulation can contribute to mitigating unethical corporate behaviour, so can formal, documented internal policies. Ethical culture and behaviour is not achieved informally just by the inclinations and personal conduct of organisations' leaders. Formal, well communicated, laid down policies can make a valuable contribution too. Staff wish to know what is expected of them. Staff are motivated to work for ethnical organisations. The challenge of documenting what conduct is expected forces are careful consideration of what it should be, and how ethical dilemmas are to be handled.

It is true that companies have often paraded their ethical statements as public relations tools, sometimes with little apparent commitment to abiding by them. A well-used tactic is to fend off external criticism by pointing to an internal code of conduct which has been crafted largely for external consumption, not for internal compliance. Of course, that is not how it should be.

Because these documented guides are so important, they should be adopted by the board as formal policies of the board. They should be reconsidered and readopted by the board regularly; otherwise they will fall into disuse and even be forgotten about.

Of course the directors and top management must lead by example, making sure that they observe these formal, laid down policies. The board and top management should must resist the temptation of deviating from these agreed policies for short term corporate gain as (a) this is likely to result in unethical conduct, and (b) it will discredit the policies across the business at all levels. They must be developed in a strongly participative way, involving many internal stakeholders. If they are not developed participatively they are unlikely to appropriate or to become embedded into the business. It should not be assumed that staff are likely by default to be familiar with them. Entity-wide training and top-up training will always be necessary.

At the apex of these formal statements are likely to be the entity's mission and vision statements. These very usefully orientate staff at all levels as well as other stakeholders to the purpose of the entity and where it is heading. All suggested initiatives should naturally be assessed against the entity's mission and vision. Below these statements can usefully be a statement of corporate principles which should articulate the values which must underpin conduct. We give an example at **A6.7**. We then envisage a series of policy statements which interpret the entity's corporate principles as expected conduct in the main areas of business activity. Security issues are likely to be some of these important policy statements adopted by the board – perhaps a fraud policy statement (**A6.30**), a whistleblowing policy statement (**A6.22**) and an internet security policy statement (**A6.29**). At **A6.8** is an example code of business conduct, and at **A6.9** an example of a code of scientific and environmental conduct.

The primacy of ethics **C6.4**

We need to rediscover the primacy of ethics in business, or perhaps it is a matter of first time discovery. Culture, ethics and behaviour need to play an important part in discouraging the effective circumvention of controls, such as with the 'three lines of defence' approach which we discuss later in this chapter. Many have drawn attention to a time before 'the Big Bang' in the City of London when 'my word is my bond' applied market participants. Then, it is said, deregulation created a 'dog-eat-dog' mentality. But it is doubtful that business ethics were better than when transparency was so much less. For instance, insider trading was rampant but 'under the counter'. There was much less transparency than today. Nevertheless, there is a view that the traditional values of the professions have become disassociated with the values of financial institutions:

> 'We have detached our appraisal of standards and behaviours from their professional roots.'[5]

It may be facile to attribute the many corporate scandals of recent times to a novel, modern collapse of morality, although it often seems like that. Greenspan's view is that:

> 'It is not that humans have become any more greedy than in generations past. It is that avenues to express greed have grown so enormously.'[6]

Lack of attention to making commercial systems secure from abuse has contributed to widening the opportunities for abuse. An appropriate business culture is one that amongst other things focuses on closing off the avenues to express greed, and challenging the sentiment that 'greed is good'.[7] Effective internal control is hugely important as an aspect of a culture that is fit for purpose. Elimination of perverse incentives that encourage the development of unethical practices, including excessive risk taking, is also hugely important. For instance, a legal department within a large corporation is incentivised to minimise court damages awarded against the company, encouraging them to suppress evidence of corporate wrongdoing. Or performance-related rewards for the head of internal audit are related to the short-term performance of the company, encouraging internal audit not to report excessive risk taking. Instead, incentives must be aligned with delivery of ethical business practices.

It has always been the case that only three ingredients have been needed to amount to an irresistible temptation for the majority to behave unethically or fraudulently:

1. opportunity;
2. perceived very little or no risk of detection;
3. modest consequences, including small degree of social disgrace, upon detection, which make the risk worthwhile.

Perhaps 25% will be ethical in all circumstances, 25% unethical whenever the opportunity presents itself, and the remaining 50% swayed according to the above three factors. If we factor in the influence of unsatisfied personal financial needs and greed, we have a cocktail that becomes irresistible. So we must close off the opportunities for unethical conduct and hence an emphasis on procedures and rules can be valuable though not enough on its own.

We should take immense trouble to recruit only trustworthy staff and to enter into business relationships only with trustworthy partners. But thereafter we should endeavour to minimise the extent that we depend upon their trustworthiness: our systems should be designed in part to confirm their ongoing trustworthiness. It is in everyone's interests that this is done: if our systems cannot demonstrate trustworthiness, then the finger of suspicion will point perhaps unjustifiably at those whom we are having to take on trust who will be unable to exonerate themselves.

We will discuss later in this chapter the declines of values of those occupational groups who still consider themselves as being professions.

On 25 November 2013, UK Business Secretary Vince Cable, Secretary of State for Business, Innovation and Skills and President of the Board of Trade, told BBC's Radio 4 programme:

> 'The authorities need to establish whether there is something worse than unethical behaviour going on here.'

He was speaking in the context of having passed to the UK 'City watchdogs' evidence relating to alleged wrong treatment of small businesses amidst allegations that a leading UK bank had been contriving to seize assets from firms to benefit its own property empire.

His stress was on the word 'worse'. It would be unfair to read too much into this spur of the moment remark. On the face of it, he was implying that breaches of regulation or law are worse than unethical behaviour. It is certainly true that from the standpoint of the authorities there may be remedies for such breaches but generally not for behaviour which, while unethical, violates neither regulation nor law. But we must not fall into the trap of allowing that unethical behaviour is considered less serious than breaches of laws and regulations.

It would be inappropriate to argue that ethical business practices rank in importance behind compliance with laws and regulations. While there is both an ethical and a statutory imperative to comply with laws and regulations, doing so is far from guaranteeing that businesses do the right things and do them right. Indeed, compliance with many laws and regulations may have a neutral or even negative impact on standards of behaviour. Furthermore, apparent non-compliance will attract no sanctions when it is not proceeded against by the authorities, or when proceedings fail on a technicality. In the absence of a focus on ethical behaviour, boards, senior executives and their professional advisors will focus on identifying the loopholes in laws and regulations.

The social responsibility of business **C6.5**

In 1970, Milton Friedman, the doyen of the Chicago free market school, famously contended that:

> 'There is one and only one social responsibility of business – to use its resources and engage in activities designed to increase its profits, so long as it stays within the rules of the game, which is to say, engages in open and free competition without deception or fraud.'[8]

Even Friedman acknowledged that breaking the rules is beyond the bounds of ethical corporate behaviour, but he seemed to expect regulations and laws to extend no further than to outlaw 'deception' and 'fraud'. He appeared to approve of companies exploiting any opportunity to increase their profits so long as deception and fraud were not involved. Indeed Friedman seemed to be claiming that maximising profits is the sole social obligation of a business, so long as it 'engages in open and free competition without deception or fraud'. For Friedman, the driver of ethical behaviour beyond mere avoidance of deception and fraud, was to increase profits. For Friedmanites, ethical behaviour that goes beyond conformance with laws and regulations, is acceptable if it adds to the profitability of the company. Social responsibility can do this – especially under pressure from the public and from ethical investment funds. Undoubtedly, businesses have a social responsibility to their providers of capital – which range from hedge funds, private equity funds, pension and other funds where the public are ultimate beneficiaries, through to small private investors. Without that capital there would be no businesses, no services, no goods, no employment. Arguably, owner return should rightly be the paramount focus of boards and top executive teams, and this focus rightly should cascade down through all levels of the business. Indeed, this shift was anticipated by the formulation of the 'enlightened shareholder value duty' of directors within s 172 of the Companies Act 2006, which acknowledges the paramount duty of directors to promote the success of the company for the benefit of its members as a whole, *but in doing so to take into account other social concerns*. Those other concerns listed in the 2006 Act are:

- the longer term;
- the interests of the company's employees;
- the need to foster the company's business relationships with suppliers, customers and others;

- the environment;
- the impact of operations on the wider community; and
- the desirability of the company maintaining a reputation for high standards of business conduct and the need to act fairly between members of the company.

The Act does not intend that this list should be regarded as exhaustive.

Mark Carney, the Governor of the Bank of England has described some bankers as socially useless and detached from reality, and only 3% in a YouGov survey strongly believe banks are changing for the better with only 4% strongly agreeing they have the needs of their customers at heart.

A strong emphasis on corporate social responsibility and business ethics will often contribute to improving the economic performance of a company especially over the medium to long term frequently in the following ways:

- attracting shareholders and other investors who are motivated by social investment considerations, thereby reducing the cost of capital;
- enhancing reputation by avoiding the need to explain non-compliance with applicable corporate governance codes (in the UK, the UK Corporate Governance Code (**App1**) and the UK Stewardship Code (**App2**);
- attracting, retaining and motivating staff who are concerned to work for a socially responsible company and who, for instance, welcome their employer's family friendly and flexible working policies and practices;
- giving a competitive advantage through differentiation from competitors not engaged in corporate social responsibility;
- aiding regulatory and legislative compliance and making it less likely that new, enhanced requirements will pose a challenge for the business;
- reducing the risk of reputational crises;
- creating an open, no blame culture, where staff and others can raise concerns without fear of retribution, making it less likely that wrongdoing will prosper.

But it is disingenuous to argue that socially responsible and other ethnical business practices automatically and always contribute to a better bottom line performance of a company in the short, medium or long term. Just as there are profits to be made from criminality, so there may be profits from social irresponsibility.

Transparency C6.6

The argument is flimsy that it is no business of the public how companies are run, but only of the owners. Sovereign wealth funds often use this argument to defend a lack of transparency in their published statements. With 58% of the top 150 world economies being companies in both 2010 and 2012, it is untenable to argue that the proper governance of companies is not in the public interest.[9] Of course, ethical behaviour includes transparent, reliable and open accountability by boards to owners so that the owners can exercise well informed control over their investment:

> 'Corporate governance lies at the heart of prospects for growth and development, and will be a key determinant of a country's success. It's very simple, if you think someone is dishonest and not telling the truth, you don't give them the money.

It's not a question of people, it's a question of intelligence. If you think someone is being honest, and is giving you a fair shake, a fair return, you do business with them.'[10]

'Open and free competition' is imperfect in all markets today and more so in some. Laws and regulations necessarily articulate 'rules of the game' to be conformed to which extend much wider than the avoidance of deception and fraud. But it is a game of 'catch up' with law makers and regulators inevitably a few steps behind practitioners. It is necessary for corporates to define and adhere to acceptable standards of ethical behavior far beyond legal requirements.

Leadership **C6.7**

The board sets the tone and should regularly review their company's culture, ethics and behaviour. It is a problem of leadership when companies fall down ethically. Frequently the wrong signals are transmitted down the line from the board and senior management.

Justin King, J Sainsbury's chief executive recently said:

> 'There is a crisis of trust … I hear too much rhetoric of 'not too much wrong was done' and to the extent that [wrong] was done, it is in the past.
>
> Bob Diamond [the former Barclays boss] famously said: "The time for apologies is finished, let's move on." Well, the time to move on is when our customers tell us that the trust that they once gave is restored.
>
> The crisis in trust is when you can still trust individuals within the organisation but you can't trust the organisation. That, therefore, must be a crisis of leadership and a failure of leadership.'[11]

While, at mid and micro levels within a company, mandatory and strong internal control procedures are important, at the regulatory level mandatory corporate governance standards should also have their place. They too can mould behaviour. The laissez faire 'comply or explain' approach to UK corporate governance is ineffectual for any company intent on sailing close to the wind in their corporate governance practices. A lesson we should learn from the recent scandals in the financial sector is that there has been a propensity to 'game' the system. The weaker the controls and regulations, the easier it is for this to be done successfully under the guise that all is well.

Duties of directors **C6.8**

The duties of directors, codified in UK statute law for the first time in the Companies Act 2006, indicate the strong, expected ethical obligation that directors have:

1. to act in accordance with the company's constitution (s 257) and to act within the company's powers (s 171);
2. to promote the success of the company for the benefit of its members as a whole, and in doing so have regard (*inter alia*) to specified matters (s 172);
3. to exercise independent judgment (s 173);

4. to exercise reasonable care, skill and diligence (as would be expected of a reasonably diligent person carrying out the functions of the director, as well as based on the director's actual knowledge, skill and experience) (s1 74);
5. to avoid conflicts of interest (s 175);
6. not to accept benefits from third parties (s 176);
7. to declare interests in a proposed transaction or arrangement with the company (s 177).

Ethical dilemmas C6.9

It is rare for there not be ethical dilemmas. Determining what is right for the client, customer, employees or society, is not always easy to do, or to be seen to do. How we handle dilemmas is an essential element in policy and training.[12]

Ethical dilemmas are likely to be multi-faceted. The Royal Bank of Scotland, for instance, has to balance its obligations to shareholders (81% of its share capital in 2013 being owned by the UK tax payer), to regulators demanding better capital adequacy and to those it does business with.

Undoubtedly, conflicting priorities result in moral dilemmas for companies and their boards. Individuals working within companies and boards themselves too easily lose their moral compass – especially when under market pressure. Perverse incentives associated with senior executive remuneration exacerbate the risk of unethical behavior. Boards are frequently kept in the dark about unethical practices being followed at executive level. Top executives have frequently claimed that their boards would have replaced them if they had settled for levels of profit available if only ethical business practices had been followed, as these profits would have been below market expectations and below competitor performance. The issue as to how boards get the assurance they need that the policies of the board are being implemented by management, is an important issue. Another important issue is that boards do not place their top executive teams under intolerable strain to balance conflicting priorities set by the board.

Filling the board's assurance vacuum C6.10

A common problem is the existence of a disconnect between the board and senior management.[13] The board may be insufficiently aware of the risks that the business is running. Management may not be implementing the policies of the board in the ways and to the extent that the board expects and believes they are. Management may be selective at feeding back information to the board, in particular with respect to 'bad news'.

A key indicator of a healthy corporate culture is the existence of open and constructive dialogue between management and the board, as well as the consistent provision of high quality, timely information to the board.

> 'There is no way a good board can function if board members don't take responsibility for getting the information that they need – and if they can't get it from the CEO, you had better be able to get it from somebody else in the company.'

and:

> 'The heart of an excellent relationship between a CEO and the board is constructive dialogue – boards that work have constructive critical dialogue among board members and senior management. Such open dialogue is the single best indication of board effectiveness.'[14]

Three lines of defence **C6.11**

Recently it has been pointed out that apparent compliance with elaborate rules can wrongly give the impression that all is well. Creation of the three lines of defence model is a case in point. We discuss this model in depth at Chapter **G4**. Under this model management the controls are the first line of defence. The risk management and compliance functions are important elements of the second line of defence while internal audit is perceived as the third line of defence. These lines of defence in practice have been described by the important UK Parliamentary Commission on Banking as 'Maginot lines',[15] a Potemkin village [16] and subject to the abuse of Goodhart's Law[17] whereby putting a name to something (in this case naming an approach as 'three lines of defence') means it tends to become a gameable box-ticking exercise rather than something truly embedded into the spirit and culture of the organisation:

> 'The financial crisis, and multiple conduct failures, have exposed serious flaws in governance. Potemkin villages were created in firms, giving the appearance of effective control and oversight without the reality. Non-executive directors lacked the capacity or incentives to challenge the executives. Sometimes those executives with the greatest insight into risks being added to balance sheets were cut off from decision-makers at board level or lacked the necessary status to speak up. Poor governance and controls are illustrated by the rarity of whistle-blowing, either within or beyond the firm, even where, such as in the case of Libor manipulation, prolonged and blatant misconduct has been evident. The Commission makes the following recommendations for improvement:
>
> 1. individual and direct lines of access and accountability to the board for the heads of the risk, compliance and internal audit functions and much greater levels of protection for their independence; …'[18] (HLHC, 2013a, p 10; HLHC, 2013b, p 138)

The CIIA (2013) guidance states that internal audit should be independent of the risk management and compliance functions, and also be independent of the finance function, not least in order to facilitate objective auditing of these activities.[19]

The UK Banking Commission of both houses of the UK's Parliament, reporting in 2013, concluded:

> 'The "three lines of defence" system for controlling risk has been adopted by many banks with the active encouragement of the regulators. It appears to have promoted a wholly misplaced sense of security. Fashionable management school theory appears to have lent undeserved credibility to some chaotic systems. Responsibilities have been blurred, accountability diluted, and officers in risk, compliance and internal audit have lacked the status to challenge front line staff effectively. Much of the system became a box-ticking exercise whereby processes

were followed, but judgement was absent. In the end, everyone loses, particularly customers.'[20]

Of course, internal and external rules and regulations are not enough on their own, but their potential to be effective has been wrongly downplayed. Other qualities such as leadership, inspiration, tone at the top and so on are also important drivers of good behaviour.

General characteristics and determinants of culture **C6.12**

Much research, often unconvincing, has been done on whether higher standards of corporate governance lead to better company performance. One of the problems of this research is that companies performing well are likely to be more inclined to invest in quality governance for the twin reasons that they are better positioned to spend resources on doing so, and they appreciate the need for successful companies to meet the expectations of a wide range of stakeholders. So, where there are correlations between governance and performance, it may be that better performance drives improvements in governance rather than vice versa. Good company performance depends upon many factors other than, but including, good corporate governance and it is not easy to isolate the impact of good governance on performance; but a well governed company is more likely to ensure that these other factors are in place and work favourably for the company.

Culture is an integral part of governance. In evaluating its corporate governance, a company should not omit to assess its culture. As with corporate governance in general, a successful company is better positioned to have a good culture as it is more likely to have the resources to do things well, and internal morale is enhanced by virtue of the company's relative success. Herzberg's motivators (**C3.14**) are more likely to be in place, resulting in positive attitudes amongst staff. To the extent that culture can be improved, a successful company is more likely to focus on making those enhancements. A company that is doing badly is likely to have an over-stressed top management team and a board pre-occupied with managing crises rather than improving culture and inclined to cut corners unethically to keep the company afloat. Of course, even successful companies can be under pressure which may suggest to their boards and top executive teams that improving culture is not a priority. Pressures impacting successful companies may be competitive, regulatory, technological, legal, takeover and other pressures. Whether culture is a focus of attention is likely to be a function of the degree of tension within the company and between the company and its stakeholders.

A company may have become successful with a culture introduced by its founding management and based on their personalities; that culture may have contributed to its early success or its success may have resulted from other factors. There may have been no conscious effort to design the culture. In extreme cases the success of these companies may have been built in part upon deception and fraud, often associated by charismatic leadership without a firm moral compass and with excessive concentration of power at the top of the business. An organisation's culture is reflected in its leaders' behaviours. There will be a subliminal bias to recruiting like-minded people. Cultural style therefore tends be self-reinforcing. When corporate success is achieved in this way it is clear that its success does not automatically drive a culture which is positive in important respects.

Culture is also likely to be influenced by the culture of the country or countries in which the company is located. This is particularly the case with respect to such issues as openness, transparency, shareholder dialogue and rights, staff relationships, honouring contractual obligations and so on. A multinational may have cultures which are distinctly different in the different locations in which it operates, though we should not under-estimate the cultural impact of the tone at the top of the group. Similarly, culture may vary within different operations of a company which may not be geographically dispersed. While the 'tone at the top' is important, culture and behaviour will be impacted by the characteristics of the managers running an operation – in terms of their personalities, competence, and management style. A key question is whether culture should be different within different operations of a company? Is it appropriate for the investment banking arm of a bank to have a different culture from its retail banking business? The short answer is that cultural norms should be universal across all parts of the business, while other cultural attributes may need to be tailored specifically to the nature of the business.

Changing culture **C6.13**

Earlier in this chapter we mentioned that social anthropologists have emphasised that cultures across the world are intricate organisms or systems comprising interrelated social, familial, legal, economic and other sub-systems which have evolved over time and tend to function in an interlocked and harmonious way.

> 'Social phenomena constitute a distinct class of natural phenomena. They are all in one way or another, connected with the existence of social structures, either being implied or resulting from them. Social structures are just as real as individual organisms.'[21]

Just as with the cultures of peoples, so business cultures evolve over time as finely tuned adjustments to circumstances. Even when some of their customs, norms and procedures may have lost some or all of their purpose, they tend to be resistant to change. Imposed changes have a high risk of failure[22] and risk a situation of anomie.[23] Great care needs to be taken to understand the intricacies of a business culture, so as to avoid changes resulting in unintended consequences. A conscious effort should be expended on creating an appropriate culture for new organisations. Old organisations will have become muscle bound with set ways of doing everything and a tendency to press every event that occurs into standard processes that have developed in detail over time. There is a likelihood that old organisations will overlook that the world has changed and some of their ways of doing things may be appropriate no longer. Even if they understand that things must change, it is hard to make those changes. This explains why new organisations can develop to supersede old organisations unwilling or incapable of making the necessary changes. It also goes some way to explaining why five out of six takeovers fail to deliver value when it becomes impossible to surmount the challenges of the culture shock, and to change the culture of the business taken over.

Shock therapy is needed to make significant culture change. It is likely to mean a change of leadership at the top. It is likely to need significant staff changes at all levels. It may mean that an acquirer takes over the assets of the company but not its organisation. But great care must be taken to understand the knock-on effects of the changes that will be made. Business process re-engineering, where the processes of the business are comprehensively re-engineered to eliminate practices that have little or no purpose, is an example of the shock therapy that may be needed. A business process re-engineering project is an ideal opportunity to redesign the culture and ethics of the organisation, and this should be part of any business process re-engineering project. Business process re-engineering risks overlooking the importance of procedures and practices which are 'engineered out'.

Hallmarks of a healthy culture **C6.14**

A healthy culture:

- is supportive of the purpose and objectives of the organisation;
- is initiated and supported from the top;
- is one where individual responsibilities and accountabilities, at board level and below, are clearly set out and applied;
- is ethical;
- is communicated internally and externally;
- is applied in practice across the organisation at all levels;
- is characterised by openness between management and the board;
- is consistent with organisational values that have been articulated and communicated and are being applied;
- is transparent to the extent feasible;
- is honest;
- results in behaviour across the organisation that is transparent;
- provides a voice and feedback mechanism across the organisation;
- uncovers inappropriate or unethical behaviour without a need to rely on whistleblowing;
- supports whistleblowing in the wider public interest where necessary;
- encourages innovation;
- supports diversity (gender, age, background, nationality, orientation, competencies, etc).

Business culture and board evaluation **C6.15**

Stilpon Nester has recently criticised the bad culture example set by many boards when they shield behind anonymity when conducting board evaluations:

> 'I cannot help but doubt the culture of a company that opts for an anonymous peer review of its directors instead of requiring the board chairman to responsibly evaluate each one of the board members on the basis of an open, one-to-one – albeit confidential – discussion. … So my advice as a board consultant: make individual responsibility the cornerstone of every board process. This approach will eventually permeate the whole organisation, underpinning a healthy company culture. After all, culture is just process over time …'[24]

The public interest and the ethics of professions C6.16

We referred earlier to a breakdown of traditional professional values in the financial and other sectors. The professions themselves have been found lacking. Here we address some of the problems of the external and internal auditing professions.

In return for the privileges that society gives to the professions, including often monopoly rights to practise, professions should place the ideal of providing a service above the monetary rewards of the professional practitioners. They should also ensure they act in the public interest. It has been unseemly to observe the aggressive lobbying of the external audit profession to preserve the market monopoly of the large audit firms.

Professions generally act in the public interest when they serve their clients well. The clients of external auditors are neither management nor boards: their clients are the shareholders which has largely been forgotten.

The issue needs to be addressed as to whether professions have a wider public interest obligation. When serving their clients in a particular way is contrary to the wider public interest, professions should be obliged to act in the wider public interest. This is particularly clear in the case of internal auditors. It is inadequate for internal auditors to take the position that serving their boards and managements loyally and well is the limit of their public interest obligation. If their boards and managements themselves are concealing significant wrongdoing, then internal auditors should consider whether there is a public interest obligation to make wider disclosure.

Five years after the eruption of the global financial crisis, the internal auditing profession is no nearer to providing mandatory guidance to internal auditors on how they should conduct themselves if their client is concealing significant misconduct where there is a public interest in wider disclosure. Examples include:

- the multinational pharmaceutical company that has been suppressing adverse data on drug trialling which is resulting in regulatory approval for a drug which will seriously harm some of those who are prescribed it;
- the drug company which is allowing a drug to be prescribed for purposes other than those that have regulatory approval;
- the financial institution that has been colluding in rate fixing of LIBOR and other key financial rates;
- oil companies colluding to manipulate key market rates. The European Commission has warned that:

  > 'even small distortions of assessed prices may have a huge impact on the prices of crude oil, refined oil products and biofuels purchases and sales, potentially harming final consumers.'

The issue arises as to what internal audit should do, if internal audit knows that these types of serious wrong practices are or have been engaged in.[25] Doing nothing when the board declines to act appropriately on a matter of acute public interest makes internal audit part of the problem that led, for instance to the 2008 global financial crisis. Another issue arises as to whether internal audit is at fault if internal audit is unaware of these types of malpractice, or insufficiently cognisant of them to be sure of their facts.

The internal audit profession should have the courage to articulate within their standards the appropriate professional behaviour of its members in such situations. It may be that the profession will conclude that its members do not have any professional obligation in making wider disclosure when their companies are engaged in significant wrongdoing about which the public has an interest in being informed. On the other hand, it is to be hoped that the internal auditing profession will be able to develop and adopt mandatory guidance which will set out the considerations that their members should weigh up in determining whether wider disclosure is appropriate. Assuming internal audit is aware of issues relating to significant wrongdoing where there is a strong public interest in wider disclosure, it would seem appropriate that internal audit should make wider disclosure as authorised within the internal audit charter and further disclosure if there is a legal, regulatory, professional or ethical obligation to do so. Whether or not there is a legal, regulatory, professional or ethical obligation to make wider disclosure will involve the exercise of professional judgement by the internal auditor. Before making wider public disclosure the internal auditors should first endeavour to ensure that the issue, including failure to respond appropriately, has been communicated clearly to all members of the board.[26] Where management and/or the board of the entity report to a parent or similar body, this should include transparent and timely disclosure at that level. It is then a professional internal audit judgement whether the matter has been satisfactorily resolved so that further action is unnecessary. In weighing up a professional obligation to make wider disclosure, internal auditors should take account of factors including:

1. the extent to which there is an overriding public interest in disclosure due to the nature, scale and/or systemic character of the issue and its societal impact;
2. the availability of sufficient, reliable evidence on the issue;
3. whether there is a realistic prospect of a satisfactory internal resolution of the issue;
4. whether the external auditor and/or the regulator if any, or other competent authority has been fully informed and whether this is sufficient;
5. whether it is a sufficient and appropriate course of action to make disclosure to one or more external stakeholders[27] of the organisation;
6. the need to ensure an effective means of wider disclosure while minimising organisational damage;
7. the legal position;
8. an obligation to balance a need for wider disclosure with due confidentiality; and
9. whether it is appropriate to notify the board of the disclosure action planned or taken.

There have been examples where quite junior internal auditors have been aware of significant wrongdoing which the chief audit executive has been aware of but has taken no action along the lines set out above. So it is necessary to formulate guidance that applies not just to the chief audit executive, notwithstanding that the primary responsibility to act appropriately is vested in the chief audit executive (CAE).

Currently the internal audit profession has no mandatory requirements along the lines of the above at the level of their standards which are mandatory for their members, though the matter is covered to some extent at the level of their less authoritative practice advisories.[28] This is one of the ethical challenges that confront many different professionals from time to time. Professionals must act in the public interest. Most of the time, this means they must serve their clients well. But if management and the board is declining to act in the public interest with respect to an important matter, it cannot be in the public interest for internal audit to effectively collude in management's and the board's deception. It becomes an ethical matter about which members of a profession can reasonably expect their profession to give clear guidance.

Suggested definitions of important terms **C6.17**

Anomie	Durkheim[29] used the term 'anomie' to refer to situations where the rules and norms of society were breaking down, a theme developed by Toffler[30] and Argenti.[31]
Behaviour, see also 'Capabilities' and 'Traits'	The conduct of individuals and groups.
Business ethics (see also 'Ethics')	'moral matters pertaining to business, industry or related activities, institutions or practices and beliefs … can also refer to the customs or standards which a particular group or community acts upon (or is supposed to act upon).'[32] 'the application of ethical values to business behaviour. It applies to any and all aspects of business conduct, from boardroom strategies and how companies treat their employees and suppliers to sales techniques and accounting practices. Ethics goes beyond the legal requirements for a company and is, therefore, about discretionary decisions and behaviour guided by values. Business ethics is relevant both to the conduct of individuals and to the conduct of the organisation as a whole.'[33]
Capabilities (see also 'Traits')	Behavioural capabilities are *learnable* components of behaviour. Examples might include facilitation, empathy (consideration of and relating to others, followers and leaders), strategic thinking behaviours such as concept formation and information search, inspirational behaviours such as influence, building confidence and communication and performance-focussed behaviours such as proactivity and continuous improvement.[34]
Codes of conduct	A statement of how business is done and how staff and others are required to behave. Usually comprises both an articulation of principles as well as rules. See Chapter **A6**, in particular A6.8.
Corporate social responsibility	'the commitment by business to behave ethically and contribute to economic development while improving the quality of life of the workforce and their families as well as of the local community and society at large.'[35]

Culture	'An overarching mental edifice that impacts all aspects of life.'[36] 'A set of historically evolved learned values and attitudes and meanings shared by members of a given community that influences their material and non-material way of life. Members of the community learn these shared characteristics through different stages of the socialization processes of their lives in institutions, such as family, religion, formal education and society as a whole.'[37] 'Ideas, values and customs that underlie behaviour'.[38] How we do things around here. How we behave when we are not being watched. 'Culture is just process over time …'[39] 'The product is the product. The culture is the next hundred products.'[40]
Ethics (see also 'Business Ethics')	'a set of moral principles or values'.[41]
Ethical behaviour (of business)	'behaviour that is consistent with the principles, norms and standards of business practice that have been agreed upon by society.'[42]
Ethical dilemmas	'The really tough choices, then, don't centre upon right versus wrong. The involve right versus right.'[43](Kidder, 1995, p 18) Kidder's four types of ethical dilemmas are based on competing values: truth versus loyalty; individual versus community; short-term versus long-term; justice versus mercy.[44]
Ethical leadership	'the demonstration of normatively appropriate conduct through personal actions and interpersonal relationships, and the promotion of such conduct to followers through two-way communication, reinforcement, and decision-making.'[45]
Goals	Targets being aimed for which, if achieved, will contribute to the achievement of objectives.
Mission statement (see also 'Vision statement')	'What we do'. 'An announcement of what your business does today and why it exists. … A Mission Statement captures the uniqueness of your company and acts as a base line for quality, service and your marketing messages. … A Mission Statement is a snapshot of what your business is today – a *vision statement* is a snapshot of what you want your business to be tomorrow.'[46]

Norms	'Not all members of a culture adhere to its expected norms; nonetheless, recognizable patterns within society can typically be discerned'[47]
Objectives	What we hope to accomplish in the next 3–5 years to move us toward vision. Targeted strategic outcomes.
Principles	'Fundamental truths, propositions or assumptions that serve as foundations for a set of beliefs or behaviours or a chain of reasoning.'[48]
Promise	Succinct commitments to stakeholders (typically to staff, customers and suppliers) relating to business conduct and outcomes to be achieved. See **A6.3–A6.4**.
Public interest	(of professional accountants, as defined by IFAC): 'The net benefits derived for, and procedural rigor employed on behalf of, all society in relation to any action, decision or policy.'[49]
Purpose	'Purpose is likely to be expressed in a "vision", or otherwise named statement of the organization's ideal impact or state, and a series of shorter-term "strategic outcomes" that define shorter term objectives.'[50]
Standards	Components of performance expected to be input and undertaken, and levels of performance expected to be achieved. 'The board should set the company's values and standards.'[51]
Traits (see also 'Capabilities')	Behavioural traits are intrinsic and innate components of behaviour. Traits might include physical vitality, stamina, eagerness to accept responsibility, need for achievement, courage, self-confidence, assertiveness, and openness to new ideas.[52]
Transparency	'visibility of governance decisions and activities that are undertaken on behalf of, and which often impact, stakeholders, and the communication of these in a clear, accurate, timely, honest, open and complete manner.'[53]
Values	'those things which people regard as good, bad, right, wrong, desirable, justifiable, etc. … It is useful to distinguish between technical, prudential and moral values.'[54] 'Standards of behaviour that are accepted as appropriate by members of a group … "the way we do things around there"'.[55] See **A6.3–A6.4**.

Vision statement (see also 'Mission statement')	'Where are we trying to go'. 'Defines what your business will do and why it will exist tomorrow and it has defined goals to be accomplished by a set date. A Vision Statement takes into account the current status of the organization, and serves to point the direction of where the organization wishes to go. … a marketing tool and a business development tool because it announces your company's goals and purpose to your employees, suppliers, customers, vendors, and the media.'[56] See **A6.3–A6.4**.

References

Argenti, J (1976) *Corporate Collapse – The Causes and Symptoms* (Maidenhead, McGraw-Hill, ISBN 0-07-084469-0).

Brown, ME, Treviño, LK and Harrison, DA (2005) 'Ethical leadership: A social learning perspective for construct development and testing', 97(2) *Organizational Behavior and Human Decision Processes*, pp 117–134.

BSI (British Standards Institution) (2013) *Code of practice for delivering effective governance of organizations*, BS13500:2013, (ISBN 978 0 580 71608 9), August 2013.

Burns, T and Stalker, GM (1961) *The Management of Innovation* (London, Tavistock Institute).

Chambers, AD (2008a) 'The board's black hole – filling their assurance vacuum: can internal audit rise to the challenge?', 12(1) *Measuring Business Excellence –The Journal of Business Performance Management*, pp 47–63.

Chambers, AD (2008c) 'Bring on the super auditors', 32(12) *Internal Auditing*, December, pp 18–21 (ISSN 1757-0999).

Chambers, AD (2009a) 'The black hole of assurance', 66(2) *The Internal Auditor*, April, pp 28–29.

Charan, R (1998) *Boards at Work – How Corporate Boards Create Competitive Advantage* (Jossey-Bass, ISBN-10: 0787910600; ISBN-13: 978-0787910600).

Collins, D (2012) *Business Ethics: How to Design and Manage Ethical Organizations* (US, Wiley, ISBN 9780470739948).

Donaldson, J (1989) *Key Issues in Business Ethics* (London and San Diego, Academic Press, ISBN 0-12-220540-5).

Durkheim, E (1893) *The Division of Labor in Society* (New York, The Free Press).

Hegel, F (1807) *The Phenomenology of Spirit* (Oxford, Clarendon Press, 1977, ISBN 0-19-824597-1).

HLHC (House of Lords and House of Commons) (2013a), *Changing Banking for Good, Report of the Parliamentary Commission on Banking Standards*, Vol I:

Summary, and Conclusions and Recommendations, HL Paper 27-I, HC 175-I, 12 June 2013, http://www.parliament.uk/business/committees/committees-a-z/joint-select/professional-standards-in-the-banking-industry/news/changing-banking-for-good-report/, accessed 14 July 2013, p 18.

HLHC (2013b), *Changing Banking for Good, Report of the Parliamentary Commission on Banking Standards,* Vol II: Chapters 1 to 11 and Annexes, together with formal minutes, HL Paper 27-II, HC 175-II, 12 June 2013, http://www.parliament.uk/business/committees/committees-a-z/joint-select/professional-standards-in-the-banking-industry/news/changing-banking-for-good-report/, accessed 14 July 2013, p 138.

IFAC (International Federation of Accountants) (2012) *A Definition of the Public Interest*, Policy Position 5, June 2012, http://www.ifac.org/sites/default/files/publications/files/PPP%205%20%282%29.pdf, accessed 14 October 2013.

Kidder, RM (1995) *How Good People Make Tough Choices* (New York, William Morrow & Company).

Nestor, S (2013) 'Responsibility and the culture of challenge', 230 *Nestor's Quarterly Advisor*, Q2, p 1, Radcliffe-Brown, AR (1952) 'On social structure', *Structure and Function in Primitive Society* (New York, Free Press).

Tayeb, M (1988) *Organizations and National Culture* (London, Sage, ISBN 0 8039 8166 X).

Toffler, A (1970) *Future Shock* (US, Random House).

Treviño, LK and Nelson, KA (2007) *Managing Business Ethics – Straight Talk About How to Do it Right* (US, Wiley, ISBN 978-0-471-75525-9).

Walle, AH (2013) *Rethinking Business Anthropology* (Sheffield, Greenleaf Publishing, ISBN 13: 978-1-906093-90-7).

Notes

1 BSI (British Standards Institution) (2013) *Code of practice for delivering effective governance of organizations*, BS13500:2013, (ISBN 978 0 580 71608 9), August 2013, §4.2.6, p 11.

2 Simon, R (2012), 'Trust in the City? The Chartered Secretary', www.charteredsceretary.net, 30 May 2012, pp 34– 35 (Richard Simon is Chairman of the City Values Forum).

3 Burns, T and Stalker, GM (1961) *The Management of Innovation* (London, Tavistock Institute).

4 Walle, AH (2013) *Rethinking Business Anthropology* (Sheffield, Greenleaf Publishing, ISBN-13: 978-1-906093-90-7), p 45.

5 Simon, R (2012), 'Trust in the City? The Chartered Secretary', www.charteredsceretary.net, 30 May 2012, pp 34–35.

6 Greenspan, A (2003), Testimony to Congress.

7 Gordon Gekko (1987), in a Wall Street speech coined the phrase 'Greed is good?', [www.americanrhetoric.com/MovieSpeeches/moviespeechwallstreet.html, accessed 27 November 2013.

8 Friedman, M (1970) 'The social responsibility of business is to increase profits', reprinted in GD Chryssides and JH Kaler (ed) (1993), *An Introduction to Business Ethics* (London, Thomson), pp 249–254.

9 Keys, TS and Malnight, T 'Corporate Clout 2013: Time for Responsible Capitalism', http://www.slideshare.net/tskeys/corporate-clout-2013-time-for-responsible-capitalism, accessed 14 October 2013.

10 President of the World Bank, 2002.

11 King, J (2013) to the CBI Annual conference, November 2013.

12 Simon, R (2012), 'Trust in the City? The Chartered Secretary', www.charteredsceretary.net, 30 May 2012, pp 34–35.

13 Chambers, AD (2008a) 'The board's black hole – filling their assurance vacuum: can internal audit rise to the challenge?', 12(1) *Measuring Business Excellence –The Journal of Business Performance Management*, pp 47–63; Chambers, AD (2008c) 'Bring on the super auditors', 32(12) *Internal Auditing*, pp 18–21; Chambers, AD (2009a) 'The black hole of assurance', 66(2) *The Internal Auditor*, pp. 28–29.

14 Charan, R (1998) *Boards at Work – How Corporate Boards Create Competitive Advantage* (Jossey-Bass, ISBN-10: 0787910600; ISBN-13: 978-0787910600).

15 Maginot Line:

> '… after the French Minister of War André Maginot, was a line of concrete fortifications, obstacles, and weapons installations that France constructed along its borders with Germany during the 1930s. … While the fortification system did prevent a direct attack, it was strategically ineffective, as the Germans invaded through Belgium, outflanking the Maginot Line. … reference to the Maginot Line is used to recall a strategy or object that people hope will prove effective but instead fails miserably.' (Wikipedia, 2013a, http://en.wikipedia.org/wiki/Maginot_Line, accessed 5 August 2013).

16 Potemkin village:

> '… originally used to describe a fake village, built only to impress. The phrase is now used, typically in politics and economics, to describe any construction (literal or figurative) built solely to deceive others into thinking that some situation is better than it really is.' (Wikipedia, 2013b, http://en.wikipedia.org/wiki/Potemkin_village, accessed 6 August 2013).

17 Goodhart's Law:

> '*When a measure becomes a target, it ceases to be a good measure.*' (Wikipedia, 2013c, Wikipedia (2013b), http://en.wikipedia.org/wiki/Goodhart's_law, accessed 9 August 2013).

18 HLHC (2013a), *Changing Banking for Good, Report of the Parliamentary Commission on Banking Standards*, Vol I: Summary, and Conclusions and Recommendations, HL Paper 27-I, HC 175-I, 12 June 2013, http://www.parliament.uk/business/committees/committees-a-z/joint-select/professional-standards-in-the-banking-industry/news/changing-banking-for-good-report/, accessed 14 July 2013, p 10; see also HLHC (2013b), *Changing Banking for Good, Report of the Parliamentary Commission on Banking Standards,* Vol II: Chapters 1 to 11 and Annexes, together with formal minutes, HL Paper 27-II, HC 175-II, 12 June 2013, http://www.parliament.uk/business/committees/committees-a-z/joint-select/professional-standards-in-the-banking-industry/news/changing-banking-for-good-report/, accessed 14 July 2013.

19 CIIA (Chartered Institute of Internal Auditors) (2013), *Effective Internal Audit in the Financial Services Sector: Recommendations from the Committee on Internal Audit Guidance for Financial Services*, July 2013, [http://www.iia.org.uk/media/354788/0758_effective_internal_audit_financial_webfinal.pdf, accessed 14 July 2013.

20 HLHC (2013a), *Changing Banking for Good, Report of the Parliamentary Commission on Banking Standards*, Vol I: Summary, and Conclusions and Recommendations, HL Paper 27-I, HC 175-I, 12 June 2013, http://www.parliament.uk/business/committees/committees-a-z/joint-select/professional-standards-in-the-banking-industry/news/changing-banking-for-good-report/, accessed 14 July 2013, p 18.

21 Radcliffe-Brown, AR (1952) 'On social structure', *Structure and Function in Primitive Society* (New York, Free Press).

22 Burns, T and Stalker, GM (1961) *The Management of Innovation* (London, Tavistock Institute).
23 Durkheim, E (1893) *The Division of Labor in Society* (New York, Free Press).
24 Nestor, S (2013) 'Responsibility and the culture of challenge', 230 *Nestor's Quarterly Advisor*, Q2, p 1.
25 Kroll's 2013 Global Fraud Report found that a whistleblower had been involved in 37% of cases where fraud was uncovered and that 52% of those cases involved senior or middle management.
26 The standards of the Institute of Internal Auditors now define 'the board' as being the highest level of governing body charged with the responsibility to direct and/or oversee the activities and management of the organisation.'
27 The Code of Professional Conduct of the Chartered Institute of Internal Auditors (April 2012), which incorporates The IIA's Code of Ethics, states that internal audit's stakeholders may include employers, employees, investors, the business and financial community, clients, regulators and government.
28 The Institute of Internal Auditors (2010) *Communicating Sensitive Information Within and Outside the Chain of Command*, Practice Advisory 2440-2, May 2010.
29 Durkheim, E (1893) *The Division of Labor in Society* (New York, The Free Press).
30 Toffler, A (1970) *Future Shock* (US, Random House).
31 Argenti, J (1976) *Corporate Collapse – The Causes and Symptoms* (Maidenhead, McGraw-Hill, ISBN 0-07-084469-0).
32 Donaldson, J (1989) *Key Issues in Business Ethics* (London and San Diego, Academic Press, ISBN 0-12-220540-5), pp xii–xiii.
33 Dando, N and Raven, W (2002) *Living up to our Values – Developing ethical assurance*, The Institute of Business Ethics, p 12.
34 The Tavistock Institute (2009) 'Psychological and behavioural elements in board performance, A review of corporate governance in UK banks and other financial industry entities – Final recommendations' ('The Walker Report'), Annex 4, November 2009.
35 The World Business Council for Sustainable Development (1998).
36 Hegel, F (1807) *The Phenomenology of Spirit* (Oxford, Clarendon Press, 1977, ISBN 0-19-824597-1).
37 Tayeb, M (1988) *Organizations and National Culture* (London, Sage, ISBN 0 8039 8166 X), p 42.
38 BSI (2013) *Code of practice for delivering effective governance of organizations*, BS13500:2013 (ISBN 978 0 580 71608 9), August 2013, p 5.
39 Nestor, S (2013) 'Responsibility and the culture of challenge', 230 *Nestor's Quarterly Advisor*, Q2, p 1.
40 Phil Libin, CEO of Evernote, quoted in McCracken, Harry (2013) 'Notes to Self', *Time Magazine*, 9 December, pp 36–39.
41 Treviño, LK and Nelson, KA (2007) *Managing Business Ethics – Straight Talk About How to Do it Right* (US, Wiley, ISBN 978-0-471-75525-9), p 13.
42 Ibid, p 16.
43 Kidder, RM (1995) *How Good People Make Tough Choices* (New York, William Morrow & Company), p 18.
44 Collins, D (2012) *Business Ethics: How to Design and Manage Ethical Organizations* (US, Wiley, ISBN 9780470739948).
45 Brown, ME, Treviño, LK and Harrison, DA (2005) 'Ethical leadership: A social learning perspective for construct development and testing', 97(2) *Organizational Behavior and Human Decision Processes*, pp 117–134, see p 120.
46 Mayhew, B (2013), http://biznik.com/articles/mission-statement-vision-statement-definition-and-purpose, accessed 27 November 2013.

47 Walle, AH (2013) *Rethinking Business Anthropology* (Sheffield, Greenleaf Publishing, ISBN-13: 978-1-906093-90-7), p 45.

48 BSI (2013) *Code of practice for delivering effective governance of organizations*, BS13500:2013 (ISBN 978 0 580 71608 9), August 2013, p 7.

49 IFAC (2012) *A Definition of the Public Interest*, International Federation of Accountants, Policy Position 5, June. http://www.ifac.org/sites/default/files/publications/files/PPP%205%20%282%29.pdf, accessed 14 October 2013. Previously IFAC defined the public interest as:

'considered to be the collective well-being of the community of people and institutions the professional accountant serves, including clients, lenders, governments, employers, employees, investors, the business and financial community and other who rely on the work of professional accountants.'

50 BSI (2013) *Code of practice for delivering effective governance of organizations*, BS13500:2013, (ISBN 978 0 580 71608 9), August 2013, p 5.

51 Corporate Governance Code (2012), Supporting Principle A.1.

52 The Tavistock Institute (2009) 'Psychological and behavioural elements in board performance, A review of corporate governance in UK banks and other financial industry entities – Final recommendations' ('The Walker Report'), Annex 4, November 2009.

53 BSI (2013) *Code of practice for delivering effective governance of organizations*, BS13500:2013 (ISBN 978 0 580 71608 9), August 2013, p 8.

54 Donaldson, J (1989) *Key Issues in Business Ethics* (London and San Diego, Academic Press, ISBN 0-12-220540-5), pp xvi–xvii.

55 Treviño, LK and Nelson, KA (2007) *Managing Business Ethics – Straight Talk About How to Do it Right* (US, Wiley, ISBN 978-0-471-75525-9), p 286.

56 Mayhew, B (2013), http://biznik.com/articles/mission-statement-vision-statement-definition-and-purpose, accessed 27 November 2013.

Part D:
Corporate Governance in Practice

Chapter D1

The UK's Companies Act 2006 – Corporate Governance Issues

Introduction D1.1

One of the achievements of the Labour administration was the reform of company law. The Company Law Review Steering Group, warmly welcomed by most parties, was set up by Margaret Beckett, President of the Board of Trade, in March 1998. It finally reported in June 2001, leading ultimately to the Companies Act 2006 receiving Royal Assent on 8 November 2006 and replacing the Acts of 1985 and 1989.

When enacted, the Companies Act 2006 was the UK's longest Act ever, amounting to some 1,300 sections divided into 47 Parts, plus 16 Schedules. In comparison by length, the US Sarbanes-Oxley Act is regarded as quite extensive in scope yet has only 77 sections divided into 11 Titles.

The Companies Act 2006 was implemented in stages and, despite its length, much of the detail was left to secondary legislation. The entire Act had been implemented by 1 October 2008, with earlier implementation of certain provisions before October 2008 in order to comply with EC Directives. For instance, the provisions on electronic communications came into force in January 2007 to bring the UK into line with the EC's First Company Law Directive.

The Act does not mention executive, non-executive or independent directors, or the chairman of the board. In the eyes of the Act, in effect a director is a director is a director – any director has the same duties etc (see **D1.5–D1.9**). As far as the Act is concerned, the chairman of the board is just a director. Indeed, a board need not have a chairman or may have a different chairman for each board meeting – the Act is silent on these matters. The chairman of the board is chosen by the board, not by the shareholders. Of course, if the shareholders disapprove, they can decline to elect or re-elect that person as a director.

Gender bias in boardrooms D1.2

The Companies Act 2006 is the last UK statute to have been drafted in the male gender – which is unfortunate in view of the relatively low level of participation of women on the boards of UK companies. For years, we can be expected to quote from the Act, tending to perpetuate the status quo of gender bias.

The percentage of women on FTSE 100 boards had climbed from 6.3% to 12.2% between 1999 and 2008, before rising to 12.2% (2009), 12.5% (2010) and 13.9% in autumn 2011.[1] By 2011, 22.7% of all new non-executive appointments within FTSE 100 companies were women.[2] In 2012, it was feared that progress had stalled but since then it has picked up. By 9 January 2014, women made up 20.4% of FTSE directors, up from 17.4% in May 2013. Only three FTSE 100 companies then had no women on their boards and a week later one of these, the London Stock Exchange, announced its appointment of two women to its board. In early 2014, the highest proportion of women on FTSE 100 boards, were to be found at Diageo (44%), Capita (40%), Royal Mail (36%) and Unilever (36%). Royal Mail was also one of only four FTSE 100 companies that then had a woman as its chief executive. It does seem that the Davies Report[3] is making a discernible impact; although, of course, there is still a long way to go. At the rate of change that applied up to the end of 2010, it had been calculated that it would take 70 years to achieve gender balance. The UK is achieving this positive result without mandatory quotas as, for instance, in Germany. Perhaps this is testimony to the effectiveness in the UK of the rather light touch 'comply or explain' approach to corporate governance. Note, however, that the new strategic report has now introduced a legal requirement for all listed companies to include quantitative information on gender diversity in their new strategic reports (see **D1.15**).

Sealy and Vinnicombe reported that by 2012, 17.3% of FTSE 100 directors were women (15% in 2011) and 13.3% of FTSE250 directors were women. In 2012, two thirds of FTSE 100 companies had more than one woman on their boards. However in 2012, only 5.8% of FTSE 100 executive directors and 5.4% of FTSE 250 directors were *executive* directors. By early 2014, this 5.8% figure had risen only to 7.2% on FTSE 100 boards, although women then made up 25.1% of non-executive directors on FTSE 100 boards.

> '[in 2012] There was a sharp increase in the percentage of new appointments going to women on both FTSE 100 and 250 boards, peaking at 44% and 36% respectively. However, those high levels were short-lived and over the past six months they have dropped to 26% and 29% respectively, showing a considerable gap from the 33% required to reach Lord Davies' target of 25% women on boards by 2015.'[4]

FTSE 250 companies are not progressing at the pace of FTSE 100 companies. Early 2014, they had only 15.1% female directors, up from 13.8% in May 2013 and 7.8% three years ago.

The UK approach, as ever very light touch with respect to corporate governance, is to rely on voluntary measures to rectify the female deficit. Following the Davies Report's 8th recommendation, there is now a Voluntary Code of Conduct for Executive Search Firms.[5] The 2010 UK Corporate Governance Code (set out in full at **App1**) referred to diversity including gender for the first time in a UK corporate governance code and, being a Supporting Principle at B.2, at a quite senior level in the hierarchy of Code statements:

> 'The search for board candidates should be conducted, and appointments made, on merit, against objective criteria and with due regard for the benefits of diversity on the board, including gender.'

Since the Davies Report, the FRC has modified the UK Corporate Governance Code with two changes to the 2010 Code. A revised Provision B.2.4 now reads:

> 'A separate section of the annual report should describe the work of the nomination committee, including the process it has used in relation to board appointments. This section should include a description of the board's policy on diversity, including gender, any measurable objectives that it has set for implementing the policy, and progress on achieving the objectives. An explanation should be given if neither an external search consultancy nor open advertising has been used in the appointment of a chairman or a non-executive director. …'

and a new Supporting Principle at B.6 reads:

> 'Evaluation of the board should consider the balance of skills, experience, independence and knowledge of the company on the board, its diversity, including gender, how the board works together as a unit, and other factors relevant to its effectiveness.'

In 2003, Norway legislated for a quota of 40% women on boards of Norwegian publicly listed companies. Norway achieved this target in 2008 following a two-year grace period. Several other countries are reported to be about to introduce quotas – for instance Netherlands, Belgium, Italy, France and Malaysia.[6] Prior to this Norwegian legislation, 470 of the 611 boards impacted by the law had no female directors at all. The proportion of women in board positions rose from 6.8% to 44.2% between 2002 and 2008 – evidence beyond doubt that the imposition of a quota can lead to impressive results[7] though it has been claimed that just a few women sit on an excessive number of Norwegian boards.

In the words of a government minister:

> 'Somebody did say … that if it had been Lehman Sisters, rather than Lehman Brothers, then there may not have been as much [turmoil]. … I do seriously think half the financial services industry is women now, … Women make up half the workforce of insurance companies and banks. Why shouldn't they have a say on boards as well?'[8]

UK Prime Minister David Cameron has argued that more women in the boardroom would lead to curbing pay. Female directors overall earn salaries 14% lower than men, rising to 20% for executive directors.[9]

The issue of female participation on boards is a sensitive one. On the one hand, it can be argued that, in an intensely competitive corporate world, companies will have prioritised recruitment of the best candidates for board positions regardless of gender. If that were so, then the diversity mix we have today would be a close reflection of the available mix within the recruitment talent pool. This point of view would argue that prioritising a modified diversity mix, which is becoming an issue for nomination committees, search firms and others, is driven by political and social considerations rather than commercial ones.

On the other hand, it is argued that boards are biased towards recruiting from a small 'old boy network', clones of themselves. There is no shortage of people who are keen to take on one or more non-executive directorship, but the majority of these are not the preferred candidates of boards or their search firms. The most preferred candidate is someone with senior executive director experience, and most of those are men, not women.

While there may be fewer women than men suitably experienced for board positions, this is a consequence of past recruitment bias as well as of a 'glass ceiling' bias against women at executive levels below the board. While currently there may be fewer women than men with the appropriate experience to be the best candidates for top executive and board positions, the proportionate availability is nowhere near the ratio of recent times. It is therefore justified, it is argued, to introduce measures which positively discriminate in favour of women and other groups. It is partly a matter of social fairness. But it is also the case that companies will benefit when participation at all levels, including at board level, more closely reflects the mix of society in general. Nobody should accept that a suitable man should be appointed to a board position when there is a better female candidate. Should a suitable woman be appointed to a board position when there is better male candidate?

More diverse boards reduce the risk of blinkered 'group think' by boards. Diversity is not just about gender.

Age (see **D1.4**), nationality, ethnicity, technical background, global experience, length of time on the board, personality, whether executive or not, and whether independent or not – may be other relevant diversity factors.

Derivative actions on gender discrimination **D1.3**

Although there are many barriers to impede shareholders taking derivative actions (see **D1.10**) in the name of the company, s 260 of the 2006 Act introduced a *statutory* right for members to launch legal actions in the name of the company – which could have the effect of making it easier for members to enforce the duties that directors owe to their companies. Bearing in mind that the 2006 Act has also codified into statute law for the first time the general duties of directors, there may even be a basis for shareholders, disgruntled about gender issues, to try their luck in court. In particular, s 172 (the 'enlightened shareholder value duty' to promote the success of the company) stipulates that a director *has a duty to the company* to …

> 'act in the way he considers, in good faith, would be most likely to promote the success of the company for the benefit of the members as a whole [ie shareholders] … having regard to … [several issues listed in the Act]'

The list is not intended to be exhaustive.

This is all a single duty rather than separate duties in relation to each of the issues and parties listed. It might be argued, in some circumstances, that gender bias on board appointments, by the nomination committee of the board or by the board itself, could breach several of the issues listed by the Act, which are:

- the longer term;
- the interests of the company's employees;
- the need to foster the company's business relationships with suppliers, customers and others;
- the environment;
- the impact of operations on the wider community; and
- the desirability of the company maintaining a reputation for high standards of business conduct and the need to act fairly between members of the company.

Before an application for a derivative action will be allowed, the court must be persuaded on a number of matters, as set out in ss 260 and 263 of the Act, one of which is that, where the act or omission has already occurred, was it authorised by the company or subsequently ratified by the company? The court will also consider any evidence of the views on the matter of members of the company. Since members vote on the election of directors, this would presumably narrow down the potential for derivative actions to be brought in cases of gender bias in the making of individual board appointments. It would seem, however, that there might be potential to bring such a case not relating to a particular board appointment which has been made and has been confirmed by the shareholders, but relating to a perceived general gender bias with respect to board appointments and also to senior executive appointments below the level of the board.

Ageism **D1.4**

The 2006 Act relaxes the law by permitting persons aged over 70 to act as directors of public companies without specific shareholder approval. This is an example of a matter previously addressed in best practice guidance being transferred into statute law. Before the Combined Code included, for the first time in 2003, a set of criteria for boards to use to assess whether a director is independent, numerous lists of criteria existed, developed by corporate governance interest groups such as PIRC, ABI, NAPF and Hermes. Invariably, these had included a criterion that, after the age of 70, a director should not be judged independent. The dubious reasoning had been that, at that age, the director had little chance of being offered further directorships and might therefore be inclined not to alienate his or her colleagues by taking an independent line on boardroom issues. When, in 2003 on the instigation of the Higgs Report, specific independence criteria were included within the Combined Code for the first time, the 'aged 70' threshold was omitted. The Higgs Review was sponsored by the Department of Trade and Industry for whom ageism would have been, at the very least, politically incorrect. Now statute law has come into line. It is no longer a legal requirement for a director over the age of 70 to stand for re-election annually. Guidance in the UK Corporate Governance Code does, however, take the line that all directors of FTSE 350 companies should be subject to annual election by shareholders (Provision B.7.1).

Codification of directors' duties **D1.5**

For the first time in the UK, the Companies Act 2006 codified directors' duties, with effect from 1 October 2008. The Act contains a statutory statement of directors' general duties (ss 170–177) which has ended the reliance the UK has previously placed on common law, developed over the years through case law. In essence, the duties of directors had been based on trustee law – to act in the best interests of the trust, and so on.

Government guidance has been issued to explain what these codified duties mean. However, in order to interpret the new codified duties, it is certain that the courts from time to time will need to make reference to old case law based on directors' traditional duties as trustees. The intended effect of the new codified duties is to make directors more accountable, and directors are exposed to increased risk of litigation. Shareholders are given extended powers to sue directors for negligence, default, breach of duty (including breach of the new codified duties) and breach of trust.

We set out here the Act's statutory statement of a director's seven general duties:

1. To act within the company's powers (s 171).
2. To promote the success of the company for the benefit of its members as a whole, and in doing so have regard (*inter alia*) to specified matters (s 172).
3. To exercise independent judgement (s 173).
4. To exercise reasonable care, skill and diligence (as would be expected of a reasonably diligent person carrying out the functions of the director, as well as based on the director's actual knowledge, skill and experience) (s 174).
5. To avoid conflicts of interest (s 175).
6. Not to accept benefits from third parties (s 176).
7. To declare interests in a proposed transaction or arrangement with the company (s 177).

(In addition, under s 257, directors are also required to ensure that they act in accordance with the company's constitution.)

These general duties are, as before, owed to the company. They apply to directors, shadow directors and, in certain cases, to former directors – whether executive or non-executive. They apply to all companies – large and small, private and public. Section 170 states that s 175 (avoiding conflicts of interest) and s 176 (not to accept benefits from third parties) continue to apply after a director has left the board.

The enlightened shareholder value duty D1.6

The second duty makes it clear that the traditional fiduciary duty in common law, for a director to act in the best interests of the company, has been replaced by a new term: 'success'. Neither 'success' nor 'having regard to' have been defined in the Act, so we can expect interpretative case law to develop over time. This second duty has become known as the 'enlightened shareholder value' duty. Under this duty, a director has a duty *to the company* to act in the way he or she considers, in good faith, would be most likely to promote the success of the company for the benefit of the members as a whole (ie shareholders in the case of a company with share capital). While 'having regard to' is not defined within the Act, the Act does state that directors must have regard to:

- the longer term;
- the interests of the company's employees;
- the need to foster the company's business relationships with suppliers, customers and others;
- the environment;
- the impact of operations on the wider community; and
- the desirability of the company maintaining a reputation for high standards of business conduct and the need to act fairly between members of the company.

When the Bill was going through Parliament, 'longer term' was explained as meaning 'long-term increase in value'.[10]

This list of considerations is not intended to be exhaustive. Clearly, it introduces into law new social responsibility factors. It is, however, a single duty rather than separate duties in relation to each of the objects listed.

It is wise for a board to be able to demonstrate, by reference to past agenda papers and/or minutes that the board had regard for each of the above matters when making a decision, except if one or more of these matters was irrelevant to the decision being made. An effective way of being able to demonstrate this is for a board agenda paper calling for a board decision to have attached to it an impact assessment covering each of the above matters as well as other matters conventionally included in impact assessments. A court would not weigh up whether it agrees with a decision the board took; but a court may find a board at fault if the court concludes that the board took a decision without having regard to the above matters. Lack of evidence that a board did have regard to these matters may therefore put the directors at risk.

The independent judgement duty D1.7

Important codified duties are that each and every director is to exercise independent judgement and to exercise reasonable care, skill and diligence. With respect to the exercise of independent judgement, this is a requirement of all directors, not just those regarded by the board as being independent. The Act does not distinguish between (a) directors who are non-executive *and* independent, (b) directors who are non-executive but *not* independent, and (c) directors who are also executives and thus certainly not to be regarded as independent. The UK Corporate Governance Code, which is discretionary even for listed companies, sets out how a board should determine whether a director is independent. But, for the 2006 Act, in effect *a director is a director is a director* and each director – whether (a) independent, (b) non-executive, or (c) executive – is required to exercise independent judgement.

The Code states at Supporting Principle B.1 that:

> 'The board should include an appropriate combination of executive and non-executive directors (and in particular independent non-executive directors) such that no individual or small group of individuals can dominate the board's decision taking.'

The 2010 Code had substituted 'an appropriate combination' for the 2008 Code wording which had said 'a balance of' and had also relegated this wording to the level of a Supporting rather than a Main Principle. Under both the Listing Rules and also the FRC guidance on the Code, companies no longer have to explain how they apply the Supporting Principles. So the FRC has now conceded that, in some circumstances, it may be appropriate for a listed company to have very few executive members on the board.

The guidance in the 2008 Code that *at least 50%* of the board, excluding the chairman in the count, should be independent directors as defined by the Code, has *not* been abandoned – even though too many boards were achieving this by cutting back on the number of executive directors on the board and thus also on the overall size of the board. The 2010 Code stated, as does the current Code at Supporting Principle B.1 (**App1**) that:

> 'The board should be of sufficient size that the requirements of the business can be met and that changes to the board's composition and that of its committees can be managed without undue disruption, and should not be so large as to be unwieldy.'[11]

For a director who is not independent (in the sense of the UK Corporate Governance Code) to meet the duty to exercise independent judgement is particularly challenging, but it is a requirement of the Act. It means, for instance, that a top executive who is also a member of the board must apply his or her independent judgement when participating in board decision taking and especially when voting at the board. Many chief executives routinely hold a pre-board meeting of their top executives who are members of the board, in order to make sure that they all 'sing from the same hymn sheet' at the full board meeting. Many executive directors would quake in their shoes at the prospect of arguing or voting against the known desire of the chief executive and the rest of the top executive team. But that is what the Act requires them to be prepared to do if, by exercising their *independent judgement*, they consider that to be the right line to take in the best interests of the company. Similarly, an executive director should not be biased in favour of his or her own executive area of responsibility in deciding how to vote at the board.

Non-executive directors who are independent have an easier time of it. Non-executive directors who are not independent are somewhere in between. The latter would include directors who are large shareholders, or who represent significant shareholders – again, they should exercise independent judgement rather than voting in the best interests of their own shareholding or of the shareholding they represent – unless their independent judgement leads them to believe that those interests are aligned with the interests of the company.

New objective standard of skill and care D1.8

Lawyers differ in their view as to whether the Act has extended directors' duties, beyond the prevailing view of the courts prior to the 2006 Act, with respect to the new statutory duty:

> 'to exercise reasonable care, skill and diligence (as would be expected of a reasonably diligent person carrying out the functions of the director, as well as based on the director's actual knowledge, skill and experience).'

Suffice it to say that this wording in the Act has concentrated directors' minds – especially when linked to the risks of derivative action (see **D1.10**), the risks associated with a generally more litigious environment, and the risks of court actions for breach of directors' duties. As a consequence, some senior executives no longer aspire to promotion to their company's board. Many senior executive directors in other companies do not consider the risk-reward ratio to be attractive enough to induce them to accept non-executive director appointments in other companies. Consider the finance director of a FTSE 100, earning £2m a year. Why would such a person consider it acceptable to join another board as a non-executive director, on some £70,000 a year, when *'a director is a director is a director'*. Joint and several liability applies to all the directors. Since the requirement to exercise reasonable care, skill and diligence is related to *'the director's actual knowledge, skill and experience'*, more (much more) on financial matters is likely to be expected of the qualified accountant who joins a board as a non-executive director. He or she is likely to be asked to chair the board's audit committee, for instance. It is not just finance directors of other companies who are reluctant now to accept non-executive directorships; retiring partners of firms of accountants and lawyers are often similarly reluctant.

'Skill' means the individual has the skill set that is usually associated with his or her professional qualification and experience, and assumes the professional has kept up to date as his or her professional body would expect. 'Care' means that these skills and other qualities are not applied fecklessly. 'Diligence' means the application of those skills, and the application of other qualities, are performed consistently over time, not just now and then when the mood takes. None of this implies that a director is regarded as infallible. The increasing burden involved with being a non-executive director is making the calling less attractive to many.

Note that the 2006 Act replaces the traditional subjective standard of skill and care by a new objective standard which assesses an individual director's conduct against the knowledge, skill and experience that may reasonably be expected of a person carrying out the director's functions. If, for instance, a professionally qualified accountant agrees to join a board, and perhaps also the audit committee, *prima facie* it will be assumed that he or she possesses the skills associated with a member of that profession who, as the profession requires, has kept up to date with professional developments. In court it would not count in the director's favour had he or she not kept up with the continued professional developments required by his or her professional body/ies, and his or her log book could well be cited in court as indicative of the extent of the director's commitment to keeping on top of professional developments relevant to his or her various professional roles, including those associated with directorships held.

As a personal protection, we can expect more use by directors of the facility to take outside advice when necessary, as a consequence of a 'Provision' within the UK Corporate Governance Code since the Cadbury Code of 1992,[12] and now reading (Provision B.5.1):

> 'The board should ensure that directors, especially non-executive directors, have access to independent professional advice at the company's expenses where they judge it necessary to discharge their responsibilities as directors. Committees should be provided with sufficient resources to undertake their duties.'

The Code Provision on insurance cover, which was introduced for the first time into the 2003 Combined Code, is also likely to receive more attention. It reads (Provision A.1.3):

> 'The company should arrange appropriate insurance cover in respect of legal action against its directors.'

Conflicts of interest **D1.9**

Note that the 2006 Act empowers the independent directors of a company to authorise a director's conflict of interest arising in respect of any property, information or opportunity that conflicts or may conflict with the interests of the company.

Derivative actions **D1.10**

Directors' statutory duties are owed to the company. However, in addition to the new codification of directors' duties, there is now a statutory basis for one or more shareholders to take action against directors by means of a new extended right for shareholders to sue directors. This is known as 'derivative action'.

Prior to the Companies Act 2006, the ability to bring a derivative action rested in a complex area of common law. Broadly speaking, this permitted a derivative action where there had been conduct amounting to a fraud on the minority; but, where the wrong was rectifiable, no action was usually possible. The 2006 Act does not displace the common law in this regard but introduces a statutory derivative action procedure in parallel. Under the Act, the cause of action must arise from negligence, default, breach of duty or breach of trust by a director. Thus it is irrelevant, for example, whether the directors have benefited from the negligence or breach.

The codified 'derivative claims' provisions within the 2006 Act make the criteria and procedure for minority shareholders to make a claim in the name of the company clearer, but include protections to ensure that lawsuits without merit are quickly dismissed and that costs will fall to the person bringing the claim. Protections include that, before a shareholder is allowed to proceed with an action, the shareholder is first required to establish a *prima facie* case of breach and, secondly, to satisfy the court that the alleged conduct was inconsistent with the director's fundamental duty to act in a way which 'promotes the success of the company'. The court will also be expected to take into account whether the petitioning shareholder is acting in good faith, whether the conduct complained of had been authorised or ratified by the company, and any views expressed by 'independent' shareholders. Furthermore, directors will only be liable to the company (or its shareholders on behalf of the company) if the company can demonstrate that it has suffered loss as a result of the breach.

Safe harbour **D1.11**

The Companies Act 2006 sets obstacles in the way of a shareholder minded to bring a derivative action. This should protect directors from having to defend themselves in court against frivolous actions or actions brought by single-issue pressure groups who perhaps have acquired just a handful of shares in order to exercise the rights of shareholders.

Directors have further protection under the Act in the form of its safe harbour provisions, that cover information in the published Directors' Reports and in the published Directors' Remuneration Reports. The Business Review (which we address below) is thus covered by the 'safe harbour' provision since it is within the Directors' Report. Where safe harbour applies, a director is liable in relation only to statements that have been proved to be untrue/misleading on a knowingly/recklessly basis, or if the director knew that an omission was a dishonest concealment.

The Business Review **D1.12**

Note that the Business Review is being replaced by amendments to the Companies Act 2006 which we introduce at **D1.15** and **D1.16**.

Building the Business Review requirement into the 2006 Act gave effect, within the UK, to requirements of EC Directives. Unlike the UK's abandoned intention for a more elaborate, mandatory Operational and Financial Review (OFR), the Business Review does, however, apply to all except small companies (see **D1.13**).

The overriding purpose of the Business Review is to help shareholders assess how the directors have performed their new fundamental statutory duty to promote the success of the company. All companies other than small ones must give a 'balanced and comprehensive analysis' of the development and performance of the company's business and of its position at the end of the year, and they must describe the principal risks and uncertainties facing the business.

The 2006 Act extends further the Business Review requirements for quoted companies. These companies must disclose information about environmental, employee, social and community matters:

> 'to the extent necessary for shareholders to understand the development, performance and position of the business,'

and also include information on the main trends and factors likely to affect the future development and performance of the business.

Small companies regime **D1.13**

The Directors' Report in the Annual Report and Accounts does not need to contain a Business Review if the company is 'subject to the small companies regime'.

The small companies regime applies to a company for a financial year in relation to which the company qualifies as small and is not excluded from the regime by s 384 of the Companies Act 2006.[13]

The qualifying conditions are met by a company for a financial year in which it satisfies two or more of the following requirements:

- Turnover – not more than £6.5m.
- Balance sheet total – not more than £3.25m.
- Number of employees – not more than 50.

These requirements, which took effect in 2008 at these levels, are subject to change from time to time, as the EC increases the permissible turnover and balance sheet limits which then need to be incorporated into UK law. Every change to date has been to increase the size limits. For instance, audit exemption was introduced in the 1990s for companies with a turnover of less than £350,000, but this is now set at £5.6m.

The qualifying conditions have, generally speaking, to be met in the relevant financial year and the preceding financial year, although the provisions are technically more complex than this.

A parent company can only qualify as a small company if the group headed by it qualifies as a small group, and the qualifying conditions for that are as set out above but with the figures for each member of the group being aggregated. The small companies regime does not apply to a company that is, or was within the relevant financial year, *inter alia*, a member of an ineligible group; and a group is ineligible if any of its members is, *inter alia*, a public company.

However, the shareholders of a small company can choose to insist that the company does not avail itself of the small company regime dispensations that may apply. For instance, a small company need not have an annual audit, but the shareholders can insist that it does.

D1.14

Section 417 of the Companies Act 2006 reads:

'Contents of directors' report: business review

(1) Unless the company is subject to the small companies' regime, the directors' report must contain a business review.

(2) The purpose of the business review is to inform members of the company and help them assess how the directors have performed their duty under section 172 (duty to promote the success of the company).

(3) The business review must contain—

  (a) a fair review of the company's business, and

  (b) a description of the principal risks and uncertainties facing the company.

(4) The review required is a balanced and comprehensive analysis of—

  (a) the development and performance of the company's business during the financial year, and

  (b) the position of the company's business at the end of that year, consistent with the size and complexity of the business.

(5) In the case of a quoted company the business review must, to the extent necessary for an understanding of the development, performance or position of the company's business, include—

  (a) the main trends and factors likely to affect the future development, performance and position of the company's business; and

(b) information about—
  (i) environmental matters (including the impact of the company's business on the environment),
  (ii) the company's employees, and
  (iii) social and community issues, including information about any policies of the company in relation to those matters and the effectiveness of those policies; and

(c) subject to subsection (11), information about persons with whom the company has contractual or other arrangements which are essential to the business of the company.

If the review does not contain information of each kind mentioned in paragraphs (b)(i), (ii) and (iii) and (c), it must state which of those kinds of information it does not contain.

(6) The review must, to the extent necessary for an understanding of the development, performance or position of the company's business, include—
  (a) analysis using financial key performance indicators, and
  (b) where appropriate, analysis using other key performance indicators, including information relating to environmental matters and employee matters.

"Key performance indicators" means factors by reference to which the development, performance or position of the company's business can be measured effectively.

(7) Where a company qualifies as medium-sized in relation to a financial year (see sections 465 to 467), the directors' report for the year need not comply with the requirements of subsection (6) so far as they relate to non-financial information.

(8) The review must, where appropriate, include references to, and additional explanations of, amounts included in the company's annual accounts.

(9) In relation to a group directors' report this section has effect as if the references to the company were references to the undertakings included in the consolidation.

(10) Nothing in this section requires the disclosure of information about impending developments or matters in the course of negotiation if the disclosure would, in the opinion of the directors, be seriously prejudicial to the interests of the company.

(11) Nothing in subsection (5)(c) requires the disclosure of information about a person if the disclosure would, in the opinion of the directors, be seriously prejudicial to that person and contrary to the public interest.'

The strategic report D1.15

The Companies Act 2006 (Strategic Report and Directors' Report) Regulations 2013[14] replace the business review and apply to financial years ending on or after 30 September 2013. The purpose and required content of the strategic report does not differ significantly from the business review and all of the Companies Act 2006 requirements relating to the content of the business review are to apply to the strategic report. All of the Companies Act 2006 requirements relating to the content of the business review continue to apply to the strategic report. The strategic report is to be presented as a separate section of the annual report, outside of the directors' report.

As with the business review, companies within the small companies regime (see **D1.13**) do not have to prepare or publish a strategic report. All other companies, and all listed companies must publish a strategic report which contains a fair and balanced analysis, consistent with the size and complexity of the business, of:

1. the development and performance of the company's business during the financial year;
2. the position of the company at the end of the year; and
3. a description of the principal risks and uncertainties facing the company.

For listed companies the strategic report introduces additional content requirements not previously within the business review. These are:

1. a description of the company's strategy and business model;
2. information on human rights issues, including the company's policy and the effectiveness of that policy, to the extent necessary for an understanding of the development, performance and position of the company's business;
3. quantitative information on gender diversity.

Note with respect to point 1. (above) that the UK Corporate Governance Code (see **App1**) already has a Provision at C.1.1 as follows:

> 'The directors should explain in the annual report their responsibility for preparing the annual report and accounts, and state that they consider the annual report and accounts, taken as a whole, is fair, balanced and understandable and provides the information necessary for shareholders to assess the company's performance, business model and strategy. There should be a statement by the auditor about their reporting responsibilities.'

The discretionary 'comply or explain' character of the UK Corporate Governance Code, which strictly speaking is only an obligation for UK quoted companies with a premium listing, has thus become a *legal* requirement for all listed companies, that is those with premium or standard listings.

The Companies Act 2006, s 426 option to provide members with summary financial statements rather than the full accounts and reports, is now replaced under the Companies Act 2006 (Strategic Report and Directors' Report) Regulations 2013 by the option to send members a copy of the strategic report.

The directors' report D1.16

The Companies Act 2006 (Strategic Report and Directors' Report) Regulations 2013 remove the requirement for a published business review and the requirements to provide information about:

1. contractual or other arrangements;
2. principal activities (but note that for listed companies this is absorbed by the requirement to disclose the business model (see above);
3. directors' value of land compared to balance sheet value (but note that relevant alternative measurements bases are covered by accounting standards);
4. the acquisition of own shares by private companies;
5. policy and practice on payment of creditors.

For quoted companies the Companies Act 2006 (Strategic Report and Directors' Report) Regulations 2013 introduce mandatory greenhouse gas emission disclosures.

Board minutes and agenda papers **D1.17**

A practical issue arising from 'the enlightened shareholder value duty' is how to ensure that the board will be able to show, after the event, that they had regard to the relevant issues in coming to a particular board decision.

A way of doing this is to ensure that each board agenda paper, that is inviting a board decision thereon, includes a written impact assessment covering the issues set out in the Act with respect to 'the enlightened shareholder value duty' (to the extent that they are relevant to the particular decision), as well as the impact on any other matters against which the board wishes the impact of its decisions to be assessed. This will be especially important in larger companies with large numbers of shareholders, due to the greater risk of 'derivative action' (**D1.10**). It is to be hoped that this will not become merely a matter of minute writing style but will reflect that boards are genuinely having regard to these matters, weighing them up before coming to decisions.

The courts will not second guess a board as to whether the board made the *right* decision; but a court may look for evidence to persuade the court that the board took account of the issues that the Act requires them to, when making the board's decision, right or wrong.

This is notwithstanding that, when the Companies Bill was going through Parliament, government gave assurances that no more would be required of directors than had previously been required:

> 'There is nothing in the Bill that says there is a need for a paper trail. I do not agree that the effect of passing this Bill will be that directors will be subject to a breach if they cannot demonstrate that they have considered every element.'[14]

and

> 'The clause does not impose a requirement on directors to keep records … in any circumstances in which they would not have to do so now.'[15]

A potential, practical snag about relying on agenda papers as evidence of what was covered at board meetings is that the Act does not specifically require that agenda papers are retained. Section 248 on 'Minutes of Directors' meetings', which is in the part of the Act on 'Records of meetings of directors', states that every company must cause minutes of all proceedings at meetings of its directors to be recorded, that these records must be kept for at least ten years from the date of the meeting, and that if a company fails to comply with this section, an offence is committed by every officer of the company who is in default. If the company can be relied upon to retain all *agenda* papers, albeit with no legal obligation to do so, then individual directors will be able to rely on impact assessments contained therein, to demonstrate that the board had regard to particular issues.

If a director is in any doubt about the company's agenda paper retention policy, then the director can retain his or her own copies of the agenda papers.

The 10-year retention requirement is an innovation in this Act. Note that it is ambiguous whether minutes of board *committee* meetings must also be retained, although it would of course be prudent to do so. Note too that *'__all__ proceedings at meetings of directors'* are to be recorded. It would be wise to interpret this as meaning that there should be a minute on each agenda item, and that each decision of the board should be minuted.

Board minutes are usually drafted defensively, with half an eye to the possibility that they may be aired in court. This means it is no longer custom and practice to draft minutes that are comprehensive of all the discussion. One risk of such comprehensive minutes is that they are more likely to include content that could be used against the directors in court. Another risk is that, if something material is not referred to in such comprehensive minutes, it will be more reasonable for the court to infer that the board had overlooked that material matter.

Audit **D1.18**

Potentially one of the most significant reforms of the Companies Act 2006 is at s 534, which introduces the possibility of negotiating limited liability for companies' auditors – if the limit of liability is authorised by the members of the company and disclosed in the company's balance sheet or director's report. The authors are not aware of this having been arranged for any UK quoted company, but it is possible that it has been. It has recently been claimed that, if all the cases pending against the 'Big Four' firms of auditors were fully successful, none of them would continue in business. Auditors are perceived as fair game, since they have deep pockets secured by professional indemnity insurance. Other means of making the auditors' risk fairer have been considered but have not been pursued – for instance, 'proportionate liability' where the court would apportion damages between various parties (particularly between the board and the auditors) in proportion to their relative negligence etc. Another means might have been a mechanistic 'cap' on auditors' liability related to, for instance, balance sheet value or a multiple of the audit fee. The opportunity is now also available to provide audit services through limited liability partnerships – which may have the effect of reducing the risk to the audit firm.

Audit committees of boards have been reluctant to concede limited liability for their auditors, as the audit firms have not promoted this possibility as a means of reducing their audit fee. In the fullness of time this approach might be implemented if the auditors' threat materialises of withdrawing audit services from clients perceived by audit firms as being high risk. UK companies also quoted in the US would be unable to negotiate limited liability arrangements with their auditors, as no such opportunity exists in the US.

Perhaps we should point out that neither in the US nor in the UK is there a statutory requirement to change the audit firm after a number of years, although the audit engagement partner has to be changed after seven years.

A notable difference between the US Sarbanes-Oxley Act (2002) and the UK Companies Act 2006 is that some non-audit services banned by the Sarbanes-Oxley Act are permitted to be provided by the external auditor under the 2006 Act and also under the UK Auditing Practices Board's ethical standards for auditors. Note that the wiggle room in the APB's Ethical Standards for external auditors has recently allowed the head of audit at one Big Four firm to contend that they are absolutely clear that also providing some internal audit services for one of their external audit clients 'falls fairly and squarely within what is expected of the ethical standards of the UK's Auditing

Practices Board'.[16] Many, including the Chartered Institute of Internal Auditors, would consider that the external auditor is seriously conflicted if the same firm also provides internal auditing services. For instance, can you imagine the external audit partner advising the audit committee of the board that the quality of internal audit services is, in his or her view, seriously deficient? Or, can you imagine the partner in charge of the internal audit service provision expressing a candid view to the audit committee that the company should consider changing their external auditor?

External auditing standards require external auditors to form a view on the extent to which they will rely on their client's system of internal control as a means of obtaining audit assurance. In a broad sense, the internal audit is a part of the company's system of internal control. This means that the external auditor would not be able to place reliance on the client's system of internal control for the duration that the audit firm provided both the external and the internal audit services. 'Chinese walls' could never be robust enough to fully mitigate this conflict. Indeed, sourcing both internal and external audit from the same service provider is usually a matter of achieving overall financial economies which are only available if the two audits collaborate with each other – hence 'Chinese walls' do not apply.

Notes

1 Prosser, David (22 September 2011), *The Independent*, p 39.

2 Treanor, J (2011) 'Boardroom Quotas for Women? Good and Bad' on The Guardian website.

3 Lord Davies (February 2011), Women on Boards, on the BIS website.

4 Sealy, Ruth and Professor Vinnicombe, Susan (2013) *The Female FTSE Board Report 2013*, Cranfield International Centre for Women Leaders, December 2013, available at http://www.som.cranfield.ac.uk/som/dinamic-content/media/Research/Research%20 Centres/CICWL/FTSEReport2013.pdf, accessed 30 December 2013.

5 For instance, at www.mwmconsulting.com.

6 GlobeWomen, a female-only lobby group (*www.globewomen.org*) reported in Valeria Criscione (22 August 2011), Norway eyes female boardroom quota, *The Financial Times, FTfm supplement*, p 5.

7 Lewis, R and Rake, K (2008) 'Breaking the Mould for Women Leaders: Could Boardroom Quotas Hold the Key?' at www.eve-olution.net.

8 Harriet Harman, 3 August 2009.

9 Institute of Directors and Croner Reward, reported in Pickard, Jim and Brian Groom (29–30 October 2011), *Financial Times*, p 1.

10 Lord Sainsbury, Hansard, col. 245, 11 January 2006.

11 Supporting Principle B.1.

12 Provision 1.5 of the 1992 Cadbury Code read: 'There should be an agreed procedure for directors in the furtherance of their duties to take independent advice if necessary, at the company's expense.'

13 For instance, s 384 excludes a company from the concessions of the small companies' regime if it is an authorised insurance company, a banking company, an e-money issuer, an ISD investment firm or a UCITS management company.

14 SI 2013/1970.

15 Lord Goldsmith, Hansard, col. 841, 9 May 2006.

16 Margaret Hodge, Hansard, col. 592, 11 July 2006.

17 KPMG now does some of Rentokil Initial's internal auditing. 'We are absolutely clear that this falls fairly and squarely within what is expected of the ethical standards by the Auditing Practices Board.' (KPMG's head of audit, quoted in *Accountancy Magazine*, September 2009, p 8).

Chapter D2

The UK Approach to Corporate Governance

Introduction D2.1

Both the Financial Reporting Council[1] and Sir David Walker[2] (see Chapter **D5**) suggested that UK corporate governance failed. It certainly failed to prevent the dysfunctionalities that allowed the global financial crisis to blow much of UK plc off course. Not surprisingly, attention has since been given by the EC to the governance of financial institutions,[3] and the UK Walker Review reported in final form in November 2009. The Vickers Report[4] appeared in September 2011 and its recommendations were largely accepted by the UK government, though with a long lead time for their full implementation by 2018. These reforms mean that bank deposits and overdrafts of ordinary consumers and small businesses will be handled only by ring-fenced parts of banks, which will not be allowed to embark on risky investment activities, and banks will have bigger cushions so they are better able to withstand losses.

In Chapters **G2** to **G5** we explore perceptions since the global financial crisis that internal audit has been part of corporate governance that has failed, and new measures in 2012 and 2013 designed to address this problem.

The UK Corporate Governance Code (set out in full at **App1**) is primarily for quoted companies with a UK premium listing, with some content designed to apply to just the largest 350 of these companies. The general intention is that other entities should also consider the applicability of the Code. Apart from strengthened regulation of financial institutions, and the 2013 introduction of a mandatory rather than advisory shareholder vote on the remuneration policy of the board, very little has so far transpired in the UK that is mandatory in nature. The Code is discretionary.

Development of the Code D2.2

The Walker Review recommended that the duties of owners should be set out in a separate Stewardship Code, which the FRC published in July 2010 with a revision in September 21012 (set out in full at **App2**). So the UK Corporate Governance Code therefore now omits this category of content. The 18 Main Principles, 25 Supporting Principles and 52 Provisions of the Code thus have extended its latest content which had been held steady in the 2006 and 2008 Code revisions. Compare this with the mere 19 provisions of the 1992 Code (see **C4.17** and **F2.1**), which had no separate Principles, and we can see how much more elaborate best practice guidelines have become since the Cadbury Code set us down this path in 1992.

The status of the Code D2.3

Even so, UK corporate governance is so light touch as to have little grip at all. It gives boards wide discretion – a lot of wiggle room. That is because the Provisions within the Code have only 'comply or explain' status under the Listing Rules. The Code and Listing Rule 9.8.6 (5) and (6)[5] (see **A2.20** and **D2.7**) now require listed companies to explain how they have applied only the Main Principles but not the Supporting Principles. Furthermore, the FSA always regarded this listing rule as merely about disclosure – they have never disciplined a company for failing to apply a Principle in the Code. Even when, in the past, Code content had later been given statutory force, as with the Companies Act 2006 (and earlier, since 2003) requirement that shareholders should vote on the board's remuneration policy, it lacks teeth as the vote is just advisory and rarely reverses remuneration decisions.

Responsibility for corporate governance **D2.4**

Indeed, who should be responsible for corporate governance? Disingenuously, much of the spin in the wake of the recent crisis has been that shareholders should be more responsible, more active and make their voices more clearly heard. But shareholders lack power, and their Exocet option of voting directors off the board will rarely be a prudent course of action for them to take. There is little evidence that shareholders will be given more powers; so, meanwhile, boards determine these things, and too many boards take their cue from management who are effectively in the driving seat.

The Code has dusted down a paragraph from the 1992 Cadbury Report to remind us that boards, not shareholders, are responsible for corporate governance:

> 'Corporate governance is the system by which companies are directed and controlled. Boards of directors are responsible for the governance of their companies. The shareholders' role in governance is to appoint the directors and the auditors and to satisfy themselves that an appropriate governance structure is in place. The responsibilities of the board include setting the company's strategic aims, providing the leadership to put them into effect, supervising the management of the business and reporting to shareholders on their stewardship. The board's actions are subject to laws, regulations and the shareholders in general meeting.'[6]

'Premium' and 'standard' listings **D2.5**

The advisory, discretionary nature of the UK Code has recently been potentially further marginalised by the FSA's replacement of 'primary' and 'secondary' listings by 'premium' and 'standard' listings. For years ending after 31 December 2009, overseas registrants with a 'premium' listing (there are fewer than 200) must, for the first time, regard Listing Rule 9.8.6 on the Code as applicable to them; but companies with a 'standard' listing can opt out of Rule 9.8.6. So, applying the Code's Main Principles and complying or explaining with respect to the Provisions of the Code need no longer concern UK companies who can now choose to opt into the 'standard' listing. Companies with a standard tier listing can also opt out of other requirements.

Prior to this new requirement, 45 out of 171 overseas primary companies already voluntarily observed the UK's Code. Whereas 'standard' tier companies are required to observe only the minimum standards required by EU Directives, 'premium' tier have to observe what are termed 'super-equivalent' standards (including the UK Corporate Governance Code etc). Companies within the standard tier still have to prepare a corporate governance statement, but it need not be in line with the Corporate Governance Code.

'Standard' tier is now available for the first time to UK companies, whereas previously it was for overseas companies only. The question must be whether it will become 'standard' practice for UK companies to opt for a 'standard' listing. Presumably that is the implication of the word. The FSA thinks not, as companies with a 'standard' listing will not feature in the FTSE indices and will thus lose market visibility; but one wonders how long it will be before indices are developed which track companies with 'standard' listings. The requirements of the new 'standard' listing equate to minimum EC requirements, whereas the requirements of the new 'premium' listing are termed 'super equivalent' and include following Rule 9.8.6 on the Code. There are 15 Indices in the FTSE UK Index Series – including the FTSE 100, FTSE 250 and the All-Share Indices. The All-Share Index represents between 98 and 99% of UK market capitalisation and is the aggregation of the FTSE 100, FTSE 250 and FTSE Small Cap Indices.

The key to these 2010 changes is the amendment to Listing Rule 14.1.1. UK companies, as well as non-UK ones, can now apply for a standard listing. LR 14.1.1 applies to a company with, or applying for, a standard listing of shares other than (1) equity shares issued by a company that is an investment entity unless it has a premium listing of a class of its equity shares; and (2) preference shares that are specialist securities. Those with a standard listing must comply with the corporate governance disclosure rules set out in this Rule.[7]

This means that only those with a premium listing have to comply with the fuller UK Corporate Governance Code disclosures set out in the Rule.[8]

Extracts from the Disclosure and Transparency Rules **D2.6**

DTR 7.2 Corporate governance statements	
DTR 7.2.1R 29/06/2008	An *issuer* to which this section applies must include a corporate governance statement in its directors' report. That statement must be included as a specific section of the directors' report and must contain at least the information set out in DTR 7.2.2 R to DTR 7.2.7 R and, where applicable, DTR 7.2.10 R.
DTR 7.2.2R 29/06/2008	The corporate governance statement must contain a reference to: (1) the corporate governance code to which the *issuer* is subject; and/or (2) the corporate governance code which the *issuer* may have voluntarily decided to apply; and/or (3) all relevant information about the corporate governance practices applied beyond the requirements under national law. [Note: Article 46a(1)(a) first paragraph of the *Fourth Company Law Directive*]
DTR 7.2.3R 29/06/2008	(1) An *issuer* which is complying with DTR 7.2.2R (1) or DTR 7.2.2R (2) must: (a) state in its directors' report where the relevant corporate governance code is publicly available; and

DTR 7.2 Corporate governance statements – *contd*	
	(b) to the extent that it departs from that corporate governance code, explain which parts of the corporate governance code it departs from and the reasons for doing so. (2) Where DTR 7.2.2R (3) applies, the issuer must make its corporate governance practices publicly available and state in its directors' report where they can be found. (3) If an issuer has decided not to apply any provisions of a corporate governance code referred to under DTR 7.2.2R (1) and DTR 7.2.2R (2), it must explain its reasons for that decision. [Note: Article 46a(1)(a) second paragraph and Article 46a(1)(b) of the *Fourth Company Law Directive*]
DTR 7.2.4G 29/06/2008	A *listed company* which complies with LR 9.8.6R (6) (the comply or explain rule in relation to the *Combined Code*) will satisfy the requirements of DTR 7.2.2 R and DTR 7.2.3 R.
DTR 7.2.5R 29/06/2008	The corporate governance statement must contain a description of the main features of the *issuer's* internal control and risk management systems in relation to the financial reporting process. [Note: Article 46a(1)(c) of the *Fourth Company Law Directive*]
DTR 7.2.6R 29/06/2008	The corporate governance statement must contain the information required by paragraph 13(2)(c), (d), (f), (h) and (i) of Schedule 7 to the Large and Medium-sized Companies and Groups (Accounts and Reports) Regulations 2008 (SI 2008/410) (information about share capital required under Directive 2004/25/EC (the Takeover Directive)) where the *issuer* is subject to the requirements of that paragraph. [Note: Article 46a(1)(d) of the *Fourth Company Law Directive*]
DTR 7.2.7R 29/06/2008	The corporate governance statement must contain a description of the composition and operation of the *issuer's* administrative, management and supervisory bodies and their committees. [Note: Article 46a(1)(f) of the *Fourth Company Law Directive*]
DTR 7.2.10R 29/06/2008	Subject to DTR 7.2.11 R, an *issuer* which is required to prepare a group directors' report within the meaning of section 415(2) of the Companies Act 2006 must include in that report a description of the main features of the group's internal control and risk management systems in relation to the process for preparing consolidated accounts. In the event that the *issuer* presents its own annual report and its consolidated annual report as a single report, this information must be included in the corporate governance statement required by DTR 7.2.1 R. [Note: Article 36(2)(f) of the *Seventh Company Law Directive*]

Extracts from Listing Rules **D2.7**

LR 9.8.6R 06/06/2011	In the case of a listed company incorporated in the United Kingdom, the following additional items must be included in its annual financial report: … (5) a statement of how the listed company has applied the Main Principles set out in the UK Corporate Governance Code, in a manner that would enable shareholders to evaluate how the principles have been applied. (6) a statement as to whether the listed company has: (a) complied throughout the accounting period with all relevant provisions set out in the UK Corporate Governance Code; or (b) not complied throughout the accounting period with all relevant provisions set out in the UK Corporate Governance Code and if so, setting out: (i) those provisions, if any it has not complied with; (ii) in the case of provisions whose requirements are of a continuing nature, the period within which, if any, it did not comply with some or all of those provisions; and (iii) the company's reasons for non-compliance.
LR 9.8.7 06/04/2010	An overseas company with a premium listing must include in its annual report and accounts the information in LR 9.8.6R (5), LR 9.8.6R (6) and LR 9.8.8R (9).
LR 9.8.7A 06/04/2010	An overseas company with a premium listing that is not required to comply with the requirements imposed by another EEA State that correspond to DTR 7.2 (Corporate governance statements) must comply with DTR 7.2 as if it were an issuer to which that section applies. An overseas company with a premium listing which complies with LR 9.8.7 R will be taken to satisfy the requirements of DTR 7.2.2 R and DTR 7.2.3 R but (unless it is required to comply with requirements imposed by another EEA State that correspond to DTR 7.2) must comply with all of the other requirements of DTR 7.2 as if it were an issuer to which that section applies.
LR 9.8.9 01/07/2005	The requirements of LR 9.8.6R (6) and LR 9.88.8 R relating to corporate governance are additional to the information required by law to be included in the listed company's annual report and accounts.

- DTR refers to the FSA's Disclosure and Transparency Rules
- The European Economic Area (EEA) comprising EU members states and Norway, Iceland, Liechtenstein and (for some purposes) Gibraltar.

2010, 2011 and 2012 changes **D2.8**

Since the UK Corporate Governance Code remains just advisory in nature, it might be seen as rather superfluous to itemise its 2010 modified features – except that many companies, whether listed or not, choose voluntarily to observe it, and under the Listing Rules all companies with a 'premium' listing must disclose their position on the Code. For 2010, the FRC moved existing content around and elevated or demoted content between the Main Principles, Supporting Principles and Provisions. Bearing in mind that the Code is discretionary, this was little more than moving the deck chairs, adding a few more deck chairs as well, and fine tuning the wording here and there. It is most unlikely to have the significant impact that the FRC hopes for, which is to alter corporate governance behaviour. FRC policy is to consider amending the Code very two years. In the event, some changes relating to diversity were brought forward to 2011. The 2012 Code (**App1**) has incorporated these changes (see **D.2.10**) and has also extended the audit provisions so that FTSE 350 companies should tender their audit at least every ten years (Provision C.3.7), disclose the significant issues the audit committee considered in relation to the financial statements (Provision C.3.8) and explain how the audit committee assessed the effectiveness of the external audit process (also Provision C.3.8).

The key role of the board's chair **D2.9**

The FRC considers that it has changed the tone of the Code by exhorting, but not for the first time, that more attention be paid to the spirit of the Code rather than the letter of it, and also by a new emphasis on the crucial and extremely demanding leadership role of the chairman, with a stress upon the chairman promoting a culture of openness and debate.[9, 10] It is interesting to note that the draft Walker Review recommended that chairmen of bank boards should have significant financial experience, though this was balanced in the final Walker Report by an acknowledgement that leadership qualities rather than banking experience might determine the selection of the chairman. No doubt between the draft and final report, Sir David Walker was lobbied to accommodate to the *status quo* of not all chairman of financial institutions having the in-depth financial experience that the draft report was expecting.

Nominating and electing directors, and evaluating performance **D2.10**

The word 'search' appeared in the 2010 Code for the first time,[11] implying the desirability to use search consultants to find new board members. Provision B.2.4 now reads:

> 'A separate section of the annual report should describe the work of the nomination committee, including the process it has used in relation to board appointments. This section should include a description of the board's policy on diversity, including gender, any measurable objectives that it has set for implementing the policy, and progress on achieving the objectives. An explanation should be given if neither an external search consultancy nor open advertising has been used in the appointment of a chairman or a non-executive director. Where an external search consultancy has been used, it should be identified in the annual

report and a statement made as to whether it has any other connection with the company.'

For the first time, the 2010 Code referred to the potential benefits of diversity on the board, including gender[12] and this was strengthened in 2011 in response to the Davies Report.[13] In line with the Walker Review, for the first time the 2010 Code advised that evaluation of FTSE 350 boards should be externally facilitated at least once every three years, and that disclosure should be made as to whether an external facilitator has any other connection with the company.[14] These requirements are continued through to the 2012 Code at Provision B.6.2 **(App1)**.

Picking up on a Walker Review recommendation, the 2012 Code recommends that directors of FTSE 350 companies should be subject to annual election,[15] a measure which most FTSE 350 boards are implementing. Some have criticised this change as encouraging short-termism; but the new Code, chiming with s 172 of the Companies Act 2006, also stresses in several places the importance of the board promoting the long-term success of the company.[16]

The board and risk management **D2.11**

The Code continues to mention the desirability of the board having a risk committee comprising exclusively independent directors unless the audit committee covers this area.[17] Now the Code recommends that the annual report discloses *all* of the board committees and the number of meetings, membership and attendance record of each.[18] Previously this guidance covered just the remuneration, nominations and audit committees.

The Walker Review's recommendation that all large financial institutions should have a board risk committee separate from the audit committee goes further than the UK Corporate Governance Code. On the other hand, Walker allows that the board's risk committee might comprise non-executive directors who are not independent and may also include the finance director. The intention of both the Code and the Walker Review is to encourage boards to take ownership of risk rather than allowing it to be dealt with just at an executive level or not at all.

On board risk committees, readers may wish to refer to Chapter **E9** and **App4.18**.

Responding to boards' failures to understand the risks their companies were running as they entered the global financial crisis, a significant change is that the Principle articulating the board's responsibility for internal control now states that the board is responsible for determining the nature and extent of the significant risks it is willing to take.[19] Risk management has been elevated above internal control, whereas in the 2008 Code it was the other way round. While the 2008 Code advised that the board's review of the effectiveness of internal control should include the risk management systems, the guidance is now that the board should review the effectiveness of the company's risk management and internal control systems.[20]

Corporate rather than financial reporting **D2.12**

A section of the Code previously titled 'Accountability and Audit' is now 'Financial and Business Reporting'.[21] Undoubtedly the current Code gives a new stress to 'business' or 'corporate' reporting, not just 'financial' reporting. For the first time, in 2010 it stated that directors should include in the Annual Report an explanation of the basis on which the company generates or preserves value over the longer term and the strategy for delivering the objectives of the company.[22] The suggestion is that this explanation should be within the Business Review required by EC Directive and by s 417 of the Companies Act 2006 (see **D1.12** to **D1.14**). It gives a new lease of life to ASB Reporting Standard No. 1 (especially §§ 30, 31 and 32) published in 2006 in anticipation of the Operating and Financial Review (OFR) requirement that was looming at that time, only to be unceremoniously dumped by Gordon Brown in the interest of cutting red tape. It was a move by the UK Chancellor that had little support from business who were geared up to implement OFR requirements; it was symptomatic of the government's light touch to regulation.

Executive remuneration D2.13

It would have been surprising if the Code had not sharpened up the guidance on executive remuneration, though the changes are very limited. The FRC must have considered that the previous guidance would hardly have struck the right chord today in stating that performance-related elements of executive remuneration should form a significant proportion of the total: so it abandoned it. A new Supporting Principle states that performance-related elements of executive directors' remuneration should be stretching and designed to promote the long-term success of the company.[23] Similar sentiment is to be found in the Code's Schedule A on remuneration which also, for the first time, suggests that challenging performance criteria might include 'non-financial performance metrics where appropriate'. It also deals obliquely with the risk of perverse incentives by using the words 'remuneration incentives should be compatible with risk policies and systems'.

Audit committees D2.14

There were no audit committee changes within the 2010 Code. The FRC's guidance on audit committees, previously known as the Smith Report, was updated in December 2010.[24] As referred to in **D2.8** above, the 2012 Code (see **App1**) extended the audit provisions so that FTSE 350 companies should tender their audit at least every ten years (Provision C.3.7), disclose the significant issues the audit committee considered in relation to the financial statements (Provision C.3.8) and explain how the audit committee assessed the effectiveness of the external audit process (also Provision C.3.8)

Principles without rules, monitoring and enforcement D2.15

The current Code, as with its most recent predecessors, has Main Principles, Supporting Principles and Provisions. By analogy, the Main Principle on our roads might be construed as being to 'drive safely'. A Supporting Principle would be that 'speed kills'. Careful enunciation, refinement and communication of these

Principles is important; but without rules, monitoring and sanctions, there would be carnage on our roads, just as there has been carnage in our financial institutions and in many other corporate entities. On one hand, improving drivers' values and ethics might impact positively on road behaviour. On the other hand, enforced rules can change behaviour and provide better assurance that important principles are observed.

Using this driving analogy, some drivers would drive safely even if there were no speed limit, no monitoring and no sanctions. Likewise, some companies would be committed always to high standards of corporate governance. It is the other companies (and, indeed, even the best of companies when they have their backs to the wall) that are the problem, and that is why mandatory rules, monitoring and sanctions should have their place.

The counter argument, which currently holds sway in the UK, is that (as with speed limits, monitoring and sanctions which might prevent a driver behaving optimally on an empty dual carriageway at 3am) mandatory corporate governance requirements might sometimes impede optimal performance. But we have not had optimal performance, have we? This is not such a significant risk compared to the risk of having no rules, no monitoring and no enforcement.

Certainly, corporate governance Principles are crucially important. But then enforceable rules (developed from carefully defined Principles) need to be introduced to raise the probability that the Principles will be followed by those who may be reluctant to do so, or by those who would claim to apply the Principles whereas in reality they do not.

As a result of its consultation on the latest Code update, the FRC concluded that the light touch 'comply or explain' approach continues to have wide support. But the majority of the respondents were companies or proxies for companies. Arguably, the wider societal viewpoint was insufficiently expressed. Perhaps the FRC is to be admired for doggedly persevering with this discretionary approach with what is now the fifth revision of the UK Code since the 1992 Cadbury Code: truly an enduring triumph of hope over experience; in reality, an example of regulatory capture. The Code, now joined by the new Stewardship Code, is more elaborate, more sophisticated and more refined than ever before, but both are still discretionary in all respects.

Whereas the FRC has standard setting, monitoring and enforcement roles with respect to its other regulatory responsibilities for financial reporting, external auditing and actuarial matters, in the field of corporate governance the FRC only crafts the wording of the entirely discretionary Code. The recent failures of corporate governance do not indicate that a lighter touch regulation is justified in contrast to financial reporting, external auditing and so on. UK corporate governance regulation is so light touch as to have little grip at all. It works to the extent that it does because of the UK propensity to voluntarily follow best practice more than might be the case in other countries. Some of the content in the UK Corporate Governance Code should be made mandatory and enforced. Departures from any part of the UK Corporate Governance Code should require shareholder approval. Neither is the case today.

This theme is developed further in Chapter **D3**.

Notes

1 Financial Reporting Council: Review of the Effectiveness of the Combined Code: Call for Evidence (March 2009), p 2; Progress report and Second Consultation (July 2009), p 3; Governance Code (December 2009), p 12.
2 Walker, Sir David (November 2009): A review of corporate governance in UK banks and other financial industry entities – Final recommendations, 'The Walker Review', p 9.
3 European Commission (June 2010): Corporate governance in financial institutions and remuneration policies, Green Paper [COM(2010) 284/3]; consultation period closed 1 September 2010.
4 Independent Commission on Banking (September 2011), Final report and Recommendations ('The Vickers Report'), ISBN 978-1-845-32-829-0.
5 Previously Listing Rule 12.43A, then 9.8.6; and, from 2010, 9.8.6 (5) and (6).
6 In Preamble to the 2010 UK Corporate Governance Code, p 1.
7 See DTR 7.2.
8 See LR 9.8.
9 Code, pp 2, 3.
10 Code, Supporting Principle at A.3.
11 Code, Supporting Principle at B.2.
12 2010 Code, Supporting Principle at B.2 read:
'The search for board candidates should be conducted, and appointments made, on merit, against objective criteria and with due regard for the benefits of diversity on the board, including gender.'
13 Women on Boards (February 2011), 'The Davies Report', on the BIS website.
14 Code, Provision B.6.2.
15 2010 and 2012 Codes, Provision B.7.1. The 2012 Code is at **App1**.
16 Code, Main Principle at A.1; first Supporting Principle at D.1; para 1 of Schedule A.
17 2010 and 2012 Codes, Provision C.3.2. The 2012 Code is at **App1**.
18 2010 and 2012 Codes, Provision A.1.2. The 2012 Codeis at **App1**.
19 2010 and 2012 Codes, Main Principle at C.2. The 2012 Code is at **App1**.
20 2010 and 2012 Codes, Provision C.2.1. The 2012 Code is at **App1**.
21 2010 and 2012 Codes, at C.1. The 2012 Code is at **App1**.
22 2010 and 2012 Codes, at C.1.2. The 2012 Code is at **App1**.
23 Code, new Supporting Principle at D.1.
24 Financial Reporting Council (December 2010), Guidance on Audit Committees, on the FRC website.

Chapter D3

Critique of UK Corporate Governance

The UK's Five Pillars of Corporate Governance D3.1

Let us start by considering the five pillars of UK corporate governance. First, there is the Financial Reporting Council (FRC), which elegantly wordsmiths the UK Corporate Governance Code (previously termed 'the Combined Code'). Unlike its remit in the fields of financial reporting, actuarial affairs and external auditing, the FRC has no corporate governance enforcement powers.

The FRC D3.2

The FRC determines the standards for financial reporting, external auditing and actuarial affairs and, for each, the FRC monitors and enforces their application. The respective professional bodies are back-up. There is no equivalent corporate governance professional body – as has now come about for remuneration consultants following recommendations first made by Sir David Walker in July 2009.[1] Indeed, due to the discretionary character of most of the UK's best practice for corporate governance, there is very little that *could* be enforced currently.

The FSA and FCA D3.3

The second pillar of corporate governance is the enforcer of the Listing Rules, which until 2012 had been the UK Listing Authority (UKLA) of the Financial Services Authority (FSA). The FSA has now been replaced by Financial Conduct Authority (FCA) in this role.[2] The UK Corporate Governance Code is not within the Listing Rules, although the Listing Rules do refer to it. The UKLA interprets Listing Rule 9.8.6 as imposing merely a disclosure obligation with respect to both the Principles and the Provisions of the Code – despite the wording of this rule which at least implies, if not specifically requires, that the Code's Principles must be applied. This listing rule at (5) is now limited to just the *main* principles, though it sued to cover *all* Principles (Main and Supporting).

The Listing Rule on the Code

9.8.6R 06/06/2011	In the case of a listed company incorporated in the United Kingdom, the following additional items must be included in its annual financial report: … (5) a statement of how the listed company has applied the Main Principles set out in the UK Corporate Governance Code, in a manner that would enable shareholders to evaluate how the principles have been applied.

	(6) a statement as to whether the listed company has: (a) complied throughout the accounting period with all relevant provisions set out in the UK Corporate Governance Code; or (b) not complied throughout the accounting period with all relevant provisions set out in the UK Corporate Governance Code and if so, setting out: (i) those provisions, if any it has not complied with; (ii) in the case of provisions whose requirements are of a continuing nature, the period within which, if any, it did not comply with some or all of those provisions; and (iii) the company's reasons for non-compliance.

Is corporate governance less important than financial reporting, external auditing and actuarial affairs, that its oversight should be so light touch as to have little grip at all? Surely not! Some 50% of the largest economies in the world are companies not countries. So the proper governance of companies is crucially important.[3] Readers may wish to refer to **C1.10**.

Owners D3.4

Currently, great stress is being placed on owners – the third pillar of corporate governance – to improve corporate governance, on the basis that if shareholders are well informed they should and must make their voices heard. Privately, everyone knows it will always be an unequal contest. To pin the blame, and the responsibility to do better in future, upon shareholders is doomed to failure and will allow management to carry on as before – which they wish to do. Managements and boards hold most of the cards. High dependence on shareholders will never work.

External Auditors D3.5

The fourth pillar of corporate governance is, or should be, the professions, notably external auditors. They have been disappointing – with little motivation to take on extra work. Cadbury's 1992 intention had been that auditors would review all directors' assertions on Code matters that were objectively verifiable. The 1992 Cadbury Report stated:

> 'Companies' statements of compliance [with the Cadbury Code] should be reviewed by the auditors before publication. The review should cover only those parts of the compliance statement which relate to provisions of the Code where compliance can be objectively verified. …'[4]

Many of both the Principles and Provisions of the Code are wholly or partially verifiable independently. It is claimed there is little or no appetite for external auditor review on the part of companies, or investors or auditors; but it could make an effective contribution to enhancing corporate governance.

Since 2003, auditors have been expected to review only nine of the growing number of Provisions of the Code, and none of the growing number of Principles. Five of the original Cadbury Provisions, which continued to be reviewed by the external auditors after the publication of the 1998 Combined Code, are now no longer reviewed. The additional Provisions that are now reviewed do not represent audit expansion into other areas – rather, they are a consequence of audit committees being addressed by a larger number of Provisions commencing with the 2003 Code; and so the overall result has been a considerable *narrowing* of auditor attention. Gone is auditor review of Provisions on (a) a formal schedule of matters reserved to the board (2003: A.1.1), on (b) directors taking independent advice (2003: A.5.2), on (c) the selection of non-executive directors (2003: A.7.1) and (d) on their terms of appointment (2003: A.7.2), and (e) on their service contracts (Cadbury: 3.1), and (f) on non-executive determination of executive remuneration (Cadbury 3.3).

In the light of (a) the development of auditing standards on assurance engagements, (b) the new possibility of limiting auditor liability, and (c) the Sarbanes-Oxley section 404 experience of auditors of US quoted companies, it should be possible for external auditors to assume an expanded role in providing assurance on directors' corporate governance assertions.

Under the UK Companies Act 2006, liability of the external auditor can be limited by contract between the company and the auditor, subject to shareholder approval.[5] This opportunity has rarely been applied, in particular because companies see little value in it for them. An alternative way of limiting auditor liability would be for UK law to allow proportionate liability to be determined by the courts, where liability would be shared for instance between the board and the auditors proportionate to their respective degrees of culpability. The disadvantage of proportionate liability is that it does not allow the auditor to know in advance the ceiling of their liability. A further way of limiting auditor liability would be to cap by law at a particular amount – as in Germany, where a cap of €4m applies. Limiting auditor liability would open the doors to auditors being more prepared to take on additional responsibilities, including attesting to directors' corporate governance assertions.

Statute and mandatory regulation **D3.6**

The fifth pillar of corporate governance is statute and mandatory regulation. Here, the UK approach has been disappointing. Even when, rarely and against vested interests, aspects of corporate governance have become mandatory by statute or by regulation, they have been successfully fabricated so as to lack teeth. Even when statute and regulation come into play, the imperative seems to have been to build in enough wiggle room for companies to be able to ignore anything they wish to ignore. Many may remember the fuss in the UK when the EC suggested that audit committees should be made mandatory for public interest entities. The UK's rearguard action led to a paragraph in the 2006 Directive which effectively avoided the mandatory requirement:

> 'Member States may allow or decide that the provisions laid down in paragraphs 1 to 4 shall not apply to any public-interest entity **that has a body performing equivalent functions to an audit committee**, established and functioning according to provisions in place in the Member State in which the entity to be audited is registered. In such a case the entity shall disclose which body carries out these functions and how it is composed.'[6] (bolding added)

Light touch D3.7

Public interest entities D3.8

True to UK form of making corporate governance very light touch, it is no surprise that 'public interest entity' (which, by EC requirement, must include all listed companies but other entities only at the discretion of individual member states) has been defined in the UK in the minimal permissible way by EU law – it excludes large privately held companies, mutuals, large professional partnerships, and so on – about all of which the public has a real interest, as the current financial crisis has clearly shown. The House of Lords Economic Affairs Select Committee's 2009–11 Inquiry into audit market concentration, leading to an Office of Fair Trading referral of the audit market to the Competition Commission, illustrates the strong public interest in the governance of large professional partnerships. In 2010 the Institute of Chartered Accountants and the FRC jointly released a governance code tailored for large accounting firms and discretionary, as with the UK Corporate Governance Code.[7]

Comply or explain D3.9

The Walker Review told us that five of the six main areas of reservation of contributors following Sir David's draft Report were calls to water it down.[8] Most contributors to both the Walker and the 2010 UK Corporate Governance Code reviews were companies or their proxies. The wider societal interest has been insufficiently sought, articulated and taken account of. A non-binding approach to corporate governance, with so much wiggle room that almost any best practice may be got around, suits the companies and other market participants well for the flexibility it provides.

So, a key question is to whom should the FRC listen? Should the FRC lead from the front or go no further than a lowest common denominator, broad consensus approach? Its progress report on the 2010 Code consultation gave its answer. It said:

> 'Almost all commentators … said that they continue strongly to support the principles-based approach of the Code and the flexibility provided by "comply or explain", and that they would not want the perceived advantages of this approach to be lost. For this reason the FRC intends to adopt three guiding principles when assessing the lessons to be learnt from the financial crisis and the case for changes to the Code and its accompanying guidance during the next phase of the review. These are:
>
> - Where there is a demonstrable need for best practice to be clarified or strengthened, this will be addressed either through amendments to the Code or additional, non-binding guidance;
>
>   …; and
>
> - We will seek to avoid an increase in the overall level of prescription in the Code and to preserve its principles-based style.'[9]

'Comply or explain' is the right approach in the sense that a company should always explain if it does not comply. But 'comply or explain' also gives complete discretion on compliance with any part of the Code. Discretion should not be as broad as it is. Consideration should be given to (a) making some current 'comply or explain' corporate governance provisions mandatory; and (b) requiring shareholder approval for departure from *any* aspect of the Corporate Governance Code. With respect to (a), possible examples would be Provision A.2.1 on separating the roles of chairman and chief executive, and Provision C.3.1 on having an audit committee.

Some might say that an approach with more mandatory rules has been shown, as with the US experience, not to be more effective. But how much worse would the US experience have been without their Securities and Exchange Act, without their Sarbanes-Oxley Act (with penalties of up to a $5m fine and prison for 20 years)[10] – and so on?

Apply or explain? Apply and explain? **D3.10**

An alternative (already adopted in the Netherlands and by King III in South Africa) would be that the requisite approach should be to 'apply or explain' rather than 'comply or explain'. This might result in even more wiggle room for a company to say they apply a principle when they probably do not. 'Apply *and* explain' would give less wiggle room. For instance, almost every company would be likely to say they avoid excessive concentration of power at the top of the business, regardless of the reality. This would work best if the principles were mandatory and if explanations were credible and informative.

Principles, not rules? **D3.11**

Sir Adrian Cadbury supported a principles-based approach to corporate governance, rather than a rules-based approach. He argued that rules could be 'got round' more easily than principles. For instance, if a rule stated that the chairman should not also be the chief executive, then a company could observe the rule by designating one person as the CEO and another as the chairman, even though the reality might be different. On the other hand, if there were a principle that excessive concentration of power at the top of the company should be avoided, then such a principle might be harder to avoid. However, to be effective this approach does require that a company discloses how it applies the principles and it also requires the principles to be mandatory. In these regards, disclosure has been inadequate and applying the principles has not been enforced. Indeed, by their nature, principles would be harder than rules to make mandatory:

> 'First, the focus has to be, not on the form of governance, but on its quality, for which legal tests are difficult to devise. The Code of Best Practice, for example, refers to the need for boards to include non-executive directors of sufficient calibre for their views to carry significant weight in the boards' decisions. A word like "calibre" may have no legal standing, but it can certainly be recognised by investors and financial commentators. When a major UK company appointed its first batch of non-executive directors, they were seen as not measuring up to this requirement of the Code. Investor pressure and press comment resulted in the appointment of a further non-executive director of sufficient bottom.
>
> To take another example, the Committee said in its report that in principle the chairman and chief executive should not be the same person. Being non-prescriptive, however, the Code did not make separation of the top two corporate

posts a recommendation. If separation were to be a legal requirement, boards could circumvent it by giving two of their members different titles, while in reality power remained in one pair of hands. If shareholders queried the balance of power on such a board, the board could reply that they complied with the law and that there was no more to be said. The [1992 Cadbury] Code, however, requires that:

"There should be a clearly accepted division of responsibilities at the head of a company … such that no one person has unfettered powers of decision."

Shareholders can demand to know precisely how powers are divided, and continue probing until they are satisfied. In that sense, a code recommendation can prove a sterner test in practice of a true separation of powers than a law to the same effect.

A further reason for backing statutory regulation with market regulation is that codes can reflect changing circumstances or new governance issues as they arise, whereas the law by its nature takes time to catch up with new situations. In the same way the law sets a floor to corporate or professional behaviour, whereas codes can promote best practice beyond lawful practice. The law is limited to the letter, while codes can put substance above form.'[1]

Light touch D3.12

The extent of wiggle room is truly amazing. The phraseology of the UK Corporate Governance Code allows companies to claim full compliance with a number of Provisions, even when they are not complying with the best practice expressed in those Provisions. Examples of excessive flexibility within the Code, allowing a company to claim compliance when it deviates from best practice, include the following:

- A company may be fully compliant with Provision A.3.1 even if the chairman was not independent when appointed to the chairmanship.
- A company may be fully compliant with Provision B.1.1 when it judges a director to be independent notwithstanding that the director 'fails' to meet some of the stated independence 'criteria'.
- A company may be fully compliant with Provision D.1.3 even when the remuneration of its non-executive directors includes share options.
- A company may be fully compliant with Provision C.3.6 even if it has no internal audit function.
- A company may be fully compliant with Provision C.3.7 when the board does not accept the advice of its audit committee on the appointment, reappointment or removal of the external auditors. This would not be possible for a company quoted in the US: section 301 of the Sarbanes-Oxley Act (2002).

Even when statute and regulation come into play, the imperative seems to have been to build in enough flexibility for companies to be able to ignore anything they wish to ignore. There is no need to get shareholder approval if a company wishes to disregard any Main or Supporting Principle or a Provision. There is no disciplinary oversight by the Listing Authority except to enforce disclosure standards.

Until 2013 there was the advisory ('non-binding') nature of members' votes on their companies' remuneration policies which the Walker Review has recommended should remain non-binding.[12] This was a classic example of apparently tightening up corporate governance but in fact not doing so. Since 2002 there has been a *statutory requirement* that shareholders vote on the remuneration policy of the board, but the vote was until 2013 just advisory. Its incorporation in the Companies Act 2006 did not change its advisory character.[13] In 2009 the almost 60% vote against by Shell's shareholders did not modify the payment of full bonuses to Shell's top executives who had failed to meet their performance targets. Also in 2009, the 90.4% vote against RBS's remuneration policy did not modify the packages given to the new top team; and 12 months earlier the vote was to prove ineffective at avoiding the severance deal for RBS's chief executive deposed a few months later.

The right of shareholders to vote on the remuneration committee report goes further than owners' powers in most other areas, but it did not work. Walker proposed that a vote of less than 75% in favour of the remuneration report should mean that the chair of the remuneration committee would be obliged to stand for re-election at the next AGM – a tentative step in the right direction but which was not expected to achieve very much, as Sir David himself inferred,[14] and which was not implemented.

Watering down **D3.13**

It could not have been a slip of the pen that the FRC's consultation on the 2010 Code revision project referred to it as the 2007 Code when its publication date was June 2008. The preamble to the 2010 Code also dates the previous review as being 2007. If any time were inopportune to water down the Code, in two detailed ways and one serious general way, surely it was June 2008. In detail, the Code was then changed to endorse company chairmen in some circumstances belonging to audit committees and also filling the chairman role for more than one FTSE 100 company. The more serious, general change was the end of the guidance that companies should explain in their annual reports their application of the 26 *Supporting* Principles in the Code[15] which has led to a more recent listing rule revision to bring it into line with the FRC's relaxation. Nowhere in the 2008 Code or subsequently has there been any guidance that the *Supporting* Principles must be applied. All of the 2008 changes outlined in this paragraph were continued in the 2010 and 2012 Codes.

A new cloud has appeared on the horizon which is a further watering down. The FSA's old two-tier listing structure ('primary' and 'secondary') continues but is re-labelled so that 'primary' becomes 'premium', and 'secondary' becomes 'standard', diminishing the influence of the UK Corporate Governance Code. We discuss this in full at **D2.5**. Let's hope that a standard listing does not become standard practice, as it carries with it no obligation to observe the UK Corporate Governance Code.

Owners or boards in charge? **D3.14**

It would be surprising indeed if companies or their suppliers of services supported the concept of more robust corporate governance requirements. It seems they will readily agree to any corporate governance guidelines so long as they are toothless and do not fetter their discretion to do whatever they like. We should be asking the question, 'Who are the real owners of corporate governance?'.

While it is now apparent that 'comply or explain' means UK corporate governance is so light touch as to have hardly any grip at all, many influential groups would like to keep it that way. The rights of owners are muted. Management hold most of the cards. Boards are too often under the thumb of top management, and shareholders lack sufficient rights to exercise effective control. The extreme option of voting directors off the board will rarely be a prudent course for shareholders to take, and their other enforcement options are very limited. And, through greed, owners are often as guilty as their companies of encouraging excessive risk taking.

But *should* owners have more corporate governance powers? The FRC thinks not. Should there be a clear separation of ownership from control? The FRC thinks so. The 2010 UK Corporate Governance Code resurrected from the 1992 Cadbury Code what the FRC calls 'the classic definition' of corporate governance, which affirms that boards, not owners, own corporate governance:

> 'Corporate governance is the system by which companies are directed and controlled. **Boards of directors are responsible for the governance of their companies. The shareholders' role in governance is to appoint the directors** and the auditors and to satisfy themselves that an appropriate governance structure is in place. The responsibilities of the board include setting the company's strategic aims, providing the leadership to put them into effect, supervising the management of the business and reporting to shareholders on their stewardship. The board's actions are subject to laws, regulations and the shareholders in general meeting.'[16] (bolding added)

This quotation from Cadbury is repeated in the preamble to the 2012 Code.

It is disingenuous to expect more active owners to solve corporate governance problems without giving owners mandatory responsibility for corporate governance or the powers to be effective. There is a lack of realism in pinning on owners most of the responsibility to enhance corporate governance. Equally, it is disingenuous to give the impression that all would be well if only shareholders were more actively engaged. This will not work. To start with, the interests of owners do not necessarily make them more responsible or more prudent than managements and boards. And the powers of owners are insufficient to call boards to account. Other than making binding, rather than advisory only, the shareholder vote on the board's remuneration policy, there have been no significant changes that increase shareholder powers.

Notes

1 A review of corporate governance in UK banks and other financial industry entities – final recommendations, 'The Walker Review' (November 2009), recommendations 38 and 39, and Annex 12.

2 In 2013, the FSA was replaced by the FCA and the Prudential Regulation Authority (PRA). The FCA, a company limited by guarantee, now regulates financial firms providing services to consumers and maintains the integrity of the UK's financial markets; it focuses on the regulation of conduct by retail and wholesale financial services firms. The PRA is a wholly owned subsidiary of the Bank of England; it carries out the prudential regulation of deposit-taking institutions, insurers and designated investment firms (financial firms, including banks, investment banks, building societies and insurance companies. The UKLA comes under the remit of the FCA.

3 Calculated based on value-added which is a similar basis to the gross domestic product of nations which is used in this comparison. Year 2000 data had it as 51/49; by 2004, it was 53/47 (www.corporations.org/system/top100.html).

4 The third recommendation of the Cadbury Report (1992), at p 54.

5 UK Companies Act 2006, ss 534–538.

6 UK lobbying led to the addition of this paragraph 5 to Article 41, chapter 10 of the Eighth Directive, European Union, 2006 (Subject: Directive of the European Parliament and of the Council on statutory audits of annual accounts and consolidated accounts, amending Council Directives 78/660/EEC and 83/349/EEC and repealing Council Directive 84/253/EEC (9.6.2006, Official Journal of the European Union, L 157/103)).

7 FRC and ICAEW (January 2010); The Audit Firm Governance Code, on the FRC website.

8 Walker Review, pp 10, 11.

9 FRC (July 2009): Second Consultation Review of the Effectiveness of the Combined Code.

10 Section 906 of the US Sarbanes-Oxley Act (2002) introduced these maximum penalties for lapses in corporate governance certification responsibilities which had also been introduced by the Act.

11 Within the text of Sir Adrian Cadbury's 1998 lecture to Gresham College in London, delivered at Mansion House, London, which was reproduced in full in the 4th edition of this Handbook (2008, ISBN 978 84766 053 4).

12 Walker Review, p 119.

13 The seven Schedule B Provisions of the 1998 Combined Code were omitted from the 2003 Combined Code in view of the separate regulations which had come into force: Directors' Remuneration Report Regulations 2002, SI 2002/1986. Initially, a statutory instrument attached to the Companies Act 1985, the requirement is now within the Companies Act 2006.

14 Walker Review, p 119.

15 Paragraph 3 of the preamble to the 2008 Combined Code reads (bolding added):

> 'The Listing Rules require UK companies listed on the Main Market of the London Stock Exchange to describe in the annual report and accounts their corporate governance from two points of view, the first dealing generally with their **adherence to the Code's main principles**, and the second dealing specifically with non-compliance with any of the Code's provisions. The descriptions together should give shareholders a clear and comprehensive picture of a company's governance arrangements in relation to the Code as a criterion of good practice.'

The equivalent paragraph in the 2006 Preamble started:

> 'The Code contains main and supporting principles and provisions. The Listing Rules require listed companies to make a disclosure statement in two parts in relation to the Code. In the first part of the statement, the company has to report on how it applies the principles in the Code. This should cover **both main and supporting principles**.'

16 Financial Reporting Council, Consultation on the Revised UK Corporate Governance Code (December 2009), within the proposed Introduction to the new Code, on p 11 (available on the FRC website).

Chapter D4

The Walker Review of Corporate Governance in UK Banks and other Financial Industry Entities

Introduction D4.1

Very few anticipated the global financial crisis of 2008. Paul Moore, head of regulatory risk at HBOS from 2002 until he was made redundant in 2004, had famously chided HBOS at the Treasury Select Committee for their excessive sales culture; but the complete collapse of the securitisation and wholesale money markets was seen as a risk by very few. In September 2008, Lord (Eddie) George, previously Governor of The Bank of England, said he knew of nobody who saw the sudden freezing up of the wholesale markets.[1] Certainly the auditors missed it – leading the Treasury Select Committee to ask 'What value audit?', and for the House of Lords Economic Affairs Select Committee to report that they considered auditors were complacent. They also considered auditors were derelict in duty. Their report said:

> 'We do not accept the defence that bank auditors did all that was required of them. In the light of what we now know, that defence appears disconcertingly complacent. It may be that the Big Four carried out their duties properly in the strictly legal sense, but we conclude that, in the wider sense, they did not do so.'

and

> 'We regard the recent paucity of meetings between bank auditors and regulators, particularly in a period of looming financial crisis as a dereliction of duty by both auditors and regulators.'[2]

The first consultation paper of the Walker Review[3] of corporate governance in large banks and other financial institutions (BOFIs) conceded that corporate governance has failed and that there is a legitimate public interest in how these entities are run:

> '… how banks are run is a matter for their boards, that is, of corporate governance. … The massive dislocation and costs borne by society justify tough regulatory action … It is clear that governance failures contributed materially to excessive risk taking in the lead up to the financial crisis.'[4]

Walker's faith in 'comply or explain' D4.2

So it is disappointing, indeed very surprising, that Sir David Walker, now chairman of Barclays Bank, concurred with the wide consensus view of interested market participants that the FRC's Corporate Governance Code is 'fit for purpose' and 'the surest route to better corporate governance practice'. If that were so, then why had it failed so drastically? There is nothing wrong with enunciating Principles and Provisions, but to expect observance of these, in substance as well as form, when all we have, by and large, is a discretionary Code, is expecting far too much of human nature – and is totally inadequate as a response to the recent acute crisis.

The UK approach to corporate governance is little more than prescribing the patient with a placebo. Over the years, it has been redesigned, enlarged and refined, but it is still a placebo. It contains trace elements of active ingredients. But it has failed to work. It can be strengthened by more prescription. And we are a long way from prescribing a dosage that would be toxic or would have significant harmful side effects, as Sir David fears.[5]

He says:

> '… undue hampering of the ability of bank boards to be innovative and to take risks would itself bring material costs. It would check the contribution of the banks to the wider economic recovery and delay restoration of investor confidence in banking as a sector capable of generating reasonable returns for shareholders.'[6]

Values and ethics, behaviour and provisions, monitoring and enforcement D4.3

In their response to the first Walker consultation, the Association of Chartered Certified Accountants (AACA) suggested that the governance failings in the banking sector were more to do with inappropriate values and behaviours at senior levels. Inappropriate values and behaviours will continue unchecked without monitoring and sanctions.

Sir David Walker says:

> '… in an array of closely related areas in which prescribed standards and processes play a necessary but insufficient part … behavioural improvement is more likely to be achieved through clearer identification of best practice and more effective but, in most areas, **non-statutory routes to implementation** so that boards and their major owners feel "ownership" of good corporate governance.'[7] (bolding added)

While focusing on behaviour, Sir David's report overlooked the fundamental importance of values and ethics,[8] relying instead on better articulation of discretionary corporate governance best practice as the means to improve behaviour. This is whistling in the wind. The UK discretionary Code approach to corporate governance, dating back to 1992, with six amended versions since 1992, has largely failed to achieve the required behavioural changes. Regular fine-tuning of this flawed approach will make no significant difference.

Sir David is convinced that more corporate governance regulation would hold little prospect of improving behaviour. We don't know. It hasn't been tried. Sir David says:

> 'The behavioural changes that may be needed are unlikely to be fostered by regulatory *fiat*.'

Inconsistently, with respect to *financial* regulation rather than to corporate governance, Sir David supports:

> 'tougher capital and liquidity requirements and a tougher regulatory stance on the part of the FSA';[9]

and he considers that:

> 'the "comply or explain" approach to guidance and provisions under the Combined Code provides **the surest route to better corporate governance practice**.' (bolding added)

Why tough, mandatory regulation on financial matters but not for corporate governance?

Active Shareholder Involvement **D4.4**

The Walker Review had proposals to encourage more active involvement of shareholders of large financial institutions, for instance:

- the annual re-election of the chairman of the board;
- the chairman of the remuneration committee to stand for re-election the following year if the remuneration committee's report gets less than 75% support of those voting;
- any executive remuneration above the median of executive board members' remuneration to be disclosed and justified in the remuneration committee's report;
- disclosure if any senior executives have received or may receive enhanced pension benefits; and
- that the FRC, with an extended remit, should develop a 'Principles of Stewardship' code for institutional investors and fund managers – which has been done, and since revised (see **App2**).

The first and the last of these are now addressed by the FRC, with all directors (including the chairman) of FTSE 350 companies standing for annual re-election if the Code, commencing with its 2010 update, is voluntarily followed.[10] How many of these proposals will be taken forward, and whether they will have any bite, remain open questions.

Sir David's proposal, accepted by the FRC, is welcome that shareholder stewardship should be separated from the Corporate Governance Code and covered more fully by a separate Code, ratified by the FRC and first published in June 2010. Sir David suggested that arrangements to monitor the extent of adherence to this Stewardship Code should be put in place by the FRC, but that this Code too should have only a 'comply or explain' status.[11] At least this would represent a move to monitoring (but not enforcing) one part of corporate governance.

Directors, Chairmen and Board Evaluation **D4.5**

Walker also recommends increased time commitment from non-executive directors – between 30 and 36 days for a major bank – and that chairmen should be at least two-thirds of full-time.[12] Both these recommendations are at best only marginal increases over what has, on average, applied in the past to medium and large companies of all sorts. Walker further recommends that board evaluations might be less frequent but should be more rigorous, with external facilitation and explained in the annual report. The UK Code now recommends external facilitation of board evaluation at least once every three years (**App1**, Provision B.6.2)[13] and that a company's annual report should state how the evaluation has been conducted (Provision B.6.1).

A 2009 study by Nestor Advisors[14] found that banks perform better when the board chairmen have banking experience, which is a Walker recommendation.

Since surveys have shown that the mean time commitment of FTSE non-executive directors is already close to 30 days, Walker's proposed increase would be hardly likely to make a significant difference even if it were enforced mandatorily, which was not Walker's intention.

Remuneration and bonuses **D4.6**

The Financial Services Authority's Code of Practice[15] on remuneration in the financial services has much common ground with the Walker and the European Commission's recommendations,[16] as well as with ACCA's highly regarded Corporate Governance Agenda and Credit Crunch policy papers.[17] ACCA's policies, which came first, may have been instrumental in influencing some of the Walker and other recommendations.

Walker recommended that bonuses should be spread over three years, that more than half of variable remuneration should amount to long-term incentives vesting in three to five years, and that there should be claw back of bonuses to reclaim amounts in circumstances of misstatement and misconduct. This is reminiscent of s 304 of the 2002 US Sarbanes-Oxley Act,[18] though that is a statutory matter, and extends to all quoted US companies.

Walker also recommended that the remuneration committee's remit should extend to all executives expected to exceed the median compensation of executive board members, and that such remuneration levels should be disclosed (in bands, not by individuals) in the remuneration committee report. Walker recommended the creation of a professional body of remuneration consultants bound by a professional code of conduct, which has been achieved.[19]

Walker recommended that the advisory ('non-binding') nature of members' votes on their companies' remuneration policies should remain non-binding.[20] More recently the vote has been made a binding vote.

Risk Committees of the Board **D4.7**

The UK's Chancellor castigated the Northern Rock bank's board in these terms:

> 'Far more attention needs to be paid to risk taking, by board members. It really is quite extraordinary that boards themselves didn't more fully understand what risks they were allowing their banks to be exposed to … The first line of defence, not just for shareholders but for everyone else, is to make sure that boards are up to the job. Now I think the regulatory system needs to ask some serious questions to ensure that people have the risk monitoring measures in place. Northern Rock didn't, for example – they weren't nearly as robust as they should have been.'[21]

On this topic the Walker Review, like the curate's egg, is good in parts. It points out that BOFI audit committees are potentially or actually overloaded, and that BOFIs should therefore have board risk committees additional to their audit committees.[22] The Walker Review also makes it clear that the UK Corporate Governance Code's implication is insufficient that boards may legitimately review just the risk management *systems* without considering the acceptability of the risks that those risk management systems have identified. On the other hand, the Walker Review is weaker than the UK Code, in that a Walkeresque board risk committee might comprise just a majority of non-executive directors and without these necessarily being independent, and with the finance director (an executive, of course) possibly being a member. The Code's risk committee of the board would comprise only independent directors. These Walkeresque board risk committees are rightly intended by Walker to be additional to the executive risk committees that the BOFIs are likely already to have, which is clearly also the intention of the UK Corporate Governance Code in view of its guidance that the members of the board risk committee should all be independent directors.

The current UK Corporate Governance Code has a Provision (C.3.2) to the effect that companies should have board risk committees unless the audit committee undertakes this work:

> 'The main role and responsibilities of the audit committee … should include:
>
> …
>
> 'To review the company's internal financial controls and, unless expressly addressed by a separate board risk committee composed of independent directors, or by the board itself, to review the company's internal control and risk management systems …'

Board Assurance, and Chief Risk Officers **D4.8**

While Sir David Walker's recommendations on chief risk officers are welcome, he addressed inadequately how boards should obtain the assurance they need that the policies of the board are being implemented by management and that there are no banana skins round the corner, known to management or otherwise, over which the company may slip in the future. External stakeholders, including shareholders, also need better and more comprehensive assurance.

It was Paul Moore, head of regulatory risk at HBOS from 2002 until 2004, who subsequently said that:

> 'people like him need to report direct not to executive management but to non-executives whose job it is to rein in management.'[23]

Sir David recommends that the removal of the chief risk officer should have the prior agreement of the board, and that the CRO's remuneration should be approved by the chairman of the board or the chairman of the board's remuneration committee. Sir David recommends that the CRO should have a status of total independence from individual business units and should serve the main board and its risk committee. Sadly, Sir David goes along with the view that the CRO may have an internal reporting line to top management, though not to the management of individual business units. The UK Corporate Governance Code is silent on these matters.

In January 2014, it was reported that the UK Prudential Regulation Authority had expressed doubts at Santander UK's intention to make a new appointment to the dual roles of deputy chief executive and also chief risk officer.

Risk management and internal audit **D4.9**

In their first response to the FRC's 2008 Combined Code consultation, ACCA recommended that the risk management and internal audit functions of companies in all sectors should be regarded as costs of running the board, and that these functions should report on their work and also for 'pay and rations' to the board or to its independent chair, so that boards thereby receive more of the assurance they need, independent of management. There have been many examples of internal audit being prevented by management from exercising their professional judgement when deciding what to report to the board or to its audit committee. 'He who pays the piper calls the tune'. Full independence from management is preferable. Arrangements such as these need not diminish the quality of assurance that risk management and internal audit would be able to give to management at all levels. Assurance is strengthened if it is provided by a party independent of the receiver of that assurance.

The board's assurance vacuum is an acute issue. Such arrangements would not diminish the quality of assurance that the risk management and internal audit functions would be able to give to management at all levels. In 2009, ACCA recommended to the FRC that internal audit should be mandatory for listed companies, which is not the policy of the Chartered Institute of Internal Auditors.[24] The Walker Review does not concur with these suggestions, but does recommend that the chief risk officer of a large financial entity should report to the board's risk committee, but not for pay and rations.

It is interesting to note that a recent draft Indian corporate governance guideline, subsequently abandoned, said:

> 'In order to ensure the independence and credibility of the internal audit process, the Board may appoint an internal auditor and such auditor, where appointed, should not be an employee of the company.'[25]

Internal Audit **D4.10**

Internal audit emerged virtually unscathed from the global financial crisis. Was it because they did a good job, or were there low expectations about their remit? The internal auditing profession succeeded in lowering expectations so that internal auditors would emerge unblamed. At least this means there is not an expectations gap for internal auditors, as there is for external auditors. That Sir David sees internal audit as no part of the solution speaks volumes. He says:

> 'Discussions in the context of this Review process suggest that failures that proved to be critical for many banks related much less to what might be characterised as conventional compliance and audit processes, including internal audit, but to **defective information flow, defective analytical tools and inability to bring insightful judgement in the interpretation of information and the impact of market events on the business model.**'[26] (bolding added)

Sir David misunderstands and understates the appropriate role of internal audit in the contemporary world. Surely internal audit has a role in identifying and communicating to the board 'defective information flow, defective analytical tools and inability to bring insightful judgement in the interpretation of information and the impact of market events on the business model'. The above reference effectively said that internal auditing is just a routine compliance function and not expected to be insightful. Put another way, if internal audit is not seen as part of the problem, there is a risk that it may not be thought to be part of the solution.

By persuading Sir David that the global financial crisis was others' fault, the profession of internal auditing has lost a once in a generation opportunity to enhance their corporate governance role for the benefit of investors, other stakeholders, boards of directors and indeed society generally. The field has been left wide open for chief risk officers to fill the board's assurance vacuum at internal audit's expense.

In the above quotation, Walker used the word 'insightful', albeit in a way that contrasts 'insightful judgement' with 'conventional' internal audit. Since Walker, the word 'insightful' has started to assume the status of a 'code word' in the context of internal auditing, with leading internal auditing figures campaigning for a more insightful approach to internal auditing.

Indeed, this is almost the only reference to internal auditing in the entire Walker report. The draft report (July 2009) had not mentioned internal auditing at all – except to include the Chartered Institute of Internal Auditors as one of the bodies that had responded to the consultation.

The House of Lords Inquiry into concentration in the audit market also inquired into the causes of the financial crisis. The Institute of Internal Auditors were excellent witnesses at an Inquiry session in December 2010,[27] but internal audit hardly featured in the report of that Inquiry. The explanation is that none of the witnesses to any of the Inquiry sessions made significant suggestions about an enhanced future role for internal audit which would contribute to filling the board's assurance vacuum.

Should it not be mandatory for boards of public interest entities to receive assurance, independent of management, that (a) the policies of the board are being implemented by management, and (b) significant internal and external risks to the company have been identified and are being mitigated?

Addressing the same concern, Lord Myners quite recently suggested that:

> 'companies should be encouraged to establish independent "secretariats" serving non-executive directors to reduce dependence on information provided by company executives and auditors'.[28]

It was Lord Smith of Clifton who said in a House of Lords debate, on 8 December 2008, that:

> 'crucially, boards, and particularly non-executive directors need assurance independent of management which requires a much greater enhancement of the role of internal audit'[29]

and then, in a further House of Lords debate eight days later, that:

> 'the function of internal audit must be strengthened.'[30]

Conclusion **D4.11**

In conclusion, it has been said that 'greed is good'[31] – if so, we have had too much of a good thing. Greenspan[32] said that it is not that folk have become more greedy, but that the avenues to express greed have become much greater. Perhaps Greenspan was being too sanguine about human nature? Certainly, many interested parties are currently demonstrating their determination not to close off Greenspan's avenues.

Sir David Walker acknowledges that corporate governance has failed.[33] This is the broad consensus, with which the FRC concurred in its 2009 progress report on the Combined Code consultation.[34] Corporate governance failed to prevent the crisis. Corporate governance failed to prevent dysfunctionalities that resulted in the crisis. It is alarming that, in view of this widely held view that corporate governance has failed, the changes made have been so anodyne as to have no prospect of succeeding.

Notes

1 Lord (Eddie) George (3 September 2008), annual lecture of The Worshipful Company of Chartered Accountants, Cass Business School.

2 House of Lords Economic Affairs Select Committee (30 March 2011), Auditors: *Market concentration and their role*, Volume 1, HL Paper 119-I, ISBN 978 0 10 847326 5 (also available on the Parliament website), see paras 142, 161 198, 201 and 142.

3 Walker, David, (July 2009): A Review of Corporate Governance in UK Banks and Other Financial Industry Entities ('Walker Review'), Draft Report [Walker Review Secretariat, www.hm-treasury.gov.uk/walker_review_information.htm].

4 Walker Review (July 2009), Draft Report, pp 6, 8. The following was also on p 6 of the final Walker Report (November 2009): '… how banks are run is a matter for their boards, that is, of corporate governance. … The massive dislocation and costs borne by society justify tough regulatory action …'.

5 Walker Review (November 2009), Final report, p 10.

6 Walker Review, p 6.

7 Walker Review (November 2009), p 9.

8 'Values' gets just two incidental mentions, once each in Annexes 4 (p 145) and 12 (p 172). 'Ethics' is referred to once in a quoted comment from a contributor, which the Walker Review did not fully endorse, and once in Annex 2 to acknowledge that the Institute of Business Ethics contributed to the review.

9 Walker Review, p 11; see also p 6.

10 Code Provision B.7.1.

11 Walker Review, pp 17 and 18: Recommendations 17 and 18.

12 Walker Review, pp 45 and 53: Recommendations 3 and 7.

13 Provision B.6.2.

14 Nestor, Stilpon and David Ladipo, (May 2009): Bank Boards and the Financial Crisis – A Corporate Governance Study of the 25 Largest European Banks, (Nestor Advisors, London, www.nestoradvisors.com).

15 Financial Services Authority (August 2009), Reforming Remuneration Practices in Financial Services – Feedback on CP09/10 and Final Rules [Policy Statement 09/15].

16 C(2009) 3177 (30.4.2009): Communication from the Commission complementing Recommendations 2004/913/EC and 2005/162/EC as regards the regime for the remuneration of directors of listed companies (SEC(2009)580 & SEC(2009)581). C(2009)3159 (30 April 2009): Commission Recommendation on remuneration policies in the financial services sector (SEC(2009)580 & SEC(2009)581). COM(2009) 211 final (30.4.2009): Communication from the Commission accompanying Commission Recommendation complementing Recommendations 2004/913/EC and 2005/162/EC as regards the regime for the remuneration of directors of listed companies (C(2009)3159) and Commission Recommendation on remuneration policies in the financial services sector (C(2009)3177). IP/09/674 (press release): Financial services sector pay: Commission sets out principles on remuneration of risk-taking staff in financial institutions. Memo/09/213 (29 April 2009): Recommendation on directors'

remuneration: Frequently Asked Questions (see PI/09/673). Memo/09/212 (29 April 2009): Recommendation on remuneration in financial services sector: Frequently Asked Questions (see PI/09/673).

17 Relevant ACCA policy and discussion papers: Corporate Governance and Risk Management Agenda (Policy paper, November 2008); Climbing out of the credit crunch (Policy paper, September 2008); Corporate Governance and the Credit Crunch (Discussion paper, November 2008).

18 Sarbanes-Oxley Act (2002): Sec. 304. Forfeiture of certain bonuses and profits.

(a) ADDITIONAL COMPENSATION PRIOR TO NONCOMPLIANCE WITH COMMISSION FINANCIAL REPORTING REQUIREMENTS.—If an issuer is required to prepare an accounting restatement due to the material noncompliance of the issuer, as a result of misconduct, with any financial reporting requirement under the securities laws, the chief executive officer and chief financial officer of the issuer shall reimburse the issuer for—

(1) any bonus or other incentive-based or equity-based compensation received by that person from the issuer during the 12-month period following the first public issuance or filing with the [Securities and Exchange] Commission (whichever first occurs) of the financial document embodying such financial reporting requirement; and

(2) any profits realized from the sale of securities of the issuer during that 12-month period.

(b) COMMISSION EXEMPTION AUTHORITY.—The Commission may exempt any person from the application of subsection (a), as it deems necessary and appropriate.

19 Walker Review, pp 103–105, Recommendations 38 and 39.

20 Walker Review, pp 119–120.

21 Alistair Darling, Chancellor of the Exchequer, Downing Street Press Conference, 13 October 2008, answering a question.

22 Walker Review, Recommendation 23.

23 Reported on BBC Radio 4's 'Today' programme, 30 October 2008. See also *The RiskMinds 2009 Risk Managers' Survey: The Causes and Implications of the 2008 Banking Crisis* (2010) by Moore, Carter & Associates with Professor Andrew Kakabadse of Cranfield School of Management.

24 Witnesses: Drs Ian Peters (Chief Executive) and Sarah Blackburn (past president) of the Chartered Institute of Internal Auditors. The House of Lords Report and their Evidence volume which starts the CIIA evidence at p 268 is available on the Parliament website.

25 The Corporate Governance Voluntary Guidelines 2009 issued by the Indian Ministry of Corporate Affairs, Part IV E AUDITORS – Appointment of Internal Auditor.

26 Walker Review, p 93.

27 Witnesses: Drs Ian Peters (Chief Executive) and Sarah Blackburn (past president) of the Chartered Institute of Internal Auditors. The House of Lords Report and their Evidence volume which starts the CIIA evidence at p 268 is available on the Parliament website.

28 Financial Times, 6 April 2009, 'Myners urges "radical" shake-up of boards'.

29 Lord Smith of Clifton, Hansard, 8 December 2008. Debate on the Queen's Speech:

> '… A preliminary start has been made by the Association of Chartered Certified Accountants. Its publication, Corporate Governance and the Credit Crunch, published last month, is a thoughtful and timely contribution as to the way forward. The ACCA identifies a failure in corporate governance as the underlying factor that led to the credit crunch. It makes nine proposals to help to remedy the situation. I shall not detail them all now but will highlight the main ones.
>
> To begin with, "boards have failed in their responsibilities", have not asked the right questions, and, "have allowed inadequate risk management and sanctioned remuneration incentives that influenced behaviour without proper consideration of risk". Furthermore: "Risk management tools have not always been fit for purpose".

This has been exacerbated by the over complexity of products in the financial sector and poor training of both executive and non-executive directors that led to a lack of understanding of the associated risks. Crucially, boards, and particularly non-executive directors need assurance independent of management, which requires a much greater enhancement of the role of internal audit, including, in the words of Professor Andrew Chambers, the creation of a cadre of "super auditors" who can relate on even terms with board members …'

30 Lord Smith of Clifton, Hansard, 16 December 2008. Debate on the Banking Bill:

'Another major defect of the Bill is that it does too little to improve corporate governance more generally. Effective regulation from the top is only one part of the solution. The other, and much more important, aspect is to try to influence individual and corporate behaviour of the main board directors. That is difficult but it must be attempted. A number of actions can be taken to improve the situation. As I said last week, the function of internal audit must be strengthened. Secondly, external auditors must be more aware that they are reporting to shareholders. As I wrote in the foreword to the fourth edition of Professor Andrew Chambers's authoritative compendium on corporate governance, one of the problems is the near-monopoly of the big four accountancy firms of the external auditing market, which is deleterious in itself because it makes for a far too cosy and complacent culture …'

31 In speech by Gordon Gekko from the film 'Wall Street'.
32 Alan Greenspan, testimony to Congress, 2003.
33 Walker Review, p 9.
34 See the FRC website.

Checklist to Benchmark Corporate Governance Practice in the Context of the UK Corporate Governance Code

Introduction D5.1

Note that this Checklist is not entirely comprehensive. The Checklist has been amended to reflect the 2012 version of the UK Corporate Governance Code (set out in full at **App1**) but should not be relied upon to be entirely comprehensive. Users of this checklist should also not overlook the three useful schedules at the end of the Code, viz:

- Schedule A: The design of performance-related remuneration for executive directors.
- Schedule B: Disclosure of corporate governance arrangements (including the Appendix on Overlap between the Disclosure and Transparency Rules and the UK Corporate Governance Code).

Note that Schedule C in the 2008 Code publication, 'Engagement Principles for Institutional Shareholders', is superseded by the Stewardship Code, first published in 2010 and updated in 2012 as set out in full at **App2**).

The Checklist contains the following sections:

1. General (**D5.2**);
2. Is the existing board effective? (**D5.3**);
3. The chairman and the chief executive (**D5.4**);
4. Board balance and independence (**D5.5**);
5. Appointments to the board (**D5.6**);
6. Information and professional development (**D5.7**);
7. Performance evaluation (**D5.8**);
8. Re-election of directors (**D5.9**);
9. Remuneration (**D5.10**);
10. Accountability and audit (**D5.11**); and
11. Relations with shareholders (**D5.12**).

General D5.2

Corporate governance component 1: General					
No	**Issue**	***Possible approach(es)***	**ABC plc reference**	**Comment**	**Conclusion**
1.1	**How does the board ensure that its constitution, composition and organisation address its responsibilities effectively?** (See also **1.2.**)	*Terms of Reference of the board, explicitly adopted by the board and reviewed periodically.* *Appropriate main board committees with Terms of Reference which have been explicitly adopted by the board and are periodically reviewed by the board.* *Appropriate mix of executive and non-executive directors as members of the board and its committees.*			

Corporate governance component 1: General					
No	**Issue**	***Possible approach(es)***	**ABC plc reference**	**Comment**	**Conclusion**
		A formal and appropriate selection and performance review process re the chair of the board, including approval by the board. *A formal and appropriate selection and performance review process of chairs for the board committees, including approval by the board of these appointments.*			
1.2	**How does the board address the matter of ensuring that its membership is suitable (in its size, composition and other respects) to the needs of the business?** (See also **1.1**.)	*Formal contracts for all directors.* *Directors' contracts are for a satisfactory fixed term.* *There is a board nominations committee which:* ❑ *determines board need;* ❑ *is responsible for succession planning; and* ❑ *recommends appointees to the board.* *A sufficient degree of independence amongst the non-executive directors.* *The record shows that the board determines that the majority of its audit committee members are regarded by the board as being independent.* *Analysis of need, and a matching of background and skills to need.* *The board itself resolves on appointments and terminations of board members.* *Periodic comparison of board composition with that of similar enterprises.* *A record is kept of attendance of directors at board and board committee meetings, tabled to the board periodically.* *Attendance has been good (better than 80%).*			
1.3	**How does the board ensure that there is not excessive concentration of power at or near the top of the business?**	*Separation of the roles of:* ❑ *chief executive; and* ❑ *chair of the business,* *or nomination of a suitable non-executive director to be the senior non-executive director.* *Non-executive directors meet alone from time to time, in addition to their time together at certain board committee meetings.* *Sufficient access for the board and its members to management, in addition to the MD.* *Close liaison between the chairs of board committees and the relevant, responsible manager(s) and/or other parties – for instance, between:* ❑ *the chair of the audit committee;* ❑ *the head of internal audit;* ❑ *the head of compliance (if applicable); and* ❑ *the external auditor.* *The record shows that board members at board meetings are encouraged to challenge management proposals.*			

Corporate governance component 1: General					
No	**Issue**	***Possible approach(es)***	**ABC plc reference**	**Comment**	**Conclusion**
1.4	**How does the board ensure it has taken charge of the ethical values of the business?**	*The board has adopted, as corporate policy statement(s), one or more of the following, as appropriate:* ❑ *statement of corporate principles;* ❑ *code of business conduct;* ❑ *code of scientific conduct;* ❑ *code of ethical conduct;* ❑ *code of environmental conduct; and* ❑ *fraud policy statement.* *The board sets an appropriate and consistent example.* *The board follows the principle of openness, and the other Nolan principles where appropriate.* *There is a satisfactory policy and procedure for taking ethical violations to the board.* *The board is in overall control of the business' policy and practices with respect to equal opportunities.*			
1.5	**How does the board ensure that its business is conducted efficiently and effectively, both at the board and in committee?**	*Scheduling of board and board committee meetings ensures that board committee minutes (at least in draft) are promptly available to the board as board agenda papers.* *Chairs of board committees speak to their committee minutes at board meetings.* *Adequate time is allowed for board and board committee meetings, and apt allocation of time between agenda items.* *There are sufficient refreshment breaks within long meetings, and between meetings which follow on from each other.* *Adequate notice of board and board committee meetings. Future schedule of meeting dates prepared and issued to members on a rolling annual basis.* *Adequate timing of distribution of agenda papers, for members to prepare thoroughly.* *Quality of agenda papers, including their reliability, sufficiency and clarity.* *Freedom of undue filtering of information placed before the board.* *Avoidance at the board of excessive involvement in detail and in management matters.*			
1.6	**How does the board ensure that the total compensation packages of executive and non-executive directors are appropriate?**	*An effective remuneration committee of non-executive directors to determine executive directors' compensation.* *Non-executive directors' compensation determined by the executive directors.*			

D5.2 *Checklist to Benchmark Corporate Government Practice*

Corporate governance component 1: General					
No	**Issue**	***Possible approach(es)***	**ABC plc reference**	**Comment**	**Conclusion**
1.7	**How does the board ensure that the right items are placed on board agendas, on a timely basis?**	*The board has an agenda committee (or a chairman's committee with, inter alia, agenda-setting responsibility).*			
1.8	**How does the board ensure that matters which require board approval are brought to the board?**	*Regular written reports from each executive director to the board, presented orally by the director and fully discussed at the board.* *Maintenance of a formal schedule of matters reserved to the board for its decision (see* **1.11***).*			
1.9	**How does the board ensure that its members are fully appraised of the continuing information they need to discharge their responsibilities as directors effectively?**	*There is a tailored, ongoing induction and training programme for each board member.* *Regular presentations are made to the board of important aspects of the business.* *Each director has a copy of a directors' manual containing, inter alia, a copy of:* ❑ *the memorandum of association;* ❑ *the articles of association;* ❑ *each director's contract;* ❑ *the terms of reference of board committees;* ❑ *delegation of authority guidelines;* ❑ *standing orders;* ❑ *all past board policy decisions not yet rescinded (see* **1.10***);* ❑ *essential extracts from all critical contracts, including significant covenants in financing and other agreements;* and ❑ *copy of policy statement on directors taking independent professional advice (see* **1.14***).*			
1.10	**How does the board ensure that earlier formal resolutions it has taken will always be recalled, when appropriate, as being board policy – until rescinded or replaced?**	*There is a complete and up-to-date guide to board policy decisions which have not been rescinded (see* **1.9***).* *Minutes are thorough.* *Matters arising from past minutes are identified and carried forward until addressed fully.*			
1.11	**How does the board ensure that it is in control of the business?**	*There is a formal schedule of matters reserved to the board for its decision (see* **1.8***).* *There is delegation of authority guidelines, and they are clear and comprehensive.* *Do the right things get placed on board and board committee agendas – in time to determine outcomes?*			

Corporate governance component 1: General					
No	**Issue**	***Possible approach(es)***	**ABC plc reference**	**Comment**	**Conclusion**
		The board receives a regular MAP (Management Accounting Pack) which allows board members to monitor performance against plan, in all areas of the business. The MAP is: ❑ *comprehensive;* ❑ *reliable;* ❑ *clear;* ❑ *timely; and* ❑ *not misleading.*			
1.12	**How does the board ensure its decisions are implemented?**	*There is a monitoring procedure for follow-up of decisions, which is applied. It includes a schedule of decisions whose implementation must be ensured. There is evidence that this monitoring procedure is being applied.*			
1.13	**How does the board ensure that its business, and that of its committees, is managed efficiently and effectively?**	*A qualified company secretariat, independent of other responsibilities, services the board and its committees.*			
1.14	**How does the board ensure that directors have adequate access to information and advice?**	*The company secretariat is available to the board, its committees and to individual board members in order to provide information and address issues of concern brought to the secretariat.* *Board members need access to members of management in addition to the chief executive.* *Board committees and individual board members are formally empowered to take independent, professional advice at the business's expense (see* **1.16***).*			
1.15	**How does the board ensure it is appraised of shareholder, customer, supplier and other stakeholder complaints and concerns?**	*There is an established reporting system through to the board on these matters.* *Non-executive directors serve on panels which deal with these matters.* *These panels have appropriate terms of reference and standing orders, and their proceedings are thoroughly minuted.* *Records of these panels show they work well.*			
1.16	**How does the board protect itself and its members against the risk of negligent performance and/or possible litigation?**	*Thorough minuting of all board and board committee meetings.* *Directors' liability insurance.* *At their own discretion, individual directors, and board committees (per their terms of reference) are authorised to take professional advice at the business's expense, on matters relating respectively to their duties as directors or to their committee responsibilities (see* **1.14***).*			

Corporate governance component 1: General					
No	**Issue**	***Possible approach(es)***	**ABC plc reference**	**Comment**	**Conclusion**
1.17	**How does the board secure its records?**	*Permanent retention of 100% of board and board committee agenda papers and minutes.* *Duplicate (separate and secure) storage of these records.* *Records are readily accessible by those who are authorised to access them, but safeguarded against unauthorised access.* *Access to records is logged, and the log is kept secure.* *Storage method(s) is (are) proof against deterioration. Archives are inspected periodically for quality. Electronic records are checked periodically for continued accessibility and are refreshed periodically to avoid deterioration.*			
1.18	**How does the board monitor that the business continues to be a going concern?**	*The MAP (see* **1.11***) covers this with respect to liquidity, solvency etc.* *The audit committee of the board regularly addresses going concern.* *The board, or the audit committee on behalf of the board, reviews the adequacy of the business's disaster recovery plan.*			
1.19	**Is the board determining effectively the nature and content of corporate information which is published?**	*The audit committee considers the reliability of all information from the directors which is published.* *The board consciously determines its policy with respect to the content of the annual report and accounts – particularly with regard to disclosures over which there is no mandatory requirement, such as:* ❑ *environmental statements* ❑ *corporate governance statements beyond minimum requirements.*			
1.20	**Is the board approaching its legal responsibilities effectively?**	*The board has appointed a senior executive as compliance officer.* *The board, through its audit committee, ensures that there is an effective internal audit, including:* ❑ *staff and other resources;* ❑ *qualifications;* ❑ *reporting relationships;* ❑ *programme of audits;* ❑ *completion of planned programme of audits; and* ❑ *content of audit reports.* *The board, through its audit committee, ensures that there is an adequate external audit, headed by an appropriate audit partner.* *In non-financial, non-accounting respects, the information and reporting system through to the board is sufficient to enable its directors to be reassured that they are meeting their legal responsibilities.*			

Corporate governance component 1: General					
No	**Issue**	***Possible approach(es)***	**ABC plc reference**	**Comment**	**Conclusion**
		The code of business conduct, approved by the board, specifically bans illegal acts by representatives of the business.			
1.21	**Is the board pro-active?**	*The board and its committees (such as the audit committee) must consider future issues.* *Significant time at meetings should be spent on future prospects.*			
1.22	**Are board members properly prepared for their duties?**	*There should be a tailored induction programme for each new board member, covering:*			
		❑ *The affairs of the business;*			
		❑ *The characteristics of this board; and*			
		❑ *The responsibilities, duties and practice of directors (except for already experienced directors).*			

Is the existing board effective? D5.3

Corporate governance component 2: Is the existing board effective?				
No	**Issue**	**ABC plc reference**	**Comment**	**Conclusion**
2.1	**Is the present board effective?**			
2.2	**For the appointment of a chairman, is there prepared a job specification, including an assessment of the time commitment expected, recognising the need for availability in the event of crises? Are a chairman's other significant commitments disclosed to the board before appointment and included in the annual report? Are changes to such commitments also reported to the board as they arise, and included in the next annual report?**			
2.3	**In the past, have all directors participated in decisions *objectively in the interests of the company*?**			
2.4	**Do the non-executive directors effectively scrutinise the performance of management in meeting agreed goals and objectives and monitor the reporting of performance? They should satisfy themselves on the integrity of financial information and that financial controls and systems of risk management are robust and defensible. They are responsible for determining appropriate levels of remuneration of executive directors and have a prime role in appointing, and where necessary removing, executive directors, and in succession planning.**			
2.5	**Do the non-executive directors satisfy themselves on the integrity of financial information and that financial controls and systems of risk management are robust and defensible? They are responsible for determining appropriate levels of remuneration of executive directors and have a prime role in appointing, and where necessary removing, executive directors, and in succession planning?**			
2.6	**Do the non-executive directors determine appropriate levels of remuneration of executive directors and have a prime role in appointing, and where necessary removing, executive directors, and in succession planning?**			
2.7	**Is there an appropriate formal schedule of matters specifically reserved for its decision, which is applied?**			

Corporate governance component 2: Is the existing board effective?				
No	**Issue**	**ABC plc reference**	**Comment**	**Conclusion**
2.8	**Does the annual report identify the chairman, the deputy chairman (where there is one), the chief executive, the senior independent director and the chairmen and members of the nomination, audit and remuneration committees?**			
2.9	**Does it also set out the number of meetings of the board and those committees and individual attendance by directors?**			
2.10	**Led by the senior independent director, do the non-executive directors meet without the chairman present at least annually to appraise the chairman's performance and on such other occasions as are deemed appropriate?**			
2.11	**Has the company arranged appropriate insurance cover in respect of legal action against its directors?**			

The chairman and the chief executive **D5.4**

Corporate governance component 3: The chairman and the chief executive				
No	**Issue**	**ABC plc reference**	**Comment**	**Conclusion**
3.1	**Is there a clear division of responsibilities at the head of the company between the running of the board and the executive responsibility for the running of the company's business?**			
3.2	**Does any one individual (or small group of individuals) have unfettered powers of decision?**			
3.3	**Is the chairman responsible for leadership of the board, ensuring its effectiveness on all aspects of its role and setting its agenda?**			
3.4	**Is the chairman responsible for ensuring that the directors receive accurate, timely and clear information?**			
3.5	**Does the chairman ensure effective communication with shareholders?**			
3.6	**Does the chairman also facilitate the effective contribution of non-executive directors in particular and ensure constructive relations between executive and non-executive directors?**			
3.7	**Is the division of responsibilities between the chairman and chief executive clearly established, set out in writing and agreed by the board?**			
3.8	**Has a senior independent non-executive director been appointed?**			

Board balance and independence **D5.5**

Corporate governance component 4: Board balance and independence				
No	**Issue**	**ABC plc reference**	**Comment**	**Conclusion**
4.1	**Is the board of the right size and balance of skills and experience appropriate for the requirements of the business?**			
4.2	**Is there a strong presence on the board of both executive and non-executive directors?**			
4.3	**Are the Combined Code's criteria of independence met by a majority of the board?**			
4.4	**Is *entitlement* to attend board committee meetings limited to their members?**			

Appointments to the board **D5.6**

Corporate governance component 5: Appointments to the board				
No	**Issue**	**ABC plc reference**	**Comment**	**Conclusion**
5.1	**Is there a formal, rigorous and transparent procedure for the appointment of new directors to the board?**			
5.2	**Are appointments to the board made on merit and against objective criteria? Is care taken to ensure that appointees have enough time available to devote to the job (especially in the case of chairmanships)?**			
5.3	**How does the board satisfy itself that plans are in place for orderly succession for appointments to the board and to senior management, so as to maintain an appropriate balance of skills and experience within the company and on the board?**			
5.4	**Does the nomination have regard to the benefits of diversity on the board, including gender (see also 10.31)?**			
5.5	**Is there a nomination committee with the right remit and appropriate chairmanship, membership and approach to its work?**			
5.6	**Does the nomination committee evaluate the balance of skills, knowledge and experience on the board and, in the light of this evaluation, prepare a description of the role and capabilities required for a particular appointment?**			
5.7	**Do letters of appointment of non-executive directors set out the expected time commitment; and do non-executive directors undertake that they will have sufficient time to meet what is expected of them? Are there other significant commitments disclosed to the board before appointment, with a broad indication of the time involved and is the board informed of subsequent changes?**			
5.8	**Does a separate section of the annual report describe the work of the nomination committee, including the process it has used in relation to board appointments? Is an explanation given if neither an external search consultancy nor open advertising has been used in the appointment of a chairman or a non-executive director (see also 10.31)?**			

Information and professional development **D5.7**

Corporate governance component 6: Information and professional development				
No	**Issue**	**ABC plc reference**	**Comment**	**Conclusion**
6.1	**Is the board supplied in a timely manner with information in a form and of a quality appropriate to enable it to discharge its duties?**			
6.2	**Does the chairman ensure that the directors receive accurate, timely and clear information? Does management provide such information? Do directors seek clarification or amplification where necessary?**			
6.3	**Does the company secretary ensure good information flows within the board and its committees and between senior management and non-executive directors, as well as facilitate induction and assisting with professional development as required?**			
6.4	**Does the company secretary discharge his or her responsibility for advising the board through the chairman on all governance matters?**			

Corporate governance component 6: Information and professional development				
No	**Issue**	**ABC plc reference**	**Comment**	**Conclusion**
6.5	**Does the company secretary ensure that board procedures are complied with?**			
6.6	**Do all directors have access to the advice and services of the company secretary?**			
6.7	**Is both the appointment and removal of the company secretary a matter for the board as a whole?**			
6.8	**Do all directors receive induction on joining the board and do they regularly update and refresh their skills and knowledge? Does the chairman ensure this? Are necessary resources provided?**			
6.9	**Are major shareholders offered the opportunity to meet a new non-executive director?**			
6.10	**Do directors, especially non-executive directors, have access to independent professional advice at the company's expense where they judge it necessary to discharge their responsibilities as directors?**			
6.11	**Are committees provided with sufficient resources to undertake their duties?**			

Performance evaluation **D5.8**

Corporate governance component 7: Performance evaluation				
No	**Issue**	**ABC plc reference**	**Comment**	**Conclusion**
7.1	**Does the board undertake a formal and rigorous annual evaluation of:** **(a) its own performance;** **(b) the performance of its committees; and** **(c) the performance of individual directors?**			
7.2	**Does the evaluation of the board consider the balance of skills, experience, independence and knowledge of the company on the board, and its diversity, including gender?**			
7.3	**What happens when individual evaluation shows a director is not contributing effectively or committedly (including commitment of time for board and committee meetings and any other duties)? Does the chairman act on the results of the performance evaluation by recognising the strengths and addressing the weaknesses of the board and, where appropriate, proposing new members be appointed to the board or seeking the resignation of directors?**			
7.4	**Does the board state in the annual report how performance evaluation of the board, its committees and its individual directors has been conducted?**			
7.5	**Do the non-executive directors, led by the senior independent director, evaluate the performance of the chairman, taking into account the views of executive directors?**			

Re-election of directors D5.9

Corporate governance component 8: Re-election of directors				
No	**Issue**	**ABC plc reference**	**Comment**	**Conclusion**
8.1	**Is there planned refreshing of the board?**			
8.2	**Does the board set out to shareholders why it believes an individual should be elected?**			
8.3	**Does the chairman confirm to shareholders when proposing re-election that, following formal performance evaluation, the individual's performance continues to be effective and to demonstrate commitment to the role?**			
8.4	**Is any term beyond six years (eg two three-year terms) for a non-executive director subject to particularly rigorous review, taking into account the need for progressive refreshing of the board?**			

Remuneration D5.10

Corporate governance component 9: Remuneration				
No	**Issue**	**ABC plc reference**	**Comment**	**Conclusion**
9.1	**Has the board established a remuneration committee of at least three members who, except for the chairman, are all independent non-executive directors and with terms of reference agreed by the board?** **(The chairman of the company may be a member of the remuneration committee if he/she was independent at the time of being appointed chairman of the company, but should not chair the remuneration committee.)**			
9.2	**Are levels of remuneration sufficient to attract, retain and motivate directors of the quality required to run the company successfully, while avoiding paying more than is necessary for this purpose?**			
9.3	**Is a significant proportion of executive directors' remuneration structured so as to link rewards to corporate and individual performance?**			
9.4	**Are external comparisons used, but with caution?**			
9.5	**Is the remuneration committee sensitive to pay and employment conditions elsewhere in 'the group', especially when determining annual salary increases?**			
9.6	**Do the performance-related elements of remuneration form a significant proportion of the total remuneration package of executive directors and is it designed to align their interests with those of shareholders and to give these directors keen incentives to perform at the highest levels, avoiding perverse incentives to take excessive risks? Do schemes of performance-related remuneration follow Schedule A of the UK Corporate Governance Code (www.frc.org.uk)?**			
9.7	**Do levels of remuneration for non-executive directors reflect the time commitment and responsibilities of the role?**			
9.8	**Are notice or contract periods set at one year or less, or if it is necessary to offer longer notice or contract periods to new directors recruited from outside, do such periods reduce to one year or less after the initial period?**			

Corporate governance component 9: Remuneration				
No	**Issue**	**ABC plc reference**	**Comment**	**Conclusion**
9.9	**Is there a formal and transparent procedure for developing policy on executive remuneration and for fixing the remuneration packages of individual directors?**			
9.10	**Is any director involved in deciding his or her own remuneration?**			
9.11	**Does the remuneration committee consult the chairman and/or chief executive about its proposals relating to the remuneration of other executive directors?**			
9.12	**Is it the remuneration committee which is responsible for appointing any consultants in respect of executive director remuneration?**			
9.13	**Does the chairman of the board ensure that the company maintains contact as required with its principal shareholders about remuneration in the same way as for other matters?**			
9.14	**Does the remuneration committee have delegated responsibility for setting remuneration for all executive directors and the chairman, including pension rights and any compensation payments?**			
9.15	**Does the committee also recommend and monitor the level and structure of remuneration for senior management?**			
9.16	**Does the board itself or, where required by the articles of association, do the shareholders, determine the remuneration of the non-executive directors within the limits set in the articles of association?**			
9.17	**Are the shareholders invited specifically to approve all new long-term incentive schemes (as defined in the Listing Rules) and significant changes to existing schemes?**			

Accountability and audit D5.11

Corporate governance component 10: Accountability and audit				
No	**Issue**	**ABC plc reference**	**Comment**	**Conclusion**
10.1	**Does the board recognise that its responsibility to present a balanced and understandable assessment extends to interim and other price-sensitive public reports and reports to regulators, as well as to information required to be presented by statutory requirements?**			
10.2	**Does the board, at least annually, conduct a review of the effectiveness of the group's system of internal controls and report to shareholders that it has done so? Does the review cover all material controls, including financial, operational and compliance controls and risk management systems?** (See following issues.)			
10.3	**In its assessment of the effectiveness of internal control and risk management, is the board assisted by an annual report from internal audit which includes an overall opinion of the effectiveness of risk management and internal control? Does that opinion correspond in scope to the oversight of the board?**			
10.4	**Does the board acknowledge its responsibility for the company's system of internal control? Has it set appropriate policies on internal control and does it seek regular assurance that will enable it to satisfy itself that the system is functioning effectively?**			

Corporate governance component 10: Accountability and audit				
No	**Issue**	**ABC plc reference**	**Comment**	**Conclusion**
10.5	**How does the board further ensure that the system of internal control is effective in managing risks in the manner which it has approved?**			
10.6	**In determining its policies with regard to internal control, and thereby assessing what constitutes a sound system of internal control in the particular circumstances of the company, have the board's deliberations included consideration of the following factors:**			
	❑ **the nature and extent of the risks facing the company;**			
	❑ **the extent and categories of risk which it regards as acceptable for the company to bear;**			
	❑ **the likelihood of the risks concerned materialising; and**			
	❑ **the company's ability to reduce the incidence and impact on the business of risks that do materialise?**			
10.7	**Is the board satisfied that management implements board policies on risk and control?**			
10.8	**In fulfilling its responsibilities, does management identify and evaluate the risks faced by the company for consideration by the board and design, operate and monitor a suitable system of internal control which implements the policies adopted by the board?**			
10.9	**Since all employees have some responsibility for internal control as part of their accountability for achieving objectives, is the board and management satisfied that staff collectively have the necessary knowledge, skills, information and authority to establish, operate and monitor the system of internal control? (This requires an understanding of the company, its objectives, the industries and markets in which it operates, and the risks it faces.)**			
10.10	**Is the system of internal control:**			
	❑ **embedded in the operations of the company and part of its culture;**			
	❑ **capable of responding quickly to evolving risks to the business arising from factors within the company and to changes in the business environment; and**			
	❑ **does the system of internal control include procedures for reporting immediately to appropriate levels of management any significant control failings or weaknesses that are identified together with details of corrective action being undertaken?**			
10.11	**Has the board satisfied itself that the embedded processes for the review of risk management and internal control are appropriate and effective? In this regard, has the board or its audit committee assessed the adequacy of the internal audit (see 10.23 *et seq*) and taken a view on whether a process of control risk self assessment should be introduced throughout the company?**			
10.12	**Does management account to the board for management's monitoring of the system, and is the review of the effectiveness of internal control part of the board's responsibilities? Does the board form its own view on effectiveness after due and careful inquiry based on the information and assurances provided to it? (The role of board committees in the review process, including that of the audit committee, is for the board to decide and will depend upon factors such as the size and composition of the**			

Corporate governance component 10: Accountability and audit					
No	**Issue**		**ABC plc reference**	**Comment**	**Conclusion**
	board; the scale, diversity and complexity of the company's operations; and the nature of the significant risks that the company faces. To the extent that designated board committees carry out tasks on behalf of the board, is the relevant committees' work reported to, and considered by, the board? (Note: the board takes responsibility for the disclosures on internal control in the annual report and accounts.)				
10.13	**Does the board regularly receive and review reports on internal control?**				
10.14	**Does the board undertake an annual assessment of risk management and internal control for the purposes of making a statement on internal control to ensure in the annual report? (In this regard, has the board considered all significant aspects of internal control for the company for the year under review and up to the date of approval of the annual report and accounts?)**				
10.15	**Has the board defined the process to be adopted for its review of the effectiveness of internal control? (This should encompass both the scope and frequency of the reports it receives and reviews during the year, and also the process for its annual assessment, such that it will be provided with sound, appropriately documented support for its statement on internal control in the company's annual report and accounts.)**				
10.16	**Do reports from management to the board provide a balanced assessment of the significant risks and the effectiveness of the system of internal control in managing those risks? Are any identified significant control failings or weaknesses discussed in the reports, including the impact that they have had, could have had or may have on the company and the actions being taken to rectify them? (It is essential that there is openness of communication by management with the board on matters relating to risk and control.)**				
10.17	**When reviewing reports during the year, does the board:**				
	❑	**consider what are the significant risks and assess how they have been identified, evaluated and managed;**			
	❑	**assess the effectiveness of the related system of internal control in managing the significant risks, having regard, in particular, to any significant failings or weaknesses in internal control that have been reported;**			
	❑	**consider whether necessary actions are being taken promptly to remedy any significant failings or weaknesses; and**			
	❑	**consider whether the findings indicate a need for more extensive monitoring of the system of internal control?**			
10.18	**Additionally, does the board's annual assessment, for the purpose of making its public statement on internal control, consider:**				
	❑	**issues dealt with in reports reviewed by it during the year; and**			
	❑	**any additional information necessary to ensure that the board has taken account of all significant aspects of internal control for the company for the year under review and up to the date of approval of the annual report and accounts?**			
	If the board becomes aware of a significant failing or weakness in internal control, does the board determine how the failing or weakness arose and reassess the effectiveness of management's ongoing processes for designing, operating and monitoring the system of internal control?				

Corporate governance component 10: Accountability and audit					
No	**Issue**		**ABC plc reference**	**Comment**	**Conclusion**
10.19	**Does the board's statement on internal control:**				
	❑	**disclose that there is an ongoing process for identifying, evaluating and managing the significant risks faced by the company;**			
	❑	**disclose that it has been in place for the year under review and up to the date of approval of the annual report and accounts;**			
	❑	**disclose that it is regularly reviewed by the board and accords with Turnbull guidance;**			
	❑	**acknowledge that the board is responsible for the company's system of internal control and for reviewing its effectiveness;**			
	❑	**explain that such a system is designed to manage rather than eliminate the risk of failure to achieve business objectives, and can only provide reasonable and not absolute assurance against material misstatement or loss;**			
	❑	**include a summary of the process the board (where applicable, through its committees) has applied in reviewing the effectiveness of the system of internal control; and**			
	❑	**disclose the process it has applied to deal with material internal control aspects of any significant problems disclosed in the annual report and accounts?**			
10.20	**Where material joint ventures and associates have not been dealt with as part of the group for the purposes of applying the Turnbull guidance, is this disclosed in the annual report?**				
10.21	**Has the board established an audit committee of at least three members, who should all be independent non-executive directors and with at least one member of the audit committee with recent and relevant financial experience?**				
10.22	**Are the role and responsibilities of the audit committee set out in written terms of reference which include:**				
	❑	**to monitor the integrity of the financial statements of the company, and any formal announcements relating to the company's financial performance, reviewing significant financial reporting judgements contained in them;**			
	❑	**to review the company's internal financial controls and, unless expressly addressed by a separate board risk committee composed of independent directors, or by the board itself, to review the company's internal control and risk management systems;**			
	❑	**to monitor and review the effectiveness of the company's internal audit function** (see **10.23** *et seq*);			
	❑	**to make recommendations to the board, for it to put to the shareholders for their approval in general meeting, in relation to the appointment, reappointment and removal of the external auditor and to approve the remuneration and terms of engagement of the external auditor;**			
	❑	**to review and monitor the external auditor's independence and objectivity and the effectiveness of the audit process, taking into consideration relevant UK professional and regulatory requirements; and**			
	❑	**to develop and implement policy on the engagement of the external auditor to supply non-audit services, taking into account relevant ethical guidance regarding the provision of non-audit services by the external audit firm; and to report to the board, identifying any matters in respect of which it considers that action or improvement is needed and making recommendations as to the steps to be taken?**			

Corporate governance component 10: Accountability and audit				
No	**Issue**	**ABC plc reference**	**Comment**	**Conclusion**
10.23	**Does the board, perhaps through its committees, at least once a year assess the adequacy of the internal audit provision (scope of work, authority and resources), having regard to factors that have increased, or are expected to increase, the risks faced by the company, such as:**			
	❑ **trends or current factors relevant to the company's activities, markets or other aspects of its external environment;**			
	❑ **internal factors such as organisational restructuring or changes in reporting processes or underlying information systems; and**			
	❑ **adverse trends or increased incidence of unexpected occurrences?**			
10.24	**Does the board assess whether other monitoring processes, together with internal audit (where present), provide sufficient and objective assurance?**			
10.25	**Where applicable, does the board disclose and justify in its annual report that there is no internal audit function, or that it has not reviewed the need for one?**			
10.26	**Does a separate section of the annual report describe the work of the committee in discharging those responsibilities?**			
10.27	**Does the audit committee review arrangements by which staff of the company may, in confidence, raise concerns about possible improprieties in matters of financial reporting or other matters? (The audit committee's objective should be to ensure that arrangements are in place for the proportionate and independent investigation of such matters and for appropriate follow-up action.)**			
10.28	**Does the audit committee monitor and review the effectiveness of the internal audit activities? (Where there is no internal audit function, the audit committee should consider annually whether there is a need for an internal audit function and make a recommendation to the board, and the reasons for the absence of such a function should be explained in the relevant section of the annual report.)**			
10.29	**Does the audit committee have primary responsibility for making a recommendation on the appointment, reappointment and removal of the external auditors? (If the board does not accept the audit committee's recommendation, it should include in the annual report, and in any papers recommending appointment or reappointment, a statement from the audit committee explaining the recommendation and should set out reasons why the board has taken a different position.)**			
10.30	**Does the board put the external audit out to tender at least once every ten years?**			
10.31	**Does the published report describing the work of the audit committee include the significant issues that the committee considered in relation to the financial statements, and how these were addressed?**			
10.32	**Does the published report describing the work of the audit committee include an explanation of how it has assessed the effectiveness of the external audit process and the approach taken to the appointment or reappointment of the external auditor, and information on the length of tenure of the current audit firm and when a tender was last conducted?**			

Corporate governance component 10: Accountability and audit				
No	**Issue**	**ABC plc reference**	**Comment**	**Conclusion**
10.33	**Does the annual report explain to shareholders how, if the auditor provides non-audit services, auditor objectivity and independence is safeguarded?**			
10.34	**Does the annual report disclose the board's policy on diversity, including gender, any measurable objectives that it has set for implementing the policy, and progress on achieving the objectives (see also 5.4 and 5.8)?**			

Relations with shareholders **D5.12**

Corporate governance component 11: Relations with shareholders				
No	**Issue**	**ABC plc reference**	**Comment**	**Conclusion**
11.1	**Is there a dialogue with shareholders based on the mutual understanding of objectives? Does the board as a whole recognise that it has a responsibility for ensuring that a satisfactory dialogue with shareholders takes place?**			
11.2	**Does the chairman (and the senior independent director and other directors as appropriate) in addition to the chief executive and finance director maintain sufficient contact with major shareholders to understand their issues and concerns?**			
11.3	**Does the chairman ensure that the views of shareholders are communicated to the board as a whole?**			
11.4	**Does the chairman discuss governance and strategy with major shareholders?**			
11.5	**Do non-executive directors have the opportunity to attend meetings with major shareholders and do they do so if requested by major shareholders?**			
11.6	**Does the senior independent director attend sufficient meetings with a range of major shareholders to listen to their views in order to help develop a balanced understanding of the issues and concerns of major shareholders?**			
11.7	**Does the board state in the annual report the steps it has taken to ensure that the members of the board, and in particular the non-executive directors, develop an understanding of the views of major shareholders about their company, for example, through direct face-to-face contact?**			

Chapter D6

British Governance Standard (2013) – Code of Practice for Delivering Effective Governance of Organizations

Introduction D6.1

Published in August 2013 after consultation, this British Standard[1] (BS 13500) is designed to be generally appropriate for most forms of organisation, unlike the UK Corporate Governance Code and its antecedents dating back to 1992 which have all been designed to be appropriate primarily for FTSE companies and in particular the FTSE 350.

BS 13500 is reasonably high-level, running to only 23 pages. Yet it costs £140; the other codes referred to within this publication are all freely available on the internet, with the exception of the QCA (2013) Code which costs £50.

Form more than substance D6.2

As with other British Standards, the emphasis of this Standard is on form rather than substance. This Standard acknowledges that conformance with its requirements may go no further than indicating that there is a system in place for delivering effective governance but does not guarantee effective governance or the achievement of objectives. This British Standard code is intended as 'a basic checklist'. It is more a matter of conformance than performance. This is unfortunate as contemporary corporate governance has been found lacking due to the stress that has been placed on complying with what the Financial Reporting Council calls the 'soft law' of their UK Corporate Governance Code, notwithstanding that the UK Code endeavours to focus on values and good behaviour.

Other Codes D6.3

Many have questioned the need for this British Standard on governance. UK entities other than listed companies already have their own governance codes. The UK public sector has had its general code since 2005.[2] More specific UK public sector codes are well established for, for instance, NHS Foundation Trusts[3] and for central government,[4] and in both these cases there were earlier versions. The former follows closely the UK Corporate Governance Code (**App1**). The UK's regulator for housing associations includes governance requirements within their regulatory framework.[5] The Quoted Companies Alliance has had a code for AIM[6] listed and other small and mid-sized quoted companies since 2010, which was updated in 2013.[7]

Casting our net wider, many countries now have their corporate governance code, and the OECD's corporate governance principles have become the basis for many of these codes, in particular of developing countries.[8] Even the Commonwealth in 1999 developed its own corporate governance code,[9] updated in 2007.[10]

Generic quality D6.4

Entering this crowded space now comes a British Standard. The plan is that the Standard will be reviewed every third year. There must be a possibility of it eventually becoming an international ISO standard. Its principal justification is its intended, wholly generic character. It eschews the phrase 'corporate governance' in preference for just 'governance', seeking to emphasise that the Code is designed for all forms of organisation, not just corporations. It uses the term 'governing body' in preference to 'board' though occasionally the British Standard lapses into 'the board' (p 2). While this is all logical, we can see from the above examples that the phrase 'corporate governance' has won acceptance by entities that are not corporations, such as in the context of UK central government.

Defining governance D6.5

BS 13500's definition of governance is based on the Cadbury definition, still widely used and still appearing in the UK Corporate Governance Code, but with useful distinctive emphasis upon the whole organisation, upon organisations of any sort, and upon accountability, core purpose and the long-term. The UK Corporate Governance Code also now emphasises the long-term, as does the UK Companies Act 2006.

BS 13500 definition of governance D6.6

> 'system by which the whole organization is directed, controlled and held accountable to achieve its core purpose over the long term.'

Cadbury and UK Code definition of corporate governance D6.7

> 'Corporate governance is the system by which companies are directed and controlled.'

The 2012 UK Corporate Governance Code describes the purpose of corporate governance as:

> 'The purpose of corporate governance is to facilitate effective, entrepreneurial and prudent management that can deliver the long-term success of the company.'[11]

Furthermore, the UK's Code's main principle on leadership stresses that the board's collective responsibility for the long-term success of the company.[12] Otherwise the UK Code uses the phrase 'long-term' in the context of executive remuneration, at supporting principle D.1:

> 'The performance-related elements of executive directors' remuneration should be stretching and designed to promote the long-term success of the company.'[13]

and at supporting principle D.2.4:

> 'Shareholders should be invited specifically to approve all new long-term incentive schemes (as defined in the Listing Rules) and significant changes to existing schemes, save in the circumstances permitted by the Listing Rules.'[14]

Governance role of stakeholders **D6.8**

A significant deficiency of BS 13500 is that it excludes from its description of the scope of governance the governance responsibilities of external stakeholders, such as owners who should be regarded as part of the whole organisation. Its early claim to distinguish the different accountabilities of different stakeholders (p 1) is not borne out in the rest of the document. The accountability of boards is designed to enable external stakeholders to exercise oversight from outside, which is itself an important element of governance.

The responsibilities of shareholders were always within the predecessors to the UK Code until the Financial Reporting Council transferred that content to their separate Stewardship Code (**App2**). BS 13500 is incorrect to aver that 'governance [is] the ultimate responsibility of the board.' (pp 2 and 3).

Accreditation **D6.9**

We can anticipate BS 13500 becoming an ISO standard in the fullness of time, and there must be a possibility that a BS 13500 accreditation scheme will be developed as a commercial opportunity for the British Standards Institution and others. The latter would marry well with one of the principles within BS 13500 that:

> 'Accountability should include recognizing and responding appropriately to governance performance' (p 11)

Whenever the word 'should' appears in BS 13500, users can claim compliance with the Standard if its recommendation(s) are being followed. BS 13500 considers that compliance with all the recommendations indicates a good governance *system* is in place, but does not guarantee effective governance behaviour. There are some 60 usages of the word 'should' in the sections of BS 13500 which relate to the requirements of a good governance system and presumably each of these will be an expectation of any future accreditation which may be developed. BS 13500 claims to be 'a basic checklist' (p 1) at a time when other codes are endeavouring to move away from a box-ticking approach to corporate governance.

Emphasis on purpose and founding documentation **D6.10**

Despite this rather mechanistic orientation, BS 13500 usefully and clearly distinguishes between management and governance, a distinction so often blurred, and suggests that governance deals with the accountability of the whole organisation to all its stakeholders and with ensuring that the organisation as a whole fulfils its full purpose. The allusion to 'purpose' reveals a 'Carver-esque' infuence[15, 16], with a repeated stress upon the importance of the governance system being 'underpinned by sound founding documentation'. Many are likely to find the emphasis within BS 13500 on 'understanding and ensuring the integrity of founding documentation' (p 18 etc) a distinctive and over-emphasised characteristic of the Standard. Founding documentation is referred to as many as two dozen times within BS 13500. It risks encouraging a backwards looking, bureaucratic orientation to governance. There is insufficient content within BS 13500 which emphasises the importance of entrepreneurial leadership by the governing body. Many corporations now define their purpose in a broad brush way so as not to inhibit their boards from taking any direction they may choose to. BS 13500 does acknowledge that expectations should be aligned not just to 'founding documentation' but also to the organisation's 'changing context' (4.3.4 on p 11).

Summarising BS 13500's requirements D6.11

We noted some two-dozen main principles within BS 13500, most of which we have attempted to summarise below. Many of these principles have several elements to them: readers will need to refer to the Standard itself as our summary here is necessarily inadequate on its own. BS 13500 also includes some useful, clear examples to illustrate some of its principles.

BS 13500 requires that a governing body is responsible to account with sufficient openness to its shareholders or other equivalent parties for the achievement of the organisation's purpose, and to other stakeholders for the organisation's impact upon them; and that the governing body should provide leadership that ensures responsible treatment of stakeholders. The governing body needs to understand the environment in which the entity operates. Its focus should be on prudent and ethical creation of value for shareholders or other equivalent parties, and on ensuring an effective culture to influence everyone's behaviour, since a good governance system on its own cannot deliver good behaviour. The governing body is responsible for its own competence and for that of its delegatees.

BS 13500 requires that the governing body ensures the organisation's governance system is underpinned by sound founding documentation converted into regularly reviewed expectations which are stated in governance policies that are in turn aligned to the founding documentation and which set appropriate standards for all aspects of organisational performance and with clear roles for all who are involved in both governance and operations, and based on an understanding of the internal and external context in which decisions are made. General principles of good delegation should be upheld.

Governance policies are to be clearly owned by the governing body, while managers should be empowered to create lower-level policies consistent with those of the governing body. The governing body should ensure that all its policies are monitored, assessed and responded to appropriately.

The governing body needs to ensure that relevant stakeholders are identified, consulted, treated responsibly and reported to. It should exhibit leadership on behalf of shareholders (or equivalent) and on behalf of other relevant stakeholders. It should determine the organisation's best long-term interests, sustaining clarity with respect to the organisation's purposes and values; it should establish an effective governance culture. It is the governing body's responsibility to establish governance competence and capacity (including diversity), to assess and respond to governance performance, and to be able to demonstrate sufficient transparency.

Notes

1 BSI (2013) *Code of Practice for Delivering Effective Governance of Organizations*, British Standards Institution, ISBN 978 0 580 71608 9, August 2013.
2 The Independent Commission on Good Governance in Public Services (2005) *The Good Governance Standard for Public Services* ('The Langlands Report'), Office for Public Management and Chartered Institute of Public Finance and Accountancy, ISBN 1 898531 86 2, January 2010.
3 Monitor (2010) *The NHS Foundation Trust Code of Governance*, The Independent Regulator of NHS Foundation Trusts, available at www.monitor-nhsft.gov.uk/sites/default/files/Code%20of%20Governance_WEB%20%282%29.pdf, accessed 21 October 2013.
4 HM Treasury and Cabinet Office (2011) *Corporate Governance in Central Government Departments: Code of Good Practice*, July 2011, available at www.gov.uk/government/uploads/system/uploads/attachment_data/file/220645/corporate_governance_good_practice_july2011.pdf, accessed 15 October 2013.
5 HCA (2012) *The Regulatory Framework for Social Housing in England from April 2012,* Homes and Communities Agency, March 2012, available at www.homesandcommunities.co.uk/sites/default/files/our-work/regfwk-2012.pdf, accessed 16 October 2013. HCA is now the regulator for housing associations, local authorities and other private social housing landlords. Governance is included in this framework. Though housing associations and other registered social landlords have to be registered, some do as Industrial and Provident Societies, some as limited companies and some as charities; so various codes of governance could apply to a housing association depending on structure and registrations. But all are covered by the HCA regulation.
6 AIM, launched in 1995 and was formerly known as the Alternative Investment Market, enables small companies to list their shares in the AIM sub-market of the London Stock Exchange, whose rules are more flexible than those of the main market.
7 QCA (2013) *Corporate Governance Code for Small and Mid-Size Quoted Companies*, Quoted Companies Alliance.
8 OECD (2004) *Principles of Corporate Governance*, Organisation for Economic Co-operation and Development, available at www.oecd.org/daf/ca/corporategovernanceprinciples/31557724.pdf, accessed 15 October 2013. In 2014, OECD is reviewing its corporate governance principles with a view to updating them (http://www.oecd.org/corporate/.
9 CACG (1999) *Principles for Corporate Governance in the Commonwealth – Towards Global Competitiveness and Economic Accountability*, Commonwealth Association for Corporate Governance, November 1999, available at www.ecseonline.com/PDF/CACG%20Guidelines%20-%20Principles%20for%20Corporate%20Governance%20in%20the%20Commonwealth.pdf, accessed 15 October 2013.
10 CBC (2007), *Business Principles*, Commonwealth Business Council, available at www.tbl.com.pk/a-way-forward-the-commonwealth-business-council-guidelines-for-corporate-citizenship/, accessed 21 October 2013.
11 FRC (2012) *The UK Corporate Governance Code*, Financial Reporting Council, September 2012, p 1, available at www.frc.org.uk/Our-Work/Publications/Corporate-Governance/UK-Corporate-Governance-Code-September-2012.pdf, accessed 21 October 2013.
12 FRC (2012), p 8.

13 FRC (2012), p 21.
14 FRC (2012), p 23.
15 Carver, J (2006) *Boards that Make a Difference: a New Design for Leadership in Public and Non-Profit Organizations*, 3rd edn (Jossey-Bass, San Francisco).
16 Carver, J and Oliver, C (2002) *Corporate Boards that Create Value: Governing Company Performance from the Boardroom* (Jossey-Bass, San Francisco).

Chapter D7

Gulf Corporate Governance[1]

Cultural diversity D7.1

> 'There is a growing recognition that the world is complex, and cultural diversity creates a need to deal with people on their own terms. In earlier times, many decision makers, embracing neoclassical principles, believed that economic reactions are universal and rational. …Today, however, the ability of culture to trigger unique responses is being recognised …' [2]

Across the world there is great diversity in corporate governance arrangements, with their respective strengths and weaknesses. At best they are tailored responses to local circumstances designed and evolved to ensure that generally accepted corporate governance principles are applied. While the principles have wide acceptance, the means to apply these principles vary according to local culture, laws and regulations. At worst, in some parts of the world, corporate governance is so light touch that it is largely or partially ineffective.

In this article we examine some of the characteristics of boards of quoted companies in the Gulf region in comparison with elsewhere, attempting to identify their strengths and weaknesses, and having regard to local circumstances.

Composition of boards D7.2

A significant difference of approach is between countries that rely on unitary boards, usually comprising non-executive as well as executive directors, and those with two-tier board structures. One example of the latter is the German supervisory board above the management board where the supervisory board comprises at least 20 non-executive members including worker representatives on the principle of 'co-determination'. In other countries where there is no requirement for two-tier boards, they may be optional.

If a company has a single, unitary board, the CEO is nevertheless likely to make use of an executive committee (EXCO) to assist in running the business, resulting informally in an arrangement which resembles a two-tier structure in some respects. This may be an important part of the CEO's approach to managing the business.

In many companies across the world with unitary boards, the CEO uses the EXCO prior to each board meeting to ensure that the executive is ready for the board meeting and that all of the executive board members 'sing from the same hymn sheet' at the board meeting. The justification for the latter is that boards may not welcome a top executive team with divergent views on important matters. On the other hand, each executive director has a responsibility to exercise independent judgement and to be frank with the board – which a sensible board should expect and welcome.

There is considerable variation *within* unitary board arrangements. In the UK there is often an approximate balance between executive and independent board members:

the UK Corporate Governance Code[3] stipulates that at least half the board (excluding the chairman in the count) should be independent directors and that there should also be a significant number of executive directors on the board. In the US the traditional practice that the chairman of the unitary board will also be the CEO is diminishing in frequency so that it now applies only to a minority of Fortune 500 companies. Where it still applies, the great power of the dual role CEO-Chairman is attempted to be counter-balanced by the rest of the board, or most of it, being independent directors. Where this dual role applies it can certainly result in strong leadership, which may be useful temporarily at times of crisis, but the concept is flawed as the chairman's role is, inter alia, to run the board and the CEO's role is to run the business. If the CEO is also the chairman of the board, the board is hampered in its oversight of the CEO as the board cannot rely on the chairman's leadership for this.

The principle to achieve is to avoid excessive power at the top of the company: hence, the guidance is often that the roles of chairman and CEO should usually be separated, and that the chairman should be independent when appointed as chairman. The preponderance of non-executive directors on the boards of companies in the Gulf region means that the region largely avoids a particular challenge which would apply if board membership was more balanced between executive and non-executive members. This is the challenge of an executive being able to transition successfully from being solely a competent executive to also being an effective board member. Every director, executive or non-executive, is expected to participate in board decision making in ways which are in the best interests of the company as a whole. This may not be the same as the best interests of the function an executive director heads. Furthermore, executive directors being expected to exercise independent judgement in the boardroom may require them to dissent from the wishes of the CEO. The region largely circumvents this challenge by having few executives on their boards.

To compensate for the relative absence of executive board members, the practice is widespread in the region for senior executives who are not board members to be in attendance at board meetings – either generally or for specific agenda items or presentations. Not having the status of being directors of the company, these executives in attendance at board meetings are even more likely to be 'under the thumb' of the CEO. Not being board members, they do not have the same legal responsibilities that directors have – to exercise independent judgement and to act in the best interests of the company.

Executive remuneration D7.3

The small extent to which executives belong to Gulf boards has facilitated keeping executive rewards in check in comparison with the Western world. This is unlikely to be as much a tribute to the effectiveness of Gulf board remuneration committees[4], as to do with the lesser influence of executives at board level. The corporate governance principle is that nobody should participate in the determination of their own rewards. Agency theory tells us that management are the agents of the owners, but that management are determined to maximise their own rewards. In the Gulf, the reward packages given to executives are generous but well under control. So it is not unusual to find that the remuneration committee of a Gulf board meets perhaps just twice a year – once to set executive targets, and secondly to decide upon the performance-related rewards. This contrasts to the multiple meetings of a typical remuneration committee in the West, valiantly but unsuccessfully endeavouring to keep under control excessive executive demands. The bargaining position of top Gulf executives, especially the majority who are from overseas, is not as strong as elsewhere. Perverse incentives are largely avoided. Deferred bonuses and claw-back arrangements to avoid excessive risk-taking are practised in the Gulf, at least as much as in the Western world.

Related parties **D7.4**

Different classes of shares are widely allowed across the world but indulged in to a varying extent from one country to another. The origin of different classes of shares is often in the founding family's reluctance to cede control of the company when the first proportion of its equity is floated. So, for instance, the family holds the 'A' shares (which constitute a small proportion of the total issued share capital) but has floated most or all of the 'B' shares: major decisions may require majority votes of both classes of shareholder. It is argued that this structure reduces the likelihood that a stronger management team can bid to take over from an incumbent, second rate management team: this protection from predatory takeover may not be in the best interests of most of the shareholders, the staff, suppliers, customers and other parties. Since such a share structure protects the company from predatory takeover bids, it allows the board to be less short-termist. Conversely, it is argued that it should be a matter of 'one share, one vote' – that is, an investor taking an equal risk should have equal participation in the company. On the other hand, those who acquired 'B' shares with fewer rights presumably did so with their eyes open.

Whether or not a share structure with different classes is resorted to, the initial public float of a family business is often not accompanied by sufficient realisation that the company is in future to be run for *all* the shareholders, not just for the family, with greater transparency and with greater commitment to corporate governance principles. Those who controlled the company when it was private may continue to engineer the appointments of chairman and 'independent' directors following the initial public offering – with, therefore, a question mark over how independent those directors are.

Possibly the greatest corporate governance strength of Gulf quoted companies is the presence of large shareholders prepared to take a long-term view and to stand behind their investments in difficult times. Even without different classes of shares with their own voting rights, vulnerability to often highly leveraged takeovers is therefore reduced. However, the risks of running a Gulf public company as if it were the private property of a few are similar to the risks which apply to old family businesses, which we discussed above.

The ownership of Gulf quoted companies is relatively closely held. Typically a few shareholders control a significant proportion of the equity. This usually carries rights to nominate one or more to be members of the board. It is not unusual for at least half the board to be members nominated by fewer than half a dozen shareholders. Widely expressed across the region is the fear that the rights of minority shareholders in quoted companies may not be sufficiently safeguarded by boards comprising perhaps a majority of directors nominated by the large shareholders. Of course, those minority shareholders know what they are buying into when they acquire their shareholdings, and in some respects they benefit from the support of the institutional and other large shareholders.

There is the additional issue that the relatively low proportion of equity that is 'free float' makes the market for shares less liquid, potentially leading to greater share price volatility as fewer and small deals may move the share price significantly. A less liquid market is less attractive to investors, resulting in higher costs of capital and lower market capitalisation than would otherwise be the case.

In other countries of the world, institutional and other large investors are usually less keen to place their nominees on the boards of companies they are invested in. It risks placing them in the position of being insiders unable at times to deal in the shares they own. It also risks an investor becoming a shadow director with the responsibilities similar to those of a director appointed formally.[5] It places the nominee director in a conflicted position as the nominee's duty to act in the best interests of the company on whose board he or she sits, may rest uneasily with the natural desire to feedback significant, perhaps price-sensitive, information to the nominator. It may impede the institutional investor from dissenting objectively from board policy since that policy will have been formulated by a board that includes one or more of the institutional investor's nominees.

Director independence D7.5

In the Gulf the distinction is made between non-executive directors who are independent and those who are not. Those regarded by the board as being independent are, in accordance with global best practice, disclosed as such within the annual reports of Gulf public companies.

The concept of director independence is important. While each director, executive or non-executive, should exercise independent judgement when participating in board decisions, there is a category of director specifically categorised as 'independent'. No executive director fits into this category, and not all non-executive directors may do so. It is widely held that a non-executive director who can be regarded as independent should not be a major shareholder, nor represent a significant shareholder. He or she should not have been an employee of the company in the recent past nor have close family ties with it, nor be associated with any parties who have material business relationships with the company, nor have cross-directorships or significant links with other directors through involvement in other companies or bodies.

Apart from receiving a fee for being a non-executive director (which may include supplements for attendance, and for committee chairmanship and attendance) independent directors are not beneficiaries of performance-related reward schemes or of pension schemes.[6] The fundamental reason is that the board needs a significant proportion of its members who can be relied upon to view these schemes impartially.

Independence is not just a matter of these and other *specific* criteria: it is also to do with whether the director has the personal qualities of character and judgement to be relied upon to be independent.

The appearance to stakeholders of a director's independence is as important as the decision the board has come to about the director's independence.

The minimum acceptable proportion of independent directors on boards in the region is less than elsewhere and the independence tests are not so rigorous. For instance, certain regional banks classify as 'independent' directors some who have been nominated to the board by major shareholders.

Whereas elsewhere best practice would suggest that chairmen of boards should be independent when appointed to that position[7], this is very frequently not the case in the region due to the common association of new chairmen with leading shareholders or with other connected parties.

Best practice elsewhere is that only non-executive directors who pass stringent independence tests should be members of board audit, risk and remuneration committees. This restriction is not always followed in the region although executive membership of these committees is readily avoided, not least due to the small number of executives with board positions.

The relative weaknesses of independence arrangements in the region can perhaps be defended on several grounds. First, since it is unusual for more than one member of the board to be an executive, the overwhelming weight of non-executive directors on boards facilitates the exercise of board judgement that is at least independent of the executive interest, if not independent of related parties. The need for independent members on boards is in part to ensure that boards have a perspective which is independent of the executive and a greater potential to challenge the executive effectively.

The role of the chairman D7.6

Likewise, the rationale for the chairman to be independent when appointed as chairman, is in large a measure to avoid excessive alignment of the chairman of the board with the executive – which might be likely had the chairman previously been a senior executive of the company. In the Gulf this is unlikely to have been the case. The chairman needs to be the chairman of the *whole* board, endeavouring to avoid alignment with any faction on the board, and indeed reducing the risk that factions develop.

Although the Gulf very effectively avoids excessive chairman alignment with the executive, there is often a built-in likelihood of an alignment bias towards the nominee directors.

While a less than objective relationship between the chairman and the CEO should always be avoided, a hallmark of a healthy company is a good, constructive relationship between these two. In view of the board structure in the region, there is a risk that the CEO may be positioned, in the eyes of the board, as an outsider rather than as an equal member of the board team. This may be counter-balanced by a board's awareness of the extreme importance of the CEO to a board otherwise bereft of executive membership.

Effectiveness of boards D7.7

There are reasons to be concerned about the competence and effectiveness of some boards in the region; although there are also some relative strengths in this regard.

The practice of large shareholders nominating directors means that the majority owners have effective 'reserve powers' to safeguard their investment. In contrast, in highly liquid capital markets where ownership is widely held, the capacity of shareholders (who, after all, are the owners) to influence their boards has been noted as often being only very marginal, slow, indecisive and inadequate.

In determining the composition of boards in the region, it would appear that undue emphasis is placed on ensuring these 'reserve powers' are in place, to the detriment of board effectiveness in other respects. Board succession planning does not always extend to ensuring that nominee directors bring to the board the qualities the board needs to oversee the executive effectively. Board nomination committees in the region may have little influence upon whom a large shareholder nominates.

It must be emphasised that it is not necessary, and may be sub-optimal for a nominee to be connected to the nominating party as an employee or otherwise: the primary driver for choosing a nominee director should be the needs of the company and the board's nomination committee should be the prime mover in this. Succession planning for the board should ensure that collectively the board is able to challenge and support the executive across the key functional areas of the business. Succession planning should extend to influencing the choice of nominee directors.

While attendance at board meetings and board committees is usually good in the region, participation at board meetings is often inadequate with many directors lacking the experience or confidence to contribute, and showing excessive deference to the chairman of the board.[8] Quality of dialogue at board meetings may be poor, not only due to the tendency to defer to the chairman of the board, but because some directors (especially some nominated ones) have insufficient experience to challenge the executive or to challenge their co-directors.

Effectiveness of directors **D7.8**

There is good disclosure of directors' other interests in most published annual reports of listed companies in the region. This rightly allows us to observe that many directors on boards in the region appear to be over-extended, and this seems to be a particularly acute problem with respect to nominee directors. Including preparation time, site visits and board committee membership, a time commitment of between 30 and 36 days a year for a non-executive director is unlikely to overstate the real need. If a company is in difficulty, is facing a takeover bid, is on the acquisition trail, is embarked upon a strategic restructuring or is grappling with a crisis, the time commitment may be significantly greater temporarily.

The time commitment of a non-executive chairmen varies greatly, is most unlikely to be less than 60 days a year and may be as much as four days a week.

Someone with a full-time executive role elsewhere would be unlikely to be able to cope properly with more than one or two non-executive directorships. Someone with a plural professional life could handle up to five non-executive directorships if he or she had no other calls upon their working time. Board chairmen should have fewer other demands on their time and should certainly not have an executive position elsewhere.

Generally, but not without exception, annual reports of quoted companies disclose membership and attendance at board and board committee meetings. The reported, good attendance levels which apply in the region may be related to the common practice of paying directors' fees in part according to meetings attended. This is equitable and may be a successful policy, but it risks directors wrongly considering they are not responsible except for matters dealt with at meetings they attended. It is not a common approach in the West where, on the other hand, supplements to the basic director fee may be paid for board committee membership and for board committee chairmanship. Other companies in the West pay no supplements for board committee chairmanship and membership, arguing that these additional responsibilities tend to be evenly spread across their independent directors over time.

A letter of appointment for a director should set out the anticipated time commitment and the skills and other qualities that the director is expected to bring to the board. Those approached to take on director roles should be confident that they will have the time and will be able, through competence and in other ways, to serve the board as the board anticipates and as set out in their letters of appointment.

Roles of boards **D7.9**

It is striking that many boards of companies in the region become heavily involved in executive matters, even though their membership is largely non-executive. Some UAE banks have EXCO committees of the board comprising largely or exclusively non-executive board members. In some cases the EXCO even includes board members indicated in the annual report as being independent. Participating in executive decisions is inimical to being an independent director.

There are examples of boards of UAE banks having risk committees of the board that may meet between 20 and 50 times a year: clearly these risk committees are making executive-type credit and other decisions, going far beyond the roles of a board risk committee to oversee the formulation of risk policy and processes, and to *oversee* their application by the executive on behalf of the board.

The conventional corporate governance model across the world is as follows:

- the members (shareholders) own the company[9];
- the chairman runs the board;
- the board runs the CEO;
- the CEO runs the business.

A sensible board sets the direction, provides the requisite resources and oversees that the CEO is implementing the direction the board has set. A sensible board does not 'tread on the toes' of the CEO as he or she runs the business. For instance, it should be possible for a bank's board, perhaps assisted by the board risk committee, to agree lending policy and risk criteria and to oversee that the policy has been discharged at executive level. Executive decision making, in line with the company's policy framework, should be a matter for the executive: if it is not, then one or more of the following probably apply:

- there is an avoidable lack of clarity on policy;
- policy is clear but the board frequently requires that the policy be overridden (perhaps in the interests of related parties);
- the board, although nominally non-executive, has assumed executive responsibilities;
- a low level of executive membership of the board makes it more likely that non-executive board members will be tempted to assume quasi-executive responsibilities.

Meetings of boards D7.10

The implicit notion that the board serves the purpose of being a 'reserve power' (so that arrangements are already in place should drastic remedial action be needed on behalf of the majority shareholders) is sometimes further borne out by an undue infrequency of board meetings. A board that meets infrequently is unlikely to be much more than a 'reserve power'. Formulation and adoption of policies and effective oversight of the executive will not be done effectively by an absentee board. For instance, one leading regional bank's board in 2012 met just four times, with a gap of almost 120 days between two adjacent board meetings. Notwithstanding that committees of the board also met, such infrequency puts in doubt that the board is able to discharge all of its responsibilities effectively, which include:

- setting the direction of the business and determining overall policies;
- determining and providing the resources needed to implement the direction set;
- overseeing that the executive is running the business so as to implement the direction the board has set;
- instigating remedial actions as and when needed.

It is hard to imagine that a board can be effective if it meets less than about ten times a year, perhaps more. The board should be the body in the company that makes the most difference.

Committees of boards D7.11

In the financial sector across the Gulf, risk committees of the board are already generally established. While financial institutions historically have had risk committees, these have in the past usually only been at an executive level – such as credit risk committees. The establishment of risk committees of boards has been a response to an awareness that boards on the whole did not understand the risks that their companies (banks and insurance companies in particular) were running at the time of the global financial crisis. So guidance has been developed that boards should establish risk committees comprising wholly or largely of independent directors.

Now it is widely accepted general practice that listed company boards should have at least *four* committees – audit, remuneration, nominations and risk. In the Gulf's financial sector all these committees are generally in place, though frequently two or three may be combined which is not ideal. In particular, the audit committee will lose some of its necessary independence if it is combined with another board committee.

In comparison with the West, it is likely that the oversight of risk by risk committees of Gulf bank boards must be at last as effective as in the West, since Gulf banks' exposure to exotic financial instruments is more modest than in the US and UK. An opposing view is that the common practice in the Gulf for board risk committees to make lending decisions threatens an inadequate focus on risk policy, risk appetite and oversight of the executive. Furthermore, a risk committee cannot effectively oversee executive-type decisions that the risk committee itself has made.

Diversity of boards **D7.12**

A contemporary issue of some importance is that of board diversity. It is much broader than gender diversity: age, nationality, background and skills are likely to be other relevant diversity hallmarks.

A non-diverse board may find it harder to 'think out of the box' and be more likely to succumb to 'group think' and staying within its 'comfort zone'.

Boards should consider the likely benefits of diversity, but avoid creating a more diverse board if this would compromise board effectiveness. It is the *business case* rather than the politically correct, social policy case that should be the driver of increased board diversity – as it should be with respect to the composition of the board generally. The experience of Norway, which has achieved its statutory proportion of 40% female directors on its large company boards, does not suggest that mandatory quotas are an unmitigated good: it has resulted in relatively few women holding an excessive number of board positions, and research has shown that Norwegian companies which had to move furthest in altering the gender composition of their boards have subsequently performed worse than the other companies.

Without quotas, the UK has achieved only about 17% female participation on large quoted company boards, with a greater proportion of women holding non-executive compared to executive directorships. Bearing in mind the higher proportion of executive directors on UK boards than on Gulf boards, to be comparable with the UK's very modest level of achievement, female board participation in the Gulf would now be between 25% and 30% of total board membership. Many Gulf companies, including banks, have one woman on the board, few have more. With a typical board size of 12 or so, the percentage of women on Gulf boards cannot be more than 10% currently.

There is a need to move beyond the 'token woman' member of the board. It is difficult for one woman to make the distinctive contribution that women can make when she is a lone voice on the board. It becomes likely she will tend to emulate the macho culture so often found in all-male boards.

A degree of international diversity on Gulf boards is often achieved through the frequent overseas status of the CEO who is generally a member of the board, and international diversity is high at executive levels below the CEO. Nominee directors, especially those who are CEOs of the nominating parties, sometimes also enhance the international element to Gulf boards.

Age diversity appears to be at least as great as with Western companies – probably more so as there are many young, nominated directors, often with family links to the nominating party.

An issue of importance for financial institutions across the world is the depth of financial experience of board members. In particular it is generally considered important for the chairman of a bank's board to have significant executive banking experience, in addition to leadership experience.[10] Even despite the general restriction of chairman appointments to nationals, Gulf banks usually succeed in appointing board chairmen with significant financial and leadership experience.

Sustainability D7.13

Gulf companies, even those such as banks that are not in more obvious exploitive sectors, are now taking sustainability seriously. Not so long ago, they tended to interpret their corporate social responsibility obligations only as a matter of making charitable donations and reporting that they had done so. Now they have a much broader understanding of their obligations especially to their local community, extending to issues relating to exploitation, pollution, global warning, staffing and social obligations. Though without any data as evidence, it appears that published sustainability reports, usually separate from the main annual reports, are now as widespread and as detailed as in the West.

Sustainability should entail concern right across the supply chain. For instance, a bank, using a scorecard approach to assist in making lending decisions, might consider assessing a potential borrower's sustainability credentials as one of a number of factors which contribute to the credit decision. The concern that this might disadvantage the bank in a competitive environment, may be counterbalanced if it is the case that sustainably responsible companies are better run. This approach would allow both the bank and the client to publicise their sustainability commitment and achievement.

Evaluation of boards D7.14

Board evaluation[11] is being introduced in the region. Its maturity varies. Sometimes it is undertaken or facilitated by an external party in accordance with best practice.[12] Some companies, but not all, include an assessment of the performance of the board chairman, and the chairmen of the board committees.

Rarely do board evaluations in the region extend to assessing the performance of individual directors. Elsewhere where this is done, it is usually overseen by the chairman of the board: its introduction has been sensitive but has been subsequently welcomed by those it impacts. This should be regarded as an important area to be addressed in the region. Directors find it helpful to learn about their strengths and weaknesses, and how they are perceived by their peers. Of course, this process flags up areas where there is a need for a director's performance to improve. Usually how to achieve the needed improvement will be self-evident, and self-knowledge is an important and effective prerequisite for achieving enhanced performance.

Companies should expect that individual director evaluation will often indicate needed personal development programmes tailored for individual directors. The best companies in the region already invest in board development programmes, though they report poor attendance levels at these programmes, and they are rarely tailored to the needs of individual directors.

We consider there is great merit in designing personal development programmes for *individual* directors, even to the extent of providing one-to-one expert mentoring of individual directors. This would be an important part of a concerted effort to 'raise the bar' in terms of the minimum competence and commitment needed from directors. Individual director 'buy-in' to a tailored personal development programme is likely to be higher than for a programme targeted only at the company's needs, but will be beneficial for both.

In the region, rarely is the board evaluation 360 degrees with directors assessing the performance of their co-directors, and with senior management below the board contributing to the board assessment process. To the extent that shareholders participate in the evaluation, it is usually only indirectly via the nominee directors, so that the voices of other shareholders are not heard.

Audit **D7.15**

Professor Mackenzie, an eminent economist at Manchester University UK, coined these immortal words as far back as 1966 in his Foreword to a book on auditing in governments by EL Normanton based on the latter's MPhil thesis which Mackenzie had supervised:[13]

> 'Without audit, no accountability; without accountability, no control; and if there is no control, where is the seat of power? … great issues often come to light only because of scrupulous verification of detail.'

Effective audit has been regarded as an essential element of corporate governance and, indeed, as price to pay for limited liability.

It is not surprising, in view of its importance, that auditing has been under the spotlight in the wake of the global financial crisis. An issue is whether the oligopoly of the 'Big 4' is impacting negatively on audit price and/or quality, whether there is sufficient choice of auditor and whether there are excessive barriers to entry into this elite by mid-tier audit firms. Both the European Commission and the UK's Competition Commission have the matter under review. A number of measures are being proposed. One is to outlaw restrictive covenants under which, for instance, a lender is able to insist that the borrower's accounts are audited by a 'Big 4' firm. Others are mandatory tendering of audit services and/or mandatory rotation of the audit firm.

In the West the 'Big 4' and also companies have been lobbying furiously against mandatory tendering or rotation of auditors, citing alleged excessive costs associated with these measures. The comparative success of the MENA region (Middle East and North Africa) in avoiding lengthy retention of the same audit firm, calls to question the resistance to mandatory audit firm tendering and rotation in the West.

In Oman, an external auditor can only audit the same bank for a maximum of four years, and in Qatar for five years. Similar requirements are in place in Algeria, Egypt, Tunisia, Saudi Arabia and elsewhere in the region, but in the UAE there is no such requirement.[14]

An excessively lengthy relationship of an audit firm with a particular audit client is subject to the same criticism as a lengthy term of office of an independent director on a board: ultimately complacency and a lack of professional scepticism are likely to creep in: the auditor (as with the independent director) is likely to have been party to so many judgements in the past that it becomes difficult or impossible to view things objectively. To some extent the audit profession, following auditing standards, has tried to surmount this difficulty by periodically rotating the audit engagement partner.

Hawkamah and the OECD carried out a survey on the governance practices of banks in the MENA region which found that 78% of the surveyed banks had internal policies on the rotation of the external auditors according to specific terms.[15]

Conclusion D7.16

The focus of this chapter has been on the corporate governance of quoted companies in the Gulf region. Markets exist by the grace of investors. Investor confidence depends upon *country factors* (such as the banking system, property rights, pressure on corruption, taxation), *capital market factors* (such as market regulation, market liquidity, accounting standards) and *corporate factors* (such as much of what we have discussed in this article).

The region has on the whole carefully adapted and applied what are generally regarded as corporate governance best practices to the extent that this has been feasible in view of the distinctive culture of the region. That distinctiveness has resulted in some elements of corporate governance that are stronger than elsewhere, and others that are not so. Many but not all of these have been explored in this chapter.

ttttthis chthis article.

Notes

1 This chapter first appeared as Chambers, AD (2013) 'Reflections on Gulf Corporate Governance', *The Hawkamah Journal*, 1 (2), pp 33–42. While the author would like to thank The Hawkamah Institute of Corporate Governance, and in particular Alec Aaltonen, for assistance in preparing this chapter, responsibility for its contents and views expressed are those of the author alone.

2 Walle, AH (2013) *Rethinking Business Anthropology* (Greenleaf Publishing, Sheffield), ISBN 13: 978-1-906093-90-7, p x.

3 The Financial Reporting Council (2012) *The UK Corporate Governance Code*, September 2012, available at http://www.frc.org.uk/Our-Work/Publications/Corporate-Governance/UK-Corporate-Governance-Code-September-2012.aspx, accessed 24 June 2013.

4 Certainly, in the Western world, the remuneration committee has been unsuccessful at containing executive remuneration.

5 A 'shadow director' being a person (or a corporate entity) whose instructions a board customarily follows.

6 While this is prima facie the case in the UK, in the US it is regarded as acceptable for independent directors to be beneficiaries of, for instance, of share option schemes.

7 This best practice elsewhere is often not followed. For instance HSBC made Stephen, now Lord, Green their Group Chairman in 2006, having previously been their Group CEO; in 2010 he was succeeded to the chairmanship by Douglas Flint who until then had been HSBC's Group Finance Director.

8 Clearly a board should have sufficient respect for its chairman to enable the chairman to discharge his/her responsibilities well on behalf of the board and the company. But

a board chairman is only *primus inter pares* (first amongst equals). In UK law, for instance, a board need not have a chairman, or may change its chairman for each board meeting. Under UK legislation the chairman has no distinctive responsibilities beyond those of being a director, and it is the board itself that determines who shall be the chairman. Of course, if the shareholders seriously dissent from the board's choice, the shareholders may vote that person off the board.

9 There are dissenting views as to whether the shareholders should run, as well as own, the company. Shareholder powers vary across the world. The UK's Financial Reporting Council, custodians of the UK Corporate Governance Code, takes the line that the board rather than the shareholders is responsible for corporate governance:

> 'The first version of the UK Corporate Governance Code (the Code) was produced in 1992 by the Cadbury Committee. Its paragraph 2.5 is still the classic definition of the context of the Code: Corporate governance is the system by which companies are directed and controlled. Boards of directors are responsible for the governance of their companies. The shareholders' role in governance is to appoint the directors and the auditors and to satisfy themselves that an appropriate governance structure is in place. The responsibilities of the board include setting the company's strategic aims, providing the leadership to put them into effect, supervising the management of the business and reporting to shareholders on their stewardship. The board's actions are subject to laws, regulations and the shareholders in general meeting.' (FRC (2012), The UK Corporate Governance Code, September 2001, p 1, available at http://www.frc.org.uk/Our-Work/Publications/Corporate-Governance/UK-Corporate-Governance-Code-September-2012.aspx, accessed 2 August 2013)

10 The UK Walker Report (2009) said:

> 'The chairman of a major bank should be expected to commit a substantial proportion of his or her time, probably around two-thirds, to the business of the entity, with clear understanding from the outset that, in the event of need, the bank chairmanship role would have priority over any other business time commitment. Depending on the balance and nature of their business, the required time commitment should be proportionately less for the chairman of a less complex or smaller bank, insurance or fund management entity.
>
> The chairman of a [bank or other financial industry] board should bring a combination of relevant financial industry experience and a track record of successful leadership capability in a significant board position. Where this desirable combination is only incompletely achievable at the selection phase, and provided that there is an adequate balance of relevant financial industry experience among other board members, the board should give particular weight to convincing leadership experience since financial industry experience without established leadership skills in a chairman is unlikely to suffice.' (Walker, D (2009) *A Review of Corporate Governance in UK banks and other Financial Industry Entities*, Final report, November 2009, p 15, available at http://webarchive.nationalarchives.gov.uk/20130129110402/http://www.hm-treasury.gov.uk/d/walker_review_261109.pdf, accessed 2 August 2013)

11 In the region this is usually termed 'board assessment'.

12 For instance, in the UK the performance of the board should be assessed at least annually; and at least once in every three years, this assessment should be externally facilitated.

13 Professor Mackenzie, an eminent economist at Manchester University, coined these words as far back as 1966 in his Foreword to a book on auditing in governments by EL Normanton based on the latter's MPhil thesis which Mackenzie had supervised: Normanton, EL (1966) *The Accountability and Audit of Governments – A Comparative Study* (Manchester University Press; also published by Frederick A Prager, New York (1966)), p vii.

14 OECD (2011), *Survey on Corporate Governance Frameworks in the Middle East and North Africa,* available at http://www.oecd.org/daf/ca/corporategovernanceprinciples/49012924.pdf, accessed 2 August 2013.

15 OECD (2009), *Policy Brief on Improving Corporate Governance of Banks in the Middle East and North Africa Region*, November 2009, available at http://www.oecd.org/mena/44186957.pdf, accessed 2 August 2013.

Part E:
Audit Committees

Chapter E1

Overview of Audit Committee Responsibilities

Introduction **E1.1**

Although audit committees are being asked to do more and more, the additional tasks may be regarded as add-ons to their four main responsibilities, which are:

1. scrutiny of financial statements (**E1.4**);
2. oversight of internal control and risk management (**E1.5**);
3. oversight of external audit (**E1.6**); and
4. oversight of internal audit and other internal review agencies (**E1.7**).

The UK's Financial Reporting Council accepted the recommendation of the Smith Committee that an audit committee should review the whistleblowing policy of the entity (Provision C.3.5 of the UK Corporate Governance Code, set out in full at **App1**). Rather than regarding this as a fifth and distinct responsibility, we regard it as part of the committee's oversight of risk management and internal control. Similarly, trends for the audit committee to both oversee significant systems changes and to become involved in mergers and acquisitions can be regarded as extensions of the committee's remit for internal control and risk management. The FRC's Smith Guidance was updated in 2010 and again in 2012.[1]

We provide practical advice for audit committees on discharging their responsibilities in each of the four (above) areas in Chapters **E4** to **E7** respectively. Here we limit ourselves to explaining the nature of the committee's responsibilities for these matters and highlighting where companies may exercise their discretion in each area, before moving on to discuss how audit committees may operate within groups and within governmental organisations. In **App4** we provide five sample terms of reference for audit committees.

There are a number of emerging issues relating to audit committees. First, there is the proposal that the report about the audit committee within a company's annual report should be a report from the audit committee and not merely a report from the board about its audit committee. Secondly, there are increasing pressures on audit committees which mean that the committee tends to meet more frequently, and site visits have become more prominent.

An important emerging issue is the rise of risk committees of the board, especially in financial institutions and other entities exposed to systemic risk, comprising independent directors (see Chapter **E9** and Appendix **App4**). Each company needs to decide how to divide responsibilities between the board risk and audit committees and to ensure that important matters fail to be addressed by either committee.

More emphasis is being placed by audit committees on assessing the independence of external and internal auditors and chief risk officers. Indeed, the audit committee's own independence and effectiveness is becoming more of a mainstream consideration within the board evaluation. Audit committees are increasingly availing themselves of additional assurances commissioned directly by the committee from external parities other than from the company's external auditors.

Are audit committees mandatory? E1.2

Since 1978, New York Stock Exchange rules had made audit committees mandatory for US domestic listed companies and, in 2002, the Sarbanes-Oxley Act gave statutory backing for mandatory audit committees in all US listed companies, and furthermore gave the audit committees of US listed company boards the responsibility to appoint the external auditors.

UK lobbying led to the addition of paragraph 5 to Article 41 of the EC Eighth Directive on Statutory Audit.[2] This rearguard action by the UK effectively avoided the mandatory requirement to have an audit committee:

> '5. Member States may allow or decide that the provisions laid down in paragraphs 1 to 4 shall not apply to any public-interest entity **that has a body performing equivalent functions to an audit committee**, established and functioning according to provisions in place in the Member State in which the entity to be audited is registered. In such a case the entity shall disclose which body carries out these functions and how it is composed.' (bolding added)

This has been reflected in the UK Disclosure and Transparency Rules.[3]

As far as the appointment of external auditors is concerned, the UK's Corporate Governance Code includes Provision C.3.7 that the audit committee should recommend to the board whom should be appointed as the external auditors; and, if the board declines to agree to its audit committee's advice, that advice should be printed in the annual report, together with an explanation as to why the board did not accept the advice. That is getting just about as close as possible to mandating the audit committee to appoint the external auditors but without quite doing so – and so it continues to preserve in all respects the authority of the board above the board's committees.

The wording of the Listing Rule (previously 12.43A, then 9.8.6; and, from 2010, 9.8.6 (5) and (6)) which sets out the requirements of UK listed companies with respect to the Corporate Governance Code could be construed as meaning that adherence to the Principles (both Main and Supporting Principles) within the Code should be regarded as mandatory, whereas the Provisions merely have a 'comply or explain' status. The wording is now:

> 'In the case of a listed company incorporated in the United Kingdom, the following additional items must be included in its annual financial report:
>
> …
>
> (5) a statement of how the listed company has applied the Main Principles set out in the UK Corporate Governance Code, in a manner that would enable shareholders to evaluate how the principles have been applied;
>
> (6) a statement as to whether the listed company has:
>
> (a) complied throughout the accounting period with all relevant provisions set out in the UK Corporate Governance Code; or

(b) not complied throughout the accounting period with all relevant provisions set out in the UK Corporate Governance Code and if so, setting out:
   (i) those provisions, if any it has not complied with;
   (ii) in the case of provisions whose requirements are of a continuing nature, the period within which, if any, it did not comply with some or all of those provisions; and
   (iii) the company's reasons for non-compliance;'

The obligation to conform to the above listing rule applies only to companies listed on the main market with a premium listing; though many other companies, listed or not, voluntarily choose to observe the Corporate Governance Code, at least to some extent.

In fact, the UK Listing Authority regards this rule as being simply a disclosure rule for premium listed companies about the extent of a company's adherence to the Main Principles and compliance with the Provisions. This interpretation of the rule is unfortunate, as it makes no distinction between the different wording of (a) and (b) within the rule. It also means that it imposes no obligation upon a company to explain why it is not observing a Principle, as this obligation is only made with respect to Provisions in section (b) of the rule.

Even were the Principles of the Code construed as mandatory, there would have been no Code requirement for a listed company to have an audit committee. No Principle within the Code mentions 'audit committee'. The single Principle in section C.3 on audit committees is worded as follows:

> 'The board should establish formal and transparent arrangements for considering how they should apply the financial reporting and internal control principles and for maintaining an appropriate relationship with the company's auditors.'

So, if a company met that Principle without having an audit committee, it would not be in breach of that Principle. Almost all UK listed companies have either decided that they cannot apply that Principle without an audit committee or that they should not do so – perhaps because of shareholder pressure to comply with the Provisions within the Code – pressure forthcoming because of the disclosure requirement of Listing Rule 9.8.6.

Audit committees are only mentioned in the Code at the level of the discretionary 'comply or explain' Provisions, for instance C.3.1:

> 'The board should establish an audit committee of at least three, or in the case of smaller companies two, members, who should all be independent non-executive directors. The board should satisfy itself that at least one member of the audit committee has recent and relevant financial experience.'

So, all that a company would need to do, should it decide not to have an audit committee ,is draw attention to the Provisions with which it is not complying and explain why not – that is Provisions C.3.1 to C.3.8.

The EC Eighth Directive **E1.3**

Articles 41 and 42 of the Directive are reproduced at **E1.16**.

Under Article 41.1, Member States must require public interest entities to have an audit committee which meets the compositional and functional requirements set out in Article 41.1–41.3. We discuss public interest entities at **E1.4**. As mentioned above, the Directive allows that certain classes of public interest entity may be exempted wholly or partly from the requirements of Article 41. In addition, under Article 41.5, Member States may disapply the requirement to have such an audit committee, providing specified conditions are met. Article 41.1 and 41.3 set out specific compositional requirements for audit committees. In particular, at least one member of the committee must be independent and have competence in accounting and/or auditing (see **E2.5**). In addition, Member States are required to determine whether such audit committees are to be composed solely of non-executives, and how they are to be appointed.

Article 41.2 sets out specific functional requirements for audit committees (without prejudice to the responsibilities of others). These requirements are that the audit committee shall, inter alia:

- monitor the financial reporting process;
- monitor the effectiveness of the company's internal control, internal audit where applicable, and risk management systems;
- monitor the statutory audit of the annual and consolidated accounts; and
- review and monitor the independence of the statutory auditor or audit firm, and in particular the provision of additional services to the audited entity.

Article 41.5, inserted at a late stage into the Directive at the instigation of the UK Department of Trade and Industry (DTI), enables Member States to choose not to apply the compositional requirements for audit committees specified in Article 41.1–41.3 to entities which have a body performing equivalent functions which is established and functions in accordance with national provisions. For the purposes of this provision, the relevant functions are those listed in Article 41.2 (see above). In such cases, the entity must disclose which body carries out these functions and how it is composed. The alternative body must obviously be composed in such a way as to enable it effectively to perform these functions and, in the Government's interpretation, this means it should in particular have within its composition sufficient independence and relevant expertise. However, the Government does not consider that the Directive requires that the national provisions prescribe rules as to what would constitute such independence and expertise. Those are matters appropriate to be judged in the individual circumstances of the company and in relation to the nature and complexity of its business.

In section 3.49 of the Consultation Document, the DTI told us that the Government was considering options for setting out the requirements in national provisions, and for ensuring adequate enforcement. In doing so, the DTI was seeking to provide the maximum flexibility available under the Directive for public interest entities to determine the composition of their audit committee, or other body performing equivalent functions, to help enable companies to establish arrangements which best suit the interests of their shareholders in the company's particular circumstances. The Companies Act 2006 (CA 2006) includes two powers which could be used for this purpose:

- CA 2006, s 1269 inserts section 890 into the Financial Services and Markets Act 2000, which enables the Financial Services Authority (FSA) to make rules

relating to corporate governance in connection with the implementation of EU obligations; and
- CA 2006, s 1273 enables the Secretary of State to make regulations for similar purposes.

The option chosen by the DTI/D-BERR was to amend the Listing Rules to make audit committees, or an equivalent way of discharging the EC responsibilities of audit committees, a listing requirement for UK quoted companies.

The UK Corporate Governance Code, promulgated by the Financial Reporting Council (FRC), already contains Provisions in relation to audit committees. These Provisions are well established, regularly reviewed by the FRC in consultation with stakeholders, and form an important plank of the corporate governance framework in the UK.

The Provisions in respect of audit committees under the UK Corporate Governance Code are more extensive and specific than the minimum requirements under Article 41.5. For example, they recommend that all members of the audit committee be independent directors, and that the committee undertakes other functions in addition to those set out in the Directive.[4] The Government's view is that it should, therefore, remain for companies to determine whether to comply with the specific recommendations of the Code in respect of audit committees. Equally, the Government considers that the Provisions of the UK Corporate Governance Code, as currently promulgated, meet the requirements in respect of audit committees set out in Article 41.1–41.3.

The current listing rules require listed companies to make disclosures in relation to their compliance with the Provisions of the Code. However, these disclosure requirements are not in themselves sufficient to implement the Directive, because the Listing Rules leave open the option of having in place no arrangements in relation to these matters at all, under the 'comply or explain' approach.

Public interest entities **E1.4**

There is no UK definition of what is construed to be a public interest entity. Public interest entities are listed companies and whatever additional entities are designated as such by Member States. The DTI released in March 2007 a Consultation Document[5] that proposed no extension of what the UK regards as public interest entities beyond the minimum requirement contained within the 2006 replacement of the Eighth Directive.[6]

Section 3.41 of the DTI (March 2007) Consultation Document pointed out that Article 2.13 of the replacement of the Eighth Directive defines 'public interest entities' as:

> 'entities which have issued transferable securities admitted to trading on a regulated market governed by a Member State, credit institutions (ie banks and building societies), and insurance undertakings (this includes Lloyds), which may be companies, friendly societies or industrial and provident societies'

but allows Member States to designate other entities as 'public interest entities' if they are of significant public relevance because of the nature of their business, their size or the number of their employees. The DTI stated (section 3.41) that the Government did not propose to go further than the EC definition, and that the Government's view is that the requirements in the implementing legislation should not apply to foreign incorporated entities listed on UK regulated markets. Entities incorporated in other Member States will, of course, be subject to those States' requirements. Clearly there are many other types of entity where there is a significant public interest and for whom the additional obligations that apply to public interest entities should also apply. Large private companies with quasi monopolies, large mutuals and large charities are examples.

Scrutiny of financial statements **E1.5**

Most audit committees had their roots in the requirement for all members of the board to approve the adoption by the board of the published financial statements, although some, particularly in the public sector, were formed initially to oversee internal control and audit arrangements.

Where the financial statements were the original, principal rationale for the audit committee, it is likely that members of the board, especially the non-executive members, would have felt the need for a forum to scrutinise draft financial statements prior to their adoption by the board as a whole for publication. This forum was known as the audit committee, and became a valuable reassurance that the audit committee was able to give to the board that the latter could safely go public with the proposed financial statements.

While the financial statements are audited, the primary responsibility for 'getting them right' is with the board. In the UK the published financial statements are the statements of the entire board, and each director shares joint and several responsibility for their reliability. This is usually not the case for governmental organisations – such as central government departments, agencies, non-departmental public bodies and so on. Independent and other non-executive directors of companies, with their lesser time commitment compared with executive directors (though with broadly the same responsibilities), have felt particularly vulnerable associating themselves so strongly with financial statements prepared under the direction of the executive finance director. Indeed, even other executive directors have also valued the reassurance that an effective audit committee can give to the board as a whole that the board can safely go public with the intended financial statements.

In other jurisdictions, the board may not have the same collective responsibility for the reliability of the financial statements. In the US, this is the responsibility of the CEO and CFO. In UK governmental organisations, it is the personal responsibility of the accounting officer – who may be the chief executive and/or the permanent secretary. Nevertheless, the board still has a concern to ensure that the financial statements are sound – even if the board's and individual directors' vulnerability to litigation may be much less.

The *primary* responsibility for the reliability of the published financial statements is vested in the board, not with the external auditors. It is not adequate for the board to rely exclusively on the fact that the financial statements are audited by independent accountants. The board should undertake its own scrutiny to satisfy itself that the financial statements are sound. Boards lean on their audit committees in this regard.

Boards and their audit committees need to establish the criteria for determining what sorts of information should be subject to audit committee scrutiny, and the approach the audit committee should follow in making this scrutiny. Audit committees are overstretched, particularly in view of their typical reluctance to meet much more than four or five times a year.

One criterion that an audit committee might apply could be that its oversight is to be limited to *information published in the name of the board*. In addition to the year-end financial statements, this would also certainly include prospectuses to raise new capital as well as interim financial statements where required. This could exclude occasional or regular, perhaps monthly, returns made by the entity to perhaps the regulator or to a sponsoring government department – where these returns do not carry the imprimatur of the board itself. However, these returns are a form of publication of information to certain categories of stakeholder of the entity. Furthermore, in UK central governmental organisations, non-departmental public bodies, NHS bodies, universities, etc, it is accepted that the audit committee has a role to provide assurance to the accounting officer – and almost certainly it will be the case that such returns are the personal responsibility of the accounting officer.

There are other issues of significance in determining the remit of the audit committee in this area. If the audit committee's brief is to be limited to information that is published, should it, for instance, extend to company briefings with large shareholders and investment analysts? The principle here is that price-sensitive information should be available to the whole market at the same time, and there is a considerable risk that briefings of this sort, if conducted carelessly, might inadvertently publish information and might place some of the market at a relative advantage.

Another borderline example would be the release of profits warnings. In practice, this will be a matter for the board as a whole. The issue here is that the company should endeavour to ensure that market expectations are in line with underlying performance – and this works both ways. The board attempts to correct misconceptions in the market that are more than, say, 10% adrift from reality. Arguably, a company that declares year-end results significantly at odds with market expectations has, deliberately or accidentally, misled the market – whether the results have turned out to be better or worse than market expectations. Shareholders who sold before better-than-expected results were declared are just as vulnerable to unanticipated losses as shareholders who held or bought before worse-than-expected results were declared.

Whether with respect to meetings with major shareholders/investment analysts or with respect to profits warnings, it is likely to be quite impractical for the audit committee to scrutinise the specific information which will be disclosed. The approach that the audit committee will need to take is to examine the *process* that the company follows. So, with respect to meetings with investment analysts, the audit committee may (perhaps as an agenda item once a year) examine the *process* that the company follows to determine the meetings which will take place and their timing, to prepare for the meetings, to conduct the meetings and to deal with the aftermath – and so on. Similarly, it is likely to be the *process* for generating profits warnings which will attract the audit committee's attention.

A further criterion which may be applied to contain the workload of the audit committee to manageable proportions could be that its oversight in this area of its responsibilities should be limited to *financial* information to be published. Consistent with this criterion, the audit committee may take a leaf out of the external auditor's book. The external auditor *audits* the financial statements, *reviews* the directors' corporate governance assertions and *reads* the rest of the content which is to appear within the published annual report and accounts; so the audit committee might restrict its purview to the financial statements themselves. The external auditor's scrutiny is progressively less as the auditor moves from *audit* to *review* to merely *read*, the last being to determine that there is no content elsewhere within the annual report which is inconsistent with the financial statements. Applying this criterion is not without its problems. First, information denominated in non-monetary units might be construed as financial information if it communicates financial messages to the reader: information within the Operational and Financial Review (OFR) or Business Review (the latter required by the amended Fourth and Seventh EC Directives and by the Companies Act 2006) might be just one example. Secondly, the board needs assurance on the reliability of non-financial information which is published: corporate social responsibility (CSR) reports might be an example of this (see **C5**).

We explore the corporate governance assertions that external auditors review at **H1.7** to **H1.16**. A decision will also need to be made whether or not to apply the criterion of '*for publication*' to the information which the audit committee reviews. Restricting the audit committee's attention to information that will be published externally is one way of containing the workload of the committee to more manageable proportions. Many boards are anxious about the quality of information which the board receives, and are asking their audit committees to provide the board with assurances on this. The quality of management information at all levels of the business, whether financial or otherwise, is of course important, and the audit committee might extend its role to enquiring into this. The quality of internal information and communication is an essential component of effective internal control and risk management, and will thus fall within that area of the audit committee's responsibilities.

Oversight of internal control and risk management E1.6

For many years, there had been a degree of ambiguity as to whether a board, including its non-executive directors, has responsibility for internal control. The US Foreign Corrupt Practices Act (FCPA 1977), sometimes termed 'the internal auditors' full employment Act', put paid to any doubt, stipulating in statute law that the board is responsible. It is notable that the US Department of Justice has been flexing its muscles in endeavouring to apply the FCPA 1977 aggressively in an extra-territorial way, as its 2007 investigation of BAE indicates; and the UK's new (2003) extradition law with the US[7] means that the US authorities need not provide *prima facie* evidence to achieve an extradition from the UK for an alleged offence under US law, even if perpetrated mainly in the UK.

A key principle of corporate governance is that where there is a responsibility there should be a matching accountability obligation – otherwise neglect, irresponsibility and even corruption may slip in over time. Hence, it is now widely understood that boards should account publicly for internal control. In the US, the Sarbanes-Oxley Act 2002, s 404 requires CEOs and CFOs of US registrants to certify in their filings (and to their audit committees and to their external auditors) that they have assessed the effectiveness of internal control over financial reporting (see Chapters **E3** and **E5**). In the UK, it was the Cadbury Code of Best Practice (for corporate governance)

(1992) which first included a provision that 'the directors should report on the effectiveness of the company's system of internal control'. 'Risk management' was first added to 'internal control' in the 1998 Combined Code revision of the Cadbury Code. Published statements on internal control (SICs) are also required across the UK public sector.

Generally there is no UK requirement, either with respect to listed companies or for public sector entities, for boards to disclose their opinion as to the effectiveness of risk management and internal control. However, it is noticeable that companies, such as Shell, who have to report on the effectiveness of internal financial control under the Sarbanes-Oxley Act (see above), are now publishing within their annual report to their UK and other shareholders their opinion of the effectiveness of internal financial control. The UK Corporate Governance Code requirement is only that they should disclose that they have reviewed the effectiveness of risk management and internal control. Optionally, entities may choose to disclose their opinion on effectiveness, but few, except those subject to Sarbanes-Oxley, do so. Nevertheless, the board should come to an opinion on the effectiveness of risk management and internal control, even though it may not publish it.

The board will be highly reliant on the audit committee to advise the board whether it considers the entity has effective risk management and internal control. We consider that there should be an annual report of the audit committee to the board and that this is the appropriate place to contain the audit committee's overall opinion on risk management and internal control. We should, however, acknowledge that there are many audit committees that do not provide an annual report to the board. We should also further acknowledge that many audit committees do not pull together all their discussions on risk management and internal control in order to consciously draw a conclusion as to whether the committee considers that risk management and internal control are effective.

Note that there are distinctions here between the US (Sarbanes-Oxley) and UK scope of the assessment of the effectiveness of internal control. The US scope is just internal control over financial reporting, whereas the UK also covers operational and compliance control *and risk management systems*:

> **'Code Provision**
>
> 'C.2.1 The board should, at least annually, conduct a review of the effectiveness of the company's risk management and internal control systems and should report to shareholders that they have done so[8]. The review should cover all material controls, including financial, operational and compliance controls.'

The US assessment is to be made within three months of the date of the annual report, whereas in the UK[9] it is an assessment of effectiveness over the whole of the year and also over the period between the year-end and the date when the board adopts the annual financial statements.

Audit committees are sub-committees of their boards, assisting boards to discharge certain board responsibilities which require time and focus beyond the practical abilities of the board in most cases. Boards ask audit committees to oversee the effectiveness of risk management and internal control not just because boards report publicly on this. Whether boards had to report or not, they would have overall responsibility for the effectiveness of risk management and internal control – and so they need to be well informed about this.

It is, however, up to each board to determine the extent to which they delegate oversight of risk management and internal control to the audit committee. As with the responsibility of the audit committee for the financial statements (see above), there is some discretion as to the extent of the audit committee's remit for risk management and internal control on behalf of the board. Whereas the 1998 Combined Code stated that the board's review should cover all of internal control (including financial, operational and compliance control) and also *risk management*, the 2003 revision to the Combined Code was amended to refer to *risk management systems* – which broadly brought it into line with the effect of the already existing Turnbull guidance on the 1998 Code Provision. Conceivably it could be argued, therefore, that the review does not have to include a consideration of the specific risks which have been identified as the critical risks of the entity, nor how they are being managed. Instead, the review could just focus on the process (or systems) used by management within the entity to identify, assess and mitigate risks. So, it could be construed as legitimate for an audit committee to have a limited remit to review, on behalf of the board, the risk management process, but not the specific risks identified by that process. However, clearly, whatever the wording of the Code, a board needs to understand the critical risks of the entity and whether they are being managed effectively. The board must obtain that understanding from its audit committee, or through its own deliberations or in some other way.

Another way that an audit committee may narrow down its remit on risk management and internal control is to restrict its oversight to internal control over financial reporting and the associated risk management elements. Apart from the challenge of audit committee overload, a rationale for this might be that a focus on published financial statements may be taken to suggest a corresponding focus on the internal controls which underpin the reliability of those financial statements, leaving the board to obtain assurance on the effectiveness of operational and compliance control/risk management in other ways. This narrow approach has been lent some support by the Sarbanes-Oxley focus on the CEO's, CFO's and audit committee's responsibilities for internal financial control. But just because the Sarbanes-Oxley Act is silent about operational control does not mean it is unimportant. The danger of a focus just on internal financial control may be that operational and compliance control/risk management fail to get the attention they warrant. Arguably, businesses achieve their objectives more through how they manage operational and compliance matters than from how they manage internal control over financial reporting.

To illustrate how this narrower remit might be applied to an audit committee's responsibilities, one large UK NHS acute hospital trust set up a further board committee – their clinical governance committee. As with their audit committee, all the members were independent directors. The committee chair was an independent director with a medical background, whereas the chair of the audit committee had an accounting background. Those in attendance (but not as members) at clinical governance committee meetings included the clinical director, the director of nursing and the clinical risk manager, whereas those in attendance at audit committee meetings included the finance director and the chief accountant. Both committees reported in a similar way to the board. That hospital trust had concluded that clinical risk and clinical control were too much for their audit committee to oversee – not least because they were highly technical matters to do with operating theatre procedures, cleanliness of wards, and so on.

For most entities, however, it is likely that the audit committee, on behalf of the board, will oversee *all* of risk management and internal control, and the backgrounds of the audit committee members are likely to mean that most of them can understand operations at least as well as they can understand financial reporting and accounting control matters.

As a means of buttressing the independence of internal audit and ensuring that the results of internal audit work are more valuable to the audit committee in its assessment of the effectiveness of risk management and internal control, it is usual practice for the audit committee to approve the planned programme of internal audit engagements to be conducted. Usually this is a matter of approving an annual plan and subsequent modifications to it. The head of internal audit will also have discussed this proposed plan of audit engagements with senior management.

As we have said, the scope of the directors' public report on internal control covers the whole of the business (including subsidiary operations) over the entire year being reported and also over the period between the year-end and the date of the annual report. The Turnbull guidance requires that the internal control report should explain whether and how joint ventures are covered in this report (see **E1.10**).

Oversight of external audit **E1.7**

In terms of its audit responsibilities, the audit committee may be compared to the conductor of an orchestra, responsible for achieving the best results from the various audit players. The players are likely to be external audit, internal audit and other review agencies.

It is not in every context that the entity chooses its own external auditor. Public bodies may be audited by a public audit office, or by an audit firm appointed by such an office, or by the stakeholder that sponsors the public body to be audited. In some legislatures, the choice of auditor for a public company is determined by the state, not by the company; in others, by the shareholders.

Where the company does not choose the external auditor, there is an inappropriate tendency for the audit committee to take less interest in the quality of the external audit. As a consequence, external auditors from public audit offices are challenged much less about the quality of their work than are auditors from public accounting firms who are auditing public companies.

Even where the choice of auditor is not made by the audited entity, the audit committee of that entity should oversee the quality of the external audit service, challenging the external auditors to defend their performance. The right objective is to ensure the best quality external audit at reasonable cost. It should *not* be the objective of the audit committee to connive to achieve the least obtrusive, least effective audit. Audit quality is largely a matter of audit effectiveness: deficiencies in audit quality are those attributes which might lead to substandard audit results, or that appearance.

Nevertheless, when it falls to the audit committee to consider a change of external auditor, there is an added reason for the audit committee to evaluate the quality of the external audit. In the UK, the Corporate Governance Code gives the audit committee the responsibility to recommend to the board who should be appointed as the external auditor. The Code states that, if a board declines to follow the advice of its audit committee, it should disclose within the annual report what was that advice and the reasons why the board chose not to follow it.

In the US, under the Sarbanes-Oxley Act, it is the audit committee that appoints the external auditor of a listed company. In the UK, the audit committee recommends to the board and, in turn, the board recommends to the shareholders – unless the shareholders have previously empowered the board to appoint the external auditors. The UK has been very careful to avoid setting up the audit committee *above* the board in any way; although, as we said earlier, the UK gets as close to it as possible without crossing the line.

While, in the UK, technically the shareholders choose the external auditors, almost invariably on the recommendation of the board, in other legislations the shareholders (or a shareholders' committee) are fully in control of the choice. After all, the external auditors report to the shareholders. The financial statements are addressed to the shareholders and the external audit is the shareholders' assurance as to their reliability. The UK position is to rely on the audit committee to safeguard the interests of the shareholders – which it can do with reasonable effectiveness if appropriate safeguards are in place. These safeguards include ensuring that audit committee members are independent directors.

The audit committee does not discharge its responsibility for overseeing the quality of the external audit simply by discussing with the external auditor its planned approach to the audit and the audit results, although they should do both of these. That dialogue is more to do with discharging the audit committee's responsibility for overseeing the financial statements. To ensure that this responsibility of the audit committee is not neglected, it should be at least a standard item on the agenda of one audit committee meeting each year.

Too many audit committees fail to seriously address whether a change of external auditor should be made: it requires consideration before the current year's audit has been completed, which can bring a touch of embarrassment to the issue, sufficient to encourage deferral of the matter to the following year. Companies may also be concerned that, if the external auditors believe this year's audit might be their last, then they will be extra thorough in their audit approach out of concern at passing on to a new audit firm any unresolved audit issues. This may explain why one UK clearing bank has kept with the same firm of external auditors for almost 190 years, although the name of the firm has changed many times due to mergers. There is, however, no mandatory requirement to change external auditors after a certain number of years, either in the UK or in the US.

Oversight of internal audit and other internal review agencies E1.8

Internal auditing has come a long way. Once a service primarily for the finance director or chief accountant, it transitioned to become a service for all of management – across all operational areas of the business and at all levels up to the chief executive. While still primarily a service for management, it is now also a service for the board via the board's audit committee. So, internal audit is an assurance and consulting service *for* management, as well as being an assurance service for the audit committee. It is an audit *for* management *and* an audit *of* management for the board. It is not easy to serve two masters.

Much of the audit committee's confidence about the effectiveness of risk management and internal control arises from its consideration of reports on the results of internal audit work. For those reports to be a reliable basis for the audit committee to depend upon, the audit committee needs to be confident that internal audit is not subordinating its judgement on professional matters to that of management or of anyone else. Inappropriate pressure may be exerted upon internal audit with respect to the planned programme of audit engagements to be conducted, the scope of individual audit engagements, auditor access to personnel and information, and the content of audit reports including those to the audit committee. In addition to satisfying itself about internal audit independence, the audit committee needs to satisfy itself that internal audit is adequately resourced and is approaching its work in a professional way.

The evidence of many of the recent corporate debacles indicates to us that there is too commonly an 'assurance vacuum' at the level of the boards of large companies. Non-executive directors (who make the board into something other than the top executive team) have no adequate, systematic way of obtaining independent assurance that the policies of the board are being implemented by the executive team. If there is a disconnect between board policy and management's implementation of it, it may take a reputational disaster to bring that disconnect to the attention of the board. *Post hoc* reviews, such as by the Baker Panel (BP),[10] by the CSHIB (BP),[11] by Lord Wolf (BAE) or by Davis Polk & Wardwell (Shell, 2004)[12] are, of course, no substitute for proactive assurance.

The Baker Report drew attention to the insufficiency of BP's almost 100% reliance on internal audits resulting in an 'internalised view of how things are done at BP' and pointed out that 'third-party reviews offer a different level of assurance'. Consequently, BP's board accepted a Baker Report recommendation that the Baker Committee identify an independent monitor to report annually to the Board (and publicly) on BP's process safety performance.

John Buchanan,[13] a respected audit committee chair, has said:

> 'When I was talking to [BP's] then head of internal audit I asked him what were the most important questions for an internal auditor. Slightly to my surprise, he responded immediately and said there were three. "Do we have policies and standards in place in the key risk areas, are these policies being implemented, and are these policies being implemented effectively?"
>
> 'If the audit committee were asking those questions and seeking deep assurance – or verification – about them, it would have a much better chance of picking up any problems.'

To provide internal audit with sufficient independence from management so that the audit committee and the board can have more confidence in the objectivity and impartiality of internal audit reports to the audit committee and to the board, we are attracted to the approach whereby the head of internal audit reports to the chairman's office, as for instance in UBS:[14]

> **'Group Internal Audit**
>
> With 275 staff members worldwide at 31 December 2005, Group Internal Audit provides an independent review of the effectiveness of UBS's system of internal controls and compliance with key rules and regulations. It specifically verifies or assesses whether the internal controls are commensurate with the corresponding risks and are working effectively, whether activities within the firm are being conducted and recorded properly, correctly and fully, and whether the organization of operations, including information technology, is efficient and information is reliable. All key issues raised by Group Internal Audit are communicated to the management responsible, to the Group CEO and to the executive members of the Board of Directors via formal Audit Reports. The Chairman's Office and the Audit Committee of the Board are regularly informed of important findings. Group Internal Audit closely cooperates with internal and external legal advisors and risk control units on investigations into major control issues.
>
> To maximize its independence from management, the head of Group Internal Audit … reports directly to the Chairman of the Board. Group Internal Audit has unrestricted access to all accounts, books and records and must be provided with all information and data needed to fulfil its auditing duties. Group Internal Audit addresses any reports with major issues to the Chairman of the Board. The Chairman's Office may order special audits to be conducted, and the Group Executive Board, with the agreement of the Chairman, may also instruct Group Internal Audit to conduct such audits.
>
> Coordination and close co-operation with the external auditors enhance the efficiency of Group Internal Audit's work.'

Internal auditing Standards of the Institute of Internal Auditors require that there should be annual internal reviews of internal audit undertaken by the internal function itself, and that there should be external reviews every five years of internal audit undertaken by independent, outside parties who are competent to do this work. It is an obligation, under internal auditing Standards, for the head of internal audit to ensure not only that these take place but also that the results of these reviews are communicated to the audit committee. The context of these reviews should be, in the main, to ascertain whether internal auditing Standards are being followed.

The quality of internal audit is not just a matter of its independence as set out in our previous paragraph. We cover other relevant issues in Chapters **E7** and **G2**.

In some entities, the audit committee's oversight of internal audit extends to appointing and dismissing the head of internal audit and setting his or her remuneration. At least it is desirable that the terms of reference of the audit committees (see **App4.1–App4.8**) require the audit committee to give prior concurrence to the appointment and dismissal of the head of internal audit, and to be informed of his or her remuneration.

In our view, the relationship between the audit committee and internal audit will be more healthy if the head of internal audit is not also the secretary to the audit committee.

Within many entities, there are other internal review functions. Within financial institutions, there may be compliance functions, usually required by the regulator. Other entities may have technical inspection, fraud investigations, risk management, quality assurance – and so on. Since an audit committee is so dependent for its effectiveness on reports from others that the audit committee considers carefully, the audit committee will need to establish an understanding with management as to which of these functional heads will report on the results of their work to the audit committee, whether they will be in attendance at audit committee meetings, and the extent to which the audit committee influences and approves their programmes of work.

Audit committees in groups and in governmental entities E1.9

The scope of UK directors' public reports on internal control covers the whole of the business (including subsidiary operations) over the entire year being reported and also over the period between the year-end and the date of the annual report. The Turnbull Report also requires that the internal control report should explain whether and how joint ventures are covered in the public report on internal control.

Many organisations have several audit committees – one in each subsidiary or division, with the minutes of more junior audit committees being agenda papers for more senior audit committees.

See the case study below for an illustration of some of the issues relating to audit committees in groups.

Case study E1.10

The query:

I work for XYZ plc, which has an Audit Committee made up of four independent non-executive directors and one non-independent non-executive director from our parent company. I am looking at various options to streamline corporate governance. One option is to make our board an executive board, comprising executive and non-independent non-executive directors, without any independent directors. The problem with this option is what to do about the audit committee. My understanding is that we would be out of line with the UK Corporate Governance Code if we were to staff it with non-independent non-executive directors. An alternative might be to merge our audit committee with that of our parent company which is overseas. Presumably, this would effectively be an outsourcing of one of the board's primary responsibilities. Have you come across such an arrangement?

The response:

I think there are quite a number of subsidiary entities within groups that do not comply at subsidiary level with the UK Corporate Governance Code in the respects implied by your note. I suppose the most fundamental issue to be decided upon is whether it is to be policy to comply with the UK Corporate Governance Code at subsidiary level. It is not obligatory.

If the subsidiary had a separate listing, then there would be much more reason (and pressure) to comply with the UK Corporate Governance Code at subsidiary level. For instance, pressure groups such as PIRC, ABI and NAPF, Hermes, etc will give black marks for non-compliance by a listed subsidiary. But I have never come across these pressure groups giving black marks at subsidiary level when the subsidiary is unlisted.

You might consider whether it is desirable to have in place best corporate governance practice if there is any possibility that the subsidiary might be floated off as an independent entity (as distinct from being acquired by another entity). IPOs go better when there is good corporate governance in place.

You should also be mindful of any requirements of the regulator of your subsidiary, the FSA.

Fundamentally, an audit committee is there to provide assurance to the board on certain matters for which the board is responsible but which the board cannot realistically cover sufficiently or effectively in sessions of the full board. In particular, the audit committee is there to provide assurances to the non-executive directors on matters that they share responsibility for along with the executive directors – such as the reliability of financial statements which will be published. If boards were entirely executive, there would not be the same emphasis upon audit committees. Executive directors are much more in the swim of things and some would argue that they do not have the same need for independent assurance. However, in central government, audit committees are seen as also providing assurance to the chief executive especially in that person's role as the accounting officer. Even executive directors can benefit from independent assurance.

The non-executive (but not independent) directors from Group on your revamped executive board will have a responsibility (shared with the executive directors on this board) for the quality of the various things typically within the remit of an audit committee. I would think they would be bound to consider that an audit committee should be there to assist them to discharge these responsibilities – as I think is the case from what you describe. While the non-executive directors on this board will not be independent, they are distinctly more so than the executive directors and therefore you are right that the membership of the new audit committee should be drawn probably exclusively from them. Referring to what I have said above, I would think that was not too unsatisfactory so long as the subsidiary is unlisted and intends to stay that way, or is not subject to any particular contrary requirements of a regulator.

One problem might be the degree of (a) time commitment, and (b) continuity of membership of these non-executive directors on the subsidiary board – and thus the effectiveness of the audit committee. Very often members from Group on subsidiary boards come and go with alarming rapidity and do not follow their duties in the same way as outside directors – who, for instance, receive a fee directly for their pains.

In contexts such as this, some entities will contemplate appointing complete outsiders (who are not members of the executive board) to the audit committee. There might be just one or two such appointments and in particular the chairman of the audit committee might be one of them. Personally I think this can be a good approach. Such a chair of the audit committee would need to attend the board to present the audit committee's report.

Whatever the membership of the audit committee, much of its effectiveness depends upon its terms of reference, including its authorities.

However your audit committee comes to be constituted, it will be important for the group audit committee to be aware of the rather novel circumstances of the subsidiary board and its audit committee – to the extent that the group audit committee is likely to need to pay more direct attention to matters within the purview of subsidiary's audit committee. This could include the group audit committee receiving direct reports from the subsidiary's audit committee (spoken to at group audit committee meetings by the chair of subsidiary's audit committee): at least an annual report would be in order. I would think it would be useful if at least one member of the subsidiary's audit committee (ie one of the non-executive members of the subsidiary's board) was someone who was habitually in attendance at the group audit committee's meeting. I would think that the subsidiary's head of internal audit should have direct access to the group audit committee (and to its chairman) at all times and that his or her appointment and dismissal should have the prior concurrence of the group audit committee.

However, you might bear in mind that stresses and strains can arise even within subsidiary companies which may be difficult to resolve. Having an audit committee comprising only independent directors might make it easier to deal with some matters in a responsible, effective way if the board is divided. But the subsidiary directors would have the parent to refer to if necessary.

In the last analysis, not even listed companies are compelled by law or regulation to comply with the UK Corporate Governance Code, and the issues covered by your note and my response are in any case substantially enshrined only within the discretionary 'comply or explain' Provisions of the UK Corporate Governance Code, rather than within the Principles. But note that the FSA's Listing Rules are being amended to make it obligatory for companies listed in the UK to have audit committees – in order to bring the UK into line with Article 41 of the amended Eighth Directive.

Audit committees in central government **E1.11**

HM Treasury has developed guidance on audit committees for central government organisations and for non-departmental public bodies (NDPBs).[15] It includes policy principles for audit committees. The guidance has been revised, in particular, to bring it into line with HM Treasury's new code of practice for corporate governance in central government.[16]

The main differences in audit committee practice within central government and NDPBs, that HM Treasury accepts may be necessary and that underpin some of its guidance, are a consequence of differences in the governance arrangements of central government entities and NDPBs compared with companies. We would summarise those differences as follows.

The role of the accounting officer E1.12

Enshrined within this sole person – the accounting officer – are many of the responsibilities which, for a company, would be held collectively by all members of the board of the company. Notable amongst these responsibilities is that the annual financial statements of the central government body are the personal responsibility of its accounting officer. It therefore follows that the audit committee has a role to play in providing assurance to the accounting officer on matters relating to the reliability of the accounts of the public body. It should go without saying that it is highly preferable that the accounting officer is not a member of the audit committee, as the assurance the accounting officer receives from the audit committee is more reassuring for the accounting officer if he or she has not been part of the audit committee process of arriving at that assurance. Notwithstanding this, there are still examples where the accounting officer is a member of the audit committee. There is the added point that the accounting officer is usually also the chief executive of the public body, and audit committees need to be independent of the chief executive if they are to be an effective oversight of the conduct of the executive. Hence, company audit committees that follow best practice comprise exclusively independent directors.

Large central government bodies, such as the Home Office or the Ministry of Defence, have more than one accounting officer, and indeed may have more than one audit committee as, for instance, does the Ministry of Defence.

The role and composition of the board E1.13

The role of the board in central government bodies varies. In some cases, the boards only provide support for the executive. In others, the boards have particular powers and responsibilities, such as the responsibility to make staff appointments perhaps other than the appointment of the chief executive.[17] In addition to providing assurance to the accounting officer, the audit committee of a central government body reports to the board. There is common ground here with audit committees of companies, in that the board relies on the audit committee to 'put in the hard graft' to keep the board well informed on matters within the remit of the audit committee. But the difference is that the members of the boards of central government bodies are not jointly and severally responsible for the reliability of the published financial statements and do not face the same risk of being sued for damages. That is the case, even when it is custom and practice for the chairman of the board, together with the accounting officer, to 'sign off' the accounts in the annual report.

Board membership E1.14

The growth of central government boards is a relatively recent development. The chief executive of a public body might have chosen to manage by having an executive committee or board. Sometimes, it is these executive boards which are evolving to become the modern board. In many cases, they have not had sufficient non-executive members to enable the audit committee to be formed exclusively from amongst these non-executive members. So, frequently, executives sat on these audit committees alongside non-executive members. This explained why, until recently, the accounting officer was sometimes still a member of the audit committee. The previous (2003) edition of HM Treasury's Guidance on audit committees had been that executive members of an audit committee, if indeed there had to be such, should have rotated so that no particular executive position developed a 'right' to be a member of the audit committee, and so as to buttress the independence and objectivity of the audit committee. HM Treasury also suggested that, where there are insufficient non-executive board members to form the audit committee, consideration should be given to inviting complete outsiders to join the committee – particularly in the role of committee chairman. In many ways, this is an excellent expedient, but it should be borne in mind that the audit committee chairman role is very important, and it is difficult for a complete outsider to have sufficient inside knowledge to appreciate where the main issues for the audit committee lie.

The new HM Treasury guidance is tightening up the requirements by excluding executives from membership of the audit committee:[18]

> 'Executive members of the organisation should not be appointed to the Audit Committee. The role of the Executive is to attend, to provide information, and to participate in discussions, either for the whole duration of a meeting or for particular agenda items.
>
> The Accounting Officer and the Finance Director should routinely attend the Audit Committee. It is also normal for the Head of Internal Audit and a representative of the External Auditor to attend. However, the Terms of Reference should also provide for the Audit Committee to sit privately without any non-members present for all or part of a meeting if they so decide.'

Focus on risk management and internal control **E1.15**

The audit committee of a central government entity proportionately tends to have a different focus from that of a company's audit committee. Traditionally, it has focused on internal control – which has now developed into a focus on *risk management and internal control*. This is usually still the main focus. Closely associated with this is the audit committee's oversight of internal audit – in terms of its quality, professionalism, independence, resources and so on. It is universally the case across this sector that there *is* an internal audit *and* that it provides the audit committee with an annual opinion on the effectiveness of risk management and internal control. But the advent of resource (accrual) accounting has extended the scope for error and creative accounting within the financial statements, as there is a greater need to exercise judgement than there had been with cash accounting – for instance on provisions, depreciation rates, contingent liabilities, etc. So it is not surprising that the audit committee's responsibility to scrutinise draft financial statements on behalf of the board and the accounting officer has assumed greater importance.

HM Treasury puts it better than the UK Corporate Governance Code when it indicates that:

> 'The Audit Committee should corporately own an appropriate skills mix to allow it to carry out its overall function.'

In comparison, the UK Corporate Governance Code for listed companies suggests that at least one person should have recent and relevant financial experience:

'Code Provision

C.3.1 The board should establish an audit committee of at least three, or in the case of smaller companies[19] two, members, who should all be independent non-executive directors. The board should satisfy itself that at least one member of the audit committee has recent and relevant financial experience.'

But it is sometimes unrealistic to expect all of the necessary financial expertise to be concentrated in just one person. For instance, the audit committee of an insurance company will require both an accounting specialist and also an actuarial specialist.

Central government bodies rarely choose their external auditors. Unfortunately, this often leads to neglect by the audit committee to oversee the quality of the external audit. The tacit assumption seems to be that, if we cannot change our auditors, then there is no point in challenging the external auditor on matters of audit quality. As a consequence, the National Audit Office is held to account much less than are the external auditors of companies.

The EC's Eighth Directive on audit committees, 2006[20] E1.16

The Eighth Directive's Chapter 10, entitled 'Special provisions for the statutory audits of public-interest entities', includes the Directive's content on audit committees:

'Article 41

Audit committee

1. Each public-interest entity shall have an audit committee. The Member State shall determine whether audit committees are to be composed of non-executive members of the administrative body and/or members of the supervisory body of the audited entity and/or members appointed by the general meeting of shareholders of the audited entity. At least one member of the audit committee shall be independent and shall have competence in accounting and/or auditing.

In public-interest entities which meet the criteria of Article 2(1), point (f) of Directive 2003/71/EC,[21] Member States may permit the functions assigned to the audit committee to be performed by the administrative or supervisory body as a whole, provided at least that when the chairman of such a body is an executive member, he or she is not the chairman of the audit committee.

2. Without prejudice to the responsibility of the members of the administrative, management or supervisory bodies, or of other members who are appointed by the general meeting of shareholders of the audited entity, the audit committee shall, *inter alia*:

(a) monitor the financial reporting process;

(b) monitor the effectiveness of the company's internal control, internal audit where applicable, and risk management systems;

(c) monitor the statutory audit of the annual and consolidated accounts;

(d) review and monitor the independence of the statutory auditor or audit firm, and in particular the provision of additional services to the audited entity.

3. In a public-interest entity, the proposal of the administrative or supervisory body for the appointment of a statutory auditor or audit firm shall be based on a recommendation made by the audit committee.

4. The statutory auditor or audit firm shall report to the audit committee on key matters arising from the statutory audit, and in particular on material weaknesses in internal control in relation to the financial reporting process.

5. Member States may allow or decide that the provisions laid down in paragraphs 1 to 4 shall not apply to any public-interest entity that has a body performing equivalent functions to an audit committee, established and functioning according to provisions in place in the Member State in which the entity to be audited is registered. In such a case the entity shall disclose which body carries out these functions and how it is composed.

6. Member States may exempt from the obligation to have an audit committee:

(a) any public-interest entity which is a subsidiary undertaking within the meaning of Article 1 of Directive 83/349/EEC if the entity complies with the requirements in paragraphs 1 to 4 of this Article at group level;

(b) any public-interest entity which is a collective investment undertaking as defined in Article 1[22] of Directive 85/611/EEC. Member States may also exempt public-interest entities the sole object of which is the collective investment of capital provided by the public, which operate on the principle of risk spreading and which do not seek to take legal or management control over any of the issuers of its underlying investments, provided that those collective investment undertakings are authorised and subject to supervision by competent authorities and that they have a depositary exercising functions equivalent to those under Directive 85/611/EEC;

(c) any public-interest entity, the sole business of which is to act as issuer of asset-backed securities as defined in Article 2(5) of Commission Regulation (EC) No 809/2004. In such instances, the Member State shall require the entity to explain to the public the reasons for which it considers it not appropriate to have either an audit committee or an administrative or supervisory body entrusted to carry out the functions of an audit committee.

(d) any credit institution within the meaning of Article 1(1) of Directive 2000/12/EC whose shares are not admitted to trading on a regulated market of any Member State within the meaning of point 14 of Article 4(1) of Directive 2004/39/EC and which has, in a continuous or repeated manner, issued only debt securities, provided that the total nominal amount of all such debt securities remains below EUR 100 000 000 and that it has not published a prospectus under Directive 2003/71/EC.

Article 42

Independence

1. In addition to the provisions laid down in Articles 22 and 24, Member States shall ensure that statutory auditors or audit firms that carry out the statutory audit of a public-interest entity:

(a) confirm annually in writing to the audit committee their independence from the audited public-interest entity;

(b) disclose annually to the audit committee any additional services provided to the audited entity; and

(c) discuss with the audit committee the threats to their independence and the safeguards applied to mitigate those threats as documented by them pursuant to Article 22(3).

2. Member States shall ensure that the key audit partner(s) responsible for carrying out a statutory audit rotate(s) from the audit engagement within a maximum period of seven years from the date of appointment and is/are allowed to participate in the audit of the audited entity again after a period of at least two years.

3. The statutory auditor or the key audit partner who carries out a statutory audit on behalf of an audit firm shall not be allowed to take up a key management position in the audited entity before a period of at least two years has elapsed since he or she resigned as a statutory auditor or key audit partner from the audit engagement.'

Notes

1 The Smith guidance suggested means of applying this part of the Code. In December 2010 and again in September 2012, the FRC updated the Smith Guidance titled 'Guidance on Audit Committees', available on the FRC website. Early 2014 the FRC had no plans to further update its guidance on audit committees, but intended to review this when the 2014 Corporate Governance and Stewardship Codes were in place, late 2014.

2 Directive 2006/43/EC of the European Parliament and of the Council on statutory audits of annual accounts and consolidated accounts, amending Council Directives 78/660/EEC and 83/349/EEC and repealing Council Directive 84/253/EEC (OJ L 157, 9.6.2006, p 103).

3 UK Disclosure and Transparency Rules:

'7.1 Audit committees

Audit committees and their functions

DTR 7.1.1 29/06/2008

An issuer must have a body which is responsible for performing the functions set out in DTR 7.1.3 R. At least one member of that body must be independent and at least one member must have competence in accounting and/or auditing.

DTR 7.1.2 29/06/2008

The requirements for independence and competence in accounting and/or auditing may be satisfied by the same member or by different members of the relevant body.

DTR 7.1.3 29/06/2008

An issuer must ensure that, as a minimum, the relevant body must:

(1) monitor the financial reporting process;

(2) monitor the effectiveness of the issuer's internal control, internal audit where applicable, and risk management systems;

(3) monitor the statutory audit of the annual and consolidated accounts;

(4) review and monitor the independence of the statutory auditor, and in particular the provision of additional services to the issuer.'

4 The Code exception is that a listed company outside the FTSE 350 may have its board chairman as a member of the audit committee, but not as its chairman, if he or she were independent when appointed to the chair. The Code does not thereafter regard the chairman as one of the independent directors (see Code Provision C.3.1 at **App1**).

5 DTI (March 2007): European Company Law and Corporate Governance, Implementation of Directive 2006/43/EC on Statutory Audits of Annual and Consolidated Accounts (replacing the Eighth Company Law Directive) – A Consultative Document.

6 Directive 2006/43/EC on Statutory Audits of Annual and Consolidated Accounts (replacing the Eighth Company Law Directive).

7 Extradition Act 2003, available at www.legislation.gov.uk.

8 In addition, FSA Rule DTR 7.2.5 R requires companies to describe the main features of the internal control and risk management systems in relation to the financial reporting process.

9 The scope required by the Turnbull guidance on the UK Corporate Governance Code Provision.

10 The Report of the BP US Refineries Independent Safety Review Panel (The Baker Report), 2007.

11 US Chemical Safety and Hazard Investigation Board Investigation Report (March 2007), Report No. 2005-04-i-tx.

12 Report of Davis Polk & Wardwell to the Shell Group Audit Committee (2004).

13 John Buchanan was CFO at BP. He then chaired the audit committee at AstraZeneca, and was deputy chairman of Vodafone, senior independent director at BHP Billiton, and chairman of Smith & Nephew. Quoted from *Internal Auditing & Business Risk,* Vol. 31, Issue 7, July 2007.

14 See the UBS website. The quoted wording has since been revised.

15 HM Treasury (March 2007): Audit Committee Handbook.

16 HM Treasury (July 2005): Corporate Governance in Central Government Departments: Code of Good Practice, updated in 2011, available on the HM Treasury website.

17 As with local Probation Service boards.

18 HM Treasury (March 2007): Audit Committee Handbook, sections 4.4, 4.5.

19 A smaller company is one that is below the FTSE 350 throughout the year immediately prior to the reporting year.

20 Directive 2006/43/EC of the European Parliament and of the Council on statutory audits of annual accounts and consolidated accounts, amending Council Directives 78/660/EEC and 83/349/EEC and repealing Council Directive 84/253/EEC (OJ L 157, 9.6.2006, p 103).

21 Directive 2003/71/EC of the European Parliament and of the Council of 4 November 2003 on the prospectus to be published when securities are offered to the public or admitted to trading (OJ L 345, 31.12.2003, p 64).

22 OJ L 149, 30.4.2004, p 1.

Chapter E2

Effective and Efficient Conduct of Audit Committee Business

Introduction E2.1

The main focus of this chapter is on audit committee agenda management. We have found it helpful to maintain a table of pro forma agenda items which are likely to be required to appear on the agendas of the particular audit committee meetings during the year, so we address this within the chapter. We also consider the qualities needed of audit committee members and discuss whether there is any conflict in belonging both to a company's audit committee and also to its remuneration committee. The chapter ends with an illustrative note to audit committee members incorporating many of the main suggestions made within this chapter.

An important general point is that, just as the chair of the board is responsible for the effectiveness of the board, so the chair of the audit committee is responsible for that committee's effectiveness. It is much more than a matter of turning up to audit committee meetings and chairing them well, although that is important. The composition of audit committee meeting agendas is one of the responsibilities of the audit committee chair, as is the content and wording of the minutes, though it is to be hoped that a good company secretary will take much of this burden from the committee chair. However, it is to be expected that each audit committee meeting will be preceded by a planning meeting between the committee chair, the committee secretary and possibly also the finance director and the head of internal audit – at which the form and content of the agenda will decided. This planning meeting is also an opportunity to revisit the action points of the previous meeting and ensure that 'matters arising' from previous meetings are properly reflected on the agenda being prepared.

Pro forma agendas for audit committees E2.2

We suggest example pro forma agendas at **E2.4**.

Audit committees should meet as frequently and for as long as necessary. The pro forma agendas at **E2.4** have been modelled on the basis that there will be four audit committee meetings each year. In practice this is likely to be inadequate and it is more typical to meet at least six times a year. The Table below shows that BP's audit committee has been meeting much more frequently, particularly accounted for by meeting twice with respect to each of the quarterly reporting obligations. The Table also provides an illuminating breakdown of how the committee has been spending its time. BP's SEEAC committee corresponds in many ways to a board risk committee.

Frequency of board and board committee meetings – BP

	2003	2004	2005	2006	2007	2008	2009	2010	2011	2012
Board	8	8	7	9	12	9	12	25	15	19
Gulf of Mexico Committee								9	16	23
Audit Committee	9	13	12	12	14	13	13	15	11	11
Remco						6	8	6	7	5
Safety, Ethics & Environment Assurance Committee (SEEAC)						?	7	9	9	6
Nomination						6	15	18	5	4
Chairman's						4	5	8	9	8
Number of directors – Chairman						1	1	1	1	1
Number of directors – NEDs						9	9	11	11	11
Number of directors – EDs						4	5	3	4	4
Number of directors – Total						14	15	15	16	16
*Allocation of audit committee agenda time – Financial reporting						34%	31%	?	?	?
– Monitoring business risk						36%	28%	?	?	?
– Internal controls and audit						26%	36?	?	?	?
– Other						4%	5%	?	?	?

* – excludes site visits by the audit committee

The Gulf of Mexico oil well failure occurred on 20 April 2010, indicating that the full BP board must have met approximately fortnightly in the latter part of 2010.

There is one joint meeting SEEAC at the start of each year to review BP's risk management and internal control systems of the previous year and to review the coming year's forward programme of audit work. The general auditor (head of internal audit) reviews his team's findings and management's actions to remedy significant issues identified in that work. His report includes information on the results of audit work undertaken by the safety and operational risk audit team and reviews by the group's finance control team.

It is preferable not to hold audit committee meetings on the same day as board meetings or the meetings of other board committees, as meeting fatigue is likely to set in. There is also the point that follow-up after an audit committee meeting may be needed before the outcomes of that meeting are reported to the board, and it is preferable that the draft audit committee minutes are an agenda paper for the board. These preferences could not be achieved if the audit committee took place on the same day as the board. But audit committee chairs are likely to find a considerable reluctance on the part of their independent director colleagues to set aside effectively two days (one for the audit committee meeting and another for the board) when both could be squeezed into a single day.

Because of the infrequency and relatively short duration of audit committee meetings, it is important that every matter is covered within their agendas in a timely way. Agendas will be drafted by the secretary to the committee, but should be approved by the committee chair who is responsible for the effectiveness of the audit committee. The chair of the committee should not accept without careful consideration whatever draft audit committee agenda is suggested by the secretary.

The chair and the committee secretary can be assisted if they maintain a set of pro forma agendas for the respective audit committee meetings during the year. Later in this chapter, we provide a table of suggested items that might be included within these pro forma agendas – on the hypothetical assumption that the committee meets four times a year and that the company year-end is 31 December (we have shown the meetings in the order which relates to a financial year ending 31 December). So, the fourth meeting is the first meeting in the calendar year and focuses mainly on matters relating to the previous financial year. The pro forma agenda items for the November meeting have been designed to avoid the need for the external auditor to attend this meeting.

We recommend dividing agendas into the following category sections, but to vary the order in which these sections appear on the agenda, in order to avoid a differential degree of audit committee attention being given over time to the different categories of agenda items:

- scrutiny of information to be published as well as important information used internally;
- oversight of risk management, internal control and governance processes, including oversight of the company's whistleblowing policy;
- oversight of external audit;
- oversight of internal audit and other review agencies; and
- audit committee business.

We further recommend including on the face of the agenda, within a text box against each agenda item, what the committee is being asked to do with the agenda item. This assists audit committee members to prepare in a more focused way for the meeting.

Risk management and internal control E2.3

We recommend that the audit committee's oversight of risk management and internal control should be spread across the year. A number of agenda items in the table below relate to risk management and internal control. We suggest that the committee receives and considers reports from the executive on the company's approach to risk management and internal control, broken down into each of the essential components of risk management and internal control. If the Committee of Sponsoring Organizations (COSO) internal control framework is the basis to be used, then there are five essential internal control components:

Control environment:	for instance, the ethical tone set by the Board
Risk assessment:	for instance, it is necessary for management to identify events which would pose a risk, assess relative risk as a prerequisite for developing and maintaining commensurate effective internal control, and then decide how to respond to the risk
Control activities:	for instance, segregation of duties
Information and communication:	for instance, exception reports
Monitoring:	for instance, by internal audit

COSO[1] defines 'internal control' as follows:

> 'Internal control is broadly defined as a process, effected by the entity's Board of directors, management and other personnel, designed to provide reasonable assurance regarding the achievement of objectives in the following categories:
>
> - Effectiveness and efficiency of operations.
> - Reliability of financial reporting.
> - Compliance with applicable laws and regulations.'

COSO[2] defines 'enterprise risk management' in a very similar way, as being:

> 'a process, effected by an entity's Board of directors, management and other personnel, applied in strategy setting and across the enterprise, designed to identify potential events that may affect the entity, and manage risks to be within its risk appetite, to provide reasonable assurance regarding the achievement of entity objectives.'

The eight essential COSO components of enterprise risk management are:

Internal environment:	for instance, the ethical tone set by the Board
Objectives:	for instance, targets to be met
Event identification:	identify events which would pose a risk
Risk assessment:	assess (measure) the risk
Risk response:	decide how to mitigate the risk
Control activities:	for instance, segregation of duties
Information and communication:	for instance, exception reports
Monitoring:	for instance, by internal audit

Pro forma agenda items **E2.4**

Meeting (in the context of company's financial year)	**Approximate date of the meeting (assuming 31 December year-end)**	**Likely agenda items**	**Comment**
1.	April	Time alone with the external auditor	It is usually best for this to be at the start of the meeting
1.	April	Time alone with the head of internal audit	It is usually best for this to be at the start of the meeting
1.	April	Review the process that the company follows to determine, prepare for and conduct meetings with investment analysts and leading shareholders and to make announcements to the market	UK Corporate Governance Code Provision C.3.2: 'Any formal announcements relating to the company's financial performance'
1.	April	Receive a report from the external auditor on their perceptions of the quality of the internal audit and of any other internal review agencies of the company	

Meeting (in the context of company's financial year)	Approximate date of the meeting (assuming 31 December year-end)	Likely agenda items	Comment
1.	April	Conclude on advice to the board on whether to reappoint the external auditors, or to invite audit firms to tender for the audit	If a decision is made to invite tenders, the incumbent auditors should only be invited to tender if there is a prospect of them being reappointed
1.	April	Receive and discuss a report from the head of internal audit on progress against the annual audit plan, and the results (in summary form) of each audit engagement completed	
1.	April	Review the company's policies which relate to risk management and internal control	This might include: Code of Business Conduct; Fraud Response Plan; Whistleblowing Policy(see Code Provision C.3.5); Harassment Policy, Risk Management Policy; IT Security Policy; Internet Usage Policy; etc
1.	April	Progress the committee's consideration of the effectiveness of risk management and internal control processes	Spread over the year's meetings, consideration of reports from the executive on each of COSO's five internal control components, or (preferably) COSO's eight enterprise risk management components[3]
1.	April	Time for committee members only	Without executives or any non-committee member being in attendance. It is usually best to end the meeting in this way
1.	April	Committee decides what should be specifically drawn attention to the next meeting of the board	
2.	July	Time alone with the external auditor	It is usually best for this to be at the start of the meeting

Meeting (in the context of company's financial year)	**Approximate date of the meeting (assuming 31 December year-end)**	**Likely agenda items**	**Comment**
2.	July	Time alone with the head of internal audit	It is usually best for this to be at the start of the meeting
2.	July	Scrutiny of interim financial results, and decision on recommending their adoption by the board	If a listed company
2.	July	Discussion with the external auditors of their review of the interim financial statements	If a listed company
2.	July	Approval of the external auditor's plan for the current year's audit	Depending on the amount of audit work planned to be done at the interim stage (ie before the year-end) this discussion may take place at the previous or following audit committee meeting
2.	July	Enquire of the external auditor about the external audit firm's approach to quality assurance of the external audit	
2.	July	Receive and consider a report from the Head of Internal Audit on the quality of the external audit	
2.	July	Conclude on whether there are any factors which compromise the independence of the external auditors in their capacity as auditors of the financial statements	

Meeting (in the context of company's financial year)	Approximate date of the meeting (assuming 31 December year-end)	Likely agenda items	Comment
2.	July	Enquire of the external auditors their view of the quality of the audit committee and its performance	
2.	July	Receive and discuss a report from the head of internal audit on progress against the annual audit plan, and the results (in summary form) of each audit engagement completed	
2.	July	Receive and consider the high-level-risk register (or similar statement on risks and their control) from the Executive	
2.	July	Progress the committee's consideration of the effectiveness of risk management and internal control processes	Spread over the year's meetings, consideration of reports from the executive on each of COSO's five internal control components, or (preferably) COSO's eight enterprise risk management components
2.	July	Receive and consider a report on changes in accounting standards which will impact the year end results	Ideally these should be modelled so that the committee can see the impact
2.	July	Receive and consider a report on proposed changes in accounting treatment which may be adopted in the year-end accounts	
2.	July	Time for committee members only	Without executives or any non-committee member being in attendance. It is usually best to end the meeting in this way

Meeting (in the context of company's financial year)	Approximate date of the meeting (assuming 31 December year-end)	Likely agenda items	Comment
2.	July	Committee decides what should be specifically drawn attention to the next meeting of the board	
3.	November (this may be a meeting which it is unnecessary for the external auditor to attend)	Time alone with the external auditor	It is usually best for this to be at the start of the meeting
3.	November	Time alone with the head of internal audit	It is usually best for this to be at the start of the meeting
3.	November	Review and approve the year-end timetable	
3.	November	Committee discusses its degree of satisfaction with the company's external auditors	
3.	November	Consider whether other services provided by the external audit firm compromise the independence and objectivity of the external audit	UK Corporate Governance Code Provision C.3.2: 'develop and implement policy on the engagement of the external auditor to supply non-audit services.'
			UK Corporate Governance Code Provision C.3.8: 'The annual report should explain to shareholders how, if the auditor provides non-audit services, auditor objectivity and independence is safeguarded.'
3.	November	Approve the external auditor's fee	Alternatively, the committee may empower the finance director to do this

Meeting (in the context of company's financial year)	**Approximate date of the meeting (assuming 31 December year-end)**	**Likely agenda items**	**Comment**
3.	November	When audit firms have been tendering for the company's eternal audit, the committee makes a decision as to which firm to recommend to the board to be the company's external auditors for the following financial year	
3.	November	Committee's review of its terms of reference (ToR), and possible formulation of amended ToR for approval by the board	Make the ToR empower the committee to (a) take outside advice, and (b) commission work to be done directly for the audit committee by the internal audit function
3.	November	Review the charter of the internal audit function	
3.	November	Receive from the head of internal audit and approve the risk-based annual plan of internal audit engagements to be conducted over the following financial year	
3.	November	Consider areas in which the Committee will particularly promote co-operation between auditors and other review bodies in the coming year	
3.	November	Review and approve the ToR of the internal audit function	

Meeting (in the context of company's financial year)	Approximate date of the meeting (assuming 31 December year-end)	Likely agenda items	Comment
3.	November	Receive a report on a quality assurance review of the internal audit function which should be conducted by internal audit on themselves at least once every year	Except in the fifth year when the *external* quality assurance review is undertaken (a requirement of the Standards – see next row)
3.	November	Receive a report on an *external* quality assurance review of the internal audit function (at least once every five years)	A requirement of the Standards both of the Institute of Internal Auditors and of the UK Public Sector Internal Audit Standards[4]
3.	November	Conclude on the adequacy of internal audit provision across the company	To do with the professionalism, independence and resources of internal audit
			The Committee should, as part of this, be satisfied that the remuneration of the head of internal audit is appropriate and some audit committees are responsible to determine what that remuneration shall be
3.	November	Receive and discuss a report from the head of internal audit on progress against the annual audit plan, and the results (in summary form) of each audit engagement completed	
3.	November	Receive and consider from management an annual fraud report, and an annual avoidable losses report	To cover frauds and avoidable losses exceptional in size of character

Meeting (in the context of company's financial year)	**Approximate date of the meeting (assuming 31 December year-end)**	**Likely agenda items**	**Comment**
3.	November	Receive an annual report from the head of internal audit, including his or her professional opinion on the effective of risk management and internal control across the whole of the business, over all of the year to date	
3.	November	Committee comes to its formal conclusion on the effective of risk management and internal control across the whole of the business, over all of the year to date, for later incorporation into the committee's annual report to the board	
3.	November	Audit committee's appraisal of its own performance and that of its chair	
3.	November	Review the training needs of audit committee members and of those in attendance at audit committee meetings.	
3.	November	Receive and consider a report, probably from external advisers, on the tax liability of the company	
3.	November	Review the directors' and officers' liability insurance	Policy, renewal and extent of cover

Meeting (in the context of company's financial year)	Approximate date of the meeting (assuming 31 December year-end)	Likely agenda items	Comment
3.	November	Time for committee members only	Without executives or any non-committee member being in attendance. It is usually best to end the meeting in this way
3.	November	Committee decides what should be specifically drawn attention to the next meeting of the board	
4.	February of the following year	Receive a report from the external auditors on the results of the annual audit for the year-end the previous 31 December	
4.	February of the following year	Receive a report from other independent advisors on material matters within the year-end financial statements	For instance, an insurance company's audit committee will be likely to take advice from independent actuaries; a property company from valuers, and so on
4.	February of the following year	Enquire whether there have been any material changes since the November audit committee meeting which impact upon the annual report and financial statements	
4.	February of the following year	Receive the finance director's 'sign off' that there are no off-balance sheet companies, partnerships, joint ventures or bank accounts, and no significant undisclosed liabilities or contingent liabilities	

Meeting (in the context of company's financial year)	**Approximate date of the meeting (assuming 31 December year-end)**	**Likely agenda items**	**Comment**
4.	February of the following year	Consider in particular material items in the financial statements which involve judgement	UK Corporate Governance Code Provision 3.2 on 'significant financial reporting judgements'. These are items where there may be scope for creative accounting
4.	February of the following year	Receive, review and approve the draft letter(s) of representation form the company to the external auditors	
4.	February of the following year	Receive a report of the 'auditor close out meeting' between the company's accountants and the external auditor	Ensure the committee understands the issues which had to be resolved between management and the external auditor
4.	February of the following year	Approve the audited financial statements, so as to commend them for adoption by the board	
4.	February of the following year	Review the wording of the corporate governance statement to be published, especially the statement on risk management and internal control	
4.	February of the following year	Approve the board's report on the audit committee which will appear within the annual report	UK Corporate Governance Code Provision C.3.8: 'A separate section of the annual report should describe the work of the committee in discharging those responsibilities.'

Meeting (in the context of company's financial year)	Approximate date of the meeting (assuming 31 December year-end)	Likely agenda items	Comment
4.	February of the following year	Agree the wording of the annual report of the audit committee to the board	Should summarise the work done by the audit committee over the year, and include its opinion on the reliability of the financial statements, the effectiveness of risk management and internal control, and the quality of internal and external audit
4.	February of the following year	Receive and discuss a report from the head of internal audit on progress against the annual audit plan, and the results (in summary form) of each audit engagement completed	
4.	February of the following year	Time for Committee members only	Without executives or any non-Committee member being in attendance. It is usually best to end the meeting in this way
4.	February of the following year	Consider the external auditor's management letter and management's responses to it	
4.	February of the following year	Committee decides what should be specifically drawn attention to the next meeting of the board	

Qualities needed of audit committee members **E2.5**

Enron's audit committee had impressive membership. Whereas even the largest UK listed company would be compliant with the UK's Corporate Governance Code with just three members, Enron's audit committee had five members.[5] They were:

1. one of the top five academic accountants in the country and dean of a leading university business school (chair of the committee);
2. a PhD in Economics, former chair of a national trade commission, and university fellow;

3. an English peer, ex-senior UK government minister and qualified chartered accountant with consider directorship experience;
4. a former company president and attorney; and
5. a multinational company chair, with an MBA.

They were not the first company, that had an apparently excellent audit committee, to have failed following creative accounting practices.

In our view, Enron's audit committee was deficient in at least one respect. In Enron's case, the accounting challenges were largely in the area of the accounting for off-balance-sheet special vehicle entities. Enron had no audit committee member who was, or had recently been, an executive finance director of another large entity that had similar accounting challenges. Such are in short supply: the risk–reward ratio does not stack up. The risk management and internal control responsibilities of the audit committee might also have led the audit committee to uncover the ultimately fatal weaknesses inherent within Enron – to do with top management style and so on.

Another potential source of suitable people with recent and relevant financial experience would be the partnerships of the 'Big Four' and mid-sized accounting firms, but on the whole they are not available until they retire, for commercial reasons associated with potential and very likely conflicts of interest. Having retired from a public accounting firm, an ex-partner is then generally precluded from joining an audit committee of a client of that public accounting firm, as to do so would violate one of the independence tests within the UK Corporate Governance Code:

> '**Code Provision**
>
> B.1.1 … has, or has had within the last three years, a material business relationship with the company either directly, or as a partner, shareholder, director or senior employee of a body that has such a relationship with the company.'

It is true that Code Provisions only have a 'comply or explain' status, so a board may explain why they have chosen not to comply; however, most boards will determine that they should comply. It is also true that, with respect to this Provision, boards have the discretion to conclude that an individual director should be regarded as 'independent' notwithstanding 'the existence of relationships or circumstance which may appear relevant', including the one we quote here. Again, most boards will decline to exercise their discretion in that way. Of course, the retiring partner may join the board of a client company as a non-executive director who is not independent and therefore who should not belong to the company's audit committee. But with small boards, there is little room for non-executive directors who do not pass the independence tests.

The UK Corporate Governance Code Provision, that each audit committee should have one member with recent and relevant financial experience, is a harsh test if taken seriously:

> 'C.3.1 The board should establish an audit committee of at least three, or in the case of smaller companies two, members, who should all be independent non-executive directors. The board should satisfy itself that at least one member of the audit committee has recent and relevant financial experience.'

It is a matter of *how much* experience and *how recent*. It is, of course, also a matter of *what experience*. The experience needs to be germane to the technical content of the financial accountants of the company.

In some companies, it will be impractical for all the necessary recent and relevant experience to be vested in just one of the audit committee members. An insurance company is likely to need an audit committee member who is at the leading edge of the actuarial profession as well as another member who is at the cutting edge of accounting standards.

Directors are required to exercise skill and care, a duty sharpened up by the UK's Companies Act 2006. If a director belongs to an audit committee by virtue of his or her professional membership of an accounting body, then this director should ensure that he or she really does have the skill usually associated with that membership – and it should then be applied very carefully.

It may be that Enron's audit committee discharged its duties with appropriate skill and care. Professional people can 'get it wrong' without being negligent; they cannot be expected to be infallible. When they are non-executive directors, they are entitled to expect to be given reliable information and explanations. It may be that audit committee members, even those with recent and relevant financial experience, may not fully understand all the complex issues which underpin the financial statements of the company. But they should at least have the competence to understand the questions that should be asked. If the answers are beyond them personally, then they should exercise their powers to obtain outside, independent advice. And they should then be able to understand the answers they get.

Audit committee members require broader competencies than we have covered above. HM Treasury puts it like this:[6]

> **'Audit Committee Competency Framework**
>
> **'All members of the Audit Committee should have, or acquire as soon as possible after appointment:**
>
> - understanding of the objectives of the organisation and current significant issues for the organisation;
> - understanding of the organisation's structure, including key relationships such as that with a sponsoring department or a major partner;
> - understanding of the organisation's culture;
> - understanding of any relevant legislation or other rules governing the organisation;
> - broad understanding of the government environment, particularly accountability structures and current major initiatives.
>
> **The Audit Committee should corporately possess:**
>
> - knowledge/skills/experience (as appropriate and required) in:
>   - accounting;
>   - risk management;
>   - audit;
>   - technical or specialist issues pertinent to the organisation's business.

- experience of managing similar sized organisations;
- understanding of the wider relevant environments in which the organisation operates;
- detailed understanding of the government environment and accountability structures.'

US definition of 'audit committee financial expert' E2.6

Section 407 of the US Sarbanes-Oxley Act (2002) 'Disclosure of Audit Committee Financial Expert' required that at least one member of a US quoted company's audit committee be a financial expert as defined by the Securities and Exchange Commission (SEC). Section 407 guided the SEC to consider incorporating into its definition whether a person has, through education and experience as a public accountant or auditor or a principal financial officer, comptroller, or principal accounting officer of an issuer, or from a position involving the performance of similar functions: (1) an understanding of generally accepted accounting principles and financial statements; (2) experience in: (a) the preparation or auditing of financial statements of generally comparable issuers; and (b) the application of such principles in connection with the accounting for estimates, accruals, and reserves; (3) experience with internal accounting controls; and (4) an understanding of audit committee functions.

Accordingly the SEC developed Final Rules that define an 'audit committee financial expert' as a person with all of the five following attributes:

1. an understanding of generally accepted accounting principles and financial statements;
2. the ability to assess the general application of such principles in connection with the accounting for estimates, accruals and reserves;
3. experience preparing, auditing, analysing or evaluating financial statements that present a breadth and level of complexity of accounting issues that are generally comparable to the breadth and complexity of issues that can reasonably be expected to be raised by the registrant's financial statements, or experience actively supervising one or more persons engaged in such activities;
4. an understanding of internal controls and procedures for financial reporting; and
5 an understanding of audit committee functions

Under the Final Rules, in order to qualify as an 'audit committee financial expert' a person must have acquired the above listed attributes through any one or more of the following:

1. education and experience as a principal financial officer, principal accounting officer, controller, public accountant or auditor or experience in one or more positions that involve the performance of similar functions;
2. experience actively supervising a principal financial officer, principal accounting officer, controller, public accountant, auditor or person performing similar functions;
3. experience overseeing or assessing the performance of companies or public accountants with respect to the preparation, auditing or evaluation of financial statements; or

4. other relevant experience; and, if other relevant experience is what qualifies the director, that experience must be described.

Is there a conflict in belonging to an audit committee and also to a remuneration committee? E2.7

There are no guidelines that discourage belonging to both committees. Since, under the UK Corporate Governance Code, each of these committees should comprise exclusively independent non-executive directors, there are bound to be many companies where there is cross-membership of both these committees. It is unrealistic, even counterproductive in some ways, to separate out everything in order to avoid potential conflicts.

In any case, we have to allow that a board member might belong to more than one board committee where there is potential overlap between the two committees. The problem would be more serious if it was the same committee which deliberated on both executive remuneration matters and also on audit matters – which nobody is suggesting.

Guidance in the Higgs Report recommended against a non-executive director belonging to all three of the principal board committees.[7] Higgs said:

> 'No one non-executive director should sit on all three principal board committees (audit, nomination and remuneration) simultaneously.'

Later, in his discussion on 'Audit and Remuneration Committees',[8] Higgs said:

> 'When appointing committee members, boards should draw on the independent non-executive directors with the most relevant skills and experience. Consideration should also be given to rotating committee members. In order not to concentrate too much influence on one individual, **I consider it undesirable for any one individual to be on all three principal board committees at the same time** (suggested Code Provision A.3.7).'

The emphasis above is Higgs', which he uses to highlight a firm recommendation. However, his suggested Code Provision A.3.7 never saw the light of day. The nearest the Code gets to it is one of the Supporting Principles at B.1 that reads:

> 'The value of ensuring that committee membership is refreshed and that undue reliance is not placed on particular individuals should be taken into account in deciding chairmanship and membership of committees.'

Higgs had not considered the idea of Supporting Principles, so they were absent from his proposed revision of the 1998 Combined Code. Supporting Principles were introduced for the first time into the 2003 Combined Code which appeared after the Higgs and Smith Reports. The Supporting Principle quoted above is clearly all that eventually became of Higgs suggested Code Provision A.3.7. His proposed Code Provision A.3.7 would have read:[9]

> 'Unless a company is small, no individual should sit on all three principal board committees at the same time.'

It is generally accepted that it is unsound for a single committee, perhaps designated *the finance and audit committee*, to have delegated authority from the board both for making certain financial decisions and also for the responsibilities of an audit committee. To be successful as an audit committee needs a measure of independence from financial decision-making.

A need for a degree of independence of the audit committee from the remuneration committee may be useful in at least two contexts. First, the audit committee gives assurance to the board that financial information which is published in the board's name is reliable – and information about executive remuneration is financial information. That is a very small area of overlap and is perhaps only of concern if there is a possibility that the information might not be accurate or complete or may be misleading. Financial information about executive remuneration is not in any case prepared by the remuneration committee: it is prepared by the finance director and accountants of the company, none of whom are members of the audit or remuneration committees.

Secondly, the audit committee has a role in advising the board on the effectiveness of risk management and internal control: in some companies, significant risks may be within the contractual terms and remuneration arrangements of directors, especially executive directors.

Being pragmatic, boards today are typically small (say seven to ten members) and typically balanced in membership between executive and non-executive directors. Under the UK Corporate Governance Code, except for small listed companies, the remuneration committee should have at least three members, and all are meant to be non-executive directors who are judged to be independent directors; and the audit committee also has to have at least three non-executive members, all of whom are meant to be independent directors. On some boards, not all non-executive directors can be classified as independent. This means that it would not be possible for most boards to find suitable directors to belong to the audit committee and another clutch of suitable directors for the remuneration committee. Companies rightly need to be concerned about total boardroom costs.

The main 'independence' issue about remuneration committees is to ensure that executive directors do not participate in decisions about their own remuneration.

Note from a new chair of an audit committee to the committee members

In the past our audit committee has felt it has met as often as necessary, but this has usually been just twice a year. Whilst we might try to contain things to three meetings a year, a fourth will almost certainly prove necessary – and more in exceptional circumstances. Much depends on the quality of agenda papers, the thoroughness of members' preparation, and, of course, on the quality of chairmanship.

The committee chair needs to be conscious that he is responsible for the effectiveness of the committee. One aspect of this is to ensure that the right executives are present for particular agenda items. Another is to ensure that committee members have the support they need and are able to access professional development opportunities as appropriate. Another is the time set aside for each meeting: it will probably be wise to indicate on the agenda the expected end time of the meeting.

It is reasonable to expect the company to pay non-executive directors additional fees for their extra committee and committee chairmanship responsibilities. However, some companies may choose not to do so if extra responsibilities of this sort tend to 'even themselves out' between board members.

This audit committee chair will not be happy for audit committee meetings in future to be scheduled to commence at, say, 9am on the days when a board meeting is scheduled to commence later on the same day – perhaps at 10am or 11am. Meeting fatigue will set in. Committee members may arrive late for the audit committee meeting and other directors are likely to meet early for the board meeting. The consequence will approximate to tokenism as far as attention to the audit committee's business is concerned.

It is preferable that audit committee meetings take place about a fortnight before a board meeting, so that the (draft) audit committee minutes can be an agenda paper for the board, with the opportunity for the chair of the audit committee to speak to those minutes at the board. Although the minutes are only draft at this stage, it is much to be preferred that the committee reports promptly to the board: other committee members present at the board can indicate if they find the minutes inadequate. It will also be essential that the audit committee's minutes are an 'A' agenda item (for discussion at the board) rather than a 'B' item (tabled for information only, not for discussion).

Agendas

A practical measure would be to group the audit committee's agenda items into the three sections already set out, with a fourth section on 'audit committee business' (which would include items such as this paper), thus:

1. scrutiny of information;
2. oversight of risk management and internal control processes;
3. oversight of 'the total audit'; and
4. audit committee business.

To aid committee members in their preparation for audit committee meetings and to facilitate focus within meetings, a further practical measure would be to show as a rubric on the face of the agenda for each agenda item what is being asked of the audit committee – such as 'The committee is being asked to express an opinion on the effectiveness of the company's risk management and internal control for communication to the board', or 'The committee is asked to approve the proposed annual plan of internal audit engagements', etc. This would not, of course, be intended to restrict members' consideration of these agenda items to the direction suggested by the rubric.

Apart from the above agenda sections, the committee should spend time alone with internal audit and also time alone with external audit. This internal audit time is certainly best at the start of the meeting. Our external auditor has a preference for their 'time alone' also to be at the start of the meeting. If the committee adopts this approach, it will allow the board members of the audit committee to have a closed session *at the end* of each meeting without attendance of anyone other than the audit committee members. Of course, each member of our audit committee is an independent non-executive director.

Agenda papers and minutes

We need to consider the style, content and retention of audit committee minutes, as well as the retention of agenda papers. Company law requires that minutes of board meetings are retained,[10] but we do not believe there is a similar stipulation for audit committee agenda papers and minutes, nor for board agenda papers. Best practice suggests indefinite retention of all of these.

In respect to how minutes are written, there is currently some concern about minutes which are comprehensive of the nuances of all the discussions that took place during the meetings. This is because minutes may be used in court to demonstrate that the audit committee or board did not discuss a matter in a very mature, comprehensive way. Minutes will rarely be used to show what a good job the audit committee did.

The best approach is probably for minutes to set out the topic areas which were discussed and then to minute the decision (if any) arrived at, but to avoid minuting the details of the discussion.

Of course, directors can ask for particular views they expressed to be minuted.

Notes

1 1992, revised 2013.

2 2004.

3 This is because, in order to assess whether risk management and internal control are effective, the committee must consider whether each of the five essential components of internal control (or eight components of enterprise risk management) are in place and working effectively. That is, the committee must consider the *process* of risk management and internal control. The committee must also consider whether any outcomes indicate that risk management and internal control have not been effective. The fraud and avoidable losses reports, the results of the external audit, and the regular reports from internal audit to the committee are examples of what will assist the committee in this regard.

4 PSIAS (2012) Public Sector Internal Audit Standards, December 2012, ISBN 978 1 84508 356 4, effective from 1 April 2013, available at http://www.iia.org.uk/media/76020/public_sector_internal_audit_standards_2012.pdf, accessed 14 July 2013.

5 A smaller listed company outside the FTSE 350 is compliant with the UK's Corporate Governance Code if its audit committee has just two members (both of whom should be independent directors) and if there are just two independent directors on the board. The Code is being complied with if the chair of the board of a listed company outside the FTSE350 may be a member but not the chair of the audit committee, if he or she was independent when appointed to the chair. A FTSE 350 company is compliant if its audit committee comprises at least three members, all of whom are independent directors,

and if at least 50% of the board, excluding its chairman in the count, are independent directors.

6 Annex G to HM Treasury's 'Audit Committee Handbook', March 2007.

7 Derek Higgs (January 2003): 'Review of the Role and Effectiveness of Non-Executive Directors', DTI, p 9.

8 Higgs Report, p 59 (section 13.2).

9 Higgs Report, p 82.

10 For ten years, under the UK's Companies Act 2006.

Chapter E3

Audit Committees and Sarbanes-Oxley in the UK

'The objective of Section 404 is to provide meaningful disclosure to investors about the effectiveness of a company's internal controls systems, without creating unnecessary compliance burdens or wasting shareholder resources'.

Christopher Cox (2007), Chair, SEC;
Congressman in 2002

Further content on the Sarbanes-Oxley Act ('the Act') is to be found in Chapter **E6**. At the end of this chapter we reproduce content from sections of the Act closely related to the annual audit and to the audit committee.

Setting auditing standards **E3.1**

The Public Companies Accounting Oversight Board (PCAOB) was established as a requirement of the Act, removing from the American Institute of Certified Public Accountants (AICPA) the setting of auditing standards for the audit of US public companies. By mid-2007, PCAOB had issued only five Standards, including the latest, which is addressed here. This tally had risen to 16 by 2014. However, *pro tem*, PCAOB has adopted as an interim measure many of the AICPA's Statements on Auditing Standards (SASs) which continue to be auditing standards to be applied to audits of unlisted US entities.

The PCAOB is, in effect, a subsidiary of the Securities and Exchange Commission. PCAOB, intendedly independent of the accounting profession, oversees the auditing of public companies in part through the development of auditing standards. This has in effect resulted in US oversight of UK auditing firms who have clients caught by requirements of the Act.

It is the PCAOB which published its Auditing Standard No 2, *'An Audit of Internal Control over Financial Reporting Performed in Conjunction with an Audit of Financial Statements'*, as the standard on attestation engagements referred to in ss 404(b) and 103(a)(2)(A) of the Act, reproduced at the end of this chapter. Auditing Standard No 2 was superseded in 2007 by Auditing Standard No 5, *'An Audit of Internal Control over Financial Reporting that is Integrated with an Audit of Financial Statements'*. It is noteworthy that neither No 2 nor No 5 gives endorsement at all to Turnbull as being an acceptable framework to use.

In the UK, the Auditing Practices Board (APB) of the Financial Reporting Council (FRC) adopted the International Standards on Auditing (ISAs) of the International Auditing and Assurance Standards Board (IAASB), which is part of the International Federation of Accountants (IFAC) based in New York. In the fullness of time, ISAs might become adopted internationally, replacing AICPA's SASs. They might also be adopted by PCAOB to cover aspects not dealt with within its own Standards, and are likely to be adopted by the European Community. But these possible developments seem some way off.

Although we would say that, generally, ISAs are 'state of the art', they are a long way from being perfect. Even after IAASB's 'clarity project', designed to make ISAs clearer without altering their intended requirements, much progress still needs to be made. For instance, ISA610, redrafted in December 2006 as part of IAASB's clarity project, on *'The Auditor's Consideration of the Internal Audit Function'* compares very poorly indeed with SAS65 *'The Auditor's Consideration of the Internal Audit Function in an Audit of Financial Statements'*, even though the latter is dated 1991, not least as the former inexplicably makes no reference to the Standards, etc of The Institute of Internal Auditors.

Changes to the external auditor's remit under the Sarbanes-Oxley Act, s 404 E3.2

Until 2007, implementation of s 404 of the Act (reproduced at the end of this chapter) had involved the external auditor in a 'triple audit' and had approximately doubled the overall cost of it,[1] as the auditors applied PCAOB's Auditing Standard No 2. This 'triple audit' had been:

(i) the traditional audit of the financial statements;
(ii) an attestation and report on *management's* assessment of internal control over financial reporting, as required by s 404(a) of the Act; and
(iii) the external auditor's own assessment of the effectiveness of internal control over financial reporting – which, however, is not specifically required by s 404(b) of the Act.

Reacting to complaints that the costs of implementing s 404 had generally far outweighed the gains, except for external auditors, the Securities and Exchange Commission (SEC) and the PCAOB, the latter responsible for the Standards to be applied to the audit of US quoted companies, devised a slimmed-down approach to implementing s 404, sometimes termed 'SOX Lite' (per PCAOB Auditing Standard No 5, 2007, etc).

Now a 'double', not a 'triple', audit? E3.3

The Sarbanes-Oxley Act remains unchanged from its introduction in 2002. The wording of s 404 is that a company's external auditors should attest to and report on management's assessment of internal control over financial reporting, not that the external auditors should undertake their own assessment of the effectiveness of internal control over financial reporting. However, it is the former that has been formally abandoned, namely their attest and report on management's assessment of internal control over financial reporting. It is impossible to escape the conclusion that PCAOB has tinkered with the auditor's obligations under s 404(b), making only a cosmetic change here, whereas they might have interpreted the Act as enabling the abandonment of their own separate audit of internal control. We cannot, therefore, expect external audit costs to reduce significantly due to this cosmetic change, since what has been abandoned was not an onerous task for the external auditors, in view of the fact that they had been undertaking their own assessment of the effectiveness of internal control over financial reporting.

The Institute of Chartered Accountants in England and Wales (ICAEW) concurs that PCAOB has misinterpreted s 404. In its response to the SEC on proposed PCAOB Auditing Standard No 5, ICAEW wrote:

> 'Section 404(a) of the Sarbanes-Oxley Act places a clear responsibility on management to assess and report on internal control over financial reporting. Section 404(b) states, in respect of the internal control assessment required of management under section 404(a), that the auditor "… . shall attest to, and report on, the assessment made by the management of the issuer." The wording of the Act does not require an audit of internal control over financial reporting.
>
> Whilst we respect the SEC's and the PCAOB's intended clarification of section 404(b) – in conjunction with section 103(a)(2)(A)(iii) – so that the wording in the Act is now interpreted to mean "the audit of internal control", we remain of the view that:
>
> - there has never been any public justification offered by the SEC or the PCAOB of why the attestation required by the Sarbanes-Oxley Act should take the form of an audit; and
> - of the two opinions required by AS 2, the wrong opinion has been eliminated.
>
> The choice of the auditors' opinion required by AS 5 will result in more testing and higher costs than would have been the case if the opinion on management's assessment had been retained and the current opinion had been removed. Such outcomes must be of concern to US authorities as they seek to enhance the effectiveness and reduce the costs of section 404 and to maintain the competitiveness of US capital markets.'[2]

PCAOB explains its Auditing Standard No 5's[3] rationale for retaining the audit of internal control, and abandoning its attest and report on management's assessment of internal control over financial reporting, in these terms:[4]

> 'Although Auditing Standard No 2 [required] the auditor to evaluate management's process, the auditor's opinion on management's assessment is not an opinion on management's internal control evaluation process. Rather, it is the auditor's opinion on whether management's statements about the effectiveness of the company's internal controls are fairly stated.
>
> …
>
> [PCAOB Auditing Standard No 5, PCAOB] attempted to address concerns that the separate opinion on management's assessment required by Auditing Standard No 2 contributed to the complexity of the standard and caused confusion regarding the scope of the auditor's work. Accordingly, to emphasize the proper scope of the audit and to simplify the reporting, [Auditing Standard No 5 requires] that the auditor express only one opinion on internal control – a statement of the auditor's opinion on the effectiveness of the company's internal control over financial reporting. The proposal eliminate[s] the separate opinion on management's assessment because it was redundant of the opinion on internal control itself

and because the opinion on the effectiveness of controls more clearly conveys the same information – specifically, whether the company's internal control is effective.

Many commenters agreed with the Board that eliminating the separate opinion on management's assessment would reduce confusion and clarify the reporting. Some commenters, however, suggested that the Board should instead require only an opinion on management's assessment. These commenters expressed their belief that the Act requires only that the auditor review management's assessment process and not the company's internal control.

…

The Board has determined, after considering these comments, to adopt the provision requiring only an opinion on internal control. The Board continues to believe that the overall scope of the audit that was described by Auditing Standard No 2 and [Standard No 5] is correct; that is, to attest to and report on management's assessment, as required by Section 404(b) of the Act, the auditor must test controls directly to determine whether they are effective.'

PCAOB also points out[5] that, in addition, s 103 of the Act (reproduced at the end of this chapter) requires PCAOB's standard on auditing internal control to include 'testing of the internal control structure and procedures of the issuer …'. PCAOB also asserts that, under s 103, PCAOB's Standard must require the auditor to present in the audit report, among other things, 'an evaluation of whether such internal control structure and procedures … provide reasonable assurance that transactions are recorded as necessary to permit preparation of financial statements in accordance with generally accepted accounting principles …'.

The SEC has also adopted corresponding changes to its own rules that require the auditor to express an opinion directly on internal control.

Small company exemption **E3.4**

Smaller quoted companies have now been exempted from s 404(b), but not from s 404(a) of the Sarbanes-Oxley Act. A smaller company is a "non-accelerated filer", ie an Exchange Act reporting company that has a public float under $75 million or that fails to meet other criteria for an "accelerated filer" (as defined in the Exchange Act Rule 12b-2) based on reporting characteristics. This temporary exemption was formalised by the Dodd-Frank Wall Street Reform and Consumer Protection Act (July 2010).

Revised definitions of 'significant deficiency' and 'material weakness' **E3.5**

More encouraging is the improved realism of the new definitions of 'significant deficiency' and 'material weakness' brought in by the 2007 changes (see table below). If management, discharging their obligations under s 404(a) (reproduced at the end of this chapter), uncover significant deficiencies or material weaknesses, they must report these in their 10-K filings and also to their audit committee and to their external auditors. They must be reported even if they have been rectified before the year-end and have not resulted in any misstatement(s) within the financial results. So it is helpful that 'more than remote' has been removed as a criterion to be applied to determine whether a deficiency is significant; and that 'remote likelihood' has been replaced by 'reasonable possibility' as a criterion to assess whether a weakness is material.

From the second table below, it can be seen that share price is depressed by having to disclose 'significant deficiencies' or 'material weaknesses' or experiencing a qualified audit opinion about the effectiveness of internal control over financial reporting. In respect of the latter, it has been shown that the percentage of clients who 'fail' has varied according to the audit firm, with a mean of 6%, as the final table in this section indicates. These figures date back to the early implementation of the requirements of s 404.

Changes of definitions between 2004 and 2007

	PCAOB Auditing Standard No 2 (2004)	**PCAOB Auditing Standard No 5 (2007)**
Significant deficiency	A control deficiency (or a combination of internal control deficiencies) should be classified as a *significant deficiency* if, by itself or in combination with other control deficiencies, it results in a more than remote likelihood of a misstatement of the company's annual or interim financial statements that is more than inconsequential will not be prevented or detected.	A *significant deficiency* is a deficiency, or a combination of deficiencies, in internal control over financial reporting that is less severe than a material weakness, yet important enough to merit attention by those responsible for oversight of the company's financial reporting.
Material weakness	A significant deficiency should be classified as a *material weakness* if, by itself or in combination with other control deficiencies, it results in more than a remote likelihood that a material misstatement in the company's annual or interim financial statements will not be prevented or detected.	A *material weakness* is a deficiency, or a combination of deficiencies, in internal control over financial reporting, such that there is a *reasonable possibility* that a material misstatement of the company's annual or interim financial statements will not be prevented or detected on a timely basis. A material weakness in internal control over financial reporting may exist even when financial statements are not materially misstated.

PCAOB Auditing Standard No 5 (2007) also defines 'significant misstatement' as 'a misstatement that is less than material yet important enough to merit attention by those responsible for oversight of the company's financial reporting.'

Average Share Price Movement, Relative to Market vs Seven Days before Announcement				
	1 day after	7 days after	30 days after	60 days after
All deficiencies	–0.72%	–0.81%	–1.50%	–3.02%
Material weaknesses	–0.67%	–0.90%	–1.96%	–4.06%
Qualified opinions	–0.23%	–0.66%	–2.30%	–3.56%
Qualified opinions, no warning	–0.04%	–0.16%	–2.49%	–3.94%

Sources: Glass Lewis, FactSet

By auditor	**10-Ks filed**	**10-Ks passed**	**Percent passed**	**10-Ks failed**	**Percent failed**
The Big Four					
Deloitte & Touche, LLP	274	266	97%	8	3%
Ernst & Young, LLP	459	439	96%	20	4%
KPMG, LLP	317	300	95%	17	5%
PriceWaterhouseCoopers, LLP	366	332	91%	34	9%
All Big Four	**1416**	**1337**	**94%**	**79**	**6%**

Source: Compliance Week/Raisch Financial Internal Control Report Scorecard

There are 66 pages and 69 sections to the US Sarbanes-Oxley Act 2002, and many of them are having a significant impact internationally, not least in the UK, and not least with respect to the audit committee's oversight of external audit (see Chapter **E6**).

Section 404 (reproduced at the end of this chapter), as interpreted in a mandatory way by the SEC, requires the CEO and CFO to assess the effectiveness of internal control over financial reporting and to certify the result of their assessment to the audit committee, the external auditors and in their SEC filings; it also requires the external auditors to attest to, or audit, that assessment. Note the narrow scope of the assessment which, unlike the 2003 UK Corporate Governance Code/Turnbull 'requirement', does not extend to aspects of operational or compliance control unrelated to the reliability of financial reporting, nor to risk management systems. In these respects, the UK is light years in front of the US.

For the purposes of s 404, the SEC has defined 'internal control over financial reporting' as:

> 'A process designed by, or under the supervision of, the registrant's principal executive and principal financial officers, or persons performing similar functions, and effected by the registrant's board of directors, management and other personnel, to provide reasonable assurance regarding the reliability of financial reporting and the preparation of financial statements for external purposes in accordance with generally accepted accounting principles and includes those policies and procedures that:

(1) Pertain to the maintenance of records that in reasonable detail accurately and fairly reflect the transactions and dispositions of the assets of the registrant;

(2) Provide reasonable assurance that transactions are recorded as necessary to permit preparation of financial statements in accordance with generally accepted accounting principles, and that receipts and expenditures of the registrant are being made only in accordance with authorizations of management and directors of the registrant; and

(3) Providing reasonable assurance regarding prevention or timely detection of unauthorized acquisition, use or disposition of the registrant's assets which could have a material effect on the financial statements.'[6]

Section 302 imposes upon management not very dissimilar responsibilities with regard to disclosures generally in the annual report, while s 906 introduces draconian criminal sanctions for failures to observe ss 302 and 404. We reproduce these sections at the end of this chapter.

The Sarbanes-Oxley Act was born out of acute public outrage at spectacular examples of fraudulent financial reporting of US listed companies. Enough was seen to be enough. After all, back in 1987, COSO[7] had published its Report of the Committee on Fraudulent Financial Reporting ('The Treadway Report'). It, together with the consequential 'Internal Control – Integrated Framework',[8] had had little or no impact upon stemming the tide of fraudulent financial reporting. If companies, their auditors, the professional bodies and regulators could not deal with the problem, then the last resort was Congress and criminal sanctions. Hence, where we find ourselves today.

While the SEC list is not intended to be comprehensive for all time, the 1992 'Internal Control – Integrated Framework' is one of just three internal control frameworks acknowledged by the SEC as being suitable to be used for the CEO's and CFO's assessment of internal control over financial reporting as required by s 404 of the Act. Note that the 1992 COSO internal control framework has now been superseded by the 2013 framework.[9] The Canadian CoCo framework is another and the Turnbull Report[10] is the third. Certainly, the assessment is required to be done using a recognised internal control framework. The UK was lucky that Turnbull was found an acceptable framework, as it can hardly be regarded as a 'framework' at all. The FRC has published guidance on using Turnbull for this purpose. Most UK companies obliged to comply with Sarbanes-Oxley are using the 1992 COSO framework rather than the 1999/2005 UK Turnbull Report, as they consider it a better framework and they need to be seen to be 'whiter than white' in a US context.

Reputedly, to date the Sarbanes-Oxley Act, as interpreted by the SEC and PCAOB, has doubled the cost of the annual audit. In effect, initially it became a 'triple audit': in addition to the audit of the financial statements, the external auditors also audited whether the CEO and CFO had followed the due process set out in the SEC's rule on s 404 on assessing the effectiveness of internal control over financial reporting. The external auditors can only do this if the CEO and CFO have ensured they have thoroughly documented what they themselves have done, or have had done on their behalf – a hugely costly and bureaucratic internal exercise, tending to lead to a greater degree of standardisation of systems of internal control over financial reporting throughout large organisations which may in the past have had disparate methods across their businesses – all the more so, we suspect, if they are non-US groups. The 'third audit' is that the external auditors have had to come to their own judgement as to whether internal control over financial reporting is effective. In coming to their respective opinions, management are not permitted to rely on the external auditors' work, nor vice versa – otherwise, it would be a matter of 'circular reliance'. While management can contract out the legwork preparatory to arriving at their opinion on the effectiveness of internal control over financial reporting, they may not contract out the conclusion, which must be their own, nor may they contract out the legwork to their external auditors. Under the 2007 'SOX Lite' programme, it is, as we have discussed earlier, the second of these audits which has been dispensed with for the future.

Research over the period 2003 to 2008 by Kinney and Shepardson[11] compared the additional disclosures made by larger and smaller companies and the extra costs of audit for larger companies. They found that all companies continued to have cost increases for the audit of their financial statements. They found that audit costs to large (non-exempt) and smaller (exempt) companies more than doubled for initial s 404(b) audits in 2004 and remain high for larger companies, while for s 404(b)-exempt smaller companies (that only had the financial statement audit) audit fees grew about 10% annually. They showed that before the introduction of the Act, the average audit fee for the sample of 379 companies was \$237k. This average had increased to \$645k by 2008. These costs were only for external audit fees and excluded all the additional, internal costs and time which are more difficult to calculate, but are very substantial.

Rather than expose themselves to the risk of criminal charges, more than 700 CEOs and CFOs of US companies had, by 2006, acknowledged in their reports on s 404 that they had not met the high threshold of effective internal control over financial reporting, thereby avoiding some of the risk of criminal charges. We understand that the SEC, at least for the present, has no plans to institute disciplinary proceedings in such cases. Perhaps, for the first time, this is an example of the famous UK approach of 'comply or explain' creeping into US corporate governance.

Section 404 applies to many UK companies: it applies to those with secondary listings in the US; it applies to UK-based operations of US parents; and it applies to UK entities that provide significant accounting services for companies with primary or secondary US listings. Overseas registrants were granted a stay of execution and the SEC, in March 2004, extended this further so that compliance is first required by these companies for company years ending on or after 15 July 2006. The majority of European SEC registrants therefore needed to be in compliance by 31 December 2006. Prudent companies used the extra year to 'dry run' their compliance programme and iron out the deficiencies.

Case study

To indicate the reach of the Sarbanes-Oxley Act, a UK-based joint venture company under the control of a UK listed company with no US listing might be caught by, for instance, s 404 of the Act. If the other party to the joint venture were a UK company which was, for instance, a subsidiary of a Swiss company, which in turn had a secondary listing in the US, then the joint venture company might be impacted by the Act. This would be the case if the services that the joint venture company provided could be said to have a significant effect upon the effectiveness of internal financial control of, in this case, the Swiss company.

It would all depend on the materiality of the joint venture to the accounts of the Swiss company.

The question would then arise as to the responsibility for where the costs of s 404 compliance should fall with respect to a joint venture.

No doubt the respective audit committees of the parties would become involved in resolving these issues. The audit committees would also benefit from the assurance they could derive from the s 404 work done within the joint venture company.

The risk of US criminal charges extends as far as CEOs and CFOs of UK companies caught by the Act. This is partly a matter of the wording of the Act itself and also of other legal developments. Alun Jones, a leading QC advising the three NatWest bankers who were extradited in connection with the Enron scandal, has said:

> 'A director of a publicly listed UK company could be extradited to the US to be tried for fraud if his company's allegedly inaccurate reports are published in a US newspaper to a solitary shareholder … Many UK companies still believe that they need a US listing or a large US shareholder base before they are subject to US laws such as Sarbanes-Oxley, but this is not the case … A UK national may now be extradited to the US where he is accused of conduct which took place mostly in the UK – even where the UK authorities have declined to prosecute him … A new treaty signed in March 2003 removed the requirement for US authorities to present evidence when making an extradition request … The allegation of fraud itself, however unfounded, is now sufficient for an extradition to be granted. Evidence of wrongdoing is simply not required.'

While Sarbanes-Oxley has undoubtedly made a US listing a less attractive proposition for UK companies, notwithstanding the liquidity of the US market, it is of course difficult to extricate a UK company from its US listing and even more difficult to end the Sarbanes-Oxley obligations.

The Act also requires each company covered by the Act to have at least one 'financial expert' on its audit committee. The Act gives guidance on what such an expert should be, and required the SEC to firm up the definition of 'financial expert', which has been done. The US 'financial expert' is more than the UK's audit committee member with 'recent and relevant financial experience', and it certainly means someone with current or recent experience in drawing up financial statements of a broadly similar character to those which the audit committee scrutinises. Again, this places demands upon UK companies that are caught by the Act.

The Sarbanes-Oxley Act and the criminalisation of corporate governance E3.6

The fervour for criminalising corporate governance violations has perhaps reached its apogee in the US, although time will tell whether there is an appetite for further extension. As Tony Blair said:

> 'The response of the US Congress to the Enron and WorldCom scandals shows what governments can do wrong. In 2002 the Sarbanes-Oxley Act was, in the words of The Economist, "designed in a panic and rushed through in a blinding fervour of moral indignation".'[12]

Congressional votes in favour of the Sarbanes-Oxley Act were 522, with only three voting 'No' and nine not voting. Compare that with other quite recent congressional votes on issues where there was a high degree of consensus:

	Yes	No	Not voting
Legalising marijuana	93	310	31
Authorising force against Iraq	373	156	12
Securities Litigation Reform Act	387	130	15
Sarbanes-Oxley Act	522	3	9

The Sarbanes-Oxley Act sets maximum penalties for certain violations at 20 years in prison *and* a fine of $5,000,000 (Appendix 7) compared to, for instance, the following penalties for other offences:

Escaping from prison:	1–2 years
Kidnapping involving ransom:	3–5 years
Second-degree murder:	11–14 years
Air piracy:	20–25 years

Tony Blair, in his quite recent speech referred to above, went on to say:

> 'Inspired by the need for Congress to be seen to do something dramatic, Sarbanes-Oxley has imposed the threat of criminal penalties on managers and substantial new costs on American business: an average of $2.4m extra for auditing for each company. The burden is especially heavy on smaller companies, the real risk-takers in the market. Firms with a revenue of less than $100m per annum now pay out more than 2.5% of turnover in compliance costs. Cumulatively the costs run into billions of dollars.
>
> There is a delicious irony in this which illustrates the unintended consequences of regulation. Sarbanes-Oxley has provided a bonanza for accountants and auditors, the very professions thought to be at fault in the original scandals.'[13]

Selected sections of the Sarbanes-Oxley Act **E3.7**

SEC. 2. DEFINITIONS.

(a) IN GENERAL.—In this Act, the following definitions shall apply:

[…]

(2) AUDIT.—The term "audit" means an examination of the financial statements of any issuer by an independent public accounting firm in accordance with the rules of the Board or the Commission (or, for the period preceding the adoption of applicable rules of the Board under section 103, in accordance with then-applicable generally accepted auditing and related standards for such purposes), for the purpose of expressing an opinion on such statements.

(3) AUDIT COMMITTEE.—The term "audit committee" means—

(A) a committee (or equivalent body) established by and amongst the board of directors of an issuer for the purpose of overseeing the accounting and financial reporting processes of the issuer and audits of the financial statements of the issuer; and

(B) if no such committee exists with respect to an issuer, the entire board of directors of the issuer.

SEC. 101. ESTABLISHMENT; ADMINISTRATIVE PROVISIONS.

(a) ESTABLISHMENT OF BOARD.—There is established the Public Company Accounting Oversight Board, to oversee the audit of public companies that are subject to the securities laws, and related matters, in order to protect the interests of investors and further the public interest in the preparation of informative, accurate, and independent audit reports for companies the securities of which are sold to, and held by and for, public investors. The Board shall be a body corporate, operate as a nonprofit corporation, and have succession until dissolved by an Act of Congress.

(b) STATUS.—The Board shall not be an agency or establishment of the United States Government, and, except as otherwise provided in this Act, shall be subject to, and have all the powers conferred upon a nonprofit corporation by, the District of Columbia Nonprofit Corporation Act. No member or person employed by, or agent for, the Board shall be deemed to be an officer or employee of or agent for the Federal Government by reason of such service.

(c) DUTIES OF THE BOARD.—The Board shall, subject to action by the Commission under section 107, and once a determination is made by the Commission under subsection (d) of this section—

(1) register public accounting firms that prepare audit reports for issuers, in accordance with section 102;

(2) establish or adopt, or both, by rule, auditing, quality control, ethics, independence, and other standards relating to the preparation of audit reports for issuers, in accordance with section 103;

(3) conduct inspections of registered public accounting firms, in accordance with section 104 and the rules of the Board;

(4) conduct investigations and disciplinary proceedings concerning, and impose appropriate sanctions where justified upon, registered public accounting firms and associated persons of such firms, in accordance with section 105;

(5) perform such other duties or functions as the Board (or the Commission, by rule or order) determines are necessary or appropriate to promote high professional standards among, and improve the quality of audit services offered by, registered public accounting firms and associated persons thereof, or otherwise to carry out this Act, in order to protect investors, or to further the public interest;

(6) enforce compliance with this Act, the rules of the Board, professional standards, and the securities laws relating to the preparation and issuance of audit reports and the obligations and liabilities of accountants with respect thereto, by registered public accounting firms and associated persons thereof; and

(7) set the budget and manage the operations of the Board and the staff of the Board.

(d) COMMISSION DETERMINATION.—The members of the Board shall take such action (including hiring of staff, proposal of rules, and adoption of initial and transitional auditing and other professional standards) as may be necessary or appropriate to enable the Commission to determine, not later than 270 days after the date of enactment of this Act, that the Board is so organized and has the capacity to carry out the requirements of this title, and to enforce compliance with this title by registered public accounting firms and associated persons thereof. The Commission shall be responsible, prior to the appointment of the Board, for the planning for the establishment and administrative transition to the Board's operation.

(e) BOARD MEMBERSHIP.—

(1) COMPOSITION.—The Board shall have 5 members, appointed from among prominent individuals of integrity and reputation who have a demonstrated commitment to the interests of investors and the public, and an understanding of the responsibilities for and nature of the financial disclosures required of issuers under the securities laws and the obligations of accountants with respect to the preparation and issuance of audit reports with respect to such disclosures.

(2) LIMITATION.—Two members, and only 2 members, of the Board shall be or have been certified public accountants pursuant to the laws of 1 or more States, provided that, if 1 of those 2 members is the chairperson, he or she may not have been a practicing certified public accountant for at least 5 years prior to his or her appointment to the Board.

(3) FULL-TIME INDEPENDENT SERVICE.—Each member of the Board shall serve on a full-time basis, and may not, concurrent with service

on the Board, be employed by any other person or engage in any other professional or business activity. No member of the Board may share in any of the profits of, or receive payments from, a public accounting firm (or any other person, as determined by rule of the Commission), other than fixed continuing payments, subject to such conditions as the Commission may impose, under standard arrangements for the retirement of members of public accounting firms.

(4) APPOINTMENT OF BOARD MEMBERS.—

(A) INITIAL BOARD.—Not later than 90 days after the date of enactment of this Act, the Commission, after consultation with the Chairman of the Board of Governors of the Federal Reserve System and the Secretary of the Treasury, shall appoint the chairperson and other initial members of the Board, and shall designate a term of service for each.

(B) VACANCIES.—A vacancy on the Board shall not affect the powers of the Board, but shall be filled in the same manner as provided for appointments under this section.

(5) TERM OF SERVICE.—

(A) IN GENERAL.—The term of service of each Board member shall be 5 years, and until a successor is appointed, except that—

(i) the terms of office of the initial Board members (other than the chairperson) shall expire in annual increments, 1 on each of the first 4 anniversaries of the initial date of appointment; and

(ii) any Board member appointed to fill a vacancy occurring before the expiration of the term for which the predecessor was appointed shall be appointed only for the remainder of that term.

(B) TERM LIMITATION.—No person may serve as a member of the Board, or as chairperson of the Board, for more than 2 terms, whether or not such terms of service are consecutive.

(6) REMOVAL FROM OFFICE.—A member of the Board may be removed by the Commission from office, in accordance with section 107(d)(3), for good cause shown before the expiration of the term of that member.

(f) POWERS OF THE BOARD.—In addition to any authority granted to the Board otherwise in this Act, the Board shall have the power, subject to section 107—

(1) to sue and be sued, complain and defend, in its corporate name and through its own counsel, with the approval of the Commission, in any Federal, State, or other court;

(2) to conduct its operations and maintain offices, and to exercise all other rights and powers authorized by this Act, in any State, without regard to any qualification, licensing, or other provision of law in effect in such State (or a political subdivision thereof);

(3) to lease, purchase, accept gifts or donations of or otherwise acquire, improve, use, sell, exchange, or convey, all of or an interest in any property, wherever situated;

(4) to appoint such employees, accountants, attorneys, and other agents as may be necessary or appropriate, and to determine their qualifications, define their duties, and fix their salaries or other compensation (at a level that is comparable to private sector self-regulatory, accounting, technical, supervisory, or other staff or management positions);

(5) to allocate, assess, and collect accounting support fees established pursuant to section 109, for the Board, and other fees and charges imposed under this title; and

(6) to enter into contracts, execute instruments, incur liabilities, and do any and all other acts and things necessary, appropriate, or incidental to the conduct of its operations and the exercise of its obligations, rights, and powers imposed or granted by this title.

(g) RULES OF THE BOARD.—The rules of the Board shall, subject to the approval of the Commission—

(1) provide for the operation and administration of the Board, the exercise of its authority, and the performance of its responsibilities under this Act;

(2) permit, as the Board determines necessary or appropriate, delegation by the Board of any of its functions to an individual member or employee of the Board, or to a division of the Board, including functions with respect to hearing, determining, ordering, certifying, reporting, or otherwise acting as to any matter, except that—

(A) the Board shall retain a discretionary right to review any action pursuant to any such delegated function, upon its own motion;

(B) a person shall be entitled to a review by the Board with respect to any matter so delegated, and the decision of the Board upon such review shall be deemed to be the action of the Board for all purposes (including appeal or review thereof); and

(C) if the right to exercise a review described in subparagraph (A) is declined or if no such review is sought within the time stated in the rules of the Board, then the action taken by the holder of such delegation shall for all purposes, including appeal or review thereof, be deemed to be the action of the Board;

(3) establish ethics rules and standards of conduct for Board members and staff, including a bar on practice before the Board (and the Commission, with respect to Board-related matters) of 1 year for former members of the Board, and appropriate periods (not to exceed 1 year) for former staff of the Board; and

(4) provide as otherwise required by this Act.

(h) ANNUAL REPORT TO THE COMMISSION.—The Board shall submit an annual report (including its audited financial statements) to the Commission, and the Commission shall transmit a copy of that report to the Committee on Banking, Housing, and Urban Affairs of the Senate, and the Committee on Financial Services of the House of Representatives, not later than 30 days after the date of receipt of that report by the Commission.

SEC. 103. AUDITING, QUALITY CONTROL, AND INDEPENDENCE STANDARDS AND RULES.

(a) AUDITING, QUALITY CONTROL, AND ETHICS STANDARDS.—

(1) IN GENERAL.—The Board shall, by rule, establish, including, to the extent it determines appropriate, through adoption of standards proposed by 1 or more professional groups of accountants designated pursuant to paragraph (3)(A) or advisory groups convened pursuant to paragraph (4), and amend or otherwise modify or alter, such auditing and related attestation standards, such quality control standards, and such ethics standards to be used by registered public accounting firms in the preparation and issuance of audit reports, as required by this Act or the rules of the Commission, or as may be necessary or appropriate in the public interest or for the protection of investors.

(2) RULE REQUIREMENTS.—In carrying out paragraph (1), the Board—

(A) shall include in the auditing standards that it adopts, requirements that each registered public accounting firm shall—

(i) prepare, and maintain for a period of not less than 7 years, audit work papers, and other information related to any audit report, in sufficient detail to support the conclusions reached in such report;

(ii) provide a concurring or second partner review and approval of such audit report (and other related information), and concurring approval in its issuance, by a qualified person (as prescribed by the Board) associated with the public accounting firm, other than the person in charge of the audit, or by an independent reviewer (as prescribed by the Board); and

(iii) describe in each audit report the scope of the auditor's testing of the internal control structure and procedures of the issuer, required by section404(b), and present (in such report or in a separate report)—

(I) the findings of the auditor from such testing;

(II) an evaluation of whether such internal control structure and procedures—

(aa) include maintenance of records that in reasonable detail accurately and fairly reflect the transactions and dispositions of the assets of the issuer;

(bb) provide reasonable assurance that transactions are recorded as necessary to permit preparation of financial statements in accordance with generally accepted accounting principles, and that receipts and expenditures of the issuer are being made only in accordance with authorizations of management and directors of the issuer; and

(III) a description, at a minimum, of material weaknesses in such internal controls, and of any material noncompliance found on the basis of such testing.

(B) shall include, in the quality control standards that it adopts with respect to the issuance of audit reports, requirements for every registered public accounting firm relating to—

(i) monitoring of professional ethics and independence from issuers on behalf of which the firm issues audit reports;

(ii) consultation within such firm on accounting and auditing questions;

(iii) Supervision of audit work;

(iv) hiring, professional development, and advancement of personnel;

(v) the acceptance and continuation of engagements;

(vi) internal inspection; and

(vii) such other requirements as the Board may prescribe, subject to subsection (a)(1).

(3) AUTHORITY TO ADOPT OTHER STANDARDS.—

(A) IN GENERAL.—In carrying out this subsection, the Board—

(i) may adopt as its rules, subject to the terms of section 107, any portion of any statement of auditing standards or other professional standards that the Board determines satisfy the requirements of paragraph (1), and that were proposed by 1 or more professional groups of accountants that shall be designated or recognized by the Board, by rule, for such purpose, pursuant to this paragraph or 1 or more advisory groups convened pursuant to paragraph (4); and

(ii) notwithstanding clause (i), shall retain full authority to modify, supplement, revise, or subsequently amend, modify, or repeal, in whole or in part, any portion of any statement described in clause (i).

(B) INITIAL AND TRANSITIONAL STANDARDS.—The Board shall adopt standards described in subparagraph (A)(i) as initial or transitional standards, to the extent the Board determines necessary, prior to a determination of the Commission under section 101(d), and such standards shall be separately approved by the Commission at the time of that determination, without regard to the procedures required by section 107 that otherwise would apply to the approval of rules of the Board.

(4) ADVISORY GROUPS.—The Board shall convene, or authorize its staff to convene, such expert advisory groups as may be appropriate, which may include practicing accountants and other experts, as well as representatives of other interested groups, subject to such rules as the Board may prescribe to prevent conflicts of interest, to make recommendations concerning the content (including proposed drafts) of auditing, quality control, ethics, independence, or other standards required to be established under this section.

(b) INDEPENDENCE STANDARDS AND RULES.—The Board shall establish such rules as may be necessary or appropriate in the public interest or for the protection of investors, to implement, or as authorized under, title II of this Act.

(c) COOPERATION WITH DESIGNATED PROFESSIONAL GROUPS OF ACCOUNTANTS AND ADVISORY GROUPS.—

(1) IN GENERAL.—The Board shall cooperate on an ongoing basis with professional groups of accountants designated under subsection (a)(3)(A) and advisory groups convened under subsection (a)(4) in the examination of the need for changes in any standards subject to its authority under subsection (a), recommend issues for inclusion on the agendas of such designated professional groups of accountants or advisory groups, and take such other steps as it deems appropriate to increase the effectiveness of the standard setting process.

(2) BOARD RESPONSES.—The Board shall respond in a timely fashion to requests from designated professional groups of accountants and advisory groups referred to in paragraph (1) for any changes in standards over which the Board has authority.

(d) EVALUATION OF STANDARD SETTING PROCESS.—The Board shall include in the annual report required by section 101(h) the results of its standard setting responsibilities during the period to which the report relates, including a discussion of the work of the Board with any designated professional groups of accountants and advisory groups described in paragraphs (3)(A) and (4) of subsection (a), and its pending issues agenda for future standard setting projects.

SEC. 204. AUDITOR REPORTS TO AUDIT COMMITTEES.

Section 10A of the Securities Exchange Act of 1934 (15 U.S.C. 78j–1), as amended by this Act, is amended by adding at the end the following:

"(k) REPORTS TO AUDIT COMMITTEES.—Each registered public accounting firm that performs for any issuer any audit required by this title shall timely report to the audit committee of the issuer—

(1) all critical accounting policies and practices to be used;

(2) all alternative treatments of financial information within generally accepted accounting principles that have been discussed with management officials of the issuer, ramifications of the use of such alternative disclosures and treatments, and the treatment preferred by the registered public accounting firm; and

(3) other material written communications between the registered public accounting firm and the management of the issuer, such as any management letter or schedule of unadjusted differences."

SEC. 301. PUBLIC COMPANY AUDIT COMMITTEES.

Section 10A of the Securities Exchange Act of 1934 (15 U.S.C. 78f) is amended by adding at the end the following:

"(m) STANDARDS RELATING TO AUDIT COMMITTEES.—

(1) COMMISSION RULES.—

(A) IN GENERAL.—Effective not later than 270 days after the date of enactment of this subsection, the Commission shall, by rule, direct the national securities exchanges and national securities associations to prohibit the listing of any security of an issuer that is not in compliance with the requirements of any portion of paragraphs (2) through (6).

(B) OPPORTUNITY TO CURE DEFECTS.—The rules of the Commission under subparagraph (A) shall provide for appropriate procedures for an issuer to have an opportunity to cure any defects that would be the basis for a prohibition under subparagraph (A), before the imposition of such prohibition.

(2) RESPONSIBILITIES RELATING TO REGISTERED PUBLIC ACCOUNTING FIRMS.—The audit committee of each issuer, in its capacity as a committee of the board of directors, shall be directly responsible for the appointment, compensation, and oversight of the work of any registered public accounting firm employed by that issuer (including resolution of disagreements between management and the auditor regarding financial reporting) for the purpose of preparing or issuing an audit report or related work, and each such registered public accounting firm shall report directly to the audit committee.

(3) INDEPENDENCE.—

(A) IN GENERAL.—Each member of the audit committee of the issuer shall be a member of the board of directors of the issuer, and shall otherwise be independent.

(B) CRITERIA.—In order to be considered to be independent for purposes of this paragraph, a member of an audit committee of an issuer may not, other than in his or her capacity as a member of the audit committee, the board of directors, or any other board committee—

(i) accept any consulting, advisory, or other compensatory fee from the issuer; or

(ii) be an affiliated person of the issuer or any subsidiary thereof.

(C) EXEMPTION AUTHORITY.—The Commission may exempt from the requirements of subparagraph (B) a particular relationship with respect to audit committee members, as the Commission determines appropriate in light of the circumstances.

(4) COMPLAINTS.—Each audit committee shall establish procedures for—

(A) the receipt, retention, and treatment of complaints received by the issuer regarding accounting, internal accounting controls, or auditing matters; and

(B) the confidential, anonymous submission by employees of the issuer of concerns regarding questionable accounting or auditing matters.

(5) AUTHORITY TO ENGAGE ADVISERS.—Each audit committee shall have the authority to engage independent counsel and other advisers, as it determines necessary to carry out its duties.

(6) FUNDING.—Each issuer shall provide for appropriate funding, as determined by the audit committee, in its capacity as a committee of the board of directors, for payment of compensation—

(A) to the registered public accounting firm employed by the issuer for the purpose of rendering or issuing an audit report; and

(B) to any advisers employed by the audit committee under paragraph (5)."

SEC. 302. CORPORATE RESPONSIBILITY FOR FINANCIAL REPORTS.

(a) REGULATIONS REQUIRED.—The Commission shall, by rule, require for each company filing periodic reports under section 13(a) or 15(d) of the Securities Exchange Act of 1934 (15 U.S.C. 78m, 78o(d)), that the principal executive officer or officers and the principal financial officer or officers, or persons performing similar functions, certify in each annual or quarterly report filed or submitted under either such section of such Act that—

(1) the signing officer has reviewed the report;

(2) based on the officer's knowledge, the report does not contain any untrue statement of a material fact or omit to state a material fact necessary in order to make the statements made, in light of the circumstances under which such statements were made, not misleading;

(3) based on such officer's knowledge, the financial statements, and other financial information included in the report, fairly present in all material respects the financial condition and results of operations of the issuer as of, and for, the period presented in the report;

(4) The signing officers—

(A) are responsible for establishing and maintaining internal controls;

(B) have designed such internal controls to ensure that material information relating to the issuer and its consolidated subsidiaries is made known to such officers by others within those entities, particularly during the period in which the periodic reports are being prepared;

(C) have evaluated the effectiveness of the issuer's internal controls as of a date within 90 days prior to the report; and

(D) have presented in the report their conclusions about the effectiveness of their internal controls based on their evaluation as of that date;

(5) the signing officers have disclosed to the issuer's auditors and the audit committee of the board of directors (or persons fulfilling the equivalent function)—

(A) all significant deficiencies in the design or operation of internal controls which could adversely affect the issuer's ability to record, process, summarize, and report financial data and have identified for the issuer's auditors any material weaknesses in internal controls; and

(B) any fraud, whether or not material, that involves management or other employees who have a significant role in the issuer's internal controls; and

(6) the signing officers have indicated in the report whether or not there are any significant changes in internal controls or in other factors that could significantly affect internal controls subsequent to the date of their evaluation, including any corrective actions with regard to significant deficiencies and material weaknesses.

SEC. 404. MANAGEMENT ASSESSMENT OF INTERNAL CONTROLS.

(a) RULES REQUIRED.—The Commission shall prescribe rules requiring each annual report required by section 13(a) or 15(d) of the Securities Exchange Act of 1934 (15 U.S.C. 78m, 78o(d)) to contain an internal control report, which shall—

(1) state the responsibility of management for establishing and maintaining an adequate internal control structure and procedures for financial reporting; and

(2) contain an assessment as of the end of the most recent fiscal year of the issuer, of the effectiveness of the internal control structure and procedures of the issuer for financial reporting.

(b) INTERNAL CONTROL EVALUATION AND REPORTING.—With respect to the internal control assessment required by subsection (a), each registered public accounting firm that prepares or issues the audit report for the issuer shall attest to, and report on, the assessment made by the management of the issuer. An attestation made under this subsection shall be made in accordance with standards for attestation engagements issued or adopted by the Board. Any such attestation shall not be the subject of a separate engagement.

SEC. 407. DISCLOSURE OF AUDIT COMMITTEE FINANCIAL EXPERT.

(a) RULES DEFINING "FINANCIAL EXPERT".—The Commission shall issue rules, as necessary or appropriate in the public interest and consistent with the protection of investors, to require each issuer, together with periodic reports required pursuant to sections 13(a) and 15(d) of the Securities Exchange Act of 1934, to disclose whether or not, and if not, the reasons therefor, the audit committee of that issuer is comprised of at least 1 member who is a financial expert, as such term is defined by the Commission.

(b) CONSIDERATIONS.—In defining the term "financial expert" for purposes of subsection (a), the Commission shall consider whether a person has, through education and experience as a public accountant or auditor or a principal financial officer, comptroller, or principal accounting officer of an issuer, or from a position involving the performance of similar functions—

(1) an understanding of generally accepted accounting principles and financial statements;
(2) experience in—
  (A) the preparation or auditing of financial statements of generally comparable issuers; and
  (B) the application of such principles in connection with the accounting for estimates, accruals, and reserves;
(3) experience with internal accounting controls; and
(4) an understanding of audit committee functions.

(c) DEADLINE FOR RULEMAKING.—The Commission shall—

(1) propose rules to implement this section, not later than 90 days after the date of enactment of this Act; and
(2) issue final rules to implement this section, not later than 180 days after that date of enactment.

SEC. 906. CORPORATE RESPONSIBILITY FOR FINANCIAL REPORTS.

(a) IN GENERAL.—Chapter 63 of title 18, United States Code, is amended by inserting after section 1349, as created by this Act, the following:

"§ 1350. Failure of corporate officers to certify financial reports

(a) CERTIFICATION OF PERIODIC FINANCIAL REPORTS.—Each periodic report containing financial statements filed by an issuer with the Securities Exchange Commission pursuant to section 13(a) or 15(d) of the Securities Exchange Act of 1934 (15 U.S.C. 78m(a) or 78o(d) shall be accompanied by a written statement by the chief executive officer and chief financial officer (or equivalent thereof) of the issuer.

(b) CONTENT.—The statement required under subsection (a) shall certify that the periodic report containing the financial statements fully complies with the requirements of section 13(a) or 15(d) of the Securities Exchange Act of 1934 (15 U.S.C. 78m or 78o(d) and that information contained in the periodic report fairly presents, in all material respects, the financial condition and results of operations of the issuer.

(c) CRIMINAL PENALTIES.—Whoever—

(1) certifies any statement as set forth in subsections (a) and (b) of this section knowing that the periodic report accompanying the statement does not comport with all the requirements set forth in this section shall

be fined not more than $1,000,000 or imprisoned not more than 10 years, or both; or

(2) Willfully certifies any statement as set forth in subsections (a) and (b) of this section knowing that the periodic report accompanying the statement does not comport with all the requirements set forth in this section shall be fined not more than $5,000,000, or imprisoned not more than 20 years, or both."

[...] (etc.)

Notes

1 More than doubled the cost for companies with an annual turnover of less than US$1 billion.

2 ICAEW's response to File No PCAOB-2007-02: 'Proposed Auditing Standard on an Audit of Internal Control over Financial Reporting that is Integrated with an Audit of Financial Statements' (12 July 2007), letter addressed to Nancy M Morris, Secretary, SEC.

3 Which replaces PCAOB Auditing Standard No 2.

4 Securities and Exchange Commission (Release No 34-55876; File No PCAOB-2007-02), 7 June 2007: Public Company Accounting Oversight Board; Notice of Filing of Proposed Rule on Auditing Standard No 5, An Audit of Internal Control over Financial Reporting that is Integrated with an Audit of Financial Statements, and Related Independence Rule and Conforming Amendments.

5 Release No 34-55876; File No PCAOB-2007-02, 7 June 2007, footnote 29.

6 The guidance for management on their implementation of s 404 is to be found in US Securities and Exchange Commission's Final Rule on 'Management's Reports on Internal Control over Financial Reporting and Certification of Disclosure in Exchange Act Periodic Reports' (11 June 2003) interpreting Section 404 (and also 302) of the Sarbanes-Oxley Act 2002. It can be downloaded from the SEC website. This definition of internal control over financial reporting is at page 83 of 93, endnote 51.

7 Committee of Sponsoring Organizations of the Treadway Commission (COSO). COSO comprises the five leading US professional bodies in this field, including AICPA, AAA and IIA.

8 COSO, 1992.

9 COSO (2013) Framework and Appendices volume, *Internal Control – Integrated Framework*, Committee of Sponsoring Organizations of the Treadway Commission, ISBN 978-1-93735-238-7, May 2013 (other volumes in the suite are: 'Internal Control over External Financial Reporting: A Compendium of Approaches and Examples', ISBN 978-1093735-240-0; 'Illustrative Tools for Assessing Effectiveness of a System of Internal Control', ISBN 978-1-93735-238-7; and 'Executive Summary', ISBN 978-1-93735-238-7).

10 *Guidance to Directors on Internal Control*, 'The Turnbull Report' (September 1999), ISBN 1 84152 010 1, The Institute of Chartered Accountants in England and Wales, Chartered Accountants' Hall, PO Box 433, Moorgate Place, London EC2P 2BJ. The report is on the ICAEW website.

11 Kinney, Jr, William R and Shepardson, Marcy L, (2011) 'Do Control Effectiveness Disclosures Require SOX 404(b) Internal Control Audits? A Natural Experiment with Small U.S. Public Companies', *Journal of Accounting Research*, 49 (2), pp 413–448, available at SSRN: http://ssrn.com/abstract=1533527.

12 Tony Blair, 26 May 2005, speech on compensation culture delivered at the Institute of Public Policy Research, University College, London.

13 See note 10 above.

Chapter E4

Audit Committee Oversight of Published Information

Introduction E4.1

In Chapter **E1**, we explained the nature of the audit committee's responsibilities for this matter and highlighted where companies may exercise their discretion in this area. Here we provide practical advice for audit committees on discharging their responsibility for the oversight of published financial information.

The audit committee's primary objective in this area is to be able to provide strong assurance to the board that the financial statements to be published are of high quality. They should be prepared in accordance with the law and applicable accounting standards. They should not be misleading.

Audit committee agenda items tend to bunch around the period which follows the financial year-end: the committee's responsibility for the scrutiny of financial statements is no exception. It is therefore sensible to bring forward as much as possible of the annual audit committee agenda to committee meetings earlier in the financial year.

Where there is a requirement to publish half-yearly or quarterly financial statements, clearly they will need to be considered by the audit committee at the appropriate time before they are adopted for publication. Even more frequent financial and perhaps other returns to regulators and to other parties will also need to be considered on a timely basis – unless the committee is opting to follow the approach of assessing the *process* which generates these returns rather than the information itself which ends up in these returns. But, either way, this should be done away from the year-end meetings at times during the year when the committee will have more time to devote to this.

Between the end of the year and the finalisation of the information that will appear in the annual report and accounts, the audit committee not only needs to scrutinise the draft annual financial statements, but also must determine or approve the wording of the directors' report on risk management and internal control, prior to the board consideration of it. It is reasonable for the board to expect the audit committee to express to the board the committee's opinion on the effectiveness of the entity's risk management and internal control, even if the board decides not to disclose that opinion publicly. Code Provision C.2.1 (**App1**) reads:

> 'The board should, at least annually, conduct a review of the effectiveness of the company's risk management and internal control systems and should report to shareholders that they have done so. The review should cover all material controls, including financial, operational and compliance controls.'

In addition, Listing Rule DTR 7.2.5 R requires companies to describe the main features of the internal control and risk management systems in relation to the financial reporting process.

Good practice is that the audit committee provides its own annual report to the board at the board meeting that signs off the annual financial statements. This annual report of the audit committee will recommend, with observations, the board's adoption of the annual financial statements, will include the committee's report and opinion on risk management and internal control, will provide the audit committee's opinion on the quality of the external audit and what arrangements should be made for external audit going forward, and will include the audit committee's opinion on the effectiveness of internal audit and other review agencies and specialist functions such as the compliance function and the risk management function.[1]

While much of the groundwork for each of these elements of the audit committee's annual report may be the subject of earlier meetings of the audit committee, there will remain much to be done during the 'window' between the end of the financial year and the board meeting that receives the audit committee's annual report. It is likely that more than one audit committee meeting will be needed during that window.

Significant issues **E4.2**

For years commencing on or after 1 October 2012, directors have to give a description of the significant issues considered by the audit committee in relation to the financial statements and how these issues were addressed. Code Provision C.3.8 (**App1**) refers to this. In their recently enhanced report to the shareholders, auditors must now draw attention to any significant issues and uncertainties in the financial statements to which the auditors consider that the audit committee has not drawn attention in a satisfactory manner. In the US, the Public Company Accounting Oversight Board (PCAOB) is in 2014 consulting on its proposal to require reporting of critical audit matters in order to identify to investors areas of uncertainty, at least where the uncertainty is known. This will impact on all companies listed in the US, including UK companies.

Items valued through the exercise of judgement **E4.3**

The committee needs a clear awareness of the items in the financial statements which are based significantly on the exercise of judgement, if they are likely to be material. The committee will probe these carefully at the year-end, but much of the committee's scrutiny of these items can be done as agenda items of meetings earlier in the year. Some examples might include:

- provisions for bad debts;
- provisions for losses on contracts;
- recognition of contingent liabilities;
- the timing of revenue recognition;
- the timing of expense recognition;
- valuations of work in progress;
- valuations based on assessments of contract progress;
- whether expenditure may be capitalised, or written off in the period incurred;
- fair value adjustments; and
- write-offs.

External auditors will challenge on matters within the financial statements which are based at least in part of the exercise of judgement. But where the judgement depends on sector-specific expertise, it is likely that the external auditors will defer to the directors' own judgement, unless it is clearly unreasonable or questionable in some way.

Since financial statements invariably contain uncertainties, the audit committee may be advised to stress test the risks inherent within them. Financial statements based on single-point estimates may disguise a wide range of possible outcomes. Towards one extreme the company may be at risk of insolvency not apparent from the figures in conventional financial statements. Confidence accounting is an approach which reveals the ranges of possible outcomes and their likelihoods. Probably at an audit committee meeting during the course of the financial year, the audit committee may wish to received and consider a set of financial statements, based on the previous year end, prepared on a confidence accounting basis.[2]

Case study

A home loans company makes a provision for mortgages in arrears. The company uses a complex algorithm to calculate the provision charge. The algorithm may factor in such criteria as:

- unemployment levels;
- interest rates;
- changes in house price indexes;
- the arrears position;
- credit ratings of customers;
- future projections concerning the above;
- future demand; and
- 'recency' – ie whether, to what extent and how recently a mortgage is performing, despite being in arrears.

It is conceivable that the results of the calculations could indicate that there is an accumulated over-provision by the company, brought forward from the previous year. Alternatively, the calculation could indicate that a further provision should be made this year. The swing between one and the other could amount to as much as 50% of the annual profits of the company. There might be a significant temptation to under-provide in order to turn in results which are up to market expectations. Or, if this year's results are good but next year may be a challenge, the finance director may wish to squirrel away additional provision which amounts to a hidden reserve to be utilised the following year.

So the audit committee will wish to examine the construction of the algorithm to determine whether it is sensitive to the right factors and whether it takes account of those factors in the right ways. The audit committee will wish to confirm that the algorithm has not changed or, if it has changed, that there is good reason for the change. It is just important that the audit committee satisfies itself that the construction of the algorithm is still up to date in view of commercial circumstances, etc. The audit committee will wish to make it clear that proposed changes to the algorithm should be brought to the attention of the audit committee in a timely way.

Of course, it is to be hoped that the external auditors take a similar interest in this matter, and it will be reassuring to the audit committee that this is so. But the audit committee should not rely on the external auditor to the extent that the audit committee fails to satisfy itself directly on these matters. Neither is the audit committee justified in assuming, without careful enquiry, that the external auditor has reviewed this thoroughly. The external auditor is likely to back off from refusing to agree with the company's predictions about, for instance, future demand for housing or future changes in house prices, since these are judgement calls which go to the heart of the expertise of management and the board. So, it will be up to the audit committee to be especially careful to consider such matters.

Smoothing E4.4

The audit committee will be alert to the issue of smoothing the financial performance of the company from one year to the next, in apparent defiance of the specific performance of the company in particular years. The opportunity to do so arises largely from the significant items in the financial statements which are valued through the exercise of judgement. To some extent, smoothing may be justified on the basis that it may provide a 'truer and fairer' view of financial performance in contexts where there are significant but uncertain judgement calls each year. Wildly fluctuating results could be misleading. But to smooth excessively is to mislead the market, and there are particular risks if smoothing involves mortgaging future financial results in the interest of this year's results. In summary, the audit committee needs to be made aware of where smoothing adjustments have been made, in order for the committee to satisfy itself that they are reasonable.

Changes in accounting practice E4.5

Changes in accounting practice are another matter of which the audit committee must be made aware. They may be justified, but changes of the creative/aggressive accounting variety need to be considered especially carefully if their rationale appears to be merely to improve the financial results.

Proposed changes in accounting practice should be brought to the early attention of the audit committee, and model sets of financial statements should be provided to show the likely impact.

Similarly, the audit committee should have early notice of changes in accounting standards and how they will impact on the financial statements. The committee should enquire whether the company will be well placed to implement the requisite changes in a timely way. There may also be a need to develop a communications strategy with the financial markets to explain the impact of the changes.

Contention between management and the auditors E4.6

The audit committee should enquire what were the main points of contention between the external auditor and those responsible for preparing the financial statements. These are likely to be issues for consideration by the audit committee. A bland question to the audit partner along these lines may not produce a very informative answer, beyond that there are no outstanding issues of concern. The audit committee should probe in more depth and enquire what the issues were which needed to be resolved before this impressive state of nirvana was arrived at. It is likely to be appropriate for the audit committee to ask to have sight of the agenda of the close-out meeting between the finance director and the external auditors. The chair of the audit committee and other audit committee members may ask to attend that close-out meeting on occasion.

Sometimes the audit committee may consider it needs to take outside advice on matters relating to its responsibilities. It should be empowered to do so by its terms of reference. Taking outside advice can, for instance, be useful in resolving a disagreement between the external auditor and management.

Certain timing issues may affect the reliability of the financial statements. We discuss these in Chapter **E6**.

Audit committees may ask the executive to provide the committee with an annual fraud report and annual avoidable losses report. These may indicate areas where the financial statements could impact on the financial statements. We discuss fraud and avoidable losses reports in Chapter **E5**.

Directors' assertions on compliance with Code Provisions which external auditors review: developments 1992–2007 **E4.7**

The Cadbury Committee (1992) proposed that external auditors should review a company's compliance with the 18 Provisions of the 1992 Cadbury Code if they were 'objectively verifiable'. This was resisted by external auditors, so that it was finally agreed that the external auditors would review only a few of the Provisions, namely those that were closest to the scope of the annual statutory audit. Over the years, the number of Provisions that external auditors review has been increased marginally, though the scope of this review has considerably narrowed. That is because auditor review has been removed from some of the Provisions, but this has been more than balanced by the expansion of the Code content in audit committees, which the auditors review.

The status quo has continued unchanged since 2003 and 2006. While the numbering of some of the Provisions in the Code has subsequently changed, the numbering of each of the Provisions which auditors continue to review remains the same in the 2010 version of the UK Corporate Governance Code (set out in full at **App1**) as is shown in columns 5 and 6 of the Table below.

Note that the auditor's review is much less than a full audit. For instance, the auditors are reviewing whether the directors' assertion that the board has an audit committee is correct, not whether the audit committee is an effective committee.

See also **H1.8** and **H1.16**.

Directors' assertions on compliance with Code Provisions which external auditors review: developments 1992 to 2007

1.	2.	3.	4.	5.	6.
1992 'Cadbury Code'[3]		1998 Combined Code		2003 and 2006 Combined Code[4,5]	
Equivalent Provision reference(s)	**Wording**	**Equivalent Provision reference(s)**	**Wording**	**Equivalent Provision reference(s)**	**Wording**
1.4	The board should have a formal schedule of matters specifically reserved to it for decision to ensure that the direction and control of the company is firmly in its hands	A.1.2	The board should have a formal schedule of matters specifically reserved to it for decision.	A1.1	No longer reviewed by the external auditors.
1.5	There should be an agreed procedure for directors in the furtherance of their duties to take independent professional advice if necessary, at the company's expense.	A.1.3	There should be a procedure agreed by the board of directors in the furtherance of their duties to take independent advice if necessary, at the company's expense.	A.5.2	No longer reviewed by the external auditors.
2.3	Non-executive directors should be appointed for specified terms and reappointment should not be automatic.	A.6.1	Non-executive directors should be appointed for specified terms subject to re-election and to Companies Act provisions relating to the removal of a director, and reappointment should not be automatic.	A.7.2	No longer reviewed by the external auditors.

1.	2.	3.	4.	5.	6.
1992 'Cadbury Code'[3]		**1998 Combined Code**		**2003 and 2006 Combined Code[4,5]**	
Equivalent Provision reference(s)	**Wording**	**Equivalent Provision reference(s)**	**Wording**	**Equivalent Provision reference(s)**	**Wording**
2.4	Non-executive directors should be selected through a formal process and both this process and their appointment should be a matter for the board as a whole.	A.6.2	All directors should be subject to election by shareholders at the first opportunity after their appointment, and to re-election thereafter at intervals of no more than three years. The names of directors submitted for election or re-election should be accompanied by sufficient biographical details to enable shareholders to take an informed decision on their election.	A.7.1	No longer reviewed by the external auditors.
3.1	Directors' service contracts should not exceed three years without shareholders' approval.				
3.2	There should be full and clear disclosure of directors' total emoluments and those of the chairman and highest-paid UK director, including pension contributions and stock options. Separate figures should be given for salary and performance-related elements and the basis on which performance is measured should be explained.				
3.3	Executive directors' pay should be subject to the recommendations of a remuneration committee made up wholly or mainly of non-executive directors.				

1.	2.	3.	4.	5.	6.
1992 'Cadbury Code'[3]		**1998 Combined Code**		**2003 and 2006 Combined Code[4,5]**	
Equivalent Provision reference(s)	**Wording**	**Equivalent Provision reference(s)**	**Wording**	**Equivalent Provision reference(s)**	**Wording**
4.4	The directors should explain their responsibility for preparing the accounts next to a statement by the auditors about their reporting responsibilities.	D.1.1	The directors should explain their responsibility for preparing the accounts and there should be a statement by the auditors about their reporting responsibilities.	C.1.1	The directors should explain in the annual report their responsibility for preparing the accounts and there should be a statement by the auditors about their reporting responsibilities.
4.5	The directors should report on the effectiveness of the company's system of internal control.	D.2.1	The directors should, at least annually, conduct a review of the effectiveness of the group's system of internal controls and should report to shareholders that they have done so. The review should cover all controls, including financial, operational and compliance controls and risk management.	C.2.1	The board should, at least annually, conduct a review of the effectiveness of the group's system of internal controls and should report to shareholders that they have done so. The review should cover all material controls, including financial, operational and compliance controls and risk management systems.

1.	2.	3.	4.	5.	6.
1992 'Cadbury Code'[3]		1998 Combined Code		2003 and 2006 Combined Code[4,5]	
Equivalent Provision reference(s)	**Wording**	**Equivalent Provision reference(s)**	**Wording**	**Equivalent Provision reference(s)**	**Wording**
4.3	The board should establish an audit committee of at least three non-executive directors with written terms which deal clearly with its authority and duties.	D.3.1	The board should establish an audit committee of at least three directors, all non-executive, with written terms of reference which deal clearly with its authority and duties. The members of the committee, a majority of whom should be independent non-executive directors, should be named in the report and accounts.	C.3.1	The board should establish an audit committee of at least three, or in the case of smaller companies, two members, who should all be independent non-executive directors. The board should satisfy itself that at least one member of the audit committee has recent and relevant financial experience.
There was no Cadbury Code Provision equivalent to the 2003 Code Provision C.3.2.		There was no 1998 Combined Code Provision equivalent to the 2003 Code Provision C.3.2.		C.3.2	The main role and responsibilities of the audit committee should be set out in written terms of reference and should include: to monitor the integrity of the financial statements of the company, and any formal announcements relating to the company's financial performance, reviewing significant financial reporting judgements contained in them; to review the company's internal financial controls and, unless expressly addressed by a

1.	2.	3.	4.	5.	6.
1992 'Cadbury Code'[3]		**1998 Combined Code**		**2003 and 2006 Combined Code[4,5]**	
Equivalent Provision reference(s)	**Wording**	**Equivalent Provision reference(s)**	**Wording**	**Equivalent Provision reference(s)**	**Wording**
					separate board risk committee composed of independent directors, or by the board itself, to review the company's internal control and risk management systems; to monitor and review the effectiveness of the company's internal audit function; to make recommendations to the board, for it to put to the shareholders for their approval in general meeting, in relation to the appointment, re-appointment and removal of the external auditor and to approve the remuneration and terms of engagement of the external auditor; to review and monitor the external auditor's independence and objectivity and the effectiveness of the audit process, taking into consideration relevant UK professional and regulatory requirements; to develop and implement policy on the engagement of the external

1.	2.	3.	4.	5.	6.
1992 'Cadbury Code'[3]		**1998 Combined Code**		**2003 and 2006 Combined Code**[4,5]	
Equivalent Provision reference(s)	**Wording**	**Equivalent Provision reference(s)**	**Wording**	**Equivalent Provision reference(s)**	**Wording**
					auditor to supply non-audit services, taking into account relevant ethical guidance regarding the provision of non-audit services by the external audit firm; and to report to the board, identifying any matters in respect of which it considers that action or improvement is needed and making recommendations as to the steps to be taken.
There was no Cadbury Code Provision equivalent to the 2003 Code Provision C.3.3		There was no 1998 Combined Code Provision equivalent to the 2003 Code Provision C.3.3		C.3.3	The terms of reference of the audit committee, including its role and the authority delegated to it by the board, should be made available. A separate section of the annual report should describe the work of the committee in discharging those responsibilities.

1.	2.	3.	4.	5.	6.
1992 'Cadbury Code'[3]		**1998 Combined Code**		**2003 and 2006 Combined Code[4,5]**	
Equivalent Provision reference(s)	**Wording**	**Equivalent Provision reference(s)**	**Wording**	**Equivalent Provision reference(s)**	**Wording**
There was no Cadbury Code Provision eqivalent to the 2003 Code Provision C.3.4		There was no 1998 Combined Code Provision equivalent to the 2003 Code Provision C.3.4		C.3.4	The audit committee should review arrangements by which staff of the company may, in confidence, raise concerns about possible improprieties in matters of financial reporting or other matters. The audit committee's objective should be to ensure that arrangements are in place for the proportionate and independent investigation of such matters and for appropriate follow-up action.
There was no Cadbury Code Provision equivalent to the 2003 Code Provision C.3.5.		There was no 1998 Combined Code Provision equivalent to the 2003 Code Provision C.3.5.		C.3.5	The audit committee should monitor and review the effectiveness of the internal audit activities. Where there is no internal audit function, the audit committee should consider annually whether there is a need for an internal audit function and make a recommendation to the board, and the reasons for the absence of such a function should be the relevant section of the annual report.

1.	2.	3.	4.	5.	6.
1992 'Cadbury Code'[3]		**1998 Combined Code**		**2003 and 2006 Combined Code[4,5]**	
Equivalent Provision reference(s)	**Wording**	**Equivalent Provision reference(s)**	**Wording**	**Equivalent Provision reference(s)**	**Wording**
There was no Cadbury Code Provision equivalent to the 2003 Code Provision C.3.6.		There was no 1998 Combined Code Provision equivalent to the 2003 Code Provision C.3.6.		C.3.6	C.3.6 The audit committee should have primary responsibility for making a recommendation on the appointment, reappointment and removal of the external auditors. If the board does not accept the audit committee's recommendation, it should include in the annual report, and in any papers recommending appointment or re-appointment, a statement from the audit committee explaining the recommendation and should set out reasons why the board has taken a different position.
There was no 'Cadbury' Code Provision equivalent to the 2003 Code Provision C.3.7.		There was no 1998 Combined Code Provision equivalent to the 2003 Code Provision C.3.7.		C.3.7	The annual report should explain to shareholders how, if the auditor provides non-audit services, auditor objectivity and independence is safeguarded.

1.	2.	3.	4.	5.	6.
1992 'Cadbury Code'[3]		1998 Combined Code		2003 and 2006 Combined Code[4,5]	
Equivalent Provision reference(s)	**Wording**	**Equivalent Provision reference(s)**	**Wording**	**Equivalent Provision reference(s)**	**Wording**
4.6	The directors should report that the business is a going concern, with supporting assumptions or qualifications as necessary.	D.1.3	The directors should report that the business is a going concern, with supporting assumptions or qualifications as necessary.	C.1.2	The directors should report that the business is a going concern, with supporting assumptions or qualifications as necessary.

Notes

1 The risk management and compliance functions are deemed to belong to the second line of defence, whereas internal audit is within the third line – see Chapter **G3**.

2 Harris, I, Mainelli, M and Onstwedder, J-P (2012) *Confidence Accounting: A Proposal*, ACCA, CISI and Long Finance, London, July 2012, available at http://www.accaglobal.com/content/dam/acca/global/PDF-technical/corporate-governance/tech-af-cap.pdf, accessed, 20 December 2013.

3 As set out in Note 14 to the 1992 Cadbury Code, which read: 'The company's statement of compliance should be reviewed by the auditors in so far as it relates to paragraphs 1.4, 1.5, 2.3, 2.4, 3.1 to 3.3 and 4.3 to 4.6 of the [Cadbury] Code.'

4 On 20 October 2004, the FSA issued instrument 2004/83 amending Listing Rule 12.43A entitled 'Listing Rules (Auditors responsibilities in relation to the Combined Code) instrument 2004'. This instrument came into force on 1 November 2004. The amendment required that: 'A company's statement under 12.43A(b) must be reviewed by the auditors before publication only insofar as it relates to Code Provisions C1.1, C2.1, C3.1, C3.2, C3.3, C3.4, C3.5, C3.6 and C3.7 of the Combined Code.' This requires the auditor to review nine of the ten objectively verifiable 2003 FRC Code Provisions relating to accountability and audit.

5 The tenth accountability and audit Code Provision (C1.2 on going concern) was covered by Listing Rule 12.43(v). The FSA had not changed the Listing Rule requirement under 12.43(v) that a statement by the directors that the business is a going concern (with supporting assumptions or qualifications as necessary) was to be included in the annual report and accounts and such a statement was to be reviewed by the auditor before publication.

Chapter E5

Audit Committee Oversight of Risk Management and Internal Control

Introduction **E5.1**

In Chapter **E1**, we explained the nature of the committee's responsibilities for this matter and highlighted where companies may exercise their discretion in this area. Here we provide practical advice for audit committees on discharging their oversight responsibility for risk management and internal control. We start with a discussion of how the audit committee may benefit from the work that internal audit does. However, there is more to it than that, and we end this chapter with a consideration of other issues important to the committee's assessment of the effectiveness of risk management and internal control.

Risk management and internal control are heavily overlapping processes. COSO's enterprise risk management framework makes it clear that ERM incorporates all of internal control:

> 'Internal control is an integral part of enterprise risk management. This enterprise risk management framework encompasses internal control, forming a more robust conceptualization and tool for management. Internal control is defined and described in Internal Control – Integrated Framework.'[1]

So, internal control is an important part of risk management. In turn, risk management is an important component of an organisation's internal governance processes. Figure 1 sets out this interconnectedness.

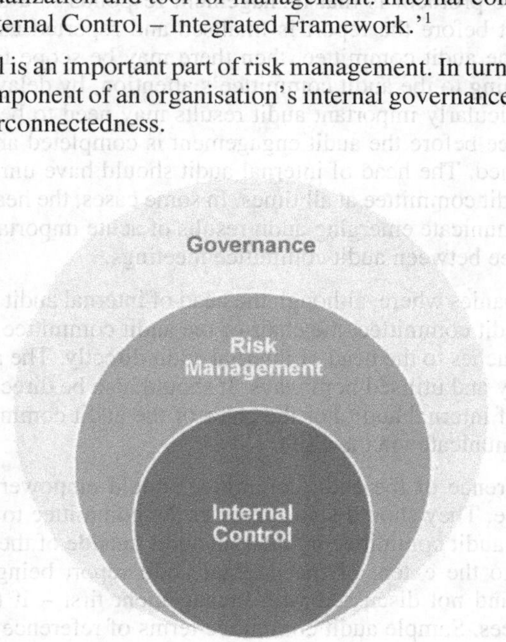

Figure 1

In assessing the effectiveness of risk management and internal control, consideration should be given to the whole of a group of companies and over the entire period that the assessment applies to. The US approach, for instance under the Sarbanes-Oxley Act, s 404 of making the assessment as of a point in time, is conceptually flawed.

Reliance on internal audit **E5.2**

Where there is an internal audit function, it is usual practice for the results of internal audit work to be reported to each audit committee meeting by the head of internal audit. This will then be the principal, regular way in which the audit committee learns about the effectiveness of risk management and internal control. Other review functions, such as the compliance function, are likely to report in a similar way to the audit committee. The audit committee should approve in advance the planned, annual programme of future internal audit engagements, and should approve subsequent variations from that agreed plan. Considering the results of internal audit work, delivered against the previously approved audit plan, therefore 'squares the circle' in enabling the audit committee to move towards formulating its own opinion on the effectiveness of risk management and internal control.

The audit committee should satisfy itself that internal audit results are not inappropriately delayed from being brought to the audit committee's attention. For instance, if the protocol is that management responds to a draft internal audit engagement report before the report is finalised and reported usually in summary form through to the audit committee, then there may be scope for management to delay matters coming to the audit committee's attention, by delaying responding to audit reports. Particularly important audit results may need to be communicated to the audit committee before the audit engagement is completed and before the draft audit report is issued. The head of internal audit should have unrestricted access to the chair of the audit committee at all times. In some cases, the head of internal audit may need to communicate emerging audit results of acute importance to the chair of the audit committee between audit committee meetings.

We know of companies where, although the head of internal audit has open access to the chair of the audit committee, the chair of the audit committee is never proactive in initiating approaches to the head of internal audit directly. The access opportunity should be two-way and utilised both ways. It should also be direct – in other words, neither the head of internal audit nor the chair of the audit committee should feel it necessary to communicate via the CEO.

The terms of reference of the audit committee should empower the committee to take outside advice. They should also empower the committee to commission work to be done for the audit committee by internal audit outside of the approved internal audit plan, even to the extent of the internal audit report being addressed to the audit committee and not discussed with management first – if that is appropriate in the circumstances. Sample audit committee terms of reference are to be found in **App4.1–App4.7**.

Overview of audit committee responsibilities **E5.3**

Case study

The importance of a direct reporting line at all times for internal audit to the audit committee is illustrated by this case which led to the chairman of the board, after conferring with the independent directors, dismissing the chief executive. The case also illustrates the importance of an audit committee having the authority and being able to meet without any executives being present at the meeting or even without the executives knowing that the meeting has taken place. The case further illustrates that the audit committee may commission internal audit engagements to be done directly for the audit committee, and that internal audit is an audit of *management* for the board, *not just an audit* for management.

The head of internal audit used his direct reporting line to the chair of the audit committee to arrange to meet the chair of the audit committee confidentially. In that meeting, he disclosed his concerns about allegations relating to the chief executive's conduct. The chair of the audit committee then convened a special meeting of the audit committee. No executives, apart from the head of internal audit, were invited to that meeting or knew that the meeting was taking place. The head of internal audit was invited to attend part of that meeting.

During that special audit committee meeting, the committee decided to ask internal audit to investigate the matter further and report back to the committee directly. Internal audit arranged for their audit fieldwork to coincide with the chief executive's annual vacation. Their audit work confirmed their fears, which they relayed to the audit committee.

The chair of the audit committee had, of course, kept the chair of the board informed throughout. When the chief executive returned from holiday, the chairman dismissed him.

Some audit committees ask that the full version of each internal audit engagement report is contained within its agenda papers. Others prefer just an executive summary of each. Still others are content with just a paragraph or two which give 'the big picture' on each completed audit engagement. Too much text makes it difficult for the reader to see the wood for the trees, and audit committees are usually overloaded with too much to do and too much to read. We consider it is preferable not to circulate the full audit engagement report if the committee member is only expected to read the executive summary at the beginning of it.

Case study

An NHS acute hospital board is approximately numerically balanced between executive and non-executive directors. Each non-executive director 'shadows' a particular executive director. It gives the non-executive director an opportunity to get more involved. A non-executive director is expected to take a special interest in the work of the executive director and, for instance, to raise in advance of a board meeting any questions he or she has about matters relating to that executive director's responsibilities or reports to the board. The non-executive director is also a source of support and counsel for the executive director.

In this case, the non-executive director who shadows the finance director is the only member of the audit committee who receives the full version of each internal audit engagement report. He is expected to have studied each in advance of the audit committee meeting and to have raised any questions with the head of internal audit in advance of the meeting.

The other members of the audit committee study a consolidated report from the head of internal audit which contains approximately two paragraphs on each internal audit completed, together with information on outstanding audit points from earlier audits, and information on audit progress against plan.

Internal audit should flag, for the audit committee's attention, outstanding issues of importance, arising from internal audit work, which have not been attended to satisfactorily by management.

The Internal Auditing Standards of the IIA (**App8**) put it like this:

> **'Communicating the Acceptance of Risks**
>
> 'When the chief audit executive concludes that management has accepted a level of risk that may be unacceptable to the organization, the chief audit executive must discuss the matter with senior management. If the chief audit executive determines that the matter has not been resolved, the chief audit executive must communicate the matter to the board.'
>
> **'Interpretation:**
>
> *'The identification of risk accepted by management may be observed through an assurance or consulting engagement, monitoring progress on actions taken by management as a result of prior engagements, or other means. It is not the responsibility of the chief audit executive to resolve the risk.'*[2]

Whenever these Standards refer to 'the board', it is legitimate to substitute 'the audit committee', as the Standards' definition of 'board' explains:

> 'The highest level of governing body charged with the responsibility to direct and/or oversee the activities and management of the organization. Typically, this includes an independent group of directors (e.g., a board of directors, a supervisory board, or a board of governors or trustees). If such a group does not exist, the "board" may refer to the head of the organization. "Board" may refer to an audit committee to which the governing body has delegated certain functions.'[3]

It is best practice for the audit committee to meet with the head of internal audit without any others who are usually in attendance at audit committee meetings being present for this private session. This should happen at each audit committee meeting. It is probably best for it to happen at the start of the meeting so as to flag issues which will arise during the meeting. This provides an opportunity for the head of internal audit to express concerns candidly to the audit committee without his or her colleague executives listening to every word being spoken. It is an opportunity for the audit committee to explore whether any scope restrictions are being placed upon internal audit which may impact upon the value of internal audit's reports to the audit committee. The audit committee will also, from time to time, have private sessions with the external auditor.

Case study

The internal audit function undertook an audit of an important operating unit in the Far East. Very quickly, they discovered that a fundamental company control was not being applied – the front office was not segregated from the back office.

Back in London, senior management asked them to tone down their report to the audit committee in order to avoid worrying the audit committee. Senior management pointed out that this Far East operating unit was very important to the company – at that time, it was earning about half the group profits. Senior management said they did not wish anything to occur which might demotivate management and staff in that Far East office. They might have said, but did not, that their year-end bonuses were also at stake.

Internal audit obliged, and toned down their report to the audit committee. Their anodyne language failed to alert the audit committee to the gravity of the problem.

Some months later, after the year-end, the company failed. A major fraud in that Far East office had been occurring at the time that the audit fieldwork had been done, and had grown considerably after the end of the audit.

The auditors had failed to discover the fraud. They had also failed to communicate effectively to the audit committee the scale of the control weakness which they had discovered. It could be argued that they had allowed their professional judgement to be subordinated to that of management's – and the audit committee had been unaware of these undercurrents.

Assessing internal control effectiveness E5.4

The 1994 Rutteman guidance, on the 1992 Cadbury Code provision on assessing internal control effectiveness, and the 1999 Turnbull guidance, on the amended Provision in the 1998 Combined Code, both stipulated that a proper assessment of internal control effectiveness should consider both *process* and *results* or *outcomes*. So, the audit committee needs to know whether there have been any *outcomes* that indicate risk management and internal control have failed. But it is not enough to consider outcomes alone. There may have been outcomes which have not yet been discovered, which (if known about) would indicate that risk management and internal control had failed significantly. On the other hand, there may be no such outcomes, known about or not, and yet it would be unsafe to consider that risk management and internal control have been effective: the system of risk management and internal control may be exceedingly flaky, hardly justifying an 'effective' conclusion – it may be just that the system's weaknesses have not yet been exploited.

So the guidance is that the audit committee needs to consider *outcomes* as well as *processes*. In terms of outcomes, at the very least the audit committee should consider whether there is anything referred to in the annual report and accounts which is a consequence, at least in part, of ineffective risk management and internal control. If so, the audit committee has to conclude that risk management and internal control have not been entirely effective.

The audit committee then needs to consider the process of risk management and internal control. Our preferred approach is for the audit committee to consider each of the five COSO essential control components in turn over the course of the year. Or, preferably, to consider each of COSO's eight essential components of *enterprise risk management* – which incorporate the five COSO control components (see **E5.9** below). The audit committee's consideration can be informed by a report on each to the audit committee provided by management, and by what else the audit committee has learnt during the course of the year. The Turnbull guidance is closely aligned to these COSO frameworks. Companies caught by the US Sarbanes-Oxley Act 2002 are required to assess the effectiveness of internal financial control using a recognised internal control framework, so there is ample justification for applying COSO to this (see Chapter **E3**).

An advantage of considering the effectiveness of each of the COSO components is that the burden is not expanded *pro rata* if the audit committee has a mandate to assess the effectiveness of *all* internal control, not just internal *financial* control. This is because the five COSO internal control components contribute to the achievement of financial, operational and compliance objectives. In the UK, the Corporate Governance Code stipulates that the board should consider the effectiveness of financial, operational and compliance control as well as risk management.

Fraud and avoidable losses reports for the audit committee E5.5

Some audit committees ask the executive to report to the committee on frauds and avoidable losses which are exceptional in size or exceptional in character. Such events may impact on the financial statements. They are also likely to be indicative of ineffective internal control. Making this a regular, standards report avoids the risk that management might fail to realise that the audit committee would wish to be informed of such matters.

Usually, this is tabled at the post year-end meeting of the audit committee. It may have a broader scope so that it covers non-fraudulent avoidable losses as well; or avoidable losses may be the subject of a separate report. The audit committee will stress diplomatically that their request should not be construed as indicating a perception that management is, or has been, reluctant to keep the audit committee properly informed in all respects.

Preparing this report is likely to fall to the finance director or to the company secretary. In turn, they are likely to need to obtain assurances from other key executives within the business, as a basis for formulating their report. No doubt the executive will ask for clarification as to the nature of the frauds and avoidable losses to which the audit committee wishes the report to refer. A short definition could be:

'Frauds and avoidable losses which have occurred and which have been exceptional in size or in character, as well as any others about which senior management considers the audit committee would wish to be informed.'

For our purposes here, 'fraud' can be defined as:

'Dishonesty for gain often with attempted concealment.'

'Avoidable loss' in this context is non-fraudulent damage to the business through a lack of effectiveness of governance processes, risk management or internal control of the enterprise (which includes the business and its business partners). Included should be material, tangible losses and also reputational ones – for instance, significant challenges to the entity's reputation with the regulator or with its shareholders. To use a tennis analogy, it is the unforced errors that the audit committee needs to know about – when they have significantly affected results or indicate significant weaknesses of approach.

Those that are 'exceptional in size' are those that make a noticeable difference to results – either the published financial statements or the narrative parts of the annual report, or to other aspects of the entity's results *even if the information is not disclosed publicly*.

Those that are 'exceptional in character' are those that the entity should not expect in the normal course of business, or which 'sound a serious alert' which needs attention.

The third category of 'others about which the audit committee would wish to be informed' is intended to encourage management to be open with the audit committee about significant events or outcomes which, while they might not literally fit into either of the above two 'exceptional' categories, are nevertheless matters about which management should realise the audit committee should be informed.

The period covered by the report should be the financial year recently ended and also the period between the end of that year and the date of the report. That is the period to be covered by the directors' review of the effectiveness of internal control, in accordance with the Turnbull Report. An interim report to an earlier meeting of the audit committee would be appropriate on matters of particular gravity.

The scope of the report should cover all businesses which are consolidated into the published results that are the oversight responsibility of the audit committee. Again, this is consistent with the Turnbull Report requirements.

The report could be very brief – it could even just say that there is nothing to report. This would still be valuable to the audit committee, as well as very reassuring.

The audit committee needs to know about these matters, especially as they could (a) impact upon the financial statements; and/or (b) indicate weaknesses in risk management and internal control to be attended to. The audit committee, on behalf of the board, has to satisfy itself on the reliability of the financial statements and the effectiveness of risk management and internal control. The audit committee needs to formally ask for this information as, were it not to do so, management inadvertently might not disclose these matters to the audit committee, presuming the audit committee were not interested. In essence, this report serves a purpose for the audit committee which is not so dissimilar from the purpose of the 'letter of representation' for the external auditor.

The external auditor's 'management letter' E5.6

While the scope of the external auditor's 'management letter' is broader than just internal control matters, covering, for instance, tax matters too, it is a report which the audit committee needs before the audit committee concludes on the effectiveness of risk management and internal control. The external audit is an audit of the financial statements, not a comprehensive audit of risk management and internal control – so we should not expect the external auditor's management letter to be a definitive guide to the effectiveness of the client's system of risk management and internal control. But it is prudent for the audit committee to check that there are no matters within the management letter which impact significantly on their assessment of effectiveness. The audit committee will also wish to ensure that management is attending to the matters raised within this management letter, as is appropriate.

A significant point is that the timing of this letter needs to be brought forward to the meeting of the audit committee which takes place shortly after the end of the financial year. This is the meeting that scrutinises the financial statements and concludes on risk management and internal control effectiveness. This conclusion has to be made before the finalisation of the wording of the statement on internal control, which appears in the directors' corporate governance statement within the annual report. It will be a responsibility of the audit committee to approve the wording of that statement.

Whistleblowing E5.7

The 2003 Combined Code included this Provision within the section on audit committees:

> 'The audit committee should review arrangements by which staff of the company may, in confidence, raise concerns about possible improprieties in matters of financial reporting or other matters. The audit committee's objective should be to ensure that arrangements are in place for the proportionate and independent investigation of such matters and for appropriate follow-up action.'[4]

The Provision continues unchanged into the 2012 UK Corporate Governance Code (Provision C.3.5, **App1**). While this can be regarded as a separate responsibility of the audit committee, we prefer to regard it as part of the committee's responsibility to oversee governance processes, risk management and internal control.

Other related audit committee responsibilities E5.8

Audit committees will need to oversee the risk and control implications of major business changes – such as significant systems changes, relocation of business, mergers and acquisitions, outsourcings, and so on.

When key processes are outsourced, some of the entity's internal control takes place within the service provider's business. The audit committee needs assurance about those parts of the system of internal control, as well as assurances that there are sufficient rights of access for audit purposes.

Comparing COSO's Internal Control and Enterprise Risk Management components **E5.9**

The table below defines the key components of internal control and enterprise risk management, according to COSO. Readers will note that COSO's 2013 revised definitions have caught the mood of the times and are more sophisticated than those of 1992.

Component	COSO: Internal Control – Integrated Framework (1992)	COSO: Internal Control – Integrated Framework (2013)[5]	COSO: Enterprise Risk Management – Integrated Framework (2004)
Environment	**'Control environment** – *The control environment sets the tone of an organization, influencing the control consciousness of its people. It is the foundation for all other components of internal control, providing discipline and structure. Control environment factors include the integrity, ethical values and competence of the entity's people; management's philosophy and operating style; the way management assigns authority and responsibility, and organizes and develops its people; and the attention and direction provided by the board of directors.*'[6]	**'Control environment** – *The control environment is the set of standards, processes, and structures that provide the basis for carrying out internal control across the organization. The board of directors and senior management establish the tone at the top regarding the importance of internal control including expected standards of conduct. Management reinforces expectations at the various levels of the organization; the parameters enabling the board of directors to carry out its governance oversight responsibilities; the organizational structure and assignment of authority and responsibility; the process for attracting, developing, and retaining competent individuals; and the rigor around performance measures, incentives, and rewards to drive accountability for performance. The resulting control environment has a pervasive impact on the overall system of internal control.*'	**'Internal environment** *– Management sets a philosophy regarding risk and establishes a risk appetite. The internal environment sets the basis for how risk and control are viewed and addressed by an entity's people. The core of any business is its people – their individual attributes, including integrity, ethical values and competence – and the environment in which they operate.*'[7] *'The internal environment encompasses the tone of an organization, influencing the risk consciousness of its people, and is the basis for all other components of enterprise risk management, providing discipline and structure. Internal environment factors include an entity's risk management philosophy; its risk appetite; oversight by the board of directors; the integrity, ethical values and competence of the entity's people; and the way management assigns authority and responsibility, and organizes and develops its people.*'[8]

Component	COSO: Internal Control – Integrated Framework (1992)	COSO: Internal Control – Integrated Framework (2013)[5]	COSO: Enterprise Risk Management – Integrated Framework (2004)
Objective setting	[not a component within the concept of the COSO Internal Control Framework]	[not a component within the concept of the COSO Internal Control Framework, but see definition in this column of 'risk assessment']	**'Objective setting** – *Objectives must exist before management can identify potential events affecting their achievement. Enterprise Risk Management ensures that management has in place a process to set objectives and that the chosen objectives support and align with the entity's mission/vision and are consistent with its risk appetite.'*[9] *'Objectives are set at the strategic level, establishing a basis for operations, reporting and compliance objectives. Every entity faces a variety of risks from external and internal sources, and a precondition to effective event identification, risk assessment and risk response is establishment of objectives. Objectives are aligned with the entity's risk appetite, which drives risk tolerance levels for the entity.'*[10]
Event identification	[Included in 'Risk assessment' – see right hand column of this table]	[Included in 'Risk assessment' – see right hand column of this table]	**'Event identification** – *Potential events that might have an impact on the entity must be identified. Event identification involves identifying potential events from internal or external sources affecting achievement of objectives. It includes distinguishing between events that represent risks, those representing opportunities, and those that may be both. Opportunities are channelled back to management's strategy or objective-setting process.'*[11]

Component	COSO: Internal Control – Integrated Framework (1992)	COSO: Internal Control – Integrated Framework (2013)[5]	COSO: Enterprise Risk Management – Integrated Framework (2004)
			'Management identifies potential events that, if they occur, will affect the entity, and determines whether they represent opportunities or whether they might adversely affect the entity's ability to successfully implement strategy and achieve objectives. Events with negative impact represent risks, which require management's assessment and response. Events with positive impact represent opportunities which management channels back into the strategy and objective-setting processes. When identifying events, management considers a variety of internal and external factors that may give rise to risks and opportunities, in the context of the full scope of the organization.'[12] *'Enterprises operate in environments where factors such as globalization, technology, restructurings, changing markets, competition and regulation create uncertainty. Uncertainty emanates from an inability to precisely determine the likelihood that events will occur and the associated impacts. Uncertainty also is presented and created by the entity's strategic choices. For example, an entity has a growth strategy based on expanding operations to another country.* *This chosen strategy presents risks and opportunities associated with the stability of the country's political*

Component	COSO: Internal Control – Integrated Framework (1992)	COSO: Internal Control – Integrated Framework (2013)[5]	COSO: Enterprise Risk Management – Integrated Framework (2004)
			environment, resources, markets, channels, workforce capabilities and costs.'[13]
Risk assessment	*'Every entity faces a variety of risks from external and internal sources that must be assessed. A precondition to risk assessment is establishment of objectives linked at different levels and internally consistent. Risk assessment is the identification and analysis of relevant risks to achievement of objectives, forming a basis for determining how risks should be managed. Because economic, industry, regulatory and operating conditions will continue to change, mechanisms are needed to identify and deal with the special risks associated with change.'*[14]	*'Every entity faces a variety of risks from external; and internal sources. Risk is defined as the possibility that an event will occur and adversely affect the achievement of objectives. Risk assessment involves a dynamic and iterative process for identifying and assessing risks to the achievement of objectives. Risks to the achievement of these objectives from across the entity are considered relative to established risk tolerances. This risk assessment forms the basis for determining how risks will be managed.'* *'A precondition to risk assessment is the establishment of objectives, linked at different levels of the entity. Management specifies objectives within categories relating to operations, reporting, and compliance with sufficient clarity to be able to identify and analyse risks to those objectives. Management also considers the suitability of the objectives for the entity. Risk assessment also requires management to consider the impact of possible changes in the external environment and within its own business model that may render internal control ineffective.'*	**'Risk assessment** – *Identified risks are analyzed in order to form a basis for determining how they should be managed. Risks are associated with objectives that may be affected. Risks are assessed on both an inherent and a residual basis, with the assessment considering both risk likelihood and impact.'*[15] *'Risk assessment allows an entity to consider the extent to which potential events have an impact on achievement of objectives.* *Management assesses events from two perspectives – likelihood and impact – and normally uses a combination of qualitative and quantitative methods. The positive and negative impacts of potential events should be examined, individually or by category, across the entity. Risks are assessed on both an inherent and a residual basis.'*[16]

Component	COSO: Internal Control – Integrated Framework (1992)	COSO: Internal Control – Integrated Framework (2013)[5]	COSO: Enterprise Risk Management – Integrated Framework (2004)
Risk response	[Arguably covered in 'Risk assessment' and 'Control activities' – see rows above and below]	[Arguably covered in 'Risk assessment' and 'Control activities' – see rows above and below]	'**Risk response** – *Personnel identify and evaluate possible responses to risks, which include avoiding, accepting, reducing and sharing risk. Management selects a set of actions to align risks with the entity's risk tolerances and risk appetite.*'[17] '*Having assessed relevant risks, management determines how it will respond. Responses include risk avoidance, reduction, sharing and acceptance. In considering its response, management assesses the effect on risk likelihood and impact, as well as costs and benefits, selecting a response that brings residual risk within desired risk tolerances. Management identifies any opportunities that might be available, and takes an entity-wide, or portfolio, view of risk, determining whether overall residual risk is within the entity's risk appetite.*'[18]

Component	COSO: Internal Control – Integrated Framework (1992)	COSO: Internal Control – Integrated Framework (2013)[5]	COSO: Enterprise Risk Management – Integrated Framework (2004)
Control activities	*'Control activities are the policies and procedures that help ensure management directives are carried out. They help ensure that risk necessary actions are taken to address risks to achievement of the entity's objectives. Control activities occur throughout the organization, at all levels and in all functions. They include a range of activities as diverse as approvals, authorizations, verifications, reconciliations, reviews of operating performance, security of assets and segregation of duties.'*[19]	*'Control, activities are the actions established through policies and procedures that help ensure that management's directives to mitigate risks to the achievement of objectives are carried out. Control activities are performed at all levels of the entity, at various stages within business processes, and over the technology environment. They may be preventive or detective in nature and may encompass a range of manual and automated activities such as authorizations and approvals, verifications, reconciliations, and business performance reviews. Segregation of duties is typically built into the selection and development of control activities. Where segregation of duties is not practical, management selects and develops alternative control activities.'*	**'Control activities –** *Policies and procedures are established and executed to help ensure that the risk responses management selected are effectively carried out.'*[20] *'Control activities are the policies and procedures that help ensure that management's risk responses are carried out. Control activities occur throughout the organization, at all levels and in all functions. They include a range of activities – as diverse as approvals, authorizations, verifications, reconciliations, reviews of operating performance, security of assets and segregation of duties.'*[21]
Information and communication	*'Pertinent information must be identified, captured and communicated in a form and timeframe that enables people to carry out their responsibilities. Information systems produce reports, containing operational, financial and compliance-related information, that make it possible to run and control the business. They deal not only with internally generated data, but also information about external; events,*	*'Information is necessary for the entity to carry out internal control responsibilities to support the achievement of its objectives. Management obtains or generates and uses relevant and quality information from both internal and external sources to support the functioning of other components of internal control. Communication is the continual, iterative process of providing, sharing, and obtaining necessary information. Internal communication*	**'Information and communication –** *Relevant information is identified, captured and communicated in a form and timeframe that enable people to carry out their responsibilities. Information is needed at all levels of an entity for identifying, assessing and responding to risk. Effective communication also occurs in a broader sense, flowing down, across and up the entity. Personnel receive clear communications regarding their role and responsibilities.'*[23]

Component	COSO: Internal Control – Integrated Framework (1992)	COSO: Internal Control – Integrated Framework (2013)[5]	COSO: Enterprise Risk Management – Integrated Framework (2004)
	activities and conditions necessary to informed business decision-making and external reporting. Effective communication also must occur in a broader sense, flowing down, across and up the organization. All personnel must receive a clear message from top management that control responsibilities must be taken seriously. They must understand their own role in the internal control system, as well as how individual activities relate to the work of others. They must have a means of communicating significant information upstream. There also needs to be effective communication with external parties, such as customers, suppliers, regulators and shareholders.'[22]	*is the means by which information is disseminated throughout the organization, flowing up, down, and across the entity. It enables personnel to receive a clear message from senior management that control responsibilities must be taken seriously. External communication is twofold: it enables inbound communication of relevant external information, and it provides information to external parties in response to requirements and expectations.'*	*'Pertinent information is identified, captured and communicated in a form and timeframe that enable people to carry out their responsibilities. Information systems use internally generated data, and information from external sources, providing information for managing enterprise risks and making informed decisions relative to objectives. Effective communication also occurs, flowing down, across and up the organization. All personnel receive a clear message from top management that enterprise risk management responsibilities must be taken seriously. They understand their own role in enterprise risk management, as well as how individual activities relate to the work of others. They must have a means of communicating significant information upstream. There is also effective communication with external parties, such as customers, suppliers, regulators and shareholders.'*[24]

Component	COSO: Internal Control – Integrated Framework (1992)	COSO: Internal Control – Integrated Framework (2013)[5]	COSO: Enterprise Risk Management – Integrated Framework (2004)
Monitoring	**Monitoring –** *'Internal control systems need to be monitored – a process that assesses the quality of the system's performance over time. This is accomplished through ongoing monitoring activities, separate evaluations or a combination of the two. Ongoing monitoring occurs in the course of operations. It includes regular management and supervisory activities, and other actions personnel take in performing their duties. The scope and frequency of separate evaluations will depend primarily on an assessment of risks and the effectiveness of ongoing monitoring activities. Internal control deficiencies should be reported upstream, with serious matters reported to top management and the board.'*[25]	**Monitoring activities –** *'Ongoing evaluations, separate evaluations, or some combination of the two are sued to ascertain whether each of the five components of internal control, including controls to effect the principles within ach component, is present and functioning. Ongoing evaluations, built into business processes at different levels of the entity, provide timely information. Separate evaluations, conducted periodically, will vary in scope and frequency depending on assessment of risks, effectiveness of ongoing evaluations, and other management considerations. Findings are evaluated against criteria established by regulators, recognised standard-setting bodies or management and the board of directors, and deficiencies are communicated to management and the board of directors.'*	**'Monitoring** – *The entire enterprise risk management process is monitored, and modifications made as necessary. In this way, it can react dynamically, changing as conditions warrant. Monitoring is accomplished through ongoing management activities, separate evaluations of the enterprise risk management processes or a combination of the two.'*[26] *'Enterprise risk management is monitored – assessing the presence and functioning of its components over time. This is accomplished through ongoing monitoring activities, separate evaluations or a combination of the two. Ongoing monitoring occurs in the normal course of management activities. The scope and frequency of separate evaluations will depend primarily on an assessment of risks and the effectiveness of ongoing monitoring procedures. Enterprise risk management deficiencies are reported upstream, with serious matters reported to top management and the board.'*[27]

Turnbull reporting on significant failings or weaknesses in the system of internal control E5.10

A comparison between section 38 of the original Turnbull Report and its equivalent section 36 of the revised Turnbull Report indicates a tightening-up of the guidance.

Original section 38 (1999):

'In relation to Code Provision D.2.1, the board should summarise the process it (where applicable, through its committees) has applied in reviewing the effectiveness of the system of internal control. It should also disclose the process it has applied to deal with material internal control aspects of any significant problems disclosed in the annual report and accounts.

Revised section 36 (2005):

'In relation to Code Provision C.2.1, the board should summarise the process it (where applicable, through its committees) has applied in reviewing the effectiveness of the system of internal control and confirm that necessary actions have been or are being taken to remedy any significant failings or weaknesses identified from that review. It should also disclose the process it has applied to deal with material internal control aspects of any significant problems disclosed in the annual report and accounts.'

The addition of the clause 'and confirm that necessary actions have been or are being taken to remedy any significant failings or weaknesses identified from that review' requires the board to report not just about significant problems disclosed in the annual report and accounts but also on significant failings and weaknesses identified in their review, even if not disclosed in the annual report and accounts. Commentators have suggested that this will help to ensure that identified weaknesses are appropriately followed up, and thereby contribute to ongoing improvement in controls.

Revised 2014 guidance on risk management, internal control and going concern **E5.11**

In November 2013, the UK's Financial Reporting Council (FRC) issued its consultation on 'Risk Management, Internal Control and the Going Concern Basis of Accounting'; it being draft guidance to the directors of companies applying the UK Corporate Governance Code and associated changes to the Code.[28] The FRC's intention is to integrate Lord Sharman's proposals on going concern ('Going Concern and Liquidity Risk: Guidance for Directors (2009))[29] with an updated version of 'Internal Control: Guidance to Directors' (often referred to as the 'Turnbull Guidance'), last updated in 2005.

Following its consultation, the FRC plans to publish revised guidance in the first half of 2014 to apply to reporting periods beginning on or after 1 October 2014 with any consequential changes to the UK Corporate Governance Code to be incorporated into the FRC's revised Corporate Governance Code which is also planned to apply to reporting periods beginning on or after 1 October 2014.

Notes

1 COSO (2004), *Enterprise Risk Management*, Framework volume, chapter 1 on 'Definition' (p 33) and also in Executive Summary (p 25). (COSO's 1992 *Internal Control – Integrated Framework* has been superseded by its 2013 version, see www.COSO.org).

2 Standard 2600.

3 **App8**, Glossary.

4 Provision C.3.5, UK Corporate Governance Code (2012) – see **App1**.
5 Text in this column is drawn from COSO (2013) Executive Summary, *Internal Control – Integrated Framework*, Committee of Sponsoring Organizations of the Treadway Commission, ISBN 978-1-93735-238-7, May 2013, pp 4–5.
6 July 1994 Printed Edition, Vol 1, p 4 – Executive Summary.
7 Framework volume, Chapter 1 on 'Definition', p 22.
8 Framework volume, summary to Chapter 2 on 'Internal Environment', p 27.
9 Framework volume, Chapter 1 on 'Definition', p 34.
10 Framework volume, summary to Chapter 3 on 'Objective Setting', p 35.
11 Framework volume, Chapter 1 on 'Definition', p 22.
12 Framework volume, summary to Chapter 4 on 'Event identification', p 41.
13 Framework volume, Chapter 1 on 'Definition', p 13.
14 July 1994 Printed Edition, Vol 1, p 4 – Executive Summary.
15 Framework volume, Chapter 1 on 'Definition', p 22.
16 Framework volume, summary to Chapter 5 on 'Risk Assessment', p 49.
17 Framework volume, Chapter 1 on 'Definition', p 22.
18 Framework volume, summary to Chapter 6 on 'Risk Response', p 55.
19 July 1994 Printed Edition, Vol 1, p 4 – Executive Summary.
20 Framework volume, Chapter 1 on 'Definition', p 22.
21 Framework volume, summary to Chapter 7 on 'Control Activities', p 61.
22 July 1994 Printed Edition, Vol 1, pp 4–5 – Executive Summary.
23 Framework volume, Chapter 1 on 'Definition', p 22.
24 Framework volume, summary to Chapter 8 on 'Information and Communication', p 67.
25 July 1994 Printed Edition, Vol 1, pp 4–5 – Executive Summary.
26 Framework volume, Chapter 1 on 'Definition', p 22.
27 Framework volume, summary to Chapter 9 on 'Monitoring', p 75.
28 http://www.frc.org.uk/Our-Work/Publications/FRC-Board/Consultation-Paper-Risk-Management,-Internal-Contr-File.pdf, accessed 21 December 2013.
29 The reports of the Sharman Panel Inquiry into going concern and liquidity risks can be found at: http://www.frc.org.uk/Our-Work/Headline-projects/The-Sharman-Inquiry.aspx, accessed 21 December 2013.

Chapter E6

Audit Committee Oversight of External Audit

Introduction E6.1

In Chapter **E1**, we covered the nature of the committee's responsibilities for overseeing the external audit. Here we provide practical advice and information for audit committees on discharging their oversight responsibility for external audit.

The new audit regime E6.2

In December 2013, the European Commission came to provisional agreement with the European Parliament and Member States on measures to reform the external audit market with the intention of increasing audit quality, particularly of banks and listed companies, and re-establishing investor confidence in financial information, an essential ingredient for investment and economic growth in Europe. The European law will come into force around 2016, with a phase-in period.

The agreement amounts to a watering down of the Commission's original proposals following concerted, very conservative lobbying by the 'Big 4' accounting firms and their representatives across Europe of parliamentarians and ministers of Members States. Nevertheless the measures amount to changes that have the potential to be effective.

For public interest entities,[1] mandatory rotation of an audit firm will now be required only after 20 or 24 years (see below). The 'Big 4' firms, having achieved this extended period for mandatory rotation, are now reflecting on whether the more frequent future mandatory tendering requirement which companies are to be saddled with is the worst of both worlds – to the extent that it will entail regular extra costs and effort for both clients and audit firms with no guarantees of successful outcomes.

In Chapter **D7** we refer to the comparative success of parts of the MENA region in avoiding lengthy retention of the same audit firm, calling to question the resistance to mandatory audit firm tendering and rotation in the West. In Oman, an external auditor can only audit the same bank for a maximum of four years, and in Qatar for five years.[2] These requirements are taken in their stride within the region and do not appear to have caused concerns about extra costs, etc. which have been the basis of the lobbying in Europe.

In essence, we consider the resistance to reforming the audit market has been driven by the audit profession's tacit misinterpretation of its client as being management rather than the shareholders. The changes are intended to have a major impact in reducing excessive familiarity between the auditors and the boards and management teams of their clients and in enhancing the professional scepticism of auditors. Commissioner Barnier is quoted in December 2013 as saying 'It is now high time for auditors to meet the challenges of their role – a societal role.'[3]

Under the new rules, the audits of public interest entities[4] must be put out to tender every ten years at a maximum. Audit tenure (ie continuing with the same audit firm) may be extended once only for a second ten-year period, upon tender; or, if there is a joint audit, the extension may be a single further period of fourteen years. Member States may introduce required periods shorter than ten years, as has already been done by the Netherlands and Italy. From 2014 a retendering period of ten years will be a UK requirement under the 'soft law' guidance of the Financial Reporting Council.[5]

Where joint auditors are in place, the period of time the auditors can serve is extended to a maximum of 24 years. The intention is to encourage the appointment of joint auditors, as is already a requirement for large public companies in France. Under a system of 'joint audit', unlike a 'shared audit', both audit firms are responsible for the audit report and opinion. Joint audits are held to be likely to increase the degree of auditor scepticism. More importantly, joint audits provide the potential to enable mid-tier audit firms to gain experience of auditing large companies, and to encourage large companies to appoint their auditors from outside the 'Big 4' thus widening choice and reducing the risks associated with the 'Big-4' oligopoly. A key risk is the inadequacy of client choice if it is considered that appointing a 'Big-4' firm is necessary. Associated with this is the risk to the audit market generally if one or more of the 'Big-4' firms were to exit the audit market.

To enhance auditor independence by limiting the risk of conflicts of interest, when auditors are involved in decisions impacting the management of a company, there will be a cap on non-audit services and a blacklist of some advisory services such as tax advice and several other non-audit services especially those linked to the financial and investment strategy of the audit client. The cap will be set at 70% of the audit fee with respect to other fees generated for non-audit services other than those prohibited, based on a three-year average at the group level.

It is possible the new arrangements will have extra-territorial reach. For instance, a branch of a US bank in London may be caught, and therefore the US, parent as well, if part of the same legal entity.

Emerging issues **E6.3**

It has become an issue of concern that companies have rarely been putting their annual statutory audit out to tender. On average, FTSE 100 companies do so once every 17 years and decide to change their auditors on average once every 48 years. Until recently, Barclays Bank has not changed its auditors for well over 100 years. The question arises as to whether this compromises the independence of the auditor. There are also concerns about the concentration of the audit market into a 'Big Four' of audit firms with the implications of restricted choice, possibly insufficient competition, possible impacts on audit price and audit quality, and the systemic risk which would materialise if one or more of these firms exited the audit market. Consequently, in the 2010–12 parliamentary session, the audit profession was the subject of a House of Lords Economic Affairs Select Committee Inquiry into 'Auditors: Market Concentration and their Role' (see Chapter **H2**) which, in late 2011, led to a referral of the profession by the UK's Office of Fair Trading to the

Competition Commission. In parallel, in November 2011 the European Commission published their White Paper on the audit profession.

Meanwhile, it is suggested that the directors' report on their audit committee, within the annual report, should explain transparently their reasoning for their audit tendering decision. If a Big Four firm was chosen, they should explain their reasoning, especially if they considered it necessary to restrict their choice to a Big Four firm. Mid-tier firms contend they are well equipped to audit even multinational companies, making use of their international networks. The Big Four are also international networks of separate partnerships. The audit committee should consider carefully the appropriateness of any restrictive covenants which oblige the company to choose a Big Four firm, and endeavour to avoid such covenants.

In response to the global financial crisis, best practice is now emerging that the published report on the audit committee should highlight the main issues which had to be resolved between the company and the external auditors before the financial statements were finalised, explaining how these were addressed. This is in response to the fact that the auditor's report itself, although addressed to the shareholders, is usually only bland text, rarely with an audit qualification and usually limited to occasional 'emphasis of matter' statements which refer to important material contained elsewhere within the annual report which the auditor is relying upon. Even the rare qualification will be expressed in an uninformative way.

Use of the external auditor to undertake additional work should also be addressed clearly in the report of the audit committee. Additional work potentially impacts upon auditor independence. There have been significant examples recently of external auditors taking on major amounts of their clients' internal auditing, on the basis that it can be classified, according to the Auditing Practices Board's Ethical Standard No 5, as extended audit work – ie work which is closely related to the annual audit but which would not be essential to be done by the external auditor for the purposes of providing an audit opinion. The policy of the Chartered Institute of Internal Auditors is that external auditors should not be asked to do internal audit work, as a clear conflict exists here. Where this has occurred, it has not always been the case that the report of the audit committee has explained how this is justified and how compromises to the auditor's independence as an external auditor have been avoided. Furthermore, the audit committee's report has often been opaque on the extent to which the previous internal audit function has been scaled back, and how the audit committee has satisfied itself that the audit of risk management and internal control – particularly in the operational areas of the business as distinct from the areas of accounting and finance – has not been marginalised.

The UK Corporate Governance Code (Provision C.3.2) recommends that the audit committee should review the company's internal control and risk management systems, unless this is done by the board itself or by a separate risk committee comprising, as with the audit committee, independent directors (see also Chapter **D5**). If there is a separate board risk committee, it should be explained, either in the audit committee report or elsewhere in the corporate governance report, how these responsibilities are divided between the two committees and how coordination between them is achieved.

A suggestion is emerging that boards of all companies exposed to systemic risk should have risk committees of the board comprising independent directors. It is also being suggested that these committees should receive external, independent advice. It is further being suggested that this advice should not be obtained from the company's external auditors. In part, this is to provide an opportunity for non-Big Four firms and others to show large companies what they are capable of. In part, it is to preserve auditor independence. Looking at this topic generally, the global financial crisis and other events have shown that boards are operating in a partial assurance vacuum. It is difficult for boards to be confident that their policies are being implemented by management and that there are no banana skins round the corner (known or not to management) over which the company may slip in the future. Boards and their committees need independent advice. This is reasonably well addressed in the UK Corporate Governance Code (set out in full at **App1**). It is becoming better understood that the board should explain its policy on its committees (including the audit, risk, nominations and remuneration committees) obtaining independent and external advice. The audit committee's published report should explain how the independence of the internal audit function is achieved. With regard to external advice to the audit committee, this may be explained in the report of the audit committee.

In all of these matters, the emphasis should be on transparency, not mere box-ticking compliance using boilerplate wording. The shareholders need to see clearly how the board is approaching these and other matters.

The UK position **E.6.4**

Recent UK developments promulgated by the Financial Reporting Council require auditors to report by exception (or explicitly confirm there is no exception) as to whether the directors' description of the work of the audit committee appropriately addresses matters communicated by the auditor to the audit committee. There is now a requirement for public explanation by an audit committee of the entity's external audit arrangements (eg continuation with the same firm, or not; tendering the audit, or not, etc), and a public description of the material issues arising from the annual audit.

E6.5

Whereas the Sarbanes-Oxley Act 2002 makes the audit committee of a US listed company 'directly responsible for the appointment, compensation and oversight' of the external auditor who reports directly to the audit committee, in the UK under the Corporate Governance Code, the audit committee makes recommendations to the board, for the board to put to the shareholders for their approval in general meeting, in relation to the appointment, reappointment and removal of the external auditor and to approve the remuneration and terms of engagement of the external auditor.

The UK audit committee should have primary responsibility for making a recommendation on the appointment, reappointment and removal of the external auditors. If the board does not accept the audit committee's recommendation, companies compliant with the UK Corporate Governance Code will include in their annual report, and in any papers recommending appointment or reappointment, a statement from the audit committee explaining its recommendation and should set out the reasons why the board has taken a different position.

The UK is also more relaxed about the provision of non-audit services by the external auditor. The guidance is merely that the audit committee should:

(a) review and monitor the external auditor's independence and objectivity and the effectiveness of the audit process, taking into consideration relevant UK professional and regulatory requirements; and

(b) develop and implement policy on the engagement of the external auditor to supply non-audit services, taking into account relevant ethical guidance regarding the provision of non-audit services by the external audit firm; and that the audit committee should report to the board, identifying any matters in respect of which it considers that action or improvement is needed and making recommendations as to the steps to be taken.

Following the adoption by the Financial Reporting Council of this guidance as part of the 2003 Combined Code, the Auditing Practices Board (a subsidiary of the FRC) developed ethical standards for auditors which specify limited categories of work which external auditors should not undertake for their external audit clients. These ethical standards are the 'relevant UK professional requirements' referred to above. For instance, it is not permissible for the external auditor to assume a management role for an audit client. However, unlike the US approach, the main thrust of these UK ethical standards is to design and apply safeguards where there may be potential conflicts, so that most categories of non-audit work can continue to be done.

This puts a particular onus on the UK audit committee to satisfy itself that the total mix and quality of work that the external auditor does for the client does not threaten the effectiveness of the external audit itself. For instance, the external auditor should not have to audit their own work. The audit committee needs to satisfy itself that the external auditor is not charged an artificially low fee for the audit[6] in anticipation of more remunerative consulting work – which may result in the audit itself being inadequately resourced. The audit committee will need to satisfy itself that the quantum of non-audit work which the audit firm does for the company is not such as to discourage the audit firm from taking a robust stand with the client on audit matters.

One issue that needs to be considered carefully is the vexed matter of whether it is acceptable for audit committees to generally frown upon their companies giving non-audit work to their external auditors. Our impression is that the 'Big Four' are lobbying hard to modify audit committees' behaviour so it becomes more liberal. Even in the US, where the Sarbanes-Oxley Act 2002 intended to outlaw most forms of non-audit work being provided by a company's external auditors, it seems that the Big Four are finding ways round this. In the UK, it appears that the Big Four are irritated that audit committees are interpreting the guidance within the Smith Report on Audit Committees (now updated as the December 2010 FRC's Guidance on Audit Committees), and the consequential wording within the UK Corporate Governance Code, as meaning that it is usually better to give non-audit work to a firm who are not the external auditors.

One of the proposals in the 2007 FRC paper on widening auditor choice[7] is that the FRC should consider developing guidance for audit committees which would have the effect, if audit committees heeded the advice, of relaxing the reluctance of audit committees to agree to their companies passing non-audit work to their external auditors. In other words, the Big Four are not supportive that audit committees are applying higher standards than the APB's Ethical Standards for auditors. It does seem unedifying to enlist the services of the FRC with the intention of lowering *de facto* standards.

US requirements E6.6

The US Sarbanes-Oxley Act 2002 identified eight categories of 'prohibited activities' which must not be sourced from the external audit firm:

1. book-keeping and related services;
2. financial information systems;
3. appraisals and valuations;
4. actuarial services;
5. internal audit outsourcing;
6. management functions or human resources;
7. broker, dealer or investment advisor services; and
8. legal services and expert services.

The Sarbanes-Oxley Act requires pre-approval by the audit committee of audit and 'other non-audit services' which are not prohibited. Pre-approval is required for *all* other non-audit services – including tax services. The audit committee may delegate pre-approval to one or more independent members; however, the full committee needs to approve this at the next scheduled meeting. Comfort letters are considered audit services and do not require pre-approval. No 'blanket approval' is permitted, and services must be specifically identified in order to be approved. Under the Sarbanes-Oxley Act, there is a *de minimis* exception to the requirement for pre-approval if:

- the aggregate amount of all such non-audit services is 5% or less of the total amounts paid by the company to the auditor in the fiscal year; and
- the company 'did not recognize the services to be non-audit services' at the time they were provided; and
- the services are promptly brought to and approved by the audit committee prior to the completion of the audit.

The Sarbanes-Oxley Act requires audit committees to disclose all approved non-audit services to be performed by the auditor to investors in periodic reports required by section 13(a) (ie 10-K and 10-Qs).

External audit quality issues E6.7

The audit committee will require the external auditor to bring to the audit committee their proposed plan for undertaking the annual audit. While the audit approach is a matter for the auditor, since it is the auditor's report and opinion which is the end product of the audit, nevertheless it is reasonable for the audit committee to challenge the auditor – especially if the audit committee considers the proposed audit emphasis is skewed away from the issues of most concern relating to the reliability of the financial statements.

The audit committee should also confirm that such matters as the following are satisfactory:

- potential auditor conflicts with work they undertake for other clients;
- the qualifications and experience of the audit staff;
- the degree of continuity of the audit team from one year to the next;
- the audit quality control mechanisms within the audit firm; and
- the timing of audit work (see below).

Timing issues **E6.8**

The audit committee should also satisfy itself on certain timing issues which may impact upon the effectiveness of the annual audit, and consequently perhaps on the reliability of the financial statements. An excessively tight deadline to disclose the financial results to the market may impact negatively on audit quality. An external audit plan which crams more of the audit into the period after the year-end, with less of the audit at the interim stage, may negatively affect audit quality, as well as delaying the finalisation of the audited accounts.

Another relevant timing issue for the audit committee to consider is the timing of the flow of information from management to the external auditor: late disclosure towards the end of the audit can mean it is effectively too late for the external auditor to deal with a matter effectively. Unscrupulous management can be manipulative in this regard. Cynics might say that audit materiality, from an external auditor's point of view, is perhaps three times the audit fee multiplied by the number of days left to complete the audit!

Notes

1 The European Directive defines a 'public interest entity' as being any company listed on the main market and also any other entities that individual Member States may wish to include in this category. The UK has included none other than their listed public companies.

2 OECD (2011), *Survey on Corporate Governance Frameworks in the Middle East and North Africa,* available at http://www.oecd.org/daf/ca/corporategovernance principles/49012924.pdf, accessed 2 August 2013.

3 See http://europa.eu/rapid/press-release_MEMO-13-1171_en.htm and http://ec.europa.eu/internal_market/auditing/reform/

4 See note 1.

5 The 2012 UK Corporate Governance Code, Provision C.3.7. See **App1**.

6 Sometimes termed 'low balling'.

7 Financial Reporting Council (April 2007), 'Choice in the UK Audit Market' (Interim Report of the Market Participants Group).

Chapter E7

Audit Committee Oversight of Internal Audit and other Review Agencies

Introduction E7.1

In Chapter **E1**, we explained the nature of the committee's responsibilities for this matter. Here we provide more detailed, practical advice for audit committees on discharging their oversight responsibility for internal audit and for other internal review agencies. Readers will find additional guidance on internal audit, including latest developments, in Chapters **G2**, **H2**, **H3** and **H4**.

The Institute of Internal Auditors (IIA), within its International Internal Auditing Standards Framework, defines internal auditing as follows:

> 'Internal auditing is an independent, objective assurance and consulting activity designed to add value and improve an organization's operations. It helps an organization accomplish its objectives by bringing a systematic, disciplined approach to evaluate and improve the effectiveness of risk management, control, and governance processes.'

Prior to the UK public sector's adoption of The IIA Standards in 2013,[1] HM Treasury's definition of internal audit within its Government Internal Auditing Standards (2011) had been consistent with the IIA, though more elaborately stated:

> 'Internal audit is an independent and objective appraisal service within an organisation:
>
> - Internal audit primarily provides an independent and objective opinion to the Accounting Officer on risk management, control and governance, by measuring and evaluating their effectiveness in achieving the organisation's agreed objectives. In addition, internal audit's findings and recommendations are beneficial to line management in the audited areas. Risk management, control and governance comprise the policies, procedures and operations established to ensure the achievement of objectives, the appropriate assessment of risk, the reliability of internal and external reporting and accountability processes, compliance with applicable laws and regulations, and compliance with the behavioural and ethical standards set for the organisation.
>
> - Internal audit also provides an independent and objective consultancy service specifically to help line management improve the organisation's risk management, control and governance. The service applies the professional skills of internal audit through a systematic and disciplined evaluation of the policies, procedures and operations that management put in place to ensure the achievement of the organisation's objectives, and through recommendations for improvement. Such consultancy work contributes to the opinion which internal audit provides on risk management, control and governance.'

The most relevant part[2] of the UK Corporate Governance Code (set out in full at **App1**) reads:

> 'The audit committee should monitor and review the effectiveness of the internal audit activities. Where there is no internal audit function, the audit committee should consider annually whether there is a need for an internal audit function and make a recommendation to the board, and the reasons for the absence of such a function should be explained in the relevant section of the annual report.'

Now that this Provision is classified within the audit committee's part of the Code, the explanatory guidance has been transferred from the Turnbull Report on Internal Control to the FRC's Guidance on Audit Committees.[3]

For governmental entities the Code of Best Practice for Corporate Governance in Central Government Departments[4] hardly needs to be taken into account. It has a single mention of internal audit:

> '5. The board should ensure that effective arrangements are in place to provide assurance on risk management, governance and internal control. In this respect, the board should be independently advised by:
>
> - an audit committee chaired by an independent non-executive member;
> - an internal audit service operating in accordance with Government Internal Audit Standards.'

Readers may also wish to refer to HM Treasury's revised 2007 guidance on audit committees, which has been aligned with the Code of Best Practice for Corporate Governance in Central Government Departments.

It is not a new practice for audit committees regularly (perhaps once a year and certainly as a significant, specific agenda item) to review the adequacy of the internal audit function. In the UK, the Turnbull Report put a new focus on this – which is carried forward into subsequent releases of the UK Code. It is important to realise that this review does not happen automatically as a by-product of the committee receiving regular reports on internal audit assignments undertaken, or even as a by-product of the committee considering the internal audit planned programme of work and then monitoring its execution and progress, or as a consequence of the committee asking for an overall report and opinion from internal audit on enterprise-wide risk management and internal control. All of these will provide helpful inputs to the committee's consideration of the adequacy of the internal audit function. But other essential considerations include:

- Is the complement of internal auditors sufficient?
- Are the experience and qualifications of the internal auditors appropriate?
- Is the scope of internal audit unrestricted?
- Is internal audit sufficiently independent of management?
- Is the charter of the internal auditing function appropriate?
- Is internal auditing conducted with due professionalism?
- What is the level of acceptability within the organisation of internal audit?
- Has the risk profile of the entity changed so as to impact on the adequacy of internal audit?

It is wise for the audit committee to review the charter or terms of reference of the internal audit function annually.

Internal audit independence **E7.2**

The audit committee will wish to answer the following questions, amongst others, in order to assess the sufficiency of internal audit independence:

- If internal audit does not report administratively to the chief executive, does internal audit report to an executive whose other responsibilities should not need to be a significant focus of internal audit attention?
- Is there any evidence that internal audit has to subordinate its judgement on professional matters to that of anyone else? For instance, with respect to designing the annual programme of audit engagements, determining the scope of each engagement, and determining the content of internal audit reports, and to whom they are addressed?
- Does the head of internal audit have direct access to the chair of the audit committee at all times?
- Is internal audit free of any management or operational responsibilities for any processes which may need to be subject to internal audit?

Quality assurance reviews of internal audit functions **E7.3**

The IIA's Internal Auditing Standards require that the internal audit function should, in effect, audit itself annually. The Standards also require that, once every five years, there should be an external assessment of the internal audit function. In the year that this occurs, the internal review may be dispensed with. Guidance from the IIA suggests that, as a temporary expedient, the requirement for a quinquennial external assessment may be met by a self-assessment with independent validation. It is not acceptable, under internal auditing Standards, for the external assessment to be undertaken by anyone who is part of the entity or, in the case of a subsidiary, who belongs to another part of the group.

It is the responsibility of the head of internal audit to ensure that the results of these internal and external assessments are reported to the audit committee. Indeed, it is best practice for the audit committee to commission the external assessment. Clearly, these assessments are a valuable means by which the audit committee can obtain assurance on the quality of internal audit. The remit of these assessments should be, primarily, to assess the extent to which internal auditing Standards are being applied successfully.

The IIA and also central government (for governmental internal audit functions) are available to assist in putting together teams to conduct these external assessments. Firms of public accountants as well as specialist management consultants also provide these services.

The Standards of the IIA (**App8**) are concise about external reviews.[5] The IIA also has Practice Advisories within their Standards Framework, which provide non-mandatory guidance on the IIA Standards – with the result that the IIA provides considerable guidance on external reviews. It should be noted that IIA Standards encourage internal auditors to report that their work is compliant with the Standards, but only if, *inter alia*, the results of quality assurance reviews indicate that this is so:

'1321 – Use of "Conforms with the International Standards for the Professional Practice of Internal Auditing"

'The chief audit executive may state that the internal audit activity conforms with the *International Standards for the Professional Practice of Internal Auditing* only if the results of the quality assurance and improvement program support this statement.'

The audit committee's responsibilities for the terms of reference of the internal audit function E7.4

A sample terms of reference, or charter, of an internal audit function, reproduced from the IIA's Standards Framework, appears at **A6.13** and **A6.14**. See also **A6.12–A6.15**. The audit committee should annually review the terms of reference of the internal audit function.

Internal audit's terms of reference should include, *inter alia*:

- A role for the head of internal audit to review the completeness and accuracy of the information the audit committee receives – not just the information pertinent to the committee's oversight of internal audit.
- That the head of internal audit reviews with the audit committee that the functional and administrative reporting lines of internal audit allow adequate independence.
- That the head of internal audit assists the audit committee to evaluate the scope, resources and results of internal audit activities, that internal audit informs the committee of internal audit coordination with and oversight of other control and monitoring functions.
- That the head of internal audit reports to the audit committee significant control issues and opportunities for improvement.
- That the head of internal audit reports progress against the approved annual audit plan and results.
- That the head of internal audit advises on sufficiency of internal audit resources.
- That the head of internal audit has a responsibility to report to audit committee on suspected frauds and assist in their investigation if significant.
- That the head of internal audit makes the audit committee aware of the external quality assessment reviews of the internal audit function (which should be done at least every five years) and the results.

Unless referred to in the audit committee's own terms of reference, the terms of reference of the internal audit function should:

- Indicate that internal audit is to function consistently with IIA Standards.
- Define the internal audit assurance and consulting roles.
- Mention that the audit committee should spend time alone with the head of internal audit.
- Mention that the audit committee should approve:
  1. The internal audit charter;
  2. The internal audit risk assessment and related audit plan;
  3. All decisions regarding the appointment or removal of the head of internal audit; and

4. The annual compensation pay adjustment of the chief audit executive;

- Receive from the head of internal audit the results of internal audit activities and other matters the head of internal audit deems necessary, including private meetings with the head of internal audit without management being present.
- Enquire of management and the head of internal audit as to scope or budgetary limitations that impede the ability of internal audit to execute its responsibilities.

Other matters for inclusion are:

- That the head of internal audit has a right to ask for items to be put on the audit committee agenda.
- That the head of internal audit (and other internal audit staff) should have open, direct access to chair and members of audit committee at all times.
- That the head of internal audit has a right to report directly to the Board.

Guidance on internal audit from the Turnbull and Smith Reports **E7.5**

The 1999 Turnbull Report had, as asked, provided guidance on both the internal control Provisions which appeared within the 1998 Combined Code and the overarching internal control Principle as well. These were expressed in the 1998 Combined Code as follows:

> **'D.2 Internal Control**
>
> **Principle**
>
> **The board should maintain a sound system of internal control to safeguard shareholders investment and the company's assets.**
>
> **Code Provisions**
>
> D.2.1 The directors should, at least annually, conduct a review of the effectiveness of the group's system of internal controls and should report to shareholders that they have done so. The review should cover all controls, including financial, operational and compliance controls and risk management.
>
> D.2.2 Companies which do not have an internal audit function should from time to time review the need for one.'

The 1999 Turnbull guidance strengthened the demands of D.2.2 (above) by (a) making the review the responsibility of the board of directors; (b) stipulating that the review should be done at least annually; and (c) indicating that a review by the board of the adequacy of a company's internal audit should be done annually even when the company had an internal audit function. Hence the revised wording of the equivalent Provision to D.2.2, as it first appeared in the 2003 Combined Code, reflecting the original Turnbull Committee's guidance, viz:

> 'C.3.5 The audit committee should monitor and review the effectiveness of the internal audit activities. Where there is no internal audit function, the audit committee should consider annually whether there is a need for an internal audit function and make a recommendation to the board, and the reasons for the absence of such a function should be explained in the relevant section of the annual report.'

Readers will note the 2003 addition at the end of this Code Provision of 'and the reasons for the absence of such a function should be explained in the relevant section of the annual report'. So this 'comply or explain' Provision thereafter had a specific 'comply or explain' clause nested within it. In essence, if a company does not have an internal audit function, it should explain why not, unless the board takes the view that it will not comply with this Provision at all – in which case, under Listing Rule 9.8.6 (previously 12.43A), the company should explain why it has decided not to comply with this Provision, or to comply with it only partly or for only part of the period being reported.

Readers may also note that this Code Provision on internal audit has, commencing 2003, belonged within the audit committees part of the UK Code, to which it has been transferred from the internal control part of the 1998 Code. The Turnbull Review decided that the Turnbull guidance on this Code Provision should therefore also be transferred out of the Turnbull Report and into the Smith Report on audit committees.[6]

While arranging the transfer of the Turnbull guidance on internal audit to the Smith Report, the Turnbull Review did not offer any guidance on the new part of the internal audit provision, namely that 'the reasons for the absence of such a function should be explained in the relevant section of the annual report'.

The 2005 Turnbull Review's impact on audit committees E7.6

The Turnbull Report was reviewed and revised during 2005 by a working group headed by Douglas Flint, Finance Director of HSBC.[7] The Turnbull Review reflected the general mood that further wholesale developments in corporate governance are not called for – at the moment, at least. Perhaps it is the case that UK corporate governance guidelines have reached a satisfactory stage of development. Perhaps it is that many leaders of business consider that the last thing they need is further demands on the corporate governance front. There are, after all, company law reform and developments coming out of the European Commission as well.

In respect of audit committees, the Turnbull Review has led to a general re-emphasis of the Turnbull guidance and also to two specific changes (see below). Audit committees need to be aware of these developments as they impact upon audit committee business. Generally, a board relies on its audit committee to undertake the 'hard graft' to place the board in a position to be able to fulfil its internal control obligations, as set out in the UK Corporate Governance Code and within the Turnbull guidance.

The specific changes are to do with internal audit and with reporting on the board's approach to significant failings or weaknesses in the system of internal control.

General re-emphasis of the Turnbull guidance E7.7

The Turnbull Review Group saw fit to discourage companies from a nominal, 'box-ticking' approach to compliance with the Code on internal control, and to discourage a boilerplate style of internal control statements in their annual reports. The Turnbull Review reiterated the view of the vast majority of their respondents to the consultation process, who emphasised 'the importance of regular and systematic assessment of the risks facing the business and the value of embedding risk management and internal control systems within business processes'. The Turnbull Review Report stressed that 'it is the board's responsibility to make sure this happens'. It says:

> 'Boards should review whether they can make more of the communication opportunity of the internal control statement in the annual report. Investors consider the board's attitude towards risk management and internal control to be an important factor when making investment decisions about a company. Taken together with the Operating and Financial Review,[8] the internal control statement provides an opportunity for the board to help shareholders understand the risk and control issues facing the company, and to explain how the company maintains a framework of internal controls to address these issues and how the board has reviewed the effectiveness of that framework. It is in this spirit that directors need to exercise their responsibility to review on a continuing basis their application of the revised guidance.'

As we have mentioned, the Turnbull guidance on internal audit has been transferred by the FRC, with some amendment, to the Smith Report from paragraphs 42 to 47 of the Turnbull Report,[9] so as to correspond with the transfer of the Code Provision on internal audit from the internal control part of the Code to the audit committees part of the Code. This guidance relates to how companies should implement Provision C.3.5 of the UK Corporate Governance Code, which reads as per 4.9 of the Smith guidance reproduced here.

From the Smith Report (para 4.9) and its successor 'Guidance on Audit Committees' (December 2010, para 4.10):

> **'The internal audit process**
>
> The audit committee should monitor and review the effectiveness of the company's internal audit function. Where there is no internal audit function, the audit committee should consider annually whether there is a need for an internal audit function and make a recommendation to the board, and the reasons for the absence of such a function should be explained in the relevant section of the annual report.'

Notes

1 PSIAS (2012) Public Sector Internal Audit Standards, ISBN 978 1 84508 356 4, December 2012, effective 1 April 2013, available at http://www.iia.org.uk/media/76020/public_sector_internal_audit_standards_2012.pdf, accessed 14 July 2013.

2 Provision C.3.6.

3 FRC (2012) *Guidance on Audit Committees*, Financial Reporting Council, September 2012, available at http://www.frc.org.uk/Our-Work/Publications/Corporate-Governance/Guidance-on-Audit-Committees-September-2012.aspx, accessed 22 December 2013.

4 HM Treasury (2005): *Corporate governance in central government departments: Code of good practice*, July 2005.

5 See Annex D – Standards 1300 to 1340.

6 FRC (2003) *Audit Committees – Combined Code Guidance, a report and proposed guidance by an FRC-appointed group chaired by Sir Robert Smith*, submitted to the Financial Reporting Council in December 2002 (January 2003).

7 FRC (2005) *Internal control – revised guidance for directors on the Combined Code*, Financial Reporting Council, October 2005.
8 Now no longer a mandatory requirement for UK listed companies, following an about-turn by the government. But the Companies Act 2006 requires all public companies to undertake and publish a business review.
9 Turnbull Review Committee, October 2005.

Chapter E8

The Development of Audit Committees over Time

E8.1

Today's focus upon audit committees may make it appear that they are a recent addition to corporate governance. Not so. An 1872 board minute of the Great Western Railway reported to the board on the work of that board's audit committee:

'Great Western Railway

Report of the Audit Committee

The auditors and Mr. Deloitte attended the Committee and explained the various matters connected with the Finances and other departments of the railway, which explanations were highly satisfactory.

The Committee consider the Auditors have performed their arduous duties with great care and intelligence and therefore confidently recommend that they be continued in office.

Benjamin Lancaster
Chairman

Paddington Station
22nd February, 1872'

In those days, Deloitte specialised in the audit of railways, and it is satisfying to note that Mr Deloitte himself attended client audit committee meetings, no doubt in his capacity as engagement partner. Three of the four contemporary responsibilities of audit committees are alluded to in the above board minute, with only the committee's responsibility for internal audit missing. Those responsibilities which correspond to present audit committee roles are the committee's scrutiny on behalf of the board of the financial statements to be published; the committee's role in advising the board on the quality of the external audit; and who should be the auditors going forward; and, finally, in the reference to 'other departments', a suggestion of an audit committee role in matters relating to internal control going beyond internal control over financial reporting.

The reliance that this audit committee placed on explanations given by the external auditors does seem to reveal that the audit committee members, doubtless non-executive directors, were rather more detached from the affairs of the company than we would approve of for them today. The minute was reproduced in a book which reported a research project by Professor Tricker sponsored by Deloitte.[1] The title of that book was perhaps in advance of its time, in coupling the independent director with the role of the audit committee, and it heralded a resurgence of interest in audit committees at around that time in the UK.

In the US, in 1939, audit committees had been proposed by the New York Stock Exchange as a direct result of the McKesson & Robbins scandal, and again by the

Securities and Exchange Commission in 1940. By 1967 the Executive Committee of the American Institute of Certified Public Accountants recommended:

> 'that publicly owned corporations appoint committees composed of outside directors (those who are not officers or employees) to nominate the independent auditors of the corporation's financial statements and to discuss the auditor's work with them.'

In the late 1960s and early 1970s, as a result of several highly publicised corporate failures (notably Atlantic Acceptance), audit committees with a *majority* of non-executive directors become mandatory under the Canadian province laws of Ontario and British Columbia and then under Canadian Federal law. But it was to take more time before audit committees became mandatory within the US. In 1978, it became required that every domestic company listed on the New York Stock Exchange should have an audit committee consisting wholly of outside (non-executive) directors with an outside chairman. Earlier, in 1972, the US Securities and Exchange Commission's Accounting Series Release No 123 (23 March 1972) had ended as follows:

> 'To this end, the Commission, in the light of the foregoing historical recital, endorses the establishment by all publicly held companies of audit committees composed of outside directors and urges the business and financial communities and all shareholders of such publicly held companies to lend their full and continuing support to the effective implementation of the above-cited recommendations in order to assist in affording the greatest possible protection to investors who rely upon such financial statements.'

Indeed, by 1975, 89% of the *Fortune* top 500 industrials had voluntarily decided to have audit committees, and we are told that 77% of heads of internal audit met regularly with them.[2] However, in the UK, only about 20% of the top 1,000 UK companies had audit committees at that time.[3]

At about the same time, in 1977 Sir Brandon Rhys Williams, MP for Kensington, unsuccessfully put to the House of Commons a 'Companies (Audit Committee) Bill' which would have applied to listed companies employing more than 1,500 people or having total net assets in excess of £5m. The 'Explanatory Memorandum' to this bill stated:

> 'In requiring major public companies to set up audit committees the Bill follows a practice now well established in Canada and the United States.'

The Bill would have required such companies to have at least three non-executive directors, and also to have had an audit committee at least half of whose members would have been three or more non-executive directors. The chairman of the audit committee was to have been chosen by the audit committee members – whereas current practice is that the board determines who shall chair its committees. The members of the audit committee were termed 'audit directors' in this Bill. The Bill set out the proposed duties of audit committees in some detail, which included a responsibility of the audit directors to make a statement, signed by each audit director, to be attached to the published balance sheet and read by the chairman of the audit committee at the AGM. The Bill proposed that, with the approval of the AGM, audit directors would be paid an additional fee. The Bill failed to be voted through into law.

Again, in 1981 Sir Brandon Rhys Williams unsuccessfully proposed amendments to the Companies (No 2) Bill, which would have required listed companies to have had at least three non-executive directors if the company turnover exceeded £25m, or the balance sheet value exceeded £50m, or the number of employees exceeded 2,500. In that Bill, Sir Brandon continued to promote the idea of audit committees, this time for listed companies with turnovers in excess of £200m, a balance sheet total in excess of £400m or having more than 50,000 employees. The Bill proposed that such companies should be required to consider the appointment of an audit committee at each AGM and, if the AGM resolved to appoint an audit committee, it would be a committee with particular characteristics as defined in the Bill, which included:

- such companies to have had at least three non-executive directors, and also to have had an audit committee at least half of whose members were to have been at least three non-executive directors;
- with the approval of the AGM, audit directors to have been paid an additional fee;
- at least two audit committee meetings per annum, convened by the committee's chairman;
- the external auditors to have been notified of the meetings, with a right to attend them, but not as members;
- a copy of the minutes of each audit committee meeting to have been given to each director of the company within seven days of the meeting;
- the audit committee to have recommended on the appointment of the auditors and their remuneration;
- the audit directors to have made a statement, signed by each audit director, to have been attached to the balance sheet and to have been read by the chairman of the audit committee at the AGM.

During the debate in the House of Commons, at 11:30pm on 19 October 1981, Sir Brandon, in apocalyptic terms, warned of the risks of inaction:

> 'I am reminded of a famous quotation from Bryce:
>
> > "But while they talked the heavens darkened, and the flood came and destroyed them all."
>
> I am afraid that while we are talking about the possibility of introducing audit committees in many of our large companies they will go bankrupt, or the whole social scene will change so much that the issue will die on its feet. Although I have had the assurances of Ministers and experts – Establishment figures particularly – that everything is going along quite all right and that there is no need for legislation, I do not think that there is any evidence that we are making significant progress in this area.'

Ten years later, in 1992, the Preface to the Cadbury Report[4] was to refer to the collapses of BCCI and Maxwell. Sir Brandon's warning was an early example of an appreciation of the value of corporate governance to deter inappropriate management practices. Unfortunately, the more recent presence of audit committees within listed and other companies has not proved to be as effective as perhaps Sir Brandon had hoped, and there have been spectacular collapses of large companies of the sort that Sir Brandon was predicting – though not, so far, of US listed companies post Sarbanes-Oxley.

The UK continues to have a preference for avoiding mandatory regulations. For instance, the audit committee is not mentioned at the level of a Principle in the UK Corporate Governance Code, and the Provisions merely have a 'comply or explain' status. Indeed, the FSA regards its Listing Rule on the UK Corporate Governance Code as requiring just disclosure rather than adherence to both Principles and Provisions. Nevertheless, best practice, even when discretionary, is widely supported by UK companies. As early as 1992, approximately two-thirds of the top UK listed companies had audit committees – even before the London Stock Exchange, commencing 1993 and in response to the 1992 Cadbury Code Provision, required UK listed companies to disclose in their annual reports if they did not have audit committees of the main board comprising at least three non-executive directors, and to explain why not.

The UK Government's Department for Business, Enterprise and Regulatory Reform (BERR, previously the DTI), after consultation, announced mid-2007 that it would be supporting an amendment to the UK Listing Rules of the FSA so as to make audit committees mandatory for UK listed companies in order to give effect to Article 41 of the amended EC Eighth Directive, which requires Member States to ensure that all listed companies are obliged to have audit committees. It is clear that introducing this mandatory requirement is merely to comply with EC Directives and will have no practical impact upon UK companies.

Arguably, Cadbury had a hidden agenda in including a Provision on audit committees within his 1992 Code. The wording was:

> '4.3 The board should establish an audit committee of at least 3 non-executive directors with written terms of reference which deal clearly with its authority and duties. (Note 11)'[5]

The effect was to increase the number of non-executive directors on many boards. By 1995, all the FTSE 100 companies had an audit committee, as had 245 of the mid 250 FTSE companies,[6] though WM Morrison was later to enter the FTSE 100 without an audit committee – now rectified.

The Sarbanes-Oxley Act 2002 gave statutory backing to the mandatory requirement for a US listed company to have an audit committee, and made audit committees of US issuers responsible for the appointment of their companies' external auditors and for approving, on an 'item by item' basis, any non-audit work undertaken by the auditor for an audit client. Certain categories of non-audit work are banned.

The 2003 Combined Code brought the UK into line with the US by 'requiring' that all (not just a majority) members of the audit committee should be independent non-executive directors. However, as we have said, the 'requirement' is not mandatory, being a 'comply or explain' obligation only. The fact that UK shareholders to some extent are able to make their voices heard within UK boardrooms partly compensates for the discretionary character of the UK Code.

The 2003 UK Combined Code, by adopting the Smith Report proposals, markedly increased content on audit committees compared to the earlier 1998 Code. No changes to the audit committees part of the Code have been made since 2003.

Notes

1 Tricker, RI (1978), *The Independent Director – The Role of the Audit Committee* (Tolley, UK, ISBN 0 510 49378 5), minute quoted on p 56.

2 Mautz, RK and Neumann, FL (1977), *Corporate Audit Committees: Policies and Practice* (Ernst & Ernst, US).

3 Chambers, AD and Snook, AJ (1978), '1978 Survey of Audit Committees in the United Kingdom', in *Proceedings of the Fourth Annual Conference on Recent Developments in Internal Auditing*, 29–30 May, 1979, The City University Business School, London, pp 77–90 and pp 211–360. Also published in the City University Business School Working Paper Series.

4 The Financial Aspects of Corporate Governance, 'The Cadbury Report' (1 December 1992) (Gee & Co, UK, ISBN 0 85258 915 8).

5 Note 11 to the Cadbury Code was the Committee's recommendations on audit committees, which read:

'(a) They should be formally constituted as sub-committees of the main board to whom they are answerable and to whom they should report regularly; they should be given written terms of reference which deal adequately with their membership, authority and duties; and they should normally meet at least twice a year.

(b) There should be a minimum of three members. Membership should be confined to the non-executive directors of the company and a majority of the non-executives serving on the committee should be independent of the company, as defined in paragraph 2.2 of the Code.

(c) The external auditor and, where an internal audit function exists, the head of internal audit should normally attend committee meetings, as should the finance director. Other board members should also have the right to attend.

(d) The audit committee should have a discussion with the auditors at least once a year, without executive board members present, to ensure that there are no unresolved issues of concern.

(e) The audit committee should have explicit authority to investigate any matters within its terms of reference, the resources which it needs to do so, and full access to information. The committee should be able to obtain outside professional advice and if necessary to invite outsiders with relevant experience to attend meetings.

(f) Membership of the committee should be disclosed in the annual report and the chairman of the committee should be available to answer questions about its work at the Annual General Meeting.'

Specimen terms of reference for an audit committee, including a list of the most commonly performed duties, are set out in the Committee's full Report.

6 Price Waterhouse Corporate Register (1995), Hamilton Scott.

Chapter E9

Board Risk Committees

> *'There are known knowns. These are things we know that we know. There are known unknowns. That is to say, there are things that we know we don't know. But there are also unknown unknowns. There are things we don't know we don't know.'*
>
> Donald Rumsfeld

Context E9.1

Readers are referred to the suggested terms of reference for a board risk committee at **App4.18** together with the footnotes to those terms of reference which provide interpretations to much of the content.

Conforming fully to all the Provisions within the UK Corporate Governance Code will mean that boards have at least three committees:

- nomination committee;
- remuneration committee;
- audit committee.

It should however be pointed out that none of these three committees are referred to within a Main Principle of the Code, and only the only remuneration committee referred to is at the level of a Supporting Principle. The other two committees are covered only at the level of the Provisions within the Code. The Listing Rules require a company with a premium listing to explain how they apply the Main Principles but not the Supporting Principles and the Provisions are only given a 'comply or explain' status by the Listing Rules.

So, apart from likely shareholder disapproval, listed companies are free to avoid having any of these committees. They could for instance reserve to the board itself all of the business that would otherwise fall within the domain of these three committees. Article 41 of the 8th European Directive permits a public interest company to have no audit committee, as do the UK Listing Rules.

Risk committees of the board in the UK Corporate Governance Code E9.2

A fourth committee is referred to within the UK Corporate Governance Code, but in an even more discretionary way – that is, the risk committee of the board. It would not be a breach of a Main or Supporting Principle nor even of a Provision if a company had no board risk committee. That is because the risk committee is referred to only as an option in a small part of one Provision. Provision C.3.2. (see **App1**) states:

> 'The main role and responsibilities of the audit committee should be set out in written terms of reference and should include:
>
> …
>
> to review the company's internal financial controls and, unless expressly addressed by a separate board risk committee composed of independent directors, or by the board itself, to review the company's internal control and risk management systems;
>
> …'

This reference in the Code to a board risk committee has been unchanged in the 2013, 2006, 2008 and 2010 Codes and dates back to Sir Derek Higgs's recommendations for changes to the 1998 Code. Sir Derek's proposed wording had been:

> 'to review the company's internal financial control system and, unless expressly addressed by a separate risk committee or by the board itself, risk management systems;'[1]

Board risk committee comprises independent directors E9.3

Note that the Financial Reporting Council's final wording was tighter in that it is clear that the risk committee must be a *board* risk committee and that it should comprise exclusively of *independent* directors. So, we are not talking about a risk committee at executive level. Furthermore, the genesis for a board risk committee is shown as being very similar to that of the audit committee – a means of providing a forum for outside directors in particular to discharge certain of their responsibilities more effectively.

Sir Alistair Darling, Chancellor of the Exchequer at the Downing Street Press Conference on 13 October 2008, which announced the capital injection of the UK banks, in answering a question said (italics added):

> '*Far more attention needs to be paid to risk taking, by board members. It really is quite extraordinary that boards themselves didn't more fully understand what risks they were allowing their banks to be exposed to.* … The first line of defence, not just for shareholders but for everyone else, is to make sure that boards are up to the job. Now I think the regulatory system needs to ask some serious questions to ensure that people have the risk monitoring measures in place. Northern Rock didn't, for example – they weren't nearly as robust as they should have been.'

It was impressive that in 2003 the UK Code promoted the possibility of board risk committees exclusively comprising independent directors five years before the global financial crisis broke. Clearly there had been earlier concerns that boards, in particular the non-executive directors, were not sufficiently cognisant of the risks their companies were exposed to. But it was less impressive that it was largely only after 2008, at the instigation of the Walker Report,[2] that banks and other financial institutions started generally to establish these board risk committees. Clearly it will be interesting to see whether the 2014 version of the Code[3] elevates board risk committees to the level of a 'comply or explain' Provision or even to the level of a Main or Supporting Principle.

Coordinating with other board committees **E9.4**

We have designed the terms of reference for a board risk committee (**App4.18**) to give effect to the need for the committee to co-ordinate with other board committees. It will need to co-ordinate with the remuneration committee in the determination of the remuneration of the heads of the functions within the 'second line of defence' (chief risk officer and head of compliance) and the 'third line of defence' (head of internal audit) and also to align executive incentives with performance, avoiding perverse incentives which encourage excessive risk taking. Depending upon the scope of the nomination committee's responsibilities, the risk committee may need to co-ordinate with the nomination committee and with the audit committee on matters relating to the appointment of these second and third line heads. Most of all, it will need to co-ordinate with the audit committee in its review of internal control and risk management systems.

A key justification for the establishment of board risk committees is the ever expanding responsibilities of board audit committees. For instance, BP's audit committee met on average more than 12 times each year between 2003 and 2012. Some heads of internal audit are suggesting that it can be better for an internal audit's sole or main reporting relationship to be transferred from the audit committee chair to the risk committee chair. This is particularly likely to be the case when the audit committee is focussed mainly on financial reporting and external auditing matters. It is an option acknowledged within the Chartered Institute of Internal Auditors 2013 guidance on internal audit in banks and insurance companies[4], guidance which is supported by the UK regulators.

Notes

1 Higgs, Sir Derek (2003) *Review of the role and effectiveness of non-executive directors*, ('The Higgs Report'), commissioned by The Department of Trade and Industry, January 2003.

2 Walker, Sir David (2009) *A review of corporate governance in UK banks and other financial industry entities*, final report ('The Walker Report'), November 2009, available at http://webarchive.nationalarchives.gov.uk/20130129110402/http://www.hm-treasury.gov.uk/d/walker_review_261109.pdf, accessed 5 December 2013.

3 Expected in October 2014, with an exposure draft earlier – www.frc.org.uk.

4 CIIA (2013) Chartered Institute of Internal Auditors, *Effective Internal Audit in the Financial Services Sector: Recommendations from the Committee on Internal Audit Guidance for Financial Services*, July 2013, available at http://www.iia.org.uk/media/354788/0758_effective_internal_audit_financial_webfinal.pdf, accessed 14 July 2013, p 9, §E.15.

Chapter E10

Board Remuneration Committees

Context E10.1

Readers are referred to the companion volume to this handbook – Cliff Weight's excellent *Directors' Remuneration Handbook.*[1]. **App4.9** provides illustrative terms of reference for a board remuneration committee.

Unlike the other board committees referred to in the UK Corporate Governance Code (**App1**), the remuneration committee gets extensive mentioning within the Code's Supporting Principles. While the Listing Rules require companies with a premium listing to explain how they apply the Main Principles of the Code, there is no specific obligation to explain how they apply the Supporting Principles; though it is generally considered that applying the Supporting Principles will be necessary if the Main Principles are applied successfully.

All the Code's board committees get extensive coverage at the level of the Code's Provisions which are intended to have only 'comply or explain' status. Strictly, this listing obligation again applies only to companies with a premium listing.

We should recognise that most UK companies conform to most of the guidance within the UK Corporate Governance Code, whether the Main or Supporting Principles or the Provisions, and this conformance extends far beyond companies with a premium listing to include many other listed and private companies, mutual and other entities. So it is appropriate that we use here the Code's guidance on remuneration.

Background to executive remuneration 'rules' E10.2

Many would consider that the UK's light touch corporate governance has been ineffective at achieving discipline with respect to executive remuneration. The 39 Provisions of the 1995 Greenbury Code[2] on executive remuneration had little impact at all, other than to further the debate inconclusively. Then, the 1998 and 2003 Code Provisions that shareholders should be invited specifically to approve all new long-term incentive schemes and the remuneration policy of the company as set out in the board's annual remuneration report, again had only modest impact as boards and their remuneration committees were not obliged to take heed of dissenting shareholders and, due to the 'comply or explain' status of Code Provisions, companies were not obliged to put these matters to shareholder vote. A further attempt was made to ratchet up the role of shareholders in determining executive remuneration by transferring the sentiment of these Code Provisions into the Companies Act 2006, s 439[3] introducing a statutory requiring that the directors' remuneration report be put to a vote by shareholders in a general meeting. But it was still a discretionary vote, the results of which boards could ignore. The intent was that if a significant proportion of shareholders, not necessarily a majority, voted down the remuneration report, then boards would be likely to take note, to enter into a dialogue with their principal shareholders, and to invite the shareholders at the next opportunity to approve a revised remuneration policy which addressed shareholders' concerns. After all, directors should be motivated to act in the best interests of shareholders, and have their own positions on the board and their reputations to worry about. However, these checks and balances have arguably not worked effectively – hence the UK government's new 2013 rules[4] requiring all UK companies listed on a main exchange to put their remuneration policy to a *binding* shareholder vote.

Paul Norris has concluded in a balanced way:[5]

> 'There is evidence that, over time, directors' pay has not outstripped shareholder returns, despite individual examples of excess. There is also evidence that although amounts paid to CEOs of top companies are large, they are insignificant when measured against the value of the business. CEOs know this and realise their negotiating position.
>
> This is good and bad: good insofar as it counters arguments of excess but potentially bad if it means that investors, as a body, are not motivated to engage at an individual company level, because overall there is no perceived problem or if a dominant CEO is able to steamroller the remuneration committee, which will not wish to fall out with the CEA about pay.
>
> The new disclosure regime will not curb fat cats, reduce complexity or introduce a greater element of fairness. But it does provide an opportunity to refresh remuneration policy for the benefit of all stakeholders. …'

A fundamental principle is that no director should be involved in deciding his or her own remuneration (**App1**, D2). Another important principle is to avoid paying either executive or non-executive directors more than necessary (**App1**, D.1.).

Determining non-executive director fees **E10.3**

The UK Code is silent on determining the rewards for non-executive directors other than Provision D.1.3. guiding that levels of remuneration for non-executive directors should reflect the time commitment and responsibilities of the role. Remuneration for non-executive directors should not include share options or other performance-related elements. If, exceptionally, options are granted, shareholder approval should be sought in advance and any shares acquired by exercise of the options should be held until at least one year after the non-executive director leaves the board (Provision B.1.1); and secondly guiding that an independent director should not receive additional remuneration from the company apart from a director's fee, nor participates in the company's share option or a performance-related pay scheme, nor is a member of the company's pension scheme. There is nothing in the Code which sets out a mechanism for determining non-executive director remuneration, and no guidance that this should be done by, for instance, a committee. On the other hand, the Code is very directive about executive remuneration.

In the absence of guidance, it would be appropriate for the chairman of the board to regularly review the fees of non-executive directors, in consultation with the executive directors and taking independent external advice where appropriate. These fees might be related to the chairman's annual evaluation of individual director performance. It is reasonable for supplementary fees to be paid to independent directors for their membership and chairmanship of board committees. As a rough rule of thumb, non-executive directors tend to be rewarded based on a multiple of the average daily rate of pay (excluding performance-related elements) that the executive directors receive, according to the time commitment associated with the non-executive role. Typically, a non-executive director is likely to spend some 30 to 36 days annually on the role.

To ensure that no executive is involved in deciding his or her own remuneration, the board's remuneration committee comprises only independent directors – at least two members for a FTSE company outside the FTSE 350, and at least three members foe a FTSE 350 company (**App1**, D.2.1.). No one other than the committee chairman and members is entitled to be present at a remuneration committee meeting, but others may attend by invitation of the committee (**App1**, B1.)

Remuneration committee composition **E10.4**

The chairman of the board may be a member of the remuneration committee, but not its chairman if he or she was independent when appointed chairman (**App1**, D.2.1.). This is similar to the guidance on audit committees except that the chairman may only be a member of the audit committee of a company outside the FTSE 350. Unlike with respect to the nomination and audit committees, the chairman of the board in no circumstances can be a member of the remuneration committee, but there is a requirement for the committee to consult the chairman and also the chief executive. The composition of nomination committees is much more relaxed because there is not the same need for independence: only a majority of members of the nomination committee need be independent non-executive directors, and the chairman or an independent non-executive director should chair the nomination committee, but the chairman should not chair the nomination committee when it is dealing with the appointment of a successor to the chairmanship.

Schedule A **E10.5**

Provision D.1.1 (**App1**) requires the remuneration committee to Apply Schedule A of the Code when designing schemes of performance-related remuneration. Schedule A reads as follows:

Schedule A

- The remuneration committee should consider whether the directors should be eligible for annual bonuses. If so, performance conditions should be relevant, stretching and designed to promote the long-term success of the company. Upper limits should be set and disclosed. There may be a case for part payment in shares to be held for a significant period.
- The remuneration committee should consider whether the directors should be eligible for benefits under long-term incentive schemes. Traditional share option schemes should be weighed against other kinds of long-term incentive scheme. Executive share options should not be offered at a discount save as permitted by the relevant provisions of the Listing Rules.

- In normal circumstances, shares granted or other forms of deferred remuneration should not vest, and options should not be exercisable, in less than three years. Directors should be encouraged to hold their shares for a further period after vesting or exercise, subject to the need to finance any costs of acquisition and associated tax liabilities.
- Any new long-term incentive schemes which are proposed should be approved by shareholders and should preferably replace any existing schemes or, at least, form part of a well-considered overall plan incorporating existing schemes. The total rewards potentially available should not be excessive.
- Payouts or grants under all incentive schemes, including new grants under existing share option schemes, should be subject to challenging performance criteria reflecting the company's objectives, including nonfinancial performance metrics where appropriate. Remuneration incentives should be compatible with risk policies and systems.
- Grants under executive share option and other long-term incentive schemes should normally be phased rather than awarded in one large block.
- Consideration should be given to the use of provisions that permit the company to reclaim variable components in exceptional circumstances of misstatement or misconduct.
- In general, only the basic salary should be pensionable. The remuneration committee should consider the pension consequences and associated costs to the company of basic salary increases and any other changes in pensionable remuneration, especially for directors close to retirement.

Meetings E10.6

It would be too optimistic to expect that an effective remuneration committee could meet only twice a year – once to set performance-related targets for executives to achieve, and secondly to determine the levels of performance-related rewards to be allocated based on whether the pre-set targets were achieved. But this does indicate the general structure of the remuneration committee's annual programme. Nevertheless, several additional meetings are likely to be needed. By way of example, BP's remuneration committee met on average more than six times in each of the five years up to 2012 and in 2008 eight times. The reward packages of new and prospective executives joining during the year will need to be addressed. Outside advice from remuneration consultants is likely to be needed in advance of remuneration committee meetings which make decisions. Committee time will be spent importantly in deciding the structure of long-term incentive schemes. Consulting the board's chairman and the chief executive may entail additional meetings. It is unlikely that performance-related elements of the executives' remuneration packages will be decided upon in a single meeting as these are likely to be negotiated hard by the top executive team. A challenge for the committee will be to determine the appropriate level of performance-related rewards when pre-set performance targets have not been met although the top executive team has performed excellently in circumstances that changed significantly after the targets were set. Meetings may be needed mid-year to consider the requirement to modify performance targets. The remit of the remuneration committee is likely to extend one or two levels below the executive board member level, although at those lower levels the remuneration committee may determine only the bands within which remuneration should be paid. In some companies there may be executives that need to be rewarded above the reward levels that apply to executive directors, and undoubtedly these will fall within the remuneration committee's remit.

Notes

1 Weight, Cliff (2013) *Directors' Remuneration Handbook*, 2nd edn (Bloomsbury, April 2014), ISBN 978 1 78043 331 8.

2 Greenbury, Sir Richard (1995) *Directors' Remuneration: Report of a Study Group chaired by Sir Richard Greenbury* ('The Greenbury Report'), 17 July 1995, available at http://www.cg.org.cn/theory/zlyz/greenbury.pdf, accessed 6 December 2013.

3 Section 439 – Quoted companies: members' approval of directors' remuneration report:

(1) A quoted company must, prior to the accounts meeting, give to the members of the company entitled to be sent notice of the meeting notice of the intention to move at the meeting, as an ordinary resolution, a resolution approving the directors' remuneration report for the financial year.

(2) The notice may be given in any manner permitted for the service on the member of notice of the meeting.

(3) The business that may be dealt with at the accounts meeting includes the resolution.

This is so notwithstanding any default in complying with subsection (1) or (2).

(4) The existing directors must ensure that the resolution is put to the vote of the meeting.

(5) No entitlement of a person to remuneration is made conditional on the resolution being passed by reason only of the provision made by this section.

(6) In this section—

'the accounts meeting' means the general meeting of the company before which the company's annual accounts for the financial year are to be laid; and

'existing director' means a person who is a director of the company immediately before that meeting.

4 Directors' Remuneration Reporting Guidelines.

5 Norris, Paul (2013) 'Directors' Remuneration – The UK State of Play', *Executive Compensation Briefing*, September 2013 (Paul Norris is Chief Executive of MM & K Limited; see http://www.executive-compensation-briefing.com/).

Part F:
The Corporate Governance Journey

Chapter F1

The Corporate Governance Framework

Short history of corporate governance developments F1.1

For the UK, the Thatcher years were tumultuous. Radical themes ran through those years and shaped policy both for the UK and elsewhere. Under the panoply of a free-market philosophy, state subsidies and 'the nanny state' were spurned, while the monopoly privileges of the professions were questioned but, in the main, left untackled. Too much government and too much red tape were identified as curses to be exorcised: determined attempts were made to roll back the frontiers of the state with the intention of liberating the entrepreneurial spirit and leading to the creation of more wealth. Self-regulation was seen as better than state control. The market should regulate itself – government should just provide a level playing field. Regulation, it was considered, should be as light touch as possible to avoid stifling enterprise and growth. 'Selling the family silver' by way of privatisations, leveraged buy-outs and demutualisations unlocked one-off spending power for the state and for its citizens in the form of windfalls. An end result was that more of the economy, for good or ill, became under the control of companies with voracious shareholders, who were often overseas parent companies, and top executives intent upon extracting the maximum possible rent for their executive services. They were heady days when unsustainable growing prosperity was partly funded by squeezing the juice out of the economy. It took time before it crashed with the global financial crisis of 2008. The economy had lost its resilience to withstand such a shock, and a freefall ensued.

Competition was perceived as not only good but also essential. On the global stage, there was seen to be no place for businesses that were internationally uncompetitive – in the UK they went to the wall in droves during the Thatcher years. Unemployment mushroomed – but not, the protagonists argued, through the loss of 'real jobs'. 'If it wasn't hurting it wasn't working', one UK government minister memorably pronounced. The interventionist approaches of the corporate state were replaced by a self-interested individualism symbolised by Margaret Thatcher's protestation that 'there is no such thing as society'. Personal ambition and self-fulfilment reigned supreme. Some would say that the UK saw the development of a more selfish society and a more distinct underclass. The unthinkable maxim that 'greed is good'[1] came to be given a sort of legitimacy and arguably contributed to the current perception of excessive levels of reward for top executives blighting the corporate governance scene today.

There is now a debate as to whether this level playing field should extend beyond the UK to the whole of the European Community, or even beyond. For instance, is it legitimate for EU countries to compete through their differences in labour and taxation laws, not to mention approaches to corporate governance approaches? The 'comply or explain' approach to corporate governance amounts to light touch regulation that gives the UK a relative advantage.

The UK chronology **F1.2**

Key UK corporate governance publications since 1992

1992 (December)	*Report of the Committee* (The Cadbury Committee) *on the Financial Aspects of Corporate Governance*, incorporating the world's first *Code of Best Practice for Corporate Governance*
1994 (December)	*Internal Control and Financial reporting – Guidance for directors of listed companies developed in response to the recommendations of the Cadbury committee* (The Rutteman Report)
1995 (July)	*Directors' Remuneration: Report of a Study Group chaired by Sir Richard Greenbury*, incorporating a *Code of Best Practice* (on Directors' Remuneration)
1998 (January)	*Final report of the Committee on Corporate Governance* (The Hampel Report)
1998 (June)	Hampel's *Combined Code* (2003 version)
1999 (September)	*Internal Control – Guidance for Directors on the Combined Code* (The Turnbull Report)
2003 (January)	*Review of the Role and Effectiveness of Non-Executive Directors* (The Higgs Report)
2003 (January)	*Audit Committees: Combined Code Guidance, a Report and Proposed Guidance by an FRC-appointed Group Chaired by Sir Robert Smith* (The Smith Report)
2003 (June)	*The Tyson Report on the Recruitment and Development of Non-Executive Directors* (DTI)
2003 (July)	*The Combined Code on Corporate Governance* (2003 version)
2005 (October)	*Internal control – Revised Guidance for Directors on the Combined Code* (The Flint Review of the Turnbull Report)
2006 (January)	ASB: *Operating and Financial Review* (Reporting Statement No 1) (FRC)
2006 (June)	*The Combined Code on Corporate Governance* (2006 version) (FRC)
2008 (June)	*The Combined Code on Corporate Governance* (2008 version) (FRC)
2008 (October)	*Guidance on Audit Committees* (an updated version of the 2003 Smith Report) (FRC)

2009 (November)	*A Review of Corporate Governance in UK Banks and Other Financial Industry Entities* (The Walker Report)
2010 (June)	*The UK Corporate Governance Code* (the designation 'Combined' was abandoned) (FRC)
2010 (July)	*The UK Stewardship Code,* 1st edition (FRC)
2010 (September)	*Corporate Governance Guidelines for Smaller Companies* (Quoted Companies Alliance)
2010 (November)	*Corporate Governance Guidance and Principles for Unlisted Companies in the UK* (Institute of Directors)
2010 (December)	Further revised *Guidance on Audit Committees* (FRC)
2011 (February)	*Women on Boards* (The Davies Report)
2011 (September)	*Boards at Risk* (FRC)
2011 (September)	*Final Report and Recommendations of the Independent Commission on Banking* (The Vickers Report)
2011 (October)	*Feedback Statement: Gender Diversity on Boards* (FRC)
2011 (October)	Amendments to the 2010 *UK Corporate Governance Code* to strengthen its diversity content
2011 (December)	*The Impact and Implementation of the UK Corporate Governance and Stewardship Codes* (FRC)
2012 (September)	*The UK Corporate Governance Code,* 2012 (FRC)
2012 (September)	*The UK Stewardship Code,* 2012 (FRC)
2012 (September)	*Further revised Guidance on Audit Committees (FRC)*
2013	*Corporate Governance Code for Small and Mid-Size Companies (Quoted Companies Alliance (2013)*
2014 (March)	*Risk Management, Internal Control and the Going Concern Basis of Accounting* (FRC). FRC consultation paper published in November 2013. Final guidance expected in March 2014 to be effective either in April 2014 or October 2014. Planned as successor guidance to the Turnbull Report and to incorporate the Sharman Committee guidance on going concern.
2014 (expected October 2014)	*The UK Corporate Governance Code,* 2014 (FRC). September 2015 year-ends will be the first expected to follow the 2014 Code.
2014 (expected October 2014)	*The UK Stewardship Code,* 2014 (FRC). September 2015 year-ends will be the first expected to follow the 2014 Code.

The Committee on the Financial Aspects of Corporate Governance (the Cadbury Committee) **F1.3**

Refer also to **App6.1**.

It was the harsh economic climate of the late 1980s and early 1990s which had exposed company reports and accounts to unusually close scrutiny, together with continuing concern about standards of financial reporting and accountability, heightened by BCCI, Maxwell and the controversy in the UK over directors' pay. All these had brought corporate governance into the public eye. It was for these reasons that the Cadbury Committee was set up in May 1991 by the Financial Reporting Council (FRC), the London Stock Exchange and the accountancy profession to address the financial aspects of corporate governance. The Committee issued a draft report for public comment on 27 May 1992. Its final report, taking account of submissions made during the consultation period and incorporating a Code of Best Practice, was published on 1 December 1992.

The Committee's central recommendation was that the boards of all listed companies registered in the UK should comply with the Code. The Committee also encouraged as many other companies as possible to aim to meet its requirements. After all, the proprietors of private companies and other entities also need full, reliable information as a basis for, for instance, rational investment decisions.

While it is unfortunate that the focus of what is now the UK Corporate Governance Code has been the listed company exclusively (and more recently those with a premium UK listing), the FRC, which is the custodian and the developer of the wording of the Code, has no formal corporate governance remit outside this constituency. Nevertheless, the FRC has been encouraging the adoption of codes based on their Code in other sectors. In the case of the life mutuals, this was recommended by Paul Myners in his report following Equitable Life, and others have done it of their own volition. These others include the Building Societies Association, NHS Foundation Trusts (via their regulator, Monitor) and some life mutuals. Links to two of these codes are as follows:

- http://www.bsa.org.uk/information/publications/industry-publications/the-uk-corporate-governance-code-bsa-guidance-for/ (accessed 29 December 2013), and.
- http://www.monitor-nhsft.gov.uk/sites/default/files/publications/CodeOfGovernanceDec13%20FINAL.pdf (accessed 29 December 2013).

In addition, The Higher Education Funding Council for England (HEFCE) first adopted the Code in 2007 for the English universities it regulates.[2]

These codes are, in the main, identical to the UK Corporate Governance Code (set out in full at **App1**), subject to the addition of some annotations where the Provisions need a degree of interpretation, and to the inevitable time delay in bringing into line these codes with updates of the UK Corporate Governance Code.

The formal scope of the Cadbury Committee's report was on the *financial* aspects of corporate governance. Some held this restriction against the Committee. For instance, some suggested that the Cadbury Code Provision that directors should report publicly on the effectiveness of internal control must have meant internal financial control in view of the intended scope of the Cadbury Committee's remit. But it was transparently clear that Cadbury meant *all* aspects of internal control, since the word 'financial' had been removed by the Cadbury Committee from their final report wherever internal control was referred to (including within the Cadbury Code itself), whereas the word 'financial' had always been present in the exposure draft of the Cadbury Report. There were good reasons why Cadbury meant that directors should report publicly on internal control 'in the round'. Internal financial control cannot be neatly differentiated from the other aspects of internal control: organisations achieve their objectives not through having effective internal financial control alone – arguably, operational control is more crucial to the achievement of objectives. Furthermore, the readers of published results already have some inkling about the effectiveness of internal financial control in view of the presence of audited financial statements; but to learn about the effectiveness of operational and legal and regulatory compliance control is to tell the readers something extra – so long as it is, and can be, reliably reported. As we have said, maximising reliable disclosure is an underlying theme of contemporary developments in corporate governance best practice.

The Greenbury Committee F1.4

In the UK, following the seminal Cadbury Code of Best Practice came the Greenbury Report[3] on directors' remuneration with its own Code on executive remuneration (reproduced at **App6.2**). Some would argue that the Greenbury Committee would not have been convened had it not been for the excesses of individual greed evidenced in particular in the 'fat cat remuneration' of senior executives within newly privatised utilities – beneficiaries of Thatcherite privatisation policies. Certainly, Greenbury had not been anticipated at the time of the Cadbury Report.

The Hampel Committee F1.5

The Cadbury Committee had recommended that its sponsors, convened by the FRC, should appoint a new Committee by the end of June 1995 to examine how far compliance with the Code had by then progressed, how far its other recommendations had been implemented, and whether the Code needed updating; and that, until then, the existing Cadbury Committee would remain responsible for reviewing the implementation of its proposals. The Hampel Committee was in fact set up in November 1995,[4] and the Cadbury Committee remained convened for a while so that it could indeed, in the meantime, review the implementation of their Code, publishing a research study thereon in May 1995.[5]

Then we had the Hampel Report[6] which consolidated, amended and added to the Cadbury and Greenbury Codes in the form of the 1998 Combined Code – so called because it combined the Cadbury and Greenbury Codes with Hampel's own additions and changes (original versions reproduced at **App6.3**). So, in the event, the Hampel Committee had been asked to roll into its review not only the functioning of the Cadbury Code, but the Greenbury Code as well. This Combined Code applied to companies listed in the UK reporting for years ending on or after 31 December 1998, until a new revised Combined Code came into effect for reporting years beginning on or after 1 November 2003. There were transitional adoption arrangements, and the 1998 Combined Code Principle D.2, together with its associated Provisions D.2.1 and D.2.2, were deferred from being implemented, pending the development and roll-out of guidance which came in the form of the Turnbull Report.

The Hampel Committee did not give us its proposed wording of the original Combined Code within its draft or final reports. Instead, it gave indications of the sort of changes it was minded to make. This undoubtedly had the effect of making it easier to get general 'buy-in' to the proposed changes – but arguably only because there was less appreciation of precisely what they would be. After the Hampel Report was accepted, the Hampel Committee quickly drew up the wording of the original Combined Code which was exposed only briefly before being adopted. In contrast, in 2003 Higgs was to give us in his report the suggested wording of a revised Combined Code, with the result that it was easier to dispute it; consequently, Higgs' proposed wording was revised before adoption by the FRC in 2003.

UK corporate governance listing requirements **F1.6**

After the adoption of the first version of the Combined Code by the London Stock Exchange, the Financial Services Authority (FSA) took over from the London Stock Exchange the regulation of UK listed companies. The Listing Rules, which used to be referred to as 'The Yellow Book', have now become 'The Purple Book'.[7]

(In 2013 the FSA was replaced by the Financial Conduct Authority (FCA) and the Prudential Regulation Authority (PRA). The FCA, a company limited by guarantee, now regulates financial firms providing services to consumers and maintains the integrity of the UK's financial markets; it focuses on the regulation of conduct by retail and wholesale financial services firms. The PRA is a wholly owned subsidiary of the Bank of England; it carries out the prudential regulation of deposit-taking institutions, insurers and designated investment firms (financial firms, including banks, investment banks, building societies and insurance companies).)

The 1998 Combined Code was appended to the Listing Rules, as had been the Cadbury and Greenbury Codes previously. The Combined Code did not form part of the Listing Rules themselves[8] and neither does the current UK Corporate Governance Code. The 'Definitions' section (May 2000) towards the start of the Listing Rules attributed the following status to the 1998 Combined Code:

> 'Combined Code: the principles of good governance and code of best practice prepared by the Committee on Corporate Governance, chaired by Sir Ronald Hampel, published in June 1998 and appended but not forming part of, the Listing Rules.'

So, as with the Cadbury Code, it is not a listing requirement for a listed company to comply with the Code. Chapter 12: Financial Information (May 2000) of the Listing Rules, the section on 'Corporate Governance and Directors' Remuneration', included obligations only requiring a company to include in its annual report two statements, namely:

> '12.43A In the case of a company incorporated in the United Kingdom, the following additional items must be included in its annual report and accounts:

(a) A narrative statement of how it has applied the principles set out in Section 1 of the Combined Code, providing sufficient explanation which enables its shareholders to evaluate how the principles have been applied;

(b) a statement as to whether or not it has complied throughout the accounting period with the Provisions set out in Section 1 of the Combined Code. A company that has not complied with the Code Provisions, or complied with only some of the Code Provisions or (in the case of Provisions whose requirements are of a continuing nature) complied for only part of an accounting period, must specify the Provisions with which it has not complied, and (where relevant) for what part of the period such non-compliance continued, and give reasons for any non-compliance; …'

Certain Provisions of the 1998 Combined Code had already been explicitly required by the Listing Rules as they were already requirements at the time of the introduction of the 1998 Combined Code.

Listing Rule 12.43A has now been replaced by 9.8.6. It continues to be the case that a consequence of the UK's discretionary approach is that the UK Corporate Governance Code is not within the UK Listing Rules. See also **D2.15** and **D3.7**.

The FSA regarded both part (a) of this listing rule (on a company's adherence to the Principles in the Code) and also part (b) on compliance or otherwise with the Provisions in the Code as being rules about *disclosure* alone, not about application. It said (September 2003):

> 'On monitoring and enforcement our powers are limited. We look at a sample of Annual Reports to check they include a corporate governance disclosure statement in line with the Code, but I expect you appreciate we make no judgement on the quality or accuracy of these statements. This is a matter for investors to determine. We could take enforcement action against companies that refused to make any disclosure but this has not proved to be necessary. We have spoken to one or two companies whose statements were considered inadequate and they have done better next time.'

So, for instance, Wm Morrison (Supermarkets) breached a number of Code Principles during its year ended in 2005 (see Table below) but was not disciplined or admonished by the FSA, the enforcer of the Combined Code, for those breaches.

When, in 1998, the Hampel Committee for the first time introduced Principles into its Combined Code, it stated that it did so for two reasons. The first was to counter criticism that some companies had been using a box-ticking approach to observance of the 1992 Cadbury Code. In other words, if the Code 'required' something, such as an audit committee, then the company would set one up so that they could claim to be complying with the Code – even if it was only token compliance and there was no intention that the committee would be effective.

So the Hampel Committee distilled from its Provisions the fundamental Principles that lay behind them. The requirement 'to include in its annual report and accounts a narrative statement of how it has applied the Principles … of the … Code, providing explanation which enables its shareholders to evaluate how the Principles have been applied' was intended to be a very robust requirement. It countenanced no discretion – all the Principles were to be applied and the company was required by the Listing Rule to explain comprehensively *how* it was doing so. This was in marked distinction to the language used about the 'comply or explain' Provisions, with respect to which the same Listing Rule required a company to publish a statement:

> 'as to whether or not it has complied throughout the accounting period with the provisions set out in Section 1 of the Combined Code. A company that has not complied with the Code provisions, or complied with only some of the Code provisions or (in the case of provisions whose requirements are of a continuing nature) complied for only part of an accounting period, must specify the provisions with which it has not complied, and (where relevant) for what part of the period such non-compliance continued, and give reasons for any noncompliance; …'[9]

The second reason was that the Hampel Committee needed to respond to concerns that the Cadbury Code was too inflexible to be appropriate in all respects for, for instance, small companies and companies in special circumstances. By focusing on mandatory 'Principles' and stressing that the Provisions were discretionary (as they had been with the Cadbury Code), the Hampel Committee considered they were introducing the needed flexibility.

It is remarkable that the emphasis in annual reports is upon Provisions and not Principles, and that many institutional shareholders and their representatives largely ignore the Principles in assessing companies' corporate governance standards. Corporate governance metrics tend to be based on compliance with the Provisions. This is largely due to the FSA's refusal to regard its Listing Rule as requiring enforcement of the application of the Principles. Neither does the FSA enforce its rule that annual report and accounts contain a narrative statement of how it has applied the Principles of the Code, providing explanation which enables its shareholders to evaluate how the Principles have been applied. They leave it to the market to enforce, and the market focuses on the Provisions, largely ignoring the Principles.

Whereas Wm Morrison (Supermarkets) plc has been exemplary at cataloguing its non-compliance with a number of Code Provisions – even specifying the Code numbers of the Provisions it failed to follow – it was less clear about its position with respect to the Principles. In the table below, we show the Principles we discern from Morrison's annual report that were not followed at particular times in the past. More recently, Morrison has come into line with the Principles – an indication that the FSA's approach of leaving it to the market to enforce can be effective.

Morrison is meant to explain *how* it applies the 'Principles'. In the table we show the narrative Morrison provided which related most closely to the Principles we believe they were breaching. Of course, this narrative is not an explanation of *how* Morrison applies these 'Principles'. Neither is it a sufficient explanation as to why it does not apply them.

The Morrison case study **F1.7**

Morrison's non-application of Code Principles (from its annual report for the year ended 30 January 2005) (Main Principles are shown in bold, supporting Principles in standard text. Numbers are as per the Code. The 2003 Code applied to Morrison at the time)

FRC 2003 Code Principle not applied by Morrison		**What Morrison says about it in its 2005 annual report**	**Our comment**
Main Principle	**Supporting Principle**		
A.1	As part of their role as members of a unitary board, non-executive directors … are responsible for determining appropriate levels of remuneration of executive directors and have a prime role in appointing, and where necessary removing, executive directors, and in succession planning.	The annual report discloses that the executive chairman and both the managing directors (one of whom is now the chief executive) comprise three of the four members of the remuneration committee, and that … 'The company's remuneration committee is chaired by David Jones and is responsible for setting the remuneration of the chairman and executive directors.' 'The company's nomination committee is responsible for the appointment of executive and non-executive directors to the board. There are no formal terms of reference for the committee, but appointments are made on the basis of selecting individuals of sufficient calibre, knowledge, and experience to fulfil the duties of a director.'	By all accounts David Jones played an active role in the search for further NEDs, but it was unlikely that he alone (being the only NED) determined who should be the executive directors on the board, or their remuneration.

FRC 2003 Code Principle not applied by Morrison			**What Morrison says about it in its 2005 annual report**	**Our comment**
Main Principle		**Supporting Principle**		
A.2	**There should be a clear division of responsibilities at the head of the company between the running of the board and the executive responsibility for the running of the company's business. No one individual should have unfettered powers of decision.**		'On 23 March 2005 Robert Stott was appointed chief executive of the company. Sir Kenneth Morrison remains executive chairman.' 'The roles of the chairman and the chief executive were not separate for the period under review (A.2.1), but have been subsequently separated.'	In what sense can Robert Stott be regarded as a true *chief* executive when there was someone above him with an executive role and who was chief executive previously? Morrison may have nominally complied with this Code requirement but they had not applied it in principle. Note that Provision A.2.2 set out that: 'The chairman should on appointment meet the independence criteria set out in A.3.1 below. A chief executive should not go on to be chairman of the same company. If exceptionally a board decides that a chief executive should become chairman, the board should consult major shareholders in advance and should set out its reasons to shareholders at the time of the appointment and in the next annual report.' It is true that Sir Ken Morrison's chairmanship predates the advent of the 2003 Code.

FRC 2003 Code Principle not applied by Morrison			**What Morrison says about it in its 2005 annual report**	**Our comment**
Main Principle		**Supporting Principle**		
A.3	**The board should include a balance of executive and non-executive directors (and in particular independent nonexecutive directors) such that no individual or small group of individuals can dominate the board's decision taking.**	To ensure that power and information are not concentrated in one or two individuals, there should be a strong presence on the board of both executive and nonexecutive directors.		The board had eight directors of whom only one was an independent NED. The board also had an executive chairman. There was no way that such a board could be described as 'balanced' or that it had a 'strong presence' of NEDs.
A.3		The value of ensuring that committee membership is refreshed and that undue reliance is not placed on particular individuals should be taken into account in deciding chairmanship and membership of committees.	'David Jones, the senior non-executive director, was appointed as non-executive deputy chairman on 23 March 2005 and will chair the recently established remuneration and audit committees, as well as the nomination committee. He will take primary responsibility for ensuring that good governance is practised within the company. He will also work with the chairman and chief executive to ensure that succession plans are in place for all board positions and that additional non-executive directors are appointed.'	There had been excessive, if temporary, reliance on David Jones, who was also chairman of the retailer Next. Best practice is that no NED belongs to all three board committees.

FRC 2003 Code Principle not applied by Morrison			What Morrison says about it in its 2005 annual report	Our comment
Main Principle		**Supporting Principle**		
A.4		Appointments to the board should be made on merit and against objective criteria. Care should be taken to ensure that appointees have enough time available to devote to the job. This is particularly important in the case of chairmanships.	'On 21 May 2004, David Jones and Duncan Davidson were appointed as non-executive directors … Duncan Davidson stood down from the board on 23 March 2005 due to the increasing time requirements of the role.' … 'The non-executive directors committed to set aside sufficient time to meet the requirements of their role.'	Jones belonged to Morrison's board for over eight months of Morrison's 2005 financial year, but managed to attend fewer than half the board meetings which took place over the complete financial year.
A.5	**The board should be supplied in a timely manner with information in a form and of a quality appropriate to enable it to discharge its duties. All directors should receive induction on joining the board and should regularly update and refresh their skills and knowledge**	The chairman is responsible for ensuring that the directors receive accurate, timely and clear information. Management has an obligation to provide such information, but directors should seek clarification or amplification where necessary.	'All directors receive appropriate information on a regular basis to assist them in fulfilling their duties and responsibilities.' [From the chairman's report]: 'Whilst the accounting problems at Safeway were not of his making, Martin Ackroyd [the finance director] has accepted full responsibility for the failure to keep full control during the year. He offered to resign from the board on 22 March due to unfounded press criticism which he believed	Four profits warnings in the space of a few months, and the surprise provision of in excess of £40m to cover the upfront payments by Safeway suppliers called to question whether the board was in possession of the information they needed on a timely basis. The ultimate responsibility for this rests with the chairman, as Supporting Principle A.5 states.

FRC 2003 Code Principle not applied by Morrison			What Morrison says about it in its 2005 annual report	Our comment
Main Principle		**Supporting Principle**		
			was damaging the reputation of the company. It was with deep regret that I accepted this request and have made it clear we would like him to remain with the company once his term of office runs out at the annual general meeting on 26 May 2005.'	
A.6	**The board should undertake a formal and rigorous annual evaluation of its own performance and that of its committees and individual directors.**		'The performance of individual directors and the whole board is evaluated by the chairman on a continual, but informal, basis. The chairman has undertaken an informal performance evaluation of David Jones, in terms of his effectiveness and commitment to the role, and believes that he should be re-elected to the board.'	Morrison's acknowledgement speaks for itself. There is therefore a greater imperative for institutional shareholders to evaluate the performance of the Morrison board.
A.6		Individual evaluation should aim to show whether each director continues to contribute effectively and to demonstrate commitment to the role (including commitment of time for board and committee meetings and any other duties).		

FRC 2003 Code Principle not applied by Morrison			What Morrison says about it in its 2005 annual report	Our comment
Main Principle		Supporting Principle		
		The chairman should act on the results of the performance evaluation by recognising the strengths and addressing the weaknesses of the board and, where appropriate, proposing new members be appointed to the board or seeking the resignation of directors.		
B.2	**There should be a formal and transparent procedure for developing policy on executive remuneration and for fixing the remuneration packages of individual directors. No director should be involved in deciding his or her own remuneration.**		The annual report discloses that the executive chairman and both the managing directors (one of whom is now the chief executive) comprise three of the four members of the remuneration committee, and that … 'The company's remuneration committee is chaired by David Jones and is responsible for setting the remuneration of the chairman and executive directors.'	With this committee membership, it would be hard for Morrison to ensure that no director was involved in determining his or her own remuneration.

FRC 2003 Code Principle not applied by Morrison			**What Morrison says about it in its 2005 annual report**	**Our comment**
Main Principle		**Supporting Principle**		
C.1	**The board should present a balanced and understandable assessment of the company's position and prospects.**	The board's responsibility to present a balanced and understandable assessment extends to interim and other price-sensitive public reports and reports to regulators as well as to information required to be presented by statutory requirements.		It is to Morrison's credit that it had not fought shy of issuing profits warnings. Yet the impression remained that Morrison was presenting an overly optimistic view of future prospects.
C.3	**The board should establish formal and transparent arrangements for considering how they should apply the financial reporting and internal control principles and for maintaining an appropriate relationship with the company's auditors.**		'An audit committee was formed during the period whose members are Sir Kenneth Morrison, David Jones (chairman of the committee) and Robert Stott. The committee does not yet have a formal constitution, nor does it comply with the Combined Code in that it does not include at least three nonexecutive directors.'	Not formal. Also a lack of transparency as the annual report did not disclose the number of occasions that the audit committee had met during the year – as Code Provision A.1.2 required: 'The annual report should identify the chairman, the deputy chairman (where there is one), the chief executive, the senior independent director and the chairmen and members of the nomination, audit and remuneration committees. It should also set out the number of meetings of the board and those committees and individual attendance by directors.'

So, if there were to be enforcement by the FSA, it would be for *failure to disclose*, not for *failure to adhere* to a Principle. The Introduction to the UK's 2006 Combined Code (p 1, section 4) took the same stance as the FSA, in that it expressed the listing rule requirement as being a disclosure requirement rather than a requirement to specifically apply the Principles:

> 'The Code contains main and supporting principles and provisions. The Listing Rules require listed companies to make a disclosure statement in two parts in relation to the Code. In the first part of the statement, the company has to report on how it applies the principles in the Code. This should cover both main and supporting principles.[10] The form and content of this part of the statement are not prescribed, the intention being that companies should have a free hand to explain their governance policies in the light of the principles, including any special circumstances applying to them which have led to a particular approach. In the second part of the statement the company has either to confirm that it complies with the Code's provisions or – where it does not – to provide an explanation. This 'comply or explain' approach has been in operation for over ten years and the flexibility it offers has been widely welcomed both by company boards and by investors. It is for shareholders and others to evaluate the company's statement.'

The 1998 Code (p 5, section 4) said likewise:

> '… companies should have a free hand to explain their governance policies in the light of the principles, including any special circumstances applying to them which have led to a particular approach. It must be for shareholders and others to evaluate this part of the company's statement.'

and, with respect to Provisions, (p 6, section 5):

> 'the company will be required either to confirm that it complies with the Code Provisions or – where it does not – provide an explanation. Again, it must be for shareholders and others to evaluate such explanations.'

The Preamble to the 1998 Code (section 4) also lent support to the approach being taken by the FSA, which is basically to depend upon the market rather than the FSA to influence enforcement of the Principles:

> 'In the first part of the [disclosure] statement, the company [is] required to report on how it applies the principles in the Combined Code … the intention being that companies should have a free hand to explain their governance policies in the light of the principles, including any special circumstances applying to them which have led to a particular approach. It must be for shareholders and others to evaluate this part of the company's statement.'

Certainly, it can be argued that leaving enforcement to the market rather that to the regulator seems to work quite well in the UK. But the problem is with the company that does not wish to conform, perhaps for unworthy reasons.

Steadily increasing burden of compliance F1.8

The tables at **C4.17** and **F2.1** summarise the extent to which adherence to UK corporate governance codes of best practice has become a more demanding business over the last decade or so.

The corporate governance framework – laws, regulations, codes of best practice etc **F1.9**

With many of the world's largest entities being corporations, not nation states, their effective governance, and in particular their accountability, become key imperatives. Sir Adrian Cadbury has described the corporate governance framework in these terms:

> 'Corporations work within a governance framework which is set first by the law and then by regulations emanating from the regulatory bodies to which they are subject. In addition, publicly quoted companies are subject to their shareholders in general meeting and all companies to the forces of public opinion. The influence of public opinion should not be underestimated; it compelled Shell to change its plans for the disposal of the Brent Star platform. Not only is public opinion a governance force, but it is one whose impact cannot be precisely foreseen in the same way as that of the law and regulations; it is not fixed in form as they are, but responds to the mood of the moment. The views of investors and public opinion reflect their current thinking, and boards of directors and members of professional bodies need to respond by being continually alert to the changing expectations of those whom they serve.
>
> Clearly the balance between these governance forces varies between countries. Where the opinions of shareholders and of the public cannot make themselves sufficiently felt, the gap needs to be filled by the law and appropriate regulations. This is why each country has to devise its own governance framework. But how effective is this framework of governance? The legal rules are clear-cut and carry known penalties if boards of directors contravene them. Regulations are equally straightforward; if quoted companies do not abide by the rules of the London Stock Exchange, they risk de-listing.'[11]

The Cadbury Committee's report also gave some emphasis to the part that internal rules should play in corporate governance, namely:

> 'It is important that all employees should know what standards are expected of them. We regard it as good practice for boards of directors to draw up Codes of ethics or statements of business practice and to publish them both internally and externally.'

The importance of disclosure **F1.10**

Sir Adrian Cadbury said of the Cadbury Code of Best Practice that its foundation, and the foundation of its equivalents elsewhere, is based on disclosure:

> 'Disclosure is the lifeblood of governance. Provided those with interests in, or responsibilities towards, companies know how they are directed and controlled, they can influence their boards constructively. A leading bank responded to the Code by including a section in its Annual Report headed "How our business is run". This covered the role of the board, the work of its committees and the responsibilities of directors; information which had never previously been accessible. Investors, lenders, employees and the public can only play their governance roles provided they have the information they need in order to do so.

Transparency is the aim. This requires clear reporting of the state of the business, of the way it is directed and controlled and of its place in the community. Openness by companies is the basis of public confidence in the corporate system. It also enables external governance forces to function as they should. Institutional investors, in particular, have the means and the incentive to use Codes to promote board effectiveness. As to whether Codes work, the degree to which the majority of quoted companies responded to the Code of Best Practice is evidence that Codes can give a lead which will be followed, provided they genuinely represent best practice and thus are going with the grain of investor and corporate opinion.'[12]

Important, related aspects of governance are accountability and disclosure:

> 'Without audit, no accountability; without accountability, no control; and if there is no control, where is the seat of power? … great issues often come to light only because of scrupulous verification of details.'[13]

Substance, not form F1.11

Sir Adrian Cadbury emphasised that the focus has to be not on the form of governance but on its quality, for which legal tests would be difficult to devise. He has pointed out that the Cadbury Code of Best Practice, for example, referred to the need for boards to include non-executive directors of sufficient calibre for their views to carry significant weight in the boards' decisions:

> 'A word like "calibre" may have no legal standing, but it can certainly be recognised by investors and financial commentators. When a major UK company appointed its first batch of non-executive directors, they were seen as not measuring up to this requirement of the Code. Investor pressure and press comment resulted in the appointment of a further non-executive director of sufficient bottom.'[14]

To take another example, the Cadbury Committee said in its report that, in principle, the chairman and chief executive should not be the same person. Being non-prescriptive, however, the Code did not make separation of the top two corporate posts a requirement for companies observing the Code:

> 'If separation were to be a legal requirement, boards could circumvent it by giving two of their members different titles, while in reality power remained in one pair of hands. If shareholders queried the balance of power on such a board, the board could reply that they complied with the law and that there was no more to be said.'[15]

The Cadbury Code, however, required that:

> 'There should be a clearly accepted division of responsibilities at the head of a company … such that no one person has unfettered powers of decision.
>
> Shareholders can demand to know precisely how powers are divided, and continue probing until they are satisfied. In that sense, a Code recommendation can prove a sterner test in practice of a true separation of powers than a law to the same effect.
>
> A further reason for backing statutory regulation with market regulation is that Codes can reflect changing circumstances or new governance issues as they arise, whereas the law by its nature takes time to catch up with new situations. In the same way the law sets a floor to corporate or professional behaviour, whereas

Codes can promote best practice beyond lawful practice. The law is limited to the letter, while Codes can put substance above form.'

Compliance **F1.12**

As Sir Adrian Cadbury has said, an important concern is that legislators may enact laws and regulators may introduce rules ('soft law') and/or guidelines, but at the end of the day what matters is that these are observed, breaches are identified and tough sanctions are consistently applied. Where there is doubt, as for instance in some countries, about the diligence or even-handedness of the authorities or the independence of the judiciary, then there will always be doubt about standards of corporate governance – however impressive might be the company law or the stock exchange regulations.

In the UK, there has been concern about flouting of aspects of the Code[16] – especially the Provisions on directors' appointments and remuneration.[17] Pensions and Investment Research Consultants (PIRC),[18] who led an early survey which highlighted these concerns, and also other bodies which represent institutional investors, have overlaid the Provisions of the Combined Code with their own more demanding interpretations and prescriptions which are not to be found in the Code and do not therefore have the authority of the Listing Rules.[19] (The Listing Rules require listed companies to explain how they are adhering to the Principles of the UK Corporate Governance Code, and to draw attention to which of the Provisions they are not adhering to, giving reasons. So it is not a Listing Rule that a listed company should necessarily comply with *any* of the Provisions; and certainly not a Listing Rule that companies should comply with the more onerous extensions promulgated in the policies of bodies which represent institutional investors.) It is, however, entirely appropriate that institutional (and other) investors should seek to exercise effective external control over the way that companies in which they invest are governed; and so, to the extent that the policies of bodies representing institutional investors are followed by the institutional investors themselves, these policies assume an authority of their own. Perhaps we should point out that these representative bodies are less inclined to draw attention to those companies that go *much further* than the Code Provisions require. It has also been pointed out that the corporate governance arrangements of many institutional investors themselves fall far short of the best practice being commended by the Code, let alone the more demanding requirements of the bodies which represent these institutional investors.

The research by PIRC, referred to above,[20] which covered 468 companies in the FTSE All Share index, found that just nine – less than 2% – put critical remuneration committee reports to the vote of shareholders at the annual general meetings. Almost half the companies had still not imposed one-year contracts on executive directors, or adopted a policy of reducing contracts to this.[21] (This recommendation dates back to the 1995 Greenbury Code on executive remuneration.) Only 77% staffed their remuneration committees with non-executives they believed to be independent. This PIRC research (December 1999) was prior to UK company law requiring the remuneration report of a listed company to be put to the vote of the shareholders – a change introduced in 2003.

PIRC found 27% of companies were happy to disclose that they had considered putting pay committee reports to an AGM vote, but most companies gave no indication either way. Stuart Bell, PIRC research director, said:

'If they are not disclosing the information, shareholders can have little confidence that they are following the Code. [It was] disappointing that compliance on pay issues is relatively low.'

Just 51% of companies reported that their practice or policy was one-year, rolling contracts for all directors. Bell said that the Code:

'represents a base-line standard.'

He expected the best companies:

'to go beyond it in providing better information to investors and improving their governance structure. This was important because it will contribute to competitiveness in the long term.'[22]

Study of the wording of the Combined Code at that time does, however, show that PIRC was taking a much more stringent line than the Code intended with respect to most of these matters. For instance, to take just one example, a reasonable interpretation of the Code at that time on 'independence' allows that it is for the board to decide whether a past or even a present relationship (with management, the business or with anyone or anything else) is an impediment to the exercise of independent judgement. In defence of PIRC, the Hampel Committee was at pains to assert that it is the spirit of the Principles contained within the Code that it is mandatory for companies to adhere to, and, of course, it becomes a matter of judgement as to how such adherence can be achieved.

Status of the Code in the UK F1.13

There are options as to the regulatory framework to be followed in order to ensure that organisations observe satisfactory standards of corporate governance. It is hard to avoid the conclusion that the route followed within the UK is typically British. The Code has not been enshrined in statute. There has been no legal requirement for listed companies to comply with the Provisions of the Code. The Code is not in the Listing Rules.[23] We should not run away with the impression that compliance with the Provisions within the Code of Best Practice has ever been a regulatory requirement. The Listing Rules themselves just require that a listed company should state within its annual report whether it complies with the Provisions of the Code and, if not, with which Provisions it does not comply and the reasons for non-compliance. That has been enough for most listed companies, most of the time, to endeavour to apply with most or all of the Provisions within the Code – few companies would wish, for instance, to have to draw attention to the absence of an audit committee and then try to explain why the company does not have an audit committee; or to the absence of a report on internal control and then try to explain that away. It is easier to comply. Excluding quite detailed disclosure requirements on directors' remuneration,[24] the listing requirements (rule 12.43A) only required a company to include in its annual report two statements, namely:

'A narrative statement of how it has applied the Principles set out in section 1 of the Combined Code providing explanation which enables its shareholders to evaluate how the Principles have been applied.'[25]

and:

> 'A statement as to whether or not it has complied throughout the accounting period with the Code provisions set out in Section 1 of the Combined Code. A company that has not complied with the Code provisions, or complied with only some of the Code provisions or (in the case of provisions whose requirements are of a continuing nature) complied for only part of an accounting period, must specify the Code provisions with which it has not complied, and (where relevant) for what part of the period such non-compliance continued, and give reasons for any non-compliance.'[26]

The wording of the listing requirement reproduced above is the post-1998 wording. This has been revised to require application of the Main Principles only, not the Supporting Principles, and to apply to companies with a Premium not a Standard listing only – see **D3.3**.

Principles, Provisions – and 'box ticking' F1.14

This raises the question as to the extent to which compliance has been nominal and superficial. Hampel referred disparagingly to this as 'box ticking' – which his committee felt was all too prevalent. This has not been the experience of the author. It could be that a listed company might have established an audit committee only because of the Cadbury Code – not because it believed in it, nor even because it had any intention that it would be effective. But, over time, the committee would tend to develop a life of its own. Its non-executive members would be unlikely to be willing to be mere ciphers for the executive. The written terms of reference would start to give teeth to the committee. Setting up the committee in the good times would mean it was already in place when bad times came along and the company was then tempted to sail closer to the wind.

The striking change, following the Hampel Report and the introduction of the Combined Code, was that *above* the level of the Code Provisions we then had higher-level Code Principles. It is interesting to observe how the Hampel Committee had forged overarching Principles from the lower level Code Provisions. The Listing Rule quoted above indicated that companies were expected to apply the Principles though not necessarily the Provisions – companies were therefore required to include a statement showing *how* they had applied the Principles, not (as with the Code Provisions) *whether*, and not *if not – why not*. Strictly, there was also no requirement to explain *how* a Provision had been complied with: *how* applied to Principles – *whether* applied to Provisions.

Although the Code Provisions were, therefore, in a sense, optional, so were those within the earlier Cadbury Code which nevertheless came to be followed in most respects by the vast majority of UK listed companies. Having to draw attention to ways in which they were not being complied with, and to give reasons for non-compliance, was enough to encourage companies to ensure compliance.

Adoption beyond listed companies F1.15

Clearly, there is more public concern about the governance of public companies than of other companies. Yet the Cadbury Committee expressed the view that their Code of Best Practice had a much broader applicability than just to the listed company sector. Indeed, it became the yardstick against which to measure the governance of other companies, enterprises incorporated not under company law, and also public sector entities.

The public sector in the UK has become one of the keenest advocates of the Code, with the encouragement in particular of HM Treasury. In the UK, just as the public sector attempts to adopt emerging accounting and auditing standards, so now this sector is keen to adopt the Corporate Governance Code.

While the major concerns which had led to the Cadbury Committee being set up were concerns within the listed company sector, and the Code was directed primarily to the boards of directors of quoted companies, the Committee said in its report that it:

> 'would encourage as many other companies as possible to aim at meeting its requirements.'

Indeed, there has been a very widespread adoption of the Code outside of the listed sector, and not least by public sector bodies (see above). There tends to be a two-year (or so) time lag before the public sector adopts newly specified best practices. This was so before most of the public sector, for instance, commenced providing directors' reports on internal control – often much more impressive ones than the private sector provides with disclosures about effectiveness. Of course, separately, the public sector has not been idle in developing its own tailor-made Codes – especially those arising from the Nolan Report (paras 9.1–9.3).

While there is more public concern about the governance of public companies than of other companies, this indicates how dated is the content of these corporate governance Codes. The general concern about environmental responsibility, sustainability and the social responsibility of corporations is a concern which is especially, but not exclusively, directed towards public, listed companies. But contemporary corporate governance codes, at least in the UK, are silent on those issues.[27] They focus on the concerns of only one stakeholder – the shareholder. Their focus on disclosure is largely on disclosures which are of value to shareholders alone.

Sir Adrian Cadbury F1.16

Perhaps the last word should be with Sir Adrian Cadbury. In 1998, he said:

> 'The Committee considered that companies as a whole would see it as in their interest to comply (with the Code of Best Practice for Corporate Governance). Compliance would publicly confirm that they met the standards expected of well-run businesses. The Code was literally based on best practice, on the way in which successful companies were directed and controlled. Meeting best practice has to be a logical aim for boards and we expect investors, especially the institutions, to encourage the companies in which they held shares to comply. In effect, the Committee was looking to market regulation, rather than strictly self-regulation, to win board acceptance for its recommendations. Provided investors, analysts and lenders valued compliance with the Code, it would confer a market advantage on companies which complied, possibly assisting their credit rating and lowering their costs of capital. In addition, good corporate governance is increasingly being linked to good corporate performance and so complying with the Code could

be expected to add to a company's competitive edge. Indeed, my continuing involvement with corporate governance is founded on the positive contribution which I am convinced it can make to board effectiveness.

Similar codes around the world have equally relied on companies seeing it as in their best interest to comply. None is mandatory and most are backed by the appropriate Stock Exchange. In sum, I believe that such codes are effective, both in assisting boards to direct their companies well and in providing some insurance against fraud and failure, provided that they are based firmly on best practice, not on what best practice in the abstract might be thought to be, and that they have some market discipline behind them. Thus Codes can usefully fill a layer below the law and regulations and help to clarify the rules of the game. But why not make compliance compulsory, on the argument that well-intentioned companies will no doubt follow the best practice lead in any case, but it is precisely the less well-intentioned who most need to be brought within the rules? There is clearly force in that argument. However, an important reason why I believe that there is a place for Codes in establishing the rules of the game is that it is hard to frame legislation which will raise governance standards.'[28]

Regulation principles **F1.17**

These days, there are standards and codes of practice for most things. We are not aware of a general code intended to cover regulation in general. So we have drafted the code suggested below as an initial suggestion of what such a code might comprise. It is not an authoritative suggested code and has not been subjected to a proper exposure process. Similar ground is covered elsewhere to some extent. For instance, the FSA has a Code of Practice for Approved Persons as well as The Fit and Proper Test for Approved Persons (www.fsa.gov.uk), which overlap with section 3 and, in particular, section 4 below.

The purpose of regulation is to ensure necessary modes of conduct and outcomes which have been agreed to by the active parties and which are consistent with the interests of the wider community. The parties to regulation are (a) those who set the rules, (b) those who enforce them, (c) those who are required to abide by them, and (d) those who may seek redress for regulatory failure of other parties.

A. Duties of those who regulate

1. To collectively possess understanding and competence of the regulated (or to be regulated) activities and the associated industry.
2. To obtain clarity as to the need for regulation.
3. To regulate when regulation is the best way of achieving the agreed upon results.
4. To liaise appropriately with other parties to the regulatory process.
5. To consult widely and carefully and to be open with respect to the nature and disposition of matters raised by parties during consultation periods.
6. To formulate regulations with impartiality and fairly with respect to the parties to regulation.
7. In determining regulations, to take account of the cost and practicality of (a) enforcement and (b) compliance.
8. To ensure that regulations are 'fit for purpose', concise and not excessive.

9. To ensure mutual consistency between regulations and an absence of ambiguity.
10. To have in place, and to follow, a suitable programme of review and revision of regulations, seeking to balance the requirement for continuity with the requirement for current and future appropriateness.
11. To ensure that the costs of regulation are borne fairly by the parties.

B. Duties of those who enforce regulations

1. To apply a 'regulatory touch' no heavier than necessary to ensure a high degree of compliance.
2. To ensure that enforcement resources are sufficient.
3. To ensure that enforcement staff are experienced in the regulated industry, are competent to discharge their enforcement responsibilities and are overseen effectively.
4. To use their best endeavours to ensure that the costs of the regulatory process are not excessive and are shared fairly between the parties.
5. To enforce regulations independently and fairly, having regard to the commercial and personal interests of those regulated.
6. To report openly to the parties.
7. To make representations to those who regulate, in the interests of proper enforcement.

C. Duties of institutions regulated

1. To be aware of the sets of regulations that apply to their businesses, and the identity of the parties who are the custodians and enforcers of those regulations.
2. To participate in the appropriate development of regulations, to the extent practical.
3. To formally undertake to follow all applicable regulations.
4. To resolve to observe the spirit as well as the letter of applicable regulations.
5. To ensure that the requirements of the regulators are met with respect to organisational, staffing, procedural and other matters.
6. To ensure compliance with applicable regulations through (a) the design and application of effective systems of control, (b) the provision of appropriate training programmes, and (c) effective compliance programmes.
7. To cause to be maintained and retained records of compliance in accordance with regulations and sufficient to demonstrate compliance.
8. To ensure timely external reporting on matters covered by regulations.
9. To exercise an appropriate openness with respect to appropriate disclosure of institutional failures to comply with regulations.
10. To ensure that there is in place an appropriate whistleblowing policy for staff and others to express concerns about perceived breaches of regulatory compliance, and that this policy is communicated effectively and applied whenever applicable.
11. To ensure that issues relating to possible non-compliance are fully investigated and appropriate action taken.
12. To review and assess conformance with these principles and to take remedial action as necessary.
13. To act with honesty and integrity at all times.

D. Duties of staff and contractors of regulated institutions

1. To be aware of the sets of regulations that apply to their work, and the identity of the parties who are the custodians of those regulations.
2. To personally commit to follow applicable regulations.
3. Through participation in a suitable programme of continuous professional development, to take personal responsibility for (a) being thoroughly appraised of the nature of regulations which apply to the conduct of one's work responsibilities, and (b) being competent to ensure observance of those regulations.
4. To ensure compliance with applicable regulations through (a) appropriate individual conduct and (b) participation in ensuring appropriate peer conduct.
5. To accept responsibility for the conduct of those for whom one has oversight responsibility and, through effective leadership and supervision, to ensure their conduct is consistent with applicable regulations.
6. Consistent with one's personal work responsibilities, to maintain and retain records of compliance in accordance with regulations and sufficient to demonstrate compliance.
7. To be active at a professional level in the appropriate development of regulations, to the extent practical.
8. To review and assess conformance with these principles, both personally and by subordinates, and to take remedial action as necessary.
9. To be open in appropriate disclosure of incidents of regulatory non-compliance encountered as a consequence of one's work.
10. Never to encourage a colleague or another to depart from regulations.
11. To act with honesty and integrity at all times.

E. Duties of those who may seek redress

1. To act with honesty and integrity at all times.
2. To understand, or seek advice on, the regulatory issues involved.
3. To use one's best endeavours to prevent non-compliance by others when this is anticipated.
4. To use one's best endeavours to mitigate loss due to perceived breaches of regulations by other parties.
5. To maintain adequate records and to cooperate with a regulatory enquiry.
6. To be prudent in communication with third parties.

Developing, disseminating and implementing codes of best practice for corporate governance F1.18

In developing codes of best practice for corporate governance, it is clearly important to arrive at a set of sentiments which have widespread support – otherwise they will fail to be implemented satisfactorily and will become discredited. Singapore found this, and had to backtrack. It is not easy to get agreement to anything. One or two exposure drafts will be necessary, as has been the case in the UK. This consultative process needs to be taken seriously, with the committee willing to make changes during the consultation phase.

It is now regarded as best practice for feedback to consultations to be in the public domain (usually on the drafter's website) and for the drafter's conclusions relating to the feedback received to be explained. It is also regarded as best practice to allow reasonable consultation period of one or two months.

Another aspect of best practice is to assess whether feedback is representative of different constituents who have a legitimate interest in the standard being developed. Arguably, the FRC has been deficient in ensuring representative feedback. Most of the responses to consultations about UK Corporate Governance Code revisions have come from a small circle of 'market participants' arguably with vested interests, whereas there is a legitimate, wider societal interest in how companies are governed. This could be construed as a serious example of regulatory capture. The FRC dismissed the wider societal interest as being 'populist', implying that it was therefore without merit.

Exposure drafts F1.19

There is a risk associated with changes at the exposure draft stage – others will not be consulted on whether they concur with the changes. In the UK, there have been instances of changes slipping in between the exposure draft and the final report which would not have had a wide consensus had they been exposed first. Thus, for instance, between the exposure draft and final versions of the Cadbury Report and Code of Best Practice, the committee removed the world *financial* from the phrase internal *financial* control – wherever it appeared in the Report and in the Code. This had the effect of broadening the scope of the directors' public reports on internal control to cover *all* aspects of internal control, not just internal *financial* control. While this was clearly Cadbury's intention (and the change was probably made due to persuasive lobbying by the Institute of Internal Auditors at the exposure draft stage), it did not have widespread support and was reversed by the Rutteman Committee when that committee developed guidance for directors in the matter. Later, the Hampel Committee was to revert to the Cadbury intention.

Implementing codes F1.20

Implementing a national corporate governance code has to be managed by the regulators with care. Of course, one expedient can be to defer the implementation of particular parts of the Code pending the development of guidance – as was the case for the 'going concern' and 'internal control' parts of the Cadbury Code, and then later for the revised 'internal control' parts of the Combined Code – or for some other reason.

In the UK, where implementation of parts of the Code has been deferred, during this deferral period, companies have been allowed to claim full compliance with the Code regardless of their practices with respect to the deferred parts of the Code. Where a revision to part of the Code is made some years later but its implementation is deferred pending the development and adoption of guidance, the original requirement (as contained within the original wording of that part of the Code) can continue to apply until the revision is adopted. This was the case with respect to the revised internal control reporting requirements within the UK's 1998 Combined Code.

In general, for companies to indicate compliance with most or all of the Provisions in the Code will only be permissible if the appropriate measures have been in place and have been followed for the whole of the year that is being reported. This means that the first annual report of a company which will be required to disclose code compliance will most likely have to be significantly more than 12 months after the publication of the Code in its final form and after its adoption as a regulatory requirement – as companies will need at least a modicum of notice to introduce the requisite measures by the commencement of that financial year. In the case of the 2003 Combined Code's internal control reporting Provision D.2.1, compliance was also required for the period between the year end date and the date that the financial statements were signed (the 'subsequent events' period).

An alternative is a particular transitional approach which allows a company to claim complete compliance with the Code in its *first* annual report after the Code has been adopted by the regulatory authorities – so long as the company had put in place the requisite measures by the end of the year being reported; but for *all* of the following year the company must have followed the requisite measures that it had put in place towards the end of the previous year if it is to claim compliance. This was the approach recommended by Turnbull for those parts of the Combined Code covered by the Turnbull guidance, and was subsequently broadly endorsed by the Stock Exchange.

The choice of the specific calendar date for implementation of the Code may be significant. In the UK, companies are allowed to vary their year end date by up to one week without obtaining shareholder approval for this. Consequently, accounting standards are often introduced with an operative date of 23 December so that companies are not readily able to defer compliance by a full year simply by varying their usual 31 December year end date by a few days. For the first time, this device was used outside of the arena of accounting standards when Turnbull set 23 December as the operative date. So, for the initial transitional period, companies with year ends on or after 23 December 1999 were able to claim compliance with the aspects of the Combined Code covered by the Turnbull Committee if they had in place the requisite measures before the end of that financial year. Twelve months later, that is for companies reporting for their first year ending on or after 23 December 2000, compliance required that the requisite measures had been in place and applied for all of that year which is being reported (as well as the 'subsequent events' period).

The dates set for implementation of a code of corporate governance, or parts of it, may need to be sympathetic to the external audit dimension. For instance, where external auditors are required to review and perhaps report on directors' compliance with aspects of the Code, allowance may need to be made for the time it will take for guidance to be developed by the auditing profession on how the auditors should undertake that review and how they should report. It will probably not be practical to develop that guidance until after such guidance as may be needed has been developed for directors with regard to what compliance means for them. This was the case with respect to both the 'going concern' and 'internal control' Provisions within the Cadbury Code.

Impact of subsequent guidance **F1.21**

When guidance is developed following the publication and/or adoption of a code of best practice for corporate governance, the guidance may have the effect of watering down the intention of a Provision in the Code. This happened with the Rutteman Guidance on directors reporting on the effectiveness of internal control – they were relieved of the obligation to disclose their opinion, if any, of effectiveness, and were permitted to restrict the scope of their report just to internal *financial* control (see **H1.7** to **H1.16**). On the other hand, guidance may have the effect of strengthening and extending the requirements of a Provision. For instance, the Turnbull Guidance on the Code Provision on internal control interpreted it to mean, in effect, that:

(a) the *board* itself should undertake this review;
(b) the review should be done at least annually; and
(c) the review should be undertaken even when there is an already existing internal audit function, so as to determine its appropriateness,

and from 2003 the Smith Guidance further strengthened this Code Provision by requiring explanation of a decision not to have an internal audit function.

Significant revisions to codes of best practice for corporate governance F1.22

It was always intended that the 1992 Cadbury Code would be revisited after a few years to review how well it had been working and to consider whether any changes were needed. In the event, as we have indicated, the review was delayed a few months and Cadbury himself declined to lead it, expressing the view that the review needed a more impartial approach. As with love and independence, there is probably no such thing as pure 100% impartiality. It was probably inevitable that the new committee, chaired by Sir Ronnie Hampel, would have been influenced by those who had been most vociferous in their opposition to aspects of the Cadbury Code, or to the whole idea of a code. Those who were content with the workings of the Cadbury Code were perhaps less likely to have expressed their views strongly to the Hampel Committee.

Hampel approached the challenge of getting consensus to his exposure draft by not revealing the wording of his intended Combined Code – even in the Committee's final report. While the intended Combined Code was exposed very briefly by the Stock Exchange later, criticism had been effectively stifled as it had not been very practical to challenge Hampel's sentiments within his Committee's final report when the precise wording of the intended Code had not been revealed.

Drafting carelessness F1.23

A further challenge in developing codes of best practice for corporate governance is to avoid carelessness or rashness. Here we give a few examples from the UK experience, in the area of internal control.

First, in the initial printing of the 1998 Combined Code Provision D.2.1 (now, with a slight amendment, 2003 Combined Code Provision C.2.1), the omission of a comma between 'financial' and 'operational' suggested to some a different meaning from that intended, namely:

> 'The directors should, at least annually, conduct a review of the effectiveness of the group's system of internal controls and should report to shareholders that they

have done so. The review should cover all controls, including financial operational and compliance controls and risk management.'

Secondly, the draft Rutteman Report did not keep entirely to the COSO framework for internal control, although comments at the exposure draft stage largely rectified this by the time the final Rutteman Report was published. Even so, there were definitions of 'internal control' and 'internal financial control' which differed somewhat from the generally accepted COSO definitions (see table at **G1.9**). More recently, the Turnbull Report moved further away from the COSO framework, by (a) suggesting that there are only four, not five, components of internal control and (b) giving a new definition of 'internal control'. It is to be questioned whether a working party with one particular brief should take upon itself to redefine key concepts already defined by another working party which had the specific brief to do so. The effect is that we are in danger of moving away from generally accepted paradigms, originally developed with great care and at risk of being overturned casually and superficially.

Thirdly, the draft Hampel Report suggested that Rutteman 'encouraged' directors to disclose their opinion on internal control 'effectiveness', but this was not so. Rutteman merely said that they might, and reserved 'encouragement' to extending the scope of their report to cover all aspects of internal control.

Fourthly, although the Hampel Report and the resulting Combined Code recommended that remuneration committees should be empowered to take outside advice, a similar recommendation for audit committees (which had been made by Cadbury) was absent, presumably inadvertently, from both the Hampel Report and also from the Combined Code. Even as recently as the 2010 UK Corporate Governance Code, there is no specific statement that audit committees should be empoowered to take independent, external advice when they require to do so.

The copyright issue F1.24

To encourage its dissemination, which can only be described as having been very successful, copyright restrictions were waived with respect to unrestricted reproduction of the original Cadbury Code. We query the appropriateness of a body such as the Stock Exchange (initially) or the FRC (currently) putting copyright protection as an obstacle in the way of wide and open circulation of the Code, waived only on payment of a significant fee.

Notes

1 Quoted from a speech by Gordon Gekko in the film 'Wall Street'.

2 HEFCE (2009) 'Guide for Members of Higher Education Governing Bodies in the UK: Incorporates the Governance Code of Practice and General Principles', Higher Education Funding Council in England, March 2009, available at http://www.hefce.ac.uk/pubs/year/2009/200914/#d.en.63808, accessed 29 December 2013.

3 Confederation of British Industry, the Greenbury Committee, chaired by Sir Richard Greenbury *Directors' Remuneration – Report of a Study Group* (July 1995).

4 Committee on Corporate Governance, chaired by Sir Ronald Hampel *Preliminary Report* (August 1997); see Foreword.

5 Report of the Committee on the Financial Aspects of Corporate Governance *Compliance with the Code of Best Practice* (24 May 1995).

6 Committee on Corporate Governance, the Hampel Committee, chaired by Sir Ronald Hampel *Final Report* (January 1998).

7 UK Listing Authority, a division of the Financial Services Authority, 25 The North Colonnade, Canary Wharf, London E14 5HS, tel: +44 (0)20 7676 1000, www.fsa.gov.uk.

8 The 'Definitions' section (May 2000) towards the start of the Listing Rules, attributed (within the definition) a status to the Combined Code, as follows:

> 'Combined Code: the principles of good governance and code of best practice prepared by the Committee on Corporate Governance, chaired by Sir Ronald Hampel, published in June 1998 and appended to, but not forming part of, the Listing Rules.'

9 This was the latest wording of the Listing Rule at that time. It was then updated later in 2004. The FSA does not seem to have noticed that, in the 2003 Code, the Principles were no longer grouped together in a separate Section 1, nor that the Code henceforth was termed the 'Combined Code'. There has over the years been a need for more timely coordination between the FRC who draft the Code and the Listing Authority. More recently, it took the Listing Authority some time to modify its listing rule to remove the requirement for companies to explain how they apply the Supporting Principles with the Code – a change that the FRC had made.

10 More recently the Listing Rule and the FRC's requirement applies only to the Main, not the Supporting, Principles.

11 Sir Adrian Cadbury 'The future of governance: the rules of the game' (1998) 1 Corporate Governance 8, September, newsletter of FTMS Consultants (S) Pte Ltd; originally delivered to a public lecture at Gresham College, London.

12 Cadbury, note 8 above.

13 Professor W J M Mackenzie in the Foreword to E L Normanton *The Accountability and Audit of Governments* (Manchester University Press, 1966), p vii. The book was based on Normanton's MPhil thesis from the University of Manchester.

14 Cadbury, note 8 above.

15 Cadbury, note 8 above.

16 Committee on Corporate Governance *The Combined Code* (June 1998).

17 December 1999 PIRC survey, email: Info@pirc.co.uk; website: www.pirc.co.uk.

18 Research by PIRC, reported in the *London Evening Standard* (26 January 1998, p 34).

19 The Listing Rules require listed companies to explain how they are adhering to the Principles of the Combined Code, and to draw attention to which of the Provisions they are not adhering to, giving reasons. So, it is not a Listing Rule that a listed company should necessarily comply with any of the Provisions; and certainly not a Listing Rule that companies should comply with the more onerous extensions promulgated in the policies of bodies which represent institutional investors.

20 See note 15 above.

21 This recommendation dates back to the 1995 Greenbury Code on executive remuneration.

22 Simon Target 'Most companies flout Code on corporate governance' (1999) Financial Times, 20 December, p 2; article on PIRC survey.

23 Previously known as 'The Yellow Book' when the London Stock Exchange, rather than the FSA, regulated listed companies.

24 The then FSA Listing Rule 12.43A (c).

25 The then FSA Listing Rule 12.43A (a).

26 London Stock Exchange, then the FSA, the then Listing Rule 12.43A (b).

27 The second King Report from South Africa (2001), while not formally adopted in South Afrfica as a corporate governance Code, does not have the same defect of neglecting the social and environmental 'triple bottom line' issues.

28 Cadbury, note 8 above.

Chapter F2

Evolution of the UK Code and the Impact of Higgs and Smith

Introduction F2.1

In Chapters **D1** to **D4** and **F1**, we explore further the development of the UK approach to corporate governance since 1992. **App6** reproduces key parts of early UK codes. We start this chapter with a brief summary of the evolution of the corporate governance code in the UK before turning our attention to the main changes made in 2003 and continued through into subsequent releases of the Code.

The Preface to the 1992 Cadbury Report mentions BCCI and Maxwell as well as 'the controversy over directors' pay'. So the genesis of the development of formal approaches to corporate governance in the UK was concern about fraudulent financial reporting and perceived executive excess. The title of the Cadbury Report was 'The Financial Aspects of Corporate Governance'. COSO's Treadway Commission report (1987) and the US Sarbanes-Oxley Act (2002) had a similar naissance.

The development of corporate governance best practice has been reactive to scandals – an on-going project of attempted catch-up. It has also been a matter of continuously increasing refinement and complexity. The Table below indicates this.

We believe the Cadbury Code was the world's first corporate governance code. By now, it has been widely emulated in developed and most developing countries across the world, and the 'comply or explain' approach has been widely adopted despite its very light touch. The Table shows that the Cadbury Code had just 19 Provisions, as Cadbury called them. The use of the term 'Provision' was to be changed with the advent of the 1998 UK Combined Code: in 1992, Cadbury's 'Provisions' were in the main similar to what, post 1998, have been termed 'Principles'.

'The controversy over directors' pay' which Cadbury had referred to remained unresolved by Cadbury (as it still does) and so the Greenbury Report was to give us in 1995 a code on executive remuneration. The origin of the title 'Combined Code' was the Hampel Committee's combining of the Cadbury Code with the Greenbury Code and with the Hampel Committee's own decisions for further changes (1998). Eventually, the word 'Combined' was dropped, as its significance had become lost in the mists of time, and so the 2010 Code became known for the first time as the UK Corporate Governance Code (the 2012 version is set out in full at **App1**).

It had always been intended that the appropriateness of the Cadbury Code would be reviewed – hence the Hampel Committee's work in 1998–99. It may seem surprising today that, immediately post 1992, the Cadbury Code, with just its 19 Provisions was criticised as being too demanding and sometimes inappropriate for companies in particular circumstances, such as smaller companies. Pressure on Hampel was to develop additional codes tailored to companies with special circumstances.

Wisely, Hampel worked his way around this pressure by distilling from the Code guidelines the fundamental Principles. He allowed that companies should 'comply or explain' with respect to the Code's guidelines (which he called 'Provisions'), but that companies should always apply the Principles and should explain in their annual reports how they were doing so. That way, Hampel created a single, flexible Code which it was considered would be appropriate for all companies in all circumstances. A consequence was increased Code complexity, both because of the inclusion of Principles as well as Provisions, and also due to the growing number of issues that were addressed in the 1998 Code. The Table indicates that this complexity has become more acute since.

It is not surprising that the ever-growing complexity of the Code has meant that there is still a perceived need for something more simple for smaller quoted companies. In 2010 the Quoted Companies Alliance responded to this need, revised in 2013.[1]

The Table understates the added complexity that has occurred over time. For instance, in 2003 the Code content on shareholders voting on the remuneration report of the board was removed from the Code as, by then, it had been incorporated into the Companies Act – in the vain hope that thereby it would be more effective. But, until 2013 it was still just an advisory vote. And, in 2010, the Code content addressed to shareholders was also removed as it had been superseded by the separate Stewardship Code (the 2012 version is set out in full at **App2**).

Although the Principles were intended to be applied by all listed companies, and the listing rule still indicates that (see **D3.3**), they have never been enforced upon a listed company by the listing authority, which regards the listing rule as merely a disclosure obligation. In essence, if a company disclosed that they applied a Principle by ignoring it, that would do no more than possibly raise the eyebrows of the listing authority.

When the 1998 Code came to be amended, an extra mezzanine level of complexity was introduced by way of Supporting Principles. Both the Supporting and the Main Principles were intended by the FRC and by the listing authority to be applied by all listed companies, but more recently both the FRC and the listing rules now require companies to explain how they have applied only the Main Principles, not the Supporting Principles; and the Listing Rules only require that companies with a Premium listing take account of the Code. Companies are also required to comply with the Provisions or explain their reasons for not complying with any of them. It is a curiosity that the Supporting Principles have fallen between the cracks as far as disclosure is concerned. First, the FRC removed the guidance that companies should explain how they apply the Supporting Principles, and now the listing rules have come into line with this (see **D3.3** and **F2.8**).

To reflect more fully the Davies Report on board diversity and gender, additional content was urgently added in 2011, between the planned 2010 and 2012 updates, to ensure more focus on these issues in the nomination process and with respect to board evaluation, with the intention that these additions would be consolidated into the planned 2012 revision of the Code, which they were. The FRC's general intention is to revise the Code bi-annually. The FRC is responsible for wordsmithing the UK Corporate Governance Code but, unlike with their other responsibilities, have no powers to monitor or enforce it.

Table

		Cadbury Code	Greenbury Code	Combined Code	Revised Combined Code	UK Corporate Governance Code	UK Corporate Governance Code	UK Corporate Governance Code
		1992	*1995*	*1998*	*2003, 06 & 08*	*2010*	*2011*	*2012*
Main principles	**General**				14	18	18	18
	Addressed to institutional investors				3	0	0*	0
	Total	**0**	**0**	**0**	**17**	**18**	**18**	**18**
Supporting principles	**General**				21	24	25	28
	Addressed to institutional investors				5	0	0*	0
	Total	**0**	**0**	**0**	**26**	**24**	**25**	**28**
Principles (Main and Supporting)	**General**			14	35	42	43	46
	Addressed to institutional investors			3	8	0	0*	0
	Total	**0**	**0**	**17**	**43**	**42**	**43**	**46**
Provisions	**General**	19	39	44	48	52	52	53
	Addressed to institutional investors	0	0	3	0	0	0	0
	Total	**19**	**39**	**47**	**48**	**52**	**52**	**53**

* Excluding (a) the seven Schedule A Provisions on the design of performance related remuneration which were part of the *Combined Code* and (b) the seven Schedule B Provisions on what should be included in the Remuneration Report which are nolonger in the *Code* but were made into separate regulations (the Directors' Remuneration Report Regulations 2002 SI 2002/986) and are now in the Companies Act 2006.

** Excluding 3 Main and 3 Supporting Principles for Institutional Shareholders at Schedule C of the FRC's UK Corporate Governance Code publication (www.frc.org.uk) which have been superseded by the separate 2010 Stewardship Code.

Status of the Turnbull and Smith Reports F2.2

Since publication of the first edition of the Turnbull Report, compliance in full with all of the guidance therein has been a prerequisite if compliance with the associated parts of the Code is to be claimed.[2] If that is still the case, then the content of the Turnbull Report could be regarded as comprising 'Supporting Principles' and/or 'Supporting Provisions'. However, the latter phrase is never used, and neither does the FRC refer to the Turnbull Report as containing 'Supporting Principles'. The status of the Turnbull guidance is now, therefore, ambiguous. The Stock Exchange's 1998 foreword to the original Turnbull Report had said:

> 'We consider that compliance with the guidance will constitute compliance with Combined Code provisions D.2.1 and D.2.2 and provide appropriate narrative disclosure of how Code principle D.2 has been applied.'

and paragraph 11 of the preamble to the 2005 revised Turnbull Report says:

> 'The guidance in this document applies for accounting periods beginning on or after 1 January 2006, and should be followed by boards of listed companies in:
>
> - assessing how the company has applied Code Principle C.2;
> - implementing the requirements of Code Provision C.2.1; and
> - reporting on these matters to shareholders in the annual report and accounts'.

The version of the Smith Report that appeared within the 2003 Combined Code publication has been watered down, in the sense that none of its guidance is expressed as being guidance which 'should' be followed. In the original Smith Report, those parts which the Smith Committee regarded should be obligatory for compliance with the Code to be claimed had been printed in bold, with the following explanation to convey their status:

> 'This guidance includes certain essential requirements that every audit committee should meet. These requirements are presented in bold in the text. Compliance with these is necessary for compliance with the Code. Listed companies that do not comply with these requirements should include an explanation as to why they have not complied with these requirements in the statement required by the Listing Rules.'[3]

The bolding had been removed, as had the above quotation, from the version of the Smith Report contained in the 2003 Combined Code publication and subsequent versions. Some, but not all, of this bold text had been promoted by the FRC, so that it became content within the 2003 and 2006 Codes. One example where this is not so is the Smith intention that:

> 'The chairman of the company should not be an audit committee member.'[4]

This became redundant, as the Code now commends that the chairman should be independent when appointed as chairman, with the possible implication that he or she should not be regarded as independent after appointment as chairman – an interpretation perhaps borne out by the Code's stipulation that companies complying with the Code, and within the FTSE 350, will ensure that at least half the board, *excluding the chairman in the count*, should be *independent* directors. Commencing 2010, the Code allows that the chairman of the board may belong to the audit committee of a quoted company outside the FTSE 350, but only if he or she were independent when appointed chairman of the board. While such a chairman may belong to the audit committee, the Code states that he or she should not chair the audit committee.

It is important to take the Code as a whole. Principles and Provisions relevant to, for instance, audit committees are not repeated within the audit committees section of the Code if they have already been stated elsewhere in the Code.

The 2005 Turnbull Review **F2.3**

In 2005 the FRC completed a review of the Turnbull Report under the chairmanship of Douglas Flint, Finance Director (now chairman) of HSBC, leading to a revised version of the Turnbull Report.[5] The main recommendations of the Turnbull Review Group were:

1. The Turnbull guidance has contributed to improvements in internal control in UK-listed companies, and significant changes are not required.
2. The guidance should continue to cover all internal controls, and not be limited to internal controls over financial reporting.
3. No changes should be made to the guidance that would have the effect of restricting a company's ability to apply the guidance in a manner suitable to its own particular circumstances.
4. The guidance should be updated to reflect changes in the Combined Code and Listing Rules since 1999 and the proposed statement of directors' duties in the draft Company Law Reform Bill.
5. Boards should review their application of the guidance on a continuing basis.
6. It would not be appropriate to require boards to make a statement in the annual report and accounts on the effectiveness of the company's internal control system, but boards should confirm that necessary action has been or is being taken to remedy any significant failings or weaknesses identified from the reviews of the effectiveness of the internal control system.
7. Boards should look on the internal control statement in the annual report and accounts as an opportunity to communicate to their shareholders how they manage risk effectively, and include such information as is considered necessary to assist shareholders' understanding of the main features of the company's risk management processes and system of internal control.
8. There should be no need for companies that are already applying the Turnbull guidance to develop additional processes in order to comply with the requirement to identify principal risks in the Operating and Financial Review (OFR), but companies are encouraged to ensure that the OFR and the internal control statement are complementary. The OFR requirement was abandoned before it came in, but a more modest requirement for a business review to be reported upon has been incorporated into the Companies Act 2006 to give effect to a European Directive requirement (see **D1.12**).
9. There should be no expansion of the external auditors' responsibilities in relation to the company's internal control statement.

The reach of the UK's Corporate Governance Code **F2.4**

The FRC's remit for corporate governance guidance does not run beyond listed companies. Thus, some would argue that there is a corporate governance deficit for much of the UK economy – such as mutuals, unlisted plcs, private companies, charities, local authorities, central government departments, non-departmental public bodies, government agencies and government-owned companies (GOCOs), which together command so much of our national economy and which thus may lack the disciplines 'enforced' by the Code. However, many entities not subject to UK Listing Rules voluntarily report that it is their policy to comply with the Code to the extent that they judge it is applicable. This is not entirely satisfactory, as such entities may be more inclined than listed companies to judge that a particular part of the Code should not be regarded as applicable for their entity. It is unsatisfactory that UK codification of corporate governance best practice is developed with the listed company in mind, with only informal and rather haphazard adaptation for the rest of the economy. In July 2005 the Association of Mutual Insurers adopted an annotated version of the 2003 Code for their members. However, not all mutual insurers are members of AMI and there are many significant mutuals that are not insurers – such as building societies or the Medical Defence Union,[6] for instance. Monitor has adopted the Combined Code too for Foundation Trusts, as has the Higher Education Funding Council for England (HEFCE). In the cases of mutuals and the NHS, minimal changes have been made to the Code to align their versions with their circumstances. See **F1.3**.

Other sectors have developed their own codes of best practice without so much direct reference to the UK Corporate Governance Code. In December 2006 the pan-European INREV finalised its corporate governance principles and guidelines relating to the corporate governance of non-listed real estate funds.[7] In July 2005, HM Treasury published its first code of good practice for corporate governance in central government departments'[8] which was revised and reissued in July 2011; and in 2007 it released the second edition of its Audit Committee Handbook with good practice principles for audit committees.[9] The 2004 Langlands Report[10] provided a good governance standard for public services outside central government: its foreword pointed out that more than 450,000 people contribute as governors to a wide range of UK public service organisations and partnerships, and that total public expenditure is well in excess of £500 billion each year. In 2013,, the British Standard Institution published its governance standard designed to be appropriate for any time of entity (see Chapter **D6**).[11]

Applicability of the Code to overseas companies F2.5

The FRC's Code has been designed for UK companies quoted on the main UK stock market. Prior to 2009 it did not have the same force for companies that are incorporated overseas but that are listed within the UK. Refer to **D2.5** for an explanation of UK 'premium' and 'standard' listings and the implications for overseas companies and for observing the UK Corporate Governance Code. Neither does the Code apply to companies listed on the UK's alternative investment market (AIM), although the experience of many AIM companies is that it is advisable to meet the 'requirements' of the Code in anticipation of seeking a listing on the main market.

There may be an issue of incompatible corporate governance requirements for companies incorporated overseas and listed in more than one country's market. UK listing rules require disclosure of the incompatibility and an explanation as to which requirement is being followed. A company with its main listing in the UK and a secondary listing in the US is confronted with differing 'requirements' on the appointment of the independent auditors. The UK Code 'requirement' is that the audit committee recommends to the board the audit firm that the board should recommend to the shareholders to be the external auditors and, if the board declines to follow that advice, the disagreement should be addressed within the annual report.[12] The US Sarbanes-Oxley Act requirement is that the audit committee appoints the external auditors.[13] The fundamental point of principle here is that the UK has been careful not to elevate the audit committee, which is a sub-committee of the board, above the board itself – which is not the case within the US. A multinational, confronted with this particular differing requirement, may attend to it in one of two ways. The company may follow the Sarbanes-Oxley requirement and ensure that its board never countermands the decision of its audit committee. Or the company may report, for US filing purposes, that it is observing the UK corporate governance practice in this regard. The former is certainly permissible due to the 'comply or explain' status of the UK Corporate Governance Code.

A company incorporated, for instance, in Malta, but listed in London, need not be caught by the UK Code if it has a Standard UK listing. However, the EU's Fourth Company Law Directive (implemented mid-2008) applies to all companies incorporated in an EU Member State and listed on a regulated market in the EU. The Directive requires them to make a 'comply or explain' statement against 'the corporate governance code to which the company is subject, and/or the corporate governance code which the company may have voluntarily decided to apply'. As this requirement has been introduced into company law rather than securities law, 'the corporate governance code to which the company is subject' will be the Code applicable in the country of incorporation. Most EU countries, including Malta, now have such a Code – but the Directive appears to allow companies the option of adopting the Code applicable in the country of listing.

However, this also means that the requirements do not bite on companies incorporated outside the EU. Different jurisdictions take different approaches to the question of third-country listings, and this can create some difficulties. For example, a Singapore-based company that is incorporated in Bermuda, has a main listing in London and a secondary listing in Singapore quite correctly, in legal terms, reports only on its adherence to the applicable requirements in Bermuda.

Background to the Code **F2.6**

The 2003 version replaced the original Combined Code, which was published in June 1998. The original Combined Code was so called because it combined the Cadbury (1992) and Greenbury (1995) Codes with the modifications and additions that the Hampel Committee had decided upon, all of which the Stock Exchange then adopted. The 2003 and 2006 Combined Codes carried forward the 1998 Combined Code, and the 2003 Code had made amendments to reflect the Higgs[14] (January 2003) and Smith[15] (January 2003) recommended Code changes – as adjusted by the FRC after consultation.

The FRC now has oversight of the Code, although not of its enforcement. To the extent that there is any regulatory enforcement of the Code, it is the responsibility of the UK Listing Authority. However, it is not clear if there is any regulatory enforcement of the Code's Principles even though they are expressed in the Listing Rules in a way which suggests they are mandatory, or of the Provisions (which the Listing Rules apply to companies on a 'comply or explain' basis). We give the listing rule at **D3.3**.

FRC addressed opposition to the Higgs Report F2.7

The opposition to Higgs' proposals, and to a lesser extent those of Smith as well, had three main thrusts:

- Although technically the Provisions have a 'comply or explain' status, the over-simplistic perception of outside parties (especially institutional investors) that non-compliance means poor corporate governance, has meant that there has been excessive and often counterproductive pressure upon companies to comply. The Hampel Committee's intention of building flexibility into the Code so that one Code could be used by companies in all circumstances and of all sizes has thus been compromised.
- The proposed strengthening of the Code, in relation to avoiding excessive concentration of power at the top of the business, had the effect of making it harder for the chairman of a company to run the board.
- The remorseless growth in size of the Code threatened to deflect the focus of boards from responsibilities other than corporate governance.

The Preamble to the 2003 and 2006 Codes had attempted to address the first two of these concerns, stressing that, while it is expected that listed companies will comply with the Code's Provisions most of the time, it is recognised that departure from the Provisions may be justified in particular circumstances, and that smaller companies, and in particular those new to listing, may judge that some of the Provisions are disproportionate or less relevant in their case. It was helpful that the FRC stressed that companies making an IPO should not necessarily be expected to have in place all the aspects of the Code. Indeed, the Code itself applies different standards to companies of different sizes, for instance:

- small companies comply with the Code if they have two independent directors, rather than 50% of the board excluding the chairman (**App1**, Provision B.1.2);
- an executive director may have only one FTSE 100 non-executive directorship and should not chair a FTSE 100 board (**App1**, Provision B.3.3); and
- small companies comply if their remuneration and audit committees have at least two, not three, members (**App1**, Provisions D.2.1 and C.3.1 respectively).

The Preamble to the 2003 and 2006 Codes stated that every company must review each Provision carefully and give a 'considered explanation if it departs from any Code Provisions'. The current Code goes into this in much more detail.[16]

The corollary of this is that shareholders, particularly institutional investors, evaluate a company's governance:

> 'with common sense in order to promote partnership and trust, based on mutual understanding [and not] in a mechanistic way and departures from the Code should not be automatically treated as breaches … Institutional shareholders and their agents should be careful to respond to the statements from companies in a

manner that supports the 'comply or explain' principle … They should put their views to the company and be prepared to enter a dialogue if they do not accept the company's position. Institutional shareholders should be prepared to put such views in writing where appropriate.'[17]

In essence, what is good for the goose is good for the gander. Boards are responsible for good governance and must account for how they are discharging their responsibility. But by the same token, institutional investors are responsible for the judgements they come to about companies and should also be held accountable. Responsibility without accountability tends to engender irresponsibility – whether by companies, institutional investors or by pressure groups.

The Preamble to the 2003 and 2006 Codes sounded a note of warning that:

> 'Nothing in this Code should be taken to override the general requirements of law to treat shareholders equally in access to information.'[18]

Higgs said that he believed that his report's principal contribution to good governance was likely to be the effect it would have on evaluating board, board committee and individual director performance. Perhaps the next significant development in governance which is needed is to iron out the potential conflicts which exist in terms of access to information. Company briefings of analysts and major shareholders almost inevitably put those parties in pole position to act ahead of small shareholders who do not have that access. When major shareholders (whether family or financial institutions) or providers of debt capital have their nominees of the board, again there are challenges. Is it acceptable for a nominee director to consult the party who nominated him with respect to how to vote at the board? A Supporting Principle in the 2003 and 2006 Combined Codes states:

> 'All directors must take decisions objectively in the interests of the company.'[19]

This is now rephrased in the Corporate Governance Code to read (Supporting Principle A.1):

> 'All directors must act in what they consider to be the best interests of the company, consistent with their statutory duties'.

Is it acceptable for the nominee director to feed back information about the company to the party who nominated him? If so, how does this square with treating shareholders equally in access to information?

2003 Changes to the Combined Code **F2.8**

Apart from the considerable significance of some of the changes and additions to the Principles and Provisions, the 2003 Code had two notable departures in style from the original Combined Code.

First, the scale of the 2003 Code was much greater. The 19 'comply or explain' Provisions in the 1992 Cadbury Code had grown to 17 Principles and 47 Provisions in the 1998 Combined Code, and reached the level of 43 Principles (including Supporting Principles) and 48 Provisions in both the 2003 and the replacement 2006 Code. The Table at **F2.1** indicates that the complexity of the Code has subsequently continued to grow. Indeed, this is an underestimate of the growing burden, as it excludes:

(a) the seven Schedule A Provisions on the design of performance-related remuneration which were part of the Combined Code and continue in the revised Combined Code; and
(b) the seven Schedule B Provisions on what should be included in the Remuneration Report, which were part of the Combined Code but are not included in the revised Combined Code as there are now separate regulations in force (the Directors' Remuneration Report Regulations 2002, SI 2002/1986) which supersede the earlier Code Provisions.

See also **C.4.17**.

Secondly, there is the introduction for the first time of Supporting Principles nesting between Main Principles and Provisions. After the introduction of Supporting Principles, the Combined Code told us that the part of the Listing Rule which applied to Principles was to apply to both Main and Supporting Principles, and that the comply or explain requirement applies to Provisions only. Now the Code and the Listing Rule restricts the requirements to Main Principles and Provisions, but not in any way to Supporting Principles, as the latest version of the Listing Rule (13 December 2013) indicates:

Listing Rule 9.8.6 (previously 12.43A, then 9.8.6; and, from 2010, 9.8.6 (5) and (6)):

'In the case of a listed company incorporated in the United Kingdom, the following additional items must be included in its annual financial report:

…

(5) a statement of how the listed company has applied the Main Principles set out in the UK Corporate Governance Code, in a manner that would enable shareholders to evaluate how the principles have been applied;
(6) a statement as to whether the listed company has:
  (a) complied throughout the accounting period with all relevant provisions set out in the UK Corporate Governance Code; or
  (b) not complied throughout the accounting period with all relevant provisions set out in the UK Corporate Governance Code and if so, setting out:
    (i) those provisions, if any it has not complied with;
    (ii) in the case of provisions whose requirements are of a continuing nature, the period within which, if any, it did not comply with some or all of those provisions; and
    (iii) the company's reasons for non-compliance;

Readers will note the current, revised Listing Rule (above) is simplified in comparison to earlier wording (below):

Listing Rule 12.43A

'In the case of a company incorporated in the United Kingdom, the following additional items must be included in its annual report and accounts:

(a) A narrative statement of how it has applied the principles set out in Section 1 of the Combined Code, providing sufficient explanation which enables its shareholders to evaluate how the principles have been applied;

(b) a statement as to whether or not it has complied throughout the accounting period with the provisions set out in Section 1 of the Combined Code. A company that has not complied with the Code provisions, or complied with only some of the Code provisions or (in the case of provisions whose requirements are of a continuing nature) complied for only part of an accounting period, must specify the provisions with which it has not complied, and (where relevant) for what part of the period such non-compliance continued, and give reasons for any non-compliance; …'

It is the case that, since 1998, boards have been challenged much more over non-compliance with Provisions than for failing to apply Principles: it has proved easier for institutional investors to box-tick company compliance with Provisions than to box-tick whether the Principles are being applied. So, classifying some aspects of the new Code as 'Supporting Principles' rather than as 'Provisions' takes some pressure off boards, notwithstanding the apparent more 'compulsory' character of Principles, per the Listing Rule. As we have pointed out, the more 'compulsory' nature now applies to Main by not Supporting Principles.

We have already discussed the modification, commencing with the 2003 version, of the Code's structure to include not only main 'Principles' and 'Provisions' but also 'Supporting Principles', allowing companies greater flexibility in how they implement the Code. KPMG complained about this, on the grounds that it was likely to result in huge swathes of disclosure in company accounts:

> 'One has to question whether it will provide a meaningful insight into how each organisation is governed, if investors will read it, and whether it will influence company behaviour?'

Apart from that, the two most profound effects of the 2003 Code were, first, the clarification of the role of the chairman vis-à-vis the board as a whole and the non-executive directors in particular; and secondly, the effect of the 2003 Code introducing more formal evaluations of board, board committee and individual director performance. In the rest of this chapter, we highlight some of the main developments, commencing with the 2003 Code, and focus on adjustments made by the FRC to Higgs' original proposals.

Duties of directors **F2.9**

Since 2003 the Code now has a Supporting Principle (A.1) that all directors must act in what they consider to be the best interests of the company. Higgs had proposed this as a Provision.[20] While this does nothing to alter the legal duties of directors (see Chapter **D1** at **D1.5** and **D1.6**), it is helpful that the Code now refers to this. The interests of the company may not always equate to the interest of maximising share value, nor to the interests of majority shareholders, nor the executive interests of particular directors.

Another duty of a director is covered where the Code includes (as Provision D.2.3 in 2003 and 2006, now E.2.3 of the 2010 and 2012 Corporate Governance Codes – see **App1**) the 1998 Provision C.2.3 that the chairman of the board should arrange for the chairmen of the audit, remuneration and nomination committees to be available to answer questions at the AGM, and for all directors to attend. Whereas Higgs had proposed, perhaps by oversight, that this be extended to include that the chairman should arrange for all non-executive directors to attend the AGM, the final wording rightly broadens this to 'all directors'. Since it has been the Provisions rather than the Principles that have caused most of the problems in the past, it is significant that there is now this additional Provision that the chairman will arrange for the directors to attend the AGM. While, as previously, the chairs of these three committees are to be available to answer questions at the AGM, it remains the case that all questions are formally put to the chairman of the AGM (who is usually the chairman of the board), who then determines whether to answer them personally or divert them to someone else of his choosing – notwithstanding the questioner's intention perhaps that the question should be answered by a particular director who chairs a board committee. The 1998 Hampel Report had this to say:

> 'Cadbury recommended that the chairman of the audit committee should be available to answer questions about its work at the AGM (report, Appendix 4, paragraph 6(f)), and Greenbury made a similar recommendation relating to the chairman of the remuneration committee (code, A8). It was suggested to us that the chairman of the nomination committee should make himself available in the same way. We believe that it should be for the chairman of the meeting to decide which questions to answer himself and which to refer to a colleague; but in general we would expect the chairman of the three committees to be available to answer questions at the AGM.'[21]

Higgs proposed[22] that:

> 'Where they have concerns about the way in which a company is being run or about a course of action being proposed by the board, directors should ensure that their concerns are recorded in the board minutes if they cannot be resolved. A written statement should be provided to the chairman, for circulation to the board, setting out the reasons where a non-executive director resigns.'

The equivalent Code wording now is (Provision A.4.3):

> 'Where directors have concerns which cannot be resolved about the running of the company or a proposed action, they should ensure that their concerns are recorded in the board minutes. On resignation, a non-executive director should provide a written statement to the chairman, for circulation to the board, if they have any such concerns.'

Clarification of the role of the chairman vis-à-vis the non-executive directors **F2.10**

Much of the debate over the Higgs proposals centred on the respective responsibilities of the chairman and the other directors. Some chairmen were concerned that the Higgs proposals would, if implemented, undermine their authority and make it more difficult for them to discharge their responsibilities to run the board. (The 2003 Code stipulation that the chairman arranges for all directors to attend the AGM was, however, an example of enhancing the chairman's authority over the board.)

Notwithstanding the much-publicised concerns of many company chairmen, most of Higgs' proposals in this area survived into the 2003 Code. In the debate, it was largely overlooked that the 1992 Cadbury Code had already established the role of the 'senior non-executive director' when the posts of chairman and chief executive were combined, and that the 1998 Code had specified the senior non-executive director position as appropriate, even when these two roles were separated.[23]

The objections to Higgs in this area were largely to do with Higgs' proposals that:

- the chairman of the company should not chair the nominations committee;
- the senior non-executive director should convene regular meetings with the other non-executive directors without the chairman of the board being present; and
- the senior non-executive director should communicate the views of institutional investors to the other non-executive directors.

Contrary to Higgs, the latest UK Corporate Governance Code at B.2.1 (**App1**) allows the board chairman to chair the nomination committee except when it is considering succession to the chair position. Provision A.4.2 (**App1**) is consistent with Higgs requiring that the senior non-executive director convenes regular meetings with the other non-executive directors without the chairman of the board being present. Section E.1 of the Code (**App1**) does not specifically require the senior independent director to be the conduit for passing shareholder views to other non-executive directors; instead it places the onus on the chairman of the board but requires that other directors, including the senior independent director, keep in touch with shareholder opinion.

The senior and other non-executive directors and institutional investors **F2.11**

There is still a requirement that the senior independent director should be identified in the annual report (Provision A.1.2), and the substance of Higgs' further proposal survived in the 2003 Code Provision A.3.3 which included the words:

> 'The senior independent director should be available to shareholders if they have concerns which contact through the normal channels of chairman, chief executive or finance director has failed to resolve or for which such contact is inappropriate.'

The FRC had added 'finance director' to Higgs' draft.

This now reads (**App1**, Provision A.4.1):

> 'The board should appoint one of the independent non-executive directors to be the senior independent director to provide a sounding board for the chairman and to serve as an intermediary for the other directors when necessary. The senior independent director should be available to shareholders if they have concerns which contact through the normal channels of chairman, chief executive or other executive directors has failed to resolve or for which such contact is inappropriate.'

Provision D.1.1 of the 2003 and 2006 Codes had been toned down to include the words:

> 'The senior independent director should attend sufficient regular meetings of management with a range of major shareholders to develop a balanced understanding of the themes, issues and concerns of shareholders.'

And now reads (**App1**, E.1.1.):

> '…
>
> The senior independent director should attend sufficient meetings with a range of major shareholders to listen to their views in order to help develop a balanced understanding of the issues and concerns of major shareholders.'

Higgs' proposal that:

> 'the senior independent director should communicate these views to the non-executive directors and, as appropriate, to the board as a whole'

had been removed and it is now the chairman who (2006 Code):

> 'should ensure that the views of shareholders are communicated to the board as a whole.'

By 2010, this had become (Supporting Principle A.3):

> 'The chairman is responsible for ensuring that the directors receive accurate, timely and clear information. The chairman should ensure effective communication with shareholders.'

Higgs' proposed Provision wording survived in the 2003 and 2006 Codes in regard to:

> 'non-executive directors should be able to attend regular meetings with major investors and should expect to attend them if requested by major shareholders.'

And this sentiment is largely carried forward to Provision E.1.2 (**App1**) of the current Code.

A Supporting Principle of the 2006 Code (D.1) read:

> 'The board should keep in touch with shareholder opinion in whatever ways are most practical and efficient.'

and this continues, with unchanged wording, into the current version of the Code (Supporting Principle E.1).

The related Main Principle on 'Dialogue with institutional investors' in 2006 (now expressed as 'Dialogue with Shareholders) included the words:

> 'The board as a whole has responsibility for ensuring that a satisfactory dialogue with shareholders takes place.'

The current version of the Code (Main Principle E.1) precedes this with an additional sentence:

> 'There should be a dialogue with shareholders based on the mutual understanding of objectives. The board as a whole has responsibility for ensuring that a satisfactory dialogue with shareholders takes place.'

Provision D.1.2 of the 2006 Code continues with almost unchanged into the current Code and now reads at Provision E.1.2 (**App1**) (with words in bold being added by the FRC to Higgs' original proposal):

> 'The board should state in the annual report the steps they have taken to ensure that the members of the board, and in particular the non-executive directors, develop an understanding of the views of major shareholders about the company, **for example through direct face-to-face contact, analysts' or brokers' briefings and surveys of shareholder opinion**.'

Higgs' proposed Provision C.1.3, which read:

> 'On appointment, non-executive directors should meet major investors, as part of the induction process.'

was changed to read, as part of Provision A.5.1 of the 2003 Code:

> '… the company should offer to major shareholders the opportunity to meet a new non-executive director.'

and broadly similar wording survived into the 2010 Code at B.4.1 and the current 2012 Code also at B.4.1. Additionally, E.1.1 of the current Code (**App1**) is important in this regard:

> 'The chairman should ensure that the views of shareholders are communicated to the board as a whole. The chairman should discuss governance and strategy with major shareholders. Non-executive directors should be offered the opportunity to attend scheduled meetings with major shareholders and should expect to attend meetings if requested by major shareholders. The senior independent director should attend sufficient meetings with a range of major shareholders to listen to their views in order to help develop a balanced understanding of the issues and concerns of major shareholders.'

Interfacing the chairman and the non-executive directors **F2.12**

Higgs suggested in his Provision B.2.5 that the remuneration committee should consult the chairman and/or chief executive about their proposals relating to the remuneration of other executive directors. This survived in the 2003 Code but as a Supporting Principle (B.2).

Whereas the Higgs proposal had been that:

> 'The non-executive directors should meet regularly as a group and at least once a year without the chairman present'[24]

Provision A.1.3 in the 2003 Code read:

> 'The chairman should hold meetings with the non-executive directors without the executives present. Led by the senior non-executive director, the non-executive

directors should meet without the chairman being present at least annually to appraise the chairman's performance and on such other occasions as are deemed appropriate.'

and this continues unchanged into the current Code (**App1**, Provision A.4.2).

Nomination committee **F2.13**

Whereas Higgs allowed that the nomination committee might include the chairman of the board, Higgs' proposed Provision would have meant that it would be chaired by an independent non-executive director (other than the chairman). The final 2003 and 2006 Codes backed down from this, allowing only that (Provision A.4.1):

> 'The chairman or an independent director should chair the committee, but the chairman should not chair the nomination committee when it is dealing with the appointment of a successor to the chairmanship.'

This has continued into the current Code (Provision B.2.1).

Higgs' proposal that the terms of reference of the nomination committee should be made publicly available was clarified in the 2003 and 2006 Codes by the addition of the words:

> 'on request and by including the information on the company's website.'

– wording used elsewhere in the 2003 and 2006 Codes – for instance, with respect to terms and conditions of appointment of non-executive directors. Similarly, the remuneration committee should make publicly available its terms of reference (by request and on the company's website), explaining its role and the authority delegated to it by the board. It is assumed that the word 'and' is intentional and that it is therefore intended that this information should always be available on a company's website. This is confirmed by the wording of the current Code, which omits 'on request'. See **App1**, B.2.1.

Whereas Higgs proposed that the nomination committee should set out in the letter of appointment the time commitment and responsibility (including in relation to chairmanship or membership of board committees or as the senior independent director) envisaged in the appointment of a non-executive director, the words 'and responsibility' did not survive into the 2003 Code. Higgs' suggestion that a new non-executive director's other commitments should be disclosed to the company has been tightened, to require that the disclosure is to the board itself.

Higgs' intended requirement that the nomination committee explain in the annual report if external advice or open advertising has not been used was restricted in the final 2003 and 2006 Codes to the appointment of a chairman or a non-executive director, which continues to today (Provision B.2.4).

Chief executives may exceptionally go on to become chairmen **F2.14**

The final 2003 and 2006 Codes persevered with Higgs' proposal that a chief executive should not go on to become chairman of the same company, but qualified this by adding words which also continue unchanged into the current Code (Provision A.3.1):

> '… If exceptionally a board decides that a chief executive should become chairman, the board should consult major shareholders in advance and should set out its reasons to shareholders at the time of the appointment and in the next annual report.'

The Code is remiss in not requiring a similar consultation if a board gives the chairmanship to another executive, other than the CEO – as did HSBC when late in 2010 it appointed as chairman its finance director, Douglas Flint. The 2003 and 2006 Codes (in Provision A.2.2) adopted Higgs' proposal that, on appointment, the chairman should meet the independence criteria set by Higgs and incorporated into the 2003 Code, and no changes have since been made to those independence criteria.

Smaller companies **F2.15**

The 2003 and 2006 Codes defined 'smaller listed companies' as those below the FTSE 350, and relaxed the rule on the number of independent non-executives to 'at least two' instead of 'at least 50% excluding the chairman'. Smaller companies also met the 2003 and 2006 Code requirements if they had two rather than three members of their remuneration and audit committees. Whereas the 1998 Combined Code allowed that the majority of members of the audit committee should be independent, although all should be non-executive, from 2003 they all should be independent[25] (as was previously the case, and continues to be the case, for remuneration committees; and as has been the case by statute since the 2002 Sarbanes-Oxley Act for US listed companies' audit committees). Also following US practice, audit committees must now have at least one member with significant, recent and relevant financial experience.

For 'recent and relevant experience of audit committee members, readers may wish to refer to **A3.4**, particularly **A3.6**, **E1.2**, **E1.15**, **E2.5** and **E3.5**.

A Supporting Principle in 2003 (A.3) stated that only committee members are entitled to attend board committees, but others may attend at the invitation of the committee; and this remains unchanged in the current Code (Supporting Principle B.1). While this is pragmatically sound, it is doubtful if it would be legally enforceable to exclude a director from any board committee meeting.

Remuneration of non-executive directors **F2.16**

Higgs intended the Code to state simply that remuneration for non-executive directors in the form of share options should be avoided, but the 2003 and 2006 Codes had added (Provision B.1.3):

> '… If, exceptionally, options are granted, shareholder approval should be sought in advance and any shares acquired by exercise of the options should be held until at least one year after the non-executive director leaves the board. Holding of share options could be relevant to the determination of a director's independence.'

and this continues unchanged into the current Code (**App1**, Provision D.1.3).

Particularly rigorous review rather than special explanation when non-executive directors are re-elected beyond six years F2.17

Higgs' intention with respect to the length of time that a non-executive director might serve, especially those whom the board relies upon to be independent, survived largely intact. The wording in the 2003 and 2006 Codes was (Provision A.7.2):

> 'Non-executive directors should be appointed for specified terms subject to re-election and to Companies Acts provisions relating to the removal of a director. The board should set out to shareholders in the papers accompanying a resolution to elect a non-executive director why they believe an individual should be elected. The chairman should confirm to shareholders when proposing re-election that, following formal performance evaluation, the individual's performance continues to be effective and to demonstrate commitment to the role. Any term beyond six years (e.g. two three-year terms) for a non-executive director should be subject to particularly rigorous review, and should take into account the need for progressive refreshing of the board. Non-executive directors may serve longer than nine years (e.g. three three-year terms), subject to annual re-election. Serving more than nine years could be relevant to the determination of a non-executive director's independence (as set out in provision A.3.1).'

All of this Provision survives into the current Code, although it has been spread around several different parts of the current Code.

Changes to audit committee, internal control and internal audit aspects F2.18

There was much more in the 2003 and 2006 Codes on audit committees than there had been in the 1998 Code, reflecting to some extent the recommendations of the Smith Committee (which Higgs had incorporated into his proposed revised Code), and also to some extent the US developing requirements under the Sarbanes-Oxley Act 2002 and the NYSE corporate governance standards. The wording of the Principle on internal control remained unchanged in 2003 and 2006 from the 1998 wording, except for the addition of the word 'systems' to the end of the old Code Provision D.2.1 on the directors' internal control review – so that it then read 'risk management systems' rather than merely 'risk management'.

The other Provision in the 1998 Code which was filed within the internal control part of that Code was moved to the audit committees part of the 2003 and 2006 Codes, as Provision C.3.5, which read:

> 'The audit committee should monitor and review the effectiveness of the internal audit activities. Where there is no internal audit function, the audit committee should consider annually whether there is a need for an internal audit function and make a recommendation to the board, and the reasons for the absence of such a function should be explained in the relevant section of the annual report.'

The 1998 Code had no requirement for the board to publicly explain the reasons for not having an internal audit function, which idea first surfaced in the Smith Report.

Commencing 2003, the audit committee's responsibilities have been stated as including:

- to review the company's internal financial control system;
- unless expressly addressed by a separate risk committee (the FRC added, in the final 2003 Code, 'composed of independent directors' to Higgs' proposal on this) or by the board itself, to review the company's internal control and risk management systems (the FRC added, in the final 2003 Code, 'internal control' to Higgs' proposal);
- to monitor and review the effectiveness of the company's internal audit function;
- to make recommendations to the board in relation to the appointment of the external auditor and to approve the remuneration and terms of engagement of the external auditor. Note the final 2003 Code wording was enhanced by the addition of the word 'removal' and the addition to the Code of Provision C.3.6, which read:

  'The audit committee should have primary responsibility for making a recommendation on the appointment and removal of the external auditors. If the board does not accept the audit committee's recommendation, it should include in the annual report, and in any papers recommending appointment or re-appointment, a statement from the audit committee explaining the recommendation and should set out reasons why the board has taken a different position.';

- to monitor and review the external auditor's independence, objectivity and effectiveness, taking into consideration relevant UK professional and regulatory requirements; and
- to develop and implement policy on the engagement of the external auditor to supply non-audit services, taking into account relevant ethical guidance regarding the provision of non-audit services by the external audit firm. The following wording was added by the FRC beyond what appeared in Higgs' proposed Code:

  'and to report to the board, identifying any matters in respect of which it considers action or improvement is needed and making recommendations as to the steps to be taken.'

None of the above Code's wording on audit committees was changed in the 2006, 2008 and 2010 Codes since the 2003 Code incorporated, with minor changes, the alterations recommended by the Smith and Higgs reports. Additional wording in the 2012 Code (App1) is that:

'… FTSE 350 companies should put the external audit contract out to tender at least every ten years' (Provision C.3.7)

and that:

'A separate section of the annual report should describe the work of the committee in discharging its responsibilities.[26] The report should include:

- the significant issues that the committee considered in relation to the financial statements, and how these issues were addressed;
- an explanation of how it has assessed the effectiveness of the external audit process and the approach taken to the appointment or reappointment of the external auditor, and information on the length of tenure of the current audit firm and when a tender was last conducted; …' (Provision C.3.8, **App1**)

Although not in the audit committees section of the 2003 and 2006 Codes, Provision A.5.2 at that time stated that all board committees should be provided with sufficient resources to undertake their duties (now expressed at Provision B.5.1). From 2003, Provision C.3.3 (now covered by Provision C.3.3) has carried the requirement that the annual report should contain a separate section that describes the role and responsibilities of the committee and the actions taken by the committee to discharge those responsibilities, and also states that the committee's terms of reference should be made available.

As mentioned earlier, the 2003 and 2006 Codes included, as Provision D.2.3, that the chairman of the board should arrange for the chairman of the audit and other board committees to be present at the AGM to answer questions, and this continues into the current Code at Provision E.2.3.

More formal evaluations of board, board committee and individual director performance F2.19

In a private conversation with the author of this handbook, Sir Derek Higgs volunteered that he considered the new material placed within the 2003 Code on performance evaluation could represent the single largest contribution to corporate governance best practice to be made by the 2003 Code, and thus his most significant contribution to UK corporate governance. Performance evaluation is expressed, commencing with the 2003 Code, as a requisite to be applied to the board as a whole, to its committees, to individual directors and to the chairman of the board. The Main Principle read:

> 'The board should undertake a formal and rigorous annual evaluation of its own performance and that of its committees and individual directors.' (2003 Code, Main Principle A.6)

and the Supporting Principle A.6:

> 'Individual evaluation should aim to show whether each director continues to contribute effectively and to demonstrate commitment to the role (including commitment of time for board and committee meetings and any other duties). The chairman should act on the results of the performance evaluation by recognising the strengths and addressing the weaknesses of the board and, where appropriate, proposing new members be appointed to the board or seeking the resignation of directors.'

Provision A.6.1 of the 2003 and 2006 Codes read:

> 'The board should state in the annual report how performance evaluation of the board, its committees and its individual directors has been conducted. The non-executive directors, led by the senior independent director, should be responsible for performance evaluation of the chairman, taking into account the views of executive directors.'

The FRC added to the 2003 and 2006 Codes (at Provision A.7.2) that no director should be re-elected unless continuing to perform satisfactorily, and that:

> 'the chairman should confirm to shareholders when proposing re-election that, following formal performance evaluation, the individual's performance

continues to be effective and to demonstrate commitment to the role. Any term of appointment beyond six years (e.g. two three-year terms) for a non-executive director should be subject to particularly rigorous review.'

Since 2003, performance evaluation has been strengthened considerably. In the current version of the Code, it is covered at B.6 and also at B.7.2 (see **App1**). The most significant enhancement since 2006 is the requirement for external facilitation at least every third year (Provision B.6.2, App1). Another significant change is that since 2011 'diversity, including gender' is part of the board evaluation (Supporting Principle B.6, **App1**).

2006 changes **F2.20**

The 2006 Code was published by the Financial Reporting Council (FRC) in June 2006, and made only modest changes to the previous Code published by the FRC in July 2003.

The 2006 Code has no additional Principles, Supporting Principles or Provisions, and the numbering of them remained therefore unchanged. The 2006 changes were:

1. Amending the existing restriction on the company chairman serving on the remuneration committee, to enable him or her to do so where considered independent on appointment as chairman (although it is recommended that he or she should not also chair the committee).
2. Providing a 'vote withheld' option on proxy appointment forms to enable shareholders to indicate if they have reservations on a resolution but do not wish to vote against it. Many listed companies already provide this option. A 'vote withheld' is not a vote in law and is not counted in the calculation of the proportion of the votes for and against the resolution.
3. Recommending that companies publish on their website the details of proxies lodged at a general meeting where votes are taken on a show of hands. The Company Law Reform Bill then before Parliament included clauses that would require companies to publish details of votes taken on a poll. This amendment to the Combined Code meant that details of all votes would be made available.
4. Enabling companies to meet the requirement to make the terms of reference of board committees available by placing them on their website.

Notes

1 Quoted Companies Alliance (2010) *Corporate Governance Guidelines for Smaller Companies*, September 2010, replaced by (2013) *Corporate Governance Code for Small and Mid-Size Companies 2013*, available at http://www.theqca.com/shop/guides/70707/corporate-governance-code-for-small-and-midsize-quoted-companies-2013.thtml, accessed 29 December 2013.

2 Old Principle D.2 and old Provisions D.2.1 and D.2.2. Both these Provisions were amended in the 2003 and 2006 Codes, in the latter case extended, but the Turnbull Guidance continued unchanged. However, the Turnbull Guidance on internal audit was transferred to the Smith Report, to mirror the transfer of the internal audit provision from the Internal Control to the Audit Committees part of the 2003 and 2006 Codes.

3 Section 1.2 of the original Smith Report (not in the version which is incorporated into the 2003 Combined Code publication).

4 Section 3.2 on p 6 of the Smith Report.

5 FRC (October 2005), at www.frc.org.uk. Internal control: Revised Guidance for Directors on the Combined Code, at www.frc.org.uk/corporate/internalcontrol.cfm.

6 At least until recently, the Medical Defence Union arranged its members' insurance through a separate joint venture company it partially owns.

7 INREV (December 2006): *Corporate Governance Principles and Guidelines Relating to Corporate Governance in Non-Listed Real Estate Funds*, www.inrev.org. INREV is the European Association for Investors in Non-listed Real Estate Vehicles.

8 HM Treasury (July 2005 and July 2011): *Corporate Governance in Central Government Departments: Code of Good Practice*. The Code and separate guidance are available on the HM Treasury website.

9 HM Treasury (March 2007): *The Audit Committee Handbook*.

10 OPM (Office for Public Management) and CIPFA (Chartered Institute of Public Finance and Accountancy) (2004): *The Good Governance Standard for Public Services* (The Independent Commission on Good Governance in Public Services, www.opm.co.uk and www.cipfa.org.uk, ISBN: 1 898531 86 2).

11 BS 13500:2013 Code of practice for delivering effective governance of organizations.

12 Provision C.3.6 of the Combined Code (2006), continued into the current Code: 'The audit committee should have primary responsibility for making a recommendation on the appointment, reappointment and removal of the external auditors. If the board does not accept the audit committee's recommendation, it should include in the annual report, and in any papers recommending appointment or re-appointment, a statement from the audit committee explaining the recommendation and should set out reasons why the board has taken a different position.'

13 Sarbanes-Oxley Act (2002), SEC. 301. PUBLIC COMPANY AUDIT COMMITTEES:

'Section 10A of the Securities Exchange Act of 1934 (15 U.S.C. 78f) is amended by adding at the end the following:

"(m) STANDARDS RELATING TO AUDIT COMMITTEES— ..

"(2) RESPONSIBILITIES RELATING TO REGISTERED PUBLIC ACCOUNTING FIRMS.—The audit committee of each issuer, in its capacity as a committee of the board of directors, shall be directly responsible for the appointment, compensation, and oversight of the work of any registered public accounting firm employed by that issuer (including resolution of disagreements between management and the auditor regarding financial reporting) for the purpose of preparing or issuing an audit report or related work, and each such registered public accounting firm shall report directly to the audit committee."'

14 *Review of the Role and Effectiveness of Non-executive Directors*.

15 *Audit Committees Combined Code Guidance* – a report and proposed guidance by an FRC-appointed committee chaired by Sir Robert Smith, still available on the FRC's website, but updated and reissued as *Guidance on Audit Committees* (December 2010).

16 Code, pp 4 and 5.

17 Preamble, section 7.

18 Preamble, section 8.

19 Under Main Principle A.1.

20 Higgs, Provision A.3.3.

21 Committee on Corporate Governance – The Hampel Committee (January 1998), Final Report, chaired by Sir Ronald Hampel, para 5.19.

22 Higgs, Provision A.1.6.

23 Provision A.2.1 of the 1998 Code had read:

'A decision to combine the posts of chairman and chief executive officer in one person should be publicly justified. Whether the posts are held by different people or the same person, there should be a strong and independent non-executive element on the board, with a recognised senior member other than the chairman to whom concerns can be conveyed. The chairman, chief executive and senior independent director should be identified in the annual report.'

24 Higgs, proposed Provision A.1.5.

25 Except that the current Code allows the chairman of a small company's board to be a member of the audit committee in certain circumstances (Provision C.3.1).

26 This provision overlaps with FSA Rules DTR 7.1.5 R and 7.2.7 R (see Schedule B).

Part G:
Risk Management and Internal Control

Chapter G1

Risk Management and Internal Control

Internal control and risk management in the UK Corporate Governance Code G1.1

The July 1998 amendment to the UK Listing Rules specified listed companies' obligations with respect to the Combined Code. The general obligations read:

> 'In the case of a company incorporated in the United Kingdom, the following additional items must be included in its annual report and accounts:
>
> (a) a narrative statement of how it has applied the principles set out in Section 1 of the Combined Code, providing explanation which enables its shareholders to evaluate how the principles have been applied;
>
> (b) a statement as to whether or not it has complied throughout the accounting period with the Code provisions set out in Section 1 of the Combined Code. A company that has not complied with the Code provisions, or complied with only some of the Code provisions or (in the case of provisions whose requirements are of a continuing nature) complied for only part of an accounting period, must specify the Code provisions with which it has not complied, and (where relevant) for what part of the period such noncompliance continued, and give reasons for any non-compliance …'

Rule 12.43A was replaced by Rule 9.8.6, which then read:

> 'In the case of a company incorporated in the United Kingdom, the following additional items must be included in its annual report and accounts:
>
> (a) a narrative statement of how it has applied the principles set out in Section 1 of the Combined Code, providing sufficient explanation which enables its shareholders to evaluate how the principles have been applied;
>
> (b) a statement as to whether or not it has complied throughout the accounting period with the provisions set out in Section 1 of the Combined Code. A company that has not complied with the Code provisions, or complied with only some of the Code provisions or (in the case of provisions whose requirements are of a continuing nature) complied for only part of an accounting period, must specify the provisions with which it has not complied, and (where relevant) for what part of the period such non-compliance continued, and give reasons for any non-compliance …'

The relevant Rule (which is now 9.8.6 (5) and (6)) reads as follows:

> 'In the case of a listed company incorporated in the United Kingdom, the following additional items must be included in its annual financial report:
>
> …
>
> (5) a statement of how the listed company has applied the Main Principles set out in the UK Corporate Governance Code, in a manner that would enable shareholders to evaluate how the principles have been applied;
>
> (6) a statement as to whether the listed company has:
> (a) complied throughout the accounting period with all relevant provisions set out in the UK Corporate Governance Code; or
> (b) not complied throughout the accounting period with all relevant provisions set out in the UK Corporate Governance Code and if so, setting out:
> (i) those provisions, if any it has not complied with;
> (ii) in the case of provisions whose requirements are of a continuing nature, the period within which, if any, it did not comply with some or all of those provisions; and
> (iii) the company's reasons for non-compliance;'

Internal control G1.2

In the March 1998 consultation document of proposed changes to the Listing Rules relating to the Combined Code,[1] the Code Provision D.3 had read:

> 'The directors should review the effectiveness of the company's system of internal control and should report to shareholders. This report should cover all controls, including financial, operational and compliance controls and risk management.'

The final form of the 1998 Combined Code used a revised numbering system for the Principles and Provisions. What had been Provision D.3 in the consultation document became Provision D.2.1 in its 1998 form. This sat beneath D.2 which was the overarching Principle on 'Internal Control', the wording of which was unchanged in its final form from the consultation draft, namely:

> 'The board should maintain a sound system of internal control to safeguard shareholders' investments and the company's assets.'

This remained unchanged in the revised 2003 and 2006 Codes. Now, in the UK Corporate Governance Code (set out in full at **App1**), it reads (Principle C.2):

> 'The board is responsible for determining the nature and extent of the significant risks it is willing to take in achieving its strategic objectives. The board should maintain sound risk management and internal control systems.'

Changes to the Code Provision on internal control G1.3

What is significant is that the wording of what had been Code Provision D.3 (see above) became amended in what became D.2.1 in the 1998 Code to read:

> 'The directors should, at least annually, conduct a review of the effectiveness of the group's system of internal controls and should report to shareholders that they have done so. The review should cover all ['material' in 2003 and 2006 versions] controls, including financial, operational and compliance controls and risk management ['risk management systems' in 2003 and 2006 versions].'

So, by 1998, there had been a tightening up in that it is now unequivocally stated that the review should be 'at least annual'.

Readers can infer what they like (or nothing at all!) from the change to the plural from 'system of internal control' to 'systems of internal controls', and the author confesses as to having no clue as to why this change was made.

The revised wording of Provision D.2.1 (1998), then C.2.1 (2003 and 2006), made it transparently clear that directors were not required to report on the results of their review of internal control – just that they had conducted a review – an approach which was not clear in the earlier wording (see above). This has been the approach taken by many listed companies in implementing this Provision. However, the Turnbull Report provides guidance on what the directors' report should contain. Now that several UK companies are having to report on the effectiveness of internal control over financial reporting, to meet Sarbanes-Oxley Act 2002, s 404 requirements, they are frequently including their opinion about internal financial control effectiveness within their public report on internal control that appears as part of their corporate governance statement within their annual report and accounts.

The further revised wording in the current Code states (**App1**, Provision C.2.1):

> 'The board should, at least annually, conduct a review of the effectiveness of the company's risk management and internal control systems and should report to shareholders that they have done so.[2] The review should cover all material controls, including financial, operational and compliance controls.'

Arguably, greater importance is now being attached to risk management, which is perhaps being given precedence over internal control. There is a suggestion in this latest wording that appropriate internal controls are there to mitigate risk and not just as a 'good thing'.

Effectiveness **G1.4**

Although the directors' review of internal control must cover 'effectiveness', their report had not in the past needed to disclose their opinion on effectiveness; and the latest UK Corporate Governance Code Provisions make no change to that. In addition, if literally interpreted, there also continues to be no requirement for directors even to come to a private (ie not for publication) opinion on effectiveness – just to *review* its effectiveness.

Nevertheless, the word 'effectiveness' has survived from Cadbury through to the current UK Corporate Governance Code notwithstanding the challenges to it along the way, and notwithstanding that, in 1994, Rutteman had given directors a way to opt out of disclosing an opinion on effectiveness, which continues until today.

Arguments for directors publicly disclosing their opinion on internal control effectiveness G1.5

- Maximum disclosure, if not misleading, is generally regarded as a desirable feature of efficient markets.
- A thorough, careful, responsible process can be followed by directors in arriving at their opinion as to internal control effectiveness. It can be thoroughly minuted. If the conclusions are consistent with what is revealed during the process, then it would be difficult to pin a charge of recklessness or negligence upon the board of directors or upon any member of the board.
- Careful wording, going beyond standard phrases such as 'reasonable assurance', can be used to avoid giving a false degree of reassurance about the effectiveness of internal control.
- Although the directors' opinions as to internal control effectiveness will always include a large degree of judgement, there is significant judgement behind many of the statements contained in companies' annual reports. Indeed, it can be argued that those statements which are entirely verifiable in an objective way are often less valuable to the readers of annual reports, as, for instance, with the historical cost of a freehold building. On the other hand, those statements which involve a large degree of subjective judgement are often more valuable, as, for instance, with respect to the chairman's report on future prospects. The external audit opinion itself is highly judgemental.

Arguments against directors publicly disclosing their opinion on internal control effectiveness G1.6

- If they have established a practice of disclosing that their systems of internal control are, in their view, effective, it would become difficult to disguise the occasion when they do not believe that such is the case.
- Making such a statement may raise the due standard of skill and care which common law expects directors to exercise, and give extra ammunition in any action alleging breach of this duty.
- Under s 214 of the Insolvency Act 1986 relating to wrongful trading, a court may require a director to contribute to a company's assets if he or she had not taken every reasonable step to minimise the loss to creditors as soon as the company had become terminally ill. A positive statement about internal control effectiveness made about a reported year during which the point of no return was passed could be construed as negligent, or that the director should have known better, or that the director may have known better – and thus make it more likely that a court order might be made. Compensation for damages might be due from a director or directors to the company itself, or to the shareholders as a body, if the annual report contained any negligent misstatements.
- Section 47(1) of the Financial Services Act 1986 makes it a criminal offence in this sector knowingly or recklessly to make a statement which is misleading, false or deceptive if it might influence someone to enter into an investment agreement – which might include the purchase of shares.
- Why disclose when there is no obligation to do so?

Understanding risk assessment and risk management **G1.7**

'The main goal of a management science must be to enable business to take the right risk. Indeed, it must be to enable business to take greater risks – by providing knowledge and understanding of alternative risks and alternative expectations; by identifying the resources and efforts needed for desired results; by mobilizing energies for contribution; and by measuring results against expectations; thereby providing means for early correction of wrong or inadequate decisions. All this may sound like mere quibbling over terms. Yet the terminology of risk minimization does induce a hostility to risk-taking and risk-making – that is, to business enterprise.'[3]

'No entity operates in a risk-free environment, and enterprise risk management does not seek to move towards such an environment. Rather, enterprise risk management enables management to operate more effectively in environments filled with risk.'[4]

Years ago, Drucker said, in effect, that it is not the task of boards to avoid risk but rather to be able to take bigger risks but more safely. While, in a sense, this is a contradictory statement, it places stress on the relationship between risk taking and the development of successful enterprises. It rightly implies that risks should be managed.

COSO frameworks **G1.8**

There is more general use of the COSO definitions and frameworks of 'internal control' and of 'enterprise risk management' than of other frameworks. The two leading alternative frameworks are the UK's Turnbull framework and the Canadian CoCo framework, but the former is based upon COSO. COSO, a standing committee of five US-based professional bodies, first convened to sponsor the 1987 Treadway Report on fraudulent financial reporting of Wall Street listed companies. Issues arising from that report led COSO to subsequently invite Coopers & Lybrand's New York office to develop, with COSO, a framework on internal control, that was published in 1992. From that point, COSO had become a standing committee and so became popularly known more simply as 'Committee of Sponsoring Organizations' although formally it is still the 'Committee of Sponsoring Organizations of the Treadway Commission'. COSO's most notable recent works have been the sponsorship of their 2004 Enterprise Risk Management – Integrated Framework and its 2013 updated Internal Control – Integrated Framework, both also developed by what was by then PwC's New York office.

COSO's internal control framework is the generally accepted framework. For instance, almost all companies complying with the Sarbanes-Oxley Act 2002, s 404 use the COSO internal control framework for that purpose. COSO's 2004 concept of enterprise risk management framework incorporates all of the COSO internal control concept and goes a bit further.

Perhaps the quickest way to gain an appreciation of these two concepts is to refer to the table and the cubes below. More detailed reference to the COSO internal control framework reveals that 'risk assessment' – one of COSO's essential components of internal control – comprises identifying events which represent risks, assessing or evaluating them, and then deciding how to respond to them. COSO's 2004 framework, focusing as it does on risk management, has opted to separate out these three elements into *three* components rather than *one*.

COSO's 2004 enterprise risk management framework differs from the COSO internal control framework in showing a fourth objective of enterprise risk management: 'strategic'. The addition of this objective (which should really be considered the first of what are now four objectives, as it comes before the others) acknowledges that risk management approaches should be applied at the time of strategy formulation and not merely after a strategy has been decided upon. Some strategic options may be too risky to be adopted; certainly, an entity should understand the risks associated with the strategic alternatives the entity is considering. Marconi is an example of a company that adopted a strategy that was too risky, and it collapsed as a consequence.

Having determined that 'strategic' should become an additional objective of enterprise risk management (in contrast to internal control), it was logical that objective setting should be added by COSO as an essential component of enterprise risk management.

In other respects the objectives of enterprise risk management are identical to those of internal control, with 'internal environment' being the preferred label rather than 'control environment'. While COSO did perhaps need to rename 'control environment' since COSO was developing an enterprise risk management framework, the use of the oxymoron 'internal environment' was unfortunate.

COSO's enterprise risk management framework therefore corresponds to the entirety of the scope of the management process, whereas its internal control framework, excluding as it did 'objective setting', does not. In that sense, COSO is correct to characterise its enterprise risk management framework as a 'more robust conceptualisation' than is its internal control framework. COSO's internal control concept is flawed, as the achievement of major objectives invariably entails the setting of subordinate objectives. Internal control is defined as providing reasonable assurance of the achievement of objectives, but the setting of objectives is excluded from the internal control framework. It is as if one exchanges one's ordinary spectacles so as to view the entire management process through risk management lenses – which gives a modified focus, a modified perspective on the management process, picking out the elements relevant to risk management. If one views the management process through the lens of internal control, it is a partial view, excluding objective setting. The concept of internal control is thus artificially circumscribed and artificially defined. While COSO's internal control definition is 'broadly defined' (as COSO states in their definition of internal control), it is nevertheless thus narrower than all of management. Internal control could have been defined even more narrowly to correspond, for instance, to what used to be termed 'internal check'.

We can use the analogy of a ship crossing an ocean. It is heading for a port the other side. It needs to have on board everything necessary to give reasonable assurance that it will reach its destination. According to the way COSO defines internal control, to pursue our analogy, we are referring not just to the navigation control system (although internal control might have been defined as narrowly as that); in addition, we are referring to the design of the hull, the strength and maintenance of the engines, the training and motivation of the crew, the quality of leadership, and so on. In other words, we are referring to everything that contributes to giving reasonable assurance that the ship will reach its destination – except for deciding what is the destination and deciding upon lesser objectives that will contribute to our arrival at our destination.

COSO: Internal Control – Integrated Framework (2013)	COSO: Enterprise Risk Management (2004)
'Internal control is broadly defined as a process, effected by the entity's board of directors, management and other personnel, designed to provide reasonable assurance regarding the achievement of objectives in the following categories: • effectiveness and efficiency of operations; • reliability of financial reporting; • compliance with applicable laws and regulations.'	'Enterprise risk management is a process, effected by an entity's board of directors, management and other personnel, applied in strategy setting and across the enterprise, designed to identify potential events that may affect the entity, and manage risks to be within its risk appetite, to provide reasonable assurance regarding the achievement of entity objectives.'[5] 'This definition is purposefully broad for several reasons. It captures key concepts fundamental to how companies and other organizations manage risk, providing a basis for application across types of organizations, industries and sectors. It focuses directly on achievement of objectives established by a particular entity. And, the definition provides a basis for defining enterprise risk management effectiveness …'[6] 'Well-designed and operated enterprise risk management can provide management and the board of directors reasonable assurance regarding achievement of an entity's objectives. Reasonable assurance reflects the notion that uncertainty and risk relate to the future, which no one can predict with certainty.'[7]

COSO's 2013 internal control 'Rubik's cube'

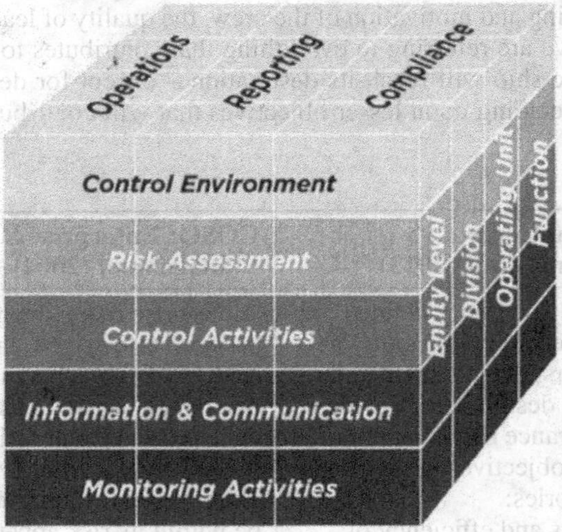

COSO's 2004 enterprise risk management 'Rubik's cube'

Key to the COSO's enterprise risk management cube:

The four objectives categories – strategic, operations, reporting and compliance – are represented by the vertical columns. The eight components are represented by horizontal rows. The entity and its units are depicted by the third dimension of the cube.[8]

It is difficult to adequately represent the concept of enterprise risk management even in COSO's three-dimensional cube, as acknowledged by COSO:

'Each component row "cuts across" and applies to all four objectives categories. For example, financial and non-financial data generated from internal and external sources, which is part of the information and communication component, is needed to set strategy, effectively manage business operations, report effectively and determine that the entity is complying with applicable laws.

'Similarly, looking at the objectives categories, all eight components are relevant to each. Taking one category, effectiveness and efficiency of operations, for example, all eight components are applicable and important to its achievement.

'Enterprise risk management is relevant to an entire enterprise or to any of its individual units. This relationship is depicted by the third dimension, which represents subsidiaries, divisions and other business units. Accordingly, one could focus on any one of the matrix's cells. For instance, one could consider the top-right back cell, representing the internal environment as it relates to compliance objectives of a particular subsidiary.

'It should be recognized that the four columns represent categories of an entity's objectives, not parts or units of the entity. Accordingly, when considering the category of objectives related to reporting, for example, knowledge of a wide array of information about the entity's operations is needed. But in that case, focus is on the right-middle column of the model – the reporting objectives – rather than the operations objectives category.'[9]

Assessing the effectiveness of internal control and risk management G1.9

Best practice advice, for instance in Turnbull as well as COSO, is that we assess the effectiveness of internal control in two ways. The same is true of assessing the effectiveness of enterprise risk management.

First, we consider whether there is any evidence of *outcomes* that indicate we have significantly failed to achieve our objectives. If so, internal control has been ineffective, since its purpose is to give us reasonable assurance that we achieve our objectives. This first test is inadequate on its own for two reasons. The first reason is that we might have failed to meet an objective although we have not noticed any evidence of that. A significant, embedded and undetected fraud might be such an example. The second reason is that we might have achieved our objectives more by luck than due to an effective system of internal control: the weaknesses in our systems of internal control might be so profound that it is likely to be only a matter of time before these defects are exploited, deliberately or accidentally.

So it would be imprudent to conclude that our internal control is effective before we had assessed the quality of our internal control *processes* – which is the second task we must do before we can conclude that our internal control is effective. This may seem a harsh requirement, as it is possible to argue that a weak system of internal control has been effective if nothing has gone wrong. However, best practice guidance demands that an evaluation of the quality of the internal control processes is also required before an 'effectiveness' conclusion can be made. Furthermore, as we have said, you cannot be sure that nothing has gone wrong.

We consider that the best way to assess the effectiveness of internal control processes is to consider the adequacy of each of COSO's five essential components of internal control (see COSO's 2013 cube). Indeed, we consider it is now preferable to consider the adequacy of each of COSO's *eight* essential components of enterprise risk management, thereby enabling a conclusion on internal control and risk management. This is the approach we recommend that audit committees follow. During the course of a year, an audit committee can ask management for reports on each of the eight essential components of enterprise risk management. Careful consideration and discussion of these reports can contribute significantly to the audit committee being able to advise the board whether the business has effective internal control and risk management.

Enterprise-wide risk management G1.10

We should add that the adjective 'enterprise' in 'enterprise risk management' reminds us that risk management should be enterprise-wide. Too much of our risk management is done in silos only.

Risks in one part of a business may be balanced out in other parts of the business. For instance, a company that manufactures sausages and ice cream is protected from the temperature vagaries of weather and seasons: folk will be buying either sausages or ice cream.

The London buses effect G1.11

We should also bear in mind that risks are like London buses – they tend all to arrive at the same time. Rather than just considering whether we are controlling risks individually, we should consider our vulnerability should several risky events occur simultaneously. Our approaches to risk management too frequently consider risks only individually. When a business fails, or almost fails, it is usually when several risky events have occurred simultaneously and the business had not planned for that to happen.

'Upside' and 'downside' risk G1.12

Finally, our approaches to risk management often dwell on what we might call 'downside risk' only – the likelihood of events occurring that constitute a threat to the business, and whether we are minimising the likelihood and putting in place what will be necessary to manage our way through the challenge should it occur. We should also think of risk management in 'upside risk' or 'opportunity' terms. When we do this, we consider in advance whether there may be events that might occur in the future that would present us with business opportunities, notwithstanding that they are not within our business plan. We should endeavour to anticipate what those future events might be and consider whether we should put in place what will be needed so that, should the event occur, we will then have the discretion to exploit that opportunity. We might even endeavour to encourage such events to occur, depending upon the nature of the events in question. By way of example (though not examples which we would encourage), a UK specialist manufacturer of high quality, sturdy, temporary buildings was not well placed to exploit the opportunity of the 2004 tsunami, and shortly afterwards missed out on a similar opportunity offered by the earthquake in Northern Pakistan. Of course, there was a 'downside risk' associated with this – the competition moved in and our manufacturer will find it hard to recover lost market share.

Defining 'risk' G1.13

Risk has been defined as:

> 'The possibility of an event occurring that will have an impact on the achievement of objectives. Risk is measured in terms of impact and likelihood.'

(This is the definition of risk in the Glossary to the Standards of the Institute of Internal Auditors, see **App8.**)

An Australian/New Zealand standard defines risk management as:

> 'The culture, processes and structures that are directed towards the effective management of potential opportunities and adverse effects.'[10]

Already, this definition of risk management is being applied in the UK, for instance in the NHS.[11]

Risk may be considered in terms of *outcomes*:

> 'A possible outcome which cannot be predicted with certainty and which would be unwelcome because it would be counterproductive.'

Or in terms of *process*:

> 'Factors which could affect the achievement of objectives, or the likelihood of unwanted consequences occurring.'

Risks in the context of *process* are often referred to as *risk factors*. In essence, the difference between risk which is viewed in terms of *outcomes* and risk which is considered in terms of *process* is a matter of the perspective of the observer. For a staff operative, a successful *outcome* of the operation may be the avoidance of an unwanted result, but for senior management and the board the risk of that unwanted outcome will be seen as a risk factor – a risk associated with the *process*.

Components of risk G1.14

Different parties have different risks, and consequently see risk as having different components. For instance, external auditors regard *audit risk* ('audit risk' for the external auditor being the risk of a significant misstatement in the financial results of the entity not being detected and corrected (or reported) as a result of the audit) as having three components: inherent risk, control risk and detection risk.[12] There is common ground that the components of risk are:

- inherent risk – the risk which is intrinsically bound up with the activity;
- control risk – the scope to reduce inherent risk through the application of control; and
- residual risk – the extent of the risk after the application of control.

The degree of residual risk which is acceptable is for the board to decide, and will depend on a number of considerations. One is the possible overall consequence to the enterprise if the risk materialises. Another is the general attitude of the entity to risk taking, which should be determined by the board. We can call this the *risk appetite*. Risk appetite may also vary between entities for a number of reasons, which can be contradictory. For instance, public entities tend to be *risk averse*, as they are custodians of the public purse. On the other hand, they often take on the management of risks which are unacceptably great for the private sector to be willing to assume.

Because it is most generally accepted that 'inherent risk' comprises the 'size' or 'impact' which is inherent in the activity and also that part of the 'system' or 'likelihood' component which is also considered to be inherent in the activity (ie uncontrollable), that is the approach we take in this handbook. Thus, for instance, trading in derivative futures may be inherently risky, both on account of how much is at risk and also because even the application of the best processes to handle these trades will not successfully control the risks.

In essence, this generally accepted view of inherent risk is subdividing the 'system' or 'process' contributor of risk into that which is deemed uncontrollable and that which is controllable; and it is bracketing the former with the 'size' risk to provide this composite measure of inherent risk. The graphical matrix approach we suggest later is an illustration of this. If this approach is followed, care must be taken not to concede with too much alacrity an inevitable, inherent vulnerability which is then not focused on with the intention of improving control. Essentially, there are these three components of risk:

- 'size' (of risk before the application of control);
- 'process' or 'system' risk; and
- residual risk – the extent of the risk after the application of control.

Risk management comprises:

- risk identification;
- risk measurement;
- risk control; and
- risk taking.

The term 'risk assessment' (one of the five COSO components of effective internal control, and thus one of the criteria for assessing the effectiveness of internal control) focuses mainly on risk identification and measurement.

Why this emphasis on 'risk'? G1.15

Spectacular corporate collapses or near collapses (Enron, Marconi, for instance) can be attributed to failures of risk management. The message of the Turnbull Report is that the board has overall responsibility for risk management – the board itself should be engaged in assessing overall risks and in effective oversight of risk management. A 'top-down' assessment of risk should feed down from the board to the businesses and operations within the entity. Secondly, the board should be satisfied about the embedded processes for the review of risk and control within the enterprise, the results of which should be fed up to the board for board consideration.

Another, less worthy, reason for the focus on risk management is the too frequent unwillingness of boards and senior management to invest in effective internal control to the extent that managements and boards would have done so in the past. It is tempting to factor into the price of the product or service the cost associated with weak control. Delayered, downsized, re-engineered entities have taken out many of the opportunities to achieve control in traditional ways. Major change, including significant redesign of systems, tends to introduce control vulnerabilities which had been progressively reduced until the reorganisation of the business. Management is less willing to invest in comprehensive internal control to reduce risk, and this has not been a priority with those who design new systems. Unwilling to lose the cost advantages of re-engineered business approaches, management seeks to justify investment in control in terms of the relative degrees of risk that control mitigates. The pursuit of annually increasing returns for the shareholders makes boards of companies reluctant to saddle the business with the costs of more watertight controls. There are, in itself, risks associated with this. The best approaches to risk assessment are highly subjective. They may overlook major risks or fail to assess them reliably. Major risks may be 'buried in the woodwork', perhaps not readily amenable to identification by top management and the board, nor to reliable assessment if they are identified. Take, for instance, the falsification of quality data by four production workers at BNFL, or the sales cut-off problem which led to the collapse of a retailer. So a 'top-down' approach to risk management is not enough on its own: intelligence about risk and control vulnerabilities needs to be gathered at the grass roots level of the business, synthesised and fed upwards to top management and the board.

Another justification for contemporary focus on risk management is that businesses are changing fast. The half-life of business systems is relentlessly getting shorter as the nature of business activities changes. It is not so much that control is costly, but that the finite resources of senior executive, systems designer and internal auditor time are limited and need to be directed to the areas of the business where the need is greatest to achieve effective internal control. It follows that a prerequisite is risk assessment – both to identify the areas of greatest need and also to identify the greatest vulnerabilities in these areas which need fixing.

Matrix and risk register approaches for the board to assess risk **G1.16**

A picture is worth a thousand words. This simple matrix allows risks to be noted down according to their potential impact as well as the probability of them occurring. When this technique has been applied at the level of the board, the number of risks plotted should be limited to perhaps the 20 to 24 major risks that the company faces, otherwise too much detail obscures the big picture. Similarly, if this matrix technique is used at divisional or departmental level, focus on just the major risks is usually desirable.

If this is done first, *before* taking account of the effectiveness of the controls upon which the company is currently relying, it can be used to indicate where and how management and the board needs to focus on implementing effective controls. A corollary of this is that it can be used to indicate where the controls upon which management and the board are currently relying are too elaborate (in view, perhaps, of the modest inherent risk) or inappropriate (in view of the characteristics of the inherent risk).

Then the risks can be plotted again on the matrix to show where the principal risks are *after* the application of internal control. Management and the board then need to judge whether the risks are acceptable in view of their 'risk appetite'.

The division of the graph into labelled quadrants suggests, in broad brush terms, the appropriate control responses to risks recorded in each of the quadrants, according to the key:

Matrix key	
Primary:	Risks which must be focused upon continuously by top management to minimise the likelihood of them occurring and the impact of them if they do occur.
Contingency:	Requires carefully pre-designed and tested contingency plans to be in place to cater for the eventuality if it occurs (but note that 'risk avoidance' might be preferred to a contingency approach to managing these risks).
Housekeeping:	Sufficiently regular and careful attention by way of effective internal control to minimise the likelihood of this unwanted outcome.
Monitoring and review:	Provision of periodic information to confirm the containment of this risk within acceptable levels, together with assigned responsibilities to keep this periodic information under review.

HM Treasury's '4 Ts' are useful as an alternative guide to the options available to manage risk:[13]

- Tolerate;
- Treat;
- Transfer; and
- Terminate.

These '4 Ts' correspond to the COSO enterprise risk management four means of managing risk which are respectively: acceptance, reduction, sharing and avoidance. These COSO terms are more accurate descriptors of the means. Some parties add 'Track' as a '5th T' referring to the need to monitor, learn and improve. Of course, there is a lot of subjectivity in this approach – as in any other approach to risk management. The identification of which risks to plot on the matrix is a matter of judgement. Where to plot them is also a matter of judgement. Revising the plotting of the risks to take account of the effectiveness of introduced controls is also a matter of judgement. Finally, it is a matter of judgement to decide whether the residual risks are acceptable.

The use of this technique *before* the application of control gives a picture which corresponds to an external auditor's view of inherent risk – which combines a consideration of the likely impact (in their case, upon the reliability of the financial statements) with a consideration of the degree of probability of it happening.

Risk assessment matrix (1) **G1.17**

(Before taking account of controls)

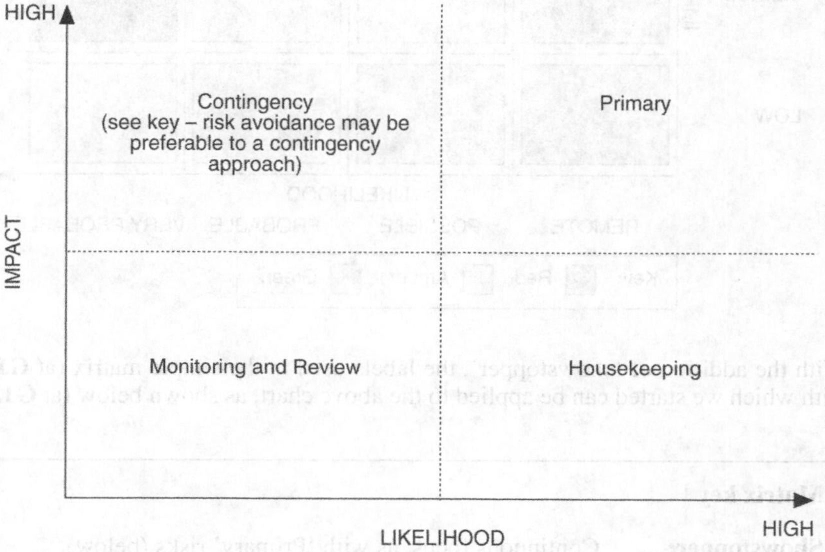

(then plot risks again after taking account of control)

A modified approach to using this graph is to (a) *possibly* omit the quadrants, and (b) use circles of varying size according to 'Impact' and of different colours according to 'Likelihood *after* control', namely:

- Green (rare) – no problem.
- Amber – some risk.
- Red – danger!

Many businesses classify or 'categorise' risks – for instance, according to whether they are funding risks, personnel risks, competitor risks, and so on. Our discussion later in this chapter of a tabular approach to top-down risk assessment, known as a 'risk register' approach, goes into this in more detail (see **G1.21** to **G1.25**). The above graphical matrix approach works well when applied to each of the classes of risks.

In the simple matrix shown above, we have encountered an elaboration of the same approach. The graph is divided into more sections and colour coding (red, amber and green) used to flag up degrees of relative seriousness, as shown in the following chart.

Risk assessment matrix (2) **G1.18**

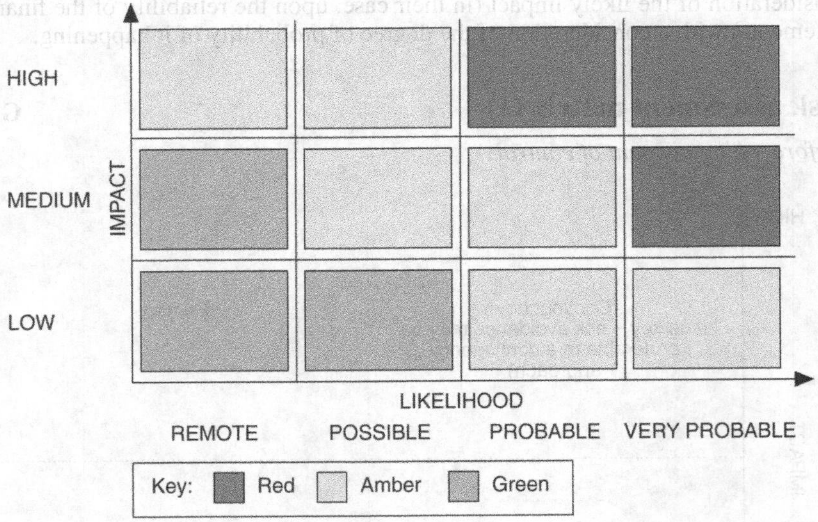

With the addition of 'showstopper', the labels used in the simple matrix (at **G1.17**) with which we started can be applied to the above chart, as shown below (at **G1.19**):

Matrix key

Showstopper:	Continuous focus, as with 'Primary' risks (below), supplemented by regular attention of the board. The intention is to eliminate as far as possible the risk of this unwanted outcome materialising, which would prudently involve avoidance of risk taking in this area.
Primary:	Risks which must be focused upon continuously by top management to minimise the likelihood of them occurring and the impact of them if they do occur.
Contingency:	Requires carefully pre-designed and tested contingency plans to be in place to cater for the eventuality if it occurs (but note that 'risk avoidance' might be preferred to a contingency approach to managing these risks).
Housekeeping:	Sufficiently regular and careful attention by way of effective internal control to minimise the likelihood of this unwanted outcome.
Monitoring and review:	Provision of periodic information to confirm the containment of this risk within acceptable levels, together with assigned responsibilities to keep this periodic information under review.

Risk assessment matrix (3) **G1.19**

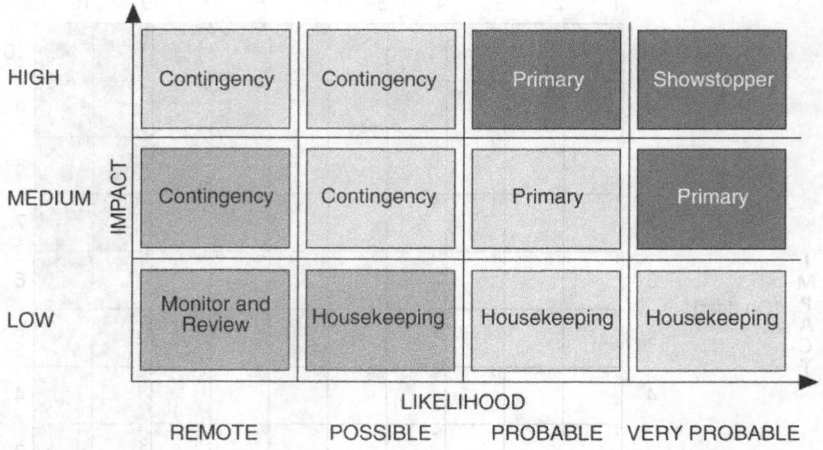

Further example of the risk matrix approach **G1.20**

Another implementation of the same concept[14] develops what is known as a 'risk map', where the vertical and horizontal axes are each divided into a ten-point scale, allowing each cell to be assigned an overall risk value resulting from multiplying its horizontal position by its vertical position (Table 1). In Table 1, four example risks are shown by the numbers 1 to 4 and described in Table 2. Thus, in this example the risks associated with the failure of a high-profile project are scored at 90, compared to a score of only ten for a plane hitting their computer centre: although the probability of the former is assessed as much greater than the probability of the latter, the assessment is that the impact of the former would be only slightly less than the impact of the latter. Table 3 shows that this business grades the risks into four levels according to the overall risk value.

That 'keying errors' comes out with a composite risk score of 27 may seem surprising, but illustrates how difficult it is to assess most risks and how easy it would be to underestimate certain risks. The significance of issues such as keying errors was illustrated well, though not for the first time, when in December 2005 a Japanese securities trader transposed two items of data that he keyed in, which resulted in his bank selling 600,000 shares in a new telecoms company for one yen each. His intention had been to sell a single share for 600,000 yen (£2,850). The Japanese Stock Exchange's computers repeatedly prevented the trader from cancelling the order. Amongst the consequences of this event were a 2% fall in Tokyo's Nikkei shares index, the closure of the world's second largest stock market for four hours, the resignation of the boss of Japan's stock exchange along with two of his senior colleagues, a cost to the Japanese Bank of £285,000 and the loss of the Christmas bonuses that the bank's staff would otherwise have received.[15, 16]

Table 1: The risk map

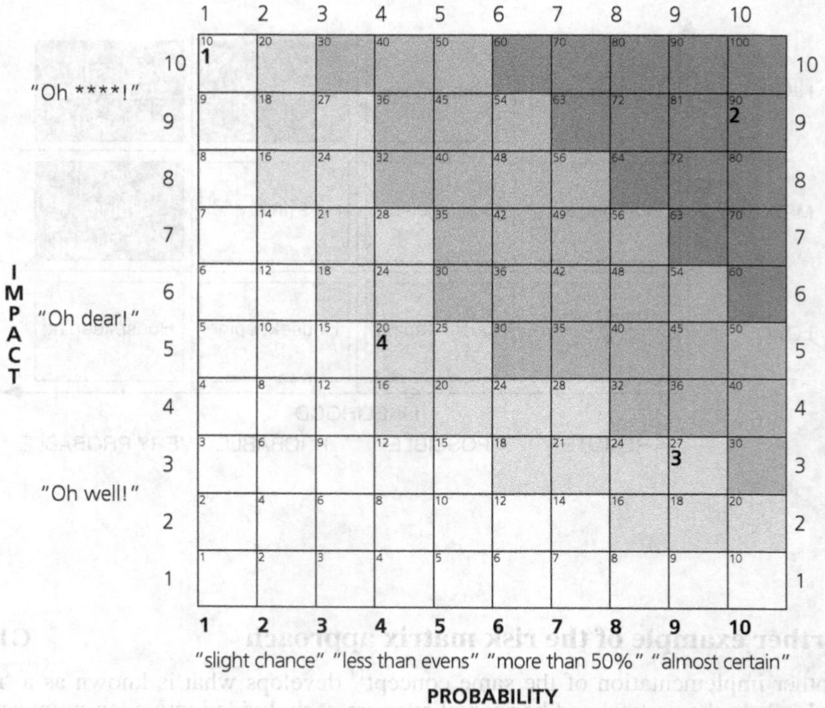

Table 2: Description of risks

Risk number	Description of risk	Probability	Impact
1	Plane hitting computer centre	1	10
2	Failure of high profile venture	10	9
3	Keying errors	9	3
4	Bad weather keeping staff from working	4	5

Table 3: Ranking of risks

Score	Risk category	Colour
60+	Critical	Red
30–59	High	Orange
16–29	Medium	Yellow
1–15	Low	White

Using a risk register approach to business risk assessment **G1.21**

In the following pages we offer four examples of risk registers, the fourth, at **G1.25**, suggesting an ideal layout. In both Examples 1 and 2 below, it is noteworthy that the company entrusted to the chief audit executive the tasks of developing these risk tables (ie 'risk register') and presenting them respectively to senior management, the audit committee and then the board. In this, he was playing a major role in the risk management of the company – a challenging role in view of the need for the risk management process to be audited independently. This is illustrative of the enhanced role that internal audit is now often playing in the wake of the Turnbull Report. In Example 3, the government agency concerned had neither a risk management function nor its own internal audit function (internal audit was centralised at sponsoring departmental level above the level of the agency), and so the task of facilitating the development of the risk register was entrusted to a member of the agency's quality assurance function.

For the board to be actively involved in oversight of risk management, an appropriate approach may be for an overall presentation to be made to the board once a year – which summarises the content of the risk tables (see below) and gives the board the opportunity to contribute to the consideration of risk management. Then, at subsequent board meetings, the subject matter of one table can be opened up in detail. The overall presentation may be made by the chief audit executive, but could be made by the chief executive. The subsequent detailed presentations could be made by the respective responsible executives – for instance, the finance director, the director of human resources, the company lawyer etc. Clearly, the board will need to balance its more detailed involvement in this way against other board priorities: time is always of the essence.

Now that colour laser and other colour printers are plentiful and economic to use, colour has arrived for internal management reports. Risk register entries can with advantage use colour coding to indicate degrees of risk – usually utilising the 'red, amber, green' indicators.

Example 1 **G1.22**

We set out below an early attempt developed by a UK listed manufacturing company to give effect to aspects of the approach for assessing internal control as set out in the Turnbull Guidance. Altogether, by considering the risks outlined in these tables, the board was considering just over 30 major risks. This was not too inconsistent with our earlier advice, in the context of the risk matrix discussed before in this section, that the number of risks the board should address needs to be limited if the board is to avoid becoming immersed in too much detail.

Although not given in this example, it is important that this exercise commences with an agreed statement of corporate objectives, and that each risk in the tables should be cross-referenced to the objective(s) it threatens. It is best that specific performance indicators (key performance indicators – KPIs) are identified and associated with each of the objectives and each of the risks in the tables wherever possible, and that the monthly management accounting pack which goes to the board should have a section showing performance against each of the KPIs so that the board can track the containment of risk.

In this example, the risks are classified into eight main areas, but they are not related directly to the stated objectives as we believe they should be – perhaps by use of an additional column to cross-reference to a separate statement of major corporate objectives. Usually, it is sufficient if major corporate objectives are expressed as between four and six objectives at the most.

An important issue is whether or not the company truly has identified the right risks. Another issue is the relative ranking by importance of each of the identified risks – which these schedules do not indicate, but a later example does.

In the full example before we abbreviated it, it was noticeable that specific controls and actions had not been identified to mitigate certain of the risks, and in some cases no review body had been identified.

Establishing ownership of risk is important. Some of the identified 'controls' referred to the monitoring role of external bodies – such as regulators or trade associations – which was inappropriate as, at best, these were 'review bodies' rather than 'controls'. These external bodies are not a front line control and at best are likely to be only an erratic 'back stop' control; and they are more by nature of *external* controls than *internal* controls. We think they should be shown in the right-hand column as a 'Review Body' rather than in the column titled 'Controls'.

The appearance again and again of the same bodies in the 'Review Body' column raises the question as to whether each of these can always be depended upon to exercise effective review of the particular risks: rules should be developed to prescribe more tightly whether it is reasonable to show a body in this column – for instance, internal audit should perhaps only be shown if an audit which covers this risk is scheduled to be conducted within the next 12 months (or has been conducted in the previous 12 months) without significant audit scope limitations.

Presenting to the board tables such as this is likely to generate the sort of discussion alluded to immediately above – which means that they are starting to work effectively to get the board involved in a top-level assessment of risk and control.

The XYZ Group plc

Business risk assessment

(date) – initial output

Following a series of discussions with the Group's senior management a range of identifiable risks have been established. Given the rate of consolidation in the sector, the intensely competitive market and the downward pressures on prices, XYZ's major risks come from the actions of both our suppliers and our competitors. The risk assessment process has therefore highlighted the need to keep a close watch on input costs as well as market and competitor developments. However, its main focus has been on areas where management actions can alleviate risks in order for the group to achieve its business objectives.

This process has resulted in eight main groups of risks which are discussed in details below. It should be noted that some risks could appear in more than one category.

The risks are summarised as:

1. strategic;
2. structural;
3. people related;
4. general systems;
5. regulatory and legal;
6. new business and markets;
7. the market and competition; and
8. funding.

1. Strategic risks

	Risk	Controls	Review Body
1.1	It is important for the group to have a clear medium/long-term strategy to avoid the danger of market initiatives being made with a short-term focus that may act against the long-term interests of the Group's shareholders.	Forecasting Budgets/variance analysis Formally documented strategy Sales and marketing strategy	Executive Operational board Internal audit Main board

	Risk	Controls	Review Body
1.3	XYZ is a medium sized operator in big markets and our strategies, structure, systems, cost base etc should reflect this: the risk being that we could be squeezed out by big competitor manufacturers.	Niche market strategy Forecasts/budgets and reviews Cost control	Executive Operational board Monthly divisional board Internal audit Main board

2. Structural issues

	Risk	Controls	Review Body
2.1	The organisation of the group's operating divisions and their management via the operational and executive boards needs constant attention to avoid the problems outlined in 1.3 above and to ensure new developments make full use of existing resources rather than duplicate management, people and processes where this may be unnecessary.	Formal documentation Budgetary reviews	Executive Operational Board Internal audit Main board
2.3	The non-executive directors (NEDs) should not become 'stale' and should continue to provide new ideas and their experience to the group as well as providing an appropriate challenge to management. The experiences of other companies (such as Marconi) indicate the importance of effective challenge by NEDs of strategic proposals of the executive.		Executive Operational Board Internal audit Main board

3. People-related risks

	Risk	Controls	Review Body
3.1	Without a medium to long-term view of succession planning and resourcing, the group faces the risks of a lack of continuity and knowledge if key individuals leave. Also there is a risk associated with making inappropriate appointments from outside the group to fill gaps that could potentially be more efficiently filled from within. Careful consideration should be given to succession planning and bolstering resourcing in key areas.	Formal consideration of succession planning Development plans for managers	Executive Operational board Business heads Internal audit Main board
3.7	Poor communication between HQ and divisional sites may impede business objectives and/or sour relations between staff in the locations.	Team Talk Databases Regular visits by Group staff to divisional sites	Executive Operational board Internal audit Main board

4. General system-related risks

	Risk	Controls	Review Body
4.1	Systems priorities may not reflect group priorities for the business lines.	Functional heads are responsible for determining their priorities clearly	Executive Operational board Internal audit Main board
4.7	Staffing requirements may not be assessed appropriately.	Cost benefit analysis	Operational board Internal audit Main board

5. Regulatory and legal risk

	Risk	Controls	Review Body
5.1	Health and safety requirements are becoming increasingly demanding and the consumer lobby is also getting stronger. Non-compliance may cause business objectives to suffer or costs to increase to ensure compliance.	Health and safety function Trade Association membership obligations and review	Executive Operational board Internal audit Main board
5.5	Empowerment has its risks. Where mandates for human resources-related issues are not clear there is a danger that local management make mistakes.	Human resources Ensure that team leaders/team directors are fully aware of their responsibilities with regards to staff issues and when they should seek advices/confirmation to be taken with HR	Executive Operational board Internal audit Main board

6. New business and markets

	Risk	Controls	Review Body
6.1	There are risks in developing new products, entering new markets or opening new distribution sources, there is a risk that product delivery is of unacceptable quality or at higher cost than anticipated.	Market analysis/research	Executive Group marketing Internal audit Main board
6.3	Staff and management in front line as well as in support areas must have sufficient skills and experience to ensure that new markets and products are fully understood, or business objectives may not be met	Ensure the relevant experience/knowledge is in place – either through recruitment of these skills or specific training programmes	Operational board Internal audit Main board

7. Market and competitive changes

	Risk	Controls	Review Body
7.1	While in the businesses we are in there are significant barriers to entry, there is relatively little customer loyalty and a need always to compete on price.	Carefully watch market developments (particularly in our niche markets) and defend our position where possible	Executive Operational board Divisional boards Internal audit Main board
7.2	Consolidation in the market brings both risks and opportunities. There is a risk of big players competing us out of the market – niche strategies can counter some of this if we can be swift and accurately identify our chosen markets and customers.	Continue to develop new niches	Executive Operational board Divisional boards Internal audit Main board

8. Funding

	Risk	Controls	Review Body
8.3	Risk of tightening of borrowing criteria leading to working capital constraints.	Optimise relationships with providers of working capital and carefully monitor performance of existing credit lines Group accounting and structured finance work together to ensure a workable solutions are achieved	Finance director Internal audit Main board

Example 2 G1.23

In this example, the listed manufacturing company sought to implement Turnbull's recommendations through a series of interviews/brainstorms with the group's directors, the creation of a risk framework or register, a series of bi-monthly reports/

presentations to formal board meetings, and the development of an operational audit plan for the following year consistent with this risk assessment. The approach is better than that shown in Example 1 in that a ranking of each risk, which takes account of impact and probability, has been attempted.

Inter alia, this assisted the board in determining:

- whether all the questions set out in the Turnbull guidance are being taken into account;
- the wording of any risk management policy document the board may wish to disseminate;
- the approval of any new procedures that need to be in place; and
- the appropriate level of disclosure in the annual report and accounts.

Risk assessment framework

The interviews/discussions with the group's directors revealed the following generic risk areas:

- Strategic
- Marketing
- People-related
- Credit
- Legal and Regulatory
- Operations
- Treasury and Funding
- Technology.

In the interests of conciseness, we show below an abstract from the first of these tables only. Of course, these are not all the risks found, but give examples and summarise the impact on objectives and the appropriate monitoring and review mechanisms.

The assessment relates primarily to the group's ability to meet its corporate objectives and has taken into consideration the potential severity of the risk to the group and also, without appropriate control processes, the likelihood of the risk occurring. Whilst this is clearly a subjective area, we have tried to create a methodology to rank both risk and security. The internal control processes relating to each risk have been established, early warning mechanisms discussed and accountable individuals/ committees identified.

In simple terms, the main and operational boards are responsible for strategic risks and marketing/people risks directly, credit committee is the point of focus for credit risks, health and safety management largely covers legal and regulatory risks, internal audit review and report on operational risks, and a finance committee oversees treasury and funding risks. Technological risks also fall to the executive directors.

The board has separate formal discussions of the different generic risk areas, and the audit committee receives regular operational reports from internal audit.

In addition to this, the board regularly reviews other standing committee minutes, as well as the group's monthly 'management accounting pack' (MAP) and market/ competitor analysis.

1	Risk Strategic risks	Control Processes	Likelihood	Severity	Review Body
1.1	Inadequate formalised (and regularly reviewed) group strategy could lead to short-term, sub-optimal decisions being made.	Regular business and strategic planning reviews, together with clear statements of group objectives to limit the scope for decisions to be made which do not fall within our strategic framework.	2	4	Main board
1.4	Share price/ sector risks. Movements in prices of either just this company or the sector as a whole create issues with regard to financing, acquisitions and even predatory activity by other players.	Close management of public relations and regular dialogue with major shareholders and brokers.	3	4	Executive

Key: 0 = Low
5 = High

Example 3 G1.24

The early Combined Code[17] Provision D.2.1 and the 'Turnbull Report'[18] Guidance on this Provision had a significant impact upon the formality with which boards and top management teams have since assessed risk and associated controls. It was the last three words of Combined Code Provision D.2.1 which jump-started this process:

> 'D.2.1 The directors should, at least annually, conduct a review of the effectiveness of the group's system of internal controls and should report to shareholders that they have done so. The review should cover all controls, including financial, operational and compliance controls and risk management.'

One consequence has been the development in many entities of risk registers. High-level risk registers are often developed in more detail, as they cascade down from the level of the board to lower levels of the business. These registers are maintained and developed further over time.

The public sector has been particularly diligent in developing these risk registers, usually taking their cue from the HM Treasury guidance.

Example 3 as an approach to developing a risk register, starting with an 'awayday'

At the end of this paragraph, we show the first two pages of a 16-page risk register which is a first attempt by an entity to develop their risk register. The extract from the register has been altered to preserve confidentiality. The approach taken was to spend a day away as a top executive team, facilitated by their designated risk management function. In their case, the risk management function, at least temporarily, is the responsibility of a nominated member of their quality assurance function. In other entities, the responsibility is often given to the internal audit function. In others, there is a separate risk management function. Of course, it is important to put across the perspective that *management* owns risk – any specialist risk management function should *facilitate* the effective ownership of risk by management.

At least one cell of their risk register format has a dual use – a simple technique which we consider quite effective. The third column is used both to indicate 'risk category' (External, Operational, Technological or Resource risk). They distinguish between 'risk sponsor' and 'risk owner', although the form only shows the 'risk owner'. All risks categorised as 'external risks' are 'sponsored' by their chief executive, whereas all their technological risks are 'sponsored' by their IT strategy group. The other categories of risk have their respective sponsors too. Sponsors may assign 'ownership' of individual risks to managers within the entity who then have the responsibility to monitor and control the risks so assigned. But overall responsibility remains with the risk sponsor.

Their awayday brainstormed (or is it more correct now to say 'word-stormed' or 'brain-showered'?) in order to identify the principal risks they consider the entity faces. During the course of the day and in the days following, they determined the ownership of each of the risks and the approach to be taken in controlling each risk. With respect to the latter, they settled on the HM Treasury's classification:

- Tolerate;
- Treat;
- Transfer; and
- Terminate.

More stress on 'likelihood' than on 'impact' in Example 3

The entity has designed a form which allows them to indicate their judgement of likelihood of the risk occurring and the probable impact if it does. These are ranked High (Red), Medium (Amber) and Low (Green), and are shown in the risk register in descending order according to Likelihood. It is ambiguous as to whether this ranking is of *inherent* risk before the application of control, or of *residual* risk after the application of control, but ideally it should be the former. The ranking takes account only of the perceived degree of *likelihood*, whereas we consider it should be based on the combined effect of 'likelihood' *and* probable 'impact'.

Further points on approach used in Example 3

Since this is the entity's first version of their risk register, and since the table ranks risks in order of priority, the serial number assigned to each stated risk and the risk priority number are the same – but this will change over time. Being the first version of their risk register, none of the risks has been closed off in the sense of no longer being a current risk on their risk register.

This entity has chosen to use the colour coding also to express their judgement of the quality of control over each of the given risks – Uncertain (Red), Inadequate (Amber) and Adequate (Green). An important column is the one where they record their agreed action – often cross-referencing to a separate 'risk assessment plan' (RAP).

A point to bear in mind is that risks, like buses, tend to arrive together: a risk register approach such as this may too easily allow management to overlook the potential challenges to the business if several risks materialise at the same time. An effective risk assessment should nevertheless assess that possibility.

The annual cycle applied by this entity to updating their risk register is intended to start with the completion of the corporate planning process for the coming year. Once the plan has been agreed, the risks associated with the plan are to be assessed using the methodology described in this article. One implication of this is that the year will be well advanced before this risk assessment is completed. Another associated implication is that the entity cannot rely upon this process to assess the risk associated with different strategic options before the annual plan for the year is settled upon.

Use of software in the context of Example 3

Currently, the entity holds this risk register as a straightforward Word file. Spreadsheet software could have been used. However, formatting the register as a Microsoft Word table does allow rows to be sorted into ascending or descending sequence according to the entries in the cells of columns selected to be sorted upon. If sorting is to be done of rows within a Word table, it is of course important to take care that the data entered in the cells to be used for the sort is capable of being interpreted as having the intended sort order. For instance, where a cell is split so that it can be used for two purposes, as is the case with the cells in row 3, it is unlikely that a useful sort could be undertaken using those cells as the basis of the sort. There would be scope for more sophisticated software to be used.

RISK REGISTER

Risk Assessor/s: Awayday | Page 1 of 16 | Date 10/9/12 | Next Review Mar-13

Date entered	Risk Serial Number	Risk Category / Owner	Description of Risk	Risk Assessment: Likelihood	Risk Assessment: Impact	Risk Priority	Adequacy of existing controls	Action [Treat/tolerate/transfer/terminate]	Closed Date
1	*2*	*3*	*4*	*5*	*6*	*7*	*8*	*9*	*10*
Sep 12	1	Op Hd Pmts 2	Postal strike with duration longer than 5 working days	H	H	1.	A	**Treatment** – Options available – management assessment of situation will dictate course of action. RAP 01	
Sep 12	2	Op Hd Rcpts	Failure to ensure that debt recovery is brought to a satisfactory and timely conclusion	H	H	2.	I	**Treatment** – Monitoring of debt level by management and escalation of causes for concern. RAP 02	
Sep 12	3	Tech Hd IT Services	Insufficient processor capacity	H	M	3.	U	**Treatment** – Scheduling meetings and routine monitoring of database capacity. RAP 03	
Sep 12	4	Op Hd Pmts 1	Change of procedures coupled with our lack of control due to external influences. Any build up of work could threaten existing targets.	H	M	4.	I	**Treatment** – Project and Quality Planning. RAP 04	
Sep 12	5	Op HEO Corp	Failure to comply with procedures resulting in poor/incorrect distribution.	H	M	5.	I	**Treatment** – Use of xyz address file to ensure consistency and % quality checks on resultants. RAP 05.	
Sep 12	6	Op Hd Pmts 2	Peaks e.g. difficulty to copy with backlog due to build up beyond our control.	H	M	6.	A	**Treatment** – Team working and mutual support between Pmts 1 & 2. RAP 06.	
Sep 12	7	Ext AMB	Other parent areas no longer need our services.	M	H	7.	U	**Toleration** – Promotion of Entity skills and monitoring of external policies potentially affecting Entity activities. RAP 07.	
Sep 12	8	Ext Hd Pmts	Reduction of supply base will reduce our workload	M	H	8.	U	**Treatment** – Monitoring and report to Entity Management Board (including nil	

Category: External, Resource, Operational, Technology

Assessment Order: Highest Likelihood first, then by Impact

Risk Assessment: High, Medium, Low

Adequacy of controls: Uncertain, Inadequate, Adequate

RISK REGISTER | **Risk Assessor/s:** Awayday | **Page 2 of 16** | **Date** 10/9/12 | **Next Review** Mar-13

Date entered	Risk Serial Number	Risk Category / Owner	Description of Risk	Risk Assessment: Likelihood	Risk Assessment: Impact	Risk Priority	Adequacy of existing controls	Action [Treat/tolerate/transfer/terminate]	Closed Date
1	*2*	*3*	*4*	*5*	*6*	*7*	*8*	*9*	*10*
		2	and may threaten our viability as a business.					return) on any significant reduction to the supply base. RAP 08.	
Sep 12	9	**Tech** Hd IT Services	Over-reliance on 3rd party suppliers.	**M**	**H**	**9.**	**I**	**Treatment** – Business Continuity Plans. RAP 09.	
Sep 12	10	**Res** Hd P&OS	Insufficient, and suitably trained, staff to achieve Entity key targets, due to factors such as recruitment and retention, 'managing attendance' and loss of skills. [HR]	**M**	**H**	**10.**	**A**	**Treatment** – Robust recruitment/promotion/advancement & managing attendance procedures. RAP 10.	
Sep 12	11	**Res** Hd Fin	Inadequate funding to meet Entity objectives in period due to HLB//Owner not agreeing bid. [Fin]	**M**	**M**	**11.**	**A**	**Treatment** – annual STP submission & renegotiation of Entity objectives if necessary. RAP 11.	
Sep 12	12	**Tech** Hd IT Services	Hardware failure causing mainframe crash or other IT downtime.	**M**	**M**	**12.**	**A**	**Treatment** – Support services in place. RAP 12.	
Sep 12	13	**Tech** Hd IT Services	Software failure causing loss of on-line service.	**M**	**M**	**13.**	**U**	**Toleration** – Service monitored via internal service level agreement. Standard management procedures in place. RAP 13.	
Sep 12	14	**Res** Hd P&OS	Failure to provide the required environment and building services for the Entity's operations.[HR]	**M**	**M**	**14.**	**U**	**Treatment** – Forward maintenance plan and routine management monitoring of progress against planned work RAP 14.	

Category: External, Operational, Technology, Resource

Assessment Order: Highest Likelihood first, then by Impact

Risk Assessment: High / Medium / Low

Adequacy of controls: Uncertain / Inadequate / Adequate

Example 4: Ideal layout for a risk register19 G1.25

In our view, this is an excellent layout to use for the risk register approach:

	Risk	Gross risk		Board accountability	Control description	Control effectiveness	Net/residual risk		Action	Responsibility	Review date
		Impact	Likelihood				Impact	Likelihood			
1.											
2.											
3.											
4.											
		Numeric scale 1–5				Strong, Good, Weak or Poor	Numeric scale 1–5				

Board approach to implementing the Turnbull Report **G1.26**

Boards of listed companies are now required to report on their compliance or otherwise with the internal control requirements of the UK Corporate Governance Code, as detailed in the Turnbull Report. In practice, this often means:

- an increase in the accountability of the board for the internal control processes and structures that exist within the company;
- the board must perform an assessment of internal controls at least annually, and consider reports relating to risk and internal control regularly during the year;
- a review process is required that enables the board to assess the risks that exist in the business and the effectiveness of the internal controls designed to limit these risks; and
- in providing a statement on internal control which complies fully with Turnbull, the directors need to be able to conclude that there is an ongoing process that has been in place for the year under review, and up to the date of approval of the annual report and accounts, which accords with the guidance.

What the board should do **G1.27**

In a well-managed business, most of the elements of risk management and internal control may already be in place through committee structures and line functions tasked with monitoring compliance with the company's risk policies. However, on an ongoing basis the board will need to:

- consider whether there are any gaps in control against significant risks;
- redirect, where necessary, monitoring and reporting; and
- consider the implications of any control failings and weaknesses.

An approach the board might take **G1.28**

Here we provide an example set of guidance notes on the process to be followed to give effect to these Turnbull requirements. They are designed with a view to being applicable for a listed group of companies which has one or more operational boards under the group board. We are assuming a 31 December year end. In our example (for instance, in the table) we are assuming that the group of companies is in the financial sector, but we suggest that a closely similar approach can be applicable for companies in other sectors.

Much of the process is likely to be facilitated by internal audit, including the discussions, the drafting of reports and the presentation of outcomes at board meetings, all of which are integral parts of the process. There is no doubt that the Turnbull initiative has often had the effect of placing internal audit more alongside the board and top management than had been the case before.

Process **G1.29**

- Summarise the group objectives and clearly identify the divisional objectives that underpin the group results.

- Conduct a series of brainstorming sessions with the executive directors, operational board members and non-executive directors to identify key risks to achieving objectives and to rank them (perhaps as 'low', 'medium' or 'high' risk). The internal control processes relating to each risk should be established, early warning mechanisms discussed and accountable individuals/committees identified.
- From this, prepare a draft paper to be presented and discussed at the board about six months before the commencement of the new company year. This should establish a clear risk management policy and formalise control strategies.
- The internal audit plan for the year will also be generated by this approach, and should be placed before the audit committee for their discussion and approval prior to the commencement of the year.
- The formal review process will then need to be established; our proposal at present would look as follows: it could follow lines similar to those suggested in the table below. In each case, the board would receive a presentation delivered by the person indicated in parentheses. It may be appropriate for the audit committee to follow the same approach before these matters come through to the main board as suggested in the table.

March board	Discussion of legal/regulatory risks (Company solicitor)
June board	Consideration of the risk assessment process (Head of internal audit)
August board	Review of credit risks (Head of credit risk)
October board	Review of treasury risks (Head of Treasury function)
December board	Review of operational risks (Internal Audit)
January/February board	Formal review of the process (Internal audit)

- Where necessary, additional resources should be put in place to ensure procedures, timetables and reviews are completed on time.
- Ahead of the year end (probably following the June board), the board should set aside time to consider:
  - whether all the questions set out in the Turnbull Guidance are being taken into account;
  - the wording of any risk management policy document the board wish to disseminate; and
  - the approval of any new procedures that need to be in place at the time of the approval of the annual report and accounts.

How non-executive directors may view risk G1.30

Turnbull is certainly impacting upon how companies consider risk. One approach is for the board to set aside time at almost every board meeting to consider one major aspect of risk – so that all aspects are reviewed over the course of the year. We discussed this under Examples 1 and 2 at **G1.22** and **G1.23**. What each of these major aspects is will depend upon the nature of the business: one might be legal risks, another might be 'regulatory', another 'funding', another 'competitive', and so on.

It is wise for the company to set aside time to be spent with each director, including especially each of the non-executive directors, to explore individual directors' own perceptions of risk. The executive involved in this can be the risk manager of the entity, the chief audit executive or the chief executive or his or her assistant. It may entail visiting the non-executive directors at their usual places of work or, occasionally, setting up a telephone or video conference where this has not been feasible.

The outcomes of these meetings will be a report to the board, which may be presented making use of risk matrices or of risk tables, as explained in this chapter.

Non-executive directors often have different perceptions of risk from those typically held by executives. A possibly not entirely anticipated consequence of the Turnbull process is the focus on external risks which non-executive directors may bring, whereas Hampel and Turnbull had both bracketed risk management with internal control, suggesting more of a focus on internal rather than external risks. It is true that an effective system of internal control provides reasonable assurance of the achievement of corporate objectives, and this includes safeguarding against external risks.

Illustrative risks from a non-executive perspective G1.31

Based on a specific case, here are some of the risks that a non-executive director identified when he participated in this process. We have amended this account to ensure confidentiality:

1. There is a risk that a top-down assessment of risk and control, emanating from the group board, will overlook key risks within the individual businesses of the group. It is important that each divisional board (etc) conducts a similar review and assessment.
2. There is a real risk that the focus on 'top-down' assessment of risk and control will overlook major risks and control weaknesses which may be concealed within the systems of the business. Detailed auditing and monitoring, with systematic coverage, remain very important.
3. We should be open to the possibility of referring in our published internal control statement to areas we have identified where there is scope for improvements which we intend to make. One of the risks a business faces is a loss of stakeholder confidence that the board really knows what is happening within the business. This is more likely if the board always reports in a bland, flawless way.
4. A critical area of risk is in that of 'competencies' – does the company have the competencies it needs, and will it do so into the future? Do we know what *are* our key competencies?
5. What is the internal audit risk? How do we measure internal audit performance?[20]
6. Any overall 'top down' assessment of risk should start by defining the objectives of the enterprise – perhaps just four to six principal objectives. Risks should be related to these objectives.
7. Where possible, Key Performance Indicators (KPIs) for each of the major risks should be established to measure whether or not these risks are under adequate

control. The board's monthly management accounting pack (MAP) should report performance against these KPIs.

8. The simple risk matrix (shown in **G1.17**) is an attractive aid to assessing and representing risks.
9. As this NED saw it, these were some of the major risks the company faced:
   - reputational risk;
   - risk of profits stagnation or decline;
   - economic cycle risks;
   - share price/sector risk;
   - board competence and succession planning risks;
   - loss of top executives (including the level(s) below the top level) risks;
   - risk of top executive exhaustion, getting into a rut, loss of enthusiasm or surrender into an 'end game' scenario for personal reasons not closely related to the company's prospects;
   - risk of irrational prejudice (eg 'anti-Microsoft', 'www a waste of time');
   - regulatory risk;
   - unprovided-for liabilities and contingent liabilities;
   - potential future impact of clauses within contracts which are unknown to the board;
   - lack of a directors' manual/insufficient board use of technology; and
   - risk from inadequate embedded monitoring of internal control.

Control environment checklist G1.32

(Based on a checklist which appears in A D Chambers and G V Rand *The Operational Auditing Handbook: Auditing Business and IT Processes* (2nd ed, Wiley, April 2010, ISBN 978 0 470 74476 5, 884 pp).)

Objectives G1.33

To ensure that management conveys the message that integrity, ethical values and commitment to competence cannot be compromised, and that employees receive and understand that message. To ensure that management continually demonstrates, by word and action, commitment to high ethical and competence standards.

Checklist G1.34

1.	Key issues
1.1	Are there in place satisfactory Codes of Conduct and other policies which define acceptable business practice, conflicts of interest and expected standards of integrity and ethical behaviour?
1.2	Does management (from the *top* of the business downwards *to all levels*) clearly conduct business on a high ethical plane, and are departures appropriately remedied?
1.3	Is the philosophy and operating style of management consistent with the highest ethical standards?

1.4	Do the human resource policies of the business adequately reinforce its commitment to high standards of business integrity, ethics and competence?
1.5	Has the level of competence needed been specified for particular jobs, and does evidence exist to indicate that employees have the requisite knowledge and skills?
1.6	Is the board and its committees sufficiently informed and independent of management such that necessary, even if difficult and probing, questions can be explored effectively?
1.7	Is the organisation structure such that (a) all fully understand their responsibilities and authorities, and (b) the enterprise's activities can be adequately monitored?
2.	**Detailed issues**
2.1	Are Codes of Conduct comprehensive, addressing conflicts of interest, illegal or other improper payments, anti-competitive guidelines and insider trading?
2.2	Are Codes of Conduct understood by and periodically subscribed to by all employees?
2.3	Do senior managers frequently visit outlying locations for which they are responsible?
2.4	Is it the impression that employees feel peer pressure 'to do the right thing'?
2.5	Is there sufficient evidence that management moves carefully in assessing potential benefits of ventures?
2.6	Does management adequately deal with signs that problems exist (eg hazardous by-products) even when the cost of identification and remedy could be high?
2.7	Are sufficient efforts made to deal honestly and fairly with business partners (eg employees, suppliers etc)?
2.8	Is disciplinary action sufficiently taken and communicated in the case of violations?
2.9	Is management override of controls appropriate when it occurs; and sufficiently authorised, documented and explained?
2.10	Are there job descriptions (which adequately define key managers' responsibilities) and performance appraisals with follow-up action to remedy deficiencies?
2.11	Is management and staff turnover not excessive?
2.12	Are staffing levels adequate but not excessive?
2.13	Do staff recruitment procedures sufficiently enhance the enterprise's commitment to high standards of integrity, ethics and competence?
2.14	Do training programmes sufficiently enhance the enterprise's commitment to high standards of integrity, ethics and competence?
2.15	Do sufficient lines of communication exist to obviate the temptation of 'whistleblowing'?

Organisation checklist G1.35

(Based on a checklist which appears in A D Chambers and G V Rand *The Operational Auditing Handbook: Auditing Business and IT Processes* (2nd ed, Wiley, April 2010, ISBN 978 0 470 74476 5, 884 pp).)

Objectives G1.36

(a) To ensure that the organisational structure is appropriate to the business and the achievement of strategic objectives.
(b) To ensure that the organisational structure is determined by the business and operational needs and avoids needless sub-divisions and excessive levels.
(c) To ensure that the structure enables the flow of key information upwards and outwards within the organisation and across all the business activities.
(d) To ensure that relevant responsibilities, authorities and functional terms of reference are defined and in place.
(e) To ensure that responsibilities and authorities are adequately segregated in order to avoid conflicts of interest and the potential for fraudulent practices.
(f) To ensure that the structure is periodically reviewed and any changes are agreed and authorised at a senior level.
(g) To ensure that each manager's span of control is optimised and avoids either over or under-utilisation.
(h) To ensure that adequate staff resources are determined, authorised and provided in order to achieve the functional and business objectives.
(i) To ensure that the prevailing organisational structure is suitably documented and communicated to all relevant staff.
(j) To ensure that the organisational structure and the related functional divisions of responsibility are accurately and adequately reflected in the accounting and management information systems.

Checklist G1.37

1.	**Key issues**
1.1	How does management ensure that the organisational structure is optimised and appropriate for the achievement of strategic objectives?
1.2	Has the prevailing structure been ratified and authorised by senior management, and are all suggested changes assessed and authorised?
1.3	Is the organisation structure regularly reviewed for its relevance and in order to rationalise and streamline its form?
1.4	Have documented terms of reference, responsibilities and authorities been agreed, authorised and implemented for all functions and departments, and are they maintained up to date?
1.5	How does management ensure that the organisational structure incorporates adequate segregation of key activities and duties?
1.6	Are management and staff establishment levels reliably determined, agreed and authorised (and what measures ensure that actual staffing levels are maintained within establishment)?

1.7	How can management be sure that the prevailing organisational structure is accurately reflected in both the accounting and management information systems?
2.	**Detailed issues**
2.1	Is the structure of the organisation based upon the operational characteristics of the underlying business activities?
2.2	Are organisation charts maintained up to date and adequately circulated?
2.3	Are reporting, functional and line relationships clearly defined?
2.4	What mechanisms enable the identification of unnecessary or superfluous structural elements (or those with the potential for amalgamation)?
2.5	Are there sufficient reporting and information channels to senior management level?
2.6	Are suitably approved authority limits (and mandates) in place?
2.7	How is the accuracy of data input from other systems (ie long-term planning considerations) confirmed?
2.8	How is the accuracy of data output to other systems (ie manpower and succession planning or the management information system) confirmed?

Management information checklist **G1.38**

(Based on a checklist which appears in A D Chambers and G V Rand *The Operational Auditing Handbook: Auditing Business and IT Processes* (2nd ed, Wiley, April 2010, ISBN 978 0 470 74476 5, 884 pp).)

Objectives **G1.39**

To ensure:

(a) that management satisfactorily utilises information (which is timely, complete, accurate, consistent, clear, concise, relevant, secure and economic) in assisting them to meet their objectives; and

(b) that opportunities are taken to gain a competitive advantage through the strategic use of information.

Checklist **G1.40**

1.	**Key issues**
1.1	Is there a clear association between (a) the *objectives* of management, and (b) the *information* available to management – so that the latter can inform management of its progress in achieving the former?
1.2	Some businesses have plentiful data but too little information derived from that data; others have plentiful information but too little analysis performed on that information; others have plentiful analysis but too little decision and action following the analysis. Is the availability and balance right in this case?

1.3	Is applicable external information (eg about the market) available – as well as internally generated information about business performance?
1.4	Is there satisfactory security over the collection, processing, retention and disposal of information?
1.5	Are data protection principles complied with, with regard to personal data?
1.6	Has the business considered the scope to develop strategic information systems (targeted at suppliers and/or staff and customers) which achieve a competitive advantage by reducing costs and/or improving service and reliability?
2.	**Detailed issues**
2.1	Has responsibility for management information been formally assigned to one or more managers who is/are formally responsible for appraising its quality and utilisation?
2.2	Is information timely – produced and distributed promptly at the most appropriate intervals from up-to-date data?
2.3	Is information clearly and reliably dated with no risk of out-of-date reports being used as if current?
2.4	Is information retained no longer than necessary?
2.5	Is the information complete enough to meet the operational needs of managers? Does it adequately inform as a basis for necessary management action? Does it cover all operational areas of the business?
2.6	Is the information *accurate* enough to be used reliably by management?
2.7	Are management reports *consistent* (a) between each edition, and (b) between different reports which relate to associated issues? Is *cut-off* handled reliably?
2.8	Is *clarity* achieved in that management reports are (a) clearly titled, dated and captioned, and (b) attractive, unambiguous and easy to use?
2.9	Where figures are presented which relate to each other, is *clarity* achieved in that comparison is facilitated?
2.10	Are management reports *concise* without being too brief? Is proper use made of reporting by exception only?
2.11	Is all the information *relevant* to the business and to those who receive it (who fully appreciate its purpose)?
2.12	Is management information satisfactorily and promptly *acted upon* by those who receive it?
2.13	Are exception reports all followed up?
2.14	*Security*: Is an inventory maintained of confidential and sensitive corporate information, and is the handling and issuance of this information subject to proper authorisation controls?
2.15	Are company secrets kept securely?
2.16	Are there satisfactory access controls to (a) the site, (b) the buildings, (c) departmental information stores and (d) computers?

2.17	Is data adequately secure while being transmitted (eg by making use of encryption)?

Risk management checklist **G1.41**

(Based on a checklist which appears in A D Chambers and G V Rand *The Operational Auditing Handbook: Auditing Business and IT Processes* (2nd ed, Wiley, April 2010, ISBN 978 0 470 74476 5, 884 pp).)

Objectives **G1.42**

(a) To ensure that management is aware of all the relevant commercial and operational risks.
(b) To ensure that an effective risk management strategy is defined, authorised and implemented in order to counteract, avoid and minimise applicable risks.
(c) To ensure that the business operations and financial success of the organisation are neither disrupted nor adversely affected by disasters and problems.
(d) To ensure that adequate precautions are taken to protect assets, persons and the organisation's reputation.
(e) To ensure that the potential for accidents and losses is prevented or reduced.
(f) To ensure that adequate contingency plans have been developed to provide continuity of the business in the event of any form of disaster.
(g) To ensure that contingency arrangements are tested to confirm their effectiveness and relevance.
(h) To ensure that adequate and cost-effective insurance cover is provided.
(i) To ensure that insurance costs are minimised.
(j) To ensure that insurance claims are made whenever relevant and duly settled.
(k) To ensure that all relevant legislation and regulations are complied with.

Checklist **G1.43**

1.	**Key issues**
1.1	What steps has management taken accurately to identify potential risks?
1.2	Has a documented business impact review been undertaken as the basis for determining the action required?
1.3	Have adequate plans been developed to counteract, reduce or avoid risks to assets, persons and the organisation's reputation?
1.4	How can management be assured that the plans in place remain relevant and adequate?
1.5	Have the risk assessment and action plans been suitably authorised (and how is this evidenced)?
1.6	Are contingency plans regularly and adequately tested in order that they remain effective?
1.7	Are all affected staff aware of their responsibilities in the event of a significant disaster or risk situation (and how is their effectiveness assessed)?

1.8	Are all insurance requirements subject to appropriate assessment and authorisation, and how can management be certain that insurance cover is appropriate and adequate?
1.9	What steps are taken to minimise and contain insurance costs?
1.10	How can management be assured that all the relevant legislation, regulations and preventative requirements are complied with?
2.	**Detailed issues**
2.1	What measures ensure that the assessment of risks is accurate and realistic?
2.2	Are all new projects and ventures adequately assessed for risks, and are action and contingency plans accordingly updated?
2.3	What mechanisms prevent any business activity or project being overlooked for risk assessment purposes?
2.4	Have the business impact review and risk management strategy been authorised, documented, and circulated?
2.5	Are non-financial risks (ie damage to commercial reputation, public image etc) also taken into account?
2.6	Are adequate measures in place to protect employees, visitors etc from injury or death?
2.7	Where the organisation is heavily dependent upon the use of information technology, has specific consideration been given to the effects on the business of a loss of computing facilities?
2.8	Have documented contingency plans been developed for all relevant business activities, and what measures ensure that the plans are maintained up to date?
2.9	Are staff made aware of their roles and responsibilities within the contingency arrangements?
2.10	Are contingency plans regularly tested for effectiveness (and how are amendments identified, authorised and applied)?
2.11	Have appropriate insurance arrangements been made to cover the following areas: ● product liability; ● loss due to business interruption; ● loss of funds due to malpractice; and ● damage and injury to persons and property?
2.12	Are all hazardous processes identified and subject to all the relevant precautions and safety measures (how is this evidenced)?
2.13	Has an effective health and safety policy been implemented? Is it suitably tested and how is it maintained up to date?
2.14	Are staff adequately trained in safety matters, and how can their understanding and proficiency be confirmed?
2.15	Are accidents and incidents fully investigated and shortcomings identified and satisfactorily addressed?

2.16	Are all claims against the organisation fully investigated and only settled when duly authorised?
2.17	What measures ensure that insurance costs are competitive?
2.18	Are insurance arrangements subject to regular review and are changes suitably authorised?
2.19	How is the accuracy of data input from other systems (ie planning) confirmed?
2.20	How is the accuracy of data output to other systems (ie insurance department) confirmed?

Notes

1 Proposed changes to the Listing Rules – Corporate Governance (principles of good governance and Code of best practice: consultation document), FRC (March 1998).

2 In addition, FSA Rule DTR 7.2.5 R requires companies to describe the main features of the internal control and risk management systems in relation to the financial reporting process.

3 Drucker, PF, *Management: Tasks, Responsibilities*, Practices (1977, 1979 Pan UK edn) p 433.

4 COSO *Enterprise Risk Management* (2004) Executive Summary, p 2.

5 Executive Summary, p 2.

6 Conceptual Framework volume, Chapter 1 on 'Composition', p 5.

7 Conceptual Framework volume, Chapter 1 on 'Composition', p 8.

8 Conceptual Framework volume, Chapter 1 on 'Composition', p 11.

9 Conceptual Framework volume, Chapter 1 on 'Composition', p 12.

10 Australia/New Zealand Standard 4360 *Risk Management – joint standard prepared by the Joint Standards Australia/Standards New Zealand Committee OB/7 on Risk Management as a revision of AS/NZS 4360: 1995 on Risk Management* (1999).

11 NHS Executive *Governance in the New NHS: Controls assurance statements 1999/2000: risk management and organisational controls* (HSC 1999/123) (May 1999).

12 Auditing Practices Board (March 1995), Statements of Auditing Standards (London, CCAB).

13 HM Treasury *Management of Risk – A Strategic Overview – With Supplementary Guidance for Smaller Bodies* (the 'Orange Book') (June 2001).

14 RiskMap© model and is used to map a prioritized list of risks. We reproduce these three tables by kind permission of Kelsey Walker Associates. KWA have a further sheet that shows the assessment of the risks. KWA can be contacted via Kelsey Walker at kelsey@kwa-risk.co.uk.

15 London Evening Standard (9 December 2005): '£285m typing error costs share traders their bonuses'.

16 Daily Mail (21 December 2005): 'Financial chief does the honourable thing'.

17 The Combined Code (July 1998), originally an appendix to The Stock Exchange Listing Rules (the 'Yellow Book') and then also available from Gee Publishing Limited, 100 Avenue Road, Swiss Cottage, London NW3 3PG, tel: +44 (0)207 393 7400, fax: +44 (0)20 7722 4762.

18 *Internal Control – Guidance to Directors on the Combined Code* (the 'Turnbull Report'), published by The Institute of Chartered Accountants in England & Wales. The guidance can be downloaded from ICAEW's website.

19 Layout suggested in Audit Committee Institute (May 2004): *Shaping the UK Audit Committee Agenda*, KPMG, 91 pages, see p 76 (contact Timothy Copnell, KPMG, 1–2 Dorset Rise, London, EC4B 0BL).

20 See February 2000 article in the Institute of Internal Auditors Inc's bi-monthly journal, *Internal Auditor*.

Chapter G2

Current Developments in Internal Auditing[1]

G2.1

Readers will find the Code of Ethics of the Institute of Internal Auditors (IIA) at **App7**. That Code is regarded by the IIA as applicable to members and candidates for IIA certifications across the world, and also as appropriate for others undertaking an internal audit role which is consistent with the IIA's definition of internal auditing. The definition is currently as shown here, though the IIA is in the process of developing a revised definition:

> 'Internal auditing is an independent, objective assurance and consulting activity designed to add value and improve an organisation's operations. It helps an organisation accomplish its objectives by bringing a systematic, disciplined approach to evaluate and improve the effectiveness of risk management, control, and governance processes.'

The UK's Chartered Institute of Internal Auditors (CIIA)[2] has incorporated this Code into its expanded Code of Professional Conduct (April 2012) which has additional principles on 'Professionalism – acting in the public interest' and on 'Courtesy and respect'.

The Standards of the IIA (**App8**) are also regarded as mandatory. The Glossary to the Standards (reproduced at the end of **App8**) explains that on the few occasions that the word 'should' rather than 'must' is used in the Standards, conformance is expected unless, when applying professional judgment, circumstances justify deviation. These Standards were revised in October 2012 and became effective from 1 January 2013. It is unlikely that further revised Standards will be effective prior to January 2016. Readers should consult the website of the global body – www.theiia.org.

Introduction

G2.2

Management may be ambivalent about what they expect from internal audit. Some management teams expect not much more than for internal audit to undertake *ad hoc* tasks to put out bush fires in the business, and have little expectation that internal audit should provide them with overall assurance about governance processes, risk management and internal control. Some management teams are resentful of the growing expectations of boards that internal audit should be an extension of the boards' eyes and ears. There can be conflicts between internal audit serving the board and internal audit serving management. Here we explore what should be the responsibilities of internal audit and how the conflicts can be mitigated. We also consider the prerequisites for internal audit to provide an effective service for the board, and also for top management – including the organisational positioning of internal audit and its independence, the scope of internal audit work and the qualities needed in internal audit staff. We draw upon recent enhanced pronouncements on internal auditing.

When the global financial crisis broke in 2008, it was quickly acknowledged at high level that boards of directors needed better assurance independent of management, and that this would mean strengthening the role of internal audit and creating of a cadre of super auditors. Never before has the internal audit profession had a better opportunity for advancement.

So it was disappointing that little of significance then happened until 2012 when the first of a number of initiatives, prompted from outside the profession, came into play. The profession, in its efforts to avoid criticism for being one of the gatekeepers who had failed, risked being seen as no part of the solution going forward. Richard Thorpe, head of accounting, audit and regulatory reporting policy at the UK's Financial Services Authority, the UK's regulator, in 2012 was quoted as saying:

> 'I can't point to the internal audit function of a single bank or insurer and say, with hand on heart, that is how we envision it being done in the future.'

and:

> 'There exist generic industry Standards and practices, but none are sufficiently robust to address the complex world of financial services firms.' (Irving, 2012, p 12 and 13)

The head of the UK's Prudential Regulatory Authority concurred:

> 'Existing standards and guidelines do not set sufficiently robust expectations for internal audit functions in firms in terms of their role, scope of work, standing within the organisation and exercise of effective challenge … [the new UK code of conduct would be a] crucial contribution in the drive to improve corporate governance in the financial services sector.' (*Financial Times*, 10 September 2012)

Three lines of defence G2.3

One initiative of potential significance, the 'three lines of defence' paradigm, was being developed (Booz, 2008; Hughes, 2011; Basel, 2012; Anderson and Daugherty, 2012; IIA, 2013), represented schematically in Figure 1.

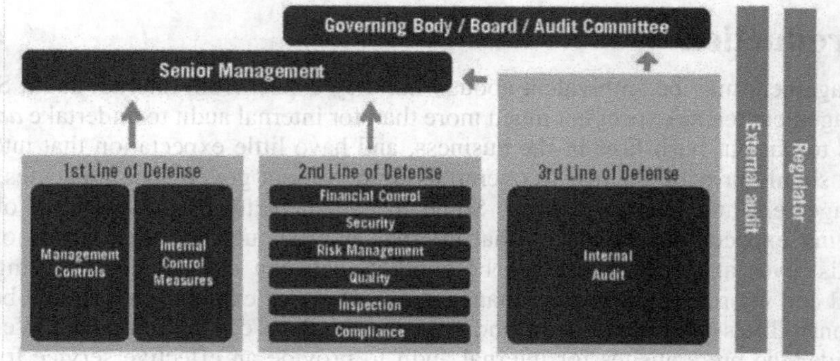

Adapted from ECIIA/FERMA *Guidance on the 8th EU Company Law Directive, article 41*

Figure 1: The Three Lines of Defense Model (IIA, 2013)

Booz (2008), possibly the first significant treatise on the three lines of defence, identified the challenges for internal audit as the third line of defence:

> 'The third line of defense—audit—has arguably failed in its role of providing independent and objective assurance of the effectiveness of the first two lines of defense. … For the third line of defense to act as an effective steward of the policies and procedures approved by the board, it needs to have not only a good understanding of the business—how the front office makes money—but also a deep understanding of risk management discipline. … For example, audit teams should investigate and validate mark-to-market positions, ensuring the integrity of information as it passes from one system to the next. … Moreover, the third line of defense must develop a strong critical approach to each functional discipline, performing more than just a "checking the checkers" role. It is not inconceivable, for example, that after reviewing the securitization process, the internal audit team could identify and bring to the board's attention potential flaws, such as overreliance on rating agencies. All too often, auditors document processes as a box-ticking exercise to ensure compliance, with limited critical review of potential weaknesses.' (Booz, 2008, p 5)

and Booz (2008) argued for:

> 'top talent within audit—to challenge the front office and risk management function' (Booz, 2008, p 3)

In 2013, the three lines of defence model has attracted serious criticism, partly because its sound theory has been sullied by unsound implementation. Terms of abuse such as 'Maginot line', 'Potemkin village' and 'Goodhart's law' have been applied to it. In essence, the criticism is that inadequate implementation of the three lines of defence, often little more than token box-ticking, has given a false sense of assurance. Boundaries have been blurred between the lines, independence of the second and third lines has been inadequate and indeed there has been uncertainty as to who belongs to which line of defence and to whom each line is accountable. There has been ambiguity as to which line should be held responsible for failures and therefore responsible to avoid them. There are also the questions as to whether internal audit is the sole occupier of the third line of defence, and whether there should also be regarded as being a further, fourth line of defence comprising external audit and others who provide assurance to owners and other stakeholders.

The UK's Parliamentary Commission on banking said this:

> 'The financial crisis, and multiple conduct failures, have exposed serious flaws in governance. Potemkin villages were created in firms, giving the appearance of effective control and oversight without the reality. Non-executive directors lacked the capacity or incentives to challenge the executives. Sometimes those executives with the greatest insight into risks being added to balance sheets were cut off from decision-makers at board level or lacked the necessary status to speak up. Poor governance and controls are illustrated by the rarity of whistle-blowing, either within or beyond the firm, even where, such as in the case of Libor manipulation, prolonged and blatant misconduct has been evident.' (HLHC, 2013, p 10)

The Commission made several recommendations for improvement, including:

'individual and direct lines of access and accountability to the board for the heads of the risk, compliance and internal audit functions and much greater levels of protection for their independence;' (HLHC, 2013, p 10)

For further discussion of the three lines of defence model, readers should refer to **G3**.

Post-2012 initiatives G2.3

Although the global Standards of the IIA were revised with effect from 1 January 2013 (IIA, 2012), a number of financial sector bodies have seen it necessary to develop enhanced guidelines for internal audit which go beyond the requirements of the Standards (Basel, 2012; Federal Reserve, 2013; CIIA, 2013). While most of this leadership has been led by the financial sector, still smarting from the global financial crisis, other sectors are weighing up the relevance of these enhancements to their own role, and in the UK the public sector has also made strides (PSIAS, 2012).

Defining internal audit G2.4

As the IIA struggles to update its definition of internal auditing, other bodies have led the way by giving internal audit a more *protective* role and, in the case of the Federal Reserve, even regarding internal audit as *part of the supervisory process* itself (Table 1). Indeed, all of these new enhanced guidances for internal audit require that there should be strong communication between internal audit and the regulator, using adjectives such as 'open', 'transparent', 'honest', 'effective', 'structured' and 'two-way', with the intention to openly share information to support their respective responsibilities.

Table 1: Definitions of internal auditing

Body/ies	Definition
IIA since 2001 (IIA, 2012). UK Government since 2008 (HMT, 2008; PSIAS, 2012).	*'Internal auditing is an independent, objective assurance and consulting activity designed to add value and improve an organization's operations. It helps an organization accomplish its objectives by bringing a systematic, disciplined approach to evaluate and improve the effectiveness of risk management, control, and governance processes'.*[a]
ISA 610 (2012)	*'A function of an entity that performs assurance and consulting activities designed to evaluate and improve the effectiveness of the entity's governance, risk management and internal control processes'.*[b]

Body/ies	Definition
Basel (2012)	*'An effective internal audit function provides independent assurance to the board of directors and senior management on the quality and effectiveness of a bank's internal control, risk management and governance systems and processes, thereby helping the board and senior management protect their organisation and its reputation'*.[c]
Federal Reserve (2013)	*'An effective internal audit function is a vehicle to advance an institution's safety and soundness and compliance with consumer laws and regulations and is therefore considered as part of the supervisory review process'*.[d]
UK Committee on Internal Audit Guidance for Financial Services (CIIA, 2013)	*'The primary role of Internal Audit should be to help the Board and Executive Management to protect the assets, reputation and sustainability of the organisation'*.[e]

[a] IIA (2012).
[b] IAASB (2012), p 6, § 12.
[c] Basel (2012), pp 2 and 4.
[d] Federal Reserve (2013), section 5, pp 14–15.
[e] CIIA (2013), p 6.

Internal audit scope **G2.5**

Attention has been drawn to inappropriate *de facto*, though usually not *de jure*, internal audit scope restrictions:

> 'While it is common for Internal Audit Charters to mandate an unrestricted scope, some Internal Audit functions do not include in their audit universe or risk assessments some of the processes, risks and events that were central to the problems … for the avoidance of doubt, [this] guidance sets out areas of scope which were found to have been restricted in some organisations, in practice even if not in principle.' (CIIA, 2013, p 12)

Basel (2012, p 2; §3 2, p 8) considers that the scope of the internal audit *plan* should cover *all* matters of regulatory interest, which is much more demanding than requiring that all these matters should merely be within the *audit universe*. The CIIA (2013, pp 6–7; § 6a–h; p 10; § [D]10) settles for the following very demanding menu of items that should be within the internal audit universe from which the audit plan will be determined:

- the design and operating effectiveness of internal governance structures;
- the information presented to the board for strategic and operational decision making;
- the setting of, and adherence to, risk appetite (though internal audit is not responsible for setting the risk appetite);

- the risk and control culture of the organisation, and whether the processes are in line with the values, ethics, risk appetite and policies of the organisation;
- risks of poor customer treatment – whether the organisation is acting with integrity in its dealings with customers and its interaction with relevant markets;
- the management of the organisation's capital and liquidity ratios;
- key corporate events (eg new products/services, outsourcing decisions, acquisitions/divestments);
- outcomes of, not mere conformance with, processes (design and operating effectiveness of policies and processes);
- the adequacy and effectiveness of the risk management, compliance and finance functions.

and recommends the IIA should develop or adopt additional guidance with respect to the less established areas of audit activity such as auditing culture, and auditing customer and other outcomes (CIIA, 2013, p 10, § 30). Evidence to the UK's parliamentary Banking Commission agreed that internal audit:

> 'should look at governance, it should look at culture, it should look at the way that the risk management departments manage risk, and it should look at compliance and how they are doing things.' (HLHC, 2013, p 355, § 739)

The Federal Reserve (2013) has extended what is usually held to be within the scope of internal audit to include significant infrastructure enhancements and governance at all management levels, and stipulates that 'all critical risk management functions' must be audited – not merely that they should all be within the internal audit universe, but that they should all be audited. Their guidance requires that the internal audit universe is documented and revised for changes at least during an annual audit planning process.

There is no mention of the audit universe in the IIA Standards, although Standard 2010 requires a risk assessment to be conducted at least annually as part of the audit planning process.

Applying the three lines of defence model, a key determinant of location within a line of defence is to whom the party within the line is accountable. Internal auditing, at the third line of defence, should be accountable to the board, as we discuss later. An implication of this is that internal audit audits up to the door of the boardroom, but does not second guess the board itself. The UK committee stated that internal audit should not second guess decisions of the board but legitimately should draw attention to information or process inadequacies which have underpinned board decisions (CIIA, 2013, p 6, § 3, 6a and 6b).

Our suggestion is that the three lines of defence paradigm should be modified to add a fourth line of defence comprising external audit and also other parties that are accountable to external stakeholders. So, for instance, in the UK the board is collectively responsible for the financial statements that are audited. On occasion regulators commission independent reports about the conduct of boards and senior management. The board itself can be construed as part of a fourth line of defence to the extent of its accountability obligation to shareholders who are external stakeholders. This illustrates the inappropriateness of regarding internal audit as part of the supervisory process (Federal Reserve, 2013, pp 14–15, section 5) as this muddies the waters of accountability for internal audit between the board and the supervisor.

While 'strategy' is now within the IIA Standards, to the extent that internal audit must evaluate risk and control exposures to meeting the organization's strategic objectives, the Standards are currently opaque as to whether internal audit has a role in challenging strategic decisions, or the processes followed and information used in formulating strategy, an opaqueness not supported by the enhanced guidances discussed in this chapter.

Cyclical approach to internal auditing **G2.6**

It is hard to escape the conclusion that the enhanced guidances, promulgated in 2012 and 2013, in effect reject an approach to drawing up a future plan of audit engagements in an *ad hoc* way that responds to and corresponds with, top management's and the board's principal concerns at the time about risk. Instead, there is a fresh promotion of the merits of a systematic, cyclical approach to auditing. Although not so clearly as the Federal Reserve, the CIIA (2013) implies that internal audit will work to both a one-year and a longer cycle for planning audit work (CIIA, 2013, p 12, § B). The Federal Reserve's guidance is that audit engagements are planned into a three- or four-year cyclical approach with high-risk areas being audited at least every 12 or 18 months (Federal Reserve, 2013, p 10, 2.C). The IIA Standards are silent on this.

The UK committee stressed that its guidance does not require internal audit to cover every area contained in the audit universe every year although they should all be considered in internal audit's risk assessment and prioritisation of audit activity (CIIA, 2013, p 12, § B).

Opinions **G2.7**

Whereas the IIA's Standards make audit opinions, at both the engagement and overall levels, discretionary for internal audit functions, the Federal Reserve prescribes that opinions should be provided at both levels. Whether or not the Federal Reserve intended that overall opinions should be restricted to just risk management processes rather than, for instance, governance processes and internal control, that is what it has specified, thus not referring to governance or control processes, though this is to include internal audit's opinion on the effectiveness of management's self-assessment and remediation of identified issues, and these overall opinions are to be provided at least annually (Federal Reserve, 2013, p 8, 2.B). We can however infer that an opinion on risk management will incorporate an opinion on internal control which is an important part of enterprise risk management (see Figure 2). COSO's enterprise risk management (ERM) framework makes it clear that ERM incorporates all of internal control:

> 'Internal control is an integral part of enterprise risk management. This enterprise risk management framework encompasses internal control, forming a more robust conceptualization and tool for management. Internal control is defined and described in Internal Control – Integrated Framework.' (COSO, 2004, Executive Summary, p 5)

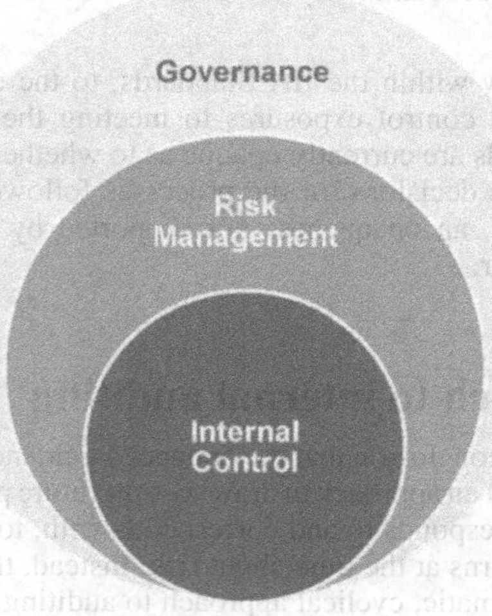

Figure 2: Integration of control, risk management and governance processes

The new UK guidance is that overall opinions by internal audit, at least annually, are to include an assessment of the overall effectiveness of the governance and risk and control framework, *together with an analysis of themes and trends impacting the organisation's risk profile* (CIIA, 2013, p 8, § [C]8). These opinions should be provided to both the organisation's audit committee and risk committee of the board (CIIA, 2013, p 8, § [C]8).

Reporting G2.8

Currently, IIA Standard 1000 requires functional reporting of internal audit to be to 'the board' which, according to how 'the board' is defined in the Glossary to the Standards, may mean that functional reporting of internal audit is to the audit committee of the board. The mandatory Interpretation to Standard 1110 explains the nature of the functional reporting relationship and mentions that it includes, *inter alia*, approving the appointment, removal and (new in 2013) remuneration of the chief audit executive (CAE).

The Standards are silent about the administrative reporting line, other than within the mandatory interpretation to Standard 1100 where it is suggested that 'a dual-reporting relationship' can be effective, though 'dual reporting' is not defined within the Standards themselves. IIA Practice Advisory 1110-1 defines this duality as comprising the functional and the administrative reporting lines and suggests that administrative reporting, including budgeting, is likely to be satisfactory if it is to the CEO.

The enhanced guidelines for internal audit which we are addressing in this chapter take a different position. The Federal Reserve prefers that CAEs report for all purposes, including administratively, to the audit committee (Federal Reserve, 2013, p 5, § 2.A), but that where there is a secondary reporting line this is best to the CEO

(Federal Reserve, 2013, p 5, § 2.A); and that if administrative reporting is other than to the audit committee, the audit committee should document the rationale for this (Federal Reserve, 2013, p 5, § 2.A). The Federal Reserve also requires that the audit committee and its chair should have on-going interaction with the CAE, separate from audit committee meetings (Federal Reserve, 2013, p 7, § 2.B).

The UK guidance loosens internal audit's ties with management, suggesting that there may be a sole reporting line to the audit committee of the board, or even to the chair of the board; and that if there is a reporting line to the executive, it should be a secondary reporting line and should be to the CEO (CIIA, 2013, p 9, § [E]15):

> 'If Internal Audit has a secondary Executive reporting line, this should be to the CEO in order to preserve independence from any particular business area or function and to establish the standing of Internal Audit alongside Executive Committee members.' (CIIA, 2013, p 9, § [E]15)

In exceptional circumstances the board may wish internal audit to report to the chairman of the board's risk committee, provided the chairman and members of this committee are all independent directors. (CIIA, 2013, p 8, § [C]7; and p 9, § [E]15). Unlike the IIA Standards which require audit committee *approval* only, the audit committee has the responsibility to appoint and remove the chief internal auditor and approve the internal audit budget. The chair of the audit committee is to set the chief internal auditor's objectives, appraise his/her performance and recommend his/her remuneration to the board's remuneration committee (CIIA (2013), p 9, § [F]16, 17, 18 and 23). The UK guidance requires that the audit committee should report publicly whether it is satisfied with the adequacy of internal audit resources, a stipulation which has caused some anxiety amongst audit committees, but must surely be appropriate:

> 'The Audit Committee … as part of the Board's overall governance responsibility, should disclose in the annual report whether it is satisfied that Internal Audit has the appropriate resources.' (CIIA, 2013, p 9, § [F]23)

The UK guidance requires internal audit to be 'present at, and to issue reports to the appropriate governing bodies, including the board audit committee, the board risk committee and any other board committees as appropriate.' (CIIA, 2013, p 8, § [C]7). Following the Basel guidance means the CAE attends at least some audit committee and board meetings to discuss internal audit views, findings and conclusions directly with both (Basel, 2012, p 4).

The UK guidance also usefully tackles the reporting line of subsidiary, branch and divisional heads of internal audit, requiring that they should report primarily to the group chief internal auditor, while recognising local legislation or regulation as appropriate. This includes the responsibility for setting budgets and remuneration, conducting appraisals and reviewing the audit plan. The group chief internal auditor should consider the independence, objectivity and tenure of the subsidiary, branch or divisional heads of internal audit when performing their appraisals (CIIA, 2013, p 9, § [E]19) just as the guidance requires the chair of the audit committee to do with respect to the appraisal of the group chief internal auditor (CIIA, 2013, p 9, § [F]16, 17, 18 and 23). The use of the word 'primarily' does not preclude a secondary reporting of a subsidiary, branch or divisional head of internal audit to the chair of the subsidiary's (etc) audit committee.

Independence G2.9

Even prior to 2013, the IIA Standards required that the board or its audit committee approve decisions relating to the appointment and removal of the CAE. 'Approval' is less than a decision-making responsibility. New in the 2013 Standards are the requirements that the board or the audit committee approves the internal audit budget and resource plan and the remuneration of the CAE.

Emulating the current debate about external auditor independence and rotation, both Basel (2012) and the UK guidance (CIIA, 2013), tackle this for internal audit. Basel requires periodic rotation of internal audit staff within the internal audit function (Basel, 2012, pp 5 and 9). The UK guidance requires that the appraisal of the CAE should consider the independence, objectivity and tenure of the chief internal auditor, implying that the CAE, as with the external auditor, may be at risk of losing his or her independence and objectivity over time (CIIA, 2013, p 9, § [E]17).

Basel, The Federal Reserve and the UK Guidance all require that there are no compensation schemes for internal auditors that introduce perverse incentives. As the UK puts it:

> 'The remuneration of the Chief Internal Auditor should be structured in a manner such that it avoids conflicts of interest, does not impair independence and objectivity and should not be directly or exclusively linked to the short term performance of the organisation'. (CIIA, 2013, p 9, § [E]18)

Quality assessments G2.10

The Federal Reserve goes further than the IIA Standards in requiring internal quality assessments of internal audit functions to be undertaken at least annually. The draft UK guidance had required that in large internal audit functions, a separate, independent team should undertake these internal quality assessments, but the final guidance was relaxed to require only that they should be undertaken by auditors independent of the audit engagements being reviewed (CIIA, 2013, p 10, § [G]26). It is clear that these enhanced guidances do not approve of the IIA Standards relaxation which, commencing from 1 January 2013, now permit external quality assessments to be done by self-assessment with independent validation – SAIVs (eg CIIA, 2013, p 10, § [G]28).

Status, standing and outsourcing G2.11

Following the Basel guidance means the CAE attends at least some audit committee and board meetings to discuss internal audit views, findings and conclusions directly with both. The UK guidance requires that the CAE has a right to attend key management fora, including attending and observing all or part of executive committee (Exco) meetings, at the professional discretion of the CAE (CIIA, 2013, p 13, § [E]). The CAE should usually be at Exco level (CIIA, 2013, p 8, § [E]12 and 13).

As more is expected of internal auditors, their status and their professionalism needs to be enhanced. The Federal Reserve requires 'gap assessments' to be undertaken at least annually to evaluate the knowledge and skills of internal audit staff members commensurate with the organisation's strategy and operations; and for internal auditors to receive at least 40 hours of training annually. The author has written elsewhere about the need to enhance the general quality of internal auditors (Chambers, 2008a, 2008b, 2009).

The extra demands on internal audit functions might suggest greater use of outsourcing internal audit to external service providers. Yet the Basel guidance considers internal auditing work should normally be undertaken by the bank's own staff while outsourcing some internal audit activities, but not the function itself, can be beneficial (Basel, 2012, p 11; Principle 15, p 14). Basel goes on to require that internal audit service providers should not be consultants to, or external auditors of, the entity (before, during or after). The Federal Reserve enunciates a series of safeguards to be applied when outsourcing is being considered:

- The internal audit charter should define the criteria for when and how outsourcing should occur.
- Outsourcing should be a matter for the audit committee and the CAE, which implies that the CAE role itself should not be outsourced.
- Vendor competence is important.
- Contingency plans for disruption of outsourced services should be made.
- Outsourced internal audit should not be to the external auditor.

Conclusion **G2.12**

The enhanced guidelines discussed in this chapter have the potential of being enforced more rigorously than the IIA Standards, coming as they do with the support of regulators with enforcement powers. These enhanced guidelines all set out to build upon rather than substitute for the IIA Standards. It is challenging for IIA to develop and enforce global internal auditing Standards that are sufficiently demanding to meet the needs of today. The Institute's enforcement powers pale into insignificance alongside those of financial regulators. Other regulated sectors have the potential to require conformance to enhanced internal auditing standards.

Where internal audit is not mandatory, or where it is not mandatory that the CAE is a member of a relevant professional body, the opportunity to enforce any internal auditing standards is marginal at best. On the one hand, it would be inappropriate for the IIA Standards to be aspirational and poorly conformed to. On the other hand, little is served by standards which correspond to the lowest common denominator of generally accepted global internal audit practice.

Jeppesen (2010, p 195) gave us a four-generation maturity framework for the setting of standards by professional bodies. In the first generation, standards are set by a standard-setting board composed of experts usually appointed by the professional body. In the second generation there is a standard-setting board organised around the principle of representation, where participants represent their firm or a geographical area. More mature professions may graduate to a third generation approach organised around the principle of *user* orientation, where outside groups are given indirect influence in the form of rights to comment on draft standards and/or observe meetings without speaking or voting rights. When the fourth generation applies, external user groups, in the public interest are directly represented on the standard-setting board and participate on equal terms with members of the profession. Currently there is insufficient public pressure on internal auditing to enhance both the standard setting process, the rigor of the *Standards* themselves, their public interest dimension and their general enforcement.

Twenty targets for CAEs

1. Replace the dual-reporting relationship with sole reporting to the non-executive chairman of the board or to the board.
2. Be determined to fill more of the board's assurance vacuum.
3. Avoid entanglement of internal audit with the first and second lines of defence
4. Ensure the internal audit Charter authorises open dialogue with regulators.
5. Audit all critical risk management functions.
6. Undertake audits of governance including culture, behaviour and customer outcomes.
7. Perform regular gap analyses of internal audit function competence.
8. Attract top talent into internal audit.
9. Invest significantly in auditor training.
10. Attend, as of right, meetings of the executive committee.
11. In addition to audit committee meetings, attend meetings of the board, the board risk committees and other board committees as appropriate.
12. Have a status equivalent to ExCo members.
13. Avoid perverse incentives in CAE remuneration.
14. Extend the scope of Quality Assurance Reviews (QARs) beyond IIA Standards to also benchmark against the enhanced guidance developed in 2012 and 2013.
15. Undertake internal quality reviews of internal audit at least annually, by personnel independent of what is being reviewed.
16. Regard self-assessment quality reviews with independent validation as an inadequate substitute for QARs of internal audit by independent parties.
17. Weigh up whether lengthy tenure in the CAE position is compromising internal audit independence and objectivity.
18. Provide the board, at least annually, an assessment of the overall effectiveness of the governance and risk and control framework, together with an analysis of themes and trends impacting the organisation's risk profile.
19. Persuade the audit committee to report publicly their opinion on the adequacy of internal audit resources, independence and professionalism.
20. Amend the 'CAE' title to avoid the possible implication that internal audit is part of the first ('executive') line of defence.

References

Anderson, U. and Daugherty, B. (2012) 'The Third Line of Defense: Internal Audit's Role in the Governance Process', *Internal Auditing,* July/August, pp 38–41.

Basel (2012) 'Basel Committee on Banking Supervision', *The Internal Audit Function in Banks*, Bank of International Settlements, June 2012, see http://www.bis.org/publ/bcbs223.pdf, accessed 14 July 2013.

Teschner, C., Golder, P. and Liebert, T. (2008) *Bringing Back Best Practices in Risk Management: Banks' Three Lines Of Defense*, Booz & Company (see http://www.booz.com/media/file/Bringing-Back-Best-Practices-in-Risk-Management.pdf, accessed 5 August 2013).

Chambers, A.D. (2008a) 'Bring on the super auditors', *Internal Auditing*, 32 (12), pp 18–21.

Chambers, A.D. (2008b) 'The board's black hole – filling their assurance vacuum: can internal audit rise to the challenge?', *Measuring Business Excellence – The Journal of Business Performance Management*, 12 (1), pp 47–63.

Chambers, A.D. (2009) 'The black hole of assurance', *The Internal Auditor*, 66 (2), pp 28–29.

CIIA (2013) *Effective Internal Audit in the Financial Services Sector: Recommendations from the Committee on Internal Audit Guidance for Financial Services*, July 2013 (see http://www.iia.org.uk/media/354788/0758_effective_internal_audit_financial_webfinal.pdf, accessed 14 July 2013).

Committee of Sponsoring Organizations (COSO) (2004) *Enterprise Risk Management*, Framework volume, chapter 1 on 'Definition' (p 33) and also in Executive Summary (p 25). (COSO's 1992 Internal Control – Integrated Framework has been superseded by their 2013 version: www.COSO.org).

Federal Reserve (2013) *Supplemental Policy Statement on the Internal Audit Function and Its Outsourcing*, Board of Governors of the Federal Reserve System, January 2013 (supplemental to 2003 *Interagency Policy Statement on the Internal Audit Function and its Outsourcing* (2003)). (See http://www.federalreserve.gov/bankinforeg/srletters/sr1301a1.pdf, accessed 14 July 2013.)

Financial Times (2012), 'Andrew Bailey, putative head of the BoE's new Prudential Regulatory Authority', 10 September 2012, p 22.

House of Lords and House of Commons (HLHC) (2013) *Changing Banking for Good, Report of the Parliamentary Commission on Banking* Standards, Volume I: Summary, and Conclusions and Recommendations, HL Paper 27-I, HC 175-I, 12 June 2013. (See http://www.parliament.uk/business/committees/committees-a-z/joint-select/professional-standards-in-the-banking-industry/news/changing-banking-for-good-report/, accessed 14 July 2013; see also Volume II.)

HM Treasury (2008) *Government Internal Audit Standards – Final Draft*, December 2008.

Hughes, P. (2011) 'Bank Internal Audit: Third Line of Defence or First Line of Attack?', *Risk Reward Risk Update*, January 2011 (see http://www.riskrewardlimited.com/admin/pdf/RU%20Jan%202011%20PH-Internal%20Audit.pdf, accessed 11 August 2013).

International Auditing and Assurance Standards Board (IAASB) (2012) Using the work of internal auditors, *International Standards on Auditing*, ISA 610, ISBN 978-1-60815-114-1, March 2012 (see http://www.ifac.org/publications-resources/isa-610-revised-2013-using-work-internal-auditors, accessed 26th July 2013).

IIA (2012) *International* Standards *for the Professional Practice of Internal Auditing (*Standards*)*, October, effective from 1 January 2013 (see https://na.theiia.org/standards-guidance/mandatory-guidance/Pages/Standards.aspx, accessed 15 July 2013).

IIA (2013) *The Three Lines of Defense in Effective Risk Management and Control*, Position Paper, January 2013 (see https://na.theiia.org/standards-guidance/Public%20Documents/PP%20The%20Three%20Lines%20of%20Defense%20in%20Effective%20Risk%20Management%20and%20Control.pdf, accessed 20 July 2013).

Irving, R. (2012) 'Not good enough', *FS Focus*, July/August, pp 12–14.

Jeppesen, K.K. (2010) 'Strategies for dealing with standard-setting resistance', *Accounting, Auditing & Accountability Journal*, 23(2), pp 175–200.

PSIAS (2012) Public Sector Internal Audit Standards, ISBN 978 1 84508 356 4, December 2012, effective from 1 April 2013 (see http://www.iia.org.uk/media/76020/public_sector_internal_audit_standards_2012.pdf, accessed 14 July 2013).

Notes

1 This chapter first appeared as Chambers, A.D. (2014) 'The current state of internal auditing: a personal perspective and assessment', *EDPACS – the EDP audit, control, and security newsletter*, 49 (1), Taylor & Francis. In that format it can be viewed or downloaded free of charge until the end of 2014 from http://www.tandfonline.com/toc/uedp20/49/1. The chapter is based on the keynote address to the annual internal auditing conference of Slovenski Inštitut Za Revizijo (The Slovenian Institute of Auditors), 14 November 2013. Except where attributed to others, the author alone is responsible for the views expressed in this chapter. Reproduced in this Handbook by permission.

2 www.iia.org.uk.

Chapter G3

Three Lines of Defence[1]

Maginot Line:

> '... after the French Minister of War André Maginot, was a line of concrete fortifications, obstacles, and weapons installations that France constructed along its borders with Germany during the 1930s. ... While the fortification system did prevent a direct attack, it was strategically ineffective, as the Germans invaded through Belgium, outflanking the Maginot Line. ... reference to the Maginot Line is used to recall a strategy or object that people hope will prove effective but instead fails miserably.' (Wikipedia, 2013a)

Potemkin village:

> '... originally used to describe a fake village, built only to impress. The phrase is now used, typically in politics and economics, to describe any construction (literal or figurative) built solely to deceive others into thinking that some situation is better than it really is.' (Wikipedia, 2013b)

Goodhart's Law:

> 'When a measure becomes a target, it ceases to be a good measure.' (Wikipedia, 2013c)

Introduction G3.1

The 'lines of defence' analogy, applied for hundreds of years especially in military contexts, has more recently acquired traction in 'management-speak'. Military lines of defence are intended to impede breaches by external forces, but in a business context the three lines of defence are in large part designed to regulate the conduct of those inside who, too often, have seemed intent upon breaching them or finding ways around.

The concept of progressive barriers to protect business is not new. It was, for instance, applied in the context of computer security over thirty years ago[2] (Chambers, 1981).

Little attention has been given by academics to the three lines of defence which had its genesis amongst practitioners. This chapter seeks to define, support and conceptually challenge the paradigm, based on a content analysis of relevant literature including 2013 pronouncements.

Focusing in particular on the third line of defence, this chapter seeks to address conceptual ambiguities in the 'three lines of defence' model and to highlight its deficiencies, while accepting that it has been, and can continue to be, a useful framework. Under this model management and management controls are the first line of defence, risk management the second and audit the third. We shall suggest that the first line of defence has been dominant in the culture of banks and other organisations and that this must be changed. There is, as we shall explore, some ambiguity as to which functions belong to which line. There is also ambiguity as to where responsibilities vest and an unclear demarcation between the three lines. Furthermore, arguably there is a fourth line.

Branding a style of management with a catchy label has contributed to a false sense of assurance and tended to lead to excessive box ticking and an externalisation of ethics. The second and third lines of defence have in practice often been insufficiently independent, and with limited scope so that major issues remain unaddressed by them. Dominance of the second and third lines of defence by executive management, and inadequate support for these lines by non-executive directors, has weakened their effectiveness.

Internal audit – a gatekeeper that failed G3.2

Risk management and internal audit have recently and enthusiastically adopted the model of three lines of defence to describe their respective positioning in the panoply of protective mechanisms that organisations should have in place.

Applied to the global, financial crisis, Booz (2008) was an early example of the current iteration of the model in a corporate context. The authors described the three major lines of defence as respectively top management and the front office, the risk management function, and audit. They were early movers in pointing a finger of blame at audit:

> 'The third line of defense—audit—has arguably failed in its role of providing independent and objective assurance of the effectiveness of the first two lines of defense. … For the third line of defense to act as an effective steward of the policies and procedures approved by the board, it needs to have not only a good understanding of the business—how the front office makes money—but also a deep understanding of risk management discipline. … For example, audit teams should investigate and validate mark-to-market positions, ensuring the integrity of information as it passes from one system to the next. … Moreover, the third line of defense must develop a strong critical approach to each functional discipline, performing more than just a "checking the checkers" role. It is not inconceivable, for example, that after reviewing the securitization process, the internal audit team could identify and bring to the board's attention potential flaws, such as overreliance on rating agencies. All too often, auditors document processes as a box-ticking exercise to ensure compliance, with limited critical review of potential weaknesses.'

They argued for:

> 'top talent within audit—to challenge the front office and risk management function'.

For a while, the common characterisation of internal audit, as the authors put it, as just 'checking the checkers' served to divert substantive blame from internal audit as one of the gatekeepers who had failed, no more so that in a major UK report on corporate governance in banks which only mentioned internal audit incidentally to absolve internal audit of blame on the grounds that:

> 'Discussions in the context of this Review process suggest that failures that proved to be critical for many banks related much less to what might be characterised as conventional compliance and audit processes, including internal audit, but

to defective information flow, defective analytical tools and inability to bring insightful judgement in the interpretation of information and the impact of market events on the business model.' (Walker, 2009, p 93, § 6.8)

The error was in suggesting that internal audit should have little or no role in 'insightful judgement in the interpretation of information and the impact of market events on the business model'.

The authors of the Booz (2008) report were not alone at that time in challenging internal audit to step up to the plate (Chambers, 2008a, 2008b; 2009) but it was not until 2013 that the challenge gained momentum.

Enhanced interpretations of the three lines of defence have appeared since 2008, for instance as indicated in Figure 1 in **G2**.

The head of accounting, audit and regulatory reporting policy at the Financial Services Authority (FSA), the UK's financial services regulator until 2013, was quoted as saying (Irving, 2012):

> 'I can't point to the internal audit function of a single bank or insurer and say, with hand on heart, that is how we envision it being done in the future.'

and:

> 'There exist generic industry standards and practices [for internal auditing], but none are sufficiently robust to address the complex world of financial services firms.'

The promotion of internal audit as the third line of defence has served to garnish internal audit with, to some extent, an undeserved aura of legitimacy. The defence analogy also has served to shift the emphasis of internal audit somewhat away from an 'add value', 'consulting' orientation to a protective, safeguarding one. Note, for instance, the dual 2013 challenge to the Institute of Internal Auditors' old (IIA, 1999) but still current definition of internal auditing (Table 1). It should be possible to define anything in a single sentence.

Table 1

	Body/Bodies	**Definition**
1.	IIA since 1999 (IIA, 1999; 2013b). UK Government since 2008 (GIAS, 2008; PSIAS, 2012).	*Internal auditing is an independent, objective assurance and consulting activity designed to add value and improve an organization's operations. It helps an organization accomplish its objectives by bringing a systematic, disciplined approach to evaluate and improve the effectiveness of risk management, control, and governance processes.*[3]
2.	Federal Reserve (2013)	*An effective internal audit function is a vehicle to advance an institution's safety and soundness and compliance with consumer laws and regulations and is therefore considered as part of the supervisory review process.*[4]

	Body/Bodies	Definition
3.	UK Committee on Internal Audit Guidance for Financial Services(CIIA, 2013b)	*The primary role of Internal Audit should be to help the Board and Executive Management to protect the assets, reputation and sustainability of the organisation.*[5]

Basel on internal audit in banks G3.3

For banks, by 2010 Basel had firmly characterised internal audit as a vital part of corporate governance, and drawn attention to the importance of internal audit independence, skills and professionalism together with effective internal audit communication with the board and with senior management. Furthermore, although the 'three lines of defence' concept was not overtly referred to in Basel (2010), it is to some extent implied in '*engaging internal auditors to judge the effectiveness of the risk management function*' (see above) and in:

> '… Sound corporate governance is evidenced, among other things, by a culture where senior management and staff are expected and encouraged to identify risk issues as opposed to relying on the internal audit or risk management functions to identify them. This expectation is conveyed not only through bank policies and procedures, but also through the 'tone at the top' established by the board and senior management.' (Basel, 2010, p 22)

The Basel (2012) internal auditing guidance has overtly adopted the three lines of defence model. As was implied by Booz (2008) it is notable that this Basel guidance regards internal audit as the *only* element in the third line of defence:

> 'The third line of defence is the internal audit function that independently assesses the effectiveness of the processes created in the first and second lines of defence and provides assurance on these processes.' (Basel, 2012, p 13)

A failure of the 2012 Basel guidance is its almost exclusive emphasis on the scope of internal auditing being the 'activities' or 'processes' of the bank; CIIA (2013b) outlines a much broader scope.

The UK Parliamentary Banking Commission and the Government's response G3.4

In July 2013, the *three lines of defence model* was strongly attacked in the report of the UK Parliamentary Commission on Banking Standards (hereinafter referred to as 'the Banking Commission') (HLHC, 2013b, p 138 et al), leading to the phrase being studiously avoided by the UK Committee on Internal Audit Guidance for Financial Services[6] (CIIA, 2013b, p 5):

> 'Wherever possible, the guidance has attempted to use layman's language to define terms open to ambiguity or differing application, e.g. "assurance", "three lines of defence" and "reporting line".'

As the UK government stated in its response in July 2013 to the Banking Commission:

> 'The Commission's final report sets out a compelling case for change and makes over 100 recommendations, which fall under four broad themes:
>
> …
>
> - reforming corporate governance: The report notes that weaknesses in corporate governance both at board level and below contributed to a lack of effective control and oversight of risks within banks, and suggests a package of recommendations to remedy these defects, including around resourcing for non-executives and provisions to strengthen the role of chief risk officer, internal audit, and compliance functions.' (HMT and DBIS, 2013, § 1.5, pp 5–6).

and:

> 'The Commission scrutinises the standard of internal risk and compliance control, and internal audit below board level. Before the crisis these systems were held as having lower importance than the front line divisions and burdened with responsibility for controlling risk, compliance or practicing internal audit for the whole company, an impossible task in most cases. The Commission recommends a strengthening of the influence and independence of the Chief of Risk, Compliance and Internal Audit, and of their role within the institution.
>
> This approach includes direct access to accountable board members, independence from the senior management, and protection from dismissal unless all NEDs agree, and sufficient remuneration to preserve independence.
>
> The Government agrees with this approach. These central functions are essential to the running of a bank in a proper and responsible fashion. The failure of HBOS revealed that without adequate information and support systems, a board is powerless to effect important change and oversight. The Government will therefore ask the PRA to consider consulting on new rules to ensure that the risk function shall be able to report directly to the management body, including the CEO, is independent from senior management and that the head of risk cannot be dismissed without approval by the management body.
>
> The Government will ask the PRA and the FCA[7] to consider the extent to which similar rules are necessary for the head of internal audit and compliance, alongside the introduction of new rules requiring the management body to ensure the integrity of the accounting and financial reporting systems, including risk, internal audit and compliance.' (HMT and DBIS, 2013, § 3.30 to 3.33, p 26)

The use of 'the management body' in the government's response (see above) was unfortunate as it clearly referred to, or at least included, the board. It is an error frequently made to refer to the board as 'management': a contributory factor in the malaise at the top of some companies has been a failure to appreciate the distinctive roles of the board and the executive.

Whereas the UK government is supporting *legislative* change[8] as well as amendments to the UK Corporate Governance Code to require directors of banks to attach the utmost importance to the safety and soundness of the firm, the UK government sees no need for legislative change to implement the Banking Commission's recommendations on internal audit but will rely on the Bank of England, the Financial Conduct Authority

(FCA), the Prudential Regulation Authority (PRA) and others to lead on these (HMT and DBIS, 2013, p 59). Indeed this is already happening (CIIA, 2013b).

The Banking Commission, which reported in July 2013, drew attention to the absence of 'substance over form',[9] although it did not use that phrase:

> 'The financial crisis, and multiple conduct failures, have exposed serious flaws in governance. Potemkin villages were created in firms, giving the appearance of effective control and oversight without the reality. Non-executive directors lacked the capacity or incentives to challenge the executives. Sometimes those executives with the greatest insight into risks being added to balance sheets were cut off from decision-makers at board level or lacked the necessary status to speak up. Poor governance and controls are illustrated by the rarity of whistle-blowing, either within or beyond the firm, even where, such as in the case of Libor manipulation, prolonged and blatant misconduct has been evident. The Commission makes the following recommendations for improvement:
>
> - individual and direct lines of access and accountability to the board for the heads of the risk, compliance and internal audit functions and much greater levels of protection for their independence; …' (HLHC, 2013a, p 10)

Problems with the three lines of defence model G3.5

The Banking Commission concluded:

> 'The "three lines of defence" system for controlling risk has been adopted by many banks with the active encouragement of the regulators. It appears to have promoted a wholly misplaced sense of security. Fashionable management school theory appears to have lent undeserved credibility to some chaotic systems. Responsibilities have been blurred, accountability diluted, and officers in risk, compliance and internal audit have lacked the status to challenge front line staff effectively. Much of the system became a box-ticking exercise whereby processes were followed, but judgement was absent. In the end, everyone loses, particularly customers.' (HLHC, 2013a, § 20, p 18)

The Commission also dismissively described the three lines of defence as 'Maginot lines' (HLHC, 2013b, p 138).

Criticism of past reliance on the 'three lines of defence' model can be summed up as follows, drawing considerably from evidence to, and conclusions of, the Banking Commission.

The first line of defence has been dominant in the culture of banks G3.6

Macho executive management have dominated the second and third lines, and have had the ear of the board to a greater extent than the second and third lines.

> 'The "three lines of defence" have not prevented banks' control frameworks failing in the past in part because the lines were blurred and the status of the front line, remunerated for revenue generation, was dominant over the compliance, risk

and audit apparatus. Mere organisational change is very unlikely, on its own, to ensure success in future. Our recommendations provide for these lines to be separate, with distinct authority given to internal control and give particular non-executive directors individual personal responsibility for protecting the independence of those responsible for key internal controls. This needs to be buttressed with rigorous scrutiny by the new regulators of the adequacy of firms' control frameworks'. (HLHC, 2013a, § 134, p 44; HLHC, 2013b, § 742, p 356)

'Goodhart's Law' biases the three lines of defence towards mere box ticking **G3.7**

'Goodhart's Law' tells us that putting a name to something (in this case naming an approach as 'three lines of defence') means it tends to become a gameable box-ticking exercise rather than something truly embedded into the spirit and culture of the organisation. Goodhart's Law is named after the banker who originated it, Charles Goodhart. Its most popular formulation is: 'When a measure becomes a target, it ceases to be a good measure.'

Exercise of judgement has been inadequate **G3.8**

The exercise of judgement, even by internal audit at the third line of defence, has been inadequate. In evidence to the Banking Commission the group head of internal audit at HSBC acknowledged that the work of his division had been characterised by a rules-based approach. He said it was very difficult for an audit unit, based on the skill sets it had and where it traditionally was positioned within the organisation, to pass an opinion on judgements or issues of strategy. He considered 'fair comment' Commissioner Baroness Kramer's challenge that HSBC's internal audit had not been looking at judgement but only whether people had taken the procedural steps (HLHC, 2013b, § 738, pp 354–356).

The three lines of defence model 'externalises ethics' **G3.9**

Three key witnesses to the Banking Commission expressed the conviction that the three lines of defence approach tended to externalise ethics. In evidence to the Commission (HLHC, 2013b, § 139, p 139 and §142, p 141), Professor John Kay volunteered:

> 'If you go into financial institution after financial institution, you will see firstly that regulation is regarded unequivocally as a nuisance, and, secondly, that regulation is largely entrusted to a department whose job it is to deal with regulation, and that department is itself regarded as a nuisance.'

Joris Luyendijk, referring to box-ticking as the second line of defence, told the Commission:

> 'Now, what the trader built was perfectly legal. It would have made money for the bank—or it seemed to make money for the bank. It stayed within all the rules. He probably went to all his compliance people and ticked all the boxes. Most traders talk about compliance as box ticking, or hurdles. They have externalised ethics:

once you have got past the priest, you are fine. Banks tend to have departments tasked with dealing with regulators, enabling the rest of the company to get on with making money.'

Sir Hector Sants, Barclays new head of compliance and previously chief executive of the FSA stated:

'Some banks' control frameworks are hardwired with an absence of personal responsibility or accountability.'

The second line of defence acts as the first line of defence G3.10

The second line of defence has often acted as if it were the first line of defence, thereby diminishing the effectiveness of the second line of defence and blurring accountabilities. If there is confusion about where responsibility is vested, there is significant risk that individuals will try to pass the buck. When responsibility is shared between different parties (eg between the first and second lines of defence) there is a possibility, even a probability, that individuals' sense of responsibility will be less keenly felt and thus that excessive risks may be taken.

The Banking Commission found it difficult to obtain clear answers from its witnesses as to whether the first or the second line of defence is responsible when things go wrong. It is difficult to determine where responsibility vests when front-line management obtains the approval of the risk management or compliance functions to a course of action it then takes: it is reasonable to conclude that front-line management is responsible as the first line of defence, and also risk management as the second. A Commissioner asked:

'Who is taking responsibility for compliance? Who ultimately has their head on the block?'

and:

'Is there ever any perception among front line staff that the control employee—the second line of defence—who approved a bad deal is the more likely to be sacked of the two people than the person who did the deal?'

to which the correct answer was given that the buck stops with the business (i.e. the front line), and to which we would add that each line of defence may be held accountable in such a situation, according to their respective responsibilities (HLHC, 2013b, § 139, pp 139–141).

A witness pointed out that if the second line, for instance the risk management or compliance functions, approves a course of action by the first line which is outside the first line's normal limits, then the second line becomes part of the decision-making process, not outside it. (HLHC, 2013b, §739, p355). In this case, if things go wrong, risk management or compliance along with front-line management would both be responsible.

Undoubtedly there is confusion as to whether the front line or the second line is responsible for control and compliance (HLHC, 2013b, § 138, pp 139–141). The departing Group Head of Compliance at Barclays, suggested that compliance was a first line responsibility:

> 'I am in charge of the compliance function, but the first line of defence has responsibility to run its business in a controlled way. It is compliance's responsibility to help that happen. Clearly, here it did not, and that is regrettable, but it is not the compliance function's responsibility to make Barclays compliant.'

Sir Hector Sants, commencing 2013 as Barclays Head of Compliance and Government and Regulatory Relations and previously chief executive of the Financial Services Authority (the regulator), told the Banking Commission that he:

> 'completely and utterly' disagreed with that statement.' (HLHC, 2013b, § 138, pp 139–141)

The third line of defence acts as the second line of defence G3.11

This has been one of the most glaring risks associated with the three lines of defence approach which can in effect mean that there are only two lines – the front line and a second line. For instance, if the compliance and internal audit functions are combined, or if both report to a single head, then there is no clear blue water between the second and third lines; likewise, if the head of internal audit is responsible for setting up the organisation's risk management function.

The third line of defence has not been sufficiently independent G3.12

Post-2008 there has been progressive development of enhanced independence of internal audit from management, and a stronger relationship with the board. There is further still to travel and in some respects risk management has sometimes gone further than internal audit.

The Walker Report (2009, p 99, § 6.22) recommended that:

> 'In support of board-level risk governance, a BOFI [bank and other financial industry] board should be served by a CRO who should participate in the risk management and oversight process at the highest level on an enterprise-wide basis and have a status of total independence from individual business units. Alongside an internal reporting line to the CEO or CFO, the CRO should report to the board risk committee, with direct access to the chairman of the committee in the event of need. The tenure and independence of the CRO should be underpinned by a provision that removal from office would require the prior agreement of the board. The remuneration of the CRO should be subject to approval by the chairman or chairman of the board remuneration committee.'

Walker's risk committee of the board should:

> 'like the audit committee, be a committee of the board and should be chaired by a NED with a majority of non-executive members, but additionally with the CFO as members or in attendance and with the CRO invariably present … Whether the CEO should be present will be for decision between the chairman of the committee and the CEO. But the CEO will invariably be involved in deliberations of the full board on risk. … The presumption in any event is that an executive risk committee structure, usually chaired by the CEO or CFO, will continue as now.' (Walker, 2009, p 95, § 6.15)

A witness to the Banking Commission (HLHC, 2013b, § 739, p 355) made the point that:

> '…it is particularly important that internal audit looks at those sorts of thing, completely independently.'

The Banking Commission concluded (HLHC, 2013b, § 739, p 355):

> 'This "complete independence" as Roger Marshall described it, reinforces again the need for this function to be protected by the non-executives to ensure their own independent challenge is informed by analysis that is also independent of the executive.'

and:

> 'Internal audit's independence is as important as that of the Chief Risk Officer and the Head of Group Compliance, and its preservation should similarly be the responsibility of a named individual non-executive director, usually the chairman of the audit committee. Dismissal or sanctions against the head of internal audit should also require the agreement of the non-executive directors. (HLHC, 2013b, § 741, pp 355–356)

Some would say that the above articulates an insufficient degree of independence from management, if not for risk management, then certainly for internal audit. The draft report of the UK Committee on Internal Audit Guidance for Financial Services advised that:

> 'The primary reporting line for the Chief Internal Auditor should be to the Chairman of the Board of Directors. The Chairman may wish to delegate responsibility for the reporting line to the Chairman of the Board Audit Committee or, exceptionally, the Chairman of the Board Risk Committee, providing this Committee is constituted exclusively of independent Non-Executive Directors. The reporting line should take into account the respective mandates of the Board Audit Committee and the Board Risk Committee, and must avoid any impairment to internal audit's objectivity. (CIIA, 2013a, § 15, pp 6–7)

and:

> 'If Internal Audit has a secondary Executive reporting line, this should be to the CEO in order to preserve independence from any particular business area or function. (CIIA, 2013a, § 21, pp 6–7)

Note that the guidance suggests that there may be no internal audit reporting line to the executive and where it exists it should only be secondary.

In response to representations during the consultation stage, the final guidance represents a watering down from the draft guidance in that the chair of the audit committee rather than the chair of the board is given as the primary reporting line:

> 'The primary reporting line for the Chief Internal Auditor should be to the Chairman of the Audit Committee. In exceptional circumstances, the Board may wish for Internal Audit to report directly to the Chairman of the Board, or delegate responsibility for the reporting line to the Chairman of the Board Risk Committee, provided the Chairman of the Board Risk Committee and all the other Committee members are independent Non-Executive Directors. The reporting line must

avoid any impairment to Internal Audit's independence and objectivity.' (CIIA, 2013b, § 15, p 9)

and:

> 'If Internal Audit has a secondary Executive reporting line, this should be to the CEO in order to preserve independence from any particular business area or function and to establish the standing of Internal Audit alongside the Executive Committee members.'(CIIA, 2013b, § 20, p 9).

Further problems with the three lines of defence model

Insufficient support for the third line of defence at independent director level **G3.13**

Chiming with our earlier observation that when responsibilities are defused and not clearly assigned, neglect is likely to ensue, it is now being more clearly understood that achieving and preserving internal audit independence should be a responsibility unambiguously assigned to an individual independent director. Evidence to the Banking Commission put it like this:

> 'Internal audit's independence is as important as that of the Chief Risk Officer and the Head of Group Compliance, and its preservation should similarly be the responsibility of a named individual non-executive director, usually the chairman of the audit committee. Dismissal or sanctions against the head of internal audit should also require the agreement of the non-executive directors.' (HLHC, 2013a, § 133, p 44)

Limited scope for the third line of defence means inadequate assurance **G3.14**

In contrast to the restrictions on the scope of internal audit work implied in the Walker Report, referred to earlier (Walker, 2009, p 93, § 6.8), there has emerged a general consensus that the scope of internal audit should be everything up to the door of the boardroom. This is particularly evident in (a) the UK guidance on internal auditing in the financial sector (CIIA, 2013b), and (b) the views expressed to, and by, the Banking Commission. With respect to the board itself, the processes and the reliability of the information that the board uses should also be within the scope of internal audit.

Evidence to the Banking Commission agreed that internal audit:

> 'should look at governance, it should look at culture, it should look at the way that the risk management departments manage risk, and it should look at compliance and how they are doing things.'

The UK financial sector guidance (CIIA, 2013b) includes, for instance, risks of poor customer treatment and key corporate events as being within internal audit scope (CIIA, 2013b, p 7, § B.6.e and f).

In response to the following question by Commissioner Baroness Kramer:

> 'So how broad would your scope be …? Would it include product suitability, HR policies for recruitment, business strategy or perception? How wide-ranging is it?'

the Head of Internal Audit at Standard Chartered Bank confirmed that:

> 'It is everything, really. We have unrestricted access to all of the bank's activities and all of the information.'

And the Confederation of British Industry said that internal audit should not be restricted to historic analysis, but elevated to a role in decision-making processes (HLHC, 2013b, § 739, p 355).

The third line of defence may be subordinate to, and eclipsed by, the second line G3.15

This was discussed by Hughes (2011):

> 'There are real grounds for concern here given that the label "third line of defence"; applied to audit implies subordination to risk management's "second line of defence"'.

Post-2008 it is certainly the case that the profile of risk management has been elevated, and it is only more recently that more attention is being given to strengthening the role of internal audit.

Close relationship of internal audit to management weakens the third line of defence G3.16

A close relationship of internal audit to management may invalidate internal audit's claim to be the third line of defence, in effect moving internal audit to the first or second line. We observe over time a steady trend to greater independence for internal audit from management. If the board is to rely on the assurance it receives from internal audit as its third line of defence, then internal audit needs to be independent of management. Indeed, the assurance that management themselves receive from internal audit will be more credible if it comes from an internal audit function which is independent of management. It is inappropriate for internal audit to be positioned within any functional area of the business, such as finance. It is also inappropriate for the determination of internal audit pay to be made at a management level.

Latest guidance (CIIA, 2013b) is:

> 'The Chairman of the Audit Committee should be accountable for setting the objectives of the Chief Internal Auditor and appraising his/her performance. It would be expected that the objectives and appraisal would take into account the views of the Chief Executive. This appraisal should consider the independence, objectivity and tenure of the Chief Internal Auditor. …
>
> The Chairman of the Audit Committee should be responsible for recommending the remuneration of the Chief Internal Auditor to the Remuneration Committee.

The remuneration of the Chief Internal Auditor and Internal Audit staff should be structured in a manner such that it avoids conflicts of interest, does not impair their independence and objectivity and should not be directly or exclusively linked to the short term performance of the organisation …

The Audit Committee should be responsible for approving the Internal Audit budget and, as part of the Board's overall governance responsibility, should disclose in the annual report whether it is satisfied that Internal Audit has the appropriate resources. (CIIA, 2013b, § s 17, 18 and 23, p 9)

Lack of agreement as to what constitutes the third line of defence **G3.17**

There is *a* legitimate question as to whether there are other parties located within the third line – such as regulators, directors,[10] external auditors and shareholders. HM Treasury (2012) defines the third line of defence as relating to:

> 'independent and more objective assurance and focuses on the role of internal audit, which carries out a programme of work specifically designed to provide the Accounting Officer with an independent and objective opinion on the framework of governance, risk management and control. Internal audit will place reliance upon assurance mechanisms in the first and second lines of defence, where possible, to enable it to direct its resources most effectively, on areas of highest risk or where there are gaps or weaknesses in other assurance arrangements. It may also take assurance from other independent assurance providers operating in the third line, such as those provided by independent regulators, for example.'[11]

and goes on to state that other sources of independent assurance in the third line of defence include, in UK government:

> 'Major Projects Authority Integrated Assurance Reviews, external system accreditation reviews/certification (e.g. ISO/Risk Management Accreditation Document Sets), European Commission/European Court of Auditors and Treasury/Cabinet Office/Parliamentary scrutiny processes.'[12]

and that:

> 'As an additional line of assurance, sitting outside of the internal assurance framework and the Three Lines of Defence model, are external auditors, chiefly the [National Audit Office], who are external to the organisation with a statutory responsibility for certification audit of the financial statements. It is important that internal audit and external audit work effectively together to the maximum benefit of the organisation and in line with international standards.'[13]

The National Audit Office (NAO) (2013) concurs with this view that internal audit may not be the only element within the third line of defence and that external audit is beyond the third line of defence, as well as providing concise definitions of each of the lines of defence, which also concur with those of HM Treasury (2012):

> 'Line 1: Business Management
>
> The processes in place at the "front line" of the business: e.g. monitoring of business controls, monitoring statistics, risk registers, other management information.

Line 2: Corporate Oversight

The processes associated with oversight over management activity: e.g. compliance assessments, reviews of policy implementation, setting and monitoring of internal guidelines. The processes are separate from those responsible for delivery, but not independent of the management chain.

Line 3: Independent Assurance

Independent assurance conducted to provide an accounting officer with an opinion on the framework of governance, risk management and control. Primarily internal audit, though also provided by other independent bodies (e.g. Major Projects Authority).

N.B. External audit is outside the internal assurance framework and the "Three Lines of Defence" model. External Audit's responsibility is for certification audit of the financial statements. It is important for internal and external audit to work effectively together for the maximum benefit to the organisation.'

But Doughty (2011) takes the view that external audit *is* part of the third line of defence:

> 'The third line of defence is that of internal and external auditors and the US Sarbanes-Oxley Act compliance team (where applicable) who report independently to the senior committee charged with the role of representing the enterprise's stakeholders relative to risk issues.'

Likewise, Sarens, *et al* (2012) combined a number of agencies within the third line:

> 'Based on the field research conducted for this report, organizations tend to group together all independent assurance providers in the third line of defense, whether they are internal or external.'

Clarifying the concept G3.18

Earlier we pointed out that military lines of defence are intended to impede breaches by external forces, but in a business context the three lines of defence are in large part designed to regulate the conduct of those *within* the organisation who, too often, have seemed intent upon breaching the defences or finding a way around them. Perhaps we need to accept that in business the enemy within is as much a threat as those without.

An important, unresolved issue is to develop definitions of each of the three lines of defence so that there is clarity as to who belongs to which and the essential attributes of those parties according to the line of defence each belongs to. We suggest a key element of these definitions is to whom the party is providing the service. If internal audit were regarded as primarily serving management rather than the board, then internal audit would be within the first or second lines of defence. Serving the board independently of management would place internal audit within the third line of defence but requires independence from management. Not all internal audit functions can legitimately claim to belong to the third line of defence: most of those are within the second line and would be within the first line if management uses them as interim executives, process designers, implementers, etc.

Consensus on the line of defence to which each party belongs is a pre-requisite to assurance mapping the totality of the assurance framework. Internal auditors have argued that they are best paced to undertake the assurance mapping exercise (Anderson and Daugherty, 2012) though other parties, such as management consultants, might compete for the same turf.

If other parties' primary mission is to provide assurance to the board rather than to management, then they too are parts of the third line of defence. It may not be appropriate for internal audit to claim exclusive occupancy of the third line of defence space.

In view of complex reporting lines, the three lines of defence model, as currently articulated, is fuzzy in respect of determining which line of defence an activity belongs to. A risk management function within a financial institution is regarded as belonging to the second line of defence and the function certainly reports to management. But the risk management function has a degree of independence from management in the sense that the CRO also reports to the board, to the risk committee of the board and to the audit committee. Furthermore, best practice is that the appointment, dismissal and remuneration of the CRO should be a matter for the board. In the case of internal audit, the best case scenario is a strong reporting relationship to the board, but nobody would deny that detailed audit engagement reports are addressed to management.

By extension, other parties, such as external auditors and regulators, may be regarded as outside the third line of defence as they exist to serve external stakeholders rather than the board: external auditors report to the shareholders, and regulators have a broad societal mission. The model should accommodate these parties as the fourth line of defence rather than representing them in a disconnected way, as in Figure 1 in **G2**.

Boards obtain *ad hoc* assurance in a number of ways. In the aftermath of the Shell oil reserves issue, Shell's audit committee commissioned a report from Davis Polk & Wardwell, the New York law firm (Chambers, 2008a). In the wake of the Texas refinery explosion, BP's commissioned James Baker to report to them (Chambers, 2008a). BAE asked Lord Wolf to report to its board on business ethics following concern about overseas contracts (Chambers, 2008a). Best practice UK corporate governance requires the board's performance to be evaluated and that at least once every three years this should be externally facilitated (FRC, 2012, § B.6). Arguably each of these is an example of the third line of defence in action.

It will sometimes be the case that outside parties, such as the regulator, demand that such *ad hoc* reviews are commissioned by a company's board, and the results of these reviews are often published for the benefit of external stakeholders. This illustrates that if we were to redefine the model as comprising four lines of defence, we would sometimes observe a positioning ambiguity between the third and fourth lines – just as we have indicated may apply between the first and second lines, and between the second and third lines.

Running a business is not just about avoiding things going wrong, important though that is. Both risk management and internal audit should contribute to the avoidance of threats and the successful mitigation of those that occur – which is the protective, defensive side of their role, which we might term 'downside risk'. Both should also contribute to maximising the organisation's potential to harness perhaps unanticipated future opportunities ('upside risk'). The 'three lines of defence' is a defensive model well adapted to the former 'protect' or 'safeguard' orientation of internal audit which we have shown is now defining internal audit in the financial sector (Basel, 2012; CIIA, 2013b), but less so for the latter.

General conclusions G3.19

While the three lines of defence model has the potential to serve business well, there is a risk that pursuit of this approach engenders complacency. This is particularly the case when responsibilities at each line are unclear, and when the approach is deviated from.

It is apparent that there has slowly emerged a general perception that internal audit is one of the gatekeepers that failed to prevent the global financial crisis. Subsequent scandals, such as the London Interbank Offered Rate (LIBOR) rate fixing saga, suggest that the internal audit house has yet to be put in order. It is not surprising that the attention of regulators and others has now turned to internal audit. Internal audit needs to raise its game.

Arguably, the new enhanced guidelines for internal audit developed recently (Basel, 2012; Federal Reserve, 2013; CIIA, 2013b) are inconsistent with the IIA Standards (IIA, 2013b) only in the sense that they build on those Standards, taking certain issues to a higher, more demanding level. For instance, overall opinions by internal audit are expressed in these enhanced guidelines as being a requirement, not merely an option. It is hard to escape the conclusion that this represents a challenge for the Institute of Internal Auditors which needs to be responded to.

The general tenor of these developments is that internal audit must be more effective at filling the board's assurance vacuum, and can be so with a stronger reporting line to the board and to the board's audit committee (Chambers, 2008a, 2008b). Loosening internal audit's reporting relationship with management so that it becomes a *secondary* reporting line at most, does not impede the level of assurance that internal audit can provide to management: the assurance is all the better if it comes from a party that has a measure of independence from those to whom the assurance is being given. The quality of assurance to the boards is seriously weak if it comes from a party whose primary reporting line is below the level of the board. Internal audit being positioned within one of the functional areas of the business, such as within finance, is now rejected as being totally unsatisfactory even though it is still common place. To use the internal audit profession's own 'three lines of defence' model, the closer internal audit is to management (whether the CFO or the CEO) the more it becomes part of the second rather than the third line of defence.

Management has its own second line of defence to provide assurance that governance, risk management and internal control are working well. Arguably, the board needs internal audit, as the third line of defence, to provide the board with independent assurance about the first and second lines of defence.

There are internal audit resource implications in these developments. Whether or not the term 'super auditors' is acceptable (Chambers, 2008a), to audit effectively with a significantly enhanced audit scope, requires in general a significantly enhanced quality of internal audit staff. When the chief audit executive has the status of a member of the executive committee,[14] which he/she attends, this implies a calibre of person in that role which exceeds common practice in many cases today.

The advent of risk committees of the board suggests that in the future those committees may sometimes assume the responsibilities for internal audit now being recommended for audit committees of the board. This is likely to be so in cases where the audit committee is so preoccupied with financial reporting and external audit matters that it is not well placed to give adequate attention to the work of internal audit.

Another future scenario is that the chief internal auditor's primary reporting line may morph to the chairman of the board, with the cost of internal audit being regarded as one of the costs of running the board.

References

Anderson, U. and Daugherty, B. (2012) 'The Third Line of Defense: Internal Audit's Role in the Governance Process', *Internal Auditing,* Boston, US, Warren Gorham Lamont, July/August, pp 38–41.

Basel Committee on Banking Supervision (Basel) (2010), *Principles for Enhancing Corporate Governance*, Bank of International Settlements, October 2010 (see http://www.bis.org/publ/bcbs176.pdf, accessed 14 July 2013).

Basel (2012) *The Internal Audit Function in Banks*, Bank of International Settlements, June 2012, (see http://www.bis.org/publ/bcbs223.pdf, accessed 14 July 2013).

Booz (2008) Teschner, C., Golder, P. and Liebert, T., *Bringing Back Best Practices in Risk Management: Banks' Three Lines Of Defense*, Booz & Company (see http://www.booz.com/media/file/Bringing-Back-Best-Practices-in-Risk-Management.pdf, accessed 5 August 2013).

Chambers, A.D. (1981) *Computer Auditing* (London: Pitman).

Chambers, A.D. (2008a) 'The board's black hole – filling their assurance vacuum: can internal audit rise to the challenge?', Measuring Business Excellence, *The Journal of Business Performance Management*, 12 (1), pp 47–63.

Chambers, A.D. (2008b) 'Bring on the super auditors', *Internal Auditing*, December, 32 (12), pp 18–21.

Chambers, A.D. (2009) 'The black hole of assurance', *The Internal Auditor*, April, 66 (2), pp 28–29.

Chambers, A.D. (2012) *Chambers' Corporate Governance Handbook* 5th edn (Haywards Heath: Bloomsbury).

Chartered Institute of Internal Auditors (CIIA) (2013a), *Effective Internal Audit in the Financial Services Sector: Draft Recommendations to the Chartered Institute of Internal Auditors* [from the Committee on Internal Audit Guidance for Financial Services], February 2013.

CIIA (2013b) *Effective Internal Audit in the Financial Services Sector: Recommendations from the Committee on Internal Audit Guidance for Financial*

Services, July 2013 (see http://www.iia.org.uk/media/354788/0758_effective_internal_audit_financial_webfinal.pdf, accessed 14 July 2013).

Doughty, K. (2011) 'The Three Lines of Defence Related to Risk Governance', *ISACA Journal* Vol 5 (see http://www.isaca.org/Journal/Past-Issues/2011/Volume-5/Pages/The-Three-Lines-of-Defence-Related-to-Risk-Governance.aspx, accessed 5 August 2013).

Federal Reserve (2013) *Supplemental Policy Statement on the Internal Audit Function and Its Outsourcing*, Board of Governors of the Federal Reserve System, January 2013 (supplemental to *Interagency Policy Statement on the Internal Audit Function and its Outsourcing* (2003)) (see http://www.federalreserve.gov/bankinforeg/srletters/sr1301a1.pdf, accessed 14 July 2013).

Federation of European Risk Management Associations, European Confederation of Institutes of Internal Auditing (FERMA/ECIIA) (2010) *Monitoring the effectiveness of internal control, internal audit and risk management systems: Guidance for boards and audit committees (*pursuant the 8th European Company Law Directive on Statutory Audit Directive 2006/43/EC, Art 41-2b, September 2010 (see http://www.eciia.eu/sites/www.eciia.org/files/guidance_on_the_8th_eu_company_law_directive_05_10_2010.pdf, accessed 20 July 2013).

Financial Reporting Council (FRC) (2012) *The UK Corporate Governance Code*, September 2012, (see https://frc.org.uk/Our-Work/Publications/Corporate-Governance/UK-Corporate-Governance-Code-September-2012.aspx, accessed 7 August 2013).

HM Treasury (2008) *Government Internal Audit Standards* (GIAS).

HM Treasury (2012) *Assurance Frameworks*, December, ISBN 978-1-84532-974-7.

HM Treasury and Department for Business Innovation and Skills (HMT and DBIS) (2013) *The Government's response to the Parliamentary Commission on Banking Standards*, Cm 8661, July 2013 (see https://www.gov.uk/government/uploads/system/uploads/attachment_data/file/211047/gov_response_to_the_parliamentary_commission_on_banking_standards.pdf, accessed 14 July 2013).

House of Lords and House of Commons (HLHC) (2013a), *Changing Banking for Good, Report of the Parliamentary Commission on Banking Standards*, Volume I: Summary, and Conclusions and Recommendations, HL Chapter 27-I, HC 175-I, 12 June 2103 (see http://www.parliament.uk/business/committees/committees-a-z/joint-select/professional-standards-in-the-banking-industry/news/changing-banking-for-good-report/, accessed 14 July 2013).

HLHC (2013b), *Changing Banking for Good, Report of the Parliamentary Commission on Banking Standards,* Volume II: Chapters 1 to 11 and Annexes, together with formal minutes, HL Chapter 27-II, HC 175-II, 12 June 2013 (see http://www.parliament.uk/business/committees/committees-a-z/joint-select/professional-standards-in-the-banking-industry/news/changing-banking-for-good-report/, accessed 14 July 2013).

Hughes, P. (2011) 'Bank Internal Audit: Third Line of Defence or First Line of Attack?', *Risk Reward Risk Update*, January 2011 (see http://www.riskrewardlimited.com/admin/pdf/RU%20Jan%202011%20PH-Internal%20Audit.pdf, accessed. 11 August 2013).

Institute of Internal Auditors (IIA) (1999) 'IIA Exposes New Internal Audit Definition', *Internal Auditor*, 56(1), February 1999.

IIA (2013a) *The Three Lines of Defense in Effective Risk Management and Control*, Position Chapter, January 2013 (see https://na.theiia.org/standards-guidance/Public%20Documents/PP%20The%20Three%20Lines%20of%20Defense%20in%20Effective%20Risk%20Management%20and%20Control.pdf, accessed 20 July 2013).

IIA (2013b) *International Standards for the Professional Practice of Internal Auditing (Standards)*, 1 January 2013 (see https://na.theiia.org/standards-guidance/mandatory-guidance/Pages/Standards.aspx, accessed 15 July 2013).

International Auditing and Assurance Standards Board (IAASB) (2012) 'Using the work of internal auditors', *International Standards on Auditing*, ISA 610, March 2012 (see http://www.ifac.org/publications-resources/isa-610-revised-2013-using-work-internal-auditors, accessed 26 July 2013).

Irving, R. (2012) 'Not good enough', *FS Focus*, July/August, pp 12–14.

National Audit Office (NAO) (2013) *Recent developments in government internal audit and assurance – Spring 2013* (see http://www.nao.org.uk/wp-content/uploads/2013/04/Recent-developments-in-internal-audit-spring-2013.pdf, accessed 30 July 2013).

(PSIAS) (2012) *Public Sector Internal Audit Standards*, ISBN 978 1 84508 356 4, December 2012, effective from 1 April 2013, (see http://www.iia.org.uk/media/76020/public_sector_internal_audit_standards_2012.pdf, accessed 14 July 2013).

Sarens, G., Decaux, L. and Lenz, R. (2012) *Combined Assurance: Case Studies on a Holistic Approach to Organizational Governance*, The Institute of Internal Auditors' Research Foundation.

Walker, D. (2009) *A review of corporate governance in UK banks and other financial industry entities*, final report, November 2009(see http://webarchive.nationalarchives.gov.uk/20130129110402/http://www.hm-treasury.gov.uk/d/walker_review_261109.pdf, accessed 2 August 2013).

Wikipedia (2013a) (see http://en.wikipedia.org/wiki/Maginot_Line, accessed 5 August 2013).

Wikipedia (2013b) (see http://en.wikipedia.org/wiki/Potemkin_village, accessed 6 August 2013).

Wikipedia (2013c) (see http://en.wikipedia.org/wiki/Goodhart's_law, accessed 9 August 2013).

Notes

1 This chapter first appeared in two parts in *Internal Auditing*, 28 (6) and 29 (1) (Thomson Reuters), as follows: Chambers, A.D. (2013) 'Maginot line, Potemkin village, Goodhart's law? Third Line of Defence – Second Thoughts Part 1', (November/December); and (2014) Part 2, (January/February).

2 '[computer centre] access control can be considered to be only one of several protective barriers. Outside perimeter control may also be appropriate. Once inside the computer area the intruder should not have it all his own way. Data should be protected in safes. Crucial data may also be encrypted. …

Is there outer perimeter control, against unauthorised access …?

Is there access control at all entry points to the computer area …?

If unauthorised access is achieved, are program and data media in safe storage?' (Chambers, 1981, pp 45 and 50).

3 IIA (2013b).

4 Federal Reserve (2013), section 5, pp 14–15.

5 CIIA (2013b), p 6.

6 'Where possible, the guidance has attempted to use layman's language to define terms open to ambiguity or differing application, e.g. "assurance", "three lines of defence" and "reporting line"' (CIIA, 2013, p5).

7 The Prudential Regulation Authority and the Financial Conduct Authority which replaced the Financial Services Authority (FSA) in 2013 as the regulatory authorities of the UK financial sector.

8 The Government proposes to amend s 172 of the Companies Act 2006 to remove shareholder primacy in respect of banks, requiring directors of banks to ensure the financial safety and soundness of the company ahead of the interests of its members.

9 'Substance' is what should be aspired to, not just 'form' (Chambers, 2012, p 349). Likewise, it is the essence of actual 'performance' which matters much more than mere 'conformance' to rules. We can say too that it is actual 'practice' which is much more significant than the laid down 'policies' of the entity:

- substance over form;
- performance over conformance;
- practice over policies.

10 'In this model, the first line consists of your business' frontline staff. They are charged with understanding their roles and responsibilities and carrying them out correctly and completely. The second line is created by the oversight function(s) made up of compliance and risk management. These functions set and police policies, define work practices and oversee the business frontlines with regard to risk and compliance. The third and final line of defence is that of auditors and directors. Both internal and external auditors regularly review both the business frontlines and the oversight functions to ensure that they are carrying out their tasks to the required level of competency. Directors receive reports from audit, oversight and the business, and will act on any items of concern from any party; they will also ensure that the three lines of defence are operating effectively and according to best practice.' (see http://www.risk.net/operational-risk-and-regulation/advertisement/1530626/the-lines-defence, accessed 14 July 2013).

11 HM Treasury, 2012, § 2.14, p 7.

12 HM Treasury, 2012, § 2.15, p 7.

13 HM Treasury, 2012, § 2.16, p 7.

14 CIIA, 2013b (§ E12 and 13) states:

'The Chief Internal Auditor should be at a senior enough level within the organisation (normally expected to be at Executive Committee or equivalent) to give him or her the appropriate standing, access and authority to challenge the Executive. Subsidiary, branch and divisional Heads of Internal Audit should also be of a seniority comparable to the senior management whose activities they are responsible for auditing.

'Internal Audit should have the right to attend and observe all or part of Executive Committee meetings and any other key management decision making fora.'

Chapter G4

New Enhanced Guidance on Internal Audit[1]

Introduction G4.1

The purpose of this chapter is to identify and compare the principal enhancements in important sets of 'guidelines' on the general practice of internal auditing that have been promulgated by respected bodies in the past year or so (Basel, 2012; IIA, 2013a; PSIAS, 2013; Federal Reserve, 2013; CIIA, 2013). The financial and public sectors are covered by these developments which amount to enhanced guidelines for internal auditing which go beyond the generally accepted global Standards of the Institute of Internal Auditors (IIA) that, in their current form, were effective from 1 January 2013. The chapter also touches on the UK's Chartered Institute of Internal Auditors' Code of Professional Conduct (CIIA, 2012).

Other sectors are starting to consider whether these enhanced guidelines have applicability beyond the financial and public sectors as a road map for strengthening internal auditing generally.

Based on a content analysis, this chapter analyses and interprets these European and US responses to the challenges facing internal auditing and compares them with the global definition of internal auditing and with the IIA's Standards whose latest changes are also reviewed (IIA, 2013a). The recent challenge to the primacy and adequacy of the IIA Standards was led by the International Federation of Accounts (IFAC) whose revised external auditing standard on using the work of internal auditors makes no mention of the IIA or its Standards (IAASB, 2012), though it uses a variant of the IIA's definition of internal auditing without attribution.

The most demanding, innovative elements of guidance in these sources are discussed in this chapter where they are cross-referenced to the tables within this chapter and provide more detail as well as precise cross-referencing to the sources.

Excluded from this chapter is an analysis of these guidelines' treatment of internal audit's interface with the regulatory process; also excluded is consideration of the IMF (2013) position, the UK's HM Treasury's Internal Audit Transformation Programme, and the UK National Audit Office's criticism of internal audit in UK central government (NAO, 2012).

Below the level of their mandatory Standards, the IIA has other material, in particular Practice Advisories, which is 'strongly recommended' rather than mandatory. While this chapter compares and contrasts a number of pronouncements by other parties which go beyond the requirements within the 'mandatory' IIA Standards, the chapter does not drill down to the level of the IIA's 'strongly recommended' guidance. Its 'strongly recommended' guidance is couched in terms that are less prescriptive than the enhanced guidelines that are the subject of this chapter and often discusses legitimate alternative approaches.

The IIA Standards are held by the IIA to be mandatory for members and candidates, and to be followed by *all* internal auditors, members or not, who perform internal audit services which correspond to the IIA definition of internal auditing. Even so, levels of conformance vary from one standard to another. At issue is whether the Standards should represent the minimum professional level of performance or should be aspirational. An aspirational yet mandatory standard is an oxymoron.

Challenge to the IIA Standards G4.2

In a 2008 debate in the House of Lords, the UK's 'senate', Lord Smith said:[2]

> 'Crucially, boards, and particularly non-executive directors need assurance independent of management, which requires a much greater enhancement of the role of internal audit, including, … the creation of a cadre of "super auditors" who can relate on even terms with board members…' (Hansard, 2008a)

A week later, in the same House, Lord Smith repeated that:[3]

> 'the function of internal audit must be strengthened.' (Hansard, 2008b)

In 2008 Lord Smith was making timely challenges which took until 2012 and 2013 to be responded to.

Now, with the emergence of the enhanced guidelines for internal auditing reviewed in this chapter, there needs to be a debate about the legitimate authority of guidelines that are more demanding than the global IIA Standards. Most of the suggested enhancements go beyond the requirements of the Standards while not being inconsistent with those Standards in most respects. For instance, overall opinions by internal audit are expressed in these enhanced guidelines as being a requirement, not merely an option as in the Standards. The question arises whether a practice that goes beyond the Standards, while not being at odds with them, should be regarded as a deviation from the Standards: an external auditor who went beyond the requirements of international Standards on auditing (ISAs) would not be held in breach of ISAs. A further issue is that where these enhanced guidelines are regarded as mandatory by regulators within the sectors to which they apply, should they have a status on a par with the IIA Standards and be incorporated into them?

Ethics and definitions

Code of Ethics G4.3

Professions have codes of ethics to be observed by their members. The IIA's Code of Ethics is unchanged since 2000 (IIA, 2000) except to update for the changed title of its Standards framework – 'International Professional Practices Framework' (IPPF). While a significant, progressive change was made in 2000 with the deletion of 'loyalty' as an ethical principle to be followed, it is concerning that the seismic corporate shockwaves since then have not led to further revision. The IIA finds it hard to break the umbilical cord which intimately connects internal auditors with management, analogous to external auditors who act as if their client is management. The concept that 'the customer is whichever party can grant or withdraw custom' is fundamental to many of the enhancements discussed in this chapter.

In the UK, spurred by the 2010 grant of a Royal Charter that carries obligations to act in the public interest, the CIIA developed a Code of Professional Conduct (CIIA, 2012) that, while incorporating verbatim the Code of Ethics (IIA, 2000), goes further by articulating the obligation of members to act in the public interest, and by defining internal audit's stakeholders as including employers, employees, investors, the business and financial community, clients, regulators and government. The grant of the Royal Charter is in itself a recognition by UK society that there is a broad public interest in internal audit that indeed extends even more broadly than to these stakeholders.

Some dispute that acting in the wider public interest is an essential tenet of a profession, or alternatively would define the professional's 'public interest' obligation in a very narrow way. For instance, Loughrey (2011, pp 48–49) recalls that in 2009 the City of London Law Society affirmed that:

> 'traditional public-interest regarding aspects of the lawyer's role … were not relevant to their members' work, and offered instead a narrow vision of the public interest that comprised protecting the interests of their business clients.'

So, for the legal profession, to act in the public interest has been interpreted as acting only in their *clients'* best interests. Even if it were legitimate for internal auditors to take such a narrow view of their public interest obligation, this would beg the question as to who is/are internal audit's client(s).

Definitions of internal auditing **G4.4**

Table 1: Definitions of internal auditing

Body/ies	Definition
IIA since 2001 (IIA, 2013a). UK Government since 2008 (HM Treasury, 2008; PSIAS 2013).	Internal auditing is an independent, objective assurance and consulting activity designed to add value and improve an organization's operations. It helps an organisation accomplish its objectives by bringing a systematic, disciplined approach to evaluate and improve the effectiveness of risk management, control, and governance processes.[1]
ISA 610 (2012)	A function of an entity that performs assurance and consulting activities designed to evaluate and improve the effectiveness of the entity's governance, risk management and internal control processes.[2]
Basel (2012)	An effective internal audit function provides independent assurance to the board of directors and senior management on the quality and effectiveness of a bank's internal control, risk management and governance systems and processes, thereby helping the board and senior management protect their organisation and its reputation.[3]

Body/ies	Definition
Federal Reserve (2013)	An effective internal audit function is a vehicle to advance an institution's safety and soundness and compliance with consumer laws and regulations and is therefore considered as part of the supervisory review process.[4]
UK Committee on Internal Audit Guidance for Financial Services (CIIA, 2013)	The primary role of internal audit should be to help the board and executive management to protect the assets, reputation and sustainability of the organisation.[5]

1 IIA (2013a).
2 ISA (2012), p 6, § 12.
3 Basel (2012), pp 2 and 4.
4 Federal Reserve (2013), section 5, pp 14–15.
5 CIIA (2013), p 6.

In view of the contemporary focus on enhancing the quality of internal audit, it is not surprising that attention is being given to whether the generally accepted definition of internal auditing adequately expresses the character of the activity (Table 1, row 1). The concept of 'protection' has been introduced into the definition of three of the enhanced guidelines (Table 1, rows 3, 4 and 5), with the protection of reputation being referred to by two of these three (Table 1, rows 3 and 5), sustainability by one (vrow 5) and internal audit as part of the supervisory process by another (Table 1, row 4).

CIIA (2013) stated:

> 'The Committee supports [the IIA's] definition, and emphasises the primary role of Internal Audit is to protect the organisation. At the discretion of the Audit Committee, Internal Audit can perform other roles and activities within the organisation, but not at the expense of helping the Board and Executive Management to protect the assets, reputation and sustainability of the organisation.'[4]

Common criticisms of the IIA definition (Table 1, row 1) are as follows:

1. It should be possible to define anything in a single sentence.
2. The definition appears to have the intention of 'selling' internal audit to stakeholders rather than solely defining what it is.
3. Although the definition is within the mandatory part of the IIA Standards, even 13 years after its introduction it reads as if it is aspirational.
4. The concept of 'protection' is at best implied only.
5. 'Risk management, control, and governance' should be rearranged (to the sequence in which they appear in the Standards themselves, starting from the largest and moving to the smallest) so as to read in this order: 'governance, risk management and control'.
6. The definition is not clear whether internal audit is concerned only with *internal* governance processes below the level of the board, or whether the board itself and the external aspects of corporate governance (eg the board's relationships with the owners) are within the scope of internal audit.

7. The definition uses dated 1990s language, such as 'add value'.
8. The definition arguably gives equal weighting to the 'assurance' and the 'consulting' roles.
9. The IIA's usage of the word 'board' does not necessarily signify the board itself, but can mean the audit committee.[5]
10. 'Governance', 'risk management' and 'control' are not mutually exclusive: internal control is an important part of risk management and risk management is an important part of governance: is there not a single term which embraces all three – eg 'governance'?
11. It is not clear whether the word 'processes' qualifies only 'governance' or is intended also to qualify 'risk management' and 'control' as well.
12. The definition uses the word 'control' rather than 'internal control' So it could construed as meaning both internal and external control, the latter being the control by stakeholders, in particular shareholders, over the entity. This construction is not intended.
13. The definition makes no suggestion that internal auditors have a public interest obligation, nor that internal auditors have a broad range of stakeholders.

Enhancements to general practice G4.5

Here we examine the principal developments in best practice promulgated recently by numerous bodies. For conciseness in this text, we refer readers to entries in the Tables accompanying this chapter. Excluded from this analysis are recommendations on the interface of internal auditors with regulators.

Basel Committee on Banking Supervision (Basel 2012) G4.6

Table 2: Basel guidance (June 2012)

1.	A bank's internal audit function must be independent of the audited activities.[1]
2.	Internal audit activities should normally be conducted by the bank's own internal audit staff.'[2]
3.	Every bank activity (including outsourced activities and a bank's subsidiaries and branches)[3] should be within the overall scope of the internal audit function.[4]
4.	Senior management should ensure that internal audit has the necessary resources.[5]
5.	The board should support the internal audit function.[6]
6.	The audit committee, or its equivalent, should oversee the bank's internal audit function on behalf of the board.[7]
7.	The internal audit function should be accountable to the board or its audit committee on all matters related to the performance of its mandate as described in the internal audit charter.[8]

8.	The audit plan should be approved by the board of directors.[9]
9.	The internal audit function should be able to discuss their views, findings and conclusions directly with the audit committee and the board of directors, thereby helping the board to oversee senior management.[10]
10.	In the interests of maintaining a capacity for critical judgement, the guidance is that internal audit staff should be periodically rotate *within* the internal audit function where practical.[11]
11.	The guidance draws attention to the risk that linking the remuneration of internal audit staff to the financial performance of the business lines may undermine internal audit independence and objectivity.[12]

1 Basel (2012), Principle 2.
2 Basel (2012), p 11; Principle 15, p 14.
3 Basel (2012), p 7.
4 Basel (2012), Principle 6. Elsewhere, the same guidance states that:
'the internal audit function must be able to perform its assignments on its own initiative in all areas and functions of the bank' (Basel, 2012, p 5).
5 Basel (2012), § 52, p 11.
6 Basel (2012), Principle 9.
7 Basel (2012), Principle 10 and Annex 2, § 1.
8 Basel (2012), Principle 12.
9 Basel (2012), p 5.
10 Basel (2012), p 4.
11 Basel (2012), pp 5 and 9.
12 Basel (2012), pp 5 and 6.

Following this guidance means that internal audit is not positioned in a part of the bank whose activities are within the scope of internal audit work (Table 2, row 1) and that its scope includes every bank activity, including bank activities that are outsourced or within subsidiaries (Table 2, row 3).

The guidance is comfortable that internal audit resources are supplied by management rather than by the board (Table 2, row 4) but requires board support and oversight of internal audit (Table 2, rows 5 and 6) and board approval of the audit plan (Table 2, row 8); in this regard Basel accepts that the board may delegate to the audit committee, but stipulates that the board of directors has final responsibility, and clearly states that internal audit is accountable to the board, not to management, for its performance as set out in the internal audit charter (Table 2, row 7).

Basel considers that internal auditing work should normally be undertaken by the bank's own staff, especially in large and international banks, but that outsourcing internal audit activities, though not the function itself, can be beneficial. Outsourced internal audit service providers are precluded by the Basel guidance from being consultants to, or external auditors of, the bank (Table 2, row 2).

Following the Basel guidance means that the head of internal audit attends at least some audit committee and board meetings to discuss internal audit views, finding and conclusions directly with both (Table 2, row 9).

Further independence issues are addressed by the guidance requiring periodic rotation of internal audit staff *within* the internal audit function (Table 2, row 10), and disapproval of internal audit remuneration being linked to the financial performance of business lines (Table 2, row 11). It is not clear whether Basel accepts that internal audit remuneration may be linked indirectly with the overall performance of the business, though it is clear that Basel acknowledges the need to avoid perverse incentives with respect to internal auditor remuneration.

IIA Standards (IIA, 2013a) G4.7

Table 3: IIA Standards 2013 changes (January 2013)

(For 'the board', read in each case 'the board of the audit committee'.)

1.	New examples of functional reporting to the board involve the board: Approving the internal audit budget and resource plan; Approving decisions regarding the appointment and removal of the chief audit executive.[1]
2.	'External assessments can be in the form of a full external assessment, or a self-assessment with independent external validation.'[2]
3.	[on developing the risk-based plan] 'after consideration of input from senior management and the board. The chief audit executive must review and adjust the plan, as necessary, in response to changes in the organization's business, risks, operations, programs, systems, and controls.'[3]
4.	New requirement for the internal audit activity to evaluate risk exposures and control adequacy with regard to 'achievement of the organization's strategic objectives'.[4]
5.	In planning an audit engagement, internal auditors must now consider the adequacy and effectiveness of the activity's governance, and opportunities to improve it.[5]
6.	When setting engagement objectives, adequate criteria are needed not just to evaluate controls but also now to evaluate governance and risk management. There is now recognition that these criteria should concern the board, not just management.[6]
7.	Better clarity that the CAE retains overall responsibility for engagement communications, even when these duties are delegated by him/her.[7]
8.	Better clarity on how the CAE should react if he/she believes management has accepted a level of risk which is unacceptable, and a new Interpretation which states: 'The identification of risk accepted by management may be observed through an assurance or consulting engagement, monitoring progress on actions taken by management as a result of prior engagements, or other means. It is not the responsibility of the chief audit executive to resolve the risk.'[8]
9.	Several changes to definitions of terms contained in the Glossary to the Standards.

[1] IIA (2013a) Std 1110, Interpretation.
[2] IIA (2013a) Std 1312, Interpretation.
[3] IIA (2013a) Std 2120.A1 and 2130.A1.
[4] IIA (2013a) Std 2010, Interpretation.
[5] IIA (2013a) Std 2201.
[6] IIA (2013a) Std 2210.
[7] IIA (2013a) Std 2440
[8] IIA (2013a) Std 2600, Interpretation.

Although the subject of a comprehensive review by the International Internal Audit Standards Board (IIASB), including a global consultation, the latest release of updated Standards by the IIA included few significant enhancements. This is not unrelated to the demanding process that any professional body has to follow in order to amend their standards, which does not apply to the same extent to the other bodies that have developed the enhanced guidelines reviewed in this chapter. It is also to do with the IIA Standards being global, tending to result in 'lowest common denominator' pronouncements. Then there is the issue of the varied degree of conformance with different IIA standards and the minimal enforcement powers of the professional body that nevertheless regards its single set of Standards as mandatory: if mandatory but unenforceable, they cannot get too far in front of current practice.

While the IIA Standards always refer to 'the board' rather than to 'the audit committee', the 2013 definition of 'the board', as this term is used in the Standards makes it clear that 'the board' can, in every case, optionally be interpreted as meaning 'the audit committee'. So there is no standard which requires any aspect of internal audit's relationship to be with the board itself rather than with the board's audit committee.

The 2013 Standards now require that the board or the audit committee approves the internal audit budget and resource plan and approves decisions relating to the appointment and removal of the chief audit executive (CAE) (Table 3, row 1). These Standards clarify that the CAE takes account of inputs from senior management and the board (or the audit committee) when drawing up a risk-based plan of audit engagements, but that the plan should be based on the CAE's own professional judgement, and should be adjusted if circumstances change (Table 3, row 3).

'Strategy' is now within the Standards to the extent that internal audit must evaluate risk and control exposures to meeting the organisation's strategic objectives (Table 3, row 4). It is therefore opaque as to whether internal audit has a role in challenging strategic decisions, or the processes followed and information used in formulating strategy.

At the level of each audit engagement, there is a new emphasis on the adequacy and effectiveness of governance and risk management and opportunities to improve these, and also an acknowledgement that internal audit may need to work with the board to develop appropriate evaluation criteria on these matters as well as on control (Table 3, rows 5 and 6).

Clarification has been given on the CAE's responsibility for engagement communications (Table 3, row 7) and for communicating internally about risks that the CAE has concluded are unacceptable (Table 3, rows 8 and 9). Despite the global financial crisis and more recent scandals, IIA Standards are still conspicuously silent on the circumstances and manner in which internal auditors might make disclosures in the public interest to parties other than management, boards and regulators (the latter as required by law).

There has been a relaxation with respect to external assessments of internal audit quality, in that these may now be in the form of self-assessment with independent external validation (Table 3, row 2).

UK public sector (PSIAS, 2013) G4.8

Table 4: UK public sector guidance (effective from 1 April 2013)

1.	(Code of Ethics) Conformance by internal auditors to the Codes of Ethics of other professional bodies to which they belong is also required.[1]
2.	(Code of Ethics) Disciplinary procedures of other professional bodies and employing organisations may apply to breaches of the Code of Ethics.[2]
3.	(Code of Ethics on Competency) Public sector internal auditors must also have regard to the UK's Seven Principles of Public Life.[3,5,6]
4.	(Interpretation to Std 1000) The internal audit charter must also: ● define the terms 'board' and 'senior management' for the purposes of internal audit activity; ● cover the arrangements for appropriate resourcing; ● define the role of internal audit in any fraud-related work; and ● include arrangements for avoiding conflicts of interest if internal audit undertakes non-audit activities.[4]
5.	(Interpretation to Std 1110) The chief audit executive must report functionally to the board. The chief audit executive must also establish effective communication with, and have free and unfettered access to, the chief executive (or equivalent) and the chair of the audit committee.
6.	(Interpretation to Std 1110) Governance requirements in the UK public sector would not generally involve the board approving the CAE's remuneration specifically. The underlying principle is that the independence of the CAE is safeguarded by ensuring that his or her remuneration or performance assessment is not inappropriately influenced by those subject to audit. In the UK public sector this can be achieved by ensuring that the chief executive (or equivalent) undertakes, countersigns, contributes feedback to or reviews the performance appraisal of the CAE and that feedback is also sought from the chair of the audit committee.
7.	(Std 1130.C2) Approval must be sought from the board for any significant additional consulting services not already included in the audit plan, prior to accepting the engagement.
8.	(Interpretation to Std 1210) The chief audit executive must hold a professional qualification (CMIIA, CCAB or equivalent) and be suitably experienced.

9.	(Interpretation to Std 1312)The chief audit executive must agree the scope of external assessments with an appropriate sponsor, eg the Accounting/Accountable Officer or chair of the audit committee as well as with the external assessor or assessment team.
10.	(Interpretation to Std 1320) Progress against any improvement plans, agreed following external assessment, must be reported in the annual report.
11.	(Std 1322) Instances of non-conformance must be reported to the board. More significant deviations must be considered for inclusion in the governance statement.
12.	(Interpretation to Std 2010)The risk-based plan must take into account the requirement to produce an annual internal audit opinion and the assurance framework. It must incorporate or be linked to a strategic or high-level statement of how the internal audit service will be delivered and developed in accordance with the internal audit charter and how it links to the organisational objectives and priorities.
13.	(Interpretation to Std 2030)The risk-based plan must explain how internal audit's resource requirements have been assessed.
14.	(Interpretation to Std 2030) Where the chief audit executive believes that the level of agreed resources will impact adversely on the provision of the annual internal audit opinion, the consequences must be brought to the attention of the board.
15.	(Std 2050) The chief audit executive must include in the risk-based plan the approach to using other sources of assurance and any work required to place reliance upon those other sources.
16.	(Std 2210.A3) In the public sector, criteria are likely to include value for money.
17.	(Interpretation to Std 2450)The chief audit executive must deliver an annual internal audit opinion and report that can be used by the organisation to inform its governance statement. The annual internal audit opinion must conclude on the overall adequacy and effectiveness of the organisation's framework of governance, risk management and control. The annual report must incorporate: ● the opinion; ● a summary of the work that supports the opinion; and ● a statement on conformance with the Public Sector Internal Audit Standards and the results of the quality assurance and improvement programme.

1 PSIAS (2013), p 10.

2 PSIAS (2013), p 10

3 PSIAS (2013), p 12.

4 Nolan (1994): The Committee on Standards in Public Life ('the Nolan Committee') was set up in October 1994 by the UK government as a standing body 'To examine concerns about standards of conduct of all holders of public office, including arrangements relating to financial and commercial activities, and make recommendations as to any

changes … to ensure the highest standards of propriety in public life.' Its first report was published in May 1995. In that report the Committee restated the general principles of conduct which the Committee considered underpin public life, and these are set out in this note in Table 1. The Committee recommended that all public bodies should draw up Codes of Conduct incorporating these seven principles. For the principle of 'Openness' the Committee suggested a standard for such a Code, which we reproduce as Table 2. It is interesting to note that in 1992 the report of the Committee on the Financial Aspects of Corporate Governance ('the Cadbury Committee') had stated that their Code of Best Practice was based on three of these principles of 'openness, integrity and accountability'.

5 The Nolan Principles are:

Selflessness

Holders of public office should act solely in terms of the public interest. They should not do so in order to gain financial or other benefits for themselves, their family or their friends.

Integrity

Holders of public office should not place themselves under any financial or other obligation to outside individuals or organisations that might seek to influence them in the performance of their official duties.

Objectivity

In carrying out public business, including making public appointments, awarding contracts, or recommending individuals for rewards and benefits, holders of public office should make choices on merit.

Accountability

Holders of public office are accountable for their decisions and actions to the public and must submit themselves to whatever scrutiny is appropriate to their office.

Openness

Holders of public office should be as open as possible about all the decisions and actions that they take. They should give reasons for their decisions and restrict information only when the wider public interest clearly demands.

Honesty

Holders of public office have a duty to declare any private interests relating to their public duties and to take steps to resolve any conflicts arising in a way that protects the public interest.

Leadership

Holders of public office should promote and support these principles by leadership and example.

Under the coordination of the CIIA, and effective from 1 April 2013, these new Standards have replaced separate sets of Standards that had applied in the UK respectively to central government, the National Health Service and local government entities.[6] Whilst those disbanded Standards inevitably had some commonality with the IIA's global Standards, they were not the same. Now these new Standards are *verbatim* identical to those of the IIA. The publication (PSIAS, 2013) incorporates a Code of Ethics, also identical to that of the IIA.

Differences are limited to new highlighted text boxes that provide interpretations tailored for the UK public sector. Sometimes these amount to enhancements of the requirements built into the IIA Standards themselves. Table 5 is a summary of the enhancements (and, arguably in some cases, modifications without enhancement) and indicates the IIA Standard to which the adjustment applies. Note that most of the enhancements relate to Interpretations already in the IIA Standards which arguably are at a lower level than the Standards they interpret – although Interpretations form part of the Standards and are held by the IIA to be equally as mandatory as the Standards they relate to.

Some additional terms have been defined in the Public Sector Internal Audit Standards (PSIAS) Glossary to the Standards. In one case a definition has been modified: 'IPPF' (International Professional Practices Framework) is defined as comprising only the mandatory and not the other parts of the IIA's IPPF, indicating that the UK public sector has adopted the definition of internal auditing, the Code of Ethics and the Standards but not the other elements of the IPPF, such as the Practice Advisories.

PSIAS elaborates the requirements of the global Code of Ethics of the IIA in a number of ways, but not by adopting the additional wording to be found in the Code of Professional Conduct (CIIA, 2012). Notably the UK's Nolan seven principles of public life are incorporated, and the authority of the codes of ethics of other bodies is recognised (Table 4, rows 1, 2, 3).

PSIAS elaborates upon the IIA Standards in respect of essential content for the internal audit charter (Table 4, row 4). There is no elaboration within PSIAS on the scope of internal audit work, other than to indicate that 'value for money' is a public sector audit consideration at the level of audit engagements (Table 4, row 16), though this is already referred to elsewhere in the IIA Standards[7]

PSIAS highlights that set out in the risk-based internal audit plan should be the approach of internal audit to making use of other sources of assurance (Table 4, row 15).

IIA Standards already require that consulting engagements must be included in the risk-based plan of audit engagements.[8] PSIAS now specifies that additional internal auditing consulting services should be approved by the board prior to acceptance (Table 4, row 7).

A key differentiation is the approach to approval of CAE remuneration. While IIA Standards already require that the board or the audit committee approves this,[9] PSIAS is content that the CEO may do so (Table 4, row 6). The weak public sector rationale for this is that the CEO, as the accounting officer, is part of the corporate governance oversight of the entity. Internal audit exists to provide assurance to the accounting officer as well as to the board.

PSIAS stipulates that CAEs must have particular professional qualifications and experience (Table 4, row 8). Requisite internal audit resources must be assessed in the light of the provision of the annual internal audit opinion which is mandatory and must be published: this opinion must conclude on the overall adequacy and effectiveness of the organisation's framework of governance, risk management and control (Table 4, rows 12, 13, 14 and 17).

There is no requirement for administrative reporting to be to the board or the audit committee rather than to management, but functional reporting is to be to the board. Since PSIAS has adopted the IIA's definition of 'board' this requirement is discharged if functional reporting by internal audit is to the audit committee. As with the Federal Reserve, there is a cogent requirement that there should be free and unfettered access to the chair of the audit committee and also to the CEO (Table 4, row 5).

Extensions of requirements with respect to external quality assessments are that the results of a quality assessment must appear in the annual report of the entity and that significant deviations from the PSIAS Standards should be considered for inclusion in the governance statement of the entity which is also published (Table 4, rows 9, 10 and 11).

Federal Reserve **G4.9**

Table 5: Federal Reserve guidance (January 2013)

1.	If the chief audit executive (CAE) reports administratively to someone other than the CEO, the audit committee should document its rationale for this reporting structure, including mitigating controls available for situations that could adversely impact the objectivity of the CAE.[1]
2.	Internal audit management should perform knowledge gap assessments at least annually to evaluate whether current staff members have the knowledge and skills commensurate with the institution's strategy and operations.[2]
3.	Internal auditors should generally receive a minimum of forty hours of training in a given year.[3]
4.	Institutions are encouraged to incorporate professional standards such as the IIA guidance into their overall internal audit architecture.[4]
5.	An institution's internal audit function should have a code of ethics that emphasizes the principles of objectivity, competence, confidentiality, and integrity, consistent with professional internal audit guidance such as the code of ethics established by the IIA.[5]
6.	The internal audit charter should define the criteria for when and how the internal audit function may outsource some of its work to external experts.[6]
7.	The audit committee and its chairperson should have on-going interaction with the CAE separate from formally scheduled meetings to remain current on any internal audit department, organisational, or industry concerns.[7]
8.	Where there is an administrative reporting of the CAE to senior management, the objectivity of internal audit is served best when the CAE reports administratively to the chief executive officer (CEO).[8]
9.	Compensation schemes for internal audit should not provide incentives for internal auditors to act contrary to the attributes and objectives of the internal audit function.[9]
10.	(The audit committee should receive an) opinion on the adequacy of risk management processes, including effectiveness of management's self-assessment and remediation of identified issues (at least annually).[10]
11.	Internal audit's risk-assessment methodology is an integral part of the evaluation of overall policies, procedures, and controls at the institution and the development of a plan to test those processes.[11]
12.	The (risk assessment) methodology should also address the role of continuous monitoring in determining and evaluating risk.[12]

13.	Internal audit should analyse the effectiveness of all critical risk management functions both with respect to individual risk dimensions (for example, credit risk), and an institution's overall risk management function.[13]
14.	Internal audit recommendations may include restricting business activity in affected lines of business until effective policies, procedures, and controls are designed and implemented.[14]
15.	Internal audit should review significant infrastructure enhancements.[15]
16.	Internal audit should evaluate governance at all management levels.[16]
17.	The audit universe should be documented and reviewed periodically as significant organisational changes occur or at least during the annual audit planning process.[17]
18.	Generally, common practice for institutions with defined audit cycles is to follow either a three- or four-year audit cycle; high-risk areas should be audited at least every twelve to eighteen months.[18]
19.	Internal audit's well-developed risk-assessment methodology should take account of risk identification techniques that the institution's management utilizes such as a risk and control self-assessment (RCSA).[19]
20.	Internal audit is encouraged to utilise formal continuous monitoring practices as part of the function's risk-assessment processes to support adjustments to the audit plan or universe as they occur.[20]
21.	A well-designed, comprehensive quality assurance program should ensure that internal audit activities conform to the IIA's professional standards and the institution's internal audit policies and procedures. The program should include both internal and external quality assessments.[21]
22.	Each institution should conduct an internal quality assessment annually and the CAE should report the results and status of internal assessments to senior management and the audit committee at least annually.[22]
23.	The audit committee and the CAE are responsible for the selection and retention of internal audit vendors and should be aware of factors that may impact vendors' competence and ability to deliver high-quality audit services.[23]
24.	When an institution relies significantly on the resources of an internal audit service provider, the institution should have contingency procedures for managing temporary or permanent disruptions in the service in order to ensure that the internal audit function can meet its intended objectives.[24]
25.	In addition and separately there is a prohibition on the external auditor providing internal audit services to the same client.[25]
26.	Audit reports must include audit's conclusions.[26]

1 Federal Reserve (2013) 2.A. p 5.
2 Federal Reserve (2013) 2.A. p 5.
3 Federal Reserve (2013) 2.A. p 6.

4 Federal Reserve (2013) p 2 and 2. at p 4.
5 Federal Reserve (2013) 2.A. p 6.
6 Federal Reserve (2013) 2.A. p 6.
7 Federal Reserve (2013) 2.B. p 7.
8 Federal Reserve (2013) 2.A. p 5.
9 Federal Reserve (2013) 2.A. p 6.
10 Federal Reserve (2013) 2.B. p 8.
11 Federal Reserve (2013) 2.C. p 8.
12 Federal Reserve (2013) 2.C. p 8.
13 Federal Reserve (2013) 1.A. p 3.
14 Federal Reserve (2013) 1.C. p 3.
15 Federal Reserve (2013) 1.D. p 3.
16 Federal Reserve (2013) 1.F. p 4.
17 Federal Reserve (2013) 2.C. p 9.
18 Federal Reserve (2013) 2.C. p 10.
19 Federal Reserve (2013) 2.C. p 8.
20 Federal Reserve (2013) 2.C. p 10.
21 Federal Reserve (2013) 2.D. p 12.
22 Federal Reserve (2013) 2.D. p 12.
23 Federal Reserve (2013) 3.A. p 15.
24 Federal Reserve (2013) 3.B. p 15.
25 SEC (March 2003).
26 Federal Reserve (2013) 2.D. p 11.

Mirroring European and UK concerns about the quality of internal auditing in the banking sector, in January 2013 the US Federal Reserve strengthened their internal audit guidance for institutions with total consolidated assets of $(US)10 billion or more.[10] The Federal Reserve starts by stating that its supplemental guidance:

> 'discusses the enhancements that an institution should incorporate into its internal audit function to address lessons learned from the recent financial crisis.'[11]

and:

> 'An institution's internal audit function should incorporate the following enhanced practices into their overall processes'

This guidance explicitly encourages those the Federal Reserve regulates to observe the Code of Ethics and Standards of the IIA (Table 5, rows 4 and 5). Concern is implicit about the quality of internal auditors with guidance that gap assessments should be made at least annually to evaluate the knowledge and skills of internal audit staff members commensurate with the organization's strategy and operations, and that internal auditors should generally have at least forty hours of training each year (Table 5, rows 2 and 3). As with other guidance discussed in this chapter (Basel, 2012; CIIA, 2013), the Federal Reserve eschews compensation schemes for internal auditors which introduce perverse incentives (Table 5, row 9).

This guidance extends what is usually within the scope of internal audit to include significant infrastructure enhancements and governance at all management levels (Table 5, rows 15 and 16). It stipulates that 'all critical risk management functions' must be audited (Table 5, row 13): the requirement is not merely that they should all be within the internal audit universe, but that they should all be audited. The guidance requires that the internal audit universe is documented and that it is revised for changes at least during the annual audit planning process (Table 5, row 17). There is no mention of the audit universe in the IIA Standards, although Std 2010 requires a risk assessment to be conducted at least annually as part of the audit planning process.

(The usage of the word 'management' in this guidance seems to embrace the board as well as management.)

The Federal Reserve's guidance is that audit engagements be planned into a three- or four-year cyclical approach with high-risk areas being audited at least every 12 or 18 months (Table 5, row 18) – again, an approach where the IIA Standards are silent. The resurgence of a cyclical approach to auditing, abandoned in the past by many internal audit functions in preference for a more *ad hoc* approach, is a noticeable feature of this guidance.

This guidance stresses the importance of internal audit's risk assessment, usefully pointing out that the methodology that internal audit uses for this should be regarded as an integral part of the evaluation of overall policies, procedures and controls (Table 5, row 11), seemingly blurring the distinction between the second and third lines in the 'three lines of defence' paradigm which, in contrast to Basel (2012), the Federal Reserve does not overtly use (Booz (2008); Hughes (2011); Anderson and Daugherty (2012); IIA (2013b).

Quite innovatively, the Federal Reserve stresses that 'continuous monitoring' should be part of internal audit's risk-assessment and be capable of adjusting the audit universe and plan (Table 5, rows 12 and 20): again, this blurs the distinction between the lines of defence as 'continuous monitoring' could be construed as being a management or a second line responsibility. It is interesting that 'continuous monitoring' is not being promoted by the Federal Reserve as being part of the performance of audit engagements, but rather as part of internal audit's risk-assessment. The Federal Reserve endorses the potential value of risk and control self-assessment (RCSA) and requires that internal audit's risk-assessment methodology takes account of this and other risk identification techniques in use by management (Table 5, row 19) – again, this is explicitly stated as part of internal audit's risk assessment, not as part of the performance of an audit engagement.

Many internal auditors will find it challenging to implement the Federal Reserve's requirement that internal audit recommendations may include advice to restrict business activity pending implementation of effective policies, procedures and controls (Table 5, row 14), but this is surely correct guidance.

The guidance requires internal audit to provide overall and engagement level opinions, in contrast to the IIA Standards which make these discretionary. The Federal Reserve requires that the audit committee should receive from internal audit an opinion on the adequacy of the organisation's risk management processes (which would include the adequacy of internal control) (Table 5, row 10); and audit engagement reports must include conclusions (Table 5, row 26). The IIA Standards are clear that a conclusion at the audit engagement level is a form of engagement opinion.[12]

This guidance prefers that CAEs may report for all purposes, including administratively, to the audit committee, but that where there is a secondary reporting line this is best to the CEO and if it is to someone else the audit committee should document the rationale for this (Table 5, rows 1 and 8). The audit committee and its chair should have ongoing interaction with the CAE, separate from audit committee meetings (Table 5, row 7).

The guidance aligns with the IIA Standards on internal audit quality assurance, except for the enhancement that internal quality assessments should be done at least annually (Table 5, rows 21 and 22).

The Federal Reserve has a lot to say about outsourcing internal audit services. Although not taking the line of Basel (2012) that internal auditing should normally be undertaken by the bank's own staff, the Federal Reserve enunciates numerous safeguards when internal audit is outsourced. First, the internal audit charter should define the criteria for when and how outsourcing may occur (Table 5, row 6). Secondly, outsourcing should be a matter for the audit committee and the CAE, implying that the CAE role should not be outsourced (Table 5, row 23). Thirdly, vendor competence is important (Table 5, row 23). Fourthly, there should be contingency plans for disruption of outsourced services (Table 5, row 24). Finally, internal audit services should not be outsourced to the external auditor (Table 5, row 25).

UK Internal Audit Guidance for Financial Services (CIIA, 2013) G4.10

Table 6: UK Financial Services guidance (July 2013)

1.	The Committee states that internal audit should not second guess decisions of the board but legitimately may draw attention to information or process inadequacies which have underpinned board decisions.[1] Internal audit scope should be unlimited. For instance the following should be within the internal audit universe: • The design and operating effectiveness of internal governance structures.[2] • The information presented to the Board for strategic and operational decision making.[3] • The setting of, and adherence to, risk appetite (though internal audit is not responsible for setting the risk appetite).[4] • The risk and control culture of the organisation, and whether the processes are in line with the values, ethics, risk appetite and policies of the organisation.[5] • Risks of poor customer treatment – whether the organisation is acting with integrity in its dealings with customers and its interaction with relevant markets.[6] • The management of the organisation's capital and liquidity ratios.[7] • Key corporate events (eg new products/services, outsourcing decisions, acquisitions/divestments).[8] • Outcomes of processes (design and operating effectiveness of policies and processes).[9] • The adequacy and effectiveness of the Risk management, Compliance and Finance functions.[10]
2.	The Institute of Internal Auditors should develop or adopt additional guidance in particular with respect to less well established areas of internal audit activity such as auditing culture and outcomes.[11]

3.	The Committee recognises the growing importance of board risk committees comprising independent directors and recommends that internal audit should issue reports to this committee, to the board audit committee and to other board committees as appropriate. In exceptional circumstances the Board may wish Internal Audit to the Chairman of the Board Risk Committee, provided the Chairman and members of this Committee are all independent directors.[12]
4.	At least annually internal audit should provide the board risk and audit committees with an assessment of the overall effectiveness of the governance and risk and control framework together with an analysis of themes and trends emerging from internal audit work and their impact on the organisation's risk profile.[13]
5.	Internal audit should be independent of the risk management, compliance and finance functions and should evaluate their effectiveness before placing reliance on them.[14].
6.	Striking recommendations are that internal audit should have a right to attend all or part of any key management fora including the Executive Committee and that the head of internal audit should usually be at Executive Committee level.[15]
7.	In response to criticism that the draft guidance had said that the primary reporting line of the chief internal auditors should be to the chairman of the board who might delegate it to the chairman of the audit committee, the final guidance now states: 'The primary reporting line for the Chief Internal Auditor should be to the Chairman of the Audit Committee. In exceptional circumstances, the Board may wish for Internal Audit to report directly to the Chairman of the Board, or delegate responsibility for the reporting line to the Chairman of the Board Risk Committee, provided the Chairman of the Board Risk Committee and all the other Committee members are independent Non-Executive Directors. … If Internal Audit has a secondary Executive reporting line, this should be to the CEO in order to preserve independence from any particular business area or function and to establish the standing of Internal Audit alongside Executive Committee members.'[16]
8.	The guidance is that the audit committee appoints and removes the chief internal auditor and approves the internal audit budget; and that the chairman of the audit committee sets the chief internal auditor's objectives, appraises his/her performance and recommends his/her remuneration.[17]
9.	The chief internal auditor may not have a secondary reporting line to the executive, but if he/she has, it should be to the CEO.[18]
10.	The final guidance has removed the requirement that large internal audit functions should have their own quality assurance function *independent of the conduct of any audit work*. Instead the guidance says that internal quality assurance of internal audit work should be done by auditors who are independent of the audit engagements being reviewed.[19]

11.	Subsidiary, branch and divisional Heads of Internal Audit should report primarily to the Group Chief Internal Auditor, while recognising local legislation or regulation as appropriate. This includes the responsibility for setting budgets and remuneration, conducting appraisals and reviewing the audit plan. The Group Chief Internal Auditor should consider the independence, objectivity and tenure of the subsidiary, branch or divisional Heads of Internal Audit when performing their appraisals.[20]
12.	The internal audit charter should be publicly available.[21]

1 CIIA (2013), p 6, § 3, 6a and 6b.
2 CIIA (2013), p 6, § 6a.
3 CIIA (2013), p 6, § 6b.
4 CIIA (2013), p 7, § 6c.
5 CIIA (2013), p 7, § 6d.
6 CIIA (2013), p 7, § 6e.
7 CIIA (2013), p 7, § 6f.
8 CIIA (2013), p 7, § 6g.
9 CIIA (2013), p 7, §6h.
10 CIIA (2013), p 10, § [D]10.
11 CIIA (2013), p 10, §30.
12 CIIA (2013), p 8, § [C]7; and p 9, §[E]15.
13 CIIA (2013), p 8, §[C]8.
14 CIIA (2013), p 8, § [D]9-11.
15 CIIA (2013), p 8, § [E]12 and 13.
16 CIIA (2013), p9, § [E]15.
17 CIIA (2013), p 9, § [F]16, 17, 18 and 23.
18 CIIA (2013), p 9, § [E]20.
19 CIIA (2013), p 10, § [G]26.
20 CIIA (2013), p9, § [E]19.
21 CIIA (2013), Guidance, [A], p 6 Basis for conclusions, [A], p 11.

This committee was set up by the CIIA in response to overtures from the regulator, the UK's Financial Services Authority (FSA), when Richard Thorpe was head of accounting, audit and regulatory reporting policy at the FSA. The committee deliberated and reported independently from the CIIA. Thorpe had been quoted as saying:

> 'I can't point to the internal audit function of a single bank or insurer and say, with hand on heart, that is how we envision it being done in the future.'

and:

> 'There exist generic industry Standards and practices, but none are sufficiently robust to address the complex world of financial services firms.' (Irving, 2012)

The committee reported in final form in July 2013 (CIIA, 2013). It is likely that the UK regulator will adopt these new guidelines as being mandatory for UK financial entities.

Because of the disquiet about the concept of 'three lines of defence' expressed by the UK Parliamentary Commission on Banking shortly before this Committee reported, references to 'three lines of defence' were removed from the Committee's final report (HLHC, 2013a; 2013b, p 138 *et al*).

The committee's 'definition' of internal audit, which we referred to earlier in this chapter, has attracted attention as it is distinctive from that of the IIA. The committee says:

> 'The primary role of Internal Audit should be to help the Board and Executive Management to protect the assets, reputation and sustainability of the organisation.' (CIIA, 2013).

Unlike PSIAS (2013), CIIA (2013) has much to say about internal audit scope. Many would glibly that internal audit scope should be unlimited. CIIA (2013) concurs[13] and acknowledges that while:

> 'While it is common for Internal Audit Charters to mandate an unrestricted scope, some Internal Audit functions do not include in their audit universe or risk assessments some of the processes, risks and events that were central to the problems faced by the financial services sector in recent years. The Committee agrees with the principle of an unrestricted scope, and, for the avoidance of doubt, the guidance set out areas of scope which were found to have been restricted in some organisations, in practice even if not in principle.'[14]

While the guidance asserts that internal audit should not second guess the boards, inadequacies of information or processes that have underpinned board decisions should be within scope (Table 6, row 1). Table 6 (row 2) sets out the most challenging of these areas, and CIIA (2013) recommends that the IIA should develop or adopt additional guidance with respect to the less established areas of audit activity such as auditing culture, and auditing customer and other outcomes (Table 6, row 3).

The guidance states that internal audit should be independent of the risk management and compliance functions, and also should be independent of the finance function (Table 6, row 6), not least in order to facilitate objective auditing of these activates.

There is no doubt that this guidance supports overall opinions by internal audit, at least annually, to include an assessment of the overall effectiveness of the governance and risk and control framework, together with an analysis of themes and trends impacting the organisation's risk profile (Table 6, row 5).

The guidance seeks to loosen internal audit's ties with management, suggesting that there may be a reporting line for all purposes to the audit committee of the board, or even to the chair of the board; and that if there is a reporting line to the executive, it should be a secondary reporting line and should be to the CEO (Table 6, rows 8, 10). The audit committee is to appoint and remove the chief internal auditor and approve the internal audit budget (Table 6, row 9); the chairman of the audit committee sets the chief internal auditor's objectives, appraises his/her performance and recommends his/her remuneration (Table 6, row 9):

> 'The Chairman of the Audit Committee should be responsible for recommending the remuneration of the Chief Internal Auditor to the Remuneration Committee.'[15]

Similar to Federal Reserve guidance:

> 'The remuneration of the Chief Internal Auditor should be structured in a manner such that it avoids conflicts of interest, does not impair independence and objectivity and should not be directly or exclusively linked to the short term performance of the organisation'.[16]

CIIA (2013) elaborated:

> 'The Committee received feedback relating to the interpretation of the recommendation relating to the remuneration of Chief Internal Auditor. The guidance is consistent with existing regulatory guidance around the remuneration of personnel working in the control functions of financial institutions. The Committee did not deem it necessary to prescribe additional guidance in this area.'[17]

The committee has taken on board the development since the global financial crisis of risk committees of the board comprising mainly or exclusively of independent directors, as distinct from risk committees at an executive level (Walker, 2009; FRC, 2012, provision C.3.2), even to the extent of support for reporting of internal audit to the risk committee of the board instead of to the audit committee in exceptional circumstances (Table 6, row 12). Justification for this might exist if the audit committee is preoccupied with financial reporting and external audit matters, if the scope of the board risk committee's oversight corresponds more closely to the scope of internal auditing, if the board's risk committee comprises exclusively independent directors, and if the board's risk committee has a maturity and an understanding of internal audit matters at a level we would expect of an audit committee.

Subsidiary, branch and divisional heads of internal audit are to report primarily to the group head of internal audit (Table 6, row 20).

An important part of this guidance is that the chief internal auditor should have a right to attend key management fora, including the executive committee (Exco), and that the chief internal auditors should usually be at Exco level (Table 6, row 7).

The final guidance removed the requirement that large internal audit functions should have their own quality assurance function *independent of the conduct of any audit work*. Instead the guidance says that internal quality assurance of internal audit work should be undertaken by auditors who are independent of the audit engagements being reviewed (Table 6, row 11).

General conclusions **G4.11**

It is impractical in these conclusions to adequately collate all the main directions of travel indicated in the enhanced guidelines we have reviewed in this chapter.

It is apparent that there has slowly emerged a general perception that internal audit is one of the gatekeepers that failed to prevent the global financial crisis. Subsequent scandals, such as the London Interbank Offered Rate (LIBOR) rate fixing saga, suggest that the internal audit house has yet to be put in order. It is not surprising that the attention of regulators has now turned to internal audit.

Internal audit needs to raise its game. The enhanced guidelines reviewed in this chapter are amongst the threats to the authority of the IIA Standards. They are signposts for the direction of travel by the IIA.

Not all is bad news. For instance, in 2007 the global Association of Chartered Certified Accountants adopted the IIA Standards as applicable to their members.

That adoption, and the 2013 adoption of the IIA Standards by the UK public sector (PSIAS, 2013), are endorsements of the IIA Standards, to be set alongside the challenges to these Standards which are the subject of this chapter. Furthermore Basel (2012) encourages bank internal auditors to comply with and contribute to the development of the IIA Standards,[24] the Federal Reserve (2013) also encourages adoption of them[25] and the UK Internal Audit Guidance for Financial Services (CIIA, 2013) states that its aim is to build on those Standards.[26] It is up to the IIA to reassert itself.

The public interest is insufficiently taken account of in the IIA Standards. There is, and has been for many years, an unaddressed public interest. The wider public is indeed showing an interest (eg Hansard, 2008a, 2008b; HLHC, 2013a, 2013b, p138 *et al*).

As internal audit matures as a profession, its Standards cannot continue to be monopolised by its members. Currently, each member of their IIASB is a member of the IIA.

Using external auditing as the case study, Jeppesen (2010, p197) noted that standard-setting processes tend to evolve over time as professions mature. Internal auditing needs to move up from the bottom rung of Jeppesen's four-rung ladder.

> 'The first generation is a standard-setting board composed of … experts, usually appointed by the professional body …' (Jeppesen, 2010, p 195)

and:

> 'In the fourth generation of auditing standard setting, external user groups … participate on equal terms with accountants in the standard-setting work … ranging from a single representative to giving users the majority. In case there is still reason to doubt whether the standard-setting board works in the public interest and/or where governments want to raise the juridical status of auditing Standards to mandatory directives, auditing standard setting may finally be relocated from the private sector to the public sector.'

From 2010, the IIA has had an IPPF Oversight Council with the majority of its members being 'representatives nominated from different organizations in the stakeholder community'. This is a step in the right direction, but this Council does not set internal auditing Standards. Furthermore its members are drawn from a narrow band of market participant bodies unlikely to represent adequately the wider public interest.

The general tenor of the developments discussed in this chapter is that internal audit must be more effective at filling the board's assurance vacuum, and can be so with a stronger reporting line to the board (Chambers, 2008a, 2008b, 2009). Loosening internal audit's reporting relationship with management so that it becomes a *secondary* reporting line at most, does not impede the level of assurance that internal audit can provide to management: the assurance is all the better if it comes from a party that has a measure of independence from those to whom the assurance is being given. The quality of assurance to boards is seriously weak if it comes from a party whose primary reporting line is below the level of the board. Internal audit being positioned within one of the functional areas of the business, such as within finance, is now rejected as being totally unsatisfactory even though it is still quite common place. To use the internal audit profession's own 'three lines of defence' model, the closer internal audit is to management (whether the CFO or the CEO) the more it becomes part of the second rather than the third line of defence.

Management has its own second line of defence to provide it assurance that governance, risk management and internal control are working well. The board needs internal audit, as the third line of defence (or at least an important part of the third line of defence), to provide the board with independent assurance about the first and second lines of defence.

There are internal audit resource implications in these developments. When the CAE has the status of a member of the Exco, which he/she attends, this implies a calibre of person in that role that exceeds common practice in many cases today. Whether or not the term 'super auditors' is acceptable (Chambers, 2008a), to audit effectively with a significantly enhanced audit scope and perhaps annual coverage of all key risk areas, requires in general a significantly enhanced quality and perhaps quantity of internal audit staff. We have noted there is no section within the IIA Standards that, for the avoidance of doubt, itemises the scope of internal audit (see, eg CIIA, 2013, pp 6–7).

Apart from implementing the new enhanced guidelines, these new guidelines themselves may need to be further extended. The advent of risk committees of the board suggests that in the future these committees may sometimes assume the responsibilities for internal audit now being recommended for audit committees of the board. Another future scenario is that the CAE's primary or sole reporting line for all purposes may morph to the chairman of the board, with the cost of the internal audit function being regarded as one of the costs of running the board. Currently, IIA Standard 1000 counsels administrative reporting to management.

References

Anderson, U. and Daugherty, B. (2012) 'The Third Line of Defense: Internal Audit's Role in the Governance Process', *Internal Auditing,* July/August, pp 38–41.

Basel Committee on Banking Supervision (Basel) (2012), *The Internal Audit Function in Banks*, Bank of International Settlements, June 2012 (see http://www.bis.org/publ/bcbs223.pdf, accessed 14 July 2013).

Booz (2008) Teschner, C., Golder, P. and Liebert, T., *Bringing Back Best Practices in Risk Management: Banks' Three Lines Of Defense*, Booz & Company, (see http://www.booz.com/media/file/Bringing-Back-Best-Practices-in-Risk-Management.pdf, accessed 5 August 2013).

Chambers, A.D. (2008a) 'Bring on the super auditors', *Internal Auditing*, 32 (12), pp 18–21.

Chambers, A.D. (2008b) 'The board's black hole – filling their assurance vacuum: can internal audit rise to the challenge?', *Measuring Business Excellence – The Journal of Business Performance Management,* 12 (1), pp 47–63.

Chambers, A.D. (2009) The black hole of assurance', *The Internal Auditor* 66 (2), pp 28–29.

Chartered Institute of Internal Auditors (CIIA) (2012) *Code of Professional Conduct,* April 2012 (see http://www.iia.org.uk/members/member-benefits/code-of-professional-conduct/, accessed 17 August 2013).

CIIA (2013) *Effective Internal Audit in the Financial Services Sector: Recommendations from the Committee on Internal Audit Guidance for Financial Services*, July 2013 (see http://www.iia.org.uk/media/354788/0758_effective_internal_audit_financial_webfinal.pdf, accessed 14 July 2013).

Federal Reserve (2013) *Supplemental Policy Statement on the Internal Audit Function and Its Outsourcing*, Board of Governors of the Federal Reserve System, January 2013 (supplemental to 2003 *Interagency Policy Statement on the Internal Audit Function and its Outsourcing* (2003)) (see http://www.federalreserve.gov/bankinforeg/srletters/sr1301a1.pdf, accessed 14 July 2013).

Financial Reporting Council (FRC) (2012) *The UK Corporate Governance Code*, September 2012.

Hansard (2008a) Smith, T. (The Lord Smith of Clifton) House of Lords Debate on the Queen's Speech, 8 December 2008.

Hansard (2008b) Smith, T. (The Lord Smith of Clifton) House of Lords Debate on the Banking Bill, 16 December, col 789–790.

House of Lords and House of Commons (HLHC) (2013a), *Changing Banking for Good, Report of the Parliamentary Commission on Banking* Standards, Volume I: Summary, and Conclusions and Recommendations, HL Paper 27-I, HC 175-I, 12 June 2013 (see http://www.parliament.uk/business/committees/committees-a-z/joint-select/professional-standards-in-the-banking-industry/news/changing-banking-for-good-report/, accessed 14 July 2013).

HLHC (2013b) *Changing Banking for Good, Report of the Parliamentary Commission on Banking* Standards, Volume II: Chapters 1 to 11 and Annexes, together with formal minutes, HL Paper 27-II, HC 175-II, 12 June 2013 (see http://www.parliament.uk/business/committees/committees-a-z/joint-select/professional-standards-in-the-banking-industry/news/changing-banking-for-good-report/, accessed 14 July 2013).

HM Treasury (2006) *Internal Audit Quality Assessment Framework – A Tool for Departments*, Version 1, December 2006.

HM Treasury (2013) *Internal Audit Quality Assessment Framework*, May 2013, ISBN 978-1-909096-17-2.

Hughes, P. (2011) 'Bank Internal Audit: Third Line of Defence or First Line of Attack?', *Risk Reward Risk Update*, January 2011 (see http://www.riskrewardlimited.com/admin/pdf/RU%20Jan%202011%20PH-Internal%20Audit.pdf, accessed 11 August 2013).

International Auditing and Assurance Standards Board of IFAC (IAASB) (2012) 'Using the work of internal auditors', *International* Standards *on Auditing*, ISA 610, ISBN 978-1-60815-114-1, March 2012 (see http://www.ifac.org/publications-resources/isa-610-revised-2013-using-work-internal-auditors, accessed 26 July 2013).

Institute of Internal Auditors (IIA) (2000) *Code of Ethics*, June 2000 (incidental revision in 2009 to reflect the altered title of the Standards framework).

IIA (2013a) *International* Standards *for the Professional Practice of Internal Auditing* (Standards), October 2013, effective from 1 January 2013 (see https://na.theiia.org/standards-guidance/mandatory-guidance/Pages/Standards.aspx, accessed 15 July 2013).

IIA (2013b) *The Three Lines of Defense in Effective Risk Management and Control*, Position Paper, January 2013 (see https://na.theiia.org/standards-guidance/Public%20Documents/PP%20The%20Three%20Lines%20of%20Defense%20in%20Effective%20Risk%20Management%20and%20Control.pdf, accessed 20 July 2013).

International Monetary Fund (IMF) (2013), *Protecting IMF Resources: Safeguards Assessments of Central Banks*, March 2013 (see http://www.imf.org/external/np/exr/facts/pdf/safe.pdf , accessed 30 July 2013).

Irving, R. (2012) 'Not good enough', *FS Focus*, July/August, pp 12–14.

Jeppesen, K.K. (2010) 'Strategies for dealing with standard-setting resistance', *Accounting, Auditing & Accountability Journal*, 23(2), pp 175–200.

Loughrey, J. (2011) *Corporate Lawyers and Corporate Governance* (Cambridge: Cambridge University Press).

National Audit Office (NAO) (2012) *The Effectiveness of Internal Audit in Central Government*, June 2012 (see http://www.nao.org.uk/wp-content/uploads/2012/06/121323.pdf, accessed 26 July 2013).

NAO (2013) *Recent developments in government internal audit and assurance – Spring 2013*, (see http://www.nao.org.uk/wp-content/uploads/2013/04/Recent-developments-in-internal-audit-spring-2013.pdf, accessed 30 July 2013).

Nolan (1994) *Standards in Public Life, First Report of the Committee on Standards in Public Life* (Chairman: Lord Nolan), Volume 1: Report, May 1995, Cm 2850-1. The second volume was evidence submitted to the Committee. Available from HMSO Publications Centre.

Public Sector Internal Audit Standards (PSIAS) (2013), ISBN 978 1 84508 356 4, December 2013, effective from 1 April 2013 (see http://www.iia.org.uk/media/76020/public_sector_internal_audit_standards_2012.pdf, accessed 14 July 2013).

Walker, D. (2009) *A review of corporate governance in UK banks and other financial industry entities*, final report (see http://www.hm-treasury.gov.uk/d/walker_review_261109.pdf), November 2009.

Notes

1 This a chapter first appeared in 2014 as 'New Guidance on Internal audit – an Analysis and Appraisal of Recent Developments' in *Managerial Auditing Journal – Assurance, Management Performance and Governance,* Emerald, and is reproduced by kind permission.

2 Lord Smith of Clifton (2008), *Hansard*, 8 December (Debate on the Queen's Speech).
3 Lord Smith of Clifton (2008), *Hansard*, 16 December (Debate on the Banking Bill).
4 CIIA (2013) Basis for conclusions [A], p 11.
5 See definition of 'Board' in the IIA's Glossary to the Standards (IIA, 2013a).
6 The PSIAS are based on the mandatory elements of the IIA's International Professional Practices Framework and will apply across the UK in central and local government and the NHS. The PSIAS were subject to a formal UK-wide consultation process during 2012, and they have been reviewed by the Internal Audit Standards Advisory Board (IASAB). The IASAB was formed in March 2012 to provide oversight and challenge for the development of the standards. The Board comprises representatives of internal audit for the CIIA, the Chartered Institute of Public Finance and Accountancy (CIPFA), HM Treasury, Scottish Government, Welsh Government, the Department of Finance and Personnel Northern Ireland and the Department of Health. Collectively these organisations are the Relevant Internal Audit Standard Setters in central government and public services, with the exception of the IIA.
7 Std 2000.
8 Std 2010.C1.
9 Std 1110.
10 Federal Reserve (2013), transmittal memo, 23 January 2013, p 2.
11 Federal Reserve (2013), p 1.
12 'Std 2410.A1 – Final communication of engagement results must, where appropriate, contain the internal auditors' opinion and/or conclusions. When issued, an opinion or conclusion must take account of the expectations of senior management, the board, and other stakeholders and must be supported by sufficient, reliable, relevant, and useful information.'

'Interpretation:

Opinions at the engagement level may be ratings, conclusions, or other descriptions of the results. Such an engagement may be in relation to controls around a specific process, risk, or business unit. The formulation of such opinions requires consideration of the engagement results and their significance.'

13 CIIA (2013), Recommendations [B] § 3, p 6: *'Internal audit's scope should be unrestricted'*.
14 CIIA (2013), Basis for conclusions, [B], p 12.
15 The Remuneration Committee (of the Board) would be termed the Compensation Committee in the US.
16 CIIA (2013) Recommendations, [E], 18, p9.
17 CIIA (2013) Basis for conclusions [E], p 13.
18 Basel (2012), Introduction, p 1, § 5.
19 Federal Reserve (2013), Purpose, p 1.
20 CIIA (2013), p 5.

Chapter G5

New Enhanced Guidance on Internal Audit's Interface with Regulators[1]

Introduction G5.1

This chapter applies a content analysis and appraisal of recent pronouncements by parties who have set out what they consider should be appropriate relationships between internal auditors and external oversight authorities (regulators/supervisors). Excluded from this analysis are recommended general rather than regulatory enhancements to internal audit practice from these and other recent pronouncements, which have been addressed in a separate chapter.

The key elements of guidance on regulation in the main sources analysed here are cross-referenced in this chapter to the tables which provide more detail as well as precise cross-referencing to the sources.

Basel (2012) and some other guidance use the terms 'supervisor' and 'head of the internal audit function', but for consistency with the rest of this chapter, the alternatives 'regulator' and 'CAE' (chief audit executive) are used here. CAE is a commonly accepted generic term although it is not ideal as it could be misconstrued as indicating that internal audit need not be independent from the executive.

Although the majority of these developments have originated within the financial sector, other sectors (such as pharma, airspace, health, oil and government) are regulated and there is interest from these other regulated sectors in the implications for them of these enhanced practices. One developer of enhanced guidance has explicitly acknowledged its wider applicability (CIIA, 2013; Table 4, row 1).

Key new guidance relating to regulation

Institute of Internal Auditors Standards (IIA, 2013a) G5.2

The Institute of Internal Auditors (IIA) Standards were effective from 1 January 2013.

Table 1: IIA Standards relating to regulation

(No changes were made in the 2013 release of these Standards)

	INTRODUCTION TO THE STANDARDS If internal auditors or the internal audit activity is prohibited by law or regulation from conformance with certain parts of the Standards, conformance with all other parts of the *Standards* and appropriate disclosures are needed.

	CODE OF ETHICS Internal auditors: … 1.2 Shall observe the law and make disclosures expected by the law and the profession. … 2.3 Shall disclose all material facts known to them that, if not disclosed, may distort the reporting of activities under review. … 3.1 Shall be prudent in the use and protection of information acuqired in the course of their duties.
	Std 2120.A1 – The internal audit activity must evaluate risk exposures relating to the organization's governance, operations, and information systems regarding the: … Compliance with laws, regulations, policies, procedures, and contracts.
	Std 2130.A1 – The internal audit activity must evaluate the adequacy and effectiveness of controls in responding to risks within the organization's governance, operations, and information systems regarding the: … Compliance with laws, regulations, policies, procedures, and contracts.
	Std 2330.A1 – The chief audit executive must control access to engagement records. The chief audit executive must obtain the approval of senior management and/or legal counsel prior to releasing such records to external parties, as appropriate.
	Std 2330.A2 – The chief audit executive must develop retention requirements for engagement records, regardless of the medium in which each record is stored. These retention requirements must be consistent with the organization's guidelines and any pertinent regulatory or other requirements.
	Std 2330.C1 – The chief audit executive must develop policies governing the custody and retention of consulting engagement records, as well as their release to internal and external parties. These policies must be consistent with the organization's guidelines and any pertinent regulatory or other requirements.
	Std 2440.A2 – If not otherwise mandated by legal, statutory, or regulatory requirements, prior to releasing results to parties outside the organization the chief audit executive must: Assess the potential risk to the organization; Consult with senior management and/or legal counsel as appropriate; and Control dissemination by restricting the use of the results.

Although the guidance on internal audit's interface with regulators in the IIA Standards was unchanged from previous releases of these Standards, this chapter starts by summarising it. Each of the three principal sets of enhanced guidance reviewed in this chapter, and also the International Monetary Fund (IMF) (2013) and HM Treasury (2013), endorse the IIA Standards in effect as the foundation upon which they have built their elaborations.

The IIA's Code of Ethics requires internal auditors to adhere to laws and regulations (Table 1, row 2). If there is a conflict between the two, the Standards give precedence to any legal and regulatory requirements, and indicate that in such cases there may be a need for appropriate disclosure (Table 1, row 1). For instance, disclosure might be necessary per Std 1322.[2]

The Standards require the internal audit activity to evaluate risk exposures regarding compliance with laws and regulations and regarding the adequacy and effectiveness of controls in responding to these risks (Table 1, rows 3 and 4).

Retention policies for audit engagement records of both assurance and consulting engagements are required to be consistent with regulatory requirements (Table 1, rows 6 and 7). The Standards make it clear that custody of consulting engagement records and their release to external parties must be consistent with regulatory requirements (Table 1, row 7), but there is no specific requirement in the same section of the Standards that the release of assurance engagement records to external parties should conform to regulatory requirements. Rather, the Standards subordinate the CAE's judgement about external release of assurance engagement records, perhaps to the regulator, to that of senior management and/or legal counsel (Table 1, row 5). Elsewhere in the Standards the CAE is empowered to release of audit results externally if 'mandated' (commanded) to do so by legal, statutory or regulatory requirements Table 1, row 8).

Looked at positively, it is clear that the IIA requires internal auditors to observe laws and regulations when they run counter to organisational preferences. But external disclosure by internal auditors, to regulators or others should only be made if there is a legal or regulatory requirement to do so, or if senior management/legal counsel approve. This curmudgeonly stance supports minimal external disclosure, gives the CAE no authority to determine external disclosure where it is not mandatory, and does not endorse external disclosure in the public interest.

There is also some lack of clarity about the respective obligations of CAEs and more junior internal auditors. Whereas the Code of Ethics and the Introduction to the Standards (Table 1, rows 1 and 2) apply to all internal auditors, most of the other Standards relied upon above (Table 1, rows 5 to 8) are addressed to CAEs, leaving unclear the position of internal auditors below the level of the CAE.

Basel Committee on Banking Supervision (Basel, 2012) G5.3

Table 2: Basel on regulatory guidance (June 2012)

1.	The internal audit function should be accountable to the board or its audit committee on all matters related to the performance of its mandate as described in the internal audit charter.[1]
2.	There should be effective two-way communication about topics of mutual interest between the supervisory authority and internal audit.[2]

3.	Supervisors and internal auditors should each ensure that enhanced communication does not undermine their respective perceived and actual independence and status, as the supervisory authority and the internal audit function each have different roles and supervisor should be able to challenge the work of the internal auditors through their continuous supervision process, including through on-site supervision.[3]
4.	Supervisory authorities should meet periodically with the bank's internal auditors to discuss their risk analysis, findings, recommendations and the audit plan. Supervisors should decide on a case per case approach whether senior management should or should not be present at these meetings. These meetings can also facilitate the understanding of how and to what extent the recommendations made by supervisors (including those made during on-site reviews) and internal auditors have been implemented. These meetings should be sufficiently frequent to enable the supervisor to ensure the effectiveness of the actions taken by the bank to carry out these recommendations. The frequency of these meetings and other communication between supervisors and internal auditors should be commensurate with the bank's size, the nature and risks of its operations and the complexity of its organisation. Supervisors may also request the internal audit reports from time to time. The analysis of these internal audit reports and information may contribute to the supervisor's assessment of the internal control system of the bank.'[4] [*Vide*: § 74, p 15]
5.	Supervisors should have regular communication with the bank's internal auditors to (i) discuss the risk areas identified by both parties, (ii) understand the risk mitigation measures taken by the bank, and (iii) monitor the bank's response to weaknesses identified. Supervisory authorities have an interest in engaging in a constructive and formalised dialogue with the internal audit function. This dialogue could be a valuable source of information on the quality of the internal control system. 'The relationship between the supervisor and the internal audit function should be established in a structured and transparent way. In principle, the supervisor will initiate this relationship.'[5]
6.	Supervisors and internal auditors should discuss the areas described in Section A – Principle 7 and related paragraphs.[6]
7.	The scope of the activities of the compliance function should be subject to periodic review by the internal audit function. Compliance laws, rules and standards include primary legislation, rules and standards issued by legislators and supervisors, market conventions, codes of practice promoted by industry associations, and internal codes of conduct applicable to the staff members of the bank. 'The audit of the compliance function should include an assessment of how effectively it fulfils its responsibilities.[7]
8.	Internal audit is well placed to provide the supervisor with insight on the institution's business model including risks in the institution's business activities, processes and functions and the adequacy of the control and oversight of these risks.[8]

9.	Bank supervisors should regularly assess whether the internal audit function has sufficient standing and authority within the bank and operates according to sound principles. The supervisory authority should consider the extent to which the board of directors, its audit committee and senior management promote a strong internal control environment supported and assessed by a sound internal audit function.[9]
10.	The appointment and replacement of the head of the internal audit function is relevant to the supervisory assessment of the bank. Therefore, the supervisory authority should be promptly informed by the audit committee (or its equivalent) or senior management of the appointment of a new head of the internal audit function, including relevant qualifications and previous experience. Similarly, whenever the head of the internal audit function ceases to act in this capacity, the supervisory authority should be informed of this fact and its circumstances. The supervisory authority should consider meeting with the former head of internal audit to discuss the reasons for his or her departure.[10]
11.	Supervisors should formally report all weaknesses they identify in the internal audit function to the board of directors and require remedial actions. When the supervisory authority concludes that a bank's internal audit function is inadequate or ineffective, it should require the board of directors to develop an appropriate written remediation plan that addresses the identified weaknesses on a timely basis. The written plan should be submitted to the supervisory authority for review. If the supervisor is not satisfied, it should require changes or additional measures to be included in the plan. The supervisor should monitor the implementation of the plan. In addition to measures relating to the performance and standing of the internal audit function, the supervisor may also recommend enhancements to the governance of the bank including the functioning of the audit committee. The audit committee and board of directors should not conclude that the internal audit function is functioning well solely because the supervisory authority has not identified any weaknesses. The supervisory review process is not a substitute for the audit committee's assessment, or an external assessment of the internal audit function.'[11]
12.	The scope of the internal audit function's activities should ensure adequate coverage of matters of regulatory interest within the audit plan.[12]
13.	'The internal audit function should independently evaluate the monitoring of compliance with laws and regulations, including any requirements from supervisors.[13]
14.	The internal audit function of a bank should have the capacity to review key risk management functions, regulatory capital adequacy and liquidity control functions, regulatory and internal reporting functions, the regulatory compliance function and the finance function.[14]

15.	Internal auditors should regularly evaluate the effectiveness of the process by which the risk and reporting functions interact to produce timely, accurate, reliable and relevant reports for both internal management and the supervisor. This includes standardised reports which record the bank's calculation of its capital resources, requirements and ratios. It may also include public disclosures intended to facilitate transparency and market discipline such as the Pillar 3 disclosures and the reporting of regulatory matters in the bank's public reports.[15]
16.	When the risk management function has not informed the board of directors about the existence of a significant divergence of views between senior management and the risk management function regarding the level of risk faced by the bank, the head of internal audit should inform the board about this divergence.[16]
17.	Banks are subject to the global regulatory framework for capital and liquidity as approved by the Committee and implemented in national regulation. This framework contains measures to strengthen regulatory capital and global liquidity. The scope of internal audit should include all provisions of this regulatory framework and in particular the bank's system for identifying and measuring its regulatory capital and assessing the adequacy of its capital resources in relation to the bank's risk exposures and established minimum ratios.[17]
18.	The internal audit function should independently evaluate the bank's systems and processes for measuring and monitoring its liquidity positions in relation to its risk profile, external environment, and minimum regulatory requirements, should fall within the audit universe.[18]

1 Basel (2012), Principle 12.
2 Basel (2012) § 69 and 75, pp 14–15.
3 Basel (2012) § 70, pp 14–15.
4 Basel (2012) § 74, p 15.
5 Basel (2012) Principle 16, p 15; § 72, p 15; §71, p 15.
6 Basel (2012) § 76–81, p 16. Section A – Principle 7 covers in some detail the five areas of risk management, capital adequacy and liquidity, regulatory and internal reporting, compliance and finance.
7 Basel (2012), § 39–41, p 9.
8 Basel (2012) § 76–81, p 16. Extensive examples are given at § 78.
9 Basel (2012) § 82–86, p 17.
10 Basel (2012) § 88, pp17–18.
11 Basel (2012) § 89–91, p 18.
12 Basel (2012), p 2.
13 Basel (2012) § 30, p 8.
14 Basel (2012) § 32, p 8.
15 Basel (2012) § 37–8, p 9.
16 Basel (2012) § 33, pp 8–9.
17 Basel (2012) § 33, pp 8–9.
18 Basel (2012) § 36, p 9.

Basel accepts that the board may delegate to the audit committee but stipulates that the board of directors has final responsibility, and clearly states that internal audit is accountable to the board, not to management, for its performance as set out in the internal audit charter (Table 2, row 1).

Basel states that, without inhibiting the regulator's ability to challenge internal audit work, there should be effective, structured and transparent two-way communication between them, initiated by the regulator (Table 2, rows 5 and 8) with regular meetings (at which the regulator has the discretion to exclude senior management) (Table 2, row 2). Regulators may also ask to see internal audit reports (Table 2, rows 2 to 4).

The regulator expects their regular communication with internal audit will discuss the risk areas identified by both parties, the risk mitigation measures, the organisation's responses to identified weaknesses (Table 2, row 5), risk management, capital adequacy and liquidity, regulatory and internal reporting, compliance and the finance function (Table 2, rows 6 and 14). The regulator expects this to be a valuable source of information on the quality of internal control (Table 2, row 5). The scope of internal audit should include the bank's system for identifying and measuring its regulatory capital and assessing the adequacy of its capital resources in relation to the bank's risk exposures and established minimum ratios (Table 2, row 17). The internal audit function should independently evaluate the bank's systems and processes for measuring and monitoring its liquidity positions in relation to its risk profile, external environment, and minimum regulatory requirements, all of which should fall within the audit universe (Table 2, row 18).

Somewhat reminiscent of Std 2600, internal audit is required to report to the board significant differences of view about risk between executive management and the risk management function, that the latter has not reported to the board (Table 2, row 16). So the regulator expects internal audit to contribute to filling the board's assurance vacuum in this way when the risk management function has failed to do so.

Internal audit should regularly review the process by which the risk and reporting functions interact to produce timely, accurate, relevant, reliable and transparent reports for management, the regulator and other stakeholders (Table 2, row 15).

Basel requires that the bank's compliance function, including the monitoring of compliance with laws and regulations and any requirements of the regulator, should be periodically reviewed by internal audit, and sets out a broad scope for this audit (Table 2, rows 7 and 13). A very significant requirement is that the scope of the internal audit plan should adequately cover *all* matters of regulatory interest (Table 2, row 12).

While no substitute for the board's and its audit committee's oversight of internal audit (Table 2, row 11), the regulator will also assess (a) the quality of internal audit; and (b) the support of the board, its audit committee and senior management for a strong internal control environment (Table 2, row 9). All weaknesses of internal audit will be reported by the regulator to the board with remedial action being required to a satisfactory written remedial plan whose implementation will be monitored by the regulator (Table 2, row 11).

The regulator should be promptly informed of the appointment of a new head of internal audit (including qualifications and experience) and his/her removal (and its circumstances). The regulator may meet the former head of internal audit to discuss the reasons for his/her departure (Table 2, row 10).

Unlike the Federal Reserve (see below), Basel (2012) does not in as many words state that internal audit is part of the regulatory process; but in effect Basel implies that point in a number of ways. For instance, Basel requires that the bank's compliance function should be periodically reviewed by internal audit (Table 2, row 6); and Basel requires that the scope of internal audit should adequately cover the matters of regulatory interest (Table 2, row 11). Likewise the UK Committee on Internal Audit Guidance for Financial Services (CIIA, 2013) is making broadly similar points.

Federal Reserve (January 2013) G5.4

Table 3: Federal Reserve on regulatory guidance (January 2013)

1.	An effective internal audit function is a vehicle to advance an institution's safety and soundness and compliance with consumer laws and regulations and is therefore considered as part of the supervisory review process.[1]
2.	If internal audit's overall processes are deemed effective, examiners may be able to rely on the work performed by internal audit depending on the nature and risk of the functions subject to examination.[2]
3.	An institution's internal audit function that does not follow the enhanced practices and supplemental guidance outlined in this policy letter generally will be considered ineffective.[3]
4.	[On at least an annual basis] examiners will supplement their examination procedures through continuous monitoring and an assessment of key elements of internal audit, including: (i) the adequacy and independence of the audit committee; (ii) the independence, professional competence, and quality of the internal audit function; (iii) the quality and scope of the audit methodology, audit plan, and risk assessment; and (iv) the adequacy of audit programs and work paper standards.[4]

1 Federal Reserve (2013) Section 5, pp 14–15.
2 Federal Reserve (2013) Section 5, pp 14–15.
3 Federal Reserve (2013) Section 5, pp 14–15.
4 Federal Reserve (2013) Section 5, pp 14–15.

The Federal Reserve's definition of internal auditing makes it explicit that internal audit is regarded as part of the supervisory process (Table 3, row 1):

> 'An effective internal audit function is a vehicle to advance an institution's safety and soundness and compliance with consumer laws and regulations and is therefore considered as part of the supervisory review process,'[3]

The Federal Reserve does not pull its punches, stating clearly that an internal audit function not following the Federal Reserve's enhanced practices will generally be considered ineffective by the regulator (Table 3, row 3). On the other hand, the regulator is likely to be able to rely on the work of an internal audit function deemed effective (Table 3, row 2). Relevant criteria are the independence, professional competence, quality and scope of the audit methodology, audit plan, risk assessment; and adequacy of audit programmes and working paper standards (Table 3, row 4).

UK Internal Audit Guidance for Financial Services (CIIA, 2013) G5.5

Table 4: UK Financial Services on regulatory guidance (July 2013)

1.	The Committee hopes that some of their recommendations will be useful outside the financial services sector. The Committee wrote to the Financial Reporting Council recommending that they consider whether additional guidance is needed on what should be expected from a good Internal Audit function. That additional guidance would be likely to reflect some of the Committee's recommendations and would be likely to appear in the planned 2014 UK Corporate Governance Code, or in the planned 2014 FRC Guidance on Audit Committees which interprets the Code content on audit committees.[1]
2.	The guidance reinforces the requirement for open, honest and constructive communication with the Regulators.[2]
3.	The Chief Internal Auditor and other senior managers within Internal Audit should have an open, constructive and co-operative relationship with regulators which supports sharing of information relevant to carrying out their respective responsibilities.[3]
4.	Internal Audit should evaluate whether Business and Risk Management are adequately designing and controlling products, services and supporting processes in line with customer interests and conduct regulation.[4]
5.	The IIA Standards require Internal Audit to be free from interference in determining the scope of their audit work. Whilst it is common for Internal Audit Charters to mandate an unrestricted scope some Internal Audit functions did not include in their audit universe or risk assessments some of the processes, risks and events that were central to the problems faced by the financial services sector in recent years.[5]
6.	The Committee agrees with the principle of an unrestricted scope and for the avoidance of doubt the guidance set out areas of scope which were found to have been restricted in some organisations in practice even if not in principle. This is not to say that these areas should take priority over more commonly audited / business-as-usual risk areas such as credit, operational or regulatory risks.[6]
7.	Subsidiary, branch and divisional Heads of Internal Audit should report primarily to the Group Chief Internal Auditor while recognising local legislation or regulation as appropriate.[7]
8.	The guidance reinforces the requirement for open, honest and constructive communication with the Regulators. In response to consultation feedback, the Committee did not see a requirement to expand on the expectations laid out in the Statements of Principle and Code of Practice for Approved Persons, and the UK Corporate Governance Code, in relation to the interaction between the Chief Internal Auditor and the Regulators.[8]

9.	The Committee received feedback relating to the interpretation of the recommendation relating to the remuneration of Chief Internal Auditor. The guidance is consistent with existing regulatory guidance around the remuneration of personnel working in the control functions of financial institutions. The Committee did not deem it necessary to prescribe additional guidance in this area.[9]

1 IIA (2013), p 4.
2 CIIA (2013) H. p 14.
3 CIIA (2013) H. 29, p 10.
4 CIIA (2013) B.5e, p 7.
5 CIIA (2013) B. p 12.
6 CIIA (2013) B. p 12.
7 CIIA (2013) E.19, p 9.
8 CIIA (2013) H, Relationships with regulators, p 14.
9 CIIA (2013) Basis for conclusions [E], p 13.

It is likely that this guidance will effectively have mandatory impact as the Prudential Regulation Authority and the Financial Conduct Authority will use this guidance as a benchmark (BoE, 2013).

The Guidance points out that there are other mandatory requirements and expectations for internal auditors within (a) the UK Statements of Principle and Code of Practice for Approved Persons (PRA, 2013), and (b) the UK Corporate Governance Code of the Financial Reporting Council (FRC, 2012a). In both cases the Committee saw no need to reiterate but clearly endorsed them (Table 4, rows 8 and 9).

The CAE role for a UK regulated entity is automatically an approved function and therefore anyone appointed to that role needs to successfully apply for approval from the PRA. Members of the CAE's top team, at the choice of the institution concerned, may also apply to be approved persons. Approved persons must observe the Statements of Principle and Code of Practice for Approved Persons (PRA, 2013). Failure to do so may lead to loss of approved person status, which for the CAE would mean removal from that position, a fine, and/or being banned from working in any responsible position within a UK financial institution. The institution is also likely to face sanctions. Of the seven Statements of Principle, the fourth is most germane to the CAE's relationship with the regulators:

> 'An approved person must deal with the FCA [Financial Conduct Authority], the PRA and other regulators in an open and cooperative way and must disclose appropriately any information of which the FCA or the PRA would reasonably expect notice.'

The Committee also expressed the hope that some of its recommendations would be useful outside the financial services sector, and wrote to the FRC recommending that it consider whether additional general guidance is needed on what should be expected from any good internal audit function (Table 4, row 1). So symbiotically, CIIA (2013) has adopted the UK Code's guidance on internal audit, and the FRC may extend its Code's guidance on internal audit to reflect CIIA (2013) recommendations.

The FRC describes its Corporate Governance Code as 'soft law'. The UK Listing Rules require companies with a premium listing of equity shares to 'comply or explain' with respect to all the provisions in the UK Code,[4] and so the Code's content on internal audit is caught by this listing rule.

However, internal audit is currently mentioned only twice in the Code itself, in the part of the Code that covers audit committees. One of the main roles and responsibilities of the audit committee is given as:

> 'to monitor and review the effectiveness of the company's internal audit function'[5]

and another Provision within the Code reads:

> 'The audit committee should monitor and review the effectiveness of the internal audit activities.
>
> Where there is no internal audit function, the audit committee should consider annually whether there is a need for an internal audit function and make a recommendation to the board, and the reasons for the absence of such a function should be explained in the relevant section of the annual report.'[6]

Below the level of the UK Corporate Governance Code is *Guidance on Audit Committees* (FRC, 2012b) designed to assist company boards to implement the relevant provisions on audit committees in the UK Corporate Governance Code, although boards are not required to follow this guidance (FRC, 2012b). It remains to be seen whether FRC adjustments on internal audit, to reflect the Committee's recommendations (CIIA, 2013) end up in the 2014 versions of the 'soft law' Code (FRC, 2012a) or in this supplementary guidance on audit committees which already has considerable content on internal audit (FRC, 2012b).

As with other guidances reviewed in this chapter, the Committee calls for an open, honest and constructive relationship with regulators, sharing information to support their respective responsibilities; and applies this to both the CAE and to senior staff within the internal audit function (Table 4, rows 2 and 3).

The Committee observed and approved that internal audit charters commonly mandate an unrestricted scope for internal audit. Because some of the processes, risks and events that were central to the problems faced by the financial services sector in recent years were not audited, the Committee sets out the scope of internal audit in some detail (Table 4, rows 5 and 6) while counselling that commonly audited areas such as conduct regulation/regulatory risks remain important (Table 4, rows 4 and 6).

This guidance accepts that different local legislation or regulation will trump their guidance that subsidiary, branch and divisional heads of internal audit should report primarily to the group chief internal auditor. The IIA Standards support the primacy of laws and regulations (Table 1, rows 1 and 2), but are silent on reporting lines of subsidiary (etc) internal auditors.

Other developments

IMF review of central banks' internal audit (IMF, 2013) G5.6

Since 2000, a due diligence exercise ('safeguards assessment') is undertaken by the IMF when the IMF provides a loan to a country, to provide assurance that the country's central bank is able to adequately manage the funds and provide reliable information to the IMF. Two of the five key areas relate to internal audit:[7]

- internal audit mechanism;
- system of internal controls.

These are described as:

> '**Internal audit mechanism:** The internal audit function helps the central bank to evaluate and improve the effectiveness of risk management, control, and governance processes. The IMF assesses whether the internal audit function is effective, and whether the central bank has sufficient staff resources and organizational independence to fulfill its mandate. Assessments also review compliance of the internal audit function with international Standards.'
>
> '**System of internal controls:** Sound policies and procedures, including effective risk management, are necessary to safeguard assets, and ensure the accuracy and completeness of accounting records and information. Assessments review the quality of oversight of external and internal audits, as well as controls over banking, accounting, and foreign exchange operations. Particular attention is paid to reserves management functions and controls over data reported to the IMF.'

It is apparent from the above that the IMF's assessments of internal audit take into account, but are not limited to, compliance with the Standards of the IIA. Furthermore, the IMF issues a 'safeguards report' which may include recommendations to enhance internal audit within a central bank that has been assessed, *viz.*:

> 'Central banks provide information—including financial statements, internal and external audit reports, and summaries of central bank controls—to the IMF on the above five areas. IMF staff review this documentation, and hold discussions with the bank's staff and external auditors; many assessments also include a visit to the central bank. A safeguards report is produced that includes recommendations to address identified vulnerabilities, and key recommendations may become part of program benchmarks.'

IMF (2013) reaffirmed the above:

- 'The IMF assesses whether the internal audit function is effective, and whether the central bank has sufficient staff resources and organizational independence to fulfill its mandate.
- Assessments also review compliance of the internal audit function with international standards. …
- [IMF] assessments review the quality of oversight of external and internal audits.'

UK National Audit Office and HM Treasury oversight of government internal audit G5.7

Included in this chapter is a summary of UK National Audit Office (NAO) and UK HM Treasury developments. As the UK's supreme public sector audit body and a member of the International Organisation of Supreme Audit Institutions (INTOSAI), the NAO has quasi-regulatory authority over UK government internal audit. HM Treasury sets and coordinates internal audit policy across UK central government.

Progress with HM Treasury's Internal Audit Transformation Programme (IATP) was delayed by the parallel developments of the NAO's very critical report on the effectiveness of internal audit in UK central government (NAO, 2012), and by the new UK Public Sector Internal Audit Standards (PSIAS, 2013).

NAO (2012) had headlined that only 40% of key internal audit users in UK central government believed that internal audit added substantial value to their organisations, but buried in the text was an acknowledgement that a further 44% believed internal audit added *some* value.[8] The NAO report estimated that expenditure on internal audit in UK central government was £70m across 400 bodies with £666bn of expenditure, of which only £13m is outsourced.[9] NAO estimated 1,000 internal auditors in all.[10]

The report complained that variations in internal audit quality and coverage meant that the NAO was often unable to rely on internal audit work to support its external audit,[11] but the report overlooked that the objectives and therefore the scope and approach of internal audit are distinctive from those of external audit. NAO stated it uses ISA 610 (IAASB, 2012) as its guide to evaluating the quality of internal audit in central government to see if it can place reliance upon it in the context of its external audit work. ISA 610 has two demerits for this purpose. First, it is designed as mandatory guidance for external auditors whose role is exclusively the audit of financial statements to be published, whereas NAO has a mandate which covers value for money auditing as well, which corresponds more closely to the internal audit mission. Secondly, ISA 610 is weak: it does not even acknowledge the existence of the IIA, as a standard setter or in any other context. Internal audit will not be good value if it is regarded as an unpaid assistant for the external auditor to reduce the amount of detailed work that the latter needs to do.

NAO (2012) made a number of recommendations.[12]

Later (NAO, 2013) NAO summarised its 2012 conclusions as:

> 'Government did not get value for money from its internal audit service. We found that internal audit needed to provide a higher level of assurance to senior management and boards across government.
>
> We recommended that:
>
> - HM Treasury set out a clear strategic view on the role of internal audit, empower a group of the most senior heads of internal audit to provide collective professional leadership and work with the Treasury to develop a plan to improve the capability of internal audit; and
> - Accounting officers and other senior users should set clear expectations for the level of service they expect. Internal audit services should adopt more detailed operational Standards, report performance and be held accountable to a set of agreed performance metrics.'

By March 2012, HM Treasury's IATP had identified a number of issues requiring to be addressed.[13]

IATP is introducing grouped internal audit services, which, it anticipates, will give the critical mass of staff needed to deliver higher quality internal audit more efficiently. The model proposes internal audit groups covering all government departments and their arm's-length bodies. Each accounting officer (eg of each government department) will retain a designated CAE, although this will often be shared. And each group will be led by a Group CAE, responsible for resource management and professional standards. Currently, the IIA Standards are silent about the implications of this innovative structure for internal audit provision.

HM Treasury has applied the IATP organisation and the adoption of the Standards of the IIA (PSIAS, 2012) to internal audit quality assessment (HM Treasury, 2013), so superseding their earlier publication on internal audit quality assessment (HM Treasury, 2006).

General conclusions G5.8

In this chapter we have reviewed the regulatory requirements of the IIA Standards, three recent sets of enhanced financial sector guidelines and a number of other developments. Two of the enhanced financial sector guidelines are published by regulators and the third (CIIA, 2013) is likely to be adopted by another regulator. It is common ground amongst them that there should be strong communication between internal audit and the regulator. Describing the nature of this relationship, adjectives such as 'open', 'transparent', 'honest', 'effective', 'structured' and 'two-way' are used. The intention is to openly share information to support their respective responsibilities.

If we accept this nature of the relationship between internal audit and regulators, there is no need to adjust IIA Std 2440.A2 (Table 1, row 8) on sharing the results of audit work with regulators: since there is a mandatory requirement to do so, it is endorsed by this Standard. It might be useful for a Standard to specifically mandate the CAE to make audit engagement and other audit reports available to the regulator.

Std 2330.A1 (Table 1, row 5) on controlling access to engagement records is problematic in two ways. First, the CAE is not authorised by this standard to disclose engagement records to regulators unless with prior approval of senior management and/or legal counsel. If this can be a continuous, general authorisation for open disclosure to the regulator, the standard should say so, but it is not clear whether such would be consistent with the intention of this standard. Secondly, in two places the Standards require that internal auditors do not subordinate their judgement on professional matters to that of others,[14] which should include management and/or legal counsel. In this context, not subordinating the auditors' judgment to that of others means that audit, usually the CAE, comes to his/her own professional judgement about whether sharing with the regulator is 'open', 'transparent', 'honest' etc, and the general presumption is that information should not be withheld if it is relevant.

It is also common ground amongst these enhanced guidelines that, although nominally the scope of internal audit may have been unlimited, in practice it has been incomplete, missing several important areas which contributed to the global banking crisis. Broadly similar omissions of audit scope doubtless have applied in other sectors. The guidelines reviewed in this chapter list categories of internal audit work important for the regulator as well as for the board and senior management. The guidance requires that all matters of regulatory interest are audited by internal audit. The IIA might consider whether its Standards should, for the avoidance of doubt, itemise in a non-exhaustive way, the categories that should be within the audit universe, and whether the Standards should stipulate that all matters of regulatory interest should be within the scope of internal audit. The Standards could also usefully address the place of audit cycles in audit planning – for instance, the need for high-risk areas to be audited annually and lesser risks less frequently.

One area of internal audit work, which is now being recognised as important, is to provide assurance to the board on the reliability of information prepared for the board (Basel 2012). This is already addressed in Stds 2110, 2120 and 2120.A1 and 2130. A1. Too many businesses rely on functional heads to prepare board reports which cover their areas of responsibility. It is better that they are generated independently, to avoid biased reporting.

There is nothing in the IIA Standards on cooperation with regulators when they assess the quality of internal audit and report the results of this assessment to the board. Basel (2012) (Table 2, row 11) states that weaknesses identified by the regulator will be reported to the board with remedial action being required to a satisfactory, written remedial plan whose implementation will be monitored by the regulator. This chapter has reviewed guidance that stipulates the appointment and removal of the CAE should be notified promptly to the regulator, again not something addressed in the IIA Standards.

Guidance discussed in this chapter requires that, subject to local legal and regulatory requirements, the primary reporting line of a CAE at subsidiary (etc) level should be to the group CAE (CIIA, 2013; Table 4, row 7): again, this is currently absent from the IIA Standards. A further nuance is that the IIA's Standards regard a relationship with the board's audit committee as satisfying any stated requirement in the Standards for internal audit to interface with the board: there is nothing in the Standards currently that makes the true board ultimately responsible. The guidances reviewed in this paper allow the board to delegate to its audit committee but make it clear that the board is ultimately responsible.

Any modification to the IIA Standards by way of responding to these enhanced guidelines will need to accommodate whether the amended obligations vest just with the CAE or also with other senior and junior internal auditors. CIIA (2013, Table 4, rows 2 and 3) are applied to CAEs and also to other senior internal auditors.

Implementing the enhanced requirements in these guidelines on the relationship between internal audit and the regulator usually requires action by both internal audit and the regulator. That does not invalidate their possible future inclusion with the IIA Standards: many existing requirements in the Standards are beyond the ability of internal audit to implement unilaterally without involvement of others – for instance, the board, the audit committee or management.

With more sectors becoming subject to regulation, these matters are assuming more general importance, to the extent that they should be considered for enhancement to the IIA's Standards. Adjustments to the Standards to accommodate more on regulation can be made without certain Standards being impossible for unregulated entities to conform to, so long as judicious wording is used.

Postscript G5.9

Two of the three sets of key pronouncements reviewed in this chapter are virtually mandatory requirements promulgated by regulators. They have a stronger potential to be followed than the Standards of the IIA, on account of the greater enforcement powers of regulators. The IIA Standards benefit as these regulators have conflated the IIA Standards with their own enhanced requirements.

The third set of guidelines reviewed in this chapter (CIIA, 2013) was developed by a committee set up by the UK Chartered Institute of Internal Auditors and is likely to be adopted by the UK financial sector regulator as well as being incorporated, in part, into the FRC's 'soft law' UK Corporate Governance Code and associated guidance (FRC, 2012a and 2012b).

The pronouncements reviewed in this chapter make no attempt to regulate how internal auditing standards are set. This may be a matter for the future, though the IIA may fend this off by moving first. By analogy, in the US and the UK responsibility for setting financial reporting and external audit standards has been removed from the professional practitioner bodies who had been perceived to have been acting in their own rather than in the public interest. In the UK this is now a responsibility of a board (the FRC) whose members are appointed by government. A broadly similar change has been made in the US (Public Company Accounting Oversight Board (PCAOB) etc).

A challenge for the IIA is to move up the continuum of standard setting processes identified by Jeppesen (2009), as follows:

1. First generation: a standard-setting board composed of experts usually appointed by the professional body.
2. Second generation: consists of a standard-setting board organised around the principle of representation, where participants represent their firm or a geographical area.
3. Third generation: organised around the principle of user orientation, where outside groups are given indirect influence in the form of rights to comment on draft standards and/or observe meetings without speaking or voting rights.
4. Fourth generation: in the public interest, external user groups are directly represented on the standard-setting board and participate on equal terms with internal auditors. They range from a single representative to giving users the majority. For instance the International Federation of Accounts' (IFAC) International Internal Audit Standards Board (IAASB) has 18 members, nine of whom are non-practitioners including three public members capable of representing the broad public interest. There are also three observers from other bodies who 'have the right of the floor' but do not vote (IFAC, 2011). Another example is the PCAOB's board of which a maximum of 40% of the members are practitioners.

Membership of the IIA's IIASB has excellent geographical spread, though its twenty-one members are not regarded as country or region representatives. Each member is appointed by the global professional body from amongst its members, and there is one observer. Remarkably, the IIA does not publish the names of IIASB members. The IIA is thus positioned near the start of the continuum, not yet adequately acknowledging the public interest. Arguably this has impacted the IIA's ability to articulate the public interest of internal auditors.

References

Bank of England (BoE) (2013), *News Release – PRA and FCA welcome Internal Audit guidance*, Prudential Regulation Authority, Bank of England, July 2013 (see http://www.bankofengland.co.uk/publications/Pages/news/2013/087.aspx, accessed 29 August 2013).

Basel Committee on Banking Supervision (Basel) (2012), *The Internal Audit Function in Banks*, Bank of International Settlements, June 2012 (see http://www.bis.org/publ/bcbs223.pdf, accessed 14 July 2013).

Chartered Institute of Internal Auditors (CIIA) (2013), *Effective Internal Audit in the Financial Services Sector: Recommendations from the Committee on Internal Audit Guidance for Financial Services*, July 2013 (see http://www.iia.org.uk/media/354788/0758_effective_internal_audit_financial_webfinal.pdf, accessed 14 July 2013).

Federal Reserve (2013) *Supplemental Policy Statement on the Internal Audit Function and Its Outsourcing*, Board of Governors of the Federal Reserve System, January 2013 (supplemental to 2003 *Interagency Policy Statement on the Internal Audit Function and its Outsourcing* (2003)) (see http://www.federalreserve.gov/bankinforeg/srletters/sr1301a1.pdf, accessed 14 July 2013).

Financial Reporting Council (FRC) (2012a) *The UK Corporate Governance Code*, September 2012, (see http://www.frc.org.uk/Our-Work/Publications/Corporate-Governance/UK-Corporate-Governance-Code-September-2012.aspx, accessed 27 August 2013).

FRC (2012b) *Guidance on Audit Committees*, September 2012 (see http://www.frc.org.uk/Our-Work/Publications/Corporate-Governance/Guidance-on-Audit-Committees-September-2012.aspx, accessed 27 August 2013).

HM Treasury (2006) *Internal Audit Quality Assessment Framework – A Tool for Departments*, Version 1, December 2006.

HM Treasury (2013) *Internal Audit Quality Assessment Framework*, May 2013, ISBN 978-1-909096-17-2 (see https://www.gov.uk/government/uploads/system/uploads/attachment_data/file/204214/internal_audit_quality_assessment_framework.pdf, accessed 28 August 2013).

International Auditing and Assurance Standards Board of IFAC (IAASB) (2012) 'Using the work of internal auditors', *International* Standards *on Auditing*, ISA 610, ISBN 978-1-60815-114-1, March 2012 (see http://www.ifac.org/publications-resources/isa-610-revised-2013-using-work-internal-auditors, accessed 26 July 2013).

Institute of Internal Auditors (IIA) (2000) *Code of Ethics*, June 2000 (incidental revision in 2009 to reflect the altered title of the Standards framework).

IIA (2013a) *International* Standards *for the Professional Practice of Internal Auditing (*Standards*)*, October 2013, effective from 1 January 2013 (see https://na.theiia.org/standards-guidance/mandatory-guidance/Pages/Standards.aspx, accessed 15 July 2013).

International Federation of Accountants Policy (IFAC) (2011) *International Standard Setting in the Public Interest*, Policy Position 3, New York, September

2011 (see http://www.ifac.org/sites/default/files/publications/files/PPP3-Standard-Setting-in-the-Public-Interest.pdf, accessed 27 August 2013).

International Monetary Fund (IMF) (2013) *Protecting IMF Resources: Safeguards Assessments of Central Banks*, March 2013 (see http://www.imf.org/external/np/exr/facts/pdf/safe.pdf, accessed 30 July 2013).

Jeppesen, K.K. (2010) 'Strategies for dealing with standard-setting resistance', *Accounting, Auditing & Accountability Journal*, 23(2), pp 175–200.

National Audit Office (NAO) (2012) *The Effectiveness of Internal Audit in Central Government*, June 2012 (see http://www.nao.org.uk/wp-content/uploads/2012/06/121323.pdf, accessed 26 July 2013).

NAO (2013) *Recent developments in government internal audit and assurance – Spring 2013*, (see http://www.nao.org.uk/wp-content/uploads/2013/04/Recent-developments-in-internal-audit-spring-2013.pdf, accessed 30 July 2013).

Prudential Regulation Authority (PRA) (2013) *Statements of Principle and Code of Practice for Approved Persons*, August 2013 (see http://fshandbook.info/FS/html/PRA/APER, accessed 29 August 2013).

Public Sector Internal Audit Standards (PSIAS) (2013), ISBN 978 1 84508 356 4, December 2013, effective from 1 April 2013 (see http://www.iia.org.uk/media/76020/public_sector_internal_audit_standards_2012.pdf, accessed 14 July 2013).

Notes

1 This chapter first appeared in 2014 as 'Guidance on Internal audit's Interface with Regulators – an Analysis and Appraisal of Recent Developments', *Managerial Auditing Journal – Assurance, Management Performance and Governance*, and is reproduced by kind permission.

2 Std 1322: Disclosure of Nonconformance:

'When non-conformance with the Definition of Internal Auditing, the Code of Ethics, or the Standards impacts the overall scope or operation of the internal audit activity, the chief audit executive must disclose the non-conformance and the impact to senior management and the board.'

3 Federal Reserve (2013), section 5, pp 14–15.

4 Listing Rules 9.8.6 R (for UK incorporated companies) and 9.8.7 R (for overseas incorporated companies) state that in the case of a company that has a Premium listing of equity shares, the following items must be included in its annual report and accounts:

- a statement of how the listed company has applied the Main Principles set out in the UK Corporate Governance Code, in a manner that would enable shareholders to evaluate how the principles have been applied;
- a statement as to whether the listed company has:
  - complied throughout the accounting period with all relevant provisions set out in the UK Corporate Governance Code; or
  - not complied throughout the accounting period with all relevant provisions set out in the UK Corporate Governance Code, and if so, setting out:
    (i) those provisions, if any, it has not complied with;
    (ii) in the case of provisions whose requirements are of a continuing nature, the period within which, if any, it did not comply with some or all of those provisions; and
    (iii) the company's reasons for non-compliance.

5 FRC (2012a), provision C.3.2, p 19.
6 FRC (2012b), provision C.3.6, p19.
7 The five key areas, under the acronym 'ELRIC', are:
   1. external audit mechanism;
   2. legal structure and autonomy;
   3. financial reporting;
   4. internal audit mechanism;
   5. system of internal controls.

8 NAO (2012), pp 4 and 6.
9 NAO (2012), p 4.
10 NAO (2012), p 5.
11 NAO (2012), pp 6 and 18.
12 NAO (2012), pp 8 & 9.
13 NAO (2012), App. 2, p29.
14 Interpretation to Std 1100 and Glossary definition of objectivity:
   '... Objectivity requires that internal auditors so not subordinate their judgment on audit matters to others. ...'

Part H:
External Oversight

Chapter H1

External Control

Introduction **H1.1**

At **C2.3** to **C2.12**, we touched on the issue of 'stakeholder control of the business'. Here we focus more on trends in the provision of independent assurance on reports to stakeholders.

'Control' divides into *external* control by external stakeholders of an entity (such as the shareholders, bond holders, creditors, the local community) and *internal* control by the board, management and other personnel. (See Chapter **G1** for a consideration of internal control.)

External control is facilitated in part by shareholder election of directors (a) to oversee the management of their interests and (b) to render an account to them:[1]

> 'Without audit, no accountability; without accountability, no control; and if there is no control, where is the seat of power? … great issues often come to light only because of scrupulous verification of details.'

This well-known quotation comes from the foreword to a book written by an auditor of the European Court of Auditors, the external auditors of the European Commission and other European institutions. It crystallises the idea that the audit is a necessary, independent attestation of the accountability to the stakeholders by the stewards (that is, the board of directors) of the enterprise. Where the stakeholders and the stewards are the same, arguably the need for the audit is less.

'Without accountability, no control' – the control being referred to here is *external* control by the stakeholders, often the shareholders, over their stake in the business. For this, a necessary prerequisite is for the shareholders to receive an account from those they have chosen to direct the business on their behalf. Today, many shareholders are more inquisitive, better informed, better organised, more assertive and more prepared to exercise this external control, as they are intent upon squeezing the last ounce of value out of their investments. Other external stakeholders are flexing their muscles too.

External auditors make a distinction between what they 'read' (all of the annual report), what they 'review' (a few of the directors' corporate governance assertions), and what they 'audit' (the financial statements).[2]

Responsible owners **H1.2**

In the wake of the 2008 global financial crisis, much attention has been given, particularly in the UK, to a perceived need for owners to be more active in influencing boards to direct and oversee their companies more effectively. There is disagreement as to whether shareholders should have more powers, centring on the philosophical debate about who is responsible for the corporate governance of a company.

Shareholder oversight **H1.3**

The FRC, responsible in the UK for developing corporate governance guidance, has come down firmly on the side of the board as being responsible for corporate governance. It seems inconsistent with this to expect shareholders to exercise a more active role in corporate governance, absent the introduction of enhanced shareholder powers. In its introduction to the current version of the UK Corporate Governance Code, the FRC reproduces and endorses the 1992 Cadbury sentiment about the respective responsibilities of boards and shareholders, which reinforces the unsatisfactory *status quo* and makes a nonsense of expecting investors to be prime movers of corporate governance improvements, which is clutching at straws. The FRC says:

> 'The first version of the UK Code on Corporate Governance (the Code) was produced in 1992 by the Cadbury Committee. Its paragraph 2.5 is still the classic definition of the context of the Code:
>
> > "Corporate governance is the system by which companies are directed and controlled. Boards of directors are responsible for the governance of their companies. The shareholders' role in governance is to appoint the directors and the auditors and to satisfy themselves that an appropriate governance structure is in place. The responsibilities of the board include setting the company's strategic aims, providing the leadership to put them into effect, supervising the management of the business and reporting to shareholders on their stewardship. The board's actions are subject to laws, regulations and the shareholders in general meeting."
>
> 'Corporate governance is therefore about what the board of a company does and how it sets the values of the company, and is to be distinguished from the day to day operational management of the company by full-time executives.'[3]

While the first sentence reproduced above is accepted as the classic definition of corporate governance, the rest of this quotation from Cadbury is highly contentious. It is still being hoped that a nod and a wink from significant shareholders will be sufficient to influence board behaviour appropriately.

The FRC's Stewardship Code (set out in full at **App2**) is designed to encourage active shareholder involvement. Without real shareholder powers, this remains questionable at least. It should not have been called a 'stewardship' code as, within corporate governance theory, it is the board and management who are the stewards for the shareholders.

There have been many examples of boards failing to modify their approach following overtures from shareholders, even though boards usually go through the motions of appearing to take shareholder concerns seriously. The 'exocet option' of declining to re-elect directors is a huge risk for shareholders to take, as it leaves the company and therefore shareholders' investment at extra risk. Furthermore, in liquid capital markets it is difficult to muster sufficient votes for shareholders to achieve an outcome at odds with the intentions of the board.

We also need to realise that many shareholders have little or no interest in these matters. Some have a vested interest in the decline of the companies in which they are invested, perhaps because they are short-term investors having 'bought short' and relying on the company's share price to decline in order to exit at a profit. Other shareholders may be content for their companies to take excessive risks if, in the short term, it is likely to pay dividends. Shareholders are not necessarily more responsible than the most irresponsible management teams. There are also significant costs involved in being an active investor.

Other stakeholders **H1.4**

The global financial crisis has highlighted that parties other than shareholders have significant stakes in companies. The Anglo-Saxon free capital markets model of corporate control has appeared very jaded compared, for instance, to the European social markets model. Millions of staff have lost their jobs and trillions of currency has been injected by states into failing financial institutions, into other failing companies and into social welfare for those displaced by failed companies. Crises of pollution, depletion of natural resources and global warming indicate that the stakeholders of companies are a much wider group than just shareholders, workers and tax payers. Now that more than half the largest 'economies' in the world are companies not countries (see **D3.3**), there is a heightened need for enhanced corporate accountability to this wider stakeholder community.

It is not just public companies that should be accountable to this wider community: for instance, sovereign wealth funds and large private companies are significant movers and shakers of global wellbeing. It is not satisfactory for disclosure requirements and standards to be determined on the basis of whether the entity is a public company or not. We discuss stakeholder theory in Chapter **C3**.

External reporting on internal control **H1.5**

But if there is external control, there is also a need for internal control. If external control is control by the stakeholders, then internal control is control by the board, management and staff. The board is at the pivotal point between these two controls, and the audit committee[4] pays attention to both. (For more discussion on this, refer to **C1.16** and Chapters **E4** and **E5**.) Indeed, there are myriad overlaps between external and internal control.

There is a whole raft of emerging requirements for external assurances on internal control, and services are emerging to fill this need. WebTrust, SysTrust and TrustGuard seals of approval are examples.[5] The WebTrust service was designed in the US by the American Institute of Certified Public Accountants and launched there and in Canada (the latter by the Canadian Institute of Chartered Accountants) in 1997. WebTrust as a 'Seal of Approval' applied to individual websites which meet strict conditions of good business practice. The service was designed to provide consumers with the confidence that using approved websites for transacting business on the Internet was as safe as doing business in the high street. In doing so, it is expected that the volume of ecommerce business undertaken will increase and benefit all those wishing to develop ecommerce activities as website operators, suppliers, service providers or consumers. In the UK, the Auditing Practices Board offered guidance on providing assurance on internal control.[6]

We believe there are no current examples of external reporting on internal control by internal audit; but it has happened before, for instance, throughout most of the 1970s by Anglian Water, later to become a UK FTSE 100 listed companies. See the following extract from Part 6 (Finance) of their 1979–80 Annual Report:

INTERNAL AUDIT

The scale and complexity of the Authority's organisation is recognised by the framework of control which is set down in Financial Regulations, Rules of Contract and the Schemes of Delegations. Within that structure management is responsible for ensuring that detailed systems of control exist to safeguard the Authority's assets, ensure reliability of records, promote operational efficiency and monitor adherence to policies and directives.

Management in turn relies on an effective internal audit to review, appraise and report on these systems of control.

During the year all major financial systems have been audited sufficiently to satisfy management on the soundness, adequacy and application of controls, and that the assets and interests of the organisation have been accounted for and protected from serious losses due to any reason, including fraud and poor value for money.

A significant change is the development of public reports progressively further and further beyond the bounds of financial statements alone, with parallel demands for attestation services to cover these extensions. A key issue is whether the auditing profession is well placed to inherit this future – or whether this future belongs to quality auditors, environmental auditors, ethics auditors, sustainability auditors and even to internal auditors. We should not overlook the Scottish Chartered Accountants' research report 'Auditing into the Twenty-first Century',[7] which floated the idea of the 'total audit', with the audit committee of the board (as it matures) becoming, in effect, the conductor of the orchestra, and today's external auditor becoming the 'assessor' of this total audit process.

On the whole, these other audits (quality, environmental and so on) have not become straitjacketed into boilerplate wordings for their audit reports, as have auditors of financial statements; and we must recognise that longer-form, discursive commentary, rather than boilerplate wording, is likely to be called for more often in the future.

Internal control in the UK Corporate Governance Code H1.6

So, the annual report of a listed company contains a narrative statement of how the company has applied Main Principle C.2 of the UK Corporate Governance Code (set out in full at **App1**). In 2003 and 2006 this read:

> 'The board should maintain a sound system of internal control to safeguard shareholders' investment and the company's assets.'

Still as a Main Principle, it now reads:

> 'The board is responsible for determining the nature and extent of the significant risks it is willing to take in achieving its strategic objectives. The board should maintain sound risk management and internal control systems.'

In our opinion, the current wording is a huge improvement. The old wording, introduced by Hampel in 1998, expressed very non-standard objectives of internal control compared to those within recognised internal control frameworks (see **G1.2**). Furthermore, this Principle now prioritises risk management, correctly implying that effective internal control is designed to mitigate the risks faced by the enterprise. 'Risk' had not previously been mentioned anywhere in the Code at the level of a Main or Supporting Principle. Thirdly, in the wake of the 2008 global financial crisis, when it became apparent that many boards had been insufficiently aware of the risks that their businesses had been running or had failed to understand those risks, the Code now makes it clear that boards are responsible for determining the nature and extent of the significant risks they are willing to take in achieving their strategic objectives. This implies that boards need to set the risk appetite(s) for their companies. It means that it is the board itself, not the executive alone, that needs to address these issues. 'Strategic objectives' implies that all categories of risk (external and internal, short and long term, etc) need to be understood and accepted by boards.

Impressively elegant as this wording is, the key question is whether excellent sentiment within the Code, which is not enforced by regulators, significantly impacts upon board behaviour. It is here that reliance is placed on responsible shareholders to make their voices heard in order to ensure appropriate board behaviour. Regrettably, many shareholders are neither responsible nor active, and shareholder powers to influence boards are not strong. The Stewardship Code (**App2**) is intended as a step forward to influence shareholder behaviour and shareholder dialogue with boards.

This narrative statement, as a minimum, is expected to disclose that there is an ongoing process for identifying, evaluating and managing the significant risks faced by the company, and that it is regularly reviewed by the board. The Turnbull Guidance also states that the board may wish to provide additional information to assist understanding of the company's risk management processes and system of internal control. The content of such narrative statements is likely, therefore, to vary widely from company to company – as, indeed, a review of subsequent published annual reports shows that it does: a standard sort of boilerplate wording is gratifyingly absent from most of these narrative statements that are appearing.

There are requirements under Auditing Standards for auditors to read the narrative statement and to seek to resolve any apparent misstatements or material inconsistencies with the audited financial statements.[8]

The Turnbull Guidance addresses all the internal control requirements of the Corporate Governance Code. This used to cover the internal control and the internal audit Provisions and the overarching internal control Principles. The internal audit Provision is no longer covered by the Turnbull guidance since it has been, post 2003, transferred into the Audit Committees and Auditors part of the Code. The Listing Rule (previously 12.43A, now 9.8.6 – see **A2.20**) requires the auditors to review only the disclosures made with respect to Provisions, not Principles, so only Provision C.2.1 is covered by the external auditor's review, which now reads:

> 'The board should, at least annually, conduct a review of the effectiveness of the company's risk management and internal control systems and should report to shareholders that they have done so. The review should cover all material controls, including financial, operational and compliance controls.'

The original Turnbull guidance (1999), at para 28, defined 'all controls' in this way:

> 'The reference to "all controls" in Code provision D.2.1 (now, in the 2003 Code, C.2.1) should not be taken to mean that the effectiveness of every internal control

(including controls designed to manage immaterial risks) should be subject to review by the board. Rather it means that, for the purposes of this guidance, internal controls considered by the board should include all types of controls including those of an operational and compliance nature, as well as internal financial controls.'

This paragraph no longer appears in the Turnbull Report, but the word 'material' was first inserted into the Code Provision in 2003.

The formal scope of the Cadbury Committee's report was on the financial aspects of corporate governance. Some held this restriction against the committee. For instance, some suggested that the Cadbury Code Provision, that directors should report publicly on the effectiveness of internal control, must have meant internal financial control in view of the intended scope of the Cadbury Committee's remit. But it was transparently clear that Cadbury meant all aspects of internal control, since the word 'financial' had been removed by the Cadbury Committee from their final report wherever internal control was referred to (including within the Cadbury Code itself), whereas the word 'financial' had always been present in the exposure draft of the Cadbury Report. There were good reasons why Cadbury meant that directors should report publicly on internal control 'in the round'. Internal financial control cannot be neatly differentiated from the other aspects of internal control; organisations achieve their objectives not through having effective internal financial control alone – arguably, operational control is more crucial to the achievement of objectives. Furthermore, the readers of published results already have some inkling about the effectiveness of internal financial control in view of the presence of audited financial statements; but to learn about the effectiveness of operational and legal and regulatory compliance control is to tell the readers something extra – so long as it is, and can be, reliably reported. Directors have oversight responsibility for all aspects of internal control – financial, operational and compliance. Maximising reliable disclosure is an underlying theme of contemporary developments in corporate governance best practice.

External audit review of corporate governance assertions H1.7

After representations made to the Hampel Committee by external auditors, that committee backed away from requiring external auditors to produce a report to shareholders on the results of their review of the board's adherence to any aspects of the Combined Code. Professional rules now require that only if the external auditor notes that there is non-compliance (which is not clearly acknowledged by the board itself within its published corporate governance statement) will the external auditor report on this non-compliance, the report of which is now incorporated into the main audit report, whereas previously it was a separate report from the auditors addressed to the directors but usually reproduced by the directors in their annual report.

The 1998 Combined Code comprised 17 Principles and 53 Provisions, compared with just 19 Provisions in the Cadbury Code.[9] The Combined Code did, however, also absorb the 29 Provisions in the Greenbury Code on executive remuneration. Although the 1998 Combined Code was much more extensive than the Cadbury Code, the requirement for the auditors to review the directors' assertions of compliance with the Provisions was not extended beyond the seven Provisions identified for this purpose within the Cadbury Report. This was a victory for the external auditing profession who were reluctant to become involved in this. Although the external auditors now review ten Provisions, including the one on going concern, in fact this is a narrowing of the scope of the review, as most of these ten Provisions concern audit committees, which were addressed by only one Provision within the Cadbury Code. External auditors no longer review directors' assertions on several matters, for instance whether there is a schedule of matters reserved to the board (see also **E4.6**).

However, in one respect the scope of the external auditor's review was extended. The external auditor's review of the internal control Provision, post-Hampel (1998), covered *all* of internal control (not just internal financial control) *and risk management*:

> 'The directors should, at least annually, conduct a review of the effectiveness of the group's system of internal controls and should report to shareholders that they have done so. The review should cover all controls, including financial, operational and compliance controls and risk management.' (1998 Code)

which was amended to (italics added):

> 'The directors should, at least annually, conduct a review of the effectiveness of the group's system of internal controls and should report to shareholders that they have done so. The review should cover all *material* controls, including financial, operational and compliance controls and risk management *systems*.' (2003 and 2006 Code Provision C.2.1)

and now reads (Provision C.2.1):

> 'The board should, at least annually, conduct a review of the effectiveness of the company's risk management and internal control systems and should report to shareholders that they have done so. The review should cover all material controls, including financial, operational and compliance controls.'

The Hampel Committee's Preamble to the 1998 Combined Code[10] stated:

> 'We have not included in the Combined Code principle D.IV in Chapter 2 of our final report, which reads as follows:
>
> > "External Auditors: The external auditors should independently report to shareholders in accordance with statutory and professional requirements and independently assure the board on the discharge of its responsibilities under D.I and D.II above in accordance with professional guidance."
>
> We say in paragraph 6.7 of the report that we recommend neither any additional prescribed requirements nor the removal of any existing requirements for auditors in relation to governance or publicly reported information, some of which derive from the Listing Rules. This recommendation is accepted by the London Stock Exchange. But the existing requirements for auditors will be kept under review, as a matter of course, by the responsible organisations.'

The table below summarises the relevant Combined Code Provisions which auditors were required to review under the 1998 Combined Code regime. In the table, we use the wording from the 1998 Combined Code:

Combined Code Provision reference	Wording (as in the 1998 Combined Code)
A.1.2	The board should have a formal schedule of matters specifically reserved to it for decision.
A.1.3	There should be a procedure agreed by the board of directors in the furtherance of their duties to take independent advice if necessary, at the company's expense.
A.6.1	Non-executive directors should be appointed for specified terms subject to re-election and to Companies Act provisions relating to the removal of a director, and re-appointment should not be automatic.
A.6.2	All directors should be subject to election by shareholders at the first opportunity after their appointment, and to re-election thereafter at intervals of no more than three years. The names of directors submitted for election or re-election should be accompanied by sufficient biographical details to enable shareholders to take an informed decision on their election.
D.1.1	The directors should explain their responsibility for preparing the accounts and there should be a statement by the auditors about their reporting responsibilities.
D.2.1	The directors should, at least annually, conduct a review of the effectiveness of the group's system of internal controls and should report to shareholders that they have done so. The review should cover all controls, including financial, operational and compliance controls and risk management.
D.3.1	The board should establish an audit committee of at least three directors, all non-executive, with written terms of reference which deal clearly with its authority and duties. The members of the committee, a majority of whom should be independent non-executive directors, should be named in the report and accounts.

Background to external audit review of corporate governance assertions **H1.8**

We should not forget that concerns about the quality of financial reporting have been key drivers of developments in corporate governance. This means that independent audit issues are not merely peripheral to the corporate governance debate. So, it was disappointing that the issues within the Cadbury Code closest to the accounting and statutory auditing professions were the issues that caused the most trouble. Indeed, it was only those two Provisions within the Cadbury Code which were closest to the accounting profession (that directors should report on 'going concern' and on the effectiveness of 'internal control'), the implementation of which had to be delayed pending the development of guidance first for directors and then for external auditors.

Guidance was needed for auditors, as Cadbury had identified certain Provisions within the Cadbury Code which the Committee considered were objectively verifiable and therefore should be reviewed by the statutory auditors during their annual audit. This was a burden (or an opportunity) which the audit profession took on with exceedingly great reluctance.

A reason for the negativity of the auditing profession to becoming involved in reviewing directors' corporate governance assertions has been the risk of litigation damages in an environment of unlimited auditor liability. Another reason has been the auditors' canny realisation that extended auditor responsibilities in the area of corporate governance attestation were unlikely to extract commensurately enhanced audit fees from reluctant clients.

As we have indicated, Cadbury had identified a number of Code Provisions which the Committee considered were objectively verifiable and they recommended that a company's compliance with these should be reviewed by the company's external auditors. The Cadbury Report, most probably as an oversight, omitted to specify that the external auditors should report on the results of their review of these matters. This allowed the external auditors to commence by addressing their report on their review to the directors and not to the shareholders, an approach now abandoned, as we shall explain. Most companies nevertheless chose to print that report from the auditors, addressed to the directors, in the annual report. Addressing the report to the directors gave an indication of the external auditors' preference that their comments on corporate governance matters should be made privately to management and the board – along the lines of the external auditor's traditional management letter on internal control and other matters.

One of the areas of directors' Code compliance that Cadbury recommended that the external auditors should review was the directors' report on the effectiveness of internal control. The external auditors led the fight to water down this requirement. It became the only Provision in the Cadbury Code which was watered down before it was implemented. Together with one other Code requirement close to the accounting profession (that directors should report on 'going concern'), implementation was also deferred. The Rutteman Working Party, which developed the watered down guidance, was convened by the main professional auditing body in the UK – the Institute of Chartered Accountants in England & Wales (ICAEW), and chaired by a senior audit partner from Ernst & Young. Later, the Turnbull Working Party, which provided the replacement guidance to the Rutteman guidance (made necessary when the wording of the relevant Code Provision was amended by the Hampel Committee), was also to be a working party of ICAEW, although it was to be chaired by a finance director and not by an external auditor. The Turnbull Working Party's deputy chairman was Roger Davies, head of professional affairs at PriceWaterhouseCoopers, who is said to have played an active part in its work. Arguably, the original Turnbull Committee was also not sufficiently independent of the issues at stake, but nevertheless it was obliged to work within the strictures of the Hampel Committee's Report which reversed some of the watering down that the Rutteman Working Party had allowed.

A key responsibility of the Hampel Committee was to review the functioning of the Cadbury Code. Since Rutteman had watered down the Code Provision on internal control, this was clearly a Provision at which the Committee would look closely. The Hampel Committee condoned the watering down which allowed directors not to disclose their opinion on the effectiveness or otherwise of internal control, but reversed the watering down which allowed the scope of the directors' internal control report to be restricted to internal financial control, insisting that it should cover the other aspects of internal control (operational and legal and regulatory compliance control) and risk management. Hampel's judgement on these matters was carried forward into the 2006 Combined Code. The scope of the board's assessment and report on the effectiveness of internal control and risk management is therefore much broader than in the US: in the UK, it covers all of internal control and also risk management, covering, therefore, operational and compliance control as well as financial control. In the US, under the Sarbanes-Oxley Act 2002, s 404, the scope is limited to internal control over financial reporting. However, in the US, the s 404 requirement is that the CEO and CFO must certify the effectiveness of internal control over financial reporting, and the external auditor attests to that certification. No similar requirement exists in the UK for a public expression of the effectiveness of internal control and risk management. However, UK companies caught by s 404 for their US reporting requirements are tending to include a public assessment of the effectiveness of internal control within their annual reports that go to UK shareholders. Royal Dutch Shell is an example.

The external auditors' report on some of the directors' corporate governance assertions has been, since Cadbury, a rather sorry and embarrassing affair. For instance, with respect to the directors' internal control report, it started as a negative assurance report. Within that report, the auditors were at pains to state that they had not done the extra work which would have been necessary for them positively to affirm that the directors' internal control assertions were justified, but only that during the course of their audit work they had stumbled across nothing which indicated to the auditors that the directors' assertions were not justified. Where the directors had gone further than the minimum watered-down requirements of Rutteman (by covering more aspects of internal control than just internal financial control, or by expressing an opinion on effectiveness, or both), the external auditors in their report were also at pains to point out that they were not reporting on any aspect of this extended scope of the directors' report.

With respect to compliance with the other Code Provisions that the auditors were required to review, the auditors have restricted themselves to a high-level confirmation of fact, without investigating the quality of compliance. For instance, the auditors were originally required to review whether there was a schedule of matters reserved to the board, or whether there was an audit committee which met at least twice a year and which had written terms of reference. If this appeared to be factually correct, then the auditors regarded their review of these items as completed.

The requirement for external auditors to review whether there is a schedule of matters reserved to the board (Provision A.1.1 in the 2006 Combined Code) has now been abandoned, replaced by Listing Rule 9.8.10 of the new Financial Conduct Authority, which we reproduce here, together with the auditors' obligations with respect to reviewing remuneration disclosures (Rule 9.8.11) and the action the auditors must take if they are of the opinion that the listed company has not complied (Rule 9.8.12). References in Rule 9.8.10 to Code Provisions correspond to those in **App1**.

LR 9.8.10 01/04/2013	A listed company must ensure that the auditors review each of the following before the annual report is published: (1) LR 9.8.6 R (3) (statement by the directors that the business is a going concern); and (2) the parts of the statement required by LR 9.8.6 R (6) (corporate governance) that relate to the following provisions of the UK Corporate Governance Code: (a) C.1.1; (b) C.2.1; and (c) C.3.1 to C.3.7.
LR 9.8.11 01/04/2013	A listed company must ensure that the auditors review the following disclosures: (1) LR 9.8.8 R (2) (amount of each element in the remuneration package and information on share options); (2) LR 9.8.8 R (3), LR 9.8.8 R (4) and (5) (details of long term incentive schemes for directors); (3) LR 9.8.8 R (11) (money purchase schemes); and (4) LR 9.8.8 R (12) (defined benefit schemes).
LR 9.8.12 01/04/2013	If, in the opinion of the auditors the listed company has not complied with any of the requirements set out in LR 9.8.11 R the listed company must ensure that the auditors report includes, to the extent possible, a statement giving details of the non-compliance.

At the time of writing this chapter, the Financial Conduct Authority's Listing Rule continued to refer to the out-of-date 2010 version of the UK Corporate Governance Code when setting out the provisions that auditors of listed companies are required to review, not reflecting the 2012 revision of the Code's provisions on audit committees (see **App1**). So the Listing Rule continued to state that a listed company's external auditor should review provisions C.3.1 to C.3.7, viz:

> '**Auditors report**
>
> LR 9.8.10
>
> 01/04/2013
>
> FCA
>
> A listed company must ensure that the auditors review each of the following before the annual report is published:
>
> (1) LR 9.8.6 R (3) (statement by the directors that the business is a going concern); and
>
> (2) the parts of the statement required by LR 9.8.6R (6) (corporate governance) that relate to the following provisions of the UK Corporate Governance Code:
>
> (a) C.1.1;
>
> (b) C.2.1; and
>
> (c) C.3.1 to C.3.7.'

New Provision C.3.8 (see **App1**) is currently excluded from the external auditor's review. It reads:

'A separate section of the annual report should describe the work of the committee in discharging its responsibilities. The report should include:

- the significant issues that the committee considered in relation to the financial statements, and how these issues were addressed;
- an explanation of how it has assessed the effectiveness of the external audit process and the approach taken to the appointment or reappointment of the external auditor, and information on the length of tenure of the current audit firm and when a tender was last conducted; and
- if the external auditor provides non-audit services, an explanation of how auditor objectivity and independence is safeguarded.'

Issues arising from this lack of alignment between the Code and the Listing Rule are as follows:

- Will it be appropriate for the external auditors to independently review all company assertions relating to Provision C.3.8 in view of the proximity of these to the matters relating to the external auditor?
- Could the Listing Rule be amended by administrative action by the FCA without a process of consultation?
- How can resolution of this lack of alignment be done in a timely way, bearing in mind that it is likely that content in the Code relating to audit committees will be further revised ion 2014.

It should be noted that companies are already reporting against the 2012 Code, and auditors are expected to look at the audit committee report under revised ISA (UK and Ireland) 700 – 'The auditor's report on financial statements' – which the FRC published at the same time as the 2012 Code.

Auditors report **H1.9**

LR 9.8.6 R (3) corresponds to UK Corporate Governance Code Provision C.1.3 on 'going concern' which now reads:

'The directors should report in annual and half-yearly financial statements that the business is a going concern, with supporting assumptions or qualifications as necessary.'

There are now, therefore, ten Code Provisions with respect to which the external auditors review the directors' 'comply or explain' assertions (C.1.1, C.1.2, C.2.1 and C.3.1 to C.3.7). While this appears to be an increase beyond what applied after the 1992 Cadbury Code had been adopted, in fact it is a narrowing down to just internal control, going concern and audit committee matters. Whereas there was only one Provision within the Cadbury Code on audit committees, there are now seven such Provisions within the 2012 Code (C.3.1 to C.3.7 at **App1**) which are included within the external auditors review. Note that Listing Rule 9.8.11 (see above) does not yet require the external auditors to review Code Provision C.3.8 which reads:

'A separate section of the annual report should describe the work of the committee in discharging its responsibilities. The report should include:

- the significant issues that the committee considered in relation to the financial statements, and how these issues were addressed;
- an explanation of how it has assessed the effectiveness of the external audit process and the approach taken to the appointment or reappointment of the

external auditor, and information on the length of tenure of the current audit firm and when a tender was last conducted; and

- if the external auditor provides non-audit services, an explanation of how auditor objectivity and independence is safeguarded.'

When the Cadbury Code came up for review by Hampel, the external auditing profession made a pitch to be excluded from any requirement to review any of the directors' corporate governance assertions. But the Hampel Committee recommended no change and the Stock Exchange agreed. That left an ambiguity, as one of these directors' corporate governance assertions had itself changed in scope – the one on internal control – and for a while it was not clear whether 'no change' meant that the auditors review continued to be based on the old, more limited, scope or should cover the new, more extended, scope.

Following publication of the final Turnbull Report, the Auditing Practices Board published its own guidance to external auditors on their review of directors' corporate governance assertions within the annual report.[11] The guidance resolved the uncertainty as to whether the auditors would restrict their review of the directors' internal control assertions to just internal financial control, or broaden it to all controls in view of the broader scope of the Combined Code's 'Provision' compared with the Rutteman interpretation of the older Provision in the Cadbury Code. In fact, the auditors cover all controls in their review.

It is also interesting that the guidance suggested that the external auditors should attend meetings of the board of directors (if there is no audit committee of the board) at which the annual report and accounts, including the statement of compliance, are considered and approved for submission to the board of directors.

It is hard to escape the conclusion that this guidance for external auditors entails additional audit work beyond what would be needed if there were no requirement for the external auditors to review certain of the directors' corporate governance assertions, although most of this additional work will have already been incorporated into external audit work plans since the implementation of Cadbury. In the US, the Sarbanes-Oxley s 404 duties of external auditors mean that there is now a much more significant extra burden upon US external auditors than upon UK auditors.

The objective of the UK auditors' review is to assess whether the company's summary of the process that the board (and, where applicable, its committees) has adopted in reviewing the effectiveness of the system of internal control is both supported by the documentation prepared by or for the directors and appropriately reflects that process.

To achieve this objective, the auditors:

(a) through inquiry of the directors obtain an understanding of the process defined by the board for its review of the effectiveness of internal control and compare their understanding with the statement made by the board in the annual report and accounts;

(b) review the documentation prepared by or for the directors to support their statement made in connection with the Code Provision on internal control and assess whether or not it provides sound support for that statement; and

(c) relate the statement made by the directors to the auditors' knowledge of the company obtained during the audit of the financial statements. The scope of the directors' review will be considerably broader than the knowledge the auditors can be expected to have based on their audit.

Points (a) to (c) (above) are in addition to the general evidence that the auditors must obtain to support each of the corporate governance disclosures which are within the scope of the auditors' review. That general evidence is as follows:

(a) reviewing the minutes of the meetings of the board of directors, and of relevant board committees;
(b) reviewing relevant supporting documents re (a) (immediately above);
(c) making inquiries of certain directors and the company secretary regarding procedure and its implementation, to satisfy the auditors; and
(d) attending meetings of the audit committee (or the full board if there is no audit committee) at which the annual report and accounts, including the statement of compliance, are considered and approved for submission to the board of directors.

External auditors' revised Code responsibilities **H1.10**

(The Table at **H1.16** traces the changes in Code Provisions that external auditors are required to review, between 1992 and the present.)

Each revision of the Code has been an opportunity to reconsider the scope of the review by auditors of directors' assertions on Code compliance. This was addressed by the Auditing Practices Board (APB) in their late-2004 Bulletin[12] which was revised further,[13] following the 2005 Turnbull Review, the latter adding the requirement that the board's statement on internal control should confirm that necessary actions have been taken, or are being taken, to remedy any significant failings or weaknesses identified from its review of the effectiveness of the system of internal control. Amongst its 29 pages, APB's Bulletin 2006/5 contained 21 pages of general and specific guidance relating to the external auditor's review of the ten statements of compliance which external auditors are now required to cover.

APB Bulletins themselves are discretionary for auditors:

> 'Practice Notes and Bulletins are persuasive rather than prescriptive and are indicative of good practice … Bulletins provide timely guidance on new or emerging issues.'[14]

On 20 October 2004 the Financial Services Authority (FSA), not the FRC, issued its instrument 2004/83 ('Listing Rules (Auditors' responsibilities in relation to the Combined Code) instrument 2004') amending part of Listing Rule 12.43A. This instrument came into force on 1 November 2004. The amendment requires that, with respect to a listed company's 'comply or explain' disclosures on the Code Provisions:

> 'A company's statement under 12.43A(b) must be reviewed by the auditors before publication only insofar as it relates to Code provisions C.1.1, C.2.1, C.3.1, C.3.2, C.3.3, C.3.4, C.3.5, C.3.6 and C.3.7 of the Combined Code.'

Listing Rule 12.43A is now to be found at Listing Rules 9.8.10 R to 9.8.12 R (reproduced at **H1.8** above).

So, apart from the separate requirement for external auditors to review the directors' assertion on going concern, there are now just nine Provisions to be reviewed, compared to seven under the 1998 Code and ten under the 1992 Cadbury Code – and they are not all identical Provisions. Hence, for instance, KPMG in its audit report on WM Morrison Supermarkets plc for the year ended 30 January 2005, stated:

> 'We review whether the corporate governance statement on pages 14 to 17 reflects the company's compliance with the nine provisions of the 2003 FRC Code specified for our review by the Listing Rules, and we report if it does not.

We are not required to consider whether the board's statements on internal control cover all risks and controls, or form an opinion on the effectiveness of the group's corporate governance procedures or its risk and control procedures.'

A narrowing of auditor focus **H1.11**

The UK and Irish Listing Rule, as it applied to the 1998 Combined Code, required the auditor to review the directors' compliance statement with respect to seven Provisions. Now the requirement is to review nine. In addition, the 1992 and 1998 requirement for the auditor to review the directors' assertions on 'going concern' continues unchanged, making ten in all.

While auditors reviewed 11 of the 19 Provisions within the 1992 Cadbury Code, they now review only nine of the 52 Provisions, and none of the Principles, in the current Code (**App1**), and none of the new Stewardship Code (**App2**). If one adds the auditors' work on going concern, we could say that auditors review ten of the Provisions in the current Code (Provision C.1.3, and see **H1.14** below). This indicates a marked reluctance by auditors to become involved in reviewing, still less auditing, aspects of corporate governance. If auditor liability were capped, or limited in some other way, we might see less reluctance by them to become involved in these important matters. Five of the original Cadbury provisions, which continued to be reviewed after the publication of the 1998 Combined Code, have not been reviewed since the introduction of the 2003 version of the Combined Code. The wording of those that continue to be reviewed has changed, and thus the specific audit review requirements, as set out in what is now APB Bulletin 2006/5, have been modified.

The additional Provisions that are now reviewed do not represent 'creep' into other areas – rather they are a consequence of audit committees being addressed by a larger number of Provisions within the 2003 and more recent versions of the Code, and the overall result has been a narrowing of auditor attention. The Code content on audit committees has not been modified between the 2003 and 2010 versions of the Code. Since Cadbury, the test as to whether a Provision falls within the remit of the auditor to review has been whether it is 'objectively verifiable'. More recently, an additional test has been added – whether the Provision relates to accountability and audit matters and is therefore close to the traditional interest and competence of the auditor. Gone is auditor review of Provisions on a formal schedule of matters reserved to the board (2006 Combined Code: Provision A.1.1), directors taking independent advice (2006: A.5.2), the selection of non-executive directors (2006: A.7.1) and their terms of appointment (2006: A.7.2), service contracts (1992 Cadbury Code: 3.1) and non-executive determination of executive remuneration (1992: 3.3).

The APB acknowledged:

> 'The scope of the auditor's review required by the Listing Rules,[15] in comparison to the totality of the Combined Code, is narrow. The auditor is not required to review the directors' narrative statement of how they have applied the Code principles and is required only to review the directors' compliance statement in relation to nine of the forty-eight Code provisions applicable to companies. Nevertheless, because the directors' narrative statement comprises other information included in a document containing audited financial statements there is a broader requirement under Auditing Standards[16] for the auditor to read such 'other information' and if the auditor becomes aware of any apparent misstatements therein, or identifies any material inconsistencies with the audited financial statements, to seek to resolve them.'[17]

The APB distinguished between the *audit* of the financial statements, the *review* of a limited number of directors' Code compliance assertions, and the auditor's duty to '*read*' all the content of the annual report:[18]

> 'The auditor has different responsibilities with respect to the various component parts of the annual report. For example, the auditor is required to "audit" the financial statements, "review" the company's compliance with certain aspects of the Combined Code and "read" all information in the annual report that is not subject to any other requirement. The auditor reads such "other information" because the credibility of the financial statements and the related auditor's report may be undermined by material inconsistencies between the financial statements and the "other information", or by apparent misstatements within the other information.'[19]

As before, there is no requirement for auditor review of directors' assertions with respect to applying any of the *Main Principles* and *Supporting Principles* of the Code, but the auditor reads these statements and:

> 'considers whether any information in either of them is apparently misstated or materially inconsistent with other information of which the auditor has become aware in the course of either the review of the company's compliance statement (insofar as it relates to the nine 2003 FRC Code provisions that the auditor is required to review under the Listing Rules) or the audit of the financial statements … If such lack of proper disclosure is considered significant by the auditor and the directors cannot be persuaded to amend the disclosure to the auditor's satisfaction, the auditor considers the implications for the auditor's reporting responsibilities and the auditor may need to take legal advice.'[20]

The auditor also has no responsibility to review or otherwise assess and comment upon a company's decision to depart from the *Provisions* of the Code: it is for shareholders and others to evaluate any such departure and the company's explanation of it.[21] But, with respect to the Provisions within the scope of the auditor's review, if the auditor concludes that an amendment is necessary to the company's Code compliance disclosures which the company refuses to make, then the auditor will consider including in the opinion section[22] of the auditor's report an 'emphasis of matter' paragraph describing the material misstatement – which *would not give rise to a qualified opinion on the financial statements*. The auditor is not required to, and does not, perform additional procedures to investigate the appropriateness of reasons given for non-compliance with any of the Code Provisions the auditor reviews.

Audit evidence **H1.12**

With respect to all of the nine 2003 (and more recent) Code Provisions that the auditor is required to review, the auditor should obtain appropriate evidence to support the company's compliance statements. Evidence is likely to be found in board committee minutes and relevant supporting documents, as well as through enquiries that the auditor makes of directors, the chairman of the board and of relevant board committees – particularly the audit committee. Usually, the auditor should attend the audit committee meeting at which the annual report and accounts, including the statement of Code compliance, are considered and approved; alternatively, if there is no audit committee, the auditor should attend the board itself. The auditor may also request that the directors provide written confirmation of oral representations made during the course of the review.

Auditor reviewing the directors' compliance statement on internal control H1.13

There is much good guidance in APB Bulletin 2006/5 on the approach the auditor should take to review compliance with Provision C.2.1. Some of the guidance is standard to any of the nine Provisions reviewed by the auditor; much of the rest applies the Turnbull Guidance.

APB took the view that the only substantial change in the wording of what is now Provision C.2.1, between the 1998 and 2003 versions of the Combined Code, was that the directors' review should cover 'all *material* controls', not 'all controls', as the 1998 Code had put it.[23] APB pointed out that the Turnbull Guidance established this, and it had been incorporated into the revised wording of the Provision as it appeared in the 2003 version of the Code.[24]

APB appears to have overlooked, or to have regarded it as an insubstantial change, that the 2003 wording also referred to the review covering 'risk management *systems*' rather than 'risk management', which could be interpreted as being significantly different. A focus on 'risk management *systems*' could appear to support that this Provision now covers only the audit committee's (or the board's) consideration of the *process* of risk management and not their consideration of the specific high-level risks themselves and whether those specific risks were sufficiently mitigated. The Turnbull Review did not clarify this matter.

APB points out that the objective of the auditor's review is to assess whether the company's summary of the processes the board (and where applicable its committees) have adopted in reviewing the effectiveness of the system of internal control, is supported by the documentation prepared by, or for, the directors and appropriately reflects that process. So, therefore, the auditor must obtain an understanding, through enquiry of the directors, of the process defined by the board for its review of the effectiveness of all material internal controls, and compare that understanding to the statement made by the board in the annual report and accounts. The auditor should also review *the documentation* prepared by, or for, the directors to support their statement made in connection with Code Provision C.2.1, and assess whether or not it provides sound support for that statement.

Since the audit of the financial statements results in the auditor obtaining knowledge of the company and an understanding of certain aspects of the company's internal control systems, the auditor should relate the directors' statement to the auditor's knowledge. However, the scope of the directors' review of internal control and risk management will be considerably broader in its scope than the knowledge on which the auditor can be expected to have based their audit.

APB recommends that material weaknesses in internal control identified by the auditor should be reported promptly to the client, so that the directors will be aware of these weaknesses and be able to take account of them in making their statements on internal control.

The auditor's review responsibility includes discussing with the directors the steps the directors have taken to determine what 'significant problems' are disclosed in the annual report and accounts; and assessing whether disclosures made by the board of the processes it has applied to deal with material internal control aspects of any significant problems disclosed in the annual report and accounts appropriately reflect those processes. The auditor is not required to assess whether the processes described by the directors will, in fact, remedy the problem described in the annual report and accounts.

The auditor might be aware of a significant problem, disclosed in the annual report and accounts, which has occurred, in large measure, because of a failure of internal control. Yet the board is not intending to disclose the material internal control aspects or has not disclosed the process it has applied to deal with those material internal control aspects, or both. If the matter cannot be resolved, there are likely to be implications for the auditor's opinion (though not necessarily for the auditor's opinion on the financial statements themselves).

Going concern H1.14

The tenth accountability and audit Code Provision (C.1.3 on 'going concern') is covered within Listing Rule 9.8.6, which requires a listed company to include in its annual financial report:

> '**Additional information**
>
> (3) a statement made by the directors that the business is a going concern, together with supporting assumptions or qualifications as necessary, that has been prepared in accordance with Going Concern and Liquidity Risk: Guidance for Directors of UK Companies 2009, published by the Financial Reporting Council in October 2009;'

and Listing Rule 9.8.10 states:

> '**Auditors report**
>
> A *listed company* must ensure that the auditors review each of the following before the annual report is published:
>
> (1) LR 9.8.6R (3) (statement by the directors that the business is a going concern); ...'

The FSA has not changed the Listing Rule requirement under 9.8.6R (3), previously LR12.43(v), that a statement by the directors that the business is a going concern (with supporting assumptions or qualifications as necessary) is included in the annual report and accounts and such a statement is reviewed by the auditor before publication.

Groups, joint ventures and associated companies H1.15

Paragraph 14 of the Turnbull Guidance established that, for groups of companies, the review of effectiveness of internal control and risk management should be from the perspective of the group as a whole. Accordingly, the auditor's consideration of the board's description of its process for reviewing the effectiveness of internal control encompasses the group as a whole. Where material joint ventures and associated companies have not been dealt with as part of the group for the purposes of applying the Turnbull Guidance, paragraph 41 of the Turnbull Guidance required that this fact should be disclosed by the board. The auditor assesses, based on the auditor's knowledge of the group obtained during the audit of the financial statements, whether any material joint ventures or associated companies have not been dealt with and, therefore, if such a disclosure is necessary.[25] If the auditor concludes that no disclosure has been made by the board that a material joint venture or associated company has not been dealt with as part of the group, they report this in the opinion section of their report on the financial statements.

Directors' assertions on compliance with Code Provisions which external auditors review: developments

See also **H1.8**. **H1.16**

1.	2.	3.	4.	5.	6.	7.	8.
1992 'Cadbury Code'[1]		**1998 Combined Code**		**2003 and 2006 Combined Codes[2, 3] and 2010 UK Corporate Governance Code**		**2012 UK Corporate Governance Code (see App1)**	
Equivalent Provision reference(s)	**Wording**	**Equivalent Provision reference(s)**	**Wording**	**Equivalent Provision reference(s)**	**Wording**	**Equivalent Provision reference(s)**	**Wording**
1.4	The board should have a formal schedule of matters specifically reserved to it for decision to ensure that the direction and control of the company is firmly in its hands.	A.1.2	The board should have a formal schedule of matters specifically reserved to it for decision.	A1.1	No longer reviewed by the external auditors.		
1.5	There should be an agreed procedure for directors in the furtherance of their duties to take independent professional advice, if necessary, at the company's expense.	A.1.3	There should be a procedure agreed by the board of directors in the furtherance of their duties to take independent advice, if necessary, at the company's expense.	A.5.2	No longer reviewed by the external auditors.	B.5.1	No longer reviewed by the external auditors.
2.3	Non-executive directors should be appointed for specified terms and reappointment should not be automatic.	A.6.1	Non-executive directors should be appointed for specified terms subject to re-election and to Companies Act provisions relating to the removal of a director, and re-appointment should not be automatic.	A.7.2	No longer reviewed by the external auditors.	B.2.3	No longer reviewed by the external auditors.

1.	2.	3.	4.	5.	6.	7.	8.
1992 'Cadbury Code'[1]		1998 Combined Code		2003 and 2006 Combined Codes[2, 3] and 2010 UK Corporate Governance Code		2012 UK Corporate Governance Code (see App1)	
Equivalent Provision reference(s)	**Wording**	**Equivalent Provision reference(s)**	**Wording**	**Equivalent Provision reference(s)**	**Wording**	**Equivalent Provision reference(s)**	**Wording**
2.4	Non-executive directors should be selected through a formal process and both this process and their appointment should be a matter for the board as a whole.	A.6.2	All directors should be subject to election by shareholders at the first opportunity after their appointment, and to re-election thereafter at intervals of no more than three years. The names of directors submitted for election or re-election should be accompanied by sufficient biographical details to enable shareholders to take an informed decision on their election.	A.7.1	No longer reviewed by the external auditors.	B.7.1	No longer reviewed by the external auditors.
3.1	Directors' service contracts should not exceed three years without shareholders' approval.						
3.2	There should be full and clear disclosure of directors' total emoluments and those of the chairman and highest-paid UK director, including pension contributions and stock options. Separate figures should be given for salary and performance-related elements and the basis on which performance is measured should be explained.					No equivalent provision	

1.	2.	3.	4.	5.	6.	7.	8.
1992 'Cadbury Code'[1]		1998 Combined Code		2003 and 2006 Combined Codes[2, 3] and 2010 UK Corporate Governance Code		2012 UK Corporate Governance Code (see App1)	
Equivalent Provision reference(s)	Wording	Equivalent Provision reference(s)	Wording	Equivalent Provision reference(s)	Wording	Equivalent Provision reference(s)	Wording
3.3	Executive directors' pay should be subject to the recommendations of a remuneration committee made up wholly or mainly of non-executive directors.					D.2.2	The remuneration committee should have delegated responsibility for setting remuneration for all executive directors and the chairman, including pension rights and any compensation payments. The committee should also recommend and monitor the level and structure of remuneration for senior management. The definition of 'senior management' for this purpose should be determined by the board but should normally include the first layer of management below board level.

1.	2.	3.	4.	5.	6.	7.	8.
1992 'Cadbury Code'[1]		1998 Combined Code		2003 and 2006 Combined Codes[2,3] and 2010 UK Corporate Governance Code		2012 UK Corporate Governance Code (see App1)	
Equivalent Provision reference(s)	**Wording**	**Equivalent Provision reference(s)**	**Wording**	**Equivalent Provision reference(s)**	**Wording**	**Equivalent Provision reference(s)**	**Wording**
4.4	The directors should explain their responsibility for preparing the accounts next to a statement by the auditors about their reporting responsibilities.	D.1.1	The directors should explain their responsibility for preparing the accounts and there should be a statement by the auditors about their reporting responsibilities.	C.1.1	The directors should explain in the annual report their responsibility for preparing the accounts and there should be a statement by the auditors about their reporting responsibilities.	C.1.1	The directors should explain in the annual report their responsibility for preparing the annual report and accounts, and state that they consider the annual report and accounts, taken as a whole, is fair, balanced and understandable and provides the information necessary for shareholders to assess the company's performance, business model and strategy. There should be a statement by the auditor about their reporting responsibilities.

1.	2.	3.	4.	5.	6.	7.	8.
1992 'Cadbury Code'[1]		1998 Combined Code		2003 and 2006 Combined Codes[2,3] and 2010 UK Corporate Governance Code		2012 UK Corporate Governance Code (see App1)	
Equivalent Provision reference(s)	**Wording**	**Equivalent Provision reference(s)**	**Wording**	**Equivalent Provision reference(s)**	**Wording**	**Equivalent Provision reference(s)**	**Wording**
4.5	The directors should report on the effectiveness of the company's system of internal control.	D.2.1	The directors should, at least annually, conduct a review of the effectiveness of the group's system of internal controls and should report to shareholders that they have done so. The review should cover all controls, including financial, operational and compliance controls and risk management.	C.2.1	The board should, at least annually, conduct a review of the effectiveness of the group's system of internal controls and should report to shareholders that they have done so. The review should cover all material controls, including financial, operational and compliance controls and risk management systems.	C.2.1	The board should, at least annually, conduct a review of the effectiveness of the company's risk management and internal control systems and should report to shareholders that they have done so[4]. The review should cover all material controls, including financial, operational and compliance controls.

1.	2.	3.	4.	5.	6.	7.	8.
1992 'Cadbury Code'[1]		1998 Combined Code		2003 and 2006 Combined Codes[2,3] and 2010 UK Corporate Governance Code		2012 UK Corporate Governance Code (see App1)	
Equivalent Provision reference(s)	**Wording**	**Equivalent Provision reference(s)**	**Wording**	**Equivalent Provision reference(s)**	**Wording**	**Equivalent Provision reference(s)**	**Wording**
4.3	The board should establish an audit committee of at least three non-executive directors with written terms of reference which deal clearly with its authority and duties.	D.3.1	The board should establish an audit committee of at least three directors, all non-executive, with written terms of reference which deal clearly with its authority and duties. The members of the committee, a majority of whom should be independent non-executive directors, should be named in the report and accounts.	C.3.1	The board should establish an audit committee of at least three, or in the case of smaller companies two, members, who should all be independent non-executive directors. The board should satisfy itself that at least one member of the audit committee has recent and relevant financial experience.	C.3.1	The board should establish an audit committee of at least three, or in the case of smaller companies[5] two, independent non-executive directors. In smaller companies the company chairman may be a member of, but not chair, the committee in addition to the independent non-executive directors, provided he or she was considered independent on appointment as chairman. The board should satisfy itself that at least one member of the audit committee has recent and relevant financial experience.

1.	2.	3.	4.	5.	6.	7.	8.
1992 'Cadbury Code'[1]		**1998 Combined Code**		**2003 and 2006 Combined Codes**[2, 3] **and 2010 UK Corporate Governance Code**		**2012 UK Corporate Governance Code (see App1)**	
Equivalent Provision reference(s)	**Wording**	**Equivalent Provision reference(s)**	**Wording**	**Equivalent Provision reference(s)**	**Wording**	**Equivalent Provision reference(s)**	**Wording**
There was no 'Cadbury' Code Provision equivalent to the 2003 Code Provision C.3.2.		There was no 1998 Combined Code Provision equivalent to the 2003 Code Provision C.3.2.		C.3.2	The main role and responsibilities of the audit committee should be set out in written terms of reference and should include: to monitor the integrity of the financial statements of the company, and any formal announcements relating to the company's financial performance, reviewing significant financial reporting judgements contained in them; to review the company's internal financial controls and, unless expressly addressed by a separate board risk committee composed of independent directors, or by the board itself, to review the company's internal control and risk management systems; to monitor and review	C.3.2	The main role and responsibilities of the audit committee should be set out in written terms of reference[6] and should include: to monitor the integrity of the financial statements of the company and any formal announcements relating to the company's financial performance, reviewing significant financial reporting judgements contained in them; to review the company's internal financial controls and, unless expressly addressed by a separate board risk committee composed of independent directors, or by the board itself, to review the company's internal control and risk management systems;

1.	2.	3.	4.	5.	6.	7.	8.
1992 'Cadbury Code'[1]		1998 Combined Code		2003 and 2006 Combined Codes[2,3] and 2010 UK Corporate Governance Code		2012 UK Corporate Governance Code (see App1)	
Equivalent Provision reference(s)	**Wording**	**Equivalent Provision reference(s)**	**Wording**	**Equivalent Provision reference(s)**	**Wording**	**Equivalent Provision reference(s)**	**Wording**
					the effectiveness of the company's internal audit function; to make recommendations to the board, for it to put to the shareholders for their approval in general meeting, in relation to the appointment, re-appointment and removal of the external auditor and to approve the remuneration and terms of engagement of the external auditor; to review and monitor the external auditor's independence and objectivity and the effectiveness of the audit process, taking into consideration relevant UK professional and regulatory requirements; to develop and implement policy on the engagement of the external auditor		to monitor and review the effectiveness of the company's internal audit function; to make recommendations to the board, for it to put to the shareholders for their approval in general meeting, in relation to the appointment, re-appointment and removal of the external auditor and to approve the remuneration and terms of engagement of the external auditor; to review and monitor the external auditor's independence and objectivity and the effectiveness of the audit process, taking into consideration relevant UK professional and regulatory requirements; to develop and implement policy on

1.	2.	3.	4.	5.	6.	7.	8.
1992 'Cadbury Code'[1]		**1998 Combined Code**		**2003 and 2006 Combined Codes**[2, 3] **and 2010 UK Corporate Governance Code**		**2012 UK Corporate Governance Code (see App1)**	
Equivalent Provision reference(s)	**Wording**	**Equivalent Provision reference(s)**	**Wording**	**Equivalent Provision reference(s)**	**Wording**	**Equivalent Provision reference(s)**	**Wording**
					to supply non-audit services, taking into account relevant ethical guidance regarding the provision of non-audit services by the external audit firm; and to report to the board, identifying any matters in respect of which it considers that action or improvement is needed and making recommendations as to the steps to be taken.		the engagement of the external auditor to supply non-audit services, taking into account relevant ethical guidance regarding the provision of non-audit services by the external audit firm; and to report to the board, identifying any matters in respect of which it considers that action or improvement is needed and making recommendations as to the steps to be taken; and to report to the board on how it has discharged its responsibilities.
There was no 'Cadbury' Code Provision equivalent to the 2003 Code Provision C.3.3.		There was no 1998 Combined Code Provision equivalent to the 2003 Code Provision C.3.3.		C.3.3	The terms of reference of the audit committee, including its role and the authority delegated to it by the board, should be made available. A separate section of the annual report should describe the work of the committee in discharging those responsibilities.	C.3.3	The terms of reference of the audit committee, including its role and the authority delegated to it by the board, should be made available.

1.	2.	3.	4.	5.	6.	7.	8.
1992 'Cadbury Code'[1]		**1998 Combined Code**		**2003 and 2006 Combined Codes[2, 3] and 2010 UK Corporate Governance Code**		**2012 UK Corporate Governance Code (see App1)**	
Equivalent Provision reference(s)	**Wording**	**Equivalent Provision reference(s)**	**Wording**	**Equivalent Provision reference(s)**	**Wording**	**Equivalent Provision reference(s)**	**Wording**
There was no 'Cadbury' Code Provision equivalent to the 2003 Code Provision C.3.4.		There was no 1998 Combined Code Provision equivalent to the 2003 Code Provision C.3.4.		C.3.4	The audit committee should review arrangements by which staff of the company may, in confidence, raise concerns about possible improprieties in matters of financial reporting or other matters. The audit committee's objective should be to ensure that arrangements are in place for the proportionate and independent investigation of such matters and for appropriate follow-up action.	C.3.5	The audit committee should review arrangements by which staff of the company may, in confidence, raise concerns about possible improprieties in matters of financial reporting or other matters. The audit committee's objective should be to ensure that arrangements are in place for the proportionate and independent investigation of such matters and for appropriate follow-up action.

1.	2.	3.	4.	5.	6.	7.	8.
1992 'Cadbury Code'[1]		**1998 Combined Code**		**2003 and 2006 Combined Codes[2,3] and 2010 UK Corporate Governance Code**		**2012 UK Corporate Governance Code (see App1)**	
Equivalent Provision reference(s)	**Wording**	**Equivalent Provision reference(s)**	**Wording**	**Equivalent Provision reference(s)**	**Wording**	**Equivalent Provision reference(s)**	**Wording**
There was no 'Cadbury' Code Provision equivalent to the 2003 Code Provision C.3.5.		There was no 1998 Combined Code Provision equivalent to the 2003 Code Provision C.3.5.		C.3.5	The audit committee should monitor and review the effectiveness of the internal audit activities. Where there is no internal audit function, the audit committee should consider annually whether there is a need for an internal audit function and make a recommendation to the board, and the reasons for the absence of such a function should be explained in the relevant section of the annual report.	C.3.6	The audit committee should monitor and review the effectiveness of the internal audit activities. Where there is no internal audit function, the audit committee should consider annually whether there is a need for an internal audit function and make a recommendation to the board, and the reasons for the absence of such a function should be explained in the relevant section of the annual report.

1.	2.	3.	4.	5.	6.	7.	8.
1992 'Cadbury Code'[1]		1998 Combined Code		2003 and 2006 Combined Codes[2, 3] and 2010 UK Corporate Governance Code		2012 UK Corporate Governance Code (see App1)	
Equivalent Provision reference(s)	**Wording**	**Equivalent Provision reference(s)**	**Wording**	**Equivalent Provision reference(s)**	**Wording**	**Equivalent Provision reference(s)**	**Wording**
There was no 'Cadbury' Code Provision equivalent to the 2003 Code Provision C.3.6.		There was no 1998 Combined Code Provision equivalent to the 2003 Code Provision C.3.6.		C.3.6	The audit committee should have primary responsibility for making a recommendation on the appointment, reappointment and removal of the external auditors. If the board does not accept the audit committee's recommendation, it should include in the annual report, and in any papers recommending appointment or re-appointment, a statement from the audit committee explaining the recommendation and should set out reasons why the board has taken a different position.	C.3.7	The audit committee should have primary responsibility for making a recommendation on the appointment, reappointment and removal of the external auditors. FTSE 350 companies should put the external audit contract out to tender at least every ten years. If the board does not accept the audit committee's recommendation, it should include in the annual report, and in any papers recommending appointment or re-appointment, a statement from the audit committee explaining the recommendation and should set out reasons why the board has taken a different position.

1.	2.	3.	4.	5.	6.	7.	8.
1992 'Cadbury Code'[1]		1998 Combined Code		2003 and 2006 Combined Codes[2, 3] and 2010 UK Corporate Governance Code		2012 UK Corporate Governance Code (see App1)	
Equivalent Provision reference(s)	**Wording**	**Equivalent Provision reference(s)**	**Wording**	**Equivalent Provision reference(s)**	**Wording**	**Equivalent Provision reference(s)**	**Wording**
There was no 'Cadbury' Code Provision equivalent to the 2003 Code Provision C.3.7.		There was no 1998 Combined Code Provision equivalent to the 2003 Code Provision C.3.7.		C.3.7	The annual report should explain to shareholders how, if the auditor provides non-audit services, auditor objectivity and independence is safeguarded.	Part of C.3.8[7]	A separate section of the annual report should describe the work of the committee in discharging its responsibilities[8]. The report should include: the significant issues that the committee considered in relation to the financial statements, and how these issues were addressed; an explanation of how it has assessed the effectiveness of the external audit process and the approach taken to the appointment or reappointment of the external auditor, and information on the length of tenure of the current audit firm and when a tender was last conducted; and if the external auditor provides non-audit services, an explanation of how auditor objectivity and independence is safeguarded.

1.	2.	3.	4.	5.	6.	7.	8.
1992 'Cadbury Code'[1]		1998 Combined Code		2003 and 2006 Combined Codes[2, 3] and 2010 UK Corporate Governance Code		2012 UK Corporate Governance Code (see App1)	
Equivalent Provision reference(s)	**Wording**	**Equivalent Provision reference(s)**	**Wording**	**Equivalent Provision reference(s)**	**Wording**	**Equivalent Provision reference(s)**	**Wording**
4.6	The directors should report that the business is a going concern, with supporting assumptions or qualifications as necessary.	D.1.3	The directors should report that the business is a going concern, with supporting assumptions or qualifications as necessary.	C.1.2	The directors should report that the business is a going concern, with supporting assumptions or qualifications as necessary.	C.1.3	The directors should report in annual and half-yearly financial statements that the business is a going concern, with supporting assumptions or qualifications as necessary.

1 As set out in Note 14 to the 1992 Cadbury Code, which read: 'The company's statement of compliance should be reviewed by the auditors in so far as it relates to paragraphs 1.4, 1.5, 2.3, 2.4, 3.1 to 3.3 and 4.3 to 4.6 of the [Cadbury] Code.'

2 On 20 October 2004, the FSA issued instrument 2004/83 amending Listing Rule 12.43A entitled 'Listing Rules (Auditors responsibilities in relation to the Combined Code) instrument 2004'. This instrument came into force on 1 November 2004. The amendment requires that, 'A company's statement under 12.43A(b) must be reviewed by the auditors before publication only insofar as it relates to Code Provisions C1.1, C2.1, C3.1, C3.2, C3.3, C3.4, C3.5, C3.6 and C3.7 of the Combined Code.' This requires the auditor to review nine of the ten objectively verifiable 2003 FRC Code Provisions relating to accountability and audit.

3 The tenth accountability and audit Code Provision (C1.2 on going concern) is covered by Listing Rule 12.43(v). The FSA has not changed the Listing Rule requirement under 12.43(v) that a statement by the directors that the business is a going concern (with supporting assumptions or qualifications as necessary) is included in the annual report and accounts and such a statement is reviewed by the auditor before publication.

4 In addition FSA Rule DTR 7.2.5 R requires companies to describe the main features of the internal control and risk management systems in relation to the financial reporting process.

5 See footnote 6.

6 This provision overlaps with FSA Rules DTR 7.1.3 R (see Schedule B).

7 Note that by the start of 2014 the Listing Rule had not been updated to explain whether the external auditor's review has been extended to all parts of 2012 Provision C.3.8; the Listing Rule still refers to the pre-2012 Provision C.3.7.

8 This provision overlaps with FSA Rules DTR 7.1.5 R and 7.2.7 R (see Schedule B).

Reviewing the performance of the external auditor H1.17

The external audit should not be viewed as a commodity to be purchased at lowest cost with splendid disregard for its quality. Still less should companies welcome external audits which are superficial. A high-quality audit is an essential part of effective corporate governance – for which the board of directors is responsible. It is an essential control in the process of disclosure to stakeholders.

Opaqueness of disclosure was blamed for much of the loss of investor confidence in Far Eastern companies during the late 1990s. Concerns were expressed about perceived variations in the quality of the main external audit brands, with the suggestion that, at times, the rigour of an external audit conducted by a 'Big Five' firm of public accountants in the Far East may not have corresponded to a similar audit conducted in the Western world – even disregarding local variations in laws, regulations and standards. In the US and the UK, concerns are frequently expressed about the quality of external audits – by no means always justifiably and usually retrospectively by damaged parties.

Practice in different countries of the world, as well as within different sectors of their respective economies, varies as to whether the external auditors are appointed by the board, by the shareholders or even by government or regulators. But in every case it should be regarded as the responsibility of top management and the board to monitor the quality of the external audit to ensure that the best quality audit is obtained commensurate with acceptable cost. It will usually fall to the audit committee of the board to undertake this on behalf of the board.

Just as the audit committee might reasonably ask the external auditors for their views on the quality of the accounting and internal audit processes within the business, so the audit committee is likely to call for reports on the quality of external audit from the accounting and internal audit functions of the business. At one meeting of the committee, the audit committee will consider the external auditor's plan for their audit and, at the later meeting which considers the year end financial statements, will receive a report from the auditors on their completed audit.

One matter to be considered by the audit committee is the external auditor's concept of materiality which, under external auditing standards, is required to be presented to be explained to the audit committee, and this will be done at the meeting which considers the plan for the audit. Here we give an example.

External auditor's statement to audit committee on audit materiality

The materiality guideline is used as a gauge of the significance of adjustments and other findings of our audit and is set out below for the Group.

	£'000
Forecast profit before tax for the Group	35,200
Effective tax rate – 30%	(10,560)
Profit after tax	24,640
	7.5%
Materiality guideline	1,848

The above materiality level is set using annualised profits before tax, based on the management accounts up to the end of October 2012, and is subject to change based on actual results for the year ended 31 December 2012.

Our audit will be designed to identify errors of a lower amount than the materiality level in order to ensure that any undetected errors do not exceed the materiality level.

Each individual subsidiary will have a materiality level based on a sliding scale of turnover, which will not exceed the group materiality level.

The future of the audit H1.18

Downwards fee pressures have threatened to turn the statutory audit of the financial statements into a commodity service, no longer attracting the levels of fees to which large external audit firms had become accustomed. Using the audit as a loss leader ('lowballing') became an attractive option, but there were concerns about independence and objectivity if the external auditor had significant additional non-audit responsibilities within audit client businesses. The 1998 Combined Code addressed this (see especially 1998 Code Provision D.3.2), and the 2003/2006 Codes developed this further. This is now addressed in part of Provision C.3.2 of the current Code, as follows:

> 'The main role and responsibilities of the audit committee should be set out in written terms of reference[26] and should include:
>
> …
>
> - to make recommendations to the board, for it to put to the shareholders for their approval in general meeting, in relation to the appointment, re-appointment and removal of the external auditor and to approve the remuneration and terms of engagement of the external auditor;
> - to review and monitor the external auditor's independence and objectivity and the effectiveness of the audit process, taking into consideration relevant UK professional and regulatory requirements;

- to develop and implement policy on the engagement of the external auditor to supply non-audit services, taking into account relevant ethical guidance regarding the provision of non-audit services by the external audit firm, and to report to the board, identifying any matters in respect of which it considers that action or improvement is needed and making recommendations as to the steps to be taken.'

The UK Auditing Practices Board's Ethical Standards for Auditors do not permit 'lowballing' to win an audit. Furthermore, the requirements imposed upon external auditors of companies caught by the Sarbanes-Oxley Act 2002 (especially s 404) have, on average, doubled the cost of the annual audit and so made audit services more attractive for the large public accounting firms.

These developing requirements have introduced greater demands upon audit committees to oversee the quality of the annual, statutory audit.

Many would say, for instance, that there is a conflict if internal auditing is outsourced to the external auditor. From 2001, the SEC's so-called '50% rule' in the US ruled against a client obtaining more than 50% of its internal auditing from the accounting firm that undertakes the external audit; but there is argument as to whether the 50% should apply to the internal auditing of operational and other matters as well as to the internal auditing of accounting aspects. Now the Sarbanes-Oxley Act outlaws internal auditing by an external auditor. There is no UK ban on external auditors providing internal audit services to their external audit clients.

In the longer term, liberalisation of trade across national frontiers can be expected to break the statutory monopoly in the provision of financial auditing services in the UK and elsewhere, leading to further fee pressures and perhaps to the relocation of the major audit practices to low-cost countries – as we have previously seen with respect to manufacturing industry. Online auditing and the use of audit software embedded into client systems will make this more feasible.

At the outset, we mentioned that, today, shareholders are more inquisitive and better informed. Rational markets require reliable and complete information. Companies already place their annual reports on their websites, and it will not be long before companies that report in real time are rewarded with a premium on their P/E ratios. Real-time reporting will require real-time auditing – a continuous, very automated audit approach with a recharged emphasis upon confirming the reliability of the system of internal financial control.

The audit expectations gap continues, and one aspect of this is the consumer's expectation that the auditor should be effective at detecting fraud.

We certainly live in an audit society.[27] Not so long ago, we called it the affluent society. Downsizing and re-engineering is intended to eliminate superfluous and inessential activities. Just as the outsourcing decision is made on unavoidable 'value for money' grounds, so the future of control and audit will essentially be determined on similar grounds. Audit needs to provide cost-effective added value. The audit itself cannot survive by offering peripheral added value extras, such as management letters, to honey the core audit. The audit has to survive on its own merit.

We explore the current controversy over external auditing in Chapter **H2**.

Notes

1 Professor W J M Mackenzie, Foreword to *The Accountability and Audit of Governments*. Also published by Frederick A Prager, New York (1966). The book was based on Normanton's MPhil thesis from the University of Manchester.
2 Auditing Practices Board of The Consultative Committee of Accounting Bodies 'Auditors' responsibility statements and auditors' reports on corporate governance' (July 1998).
3 Reproduced in the preamble to the 2012 UK Corporate Governance Code at p1. Not reprinted in **App1**.
4 See Auditing Practices Board 'Communication between external auditors and audit committees' Audit Briefing Paper (June 1998).
5 See www.webtrust.org.
6 Auditing Practices Board 'Providing assurance on the effectiveness of internal control' (July 2001).
7 The Institute of Chartered Accountants of Scotland 'Auditing into the twenty-first century' (1993).
8 'Other information in documents containing audited financial statements' (SAS 160, revised), paras 22–23.
9 The Combined Code did, however, also absorb the 29 provisions in the Greenbury Code on executive remuneration.
10 June 1998, reproduced in an Appendix to the Listing Rules (May 2000).
11 Auditing Practices Board 'The Combined Code: Requirements of Auditors under the Listing Rules of The London Stock Exchange' Bulletin 1999/5 (November 1999).
12 APB Bulletin 2004/3 (November 2004): 'The Combined Code on Corporate Governance: Requirements of Auditors under the Listing Rules of the Financial Services Authority'; see section 7. This Bulletin replaced Bulletin 1999/5 (above).
13 APB Bulletin 2006/5 (2006): 'The Combined Code on Corporate Governance: Requirements of Auditors under the Listing Rules of the Financial Services Authority and The Irish Stock Exchange'.
14 Auditing Practices Board (2007): Standards and Guidance 2007, p 15 (Scope and authority of Pronouncements, section 13).
15 FSA LR 9.8.10 R; ISE LR 6.8.9.
16 ISA (UK and Ireland) 720 (Revised) Section A, 'Other information in documents containing financial statements'.
17 Section 11, APB Bulletin 2006/5.
18 Sections 15, 25, 34 and 37, APB Bulletin 2004/3.
19 Section 24, APB Bulletin 2006/5.
20 Sections 21 and 22, APB Bulletin 2006/5.
21 Section 19, APB Bulletin 2006/5.
22 Sections 12 and 55, APB Bulletin 2006/5.
23 Section 35, APB Bulletin 2004/3.
24 Sections 45–47, APB Bulletin 2006/5.
25 Section 53, APB Bulletin 2004/3.
26 This provision overlaps with FSA Rules DTR 7.1.3 R (see Schedule C).
27 Power, Michael (1997) *The Audit Society: Rituals of Verification* (Oxford University Press).

Chapter H2

Is Audit failing the Global Capital Markets?[1]

Introduction H2.1

This chapter challenges the fitness for purpose of auditing today. The author draws together and critiques a wide range of available research, professional and independent sources to argue that fundamental changes are required to both external and internal auditing in order for them to provide the public service so badly needed.

The current problems cited are manifold. They include a lack of independence, regulatory capture by the profession, the pursuit of profit maximisation above the public interest, a confusion as to identity of the auditor's client, and a lack of value in the products that auditors provide.

The chapter argues that solutions are available and are within the grasp of the profession to apply.

At a time when the future of the audit profession is a lively issue in Europe, the UK and the US, this chapter is important for professional leaders, regulators and legislators; and it will suggest many areas for further research. Doubtless the conclusions drawn within will fail to convince everyone, and no doubt the evidence behind many of the findings expressed could be stronger.

An implicit thread woven through this chapter is that the audit profession is too comfortable with the *status quo* and with their business model which serves them well. Their attention needs to become more focused on the wider public interest. Otherwise in time others will enforce this adjustment.

Early attention was given to the role of several 'gatekeepers' in enabling, or failing to mitigate, the global financial crisis, but it is only more recently that the role of auditors has started to be given concerted attention by some commentators. The entrenched privileges of auditors, associated with the mandatory audit requirement which can only be fulfilled by members of the profession, requires us to ask whether the balance between serving the public and the auditors' own interests is correctly calibrated. While it is understandable that accountancy and auditing are inextricably linked, it would be better for the global economy if the auditing profession were to cut its umbilical cord connecting it to accountancy.

This chapter also suggests that neither have internal auditors, as one of the 'gatekeepers', been blameless for the global financial crisis although they have emerged largely unscathed. The price they have paid is that so far they are not perceived as being a significant part of the solution going forward.

This chapter sets out and draws together many of the disparate strands of research and thought relevant to the state of health of the auditing profession and the challenges it faces in serving the public interest. The chapter has the intention of debating these in a critical way.

Most categories of gatekeeper failed to warn of the 2007 impeding global financial crisis. Auditors, both external and internal auditors, were such gatekeepers. In their defence they were not alone. External auditors take refuge in their remit which requires them to audit only against financial reporting standards – standards that continue to allow dangerously misleading results to be reported and relied upon. They are standards developed largely by members of the same profession that the auditors belong to. Indeed it is unclear whether it is an accounting or an auditing profession, and whether it is wise to be both. The ambiguity is exacerbated by the extent to which regulatory capture by the profession has been achieved.

In other important ways conflicts of interest threaten both external and internal auditor independence and, equally important, the perception of independence. In particular, professional scepticism of external auditors is likely to be dulled by excessively long-term relationships with the entities they audit, by additional fee income for non-audit work and by the closeness of their relationships with managements and boards as distinct from their client shareholders to whom they report. Whatever their knowledge, they are not required to warn shareholders of future going concern issues so long as they are confident the company will be in business next time they report to the shareholders, since 'going concern' is only an audit concern to the extent that it impacts upon the reliability of the historic financial statements being audited.

External auditors are an occupational group, now a global oligopoly, having monopoly rights to practise upon a captive client base unable to opt out of buying the service. Oligopolies usually impact negatively on price and quality, and always negatively on client choice. The globalisation of business, with more than half the largest one-hundred world economies being companies not countries, has required the development of global audit firms; yet even the best are only loose global audit networks. Even so, they conduct themselves anti-competitively, failing to appreciate the distinction between a multi-national commercial business set to maximise return to the owners, and a profession committed to putting the public interest first.

The audit of the financial statements is widely regarded as an essential element of the efficient functioning of the global financial markets. If that is so, might it not be left to the market to decide whether an entity should be audited? And does this not presuppose a consistent and high standard of auditing across the world?

Internal auditors have not been blamed significantly for the global financial crisis, but only at the price of portraying themselves as peripheral to it. Consequently they have missed a strong opportunity to raise their profile and provide a higher level of assurance to both boards and to external stakeholders. To a large extent risk managers have seized the opportunity to fill this vacuum.

The audit oligopoly **H2.2**

Using UK data as an example,[2] in 2012 the Big 4 audited 99 of the FTSE 100 companies. Randgold, the FTSE 100 gold mining company which has shot into the FTSE 100 due to the current price of gold, is the exception as it has kept its audit firm (BDO). Randgold replaced PartyGaming, no longer a FSTE 100 company, as the sole FTSE 100 company audited by a non-Big 4 firm: again it had been BDO who saw PartyGaming through its initial public offering. Table 1, which shows the audit fee incomes of the five firms auditing FTSE 100 companies, tentatively supports the view that the audit fees of non-Big 4 firms are less costly, though the sample is much too small to be significant.

A total of 240 out of 250 FTSE 250 companies, ie those immediately below the FTSE 100, are audited by the Big 4 firms, with three mid-tier firms auditing the remaining ten. The mid-tier firms argue that they are well placed to take on FTSE 250 audit work and, where those companies require an international audit firm, the mid-tier firms' international networks, as with the international networks of the Big 4, are adequate for the purpose. At present non-Big 4 firms have an insignificant audit client base amongst the FTSE 350 (see Table 3). Understandably, the larger the company, the less likely it is to use a non-Big 4 firm for their audit (see Tables 4, 5 and 6), though complexity rather than sheer size is more likely to be a reasonable determinant for using a Big 4 firm. In reality, it is more usually brand image and inertia rather than quality that impede large companies from considering the use of a non-Big 4 firm for their audits. Recent studies (Boone *et al,* 2010; Lawrence *et al,* 2012) have found little difference in actual audit quality between Big 4 and non-Big 4 firms, but a pronounced difference in perceived audit quality.[3]

Table 1: Sum of FTSE 100 audit fees (£m)

	Total	%
BDO	0.47	0%
Deloitte	100.26	16%
EY	91.05	15%
KPMG	150.44	25%
PWC	270.89	44%
Grand Total	613.11	

Table 2: Sum of FTSE 250 audit fees (£m)

	Total	%
BDO	1.01	1%
Deloitte	50.34	29%
EY	31.28	18%
Grant Thornton	0.98	1%
KPMG	40.46	23%
PKF (UK)	0.08	0%
PWC	50.68	29%
Grand Total	174.83	

Table 3: Sum of FTSE 350 audit fees (£m)

	FTSE100	FTSE250	Total	%
Deloitte	100.26	50.34	150.60	19%
EY	91.05	31.28	122.33	16%
KPMG	150.44	40.46	190.90	24%
PwC	270.89	50.68	321.57	41%
		Grand Total	785.40	

Table 4: Sum of Top 20 audit fees (£m)

	Total	%
Deloitte	16.54	5%
EY	38.96	12%
KPMG	84.30	27%
PWC	177.61	56%
Grand Total	317.41	

Table 5: Sum of Next 30 audit fees (£m)

	Total	%
Deloitte	66.74	35%
EY	23.25	12%
KPMG	49.73	26%
PWC	48.95	26%
Grand Total	188.67	

Table 6: Sum of other 50 in FTSE 100 audit fees (£m)

	Total	%
BDO	0.47	0%
Deloitte	16.98	16%
EY	28.84	27%
KPMG	16.41	15%
PWC	44.33	41%
Grand Total	107.03	

The tables highlight that 77.8% of total FTSE 350 income is in FTSE 100 audits and 64.2% of the total for the FTSE 350 is in the top 60 audits – highlighting that if one is to tackle concentration one has to tackle it at the top end of the FTSE 100 – which leads one directly towards joint audits with one of the two joint auditors being a mid-tier firm, in order to develop the capability of non-Big 4 firms to audit the largest companies and to develop their credibility with boards and audit committees of these largest companies. Prima facie, joint audits will be more robust on account of the 'two sets of eyes', but they are more costly. Joint audits are mandatory in France for the largest companies.

Joint audits[4] were proposed in the widely leaked European Commission's early-2011 draft white paper but, following concerted lobbying against joint audits by Big 4 firms, survives only in the extent that the Commission is proposing that the interval between the proposed mandatory rotation of auditors is extended from six to nine years if joint auditors are in place; but the Commission is not proposing that one of the joint audit firms should be a non-Big 4 firm, and so an opportunity is missed to tackle the problem of audit market concentration. The UK Financial Reporting Council's (FRC) proposals for 2012 changes to its UK Corporate Governance Code, itself merely discretionary, includes a 'request' (FRC's word) that FTSE 350 companies put the external audit contract out to tender at least every ten years. The UK approach to corporate governance is exceedingly light touch.[5]

The gatekeepers **H2.3**

Writing before the global financial crisis, Coffee (2006) pointed out that his so-called gatekeepers – the professional agents of the board and of the shareholders – had been ineffective at preventing corporate debacles such as Enron. His gatekeepers were auditors, attorneys, securities analysts, credit-rating agencies, investment advisors and proxy advisors. More recently, Loughrey (2011) pointed the finger at lawyers. For a while it appeared that auditors were emerging relatively unscathed from the financial crisis until a key committee of the UK's House of Commons (2009) noted that the audit process had failed to highlight developing problems in the banking sector, leading it to question how useful audit currently is. It said:

> 'We have received very little evidence that auditors failed to fulfil their duties as currently stipulated. The fact that some banks failed soon after receiving unqualified audits does not necessarily mean that these audits were deficient. But the fact that the audit process failed to highlight developing problems in the banking sector does cause us to question exactly how useful audit currently is. We are perturbed that the process results in 'tunnel vision', where the big picture that shareholders want to see is lost in a sea of detail and regulatory disclosures.'

The House of Lords (2011) was to be less reticent. It said:

> 'We do not accept the defence that bank auditors did all that was required of them. In the light of what we now know, that defence appears disconcertingly complacent. It may be that the Big Four carried out their duties properly in the strictly legal sense, but we conclude that, in the wider sense, they did not do so'.[6]

and:

'We regard the recent paucity of meetings between bank auditors and regulators, particularly in a period of looming financial crisis as a dereliction of duty by both auditors and regulators'.[7]

A quick, superficial riposte by the CEO of the Institute of Chartered Accountants in England and Wales (ICAEW)[8] drew attention to the serious expectations gap which has bedevilled auditing for so long (Liggio, 1974; Porter, 1990):[9]

'We do not accept that auditors contributed to the severity of the financial crisis. They did the job that they were expected to do: provide an audit opinion on banks' financial statements.'

Auditors serving the owners **H2.4**

In essence, the auditor makes an assessment of future going concern because it is significant to whether figures in the financial statements are correctly stated, for instance whether assets should be revalued downwards at break-up value. The auditor currently takes a forward view on this basis of approximately just one year which, arguably, is not long enough especially for financial institutions. If there are significant uncertainties about going concern, the auditor will refer to them in 'emphasis of matter' text within their audit report which cross references to narrative provided by the board elsewhere within the annual report. The value of the auditor's assessment is reduced as it will frequently rely in part on management's assessment (for instance, management's judgement as to whether a loan facility will be renewed) which the auditor may refer to in an 'emphasis of matter' statement within the audit report. Auditors, especially of banks, have a problem as any hint that a bank is not a going concern will almost inevitably lead to the collapse of the bank since banks are viable only if confidence stays. Hence, towards the end of 2008 a UK Treasury minister's reassurance to the Big 4 that the UK government would stand behind the banks was sufficient for the auditors to conclude their banking clients were going concerns. [10] If this excuses auditor obfuscation it can only do so by reinforcing the query about the value of the audit. The Lords Inquiry also concluded:

'It cannot (or at least should not) be taken for granted by auditors that banks in difficulties will be bailed out by the authorities and the taxpayers. We do not accept therefore that this should at any time be a decisive consideration in making the 'going concern' judgment.'[11]

The shareholders were not alerted to the likelihood that, in several cases, the banks they owned were then going concerns only if ownership were shortly thereafter to pass substantially from the existing shareholders to the state (in the case of RBS), or to others (as with HBOS), Clearly this reduces the value of the audit for those who nominally appoint the auditors and to whom the auditor reports.

Since the Sarbanes-Oxley Act (2002) it is the audit committee of the board of a US listed company that appoints the auditors. Previously it was the board. In the UK it has always been the shareholders who nominally make the appointment but almost always on the recommendation of the board. Although there are indications that UK audit committees are flexing their muscles, it is still very common for the preferences of the UK CEO and CFO to prevail in auditor appointment decisions. So the reality is different from the nominal position. There is a good case for shareholders' panels to appoint the auditors, and the 'financial statements insurance' alternative to a conventional audit (which we discuss later) would also better align the auditors with the shareholders.

The auditor's close relationship with management is made worse by the length of time that auditors typically serve. On average large UK companies keep the same audit firm for 48 years and only put the audit out to tender once every 17 years. No wonder the EC Commissioner Barnier has said:

> 'the key word for the profession is independence'

and

> 'we see auditors who are too closely linked to clients.'[12]

As part of its current review of the UK Corporate Governance Code, the FRC is considering 'requesting' FTSE 350 companies to put the external audit contract out to tender at least every ten years – a timid half step in the right direction.[13] So long as the perception of most companies is that they must have a Big 4 auditor, an issue we discuss later, excessively long audit appointments are likely to persist as there is such limited choice and, in particular cases, perhaps no alternative to the incumbent auditor when the other firms are conflicted. Clearly this is a competition issue currently being investigated in the UK by the Competition Commission.

Auditors and accounting standards **H2.5**

International Financial Reporting Standards (IFRS) have given the Big 4 an opportunity to strengthen their monopoly. The commendable pursuit of IFRS, so that accounts are prepared on a common and comparable basis globally, has resulted in the accounting battalions nailing their colours to the mast so firmly that they are no longer able to concede their error and beat a tactical retreat. The IASB,[14] itself with an inadequate democratic or global mandate, has tended to adopt a US approach within its IFRS, mindful of how important it will be for IFRS that the US adopt these Standards – a move the US has yet to make.

A key IFRS policy has been to substitute the principle of 'prudence', which was present in UK GAAP, by the principle of 'neutrality' which underpins IFRS. Superficially that makes some sense on the basis that the financial statements fairly present the position as of, and up to, a point in time. For instance, IFRS does not allow so-called 'cookie jar reserves' to be set aside for some vague future rainy day: such provisioning would have a high potential to mean that the financial results would not be 'true and fair' or, in the new parlance, would not 'fairly represent in accordance with IFRS' the results of operations and the state of affairs of the entity as of the year end. But this has had unanticipated consequences. For instance, a new mortgage bank might have a sub-prime mortgage book whose mortgagees have been granted 125% of their properties' values. For a while the mortgage book performs perfectly with repayments partly serviced initially by the generous advances made, assisted by rising property prices. The board, management and the auditors all know that future problems are stacking up, but IFRS 39 does not allow for those problems to be provided for on an expected basis. This led to Mr Adam Applegarth, the CEO of Northern Rock at the time of its 2007 collapse, to state in 2005 that moving to IFRS had introduced more volatility and led to 'faintly insane' profits growth.[15] Another example:[16]

> On 1 January 2010, Bank X grants a ten-year rolled up loan for Euro 10,000,000 to a property developer. Interest is agreed at 10%. The developer agrees to pay 10,000,000 X (1+10%)^10 = Euro 25,937,423 in ten years' time (the interest is effectively rolled up). The bank does not look for collateral and the documentation is very weak. On 31 December 2010, it becomes clear that the property developer is in difficulty and there is only a 70% chance that the principal will be repaid. Under the Incurred Loss rules, the bank is required to record a profit (ie interest income of 10% = 1,000,000) but under the Prudent rules, the bank would probably be required to show a loss of approximately Euro 3,300,000.

A further example would be a lender who periodically makes further loans to the borrower which are sufficient for the borrower to make the interest payments on the original loan when they fall due, so that the loan is accounted for as fully performing.[17]

The volatility introduced by IFRS has tended to make IFRS-prepared financial results procyclical, recording excessively good performance when the economy is doing well and the opposite at other times. It is not just a matter of provisioning, it is also a matter of valuing sometimes complex financial assets by 'marking them to market' or, where there is no market 'marking to model' where judgemental latitude is wide. Anecdotal evidence suggests that finance directors ask their auditors what range of values would be acceptable and then choose to apply the top of the range valuation.

Defenders of IFRS point out that the US experienced the problems of the banking crisis even though it had not adopted IFRS, whereas Australia emerged relatively unscathed even though it had adopted IFRS.[18] This misses the points that IFRS has been designed to be close to US GAAP and that Australia had much tighter regulatory requirements for its banks.

Excessive, imprudent bottom-line profit figures have been the starting point for determining distributions to shareholders and bonuses to executives, even though of course boards are not obliged to follow them slavishly and, hopefully, regulators will not allow them to do so. IFRS profits have been so wildly off the mark that it is now being suggested by those close to IFRS that a second, different set of financial statements should be prepared for use as a guide to determining distributions and bonuses. This would be a bonanza for accountants and auditors who are a cause of this crisis and an absurdity of huge proportions, being an acknowledgement that IFRS accounts can be of little value, indeed may be profoundly misleading.

The International Accounting Standards Board (IASB) is working on a modification to IFRS 39 (to be IAS 9) but this is not expected to be finalised until 2015 and will then be further delayed before the EC and other bodies approve its adoption.

The issue arises as to whether it is acceptable for auditors to limit themselves to expressing an opinion that a client's financial statements fairly present in accordance with IFRS when IFRS-prepared accounts may be so deeply flawed. It is a problem that the accounting and auditing professions are so enmeshed that auditors subordinate themselves to financial reporting standards, expressing audit opinions that are limited to whether their clients' financial statements fairly present in accordance with IFRS. Professor David Myddleton has said this:

> 'When I was a young accountant, we had what were called recommendations: voluntary guidelines. … We didn't have 2,000 pages of regulations as we have now. We had 150 pages. I think it worked perfectly well, because it enabled, indeed it required, accountants and auditors to use their professional judgement. It was up to them – ultimately the courts, not the standard setters – to decide what a true and fair view consisted of. I think that could work perfectly well. …'[19]

The House of Lords Inquiry report recommended that auditors should apply the prudence principle when necessary even when it is absent from accounting standards. Those many who interpreted this as an error of principle were clearly set on the notion that auditors could not think for themselves but were merely box ticking whether detailed prescriptions within elaborate and flawed financial reporting standards were being applied.[20]

It is often said that much of the value of audit is to do with the adjustments to the financial statements that the auditor insists upon but which are not apparent although they have been made; hence FRC proposals for the report of the audit committee to be more informative of the dialogue between the auditor and the company. Such a measure would not place additional obligations upon the auditor. Neither would it amount to much, so long as the auditors are willing to accept financial statements which are intrinsically flawed, merely because they comply with financial reporting standards, albeit deficient ones.

The audit market **H2.6**

Economists argue that monopolies and oligopolies raise prices and reduce quality. In 1986, Peat Marwick merged with KMG to form KPMG, one of the Big 4 today. Two significant mergers took place in 1989 which created Ernst & Young and Deloitte & Touche (now Deloitte). By then the Big 8 had reduced to the Big 6. In 1998, Price Waterhouse merged with Coopers & Lybrand to form PricewaterhouseCoopers, and then there were five: research evidence indicated that audit prices rose following this merger (Oxera, 2006). Then Arthur Andersen collapsed in 2002 leaving just the Big 4. In particular sectors there may be only three active large audit firms. For instance, Ernst & Young do not audit UK banks. Market choice is insufficient and may effectively be absent – if it is assumed that a Big 4 firm is required. One clearing bank has told the author it would be impossible to change their auditors as the other two large audit firms active in auditing banks are conflicted. Barclays Bank has never changed its auditors in well over 100 years.

There would be a systemic risk to the global financial markets if one of the Big 4 exited the audit market by choice or as Arthur Andersen did. When large companies are engaged in takeovers entailing due diligence and defence activities, there may be no Big 4 audit firm to turn to as the others are likely to be conflicted – so new entrants must be involved at the top end of the market.

The Big 4 claim that the audit market is intensely competitive. The problem is that their opportunity to compete for audit work is infrequent as it is most commonly linked to rare tendering opportunities. Large UK companies put their audits out to tender once every 17 years. FTSE 100 companies change their auditors on average once in 48 years, FTSE 250 every 36 years and all listed companies every 25 years (Oxera, 2006). As a consequence, arguably auditors develop too cosy a relationship with management and auditor scepticism may be dulled: the FRC has expressed concerns about this.

In view of competition concerns, the issue arises as to whether it is wise of the six largest firms to meet as the Global Public Policy Committee and as the UK Policy and Regulatory Group – notwithstanding they are careful not to use these forums to secure or enhance their competitive position.

Challenges facing international audit networks H2.7

Arthur Andersen espoused a global one-firm philosophy. When it imploded in 2002 in the wake of the Enron scandal, it became apparent that this espousal was more a matter of spin than substance, as its different national partnerships went their separate ways looking for safe havens within other firms. The present Big 4 firms are also collectivities of largely autonomous national partnerships. This presents challenges for the consistent application of similar high auditing standards across these networks between countries. Furthermore, Carlin, *et al* (2009) have shown that contrary to the view within the extant literature that there is homogeneity in audit quality among Big 4 firms, there is substantial cross-sectional variation and distinctly poor compliance levels. Their research raises questions about audit quality among the firms.

The organisation of auditing firms into networks makes it easier for the Big 4 to acquire smaller firms, thus making it more difficult for smaller firms to grow to become competitors of the largest firms. The limited success of joint audits in France to widen choice cannot be unconnected to the absorption by Big 4 firms over the last fifteen years of three firms that were each number 6 in France when they were acquired, with only Mazars at number 5 holding out. It is noticeable that the Big 4 firms across the world have acquired significant firms that challenged their dominance.[21] In 2010 and 2011, the fifth and sixth Brazilian firms joined forces with the Big 4 firms, depriving Grant Thornton and BDO of their network partners.[22] International networks take time to build and are essential for non-Big 4 firms bidding for most large client work. While Grant Thornton replaced its Brazilian partner by another, it is half the size of the firm it lost. Late 2011, Grant Thornton's Danish firm was absorbed into a Big 4 firm.[23] These are just a few of many examples which are recorded well elsewhere (Basioudis and Steele, 2001; Boys, 1989, 1990;[24] Coopers & Lybrand, 1984; Habgood, 1994; Jones, 1981, 1995; Kettle, 1958; Richards, 1981; Spacek, 1974; Wise, 1982).[25]

Leave it to the market to decide? H2.8

It can be argued that liberating companies from the mandatory audit requirement would invigorate competition in the audit market, improving quality and reducing price. Might not the requirement for an audit even of large companies be left to the market (shareholders, banks, other creditors, tax authorities etc) to demand? In evidence to the House of Lords Inquiry, Ed Davey, MP – the Department for Business, Innovation and Skills (DBIS) government minister, supported the EC's proposal to end mandatory audits for mid-tier companies, as they have already been ended for companies within the small companies' regime, though this proposal has now been abandoned for now, due to opposition from most member states. He said to the Inquiry:

> '…the Government believes there is a strong case for taking away the mandatory requirement for an audit from medium-sized companies, and I think that would have a real advantage. If a company decides to go for an audit voluntarily, I think this sends a strong signal to investors and to the market. So I don't see some systems risk for deregulating here and taking away mandation [sic] from [the 32,385 UK] medium-sized companies.'[26]

Not only is choice of auditor currently perceived to be limited to the Big 4, but so long as audits are mandatory, companies have no option to avoid audits which have to be conducted by approved professionals. Optional audits would, in that sense, give companies more choice. They would also make it more necessary for audit firms to 'sell' their services as economically desirable.

It may be argued that if the size of the conventional audit market were to decline as a consequence of ending, at least in some cases, the mandatory audit requirement, or by introducing an alternative financial statements insurance approach (see below) then the Big 4 may find a need for even further consolidation. The indications are that this would be entirely unnecessary. The Big 4 are truly massive. Based on latest information available at end 2011, total Big 4 revenue is over $103 billion. Converting this (using $:£ at 31 December 2011 rate of 1.60) gives around £65 billion. The total turnover for Tesco for its 2011 year end was £60.9 billion.

A financial statements insurance approach **H2.9**

A possible solution to the problems of audit market concentration would be to introduce an alternative audit market. One alternative is financial statements insurance (FSI) (Ronen, 2010). Under FSI a board audit committee (with the approval of its shareholders) would approach an insurer to quote to cover the reliability of the financial statements which would otherwise be subject to a conventional audit. By arrangement, FSI could cover additional assertions made by management beyond those currently embraced by the conventional audit. The financial limit of FSI cover, on behalf of those who might sue, would be at least equal to any cap on auditor liability which might be introduced, but could be higher by arrangement. As with other forms of insurance, the insurer would be likely to review the company and set conditions before providing the cover: this review might be done by the insurer's staff or by a firm of accountants chosen from a panel approved by the audit regulator. The insurance premium and the limit of the cover would be published. Then the insurer would appoint an auditor, also from the approved list, whose scope of work would be determined by the degree of risk that the insurer was willing to bear. Since the board and management would have no influence over the choice of auditor, better alignment with the interests of the shareholders would be achieved. If the company failed this audit, it would have two options for the following year: first, to revert to a conventional audit; or to renegotiate the FSI cover. If a claim were made against an FSI policy it would be assessed by an arbitration process.

Capping the liability of auditors (as applies, for instance, in Germany where the cap is set at €4m) has little current support as little goodwill is felt towards auditors. A cap would encourage non-Big 4 audit firms to be willing to audit larger companies. It might also encourage the audit profession to extend the assurances they are willing to give beyond the audit of the historic financial statements, for instance to the audit of directors' corporate governance, risk and internal control assertions and to statements about future prospects which interest investors most. A cap might serve also to reduce the cost of audit. While the 2006 UK Companies Act allows that auditor liability can be negotiated contractually, this rarely if ever occurs at the level of large company audits as clients do not see the point of conceding on auditor liability. Alternatives to contractual liability have been suggested: proportionate liability (where liability is apportioned between the various parties held to be culpable, including the directors and auditors) has the disadvantage of leaving the scale of the audit firm's liability uncertain until any court case is concluded.

The necessary primacy of professionalism **H2.10**

The auditing profession, most recently in its fierce lobbying against UK and European proposed changes, gives the impression of elevating its pursuit of profit maximisation above professional obligations. Professional behaviour should be much more than technical excellence, but even the technical quality of audits is in question. It should also not be a matter of pursuing of profit maximisation.

This attitude was memorably illustrated by Lord Sharman in 2000. After Arthur Levitt was made chairman in 1993, the Securities and Exchange Commission (SEC) became increasingly concerned about auditor independence through increased in-roads into non-audit work. The auditing profession in turn became increasingly concerned about the SEC. Lord Sharman, then former chairman of KPMG International, issued a challenge at ICAEW's annual dinner in June 2000 (Perry, 2000). He said:

> 'I say to chairman Levitt: get your tanks off our lawn.'

Arthur Levitt resigned prematurely a few months later.[27] Enron collapsed a few months thereafter.[28] Arthur Andersen had provided many non-audit services to Enron, its audit client, including most of Enron's internal auditing. Then, in a short space of time, we had the Sarbanes-Oxley Act of 2002 which set out, not entirely successfully, to outlaw most non-audit services being provided by a US issuer's external auditors; and in the UK the FRC's Auditing Practices Board devised some subtle ethical standards so that audit firms could continue to provide non-audit services where they would otherwise be conflicted.

The House of Lords Inquiry report had these words:

> 'Appeal to the Big 4 as professional entities to put the public interest first and voluntarily break up their firms to form a Big 6 or Big 8. The quid pro quo for society ceding monopoly rights to practise and other privileges, is that professionals place the ideal of public service above other considerations. A clear ultimatum, time-defined, might be set for the Big 4.'[29]

It is overdue to address the folly of an occupational group, now an oligopoly, having monopoly rights to practise upon a captive client base which, through law and regulation, has no choice but to buy the audit service. The profession should end its self-interested lobbying and put service and public interest in front of profit. Competition authorities must act in the wider societal interest, moving far beyond endorsing measures with insufficient potential to remedy the situation. It is not too late for the profession to lead with its own radical proposals. Sociological research into the hallmarks of a profession has demonstrated the essential professional ideal of placing the concept of service above monetary reward as a *quid pro quo* for society giving the profession privileges including monopoly rights to practise (Abbott, 1988; Cowton, 2008 & 2009; Duska and Duska, 2003; Greenwood, 1957).

Some would dispute that acting in the wider public interest is an essential tenet of a profession, or alternatively would define the professional's 'public interest' in a very narrow way. Expressing sentiment which seemingly corresponds to that of the Big 4 but writing about the legal profession, Loughrey (2011, pp 48-49) recalls that in 2009 the City of London Law Society affirmed that:

> 'traditional public-interest regarding aspects of the lawyer's role …were not relevant to their members' work, and offered instead a narrow vision of the public interest that comprised protecting the interests of their business clients.'

It is widely held that the hallmarks of a profession are: (a) specialised body of knowledge, (b) recognised formal education process for acquiring the requisite specialised knowledge, (c) standard professional qualifications governing admission to the profession, (d) a standard of conduct governing the relationship of the practitioner with clients, colleagues and the public, (e) recognition of status, (f) an acceptance of social responsibility inherent in an occupation endowed with the public interest, (g) an organisation devoted to the advancement of the social obligations of a group, and (h) a profession is represented in three forums – the professional body, the universities and the units that practise – with cross-membership between these three. Society cedes professional status to an occupational group when it is in society's best interests to do so; in return the occupational group is expected to place the concept of service above that of personal financial gain. This is relevant to the conduct of the large public accounting practices and the appropriate action they might take and support to deal with concentration in the audit market.

It should be feasible to appeal successfully to the better nature of the professionals within the Big 4 to do the decent thing in the public interest. This would avoid the need for a UK Competition Commission ruling, or for action by way of the Competition Directorate of the EC and changes to the European Directive, thus avoiding any subsequent requirements that might then be imposed on the existing large firms. It would allow the large firms a much greater degree of control over the process to be followed and the formats of the large firms that would emerge. It would utlilise the understanding of the Big 4 firms to engineer an optimal solution at minimal cost. It would be the most effective way to deal with the desirability that change is implemented globally. It would modify the behaviour of clients who at present are said to most frequently demand the services of the Big 4. Importantly for the firms, the total fee income per partner would remain unchanged. It may be that the annual rewards of the top partners might be ameliorated to some extent since they would be running smaller, though still very large, businesses. There would be some extra costs as economies of scale in 'back office' and technical functions would not be as great as at present. Weighed against that are the efficiency gains that would be encouraged through greater competition between the larger number of large firms that would emerge. The firms would regain the goodwill of society as they would be seen to be placing their duties as professionals above the pursuit of profit maximisation. Furthermore, the Big 4 are experienced in this process– three of them spun off their consulting firms a few years ago, before rebuilding their in-house consulting competence.

The conflict of non-audit services for audit clients H2.11

The House of Lords recommended that external auditors should not be permitted to undertake internal auditing work for their audit clients. The FRC responded that internal audit services are already prohibited save in the most minor circumstances – which chimes discordantly with one Big 4 firm's recent successful tendering for the external *and* most of the internal audit of a large listed company, subsequently approved by the FRC's Audit Inspection Unit in its 2009/10 report. Legalistic reliance on the detailed wording of the UK FRC's Auditing Practices Board's *Ethical Standards for Auditors* gives too much wiggle room to engage in work that is conflicted in reality or in perception. There is insufficient understanding that perception is part of reality. Nevertheless, due to active oversight by audit committees, whereas in year the 2000 fee income for non-audit work from FTSE 100 audit clients was more than three times the fee income for audit work, by 2006 non-audit fees were about 0.75 of audit fees from these clients (APB, 2009).

Regulatory capture H2.12

Traditionally, one of the hallmarks of a profession is that it regulates itself. While the professional accounting bodies have disciplinary oversight of their members, due to a perception that these bodies acted more as trade associations in the interests of their members, regulation has now been transferred to independent regulatory bodies – for instance, in the UK the FRC's Auditing Practices Board and Audit Inspection Unit, and in the US the Public Company Accounting Oversight Board. In 2010 of the 15 members of APB, five were current and a further four were ex-Big 4: the FRC was not applying its own independence criteria as contained within its UK Corporate Governance Code. Many of the staff of the Public Company Accounting Oversight Board (PCAOB) have been recruited from the Big 4 firms. In many other influential forums the profession dominates. The audit diaspora is nationally and globally too powerful.

Kay (2012) has recently drawn attention to the regulatory capture issue in the financial sector generally, and of course there are intimate crossovers between that sector and the auditing profession:

> 'The outcome is regulation that is at once extensive and intrusive, yet ineffective and largely captured by financial sector interests.'

> 'Such capture is sometimes crudely corrupt, as in the US where politics is in thrall to Wall Street money. The European position is better described as intellectual capture. Regulators come to see the industry through the eyes of market participants rather than the end users they exist to serve, because market

participants are the only source of the detailed information and expertise this type of regulation requires. This complexity has created a financial regulation industry – an army of compliance officers, regulators, consultants and advisors – with a vested interest in the regulation industry's expansion.'

Internal audit has also failed H2.13

The UK's Chartered Institute of Internal Auditors (CIIA) were very effective witnesses to the House of Lords Inquiry on audit market concentration although the Committee's report makes little mention of internal auditing. As mentioned above, the Committee adopted advice of CIIA and others that internal audit services should not be provided by the company's external auditors.[30] The Committee also recommended that tax advisory services should not be provided by the external auditor. In the US the Sarbanes-Oxley Act bans by statute most non-audit services from being provided by a quoted company's auditor. The Committee stopped short of recommending that no non-audit services should be provided by external auditors, or that 'pure' audit firms should be created. The CIIA explained that its opposition to making internal audit mandatory was to do with its desire to align itself with the UK principles-based 'comply or explain' approach.[31]

It is pertinent to ask why CIIA's very strong written and oral testimony impacted only marginally on the Committee's report. Before addressing the question directly, it must be said that it is reminiscent of the earlier failure of internal audit to feature significantly in another important recent report. Internal audit received no mention at all in the draft Walker (2009a) report except for an acknowledgement that the CIIA had responded to the consultation. Within the 181 pages of his final report (Walker, 2009b) there was only one significant reference to internal audit:

> 'Discussions in the context of this Review process suggest that failures that proved to be critical for many banks related much less to what might be characterised as conventional compliance and audit processes, including internal audit, but to defective information flow, defective analytical tools and inability to bring insightful judgement in the interpretation of information and the impact of market events on the business model.'[32]

To paraphrase Walker, internal audit cannot be blamed for the financial crisis as internal audit is perceived as being a compliance checking process with no remit to provide assurance on information flow, analytical tools, the interpretation of information or the impact of market events on the business model. So, internal audit escaped blame for the financial crisis at the cost of being characterised as being a bit player. If no part of the problem, internal audit can hardly be regarded as part of the solution. Many internal auditors would not accept this modest role for internal audit.

Had the representatives of the internal auditing profession proposed to the Inquiry that internal audit should serve the board in a way that is truly independent of management, and that internal audit could be the provider of independent assurance to board risk committees, then the Inquiry might have sat up and taken notice, and internal audit might have featured much more prominently in the Inquiry's report and recommendations.

Over the years internal audit has transformed itself several times to meet changing needs, but this progressive, pioneering spirit seems to have been lost and internal audit is now locked into a conservative time warp. Internal auditing is missing out on an unprecedented opportunity to enhance its status and provide a badly needed service in filling the board's assurance vacuum. Around the year 1900, internal audit was the reperformance of certain accounting processes, as a service to mid-level accounting management (Collins, 1904). By the 1940s the approach had morphed to providing assurance about the *systems* of internal control over accounting processes – on the basis that audit assurance by reperformance was no longer feasible when processes had become more complex and the volume of transactions had become so much greater (Smith, 1953; Bigg and Davies, 1953). Overlapping with this transition was a change to internal audit providing assurance over *all* operational processes, not just accounting processes (Brink, 1941; Chambers, 1981). Then the 1980s saw the development of a risk-based approach to internal auditing – on the basis that, since internal audit resources are limited and business processes are ever more complex, it is more important to provide reliable assurance about the business processes that mitigate the principal risks of the business (McNamee and Selim, 1998).

In parallel with this evolution of internal auditing, it became appropriate for internal auditing to progress from reporting to mid-level accounting management to reporting to the finance director and then to the chief executive (who is at the apex of all business processes). Now there is a need for internal audit to report for all purposes to the independent chairman of the board or to the board itself, so that internal auditors can provide independent assurance to the board on both the internal and external risks facing the business.

Internal auditors acknowledged to the House of Lords' Inquiry that they share collective responsibility with other parties for the financial crisis, as indeed did most other parties who appeared before the Inquiry – almost always without accepting specific responsibility. CIIA's remarks to the Inquiry chime with this willingness to share collective responsibility, but also go further by implicitly rejecting the Walker Review's diminutive characterisation of the internal audit role:

> '… not surprisingly, we would take the view that internal audit does a very effective job in most instances.'
>
> 'However, in the case of the financial crisis and in the case of the banks and the financial institutions, it is clear that internal audit was part of the structure that went wrong. I think there are many lessons that we need to learn from that and that we are still learning. But I think particularly important is the fact that internal audit and audit committees were very much focused on process and on internal controls within the organisation, and were not looking beyond that; were not looking at the wider picture as much as, clearly with the benefit of hindsight, they should have been doing. That would suggest that, going forward, internal audit needs to play a much broader role, in looking at the governance of the organisation, looking at the behaviour in governance, the behaviour of management and the board, the skills, the abilities, the capabilities of the board and the non-executives in particular, to ensure that they are able to play their role effectively in identifying and ensuring that the organisation is mitigating risk.'[33]

One thing that is missing from this is a recognition that to be a reliable provider of assurance to the board, internal audit needs to report for all purposes, including 'pay and rations', to the board or to the independent chairman of the board. He who pays the piper calls the tune. Internal audit should be regarded as one of the costs of running the board. Internal audit in general has not yet reached this conclusion, and hence it is not being seen as a significant part of the solution to the problems we have been experiencing. CIIA told the Inquiry:

> '… [Internal audit] needs a relationship with internal management – it is internal – and pay and rations, if you like, in terms of where the money comes from;'[34]

But it has traditionally been called 'internal' because it provides assurance on internal matters.

The financial crisis has been an unprecedented opportunity foregone for internal audit to make a pitch for enhancing their role to fill the board's assurance vacuum. Yet, there is some light at the end of the tunnel. The UBS website stated until recently:

> 'To maximize its independence from management, the head of Group Internal Audit … reports directly to the Chairman of the Board. Group Internal Audit has unrestricted access to all accounts, books and records and must be provided with all information and data needed to fulfill its auditing duties. Group Internal Audit addresses any reports with major issues to the Chairman of the Board. The Chairman's Office may order special audits to be conducted, and the Group Executive Board, with the agreement of the Chairman, may also instruct Group Internal Audit to conduct such audits.'

A further example is that the head of internal audit at Novartis reports to the non-executive chairman of the board and management does not determine the audit plan. 'Pay and rations' for the Novartis internal audit function is a matter for the chairman of the supervisory board and for the audit committee of the supervisory board. If this approach is achievable where a two-tier board structure is in place, it should be even more feasible in the case of unitary boards.

By strengthening internal audit's relationship with the board, internal audit would be able to provide stronger assurance to the board, while still being able to provide at least as strong assurance to management. Indeed, assurance is all the better if it is provided by a party that is not subordinate to those to whom the assurance is being given. In none of the extensive evidence presented to the Inquiry was there any suggestion that internal audit could satisfy a board risk committee's need for independent assurance. Currently, most internal auditors cherish their close bond with the top management team and do not wish to move out of that comfort zone.[35]

A crucial issue is 'how do boards get the assurance they need?' There have been so many examples of internal audit trimming their reporting to the audit committee of the board in order to accommodate to pressure from top management. This issue is discussed further elsewhere (Chambers, 2008a; 2008b; 2009).

Conclusion **H2.14**

Whether or not an insufficiently competitive external audit market is a consequence in part of anti-competitive conduct, in most developed countries of the world competition authorities are empowered to act to rectify insufficient competition however it came about The 2011 referral of the audit profession by the UK Office of Fair Trading to the Competition Commission was made after the former concluded that potential remedies were available; and a European Commission White Paper and draft Audit Regulation, designed largely to address these issues, has to complete its path through the European Parliament and the Council of Ministers. Most importantly, the audit profession, and in particular the Big 4 firms who dominate the profession, need to rediscover an understanding of the meaning of professionalism – in particular placing service above monetary reward. Earlier concerns that this had been lost led to the regulation of auditing being largely removed from the profession, although regulatory capture has meant that this had not been entirely effective. Contemporary concerns may lead to marginalising audit and to continued downward pressures on audit price until costs and benefits are in better balance. Technically, and in terms of work efficiency, the audit profession is generally in quite good heart. In a broader sense its loss of most other attributes of a profession is the key to understanding the current malaise. The subservience of the auditing profession to accounting standards is a particular concern, making auditing more of a box ticking exercise where auditors relegate their professional judgement to whether accounting standards have been followed, whatever the result. It should be within the grasp of the profession itself, without assistance from competition authorities, to address these concerns; and it is not too late for it to do so.

It is apparent that external auditing can change to better serve the global financial markets. Likewise, internal audit can evolve to fill more of the board's assurance vacuum.

Suggestions for further research **H2.15**

There are many lines of research suggested by this chapter. Further research to update the generally accepted tenets of a profession and their relevance to auditing would be valuable. Related to this is the issue as to whether breaking up the Big 4 would on balance benefit society and whether it would enhance competition, quality and choice in the audit market. It would be worthwhile to explore the impacts on the audit market and on market participants of withdrawing from some companies the mandatory requirement for an audit.

References

Abbott, A. (1988) *The System of Professions: An Essay on the Division of Expert Labor*, Chicago: The University of Chicago Press.

Auditing Practices Board (2009) *Consultation on Audit Firms Providing Non-audit Services to Listed Companies that they Audit*, London, Financial Reporting Council, October 2009.

Basioudis, I.G. and Steele, A. (2001) *Accountancy*, July 2001, pp 135–136.

Bigg, W.W. and Davies, J. (1953) *Internal Auditing*, 1st edn, London: HFL (Publishers).

Boone, J.P., Khurana, I.K. and Raman, K.K. (2010) 'Do the Big 4 and second-tier firms provide audits of similar quality?', Journal of Accounting and Public Policy, 29 (4), pp 330–352.

Boys, P. (1989, 1990) 'What's in a name', Accountancy.

Brink, V.Z. (1941) *Internal Auditing*, New York: The Ronald Press.

Carlin, T.M., Finch, N. and Laili, N.H. (2009) 'Investigating audit quality among Big 4 Malaysian firms', *Asian Review of Accounting*, 17 (2), Emerald, pp 96–114.

Chambers, A.D. (1981*) Internal Auditing: Theory and Practice*, London: Pitman.

Chambers, A.D. (2008a) 'The Board's Black Hole – Filling their Assurance Vacuum: Can Internal Audit Rise to the Challenge?', *Measuring Business Excellence: the Journal of Organizational Performance Management*, 12 (1), Emerald, pp 47–63.

Chambers, A.D. (2008b) 'Bring on the Super Auditors', *Internal Auditing*, CIIA (UK), December, pp 18–21.

Chambers, A.D. (2009) 'The Black Hole of Assurance', *Internal Auditor*, IIA Inc, April, pp 28–29.

Coffee, J. (2006) *Gatekeepers: the Professions and Corporate Governance*, Oxford: Oxford University Press.

Collins, A. (1904) *A Municipal Internal Audit*, London: Gee & Co.

Coopers & Lybrand (1984) *The Early History of Coopers & Lybrand*, Coopers & Lybrand, London.

Cowton, C.J. (2009) 'Accounting and the ethics challenge: re-membering the professional body', *Accounting and Business Research*, 39 (3), International Accounting Policy Forum, pp 177–189 (paper-based on the P.D. Leake Lecture 2007).

Cowton, C.J. (2008) 'Governing the corporate citizen: reflections on the role of professionals', in J. Conill, C. Luetge and T. Schönwälder-Küntze (eds), *Corporate Citizenship, Contractarianism and Ethical Theory: On Philosophical Foundations of Business Ethics*, Aldershot: Ashgate, pp 29–47.

Duska, R.F. and Duska, B.S. (2003) *Accounting Ethics*, Malden, Mass: Blackwell.

Greenwood, E. (1957) 'Attributes of a Profession', *Social Work*, July, pp 45–55 (also as (1966) H. Vollmer and D. Mills (eds), *The Elements of Professionalisation, Professionalisation*, New Jersey: Prentice-Hall).

House of Commons (2009) *Banking Crisis: Reforming Corporate Governance and Pay in the City*, Treasury Select Committee, Ninth Report of Session 2008–09, 15 May 2009, p 5 and para 221.

Habgood, W. (1994), *Chartered Accountants in England and Wales: A Guide to Historical Records*, Manchester: Manchester University Press.

House of Lords (2011*) Auditors: Market Concentration and their Role*, Select Committee on Economic Affairs, 30 March 2011, Volume I: Report, HL Paper 119-I at http://www.publications.parliament.uk/pa/ld201011/ldselect/ldeconaf/119/11902.htm (accessed 23 June 2012); Volume II: Evidence, HL Paper 119-II at http://www.publications.parliament.uk/pa/ld201011/ldselect/ldeconaf/119/11902.htm#evidence (accessed 23 June 2012); further online evidence (not available in hard copy at http://www.parliament.uk/business/committees/committees-a-z/lords-select/economic-affairs-committee/Publications/previous-sessions/Session-2010-12/ (accessed 23 June 2012).

Jones, E. (1981) *Accountancy and the British Economy 1840-1980: The evolution of Ernst & Whinney*, London: Batsford B.T. Ltd.

Jones, E. (1995), *True and Fair: A History of Price Waterhouse*, London: Hamish Hamilton.

Kay, J. (2012), 'Finance needs trusted stewards, not toll collectors', *Financial Times*, 23 July 2012, p 11.

Kettle, R. (1958) *Deloitte & Co. 1845-1956*, Oxford: Oxford University Press.

Lawrence, A., Minutti-Meza, M. and Zhang,P. (2011) 'Can Big 4 versus non-Big 4 differences in audit-quality proxies be attributed to client characteristics?', *Accounting Review*, 86 (1), pp 259–268.

Liggio, C.D. (1974) 'The Expectation Gap: The Accountant's Legal Waterloo', *Journal of Contemporary Business*, 3 (3), pp 27–44.

Loughrey, J. (2011) *Corporate Lawyers and Corporate Governance*, Cambridge: Cambridge University Press.

McNamee, D. and Selim, G. (1998) *Risk Management: Changing the Internal Auditor's Paradigm*, Florida, IIA Research Foundation.

Oxera Consulting (2006) *Competition and Choice in the UK Audit Market*, prepared for the Department of Trade and Industry and the Financial Reporting Council, April 2006.

Perry, M. (2000) *Accountancy Age*, 22 June 2000.

Porter, B.A. (1990) 'The Audit Expectation-Performance Gap and the Role of External Auditors in Society', PhD thesis, Massey University, New Zealand.

Richards, A B. (1981) *Touche Ross & Co 1899-1981: The Origins and Growth of the UK Firm*, Touche & Ross & Co, London.

Ronen, J. (2010) 'Corporate Audits and How to Fix Them', *Journal of Economic Perspectives*, (24) 2, pp 189–210.

Smith, A.C. (1953) *Internal Auditing – An Introduction to the Audit of Industrial Management Accounts*, London: Pitman.

Spacek, L. (1974) *The Growth of Arthur Andersen & Co,* New York: Garland.

Walker, D. (2009a) *A review of corporate governance in UK banks and other financial industry entities*, draft report, http://www.hm-treasury.gov.uk/walker_review_information.htm, 16 July 2009.

Walker, D. (2009b) *A review of corporate governance in UK banks and other financial industry entities*, final report, http://www.hm-treasury.gov.uk/d/walker_review_261109.pdf, November 2009.

Wise, T.A. (1982), *Peat, Marwick, Mitchell & Co: 85 years*, Peat, Marwick, Mitchell & Co.

Notes

1 This chapter is based on a paper that appeared as Chambers, A.D. (2013) 'Is Audit Failing the Global Capital Markets?', *International Journal of Disclosure and Governance*, 10 (3), pp 195–212, copyright Macmillan Publishers Ltd. In working paper form it was presented at the Centre for Corporate Governance Research (CCGR) 10th International Conference on Corporate Governance, Birmingham University, UK, 25 June 2012. The author is grateful for assistance from Dr Ilias Basioudis, Cormac Butler and Anthony Carey.

2 The tables are based on the latest data available at the end of 2012, being in the main data relating to years ended 31 December 2011.

3 Refer also to Memorandum by Mr Iain Richards of Aviva in HL paper 119-II (note 10), pp 313–328.

4 Unlike a 'shared audit', under a 'joint audit' arrangement both audit firms are responsible for the full audit report and opinion.

5 Examples are the shareholders' vote on the remuneration report which has been only advisory. Until 2003, this was a provision within the UK Combined Code: since it was clearly not working, it was taken out of the Code and attached to the Companies Act of the day; it is now a section within the Companies Act 2006, but still only an advisory vote. Similarly the Davies Report on women on boards has not led to a mandatory quota approach, appealing instead to boards to voluntarily make their boards more diverse.

6 House of Lords Report (2011) *Auditors: Market Concentration and their Role,* Volume 1, HL paper 119-I, 30 March 2001, pp 39 and 51, paras 198 and 142.

7 HL paper 119-I, *ibid*, paras 201 and 161.

8 Izza, M., reported widely, for instance in *The Times*, 31 March 2011, p 53.

9 Liggio (1974) defined the 'auditor's expectations gap' as:

'A factor of the levels of expected performance as envisioned both by the independent accountants and by the use of financial statements. The difference between these levels of expected performance is the expectation gap.'

Porter (1990) elaborated upon the 'audit expectation-performance gap':

'Gap between what society expects auditors to achieve and what they can reasonably be expected to accomplish ("reasonableness gap");

Gap between what society can reasonably expect auditors to accomplish and what they are perceived to achieve ("performance gap")

– a gap between what can reasonably be expected of auditors and auditors' existing duties, as defined by the law and professional promulgations ("deficient standards"); and

– a gap between auditors' existing duties and auditors' performance, as perceived by society ("deficient performance").'

10 House of Lords Evidence (2011) *Auditors: Market Concentration and their Role,* Volume II, HL paper 119-II, 30 March 2011, Q466, p 346.

11 HL paper 119-I (note 6), pp 40 and 51, paras 144 and 199.

12 At the June 30 2011 FEE conference in Brussels.

13 http://www.frc.org.uk/press/pub2764.html.

14 IASB sets IFRSs.

15 See discussion at para 126 of the HL paper 119-I (note 6), p 35.

16 The author is grateful to Cormac Butler (ctbutler@aol.com) for use of this example. He is author of *Accounting for Financial Instruments*, Chichester: Wiley.

17 http://namawinelake.wordpress.com/2012/01/05/nama-reveals-new-practice-in-irish-banks-give-a-borrower-a-loan-give-the-borrower-a-second-loan-to-pay-interest-on-the-first-loan-and-classify-the-first-loan-as-performing/.

18 HL paper 119-I (note 6), p.35, para 125.

19 HL paper 119-II (note 10), p 340.

20 Some have queried whether the Lords' report should have linked 'prudence' to accounting standards rather than to audit. The point the Committee was making

was that they considered prudence should be reasserted as the guiding principle of accounting standards but that, even if it were not, the auditor's true and fair override should always apply the principle of prudence. Concern was expressed to the Inquiry that audit had become too much of a box-ticking exercise of compliance with financial reporting standards, with too little regard for substance over form and too little scope for the application of auditor scepticism. The Inquiry heard that the FRC had taken advice from a financial QC whose opinion was that IFRSs' 'fairly present' (IAS 1) is the same as 'true and fair' under UK GAAP.

21 BDO Marque Gendrot acquired by Deloitte in 2006; BDO Marque Gendrot was at that time the 6th largest audit firm in France with interesting listed clients in joint audits. Salustro acquired by KPMG in 2004; Salustro was at the time the sixth largest audit firm in France with a very enviable portfolio of listed audit clients, including a number listed in the CAC40 index. Calan Ramolino in 1997 acquired by Deloitte in 1997: Calan Ramolino was at the time the sixth largest audit firm in France with 60 listed audit clients.

22 Terco, the Brazilian Grant Thornton firm, joined forces with E&Y, 2010; BDO's member firm in Brazil defected to KPMG, 2011. See: http://www.big4.com/blog/brazil-merry-go-round-%E2%80%93-kpmg-acquires-bdo-who-acquires-crowe-howarth%E2%80%A6-707; https://zephyr2.bvdep.com/version-201138/FullEditorialNews.serv?product=zephyrneo&databasecontext=Deals&newsid=9176; http://www.accountingtoday.com/news/BDO-KPMG-Crowe-Horwath-Change-Member-Firms-Brazil-57798-1.html.

23 Grant Thornton in Denmark (fifth largest in Denmark) acquired by PricewaterhouseCoopers (PwC), 2011.

24 A series of articles published in the *Accountancy* magazine that charted the changes in the names of accounting firms through a maze of mergers from 1780 to 1990. In that way the family trees of the largest accounting firms in British practice in 1989 were followed to their beginnings.

25 Basiousis, I.G: PhD (2000), he quotes: '604 different accounting firms appear in my dataset between 1953-1991, and many (if not the majority) of them have now disappeared mainly due to a wave of mergers during the last 40-50 years … the merger activities were accelerating during the 60s, 70s and 80s, and that mergers have been prevalent throughout the history of the British accounting firms.'

26 HL paper 119-I (note 6), p 369, Q522.

27 Arthur Levitt resigned as chairman of the SEC in February 2001.

28 Enron collapsed in November 2001.

29 Appendix 3, item 31, p 65.

30 HL paper 119-I (note 6), pp 281-282, Q380.

31 HL paper 119-I (note 6), p.287, Q392.

32 Walker (2009b), p93, para 6.8.

33 HL paper 119-II (note 10), p 276, Q357 (see also HL paper 119-II,op cit, Dr Peters' answer to Q381 at p 282).

34 HL paper 119-II (note 10), p 286, Q390.

35 See Dr Blackburn's answer to Q383 at p 282 of HL paper 119-II (note 10), which implies an advantage of a close relationship between internal audit and management.

The UK Corporate Governance Code

Here we reproduce the September 2012 version of the UK Corporate Governance Code of the Financial Reporting Council. The FRC's Stewardship Code is set out in full at **App2**.

The Code, together with additional material, is available on the Financial Reporting Council website (www.frc.org.uk).

The general intention of the FRC is to update the Corporate Governance Code every two years, with the next update expected to be published in July 2014 and to apply to financial years beginning on or after 1 October 2012.

The review on gender diversity by Lord Davies of Abersoch, commissioned by the Government and published in February 2011, resulted in diversity being addressed for the first time in the 2012 version of the UK Corporate Governance Code at revised Provision B.2.4 and at new Supporting Principle B.6 (see below). These Code requirements on diversity applied from the same date as the Government's regulations requiring companies to disclose information about the percentage of women at different levels of the organisation. The Davies Review was designed to identify barriers preventing more women from reaching the boardroom, and to make recommendations regarding what government and business could do to increase the proportion of women on boards.

The FRC's publication on the Code also includes an introduction on governance and the Code, a preface, a note on 'comply or explain', and two supporting schedules on the design of performance-related remuneration for executive directors (Schedule A), and on disclosure of corporate governance arrangements (Schedule B) and an Appendix on the overlap between the disclosure and transparency rules and the UK Corporate Governance Code. Schedule C, on engagement principles for institutional shareholders, was removed from later FRC reprints of the earlier 2010 Code, and from the FRC's online version, as since 2010 this has been addressed more fully in the FRC's Stewardship Code (see **App2**).

The listing obligation for companies with a UK premium listing is to apply the main principles of the Code and top comply or explain with respect to the Code's provisions.

Note that the numbering of the footnotes in this reproduction of the Code is different from the FRC's numbering, since we are reproducing only the Code itself and not other material which appears within the FRC's publication.

THE MAIN PRINCIPLES OF THE CODE

Section A: Leadership

Every company should be headed by an effective board which is collectively responsible for the long-term success of the company.

There should be a clear division of responsibilities at the head of the company between the running of the board and the executive responsibility for the running of the company's business. No one individual should have unfettered powers of decision.

The chairman is responsible for leadership of the board and ensuring its effectiveness on all aspects of its role.

As part of their role as members of a unitary board, non-executive directors should constructively challenge and help develop proposals on strategy.

Section B: Effectiveness

The board and its committees should have the appropriate balance of skills, experience, independence and knowledge of the company to enable them to discharge their respective duties and responsibilities effectively.

There should be a formal, rigorous and transparent procedure for the appointment of new directors to the board.

All directors should be able to allocate sufficient time to the company to discharge their responsibilities effectively.

All directors should receive induction on joining the board and should regularly update and refresh their skills and knowledge.

The board should be supplied in a timely manner with information in a form and of a quality appropriate to enable it to discharge its duties.

The board should undertake a formal and rigorous annual evaluation of its own performance and that of its committees and individual directors.

All directors should be submitted for re-election at regular intervals, subject to continued satisfactory performance.

Section C: Accountability

The board should present a fair, balanced and understandable assessment of the company's position and prospects.

The board is responsible for determining the nature and extent of the significant risks it is willing to take in achieving its strategic objectives. The board should maintain sound risk management and internal control systems.

The board should establish formal and transparent arrangements for considering how they should apply the corporate reporting, risk management and internal control principles and for maintaining an appropriate relationship with the company's auditor.

Section D: Remuneration

Levels of remuneration should be sufficient to attract, retain and motivate directors of the quality required to run the company successfully, but a company should avoid paying more than is necessary for this purpose. A significant proportion of executive directors' remuneration should be structured so as to link rewards to corporate and individual performance.

There should be a formal and transparent procedure for developing policy on executive remuneration and for fixing the remuneration packages of individual directors. No director should be involved in deciding his or her own remuneration.

Section E: Relations with Shareholders

There should be a dialogue with shareholders based on the mutual understanding of objectives. The board as a whole has responsibility for ensuring that a satisfactory dialogue with shareholders takes place.

The board should use the AGM to communicate with investors and to encourage their participation.

SECTION A: LEADERSHIP

A.1: The Role of the Board

Main Principle

Every company should be headed by an effective board which is collectively responsible for the long-term success of the company.

Supporting Principles

The board's role is to provide entrepreneurial leadership of the company within a framework of prudent and effective controls which enables risk to be assessed and managed. The board should set the company's strategic aims, ensure that the necessary financial and human resources are in place for the company to meet its objectives and review management performance. The board should set the company's values and standards and ensure that its obligations to its shareholders and others are understood and met.

All directors must act in what they consider to be the best interests of the company, consistent with their statutory duties[1].

Code Provisions

A.1.1. The board should meet sufficiently regularly to discharge its duties effectively. There should be a formal schedule of matters specifically reserved for its decision. The annual report should include a statement of how the board operates, including a high level statement of which types of decisions are to be taken by the board and which are to be delegated to management.

A.1.2. The annual report should identify the chairman, the deputy chairman (where there is one), the chief executive, the senior independent director and the chairmen and members of the board committees[2]. It should also set out the number of meetings of the board and those committees and individual attendance by directors.

A.1.3. The company should arrange appropriate insurance cover in respect of legal action against its directors.

A.2: Division of Responsibilities

Main Principle

There should be a clear division of responsibilities at the head of the company between the running of the board and the executive responsibility for the running of the company's business. No one individual should have unfettered powers of decision.

Code Provision

A.2.1 The roles of chairman and chief executive should not be exercised by the same individual. The division of responsibilities between the chairman and chief executive should be clearly established, set out in writing and agreed by the board.

A.3: The Chairman

Main Principle

The chairman is responsible for leadership of the board and ensuring its effectiveness on all aspects of its role.

Supporting Principle

The chairman is responsible for setting the board's agenda and ensuring that adequate time is available for discussion of all agenda items, in particular strategic issues. The chairman should also promote a culture of openness and debate by facilitating the effective contribution of non-executive directors in particular and ensuring constructive relations between executive and non-executive directors.

The chairman is responsible for ensuring that the directors receive accurate, timely and clear information. The chairman should ensure effective communication with shareholders.

Code Provisions

A.3.1. The chairman should on appointment meet the independence criteria set out in B.1.1 below. A chief executive should not go on to be chairman of the same company. If exceptionally a board decides that a chief executive should become chairman, the board should consult major shareholders in advance and should set out its reasons to shareholders at the time of the appointment and in the next annual report[3].

A.4: Non-executive Directors

Main Principle

As part of their role as members of a unitary board, non-executive directors should constructively challenge and help develop proposals on strategy.

Supporting Principles

Non-executive directors should scrutinise the performance of management in meeting agreed goals and objectives and monitor the reporting of performance. They should satisfy themselves on the integrity of financial information and that financial controls and systems of risk management are robust and defensible. They are responsible for determining appropriate levels of remuneration of executive directors and have a prime role in appointing and, where necessary, removing executive directors, and in succession planning.

Code Provisions

A.4.1. The board should appoint one of the independent non-executive directors to be the senior independent director to provide a sounding board for the chairman and to serve as an intermediary for the other directors when necessary. The senior independent director should be available to shareholders if they have concerns which contact through the normal channels of chairman, chief executive or other executive directors has failed to resolve or for which such contact is inappropriate.

A.4.2. The chairman should hold meetings with the non-executive directors without the executives present. Led by the senior independent director, the non-executive directors should meet without the chairman present at least annually to appraise the chairman's performance and on such other occasions as are deemed appropriate.

A.4.3. Where directors have concerns which cannot be resolved about the running of the company or a proposed action, they should ensure that their concerns are recorded in the board minutes. On resignation, a non-executive director should provide a written statement to the chairman, for circulation to the board, if they have any such concerns.

SECTION B: EFFECTIVENESS

B.1: The Composition of the Board

Main Principle

The board and its committees should have the appropriate balance of skills, experience, independence and knowledge of the company to enable them to discharge their respective duties and responsibilities effectively.

Supporting Principles

The board should be of sufficient size that the requirements of the business can be met and that changes to the board's composition and that of its committees can be managed without undue disruption, and should not be so large as to be unwieldy.

The board should include an appropriate combination of executive and non-executive directors (and, in particular, independent non-executive directors) such that no individual or small group of individuals can dominate the board's decision taking.

The value of ensuring that committee membership is refreshed and that undue reliance is not placed on particular individuals should be taken into account in deciding chairmanship and membership of committees.

No one other than the committee chairman and members is entitled to be present at a meeting of the nomination, audit or remuneration committee, but others may attend at the invitation of the committee.

Code Provisions

B.1.1. The board should identify in the annual report each non-executive director it considers to be independent[4]. The board should determine whether the director is independent in character and judgement and whether there are relationships or circumstances which are likely to affect, or could appear to affect, the director's judgement. The board should state its reasons if it determines that a director is independent notwithstanding the existence of relationships or circumstances which may appear relevant to its determination, including if the director:

- has been an employee of the company or group within the last five years;
- has, or has had within the last three years, a material business relationship with the company either directly, or as a partner, shareholder, director or senior employee of a body that has such a relationship with the company;
- has received or receives additional remuneration from the company apart from a director's fee, participates in the company's share option or a performance-related pay scheme, or is a member of the company's pension scheme;
- has close family ties with any of the company's advisers, directors or senior employees;
- holds cross-directorships or has significant links with other directors through involvement in other companies or bodies;
- represents a significant shareholder; or
- has served on the board for more than nine years from the date of their first election.

B.1.2. Except for smaller companies[5], at least half the board, excluding the chairman, should comprise nonexecutive directors determined by the board to be independent. A smaller company should have at least two independent non-executive directors.

B.2: Appointments to the Board
Main Principle

There should be a formal, rigorous and transparent procedure for the appointment of new directors to the board.

Supporting Principles

The search for board candidates should be conducted, and appointments made, on merit, against objective criteria and with due regard for the benefits of diversity on the board, including gender.

The board should satisfy itself that plans are in place for orderly succession for appointments to the board and to senior management, so as to maintain an appropriate balance of skills and experience within the company and on the board and to ensure progressive refreshing of the board.

Code Provisions

B.2.1. There should be a nomination committee which should lead the process for board appointments and make recommendations to the board. A majority of members of the nomination committee should be independent non-executive directors. The chairman or an independent non-executive director should chair the committee, but the chairman should not chair the nomination committee when it is dealing with the appointment of a successor to the chairmanship. The nomination committee should make available its terms of reference, explaining its role and the authority delegated to it by the board[6].

B.2.2. The nomination committee should evaluate the balance of skills, experience, independence and knowledge on the board and, in the light of this evaluation, prepare a description of the role and capabilities required for a particular appointment.

B.2.3. Non-executive directors should be appointed for specified terms subject to re-election and to statutory provisions relating to the removal of a director. Any term beyond six years for a nonexecutive director should be subject to particularly rigorous review, and should take into account the need for progressive refreshing of the board.

B.2.4. A separate section of the annual report should describe the work of the nomination committee[7], including the process it has used in relation to board appointments. This section should include a description of the board's policy on diversity, including gender, any measurable objectives that it has set for implementing the policy, and progress on achieving the objectives. An explanation should be given if neither an external search consultancy nor open advertising has been used in the appointment of a chairman or a non-executive director. Where an external search consultancy has been used, it should be identified in the annual report and a statement made as to whether it has any other connection with the company.

B.3: Commitment

Main Principle

All directors should be able to allocate sufficient time to the company to discharge their responsibilities effectively.

Code Provisions

B.3.1. For the appointment of a chairman, the nomination committee should prepare a job specification, including an assessment of the time commitment expected, recognising the need for availability in the event of crises. A chairman's other significant commitments should be disclosed to the board before appointment and included in the annual report. Changes to such commitments should be reported to the board as they arise, and their impact explained in the next annual report.

B.3.2. The terms and conditions of appointment of non-executive directors should be made available for inspection[8]. The letter of appointment should set out the expected time commitment. Non-executive directors should undertake that they will have sufficient time to meet what is expected of them. Their other significant commitments should be disclosed to the board before appointment, with a broad indication of the time involved and the board should be informed of subsequent changes.

B.3.3. The board should not agree to a full time executive director taking on more than one non-executive directorship in a FTSE 100 company nor the chairmanship of such a company.

B.4: Development

Main Principle

All directors should receive induction on joining the board and should regularly update and refresh their skills and knowledge.

Supporting Principles

The chairman should ensure that the directors continually update their skills and the knowledge and familiarity with the company required to fulfil their role both on the board and on board committees.

The company should provide the necessary resources for developing and updating its directors' knowledge and capabilities.

To function effectively all directors need appropriate knowledge of the company and access to its operations and staff.

Code Provisions

B.4.1. The chairman should ensure that new directors receive a full, formal and tailored induction on joining the board. As part of this, directors should avail themselves of opportunities to meet major shareholders.

B.4.2. The chairman should regularly review and agree with each director their training and development needs.

B.5: Information and Support

Main Principle

The board should be supplied in a timely manner with information in a form and of a quality appropriate to enable it to discharge its duties.

Supporting Principles

The chairman is responsible for ensuring that the directors receive accurate, timely and clear information. Management has an obligation to provide such information but directors should seek clarification or amplification where necessary.

Under the direction of the chairman, the company secretary's responsibilities include ensuring good information flows within the board and its committees and between senior management and non-executive directors, as well as facilitating induction and assisting with professional development as required. The company secretary should be responsible for advising the board through the chairman on all governance matters.

Code Provisions

B.5.1. The board should ensure that directors, especially non-executive directors, have access to independent professional advice at the company's expense where they judge it necessary to discharge their responsibilities as directors. Committees should be provided with sufficient resources to undertake their duties.

B.5.2. All directors should have access to the advice and services of the company secretary, who is responsible to the board for ensuring that board procedures are complied with. Both the appointment and removal of the company secretary should be a matter for the board as a whole.

B.6: Evaluation

Main Principle

The board should undertake a formal and rigorous annual evaluation of its own performance and that of its committees and individual directors.

Supporting Principles

Evaluation of the board should consider the balance of skills, experience, independence and knowledge of the company on the board, its diversity, including gender, how the board works together as a unit, and other factors relevant to its effectiveness.

The chairman should act on the results of the performance evaluation by recognising the strengths and addressing the weaknesses of the board and, where appropriate, proposing new members be appointed to the board or seeking the resignation of directors.

Individual evaluation should aim to show whether each director continues to contribute effectively and to demonstrate commitment to the role (including commitment of time for board and committee meetings and any other duties).

Code Provisions

B.6.1. The board should state in the annual report how performance evaluation of the board, its committees and its individual directors has been conducted.

B.6.2. Evaluation of the board of FTSE 350 companies should be externally facilitated at least every three years. The external facilitator should be identified in the annual report and a statement made as to whether they have any other connection with the company.

B.6.3. The non-executive directors, led by the senior independent director, should be responsible for performance evaluation of the chairman, taking into account the views of executive directors.

B.7: Re-election

Main Principle

All directors should be submitted for re-election at regular intervals, subject to continued satisfactory performance.

Code Provisions

B.7.1. All directors of FTSE 350 companies should be subject to annual election by shareholders. All other directors should be subject to election by shareholders at the first annual general meeting after their appointment, and to re-election thereafter at intervals of no more than three years. Non-executive directors who have served longer than nine years should be subject to annual re-election. The names of directors submitted for election or re-election should be accompanied by sufficient biographical details and any other relevant information to enable shareholders to take an informed decision on their election.

B.7.2. The board should set out to shareholders in the papers accompanying a resolution to elect a non-executive director why they believe an individual should be elected. The chairman should confirm to shareholders when proposing re-election that, following formal performance evaluation, the individual's performance continues to be effective and to demonstrate commitment to the role.

SECTION C: ACCOUNTABILITY

C.1: Financial And Business Reporting

Main Principle

The board should present a fair, balanced and understandable assessment of the company's position and prospects.

Supporting Principle

The board's responsibility to present a fair, balanced and understandable assessment extends to interim and other price-sensitive public reports and reports to regulators as well as to information required to be presented by statutory requirements.

The board should establish arrangements that will enable it to ensure that the information presented is fair, balanced and understandable.

Code Provisions

C.1.1. The directors should explain in the annual report their responsibility for preparing the annual report and accounts, and state that they consider the annual report and accounts, taken as a whole, is fair, balanced and understandable and provides the information necessary for shareholders to assess the company's performance, business model and strategy. There should be a statement by the auditor about their reporting responsibilities[9].

C.1.2. The directors should include in the annual report an explanation of the basis on which the company generates or preserves value over the longer term (the business model) and the strategy for delivering the objectives of the company[10]

C.1.3. The directors should report in annual and half-yearly financial statements that the business is a going concern, with supporting assumptions or qualifications as necessary[11].

C.2: Risk Management and Internal Control[12]

Main Principle

The board is responsible for determining the nature and extent of the significant risks it is willing to take in achieving its strategic objectives. The board should maintain sound risk management and internal control systems.

Code Provision

C.2.1. The board should, at least annually, conduct a review of the effectiveness of the company's risk management and internal control systems and should report to shareholders that they have done so[13]. The review should cover all material controls, including financial, operational and compliance controls.

C.3: Audit Committee and Auditors[14].

Main Principle

The board should establish formal and transparent arrangements for considering how they should apply the corporate reporting and risk management and internal control principles and for maintaining an appropriate relationship with the company's auditors.

Code Provisions

C.3.1. The board should establish an audit committee of at least three, or in the case of smaller companies[15] two, independent non-executive directors. In smaller companies the company chairman may be a member of, but not chair, the committee in addition to the independent non-executive directors, provided he or she was considered independent on appointment as chairman. The board should satisfy itself that at least one member of the audit committee has recent and relevant financial experience[16].

C.3.2. The main role and responsibilities of the audit committee should be set out in written terms of reference[17] and should include:

- to monitor the integrity of the financial statements of the company and any formal announcements relating to the company's financial performance, reviewing significant financial reporting judgements contained in them;
- to review the company's internal financial controls and, unless expressly addressed by a separate board risk committee composed of independent directors, or by the board itself, to review the company's internal control and risk management systems;
- to monitor and review the effectiveness of the company's internal audit function;

- make recommendations to the board, for it to put to the shareholders for their approval in general meeting, in relation to the appointment, re-appointment and removal of the external auditor and to approve the remuneration and terms of engagement of the external auditor;
- to review and monitor the external auditor's independence and objectivity and the effectiveness of the audit process, taking into consideration relevant UK professional and regulatory requirements;
- to develop and implement policy on the engagement of the external auditor to supply non-audit services, taking into account relevant ethical guidance regarding the provision of non-audit services by the external audit firm; and to report to the board, identifying any matters in respect of which it considers that action or improvement is needed and making recommendations as to the steps to be taken; and
- to report to the board on how it has discharged its responsibilities.

C.3.3. The terms of reference of the audit committee, including its role and the authority delegated to it by the board, should be made available[18].

C.3.4. Where requested by the board, the audit committee should provide advice on whether the annual report and accounts, taken as a whole, is fair, balanced and understandable and provides the information necessary for shareholders to assess the company's performance, business model and strategy.

C.3.5. The audit committee should review arrangements by which staff of the company may, in confidence, raise concerns about possible improprieties in matters of financial reporting or other matters. The audit committee's objective should be to ensure that arrangements are in place for the proportionate and independent investigation of such matters and for appropriate follow-up action.

C.3.6. The audit committee should monitor and review the effectiveness of the internal audit activities. Where there is no internal audit function, the audit committee should consider annually whether there is a need for an internal audit function and make a recommendation to the board, and the reasons for the absence of such a function should be explained in the relevant section of the annual report.

C.3.7. The audit committee should have primary responsibility for making a recommendation on the appointment, reappointment and removal of the external auditors. FTSE 350 companies should put the external audit contract out to tender at least every ten years. If the board does not accept the audit committee's recommendation, it should include in the annual report, and in any papers recommending appointment or re-appointment, a statement from the audit committee explaining the recommendation and should set out reasons why the board has taken a different position.

C.3.8. A separate section of the annual report should describe the work of the committee in discharging its responsibilities[19]. The report should include:

- the significant issues that the committee considered in relation to the financial statements, and how these issues were addressed;
- an explanation of how it has assessed the effectiveness of the external audit process and the approach taken to the appointment or

reappointment of the external auditor, and information on the length of tenure of the current audit firm and when a tender was last conducted; and

- if the external auditor provides non-audit services, an explanation of how auditor objectivity and independence is safeguarded.

SECTION D: REMUNERATION

D.1: The Level and Components of Remuneration

Main Principle

Levels of remuneration should be sufficient to attract, retain and motivate directors of the quality required to run the company successfully, but a company should avoid paying more than is necessary for this purpose. A significant proportion of executive directors' remuneration should be structured so as to link rewards to corporate and individual performance.

Supporting Principle

The performance-related elements of executive directors' remuneration should be stretching and designed to promote the long-term success of the company.

The remuneration committee should judge where to position their company relative to other companies. But they should use such comparisons with caution, in view of the risk of an upward ratchet of remuneration levels with no corresponding improvement in performance.

They should also be sensitive to pay and employment conditions elsewhere in the group, especially when determining annual salary increases.

Code Provisions

D.1.1. In designing schemes of performance-related remuneration for executive directors, the remuneration committee should follow the provisions in Schedule A to this Code.

D.1.2. Where a company releases an executive director to serve as a non-executive director elsewhere, the remuneration report[20] should include a statement as to whether or not the director will retain such earnings and, if so, what the remuneration is.

D.1.3. Levels of remuneration for non-executive directors should reflect the time commitment and responsibilities of the role. Remuneration for non-executive directors should not include share options or other performance-related elements. If, exceptionally, options are granted, shareholder approval should be sought in advance and any shares acquired by exercise of the options should be held until at least one year after the non-executive director leaves the board. Holding of share options could be relevant to the determination of a non-executive director's independence (as set out in provision B.1.1).

D.1.4. The remuneration committee should carefully consider what compensation commitments (including pension contributions and all other elements) their directors' terms of appointment would entail in the event of early termination.

The aim should be to avoid rewarding poor performance. They should take a robust line on reducing compensation to reflect departing directors' obligations to mitigate loss.

D.1.5. Notice or contract periods should be set at one year or less. If it is necessary to offer longer notice or contract periods to new directors recruited from outside, such periods should reduce to one year or less after the initial period.

D.2: Procedure

Main Principle

There should be a formal and transparent procedure for developing policy on executive remuneration and for fixing the remuneration packages of individual directors. No director should be involved in deciding his or her own remuneration.

Supporting Principles

The remuneration committee should consult the chairman and/or chief executive about their proposals relating to the remuneration of other executive directors. The remuneration committee should also be responsible for appointing any consultants in respect of executive director remuneration. Where executive directors or senior management are involved in advising or supporting the remuneration committee, care should be taken to recognise and avoid conflicts of interest.

The chairman of the board should ensure that the company maintains contact as required with its principal shareholders about remuneration.

Code Provisions

D.2.1. The board should establish a remuneration committee of at least three, or in the case of smaller companies[21] two, independent non-executive directors. In addition the company chairman may also be a member of, but not chair, the committee if he or she was considered independent on appointment as chairman. The remuneration committee should make available its terms of reference, explaining its role and the authority delegated to it by the board[22]. Where remuneration consultants are appointed, they should be identified in the annual report and a statement made as to whether they have any other connection with the company.

D.2.2. The remuneration committee should have delegated responsibility for setting remuneration for all executive directors and the chairman, including pension rights and any compensation payments. The committee should also recommend and monitor the level and structure of remuneration for senior management. The definition of 'senior management' for this purpose should be determined by the board but should normally include the first layer of management below board level.

D.2.3. The board itself or, where required by the Articles of Association, the shareholders should determine the remuneration of the non-executive directors within the limits set in the Articles of Association. Where permitted by the Articles, the board may however delegate this responsibility to a committee, which might include the chief executive.

D.2.4. Shareholders should be invited specifically to approve all new long-term incentive schemes (as defined in the Listing Rules[23]) and significant changes to existing schemes, save in the circumstances permitted by the Listing Rules.

SECTION E: RELATIONS WITH SHAREHOLDERS

E.1: Dialogue with Shareholders

Main Principle

There should be a dialogue with shareholders based on the mutual understanding of objectives. The board as a whole has responsibility for ensuring that a satisfactory dialogue with shareholders takes place[24].

Supporting Principles

Whilst recognising that most shareholder contact is with the chief executive and finance director, the chairman should ensure that all directors are made aware of their major shareholders' issues and concerns.
The board should keep in touch with shareholder opinion in whatever ways are most practical and efficient.

Code Provisions

E.1.1. The chairman should ensure that the views of shareholders are communicated to the board as a whole. The chairman should discuss governance and strategy with major shareholders. Nonexecutive directors should be offered the opportunity to attend scheduled meetings with major shareholders and should expect to attend meetings if requested by major shareholders. The senior independent director should attend sufficient meetings with a range of major shareholders to listen to their views in order to help develop a balanced understanding of the issues and concerns of major shareholders.

E.1.2. The board should state in the annual report the steps they have taken to ensure that the members of the board, and in particular the non-executive directors, develop an understanding of the views of major shareholders about the company, for example through direct face-to-face contact, analysts' or brokers' briefings and surveys of shareholder opinion.

E.2: Constructive Use of the AGM

Main Principle

The board should use the AGM to communicate with investors and to encourage their participation.

Code Provisions

E.2.1. At any general meeting, the company should propose a separate resolution on each substantially separate issue, and should in particular propose a resolution at the AGM relating to the report and accounts. For each resolution, proxy appointment forms should provide shareholders with the option to direct their proxy to vote either for or against the resolution or to withhold their vote. The proxy form and any announcement of the results of a vote should make it clear that a 'vote withheld' is not a vote in law and will not be counted in the calculation of the proportion of the votes for and against the resolution.

E.2.2. The company should ensure that all valid proxy appointments received for general meetings are properly recorded and counted. For each resolution, where a vote has been taken on a show of hands, the company should ensure that the following information is given at the meeting and made available as soon as reasonably practicable on a website which is maintained by or on behalf of the company:

- the number of shares in respect of which proxy appointments have been validly made;
- the number of votes for the resolution;
- the number of votes against the resolution; and
- the number of shares in respect of which the vote was directed to be withheld.

E.2.3. The chairman should arrange for the chairmen of the audit, remuneration and nomination committees to be available to answer questions at the AGM and for all directors to attend.

E.2.4. The company should arrange for the Notice of the AGM and related papers to be sent to shareholders at least 20 working days before the meeting.

Notes

1 For directors of UK incorporated companies, these duties are set out in the Sections 170 to 177 of the Companies Act 2006.

2 Provisions A.1.1 and A.1.2 overlap with FSA Rule DTR 7.2.7 R; Provision A.1.2 also overlaps with DTR 7.1.5 R (see Schedule B).

3 Compliance or otherwise with this provision need only be reported for the year in which the appointment is made.

4 A.3.1 states that the chairman should, on appointment, meet the independence criteria set out in this provision, but thereafter the test of independence is not appropriate in relation to the chairman.

5 A smaller company is one that is below the FTSE 350 throughout the year immediately prior to the reporting year.

6 The requirement to make the information available would be met by including the information on a website that is maintained by or on behalf of the company.

7 This provision overlaps with FSA Rule DTR 7.2.7 R (see Schedule B).

8 The terms and conditions of appointment of non-executive directors should be made available for inspection by any person at the company's registered office during normal business hours and at the AGM (for 15 minutes prior to the meeting and during the meeting).

9 This requirement may be met by the disclosures about the audit scope and responsibilities of the auditor included, or referred to, in the auditor's report pursuant to the requirements of ISA (UK and Ireland) 700, 'The Auditor's Report on Financial Statements'.

10 It would be desirable if the explanation were located in the same part of the annual report as the Business Review required by Section 417 of the Companies Act 2006. Guidance as to the matters that should be considered in an explanation of a business model is provided in 'Reporting Statement: Operating And Financial Review'. Copies are available from the FRC website.

11 'Going Concern and Liquidity Risk: Guidance for Directors of UK Companies 2009' suggests means of applying this part of the Code. Copies are available from the FRC website.

12 'Internal Control: Guidance to Directors' suggests means of applying this part of the Code. Copies are available from the FRC website.

13 In addition FSA Rule DTR 7.2.5 R requires companies to describe the main features of the internal control and risk management systems in relation to the financial reporting process.

14 'Guidance on Audit Committees' suggests means of applying this part of the Code. Copies are available from the FRC website.

15 See footnote 6.

16 This provision overlaps with FSA Rule DTR 7.1.1 R (see Schedule B).

17 This provision overlaps with FSA Rules DTR 7.1.3 R (see Schedule B).

18 See footnote 7.

19 This provision overlaps with FSA Rules DTR 7.1.5 R and 7.2.7 R (see Schedule B).

20 As required for UK incorporated companies under the Large and Medium-Sized Companies and Groups (Accounts and Reports) Regulations 2008.

21 See footnote 6.

22 This provision overlaps with FSA Rule DTR 7.2.7 R (see Schedule B).

23 Listing Rules LR 9.4. Copies are available from the FSA website.

24 Nothing in these principles or provisions should be taken to override the general requirements of law to treat shareholders equally in access to information.

Appendix 2

The UK Stewardship Code

Here we reproduce the second edition of the UK Stewardship Code, which was published in September 2012 by the Financial Reporting Council.

This Code, together with additional material, is available on the Financial Reporting Council website (www.frc.org.uk).

The UK is in the lead in having developed an authoritative Code designed to address the responsibilities of shareholders. The UK Corporate Governance Code is set out in full at **App1**.

The FRC's publication of this Code also includes introductory material which is not reproduced here, being a statement on 'Stewardship and the Code', an explanation of the 'Application of the Code' and a consideration of 'Comply or Explain'.

Schedule C of the UK Corporate Governance Code, on engagement principles for institutional shareholders, has been removed from later FRC publications of that Code, as this is now addressed more fully in this UK Stewardship Code.

Some readers may be curious about the choice of title for this Code. 'Stewards', under 'stewardship theory', are the management and the board, who are the stewards (ie trustees) on behalf of the shareholders as owners, and perhaps also on behalf of other stakeholder groups. This Code focuses on the responsibilities of the owners rather than the stewards.

THE UK STEWARDSHIP CODE

The Principles of the Code

So as to protect and enhance the value that accrues to the ultimate beneficiary, institutional investors should:

1. publicly disclose their policy on how they will discharge their stewardship responsibilities.
2. have a robust policy on managing conflicts of interest in relation to stewardship which should be publicly disclosed.
3. monitor their investee companies.
4. establish clear guidelines on when and how they will escalate their stewardship activities.
5. be willing to act collectively with other investors where appropriate.
6. have a clear policy on voting and disclosure of voting activity.
7. report periodically on their stewardship and voting activities.

The UK Stewardship Code

Principle 1

Institutional investors should publicly disclose their policy on how they will discharge their stewardship responsibilities.

Guidance

Stewardship activities include monitoring and engaging with companies on matters such as strategy, performance, risk, capital structure, and corporate governance, including culture and remuneration. Engagement is purposeful dialogue with companies on those matters as well as on issues that are the immediate subject of votes at general meetings.

The policy should disclose how the institutional investor applies stewardship with the aim of enhancing and protecting the value for the ultimate beneficiary or client.

The statement should reflect the institutional investor's activities within the investment chain, as well as the responsibilities that arise from those activities. In particular, the stewardship responsibilities of those whose primary activities are related to asset ownership may be different from those whose primary activities are related to asset management or other investment-related services.

Where activities are outsourced, the statement should explain how this is compatible with the proper exercise of the institutional investor's stewardship responsibilities and what steps the investor has taken to ensure that they are carried out in a manner consistent with the approach to stewardship set out in the statement.

The disclosure should describe arrangements for integrating stewardship within the wider investment process.

Principle 2

Institutional investors should have a robust policy on managing conflicts of interest in relation to stewardship which should be publicly disclosed.

Guidance

An institutional investor's duty is to act in the interests of its clients and/or beneficiaries.

Conflicts of interest will inevitably arise from time to time, which may include when voting on matters affecting a parent company or client.

Institutional investors should put in place, maintain and publicly disclose a policy for identifying and managing conflicts of interest with the aim of taking all reasonable steps to put the interests of their client or beneficiary first. The policy should also address how matters are handled when the interests of clients or beneficiaries diverge from each other.

Principle 3

Institutional investors should monitor their investee companies.

Guidance

Effective monitoring is an essential component of stewardship. It should take place regularly and be checked periodically for effectiveness.

When monitoring companies, institutional investors should seek to:

- keep abreast of the company's performance;
- keep abreast of developments, both internal and external to the company, that drive the company's value and risks;
- satisfy themselves that the company's leadership is effective;
- satisfy themselves that the company's board and committees adhere to the spirit of the UK Corporate Governance Code, including through meetings with the chairman and other board members;
- consider the quality of the company's reporting; and
- attend the General Meetings of companies in which they have a major holding, where appropriate and practicable.

Institutional investors should consider carefully explanations given for departure from the UK Corporate Governance Code and make reasoned judgements in each case. They should give a timely explanation to the company, in writing where appropriate, and be prepared to enter a dialogue if they do not accept the company's position.

Institutional investors should endeavour to identify at an early stage issues that may result in a significant loss in investment value. If they have concerns, they should seek to ensure that the appropriate members of the investee company's board or management are made aware.

Institutional investors may or may not wish to be made insiders. An institutional investor who may be willing to become an insider should indicate in its stewardship statement the willingness to do so, and the mechanism by which this could be done.

Institutional investors will expect investee companies and their advisers to ensure that information that could affect their ability to deal in the shares of the company concerned is not conveyed to them without their prior agreement.

Principle 4

Institutional investors should establish clear guidelines on when and how they will escalate their stewardship activities.

Guidance

Institutional investors should set out the circumstances in which they will actively intervene and regularly assess the outcomes of doing so. Intervention should be considered regardless of whether an active or passive investment policy is followed. In addition, being underweight is not, of itself, a reason for not intervening. Instances when institutional investors may want to intervene include, but are not limited to, when they have concerns about the company's strategy, performance, governance, remuneration or approach to risks, including those that may arise from social and environmental matters.

Initial discussions should take place on a confidential basis. However, if companies do not respond constructively when institutional investors intervene, then institutional investors should consider whether to escalate their action, for example, by:

- holding additional meetings with management specifically to discuss concerns;
- expressing concerns through the company's advisers;
- meeting with the chairman or other board members;
- intervening jointly with other institutions on particular issues;
- making a public statement in advance of General Meetings;
- submitting resolutions and speaking at General Meetings; and
- requisitioning a General Meeting, in some cases proposing to change board membership.

Principle 5

Institutional investors should be willing to act collectively with other investors where appropriate.

Guidance

At times collaboration with other investors may be the most effective manner in which to engage. Collective engagement may be most appropriate at times of significant corporate or wider economic stress, or when the risks posed threaten to destroy significant value.

Institutional investors should disclose their policy on collective engagement, which should indicate their readiness to work with other investors through formal and informal groups when this is necessary to achieve their objectives and ensure companies are aware of concerns. The disclosure should also indicate the kinds of circumstances in which the institutional investor would consider participating in collective engagement.

Principle 6

Institutional investors should have a clear policy on voting and disclosure of voting activity.

Guidance

Institutional investors should seek to vote all shares held. They should not automatically support the board.

If they have been unable to reach a satisfactory outcome through active dialogue then they should register an abstention or vote against the resolution. In both instances, it is good practice to inform the company in advance of their intention and the reasons why.

Institutional investors should disclose publicly voting records.

Institutional investors should disclose the use made, if any, of proxy voting or other voting advisory services. They should describe the scope of such services, identify the providers and disclose the extent to which they follow, rely upon or use recommendations made by such services.

Institutional investors should disclose their approach to stock lending and recalling lent stock.

Principle 7

Institutional investors should report periodically on their stewardship and voting activities.

Guidance

Institutional investors should maintain a clear record of their stewardship activities.

Asset managers should regularly account to their clients or beneficiaries as to how they have discharged their responsibilities. Such reports will be likely to comprise qualitative as well as quantitative information. The particular information reported and the format used, should be a matter for agreement between agents and their principals.

Asset owners should report at least annually to those to whom they are accountable on their stewardship policy and its execution.

The Chartered Director (C Dir) Qualification

This was introduced by the Institute of Directors (IoD) in 1998 as the first professional qualification for directors governed under Royal Charter. It has received international recognition as the pre-eminent award for those (both executive and non-executive) directors who seek to achieve excellence at board level in company direction and governance.

Summary

The Chartered Director qualification is available to directors who have demonstrated the requisite knowledge and experience to act as a member of a formally constituted, accountable board, having passed the Certificate and Diploma in Company Direction examinations. The IoD regards this to be the only award that comprehensively and rigorously assesses the capabilities of individual directors. Chartered Directors must demonstrate the attributes and qualities of a steward of their organisation, and show that they possess the key skills to be a critical, effective and dynamic member of a board who is able to challenge with confidence. The IoD continuously works with government, regulators, executive search agencies, the public and charitable sectors to promote the value of the Chartered Director qualification and its benefits to all boards. In building on more than a century of supporting directors, the IoD also works with organisations to assess the effectiveness of their boards – and raises the standards for all who will benefit from its wealth of experience.

Eligibility

Candidates must be:

- a member or fellow of the IoD;
- a practising director, and must have been so for at least three years (five if the candidate does not have a degree or professional qualification). The experience will include at least one recent role, undertaken within the last five years;
- proposed and verified, and
- a fully participating member of a board that meets at least four times a year, having at least three directors and focusing on the direction and governance of the organisation.

The Chartered Director Programme

There are two taught programme elements for the Certificate in Company Direction (four modules) and the Diploma in Company Direction (one module).

As an initial test of eligibility, candidates must pass the two formal examinations associated with these two programmes. The third stage comprises the submission of a portfolio of experience and a peer review interview, in addition to being a full member or Fellow of the IoD. The criteria for eligibility for Chartered Director applicants are several, but include *inter alia* being a full (director) member of a fully constituted board (or equivalent) of an qualifying entity (repeated – see above), determined by turnover (or equivalent), board composition and constitution, including board meeting frequency and agenda items. The candidate will need to demonstrate clarity in relation to their functions, both in terms of their board context and their impact, as a director, on their organisation, in satisfying the dimensions of the Professional Review which reflect the key tasks of a board.

It is the IoD's expectation that Chartered Directors should:

- secure the confidence of financiers, investors, suppliers, customers and all other stakeholders;
- demonstrate to clients or customers that their organisation's governance, exposure to risk, compliance and sustainability is professionally managed through the board, taking account of its stewardship responsibilities;
- operate at a strategic level to lead effectively to establish and sustain growth and demonstrate appropriate values based behaviours – and in so doing, to challenge rigorously and impartially to ensure that the best outcomes are obtained to secure the organisation's future and to sustain its strategic and stakeholder strategies;
- appreciate all aspects of effective business leadership and sound, broadly based approaches to corporate governance and to enable significant benefits to the organisation in securing its future capabilities; and
- improve the board's effectiveness and the personal contribution of its members through a professional development process.

Syllabus content

The syllabus for the examination in company direction assesses competence in:

- director duties, liabilities and responsibilities;
- finance;
- strategy and setting strategic direction;
- leading the organisation through the implementation of its strategy, utilising its capabilities and skills, through periods of transformation and change;
- decision-making; and
- performance management and control through effective top-down behavioural, values-based and objective-setting measures that ensure the organisation's strategy will be delivered.

Study

Candidates decide for themselves how to prepare for the examinations with the assistance of the programmes. There are interactive exercises and practice examinations to help in assessing knowledge in all areas of the programmes.

Certificate level

The Certificate offers a number of routes as follows:

- the study route (all four courses);

- the MBA route (Role of the Director and the Board and any other programmes deemed appropriate in discussion with the candidate);
- partial study route (this allows an exemption from attending the Finance for non-Finance Directors' course for those who hold a professional accountancy qualification. However this dispensation does not exempt the candidate from any part of the Certificate examination).

Diploma level

The Diploma programme (Developing Board Performance) is compulsory for entry to the examination.

The IoD offers the four Certificate and the one Diploma in Company Direction programmes over the calendar year in London and in regional franchise centres. The total attended time commitment to study the Certificate comprises ten days and, for the Diploma, three days. Alternatively, there is a five and a half day intensive (resident) Certificate programme offered several times per year. Additionally, it is expected that candidates will undertake personal study following the programmes; on average, this will amount to around 80 hours per subject.

Registration and fees

For further information on programmes and their availability, please contact the Professional Development programme team on +44 (0)20 7766 2601; email: professionaldev@iod.com.

For information on Chartered Director, please contact the team on +44 (0)20 7766 2602; email: chartered.director@iod.com; website: www.iod.com/chartered.

Appendix 4

Board Committees – Terms of Reference

This appendix carries sample terms of reference for board committees as follows:

- Audit committee: **App4.1–App4.7**;
- Remuneration committee: **App4.8–App4.10**;
- Nominations committee: **App4.11–App4.12**;
- Finance committee: **App4.13–App4.14**;
- HR/personnel committee: **App4.15–App4.16**;
- Standing orders committee: **App4.17; and**
- Risk committee: **App4.18**.

Audit committee terms of reference **App4.1**

Readers intending to use any of these samples as templates for developing their own terms of reference for audit committees may wish to consider three recent innovations in audit committee practice which are not fully covered in these sample terms of reference. First, audit committees, especially in the US, are increasingly being charged with the responsibility to consider the quality of information which the board receives, and to advise the board on the conclusions of this consideration. Secondly, audit committees, especially in the UK following the adoption of Turnbull, now more frequently have responsibility to advise the board on the quality of the entity's risk management and, on behalf of the board, to consider the major risks facing the entity and their management. Thirdly, again, particularly in the US, it is becoming accepted that the audit committee may have the responsibility proactively and specifically to consider the likely impact on risk, control and financial reporting of major changes planned, or being implemented by, the entity.

Sample terms of reference for an audit committee **App4.2**

It is good practice for an audit committee to review its terms of reference annually. This ensures that committee members are reminded of their responsibilities and powers. It also provides an opportunity for the committee to draw the board's attention to desirable modifications. In particular, observance of the latest versions of the Combined Code and implementation of The Turnbull Report are likely to suggest changes from time to time. Here we show the sample sets of terms of reference. First, a model terms of reference; secondly one adopted by a listed company has for its audit committee; and thirdly one developed by the Institute of Internal Auditors to be applicable to a company that is subject to the Sarbanes-Oxley Act 2002 – that is, principally a company with a primary or secondary listing in the US.

Example 1: Sample terms of reference for an audit committee taken from the Smith Report[1] **App4.3**

Constitution

1. The board hereby resolves to establish a committee of the board to be known as the Audit [*and Risk*] Committee.

Membership

2. The committee shall be appointed by the board. All members of the committee shall be independent non-executive directors of the company. The committee shall consist of not less than three members. A quorum shall be two members.
3. The chairman of the committee shall be appointed by the board from amongst the independent non-executive directors.

Attendance at meetings

4. The finance director, head of internal audit and a representative of the external auditors shall attend meetings at the invitation of the committee.
5. The chairman of the board, the CEO and other board members shall attend if invited by the committee.
6. There should be at least one meeting a year, or part thereof, where the external auditors attend without management present.
7. The company secretary shall be secretary of the committee.

Frequency of meetings

8. Meetings shall be held not less than [three] times a year, and where appropriate should coincide with key dates in the company's financial reporting cycle.
9. External auditors or internal auditors may request a meeting if they consider that one is necessary.

Authority

10. The committee is authorised by the board to:
    (a) investigate any activity within its terms of reference;
    (b) seek any information that it requires from any employee of the company, and all employees are directed to cooperate with any request made by the committee; and
    (c) obtain outside legal or independent professional advice and such advisors may attend meetings as necessary.

Responsibilities

11. The responsibilities of the committee shall be:
    (a) to consider the appointment of the external auditor and assess independence of the external auditor, ensuring that key partners are rotated at appropriate intervals;
    (b) to recommend the audit fee to the board and pre-approve any fees in respect of non-audit services provided by the external auditor and to ensure that the provision of non-audit services does not impair the external auditors' independence or objectivity;

(c) to discuss with the external auditor, before the audit commences, the nature and scope of the audit and to review the auditors' quality control procedures and steps taken by the auditor to respond to changes in regulatory and other requirements;

(d) to oversee the process for selecting the external auditor and make appropriate recommendations through the board to the shareholders to consider at the AGM;

(e) to review the external auditor's management letter and management's response;

(f) to review the internal audit programme and ensure that the internal audit function is adequately resourced and has appropriate standing within the company;

(g) to consider management's response to any major external or internal audit recommendations;

(h) to approve the appointment or dismissal of the head of internal audit;

(i) to review the company's procedures for handling allegations from whistleblowers;

(j) to review management's and the internal auditor's reports on the effectiveness of systems for internal financial control, financial reporting and risk management;

(k) to review, and challenge where necessary, the actions and judgements of management, in relation to the interim and annual financial statements before submission to the board, paying particular attention to:

- (i) critical accounting policies and practices, and any changes in them;
- (ii) decisions requiring a major element of judgement;
- (iii) the extent to which the financial statements are affected by any unusual transactions in the year and how they are disclosed;
- (iv) the clarity of disclosures;
- (v) significant adjustments resulting from the audit;
- (vi) the going concern assumption;
- (vii) compliance with accounting standards;
- (viii) compliance with stock exchange and other legal requirements; and
- (ix) reviewing the company's statement on internal control systems prior to endorsement by the board and to review the policies and process for identifying and assessing business risks and the management of those risks by the company; and

(l) to consider other topics, as defined by the board.

Reporting procedures

12. The secretary shall circulate the minutes of meetings of the committee to all members of the board, and the chairman of the committee or, as a minimum, another member of the committee, shall attend the board meeting at which the accounts are approved.
13. The committee members shall conduct an annual review of their work and these terms of reference and make recommendations to the board.
14. The committee's duties and activities during the year shall be disclosed in the annual financial statements.

15. The chairman shall attend the AGM and shall answer questions, through the chairman of the board, on the audit committee's activities and their responsibilities.

Example 2: Sample terms of reference for an audit committee of a UK listed company **App4.4**

XYZ plc

AUDIT COMMITTEE

TERMS OF REFERENCE

The Audit Committee (hereinafter 'the committee') is a committee of the Group Board (hereinafter "the board"), comprising at least three non-executive directors with a quorum being any two committee members. Committee members are appointed by the board, the majority being directors independent of management and free of any relationship that, in the opinion of the board, would interfere with the exercise of independent judgement as committee members. The chair of the committee, who shall not also be the chair of the board, is nominated by the chair of board and approved by the board.

At the request of the chair of the committee, the financial and other executive directors and further executives (in particular the chief audit executive) will be in attendance at committee meetings or for selected agenda items; and representatives of the external auditors may also be invited. The chief audit executive and the external auditor at their respective discretions also have direct access to the board.

The external auditor and the chief audit executive shall each, on separate occasions, have time alone with the committee at least once a year without members of the Executive being present.

The committee meets at least three times a year (to scrutinise the interim and final accounts with the principal focus of the other meeting(s) being risk management, the quality of information the board receives, management control, internal audit and external audit).

The committee's minutes are an 'above the line' agenda paper for the next board meeting at which they are spoken to by the committee's chair.

The committee's purview extends to all the operations within the XYZ group of companies.

The committee at its own discretion is empowered to seek outside advice in the furtherance of its responsibilities, at the company's expense.

The secretary to the board shall also be secretary to this committee.

Consistent with *The Combined Code* [see Attachment[2]], the committee's responsibilities, on behalf of the board, are to:

1. ensure the board presents a balanced and understandable assessment of the company's position and prospects in all financial information which is published;

2. ensure the board maintains a sound approach to risk management and to internal control;
3. ensure that formal and transparent arrangements are established and followed for applying 1. and 2. (above) and for maintaining an appropriate relationship with the company's auditors, including keeping under review the scope and results of the external audit, its cost effectiveness and the independence and objectivity of the auditors; and
4. approve in advance the appointment and termination of employment of the chief audit executive who shall have a right of direct access to the chair of the committee at all times; review the quality, adequacy, resources, scope and nature of the work of the internal auditing function; recommend to whom it should report; receive and review reports (usually in summary form) from the chief audit executive; and on occasion commission audit assignments to be conducted on the committee's behalf.

Formally adopted by the board of XYZ plc, [date]

Example 3: Audit committee charter **App4.5**

The following sample charter captures many of the best practices used today and complies with the requirements of the Sarbanes-Oxley Act and the US Stock Exchanges. Of course, no sample charter encompasses all activities that might be appropriate to a particular audit committee, nor will all activities identified in a sample charter be relevant to every committee. Accordingly, this charter must be tailored to each committee's needs and governing rules. The footnotes identify Sarbanes-Oxley and related stock exchange requirements that were addressed in the most recent update of this charter. These footnotes would not be included in a company's actual charter.

AUDIT COMMITTEE CHARTER

Purpose

To assist the board of directors in fulfilling its oversight responsibilities for (1) the integrity of the company's financial statements, (2) the company's compliance with legal and regulatory requirements, (3) the independent auditor's qualifications and independence, and (4) the performance of the company's internal audit function and independent auditors. The audit committee will also prepare the report that SEC rules require be included in the company's annual proxy statement.

Authority

The audit committee has authority to conduct or authorise investigations into any matters within its scope of responsibility. It is empowered to:

- Appoint, compensate, and oversee the work of the public accounting firm employed by the organisation to conduct the annual audit. This firm will report directly to the audit committee.
- Resolve any disagreements between management and the auditor regarding financial reporting.
- Pre-approve all auditing and permitted non-audit services performed by the company's external audit firm.

- Retain independent counsel, accountants, or others to advise the committee or assist in the conduct of an investigation.
- Seek any information it requires from employees – all of whom are directed to cooperate with the committee's requests – or external parties.
- Meet with company officers, external auditors, or outside counsel, as necessary.
- The committee may delegate authority to subcommittees, including the authority to pre-approve all auditing and permitted non-audit services, providing that such decisions are presented to the full committee at its next scheduled meeting.

Composition

The audit committee will consist of at least three and no more than six members of the board of directors. The board nominating committee will appoint committee members and the committee chair.

Each committee member will be both independent and financially literate. At least one member shall be designated as the 'financial expert', as defined by applicable legislation and regulation. No committee member shall simultaneously serve on the audit committees of more than two other public companies.

Meetings

The committee will meet at least four times a year, with authority to convene additional meetings, as circumstances require. All committee members are expected to attend each meeting, in person or via tale – or video-conference. The committee will invite members of management, auditors or others to attend meetings and provide pertinent information, as necessary. It will meet separately, periodically, with management, with internal auditors and with external auditors. It will also meet periodically in executive session. Meeting agendas will be prepared and provided in advance to members, along with appropriate briefing materials. Minutes will be prepared.

Responsibilities

The committee will carry out the following responsibilities:

Financial statements

- Review significant accounting and reporting issues and understand their impact on the financial statements. These issues include:
  - complex or unusual transactions and highly judgmental areas;
  - major issues regarding accounting principles and financial statement presentations, including any significant changes in the company's selection or application of accounting principles; and
  - the effect of regulatory and accounting initiatives, as well as off-balance sheet structures, on the financial statements of the company.
- Review analyses prepared by management and/or the independent auditor setting forth significant financial reporting issues and judgments made in connection with the preparation of the financial statements, including analyses of the effects of alternative GAAP methods on the financial statements.
- Review with management and the external auditors the results of the audit, including any difficulties encountered. This review will include any restrictions

on the scope of the independent auditor's activities or on access to requested information, and any significant disagreements with management.

- Discuss the annual audited financial statements and quarterly financial statements with management and the external auditors, including the company's disclosures under 'Management's Discussion and Analysis of Financial Condition and Results of Operations'.
- Review disclosures made by CEO and CFO during the Forms 10-K and 10-Q certification process about significant deficiencies in the design or operation of internal controls or any fraud that involves management or other employees who have a significant role in the company's internal controls.
- Discuss earnings press releases (particularly use of 'pro forma', or 'adjusted' non-GAAP, information), as well as financial information and earnings guidance provided to analysts and rating agencies. This review may be general (ie the types of information to be disclosed and the type of presentations to be made). The audit committee does not need to discuss each release in advance.

Internal control

- Consider the effectiveness of the company's internal control system, including information technology security and control.
- Understand the scope of internal and external auditors' review of internal control over financial reporting, and obtain reports on significant findings and recommendations, together with management's responses.

Internal audit

- Review with management and the chief audit executive the charter, plans, activities, staffing, and organisational structure of the internal audit function.
- Ensure there are no unjustified restrictions or limitations, and review and concur in the appointment, replacement, or dismissal of the chief audit executive.
- Review the effectiveness of the internal audit function, including compliance with the Institute of Internal Auditors' *Standards for the Professional Practice of Internal Auditing*.
- On a regular basis, meet separately with the chief audit executive to discuss any matters that the committee or internal audit believes should be discussed privately.

External audit

- Review the external auditors' proposed audit scope and approach, including coordination of audit effort with internal audit.
- Review the performance of the external auditors, and exercise final approval on the appointment or discharge of the auditors. In performing this review, the committee will:
  - At least annually, obtain and review a report by the independent auditor describing: the firm's internal quality-control procedures; any material issues raised by the most recent internal quality-control review, or peer review, of the firm, or by any inquiry or investigation by governmental or professional authorities, within the preceding five years, respecting one or more independent audits carried out by the firm, and any steps taken to deal with any such issues; and (to assess the auditor's independence) all relationships between the independent auditor and the company.

  - Take into account the opinions of management and internal audit.
  - Review and evaluate the lead partner of the independent auditor.
  - Present its conclusions with respect to the external auditor to the board.
- Ensure the rotation of the lead audit partner every five years and other audit partners every seven years, and consider whether there should be regular rotation of the audit firm itself.
- Present its conclusions with respect to the independent auditor to the full board.
- Set clear hiring policies for employees or former employees of the independent auditors.
- On a regular basis, meet separately with the external auditors to discuss any matters that the committee or auditors believe should be discussed privately.

Compliance

- Review the effectiveness of the system for monitoring compliance with laws and regulations and the results of management's investigation and follow-up (including disciplinary action) of any instances of non-compliance.
- Establish procedures for: (i) The receipt, retention, and treatment of complaints received by the listed issuer regarding accounting, internal accounting controls, or auditing matters; and (ii) The confidential, anonymous submission by employees of the listed issuer of concerns regarding questionable accounting or auditing matters.
- Review the findings of any examinations by regulatory agencies, and any auditor observations.
- Review the process for communicating the code of conduct to company personnel, and for monitoring compliance therewith.
- Obtain regular updates from management and company legal counsel regarding compliance matters.

Reporting responsibilities

- Regularly report to the board of directors about committee activities and issues that arise with respect to the quality or integrity of the company's financial statements, the company's compliance with legal or regulatory requirements, the performance and independence of the company's independent auditors, and the performance of the internal audit function.
- Provide an open avenue of communication between internal audit, the external auditors, and the board of directors.
- Report annually to the shareholders, describing the committee's composition, responsibilities and how they were discharged, and any other information required by rule, including approval of non-audit services.
- Review any other reports the company issues that relate to committee responsibilities.

Other responsibilities

- Discuss with management the company's major policies with respect to risk assessment and risk management.
- Perform other activities related to this charter as requested by the board of directors.
- Institute and oversee special investigations as needed.

- Review and assess the adequacy of the committee charter annually, requesting board approval for proposed changes, and ensure appropriate disclosure as may be required by law or regulation.
- Confirm annually that all responsibilities outlined in this charter have been carried out.
- Evaluate the committee's and individual members' performance at least annually.

Example 4: Sample terms of reference for a charity's audit committee **App4.6**

We are grateful to Michael Colin for providing this sample terms of reference. Michael was President of the Manchester Society of Chartered Accountants. He can be contacted by email at michael@mcolin.com; and http://www.mcolin.com/.

XYZ charity

1. The audit committee shall consist of no less than three members of the board of trustees, one of whom will be nominated as chair of the committee. Suitably experienced or qualified independent persons may be appointed to the audit committee with the approval of the board of trustees and who will have all the authority of trustee members of the committee.
2. Members of the audit committee shall be independent of all other functions relating to the management of the entity.
3. To determine the frequency of tendering for external auditing services.
4. To consider tenders for the external auditing services and recommend to the board of trustees which firm should carry out the annual external audit of The XYZ charity's statutory accounts.
5. To scrutinise and advise the board on the contents of the draft audit report and of any management letter that the auditors may wish to present to the board, and to formulate for board use any written representations that may be needed by the auditors in connection with he XYZ charity's statutory accounts or any other financial statements.
6. To discuss with the external auditors any problems or reservations arising from the draft external audit report and draft management letter, reporting relevant issues back to the board, and advising the board accordingly.
7. To recommend to the board of trustees the remuneration of the auditors for work carried out during the year.
8. To review the performance of The XYZ charity's auditors and advise the board on any changes that ought to be made to their terms of engagement.
9. To ensure that appropriate internal control procedures are in place for the appropriate application and protection of the assets of the entity.
10. To ensure that appropriate internal auditing arrangements are introduced by the executive of the entity as appropriate, and to review them annually (in conjunction with and subject to any audit committee established by the board). To receive reports (not less than once a year) from the internal auditors on their work.
11. Review procedures in the entity for the effective acquisition and deployment of all the entity's resources.

12. To investigate on behalf of the board any financial or administration matter, which may put the financial position of The XYZ charity at risk.
13. To receive reports directly from members of staff about issues that they feel are of concern in the management of The XYZ charity in conformity with the procedures currently referred to as 'whistle blowing'.
14. To ensure that The XYZ charity has appropriate risk assessment procedures, disaster recovery and business continuity plans in place, reviewed annually.
15. Minutes of all proceedings of the Committee will be made available to the board of trustees at the next available meeting and where deemed advisable by the Chair of the Committee and the Chair of the board of trustees, such minutes or reports expanding on the minutes may be given orally to the Trustees alone.

To enable the committee to discharge its duties, it shall have the authority to interview any trustee or member of staff on matters relevant to their remit and to obtain independent professional advice as necessary. A budget of £5,000 shall be made available to the committee for costs necessarily incurred in independent advice without reference to the board but in consultation with the treasurer.

Example 5: Sample terms of reference for the audit committee of a large private company **App4.7**

Readers may like to consult **App5** for a summary of the principal duties of remuneration committees.

Possibly, at about 8.6.1 this audit committee should also make an annual report to the board which would summarise what the committee has achieved over the year and would include:

1. The committee's recommendation to the board re. the adoption of the annual financial statements;
2. The committee's recommended wording of the statement on internal control to appear in the annual report;
3. The committee's overall opinion on the effectiveness of risk management and internal control;
4. The committee's recommended wording of the statement about the audit committee to appear in the annual report;
5. The committee's recommendation to the board on the company's future external audit arrangements;
6. The committee's advice to the board as to the adequacy of the company's internal audit function.

1 Membership

1.1 Members of the committee shall be appointed by the board, on the recommendation of the nomination committee in consultation with the chairman of the audit committee. The committee shall be made up of at least 3 members and rotated when requested by main board.

1.2 All members of the committee shall be independent non-executive directors at least one of whom shall have recent and relevant financial experience. The chairman of the board shall not be a member of the committee[3].

1.3 Only members of the committee have the right to attend committee meetings. However, other individuals such as the chairman of the board, chief executive, finance director, other directors, the heads of risk management, compliance and internal control and representatives from the finance function may be invited to attend all or part of any meeting as and when appropriate.

1.4 The external auditors will be invited to attend meetings of the committee on a regular basis.

1.5 Ordinarily, appointments to the committee shall be for a period of up to three years, which may be extended for two further three year periods, provided the director remains independent.

1.6 The board shall appoint the committee chairman who shall be an independent non-executive director. In the absence of the committee chairman and/or an appointed deputy, the remaining members present shall elect one of themselves to chair the meeting.

2 Secretary

2.1 The company secretary or their nominee shall act as the secretary of the committee.

3 Quorum

3.1 The quorum necessary for the transaction of business shall be 2 members. A duly convened meeting of the committee at which a quorum is present shall be competent to exercise all or any of the authorities, powers and discretions vested in or exercisable by the committee.

4 Frequency of meetings

4.1 The committee shall meet at least three times a year at appropriate times in the reporting and audit cycle and otherwise as required.

5 Notice of meetings

5.1 Meetings of the committee shall be called by the secretary of the committee at the request of any of its members or at the request of external or internal auditors if they consider it necessary

5.2 Unless otherwise agreed, notice of each meeting confirming the venue, time and date together with an agenda of items to be discussed, shall be forwarded to each member of the committee, any other person required to attend and all other non-executive directors. Supporting papers shall be sent to committee members and to other attendees as appropriate, at the same time.

6 Minutes of meetings

6.1 The secretary shall minute the proceedings and resolutions of all meetings of the committee, including recording the names of those present and in attendance

6.2 The secretary shall ascertain, at the beginning of each meeting, the existence of any conflicts of interest and minute them accordingly

6.3 Minutes of committee meetings shall be circulated promptly to all members of the committee and, once agreed, to all members of the board, unless a conflict of interest exists.

7 General Meetings

7.1 The chairman of the committee shall attend the General Meetings of the Company prepared to respond to any shareholder questions on the committee's activities[4].

8 Duties

The committee should carry out the duties below for the parent company, major subsidiary undertakings and the group as a whole, as appropriate.

8.1 *Financial reporting*

8.1.1 The committee shall monitor the integrity of the financial statements of the company, including its annual and half-yearly reports, preliminary results' announcements and any other formal announcement relating to its financial performance, reviewing significant financial reporting issues and judgements which they contain. The committee shall also review summary financial statements and any financial information contained in certain other documents, such as announcements of a price sensitive nature

8.1.2 The committee shall review and challenge where necessary:

8.1.2.1 the consistency of, and any changes to, accounting policies both on a year on year basis and across the company/group

8.1.2.2 the methods used to account for significant or unusual transactions where different approaches are possible

8.1.2.3 whether the company has followed appropriate accounting standards and made appropriate estimates and judgements, taking into account the views of the external auditor

8.1.2.4 the clarity of disclosure in the company's financial reports and the context in which statements are made; and

8.1.2.5 all material information presented with the financial statements, such as within the business review and the corporate governance statement (insofar as it relates to the audit and risk management)

8.2 *Internal controls and risk management systems*

The committee shall:

8.2.1 keep under review the effectiveness of the company's internal controls and risk management systems; and

8.2.2 review and approve the statements to be included in the annual report concerning internal controls and risk management

8.2.3 highlight major new risks relating to the business or matters of control as a result of new legislation

8.3 *Whistle-blowing and fraud*

The committee shall:

8.3.1 review the company's arrangements for its employees to raise concerns, in confidence, about possible wrongdoing in financial reporting or other matters The committee shall ensure that these arrangements allow proportionate and independent investigation of such matters and appropriate follow up action; and

8.3.2 review the company's procedures for detecting fraud

8.4 *Internal audit*

The committee shall:

8.4.1 monitor and review the effectiveness of the company's internal control function[5] in the context of the company's overall risk management system

8.4.2 approve the appointment and removal of the head of the internal control function

8.4.3 consider and approve the remit of the internal control function and ensure it has adequate resources and appropriate access to information to enable it to perform its function effectively and in accordance with the relevant professional standards. The committee shall also ensure the function has adequate standing and is free from management or other restrictions

8.4.4 review and assess the annual internal control plan

8.4.5 review promptly all reports on the company from the internal control function

8.4.6 review and monitor management's responsiveness to the findings and recommendations of the internal control function; and

8.4.7 meet the head of internal control at least once a year, without management being present, to discuss their remit and any issues arising from the internal audits carried out. In addition, the head of internal control shall be given the right of direct access to the chairman of the board and to the committee.

8.4.8 Require the head of the internal audit function to express an overall opinion at least annually on the effectiveness of internal governance processes, risk management and internal control.

8.5 *External audit*

The committee shall:

8.5.1 consider and make recommendations to the board, to be put to shareholders for approval at the AGM, in relation to the appointment, re-appointment and removal of the company's external auditor. The committee shall oversee the selection process for new auditors and if an auditor resigns the committee shall investigate the issues leading to this and decide whether any action is required

8.5.2 oversee the relationship with the external auditor including (but not limited to)

8.5.2.1 the review and making recommendations to the board on their remuneration, whether fees for audit or non-audit services and that the level of fees is appropriate to enable an adequate audit to be conducted

8.5.2.2 the review and making recommendations to the board on their terms of engagement, including any engagement letter issued at the start of each audit and the scope of the audit

8.5.2.3 assessing annually their independence and objectivity taking into account relevant UK professional and regulatory requirements and the relationship with the auditor as a whole, including the provision of any non-audit services

8.5.2.4 satisfying itself that there are no relationships (such as family, employment, investment, financial or business) between the auditor and the company that might interfere with the external auditor's independence.

8.5.2.5 agreeing with the board a policy on the employment of former employees of the company's auditor, then monitoring the implementation of this policy

8.5.2.6 monitoring the auditor's compliance with relevant ethical and professional guidance on the rotation of audit partners, the level of fees paid by the company compared to the overall fee income of the firm, office and partner and other related requirements

8.5.2.7 assessing annually their qualifications, expertise and resources and the effectiveness of the audit process which shall include a report from the external auditor on their own internal quality procedures

8.5.2.8 seeking to ensure co-ordination with the activities of the internal audit function

8.5.3 meet regularly with the external auditor, including once at the planning stage before the audit and once after the audit at the reporting stage. The committee shall meet the external auditor at least once a year, without management being present, to discuss their remit and any issues arising from the audit

8.5.4 review and approve the annual audit plan and ensure that it is consistent with the scope of the audit engagement

8.5.5 review the findings of the audit with the external auditor. This shall include but not be limited to, the following

8.5.5.1 a discussion of any major issues which arose during the audit

8.5.5.2 any accounting and audit judgements

8.5.5.3 levels of errors identified during the audit

The committee shall also review the effectiveness of the audit

8.5.6 review any representation letter(s) requested by the external auditor before they are signed by management

8.5.7 review the management letter and management's response to the auditor's findings and recommendations and past accounting errors (Ref SAS610)

8.5.8 develop and implement a policy on the supply of non-audit services by the external auditor, taking into account any relevant ethical guidance on the matter

8.6 *Reporting responsibilities*

8.6.1 The committee chairman shall report formally to the board on its proceedings after each meeting on all matters within its duties and responsibilities

8.6.2 The committee shall make whatever recommendations to the board it deems appropriate on any area within its remit where action or improvement is needed

8.6.3 The committee shall compile a report to shareholders on its activities to be included in the company's annual report

8.7 *Other matters*

The committee shall

8.7.1 have access to sufficient resources in order to carry out its duties, including access to the company secretariat for assistance as required

8.7.2 be provided with appropriate and timely training, both in the form of an induction programme for new members and on an ongoing basis for all members

8.7.3 give due consideration to laws and regulations, the provisions of the Combined Code and the requirements of the UK Listing Authority's Listing, Prospectus and Disclosure and Transparency Rules as appropriate

8.7.4 be responsible for co-ordination of the internal and external auditors

8.7.5 oversee any investigation of activities which are within its terms of reference and act for internal purposes as a court of the last resort on such matters

8.7.6 at least once a year, review its own performance, constitution and terms of reference to ensure it is operating at maximum effectiveness and recommend any changes it considers necessary to the board for approval.

9 Authority

The committee is authorised

9.1 to seek any information it requires from any employee of the company in order to perform its duties

9.2 to obtain, at the company's expense, outside legal or other professional advice on any matters within its terms of reference.

9.3 to call any employee to be questioned at a meeting of the committee as and when required.

Remuneration committee sample terms of reference[6] App4.8

There is some overlap of responsibilities between the nomination, personnel and remuneration committees, as set out in the sample terms of reference for those committees given in **App4.8–App4.12** and **App4.15–App4.16**. The overlap is set out in **A5.25**.

In a listed company the remuneration committee would always have responsibility for advising the board on the remuneration of the executive directors in all its forms, and would also frequently provide similar advice with regard to the most senior executives who are not board members. In the family-controlled, non-listed company for whom these sample terms of reference were developed, we have drafted the terms with a view to the remuneration committee also providing similar advice with regard to the compensation of members of the board and the remuneration in all its forms of the senior executives.

Example 1: Sample terms of reference for a remuneration committee App4.9

A Introduction

The remuneration committee is a main committee of the group board, without executive powers. The committee will comprise only non-executive directors (preferably at least three) each appointed by the group board. It will select its own chairman and its secretary will be the company secretary.

The committee may require the group's chairman and/or chief executive (and other executives) to attend its meetings and may draw on outside advice as necessary. No executive should take any part on decisions on his or her own remuneration.

The committee determines the company's policy on executive remuneration and specific compensation packages for each of the executive directors and company secretary.

B Committee's purpose

- To ensure that the group directors and senior executives are suitably motivated and fairly rewarded for their individual contributions to overall performance.

- To demonstrate that the remuneration of the group directors and senior executives is set by directors who have no personal interest in the outcome of their decisions and who will give due regard to the interests of the shareholders and to the financial and commercial needs of the group.

C Committee's responsibilities

- To determine on all forms of remuneration (including pension arrangements within the discretion of the company's schemes) of the group chairman, chief executive and other executive directors and senior executives, as defined from time to time. This will bear in mind the relativity between board members and other levels of management.
- To see that, in exercising the rights under the group's long-term incentives plan, senior executive share option schemes and the ESOP, benefits are related to the performance of both the members, where appropriate, and the group and that they provide a long term incentive.
- To determine and agree with the board the framework or broad policy, including performance targets, for the remuneration of the executive directors and senior executives.
- To ensure that contractual terms on termination, and any payments made, are fair to the individual and the Company, that failure is not rewarded and that the duty to mitigate loss is fully recognised.
- To be aware of and advise on any major changes in employment benefit structures throughout the company or group.
- Agree the policy for authorising claims for expenses from the chief executive and chairman.
- Ensure the provisions regarding disclosure of remuneration, including pensions, as set out in the Directors' Remuneration Report Regulations 2002[7] and the [Combined] Code, are fulfilled.
- Be exclusively responsible for establishing the selection criteria, selecting, appointing and setting the terms of reference for any remuneration consultants who advise the committee.
- To ensure that the committee only makes recommendations which it can justify to shareholders and staff alike and that the criteria on which performance is measured can be clearly explained.

D Frequency of meetings

- The committee meets twice yearly; to consider the appropriateness of current remuneration policy; and to agree the yearly remuneration package of the chairman and relevant executives.
- The committee also meets on an ad hoc basis should the group or committee chairman require it.

Example 2: Sample terms of reference for a remuneration committee App4.10

1. Constitution

At a meeting held at [location] on [date] the board of directors of [company name] resolved to establish a standing committee of the board without executive powers to be known as the remuneration committee, in accordance with these terms of reference which were adopted.

2. Membership

2.1 The membership of the committee shall be appointed by the board by formal resolution from amongst the independent[8], non-executive directors of the company and shall consist of a minimum of three members. A quorum shall be two members.

2.2 The duties and responsibilities of a member of the remuneration committee are in addition to those set out for a member of the board of directors.

2.3 The chairman of the committee shall be appointed by the board by formal resolution.

3. Attendance at meetings

3.1 The committee may require the group's chief executive (and other executives) to attend its meetings for certain agenda items. No executive shall take part in decisions on his or her own remuneration.

3.2 At the discretion of the chairman of this committee, outside professional advisors may be in attendance for certain agenda items.

3.3 The company secretary shall be secretary to this committee.

4. Frequency of meetings

4.1 The committee shall meet at least twice a year and as frequently as is required.

4.2 The timing and agenda of meetings is the responsibility of the committee chairman, subject to the expressed wishes of committee members.

5. Authority

5.1 The committee is authorised to require the provision of such information[9], and access to such personnel, as it requires to discharge its responsibilities.

5.2 The committee is authorised to take outside professional advice as appropriate in particular to make external comparisons.

6. Duties

6.1 The committee's purpose is to ensure that the group directors and senior executives are fairly rewarded for their individual contributions to overall performance, and to demonstrate that the remuneration of senior executives is set by directors who have no personal; interest in the outcome of their decisions and who will give due regard to the interests of the shareholders and to the financial and commercial needs of the group.

6.2 The duties of the committee shall be to recommend to and advise the board on the remuneration (in all its forms) and associated matters of the directors and senior executives. This requires the committee to:

1. Determine appropriate remuneration in all its forms (including pension arrangements within the discretion of the company's scheme) of the group chairman, directors, chief executive and senior executives, as defined from time to time. This will bear in mind differentials between levels of personnel and market relativities.
2. Ensure there is good succession planning and management development at senior executive levels, and to review specific development plans for the top *n*[10] executives in the group[11].
3. Measure the performance of key senior executives as a prelude to determining their annual remuneration, bonus rewards and award of long term incentives.

4. See that, in exercising the rights to performance related compensation, benefits are related to the performance both of individuals and the group, and that they provide a long term incentive.
5. Ensure that the committee only makes recommendations which it can justify to shareholders and staff alike and that the criteria on which performance is measured can be clearly explained.

7. Reporting

7.1 The committee makes recommendations to the group board which either approves them or, stating its reasons for not doing so, asks the committee to reconsider them.

7.2 The chairman of the committee shall be available to answer members' questions at the annual general meeting.

Nominations committee sample terms of reference[12] App4.11

There is some overlap of responsibilities between the nomination, personnel and remuneration committees, as set out in the sample terms of reference for those committees given in **App4.8–App4.12** and **App4.15–App4.16**. The overlap is set out in **A5.25**.

Readers may like to consult **App5** for a summary of the principal duties of nomination committees.

A few director search firms are listed in **A3.43**.

The terms of reference for the nominations committee give to it responsibility for succession planning at board level while leaving to the remuneration committee the responsibility for ensuring that there is good succession planning and management development at senior executive levels. Alternative approaches would be to settle all these duties upon the nominations committee or to split them between the nominations committee and the senior executive team.

Sample terms of reference for a nominations committee App4.12

1. Constitution

At a meeting held at [location] on [date] the board of directors of [company name] resolved to establish a standing committee of the board to be known as the nominations committee, in accordance with these terms of reference which were adopted.

2. Membership

2.1 Membership of the committee shall comprise a majority of the non-executive directors of the board with an emphasis on seniority[13], to be appointed to this committee by resolution of the board.

2.2 The chairman of the board shall be chairman of this committee.

3. Attendance at meetings

3.1 The chairman of the committee may co-opt other directors to join the committee temporarily for particular specified purposes.

3.2 The committee may require the group's chief executive (and other executives) to attend its meetings for certain agenda items.

3.3 Directors (and senior executives in attendance) may be required by the chairman to leave the meetings of this committee when open discussion might be inhibited by their presence.

3.4 At the discretion of the chairman of this committee, outside professional advisors may be in attendance for certain agenda items.

3.5 The company secretary shall be secretary to this committee[14].

4. Frequency of meetings

4.1 The committee shall meet at least twice a year and as frequently as is required.

4.2 The timing and agenda of meetings is the responsibility of the committee chairman, subject to the expressed wishes of committee members.

5. Authority

5.1 The committee is authorised to require the provision of such information, and access to such personnel, as it requires to discharge its responsibilities.

5.2 The committee is authorised to take outside professional advice as appropriate.

6. Duties

The committee is responsible for:

6.1 proposing to the board the responsibilities of non-executive directors, including membership and chairmanship of board committees;

6.2 ensuring that there is a satisfactory, formal process for the selection of non-executive directors which it is the responsibility of this committee to follow;

6.3 proposing to the board any new board appointments, whether of executive or non-executive directors;

6.4 ensuring there is good succession planning at board level;

6.5 reviewing the effectiveness of non-executive directors; and

6.6 nominating suitable people for the most senior executive positions, including that of chief executive.

7. Reporting

7.1 The committee makes recommendations to the group board which either approves them or, stating its reasons for not doing so, asks the committee to reconsider them[15].

Finance committee sample terms of reference[16]

Example 1: Sample terms of reference for a finance committee **App4.13**

1. Constitution

At a meeting held at [location] on [date] the board of directors of [company name] resolved to establish a standing committee of the board to be known as the finance committee, in accordance with these terms of reference which were adopted.

2. Membership

2.1 The membership of the committee shall be appointed by the board from amongst the directors of the company and shall consist of a minimum of three members. A quorum shall be two members.

2.2 The duties and responsibilities of a member of the finance committee are in addition to those set out for a member of the board of directors.

2.3 The chairman of the committee, who shall not be the chairman of the company, shall be appointed by the board by formal board resolution.

3. Attendance at meetings

3.1 The chief executive officer and the chief financial officer shall normally attend meetings. All board members shall also normally have the right to attend.

3.2 The committee may instruct any officer or employee of the company to attend any meeting and provide pertinent information as necessary.

3.3 The company secretary shall be the secretary of the committee.

4. Frequency of meetings

4.1 Meetings shall be held at least three times yearly or more frequently as circumstances require.

4.2 The committee chairman shall convene a meeting upon request of any committee member who considers it necessary.

4.3 Whenever possible committee meetings shall be scheduled to allow for adequate time for committee business, and so that they can be reported promptly and effectively to the board.

5. Authority

5.1 The committee is authorised by the board to investigate any activity it deems appropriate. It is authorised to seek any information from any officer or employee of the company all of whom are directed to co-operate with any request made by the committee.

5.2 The committee is authorised to engage any firm of accountants, merchant bankers, lawyers or other professionals as the committee sees fit to provide independent council and advice and to assist in any review or investigation on such matters as the committee deems appropriate.

6. Duties

The purpose of this committee is to monitor the financial arrangements of the company; to decide upon financial issues of importance which have been delegated to this committee by the board; and to recommend to the board as appropriate on financial issues of more major importance which are reserved for board decision.

The duties of the committee include, but are not limited to the following.

Going concern

6.1 Formally considering and concluding upon whether the company remains a going concern.

Capital issues

6.2 Recommending to the board (a) any changes to the capital structure of the business and (b) any arrangements with bankers and/or others for rescheduling long-term debt.

6.3 Recommending to the board appropriate dividend policy and appropriate dividends to be declared.

6.4 Approving borrowing limits of less than $50 million and recommending for board approval of borrowing limits greater than $50 million.

6.5 Recommending to the board approval of investments and expenditure of a capital nature greater or equal to $5 million, and approving similar expenditures between $1 million and £5 million.

Liquidity and solvency

6.6 Reviewing and determining cash flow assumptions and projections.

6.7 Reviewing asset and liability positions.

Treasury policies and treasury risk

6.8 Approving treasury policies including the management of funds and investment policies, exposures to counter party risk, interest rate risk, liquidity risk, exchange risk, legal or compliance risk.

6.9 Reviewing currency positions.

Variances

6.10 Considering negative variances of more than 5 per cent from the net income of an approved budget or business plan where these are greater than, or equal to, $1 million; and determining or approving appropriate action to be taken.

6.11 Considering overruns on approved capital investment budgets of more than 20 per cent.

Contracts

6.12 Approving (a) major contracts and agreements for services and consultancy (excluding those relating to directors and staff); (b) recommending to the board approval of commitment to spend which amount to $500,000 or greater; and (c) approving commitments to spend of between $100,000 and $500,000.

6.13 Monitoring major arrangements and contracts to ensure that company is not in default of significant financial and other contract terms; and decisions for remedial action where necessary.

7. Reporting

7.1 The chairman of the committee shall report on committee business to the board of directors with such recommendations as the committee may deem appropriate.

7.2 The secretary shall distribute copies of the minutes of meetings of the committee to all members of the board of directors, and the minutes shall be an agenda paper of next following board meeting.

Example 2: Sample terms of reference for a finance committee App4.14

We are grateful to Michael Colin for providing this sample terms of reference. Until recently Michael was President of the Manchester Society of Chartered Accountants. He can be contacted by email at michael@mcolin.com.

XYZ charity

Main duties

1. Financial

1. To ensure that The XYZ charity operates within the financial guidelines set out in current legislation, accounting standards, the Charity Commission, The XYZ charity's memorandum and articles of association and by the board of trustees.
2. On behalf of the board of trustees to ensure that The XYZ charity's financial obligations are met.
3. To regularly review and advise the board of trustees on the regulatory framework within which XYZ charity must function.
4. To advise the board of trustees on the financial implications and operational risks arising from board decisions – especially the board's strategic and policy decisions.
5. To review longer-term forecasts of capital resources and of income and expenditure, and to review and monitor financial trends within The XYZ charity and the sector within which it operates.
6. To formulate, for the board to approve and agree, and regularly to review and monitor, a financial strategy and a reserves policy that will help to achieve The XYZ charity's objectives, as set out in The XYZ charity's current strategic plan.
7. To scrutinise and evaluate draft annual budgets for the approval of the board, ensuring that it is compatible with, and supports, The XYZ charity's objects and the strategic plans.
8. To work with the chief executive, resources director and other senior executive staff to ensure that financial information is both accurate and presented in such a way that it facilitates good governance and management.
9. To consider no less than every three months, The XYZ charity's management accounts and monitor performance against the approved budget.
10. To scrutinise and evaluate regularly The XYZ charity's current and forecast cash flow and to inform the board of any concerns.
11. To approve, within the limits laid down by the board, emergency unbudgeted expenditure.
12. To approve, within the criteria specified by the board, expenditure of a significant.
13. To formulate for board approval and regularly to review an appropriate investment policy; to ensure that it is adhered to and to monitor investment performance against policy and report back to the board accordingly.
14. To periodically review the need for and appointment of investment advisers.

2. General

1. To provide minutes of all finance committee meetings for review by the board of trustees.

HR/personnel committee sample terms of reference **App4.15**

There is some overlap of responsibilities between the nomination, personnel and remuneration committees, as set out in the sample terms of reference for those committees given in **App4.8–App4.12** and **App4.15–App4.16**. The overlap is set out in **A5.25**.

Sample terms of reference for an HR committee **App4.16**

1. Constitution

At a meeting held at [location] on [date] the board of directors of [company name] resolved to establish a standing committee of the board to be known as the personnel committee, in accordance with these terms of reference which were adopted.

2. Membership

2.1 The membership of the committee shall be appointed by the board from amongst the directors of the company and shall consist of a minimum of three members. A quorum shall be two members.

2.2 The duties and responsibilities of a member of the personnel committee are in addition to those set out for a member of the board of directors.

2.3 The chairman of the committee, who shall not be the chairman of the company, shall be appointed by the board by formal board resolution.

3. Attendance at meetings

3.1 The chief executive officer and the chief personnel officer shall normally attend meetings. All board members shall also normally have the right to attend.

3.2 The committee may instruct any officer or employee of the company to attend any meeting and provide pertinent information as necessary.

3.3 The company secretary shall be the secretary of the committee.

4. Frequency of meetings

4.1 Meetings shall be held at least three times yearly or more frequently as circumstances require.

4.2 The committee chairman shall convene a meeting upon request of any committee member who considers it necessary.

4.3 Whenever possible committee meetings shall be scheduled to allow for adequate time for committee business, and so that they can be reported promptly and effectively to the board.

5. Authority

5.1 The committee is authorised by the board to investigate any activity it deems appropriate and within its terms of reference. It is authorised to seek any information from any officer or employee of the company all of whom are directed to co-operate with any request made by the committee.

5.2 The committee is authorised to engage any firm of personnel consultants, management consultants, lawyers or other professional advisors as the committee sees fit to provide independent council and advice and to assist in any review or investigation on such matters as the committee deems appropriate.

6. Duties

The committee is responsible to ensure that the company follows best practice with regard to personnel matters. To this end it will:

6.1 ensure that the company has a satisfactory personnel function covering all aspects of personnel management including succession planning and career development;

6.2 approve all personnel policies of the company, including health and safety policies;

6.3 review to ensure that the company does not discriminate unfairly in personnel matters;

6.4 review to ensure that the company complied with all legal and regulatory requirements impacting upon personnel;

6.5 recommend to the board for board approval all significant staff redundancy plans;

6.6 ensure there is good succession planning and management development at senior executive levels; and review specific development plans for the top executives in the group;

6.7 recommend to and advise the board on the remuneration (in all its forms) and associated matters of the senior executives;

6.8 review the performance of key senior executives;

6.9 ensure that, in exercising the rights to performance related compensation, benefits are related to the performance both of individuals and the group, and that they provide a long-term incentive;

6.10 ensure that the committee only makes recommendations which it can be justified to shareholders and staff alike and that the criteria on which performance is measured can be clearly explained; and

6.11 nominate suitable people for senior executive positions.

7. Reporting

7.1 The chairman of the committee shall report on committee business to the board of directors with such recommendations as the committee may deem appropriate.

7.2 The secretary shall distribute copies of the minutes of meetings of the committee to all members of the board of directors, and the minutes shall be an agenda paper of next following board meeting.

Standing orders committee[17] sample terms of reference

Terms of reference

App4.17

1. Constitution

At a meeting held at [location] on [date] the board of directors of [company name] resolved to establish a standing committee of the board to be known as the standing orders committee, in accordance with these terms of reference which were adopted.

2. Membership

2.1 The membership of the committee shall be appointed by the board from amongst the directors of the company and shall consist of a minimum of three members. A quorum shall be two members.

2.2 The duties and responsibilities of a member of the standing orders committee are in addition to those set out for a member of the board of directors.

2.3 The chairman of the committee, who shall not be the chairman of the company, shall be appointed by the board by formal board resolution.

3. Attendance at meetings

3.1 The chairman, the chief executive officer, the company secretary and the deputy company secretary shall normally attend meetings. All board members shall also normally have the right to attend.

3.2 The committee may instruct any officer or employee of the company to attend any meeting and provide pertinent information as necessary.

3.3 The company secretary shall be in attendance as secretary to the committee[18] except, at the discretion of the committee chairman, for agenda items where a frank discussion might be impeded by the company secretary's presence.

4. Frequency of meetings

4.1 Meetings shall be held at least twice yearly or more frequently as circumstances require.

4.2 The committee chairman shall convene a meeting upon request of any committee member who considers it necessary.

4.3 Whenever possible committee meetings shall be scheduled to allow for adequate time for committee business, and so that they can be reported promptly and effectively to the board.

5. Authority

5.1 The committee is authorised by the board to initiate any activity it deems appropriate and within its terms of reference. It is authorised to seek any information from any director, officer or employee of the company all of whom are directed to co-operate with any request made by the committee.

5.2 The committee is authorised to engage any firm of lawyers, accountants, merchant bankers, or other professionals as the committee sees fit to provide independent council and advice as the committee deems appropriate.

6. Duties

The committee is responsible to ensure that board business is conducted in an orderly way consistent with (a) best corporate governance practices and (b) the memorandum and articles of association of the company (or equivalent) and all existing resolutions of the board.

To these ends, the committee shall:

6.1 Ensure that there is maintained an up-to-date board manual, available to all board directors, comprising:

- the memorandum and articles of association of the company;
- a copy of all past formal resolutions of the board which have continuing applicability;
- the terms of reference of all board committees;
- the terms of appointment of all current directors;
- the duties and responsibilities of members of the board;
- the authorities of individual directors to take advice at the company's expense;
- organisation charts of corporate structure and senior executive positions; and
- any other matters of constitution and procedure which directors need to continue to be aware of.

6.2 Advise the board on the appointment of members to, and chairmen of, board committees; and advise the board on changes to the terms of reference of board committees.

6.3 Ensure that due consideration is given to the implications for the company of developments in generally accepted approaches to corporate governance.

6.4 Advise the board on policy relating to the seeking by directors of independent professional advice, and the payment for such advice.
6.5 Ensure that there is an acknowledged senior member of the board.
6.6 Advise the chairman as appropriate on any matters relating to the orderly conduct of board and board committee meetings.
6.7 Advise the board on amendments to the schedule of matters reserved to the board for the board to decide upon.
6.8 Advise the board on delegation of authority ('Concurrence Guidelines').
6.9 Monitor the performance of the company secretariat function.

7. Reporting

7.1 The chairman of the committee shall report on committee business to the board of directors with such recommendations as the committee may deem appropriate.
7.2 The secretary shall distribute copies of the minutes of meetings of the committee to all members of the board of directors, and the minutes shall be an agenda paper of next following board meeting.

Board risk committee sample terms of reference

Terms of reference App4.18

Purpose

The board's risk committee is to enable the whole board to effectively discharge its responsibility to oversee, govern and be accountable for the entity's management of both internal; and external risks.

Responsibilities

To approve:

subject to board confirmation, the risk policies and limits on exposures to be applied by management;
individual variations from these policies and limits, in a timely manner.[19]

To monitor:

the level and character of risks being incurred;
the quality of due diligence appraisals of risks associated with key business events and transactions;
the effectiveness of company risk committees at executive level.

To advise the board on:

the entity's overall risk appetite,[20] risk tolerance,[21] risk strategy[22] and risk exposure[23] through the business cycle;
the extent to which 'perverse incentives' with respect to executive incentive schemes, are under control;
the risks inherent in proposed and/or agreed future corporate strategies and key business events;

the appropriateness and effective functioning of the company's internal control and risk management processes;
the appointment, tenure, professionalism, independence and removal of the chief risk officer;
with the remuneration committee of the board, the remuneration of the chief risk officer;
the content of the board's report on risk to appear in the Annual Report and Accounts.[24]

External advice

The committee is empowered by the board to take external advice at the company's expense as necessary on matters to do with the committee's responsibilities, in particular to ensure that the board has up-to-date access to perspectives on product, market and other relevant developments.

Co-ordination with other board committees

The board risk committee co-ordinates with other board committees as necessary.

Co-ordination with the board's remuneration committee is facilitated by cross-membership of at least one independent director who serves on both committees, and is necessary *inter alia* with respect to (a) oversight of the risk of perverse incentives,[25] (b) risk adjustments to be applied to performance objectives set in the context of incentive packages, and (c) determination of the appropriate remuneration of the head of compliance, the head of internal audit and the chief risk officer.

Co-ordination with the board's audit committee is similarly facilitated, and additionally by at least one joint meeting of the two committees annually. It is necessary in particular due to the overlapping responsibilities with respect to risk management and internal control.

Membership

The board risk committee comprises three[26] board directors, chosen by the board, each considered by the board to be independent[27] and to collectively have the expertise to understand the risks faced by the company, and contemporary approaches to risk management. The board determines which of these three shall be the committee's chair.

Neither the chairman of the board nor any executive shall be a member of this committee.

Development of committee members

Requisite professional development of committee members will be assessed annually as part of the board evaluation process, and appropriate arrangements made by the company secretary, overseen by the committee chairman.

Committee members are empowered to take individual external advice at the company's expense on matters relating to their duties as directors, in accordance with the policy adopted by the board.

Attendance at meetings

One other than the committee's members has a right to attend the committee's meetings. The chair of the committee shall determine who, other than the committee members, is in attendance for which agenda items.

Subject to the above, the following will usually be in attendance at board risk committee meetings:

- the chief executive;
- the finance director;
- the director of operations;
- the chief risk officer;
- the head of internal audit;
- the head of compliance;
- the company secretary.

Representatives of the external auditor, as well as external advisors to the committee, may also attend from time to time by invitation.

The committee should spend time alone with the chief risk officer, and separate time alone with the head of internal audit and with the head of compliance. These officers also should have unrestricted access to the chair of the board risk committee between committee meetings.

Meetings

The committee meets at least four times a year, and more frequently as necessary. Meetings are usually arranged to take place approximately ten days before a board meeting.[28]

Agenda papers and minutes

The committee's chair is responsible to ensure that committee agenda papers are of high quality and are circulated to committee members at least five days before meetings. Pro forma agendas for each of the standard four meetings of this committee will be the basis for preparing meeting agendas. Minutes of the board's remuneration and audit committees will usually be within the agenda papers of this committee.

Agenda papers and minutes will be retained indefinitely.

Reporting of the committee to the board

The chair of the committee prepares a report of the committee's business as an agenda paper for the board, and speaks to this report at the board meeting. In addition, the draft minutes of the committee are a board agenda paper.

Reports to the board of the committee's business address the committee's responsibilities. In particular they constitute advice to the board on:

- current risk exposures;
- future risk strategy;
- embedding and maintenance throughout the entity of a supportive culture in relation to the management of risk;

advice on prescriptive rules and procedures;
qualitative and also quantitative metrics.

Public reporting about the committee

The committee approves a separate report to appear within the annual report and accounts[29] covering:

the entity's risk management strategy;
information on key risk exposures, risk appetite and risk tolerance;
how actual risk appetite is assessed over time;
high-level information on the scope and outcome of the stress-testing programme;
membership, frequency of meetings and attendance record of members at board risk committee meetings;
whether external advice has been sought and, if so, its source.

Committee secretarial services

Secretariat support for this committee comes from the company secretariat function.[30]

Notes

1 'Audit committees: Combined code guidance' (January 2003); a report and guidance by an FRC-appointed group chaired by Sir Robert Smith, Financial Reporting Council, Holborn Hall, 100 Gray's Inn Road, London WC1X 8AL, Tel: +44 (0)20 7611 9700, Fax: +44 (0)20 7404 4497. The related report is by Derek Higgs, 'Review of the role and effectiveness of non-executive directors'.

2 The company shows this part of the Combined Code as an attachment to the audit committee's terms of reference.

3 The UK Corporate Governance Code (set out in full at **App1**), commencing 2008, allows a company smaller than a FTSE 350 to have the chairman of the board as a member of its audit committee – so long as he or she was independent when appointed chairman of the board.

4 Technically, a shareholder question has to be put to the chairman of the general meeting who then decides who is the appropriate person to answer.

5 'Internal control function' is this company's name for its 'internal audit function' (here and in following paragraphs). If would be better if it were renamed 'internal audit function', since management should be responsible for internal control, with internal audit being responsible for reviewing the effectiveness of internal control.

6 Generally, the remuneration committee comprises non-executive directors whose main mission is to recommend to the board the appropriate compensation for (a) the executive directors, and (b) most probably the executives immediately below the board level (who may be board members of group operating companies). Non-executive directors' fees would normally be recommended to the board by an executive committee of executive directors. In a case where the entire board is non-executive, the remuneration committee is still an appropriate vehicle to arrive at recommendations on senior executive compensation; in the absence of executive directors on the board, it is also the best way of arriving at appropriate fee levels for the non-executive directors, but there is a special need for the committee to take independent professional advice before reaching its conclusions. These terms of reference have been designed for a large, private company with a strong family element on a board which is entirely non-executive.

7 SI 2002/1986.

8 In the case of a private company where the majority of the shares are held by family or family trusts, it may not be feasible, even though desirable, to restrict membership of this committee to non-executive directors who are genuinely independent. This will depend upon the composition of membership of the board. Independence for a non-executive director implies a freedom of relationships (such as family ties) with other directors and an absence of other business associations with the enterprise except for one's directorship.

9 Required information is likely to include a spreadsheet schedule which specifies the monetary value, for each director and senior executive within the purview of this committee, of the following components of compensation met by the company (as appropriate):
- basic pay (or fee);
- national insurance;
- tax paid by company on fees etc;
- pension contribution;
- private medical insurance premium;
- mortgage;
- car;
- free petrol;
- last bonus;
- ESOP (applicable for a quoted company);
- share options allocated; and
- their current notional value.

10 By way of illustration, the number here in the latter days of Grandmet was 250.

11 The duty of nominating people for the most senior executive positions (including that of chief executive) has been accorded to the nominations committee in these terms of reference.

12 In these terms of reference, responsibility for succession planning at non-board senior executive level has been given to the remuneration committee. Alternatively, it could be a responsibility of the nominations committee. However, the specific duty of nominating someone for one of the most senior executive positions (including that of chief executive) has been accorded to the nominations committee.

13 'Seniority' may be determined by (a) existing role on the board – such as that of chairman or deputy chairman, (b) length of service as a non-executive director, (c) general reputation or (d) through being formally nominated by the board to be regarded as the senior non-executive director.

14 In view of the sensitivity and confidentiality of issues discussed, the company may take the view that the committee should appoint a secretary from amongst its members. However, on the whole, boards operate better if the secretary to the board is also privy to the business of, and secretary to, the board committees. If the view is taken that the company secretary should not be privy to the business of this committee, it follows that the committee's secretary (a non-executive director of the company) should circulate the minutes privately to all the other board directors. Being a board committee, all directors have a right and need to see the minutes.

15 The way this is handled will need to be considered if it is decided that the company secretary should not be secretary to this committee.

16 Some companies would have an assets and liabilities committee (ALCO) covering broadly similar issues. It would be unlikely to be appropriate to have both a finance and an ALCO committee.

17 This committee could alternatively be called 'the chairman's committee' (though this sometimes has a different meaning) or 'board business committee'.

18 If it is accepted that a duty of this committee is to review the company secretariat function, it may be desirable that the secretary of this committee is not a member of that function. Instead, the committee may appoint its secretary from amongst its members.

This is analogous to the secretary of the audit committee not being the chief internal auditor, since the audit committee has to review the effectiveness of the internal audit function. However, it is always more difficult to exclude the company secretary from knowledge of, and influence over, board and board committee business: the decisions and recommendations of the standing orders committee ultimately reach the board for consideration.

19 Care must be taken to ensure that risk policies are clear and can be applied by management. The board risk committee is not an executive committee and should not routinely be taking operational risk decisions. Exceptions should be few and far between.

20 Risk appetite is the level of risk an entity is willing to take in order to execute a strategy.

21 Risk tolerance is the capacity to accept or absorb risk.

22 A risk management strategy provides a structured and coherent approach to identifying, assessing and managing risk.

23 The amount of risk that is being taken.

24 As with audit committee reports, some companies may make this a report from the board's risk committee, rather than a report from the board itself.

25 Apart from the risk of perverse incentives applying to other senior executives, this oversight includes obtaining satisfaction that the reward package of the head of internal audit is not tied to the short-term performance of the company.

26 According to Provision C.3.1 of the UK Corporate Governance Code (see **App1**) a company outside the FTSE 350 may choose to have only two independent directors as the members of their audit committee. A similar practice could reasonably be followed with respect to the board's risk committee.

27 This applies the criteria set out in Provision B.1.1 of the UK Corporate Governance Code (see **App1**). The Walker Report (Walker, D (2009) *A review of corporate governance in UK banks and other financial industry entities*, final report, (see http://webarchive.nationalarchives.gov.uk/20130129110402/http://www.hm-treasury.gov.uk/d/walker_review_261109.pdf, accessed 5 December 2013), November 2009, §6.15) recommended not that all members of the board risk committee of a BOFI (bank or financial institution) should be *independent* directors, but that each should be *non-executive* with the exception of the finance director who should also be a member. It is likely that the recommendation that the members (other than the finance director) should be non-executive rather than non-executive *and independent* was an acknowledgement that some UK BOFIs are subsidiaries of overseas parents whose boards have an inadequate number of directors who pass the UK Code's independence tests. UK BOFIs that are subsidiaries of overseas parents often have representatives (executive or non-executive) from the overseas parent on their boards: while these are non-executive, they fail to meet the UK Code's independence tests.

28 This interval allows the minutes to be drafted to become an agenda paper for the board meeting, and for the report of the committee chairman to be prepared also in time to be a board agenda paper. It is not good practice for board committee meetings to take place on the same day as board meetings, as meeting fatigue sets in, and only impromptu, oral reports of the committee business can be made at the board meeting.

29 As with audit committee reports, some companies may make this a report from the board's risk committee, rather than a report from the board itself.

30 Just as the head of internal audit should not be the secretary to the audit committee, so the chief risk officer should not be the secretary to the board's risk committee. Being a board committee it should receive its secretariat services from the company secretariat. The committee needs to be able to form an objective view about the effectiveness of the chief risk officer and the function he/she heads up, and this is likely to be impeded if that person acts as secretary to the committee.

Appendix 5

Suggestions for Good Practice from the Higgs Report

Introduction **App5.1**

In March 2010, the FRC published new guidance entitled 'Guidance on Board Effectiveness', which relates primarily to Sections A and B of the Code on the leadership and effectiveness of the Board. The guidance was developed by the Institute of Chartered Secretaries and Administrators on the FRC's behalf, and replaces 'Suggestions for Good Practice from the Higgs Report' (known as the Higgs guidance). We reproduce below annexes from the original 2003 Higgs Report, as they remain excellent guidance on these matters.

Suggestions for Good Practice from the Higgs Report **App5.2**

Reproduced by kind permission of the copyright holder, the Financial Reporting Council.

Contents

GUIDANCE ON THE ROLE OF THE CHAIRMAN

The chairman is pivotal in creating the conditions for overall board and individual director effectiveness, both inside and outside the boardroom. Specifically, it is the responsibility of the chairman to:

- run the board and set its agenda. The agenda should take full account of the issues and the concerns of all board members. Agendas should be forward looking and concentrate on strategic matters rather than formulaic approvals of proposals which can be the subject of appropriate delegated powers to management;

- ensure that the members of the board receive accurate, timely and clear information, in particular about the company's performance, to enable the board to take sound decisions, monitor effectively and provide advice to promote the success of the company;
- ensure effective communication with shareholders and ensure that the members of the board develop an understanding of the views of the major investors;
- manage the board to ensure that sufficient time is allowed for discussion of complex or contentious issues, where appropriate arranging for informal meetings beforehand to enable thorough preparation for the board discussion. It is particularly important that non-executive directors have sufficient time to consider critical issues and are not faced with unrealistic deadlines for decision-making;
- take the lead in providing a properly constructed induction programme for new directors that is comprehensive, formal and tailored, facilitated by the company secretary;
- take the lead in identifying and meeting the development needs of individual directors, with the company secretary having a key role in facilitating provision. It is the responsibility of the chairman to address the development needs of the board as a whole with a view to enhancing its overall effectiveness as a team;
- ensure that the performance of individuals and of the board as a whole and its committees is evaluated at least once a year; and
- encourage active engagement by all the members of the board.

The effective chairman:

- upholds the highest standards of integrity and probity;
- sets the agenda, style and tone of board discussions to promote effective decision-making and constructive debate;
- promotes effective relationships and open communication, both inside and outside the boardroom, between non-executive directors and executive team;
- builds an effective and complementary board, initiating change and planning succession in board appointments, subject to board and shareholders' approval;
- promotes the highest standards of corporate governance and seeks compliance with the provisions of the Code wherever possible;
- ensures clear structure for and the effective running of board committees;
- ensures effective implementation of board decisions;
- establishes a close relationship of trust with the chief executive, providing support and advice while respecting executive responsibility; and
- provides coherent leadership of the company, including representing the company and understanding the views of shareholders.

GUIDANCE ON THE ROLE OF THE NON-EXECUTIVE DIRECTOR

As members of the unitary board, all directors are required to:

- provide entrepreneurial leadership of the company within a framework of prudent and effective controls which enable risk to be assessed and managed;
- set the company's strategic aims, ensure that the necessary financial and human resources are in place for the company to meet its objectives, and review management performance; and

- set the company's values and standards and ensure that its obligations to its shareholders and others are understood and met.

In addition to these requirements for all directors, the role of the non-executive director has the following key elements:

- **Strategy.** Non-executive directors should constructively challenge and help develop proposals on strategy.
- **Performance.** Non-executive directors should scrutinise the performance of management in meeting agreed goals and objectives and monitor the reporting of performance.
- **Risk.** Non-executive directors should satisfy themselves on the integrity of financial information and that financial controls and systems of risk management are robust and defensible.
- **People.** Non-executive directors are responsible for determining appropriate levels of remuneration of executive directors, and have a prime role in appointing, and where necessary removing, executive directors and in succession planning.

Non-executive directors should constantly seek to establish and maintain confidence in the conduct of the company. They should be independent in judgement and have an enquiring mind. To be effective, non-executive directors need to build a recognition by executives of their contribution in order to promote openness and trust.

To be effective, non-executive directors need to be well-informed about the company and the external environment in which it operates, with a strong command of issues relevant to the business. A non-executive director should insist on a comprehensive, formal and tailored induction. An effective induction need not be restricted to the boardroom, so consideration should be given to visiting sites and meeting senior and middle management. Once in post, an effective non-executive director should seek continually to develop and refresh their knowledge and skills to ensure that their contribution to the board remains informed and relevant.

Best practice dictates that an effective non-executive director will ensure that information is provided sufficiently in advance of meetings to enable thorough consideration of the issues facing the board.

The non-executive should insist that information is sufficient, accurate, clear and timely.

An element of the role of the non-executive director is to understand the views of major investors both directly and through the chairman and the senior independent director.

The effective non-executive director:

- upholds the highest ethical standards of integrity and probity;
- supports executives in their leadership of the business while monitoring their conduct;
- questions intelligently, debates constructively, challenges rigorously and decides dispassionately;
- listens sensitively to the views of others, inside and outside the board;
- gains the trust and respect of other board members; and

- promotes the highest standards of corporate governance and seeks compliance with the provisions of the Code wherever possible.

SUMMARY OF THE PRINCIPAL DUTIES OF THE REMUNERATION COMMITTEE

The Code provides that the remuneration committee should consist exclusively of independent non-executive directors and should comprise at least three or, in the case of smaller companies[1] two, such directors.

Duties

The committee should:

- determine and agree with the board the framework or broad policy for the remuneration of the chief executive, the chairman of the company and such other members of the executive management as it is designated to consider[2]. At a minimum, the committee should have delegated responsibility for setting remuneration for all executive directors, the chairman and, to maintain and assure their independence, the company secretary. The remuneration of non-executive directors shall be a matter for the chairman and executive members of the board. No director or manager should be involved in any decisions as to their own remuneration;
- determine targets for any performance-related pay schemes operated by the company;
- determine the policy for and scope of pension arrangements for each executive director;
- ensure that contractual terms on termination, and any payments made, are fair to the individual and the company, that failure is not rewarded and that the duty to mitigate loss is fully recognised[3];
- within the terms of the agreed policy, determine the total individual remuneration package of each executive director including, where appropriate, bonuses, incentive payments and share options;
- in determining such packages and arrangements, give due regard to the contents of the Code as well as the UK Listing Authority's Listing Rules and associated guidance;
- be aware of and advise on any major changes in employee benefit structures throughout the company or group;
- agree the policy for authorising claims for expenses from the chief executive and chairman;
- ensure that provisions regarding disclosure of remuneration, including pensions, as set out in the Directors' Remuneration Report Regulations 2002 and the Code, are fulfilled;
- be exclusively responsible for establishing the selection criteria, selecting, appointing and setting the terms of reference for any remuneration consultants who advise the committee; and
- report the frequency of, and attendance by members at, remuneration committee meetings in the annual reports; and make available the committee's terms of reference. These should set out the committee's delegated responsibilities and be reviewed and, where necessary, updated annually.

This guidance has been compiled with the assistance of ICSA which has kindly agreed to produce updated guidance on its website www.icsa.org.uk in the future.

SUMMARY OF THE PRINCIPAL DUTIES OF THE NOMINATION COMMITTEE

There should be a nomination committee which should lead the process for board appointments and make recommendations to the board.

A majority of members of the committee should be independent non-executive directors. The chairman or an independent non-executive director should chair the committee, but the chairman should not chair the nomination committee when it is dealing with the appointment of a successor to the chairmanship.

Duties

The committee should:

- be responsible for identifying and nominating for the approval of the board, candidates to fill board vacancies as and when they arise;
- before making an appointment, evaluate the balance of skills, knowledge and experience on the board and, in the light of this evaluation, prepare a description of the role and capabilities required for a particular appointment;
- review annually the time required from a non-executive director. Performance evaluation should be used to assess whether the non-executive director is spending enough time to fulfil their duties;
- consider candidates from a wide range of backgrounds and look beyond the "usual suspects";
- give full consideration to succession planning in the course of its work, taking into account the challenges and opportunities facing the company and what skills and expertise are therefore needed on the board in the future;
- regularly review the structure, size and composition (including the skills, knowledge and experience) of the board and make recommendations to the board with regard to any changes;
- keep under review the leadership needs of the organisation, both executive and non-executive, with a view to ensuring the continued ability of the organisation to compete effectively in the marketplace;
- make a statement in the annual report about its activities; the process used for appointments and explain if external advice or open advertising has not been used; the membership of the committee, number of committee meetings and attendance over the course of the year;
- make available its terms of reference explaining clearly its role and the authority delegated to it by the board; and
- ensure that on appointment to the board, non-executive directors receive a formal letter of appointment setting out clearly what is expected of them in terms of time commitment, committee service and involvement outside board meetings.

The committee should make recommendations to the board:

- as regards plans for succession for both executive and non-executive directors;
- as regards the re-appointment of any non-executive director at the conclusion of their specified term of office;

- concerning the re-election by shareholders of any director under the retirement by rotation provisions in the company's articles of association;
- concerning any matters relating to the continuation in office of any director at any time; and
- concerning the appointment of any director to executive or other office other than to the positions of chairman and chief executive, the recommendation for which would be considered at a meeting of the board.

This guidance has been compiled with the assistance of ICSA which has kindly agreed to produce updated guidance on its website www.icsa.org.uk in the future.

PRE-APPOINTMENT DUE DILIGENCE CHECKLIST FOR NEW BOARD MEMBERS

Why?

Before accepting an appointment a prospective non-executive director should undertake their own thorough examination of the company to satisfy themselves that it is an organisation in which they can have faith and in which they will be well suited to working.

The following questions are not intended to be exhaustive, but are intended to be a helpful basis of the pre-appointment due diligence process that all non-executive directors should undertake.

Questions to ask

What is the company's current financial position and what has its financial track record been over the last three years?

What are the key dependencies (e.g. regulatory approvals, key licences, etc)?

What record does the company have on corporate governance issues?

If the company is not performing particularly well is there potential to turn it round and do I have the time, desire and capability to make a positive impact?

What are the exact nature and extent of the company's business activities?

Who are the current executive and non-executive directors, what is their background and their record, and how long have they served on the board?

What is the size and structure of the board and board committees and what are the relationships between the chairman and the board, the chief executive and the management team?

Who owns the company i.e. who are the company's main shareholders and how has the profile changed over recent years? What is the company's attitude towards, and relationship with, its shareholders?

Is any material litigation presently being undertaken or threatened, either by the company or against it?

Is the company clear and specific about the qualities, knowledge, skills and experience that it needs to complement the existing board?

What insurance cover is available to directors and what is the company's policy on indemnifying directors?

Do I have the necessary knowledge, skills, experience and time to make a positive contribution to the board of this company?

How closely do I match the job specification and how well will I fulfil the board's expectations?

Is there anything about the nature and extent of the company's business activities that would cause me concern both in terms of risk and any personal ethical considerations?

Am I satisfied that the internal regulation of the company is sound and that I can operate effectively within its stated corporate governance framework?

Am I satisfied that the size, structure and make-up of the board will enable me to make an effective contribution?

Would accepting the non-executive directorship put me in a position of having a conflict of interest?

Sources of information

- Company report and accounts, and/or any listing prospectus, for the recent years.
- Analyst reports.
- Press reports.
- Company website.
- Any corporate social responsibility or environmental report issued by the company.
- Rating agency reports.
- Voting services reports.

Published material is unlikely to reveal wrong-doing. However, a lack of transparency may be a reason to proceed with caution.

This guidance has been compiled with the assistance of ICSA which has kindly agreed to produce updated guidance on its website www.icsa.org.uk in the future.

SAMPLE LETTER OF NON-EXECUTIVE DIRECTOR APPOINTMENT

On [date], upon the recommendation of the nomination committee, the board of [company] ('the Company') has appointed you as non-executive director. I am writing to set out the terms of your appointment. It is agreed that this is a contract for services and is not a contract of employment.

Appointment

Your appointment will be for an initial term of three years commencing on [date], unless otherwise terminated earlier by and at the discretion of either party upon [one month's] written notice. Continuation of your contract of appointment is contingent on satisfactory performance and re-election at forthcoming AGMs.

Non-executive directors are typically expected to serve two three-year terms, although the board may invite you to serve an additional period.

Time commitment

Overall we anticipate a time commitment of [number] days per month after the induction phase. This will include attendance at [monthly] board meetings, the AGM, [one] annual board awayday, and [at least one] site visit per year. In addition, you will be expected to devote appropriate preparation time ahead of each meeting.

By accepting this appointment, you have confirmed that you are able to allocate sufficient time to meet the expectations of your role. The agreement of the chairman should be sought before accepting additional commitments that might impact on the time you are able to devote to your role as a non-executive director of the company.

Role

Non-executive directors have the same general legal responsibilities to the company as any other director. The board as a whole is collectively responsible for the success of the company. The board:

- provides entrepreneurial leadership of the company within a framework of prudent and effective controls which enable risk to be assessed and managed;
- sets the company's strategic aims, ensures that the necessary financial and human resources are in place for the company to meet its objectives, and reviews management performance; and
- sets the company's values and standards and ensure that its obligations to its shareholders and others are understood and met.

All directors must take decisions objectively in the interests of the company.

In addition to these requirements of all directors, the role of the non-executive director has the following key elements:

- **Strategy.** Non-executive directors should constructively challenge and help develop proposals on strategy;
- **Performance.** Non-executive directors should scrutinise the performance of management in meeting agreed goals and objectives and monitor the reporting of performance;
- **Risk.** Non-executive directors should satisfy themselves on the integrity of financial information and that financial controls and systems of risk management are robust and defensible; and
- **People.** Non-executive directors are responsible for determining appropriate levels of remuneration of executive directors and have a prime role in appointing, and where necessary removing, executive directors and in succession planning.

Fees

You will be paid a fee of £[amount] gross per annum which will be paid monthly in arrears, [plus [number] ordinary shares of the company per annum, both of] which will be subject to an annual review by the board. The company will reimburse you for all reasonable and properly documented expenses you incur in performing the duties of your office.

Outside interests

It is accepted and acknowledged that you have business interests other than those of the company and have declared any conflicts that are apparent at present. In the event that you become aware of any potential conflicts of interest, these should be disclosed to the chairman and company secretary as soon as apparent.

[The board of the Company have determined you to be independent according to provision A.3.1 of the Code.]

Confidentiality

All information acquired during your appointment is confidential to the Company and should not be released, either during your appointment or following termination (by whatever means), to third parties without prior clearance from the chairman.

Your attention is also drawn to the requirements under both legislation and regulation as to the disclosure of price sensitive information. Consequently you should avoid making any statements that might risk a breach of these requirements without prior clearance from the chairman or company secretary.

Induction

Immediately after appointment, the Company will provide a comprehensive, formal and tailored induction. This will include the information pack recommended by the Institute of Chartered Secretaries and Administrators (ICSA), available at www.icsa.org.uk. We will also arrange for site visits and meetings with senior and middle management and the Company's auditors. We will also offer to major shareholders the opportunity to meet you.

Review process

The performance of individual directors and the whole board and its committees is evaluated annually. If, in the interim, there are any matters which cause you concern about your role you should discuss them with the chairman as soon as is appropriate.

Insurance

The Company has directors' and officers' liability insurance and it is intended to maintain such cover for the full term of your appointment. The current indemnity limit is £[amount]; a copy of the policy document is attached.

Independent professional advice

Occasions may arise when you consider that you need professional advice in the furtherance of your duties as a director. Circumstances may occur when it will be appropriate for you to seek advice from independent advisors at the company's expense. A copy of the board's agreed procedure under which directors may obtain such independent advice is attached. The Company will reimburse the full cost of expenditure incurred in accordance with the attached policy.

Committees

This letter refers to your appointment as a non-executive director of the Company. In the event that you are also asked to serve on one or more of the board committees this will be covered in a separate communication setting out the committee(s)'s terms of reference, any specific responsibilities and any additional fees that may be involved.

This sample appointment letter has been complied with the assistance of ICSA which has kindly agreed to produce updated guidance on its website www.icsa.org.uk in the future.

INDUCTION CHECKLIST

[*Readers may also wish to refer to Chapter A2, especially **A2.19**.*]

Guidance on Induction

Every company should develop its own comprehensive, formal induction programme that is tailored to the needs of the company and individual non-executive directors. The following guidelines might form the core of an induction programme.

As a general rule, a combination of selected written information together with presentations and activities such as meetings and site visits will help to give a new appointee a balanced and real-life overview of the company. Care should be taken not to overload the new director with too much information. The new non-executive director should be provided with a list of all the induction information that is being made available to them so that they may call up items if required before otherwise provided.

The induction process should:

1. Build an understanding of the **nature of the company, its business and the markets in which it operates**. For example, induction should cover:
   - the company's products or services;
   - group structure/subsidiaries/joint ventures;
   - the company's constitution, board procedures and matters reserved for the board;
   - summary details of the company's principal assets, liabilities, significant contracts and major competitors;
   - the company's major risks and risk management strategy;
   - key performance indicators; and
   - regulatory constraints.
2. Build a link with the **company's people** including;
   - meetings with senior management;
   - visits to company sites other than the headquarters, to learn about production or services and meet employees in an informal setting. It is important, not only for the board to get to know the new non-executive director, but also for the non-executive director to build a profile with employees below board level; and
   - participating in board strategy development. Awaydays enable a new non-executive director to begin to build working relationships away from the formal setting of the boardroom.

3. Build an understanding of the **company's main relationships,** including meeting with the auditors and developing a knowledge of in particular:
   - who are the major customers;
   - who are the major suppliers; and
   - who are the major shareholders and what is the shareholder relations policy – participation in meetings with shareholders can help give a firsthand feel, as well as letting shareholders know who the non-executive directors are.

The induction pack

On appointment, or during the weeks immediately following, a new non-executive director should be provided with certain basic information to help ensure their early effective contribution to the company. ICSA has produced, and undertaken to maintain, on its website www.icsa.org a guidance note detailing a full list of such material.

PERFORMANCE EVALUATION GUIDANCE

Guidance on performance evaluation

The Code provides that the board should undertake a formal and rigorous annual evaluation of its own performance and that of its committees and individual directors. Individual evaluation should aim to show whether each director continues to contribute effectively and to demonstrate commitment to the role (including commitment of time for board and committee meetings and any other duties). The chairman should act on the results of the performance evaluation by recognising the strengths and addressing the weaknesses of the board and, where appropriate, proposing new members be appointed to the board or seeking the resignation of directors. The board should state in the annual report how such performance evaluation has been conducted.

It is the responsibility of the chairman to select an effective process and to act on its outcome. The use of an external third party to conduct the evaluation will bring objectivity to the process.

The non-executive directors, led by the senior independent director, should be responsible for performance evaluation of the chairman, taking into account the views of executive directors.

The evaluation process will be used constructively as a mechanism to improve board effectiveness, maximise strengths and tackle weaknesses. The results of board evaluation should be shared with the board as a whole while the results of individual assessments should remain confidential between the chairman and the non-executive director concerned.

The following are some of the questions that should be considered in a performance evaluation. They are, however, by no means definitive or exhaustive and companies will wish to tailor the questions to suit their own needs and circumstances.

The responses to these questions and others should enable boards to assess how they are performing and to identify how certain elements of their performance areas might be improved.

Performance evaluation of the board

How well has the board performed against any performance objectives that have been set?

What has been the board's contribution to the testing and development of strategy?

What has been the board's contribution to ensuring robust and effective risk management?

Is the composition of the board and its committees appropriate, with the right mix of knowledge and skills to maximise performance in the light of future strategy? Are inside and outside the board relationships working effectively?

How has the board responded to any problems or crises that have emerged and could or should these have been foreseen?

Are the matters specifically reserved for the board the right ones?

How well does the board communicate with the management team, company employees and others?

How effectively does it use mechanisms such as the AGM and the annual report?

Is the board as a whole up to date with latest developments in the regulatory environment and the market?

How effective are the board's committees? [Specific questions on the performance of each committee should be included such as, for example, their role, their composition and their interaction with the board.]

The processes that help underpin the board's effectiveness should also be evaluated e.g.:

- Is appropriate, timely information of the right length and quality provided to the board and is management responsive to requests for clarification or amplification? Does the board provide helpful feedback to management on its requirements?
- Are sufficient board and committee meetings of appropriate length held to enable proper consideration of issues? Is time used effectively?
- Are board procedures conducive to effective performance and flexible enough to deal with all eventualities?

In addition, there are some specific issues relating to the chairman which should be included as part of an evaluation of the board's performance e.g.:

- Is the chairman demonstrating effective leadership of the board?
- Are relationships and communications with shareholders well managed?
- Are relationships and communications within the board constructive?
- Are the processes for setting the agenda working? Do they enable board members to raise issues and concerns?
- Is the company secretary being used appropriately and to maximum value?

Performance evaluation of the non-executive director

The chairman and other board members should consider the following issues and the individual concerned should also be asked to assess themselves. For each non-executive director:

- How well prepared and informed are they for board meetings and is their meeting attendance satisfactory?
- Do they demonstrate a willingness to devote time and effort to understand the company and its business and a readiness to participate in events outside the boardroom such as site visits?
- What has been the quality and value of their contributions at board meetings?
- What has been their contribution to development of strategy and to risk management?
- How successfully have they brought their knowledge and experience to bear in the consideration of strategy?
- How effectively have they probed to test information and assumptions? Where necessary, how resolute are they in maintaining their own views and resisting pressure from others?
- How effectively and proactively have they followed up their areas of concern?
- How effective and successful are their relationships with fellow board members, the company secretary and senior management?
- Does their performance and behaviour engender mutual trust and respect within the board?
- How actively and successfully do they refresh their knowledge and skills and are they up to date with:
  - the latest developments in areas such as corporate governance framework and financial reporting?
  - the industry and market conditions?
- How well do they communicate with fellow board members, senior management and others, for example shareholders? Are they able to present their views convincingly yet diplomatically and do they listen and take on board the views of others?

Notes

1 A smaller company is one that is below the FTSE 350 throughout the year immediately prior to the reporting year.

2 Some companies require the remuneration committee to consider the packages of all executives at or above a specified level such as those reporting to a main board director whilst others require the committee to deal with all packages above a certain figure.

3 Remuneration committees should consider reviewing and agreeing a standard form of contract for their executive directors, and ensuring that new appointees are offered and accept terms within the previously agreed level.

Appendix 6

Cadbury, Greenbury and 1998 Combined Codes

In this Appendix we reproduce three early Codes:

- the Cadbury Code: **App6.1**;
- the Greenbury Code: **App6.2**; and
- the 1998 Combined Code: **App6.3**.

The 1992 'Cadbury Code' **App6.1**

Report of the Committee on the Financial Aspects of Corporate Governance (The 'Cadbury Committee')

The Code of Best Practice

Introduction

1. The Committee was set up in May 1991 by the Financial Reporting Council, the London Stock Exchange, and the accountancy profession to address the financial aspects of corporate governance.
2. The Committee issued a draft report for public comment on 27 May 1992. Its final report, taking account of submissions made during the consultation period and incorporating a Code of Best Practice, was published on 1 December 1992. This extract from the report sets out the text of the Code. It also sets out, as Notes, a number of further recommendations on good practice drawn from the body of the report.
3. The Committee's central recommendation is that the board of all listed companies registered in the United Kingdom should comply with the Code. The Committee encourages as many other companies as possible to aim at meeting its requirements.
4. The Committee also recommends:
   (a) that listed companies reporting in respect of years ending after 30 June 1993 should make a statement in their report and accounts about their compliance with the Code and identify and give reasons for any areas of non-compliance;
   (b) that companies' statements of compliance should be reviewed by the auditors before publication. The review by the auditors should cover only those parts of the compliance statement which relate to provisions of the Code where compliance can be objectively verified (see Note 14).
5. The publication of a statement of compliance, reviewed by the auditors, is to be made a continuing obligation of listing by the London Stock Exchange.
6. The Committee recommends that its sponsors, convened by the Financial Reporting Council, should appoint a new Committee by the end of June 1995 to examine how far compliance with the Code has progressed, how far its

other recommendations have been implemented, and whether the Code needs updating. In the meantime the present Committee will remain responsible for reviewing the implementation of its proposals.

7. The Committee has made clear that the Code is to be followed by individuals and boards in the light of their own particular circumstances. They are responsible for ensuring that their actions meet the spirit of the Code and in interpreting it they should give precedence to substance over form.

8. The Committee recognises that smaller listed companies may initially have difficulty in complying with some aspects of the Code. The boards of smaller listed companies who cannot, for the time being, comply with parts of the Code should note that they may instead give their reasons for noncompliance. The Committee believes, however, that full compliance will bring benefits to the boards of such companies and that it should be their objective to ensure that the benefits are achieved. In particular, the appointment of appropriate non-executive directors should make a positive contribution to the development of their businesses.

The Code of Best Practice (The 'Cadbury Code')

1. The board of directors

1.1 The board should meet regularly, retain full and effective control over the company and monitor the executive management.

1.2 There should be a clearly accepted division of responsibilities at the head of a company, which will ensure a balance of power and authority, such that no one individual has unfettered powers of decision. Where the chairman is also the chief executive, it is essential that there should be a strong and independent element on the board, with a recognised senior member.

1.3 The board should include non-executive directors of sufficient calibre and number for their views to carry significant weight in the board's decisions. (Note 1.)

1.4 The board should have a formal schedule of matters specifically reserved to it for decision to ensure that the direction and control of the company is firmly in its hands. (Note 2.)

1.5 There should be an agreed procedure for directors in the furtherance of their duties to take independent professional advice if necessary, at the company's expense. (Note 3.)

1.6 All directors should have access to the advice and services of the company secretary, who is responsible to the board for ensuring that board procedures are followed and that applicable rules and regulations are complied with. Any question of the removal of the company secretary should be a matter for the board as a whole.

2. Non-executive directors

2.1 Non-executive directors should bring an independent judgement to bear on issues of strategy, performance, resources, including key appointments, and standards of conduct.

2.2 The majority should be independent of management and free from any business or other relationship which could materially interfere with the exercise of their independent judgement, apart from their fees and shareholding. Their fees should reflect the time which they commit to the company. (Notes 4 and 5.)

2.3 Non-executive directors should be appointed for specified terms and reappointment should not be automatic. (Note 6.)

2.4 Non-executive directors should be selected through a formal process and both this process and their appointment should be a matter for the board as a whole. (Note 7.)

3. Executive directors

3.1 Directors' service contracts should not exceed three years without shareholders' approval. (Note 8.)

3.2 There should be full and clear disclosure of directors' total emoluments and those of the chairman and highest-paid UK director, including pension contributions and stock options. Separate figures should be given for salary and performance-related elements and the basis on which performance is measured should be explained.

3.3 Executive directors' pay should be subject to the recommendations of a remuneration committee made up wholly or mainly of non-executive directors. (Note 9.)

4. Reporting and controls

4.1 It is the board's duty to present a balanced and understandable assessment of the company's position. (Note 10.)

4.2 The board should ensure that an objective and professional relationship is maintained with the auditors.

4.3 The board should establish an audit committee of at least three non-executive directors with written terms of reference which deal clearly with its authority and duties. (Note 11.)

4.4 The directors should explain their responsibility for preparing the accounts next to a statement by the auditors about their reporting responsibilities. (Note 12.)

4.5 The directors should report on the effectiveness of the company's system of internal control. (Note 13.)

4.6 The directors should report that the business is a going concern, with supporting assumptions or qualifications as necessary. (Note 13.)

Notes

These notes include further recommendations on good practice. They do not form part of the Code.

1. To meet the Committee's recommendations on the composition of subcommittees of the board, boards will require a minimum of three non-executive directors, one of whom may be the chairman of the company provided he or she is not also its executive head. Additionally, two of the three non-executive directors should be independent in the terms set out in paragraph 2.2 of the Code.
2. A schedule of matters specifically reserved for decision by the full board should be given to directors on appointment and should be kept up to date. The Committee envisages that the schedule would at least include:
   (a) acquisition and disposal of assets of the company or its subsidiaries that are material to the company;
   (b) investments, capital projects, authority levels, treasury policies and risk management policies.

The board should lay down rules to determine materiality for any transaction, and should establish clearly which transactions require multiple board signatures. The board should also agree the procedures to be followed when, exceptionally, decisions are required between board meetings.

3. The agreed procedure should be laid down formally, for example in a Board Resolution, in the Articles, or in the Letter of Appointment.
4. It is for the board to decide in particular cases whether this definition of independence is met. Information about the relevant interest of directors should be disclosed in the Directors' Report.
5. The Committee regards it as good practice for non-executive directors not to participate in share option schemes and for their service as non-executive directors not to be pensionable by the company, in order to safeguard their independent position.
6. The Letter of Appointment for non-executive directors should set out their duties, term of office, remuneration and its review.
7. The Committee regards it as good practice for a nomination committee to carry out the selection process and to make proposals to the board. A nomination committee should have a majority of non-executive directors on it and be chaired either by the chairman or a non-executive director.
8. The Committee does not intend that this provision should apply to existing contracts before they become due for renewal.
9. Membership of the remuneration committee should be set out in the Directors' Report and its chairman should be available to answer questions on remuneration principles and practice at the Annual General Meeting. Best practice is set out in PRO NED's Remuneration Committee guidelines, published in 1992. (Available at the price of £5 from PRO NED, 1 Kingsway, London WC2B 6XF, telephone 020 7240 8305.)
10. The report and accounts should contain a coherent narrative, supported by the figures, of the company's performance and prospects. Balance requires that setbacks should be dealt with as well as successes. The need for the report to be readily understood emphasises that words are as important as figures.
11. The Committee's recommendations on audit committees are as follows:
    (a) They should be formally constituted as sub-committees of the main board to whom they are answerable and to whom they should report regularly; they should be given written terms of reference which deal adequately with their membership, authority and duties; and they should normally meet at least twice a year.
    (b) There should be a minimum of three members. Membership should be confined to the non-executive directors of the company and a majority of the non-executives serving on the committee should be independent of the company, as defined in paragraph 2.2 of the Code.
    (c) The external auditor and, where an internal audit function exists, the head of internal audit should normally attend committee meetings, as should the finance director. Other board members should also have the right to attend.
    (d) The audit committee should have a discussion with the auditors at least once a year, without executive board members present, to ensure that there are no unresolved issues of concern.

(e) The audit committee should have explicit authority to investigate any matters within its terms of reference, the resources which it needs to do so, and full access to information. The committee should be able to obtain outside professional advice and if necessary to invite outsiders with relevant experience to attend meetings.

(f) Membership of the committee should be disclosed in the annual report and the chairman of the committee should be available to answer questions about its work at the Annual General Meeting.

Specimen terms of reference for an audit committee, including a list of the most commonly performed duties, are set out in the Committee's full report.

12. The statement of directors' responsibilities should cover the following points:

- the legal requirement for directors to prepare financial statements for each financial year which give a true and fair view of the state of affairs of the company (or group) as at the end of the financial year and of the profit and loss for that period;
- the responsibility of the directors for maintaining adequate accounting records, for safeguarding the assets of the company (or group), and for preventing and detecting fraud and other irregularities;
- confirmation that suitable accounting policies, consistently applied and supported by reasonable and prudent judgements and estimates, have been used in the preparation of the financial statements;
- confirmation that applicable accounting standards have been followed, subject to any material departures disclosed and explained in the notes to the accounts. (This does not obviate the need for a formal statement in the notes to the accounts disclosing whether the accounts have been prepared in accordance with applicable accounting standards.)

The statement should be placed immediately before the auditors' report which in future will include a separate statement (currently being developed by the Auditing Practices Board) on the responsibility of the auditors for expressing an opinion on the accounts.

13. The Committee notes that companies will not be able to comply with paragraphs 4.5 and 4.6 of the Code until the necessary guidance for companies has been developed as recommended in the Committee's report.

14. The company's statement of compliance should be reviewed by the auditors in so far as it relates to paragraphs 1.4, 1.5, 2.3, 2.4, 3.1 to 3.3 and 4.3 to 4.6 of the Code.

The 1995 'Greenbury Code' **App6.2**

Note that this Code was superseded by some of the contents of the 1998 Combined Code (see **App6.3**). The Code printed here incorporates the two late corrections made after the Greenbury Report was printed, which had been shown on a loose erratum slip in the first printing of the Report. Code references to paragraphs relate to the Greenbury Report itself.

Directors' remuneration

Report of a study group chaired by Sir Richard Greenbury

17 July 1995

The Code

A The remuneration committee

A1 To avoid potential conflicts of interest, boards of directors should set up remuneration committees of non-executive directors to determine on their behalf, and on behalf of the shareholders, within agreed terms of reference, the company's policy on executive remuneration and specific remuneration packages for each of the executive directors, including pension rights and any compensation payments (paragraphs 4.3–4.7).

A2 Remuneration committee chairmen should account directly to the shareholders through the means specified in this Code for the decisions their committees reach (paragraph 4.4).

A3 Where necessary, companies' Articles of Association should be amended to enable remuneration committees to discharge these functions on behalf of the board (paragraph 4.3).

A4 Remuneration committees should consist exclusively of non-executive directors with no personal financial interest other than as shareholders in the matters to be decided, no potential conflicts of interest arising from cross-directorships and no day-to-day involvement in running the business (paragraphs 4.8 and 4.11).

A5 The members of the remuneration committee should be listed each year in the committee's report to shareholders (B1 below). When they stand for reelection, the proxy cards should indicate their membership of the committee (paragraphs 4.12 and 5.25).

A6 The board itself should determine the remuneration of the non-executive directors, including members of the remuneration committee, within the limits set in the Articles of Association (paragraph 4.13).

A7 Remuneration committees should consult the company chairman and/or chief executive about their proposals and have access to professional advice inside and outside the company (paragraphs 4.14–4.17).

A8 The remuneration committee chairman should attend the company's Annual General Meeting (AGM) to answer share-holders' questions about directors' remuneration and should ensure that the company maintains contact as required with its principal shareholders about remuneration in the same way as for other matters (paragraph 5.27).

A9 The committee's annual report to shareholders (B1 below) should not be a standard item of agenda for AGMs. But the committee should consider each year whether the circumstances are such that the AGM should be invited to approve the policy set out in their report and should minute their conclusions (paragraphs 5.28–5.32).

B Disclosure and approval provisions

B1 The remuneration committee should make a report each year to the shareholders on behalf of the board. The report should form part of, or be annexed to, the company's Annual Report and Accounts. It should be the main vehicle through which the company accounts to shareholders for directors' remuneration (paragraph 5.4).

B2 The report should set out the company's policy on executive directors' remuneration, including levels, comparator groups of companies, individual components, performance criteria and measurement, pension provision, contracts of service and compensation commitments on early termination (paragraphs 5.5–5.7).

B3 The report should state that, in framing its remuneration policy, the committee has given full consideration to the best practice provisions set out in sections C and D below (paragraph 5.25).

B4 The report should also include full details of all elements in the remuneration package of each individual director by name, such as basic salary, benefits in kind, annual bonuses and long-term incentive schemes including share options (paragraphs 5.8–5.12).

B5 Information on share options, including SAYE options, should be given for each director in accordance with the recommendations of the Accounting Standards Board's Urgent Issues Task Force Abstract 10 and its successors (paragraphs 5.13–5.16).

B6 If grants under executive share option or other long-term incentive schemes are awarded in one large block rather than phased, the report should explain and justify (paragraph 6.29).

B7 Also included in the report should be pension entitlement earned by each individual director during the year, calculated on a basis to be recommended by the Faculty of Actuaries and the Institute of Actuaries (paragraphs 5.17–5.23).

B8 If annual bonuses or benefits in kind are pensionable, the report should explain and justify (paragraph 6.44).

B9 The amounts received by, and commitments made to each director under B4, B5 and B7 should be subject to audit (paragraph 5.4).

B10 Any service contracts which provide for, or imply, notice periods in excess of one year (or any provisions for predetermined compensation on termination which exceed one year's salary and benefits) should be disclosed and the reasons for the longer notice periods explained (paragraph 7.13).

B11 Shareholdings and other relevant business interests and activities of the directors should continue to be disclosed as required in the Companies Acts and London Stock Exchange Listing Rules (paragraph 5.24).

B12 Shareholders should be invited specifically to approve all new long-term incentive schemes (including share option schemes) whether payable in cash or shares in which directors and senior executives will participate which potentially commit shareholders' funds over more than one year or dilute the equity (paragraph 5.33).

C Remuneration policy

C1 Remuneration committees must provide the packages needed to attract, retain and motivate directors of the quality required but should avoid paying more than is necessary for this purpose (paragraphs 6.5–6.7).

C2 Remuneration committees should judge where to position their company relative to other companies. They should be aware what other comparable companies are paying and should take account of relative performance (paragraphs 6.11–6.12).

C3 Remuneration committees should be sensitive to the wider scene, including pay and employment conditions elsewhere in the company, especially when determining annual salary increases (paragraph 6.13).

C4 The performance-related elements of remuneration should be designed to align the interests of directors and shareholders and to give directors keen incentives to perform at the highest levels (paragraph 6.16).

C5 Remuneration committees should consider whether their directors should be eligible for annual bonuses. If so, performance conditions should be relevant, stretching and designed to enhance the business. Upper limits should always be considered. There may be a case for part-payment in shares to be held for a significant period (paragraphs 6.19–6.22).

C6 Remuneration committees should consider whether their directors should be eligible for benefits under long-term incentive schemes. Traditional share option schemes should be weighed against other kinds of long-term incentive scheme. In normal circumstances, shares granted should not vest, and options should not be exercisable, in under three years. Directors should be encouraged to hold their shares for a further period after vesting or exercise subject to the need to finance any costs of acquisition and associated tax liability (paragraphs 6.23–6.34).

C7 Any new long-term incentive schemes which are proposed should preferably replace existing schemes or at least form part of a well-considered overall plan, incorporating existing schemes, which should be approved as a whole by shareholders. The total rewards potentially available should not be excessive (paragraph 6.35). (See also B12.)

C8 Grants under all incentive schemes, including new grants under existing share option schemes, should be subject to challenging performance criteria reflecting the company's objectives. Consideration should be given to criteria which reflect the company's performance relative to a group of comparator companies in some key variables such as total shareholder return (paragraphs 6.38–6.40).

C9 Grants under executive share option and other long-term incentive schemes should normally be phased rather than awarded in one large block (paragraph 6.29). (See B6.)

C10 Executive share options should never be issued at a discount (paragraph 6.29).

C11 Remuneration committees should consider the pension consequences and associated costs to the company of basic salary increases, especially for directors close to retirement (paragraphs 6.42–6.45).

C12 In general, neither annual bonuses nor benefits in kind should be pensionable (paragraph 6.44). (See B8.)

D Service contracts and compensation

D1 Remuneration committees should consider what compensation commitments their directors' contracts of service, if any, would entail in the event of early termination, particularly for unsatisfactory performance (paragraph 7.10).

D2 There is a strong case for setting notice or contract periods at, or reducing them to, one year or less (see B10). Remuneration committees should, however, be sensitive and flexible, especially over timing. In some cases notice or contract periods of up to two years may be acceptable. Longer periods should be avoided wherever possible (paragraphs 7.11–7.15).

D3 If it is necessary to offer longer notice or contract periods, such as three years, to new directors recruited from outside, such periods should reduce after the initial period (paragraph 7.16).

D4 Within the legal constraints, remuneration committees should tailor their approach in individual early termination cases to the wide variety of circumstances. The broad aim should be to avoid rewarding poor performance while dealing fairly with cases where departure is not due to poor performance (paragraphs 7.17–7.18).

D5 Remuneration committees should take a robust line on payment of compensation where performance has been unsatisfactory and on reducing compensation to reflect departing directors' obligations to mitigate damages by earning money elsewhere (paragraphs 7.19–7.20).

D6 Where appropriate, and in particular where notice or contract periods exceed one year, companies should consider paying all or part of compensation in instalments rather than one lump sum and reducing or stopping payment when the former director takes on new employment (paragraph 7.20).

The 1998 Combined Code

App6.3

The 1998 Combined Code

Part 1: Principles of good governance

Section 1: Companies

A. Directors

The board

1. Every listed company should be headed by an effective board which should lead and control the company.

Chairman and CEO

2. There are two key tasks at the top of every public company – the running of the board and the executive responsibility for the running of the company's business. There should be a clear division of responsibilities at the head of the company which will ensure a balance of power and authority, such that no one individual has unfettered powers of decision.

Board balance

3. The board should include a balance of executive and non-executive directors (including independent non-executives) such that no individual or small group of individuals can dominate the board's decision taking.

Supply of information

4. The board should be supplied in a timely manner with information in a form and of a quality appropriate to enable it to discharge its duties.

Appointments to the board

5. There should be a formal and transparent procedure for the appointment of new directors to the board.

Re-election

6. All directors should be required to submit themselves for re-election at regular intervals and at least every three years.

B. Directors' remuneration

The level and make-up of remuneration

1. Levels of remuneration should be sufficient to attract and retain the directors needed to run the company successfully, but companies should avoid paving more than necessary for this purpose. A proportion of executive directors' remuneration should be structured so as to link rewards to corporate and individual performance.

Procedure

2. Companies should establish a formal and transparent procedure for developing policy on executive remuneration and for fixing the remuneration packages of individual directors. No director should be involved in deciding his or her own remuneration.

Disclosure

3. The company's annual report should contain a statement of remuneration policy and details of the remuneration of each director.

C. Relations with shareholders

Dialogue with institutional shareholders

1. Companies should be ready, where practicable, to enter into a dialogue with institutional shareholders based on the mutual understanding of objectives.

Constructive use of the AGM

2. Boards should use the AGM to communicate with private investors and encourage their participation.

D. Accountability and audit

Financial reporting

1. The board should present a balanced and understandable assessment of the company's position and prospects.

Internal control

2. The board should maintain a sound system of internal control to safeguard shareholders' investment and the company's assets.

Audit committee and auditors

3. The board should establish formal and transparent arrangements for considering how they should apply the financial reporting and internal control principles and for maintaining an appropriate relationship with the company's auditors.

Section 2: Institutional investors

E. Institutional investors

Shareholder voting

1. Institutional shareholders have a responsibility to make considered use of their votes.

Dialogue with companies

2. Institutional shareholders should be ready, where practicable, to enter into a dialogue with companies based on the mutual understanding of objectives.

Evaluation of governance disclosures

3. When evaluating companies' governance arrangements, particularly those relating to board structure and composition, institutional investors should give due weight to all relevant factors drawn to their attention.

Part 2: Code of best practice

Section 1: Companies

A. Directors

A.1 The board

Principle

Every listed company should be headed by an effective board which should lead and control the company.

Code provisions

A.1.1 The board should meet regularly.

A.1.2 The board should have a formal schedule of matters specifically reserved to it for decision.

A.1.3 There should be a procedure agreed by the board for directors in the furtherance of their duties to take independent professional advice if necessary at the company's expense.

A.1.4 All directors should have access to the advice and services of the company secretary, who is responsible to the board for ensuring that board procedures are followed and that applicable rules and regulations are complied with. Any question of the removal of the company secretary should be a matter for the board as a whole.

A.1.5 All directors should bring an independent judgement to bear on issues of strategy performance, resources (including key appointments) and standards of conduct.

A.1.6 Every director should receive appropriate training on the first occasion that he or she is appointed to the board of a listed company, and subsequently as necessary.

A.2 Chairman and CEO

Principle

There are two key tasks at the top of every public company – the running of the board and the executive responsibility for the running of the company business. There should be a clear division of responsibilities at the head of the company which will ensure a balance of power and authority, such that no one individual has unfettered powers of decision.

Code provision

A.2.1 A decision to combine the posts of chairman and chief executive officer in one person should be publicly justified. Whether the posts are held by different people or the same person, there should be a strong and independent non-executive element on the board, with a recognised senior member other than the chairman to whom concerns can be conveyed. The chairman, chief executive and senior independent director should be identified in the annual report.

A.3 Board balance

Principle

The board should include a balance of executive and non-executive directors (including independent non-executives) such that no individual or small group of individuals can dominate the board's decision taking.

Code provisions

A.3.1 The board should include non-executive directors of sufficient calibre and number for their views to carry significant weight in the board's decisions. Non-executive directors should comprise not less than one third of the board.

A.3.2 The majority of non-executive directors should be independent of management and free from any business or other relationship which could materially interfere with the exercise of their independent judgement. Non-executive directors considered by the board to be independent in this sense should be identified in the annual report.

A.4 Supply of information

Principle

The board should be supplied in a timely manner with information in a form and of a quality appropriate to enable it to discharge its duties.

Code provision

A.4.1 Management has an obligation to provide the board with appropriate and timely information, but information volunteered by management is unlikely to be enough in all circumstances and directors should make further enquiries where necessary. The chairman should ensure that all directors are properly briefed on issues arising at board meetings.

A.5 Appointments to the board

Principle

There should be a formal and transparent procedure for the appointment of new directors to the board.

Code provision

A.5.1 Unless the board is small, a nomination committee should be established to make recommendations to the board on all new board appointments. A majority of the members of this committee should be non-executive directors and the chairman should be either the chairman of the board or a non-executive director. The chairman and members of the nomination committee should be identified in the annual report.

A.6 Re-election

Principle

All directors should be required to submit themselves for re-election at regular intervals and at least every three years.

Code provisions

A.6.1 Non-executive directors should be appointed for specified terms subject to re-election and to Companies Act provisions relating to the removal of a director, and reappointment should not be automatic.

A.6.2 All directors should be subject to election by shareholders at the first opportunity after their appointment, and to re-election thereafter at intervals of no more than three years. The names of directors submitted for election or re-election should be accompanied by sufficient biographical details to enable shareholders to take an informed decision on their election.

B. Directors' remuneration

B.1 The level and make-up of remuneration

Principle

Levels of remuneration should be sufficient to attract and retain the directors needed to run the company successfully, but companies should avoid paying more than is necessary for this purpose. A proportion of executive directors' remuneration should be structured so as to link rewards to corporate and individual performance.

Code provisions

Remuneration policy

B.1.1 The remuneration committee should provide the packages needed to attract, retain and motivate executive directors of the quality required, but should avoid paying more than is necessary for this purpose.

B.1.2 Remuneration committees should judge where to position their company relative to other companies. They should be aware what comparable companies are paying and should take account of relative performance. But they should use such comparisons with caution, in view of the risk that they can result in an upward ratchet of remuneration levels with no corresponding improvement in performance.

B.1.3 Remuneration committees should be sensitive to the wider scene, including pay and employment conditions elsewhere in the group, especially when determining annual salary increases.

B.1.4 The performance-related elements of remuneration should form a significant proportion of the total remuneration package of executive directors and should be designed to align their interests with those of shareholders and to give these directors keen incentives to perform at the highest levels.

B.1.5 Executive share options should not be offered at a discount save as permitted by paragraphs 13.30 and 13.31 of the Listing Rules.

B.1.6 In designing schemes of performance-related remuneration, remuneration committees should follow the provisions in Schedule A to this Code.

Service contracts and compensation

B.1.7 There is a strong case for setting notice or contract periods at, or reducing them to, one year or less. Boards should set this as an objective, but they should recognise that it may not be possible to achieve it immediately.

B.1.8 If it is necessary to offer longer notice or contract periods to new directors recruited from outside, such periods should reduce after the initial period.

B.1.9 Remuneration committees should consider what compensation commitments (including pension contributions) their directors' contracts of service, if any, would entail in the event of early termination. They should, in particular, consider the advantages of providing explicitly in the initial contract for such compensation commitments except in the case of removal for misconduct.

B.1.10 Where the initial contract does not explicitly provide for compensation commitments, remuneration committees should, within legal constraints, tailor their approach in individual early termination cases to the wide variety of circumstances. The broad aim should be to avoid rewarding poor performance while dealing fairly with cases where departure is not due to poor performance and to take a robust line on reducing compensation to reflect departing directors' obligations to mitigate loss.

B.2 Procedure

Principle

Companies should establish a formal and transparent procedure for developing policy on executive remuneration and for fixing the remuneration packages of individual directors. No director should be involved in deciding his or her own remuneration.

Code provisions

B.2.1 To avoid potential conflicts of interest, boards of directors should set up remuneration committees of independent non-executive directors to make recommendations to the board, within agreed terms of reference, on the company's framework of executive remuneration and its cost: and to determine on their behalf specific remuneration packages for each of the executive directors, including pension rights and any compensation payments.

B.2.2 Remuneration committees should consist exclusively of non-executive directors who are independent of management and free from any business or other relationship which could materially interfere with the exercise of their independent judgement.

B.2.3 The members of the remuneration committee should be listed each year in the board's remuneration report to shareholders (B.3.1 below).

B.2.4 The board itself or, where required by the Articles of Association, the shareholders should determine the remuneration of the non-executive directors, including members of the remuneration committee, within the limits set in the Articles of Association. Where permitted by the Articles, the board may, however, delegate this responsibility to a small sub-committee, which might include the chief executive officer.

B.2.5 Remuneration committees should consult the chairman and/or chief executive officer about their proposals relating to the remuneration of other executive directors and have access to professional advice inside and outside the company.

B.2.6 The chairman of the board should ensure that the company maintains contact as required with its principal shareholders about remuneration in the same way as for other matters.

B.3 Disclosure

Principle

The company's annual report should contain a statement of remuneration policy and details of the remuneration of each director.

Code provisions

B.3.1 The board should report to the shareholders each year on remuneration. The report should form part of, or be annexed to, the company's annual report and accounts. It should be the main vehicle through which the company reports to shareholders on directors' remuneration.

B.3.2 The report should set out the company's policy on executive directors' remuneration. It should draw attention to factors specific to the company.

B.3.3 In preparing the remuneration report, the board should follow the provisions in Schedule B to this Code.

B.3.4 Shareholders should be invited specifically to approve all new long-term incentive schemes (as defined in the Listing Rules) save in the circumstances permitted by paragraph 13.13A of the Listing Rules.

B.3.5 The board's annual remuneration report to shareholders need not be a standard item of agenda for AGMs. But the board should consider each year whether the circumstances are such that the AGM should be invited to approve the policy set out in the report and should minute their conclusions.

C. Relations with shareholders

C.1 Dialogue with institutional shareholders

Principle

Companies should be ready, where practicable, to enter into a dialogue with institutional shareholders based on the mutual understanding of objectives.

C.2 Constructive use of the AGM

Principle

Boards should use tile AGM to communicate with private investors and encourage their participation.

Code provisions

C.2.1 Companies should count all proxy votes and, except where a poll is called, should indicate the level of proxies lodged on each resolution, and the balance for and against the resolution, after it has been dealt with on a show of hands.

C.2.2 Companies should propose a separate resolution at the AGM on each substantially separate issue and should in particular propose a resolution at the AGM relating to the report and accounts.

C.2.3 The chairman of the board should arrange for the chairmen of the audit, remuneration and nomination committees to be available to answer questions at the AGM.

C.2.4 Companies should arrange for the Notice of the AGM and related papers to be sent to shareholders at least 20 working days before the meeting.

D. Accountability and audit

D.1 Financial reporting

Principle

The board should present a balanced and understandable assessment of the company's position and prospects.

Code provisions

D.1.1 The directors should explain their responsibility for preparing the accounts and there should be a statement by the auditors about their reporting responsibilities.

D.1.2 The board's responsibility to present a balanced and understandable assessment extends to interim and other price-sensitive public reports and reports to regulators as well as to information required to be presented by statutory requirements.

D.1.3 The directors should report that the business is a going concern, with supporting assumptions or qualifications as necessary.

D.2 Internal control

Principle

The board should maintain a sound system of internal control to safeguard shareholders investment and the company's assets.

Code provisions

D.2.1 The directors should, at least annually, conduct a review of the effectiveness of the group's system of internal controls and should report to shareholders that they have done so. The review should cover all controls, including financial, operational and compliance controls and risk management.

D.2.2 Companies which do not have an internal audit function should from time to time review the need for one.

D.3 Audit committee and auditors

Principle

The board should establish formal and transparent arrangements for considering how they should apply the financial reporting and internal control principles and for maintaining an appropriate relationship with the company's auditors.

Code provisions

D.3.1 The board should establish an audit committee of at least three directors, all non-executive, with written terms of reference which deal clearly with its authority and duties. The members of the committee, a majority of whom should be independent non-executive directors, should be named in the report and accounts.

D.3.2 The duties of the audit committee should include keeping under review the scope and results of the audit and its cost effectiveness and the independence and objectivity of the auditors. Where the auditors also supply a substantial volume of non-audit services to the company, the committee should keep the nature and extent of such services under review, seeking to balance the maintenance of objectivity and value for money.

Section 2: Institutional shareholders

E. Institutional investors

E.1 Shareholder voting

Principle

Institutional shareholders have a responsibility to make considered use of their votes.

Code provisions

E.1.1 Institutional shareholders should endeavour to eliminate unnecessary variations in the criteria which each applies to the corporate governance arrangements and performance of the companies in which they invest.

E.1.2 Institutional shareholders should, on request, make available to their clients information on the proportion resolutions on which votes were cast and nondiscretionary proxies lodged.

E.1.3 Institutional shareholders should take steps to ensure that their voting intentions are being translated into practice.

E.2 Dialogue with companies

Principle

Institutional shareholders should be ready, where practicable, to enter into a dialogue with companies based on the mutual understanding of objectives.

E.3 Evaluation of governance disclosures

Principle

When evaluating companies' governance arrangements, particularly those relating to board structure and composition, institutional investors should give due weight to all relevant factors drawn to their attention.

Schedule A: Provisions on the design of performance-related remuneration

1. Remuneration committees should consider whether the directors should be eligible for annual bonuses. If so, performance conditions should be relevant, stretching and designed to enhance the business. Upper limits should always be considered. There may be a case for part payment in shares to be held for a significant period.

2. Remuneration committees should consider whether the directors should be eligible for benefits under long-term incentive schemes. Traditional share option schemes should be weighed against other kinds of long-term incentive schemes. In normal circumstances, shares granted or other forms of deferred remuneration should not vest, and options should not be exercisable, in under three years. Directors should be encouraged to hold their shares for a further period after vesting or exercise, subject to the need to finance any costs of acquisition and associated tax liability.

3. Any new long-term incentive schemes which are proposed should be approved by shareholders and should preferably replace existing schemes or at least form part of a well considered overall plan, incorporating existing schemes. The total rewards potentially available should not be excessive.

4. Payouts or grants under all incentive schemes, including new grants under existing share option schemes, should be subject to challenging performance criteria reflecting the company's objectives. Consideration should be given to criteria which reflect the company's performance relative to a group of comparator companies in some key variables such as total shareholder return.

5. Grants under executive share option and other long-term incentive schemes should normally be phased rather than awarded in one large block.

6. Remuneration committees should consider the pension consequences and associated costs to the company of basic salary increases and other changes in remuneration, especially for directors close to retirement.

7. In general, neither annual bonuses nor benefits in kind should be pensionable.

Schedule B: Provisions on what should be included in the remuneration report

1. The report should include full details of all elements in the remuneration package of each individual director by name, such as basic salary, benefits in kind, annual bonuses and long-term incentive schemes including share options.

2. Information on share options, including SAYE options, should be given for each director in accordance with the recommendations of the Accounting Standards Boards Urgent Issues Task Force Abstract 10 and its successors.

3. If grants under executive share option or other long-term incentive schemes are awarded in one large block rather than phased, the report should explain and justify.

4. Also included in the report should be pension entitlements earned by each individual director during the year, disclosed on one of the alternative bases recommended by the Faculty of Actuaries and the Institute of Actuaries and included in the Stock Exchange Listing Rules. Companies may wish to make clear that the transfer value represents a liability of the company, not a sum paid or due to the individual.

5. If annual bonuses or benefits in kind are pensionable the report should explain and justify.

6. The amounts received by, and commitments made to, each director under 1, 2 and 4 above should be subject to audit.

7. Any service contracts which provide for, or imply, notice periods in excess of one year (or any provisions for predetermined compensation on termination which exceed one year's salary and benefits) should be disclosed and the reasons for the longer notice periods explained.

Appendix 7

Code of Ethics

The Code of Ethics of the Institute of Internal Auditors is as follows:

Introduction

The purpose of the Institute's Code of Ethics is to promote an ethical culture in the profession of internal auditing:

> 'Internal auditing is an independent, objective assurance and consulting activity designed to add value and improve an organisation's operations. It helps an organisation accomplish its objectives by bringing a systematic, disciplined approach to evaluate and improve the effectiveness of risk management, control, and governance processes.'

A code of ethics is necessary and appropriate for the profession of internal auditing, founded as it is on the trust placed in its objective assurance about risk management, control, and governance. The Institute's Code of Ethics extends beyond the definition of internal auditing to include two essential components:

- Principles that are relevant to the profession and practice of internal auditing.
- Rules of Conduct that describe behaviour norms expected of internal auditors. These rules are an aid to interpreting the Principles into practical applications and are intended to guide the ethical conduct of internal auditors.

The Code of Ethics together with the Institute's Professional Practices Framework and other relevant Institute pronouncements provide guidance to internal auditors serving others. 'Internal auditors' refers to Institute members, recipients of or candidates for IIA professional certifications and those who provide internal auditing services within the definition of internal auditing.

Applicability and enforcement

This Code of Ethics applies to both individuals and entities that provide internal auditing services.

For Institute members and recipients of or candidates for IIA professional certifications, breaches of the Code of Ethics will be evaluated and administered according to the Institute's Bylaws and Administrative Guidelines. The fact that a particular conduct is not mentioned in the Rules of Conduct does not prevent it from being unacceptable or discreditable, and therefore the member, certification holder or candidate can be liable for disciplinary action.

Principles

Internal auditors are expected to apply and uphold the following principles:

Integrity

The integrity of internal auditors establishes trust and thus provides the basis for reliance on their judgment.

Objectivity

Internal auditors exhibit the highest level of professional objectivity in gathering, evaluating and communicating information about the activity or process being examined. Internal auditors make a balanced assessment of all the relevant circumstances and are not unduly influenced by their own interests or by others in forming judgments.

Confidentiality

Internal auditors respect the value and ownership of information they receive and do not disclose information without appropriate authority unless there is a legal or professional obligation to do so.

Competency

Internal auditors apply the knowledge, skills and experience needed in the performance of internal auditing services.

Rules of conduct

1. Integrity

Internal auditors:

1.1. shall perform their work with honesty, diligence, and responsibility;

1.2. shall observe the law and make disclosures expected by the law and the profession;

1.3. shall not knowingly be a party to any illegal activity, or engage in acts that are discreditable to the profession of internal auditing or to the organisation; and

1.4. shall respect and contribute to the legitimate and ethical objectives of the organisation.

2. Objectivity

Internal auditors:

2.1. Shall not participate in any activity or relationship that may impair or be presumed to impair their unbiased assessment. This participation includes those activities or relationships that may be in conflict with the interests of the organisation.

2.2 Shall not accept anything that may impair or be presumed to impair their professional judgment.

2.3 Shall disclose all material facts known to them that, if not disclosed, may distort the reporting of activities under review.

3. Confidentiality

Internal auditors:

3.1 Shall be prudent in the use and protection of information acquired in the course of their duties.

3.2 Shall not use information for any personal gain or in any manner that would be contrary to the law or detrimental to the legitimate and ethical objectives of the organisation.

4. Competency

Internal auditors:

4.1. Shall engage only in those services for which they have the necessary knowledge, skills, and experience.

4.2 Shall perform internal auditing services in accordance with the *International Standards for the Professional Practice of Internal Auditing*.

4.3 Shall continually improve their proficiency and the effectiveness and quality of their services.

Adopted by The IIA Board of Directors, June 17, 2000. [Still current in 2014.]

Appendix 8

International Standards for the Professional Practice of Internal Auditing

The International Standards of the Institute of Internal Auditors are as follows:

Introduction to the International Standards

Internal auditing is conducted in diverse legal and cultural environments; within organizations that vary in purpose, size, complexity, and structure; and by persons within or outside the organization. While differences may affect the practice of internal auditing in each environment, conformance with The IIA's *International Standards for the Professional Practice of Internal Auditing (Standards)* is essential in meeting the responsibilities of internal auditors and the internal audit activity. If internal auditors or the internal audit activity is prohibited by law or regulation from conformance with certain parts of the *Standards*, conformance with all other parts of the *Standards* and appropriate disclosures are needed.

If the *Standards* are used in conjunction with standards issued by other authoritative bodies, internal audit communications may also cite the use of other standards, as appropriate. In such a case, if inconsistencies exist between the *Standards* and other standards, internal auditors and the internal audit activity must conform with the *Standards,* and may conform with the other standards if they are more restrictive.

The purpose of the *Standards* is to:

1. Delineate basic principles that represent the practice of internal auditing.
2. Provide a framework for performing and promoting a broad range of value-added internal auditing.
3. Establish the basis for the evaluation of internal audit performance.
4. Foster improved organizational processes and operations.

The *Standards* are principles-focused, mandatory requirements consisting of:

- Statements of basic requirements for the professional practice of internal auditing and for evaluating the effectiveness of performance, which are internationally applicable at organizational and individual levels.
- Interpretations, which clarify terms or concepts within the Statements.

The *Standards* employ terms that have been given specific meanings that are included in the Glossary. Specifically, the *Standards* use the word "must" to specify an unconditional requirement and the word "should" where conformance is expected unless, when applying professional judgment, circumstances justify deviation.

It is necessary to consider the Statements and their Interpretations as well as the specific meanings from the Glossary to understand and apply the *Standards* correctly.

The structure of the *Standards* is divided between Attribute and Performance Standards. Attribute Standards address the attributes of organizations and individuals performing internal auditing. The Performance Standards describe the nature of internal auditing and provide quality criteria against which the performance of these services can be measured. The Attribute and Performance Standards are also provided to apply to all internal audit services.

Implementation Standards are also provided to expand upon the Attribute and Performance standards, by providing the requirements applicable to assurance (A) or consulting (C) activities.

Assurance services involve the internal auditor's objective assessment of evidence to provide an independent opinion or conclusions regarding an entity, operation, function, process, system, or other subject matter. The nature and scope of the assurance engagement are determined by the internal auditor. There are generally three parties involved in assurance services: (1) the person or group directly involved with the entity, operation, function, process, system, or other subject matter — the process owner, (2) the person or group making the assessment — the internal auditor, and (3) the person or group using the assessment — the user.

Consulting services are advisory in nature, and are generally performed at the specific request of an engagement client. The nature and scope of the consulting engagement are subject to agreement with the engagement client. Consulting services generally involve two parties: (1) the person or group offering the advice — the internal auditor, and (2) the person or group seeking and receiving the advice — the engagement client. When performing consulting services the internal auditor should maintain objectivity and not assume management responsibility.

The Standards apply to individual internal auditors and internal audit activities. All internal auditors are accountable for conforming with the Standards related to individual objectivity, proficiency, and due professional care. In addition, internal auditors are accountable for conforming with the Standards, which are relevant to the performance of their job responsibilities. Chief audit executives are accountable for overall conformance with the Standards.

The review and development of the *Standards* is an ongoing process. The International Internal Audit Standards Board engages in extensive consultation and discussion prior to issuing the *Standards*. This includes worldwide solicitation for public comment through the exposure draft process. All exposure drafts are posted on The IIA's Web site as well as being distributed to all IIA institutes.

Suggestions and comments regarding the *Standards* can be sent to:

The Institute of Internal Auditors

Standards and Guidance

247 Maitland Avenue

Altamonte Springs, FL 32701-4201, USA

E-mail: guidance@theiia.org

Web: www.globaliia.org

***

INTERNATIONAL STANDARDS FOR THE PROFESSIONAL PRACTICE OF INTERNAL AUDITING (STANDARDS)

Attribute Standards

1000 – Purpose, Authority, and Responsibility

The purpose, authority, and responsibility of the internal audit activity must be formally defined in an internal audit charter, consistent with the Definition of Internal Auditing, the Code of Ethics, and the Standards. The chief audit executive must periodically review the internal audit charter and present it to senior management and the board for approval.

Interpretation:

The internal audit charter is a formal document that defines the internal audit activity's purpose, authority, and responsibility. The internal audit charter establishes the internal audit activity's position within the organization, including the nature of the chief audit executive's functional reporting relationship with the board; authorizes access to records, personnel, and physical properties relevant to the performance of engagements; and defines the scope of internal audit activities. Final approval of the internal audit charter resides with the board.

1000.A1 – The nature of assurance services provided to the organization must be defined in the internal audit charter. If assurances are to be provided to parties outside the organization, the nature of these assurances must also be defined in the internal audit charter.

1000.C1 – The nature of consulting services must be defined in the internal audit charter.

1010 – Recognition of the Definition of Internal Auditing, the Code of Ethics, and the Standards in the Internal Audit Charter

The mandatory nature of the Definition of Internal Auditing, the Code of Ethics, and the Standards must be recognized in the internal audit charter. The chief audit executive should discuss the Definition of Internal Auditing, the Code of Ethics, and the Standards with senior management and the board.

1100 – Independence and Objectivity

The internal audit activity must be independent, and internal auditors must be objective in performing their work.

Interpretation:

Independence is the freedom from conditions that threaten the ability of the internal audit activity to carry out internal audit responsibilities in an unbiased manner. To achieve the degree of independence necessary to effectively carry out the responsibilities of the internal audit activity, the chief audit executive has direct and unrestricted access to senior management and the board. This can be achieved through a dual-reporting relationship. Threats to independence must be managed at the individual auditor, engagement, functional, and organizational levels.

Objectivity is an unbiased mental attitude that allows internal auditors to perform engagements in such a manner that they believe in their work product and that no quality compromises are made. Objectivity requires that internal auditors do not subordinate their judgment on audit matters to others. Threats to objectivity must be managed at the individual auditor, engagement, functional, and organizational levels.

1110 – Organizational Independence

The chief audit executive must report to a level within the organization that allows the internal audit activity to fulfill its responsibilities. The chief audit executive must confirm to the board, at least annually, the organizational independence of the internal audit activity.

Interpretation:

Organizational independence is effectively achieved when the chief audit executive reports functionally to the board. Examples of functional reporting to the board involve the board:

- *Approving the internal audit charter;*
- *Approving the risk based internal audit plan;*
- *Approving the internal audit budget and resource plan;*
- *Receiving communications from the chief audit executive on the internal audit activity's performance relative to its plan and other matters;*
- *Approving decisions regarding the appointment and removal of the chief audit executive;*
- *Approving the remuneration of the chief audit executive; and*
- *Making appropriate inquiries of management and the chief audit executive to determine whether there are inappropriate scope or resource limitations.*

1110.A1 – The internal audit activity must be free from interference in determining the scope of internal auditing, performing work, and communicating results.

1111 – Direct Interaction with the Board

The chief audit executive must communicate and interact directly with the board.

1120 – Individual Objectivity

Internal auditors must have an impartial, unbiased attitude and avoid any conflict of interest.

Interpretation:

Conflict of interest is a situation in which an internal auditor, who is in a position of trust, has a competing professional or personal interest. Such competing interests can make it difficult to fulfill his or her duties impartially. A conflict of interest exists even if no unethical or improper act results. A conflict of interest can create an appearance of impropriety that can undermine confidence in the internal auditor, the internal audit activity, and the profession. A conflict of interest could impair an individual's ability to perform his or her duties and responsibilities objectively.

1130 – Impairment to Independence or Objectivity

If independence or objectivity is impaired in fact or appearance, the details of the impairment must be disclosed to appropriate parties. The nature of the disclosure will depend upon the impairment.

Interpretation:

Impairment to organizational independence and individual objectivity may include, but is not limited to, personal conflict of interest, scope limitations, restrictions on access to records, personnel, and properties, and resource limitations, such as funding.

The determination of appropriate parties to which the details of an impairment to independence or objectivity must be disclosed is dependent upon the expectations of the internal audit activity's and the chief audit executive's responsibilities to senior management and the board as described in the internal audit charter, as well as the nature of the impairment.

1130.A1 – Internal auditors must refrain from assessing specific operations for which they were previously responsible. Objectivity is presumed to be impaired if an internal auditor provides assurance services for an activity for which the internal auditor had responsibility within the previous year.

1130.A2 – Assurance engagements for functions over which the chief audit executive has responsibility must be overseen by a party outside the internal audit activity.

1130.C1 – Internal auditors may provide consulting services relating to operations for which they had previous responsibilities.

1130.C2 – If internal auditors have potential impairments to independence or objectivity relating to proposed consulting services, disclosure must be made to the engagement client prior to accepting the engagement.

1200 – Proficiency and Due Professional Care

Engagements must be performed with proficiency and due professional care.

1210 – Proficiency

Internal auditors must possess the knowledge, skills, and other competencies needed to perform their individual responsibilities. The internal audit activity collectively must possess or obtain the knowledge, skills, and other competencies needed to perform its responsibilities.

Interpretation:

Knowledge, skills, and other competencies is a collective term that refers to the professional proficiency required of internal auditors to effectively carry out their professional responsibilities. Internal auditors are encouraged to demonstrate their proficiency by obtaining appropriate professional certifications and qualifications, such as the Certified Internal Auditor designation and other designations offered by The Institute of Internal Auditors and other appropriate professional organizations.

1210.A1 – The chief audit executive must obtain competent advice and assistance if the internal auditors lack the knowledge, skills, or other competencies needed to perform all or part of the engagement.

1210.A2 – Internal auditors must have sufficient knowledge to evaluate the risk of fraud and the manner in which it is managed by the organization, but are not expected to have the expertise of a person whose primary responsibility is detecting and investigating fraud.

1210.A3 – Internal auditors must have sufficient knowledge of key information technology risks and controls and available technology-based audit techniques to perform their assigned work. However, not all internal auditors are expected to have the expertise of an internal auditor whose primary responsibility is information technology auditing.

1210.C1 – The chief audit executive must decline the consulting engagement or obtain competent advice and assistance if the internal auditors lack the knowledge, skills, or other competencies needed to perform all or part of the engagement.

1220 – Due Professional Care

Internal auditors must apply the care and skill expected of a reasonably prudent and competent internal auditor. Due professional care does not imply infallibility.

1220.A1 – Internal auditors must exercise due professional care by considering the:

- Extent of work needed to achieve the engagement's objectives;
- Relative complexity, materiality, or significance of matters to which assurance procedures are applied;
- Adequacy and effectiveness of governance, risk management, and control processes;
- Probability of significant errors, fraud, or noncompliance; and
- Cost of assurance in relation to potential benefits.

1220.A2 – In exercising due professional care internal auditors must consider the use of technology-based audit and other data analysis techniques.

1220.A3 – Internal auditors must be alert to the significant risks that might affect objectives, operations, or resources. However, assurance procedures alone, even when performed with due professional care, do not guarantee that all significant risks will be identified.

1220.C1 – Internal auditors must exercise due professional care during a consulting engagement by considering the:

- Needs and expectations of clients, including the nature, timing, and communication of engagement results;

- Relative complexity and extent of work needed to achieve the engagement's objectives; and
- Cost of the consulting engagement in relation to potential benefits.

1230 – Continuing Professional Development

Internal auditors must enhance their knowledge, skills, and other competencies through continuing professional development.

1300 – Quality Assurance and Improvement Program

The chief audit executive must develop and maintain a quality assurance and improvement program that covers all aspects of the internal audit activity.

Interpretation:

A quality assurance and improvement program is designed to enable an evaluation of the internal audit activity's conformance with the Definition of Internal Auditing and the Standards and an evaluation of whether internal auditors apply the Code of Ethics. The program also assesses the efficiency and effectiveness of the internal audit activity and identifies opportunities for improvement.

1310 – Requirements of the Quality Assurance and Improvement Program

The quality assurance and improvement program must include both internal and external assessments.

1311 – Internal Assessments

Internal assessments must include:

- Ongoing monitoring of the performance of the internal audit activity; and-
- Periodic self-assessments or assessments by other persons within the organization with sufficient knowledge of internal audit practices.

Interpretation:

Ongoing monitoring is an integral part of the day-to-day supervision, review, and measurement of the internal audit activity. Ongoing monitoring is incorporated into the routine policies and practices used to manage the internal audit activity and uses processes, tools, and information considered necessary to evaluate conformance with the Definition of Internal Auditing, the Code of Ethics, and the Standards.

Periodic assessments are conducted to evaluate conformance with the Definition of Internal Auditing, the Code of Ethics, and the Standards.

Sufficient knowledge of internal audit practices requires at least an understanding of all elements of the International Professional Practices Framework.

1312 – External Assessments

External assessments must be conducted at least once every five years by a qualified, independent assessor or assessment team from outside the organization.

The chief audit executive must discuss with the board:

- The form and frequency of external assessment; and
- The qualifications and independence of the external assessor or assessment team, including any potential conflict of interest.

Interpretation:

External assessments can be in the form of a full external assessment, or a self-assessment with independent external validation.

A qualified assessor or assessment team demonstrates competence in two areas: the professional practice of internal auditing and the external assessment process. Competence can be demonstrated through a mixture of experience and theoretical learning. Experience gained in organizations of similar size, complexity, sector or industry, and technical issues is more valuable than less relevant experience. In the case of an assessment team, not all members of the team need to have all the competencies; it is the team as a whole that is qualified. The chief audit executive uses professional judgment when assessing whether an assessor or assessment team demonstrates sufficient competence to be qualified.

An independent assessor or assessment team means not having either a real or an apparent conflict of interest and not being a part of, or under the control of, the organization to which the internal audit activity belongs.

1320 – Reporting on the Quality Assurance and Improvement Program

The chief audit executive must communicate the results of the quality assurance and improvement program to senior management and the board.

Interpretation:

The form, content, and frequency of communicating the results of the quality assurance and improvement program is established through discussions with senior management and the board and considers the responsibilities of the internal audit activity and chief audit executive as contained in the internal audit charter. To demonstrate conformance with the Definition of Internal Auditing, the Code of Ethics, and the Standards, the results of external and periodic internal assessments are communicated upon completion of such assessments and the results of ongoing monitoring are communicated at least annually. The results include the assessor's or assessment team's evaluation with respect to the degree of conformance.

1321 – Use of "Conforms with the International Standards for the Professional Practice of Internal Auditing"

The chief audit executive may state that the internal audit activity conforms with the International Standards for the Professional Practice of Internal Auditing only if the results of the quality assurance and improvement program support this statement.

Interpretation:

The internal audit activity conforms with the Standards when it achieves the outcomes described in the Definition of Internal Auditing, Code of Ethics, and Standards.

The results of the quality assurance and improvement program include the results of both internal and external assessments. All internal audit activities will have the results of internal assessments. Internal audit activities in existence for at least five years will also have the results of external assessments.

1322 – Disclosure of Nonconformance

When nonconformance with the Definition of Internal Auditing, the Code of Ethics, or the Standards impacts the overall scope or operation of the internal audit activity, the chief audit executive must disclose the nonconformance and the impact to senior management and the board.

Performance Standards

2000 – Managing the Internal Audit Activity

The chief audit executive must effectively manage the internal audit activity to ensure it adds value to the organization.

Interpretation:

The internal audit activity is effectively managed when:

- *The results of the internal audit activity's work achieve the purpose and responsibility included in the internal audit charter;*
- *The internal audit activity conforms with the Definition of Internal Auditing and the Standards; and*
- *The individuals who are part of the internal audit activity demonstrate conformance with the Code of Ethics and the Standards.*

The internal audit activity adds value to the organization (and its stakeholders) when it provides objective and relevant assurance, and contributes to the effectiveness and efficiency of governance, risk management, and control processes.

2010 – Planning

The chief audit executive must establish a risk-based plan to determine the priorities of the internal audit activity, consistent with the organization's goals.

Interpretation:

The chief audit executive is responsible for developing a risk-based plan. The chief audit executive takes into account the organization's risk management framework, including using risk appetite levels set by management for the different activities or parts of the organization. If a framework does not exist, the chief audit executive uses his/her own judgment of risks after consideration of input from senior management and the board. The chief audit executive must review and adjust the plan, as necessary, in response to changes in the organization's business, risks, operations, programs, systems, and controls.

2010.A1 – The internal audit activity's plan of engagements must be based on a documented risk assessment, undertaken at least annually. The input of senior management and the board must be considered in this process.

2010.A2 – The chief audit executive must identify and consider the expectations of senior management, the board, and other stakeholders for internal audit opinions and other conclusions.

2010.C1 – The chief audit executive should consider accepting proposed consulting engagements based on the engagement's potential to improve management of risks, add value, and improve the organization's operations. Accepted engagements must be included in the plan.

2020 – Communication and Approval

The chief audit executive must communicate the internal audit activity's plans and resource requirements, including significant interim changes, to senior management and the board for review and approval. The chief audit executive must also communicate the impact of resource limitations.

2030 – Resource Management

The chief audit executive must ensure that internal audit resources are appropriate, sufficient, and effectively deployed to achieve the approved plan.

Interpretation:

Appropriate refers to the mix of knowledge, skills, and other competencies needed to perform the plan. Sufficient refers to the quantity of resources needed to accomplish the plan. Resources are effectively deployed when they are used in a way that optimizes the achievement of the approved plan.

2040 – Policies and Procedures

The chief audit executive must establish policies and procedures to guide the internal audit activity.

Interpretation:

The form and content of policies and procedures are dependent upon the size and structure of the internal audit activity and the complexity of its work.

2050 – Coordination

The chief audit executive should share information and coordinate activities with other internal and external providers of assurance and consulting services to ensure proper coverage and minimize duplication of efforts.

2060 – Reporting to Senior Management and the Board

The chief audit executive must report periodically to senior management and the board on the internal audit activity's purpose, authority, responsibility, and performance relative to its plan. Reporting must also include significant risk exposures and control issues, including fraud risks, governance issues, and other matters needed or requested by senior management and the board.

Interpretation:

The frequency and content of reporting are determined in discussion with senior management and the board and depend on the importance of the information to be communicated and the urgency of the related actions to be taken by senior management or the board.

2070 – External Service Provider and Organizational Responsibility for Internal Auditing

When an external service provider serves as the internal audit activity, the provider must make the organization aware that the organization has the responsibility for maintaining an effective internal audit activity.

Interpretation

This responsibility is demonstrated through the quality assurance and improvement program which assesses conformance with the Definition of Internal Auditing, the Code of Ethics, and the Standards.

2100 – Nature of Work

The internal audit activity must evaluate and contribute to the improvement of governance, risk management, and control processes using a systematic and disciplined approach.

2110 – Governance

The internal audit activity must assess and make appropriate recommendations for improving the governance process in its accomplishment of the following objectives:

- Promoting appropriate ethics and values within the organization;
- Ensuring effective organizational performance management and accountability;
- Communicating risk and control information to appropriate areas of the organization; and
- Coordinating the activities of and communicating information among the board, external and internal auditors, and management.

2110.A1 – The internal audit activity must evaluate the design, implementation, and effectiveness of the organization's ethics-related objectives, programs, and activities.

2110.A2 – The internal audit activity must assess whether the information technology governance of the organization supports the organization's strategies and objectives.

2120 – Risk Management

The internal audit activity must evaluate the effectiveness and contribute to the improvement of risk management processes.

Interpretation:

Determining whether risk management processes are effective is a judgment resulting from the internal auditor's assessment that:

- Organizational objectives support and align with the organization's mission;
- Significant risks are identified and assessed;
- Appropriate risk responses are selected that align risks with the organization's risk appetite; and
- Relevant risk information is captured and communicated in a timely manner across the organization, enabling staff, management, and the board to carry out their responsibilities.

The internal audit activity may gather the information to support this assessment during multiple engagements. The results of these engagements, when viewed together, provide an understanding of the organization's risk management processes and their effectiveness.

Risk management processes are monitored through ongoing management activities, separate evaluations, or both.

2120.A1 – The internal audit activity must evaluate risk exposures relating to the organization's governance, operations, and information systems regarding the:

- Achievement of the organization's strategic objectives;
- Reliability and integrity of financial and operational information;
- Effectiveness and efficiency of operations and programs;
- Safeguarding of assets; and
- Compliance with laws, regulations, policies, procedures, and contracts.

2120.A2 – The internal audit activity must evaluate the potential for the occurrence of fraud and how the organization manages fraud risk.

2120.C1 – During consulting engagements, internal auditors must address risk consistent with the engagement's objectives and be alert to the existence of other significant risks.

2120.C2 – Internal auditors must incorporate knowledge of risks gained from consulting engagements into their evaluation of the organization's risk management processes.

2120.C3 – When assisting management in establishing or improving risk management processes, internal auditors must refrain from assuming any management responsibility by actually managing risks.

2130 – Control

The internal audit activity must assist the organization in maintaining effective controls by evaluating their effectiveness and efficiency and by promoting continuous improvement.

2130.A1 – The internal audit activity must evaluate the adequacy and effectiveness of controls in responding to risks within the organization's governance, operations, and information systems regarding the:

- Achievement of the organization's strategic objectives;
- Reliability and integrity of financial and operational information;

- Effectiveness and efficiency of operations and programs;
- Safeguarding of assets; and
- Compliance with laws, regulations, policies, procedures, and contracts.

2130.C1 – Internal auditors must incorporate knowledge of controls gained from consulting engagements into evaluation of the organization's control processes.

2200 – Engagement Planning

Internal auditors must develop and document a plan for each engagement, including the engagement's objectives, scope, timing, and resource allocations.

2201 – Planning Considerations

In planning the engagement, internal auditors must consider:

- The objectives of the activity being reviewed and the means by which the activity controls its performance;
- The significant risks to the activity, its objectives, resources, and operations and the means by which the potential impact of risk is kept to an acceptable level;
- The adequacy and effectiveness of the activity's governance, risk management, and control processes compared to a relevant framework or model; and
- The opportunities for making significant improvements to the activity's governance, risk management, and control processes.

2201.A1 – When planning an engagement for parties outside the organization, internal auditors must establish a written understanding with them about objectives, scope, respective responsibilities, and other expectations, including restrictions on distribution of the results of the engagement and access to engagement records.

2201.C1 – Internal auditors must establish an understanding with consulting engagement clients about objectives, scope, respective responsibilities, and other client expectations. For significant engagements, this understanding must be documented.

2210 – Engagement Objectives

Objectives must be established for each engagement.

2210.A1 – Internal auditors must conduct a preliminary assessment of the risks relevant to the activity under review. Engagement objectives must reflect the results of this assessment.

2210.A2 – Internal auditors must consider the probability of significant errors, fraud, noncompliance, and other exposures when developing the engagement objectives.

2210.A3 – Adequate criteria are needed to evaluate governance, risk management, and controls. Internal auditors must ascertain the extent to which management and/or the board has established adequate criteria to determine whether objectives and goals have been accomplished. If adequate, internal auditors must use such criteria in their evaluation. If inadequate, internal auditors must work with management and/or the board to develop appropriate evaluation criteria.

2210.C1 – Consulting engagement objectives must address governance, risk management, and control processes to the extent agreed upon with the client.

2210.C2 – Consulting engagement objectives must be consistent with the organization's values, strategies, and objectives.

2220 – Engagement Scope

The established scope must be sufficient to achieve the objectives of the engagement.

2220.A1 – The scope of the engagement must include consideration of relevant systems, records, personnel, and physical properties, including those under the control of third parties.

2220.A2 – If significant consulting opportunities arise during an assurance engagement, a specific written understanding as to the objectives, scope, respective responsibilities, and other expectations should be reached and the results of the consulting engagement communicated in accordance with consulting standards.

2220.C1 – In performing consulting engagements, internal auditors must ensure that the scope of the engagement is sufficient to address the agreed-upon objectives. If internal auditors develop reservations about the scope during the engagement, these reservations must be discussed with the client to determine whether to continue with the engagement.

2220.C2 – During consulting engagements, internal auditors must address controls consistent with the engagement's objectives and be alert to significant control issues.

2230 – Engagement Resource Allocation

Internal auditors must determine appropriate and sufficient resources to achieve engagement objectives based on an evaluation of the nature and complexity of each engagement, time constraints, and available resources.

2240 – Engagement Work Program

Internal auditors must develop and document work programs that achieve the engagement objectives.

2240.A1 – Work programs must include the procedures for identifying, analyzing, evaluating, and documenting information during the engagement. The work program must be approved prior to its implementation, and any adjustments approved promptly.

2240.C1 – Work programs for consulting engagements may vary in form and content depending upon the nature of the engagement.

2300 – Performing the Engagement

Internal auditors must identify, analyze, evaluate, and document sufficient information to achieve the engagement's objectives.

2310 – Identifying Information

Internal auditors must identify sufficient, reliable, relevant, and useful information to achieve the engagement's objectives.

Interpretation:

Sufficient information is factual, adequate, and convincing so that a prudent, informed person would reach the same conclusions as the auditor. Reliable information is the best attainable information through the use of appropriate engagement techniques. Relevant information supports engagement observations and recommendations and is consistent with the objectives for the engagement. Useful information helps the organization meet its goals.

2320 – Analysis and Evaluation

Internal auditors must base conclusions and engagement results on appropriate analyses and evaluations.

2330 – Documenting Information

Internal auditors must document relevant information to support the conclusions and engagement results.

2330.A1 – The chief audit executive must control access to engagement records. The chief audit executive must obtain the approval of senior management and/or legal counsel prior to releasing such records to external parties, as appropriate.

2330.A2 – The chief audit executive must develop retention requirements for engagement records, regardless of the medium in which each record is stored. These retention requirements must be consistent with the organization's guidelines and any pertinent regulatory or other requirements.

2330.C1 – The chief audit executive must develop policies governing the custody and retention of consulting engagement records, as well as their release to internal and external parties. These policies must be consistent with the organization's guidelines and any pertinent regulatory or other requirements.

2340 – Engagement Supervision

Engagements must be properly supervised to ensure objectives are achieved, quality is assured, and staff is developed.

Interpretation:

The extent of supervision required will depend on the proficiency and experience of internal auditors and the complexity of the engagement. The chief audit executive has overall responsibility for supervising the engagement, whether performed by or for the internal audit activity, but may designate appropriately experienced members of the internal audit activity to perform the review. Appropriate evidence of supervision is documented and retained.

2400 – Communicating Results

Internal auditors must communicate the results of engagements.

2410 – Criteria for Communicating

Communications must include the engagement's objectives and scope as well as applicable conclusions, recommendations, and action plans.

2410.A1 – Final communication of engagement results must, where appropriate, contain the internal auditors' opinion and/or conclusions. When issued, an opinion or conclusion must take account of the expectations of senior management, the board, and other stakeholders and must be supported by sufficient, reliable, relevant, and useful information.

Interpretation:

Opinions at the engagement level may be ratings, conclusions, or other descriptions of the results. Such an engagement may be in relation to controls around a specific process, risk, or business unit. The formulation of such opinions requires consideration of the engagement results and their significance.

2410.A2 – Internal auditors are encouraged to acknowledge satisfactory performance in engagement communications.

2410.A3 – When releasing engagement results to parties outside the organization, the communication must include limitations on distribution and use of the results.

2410.C1 – Communication of the progress and results of consulting engagements will vary in form and content depending upon the nature of the engagement and the needs of the client.

2420 – Quality of Communications

Communications must be accurate, objective, clear, concise, constructive, complete, and timely.

Interpretation:

Accurate communications are free from errors and distortions and are faithful to the underlying facts. Objective communications are fair, impartial, and unbiased and are the result of a fair-minded and balanced assessment of all relevant facts and circumstances. Clear communications are easily understood and logical, avoiding unnecessary technical language and providing all significant and relevant information. Concise communications are to the point and avoid unnecessary elaboration, superfluous detail, redundancy, and wordiness. Constructive communications are helpful to the engagement client and the organization and lead to improvements where needed. Complete communications lack nothing that is essential to the target audience and include all significant and relevant information and observations to support recommendations and conclusions. Timely communications are opportune and expedient, depending on the significance of the issue, allowing management to take appropriate corrective action.

2421 – Errors and Omissions

If a final communication contains a significant error or omission, the chief audit executive must communicate corrected information to all parties who received the original communication.

2430 – Use of "Conducted in Conformance with the International Standards for the Professional Practice of Internal Auditing"

Internal auditors may report that their engagements are "conducted in conformance with the International Standards for the Professional Practice of Internal Auditing", only if the results of the quality assurance and improvement program support the statement.

2431 – Engagement Disclosure of Nonconformance

When nonconformance with the Definition of Internal Auditing, the Code of Ethics or the Standards impacts a specific engagement, communication of the results must disclose the:

- Principle or rule of conduct of the Code of Ethics or Standard(s) with which full conformance was not achieved;
- Reason(s) for nonconformance; and
- Impact of nonconformance on the engagement and the communicated engagement results.

2440 – Disseminating Results

The chief audit executive must communicate results to the appropriate parties.

Interpretation:

The chief audit executive is responsible for reviewing and approving the final engagement communication before issuance and for deciding to whom and how it will be disseminated. When the chief audit executive delegates these duties, he or she retains overall responsibility.

2440.A1 – The chief audit executive is responsible for communicating the final results to parties who can ensure that the results are given due consideration.

2440.A2 – If not otherwise mandated by legal, statutory, or regulatory requirements, prior to releasing results to parties outside the organization the chief audit executive must:

- Assess the potential risk to the organization;
- Consult with senior management and/or legal counsel as appropriate; and
- Control dissemination by restricting the use of the results.

2440.C1 – The chief audit executive is responsible for communicating the final results of consulting engagements to clients.

2440.C2 – During consulting engagements, governance, risk management, and control issues may be identified. Whenever these issues are significant to the organization, they must be communicated to senior management and the board.

2450 – Overall Opinions

When an overall opinion is issued, it must take into account the expectations of senior management, the board, and other stakeholders and must be supported by sufficient, reliable, relevant, and useful information.

Interpretation:

The communication will identify:

- *The scope, including the time period to which the opinion pertains;*
- *Scope limitations;*
- *Consideration of all related projects including the reliance on other assurance providers;*
- *The risk or control framework or other criteria used as a basis for the overall opinion; and*
- *The overall opinion, judgment, or conclusion reached.*

The reasons for an unfavorable overall opinion must be stated.

2500 – Monitoring Progress

The chief audit executive must establish and maintain a system to monitor the disposition of results communicated to management.

2500.A1 – The chief audit executive must establish a follow-up process to monitor and ensure that management actions have been effectively implemented or that senior management has accepted the risk of not taking action.

2500.C1 – The internal audit activity must monitor the disposition of results of consulting engagements to the extent agreed upon with the client.

2600 – Communicating the Acceptance of Risks

When the chief audit executive concludes that management has accepted a level of risk that may be unacceptable to the organization, the chief audit executive must discuss the matter with senior management. If the chief audit executive determines that the matter has not been resolved, the chief audit executive must communicate the matter to the board.

Interpretation:

The identification of risk accepted by management may be observed through an assurance or consulting engagement, monitoring progress on actions taken by management as a result of prior engagements, or other means. It is not the responsibility of the chief audit executive to resolve the risk.

Glossary

Add Value

The internal audit activity adds value to the organization (and its stakeholders) when it provides objective and relevant assurance, and contributes to the effectiveness and efficiency of governance, risk management, and control processes.

Adequate Control

Present if management has planned and organized (designed) in a manner that provides reasonable assurance that the organization's risks have been managed effectively and that the organization's goals and objectives will be achieved efficiently and economically.

Assurance Services

An objective examination of evidence for the purpose of providing an independent assessment on governance, risk management, and control processes for the organization. Examples may include financial, performance, compliance, system security, and due diligence engagements.

Board

The highest level of governing body charged with the responsibility to direct and/or oversee the activities and management of the organization. Typically, this includes an independent group of directors (e.g., a board of directors, a supervisory board, or a board of governors or trustees). If such a group does not exist, the "board" may refer to the head of the organization. "Board" may refer to an audit committee to which the governing body has delegated certain functions.

Charter

The internal audit charter is a formal document that defines the internal audit activity's purpose, authority, and responsibility. The internal audit charter establishes the internal audit activity's position within the organization; authorizes access to records, personnel, and physical properties relevant to the performance of engagements; and defines the scope of internal audit activities.

Chief Audit Executive

Chief audit executive describes a person in a senior position responsible for effectively managing the internal audit activity in accordance with the internal audit charter and the Definition of Internal Auditing, the Code of Ethics, and the Standards. The chief audit executive or others reporting to the chief audit executive will have appropriate professional certifications and qualifications. The specific job title of the chief audit executive may vary across organizations.

Code of Ethics

The Code of Ethics of The Institute of Internal Auditors (IIA) are Principles relevant to the profession and practice of internal auditing, and Rules of Conduct that describe behavior expected of internal auditors. The Code of Ethics applies to both parties and entities that provide internal audit services. The purpose of the

Code of Ethics is to promote an ethical culture in the global profession of internal auditing.

Compliance

Adherence to policies, plans, procedures, laws, regulations, contracts, or other requirements.

Conflict of Interest

Any relationship that is, or appears to be, not in the best interest of the organization. A conflict of interest would prejudice an individual's ability to perform his or her duties and responsibilities objectively.

Consulting Services

Advisory and related client service activities, the nature and scope of which are agreed with the client, are intended to add value and improve an organization's governance, risk management, and control processes without the internal auditor assuming management responsibility. Examples include counsel, advice, facilitation, and training.

Control

Any action taken by management, the board, and other parties to manage risk and increase the likelihood that established objectives and goals will be achieved. Management plans, organizes, and directs the performance of sufficient actions to provide reasonable assurance that objectives and goals will be achieved.

Control Environment

The attitude and actions of the board and management regarding the importance of control within the organization. The control environment provides the discipline and structure for the achievement of the primary objectives of the system of internal control. The control environment includes the following elements:

- Integrity and ethical values.
- Management's philosophy and operating style.
- Organizational structure.
- Assignment of authority and responsibility.
- Human resource policies and practices.
- Competence of personnel.

Control Processes

The policies, procedures (both manual and automated), and activities that are part of a control framework, designed and operated to ensure that risks are contained within the level that an organization is willing to accept.

Engagement

A specific internal audit assignment, task, or review activity, such as an internal audit, control self-assessment review, fraud examination, or consultancy. An engagement may include multiple tasks or activities designed to accomplish a specific set of related objectives.

Engagement Objectives

Broad statements developed by internal auditors that define intended engagement accomplishments.

Engagement Opinion

The rating, conclusion, and/or other description of results of an individual internal audit engagement, relating to those aspects within the objectives and scope of the engagement.

Engagement Work Program

A document that lists the procedures to be followed during an engagement, designed to achieve the engagement plan.

External Service Provider

A person or firm outside of the organization that has special knowledge, skill, and experience in a particular discipline.

Fraud

Any illegal act characterized by deceit, concealment, or violation of trust. These acts are not dependent upon the threat of violence or physical force. Frauds are perpetrated by parties and organizations to obtain money, property, or services; to avoid payment or loss of services; or to secure personal or business advantage.

Governance

The combination of processes and structures implemented by the board to inform, direct, manage, and monitor the activities of the organization toward the achievement of its objectives.

Impairment

Impairment to organizational independence and individual objectivity may include personal conflict of interest, scope limitations, restrictions on access to records, personnel, and properties, and resource limitations (funding).

Independence

The freedom from conditions that threaten the ability of the internal audit activity to carry out internal audit responsibilities in an unbiased manner.

Information Technology Controls

Controls that support business management and governance as well as provide general and technical controls over information technology infrastructures such as applications, information, infrastructure, and people.

Information Technology Governance

Consists of the leadership, organizational structures, and processes that ensure that the enterprise's information technology supports the organization's strategies and objectives.

Internal Audit Activity

A department, division, team of consultants, or other practitioner(s) that provides independent, objective assurance and consulting services designed to add value and improve an organization's operations. The internal audit activity helps an organization accomplish its objectives by bringing a systematic, disciplined approach to evaluate and improve the effectiveness of governance, risk management and control processes.

International Professional Practices Framework

The conceptual framework that organizes the authoritative guidance promulgated by The IIA. Authoritative Guidance is comprised of two categories – (1) mandatory and (2) strongly recommended.

Must

The Standards use the word "must" to specify an unconditional requirement.

Objectivity

An unbiased mental attitude that allows internal auditors to perform engagements in such a manner that they believe in their work product and that no quality compromises are made. Objectivity requires that internal auditors do not subordinate their judgment on audit matters to others.

Overall Opinion

The rating, conclusion, and/or other description of results provided by the chief audit executive addressing, at a broad level, governance, risk management, and/or control processes of the organization. An overall opinion is the professional judgment of the chief audit executive based on the results of a number of individual engagements and other activities for a specific time interval.

Risk

The possibility of an event occurring that will have an impact on the achievement of objectives. Risk is measured in terms of impact and likelihood.

Risk Appetite

The level of risk that an organization is willing to accept.

Risk Management

A process to identify, assess, manage, and control potential events or situations to provide reasonable assurance regarding the achievement of the organization's objectives.

Should

The Standards use the word "should" where conformance is expected unless, when applying professional judgment, circumstances justify deviation.

Significance

The relative importance of a matter within the context in which it is being considered, including quantitative and qualitative factors, such as magnitude, nature, effect, relevance, and impact. Professional judgment assists internal auditors when evaluating the significance of matters within the context of the relevant objectives.

Standard

A professional pronouncement promulgated by the Internal Audit Standards Board that delineates the requirements for performing a broad range of internal audit activities, and for evaluating internal audit performance.

Technology-based Audit Techniques

Any automated audit tool, such as generalized audit software, test data generators, computerized audit programs, specialized audit utilities, and computer-assisted audit techniques (CAATs).

Appendix 9

Independent External Board Evaluations Code of Practice

INDEPENDENT EXTERNAL BOARD EVALUATIONS

CODE OF PRACTICE

January 2014

A. PREFACE

An effective board creates value. It is more likely to make the high-quality decisions which will help the company achieve its objectives, manage its risks, and safeguard its reputation. Effective boards – and successful companies – build trust and confidence among investors, employees, customers and all those who have a stake in the company's on-going success.

Board evaluations – as set out in the UK Corporate Governance Code – are one of the principal methods for building board effectiveness. The activity must be owned by the company, and tailored to suit the needs of the business, and its board. The evaluation should be professionally delivered, and its outcomes implemented.

There is a perception, however, that the scope and service quality of evaluations is variable, and a there is a concern about standards. It is an appropriate time to reflect on what can be done to increase the effectiveness of board evaluations, particularly those conducted by independent, external consultants.

This draft Code of Practice on Board Evaluation seeks to begin a discussion to address and resolve this perceived lack of market confidence, and install a more coherent framework to allow companies and consultants to work more effectively together.

We would like to acknowledge the valuable contribution of a number of market participants, whose views and comments we have used to inform the document.

Evaluations provide a unique opportunity to improve board performance and shape corporate success. We look forward to working together to strengthen the sector to realise our shared aspiration – to help UK companies, the primary source of wealth creation in our economy, succeed and excel.

Helen Pitcher

Chairman
Advanced Boardroom Excellence

Seamus Gillen

CEO, Board Evaluation and Governance
Advanced Boardroom Excellence

B. INTRODUCTION

This Code of Practice on Board Evaluation ('Code') has been created to provide a framework within which independent external board evaluations can be conducted. Its aim is to introduce high professional standards in a rapidly-developing sector, and to give chairmen, company secretaries and key stakeholders assurance, and greater clarity, on the service, and standards, they should be able to expect from consultants; and consultants confidence in the degree of commitment they can expect from companies.

This Code should help the sector achieve higher levels of performance, while maintaining a flexible framework which retains the scope for diversity of approach and methodology, and further innovation.

C. GUIDANCE

1. PROFESSIONALISM OF APPROACH

The consultants will regard the client's requirements and interests as paramount at all times, and will conduct themselves in such a way as to maximise the value generated by the board evaluation. The consultants should display the following behaviours at all times.

1.1 Independence

The consultants will freely express their own opinion without any control or influence from others inside or outside the (consulting) organisation, and without the need to consider the impact of such opinion on the consultants' own interests.

1.2 Integrity

The consultants will avoid any action or situation inconsistent with their professional obligations, or which in any way could be seen to impair their integrity. In formulating advice and recommendations, the consultants will be guided solely by the objective view of the client's best interests.

1.3 Competence

The consultants will only accept work that they are qualified to perform and in which the client can be served effectively. The consultants will not make any misleading claims concerning capability, competence or experience, and will facilitate access to selected clients to allow a prospective new client to talk to them and collect references.

1.4 Respect

The consultants will act with courtesy and consideration toward the individuals contacted in the course of undertaking assignments.

1.5 Objectivity

The consultants will not pursue more than two consecutive assignments with the same client.

The consultants, and their organisation, will not pursue any other work elsewhere in the company, such as non-audit work, where there may be a perception that the outcomes of one assignment might potentially affect the approach conducted in relation to the other assignment.

The consultants will advise the client of any significant reservations the consultants may have about the client's expectation of benefits from an engagement.

The consultants will not pursue any short-term benefit at the expense of the long-term welfare of the client, without advising the client of the implications.

1.6 Tact

The consultants will appreciate the sensitive nature of the assignment and will always act with tact, discretion and diplomacy. The consultants will understand that significant insights will potentially be generated by directors being prepared to talk frankly, and will make clear, and ensure, that such conversations take place in a secure environment.

1.7 Personal conduct

The consultants will be fit and proper persons to carry out the independent external board evaluation. The consultants will at all times be of a good reputation, character and standing. Particular matters for concern might include:

- conviction of a criminal offence, or committal under bankruptcy proceedings
- censure or disciplining by a court or regulatory authority
- unethical or improper behaviour towards clients, employees or other stakeholders

2. COMPETENCIES AND CAPABILITIES

Consultants should be highly qualified, with appropriate levels of technical and behavioural expertise.

2.1 Scope

The FRC's Guidance on Board Effectiveness (Appendix) suggests a non-exhaustive and non-prescriptive list of topics to be covered during an evaluation. The consultants should be competent to cover any or all of these areas.

Depending on client need, and the board's current cycle and circumstances, the consultants should recommend a scope of work which will be sufficiently rigorous, and comprehensive, avoids a one-size-fits-all approach, and provides reassurance that all priority areas are being covered.

2.2 Additional coverage

The consultants should be willing to discuss client requests which go beyond the areas identified in the Appendix, or otherwise identify the limits of their capability and competence.

The consultants should be able to confirm whether they have the expertise, depth of knowledge and suitable experience to meet more challenging client requests including, for example, the ability to: assess the behavioural dynamics of the board; conduct deep-dive observations and reviews across the board and its committees; assess wider succession issues, such as that of the executive team; analyse the effectiveness of particular decisions made over time which were critical to the success of the business; review board and committee documentation and; provide action planning for the board.

The consultants should appreciate the critical importance of diversity on a board, which should be understood to be broader than issues of genetics, e.g. gender, ethnicity etc. In the course of an evaluation, consultants should be able to assess the degree to which, individually and collectively, the board and its directors display rigorous thought processes leading to breadth, depth and independence of thinking, in addition to attributes such as skill, experience, knowledge and capability.

2.3 Required skill sets

Consultants should display the required levels of competence to ensure their contributions are meaningful, informed and constructive. Areas of capability should include:

- Direct experience of board practice – derived from being a director, company secretary or other professional
- Knowledge of, and expertise in, governance and behavioural issues
- Management and commercial experience
- Financial expertise
- Communication, personal and interpersonal skills
- Political sensitivity and nous
- Possession of relevant professional qualifications and up-to-date professional knowledge

2.4 Understanding of commercial context

The consultants should develop an understanding of the company's business model, strategy, approach to risk and other relevant issues, to understand how effectively the board challenges itself on the key issues. This will require access to documents which will not be in the public domain, and to which the provisions of a confidentiality agreement, and insider restrictions, will apply.

2.5 Commercial and personal sensitivity

The consultants will understand (section 1.6) that significant insights will potentially be generated by directors being prepared to talk frankly, and will display the required qualities to ensure the directors feel comfortable that such conversations will take place in a way that allows confidentiality to be preserved, if appropriate, while ensuring the discussions are incorporated tactfully into the report back to the chairman and board.

2.6 Customer awareness

Without demonstrating any unjustifiable bias in favour of the client, or the principal person leading the assignment (such as the chairman or company secretary), the consultants should nevertheless work closely with the client to ensure the evaluation achieves the client's objectives. The consultants should be able to display the flexibility of style, approach and methodology to suit the client's needs.

2.7 Managing outcomes

An effective independent external evaluation should generate insights which a board will not have been able, or willing, to identify for itself. The consultants will be able to demonstrate the skills required to advise a board on how to address and resolve the issues identified in the evaluation.

2.8 Measuring progress

The consultants should be willing to return to the client six months, or a mutually-agreed period, after the evaluation has been completed, to assess what progress has been made in terms of implementing outcomes. This visit would form part of the scope of the engagement.

3. EXPECTATIONS OF THE CLIENT BY THE CONSULTANTS

It is important that the client – who owns the board evaluation process – enters into the exercise with commitment.

3.1 Commitment from the whole board to the evaluation process

The consultants should work closely with the chairman, or company secretary, or the person responsible for the evaluation, to engage the interest of the whole board, and encourage appropriate levels of participation.

3.2 Director involvement

The client and the consultants should consider the appropriate level of interaction with each director, and particularly the need for each director to be interviewed, to ensure the full range of board views and sentiments are taken into account during the evaluation process.

3.3 Board observation

The client should accept that the consultants may wish to observe meetings of the board and/or its committees, to maximise the value of the exercise. In appointing consultants to an assignment, the client will be satisfied that they are sufficiently experienced, and of the required calibre and character, to attend meetings.

3.4 Provision of company information

The quality of the consultants' intervention will partly be driven by the extent to which they understand the commercial context within which the company operates. In this respect, the consultant is in the same position as other trusted advisors who are insiders, and the company should consider what information of a confidential nature

– board papers, minutes and other documents – it will pass to the consultants so that they can operate effectively. The supply of such information will be subject to the provisions of a confidentiality agreement, and inclusion in an insider trading register.

3.5 Reporting back to the board

The consultants should be capable of feeding back to the members of the board in a discreet, balanced and informative manner, providing clear, constructive and objective feedback. The client, for its part, should make the necessary preparations to allow feedback to be delivered in as open a way as possible, to maximise the benefits derived from the evaluation. The client should be willing to let the consultants be 'courageous', and offer feedback which may not be viewed by all board members as welcome, as long as the process is carefully handled.

3.6 Reporting of outcomes

The client will acknowledge that the outcome of a board evaluation process is of material interest to key stakeholders, notably investors. The client will consider how to disclose the outcomes of an evaluation in an appropriate way in the Annual Report and Accounts, and may wish to seek the consultants' view on how to do so with maximum effect, while maintaining issues of confidentiality and sensitivity.

Both the company and the consultants should agree the content to be disclosed, so that both parties are comfortable with what subsequently appears in the public domain. Both parties should accept that reputational damage can be caused if there is inappropriate or inaccurate reporting of the outcome of a board evaluation.

The company should consider whether there are other approaches for building shareholder confidence in the company as a result of an evaluation. For example, it might be deemed worthwhile for either the chairman or the senior independent director to discuss the most recent evaluation, and its outcomes, with the company's principal shareholders in the course of their routine engagement activity.

3.7 Measuring progress

As part of the scope of the engagement, the company should be prepared to enter into an arrangement with the consultants (see section 2.8), for a return visit six months, or a mutually- agreed period, after the evaluation has been completed, to discuss progress made in implementing outcomes.

4. CLARIFYING THE TERMS OF THE ENGAGEMENT

The consultants and client should be clear about the levels of expectation associated with the assignment. This is most likely to happen if both parties communicate openly and transparently to avoid the risk of misunderstandings, and maximise the benefits of the engagement. Agreements in the following areas should be set out formally and in writing.

4.1 Clarity of engagement and scope

There should be agreement on the scope of the assignment, in advance of commencing work. Any subsequent revisions will be subject to prior discussion and agreement with the client.

There should be agreement on the process which will be followed to deliver the assignment, in advance of commencing work. Any subsequent revisions will be subject to prior discussion and agreement with the client.

4.2 Agreement on timing, deliverables and fees

There should be agreement on the nature of the services to be provided. The agreement should clearly identify the timescale for completing the assignment, the deliverables, and the basis of remuneration, in advance of commencing work. Any subsequent revisions will be subject to prior discussion and agreement with the client.

4.3 Assignment of personnel

There should be agreement on the client-consultant relationship, the principal contact points on either side within that relationship, and the process for communication between those principal contacts. The terms of this relationship should not be changed without the prior agreement of both the client and the consultants.

There should be agreement on who will carry out the assignment. The consultants should not substitute or sub-contract or assign work without the prior agreement of the client.

The consultants should make clear whether any person working on the assignment is employed by the firm, or is working under contract. The consultants will ensure that, whatever their status, they meet all the standards required under the Code. Except where otherwise agreed, the consultants will remain responsible for the performance of the work.

4.4 Communication and feedback

The consultants will ensure that the client is kept fully informed about the progress of the assignment.

The consultants will take note of any feedback provided by the client on the performance of the consultants' services, and will seek formal feedback from the client after the process not just on the outcomes, but on the overall approach pursued by the consultants, and how they could be more effective.

4.5 Public reporting of outcomes

There should be clarity in the agreement between the client and the consultants on the degree and extent to which the consultants' assent to public reporting by the company will be required.

4.6 Post-evaluation review of the assignment

The client and the consultants should agree on whether there will be a review of the evaluation exercise, and how the lessons learned can be shared to the participants' mutual benefit.

4.7 Post-evaluation review of the assignment outcomes

The client and the consultants should agree on whether, and how, there should be a review of what actions have been taken in response to the evaluation, and the effectiveness of the outcomes. (See also 2.8 and 3.7).

4.8 References

The consultants will offer the names of, and facilitate access as necessary to, selected clients to allow a prospective new client to talk to them and collect references.

4.9 Professional indemnity insurance

The consultants will carry adequate Professional Indemnity Insurance (PII) to cover any work undertaken.

4.10 Administration

The consultants will operate an efficient back-office function to ensure that basic housekeeping issues – setting up meetings, replying to queries, billing and so on – are conducted in a timely and effective manner.

5. EFFICIENT PROCESS

The consultants should be able to reassure the client that all activities will be undertaken at the highest level of professionalism.

5.1 Confidentiality

The consultants will sign a confidentiality agreement with the client. The confidentiality agreement will apply to the overall assignment, and to every intervention and interview which takes place during the assignment.

The consultant will hold all information concerning the affairs of the client in the strictest confidence, and will not disclose proprietary information obtained during the course of assignments. Consent will be specifically sought for any derogation from the terms of the confidentiality agreement.

The consultant will not reveal the name of the client to any other party, unless with the agreement of the client, the nature and terms of such agreement to be set out in the confidentiality agreement.

5.2 Confidential interviewing process

The consultants will, in liaison with the client, take all necessary steps to ensure that any interviews – whether face-to-face, over the phone, or by any other means – are conducted in confidential circumstances, and that the outputs of the interviews are adequately protected.

5.3 Privacy of information

The consultants will not use any confidential information about a client's affairs, elicited during the course of an assignment, for personal benefit, professional benefit, or for the benefit of others outside the client organisation. An example where this provision applies is in the area of board and executive search.

When required, or appropriate, the consultants will establish specific methods of working which preserve the privacy of the client's information, such as where the conditions concerning conflicts of interest apply.

5.4 Sensitivity of information

The consultants should acknowledge that they may become privy to sensitive information that should not be attributed or, on occasion, appear in the main report. The evaluator should agree with the chairman how such information should be brought to the chairman's, or board's, attention in a way that ensures matters are aired, but without compromising the information concerned.

5.5 Sensitivity of views

The consultants should acknowledge that, if individual directors are to be fully involved in the evaluation process (section 3.2), the consultants may become privy to differences of view, attitude and approach that should be respected and, again, should not be attributed or, on occasion, appear in the main report. The evaluator should agree with the chairman how such information should be brought to the chairman's, or board's, attention in a way that ensures matters are aired, but without compromising the individual(s) concerned.

5.6 Insider status

The consultants are likely to acquire insider status as a consequence of being made privy to confidential company, especially board, information. This issue should be covered in the appointment process, with the consultants registered on any relevant insider trading register.

5.7 Due care, skill and diligence

The consultants will make certain that advice, solutions and recommendations are based on thorough, impartial consideration and the analysis of all available pertinent facts and relevant experience, and are realistic, practicable and clearly understood by the client.

5.8 Professional disclosure

The consultants will disclose, at the earliest opportunity, any special relationships, circumstances, or business interests, which might influence or impair, or could be seen by the client or others to influence or impair, the consultants' judgment or objectivity on a particular assignment. This will require the prior disclosure of all relevant personal, financial or other business interests which could not be inferred from the description of services offered.

5.9 Conflicts of interest

The consultants will not serve a client under circumstances which are inconsistent with the consultants' primary duty to the client, or which in any way might be seen to impair the consultants' integrity.

Wherever a conflict, or potential conflict of interest, arises, the consultants will, as the circumstances require, either withdraw from the assignment, remove the source of conflict, or disclose and obtain the agreement of the parties concerned, to the performance or continuation of the engagement.

5.10 Inducements

The consultants will not accept discounts, hospitality, commissions or gifts as an inducement to show favour to any person or body, nor attempt to obtain advantage by giving the same to clients or client staff, or potential clients or their staff.

5.11 Assurance review

The consultants should have systems in place to ensure quality control during the assignment, as well as undertake an internal post-evaluation review to reflect on how well the assignment was executed.

D. INDEPENDENT OVERSIGHT OF THE CODE

Independent oversight body

It is proposed that consideration be given to creation of an independent oversight body, comprising senior market participants meeting on a periodic basis, to review adherence to the Code by consultants, and to make recommendations for improvement and further actions. The independent oversight body will help ensure appropriate levels of accountability, and build confidence among market participants, and wider groups of stakeholders.

Secretariat

The independent oversight body would be serviced by a secretariat which would put into place appropriate governance arrangements, including a meetings schedule and budget, and arrangements for the publication of an annual report. The Institute of Chartered Secretaries and Administrators has indicated that it would be willing to undertake this task, at least initially.

Costs

The costs of the independent oversight body, and the secretariat, would be met from a levy on consultants. It is not expected that the costs would be significant. A method for calculating the levy would be agreed with reference to other sector models.

Register

The secretariat would maintain a Register of consultants. Early issues for consideration would be whether consultants would be expected to sign up to the Code, what systems of quality control would be introduced to determine whether a consultants should be entitled to join, and subsequently remain, on the Register, and the role of the oversight body in maintaining standards.

Revisions

The Code will be revised periodically, and revised as necessary, to reflect innovations in approach and methodology, the development of customer need, and other issues.

Any comments on this document should be addressed to policy@icsa.org.uk

APPENDIX

FRC Guidance on Board Effectiveness – evaluating the performance of the board and directors

- Board composition: the mix of skills, experience, knowledge and diversity on the board, in the context of the challenges facing the company
- Board leadership: clarity of, and leadership given to, the purpose, direction and values of the company
- Succession planning: succession and development plans
- How the board works together as a unit, and the tone set by the chairman and the CEO
- Board relations: key board relationships, particularly chairman/CEO, chairman/senior independent director, chairman/company secretary and executive/non-executive
- Individual director effectiveness: effectiveness of individual non-executive and executive directors
- Role of the Senior Independent Director: clarity of the senior independent director's role
- Board committee effectiveness: effectiveness of board committees, and how they are connected with the main board
- Board information management: quality of the general information provided on the company and its performance
- Quality of board papers and presentations: quality of papers and presentations to the board
- Quality of board debate: quality of discussions around individual proposals
- The challenge process: the process the chairman uses to ensure sufficient debate for major decisions or contentious issues
- The company secretariat: effectiveness of secretariat
- The decision-making process: clarity of the decision processes and authorities
- The risk process: processes for identifying and reviewing risks
- Shareholders and stakeholders communication: how the board communicates with, and listens and responds to, shareholders and other stakeholders

ABOUT ADVANCED BOARDROOM EXCELLENCE

Advanced Boardroom Excellence is a new organisation, though with a significant track record built on the expertise, experience and capabilities of the founder directors.

The consultancy is led by Helen Pitcher, supported by an experienced team who have worked together for over 20 years, bringing expertise, knowledge and skills to a dedicated range of board effectiveness and developmental services for board and senior leaders, at a collective and individual level.

We are committed to building the new organisation based on our values of client service, creativity, innovation and integrity.

Over the past five years, in particular, we have had direct experience of creating a leading board effectiveness consultancy, undertaking external independent reviews for clients from a range of sectors, from the FTSE100 and FTSE250, and from large global organisations to private equity and smaller family-owned companies. They have included Old Mutual, the Royal Bank of Scotland, Hunting, Miller Group and many others not yet in the public domain. The team has completed reviews for a major telecoms company, a professional association, a major financial services mutual, and is currently undertaking a review for a FTSE100 financial services organisation, and a privately owned mid-cap general insurance organisation.

We have created a unique Board Leadership Effectiveness Model, which blends formal evaluation with organisational behavioural engagement, providing an accelerated high-impact engagement strategy for the director team. Built into our DNA is the desire to provide elegant, rigorous and action-focused solutions which support and make a difference to our clients.

We will happily provide reference points to potential new clients through our extensive network. Most clients come to us by referral and endorsement:

> "They create great client solutions by listening and interpreting needs very well and developing creative resolutions."
>
> "Their approach to board review is profoundly different, with a development focus which provides a real opportunity for creating value and improvement in the board's effectiveness."
>
> "They are innovative and robust thinkers who deliver potentially tough messages in an elegant but irresistible way."

Please visit us at www.abexcellence.com. We would be pleased to hear from you.

Index

References are to paragraph number and Appendix.